109th Congress
2nd Session

SPECIAL REPORT

S. Rept. 109-322

HURRICANE KATRINA: A NATION STILL UNPREPARED

SPECIAL REPORT

OF THE

COMMITTEE ON HOMELAND SECURITY AND GOVERNMENTAL AFFAIRS

UNITED STATES SENATE

TOGETHER WITH

ADDITIONAL VIEWS

Printed for the Use of the Committee on Homeland Security and Governmental Affairs
http://hsgac.senate.gov/

ORDERED TO BE PRINTED
U.S. GOVERNMENT PRINTING OFFICE
WASHINGTON : 2006
FOR SALE BY THE SUPERINTENDENT OF DOCUMENTS

Cover Photo: Helicopter Rescue, New Orleans (Courtesy of U.S. Coast Guard)

For sale by the Superintendent of Documents, U.S. Government Printing Office
Internet: bookstore.gpo.gov Phone: toll free (866) 512-1800; DC area (202) 512-1800
Fax: (202) 512-2250 Mail: Stop IDCC, Washington, DC 20402-0001

ISBN 0-16-076749-0

Committee on Homeland Security and Governmental Affairs

SUSAN M. COLLINS, Maine, *Chairman*

TED STEVENS, Alaska

GEORGE V. VOINOVICH, Ohio

NORM COLEMAN, Minnesota

TOM COBURN, M.D., Oklahoma

LINCOLN D. CHAFEE, Rhode Island

ROBERT F. BENNETT, Utah

PETE V. DOMENICI, New Mexico

JOHN W. WARNER, Virginia

JOSEPH I. LIEBERMAN, Connecticut

CARL LEVIN, Michigan

DANIEL K. AKAKA, Hawaii

THOMAS R. CARPER, Delaware

MARK DAYTON, Minnesota

FRANK LAUTENBERG, New Jersey

MARK PRYOR, Arkansas

Michael D. Bopp, Majority Staff Director and Chief Counsel
David T. Flanagan, Majority General Counsel, Katrina Investigation
Joyce A. Rechtschaffen, Minority Staff Director and Counsel
Laurie R. Rubenstein, Minority Chief Counsel
Robert F. Muse, Minority General Counsel, Katrina Investigation
Trina Driessnack Tyrer, Chief Clerk

Majority Staff

Arthur W Adelberg, Senior Counsel

Melvin D. Albritton, Counsel

Kate C. Alford, Research Assistant

Jennifer C. Boone, FBI Detailee

Erin M. Bouchard, Intern

Allison J. Boyd, Counsel

Codias M. Brown, Legislative Correspondent

Donald L. Bumgardner, GAO Detailee

Jennifer S. Burita, Communications Director

Cyrus E. Cheslak, Intern

John H. Cobb, Senior Counsel

Thomas R. Eldridge, Senior Counsel

Ann C. Fisher, Deputy Staff Director

Keith A. Fleming, CBP Detailee

Jennifer E. Gagnon, Executive Assistant

Amy L. Hall, Professional Staff Member

Catherine A. Harrington, Intern

Jennifer A. Hemingway, Professional Staff Member

David E. Hunter, Staff Scientist

Clark T. Irwin, Editor/Professional Staff Member

Keith B. Janssen, USCG Detailee

Kathleen L. Kraninger, Professional Staff Member

Gordon N. Lederman, Special Counsel

Brian J. Lepore, GAO Detailee

Mira L. Lezell, Intern

Jay W. Maroney, Counsel

Asha A. Mathew, Counsel

James R. McKay, Counsel

Jonathan T. Nass, Counsel

David K. Porter, Counsel

Chad T. Sarchio, DOJ Detailee

Debra J. Schlagenhauf, Assistant Clerk

Kurt A. Schmautz, Counsel

Robert L. Strayer, Counsel

Jennifer L. Tarr, Research Assistant

Sarah V. Taylor, Research Assistant

Debra M. Thomas, Executive Assistant

Larry F. Vigil, Professional Staff Member

Monica A. Wickey, Legislative Correspondent

Minority Staff

Michael L. Alexander, Professional Staff Member*

Alistair F. Anagnostou, Staff Assistant

Eric P. Andersen, Professional Staff Member

David M. Berick, Professional Staff Member

Dan M. Berkovitz, Counsel, PSI

Stacey M. Bosshardt, Counsel

Janet L. Burrell, Office Manager/Executive Assistant

Scott G. Campbell, Communications Advisor

William E. Corboy, Professional Staff Member

Troy H. Cribb, Counsel

Heather R. Fine, Counsel

Boris Y. Fishman, Editor

Susan A. Fleming, GAO Detailee

Jeffrey E. Greene, Counsel

Elyse F. Greenwald, Staff Assistant

Beth M. Grossman, Counsel

R. Denton Herring, GAO Detailee

Holly A. Idelson, Counsel

Kristine V. Lam, Staff Assistant

Kevin J. Landy, Senior Counsel

Joshua A. Levy, Counsel

Alysha S. Liljeqvist, Staff Assistant

F. James McGee, Professional Staff Member

Lawrence B. Novey, Senior Counsel

Siobhan C. Oat-Judge, Deputy Press Secretary

Leslie J. Phillips, Communications Director

A. Patricia Rojas, Professional Staff Member

Mary Beth Schultz, Counsel

Adam R. Sedgewick, Professional Staff Member

Todd M. Stein, Counsel, Office of Senator Lieberman

Traci L. Taylor, DOI Detailee

Donny Ray Williams, Jr., Professional Staff Member

Jason M. Yanussi, Professional Staff Member

Elisabeth F. Butler, Archivist
John S. Gleason, Financial Clerk
Megan T. Gorski, Documents Manager
Patricia R. Hogan, Publications Clerk/GPO Detailee
Daniel M. Muchow, Systems Administrator

* Succeeded Ms. Rechtschaffen as Minority Staff Director on May 1, 2006.

Note to Readers

Fellow Citizens:

In the late summer of 2005, millions of us watched the satellite images of Hurricane Katrina as it moved through the Gulf of Mexico and drove menacing swells of water toward the American coastline.

We watched in sympathy as hundreds of thousands of lives were upended when the hurricane struck the coasts of Louisiana, Mississippi, and Alabama. We watched in horror as hundreds died in collapsed or flooded houses and nursing homes.

We were heartened by acts of initiative, perseverance, and heroism by local responders and the U.S. Coast Guard but, to add bewilderment and outrage to our sense of tragedy, we were horrified when the response to the Katrina catastrophe revealed – all too often, and for far too long – confusion, delay, misdirection, inactivity, poor coordination, and lack of leadership at all levels of government.

Meanwhile, thousands languished in heat and squalor on islands of concrete highway, in darkened stadiums, in nursing homes, or on rooftops, waiting for rescue, sometimes dying before help arrived.

All of this unfolded nearly four years after the terror attacks of September 11, 2001; after a massive reorganization of federal plans and organizations for disaster response and billions of dollars of expenditures; and after a closely observed hurricane struck when and where forecasters said it would.

We knew Katrina was coming. How much worse would the nightmare have been if the disaster had been unannounced – an earthquake in San Francisco, a burst levee near St. Louis or Sacramento, a biological weapon smuggled into Boston Harbor, or a chemical-weapon terror attack in Chicago?

Hurricane Katrina found us – still – a nation unprepared for catastrophe.

The United States Senate Committee on Homeland Security and Governmental Affairs has prepared this bipartisan report to acknowledge what was done well, to identify what was done poorly or not at all, and to recommend changes in our national system for emergency response that will put local, state, federal, and private responders in a better position to provide prompt and effective relief when disaster strikes again. The Committee conducted a long and thorough investigation of these issues, and is grateful for the work of its staff of investigators, writers, researchers, and other professionals that made this report possible.

We hope you find it informative and, above all, useful.

Senator Susan M. Collins   Senator Joseph I. Lieberman
Maine, Chairman   Connecticut, Ranking Member

Hurricane Katrina: A Nation Still Unprepared

Contents   Page

Results

Appendices

Hurricane Katrina: A Nation Still Unprepared

Executive Summary

Executive Summary

Hurricane Katrina was an extraordinary act of nature that spawned a human tragedy. It was the most destructive natural disaster in American history, laying waste to 90,000 square miles of land, an area the size of the United Kingdom. In Mississippi, the storm surge obliterated coastal communities and left thousands destitute. New Orleans was overwhelmed by flooding. All told, more than 1,500 people died. Along the Gulf Coast, tens of thousands suffered without basic essentials for almost a week.

But the suffering that continued in the days and weeks after the storm passed did not happen in a vacuum; instead, it continued longer than it should have because of – and was in some cases exacerbated by – the failure of government at all levels to plan, prepare for, and and respond aggressively to the storm. These failures were not just conspicuous; they were pervasive. Among the many factors that contributed to these failures, the Committee found that there were four overarching ones:

Hurricane Katrina over the Gulf Coast, August 2005

NOAA photo

1. Long-term warnings went unheeded and government officials neglected their duties to prepare for a forewarned catastrophe;

2. Government officials took insufficient actions or made poor decisions in the days immediately before and after landfall;

3. Systems on which officials relied on to support their response efforts failed; and

4. Government officials at all levels failed to provide effective leadership.

These individual failures, moreover, occurred against a backdrop of failure, over time, to develop the capacity for a coordinated, national response to a truly catastrophic event, whether caused by nature or man-made.

The results were tragic loss of life and human suffering on a massive scale, and an undermining of confidence in our governments' ability to plan, prepare for, and respond to national catastrophes.

Effective response to mass emergencies is a critical role of every level of government. It is a role that requires an unusual level of planning, coordination, and dispatch among governments' diverse units. Following the terrorist attacks of September 11, 2001, this country went through one of the most sweeping reorganizations of the federal government in history. While driven primarily by concerns of terrorism, the reorganization was designed to strengthen our nation's ability to address the consequences of both natural and man-made disasters. In its first major test, this reorganized system failed. Katrina revealed that much remains to be done.

The Committee began this investigation of the preparations for and response to Hurricane Katrina within two weeks of the hurricane's landfall on the Gulf Coast. The tragic loss of life and human suffering in Katrina's wake would have been sufficient in themselves to compel the Committee's attention. But the conspicuous failures in governments' emergency preparedness and response added a sense of urgency to the investigation – not only because of our heightened national awareness of the dangers of both terrorist acts and natural disasters, but because so much effort had been directed towards improvement.

The Committee's investigation has been bipartisan, and has examined in detail the actions of officials of local, state, and federal government departments and agencies. Though suffering was pervasive across the Gulf Coast, the Committee focused most of its efforts on the response in New Orleans, where massive flooding presented extraordinary challenges to responders and victims alike. In addition, the investigation centered largely on the initial response to the hurricane in the critical week or so after the storm hit. We have conducted formal interviews of more than 325 witnesses, reviewed over 838,000 pages of documentation, and conducted 22 public hearings with 85 witnesses in the course of our information gathering efforts.

Most of the hearings focused on what went wrong in Katrina. Two of the hearings, however, examined the successes: the effective and heroic search-and-rescue efforts by the U.S. Coast Guard; and the outstanding performance of certain members of the private sector in restoring essential services to the devastated communities and providing relief to the victims.

These successes shared some important traits. The Coast Guard and certain private-sector businesses both conducted extensive planning and training for disasters, and they put that preparation into use when disaster struck. Both moved material assets and personnel out of harm's way as the storm approached, but kept them close enough to the front lines for quick response after it passed. Perhaps most important, both had empowered front-line leaders who were able to make decisions when they needed to be made.

The Roles of the Different Levels of Government in Disaster Response

Assessing the government's response to Katrina requires, at the outset, an understanding of the roles of government entities and their leaders and the framework within which they operate. Every level of government, and many components within each level, play important roles. At every level of government, the chief executive has the ultimate responsibility to manage an emergency response.

It has long been standard practice that emergency response begins at the lowest possible jurisdictional level – typically the local government, with state government becoming involved at the local government's request when the resources of local government are (or are expected to be) overwhelmed. Similarly, while the federal government provides ongoing financial support to state and local governments for emergency preparedness, ordinarily it becomes involved in responding to a disaster at a state's request when resources of state and local governments are (or are expected to be) overwhelmed. Louisiana's Emergency Operations Plan explicitly lays out this hierarchy of response.

During a catastrophe, which by definition almost immediately exceeds state and local resources and significantly disrupts governmental operations and emergency services, the role of the federal government is particularly vital, and it would reasonably be expected to play a more substantial role in response than it would in an "ordinary" disaster.

Long-Term and Short-Term Warnings Went Unheeded

The Committee has worked to identify and understand the sources of the government's inadequate response and recovery efforts. And while this Report does not purport to have identified every such source, it is clear that there was no lack of information about the dev-astating potential of Katrina, or the uncertain strength of the levees and floodwalls protect-ing New Orleans, or the likely needs of survivors. Nonetheless, top officials at every level of government – despite strongly worded advisories from the National Hurricane Center (NHC) and personal warnings from NHC Director Max Mayfield – did not appear to truly grasp the magnitude of the storm's potential for destruction before it made landfall.

The potentially devastating threat of a catastrophic hurricane to the Gulf Coast has been known for 40 years: New Orleans experienced flooding in some areas of remarkably similar proportions from Hurricane Betsy in 1965, and Hurricane Camille devastated the Gulf Coast in 1969. More recently, numerous experts and governmental officials had been an-ticipating an increase in violent hurricanes, and New Orleans' special and growing vulner-ability to catastrophic flooding due to changing geological and other conditions was widely described in both technical and popular media.

Hurricane Georges hit the Gulf Coast in 1998, spurring the State of Louisiana to ask Federal Emergency Management Agency (FEMA) for assistance with catastrophic hurricane plan-ning. Little was accomplished for the next six years. Between 2000 and 2003, state authori-

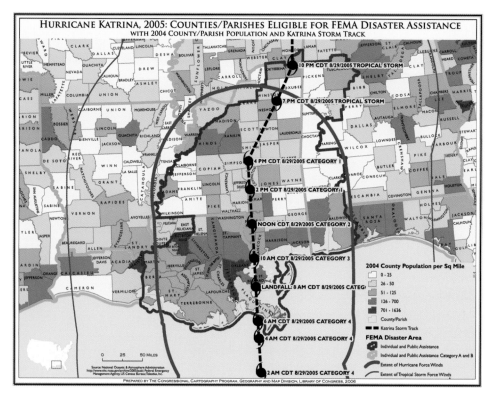

Katrina's track of disaster

Geography and Map Division,
The Library of Congress

ties, an emergency-preparedness contractor, and FEMA's own regional staff repeatedly advised FEMA headquarters in Washing-ton that planning for evacuation and shelter for the "New Orleans scenario" was incomplete and inadequate, but FEMA failed to approach other federal agencies for help with transportation and shelter or to ensure that the city and state had the matters in hand.

Then, in 2004, after a White House aide received a briefing on the catastrophic consequences of a Category 3 hurricane hitting New Orleans, the federal gov-ernment sponsored a planning exercise, with participation from federal, state, and local officials, based on a scenario whose char-acteristics foreshadowed most of Katrina's impacts. While this hy-pothetical "Hurricane Pam" exercise resulted in draft plans beginning in early 2005, they were incomplete when Katrina hit. Nonetheless, some officials took the initiative to use concepts developed in the drafts, with mixed success, in the critical aspects of the Katrina response. However, many of its admonitory lessons were either ignored or inadequately applied.

During the Hurricane Pam exercise, officials determined that massive flooding from a cata-strophic storm in New Orleans could threaten the lives of 60,000 people and trap hundreds of thousands more, while incapacitating local resources for weeks to months. The Pam exercise gave all levels of government a reminder that the "New Orleans scenario" required more forethought, preparation, and investment than a "typical" storm. Also, it reinforced the importance of coordination both within and among federal, state, and local governments for an effective response.

The specific danger that Katrina posed to the Gulf Coast became clear on the afternoon of Friday, August 26, when forecasters at NHC and the National Weather Service (NWS) saw that the storm was turning west. First in phone calls to Louisiana emergency-management officials and then in their 5 p.m. ET Katrina forecast and accompanying briefings, they alerted both Louisiana and Mississippi that the track of the storm was now expected to shift significantly to the west of its original track toward the Florida panhandle. NHC warned that Katrina could be a Category 4 or even a Category 5 by landfall. By the next morning, NWS officials directly confirmed to the Governor of Louisiana and other state and local officials that New Orleans was squarely at risk.

Over the weekend, there was a drumbeat of warnings: FEMA held video-teleconferences on both days, where the danger of Katrina and the particular risks to New Orleans were discussed; NHC's Max Mayfield called the governors of the affected states, something he had only done once before in his 33-year career; President Bush took the unusual step of declaring, in advance, an emergency for the states in the impact zone; numerous media reports noted that New Orleans was a "bowl," and could be left submerged by the storm; the Department of Homeland Security's Simulation and Analysis group generated a report stating that the levees protecting New Orleans were at risk of breaching and overtopping; and internal FEMA slides stated that the projected impacts of Katrina could be worse than those in the Hurricane Pam exercise. The warnings were as widespread as they were dire.

Preparation Proved Insufficient

Katrina was not a "typical" hurricane as it approached landfall; it was much larger, more powerful, and was capable of producing catastrophic damage.

In some respects, officials did prepare for Katrina with the understanding that it could be a catastrophe. Some coastal towns in Mississippi went to extraordinary lengths to get citizens to evacuate, including sending people door-to-door to convince and cajole people to move out of harm's way. The State of Louisiana activated more than twice the number of National Guard troops called to duty in any prior hurricane, and achieved the largest evacuation of a threatened population ever to occur. The City of New Orleans issued its first ever mandatory evacuation order. The Coast Guard readied its personnel, pre-positioned its equipment, and stood by to begin search-and-rescue operations as quickly as humanly possible. Departing from usual practice, the governors of the three affected states requested, and President Bush issued, emergency declarations before the storm made landfall.

But however vigorous these preparations, ineffective leadership, poor advance planning, and an unwillingness to devote sufficient resources to emergency management over the long term doomed them to fail when Katrina struck. Despite the understanding of the Gulf Coast's particular vulnerability to hurricane devastation, officials braced for Katrina with full awareness of critical deficiencies in their plans and gaping holes in their resources. While Katrina's destructive force could not be denied, state and local officials did not marshal enough of the resources at their disposal.

In addition, years of short-changing federal, state, and local emergency functions left them incapable of fully carrying out their missions to protect the public and care for victims. For example, the lack of survivable, interoperable communications, which Governor Haley Barbour of Mississippi said was the most critical problem in his state, occurred because of an accumulation of decisions by federal, state, and local officials that left this long-standing problem unsolved.

The Committee believes that leadership failures needlessly compounded these losses. New Orleans Mayor Ray Nagin and Louisiana Governor Kathleen Blanco – who knew the limitations of their resources to address a catastrophe – did not specify those needs adequately to the federal government before landfall. For example, while Governor Blanco stated in a letter to President Bush, two days before landfall, that she anticipated the resources of the state would be overwhelmed, she made no specific request for assistance in evacuating the known tens of thousands of people without means of transportation, and a senior State official identified no unmet needs in response to a federal offer of assistance the following day. The State's transportation secretary also ignored his responsibilities under the state's emergency operations plan, leaving no arm of the State government prepared to obtain and deliver additional transportation to those in New Orleans who lacked it when Katrina struck. In view of the long-standing role of requests as a trigger for action by higher levels of government, the State bears responsibility for not signaling its needs to the federal government more clearly.

Compounded by leadership failures of its own, the federal government bears responsibility for not preparing effectively for its role in the post-storm response.

FEMA was unprepared for a catastrophic event of the scale of Katrina. Well before Katrina, FEMA's relationships with state and local officials, once a strength, had been eroded in part because certain preparedness grant programs were transferred elsewhere in the Department of Homeland Security (DHS). With its importance to state and local preparedness activities reduced, FEMA's effectiveness was diminished. In addition, at no time in its history, including in the years before it became part of DHS, had FEMA developed – nor had it been designed to develop – response capabilities sufficient for a catastrophe, nor had it developed the capacity to mobilize sufficient resources from other federal agencies, and the private and nonprofit sectors.

Moreover, FEMA's former Director, Michael Brown, lacked the leadership skills that were needed. Before landfall, Brown did not direct the adequate pre-positioning of critical personnel and equipment, and willfully failed to communicate with DHS Secretary, Michael Chertoff, to whom he was supposed to report. Earlier in the hurricane season, FEMA had pre-positioned an unprecedented amount of relief supplies in the region. But the supplies were not enough. Similarly, while both FEMA and the Department of Health and Human Services (HHS) made efforts to activate the federal emergency health capabilities of the National Disaster Medical System (NDMS) and the U.S. Public Health Service (PHS), only a limited number of federal medical teams were actually in position prior to landfall to deploy into the affected area. Only one such team was in a position to provide immediate medical care in the aftermath of the storm.

More broadly, DHS – as the Department charged with preparing for and responding to domestic incidents, whether terrorist attacks or natural disasters – failed to effectively lead the federal response to Hurricane Katrina. DHS leadership failed to bring a sense of urgency to the federal government's preparation for Hurricane Katrina, and Secretary Chertoff himself should have been more engaged in preparations over the weekend before landfall. Secretary Chertoff made only top-level inquiries into the state of preparations, and accepted uncritically the reassurances he received. He did not appear to reach out to the other Cabinet secretaries to make sure that they were readying their departments to provide whatever assistance DHS – and the people of the Gulf Coast – might need.

Similarly, had he invoked the Catastrophic Incident Annex of the National Response Plan (NRP-CIA), Secretary Chertoff could have helped remove uncertainty about the federal government's need and authority to take initiative before landfall and signaled that all federal government agencies were expected to think – and act – proactively in preparing for and responding to Katrina. The Secretary's activation of the NRP-CIA could have increased the urgency of the federal response and led the federal government to respond more pro-actively rather than waiting for formal requests from overwhelmed state and local officials.

Because delay may preclude meaningful assistance and state and local resources may be quickly overwhelmed and incapacitated, the NRP-CIA directs federal agencies to pre-position resources without awaiting requests from the state and local governments. Even then, except in certain prescribed circum-stances, the NRP-CIA holds these resources at mobilization sites until requested by state and local officials.

The military also had a role to play, and ulti-mately, the National Guard and active-duty military troops and assets deployed during Katrina constituted the largest domestic deployment of military forces since the Civil War. And while the Department of Defense (DOD) took additional steps to prepare for Katrina beyond those it had taken for prior civil-support missions, its preparations were not sufficient for a storm of Katrina's mag-nitude. Individual commanders took actions that later helped improve the response, but these actions were not coordinated by the Department. The Department's preparations were consistent with how DOD interpreted its role under the NRP, which was to provide support in response to requests for assistance from FEMA. However, additional preparations in advance of specific requests for support could have enabled a more rapid response.

Waiting for help, New Orleans

In addition, the White House shares responsibility for the inadequate pre-landfall prepara-tions. To be sure, President Bush, at the request of Brown, did take the initiative to person-ally call Governor Blanco to urge a mandatory evacuation. As noted earlier, he also took the unusual step of declaring an emergency in the Gulf Coast States prior to Katrina's landfall. On the other hand, the President did not leave his Texas ranch to return to Washington until two days after landfall, and only then convened his Cabinet, as well as a White House task force, to oversee federal response efforts.

Response at all Levels of Government Was Unacceptable

The effect of the long-term failures at every level of government to plan and prepare ad-equately for a catastrophic hurricane in the Gulf of Mexico was evident in the inadequate preparations before Katrina's landfall and then again in the initial response to the storm.

Search and Rescue

Flooding in New Orleans drove thousands of survivors to attics and rooftops to await rescue. Some people were trapped in attics and nursing homes and drowned as the dirty waters rose around them. Others escaped only by chopping their way through roofs. Infrastructure damage complicated the organization and conduct of search-and-rescue missions in New Orleans and elsewhere. Destruction of communications towers and equipment, in particular, limited the ability of crews to communicate with one another, undermining coordination and efficiency. Rescuers also had to contend with weapons fire, debris, and polluted water. The skill and dedication of Louisiana Department of Wildlife and Fisheries (W&F) officials and others working in these adverse conditions stand out as a singular success story of the hurricane response.

Applying a model developed in the Hurricane Pam exercise, rescue teams in Louisiana brought hurricane victims to high ground, where they were supposed to receive food, water, medical attention, and transport to shelters. Here, too, there were problems. Poor communications delayed state and federal officials' learning about where rescuees had been dropped, in turn slowing shipments of food and water to those areas. The City of New Orleans was unprepared to help people evacuate, as many buses from the city's own fleet were submerged, while officials had not arranged in advance for drivers for those buses that were available.

The storm also laid waste to much of the city's police, whose headquarters and several district offices, along with hundreds of vehicles, rounds of ammunition, and uniforms were all destroyed within the first two days of landfall.

Planning for search and rescue was also insufficient. FEMA, for instance, failed to provide boats for its search-and-rescue teams even though flooding had been confirmed by Tuesday. Moreover, interagency coordination was inadequate at both the state and federal levels. While the Louisiana W&F and FEMA are responsible for interagency search-and-rescue coordination at the state and federal levels, respectively, neither developed adequate plans for this mission. Staggeringly, the City of New Orleans Fire Department (NOFD) owned no boats, and the New Orleans Police Department (NOPD) owned five. Meanwhile, widespread communications failures in Louisiana and Mississippi were so bad that many officers reverted to either physically running messages from one person to another, or passing messages along a daisy chain of officers using radios with limited range.

Situational Awareness

While authorities recognized the need to begin search-and-rescue missions even before the hurricane winds fully subsided, other aspects of the response were hindered by a failure to quickly recognize the dimensions of the disaster. These problems were particularly acute at the federal level. The Homeland Security Operations Center (HSOC) – charged with providing reliable information to decision makers including the Secretary of DHS and the President – failed to create a system to identify and acquire all available, relevant information, and as a result situational awareness was deeply flawed.

With local and state resources immediately overwhelmed, rapid federal mobilization of resources was critical. Yet reliable information on such vital developments as the levee failures, the extent of flooding, and the presence of thousands of people in need of life-sustaining assistance at the New Orleans Convention Center did not reach the White House, Secretary Chertoff, or other key officials for hours, and in some cases more than a day. Brown, then in Louisiana, contributed to the problem by refusing to communicate with Secretary Chertoff, opting instead to pass information directly to White House staff. Moreover, even though senior DHS officials did receive, on the day of landfall, numerous reports that should have led to an understanding of the increasingly dire situation in New Orleans, many indicated they were not aware of the crisis until sometime Tuesday morning.

DHS was slow to recognize the scope of the disaster or that FEMA had become overwhelmed. On the day after landfall, DHS officials were still struggling to determine the "ground truth" about the extent of the flooding despite the many reports they had received about the catastrophe; key officials did not grasp the need to act on the less-than-complete information that is to be expected in a disaster. DHS leaders did not become fully engaged in recovery efforts until Thursday, when in Deputy Secretary Michael Jackson's words, they "tried to kick it up a notch"; after that, they did provide significant leadership within DHS (and FEMA) as well as coordination across the federal government. But this effort should have begun sooner.

DOD also was slow to acquire information regarding the extent of the storm's devastation. DOD officials relied primarily on media reports for their information. Many senior DOD officials did not learn that the levees had breached until Tuesday; some did not learn until Wednesday. As DOD waited for DHS to provide information about the scope of the damage, it also waited for the lead federal agency, FEMA, to identify the support needed from DOD. The lack of situational awareness during this phase appears to have been a major reason for DOD's belated adoption of the forward-looking posture necessary in a catastrophic incident.

Post-Storm Evacuation

Overwhelmed by Katrina, the city and state turned to FEMA for help. On Monday, Governor Blanco asked Brown for buses, and Brown assured the state the same day that 500 buses were en route to assist in the evacuation of New Orleans and would arrive within hours. In spite of Brown's assurances and the state's continued requests over the course of the next two days, FEMA did not direct the U.S. Department of Transportation to send buses until very early on Wednesday, two days after landfall. The buses did not begin to arrive until Wednesday evening, and not in significant numbers until Thursday. Concerned over FEMA's delay in providing buses – and handicapped by the Louisiana Department of Transportation and Development's utter failure to make any preparation to carry out its lead role for evacuation under the state's emergency plan – Governor Blanco directed members of her office to begin locating buses on Tuesday and approved an effort to commandeer school buses for evacuation on Wednesday. But these efforts were too little, too late. Tens of thousands of people were forced to wait in unspeakably horrible conditions until as late as Saturday to be evacuated.

Logistics and Military Support

Problems with obtaining, communicating, and managing information plagued many other aspects of the response as well. FEMA lacked the tools to track the status of shipments, interfering with the management of supplying food, water, ice, and other vital commodities to those in need across the Gulf Coast. So, too, did the incompatibility of the electronic systems used by federal and state authorities to manage requests for assistance, which made it necessary to transfer requests from the state system to the federal system manually.

Supplies of commodities were especially problematic. Federal shipments to Mississippi did not reach adequate levels until 10 days after landfall. The reasons for this are unclear, but FEMA's inadequate "surge capacity" – the ability to quickly ramp up the volume of shipments – is a likely cause. In both Mississippi and Louisiana, there were additional problems in getting the supplies the "last mile" to individuals in need. Both states planned to make supplies available for pickup at designated distribution points, but neither anticipated the problems people would face in reaching those points, due to impassable roads or other issues. And in Louisiana, the National Guard was not equipped to assume this task. One of

Louisiana's greatest shortages was portable toilets, which were requested for the Superdome but never arrived there, as more than 20,000 people were forced to stay in the Superdome without working plumbing for nearly a week.

For their part, Louisiana and Mississippi relied heavily on support from other states to supplement their own emergency resources. Both states were parties to an interstate agreement known as the Emergency Management Assistance Compact (EMAC), which provides a system for sharing National Guard troops and other resources in natural disasters. As in many other areas of the Katrina response, however, the magnitude of the demands strained the EMAC process and revealed limitations in the system. Paperwork burdens proved overwhelming. Louisiana experienced difficulties processing the volume of incoming resources. On Wednesday, August 31, the federal National Guard Bureau, which ordinarily serves a coordinating function within DOD, relieved Louisiana and Mississippi of many of the bureaucratic responsibilities by making direct requests for available troops to state adjutants general.

This process quickly resulted in the largest National Guard deployment in U.S. history, with 50,000 troops and supporting equipment arriving from 49 states and four territories within two weeks. These forces participated in every aspect of emergency response, from medical care to law enforcement and debris removal, and were considered invaluable by Louisiana and Mississippi officials.

Although this process successfully deployed a large number of National Guard troops, it did not proceed efficiently, or according to any pre-existing plan or process. There is, in fact, no established process for the large-scale, nation-wide deployment of National Guard troops for civil support. In addition, the deployments of National Guard troops were not coordinated with the federal Northern Command, which was overseeing the large-scale deployments and operations of the active-duty military (i.e., Regular and activated Reserve forces).

While the NRP has specific procedures for active-duty involvement in natural disasters, the deployment of these troops raised unforeseen issues and was initially a source of frustration to Governor Blanco. The Governor directed her adjutant general to secure additional troops on the day after landfall, but federal and state officials did not coordinate her requests well, and ground troops didn't arrive in significant numbers for several days. DOD chose to rely primarily on the deployment of National Guard troops (versus federal active-duty troops) pursuant to its declared strategy and because it believed they were best suited to the required tasks, including performing law enforcement. In addition, the need to resolve command issues between National Guard and active-duty forces – an issue taken up (but not resolved) in a face-to-face meeting between President Bush and the Governor on Air Force One on the Friday after landfall – may have played a role in the timing of active-duty troop deployments. The issue became moot as the two forces stayed under their separate commands, an arrangement that turned out to work well in this case, thanks to the cooperation of the respective commanders.

While the large numbers of active-duty troops did not arrive until the end of the first week following landfall, National Guard troops did, and DOD contributed in other important ways during that period. Early in the week, DOD ordered its military commanders to push available assets to the Gulf Coast. They also streamlined their ordinarily bureaucratic processes for handling FEMA requests for assistance and emphasized movement based on vocal commands with the paperwork to follow, though some FEMA officials believe that DOD's approval process continued to take too long. They provided significant support to search-and-rescue missions, evacuee airlifts, logistics management of buses arriving in the state for evacuation, and other matters.

Toward the end of the week, with its own resources stretched thin, FEMA turned to DOD to take over logistics for all commodity movements. DOD acceded to the request, and provided some logistics assistance to FEMA. However, it did not undertake the complete logistical take-over initially requested by FEMA because that was not needed.

By Tuesday afternoon, the New Orleans Superdome had become overcrowded, leading officials to turn additional refugees away. Mayor Nagin then decided to open the Morial Convention Center as a second refuge of last resort inside the city, but did not supply it with food or water. Moreover, he communicated his decision to open the Convention Center to state and federal officials poorly, if at all. That failure, in addition to the delay of shipments due to security concerns and DHS's own independent lack of awareness of the situation, contributed to the paucity of food, water, security, and medical care at the Convention Center, as a population of approximately 19,000 gathered there. Those vital commodities and services did not arrive until Friday, when the Louisiana National Guard, assisted by National Guard units from five other states, brought in relief supplies provided by FEMA, established law and order, and then evacuated the Convention Center on Saturday within eight hours.

Law Enforcement

Law enforcement outside the Superdome and the Convention Center was a problem, and was fueled by several contributing factors, including erroneous statements by top city officials that inflamed the public's perception of lawlessness in New Orleans.

Without effective law enforcement, real or imagined safety threats interrupted virtually every aspect of the response. Fearing for their personal safety, medical and search-and-rescue teams withdrew from their missions. FEMA and commercial vendors of critical supplies often refused to make deliveries until military escorts could be arranged. In fact, there was some lawlessness, yet for every actual act there were rumors of dozens more, leading to widespread and inaccurate reporting that severely complicated a desperate situation. Unfortunately, local, state, and federal officials did little to stanch this rumor flow. Police presence on the streets was inadequate, in part because in a matter of hours Katrina turned the NOPD from protectors of the public to victims of the storm. Nonetheless, most New Orleans police officers appear to have reported for duty, many setting aside fears about the safety of their families or the status of their homes.

Even so, the ability of the officers who remained to perform their duties was significantly hampered by the lack of basic supplies. While supplies such as weapons and ammunition were lost to flooding, the NOPD leadership did not provide its officers with basic necessities such as food; nor did the department have logistics in place to handle supplies. Members of the NOPD also identified the lack of a unified command for this incident as a major problem; eight members of the command staff were extremely critical of the lack of leadership from the City's Office of Emergency Preparedness (OEP). The department's rank and file were unfamiliar with both the department's and the city's emergency-operations manuals and other hurricane emergency procedures. Deficiencies in the NOPD's manual, lack of training on this manual, lack of familiarity with it, or a combination of the three resulted in inadequate protection of department resources.

Federal law-enforcement assistance was too slow in coming, in large part because the two federal departments charged under the NRP with providing such assistance – DHS and the Department of Justice (DOJ) – had done almost no pre-storm planning. In fact, they failed to determine even well into the post-landfall period which of the two departments would assume the lead for federal law enforcement under the NRP. As a result, later in the week, as federal law-enforcement officers did arrive, some were distracted by a pointless "turf war" between DHS and DOJ over which agency was in the lead. In the end, federal assistance was crucial, but should have arrived much sooner.

Health Care

Safety concerns were only one of numerous challenges faced by health-care providers. There were numerous other challenges, including the following:

• Medical teams had to triage more than 70,000 rescuees and evacuees and provide acute care to the sick and wounded. While officials used plans developed in the Hurricane Pam exercise as a helpful framework for managing this process, existing emergency-room facilities were overwhelmed by the volume of patients. Local and state officials quickly set up temporary field hospitals at a sports arena and a K-Mart in Baton Rouge to supplement hospital capacity.

• New Orleans had a large population of "special-needs patients," individuals living at home who required ongoing medical assistance. Before Katrina struck, the City Health Department activated a plan to establish a care facility for this population within the Superdome and provided transportation to evacuate several hundred patients and their caregivers to Baton Rouge. While Superdome facilities proved useful in treating special-needs patients who remained behind, they had to contend with shortages of supplies, physical damage to the facility necessitating a post-landfall relocation of patients and equipment to an area adjacent to the Superdome, and a population of more than 20,000 people using the Superdome as a refuge of last resort. Also, FEMA's Disaster Medical Assistance Teams (DMATs) which provide the invaluable resources of pharmacies and hospital equipment, arrived at the Superdome on the night following landfall, but left temporarily on Thursday, before the evacuation of the Superdome's special-needs population was completed, because of security concerns.

• In Louisiana, hospitals had to evacuate after landfall on short notice, principally due to loss of electrical power. While hospitals had evacuated some of their patients before landfall, they had retained others thought to be too frail for transport, and believed that by staying open they would be available to serve hurricane victims. Their strategy became untenable after landfall when power was lost, and their backup generators were rendered inoperable by flooding and fuel shortages. The Louisiana Department of Health and Hospitals (DHH) stepped in to arrange for their evacuation; while successful, it had to compete with search-and-rescue teams for helicopters and other needed resources.

• Many nursing homes in and around New Orleans lacked adequate evacuation plans. Although they were required to have plans on file with local government, there was no process to ensure that there were sufficient resources to evacuate all the nursing homes at once, and dozens of patients who were not evacuated died. When evacuation became necessary, some sent their patients to the Superdome, where officials, struggling to handle the volume of patients already there, were obliged to accept still more.

Long-Term Factors Contributed to the Poor Response

Actions taken – and failures to act – well before Katrina struck compounded the problems resulting from the ineffective leadership that characterized the immediate preparations for the hurricane and the post-landfall response. A common theme of these earlier actions is underfunding emergency preparedness. While the Committee did not examine the conflicting political or budget priorities that may have played a role, in many cases the short-sightedness associated with the underfunding is glaring. Among notable examples are the following:

• The Louisiana Office of Homeland Security and Emergency Preparedness (LOHSEP), the state counterpart to FEMA, suffered chronic staffing problems and employee turnover due to underfunding. LOHSEP's planning chief also testified that lack of resources prevented the agency from meeting its schedule for periodic review and updates of state emergency plans.

• The Office of Emergency Preparedness for New Orleans, a city long known to be among the nation's most vulnerable to a catastrophic hurricane, had a staff of only three. Its police and fire departments, responsible for search-and-rescue activities, had five boats and no boats, respectively. In 2004, the city turned down a request by the NOFD to fund the purchase of six additional boats.

• The Hurricane Pam exercise faced repeated delays due to funding constraints. It took nearly five years for the federal government to approve the state's initial funding request, and the limited funding finally granted necessitated last-minute cutbacks in the scope of the exercise. Follow-up workshops were delayed by funding shortfalls – some as small as the $15,000 needed for participants' travel expenses – that either the state or federal government should have remedied.

• Numerous witnesses testified that FEMA's budget was far short of what was needed to accomplish its mission, and that this contributed to FEMA's failure to be prepared for a catastrophe. FEMA witnesses also universally pointed out that the agency has suffered for the last few years from a vacancy rate of 15 to 20 percent (i.e., between 375 to 500 vacant positions in a 2,500-person agency), including several at key supervisory levels. FEMA sought additional funding but did not receive it. The Committee found that FEMA's budget shortages hindered its preparedness.

The Committee also found that inadequate training in the details of the recently promulgated NRP was a contributing factor in shortcomings in the government's performance. Louisiana emergency-management officials and National Guardsmen were receiving basic NRP and Incident Command System (ICS) training two days after the storm hit. Certain FEMA officials, also, were inadequately trained on the NRP and ICS. Only one large-scale federal exercise of the NRP took place before Katrina, the DHS's Top Officials 3 (TOPOFF 3) exercise in April 2005, approximately three months after the NRP was issued. TOPOFF 3, sponsored by DHS, involved responders from all levels of government. A November 2005 report by the DHS Inspector General, echoing the findings of an earlier report by DHS itself in May 2005, found that the exercise, which involved federal, state and local responders, "highlighted – at all levels of government – a fundamental lack of understanding for the principles and protocols set forth in the NRP and [National Incident Management System]." The lack of familiarity with emergency-management principles and plans hampered the Katrina response.

The Committee also identified significant planning failures that predated Katrina. One of the most remarkable stories from this investigation is the history of planning for the 100,000 people in New Orleans believed to lack the means to evacuate themselves. Local and state officials have known since at least 1994 about the need to address this problem. For its part, the federal government, which knew about this problem for some time, neither monitored their planning nor offered assistance. This evacuation problem was not included in the Hurricane Pam exercise and, during follow-up meetings in the summer of 2005, New Orleans officials informed counterparts from FEMA, other federal agencies, and the state preparedness agency that the city was not able to provide for the necessary pre-storm evacuation, but nothing was done to resolve the issue.

• The City of New Orleans, with primary responsibility for evacuation of its citizens, had language in its plan stating the city's intent to assist those who needed transportation for pre-storm evacuation, but had no actual plan provisions to implement that intent. In late 2004 and 2005, city officials negotiated contracts with Amtrak, riverboat owners, and others to pre-arrange transportation alternatives, but received inadequate support from the City's Director of Homeland Security and Emergency Preparedness, and contracts were not in place when Katrina struck. As Katrina approached, notwithstanding the city's evacuation plans on paper, the best solution New Orleans had for people without transportation was a private-citizen volunteer carpool initiative called Operation Brothers' Keepers and transit buses taking people – not out of the city, but to the Superdome. While the Superdome provided shelter from the devastating winds and water, conditions there deteriorated quickly. Katrina's "near miss" ripped the covering off the roof, caused leaking, and knocked out the power, rendering the plumbing, air conditioning, and public announcement system totally useless.

Trapped by floodwaters, New Orleans

AP/Wide World Photo

• The Louisiana Department of Transportation and Development (DOTD), whose Secretary had personally accepted departmental responsibility under the state's emergency operations plan to arrange for transportation for evacuation in emergencies, had done nothing to prepare for that responsibility prior to Katrina. While the Secretary attempted to defend his inaction in a personal appearance before the Committee, the Committee found his explanations rang hollow, and his account of uncommunicated doubts and objections to state policy disturbing. Had his Department identified available buses or other means of transport for evacuation within the state in the months before the hurricane, at a minimum the state would have been prepared to evacuate people stranded in New Orleans after landfall more quickly than it did.

• FEMA and the U.S. Department of Transportation (DOT), charged under the NRP with supporting state and local government transportation needs (including evacuation) in emergencies, did little to plan for the possibility that they would be called on to assist with post-landfall evacuation needs, despite being on notice for over a month before Katrina hit that the state and local governments needed more buses and drivers – and being on notice for years that tens of thousands of people would have no means to evacuate.

• Though much attention had been paid to addressing communications shortfalls, efforts to address interoperability – as well as simply operability – were inadequate. There was little advance preparation for responders operating in an area with no power and where virtually all forms of pre-existing communications were destroyed. And while satellite phones were available to some, either they did not function properly or officials were not trained to use these relatively complex devices. Moreover, the National Communications System, the DHS agency primarily responsible under the NRP for providing communications support to first responders during disasters, had no plans to do so.

These planning failures would have been of far less consequence had the system of levees built to protect New Orleans from flooding stayed intact, as they had in most prior hurricanes. But they did not, and the resulting inundation was catastrophic. The levee failures themselves turned out to have roots long predating Katrina as well. While several engineering analyses continue, the Committee found deeply disturbing evidence of flaws in the design and construction of the levees. For instance, two major drainage canals – the 17th Street and London Avenue Canals – failed at their foundations, prior to their flood walls being met with the water heights for which they were designed to protect central New Orleans.

Moreover, the greater metropolitan New Orleans area was literally riddled with levee breaches caused by massive overtopping and scouring of levees that were not "armored," or properly designed, to guard against the cascading waters that would inevitably accompany a storm of the magnitude of Hurricane Katrina. The Committee also discovered that the inspection-and-maintenance regime in place to ensure that the levees, floodwalls, and other structures built to protect the residents of the greater New Orleans area was in no way commensurate with the risk posed to these persons and their property.

Equally troubling was the revelation of serious disagreement – still unresolved months after Katrina – among officials of several government entities over who had responsibility, and when, for key levee issues including emergency response and levee repair. Such conflicts prevented any meaningful emergency plans from being put in place and, at the time of Katrina, none of the relevant government agencies had a plan for responding to a levee breach. While the deadly waters continued to pour into the heart of the city after the hurricane had passed, the very government agencies that were supposed to work together to protect the city from such a catastrophe not only initially disagreed about whose responsibility it was to repair the levee breaches, but disagreed as to how the repairs should be conducted. Sadly, due to the lack of foresight and overall coordination prior to the storm, such conflicts existed as the waters of Lake Pontchartrain continued to fill central New Orleans.

Taking refuge on an Interstate island, Louisiana

FEMA

Waste, Fraud, and Abuse

Besides overwhelming many government emergency-response capabilities, Katrina severely affected the government's ability to properly track and verify its costs when it contracted for disaster relief goods and services. While the Committee did not specifically include this issue in its investigation, the Committee became aware of wasteful, and sometimes fraudulent and abusive spending practices, and held two hearings on the subject.

It takes money to prepare, respond, and recover from a disaster, and typically the bigger the disaster, the more money it takes. As of March 8, 2006, the federal government had committed $88 billion to the response, recovery, and rebuilding efforts. Unfortunately, not all of this money has been wisely spent. Precious taxpayer dollars have been lost due to waste, fraud, and abuse.

Among the problems that have come to the Committee's attention are FEMA's lack of financial controls, failures to ensure eligibility of individuals receiving disaster-related assistance, and poor contracting practices, including the use of no-bid contracts. A notable example of the resulting wastefulness was FEMA's purchase of 25,000 manufactured homes that are virtually useless because FEMA's own regulations prohibit their installation in a flood plain. In a similar vein, FEMA's lack of controls in dealing with hotels providing temporary housing for evacuees resulted in instances where hotels charged for empty rooms; individuals held multiple rooms; hotel rooms were used as storage units for personal goods; individuals stayed at resorts; and hotels charged rates as high as $400 per night.

Recommendations: A New National Emergency-Management System for the 21ST Century

The Committee's Report sets out seven core recommendations together with a series of supporting tactical recommendations, all designed to make the nation's emergency-preparedness and response system strong, agile, effective, and robust.

Hurricane Katrina exposed flaws in the structure of FEMA and DHS that are too substantial to mend. **Our first core recommendation is to abolish FEMA and replace it with a stronger, more capable structure, to be known as the National Preparedness and Response Authority (NPRA).** To take full advantage of the substantial range of resources DHS has at its disposal, NPRA will remain within DHS. Its Director would be assured of having sufficient access and clout by having the rank of Deputy Secretary, and having a direct line of communication to the President during catastrophes. The Director would also serve as the Advisor to the President for national emergency management, in a manner akin to the Chairman of the Joint Chiefs of Staff. To ensure capable and qualified leadership, senior NPRA officials would be selected from the ranks of professionals with experience in crisis management, in addition to substantial management and leadership experience, whether in the public, private, or non-profit sector.

Our second core recommendation is to endow the new organization with the full range of responsibilities that are core to preparing for and responding to disasters. These include the four central functions of comprehensive emergency management – mitigation, preparedness, response, and recovery – which need to be integrated. In addition, NPRA would adopt an "all-hazards plus" strategy for preparedness. In preparing our nation to respond to terrorist attacks and natural disasters, NPRA must focus on building those common capabilities – for example survivable, interoperable communications and evacuation plans – that are necessary regardless of the incident. At the same time, it must not neglect to build those unique capabilities – like mass decontamination in the case of a radiological attack or water search and rescue in the case of flooding – that will be needed for particular types of incidents. NPRA's mandate should also include overseeing protection of critical infrastructure, such as energy facilities and telecommunications systems, both to protect such infrastructure from harm and to ensure that such infrastructure is restored as quickly as possible after a natural disaster or terrorist attack.

Our third core recommendation is to enhance regional operations to provide better coordination between federal agencies and the states and establish regional strike teams. Regional offices should be adequately staffed, with representation from federal agencies outside DHS that are likely to be called on to respond to a significant disaster in the region. They should provide coordination and assist in planning, training, and exercising of emergency-preparedness and response activities; work with states to ensure that grant funds are spent most effectively; coordinate and develop inter-state agreements; enhance coordination with non-governmental organizations and the private sector; and provide personnel and assets, in the form of Strike Teams, to be the federal government's first line of response to a disaster.

The Strike Teams would consist of, at a minimum, a designated Federal Coordinating Officer (FCO); personnel trained in incident management, public affairs, relief and recovery, and communications support; a Defense Coordinating Officer (DCO); and liaisons to other federal agencies. These regional Strike Teams should coordinate their training and exercises with the state and local officials and the private sector entities they will support when disasters occur.

Our fourth core recommendation is to build a true, government-wide operations center to provide enhanced situational awareness and manage interagency coordination in a disaster. Currently, there is a multiplicity of interagency coordinating structures, with overlapping missions, that attempt to facilitate an integrated federal response. Three of these structures – the Homeland Security Operations Center (HSOC), the National Response Coordination Center (NRCC), and the Interagency Incident Management Group (IIMG) – should be consolidated into a single, integrated entity – a new National Operations Center (NOC). The NOC would include representatives of all relevant federal agencies, and should provide for one clearly defined, emergency-management line of communication from the states to the federal government, and from the federal government to the states. It would also include a strong analytic team capable of sorting through and assessing information and determining which pieces would become part of the common operating picture.

To improve its performance in future disasters, the NOC should establish clear protocols and procedures to ensure that reports are received and reviewed at appropriate levels and in a timely manner. When there is notice of a potential major disaster, the NOC should implement plans, including one for obtaining information from DOD, for obtaining post-disaster situational awareness, including identifying sources of information and data particular to the region in which the disaster may occur and, where appropriate, bringing in individuals with particular knowledge or expertise about that region.

Our fifth core recommendation is to renew and sustain commitments at all levels of government to the nation's emergency core management system. FEMA emergency-response teams have been reduced substantially in size, are inadequately equipped, and training for these teams has been all but eliminated. If the federal government is to improve its performance and be prepared to respond effectively to the next disaster, we must give NPRA – and the other federal agencies with central responsibilities under the NRP – the necessary resources to accomplish this. We must fund NPRA commensurate with the significance of its mission and ensure that those funds are well spent. To be full partners in the national preparedness effort, states, and localities will need additional resources as well.

The Administration and DHS must also ensure that federal leaders of all agencies with an emergency-support role understand their key responsibilities under the NRP and the resources they need to effectively carry out the comprehensive planning required, while also training and exercising on NIMS, NRP, and other operational plans. To fully integrate state and local officials into the system, there should be established an advisory council to NPRA made up of state and local officials and first responders. The advisory council should play an integral role in ensuring that the full range of activities of the new organization – including developing response plans, conducting training and exercises, formulating preparedness goals, effectively managing grants and other resources – are done in full consultation and coordination with, and take into account the needs and priorities of, states and localities.

DHS and the NPRA should more fully integrate the private and nonprofit sectors into their planning and preparedness initiatives. Among other things, they should designate specific individuals at the national and regional levels to work directly with private-sector organizations. Where appropriate, private-sector representatives should also be included in planning, training, and exercises.

Our sixth core recommendation is to strengthen the underpinning of the nation's response to disasters and catastrophes. Despite their shortcomings and imperfections, the NRP and National Incident Management System (NIMS), including the Emergency Support Function (ESF) structure currently represent the best approach available to respond to multi-agency, multi-jurisdictional emergencies. Federal, state, and local officials and other responders must commit to supporting the NRP and NIMS and working together to improve the performance of the national emergency management system. We must undertake further refinements of the NRP and NIMS, develop operational plans, and engage in training and exercises to ensure that everyone involved in disaster response understands them and is prepared to carry them out. In particular, the NRP should be strengthened to make the unity of effort concept very clear, so that everyone understands the concept and their roles in establishing unity, and there should be clarification of the importance of integrating agencies with ESF responsibilities into the ICS, rather than their operating in "stovepipes."

The roles and responsibilities of the Principal Federal Official (PFO) and FCO overlap, and were a source of confusion during Hurricane Katrina. The Stafford Act should be amended to clarify the roles and responsibilities of the FCO, and the NRP should be revised to eliminate the PFO position for Stafford Act-declared emergencies and disasters. It should also be amended to ensure that the Act addresses response to all disasters and catastrophes, whether natural or man-made.

Our seventh core recommendation is to improve the nation's capacity to respond to catastrophic events. DHS should ensure that the Catastrophic Incident Annex (CIA) is fully understood by the federal departments and agencies with responsibilities associated with it. The Catastrophic Incident Supplement (CIS) should be completed and published, and the supporting operational plans for departments and agencies with responsibilities under the CIA should be completed. These plans should be reviewed and coordinated with the states, and on a regional basis, to ensure they are understood, trained and exercised prior to an emergency.

DHS must also develop the national capabilities – especially surge capacity – it needs to respond to catastrophic disasters, ensuring it has sufficient full-time staff, response teams, contracting personnel, and adequately trained and sufficiently staffed reserve corps to ramp up capabilities, as needed. These capabilities must be scalable so that NPRA can draw on the appropriate resources from supporting ESF agencies to respond to a disaster irrespective of cause, size, or complexity.

Conclusion

The Committee's Report can do justice neither to the human suffering endured during and after Katrina nor to the dimensions of the response. As to the latter, we have identified many successes and many failures; no doubt there are others in both categories we have missed. The Committee shares the view expressed by President Bush shortly after Katrina that our nation can do better.

Avoiding past mistakes will not suffice. Our leadership and systems must be prepared for catastrophes we know will be unlike Katrina, whether due to natural causes or terrorism. The Committee hopes to help meet that goal through the recommendations in this Report, because almost exactly four years after 9/11, Katrina showed that the nation is still unprepared.

Ruins of apartment building,
Long Beach, MS
Denton Herring photo

Searchers above the flood,
New Orleans
Louisiana Army National Guard photo

Introduction

In the early morning of Monday, August 29, 2005, Hurricane Katrina came ashore in southern Louisiana, changing American history. Since September 11, 2001, when two American cities suffered devastating attacks, the United States had been working to better protect itself. Almost four years and billions of dollars later, Katrina destroyed an entire region, killing more than 1,500, leaving hundreds of thousands homeless, and ravaging one of America's most storied cities.

Katrina revealed that this country remains ill-prepared to respond to a catastrophe. More should have been done to prepare before the storm and to mitigate the suffering that followed: more to save lives; more to evacuate the most vulnerable citizens; more to move the victims to safety earlier; more to get aid to affected areas sooner.

Before the storm, government planning was incomplete and preparation was often ineffective, inadequate, or both. Afterward, government responses were often tentative, bureaucratic, or inert. These failures resulted in unnecessary suffering.

Katrina's damage unnerved even hardened search-and-rescue professionals. "Federal Urban Search and Rescue teams that had been to earthquakes in California, 9/11, Oklahoma City, I mean, extremely knowledgeable professionals, and even they said they hadn't seen a disaster area that large," Jim Brinson of the Mississippi Office of Homeland Security recalled. "9/11 was blocks. [Here] we were talking miles after miles after miles of complete devastation."

Hurricane Katrina laid waste to 90,000 square miles of land, an area the size of the United Kingdom. At its fiercest, the storm extended for 460 miles, nearly the distance from Kansas City to Dallas. As the Mississippi Gulf Coast's *Sun-Herald* pointed out, "the world's fastest river rapids move at about 10 to 12 feet per second," challenging even experienced athletes protected by kayaks and life jackets. At about only a third of its strength, Katrina's storm surge – the swell of water snowballed by a storm approaching shore – "could have been moving as fast as 16 feet per second."

Though Katrina made landfall as a Category 3 storm (on the 1-5 Saffir-Simpson scale), it had begun driving its storm surge in the Gulf of Mexico when it was a Category 5. As a result, Katrina brought ashore surge that reached as high as 27 feet above normal sea levels in Mississippi and between 18 and 25 feet in Louisiana. By contrast, New Orleans had no levees or flood walls higher than 17 feet. Though levees had begun to breach as early as landfall, overtopping of the levees may have caused an equal amount of damage.

Citizens and government officials alike knew that it was only a matter of time before a hurricane inundated the Gulf Coast – especially New Orleans, which lies as much as 10 feet below sea level, and continues to sink an inch every three years. (Meanwhile, wave-slowing marshlands and barrier islands in coastal Louisiana erode by 10 square miles a year – losing the area of a football field every 30 minutes – due to flood-control constraints on the Mississippi River, which prevent it from depositing sediments to replenish the subsiding soils.)

For years, meteorologists, emergency-management, and government officials had referred to it, simply, as the "New Orleans scenario." In 1965, Hurricane Betsy, also a Category 3, had provided a preview of Katrina when, in the memorable words of Louisiana's then-U.S. Senator Russell Long, it "picked up the lake [Pontchartrain] … and put it inside New Orleans and Jefferson Parish." When Hurricane Andrew leveled parts of south Florida in 1992, Robert Sheets, Ph.D., then head of the National Weather Service, reminded Congressional investigators that the country had actually been lucky – for a while afterward, the storm looked like it was making its way toward New Orleans.

"People think Andrew was the big one," he told the Committee on Governmental Affairs, as it was then named, in 1993. Andrew had come "within a gnat's eyelash of being our nightmare and the big one," he went on. Sheets displayed a computer projection of what Andrew's storm surge would have done had the hurricane's track shifted slightly and hit New Orleans directly. It showed the hurricane whipping the waters of Lake Borgne, on the eastern side of the city, and Lake Pontchartrain, on the northern edge of the city, over the city's levees. Katrina would follow this very pattern 12 years later. "The city will be under 20 feet of water," Sheets predicted.

In 1998, Hurricane Georges narrowly missed New Orleans, striking Mississippi and Alabama instead. Roused by the close call, local emergency-management planners began to seek federal funding for a massive exercise to consider the potential impact of a direct strike on New Orleans by a slow-moving – and, therefore, more damaging, by virtue of its longer duration – Category 3 hurricane. That funding did not arrive for five years. The effort, known as the Hurricane Pam exercise, finally began in 2004, and tried to address the consequences of a Katrina-like hurricane as developed by government scientists and emergency-management officials and contractors: Widespread flooding; 67,000 dead; 200,000 to 300,000 in need of evacuation after landfall, and hundreds of thousands displaced in need of shelter, exceeding state and local capabilities; hospitals and nursing homes overcrowded and short on critical resources; and incapacitated first responders. Sadly, Katrina proved many of these predictions true.

Near the beach, Biloxi, MS
Denton Herring photo

Katrina formed on August 23, 2005, 200 miles southeast of the Bahamas. Within 24 hours, it had been designated Tropical Storm Katrina by the National Hurricane Center. Two days later, it became a Category 1 hurricane, just two hours before striking the Florida coast between Fort Lauderdale and Miami. By early afternoon on Friday, August 26, Max Mayfield, the director of the National Hurricane Center, and fellow forecasters in the Miami headquarters and regional offices throughout the Gulf Coast believed Katrina might be heading toward New Orleans.

Mayfield called his friend Walter Maestri, Ph.D., the emergency-preparedness director of Jefferson Parish, on the western edge of New Orleans. "This is it," Maestri recalled Mayfield saying. "This is what we've been talking about all of these years. It's a 30-90 storm," Maestri said Mayfield told him. "That's the longitude and latitude of the city of New Orleans," Maestri explained. Beginning with that phone call, Mayfield and other forecasters embarked on a round of urgent communications with local, state, and federal officials to alert them to the encroaching threat.

Ordinary citizens, as well as their leaders in local, state, and federal government knew that Katrina was coming. But few could imagine the impact. By the time Katrina subsided, it had taken with it the Gulf Coast as its 9.5 million residents knew it.

"You could easily identify what building east of you was [floating] by," recalled D. J. Ziegler, the Gulfport, Mississippi, harbormaster, who weathered the storm at a parking garage not far from shore. "You could see church pews and knew what church it was and you could see doors from the motels with room numbers on it."

Katrina carried away not only police cruisers and homes, but also the instruments of daily life. "All our medical records, all the legal documents," Lynn Christiansen, a housewife in St. Bernard Parish, recounted. "My safety deposit was under water for three weeks." As Jim Brinson, of the Mississippi Office of Homeland Security, traveled toward the coast from his headquarters in Jackson shortly after the storm, he encountered scenes of near-apocalyptic destruction and bewilderment. "Going down [Route] 49 and seeing all these people just dazed and confused – you know, I've been to bad areas all over the world in the military; I've seen, you know, entire cities that have been bombed out … and these folks are just dazed. … They're trying to get anything and everything they possibly can. … The further south we went, the worse and worse it got."

Katrina turned first responders – police, medical personnel, etc. – into some of the storm's first victims. As the storm pummeled New Orleans, some 80 police officers – 5 percent of the city's force – were stranded at home, according to Warren Riley, then Deputy Superintendent of the New Orleans Police Department (NOPD). In New Orleans East, Riley said, an officer named Chris Abbott moved to the attic of his home to avoid the rising water, but it continued to climb. Abbott tried to break his way out, but couldn't. In desperation, he attempted to raise colleagues on his police radio even though the storm had knocked out most of the region's communications network.

Abbott lucked out, eventually reaching Captain Jimmy Scott, one of the city's eight district commanders. Captain Scott asked if Abbott had his service weapon and advised him to fire rounds through the base of the attic vent until he could knock it out. Abbott agreed to try,

Stories from Southeast Louisiana

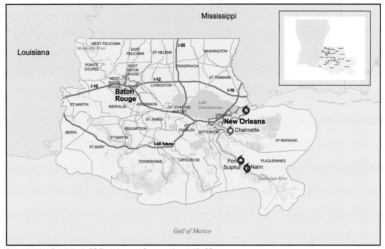

Southeastern Louisiana

Sources: Louisiana State University GIS Clearinghouse and Government Accountability Office

Sara Faulkner, Coast Guard   Larry Ingargiola   Laurence Nettles, Coast Guard   Bobbie Jean Moreau

New Orleans

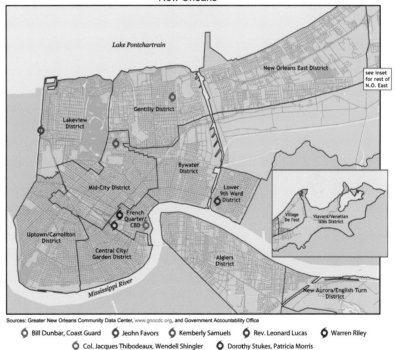

Sources: Greater New Orleans Community Data Center, www.gnocdc.org, and Government Accountability Office

Bill Dunbar, Coast Guard   Jeohn Favors   Kemberly Samuels   Rev. Leonard Lucas   Warren Riley
Col. Jacques Thibodeaux, Wendell Shingler   Dorothy Stukes, Patricia Morris

Witnesses' locations, Louisiana
GAO

but then communication ceased. Officers listening in on the conversation called for him, but there was no reply. Finally, five minutes later, Abbott's voice broke through the air: "I'm halfway out, and I'm going to make it!" The water had been chest-high when he finally scrambled onto his roof, where he was rescued.

Even headquarters could do little. At 7 a.m. on Monday, August 29, just 50 minutes after the storm had made landfall in Plaquemines Parish, southeast of New Orleans, Deputy Superintendent Riley visited the communication section of the department's emergency operations center. "Almost every dispatcher and 911 operator was crying," he recalled. "I did not know that only moments earlier, the Industrial Street Canal levee breached and had an almost 200-yard opening and water was now pouring into the Lower Ninth Ward. … It went from nothing to as high as 14 feet within 23 minutes. We had 600 911 calls within the first 23 minutes. … But [the 911 dispatchers and operators] were powerless to assist. … We still had sustained winds in excess of 100 miles per hour."

Similar calls were arriving at the fire department office in St. Bernard Parish, in eastern New Orleans, from where Larry Ingargiola, the Parish Director of Homeland Security and Emergency Preparedness, was operating a makeshift response center with his wife and his secretary. "I am in the attic, I have my child with me in my attic, I need somebody to come get me out," he recalled a typical plea. "And they are crying. Let me tell you, it got to the point where my secretary and wife couldn't answer the phones anymore. … We knew that the majority of these people we are talking to now were going to die and we were the last people they were talking to. There was nothing we could do. Nothing physically possible for us to do."

Most of the people in the area, civilians and officials alike, could talk to no one at all. Telephone lines were down. Switching stations were flooded. Radio and cell-phone towers had been knocked out. Some emergency personnel had to rely on runners to relay messages. As Mississippi Governor Haley Barbour described it, "My head of the National Guard might as well been a Civil War general for the first two or three days, because he could only find out what was going on by sending somebody."

On Saturday, a day before New Orleans Mayor Ray Nagin would order the first mandatory evacuation of New Orleans in the city's history, city residents had begun to evacuate using a system known as contraflow, which converts incoming highway lanes to outbound to expedite evacuation. More than a million residents of southeastern Louisiana left the area in just over 24 hours, a marked improvement over the 12-15 hour bottlenecks that stalled the evacuation before Hurricane Ivan in 2004. Those delays, coupled with the fact that Ivan – initially a Category 5 storm that came within 135 miles of New Orleans – banked eastward at the last moment, persuaded some to remain behind this time.

Gulf Coast residents call it "hurricane roulette." Some who had endured 1969's Category 5 Hurricane Camille, the region's benchmark for catastrophic storms, thought that no other storm could come close. But Katrina ended lifetimes of successful storm-dodging. Jeff Elder, an insurance rep, had ridden out 20 years of hurricanes with his family in a two-story, wood-frame home three miles north of the Biloxi, Mississippi, beachfront and 14 feet above sea level. "The eye of Hurricane Georges passed directly over our home," he wrote in an e-mail, "and, while the bay [just south of the Elders' home] rose to a level of about ten feet above normal, the water never reached our property. In fact, during Hurricane Camille… the water in Back Bay only rose to a level approximately 12 feet above normal." By early afternoon on Monday, August 29, the day Katrina made landfall, the Elders had six feet of water in their living room.

Stories from the Mississippi Gulf Coast

Courtesy of Mississippi Department of Transportation and Government Accountability Office

As Biloxi city spokesman Vincent Creel said of Hurricane Camille survivors lulled into a false sense of security, Camille killed more people in 2005 than it did in 1969.

Witnesses' locations, Mississippi
GAO

In many cases, however, hubris or miscalculation had nothing to do with why some stayed behind. Katrina struck in the very last days of August, when those living check-to-check were running out of their bi-weekly or monthly allotments. Tens of thousands didn't have cars. Even many who did may not have been able to shoulder the costs of evacuation; the average cost for three days for a family of four, including lodging, food, and transportation, could easily exceed a thousand dollars, according to an analysis of Hurricane Ivan prepared for the Federal Emergency Management Agency (FEMA). For the poor of neighborhoods like the Lower Ninth Ward, one of the city's lowest-lying areas, this was an impossible sum, though they had an alternative in the Superdome, the city's "refuge of last resort."

Nearly 100,000 New Orleanians either couldn't or didn't comply with Mayor Nagin's evacuation order. The city had no plan for evacuating them, and the Louisiana Department of Transportation and Development, the state agency responsible for transportation during a disaster, had done nothing by the time of landfall. New Orleans' enterprising health department director, Dr. Kevin Stephens, had begun negotiating agreements with several transportation agencies, but they remained incomplete at the time of landfall. Federal officials, who had participated in the Hurricane Pam exercise and knew that state and local authorities would need evacuation help, had no plans in place, either.

Bobbie Moreau, a legal secretary in Nairn, a small town in Plaquemines Parish, stayed at home because she didn't have the means to evacuate. She was with her daughter Tasha and Tasha's four-month-old daughter, who was born prematurely and required a heart monitor. Moreau woke up at 4 a.m. on Monday, just as the wind and storm surge preceding Katrina's eye were reaching shore. "The pressure was so bad in the house, I opened a crack in the living room window," she recalled. When she walked into the den, she saw water pouring through the grout in the marble tile that lined a part of the wall. By the time she had climbed to the second floor, the water had risen halfway up the stairs. Moreau could see her living-room furniture floating.

"I shut the door upstairs, I guess thinking I could shut the water out," she said. "From then on, it was a nightmare. I held the baby at the foot of the bed fanning her. The pressure was awful; we thought the windows were going to pop. We got on our knees and prayed and begged God to save us. Then I felt the water under me on the second floor. … I got up and walked to the window and the water was right under the window. My legs felt like Jell-O, I staggered. My daughter screamed, 'Mama, what's wrong?' I knew at that moment we were going to die."

But "in an instant, survival kicked in." Moreau tore the canopy from the bed and tied knots so that she and Tasha could hold on to each other. She used a belt to create a makeshift life jacket for the baby. With the water halfway up the bed, they climbed out onto the roof, managing to take along Moreau's three dogs. "The eye of the hurricane was on us," Moreau recalled. "I told my daughter, you will have to swim and get a boat, I am too weak. She said, 'Mama, I'm scared.' There was dead animals floating by, snakes, debris, oil. I told her, 'We will die if you don't.' She handed me the baby and slipped into the water. … Then I lost sight of her and called and called because the wind was picking up. And then I knew it was the eye. Nothing but silence. I thought she had drowned. I was crying and praying. And then I heard an outboard motor start up. And I knew she was alive.

"Where she pulled [up] the boat, the power lines to the house was between us," Moreau continued. "I had to drop the baby through the power lines to her and the dogs and then myself. By then, the wind was so hard, we could not control the boat with the motors. … We came to a stop in the top of some little trees. We huddled under the steering wheel with the baby because a window was broke out of the cabin. We stayed there for about 6-7 hours. The wind would almost turn the boat over and we sang and prayed. … It was so weird. Felt like we were the only people left in the world, everything covered by water."

Around the same time, at Hancock Medical Center in Bay St. Louis, Mississippi, the first floor was beginning to flood. Patients would have to be moved upstairs. Staffers managed to use the elevator to move a 600-pound, non-ambulatory patient to safety before flood waters damaged the hospital generators. Physicians and service staff carried the remaining patients upstairs on their backs. The first floor quickly filled with three feet of water, disabling and washing away equipment.

The Hancock staff had considered evacuating its 34 patients, but eventually decided to "shelter in place." In the past, patients had deteriorated and even died while languishing in evacuation gridlock, some of it in response to storm warnings that turned out to be false alarms. But few hospitals had the resources to withstand the assault of a storm like Katrina, and, as the Hurricane Pam exercise predicted, became victims themselves. State governments had failed to address the problem prior to the storm. In Louisiana, the Department of Health and Hospitals required nursing homes to have evacuation plans, but did not require the institutions to actually follow them.

On the second floor of Hancock, patients were treated in the hall, as wind and rain prevented the use of patient rooms. Because the water pumps failed, staff had to use buckets of water to flush toilets. Maintenance staff hung multi-colored emergency glow-lights to mark the way down corridors and stairwells. Because communications were down, no one knew whether their loved ones had made it.

Forty miles away, at Ocean Springs Hospital, physicians struggled with dwindling supplies and an increasing number of patients. "We couldn't sterilize anything because there was no power," said Dr. Bill Passarelli, a cardiologist who was on duty as Katrina came ashore. "There were only like two surgical packets left. So unless somebody was absolutely going to die, you weren't going to surgery."

"It got so hot that the laboratory computers had to be shut down to prevent them from overheating," Dr. Passarelli's colleague and friend Dr. Jeff Bass, an emergency-room doctor, recalled. "We were able to do only extremely basic lab tests. I could not even get a basic test of kidney function." The first fatalities arrived at around 5 p.m., before the wind had died down. "A friend who was a police officer told me that every bayou and every waterway had bodies in them, and that they were pulling bodies from the trees. … Our morgue only holds two people. We had living people to worry about. At about 6 o'clock I wrote on [a wipe board facing the emergency room door] 'DON'T BRING US ANY MORE DEAD BODIES. WE DON'T HAVE ENOUGH ROOM FOR THE LIVING PEOPLE.'"

"I had always dreamed of working for Doctors Without Borders and going to a Third World country right after a disaster," Dr. Bass said. "Never in my wildest dreams did I think I would experience that without leaving my home."

At Hancock, survivors who had injured themselves clinging to trees or breaking out of their attics were also beginning to trickle in, many after walking for miles, others on makeshift stretchers, as ambulances had been washed away. Staff treated 850 new patients during the next 48 hours. Though a Hancock medical specialist had e-mailed the director of the National Disaster Medical System less than 24 hours after landfall that county authorities were "pulling bodies from trees," a federal Disaster Medical Assistance Team did not arrive until Wednesday evening. It had been pre-staged in Memphis, Tennessee, 350 miles away. Hancock general surgeon Brian Anthony repaired a man's severed radial artery while a scrub tech held a flashlight overhead. Coast Guard helicopters refueling between rescues airlifted critical patients to fully functional hospitals further inland.

The Coast Guard performed heroically during Katrina, rescuing more than half of the 60,000 survivors who were stranded by the storm. (The Louisiana Department of Wildlife & Fisheries, the state's lead agency for search-and-rescue, similarly distinguished itself, rescuing much of the rest.) Coast Guard rescue swimmer Sara Faulkner's first rescue was in East New Orleans: "My first hoist was down to the second story of [an] apartment building. And they handed me their baby like it was nothing, you know. … And I was so terrified for that baby, of him starting to squirm or wiggle, you know, for not knowing any better. And making it hard for me to hold him because the rescue, the quick strap is too small for him and he didn't fit, so you just have to hold him in your arms. And I'm already two stories up and I have to go up a hundred feet, you know, on a cable. I was holding on to him so tight, I had to check him to make sure I wasn't crushing him 'cause, you know, I was just holding on to him so tight. And, uh, he was fine. I don't even think he was scared. I think he was too young to be scared. But the flight mech[anic] said when I came out from underneath the roof that he got chills because his son was about that same size, same age, so. … That, uh, that was bad, that one, but then I did three more and they weren't as bad as that one, but, um, I don't think I'll forget that first baby."

Another typical rescue took place several days later in Gentilly, in north-central New Orleans. Coast Guard rescuer Bill Dunbar was leaving to refuel when an older man flagged him down. "This guy was 86 years old and had climbed up… two 17-rung straight-up ladders after being without water for three or four days," Dunbar recalled. And he's laughing, he's in [a] good mood. I thought he was delirious." Back at the Coast Guard station, the man asked Dunbar to call his son Jeff, who was a Marine. "So I dialed the phone number and I asked for Jeff and he says, 'Yeah, who's this?' and I say, 'Well, my name is Lieutenant Bill Dunbar and I'm calling from the Coast Guard. We just saved your father. We just pulled him off a roof.' And the guy broke down crying. And I got a little weepy, 'cause, you know, after that you're a little tired. He said that every day of … 26 years in the Marine Corps was worth that one moment knowing that his Dad was alright. So we put a little money in his dad's wallet, put some food in his pockets, and we flew him out to Armstrong [Airport] and put him with a doctor. And the doctor said that he'd make sure he got to Houston where his son was coming to meet him to take him home."

But the Coast Guard's first Katrina rescue, at 2:50 p.m. on the day of landfall, came in response to "a Mayday from a frantic woman saying that her and her daughter … and her grandchild were stuck on a small boat in the middle of the city of Port Sulphur." It was Bobbie Moreau, who had managed to use the radio in the boat her daughter had found to summon the Coast Guard. A direct hoist was impossible because the boat was under trees, so rescue swimmer Laurence Nettles was lowered into the water by the side of the boat. A Coast Guard video of the rescue records what happened next:

Pilot: You want me to come to the right?

Nettles: No, hold position. … On deck, picking up slack, waiting for the survivor to get in basket. Hold position. Woman and baby are getting in the basket. Ready for pickup. Picking up slack. Start taking the load. … Clear vessel, clear back to the left.

Pilot: Okay, I can move it to the right, if I can.

Nettles: Roger, that's fine. … Basket's coming up … basket's halfway up. … Roger, she's got a dog with her, too. [Pause]

Pilot: That's fine. Let her bring the dog, it's fine.

Waiting, New Orleans
AP/Wide World Photo

As for many survivors of Katrina, the rescue hardly brought Moreau's ordeal to a close. The Coast Guard crew dropped off her and her family at West Jefferson Hospital in Jefferson Parish. "Barefoot, no purse, no money, no shoes," Moreau recalled. "My daughter went in with the baby. I sat on the curb crying." Soon, they were moved to a shelter. "There was over 100 people in one room. The heat was incredible, could not go outside with the baby for mosquitoes. We fanned her all night." Moreau appealed to a National Guardsman, but she said he told her they would be at the shelter for another week. "My daughter said, 'I am not going to let my baby die. We are going to walk out of here and get help.'"

According to Moreau, Jefferson Police tried to prevent her from leaving, presumably for her safety, but "I said, 'Do what you want to do, I have nothing left anyway.'" Moreau and her family snuck out when the police were distracted by a scuffle and hitched a ride to West-wego, on the west bank of the Mississippi River, where a friend lived. He had evacuated. "I broke into his house, cooled the baby off, we took a shower and ate can food," Moreau said. "He had left his truck in the driveway. … [It] had no gas in it, and there was nowhere to buy gas, so I siphoned gas out of his boat, two gallons at a time, and put [it] into his truck. I left him a letter with my nephew's phone number [in Arkansas]. The only clothes he had that would fit us was boxer shorts and t-shirt, so that is what we left in. … We went across the Sunshine Bridge [across the Mississippi River], got to Prairieville, and my nephew picked us up. We had a hard time since then, but we made it."

In the Lower Ninth Ward, Reverend Leonard Lucas of Light City Church was trying to persuade dazed survivors to leave their homes. Parts of the neighborhood had flooded to the rooftops after weak levees on its west side gave way in two spots to water from Lake Borgne rushing down the Mississippi River Gulf Outlet. "We went house to house telling people they had to leave," Reverend Lucas recalled. "They kept coming and coming and coming. People were leaving everything and only taking a packed bag and their kids. Some people had pets and wouldn't leave them. I don't know how many people told me that their pet 'was all they had.' We kept telling everyone to go to Stallings Park in the Upper Ninth [west of the Lower Ninth, across the Industrial Canal]. It was a steady flow of people marching like zombies to the park." The less fortunate who were stranded on rooftops sometimes remained there for days awaiting rescue.

Some of the rescues were performed by volunteers who came to help in the wake of the storm. The assistance was unorganized and frustrated authorities trying to streamline response. Groups of volunteers in civilian clothes converged, frequently armed and without coordination, on the same areas of a sometimes lawless city, adding to the tension. But they also performed an invaluable service. Among them was Jeohn Favors, an emergency management technician (EMT) from Franklin, an hour west of New Orleans, who joined a group of fellow firefighters and police heading to the city.

"The first five minutes into New Orleans, someone came out and asked for a medic," he recalled. "[We] rode up to the water's edge and then waded through water till we got to the boat. A R[egistered] N[urse] … had just finished delivering a baby. The girl was 16 years old, had been taken off her roof, and was having her first child and actually delivered in the boat. The nurse had just cut the umbilical cord, and they handed me the baby to check it out. It was my first delivery."

Favors's crew hotwired empty boats, rescuing 350 people from rooftops by the end of the day. By his account, they were the first rescuers in Lakeview, a neighborhood in western New Orleans. They traveled through water riddled with six-foot plumes of flames rising from what must have been gas leaks. Power lines – some still active – hung above the water; beneath, submerged obstructions threatened to puncture the boats.

"The thing I'll never forget was the look on people's faces, you know, Could this really happen?" Favors recalled. "People were so happy to see us there." He mentioned a boat that ran out of gas on its way to a hospital, for a passenger whose blood pressure was dangerously elevated. "We gave them gas and tried to direct them to a hospital. … They had nothing, house destroyed, just wearing cutoffs, nothing left, and they tried to pay us for the gas. We couldn't believe it. People were so grateful."

Someone like Favors helped Kemberly Samuels, a teacher who sheltered from the storm with her husband at a housing development in St. Bernard Parish, where he worked. The building flooded. "You know, everyone heard about all the young gang bangers in New Orleans, but you didn't hear about the young men who came and found us," she said. "They had to be in their teens or early twenties. … They came … on Tuesday night with boats. They brought us food and drinks. I asked them where they got it from, they said, 'Don't worry about that, just eat it.' They also said the boats were 'borrowed.'"

The rescuers took Samuels and her husband to Interstate 610, a highway overpass in downtown New Orleans where rescuers had begun depositing survivors. (Local authorities had identified only one official drop-off point, at an intersection of Interstate 10 and the Lake Pontchartrain Causeway known as the Cloverleaf, about two miles away. It was also the only rescue point where they had positioned food, water, and medicine.) "There were people lined up as far as I could see," Samuels recalled. "I saw one 9-year-old boy try to drag his grandmother up the interstate on a blanket. She was too weak to make it on her own. I tried to get them help, but none of the officials would help them. It was so hot you wouldn't believe. … We went for a while without water and when it finally did get there they just started throwing it at the crowd. People were fighting over it and I did not want to get in the middle of that. They did the same thing with the MREs [Meals Ready to Eat]," the military-style rations.

Though the Federal Emergency Management Agency (FEMA) positioned resources in the area before the start of the hurricane season, the food and water – critical supplies when a disaster has disrupted local services – were insufficient. Mississippi received only a fifth of the water and ice that state officials estimated was necessary; shipments didn't meet demand in Mississippi until September 9, 12 days after landfall.

FEMA, the federal government's primary disaster-response agency, had no effective supply-tracking system, so replenishing provisions turned out to be complicated. Planning and coordination were so poor that truck drivers didn't know where to go, and emergency-management officials didn't know what was en route, or when it might show up. Phone lines were down, so it was hard to clarify. "We'd find [the trucks] parked along [Highway] 49," Mike Beeman, FEMA's liaison to coastal Harrison County in Mississippi, said. "[We'd] go over and find out who he was, what he had in the back end, because … many times [we] knew items were sent to us, but we didn't know where they were. … We'd finally find maybe five or six truckloads of water or ice that were sitting off the roadway in some apron at a supermarket. … Some of them sat sometimes two or three days. I found 25 trucks one day. … They were just sitting there, waiting for somebody to tell them where to go. … I have no idea where they came from."

The situation called for occasionally morbid forms of improvisation. In Bay St. Louis, Mississippi, Bill Carwile, FEMA's lead representative in Mississippi, and Robert Latham, the head of the state's emergency-management agency, encountered a funeral home director "in tears. And he says, you know, I have no more room for bodies. … My funeral home is full and I'm fixing to have to start putting people in the parking lot and on the sidewalk," Latham recalled. FEMA had ordered several refrigerator, or reefer, trucks as temporary morgues, but they hadn't arrived.

Just then, a tractor-trailer pulled up. "I said, What are you hauling?" Latham continued. "[The driver] said, Well, I'm hauling ice. … I said, Well, can I rent your truck? … We need to use it as a morgue. And he said, No, this is the way I make my living. If I give you that, I won't ever be able to use that trailer again for hauling ice or anything else refrigerated. I says, can we buy your truck? I'll buy it. I looked at Bill and I said, Bill, can I do this? He said, Yeah, we're going to do what we have do." Carwile and Latham negotiated a price ($25,000) and started loading bodies. The reefer trucks finally showed up five days later.

Supplies also were stretched at the New Orleans Superdome, the "refuge of last resort" for city residents who did not evacuate. It saved many lives during the hurricane, but at a dismaying cost. Lighting and plumbing failed. As 25,000 evacuees waited in heat and humidity for evacuation buses that wouldn't arrive for days, the Superdome deteriorated into nightmarish squalor. Though conditions were often worse at spontaneous rescue points like the one where Kemberly Samuels found herself, the Superdome became a center of the crisis, a symbol of the ways in which America failed New Orleans.

Dorothy Stukes rode out the hurricane at 1517

Heading for airlift from the Superdome, New Orleans
U.S. Coast Guard photo

Virginia Marie Place, her home in Gentilly. She didn't evacuate because her sister, who had recently undergone surgery, was at Charity Hospital, in the Central Business District. After the storm had passed, she went outside and walked for several miles until city police officers picked her up and drove her to the Superdome.

"A female officer searched us before we went inside," she recalled. "She took some medicine I had, but she also took some insulin from an elderly woman behind me because it was not in its proper box. I don't know how they expected her to make it without her insulin. When we got in, we found a chair and just sat there. All I could think about was my daughter. The last time I talked to her, water was coming through the walls and roof of her house. I didn't know if she was dead or alive.

"The Dome was horrible; it was like jail or something," she went on. "One guy jumped from a balcony and committed suicide. We saw some people having sex under a blanket. There were kids all around. Some kids found where they were hiding the ice and stole some of it and started selling it. Most of the supplies were going to the people [special-needs patients] up in the suites. Some folks found a newborn baby in a trash can; they ended up taking care of it. People were sleeping in the halls on cardboard boxes in the middle of all that waste. And it stank; it was past stink due to all the urine and feces all over the floor. We just sat there and put our shirts over our face to mask the smell. We used an empty MRE bag and a box to go in. We would try to hide ourselves but you couldn't really get away. They wouldn't open any extra doors to let us get fresh air."

Among Stukes' fellow refugees was Patricia Morris, a home-care nurse who had passed up the chance to evacuate to Mississippi with her daughter because she wanted to help at the Superdome. "I kept telling [the] National Guard that I'm a registered nurse, and disaster-certified," she said. "Finally they got angry with me, and told me, Look, woman, Red Cross didn't even show," referring to the Red Cross' refusal to certify and staff the Superdome because it was in the flood zone. Morris says she offered her help to FEMA medics, as well as representatives of the state health department. "I could not understand with all the need they had how they could refuse help," she said. (Generally, medical personnel turned away volunteers because there was no way to evaluate their skills.) Meanwhile, Morris had to find ways around the same indignities as Dorothy Stukes. "After the second day I decided that if I didn't eat, I wouldn't have to go to the bathroom," she said.

As conditions at the Superdome deteriorated, officials scrambled to find a way to evacuate the population. Prior to landfall, city authorities had failed to position buses outside the flood zone. The Regional Transit Authority, the city's transit system, pre-positioned two fleets of buses on high ground within New Orleans, but no level of government attempted to send drivers until three days after landfall.

On Monday, the day of landfall, Louisiana Governor Kathleen Blanco had turned to FEMA Director Michael Brown with a request for 500 buses. He promised they would come. For reasons that have never been explained, those buses did not begin to arrive at the Superdome until Wednesday evening. By Katrina's impossible clock, two and a half days was a lifetime. Waiting, even if because the facts on the ground weren't clear, was an unconscionable luxury. If ever there was a time to overreact, this was it.

"We kept being told that the buses were coming," Dorothy Stukes said. "They promised they were coming on Monday, and then Tuesday, and then Wednesday. Thursday they finally got us to line up to load on the buses. At first they said [to] make a single-file line, and then someone said women and children first. Some of the men started snatching kids away from women so they could get on the bus."

"After we got on the bus they wouldn't tell us where they were taking us, and they said they forgot to load water for us," Kemberly Samuels recalled. "Once we got settled we started reading signs and realized we were going to Houston. We found out that there were kids on the bus that had been separated from their parents. There were at least four. I was asked to take care of one of them. Once we got to Houston, I took the kid to a Red Cross official and let them know that the kid had gotten lost. By that time, a lot of people had gotten sick. People were bathing in the sinks. We hadn't had a bath since Sunday. It was now Friday."

The Louisiana National Guard troops who developed the Superdome evacuation plan were assisted by members of a 50,000-strong Guard deployment from all 50 states, as well as the District of Columbia, Puerto Rico, the Virgin Islands, and Guam. After initiating the Superdome evacuation on Thursday, they moved on to the Ernest N. Morial Convention Center.

Tuesday evening, Mayor Nagin had opened the Convention Center as an alternate refuge. Before landfall, the city had not intended to use the Convention Center for this purpose, so no food or water had been positioned, and few law enforcement, medical or government personnel were present. Over the next two days, 19,000 people converged on the facility, but all levels of government were slow to grasp the gravity of the unfolding crisis. The first supplies may not have arrived until Thursday. The first media reports of the crowds at the Convention Center appeared Wednesday evening; by the next day there was video of thousands of stranded, desperate victims chanting "We want help."

The National Guard moved in on Friday, restoring order, distributing provisions, and evacuating the entire population in just over a day. Louisiana National Guard Colonel Jacques Thibodeaux recalled his first encounter with the people inside: "The first time I went into the building … groups of people just lying there immobile, and when I say immobile, they assume that several were deceased because they actually kicked a couple to see if they were, 'Hey, are you okay?,' just to see, to get an assessment, and they didn't move." The people Thibodeaux saw were alive, but so malnourished that they did not respond to physical stimuli.

"They're hot, they're tired, they're hungry," Wendell Shingler, the head of the Federal Protective Service, who assessed the situation at the Convention Center for the Department of Homeland Security (DHS), recalled. "They had no place to go to the bathroom. They – some of these folks could not walk, so they were relieving themselves in their pants, and they had just lost their sense of humanity, they had lost their sense of dignity, and that was something that you could just see, they were just so distraught. They had now gone from a retired person with a home and probably some income to a homeless person sitting on a sidewalk, owning everything they had in the bag."

Though initial reports like Colonel Thibodeaux's suggested that as many as a hundred had died at the Convention Center, the actual toll was far lower. But this was cold comfort. One of Katrina's most enduring images was that of 91-year-old Ethel Freeman, whose lifeless body, partially covered by a poncho, sat in a wheelchair at the Convention Center for days.

The evacuation of most of the city was complete by Saturday, when 8,800 active-duty ground troops began to arrive. It's unclear why President Bush waited until Saturday to deploy federal ground troops – whether because of delay in settling command issues with state officials, because of the Defense Department's doctrine of relying on National Guard units first, because of federal units' inability to take on law-enforcement duties, or other reasons. The National Response Plan, the document meant to guide federal response to a disaster like Katrina, assigns a supporting role to the Department of Defense, to be called on by FEMA as necessary. On Thursday evening, three and a half days after landfall, FEMA asked the Department of Defense to take over its logistics operation. By that time, the Department had already begun to mobilize a significant amount of its resources, including ships, aircraft, and medical support. Some commanders had seized the initiative to mobilize assets so that they would be ready to deploy when the orders finally came.

Perhaps the most visible among them was Lieutenant General Russel Honoré, Commander of U.S. First Army, based in Atlanta, Georgia. Military commanders have limited authority to deploy their troops without orders from above as part of an "exercise." A native Louisianan who had assisted FEMA during the 2004 hurricane season, Honoré decided to stage an "exercise" that took his command element to Camp Shelby, Mississippi. Once Katrina subsided, Honoré was ideally positioned to take charge, and was named head of Joint Task Force Katrina by U.S. Northern Command, the headquarters for domestic military operations.

"When you landed here, with everybody walking with these red berets, in 45 minutes everybody's attitude changed," said Colonel Terry Ebbert, a former Marine who was New Orleans' head of Homeland Security when Katrina struck. "Nothing really changed but their attitude. Everybody, instantaneously, when they saw these guys walking down the street, you know, they're all good-looking, slim, tough guys that walk with a swagger, and it was over. Everybody felt good. Had that response come in on Tuesday," Colonel Ebbert said, the situation may have improved sooner.

The Gulf Coast has been trying to find its way back to normalcy. In the days after the storm "the weather was beautiful, … but you'd smell rotting flesh in the air," Dr. Bill Passarelli, the cardiologist from Ocean Springs, Mississippi, recalled. "Whether it was animal or human you didn't know, but it was everywhere. The closer you got to water the more intense it was."

"Just the devastation that was seen, it causes extreme – sudden and extreme duress," Passarelli continued. "And we saw people who had heart attacks just from seeing their houses. One lady in particular, my daughter's Spanish teacher, died that way. She was away for the storm, she survived the storm, and two days after the storm came back and died on her property."

"Every little detail of life as I knew it here on the Gulf Coast before the storm has changed," Dr. Jeff Bass, Passarelli's colleague, wrote in an e-mail to friends in late September. "The schools are damaged, most of the local businesses are closed, and almost all of the police cars are from out of state because virtually all of the local cruisers were washed away. On the street, instead of greeting people with, 'Hi, how are you?' the greeting is 'Hi, do you have a home, and is it livable?'"

Some 17,000 people lost jobs when the storm wiped out the local off-shore casinos, Bass continued. The destruction of Keesler Air Force Base in Biloxi unemployed 50,000 more, he wrote. "Almost all of the nice local restaurants have been destroyed … along with many of the small Mom and Pop businesses. I doubt that they carried adequate insurance."

Katrina destroyed or made uninhabitable 300,000 homes and caused as much as $150 billion in damage. In three Mississippi coastal counties alone, it left behind more debris than the 9/11 attacks and Hurricane Andrew, the most destructive recent hurricane, combined.

At Hancock Medical Center, the storm left three-quarters of the staff homeless. Hal Leftwich, the hospital administrator, and Hank Wheeler, the facilities-services director, spent the first two weeks after the storm on air mattresses in the business office and the next month in patient rooms. The numbers were similar at Ocean Springs. In some cases, the survivors have chosen to rebuild elsewhere. As of late January, half of New Orleans' population had not returned.

In the days after the magnitude of government's failure to respond became apparent, the Homeland Security and Governmental Affairs Committee initiated an investigation to "thoroughly examine what appears to be breakdowns in preparedness for and responses to" Hurricane Katrina and to "demand answers as to how this immense failure occurred," according to a statement by Senators Susan Collins and Joseph Lieberman, Chairman and Ranking Member, respectively.

For the past seven months, the Committee has worked to discharge this obligation. It has held 22 days of hearings, interviewed or heard testimony from more than 400 witnesses, and reviewed in excess of 800,000 pages of documents. It has found failings at all levels of government. Preparations that were adequate in the past and that might have been sufficient had Katrina been a "typical" hurricane proved to be grievously inadequate. The National Response Plan had its first real-world test, revealing shortcomings. Katrina began as a human tragedy, but in the weeks after the storm, the fecklessness of the government response became a story unto itself.

This Report is a study of a catastrophe, an "ultra-catastrophe," in the words of Department of Homeland Security Secretary Michael Chertoff. The National Response Plan defines a catastrophe as "any natural or man-made incident, including terrorism, that results in extraordinary levels of mass casualties, damage, or disruption severely affecting the population, infrastructure, environment, economy, national morale, and/or government functions." By definition, they are rare, but the age of terrorism and climate change has ensured that the next occurrence is mainly a question of *how* and *where*, not *when*.

For that reason, the Committee intends this Report to serve as a catalyst for constructive reform before the next catastrophe, whatever shape it might take. Ironically, many of this

Report's findings have an alarming resemblance to the General Accounting Office's analysis of the government's inadequate response to 1992's Hurricane Andrew. The Committee hopes that this Report will never become part of a compendium of warnings similarly, and tragically, ignored.

This is why the Committee's report includes not only an analysis of the response at all levels of government, but assessments and recommendations as well. The Committee has found:

- A failure on the part of all levels of government to plan and prepare for the consequences of Katrina.

- A failure to heed the warnings of a looming catastrophe during the weekend preceding the storm, and a failure on the day of landfall to recognize that the worst predictions had come true.

- A failure on the part of government leaders to think "big" before Katrina struck and to challenge existing planning assumptions in the face of what was known to be a "nightmare scenario."

- A failure on the part of all levels of government to plan and provide for the timely and effective evacuation of the elderly, the sick, and the disabled from New Orleans, and the evacuation of tens of thousands of able-bodied residents who did not have personal transportation.

- A failure to act on the lessons of past catastrophes, both man-made and natural, that demonstrated the need for a large, well-equipped, and coordinated law enforcement response to maintain or restore civil order after catastrophic events.

- A failure to plan for and provide in a timely manner mass medical care and temporary shelter for tens of thousands of Katrina victims that all levels of government knew were likely to be impacted by a catastrophic hurricane.

The Committee has not used the power to judge lightly. This investigation has benefited from hindsight, which revealed that, for all the warnings and predictions, there had been too little foresight, after all. Though many understood and acknowledged the risks to the Gulf Coast, it seems few could imagine a major American city destroyed.

The Committee has not assembled the complete record of what happened before, during, and after Hurricane Katrina. Areas for further study and clarification remain. The issues raised by the response to Hurricane Katrina could not be more critical to America's sense of itself in this moment in history, its security, prosperity, and honor.

Revisiting stories like those above recalls that endless week in late August and early September when the entire nation watched with frustration, anger, and despair as the disaster unfolded. It is the hope of this Committee that changes prompted by this Report will ensure that the anguish that might have been avoided or relieved sooner in America's response to Hurricane Katrina will never come to pass again.

Katrina on the Gulf Coast
NASA photo

Hurricane Katrina: Indicators of Impact

Deaths caused by Hurricane Katrina, as of May 23, 2006[1]   1,577
Deaths caused by 20th century's most lethal hurricane,
       1935's "Labor Day Hurricane" in Florida[2]   400+

Land area damaged by Hurricane Katrina[3]   90,000 sq. miles
Ratio of area damaged by Katrina to area of United Kingdom   1:1

Homes destroyed or made unlivable by Hurricane Katrina[4]   300,000
Ratio of homes damaged or made unlivable by Katrina to
       the number similarly affected by 1992's Hurricane
       Andrew, the most destructive recent hurricane[5]   10:1

Estimated economic loss related to Hurricane Katrina[6] $125 - $150 billion

Estimated economic loss related to 20th century's previous
       most destructive hurricane (Andrew, FL, 1992)[7] $48.4 billion (2005 dollars)
Economic losses from 9/11 terror attacks, 2001[8] $87 billion (2005 dollars)

Louisiana unemployment rate, August 2005   5.6 percent[9]
Louisiana unemployment rate, September 2005   12.1 percent[10]

Widest extent of Katrina's tropical-storm force winds the
       day before landfall[11]   460 miles
Approximate ratio to distance from Kansas City to Dallas   1:1
Sustained-wind speed at landfall, August 29, near Buras, LA[12]   125 miles per hour

Rainfall accumulation along Gulf Coast from Katrina[13]   8 to 10 inches
Storm surges above normal ocean levels, various locations[14]   20 to 30 feet

Electric customers, all types, left without power by storm[15]   1.7 million
Gulf of Mexico daily oil output shut down by Katrina[16]   95 percent

Number of oil spills caused by Katrina[17]   142
Gallons of oil spilled[18]   8 million
Gallons of oil recovered by Coast Guard as of Dec. 7, 2005[19]   3.8 million

Estimated debris created by Hurricane Katrina[20]   118 million cu. yds
Ratio to debris created by Hurricane Andrew[21]   6:1

Number of children reported displaced/missing[22]   5,088
Number reunited with families or guardians[23]   5,088

Last date at which bodies have been found in New Orleans[24]   April 17, 2006
Number of bodies unclaimed or unidentified[25]   200

Approximate ratio of New Orleans population in 2000 to
January 2006[26]   3:1

Ratio of tons of debris created by Katrina in the three coastal
Mississippi counties, as compared to the combined
debris of the 9/11 attacks and Hurricane Andrew[27]   1:1

---

1 Michelle Hunter, "Deaths of evacuees push toll to 1,577," New Orleans *Times-Picayune*, May 19, 2006, p. 1. The article indicates that the Louisiana Department of Health and Hospitals added 281 victims to earlier counts on May 18, 2006, after officials concluded from a review of evacuees' out-of-state death certificates that many were Katrina-related, such as from stress or loss of access to essential medications.

2 National Oceanic and Atmospheric Administration (NOAA), "NOAA's Top U.S. Weather, Water and Climate Events of the 20th Century," Dec. 13, 1999. http://www.noaanews.noaa.gov/stories/s334c.htm. Accessed on Mar. 26, 2006.

3 Written Statement of Sec. Michael Chertoff, U.S. Department of Homeland Security, for the U.S. Senate, Committee on Homeland Security and Governmental Affairs, hearing on *Hurricane Katrina: The Homeland Security Department's Preparation and Response*, Feb. 15, 2006, p. 1.

4 Written Statement of Sec. Chertoff, Senate Committee hearing, Feb. 15, 2006, p. 1.

5 Written Statement of Walter Isaacson, Vice Chairman, Louisiana Recovery Authority, for the U.S. House, Committee on Financial Services, hearing on *H.R. 4100, the Louisiana Recovery Corporation Act,* Nov. 17, 2005, p. 1.

6 Federal Deposit Insurance Corporation, "Bank Performance After Natural Disasters: A Historical Perspective," Jan. 16, 2006. http://www.fdic.gov/bank/analytical/regional/ro20054q/na/2005_winter01.html. Accessed on Mar. 26, 2006.

7 Federal Deposit Insurance Corporation, "Bank Performance After Natural Disasters: A Historical Perspective," Jan. 16, 2006. http://www.fdic.gov/bank/analytical/regional/ro20054q/na/2005_winter01.html. Accessed on Mar. 26, 2006.

8 Written Statement of Douglas Holtz-Eakin, Director, Congressional Budget Office, for the U.S. House, Committee on the Budget, hearing on *After the Hurricanes: Impact on the Fiscal Year 2007 Budget*, Oct. 6, 2005.

9 U.S. Department of Labor, U.S. Bureau of Labor Statistics, "State Unemployment Rates in September 2005," Oct. 24, 2005. http://www.bls.gov/opub/ted/2005/oct/wk4/art01.htm. Accessed on Mar. 29, 2006.

10 U.S. Department of Labor, U.S. Bureau of Labor Statistics, "State Unemployment Rates in September 2005," Oct. 24, 2005. http://www.bls.gov/opub/ted/2005/oct/wk4/art01.htm. Accessed on Mar. 29, 2006.

11 Richard D. Knabb, Jamie Rhome, and Daniel Brown, National Hurricane Center, "Tropical Cyclone Report, Hurricane Katrina," Dec. 20, 2005.

12 NOAA, National Climatic Data Center, "Climate of 2005: Summary of Hurricane Katrina," Dec. 29, 2005. http://www.ncdc.noaa.gov/oa/climate/research/2005/katrina.html. Accessed on Feb. 17, 2006.

13 NOAA, National Climatic Data Center, "Climate of 2005: Summary of Hurricane Katrina," Dec. 29, 2005. http://www.ncdc.noaa.gov/oa/climate/research/2005/katrina.html. Accessed on Feb. 17, 2006.

14 NOAA, National Climatic Data Center, "Climate of 2005: Summary of Hurricane Katrina," Dec. 29, 2005. http://www.ncdc.noaa.gov/oa/climate/research/2005/katrina.html. Accessed on Feb. 17, 2006.

15 NOAA, National Climatic Data Center, "Climate of 2005: Summary of Hurricane Katrina," Dec. 29, 2005. http://www.ncdc.noaa.gov/oa/climate/research/2005/katrina.html. Accessed on Feb. 17, 2006.

16 NOAA, National Climatic Data Center, "Climate of 2005: Summary of Hurricane Katrina," Dec. 29, 2005. http://www.ncdc.noaa.gov/oa/climate/research/2005/katrina.html. Accessed on Feb. 17, 2006.

17 Cmdr. Anthony Popiel, e-mail to Jason Yanussi, Senate Committee staff member, Apr. 6, 2006, 2 pm.

18 Cmdr. Anthony Popiel, e-mail to Jason Yanussi, Senate Committee staff member, Apr. 6, 2006, 2 pm.

19 Cmdr. Anthony Popiel, e-mail to Jason Yanussi, Senate Committee staff member, Apr. 6, 2006, 2 pm.

20 Written Statement of Sec. Chertoff, Senate Committee hearing, Feb. 15, 2006, p. 2.

21 Written Statement of Sec. Chertoff, Senate Committee hearing, Feb. 15, 2006, p. 2.

22 National Center for Missing and Exploited Children, "National Center for Missing and Exploited Children Reunites Last Missing Child Separated by Hurricane Katrina and Rita," press release, Mar. 17, 2006. http://www.missingkids.com/missingkids/servlet/NewsEventServlet?LanguageCountry=en_US&PageId=2317. Accessed on Mar. 30, 2006.

23 National Center for Missing and Exploited Children, "National Center for Missing and Exploited Children Reunites Last Missing Child Separated by Hurricane Katrina and Rita," press release, Mar. 17, 2006. http://www.missingkids.com/missingkids/servlet/NewsEventServlet?LanguageCountry=en_US&PageId=2317. Accessed on Mar. 30, 2006.

24 "Never-ending Sorrow," New Orleans *Times-Picayune*, Apr. 19, 2006, p. 6.

25 Michele Norris, All Things Considered, NPR, "New Orleans Seeks Final Home for Nameless Victims," Feb. 13, 2006, 9 p.m. Transcript accessed on LexisNexis.

26 City of New Orleans, Emergency Operations Center, *Rapid Population Estimate Project*, Jan. 28-29, 2006. http://www.gnocdc.org/reports/NOLAPopEstimate.pdf. Accessed on Apr. 6, 2006.

27 Testimony of Don Powell, Coordinator of Recovery and Rebuilding in the Gulf Coast Region, U.S. Department of Homeland Security, before the U.S. Senate, Committee on Homeland Security and Governmental Affairs, hearing on *Mississippi's Recovery from Hurricane Katrina*, Jan. 17, 2006.

New Orleans, flooded
U.S. Coast Guard photo

Hurricanes and the Gulf Coast

How Hurricanes Form

A hurricane is the strongest form of a "tropical cyclone," the term used to describe weather systems that develop over tropical or sub-tropical waters with organized thunderstorms and a well-defined central "eye."

Most Atlantic hurricanes begin as atmospheric waves that move westward from Africa across the tropical North Atlantic and Caribbean Sea. This stretch of ocean is known as the main development region. Here, warm sea-surface temperatures pass moisture into the atmosphere, increasing humidity levels. Winds moving in from different directions collide with the atmospheric waves and force air upwards. If there is low wind shear the air will continue to rise. The storm's energy comes from the continuous exchange of heat between the ocean and the atmosphere, which is released through the formation of clouds concentrated in the center of the forming cyclone.

Scouting Katrina from above
U.S. Air Force photo

The appearance of a high-pressure system provides the final ingredient. The high-pressure system floats above the storm and draws the warm ocean air upward, pushing it outward from the top of the gathering storm in a continuous cycle. At this point the Earth's rotation gives the incoming air a counter-clockwise spin and, propelled by the warm wind currents, the storm moves toward the coast.[1]

Tracking and Predicting Hurricanes

Not all storms in the main development region become hurricanes. Often, preexisting winds will tear apart the storm as it forms. If conditions are favorable, however, scientists will reclassify these "tropical disturbances" into more severe storms as their sustained wind speed rises:

- At 23 miles per hour, the disturbance becomes a "tropical depression."

- At 39 miles per hour, the depression becomes a "tropical storm" and gets a name.

- At 74 miles per hour, the tropical storm is classified as a hurricane (in the Pacific, a typhoon).[2]

A hurricane needs a constant source of energy. In this case, from June to November, the warm, humid waters of the Atlantic fuel the storm as trade winds from the east and ocean currents direct its path.[3] The storm weakens if it happens to move across cool water or land, losing its thermal energy source.[4]

The National Hurricane Center (NHC) in Miami, Florida, determines the track, intensity, and landfall effects of a storm. The NHC issues 72-hour tropical cyclone track and intensity forecasts four times a day for all storms in the north Atlantic and northeastern Pacific.[5]

A hurricane watch is issued 36 hours before hurricane conditions are expected to affect coastal areas. A warning is issued 24 hours beforehand and may remain in effect even if wind speeds drop below hurricane force to account for the possibility of hurricane-level storm surge.

Storm surge is wind-driven water.[6] As a hurricane churns in the atmosphere, its winds snowball the water below toward the shoreline. Combined with normal tides, this surge can increase the mean water level 15 feet and push up to 100 miles inland.[7] Even if a hurricane has weakened by the time it has reached shore, it has been building up storm surge since a much earlier time, when it was much stronger.

Though hurricanes are measured by their wind speeds, many scientists have come to believe that storm surge is far more deadly than wind, especially considering that the highly populated areas of the Atlantic seaboard and the Gulf Coast lie only 10 feet above mean sea level.[8] Hurricane Andrew (1992), which carried a 17-foot storm surge into Miami's Biscayne Bay, illustrated the danger. Its storm surge shoved the Belzona Barge – a 215-foot, 350-ton barge that had been deliberately sunk 68 feet below the surface, with a thousand tons of concrete resting on deck, off the coast of Florida to establish an artificial reef – 700 feet to the west along the ocean floor.[9] "The greatest potential for loss of life related to a hurricane is from the storm surge," according to an official with the National Oceanic and Atmospheric Administration (NOAA).[10]

Significant progress in hurricane forecasting has prevented major loss of life in areas prone to hurricanes.[11] The National Weather Service (NWS) uses the Sea, Lake, and Overland Surges from Hurricanes (SLOSH) computer program to predict the storm surge of an inbound hurricane and to map the likely impact of hurricanes of different sizes, speeds, strengths, and tracks. The SLOSH program uses a storm's barometric pressure, overall size, forward speed, track, and wind speed, as well as prior hurricane information and other models.[12]

During Hurricane Andrew in 1992, alarmed by scenes in South Florida, approximately 1.2 million people evacuated from the New Orleans metropolitan area. While the evacuation almost certainly saved lives, federal hurricane experts were alarmed that officials in New Orleans expected 60 to 80 hours' warning to complete an evacuation. During testimony before a Congressional committee in 1993, Robert Sheets, Ph.D., then the director of the NHC, warned that "We don't have the skill meteorologically speaking to provide a sufficient warning for those long lead times. There is no way I am going to have 70 hours of lead time for New Orleans to respond to a hurricane."[13]

By 2005, advances in technology, such as refinement of satellite capabilities and improvement of pressure-measuring sensors in reconnaissance planes, had drastically increased the NHC's lead times.[14] By 2 p.m. ET Friday, August 26, 65 hours before Katrina made landfall, NHC Director Max Mayfield, Ph.D., was making calls to emergency officials in the Gulf Coast alerting them that a rapidly strengthening storm was heading directly for New Orleans.[15]

Hurricanes and the Gulf Coast

The same warm waters that give the Gulf Coast its marshy topography and humid climate make it a prime target for hurricanes, while demographic and economic trends have multiplied their potential impact.[16] In earlier periods of our history, the physical impact of major hurricanes in the Gulf was softened by swamps, marshes, and barrier islands, while the societal impact was limited by its relatively small concentrations of buildings and people.

In more recent times, however, the population in the coastal counties from Texas to the Florida Keys has soared. The U.S. Census Bureau reports that 9.46 million people live along

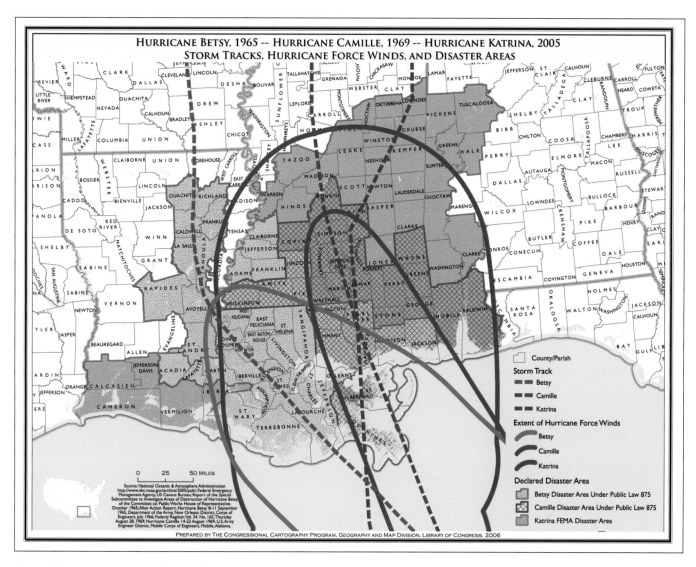

HURRICANE BETSY, 1965 -- HURRICANE CAMILLE, 1969 -- HURRICANE KATRINA, 2005
STORM TRACKS, HURRICANE FORCE WINDS, AND DISASTER AREAS

the Gulf Coast – 3.5 times the number in 1950 – and their numbers are growing by nearly 7 percent a year.[17] From 1970 to 1994, the Gulf Coast averaged less than one hurricane land-fall per season, and the East Coast averaged one hurricane landfall every five years. This is in sharp contrast to the average of three U.S. hurricane landfalls during very active seasons. Unfortunately, decisions about land use, construction standards, etc. were based on an erroneous assumption, growing out of that period, that hurricanes would no longer affect the United States as frequently or as strongly as they had in earlier decades.[18]

Besides economic and population growth – including the swelling numbers of retirees drawn to warm-winter locales – engineering projects intended to prevent or reduce flood damage increased the appeal of the Gulf Coast. Here, as in the Southwest and the West Coast, "We are pushing toward the very areas where nature puts us most at risk from tropical storms, mudslides, and forest fires," Princeton University researcher Edward Tenner wrote in 1996. One of Tenner's examples: "A big storm could leave 20 feet of water in downtown New Orleans and flood evacuation routes."[19]

Ten years before Hurricane Katrina struck New Orleans, NOAA saw signs that the Atlantic Ocean had entered a 10 to 40-year cycle of intense hurricanes that would present an especially serious threat to the Gulf Coast.[20] From 1970 through 1994, the United States enjoyed what meteorologists viewed as "normal" Atlantic hurricane seasons, a period of relatively

Hurricanes Betsy, Camille, and Katrina
Geography and Map Division,
The Library of Congress

mild activity that had produced few major hurricanes, That period averaged five hurricanes annually and 1.5 major hurricanes.[21]

Since 1995, however, hurricane seasons have averaged 7.6 hurricanes each year and 3.6 major hurricanes, with reported increases in their destructive power.[22] Historically, the number of major hurricanes and the number of Caribbean hurricanes tended to follow the multi-decade cycle, according to a 2001 analysis by a team of hurricane experts, who said: "The late 1920s to the 1960s were very active, while both the 1900s and the 1970s through the early 1990s were quiescent." [23]

New Orleans was not the only major U.S. population center that was in greater danger of a catastrophic storm. Analysis of historical data showed that two regions of the United States – the East Coast from South Carolina to Maine and the Gulf Coast from Florida to Texas – faced a much greater risk of catastrophic hurricanes and storm surges.

Marking the beginning of a new multi-decade period of hurricanes activity involves extensive analysis of historical trends, conditions in the Atlantic and the atmosphere.[24] Even so, there are no guarantees. Catastrophic hurricanes have occurred in years of normal or even below-normal hurricane activity. In 1972, Hurricane Agnes never got beyond Category 1 strength, but still caused 122 deaths in the United States, with severe flooding in Virginia and the Carolinas.[25] Hurricane Andrew, the most damaging hurricane in U.S. history before Katrina, formed during a season (and cycle, lasting until 1994) of below-normal activity.[26]

Between 1995 and 2000, however, the North Atlantic had the highest level of hurricanes on record, including several that threatened New Orleans.[27] Among them was Hurricane Georges in 1998, a Category 3 storm that caused 602 deaths in the Caribbean, set a track for New Orleans, but turned toward Mississippi before making landfall. [28] By 2000, hurricane experts had concluded that the Atlantic was undergoing "multi-decadal conditions" that favored more major hurricanes. Scientists began calling for improvements in hurricane preparedness.[29] The NWS was issuing annual Atlantic Hurricane Outlooks, long-range forecasts of hurricane activity and severity.[30] Released each May before the June 1 start of the hurricane season, the Outlooks relied on a yardstick known as the Accumulated Cyclone Energy (ACE) Index.[31]

The agency's 2003 Outlook predicted a 55 percent likelihood of above-normal hurricane activity, with an estimated range of two to four major hurricanes. However, the projected ACE value of the season had a staggering range: 110-180 percent of the median, which was much higher than 2002 and the 1971-1994 period.[32] Two months later, the agency increased the probability for an above-normal hurricane season to 60 percent and projected that three to four major hurricanes would threaten the United States.[33] The assessment was correct: By November, the Atlantic had spawned three major hurricanes, including Isabel, a storm that reached Category 5 strength before striking North Carolina as a Category 2.[34]

A year later, the Outlook for 2004 predicted a 50 percent chance of an above-normal hurricane season, with two to four major hurricanes and an ACE index in the range of 100-160 percent. That year, four major storms roared through the Gulf, including Hurricane Ivan. This Category 5 storm produced at least 34 tornadoes and was the most destructive hurricane to strike the Florida Panhandle and Alabama coast in a hundred years.[35]

The NWS's 2005 Outlook, issued in May, predicted yet another above-normal hurricane season with twice the usual number of major hurricanes.[36] This time, the pre-season estimate called for three to five major storms and made it clear that the odds of a catastrophic storm were increasing. "The main uncertainty in this outlook is not whether the season will be above normal, but how much above normal it will be," the report said.[37]

During the next 60 days, the Atlantic spawned seven tropical storms and two major hurricanes, Dennis and Emily.[38] On August 2, the NWS issued an update of its 2005 Outlook that predicted a "95% to 100% chance" of an above-normal hurricane season and increased its estimated range from three to five, to five to seven storms. [39]

Twenty-one days later, on August 23, Tropical Depression 12 developed about 175 nautical miles southeast of Nassau, in the Bahamas. The following day, it was designated Tropical Storm Katrina.[40]

---

1 Christopher Landsea et al., "Atlantic Basin Hurricanes: Indices of Climatic Changes," *Climatic Change* 42:1, May 1999, pp. 89-129; Stanley B. Goldenberg et al., "The Recent Increase in Atlantic Hurricane Activity: Causes and Implications," *Science*, July 20, 2001, pp. 475-467 [hereinafter Goldenberg, "The Recent Increase in Atlantic Hurricane Activity"]; and Lloyd J. Shapiro and Stanley B. Goldenberg, "Atlantic Sea Surface Temperatures and Tropical Cyclone Formation," *Journal of Climate* 11, 1997, pp. 578-590; National Aeronautics and Space Administration, Earth Observatory "Hurricanes: The Greatest Storms on Earth." http://earthobservatory.nasa.gov/Library/Hurricanes/index.html. Accessed on Mar. 31, 2006 [hereinafter NASA, "Hurricanes: The Greatest Storms on Earth"] ("Hurricanes form over tropical waters (between 8° and 20° latitude) in areas of high humidity, light winds, and warm sea surface temperatures (typically 26.5°C [80°F] or greater). These conditions usually prevail in the summer and early fall months of the tropical North Atlantic and North Pacific Oceans and for this reason, hurricane 'season' in the northern hemisphere runs from June through November.").

2 NASA, "Hurricanes: The Greatest Storms on Earth."

Hurricanes are sorted into categories on the Saffir-Simpson Scale, named for the engineer and the meteorologist who developed it in the 1970s. Its five categories are now the standard method for classifying hurricanes:

Category	1	2	3	4	5
Wind speed (mi/hr)	74–95	96–110	111–130	131–155	155+
Storm surge (ft)	4–5	6–8	9–12	13–18	18+
Damage	Minimal	Moderate	Extensive	Extreme	Catastrophic

3 National Oceanic and Atmospheric Administration, Hurricane Research Division, "When is Hurricane Season?" http://www.aoml.noaa.gov/hrd/tcfaq/G1.html. Accessed on Jan. 24, 2006 ("The Atlantic hurricane season is officially from 1 June to 30 November. There is nothing magical in these dates, and hurricanes have occurred outside of these six months, but these dates were selected to encompass over 97% of tropical activity. The Atlantic basin shows a very peaked season from August through October, with 78% of the tropical storm days, 87% of the minor (Saffir-Simpson Scale categories 1 and 2 – see Subject D1) hurricane days, and 96% of the major (Saffir-Simpson categories 3, 4 and 5) hurricane days occurring then (*Landsea 1993*). Maximum activity is in early to mid September.").

4 *Technical Data Report: Southeast Louisiana Hurricane Preparedness Study*, prepared by U.S. Army Corps of Engineers, New Orleans District for Federal Emergency Management Agency, Aug. 1994, p. 2–12 [hereinafter *Southeast Louisiana Hurricane Preparedness Study*, Aug. 1994] ("Most hurricanes weaken after landfall because the central pressure increases and the radius of maximum winds tends to increase. The terrain of southern Louisiana is very low, flat, and marshy and the transition to land from water is not abrupt.").

5 *See:* National Weather Service, National Hurricane Center, Tropical Prediction Center. http://www.nhc.noaa.gov.

6 *Southeast Louisiana Hurricane Preparedness Study*, Aug. 1994, p. 2–2 ("A hurricane moving over the continental shelf produces a buildup of water at the coastline which is commonly referred to as storm surge. Storm surge is the increase in height of the surface of the sea due to the forces of an approaching hurricane. Storm surge normally occurs over a coastline for distances of 100 miles or more. The winds associated with a hurricane are the largest single component responsible for the buildup of storm surge within a basin. The wind blowing over the surface of the water exerts a horizontal force which induces a surface current in the general direction of the wind. The surface current, in turn, induces currents in subsurface water. This process of current creation continues to a depth which is determined by the depth of the water and by the intensity and forward motion of the hurricane. For example, a fast moving hurricane of moderate intensity may only induce currents to a depth of a hundred feet, whereas a slow moving hurricane of moderate intensity might induce currents to several hundred feet. These horizontal currents are impeded by a sloping continental shelf as the hurricane approaches the coastline, thereby causing the water level to rise. A wide gently sloping continental shelf is particularly conducive to the formation of large storm surges. The amount of rise increases shoreward to a maximum level at, or some distance inland from the shoreline.").

7 Louisiana Office of Homeland Security and Emergency Preparedness and Louisiana State Hazard Mitigation Planning Committee, *State of Louisiana Hazard Mitigation Plan*, Apr. 15, 2005, p. I–46 [hereinafter *State of Louisiana Hazard Mitigation Plan*, Apr. 15, 2005] ("In Louisiana, storm surges are large waves of Gulf waters that sweep across coastlines where a tropical storm makes landfall. Generally the more intense the storm, the greater the height of the storm surge; the higher the storm surge, the greater the damage to the coastline. Storm surges inundate coastal floodplains, wash out dunes, cause backwater flooding through coastal river mouths, generate large waves that run up and flood coastal beach-

es, and can flood streets and buildings in coastal communities….The coastal bathymetry of southeastern Louisiana, with its low, flat topography and land surface elevations that in many places dip below sea level, can experience storm surges up to 100 miles inland. Category 3 storms can bring depths up to 24 feet as far north as the City of New Orleans. Category 5 storms can produce depths as high as 36 feet. Furthermore, lakes along the coast, namely, Lake Maurepas, Lake Borgne, and Lake Pontchartrain, exacerbate the effects of coastal flooding because of wave effects that can regenerate over inland lakes. It is important to note that the map represents the cumulative storm surges for hundreds of modeled hypothetical hurricane tracks; no single hurricane event would produce the inundation pattern depicted on the map.").

8 National Hurricane Center, Hurricane Preparedness, "Hurricane Preparedness Week." http://www.nhc.noaa.gov/HAW2/english/intro.shtml. Accessed on Jan. 16, 2006.

9 Ed Rappaport, National Hurricane Center, *Preliminary Report: Hurricane Andrew, 16-28 August 1992*, Dec. 10, 1993. http://www.nhc.noaa.gov/1992andrew.html. Accessed on Apr. 26, 2006 [hereinafter Rappaport, *Preliminary Report: Hurricane Andrew*].

10 Brian Jarvinen, National Hurricane Center, Hurricane Preparedness, "Storm Surge." http://www.nhc.noaa.gov/HAW2/english/storm_surge.shtml. Accessed on Apr. 27, 2006.

11 Written Statement of Brig. Gen. David L. Johnson, U.S. Air Force (Ret.), Assistant Administrator for Weather Services, and Director, National Weather Service, National Oceanic and Atmospheric Administration, for the U.S. House of Representatives, Committee on Science, hearing on *NOAA Hurricane Forecasting*, Oct. 7, 2005, p. 3 ("The mission of the National Weather Service (NWS) is to issue weather, water and climate forecasts and warnings for the protection of life and property and the enhancement of the national economy. Nowhere is that more evident than in the hurricane program."). *Source:* Written Statement of Brig. Gen. Johnson, House Committee on Science hearing, Oct. 7, 2005, p.1. In 1943, aircraft reconnaissance of the hurricanes began. In 1959, land-based weather radars were placed at Lake Charles and Slidell, Louisiana and Pensacola, Florida. In the 1960s scientists gained the ability to observe tropical storm behavior through the use of satellite photography. *Source*: *Southeast Louisiana Hurricane Preparedness Study*, Aug. 1994, p. 1-9.

12 Written Statement of Brig. Gen. Johnson, House Committee on Science hearing, Oct. 7, 2005, p. 4 ("Following Hurricane Camille in 1969, NOAA established a group that developed and implemented a storm surge model called SLOSH (Sea, Lake, and Overland Surges from Hurricanes) The SLOSH model calculates storm surge heights resulting either from historical, hypothetical or actual hurricanes. SLOSH incorporates bathymetry and topography, including bay and river configurations, roads, levees, and other physical features that can modify the storm surge flow pattern."). *See also: Southeast Louisiana Hurricane Preparedness Study*, Aug. 1994, p. 2-6 ("In addition to furnishing surge heights for the open coast, the SLOSH model has the added capability to compute the routing of storm surge into bays, estuaries, or coastal river basins as well as calculating surge heights for overland locations. Significant natural and man-made barriers are represented in the model and their effects simulated in the calculations of surge heights within a basin."); *State of Louisiana Hazard Mitigation Plan*, Apr. 15, 2005, p. I–46 ("Storm surge areas can be mapped by the probability of storm surge occurrences using Sea, Lake and Overland Surges from Hurricanes modeling (referred to as SLOSH modeling)… SLOSH models represent the storm surge of hundreds of simulated hurricanes, taking into account storm wind intensities, forward speeds, directions of motion, and radius of maximum winds.").

13 Testimony of Robert Sheets, Ph.D., Director, National Hurricane Center, before the U.S. Senate, Committee on Governmental Affairs, hearing on *Rebuilding FEMA: Preparing for the Next Disaster*, May 18, 1993, p. 45.

14 Written Statement of Max Mayfield, Ph.D., Director, National Hurricane Center, for the U.S. House, Select Bipartisan Committee to Investigate the Preparation for and Response to Hurricane Katrina, hearing on *Predicting Hurricanes: What We Knew About Katrina and When*, Sept. 22, 2005, p. 5. For instance, the NWS used reconnaissance aircraft equipped with Stepped Frequency Microwave Radiometer (SFMR) that collects data about hurricane structure, surface wind and rain rate. *See also:* Written Statement of Brig. Gen. Johnson, House Committee on Science hearing, Oct. 7, 2005, p. 3 NWS also uses hurricane monitoring buoys deployed in the Caribbean.

15 Committee staff interview of Max Mayfield, Ph.D., Director, National Hurricane Center, conducted on Jan. 27, 2006, transcript pp. 29-40.

16 For a detailed description of topography and economic development of the Louisiana Gulf Coast, *see: Southeast Louisiana Hurricane Preparedness Study*, Aug. 1994, pp. 1–2 through 1–5.

17 U.S Census Bureau, U.S. Census Bureau News, Newsroom "Almost 10 Million Gulf Coast Residents Bracing for Hurricane Dennis," press release, July 8, 2005. http://www.census.gov/PressRelease/www/releases/archives/hurricanes_tropical_storms/005345.html. Accessed on Jan. 27, 2006.

18 National Oceanic and Atmospheric Administration, "NOAA Attributes Recent Increase in Hurricane Activity to Naturally Occurring Multi-Decadal Climate Variability," *NOAA Magazine*, Nov. 29, 2005. http://www.magazine.noaa.gov/stories/mag184.htm. Accessed on Mar. 8, 2006 [hereinafter NOAA, "NOAA Attributes Recent Increase in Hurricane Activity to Naturally Occurring Multi-Decadal Climate Variability"].

19 Edward Tenner, *Why Things Bite Back: Technology and the Revenge of Unintended Consequences*, New York: Knopf, 1996, pp. 93-94.

20 Goldenberg, "The Recent Increase in Atlantic Hurricane Activity" pp. 474-479 ("The years 1995 to 2000 experienced the highest level of North Atlantic hurricane activity in the reliable record. Compared with the generally low activity of the previous 24 years (1971 to 1994), the past 6 years have seen a doubling of overall activity for the whole basin, a 2.5-fold increase in major hurricanes … five-fold increase in hurricanes affecting the Caribbean.").

21 National Weather Service, Climate Prediction Center, "Background Information: The North Atlantic Hurricane

Season." http://www.cpc.ncep.noaa.gov/products/outlooks/background_information.shtm. Accessed on Apr. 6, 2006. ("An average hurricane season features ten tropical storms (maximum sustained winds between 39-73 mph), of which an average of six become hurricanes (maximum sustained winds of at least 74 mph) and two become major hurricanes (maximum sustained winds exceeding 110 mph, categories 3-5 on the Saffir-Simpson scale).").

22 National Oceanic and Atmospheric Administration, National Climatic Data Center, National Environmental Satellite, Data, and Information Service, "Climate of 2005, Atlantic Hurricane Season." http://www.ncdc.noaa.gov/oa/climate/research/2005/hurricanes05.html. Accessed on Apr. 30, 2006. ("Tropical cyclone activity in the Atlantic basin has been above normal since 1995. This has been largely in response to the active phase of the multi-decadal signal. The average number of named storms since 1995 has been 13, compared to 8.6 during the preceding 25 years during which time the multi-decadal signal was in an inactive phase. An average of 7.7 hurricanes and 3.6 major hurricanes since 1995 compares to 5 hurricanes and 1.5 major hurricanes from 1970-1994. Characteristics of an active multi-decadal signal in the Atlantic include: warmer SSTs in the tropical Atlantic region, an amplified sub-tropical ridge at upper levels across the central and eastern North Atlantic, reduced vertical wind shear in the deep tropics over the central North Atlantic, and an African Easterly Jet (AEJ) that is favorable for promoting the development and intensification of tropical disturbances moving westward off the coast of Africa. Recent studies also indicate that in addition to this multi-decadal oscillation the destructive power of hurricanes has generally increased since the mid-1970s, when the period of the most rapid increase in global ocean and land temperatures began.").

23 Goldenberg, "The Recent Increase in Atlantic Hurricane Activity," pp. 476-477 ("The Caribbean Sea has shown dramatic changes in hurricane activity – averaging 1.7 occurrences per year during the warm periods compared with only 0.5 per year during the cold period (34). The current warm period has produced an average of 2.5 occurrences per year with an unprecedented (since 1944) six hurricanes in the region during 1996. … This means that during the next 10 to 40 years or so, most of the Atlantic hurricane seasons are likely to have above average activity, with many hyperactive, some around average, and only a few below average. Furthermore, consistent with experience since the active phase began in 1995, there would be a continuation of significantly increased numbers of hurricanes (and major hurricanes) affecting the Caribbean Sea and basin-wide numbers of major hurricanes.").

24 Goldenberg, "The Recent Increase in Atlantic Hurricane Activity," pp. 474-479 ("The greater activity results from simultaneous increases in North Atlantic sea-surface temperatures and decreases in vertical wind shear."). *See also:* NOAA, "NOAA Attributes Recent Increase in Hurricane Activity to Naturally Occurring Multi-Decadal Climate Variability" ("This era has been unfolding in the Atlantic since 1995, and is expected to continue for the next decade or perhaps longer. NOAA attributes this increased activity to natural occurring cycles in tropical climate patterns near the equator. These cycles, called 'the tropical multi-decadal signal,' typically last several decades (20 to 30 years or even longer). As a result, the North Atlantic experiences alternating decades long (20 to 30 year periods or even longer) of above normal or below normal hurricane seasons.").

25 National Oceanic and Atmospheric Administration, NOAA Coastal Services Center, "Hurricane History." http://www.nhc.noaa.gov/HAW2/english/history.shtml. Accessed on Apr. 16, 2006. Agnes was barely a hurricane at landfall in Florida, and the effects of winds and storm surges were relatively minor. The major impact was over the northeastern United States, where Agnes combined with the non-tropical low to produce widespread rains of 6 to 12 inches with local amounts of 14 to 19 inches. These rains produced widespread severe flooding from Virginia northward to New York, with other flooding occurring over the western portions of the Carolinas. Agnes caused 122 deaths in the United States. Nine of these were in Florida (mainly from severe thunderstorms) while the remainder were associated with the flooding. The storm was responsible for $2.1 billion in damage in the United States, the vast majority of which came from the flooding. Agnes also affected western Cuba, where seven additional deaths occurred.

26 Rappaport, *Preliminary Report: Hurricane Andrew* ("Andrew was a small and ferocious Cape Verde hurricane that wrought unprecedented economic devastation along a path through the northwestern Bahamas, the southern Florida peninsula, and south-central Louisiana. Damage in the United States is estimated to be near 25 billion, making Andrew the most expensive natural disaster in U.S. history.[1] The tropical cyclone struck southern Dade County, Florida, especially hard, with violent winds and storm surges characteristic of a category 4 hurricane (see addendum on upgrade to category 5) on the Saffir/Simpson Hurricane Scale, and with a central pressure (922 mb) that is the third lowest this century for a hurricane at landfall in the United States. In Dade County alone, the forces of Andrew resulted in 15 deaths and up to one-quarter million people left temporarily homeless. An additional 25 lives were lost in Dade County from the indirect effects of Andrew. The direct loss of life seems remarkably low considering the destruction caused by this hurricane.").

27 Goldenberg, "The Recent Increase in Atlantic Hurricane Activity," pp. 474-479.

28 John L. Guiney, National Hurricane Center, Preliminary Report: Hurricane George, 15 September – 01 October 1998, Jan. 5, 1999. http://www.nhc.noaa.gov/1998georges.html. Accessed on Apr. 26, 2006. ("Georges (pronounced Zhorzh) was the second deadliest and second strongest hurricane within the Atlantic basin during the 1998 season. Its 17 day journey resulted in seven landfalls, extending from the northeastern Caribbean to the coast of Mississippi, and 602 fatalities – mainly in the Dominican Republic and Haiti.").

29 Goldenberg, "The Recent Increase in Atlantic Hurricane Activity" p. 474 ("The years 1995 to 2000 experienced the highest level of North Atlantic hurricane activity in the reliable record. Compared with the generally low activity of the previous 24 years (1971 to 1994), the past 6 years have seen a doubling of overall activity for the whole basin, a 2.5-fold increase in major hurricanes (≥50 meters per second), and a twofold increase in hurricanes affecting the Caribbean. The greater activity results from simultaneous increases in North Atlantic sea-surface temperatures and decreases in vertical wind shear. Because these changes exhibit a multidecadal time scale, the present high level of hurricane activity is likely to persist for an additional ~ 10 to 40 years. The shift in climate calls for a reevaluation of preparedness and mitigation strategies.").

30 *See:* National Weather Service, Climate Prediction Center, "August 2004 Update to Atlantic Hurricane Season Outlook," Aug. 10, 2004. http://www.cpc.noaa.gov/products/outlooks/hurricane2004/August/hurricane.html.

31 National Oceanic and Atmospheric Administration, National Climatic Data Center, "Hurricane Katrina A Climatological Perspective," Oct. 2005, p. 23 ("The Accumulated Cyclone Energy Index is one method to describe trends in tropical cyclone activity. This index is a combination of the tropical cyclone's duration in a particular ocean basin, along with the strength of each storm.").

32 National Weather Service, Climate Prediction Center, "NOAA: 2003 Atlantic Hurricane Outlook," May 19, 2003. http://www.cpc.noaa.gov/products/outlooks/hurricane2003/May/hurricane.html. Accessed on April 5, 2006 ("This expected activity is considerably more than the four hurricanes and ACE value of 74% of the median observed during 2002. It is also much larger than the seasonal average of five hurricanes and ACE value of 75% of the median observed during the relatively quiet period 1970-1994.").

33 National Weather Service, Climate Prediction Center, "NOAA: 2003 Atlantic Hurricane Outlook Update," Aug, 7, 2003. http://www.cpc.noaa.gov/products/outlooks/hurricane2003/August/hurricane.html. Accessed on Apr. 4, 2006.

34 Isabel is considered to be one of the most significant tropical cyclones to affect portions of northeastern North Carolina and east-central Virginia since Hurricane Hazel in 1954 and the Chesapeake-Potomac Hurricane of 1933. Jack Bevin and Hugh Cobb, National Oceanic and Atmospheric Administration, "Tropical Cyclone Report for Hurricane Isabel 6 – 19 September 2003." Jan. 16, 2004. http://www.nhc.noaa.gov/2003isabel.shtml. Accessed on Apr. 14, 2006.

35 Gerald Bell, et al., "The 2004 North Atlantic Hurricane Season: A Climate Perspective," pp. 1-4. http://www.cpc.ncep.noaa.gov/products/expert_assessment/hurrsummary_2004.pdf#search='The%202004%20North%20Atlantic%20Hurricane%20Season%3A%20A%20Climate%20Perspective'. Accessed on Apr. 26, 2006 ("The 2004 Atlantic hurricane season had well above-normal activity, with 15 named storms, 9 hurricanes (H), and 6 major hurricanes [MH, defined as categories 3-5 on the Saffir-Simpson scale, Simpson (1974)]. Nine of these systems struck the continental United States, three as tropical storms (Bonnie, Hermine, and Matthew) and six as hurricanes (Alex, Charley, Frances, Gaston, Ivan, and Jeanne). Three of the hurricanes (Charley, Ivan, and Jeanne) hit as major hurricanes… MH Ivan, the strongest of the 2004 hurricanes, eventually made landfall in Alabama and produced the largest storm total ACE value (70.4 x 104 kt2) in the reliable record.").

36 National Weather Service, Climate Prediction Center, "NOAA: 2005 Atlantic Hurricane Outlook," May 16, 2005. http://www.cpc.noaa.gov/products/outlooks/hurricane2005/May/hurricane.html. Accessed on Apr. 4, 2006; Written Statement of Max Mayfield, Ph.D., Director, National Hurricane Center, for the U.S. Senate, Committee on Commerce, Science, and Transportation, hearing on *The Life Saving Role of Accurate Hurricane Prediction*, Sept. 20, 2005, p. 6 ("The natural cycles are quite large with on average 3-4 major hurricanes a year in active periods and only about 1-2 major hurricanes annually during quiet periods, with each period lasting 25-40 years.").

37 National Weather Service, Climate Prediction Center, "NOAA: 2005 Atlantic Hurricane Outlook," May 16, 2005. http://www.cpc.noaa.gov/products/outlooks/hurricane2005/May/hurricane.html. Accessed on Apr. 4, 2006.

38 National Weather Service, Climate Prediction Center, "NOAA: August 2005 Update to Atlantic Hurricane Season Outlook," Aug. 2, 2005. http://www.cpc.noaa.gov/products/outlooks/hurricane2005/August/hurricane.html. Accessed on Apr. 4, 2006 ("The predicted seasonal totals include the considerable activity that has already occurred prior to this update (7 tropical storms and 2 major hurricanes)...Of particular relevance to this outlook is that two July tropical systems, Major Hurricanes Dennis and Emily, formed over the eastern Caribbean Sea and over the central tropical Atlantic (near 10°N), respectively. It is rare for hurricanes to develop in these regions during July because the wind patterns are normally so unfavorable.").

39 National Oceanic and Atmospheric Administration, "August 2005 Update to Atlantic Hurricane Season Outlook," Aug. 2, 2005. http://www.cpc.noaa.gov/products/outlooks/hurricane2005/August/hurricane.html. Accessed on Apr. 4, 2006 ("The updated outlook calls for an extremely active season, with an expected seasonal total of 18-21 tropical storms (mean is 10), with 9-11 becoming hurricanes (mean is 6), and 5-7 of these becoming major hurricanes (mean is 2-3). The likely range of the ACE index for the season as a whole is 180%-270% of the median. The predicted seasonal totals include the considerable activity that has already occurred prior to this update (7 tropical storms and 2 major hurricanes). Therefore, for the remainder of the season, we expect an additional 11-14 tropical storms, with 7-9 becoming hurricanes, and 3-5 of these becoming major hurricanes. The expected ACE range during August-November is 110%-200% of the median. These very high levels of activity are comparable to those seen during August-November 2003 and 2004.").

40 Richard D. Knabb, Jamie R. Rhome, and Daniel P. Brown, National Hurricane Center, "Tropical Cyclone Report Hurricane Katrina 23-30 August 2005," Dec. 20, 2005, p. 1. http://www.nhc.noaa.gov/pdf/TCR-AL122005_Katrina.pdf#search='Tropical%20Cyclone%20Report%20Hurricane%20Katrina'. Accessed on Apr. 26, 2006.

A city become a lake, New Orleans
U.S. Coast Guard photo

Katrina Strikes

Louisiana

On August 23, 2005, Tropical Depression 12 developed about 200 miles southeast of Nassau. Within 24 hours, it was designated Tropical Storm Katrina.[1] Over the next two days, the storm strengthened and set a course for Florida. On August 25, Tropical Storm Katrina became a Category 1 hurricane, just hours before striking the Florida coast between Fort Lauderdale and Miami.[2] (See Chapter 3 for information about how hurricanes form and grow, and other relevant data.)

Katrina's six-hour march across land diminished its winds, but – atypically – left it with a more concentrated eye because it continued taking up heat and moisture as it passed over a marshy part of Florida's Everglades before entering the Gulf of Mexico.[3] There, the storm strengthened further, turned north and headed for the Florida Panhandle.[4]

Friday, August 26

By early Friday morning, August 26, Katrina was well into the Gulf of Mexico, just off the Florida Keys, 365 miles southeast of the mouth of the Mississippi River. It continued to grow and became more powerful.[5] Until now, the different modeling programs used by the National Weather Service's (NWS) National Hurricane Center (NHC) had projected the hurricane's track making landfall in the Florida Panhandle.[6]

By midday, however, the models began to converge on a course that showed a marked shift westward, toward Louisiana.[7] The NHC did not immediately issue a new advisory, but it now appeared that the agency's long-time fear – that New Orleans would take a direct hit from a major hurricane – was increasingly likely to come true.[8]

The 5 p.m. NHC advisory made the new track official: Katrina, still growing, had shifted 170 miles west.[9] It would soon become a major Category 3 hurricane, and, as reported by the NHC, conditions in the Gulf of Mexico "should allow the hurricane to reach Category 4 status before landfall occurs."[10]

Max Mayfield, Director of the NHC, phoned Walter Maestri, an old friend and the Emergency Preparedness Director in Jefferson Parish, Louisiana. Maestri recalled Mayfield's words: "This is it. This is what we've been talking about all of these years. You are going to take it. … It's a 30, 90 storm." Maestri explained, "That's the longitude and latitude of the City of New Orleans."[11] Other forecasters made similar calls to officials in Louisiana and Mississippi warning that Katrina was shifting their way.[12]

This new information was shared in a 5 p.m. CT (all subsequent times are Central Time) statewide conference call run by Colonel Jeff Smith, Deputy Director of the Louisiana Office of Homeland Security and Emergency Preparedness (LOHSEP). Katrina would be striking the eastern portion of the Mississippi coast in approximately 72 hours with Category 4 winds, a NWS forecaster informed officials.[13]

The forecaster reminded emergency managers that landfall was extremely difficult to predict with precision three days in advance.[14] But, the forecaster added, referring to the computer model used to measure storm surge, "If you look at a Category 4 storm surge, looking at the SLOSH models, you'd get into the 15 to 20-foot range quite easily."[15]

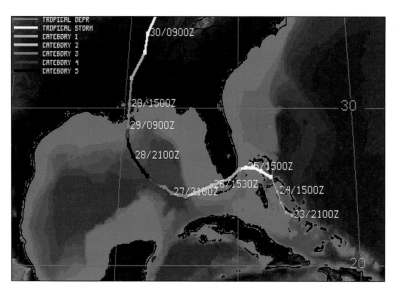

Katrina's storm track by day, time, and severity

Courtesy of University of Wisconsin Space Science and Engineering Center

Saturday, August 27

Throughout Saturday, August 27, Katrina nearly doubled in size. Its tropical storm-force winds extended outward about 160 miles from the center.[16]

At the NHC, officials were increasingly confident that Katrina would make landfall at or near New Orleans; a level of geographic precision was required for more accurate predictions of storm surge.[17] On a 7:30 a.m. conference call, a federal forecaster told Louisiana Governor Kathleen Blanco and state and parish emergency officials that by 9 a.m. Monday, southeast Louisiana could expect hurricane-force winds and a storm surge of 15 to 18 feet. The latest track prediction put the hurricane "smack dab through the metropolitan New Orleans areas."[18]

On Saturday evening, Max Mayfield made another round of telephone calls to assure himself that local and state officials understood what was coming. At approximately 7:25 p.m., he spoke with Governor Blanco, who suggested he call New Orleans Mayor C. Ray Nagin. Twenty minutes later, he spoke with Governor Haley Barbour in Mississippi. By 8 p.m., he had spoken with Mayor Nagin.[19]

Sunday, August 28

At 7 a.m., August 28, the NHC announced that Katrina was a "potentially catastrophic Category 5 hurricane."[20] The storm's tropical-force winds extended 230 miles from the center, "making Katrina not only extremely intense but also exceptionally large."[21] At that point, Katrina was twice as wide as 1992's Hurricane Andrew. Superimposed over the United States, it would have reached from Boston to Washington, D.C.

Less than an hour later, at 7:50 a.m., a NWS forecaster advised the St. Bernard Parish Office of Emergency Management to expect a direct strike from the hurricane with "[m]ajor overtopping" of the levees. He advised officials that "Residents should leave now before the onset of tropical force winds and rising tides cut off evacuation routes."[22]

Throughout the afternoon and evening, local forecasters advised local emergency managers about the intensifying storm. At 4:45 p.m., Hancock County, Mississippi, emergency managers were warned that Category 5 winds could produce a 28-foot storm surge in Waveland, on the coast. The City of New Orleans was warned to expect 18 to 22 feet.[23]

By early evening, storm-surge projections had grown more worrying. To underscore the danger, the NWS office in Slidell, Louisiana, issued a 5:45 p.m. advisory that called Katrina a "catastrophic" Category 5 hurricane and warned that "a few areas may experience storm surge flooding as high as 28 feet along with large and dangerous battering waves."[24] For the first time, the weather agency publicly warned of levee overtopping.[25]

The Geography of the Metropolitan New Orleans Region

While the New Orleans metropolitan area has been referred to as a "bowl," it would be more accurately described as three distinct, large, urban bowls, and one very thin, elongated, predominantly rural bowl.

A flood-control system surrounds these four areas, known as "polders": (1) Orleans East Bank, (2) New Orleans East, (3) Ninth Ward/St. Bernard, and (4) Plaquemines Parish.

The Orleans East Bank polder includes the downtown district, the French Quarter, the Garden District, and several other central New Orleans neighborhoods. It borders Lake Pontchartrain to the north and the Mississippi River to its south; the Industrial Canal forms its eastern border. Three large drainage canals penetrate the Orleans East Bank polder, emptying out into Lake Pontchartrain: the 17th Street, Orleans Avenue, and London Avenue Canals.

The New Orleans East polder also borders Lake Pontchartrain to the north; the Industrial Canal forms the west edge. To the south is the Gulf Intracoastal Waterway/Mississippi River Gulf Outlet (MRGO). Undeveloped swampland contained within the levee ring takes up the eastern edge. To the southeast is Lake Borgne.

The Ninth Ward/St. Bernard polder also borders the Industrial Canal to the west; the Gulf Intracoastal Waterway/MRGO channel is to the north and northeast. Lake Borgne is east, separated from the polder by the MRGO channel and undeveloped marshland. The polder's primary urban areas are in the south (St. Bernard Parish) and west (Ninth Ward).

Plaquemines Parish is a thin strip of land along the Mississippi River, which runs south-southeast from St. Bernard Parish to the mouth of the Mississippi River at the Gulf of Mexico. This strip, less than a mile wide in many areas, has levees fronting the Mississippi River and a second set of hurricane levees on its other side to protect against Gulf waters. The levees surround several small communities, utilities, and pipelines.[26]

Monday, August 29

Late Sunday, August 28, hurricane-force winds reached more than 100 miles from Katrina's eye.[27] The winds and, later, the accompanying storm surge would strike land well before the official landfall event of the eye's arrival. By 5 a.m. on Monday, with the wind field already over land, but the eye's landfall an hour away, Katrina was at Category 4 strength with maximum sustained winds of more than 130 miles an hour.[28] The NHC reported that with the storm's radius of maximum winds extending out roughly 30 to 35 miles from its center, "It is possible that sustained winds of Category 4 strength briefly impacted the extreme southeastern tip of Louisiana in advance of landfall."[29]

As the eye approached New Orleans, Katrina shoved a 14 to 17-foot storm surge up a "funnel" created by the hurricane protection levees at the convergence of the south bank of the MRGO and the north bank of the Gulf Intracoastal Waterway, and focused a torrent of water on the Inner Harbor Navigation Canal.[30] The eye of Hurricane Katrina made landfall at Buras, Plaquemines Parish, Louisiana, at 6:10 a.m. The storm was at the high end of Category 3 strength, with estimated maximum sustained winds of 127 miles an hour.[31] It tore through the Mississippi River and hurricane protection levees of the Plaquemines Parish polder.[32] By 10 a.m. the northward-moving eye had reached the mouth of the Pearl River at the Louisiana/Mississippi border.[33]

As the storm continued north – just east of downtown New Orleans – its strongest winds likely existed over the Gulf of Mexico to the east of the eye. Winds over the greater New Orleans metropolitan area were most likely weaker than Category 3,[34] but were probably stronger several hundred feet above ground, where brutal wind punched out windows in hotels and office buildings.[35]

As the counterclockwise-moving hurricane passed over Lake Borgne on the eastern side of the city with a storm surge estimated at 18 to 25 feet, it shoved water westward onto an edge of the levee that protected the northern edge of the Ninth Ward and St. Bernard Parish; 5 to 10 feet of excess surge easily slid over the levee walls.[36] Upon reaching Lake Pontchartrain, Katrina's winds produced a southward surge of lakewater along the northern edges of the

Orleans East Bank and New Orleans East polders, with overtopping and a breach in New Orleans East, adjacent to the Lakefront Airport.[37]

The surge from Lake Pontchartrain and Lake Borgne streamed into the Industrial Canal and the MRGO channel. Here, too, the floodwaters easily overflowed the levees. In time, the erosion of the earthen levees by overtopping led to numerous breaches that added to the torrent of water quickly filling the "bowls" that included the New Orleans East and Ninth Ward/St. Bernard polders.[38]

The inundation of New Orleans happened in two stages. A "surge funnel" that attacked the levees and floodwalls along the MRGO, the Gulf Intracoastal Waterway and the Inner Harbor Navigation Canal caused the first flooding. The second stage began when Katrina's storm surge muscled into Lake Pontchartrain.[39] "Both events caused overtopping, or flow over intact levees and floodwalls, as well as breaching that resulted in flow under and through levees and floodwalls,"[40] according to a report by the Center for the Study of Public Health Impacts of Hurricanes at Louisiana State University. "In some cases, overtopping preceded or led to breaching, while in other places breaches opened before surge levels rose high enough to cause overtopping."[41]

A report by the American Society of Civil Engineers and the National Science Foundation reached a similar conclusion, noting that "Most of the levee and floodwall failures were caused by overtopping, as the storm surge rose over the tops of the levees and/or their floodwalls and produced erosion that subsequently led to failures and breaches."[42]

First image of breaching, New Orleans

Courtesy of National Geographic Channel's "Explorer: Drowning New Orleans." Photo by Paul Hellmers © Paul Hellmers

Because the storm surge arrived ahead of the hurricane, some residential areas in the greater New Orleans area began to flood just after 4 a.m.[43] Between 4 and 5 a.m., minor breaches opened in the levees at the intersection of the CSX Railroad and the northern arm of the Industrial Canal (adjacent and parallel to I-10) sending water into the New Orleans East polder to the east and the Orleans East Bank polder to the west. The flooding continued for over 12 hours.[44] At approximately 6:50 a.m., the levees along all reaches of the Industrial Canal began to be overtopped and water started to pour into the city both to the east and the west.[45]

Between 5 and 7 a.m., the storm surge coming through Lake Borgne struck and destroyed several levee reaches along the MRGO channel and the Industrial Canal, flooding portions of the New Orleans East, Orleans East Bank and the Ninth Ward/St. Bernard polders.[46] In some places, flooding continued for days.[47] Levees along several reaches of the Industrial Canal were overtopped, resulting in water gushing to the west into the Orleans East Bank polder and to the east into the New Orleans East and Ninth Ward/St. Bernard polders.[48]

At about 7 a.m., the 18-foot Lake Borgne storm surge peaked and almost certainly caused the rapid flooding at the Louisiana National Guard's Jackson Barracks in St. Bernard Parish.[49] For years, the Louisiana National Guard had used this compound to deploy a small group of soldiers and officers close to the area where a major hurricane was likely to strike. The facility had stood up to numerous strong storms, including 1965's Hurricane Betsy. Brigadier General Brod Veillon, who was in command at Jackson Barracks on the night of August 28, said that, by dawn, Jackson Barracks had 6 to 12 inches of water in the parking lot, a typical amount from heavy rainfall. Within 30 minutes, however, the compound was engulfed by 10 feet of water. "It rose about a foot every 3 minutes. We watched it climb the stairs. … I knew it was significant when the walls of Jackson Barracks, which are brick walls, began to collapse."[50]

By 7:30 a.m., levees along the west side of the Industrial Canal (at the railroad yard) failed and began a flood of the Orleans East Bank polder that continued for about 12 to 15 hours.[51] By this time, there was massive flooding in much of the city, and the pumping stations had died.[52]

At approximately 7:45 a.m., the levees along the east side of the southeastern section of the Industrial Canal failed, sending a wall of water into the neighborhoods of the Ninth Ward/St. Bernard polder, especially the Lower Ninth Ward.[53] The National Weather Service reported that 3 to 8 feet of flooding was possible.[54] Then, at 8:30 a.m., a continuous wave of storm surge poured over a one-mile section of levee along Lake Pontchar-

A canal breached, New Orleans

train behind the Lakefront Airport. The water kept coming for another two to three hours.[55] In the Ninth Ward/St. Bernard polder,[56] floodwaters were reaching the second stories of bigger buildings and residents were fleeing to their attics.[57]

To the west – along the northern edge of the Orleans East Bank polder – the storm surge that hit the southern lakefront of Lake Pontchartrain did not produce waters high enough to overtop the concrete floodwalls lining the three major drainage canals: the 17th Street, Orleans Avenue, and London Avenue Canals. Nevertheless, three major breaches occurred along these canals. Based on two very detailed eyewitness accounts in the area, it is estimated that the initial breach on the east side of the 17th Street Canal occurred at approximately 6:30 a.m.,[58] and that the catastrophic failure of the levee took place somewhere between 9 and 10 a.m. [59] Similarly, sometime between 7 and 9:30 a.m., a section on the east side of the London Avenue Canal (close to the Mirabeau Bridge) failed;[60] sometime between 7:30 and 10:30 a.m., a section on the west side of the London Avenue Canal breached, "sen[ding] an 8 foot high wall of water cascading into the surrounding neighborhoods."[61] All three of these breaches caused catastrophic flooding in the Orleans East Bank polder, which includes (among others) the Central Business District, Lakeview, Mid City, and Lakewood areas of the city.

Captains Paul Hellmers and Joe Fincher, two New Orleans Fire Department firemen located at a department refuge in the Lakefront area of the city, videotaped the 17th Street Canal breach. In the video, which captures the breach at 11:11 a.m., Capt. Hellmers said:[62]

> You can … see the water pouring through the [inaudible] wall. There's a … concrete wall on top of the dirt levee. And you can see that the … wall is gone – you can see the water pouring through, it looks like about a 200-foot section of wall that's gone! The water is continuing to rise – very slowly.[63]

While Capt. Hellmers observed that the water in the entire area was rising "very slowly," it is clear from the video that the water from the 17th Street Canal breach is pouring through the gaping hole with enormous pressure and speed.[64] A second video of the New Orleans area, shot from a Coast Guard helicopter during the early afternoon of August 29, helps explain the different impressions.[65] From the vantage point of the helicopter's bay window, it is evident that the inflow from Lake Pontchartrain was spreading out rapidly into a vast area of land, so the water level rose slowly despite the power of the flow.

Later in the day, between approximately 5:15 and 7 p.m., Marty Bahamonde, a public- affairs official with the Federal Emergency Management Agency (FEMA) who had spent the night at the New Orleans City Hall Emergency Operations Center, joined a Coast Guard helicopter crew to conduct a visual inspection. The first of his two rides began with a quick pass over the 17th Street Canal. A second flight of approximately 45 minutes covered most of the metropolitan area of New Orleans. Bahamonde described the scene:

> As far as the eye could see in either direction was completely covered with water. There was no dry land. I saw no dry land the moment I left, other than around the Superdome. … It was varying in depth. There were houses that were completely under water. All you saw was rooftops. … It was obvious that there was massive flooding throughout the city. … And we went out and flew over the [I-10] twin span and it was completely destroyed. … We flew over the canal area, may have even been the Mississippi, where a huge tanker had been run aground. … Chalmette, the Ninth Ward, all completely flooded … the Intracoastal Industrial Canal. You didn't really know it was a canal because it was just one sheet of water. … And as we got back toward the city, it became obvious now that – it's close to 7 o'clock – that there are literally hundreds of people on rooftops, standing in balconies in apartments, and that there was a desperate need for a rescue mission because it was now getting dark.[66]

Around the same time that Bahamonde was observing the devastation from a Coast Guard helicopter, Colonel Richard P. Wagenaar, Commander of the Army Corps of Engineers district office in New Orleans, was conducting a similar reconnaissance in a four-wheel-drive vehicle. Col. Wagenaar told the Committee that between 5 and 5:30 p.m. he reached an elevated overpass on Interstate 10 near downtown New Orleans:

> Then we saw the water, and the water was – all you could see were the trees sticking out of the water. … That's probably 10 or 15 feet of water … a sight to behold, because, literally, I mean, you just drive on an interstate and there is a lake. I mean, it literally was a lake." [67]

Mississippi

Hurricanes are part of life on the Mississippi Gulf Coast. Every year there are hurricane warnings, evacuations, and scares; some years the coast gets hit. Before Katrina, the gold standard for storms in the region was Hurricane Camille,[68] a Category 5 hurricane that struck Mississippi on August 17-18, 1969, killing 143 along the coast, bringing with it about 10 inches of rain and a storm tide as high as 24 feet.[69]

The area's familiarity with hurricanes – and with the inevitable false alarms generated as the storms wander toward land – gives coastal residents both a healthy respect for storms and a degree of nonchalance toward dire warnings. False alarms during previous seasons – including an evacuation in 2004 before Hurricane Ivan, which ultimately veered away from the Mississippi coast – may have contributed to this attitude. Surviving Camille, widely viewed as the worst storm imaginable, may have led some to believe that future storms would be no worse.

Katrina changed all that. As Governor Barbour recounted at a February 2, 2006, hearing of the Senate Homeland Security and Governmental Affairs Committee:

> On Aug. 29, 2005, Hurricane Katrina struck our state a grievous blow. Although the eye of the storm landed at the Mississippi-Louisiana line, that eye was more than 30 miles wide, and Katrina completely devastated our entire coastline, from Pearlington to Pascagoula. The miles and miles of utter destruction is unimaginable. … But this hurricane wasn't just a calamity for the Mississippi Gulf Coast. Its impact extended inland with hurricane force more than 200 miles from the coast. In her wake, Katrina left literally tens of thousands of uninhabitable, often obliterated homes; thousands of small businesses in shambles; dozens of schools and public buildings ruined and unusable; highways, ports and railroads, water and sewer systems, all destroyed.[70]

The Region

In 2005, the State of Mississippi had a population of approximately 2.9 million people. The state comprises 82 counties, with three (Hancock, Harrison, and Jackson) located directly on the Gulf of Mexico, and three directly to the north of them (Pearl River, Stone, and George). The three counties that lie directly on the Gulf are generally referred to as the Mississippi Gulf Coast, and have a combined population of approximately 374,000 people (with populations of 46,000 in Hancock, 193,000 in Harrison, and 135,000 in Jackson). The Mississippi Gulf Coast extends for some 90 miles between Louisiana and Alabama. With the three counties to the north (Pearl River has 52,000, Stone has 14,000, and George has 21,000), that number rises to 461,000.[71]

The largest cities of the southernmost six counties are Gulfport and Biloxi, both located in Harrison County. They are the second and third largest cities in the state after the capital, Jackson, with populations of 71,000 and 50,000 respectively. The next largest in the region are the cities of Pascagoula in Jackson County (26,000), Laurel in Jones County (18,000), and Long Beach in Harrison County (17,000). Other cities in Hancock County include Bay St. Louis (8,000) and Waveland (6,000). [72]

The Mississippi coastal area had a varied economy before Katrina struck. Major sectors included oil-and-gas refining and distribution, light manufacturing, and tourism. The area's beaches and casino resorts were a mainstay of the tourism industry. Recent years had seen development of a number of casino/hotel complexes, including the Hard Rock Casino, the Beau Rivage, the Palace Casino, and the Grand Casino. To comply with Mississippi law, the casino operations were offshore, on barges arrayed along the coast.[73] The casino industry was an important source of jobs and tax revenue for the region.[74]

Katrina Approaches

At about 10 a.m. on Wednesday, August 24, the Mississippi Emergency Management Agency (MEMA) activated the state Emergency Operations Center (EOC) in Jackson, Mississippi. At this point Katrina was just a tropical storm in the Atlantic.[75] By 4 p.m. the next day, Katrina was bearing down on Florida and its entry into the Gulf of Mexico was increasingly likely.[76]

At 10 a.m. on Friday, August 26, MEMA's situation report reported that Katrina was likely to make a gradual turn to west-northwest and northwest from Florida and noted, "This longer westerly motion is significant in that it indicates an increasing threat farther west along the northern Gulf Coast."[77] By 4:30 p.m. that day, MEMA reported, "Landfall is now projected for near the Alabama/Mississippi border on Monday morning" as a Category 4 hurricane.[78] On August 26, the Governor declared a State of Emergency and signed Executive Order #939, activating the National Guard.[79] By 9 a.m. the next day, Katrina was forecasted to make landfall in the Mississippi Delta/New Orleans area as a Category 4 hurricane.[80]

By noon on Saturday, August 27, Harrison County and the City of Pass Christian issued Proclamations of Local Emergency.[81] These proclamations meant that these localities felt it was beyond their capacity to respond to the threat Hurricane Katrina posed and that they required help from other counties and the state.[82] By 4 p.m., they had been joined by Hancock County and the City of Waveland.[83] By 8 a.m. the next day, Jackson County did as well.[84]

On the morning of Sunday, August 28, MEMA issued a situation report describing Katrina as an "extremely dangerous" Category 5 storm and stating that the entire Mississippi coast was subject to a hurricane warning.[85] By noon that day, Katrina had been upgraded to "potentially catastrophic," with expected storm surges of up to 25 feet.[86]

As recounted more fully elsewhere in this report, federal, state, and local governments made various preparations and preliminary deployments in the days leading up to Katrina's landfall on August 29. The Governor called up Mississippi National Guard units, which had begun deploying August 27, with some units positioned in the coastal counties while others formed up at Camp Shelby, near Hattiesburg, Mississippi. By noon on Sunday, August 28, MEMA's State Emergency Response Team (SERT) had deployed to Camp Shelby.[87] FEMA representatives arrived as well.

The Storm Hits

Katrina weakened from a Category 5 to a Category 3 storm as it made landfall on the Mississippi Gulf Coast, but its magnitude was still extraordinary. No one the Committee staff spoke to had ever seen a comparable storm. On August 29, Katrina's radius of maximum winds stretched out 25 to 30 nautical miles from its center, and hurricane-force winds extended out at least 75 nautical miles eastward from its center, making it a storm of unprecedented size on the Mississippi Gulf Coast.[88]

The Surge: Witnesses from the Gulf Coast have told of the horrible, overwhelming storm surge driven ashore by Katrina, a surge that caused significant flooding the length of the coast. Yet, as the NWS has observed, "A precise measure of the storm surge . . . is complicated by many factors, including the widespread failure of tide gauges. Additionally, in many locations, most of the buildings along the coast were completely destroyed, leaving few structures within which to identify still-water marks."[89]

Whatever its exact surge level, Katrina battered Mississippi with a deadly and unprecedented wall of water. Unofficial measurements hint at its power. The Hancock County Emergency Operations Center recorded a 28-foot storm tide.[90] The Harrison County emergency director estimates that a tidal surge of 25 to 35 feet hit that part of the coast.[91] Across the Mississippi Gulf Coast in Pascagoula, the Jackson County EOC recorded a high water mark of 16.2 feet.[92]

The NWS reports that Katrina's ferocity in the Gulf of Mexico, combined with its enormous size at landfall, caused the extraordinary surges. "Overall, Katrina's very high water levels are attributable to a large Category 3 hurricane's storm surge being enhanced by waves generated not long before by a Category 5 strength storm."[93]

Katrina's waves and high waters lasted for hours, compounding the destruction. D.J. Ziegler, the Gulfport Harbormaster, rode out the storm in a parking deck near the ocean:

> The word "surge" irritates me a little. … People want to act like there's one sudden … surge that comes in, and it's not the case. The water just keeps getting deeper and the swells getting larger. So what you really have is a constant pounding. … So it's more like somebody's got a sledge hammer … and keeps hitting.[94]

Devastated neighborhood, Waveland, MS
Sun Herald news photo, Biloxi/Gulfport, MS

The surge penetrated at least six miles inland along many portions of coastal Mississippi, and up to 12 miles along bays and rivers.[95]

The Rain: Even without the storm surge, Katrina's rain was enough to flood many communities along the coast. Eight to 10 inches of rain fell across a large swath of southwestern Mississippi.[96] Estimates gathered by the NWS indicate that Hancock County received more than 10 inches of rain. Even Jackson, almost 150 miles north of the coast, still received nearly four inches of rain.[97]

The Wind: Katrina's winds were strong, broad in reach, and long-lasting. As a Category 3 hurricane, Katrina had sustained winds of 111 to 130 miles per hour. In Jackson County, the reported winds were even higher.[98]

Katrina's Reach: Katrina remained a destructive storm well north of the Gulf Coast. It weakened to a tropical storm late in the day on August 29 just northwest of Meridian, Mississippi.[99] Winds of over 56 m.p.h. were registered in the state capital of Jackson, and as far north as Columbus, Mississippi, there were winds of over 50 m.p.h.[100] Mayor Bob Massengill of Brookhaven, Mississippi, located 135 miles northwest of the Mississippi Gulf Coast, recalled that his community received wind gusts of up to 85 miles per hour and had several hours of sustained winds of over 50 miles per hour. This resulted in hundreds of downed trees and dozens of severely damaged or destroyed homes.[101]

As if the destructive force of the hurricane winds alone were not enough, Katrina produced a total of 11 reported tornados in Mississippi during August 29 and 30.[102]

Immediate Impact on Mississippi

Within hours, Katrina brought the coast to a halt. By 4 p.m. on Monday, all of Highway 90 along the Gulf Coast had flooded, along with parts of I-10.[103] The two main bridges on Highway 90, the Biloxi-Ocean Springs Bridge and the Bay St. Louis Bridge, collapsed. The Bay St. Louis Bridge fell into the bay, between supports that had withstood the storm. The storm rendered roads completely impassable, and rail service was discontinued.[104]

The most basic of community services were totally disrupted, in some cases for weeks. Water and sewer service failed. Local schools closed. Gulfport Memorial Hospital and other hospitals along the coast were damaged and forced to relocate hundreds of patients.[105] Katrina knocked out power to hundreds of thousands of Mississippi residents. At its peak, as of August 30, almost one million energy customers were without power.[106]

The physical damage was staggering. According to estimates, 65,380 homes were destroyed in southern Mississippi – over 95 percent of the statewide total of 68,641 destroyed homes. Katrina left 44 million cubic yards of debris and caused billions of dollars in property damage.[107]

The impact on many communities along the coast is difficult to conceive. In Waveland and Bay St. Louis, communities of thousands of homes on the westernmost part of the Mississippi Gulf Coast, Katrina left only a few dozen habitable residences. Mayor Brent Warr of Gulfport estimates that 80 to 90 percent of the residential and commercial properties of his city sustained heavy damage or were destroyed.[108] In Gulfport and Biloxi, the big casino barges so significant to the region's economy were destroyed. In many instances, the casinos were lifted off of their anchoring stanchions by the powerful water and dumped hundreds of yards away. At one casino, boats from nearby Gulfport Harbor were wedged between the girders of what was left of the structure, like nails hammered in by some unseen hand.[109]

According to recent figures, 231 identified victims perished in Mississippi as a result of Katrina, with 5 other unidentified dead and 67 missing.[110]

Alabama

While Alabama did not suffer the same level of damage as Louisiana and Mississippi, Hurricane Katrina gave the state a battering, especially coastal Baldwin and Mobile counties. Dauphin Island, a barrier island, faced 100 m.p.h. wind gusts; Mobile had gusts exceeding 80 m.p.h.[111] An oil rig under construction along the Mobile River in Alabama was dislodged, floated 1.5 miles northward, and struck the Cochrane Bridge, causing significant damage just north of downtown Mobile.[112] Another offshore oil rig washed up near the beach of Dauphin Island.[113] Katrina also reportedly caused significant beach erosion and significant tree damage throughout the state.[114]

Hurricane Katrina produced a large storm surge along the Alabama coast. A Dauphin Island town-council member described the damage:

> The West End of our island … was ravaged by Katrina. Visual inspections of this area show 190 homes totally swept away, another 96 homes totally destroyed or severely damaged, roads completely obliterated, and water, sewer, phone, and power are non-existent. No home was left unscathed by Katrina in this area.[115]

According to a study published by the National Hurricane Center, the storm surge was as high as 10 feet as far east as Mobile, Alabama, and caused flooding several miles inland from the Gulf Coast along Mobile Bay.[116] In addition, the Alabama Emergency Management Agency (AEMA) reported that the highest storm surge, 15 feet, was in Bayou La Batre, approximately 30 miles south of Mobile on the Gulf Coast.[117]

In addition to the storm surge and wind damage, there were four confirmed tornadoes, in Montgomery, Macon, Tallapoosa, and Calhoun counties in the eastern half of the state. AEMA described rainfall during Katrina as "insignificant."[118]

Two indirect fatalities occurred in Alabama during Hurricane Katrina as a result of a car accident in heavy rain during the storm. These fatalities, Alabama's only fatalities in Katrina, occurred in Washington County, directly north of Mobile County on the Mississippi border.[119] The Federal Emergency Management Agency (FEMA) registered a total of 25,454 evacuees in the state. Nearly 112,000 individuals registered for federal assistance in the state.[120]

Texas

Despite ominous early signs, Katrina ultimately inflicted minimal direct damage on Texas.[121] In the days that followed, however, Texas took in an estimated 400,000 evacuees, stretching the capacity of shelters and relief workers across the state.[122]

---

1 Richard D. Knabb, Jamie Rhome, and Daniel Brown, National Hurricane Center, "'Tropical Cyclone Report, Hurricane Katrina,' Hurricane Katrina 23-30 Augusta 2005," Dec. 20, 2005, p. 1. http://www.nhc.noaa.gov/pdf/TCR-L122005_Katrina.pdf. Accessed on Mar. 30, 2006 [hereinafter NHC, "Tropical Cyclone Report, Hurricane Katrina,"] ("The complex genesis of Katrina involved the interaction of a tropical wave, the middle tropospheric remnants of Tropical Depression Ten, and an upper tropospheric trough" that created a "tropical depression by 1800 UTC 23 August over the southeastern Bahamas about 175 nautical miles (n mi) southeast of Nassau" that eventually became "designated Tropical Depression Twelve.").

2 NHC, "Tropical Cyclone Report, Hurricane Katrina," Hurricane Katrina," p. 2 ("Further strengthening ensued, and Katrina is estimated to have reached hurricane status near 2100 UTC 25 August, less than two hours before its center made landfall on the southeastern coast of Florida.").

3 NHC, "Tropical Cyclone Report, Hurricane Katrina," p. 2 ("In fact, the eye feature actually became better defined while Katrina moved inland, and it remained intact during its entire track across the peninsula. … Katrina continued west-southwestward overnight and spent only about six hours over land, mostly over the water-laden Everglades.").

4 NHC, "Tropical Cyclone Report, Hurricane Katrina," p. 2 ("The center of Tropical Storm Katrina then emerged into the southeastern Gulf of Mexico at approximately 0500 UTC on 26 August just north of Cape Sable. Once back over water, Katrina quickly regained hurricane status at 0600 UTC with maximum sustained winds of 65 knots. … The center of Katrina continued west-southwestward over the southeastern Gulf of Mexico and away from the southern Florida peninsula.").

5 NHC, "Tropical Cyclone Report, Hurricane Katrina," p. 3 (On August 27, "Katrina became a Category 3 hurricane with 100 kt winds at 1200 UTC that morning about 365 n mi southeast of the mouth of the Mississippi River. … Accompanying the intensification…was a significant expansion of the wind field on 27 August. Katrina nearly doubled in size on 27 August, and by the end of that day tropical storm-force winds extended up to about 140 n mi from the center.").

6 NHC, "Tropical Cyclone Report, Hurricane Katrina," p. 3 ("The strong middle- to upper-tropospheric ridge that had kept Katrina on a west-southwestward track over the Florida peninsula and southeastern Gulf of Mexico began to shift eastward toward Florida, while a mid-latitude trough amplified over the north-central United States. This evolving pattern resulted in a general westward motion on 27 August and a turn toward the northwest on 28 August when Katrina moved around the western periphery of the retreating ridge.").

7 Committee staff interview of Max Mayfield, Ph.D., Director, National Hurricane Center, conducted on Jan. 27, 2005, transcript pp. 40-41 ("By that Friday afternoon, the models have come into much, much better agreement. … So when all these models started to finally converge – I mean, still not on top of each other; I mean, there's still some scatter, but they were in much, much better agreement than we had seen up to that time, and they started converging towards the Mississippi and Southeast Louisiana coast, yeah, you bet the alarm bells started sounding.").

8 Mayfield interview, Jan. 27, 2006, p. 40 ("At least for the 34 years that I've been at the National Hurricane Center, we've always been saying that the greatest concern from a hurricane anywhere in the Gulf of Mexico is Southeastern Louisiana and the great New Orleans area.").

9 National Hurricane Center, Hurricane Advisory, Aug. 26, 2005, 5 p.m.

10 National Weather Service, Hurricane Katrina Discussion Number 14, Aug. 26, 2005, 5 p.m.

11 Committee staff interview of Walter Maestri, Ph.D., Director, Jefferson Parish Office of Emergency Management, LA, conducted on Oct. 25, 2005, transcript p. 119.

12 Mayfield interview, Jan. 27, 2006, pp. 35-36 ("And they were doing a very good job, in my opinion, of reaching out. … So they were indeed making their local officials aware that, hey, you're in the cone.").

13 Louisiana Office of Homeland Security and Emergency Preparedness (LOHSEP), Katrina Conference Call Number 1, Aug. 26, 2005, 5 p.m. CT, pp. 4-5. Provided to Committee.

14 LOHSEP, Katrina Conference Call Number 1, Aug. 26, 2005, 5 p.m. CT, p. 5. Provided to Committee. ("There is still a lot of uncertainty here, so I don't want to really say what area has the highest landfall threat. Certainly with Plaquemines Parish sticking out into the Gulf, it typically has the highest threat, but I don't want to focus on one specific region right now.").

15 LOHSEP, Katrina Conference Call Number 1, Aug. 26, 2005, 5 p.m. CT, p. 6. Provided to Committee.

16 NHC, "Tropical Cyclone Report, Hurricane Katrina," p. 3 ("Accompanying the intensification and the subsequent deterioration of the inner eyewall was a significant expansion of the wind field on 27 August. Katrina nearly doubled in size on 27 August, and by the end of that day tropical storm-force winds extended up to about 140 n mi from the center.").

17 Mayfield interview, Jan. 27, 2006, p. 60 ("There is indeed a storm surge model that the National Weather Service runs. We have agreed to do that about 24 hours before landfall to let people see what might happen, what the storm surge might be, if we had that perfect forecast.").

18 LOHSEP, Katrina Conference Call Number 2, Aug. 27, 2005, 7:30 a.m. CT, p. 10. Provided to Committee.

19 Mayfield interview, Jan. 27, 2006, pp. 56-57 ("I wanted to make sure that they understood the severity of the situation. … And I should say, too, that when I called Governor Blanco, she's the one that suggested that I call Mayor Nagin, which I did. I left a message, and he called me back very quickly. … This is Saturday. The log here shows – the HLT log shows 7:25 Central daylight time, called Governor Blanco."). See also: National Hurricane Center, Hurricane Katrina Forecast Timeline, 2006, p. 3. Provided to Committee [hereinafter NHC Timeline].

20 National Hurricane Center, Hurricane Advisory, Aug. 28, 2005, 7 a.m. CT. The New Orleans NWS office broadcast a similar warning at 8 a.m., stating "direct strike of catastrophic hurricane expected … rush protective measures to completion and leave area as soon as possible." National Weather Service, Hurricane Katrina Local Statement, New Orleans, Aug. 28, 2005, 8 a.m. CT.

21 NHC, "Tropical Cyclone Report, Hurricane Katrina," p. 3 ("Katrina strengthened from a low-end Category 3 hurricane to a Category 5 in less than 12 h, reaching an intensity of 145 kt by 1200 UTC 28 August. Katrina attained its peak intensity of 150 kt at 1800 UTC 28 August about 170 n mi southeast of the mouth of the Mississippi River. The wind field continued to expand on 28 August, and by late that day tropical stormforce winds extended out to about 200 n mi from the center, and hurricane-force winds extended out to about 90 n mi from the center, making Katrina not only extremely intense but also exceptionally large.").

22 National Oceanic and Atmospheric Administration, Briefing to Committee, Dec. 21, 2005 [hereinafter NOAA Briefing to Committee].

23 NOAA Briefing to Committee, Dec. 21, 2005.

24 National Weather Service, Hurricane Katrina Local Statement, New Orleans, Aug. 28, 2005, 5:45 p.m.

25 National Hurricane Center, Hurricane Advisory, Aug. 28, 2005, 4 p.m. CT.

26 R. B. Seed et al., ASCE/NSF, Preliminary Report on the Performance of the New Orleans Levee Systems in Hurricane Katrina on August 29, 2005, Nov. 2, 2005, pp. 1–2, 1–3 [hereinafter ASCE/NSF, Preliminary Report].

27 NHC, "Tropical Cyclone Report, Hurricane Katrina," p. 3.

28 NHC, "Tropical Cyclone Report, Hurricane Katrina," p. 7.

29 NHC, "Tropical Cyclone Report, Hurricane Katrina," p. 7.

30 Ivor Ll. van Heerden, G. Paul Kemp, Wes Shrum, Ezra Boyd and Hassan Mashriqui, Louisiana State University, Center for the Study of Public Health Impacts of Hurricanes, Initial Assesment of the New Orleans' Flooding Event during the Passage of Hurricane Katrina, p. 4 [hereinafter LSU, Initial Assessment of New Orleans Flooding] ("The 'Funnel' effects: As the eye of the storm approached the latitude of New Orleans a 14-17 foot surge was pushed into the western apex of a triangle known as the 'Funnel', so called because the hurricane protection levees that form the south bank of the MRGO and the north bank of the GIWW converge from being about 10 m miles apart to a few hundred yards as the banks of the GIWW where it separates the East Orleans and St. Bernard polders. The Funnel is a 6-mile long section of the GIWW where the cross-section was enlarged by a factor of three when the MRGO was built to expand it from a barge channel to accommodate ocean-going vessels. At the western end, the funnel focused a jet into the IHNC. The US Army Corps of Engineers had inadvertently designed an excellent storm surge delivery system – nothing less – to bring this mass of water with simply tremendous 'load' – potential energy – right into the middle of New Orleans.").

31 NHC, "Tropical Cyclone Report, Hurricane Katrina," p. 3.

32 NHC, "Tropical Cyclone Report, Hurricane Katrina," p. 3.

33 NHC, "Tropical Cyclone Report, Hurricane Katrina," p. 3.

34 NHC, "Tropical Cyclone Report, Hurricane Katrina," p. 8.

35 NHC, "Tropical Cyclone Report, Hurricane Katrina," p. 8 ("[W]inds in a hurricane generally increase from the ground upward to a few hundred meters in altitude, and the sustained winds experienced on upper floors of high-rise buildings were likely stronger than the winds at the same location near the ground. For example, on average the 25th story of a building would experience sustained winds corresponding to one Saffir-Simpson category stronger than that experienced at the standard observing height of 10 m[eters].").

36 ASCE/NSF, Preliminary Report, pp. 1–4, 1–5.

37 ASCE/NSF, Preliminary Report, pp. 1–4, 1–10 (Figure 1.4); See also: LSU, Initial Assessment of New Orleans Flooding, p. 7 ("Lake Pontchartrain levee overtopping: Between 8:30 and 11:00 am, flood water poured into Orleans East from Lake Pontchartrain where a section of concrete levee wall at the Lakefront Airport that strangely was almost two feet lower than the earthen walls it was attached to served as a spillway when it was overtopped. Otherwise, no significant overtopping occurred anywhere along the south shore of Lake Pontchartrain.").

38 ASCE/NSF, Preliminary Report, p. 1–5.

39 LSU, Initial Assessment of New Orleans Flooding, p. 1.

40 LSU, Initial Assessment of New Orleans Flooding, p. 1.

41 LSU, *Initial Assessment of New Orleans Flooding*, p. 1.

42 ASCE/NSF, *Preliminary Report*, p. iv.

43 Ivor van Heerden, Ph.D., Timeline for Hurricane Katrina, 2006. Provided to Committee. There are numerous reports and oral reflections regarding the timing on Monday, August 29, 2005, of the overtopping and breaching of levees and floodwalls, and subsequent flooding, in the metropolitan New Orleans region. The Committee, through numerous interviews, copious documents, and scientific analyses received from experts, has done its best to construct a tentative timeline with respect to these events. To this end, the Committee has depended to a large degree on the information provided by van Heerden, and from information contained in the ASCE/NSF, *Preliminary Report* and U.S. Army Corps of Engineers, Interagency Performance Evaluation Task Force, *Performance Evaluation Status and Interim Results, Report 2 of a Series*, Mar. 10, 2006 [hereinafter IPET, *Report 2 of a Series*].

Van Heerden is the Deputy Director of the LSU Hurricane Center and the Director of the LSU Center for the Study of Public Health Impacts of Hurricanes. Van Heerden was also designated by the State of Louisiana to lead its Forensic Data Gathering Team in its efforts to learn more about the causes of the levee failures in the metropolitan New Orleans area. As part of his work, van Heerden and his colleagues at LSU have reviewed video camera footage and conducted several first-responder and survivor interviews. The team of LSU scientists also implemented the "stopped clock program," in which they collected stopped battery-operated and mechanical hand-dial clocks from flooded homes, noting both the time and elevation. The data is compiled in a report provided to the Committee entitled, *Initial Assessment of the New Orleans' Flooding Event During the Passage of Hurricane Katrina*.

It should also be noted that two scientists who testified before the Committee – Raymond Seed, Ph.D., who led the National Science Foundation sponsored forensic gathering and analysis team, and Peter Nicholson, P.F., head of the American Society of Civil Engineer's data gathering team – stated that they not only funneled information regarding witnesses' statements to Dr. van Heerden, but that "The time lines described by Dr. van Heerden would make sense with the geotechnical observations we see in the field … they are consistent." Testimony of Raymond Seed, Team Leader, National Science Foundation, before the U.S. Senate, Committee on Homeland Security and Governmental Affairs, hearing on *Hurricane Katrina, Why Did the Levees Fail?*, Nov. 2, 2005.

Similarly, the IPET observed over 200 high-water marks, contacted over 600 people for eyewitness accounts and interviewed over 175 persons who observed flooding induced by Hurricane Katrina. See, IPET, *Report 2 of a Series*, p. V-5. The IPET also employed the use of stopped clocks in houses, and gathered videos and still photos. See, IPET, *Report 2 of a Series*, p. V-5.

44 LSU, *Initial Assessment of New Orleans Flooding*, p. 11; IPET, *Report 2 of a Series*, p. V–9.

45 LSU, *Initial Assessment of New Orleans Flooding*, p. 4.

46 Ivor van Heerden, Timeline for Hurricane Katrina, 2006. Provided to Committee; LSU, *Initial Assessment of New Orleans Flooding*, p. 3; IPET, *Report 2 of a Series*, pp. V–9 through V–11.

47 Van Heerden, Timeline for Hurricane Katrina, 2006. Provided to Committee.

48 Van Heerden, Timeline for Hurricane Katrina, 2006. Provided to Committee; LSU, *Initial Assessment of New Orleans Flooding*, pp. 3-7.

49 LSU, *Initial Assessment of New Orleans Flooding*, p. 4.

50 Committee staff interview of Brig. Gen. Brod Veillon, Assistant Adjutant General, Louisiana National Guard, conducted on Nov. 29, 2005, transcript p. 18.

51 LSU, *Initial Assessment of New Orleans Flooding*, p. 11.

52 Col. Terry Ebbert, LOHSEP, Katrina Conference Call Number 10, Aug. 29, 2005, 7:30 a.m. CT, p. 13.

53 Van Heerden, Timeline for Hurricane Katrina, 2006. Provided to Committee; LSU, *Initial Assessment of New Orleans Flooding*, pp. 5, 11.

54 Transportation Security Administration, Katrina Brief, Aug. 29, 2005, 9 a.m. Provided to Committee; files as Bates no. DHS-HSOC-0002-0000190.

55 LSU, *Initial Assessment of New Orleans Flooding*, pp. 7, 11.

56 At 9 a.m., the local weather office issued a "Hurricane Katrina Local Statement: "Levees overtopped in Orleans and St. Bernard Parishes….Extensive and life threatening storm surge flooding occurring along the Louisiana and Mississippi coast at this time….Significant and life threatening storm surge 18 to 22 feet above normal is occurring." National Weather Service, Hurricane Katrina Local Statement, New Orleans, Aug. 29, 2005, 9 a.m. CT.

57 Michael Heath, e-mail to Michael Lowder, Aug. 29, 2005, 10:43 a.m. Provided to Committee; filed as Bates no. DHS-FEMA-0029-0002963.

58 IPET, *Report 2 of a Series*, pp. V–5 through V–7.

59 LSU, *Initial Assessment of New Orleans Flooding*, pp. 8, 11. *See also*: IPET, *Report 2 of a Series*, p. V–5 through V–7.

60 Van Heerden, Timeline for Hurricane Katrina, 2006. Provided to Committee; and LSU, *Initial Assessment of New Orleans Flooding*, p. 9. *See also*: IPET, *Report 2 of a Series*, p. V–5 through V–7.

61 LSU, *Initial Assessment of New Orleans Flooding*, p. 9. *See also*: IPET, *Report 2 of a Series*, pp. V–5 through V–7.

62 Moreover, the NOFD Hurricane Katrina Log (Fire Communications) produced to the Committee by the NOFD,

reflects that at 11:15 a.m. CT, the "first report of levee either being breeched [sic] or topped at 17th Ave. Canal." New Orleans Fire Department, Hurricane Katrina Fire Communications Log, 2005. Provided to Committee.

63 NOFD, Capt. Paul Hellmers, Lake Marina Towers Video, Aug. 29, 2005. Provided to Committee.

64 LSU, *Initial Assessment of New Orleans Flooding*, p. 8 ("Eye witnesses reported the flood waters rose rapidly.").

65 U.S. Coast Guard, Initial Helicopter Overflight Video, Aug. 29, 2005. Provided to the Committee.

66 Committee staff interview of Marty Bahamonde, Region I Director, External Affairs, FEMA, conducted on Oct. 7, 2005, transcript pp. 106-110.

67 Committee staff interview of Col. Richard P. Wagenaar, U.S. Army, District Commander, New Orleans District, U.S. Army Corps of Engineers, conducted on Nov. 15, 2005, transcript pp. 56-58.

68 Written Statement of Robert Latham, Executive Director, Mississippi Emergency Management Agency, for the U.S. House Select Bipartisan Committee to Investigate the Preparation for and Response to Hurricane Katrina, hearing on *Hurricane Katrina: Preparedness and Response by the State of Mississippi*, Dec. 7, 2005, p. 1.

69 National Hurricane Center, "Hurricane History." http://www.nhc.noaa.gov/HAW2/english/history.shtml#camille. Accessed on Mar. 30, 2006. Camille is only one of three Category 5 hurricanes to make landfall on the United States coast since records have been kept. National Hurricane Center, The Saffir-Simpson Scale. http://www.nhc.noaa.gov/aboutsshs.shtml. Accessed on Apr. 3, 2006.

70 Written statement of Gov. Haley Barbour, Mississippi, before the U.S. Senate, Committee on Homeland Security and Governmental Affairs, hearing on *Hurricane Katrina: The Role of Governors in Managing the Catastrophe*, Feb. 2, 2006, p. 1.

71 U.S. Census Bureau, American Factfinder, 2006. http://factfinder.census.gov. Accessed on Mar. 30, 2006.

72 U.S. Census Bureau, American Factfinder, 2006. http://factfinder.census.gov. Accessed on Mar. 30, 2006.

73 Richard Fausset, "Mississippi Casinos Trump Katrina," *Los Angeles Times*, Feb. 25, 2006.

74 Committee staff interview of Mayor A.J. Holloway, City of Biloxi, MS, conducted on Jan. 5, 2006 (untranscribed).

75 Mississippi Emergency Management Agency (MEMA), Hurricane Situation Report: Tropical Storm Katrina, Aug. 24, 2005, 10 a.m. CT, p. 1. Provided to Committee; filed as Bates no. MEMA-0010808.

76 MEMA, Hurricane Situation Report: Hurricane Katrina, Aug. 25, 2005, 4 p.m. CT, p. 1. Provided to Committee; filed as Bates no. MEMA-0010820.

77 MEMA, Hurricane Situation Report: Hurricane Katrina, Aug. 26, 2005, 10 a.m. CT, p. 1. Provided to Committee; filed as Bates no. MEMA-0010824.

78 MEMA, Hurricane Situation Report: Hurricane Katrina, Aug. 26, 2005, 4:30 p.m. CT, p. 1. Provided to Committee; filed as Bates no. MEMA-0010828.

79 MEMA, Hurricane Situation Report: Hurricane Katrina, Aug. 27, 2005, noon CT, p. 2. Provided to Committee; filed as Bates no. MEMA-0010832.

80 MEMA, Hurricane Situation Report: Hurricane Katrina, Aug. 27, 2005, 9 a.m. CT. Provided to Committee; filed as Bates no. MEMA-0010831.

81 MEMA, Hurricane Situation Report: Hurricane Katrina, Aug. 27, 2005, noon CT, p. 2. Provided to Committee; filed as Bates no. MEMA-0010835.

82 Miss. Code Ann. § 33-15-5 (g).

83 MEMA, Hurricane Situation Report: Hurricane Katrina, Aug. 27, 2005, 4 p.m. CT, p. 2. Provided to Committee; filed as Bates no. MEMA-0010838.

84 MEMA, Hurricane Situation Report #5: Hurricane Katrina, Aug. 28, 2005, 8 a.m. CT, p. 2. Provided to Committee; filed as Bates no. MEMA-0010859.

85 MEMA, Hurricane Situation Report #5: Hurricane Katrina, Aug. 28, 2005, 8 a.m. CT, p. 1. Provided to Committee; filed as Bates no. MEMA-0010858.

86 MEMA, Hurricane Situation Report #6: Hurricane Katrina, Aug. 28, 2005, noon CT, p. 1. Provided to Committee; filed as Bates no. MEMA-0010864.

87 MEMA, Hurricane Situation Report #6: Hurricane Katrina, Aug. 28, 2005, noon CT. Provided to Committee; filed as Bates nos. MEMA-0010864 through 0010869.

88 NHC, "Tropical Cyclone Report, Hurricane Katrina," p. 9.

89 NHC, "Tropical Cyclone Report, Hurricane Katrina," p. 8. In an interview with Committee staff, Brian Adam, the Hancock County Director of Emergency Management, recounted that the Hancock County EOC sits 27 feet above sea level but was flooded by 3.5 feet of water during Katrina. Committee staff interview of Brian Adam, Director of Emergency Management, Hancock County, MS, conducted on Nov. 16, 2005 (untranscribed).

90 NHC, "Tropical Cyclone Report, Hurricane Katrina," p. 8.

91 Testimony of Col. Joe Spraggins, Director of Emergency Management, Harrison County, MS, for the U.S. House, Se-

lect Bipartisan Committee to Investigate the Preparation for and Response to Hurricane Katrina, hearing on *Hurricane Katrina: Preparedness and Response by the State of Mississippi*, Dec. 7, 2005.

92 Committee staff interview of Butch Loper, Emergency Management Director, Jackson County, MS, conducted on Dec. 6, 2005, transcript pp. 64-65.

93 NHC, "Tropical Cyclone Report, Hurricane Katrina," p. 9. The expected storm surge for a Category 3 hurricane would normally be between 9-12 feet, according to the Saffir-Simpson Hurricane Scale. An introduction to the scale may be found at http://www.nhc.noaa.gov/aboutsshs.shtml.

94 Committee staff interview of D.J. Ziegler, Harbor Master, Gulfport Harbor, MS, conducted on Dec. 8, 2005, transcript, p. 30.

95 NHC, "Tropical Cyclone Report, Hurricane Katrina," pp. 8-9.

96 NHC, "Tropical Cyclone Report, Hurricane Katrina," p. 10.

97 NHC, "Tropical Cyclone Report, Hurricane Katrina," pp. 27-28.

98 Loper interview, Dec. 6, 2005, p. 64. This is consistent with wind speeds noted in the MEMA situation reports. MEMA, Hurricane Situation Report #13: Hurricane Katrina, Aug. 29, 2005, 4 p.m. CT. Provided to Committee; filed as Bates no. MEMA-0010924.

99 NHC, "Tropical Cyclone Report, Hurricane Katrina," p. 4.

100 NHC, "Tropical Cyclone Report, Hurricane Katrina," pp. 27-28.

101 Written Statement of Mayor Robert V. Massengill, Brookhaven, MS, for the U.S. Senate, Committee on Homeland Security and Governmental Affairs, hearing on *Recovering from Hurricane Katrina: Responding to the Immediate Needs of Its Victims*, Sept. 28, 2005, p. 1.

102 NHC, "Tropical Cyclone Report, Hurricane Katrina," p. 10.

103 MEMA, Hurricane Situation Report #13: Hurricane Katrina, Aug. 29, 2005, 4 p.m. CT, p. 6. Provided to Committee; filed as Bates no. MEMA-0010929.

104 MEMA, Hurricane Situation Report #19 Hurricane Katrina, Aug. 30, 2005 at 4:30 p.m. CT, p. 6. Provided to Committee; filed as Bates no. MEMA-0010989.

105 MEMA, Hurricane Situation Report #19 Hurricane Katrina, Aug. 30, 2005 at 4:30 p.m. CT, p. 8. Provided to Committee; filed as Bates nos. MEMA-0010990 through 0010991.

106 MEMA, Hurricane Situation Report #20 Hurricane Katrina, Aug. 31, 2005 at 1:30 a.m. CT, p. 9. Provided to Committee; filed as Bates no. MEMA-0011002.

107 "Mississippi's Invisible Coast," Biloxi *Sun-Herald*, Dec. 14, 2005. http://www.sunherald.com/mld/sunherald/13402585.htm. Accessed on Apr. 24, 2006; MEMA, Red Cross Damage Assessments. http://www.msema.org/redcrossassessments.htm. Accessed on Apr. 24, 2006.

108 Committee staff interview of Bret Warr, Mayor, City of Gulfport, MS, conducted on Jan. 9, 2006 (untranscribed).

109 Ziegler interview, Dec. 8, 2005, p. 27.

110 "Mississippi's Invisible Coast," Biloxi *Sun-Herald*, Dec. 14, 2005. http://www.sunherald.com/mld/sunherald/13402585.htm. Accessed on Apr. 24, 2006.

111 Alabama Emergency Management Agency, Hurricane Katrina Situation Report #7, Aug. 31, 2005, 7 p.m. CT.

112 Written Statement of Don Vaughn, Chief Engineer, Alabama Department of Transportation, for the U.S. House, Committee on Transportation and Infrastructure, hearing on *Rebuilding Transit Infrastructure in the Gulf Coast Area*, Oct. 27, 2005.

113 NHC, "Tropical Cyclone Report, Hurricane Katrina," p. 12.

114 NHC, "Tropical Cyclone Report, Hurricane Katrina," p. 12.

115 Jackie Previto, Dauphin Island, Alabama Town Council Member, letter to Governor Bob Riley, Alabama, Sept. 7, 2005.

116 NHC, "Tropical Cyclone Report, Hurricane Katrina," p. 9.

117 Alabama Emergency Management Agency, Hurricane Katrina Situation Report #7, Aug. 31, 2005, 7 p.m. CT.

118 Alabama Emergency Management Agency, Hurricane Katrina Situation Report #7, Aug. 31, 2005, 7 p.m. CT.

119 NHC, "Tropical Cyclone Report, Hurricane Katrina," pp. 10-11; Garry Mitchell, "Massive Storm Damage Found in Alabama," Associated Press Online, Aug. 30, 2005. Accessed on LexisNexis.

120 Garry Mitchell, "Katrina's painful blow to coast Alabama's top story in 2005," *Montgomery Advisor*, Dec. 21, 2005.

121 Texas State Operations Center, Hurricane Katrina Situation Report #10, Aug. 29, 2005, 4 p.m.

122 Final Report to the Governor, Governor's Task Force on Evacuation, Transportation, and Logistics, Texas, Feb. 14, 2006.

Rescued, New Orleans

Hurricane Katrina: Timeline of Key Events

Dates (all 2005) and Times (all Central) of Event

Tuesday, August 23

4 p.m.: Tropical Depression 12 develops about 200 miles southeast of Nassau in the Bahamas.[1]

Thursday, August 25

2:30 p.m.: The tropical storm is elevated to a hurricane and is named "Katrina."[2]

4 p.m.: The National Hurricane Center, for the first time, reports that some models show Katrina coming ashore "between Mobile, Alabama, and Grand Isle, Louisiana." Katrina, still about 15 miles east of Florida, is expected to gradually strengthen once in the Gulf of Mexico.[3]

5:30 p.m.: Katrina makes landfall in Florida as a Category 1 hurricane.[4]

Friday, August 26

10:30 a.m.: Katrina, still moving westward, is elevated to a Category 2 hurricane, with note that the storm "could become a category three or major hurricane on Saturday."[5]

11 a.m.: National Hurricane Center officials state in a video teleconference that their prediction models indicate a shift in Katrina's path west "towards New Orleans." Prior models had predicted a probable strike in the Florida panhandle.[6]

1 p.m.: Louisiana Governor Kathleen Blanco declares a State of Emergency and activates her state's National Guard.[7]

Afternoon-Evening: Mississippi Governor Haley Barbour declares a State of Emergency and activates his state's National Guard.[8]

4 p.m.: NHC issues an official forecast shifting Katrina's track 170 miles west, predicting a probable Category 4 hurricane striking the Mississippi coast near the Alabama border with landfall on Monday, August 29.[9]

10 p.m.: NHC issues a forecast shifting the track farther west and predicting a probable strike at or near the Louisiana-Mississippi border, east of New Orleans, on Monday, August 29.[10]

Saturday, August 27

4 a.m.: NHC issues a forecast stating that Katrina is a Category 3 hurricane and predicting a direct hit on New Orleans.[11]

6 a.m.: FEMA headquarters begins 24-hour operations in Washington, D.C.[12]

7:30 a.m.: National Weather Service, in teleconference, informs Louisiana state and local officials that the probable path of the storm is "smack dab through the metropolitan New Orleans area."[13]

9 a.m.: The first phase of the Louisiana Emergency Evacuation Plan begins. Under Phase I, citizens in coastal areas, south of the Intracoastal Waterway, would evacuate 50 hours before a Category 3 or stronger hurricane hits.[14]

11:41 a.m.: Governor Blanco requests a declaration of a federal state of emergency for Louisiana under the Stafford Act. President Bush issues the declaration later in the day.[15]

12 p.m.: Phase II of the Louisiana Emergency Evacuation Plan is initiated.[16]

1 p.m.: (approximately) New Orleans Mayor C. Ray Nagin, in a joint press conference with Governor Blanco, declares a State of Emergency, announces he will issue a voluntary evacuation order, and announces that the Superdome will open at 8 a.m. on Sunday as a special-needs shelter.[17]

2 p.m.: Louisiana Emergency Operations Center in Baton Rouge goes to 24-hour operations.[18]

4 p.m.: The final phase of the Louisiana Emergency Evacuation Plan is initiated and contraflow evacuation by highway begins.[19]

7 p.m.: National Weather Service advises City of New Orleans Office of Emergency Preparedness that the New Orleans levees could be overtopped.[20]

7:25-8 p.m.: NHC Director Max Mayfield briefs Governor Blanco, Governor Barbour, and Mayor Nagin about Katrina's potential impact.[21] Late evening traffic from Louisiana's evacuation into Mississippi subsides, allowing Mississippi to issue mandatory evacuations for three coastal counties – Hancock, Harrison, and Jackson.[22]

10 p.m.: NHC issues first official storm-surge forecast for Katrina, predicting surge flooding of 15 to 20 feet above normal tides and locally as high as 25 feet. NHC issues Hurricane Warning for north-central Gulf Coast from Morgan City, Louisiana, eastward to the Alabama-Florida border, including the City of New Orleans. Hurricane-force winds are expected within 24 hours.[23]

Sunday, August 28

President Bush issues federal emergency declarations for Mississippi and Alabama, and declares Florida a federal disaster area.[24] Alabama, Mississippi, and Louisiana Governors request Presidential Major Disaster Declarations; they are signed the next day.[25]

1 a.m.: NHC issues Special Advisory: "Katrina Strengthens to Category 4 with 145 mph winds."[26]

7 a.m.: NHC issues Special Advisory stating that Katrina is "now a potentially catastrophic category 5 hurricane" with maximum sustained winds near 160 mph.[27]

8 a.m.: The Superdome is opened as a special-needs shelter.[28]

9:30 a.m.: Mayor Nagin orders a mandatory evacuation of Orleans Parish.[29]

10 a.m.: NHC increases storm-surge forecast to 18 to 22 feet above normal tide levels and locally as high as 28 feet.[30]

11 a.m.: During a daily video teleconference with the President, DHS headquarters, FEMA headquarters, FEMA's regional offices, and representatives from Louisiana and Mississippi, National Hurricane Center Director Max Mayfield states, "I don't think any model can tell you with any confidence right now whether the levees will be topped or not, but that's obviously a very, very grave concern." FEMA Director Michael Brown says, "Just keep jamming those lines full as much as you can with commodities."[31]

12 p.m.: The Superdome is opened as a "refuge of last resort" for the general population.[32]

4 p.m.: NHC issues first official forecast addressing New Orleans levees which states, "Some levees in the greater New Orleans area could be overtopped."[33]

5 p.m.: Contraflow highway evacuation in Louisiana ends.[34]

Monday, August 29

12:47 a.m.: A Department of Homeland Security assessment detailing the storm's likely impact is e-mailed to the White House's Homeland Security Operations Center (HSOC).[35]

6:10-7 a.m.: On August 29, at approximately 6:10 a.m. CT, Hurricane Katrina's eye makes landfall at Buras on the Louisiana coast between Grand Isle and the mouth of the Mississippi River. Storm surge overtops the levees on the east bank of the river, "crosses" the river, overtops the levees on the west bank, and sends additional water into neighborhoods in Plaquemines Parish. The center of Hurricane Katrina moves ashore into southeast Louisiana just east of Grand Isle.[36] Morning Catastrophic flooding begins in New Orleans resulting from massive overtopping of levees in east Orleans and St. Bernard Parishes, overtopping and breaking of the Industrial Canal levees, and breaks in the 17th Street and London Avenue Canal floodwalls.[37] The Superdome's roof begins to leak; it loses air conditioning, plumbing in all but the first floor, and its communication system. A backup generator provides minimal lighting.[38]

10 a.m.: Hurricane Katrina makes landfall in Mississippi. Storm surge reported 20 feet above normal in Biloxi area.[39]

Afternoon: State and local first responders' communications begin to fail in the Greater New Orleans area and Mississippi.[42]

Mid–afternoon: Search-and-rescue operations begin by the U.S. Coast Guard, the New Orleans Police and Fire Departments, the Louisiana National Guard, and the Louisiana Department of Wildlife and Fisheries.[40]

2-3 p.m.: Local officials in Mississippi begin search and rescue.[41]

Evening: FEMA Director Brown assures Governor Blanco that FEMA will send 500 buses to New Orleans the next day.[43]

10 p.m.: MEMA search-and-rescue teams arrive and immediately begin life-saving operations.[44]

Tuesday, August 30

Mayor Nagin opens the New Orleans Convention Center as a refuge for the general population.[45]

10:30 a.m.: Acting Deputy Secretary of Defense orders U.S. Northern Command to move all necessary assets to the Gulf Coast, giving blanket authority for forces to provide military assistance.[46]

4 p.m.: U.S. Army Lieutenant General Russel Honoré is designated Commander of Joint Task Force Katrina.[47] Evening Plumbing fails completely at the Superdome. Conditions at the stadium deteriorate due to the massive crowds and lack of air conditioning and sanitation.[48] DHS Secretary Michael Chertoff declares Katrina an "incident of national significance." Chertoff designates Michael Brown as the Principal Federal Official (PFO) to manage the response and recovery operations for Hurricane Katrina.[49]

Late evening: Governor Blanco directs the Department of Social Services to find a shelter by 6 a.m. Wednesday for at least 25,000 people.[50]

Wednesday, August 31

Health and Human Services Secretary Michael Leavitt declares a public-health emergency for Louisiana, Mississippi, Florida, and Alabama.[51] Governor Blanco issues an Executive Order to commandeer school buses.[52]

1:30-1:45 a.m.: FEMA, for the first time, mission-assigns DOT to send buses to New Orleans.[53]

8:30-9:30 a.m.: Governor Blanco calls Governor Rick Perry of Texas to request that the Houston Astrodome open to house New Orleans evacuees.[54]

11 a.m.: Chief of the federal National Guard Bureau directs all state Adjutants General to rapidly deploy available National Guard troops to Louisiana and Mississippi.[55]

2:30 p.m.: Governor Blanco and President Bush discuss by telephone the need for military assistance and the Governor's command of the Louisiana National Guard in a unified-command structure.[56]

4:11 p.m.: President Bush holds a Cabinet meeting at the White House and speaks publicly to outline federal relief efforts.[57]

Evening: Some federally contracted buses arrive in New Orleans and begin evacuation of overpasses and special-needs shelter.[58]

Thursday, September 1

10 a.m.: Bus evacuation of the general population begins at the Superdome.[59]

Late Evening: Colonel Terry Ebbert, New Orleans Director of Homeland Security and Public Safety, requests assistance from Louisiana National Guard commander Major General Bennett Landreneau to secure and evacuate the Convention Center in conjunction with the New Orleans Police Department.[60]

Friday, September 2

President Bush makes his first visit to the Gulf States after Katrina and meets with the governors of Louisiana, Alabama, and Mississippi; and Mayor Nagin in New Orleans. [61]

Late Morning: In a private meeting, the President and Governor Blanco discuss command and control for the military response.[62]

12-12:30 p.m.: 1,000 National Guard forces (LA, TX, OK, NV, and AR) move toward the Convention Center and secure the building to begin relief operations.[63]

11:20 p.m.: White House faxes proposal to Governor Blanco under which there would be appointed a dual-status commander who would be an active-duty military officer and who would exercise command and control on behalf of the Governor over National Guard forces and on behalf of the President over federal active-duty forces.[64]

Saturday, September 3

8:56 a.m.: Governor Blanco declines the White House proposal to appoint a dual-status commander and retains sole command of National Guard troops in Louisiana.[65]

9:06 a.m.: President Bush orders 7,200 active-duty troops to the Gulf Coast.[66]

10 a.m.: Convention Center evacuation begins.[67]

1 p.m.: Superdome evacuation is complete.[68]

6:30 p.m.: Convention Center evacuation is complete.[69]

Monday, September 5

I-10 Cloverleaf and Causeway Boulevard evacuations are complete.[70] Coast Guard Admiral Thad Allen is appointed Deputy PFO.[71]

Tuesday, September 6

5 a.m.: Search and recovery efforts in New Orleans continue.[72]

---

1 National Hurricane Center, Tropical Depression 12, Advisory #1, Aug. 23, 2005, 5 p.m. ET. Provided to Committee; National Hurricane Center, Tropical Depression 12, Forecast/Advisory #1, Aug. 23, 2005, 2100 Z. Provided to Committee. Both documents filed as Bates nos. DHS-FEMA-0037-0000014 through 0000017.

2 National Hurricane Center, Hurricane Katrina Forecast Timeline, 2006, p. 1. Provided to Committee [hereinafter NHC Timeline].

3 National Hurricane Center, Hurricane Katrina Discussion #9, and Hurricane Katrina Advisory #9, both Aug. 25, 2005, 5 p.m. ET. Provided to Committee; filed as Bates nos. DHS-FEMA-0037-0000147 through 0000150.

4 NHC Timeline, p. 1.

5 National Hurricane Center, Hurricane Katrina Special Advisory #13, Aug. 26, 2005, 11:30 a.m. ET. Provided to Committee; filed as Bates no. DHS-FEMA-0037-0000217.

6 Bill Reed, FEMA Daily Video Teleconference, Aug. 26, 2005, transcript p. 7. Provided to Committee; filed as Bates no. DHS-FEMA-0105-0000028; NHC Timeline, p. 1.

7 Louisiana's Preparation and Response to Hurricane Katrina, Integrated Timeline, p. 6. Provided to Committee; State of Louisiana, Office of the Governor, Proclamation No. 48 KBB 2005, Aug. 26, 2005; Louisiana Office of the Governor, Response to the U.S. Senate Committee on Homeland Security and Governmental Affairs Document and Information Request Dated October 7, 2005 and to the U.S. House of Representatives Select Committee to Investigate the Preparation for and Response to Hurricane Katrina, Overview of Governor Kathleen Babineaux Blanco's Actions in Preparation for and Response to Hurricane Katrina, Dec. 2, 2005, p. 2 [hereinafter Louisiana Office of the Governor, Governor's Timeline].

8 State of Mississippi, Office of the Governor, Executive Order No. 939, Aug. 26, 2005. Provided to Committee; filed as Bates nos. MEMA 0009765 through 0009766; Mississippi Emergency Management Agency (MEMA), Preparedness and Response Timeline – Hurricane Katrina, p. 1. Provided to Committee; filed as Bates no. MEMA 0010678 [hereinafter MEMA, Hurricane Katrina Timeline].

9 National Hurricane Center, Hurricane Katrina Advisory #14, Hurricane Katrina Discussion #14, and Hurricane Katrina Probabilities #14, all Aug. 26, 2005, 5 p.m. ET. Provided to Committee. All documents filed as Bates nos. DHS-FEMA-0037-0000229 through 0000234. *See also*: National Hurricane Center, "Katrina Graphics Archive," Aug. 30, 2005. http://www.nhc.noaa.gov/archive/2005/KATRINA_graphics.shtml. Accessed on Apr. 30, 2006.

10 National Hurricane Center, Hurricane Katrina Forecast/Advisory #15, Aug. 26, 2005, 0300 Z; Hurricane Katrina Advisory #15, Aug. 26, 2005, 11 p.m. ET; Hurricane Katrina Discussion #15, Aug. 26, 2005, 11 p.m. ET; and Hurricane Katrina Probabilities #15, Aug. 26, 2005, 11 p.m. ET. Provided to Committee. All documents filed as Bates nos. DHS-FEMA-0037-0000238 through 0000245; NHC Timeline, p. 2; National Hurricane Center, "Katrina Graphics Archive," Aug. 30, 2005. Provided to Committee; filed as Bates no. DHS-FEMA-0037-0000237; National Hurricane Center, "Katrina Graphics Archive," Aug. 30, 2005. http://www.nhc.noaa.gov/archive/2005/KATRINA_graphics.shtml. Accessed on Apr. 30, 2006.

11 NHC Timeline, p. 2; National Hurricane Center, Hurricane Katrina Forecast/Advisory #16, Aug. 27, 2005, 0900 Z; Hurricane Katrina Advisory #16, Aug. 27, 2005, 5 a.m. ET; Hurricane Katrina Discussion #16, Aug. 27, 2005, 5 a.m. ET; and Hurricane Katrina Probabilities #16, Aug. 27, 2005, 5 a.m. ET. Provided to Committee; Federal Emergency Management Agency (FEMA), National Situation Report, Aug. 27, 2005, 5:30 a.m. Provided to Committee. All documents filed as Bates nos. DHS-FEMA-0037-0000253 through 0000261; National Hurricane Center, "Katrina Graphics Archive," Aug. 30, 2005. http://www.nhc.noaa.gov/archive/2005/KATRINA_graphics.shtml. Accessed on Apr. 30, 2006.

12 U.S. Department of Homeland Security, Situation Report #4, Aug. 27, 2005, 6 a.m., p. 11. Provided to Committee; filed as Bates no. DHS 0001123.

13 Louisiana Office of Homeland Security and Emergency Preparedness (LOHSEP), Hurricane Katrina Conference Call #2, Aug. 27, 2005, 7:30 a.m. CT, transcript p. 10. Provided to Committee.

14 Louisiana's Preparation and Response to Hurricane Katrina, Integrated Timeline, p. 10. Provided to Committee; State of Louisiana and U.S. Department of Homeland Security, Louisiana Citizen Awareness Disaster and Evacuation Guide [hereinafter Louisiana Citizen Awareness Guide].

15 LOHSEP, Letter to President George W. Bush, Aug. 27, 2005. Provided to Committee; Louisiana Office of the Governor, Governor's Timeline, pp. 3-4; The White House, "Statement on Federal Emergency Assistance for Louisiana," press release, Aug. 27, 2005. http://www.whitehouse.gov/news/releases/2005/08/20050827-1.html. Accessed on Jan. 17, 2006.

16 Louisiana's Preparation and Response to Hurricane Katrina, Integrated Timeline, p. 11; Louisiana Citizen Awareness Guide.

17 City of New Orleans, Mayors Press Office, "Mayor Nagin Urges Citizens to Prepare for Hurricane Katrina," press release, Aug. 27, 2005. Provided to Committee.

18 Louisiana's Preparation and Response to Hurricane Katrina, Integrated Timeline, p. 12. Provided to Committee; Louisiana Office of Homeland Security and Emergency Preparedness, Emergency Operations Plan, Apr. 2005, p. 5 [hereinafter Louisiana Emergency Operations Plan].

19 Louisiana's Preparation and Response to Hurricane Katrina, Integrated Timeline, p. 13. Provided to Committee; Louisiana Citizen Awareness Guide.

20 National Oceanic and Atmospheric Administration (NOAA), briefing on National Weather Service Products and Services During Katrina, given to Senate Committee staff, Feb. 7, 2006, p. 12.

21 NHC Timeline, p. 3; Testimony of Max Mayfield, Director, Tropical Prediction Center and National Hurricane Center, National Weather Service, NOAA, before the U.S. House, Select Bipartisan Committee to Investigate the Preparation for and Response to Hurricane Katrina, hearing on Predicting Hurricanes: What We Knew About Katrina When?, Sept. 22, 2005; Committee staff interview of Max Mayfield, Director, Tropical Prediction Center and National Hurricane Center, National Weather Service, NOAA, conducted on Jan. 27, 2006, transcript pp. 57-58.

22 MEMA, Director's Brief, Aug. 28, 2005, 7 p.m. CT, p. 3. Provided to Committee; filed as Bates no. MEMA 0010690; MEMA, Hurricane Katrina Situation Report #6, Aug. 28, 2005, 8 a.m. CT. Provided to Committee; filed as Bates nos. MEMA 0010864 through 0010869.

23 National Hurricane Center, Hurricane Katrina Advisory #19, Aug. 27, 2005, 10 p.m. CT. Provided to Committee; National Hurricane Center, Hurricane Katrina Discussion #19, Aug. 27, 2005, 10 p.m. CT. Provided to Committee. Both documents filed as Bates nos. DHS-FEMA-0037-0000314 through 0000317.

24 The White House, "Statement on Federal Emergency Assistance for Mississippi," press release, Aug. 28, 2005. http://www.whitehouse.gov/news/releases/2005/08/20050828.html. Accessed on Nov. 8, 2005; The White House, "Statement on Federal Emergency Assistance for Alabama," press release, Aug. 28, 2005. http://www.whitehouse.gov/news/releases/2005/08/20050828-3.html. Accessed on Nov. 8, 2005; The White House, "Statement on Federal Disaster Assistance for Florida," press release, Aug. 28, 2005. http://www.whitehouse.gov/news/releases/2005/08/20050828-2.html. Accessed on Nov. 8, 2005.

25 U.S. Department of Homeland Security, Situation Report #9, Aug. 30, 2005, 6 p.m., p. 3. Provided to Committee; filed as Bates no. DHS 0001234.

26 National Hurricane Center, Special Advisory #20, Aug. 28, 2005, 1 a.m. CT. Provided to Committee; filed as Bates nos. DHS-FEMA-0037-0000323 through 0000324.

27 National Hurricane Center, Special Advisory #22, Aug. 28, 2005, 7 a.m. CT. Provided to Committee; filed as Bates nos. DHS-FEMA-0037-0000367 through 0000368.

28 City of New Orleans, Mayor's Press Office, "Mayor Nagin Urges Citizens to Prepare for Hurricane Katrina," press release, Aug. 27, 2005. Provided to Committee; Mayor Ray Nagin and Kevin Stephens, City of New Orleans Health Department, Response to the U.S. Senate, Committee on Homeland Security and Governmental Affairs, hearing on Challenges in a Catastrophe: Evacuating New Orleans in Advance of Hurricane Katrina, Jan. 31, 2006, pp. 4-5.

29 City of New Orleans, Mayor's Press Office, "Mayor Nagin Issues Mandatory Evacuation," press release, Aug. 28, 2005. Provided to Committee; Mayor Ray Nagin, CNN, "New Orleans Mayor, Louisiana Governor Hold Press Conference," Aug. 28, 2005. http://transcripts.cnn.com/TRANSCRIPTS/0508/28/bn.04.html. Accessed on Mar. 17, 2006.

30 National Hurricane Center, Hurricane Katrina Advisory #23, Aug. 28, 2005, 10 a.m. CT. Provided to Committee; filed as Bates nos. DHS-FEMA-0037-0000379 through 0000380.

31 Max Mayfield, FEMA Daily Video Teleconference, Aug. 28, 2005, transcript p. 6. Provided to Committee; filed as Bates no. DHS-FEMA-0105-0000071. Michael Brown, FEMA Daily Video Teleconference, Aug. 28, 2005, transcript p. 29. Provided to Committee; filed as Bates no. DHS-FEMA-0105-0000094.

32 Louisiana's Preparation and Response to Hurricane Katrina, Integrated Timeline, p. 1. Provided to Committee; Written Statement of Marty Bahamonde, Director, External Affairs, Region I, FEMA, for the U.S. Senate, Committee on Homeland Security and Governmental Affairs, hearing on Hurricane Katrina in New Orleans: A Flooded City, a Chaotic Response, Oct. 20, 2005, p. 1.

33 National Hurricane Center, Hurricane Katrina Advisory #24, Aug. 28, 2005, 4 p.m. CT. Provided to Committee; filed

as Bates nos. DHS-FEMA-0037-0000395 through 0000396.

34 Committee staff interview of Lt. Col. Mark S. Oxley, Chief of Staff, Louisiana State Police, and Lt. Col. Joseph Booth, Deputy Superintendent, Crisis Response and Special Operations, Louisiana State Police, conducted on Dec. 9, 2005, transcript pp. 202-204.

35 Andrew Akers, e-mail to HSOC SWO and others, Aug. 29, 2005, 1:47 a.m. Provided to Committee; filed as Bates nos. WHK 15399 through 15404.

36 National Space and Aeronautics Agency, "Katrina Intensifies Into a Powerful Hurricane, Strikes Northern Gulf Coast," Aug. 30, 2005. http://www.nasa.gov/vision/earth/lookingatearth/katrina_trmm_0828_0829.html. Accessed on Jan. 17, 2006; Richard D. Knabb, Jamie Rhome, and Daniel Brown, National Hurricane Center, "Tropical Cyclone Report: Hurricane Katrina," Dec. 20, 2005, pp. 8-9 [hereinafter NHC, "Tropical Cyclone Report, Hurricane Katrina"]; MEMA, Hurricane Katrina Situation Report #11, Aug. 29, 2005, 9 a.m. CT. Provided to Committee; filed as Bates no. MEMA 0010905.

37 NHC, "Tropical Cyclone Report, Hurricane Katrina," p. 9.

38 Louisiana National Guard, Timeline of Significant Events, Hurricane Katrina, Dec. 7, 2005, pp. 4-5. Provided to Committee [hereinafter LANG Timeline]; Committee staff interview of Lonnie Swain, Assistant Superintendent, New Orleans Police Department, LA, conducted on Nov. 9, 2005, transcript pp. 49-52.

39 MEMA, Hurricane Katrina Timeline, p. 4.

40 Written Statement of Capt. Bruce C. Jones, U.S. Coast Guard, Commanding Officer, Coast Guard Air Station New Orleans, for the U.S. Senate, Committee on Homeland Security and Governmental Affairs, hearing on *Always Ready: The Coast Guard's Response to Hurricane Katrina*, Nov. 9, 2005, pp. 24-25; Committee staff interview of Lt. Col. Keith LaCaze, Assistant Administrator, Law Enforcement Division, Louisiana Department of Wildlife and Fisheries, conducted on Nov. 30, 2005, transcript pp. 46-47; Committee staff interview of Capt. Tim Bayard, Commander, Vice Crimes and Narcotics Section, New Orleans Police Department, LA, conducted on Nov. 21, 2005, transcript pp. 30-33; Committee staff interview of Capt. Paul Hellmers, Engine 18, Second Platoon, Sixth District, New Orleans Fire Department, LA, and Capt. Joseph Fincher, Engine 18, Third Platoon, Sixth District, New Orleans Fire Department, LA, conducted on Nov. 7, 2005, transcript pp. 92-93, 95-96.

41 Committee staff interview of Paul Bennett, Deputy Chief of Police, Gulfport Police Department, MS, conducted on Dec. 8, 2005, transcript pp. 32-33.

42 Capt. Bayard interview, Nov. 21, 2005, p. 40; Lt. Col. LaCaze interview, Nov. 30, 2005, pp. 14-17; James L. Barksdale, Governor's Commission on Recovery, Rebuilding, and Renewal, *After Katrina: Building Back Better than Ever*, Dec. 31, 2005, p. 9; Testimony of Gov. Haley Barbour, Mississippi, before the U.S. Senate, Committee on Homeland Security and Governmental Affairs, hearing on *Hurricane Katrina: The Role of Governors in Managing the Catastrophe in the Response*, Feb. 2, 2006; Written Statement of Gov. Haley Barbour, Mississippi, for the U.S. Senate, Committee on Homeland Security and Governmental Affairs, hearing on *Hurricane Katrina: The Role of Governors in Managing the Catastrophe in the Response*, Feb. 2, 2006, pp. 1-4.

43 Louisiana Office of the Governor, Governor's Timeline, p. 7; Testimony of Maj. Gen. Bennett Landreneau, Adjutant General, Louisiana, before the U.S. Senate, Committee on Homeland Security and Governmental Affairs, hearing on *Hurricane Katrina: The Defense Department's Role in the Response*, Feb. 9, 2006; Committee staff interview of Maj. Gen. Bennett Landreneau, Adjutant General, Louisiana, conducted on Jan. 11, 2006, transcript pp. 33-34, 140-141, 273-274.

44 Committee staff interview of Pat Sullivan, Chief, Gulfport Fire Department, MS, conducted on Dec. 7, 2005, transcript pp. 97-98.

45 Written Statement of Mayor C. Ray Nagin, City of New Orleans, LA, for the U.S. Senate, Committee on Homeland Security and Governmental Affairs, hearing on *Hurricane Katrina: Managing the Crisis and Evacuating New Orleans*, Feb. 1, 2006, p. 4; Penya Moses-Fields, letter to The Honorable Susan M. Collins and The Honorable Joseph I. Lieberman, Jan. 30, 2006, "Attachment A: Timeline of Mayor Nagin's Activities, Aug. 26, 2005 – Sept. 6, 2005."

46 Clair Blong, e-mail to Fema-NRCC and others, Aug. 30, 2005, 10:51 p.m. Provided to Committee; Col. David Rhodes, e-mail to Tom Eldridge, Dan Berkovitz, and Eric Andersen, Senate Committee staff members, Apr. 19, 2006, 2:32 p.m.; Committee staff interview of Gen. Richard Myers, former Chairman of the Joint Chiefs of Staff, conducted on Feb. 28, 2006, transcript p. 9.

47 U.S. Department of Defense, First U.S. Army, Joint Task Force Katrina, Hurricane Katrina Chronology. Provided to Committee.

48 LANG Timeline, p. 6; Swain interview, Nov. 9, 2005, p. 73.

49 Sec. Michael Chertoff, memorandum to various DHS officials, "Designation of Principal Federal Official for Hurricane Katrina," Aug. 30, 2005. Provided to Committee; U.S. Department of Homeland Security, Situation Report #11, Aug. 31, 2005, 6 p.m. ET, p. 2. Provided to Committee; filed as Bates no. DHS 0001266.

50 Louisiana Office of the Governor, Governor's Timeline, p. 9; Committee staff interview of Sec. Ann Williamson, Louisiana Department of Social Services, conducted on Dec. 12, 2005, transcript pp. 98-99.

51 U.S. Department of Health and Human Services, "Disasters & Emergencies: Hurricanes, HHS Declares Public Health Emergency for Hurricane Katrina," Aug. 31, 2005. http://www.hhs.gov/emergency/determination.html. Accessed on Dec. 9, 2005.

52 Louisiana Office of the Governor, Governor's Timeline, p. 11; State of Louisiana, Executive Order No. KBB 2005-31.

53 U.S. Department of Transportation, Actions for Hurricane Katrina: Annotated Chronology of Significant Events, Oct. 6, 2005, p. 4. Provided to Committee; FEMA, Tasking Request and Assignment Form, LRC-Katrina-378, Aug. 31, 2005. Provided to Committee.

54 Louisiana Office of the Governor, Governor's Timeline, p. 10; Sec. Williamson interview, Dec. 12, 2005, pp. 105-106.

55 National Guard Bureau, *After Action Review, Hurricane Response September 2005*, Dec. 21, 2005, p. 14. Provided to Committee.

56 Louisiana Office of the Governor, Governor's Timeline, pp. 9-10; Testimony of Gov. Kathleen Babineaux Blanco, Louisiana, before the U.S. Senate, Committee on Homeland Security and Governmental Affairs, hearing on *Hurricane Katrina: The Role of the Governors in Managing the Catastrophe*, Feb. 2, 2006; Committee staff interview of Terry Ryder, Executive Counsel, Office of the Governor, LA, conducted on Jan. 10, 2006, transcript pp. 200-203.

57 The White House, "President Outlines Hurricane Katrina Relief Efforts," press release, Aug. 31, 2005. http://www.whitehouse.gov/news/releases/2005/08/20050831-3.html. Accessed on Mar. 7, 2006.

58 U.S. Department of Transportation, Actions for Hurricane Katrina, Annotated Chronology of Significant Events, Oct. 6, 2005, pp. 3-4.

59 U.S. Department of Transportation, Actions for Hurricane Katrina, Annotated Chronology of Significant Events, Oct. 6, 2005, p. 5; LANG Timeline, p. 7; Committee staff interview of Brig. Gen. Mark Graham, U.S. Army, Deputy Commanding General, Fifth U.S. Army, U.S. Department of Defense, conducted on Jan. 12, 2006, transcript pp. 76-80; Committee staff interview of Dolph Diemont, Region X Regional Emergency Transportation Representative, Office of Intelligence, Security and Emergency Response, U.S. Department of Transportation, conducted on Jan. 6, 2006, transcript pp. 57-59; Committee staff interview of Col. Jacques Thibodeaux, Joint Director of Military Support to Civilian Authorities, Louisiana National Guard, conducted on Jan. 12, 2006, transcript p. 24.

60 LANG Timeline, p. 7; Maj. Gen. Landreneau interview, Jan. 11, 2006, pp. 265-266.

61 The White House, "President Heads to Hurricane Katrina Affected Areas," press release, Sept. 2, 2005. http://www.whitehouse.gov/news/releases/2005/09/print/20050902.html. Accessed on Apr. 24, 2006;

The White House, "President Remarks on Hurricane Recovery Efforts," press release, Sept. 2, 2005. www.whitehouse.gov/news/releases/2005/09/20050902-8.html. Accessed on Mar. 6, 2006; Louisiana Office of the Governor, Governor's Timeline, p. 14.

62 Louisiana Office of the Governor, Governor's Timeline, p. 14; Gov. Blanco, Senate Committee hearing, Feb. 2, 2006.

63 Louisiana's Preparation and Response to Hurricane Katrina, Integrated Timeline, p. 46. Provided to Committee; LANG Timeline, p. 8.

64 The White House, memorandum to Governor Blanco, "Memorandum of Agreement Concerning Authorization, Consent, and Use of Dual Status Commander for JTF-Katrina," Sept. 2, 2005. Provided to Committee; Ryder interview, Jan. 6, 2006, pp. 234-235; Committee staff interview of Andy Kopplin, then Chief of Staff, Office of the Governor, LA, conducted on Jan.10, 2006, transcript p. 148.

65 Ryder interview, Jan. 10, 2006, pp. 248-252; Terry Ryder, Handwritten Notes, Sept. 3, 2005. Provided to Committee.

66 U.S. Department of Defense, Hurricane Katrina/Rita Comprehensive Timeline, p. 16. Provided to Committee; The White House, "President Addresses Nation: Discusses Hurricane Katrina Relief Efforts," press release, Sept. 3, 2005. http://www.whitehouse.gov/news/releases/2005/09/20050903.html. Accessed on Mar. 6, 2006.

67 Col. Thibodeaux interview, Jan. 12, 2006, pp. 33-35; Col. Jacques Thibodeaux, Timeline, p. 9. Provided to Committee; Louisiana's Preparation and Response to Hurricane Katrina, Integrated Timeline, p. 49. Provided to Committee.

68 Louisiana's Preparation and Response to Hurricane Katrina, Integrated Timeline, p. 49. Provided to Committee.

69 Col. Thibodeaux interview, Jan. 12, 2006, pp. 34-35; Col. Jacques Thibodeaux, Timeline, p. 9. Provided to Committee.

70 Louisiana's Preparation and Response to Hurricane Katrina, Integrated Timeline, p. 52. Provided to Committee.

71 U.S. Assistant to the President for Homeland Security and Counterterrorism, *The Federal Response to Hurricane Katrina: Lessons Learned*. Washington: Government Printing Office, Feb. 2006, p. 47.

72 U.S. Department of Homeland Security, Situation Report #22, Sept. 6, 2005, 6 a.m., p. 2. Provided to Committee; filed as Bates no. DHS 0001462.

LOUISIANA EMERGENCY EVACUATION MAP

LEGEND

— Interstate Highways
— US Highways
— Louisiana Evacuation Routes
— Mississippi State Highways
— Mississippi River
— Intracoastal Waterway
▨ Urban Areas
⬚ Parishes/Counties
🛡 Interstate Highway Shield
🛡 US Highway Shield
◯ State Highway Shield
① Shelter Information Points

Gulf of Mexico

N
W — S
E

0 5 10   20   30   40
Miles

Phased Evacuation

During a threat of a hurricane, a phased evacuation will be based on geographic location and time in which tropical storm winds are forecasted to reach the affected areas.

Phase I - 50 Hours before onset of tropical storm winds. Includes areas south of the Intracoastal Waterway. These areas are outside any levee protection system and are vulnerable to Category 1 and 2 storms. These areas are depicted in RED on the Evacuation Map. During Phase I there are no route restrictions.

Phase II - 40 Hours before onset of tropical storm winds. Includes areas south of the Mississippi River which are levee protected but remain vulnerable to Category 2 or higher storms. These areas are depicted in ORANGE on the Evacuation Map. During Phase II there are no route restrictions.

Phase III - 30 Hours before onset of tropical storm winds. Includes areas on the East Bank of the Mississippi River in the New Orleans Metropolitan Area which are within the levee protection system but remain vulnerable to a slow-moving Category 3 or any Category 4 or 5 storm. These areas are depicted in YELLOW on the Evacuation Map. During Phase III, certain routes will be directed and the Contraflow Plan implemented.

Phased evacuation procedures are for traffic management purposes only. Consult your local Office of Emergency Preparedness Director for further evacuation information.

Louisiana is blessed with some of the Nation's greatest resources. When a crisis threatens, we must take steps to protect the most precious of those resources — our people. State and local agencies have worked together on a plan to evacuate Louisiana citizens from harm's way. Regardless of the location or nature of the threat, this evacuation plan is your guide to a safe and efficient evacuation. Please take the time to familiarize yourself with the contents of this guide, and discuss evacuation preparedness with your family. Working together, we can assure the safety of all our citizens during times of crisis. For more information, please visit my web site at: www.gov.la.gov.

Sincerely,

Kathleen Babineaux Blanco
Governor

Citizens' evacuation
map and message
from Gov. Blanco

State of Louisiana

Emergency Management: Louisiana

The Threat

Like its Gulf Coast neighbor states, Louisiana repeatedly finds itself the target of tropical storms and hurricanes coming ashore from the Gulf of Mexico. Louisiana has the added problems of having large tracts of low-lying land that are sinking while sea levels are rising, and of being home to a major city that, on average, lies below sea level.

As the Congressional Research Service (CRS) has noted, "New Orleans' location on the Gulf Coast with water on three sides and below-sea-level terrain makes this densely populated section of Louisiana highly susceptible to flooding from hurricane storm surges" – not to mention the risks it faces from river flooding and trapped rainwater.[1]

The need to protect New Orleans is old and pressing. And it is getting more severe. Three researchers presenting at a U.S. Geological Survey conference observed that "Considering the rate of subsidence [sinking soil levels] and the mid-range estimate of sea-level rise during the next 100 years (480 millimeters) [about 1.9 inches] the areas of New Orleans and vicinity that are presently 1.5 to 3 meters [about 5 to 10 feet] below mean sea level will likely be 2.5 to 4.0 meters [about 8 to 13 feet] or more below mean sea level by 2100."[2] Like other researchers, they also note that the New Orleans area's vulnerability is "aggravated owing to flood-protection measures and disruption of natural drainageways that reduce sediment deposition" that would otherwise compensate for some of the subsidence.[3]

The desire to protect New Orleans is old and powerful. And it continues. French settlers in the early 1700s built earthen levees to protect their high-ground settlement from flood waters rising in the Mississippi River. After Louisiana had passed into American hands in 1803, a succession of private landowners, local levee boards, and later the Army Corps of Engineers (the Corps) added to the protective works.[4] The Corps got its first Mississippi flood-control mandate from Congress in 1850; its authority expanded through major flood-control legislation of 1936, 1944, and 1950, among others.[5]

Most of the current hurricane-protection system around the metropolitan New Orleans area has been built since 1879 by local sponsors or by the Corps.[6] The most intense and protracted program of protection, however, was launched after the 1965 assault by Hurricane Betsy.

On the night of September 9, 1965, Hurricane Betsy made landfall near New Orleans, driving before it a storm surge of water that easily overran levees and flooded more than 5,000 square miles of land, including densely populated areas in Orleans and St. Bernard Parishes, and more rural areas in Plaquemines Parish. The hurricane was the worst up to that point in Louisiana's history: it killed 81 people, injured over 17,600, and drove more than 250,000 to shelters.[7]

President Lyndon Johnson visited New Orleans the next day. He praised the work of state and local first responders – "The agony and the loss of Louisiana would have been far greater without the cooperation, effective work of the Weather Bureau, the Civil Defense Authorities of Louisiana, the Red Cross and other local groups" – then added, "[Y]ou can be sure that the federal government's total resources, with the help of the fine Louisiana Delegation, will be turned toward helping this state and its citizens find its way back from this tragedy."[8]

Congress responded with the Lake Pontchartrain and Vicinity Hurricane Protection Project in the Flood Control Act of 1965. The project envisioned a series of control structures, floodwalls, and levees to provide hurricane protection to areas around Lake Pontchartrain, the large lake lying north of New Orleans. Originally expected to be completed in about 13 years, the project was delayed by technical issues, environmental and legal challenges, and some local opposition that ultimately led to design changes. When Hurricane Katrina struck, the project included some 125 miles of levees, and the completion date had been extended to 2015. The drainage-canal floodwalls that failed during Katrina, however, were complete at that point.[9]

During the 40 years of construction that followed the Flood Control Act of 1965, a succession of powerful hurricanes – Camille in 1969, Andrew in 1992, Georges in 1998, Isadore and Lili in 2002, and Ivan in 2004 – supplied grim reminders of the need to protect the Louisiana coast and the low-lying City of New Orleans, and to perfect evacuation plans to remove people from the impact areas.

The Army Corps of Engineers had built the New Orleans levee system to handle a "standard project hurricane" – a notional, hybrid storm that engineers later described, in terms of the Saffir-Simpson scale adopted in 1977, as "equivalent to a fast-moving Category 3 hurricane."[10] On its five-category scale, the National Weather Service (NWS) classifies Category 3, 4, and 5 hurricanes as "major," and the damage from a Category 5 storm as "catastrophic."[11] Compared to the Saffir-Simpson standards, the Standard Project Hurricane's winds were as fast as a Category 2 hurricane, its storm surge as high as a Category 3, and its central atmospheric pressure as low as a Category 4 – hence the rough description as a fast-moving Category 3 storm.[12]

Assessing the protective strength of the New Orleans-area system was complicated by the region's soil subsidence. Though the Corps periodically "lifted" the levees to compensate for subsiding soils, the levels of the lifts varied, resulting in a system as vulnerable as its lowest component. A Corps of Engineers fact sheet of 2003, "How Safe is New Orleans from Flooding?" took note of these uncertainties about the Lake Pontchartrain project:

> This level of protection [against a fast-moving Category 3 hurricane] was based on the science of storm prediction as it existed in the 1960s. The question remains, however, whether this level of protection would be sufficient to protect the city from a category 4 or 5 hurricane today – or even a category 3 storm that lingered over the city [i.e., a "slow-moving" storm]. Since the 1960s, New Orleans has been sinking – in some areas at the rate of ½ inch per year. The distance from the Gulf Coast to New Orleans has also been shrinking. A century ago, a hurricane would have to cross 50 miles of marshland able to reduce the storm's energy; today only half as much.[13]

By 2003 – 10 years after the start of a new cycle of more active hurricane formation in the Atlantic – new research suggested that the combination of sinking soil and rising ocean water around the Mississippi Delta meant that even some Category 2 storms could produce devastating floods in the New Orleans area. Director Marc Levitan of the Louisiana State University Hurricane Center wrote a paper analyzing the computerized, multi-storm flooding projections of the National Oceanic and Atmospheric Administration's SLOSH (Sea, Lake, and Overland Surges from Hurricanes) program. Examining the mapping results of the program, he wrote,

> clearly demonstrates that New Orleans is at significant risk of flooding from Category 2 and 3 hurricanes. All locations on the West Bank and many points on the East Bank could flood even in Category 2 intensity storms from certain

directions … locations anywhere within Orleans and Jefferson Parishes can experience significant storm surge flooding in a Category 3 storm. … The situation deteriorates rapidly if Category 4 and 5 storms are considered. Any single storm can easily flood broad areas of both parishes to depths over land of 10 feet or more.[14]

The historic record shows the concern over extreme or catastrophic storms was not idle fretting about some remote possibility. The National Hurricane Center's list of "Most Intense Hurricanes in the United States, 1851-2004" includes six hurricanes measured or estimated as Category 4 or 5 that have struck Louisiana:

Hurricane Andrew	1992	Category 5
Hurricane Camille	1969	Category 5
Hurricane Audrey	1957	Category 4
Unnamed storm	1947	Category 4
Unnamed storm	1915	Category 4
"Last Island" storm	1856	Category 4[15]

Hurricane Betsy, which devastated New Orleans and other Louisiana communities in 1965, had reached Category 5 strength while still in the Gulf of Mexico, though it weakened before landfall. Hurricane Katrina reached the same strength in 2005, and faced a protective system with newly recognized vulnerabilities.

Just as the hurricane-protection system reflected coordinated efforts at different levels of government, Louisiana's response capability for disasters like Katrina is vested in an emergency-management system that coordinates preventive and remedial actions by local, state, and federal governments. As will be seen, that system had deficiencies in its structure and operation.

The State

Louisiana's Emergency-Management Structure

Louisiana law entrusts the Governor with "overall responsibility for emergency management in the state." [16] The Governor delegated her authority to direct emergency operations to the state Adjutant General.[17] As in many other states, when Katrina struck, the Adjutant General was serving both as director of the state emergency-preparedness office and as commander of the National Guard.

The state's lead agency for emergencies is the Governor's Office of Homeland Security and Emergency Preparedness. From 2003 to March 2006 – and therefore during the Katrina disaster – it was known as the Louisiana Office of Homeland Security and Emergency Preparedness (LOHSEP), and will be referred to by that title in this discussion. Since its creation in 1950, the agency has been variously assigned to the Department of Public Safety, the Military Department, and finally the Governor's Office.[18]

LOHSEP says it "has managed over 16 Federal Disaster Declarations and has coordinated several hundred State Disaster Declarations authorized under the Governor's signature" since 1990.[19] Based in Baton Rouge, LOHSEP was directed at the time of Katrina by the

Adjutant General of the Louisiana National Guard, Major General Bennett C. Landreneau; its current Acting Director is Colonel Jeff Smith.

Allocation of disaster-response responsibilities is governed primarily by the Louisiana Constitution, the Louisiana Homeland Security and Emergency Assistance and Disaster Act, and the State Emergency Operations Plan (EOP).

The State's EOP comprises a 21-page "Basic Plan," four Attachments, 15 Emergency Support Function (ESF) Annexes, and seven Supplements. Its purpose is to "establish the policies and structure for state government management of emergencies and disasters."[20] It prescribes phases of emergencies and disasters, and assigns responsibilities for actions the state will take to provide for the safety and welfare of its citizens.[21]

The general principles underlying the EOP's allocation of responsibilities exemplify the long-standing, federal-system approach to disaster planning. The EOP's "Assumptions" section reads, in part:

> 5. The initial actions of prevention, mitigation, preparedness, response and recovery operations are conducted by local government. Local authorities will exhaust their resources, and then use mutual aid agreements with volunteer groups, the private sector and/or neighboring parishes.

> 6. State assistance will supplement local efforts and federal assistance will supplement State and local efforts when it is clearly demonstrated that it is beyond local and State capability to cope with the emergency/disaster.[22]

Following the template of the National Response Plan (NRP), the EOP identifies 15 Emergency Support Functions (ESFs), for which 28 state departments, offices and agencies have primary and/or supporting roles. LOHSEP has primary responsibility for five ESFs; the Department of Agriculture and Forestry, the State Police, and the Department of Transportation and Development have responsibility for two; and 10 agencies have a single primary responsibility. The National Guard is unique in being assigned supporting responsibility for all 15 ESFs, but no primary responsibilities.[23]

While most of those departments and agencies took their responsibilities seriously, as discussed elsewhere in this report, the Louisiana Department of Transportation and Development, which acquired primary responsibility for the emergency support function relating to evacuation in 2004, did not. Colonel Smith also acknowledged LOHSEP's shortcomings in this area, saying the agency needed to do more to ensure that all entities assigned lead responsibilities for emergency support functions are "completely aware of what those responsibilities mean."[24]

Governor Blanco failed to provide sufficient resources to LOHSEP. However, the inadequacy of LOHSEP's resources was a chronic issue, known to Louisiana officials well before Katrina. LOHSEP had a pre-Katrina staff of 43 to 45, some of whom were detailed from other offices. Only about 15 agency staff had emergency-management leadership experience.[25] Depressed pay scales both prevented the agency from hiring experienced candidates and led to high turnover.[26] Planning in particular suffered. When the New Orleans medical director sought to put in place memoranda of understanding with Amtrak and other carriers for pre-landfall evacuation in the summer of 2005, LOHSEP was too short-staffed to help finalize the plan.[27]

When Colonel Smith became Acting Deputy Director in late 2004, General Landreneau directed him to undertake a staffing study.[28] While the resulting study showed that LOHSEP's staffing was only about 60 percent of the national average, efforts to persuade the legislature to fund additional positions – which had the support of the Governor's staff – met with little success. [29]

LOHSEP was also well aware long before Katrina that its emergency plan was not adequate to deal with a catastrophic hurricane, and that it lacked the resources to remedy that inadequacy. It was that very awareness that led to its efforts beginning in 1999 to secure federal assistance in developing a more comprehensive plan (eventually leading to the Hurricane Pam exercise).[30] The extent of that inadequacy only became more apparent as LOHSEP wrestled with the overwhelming problems of responding to the devastation of Katrina.

The State Updates its EOP

In addition to the issues that led to the Hurricane Pam exercise, the state and federal agencies addressed other concerns related to evacuation.

In 2000, the State's Office of Emergency Preparedness finished an update of the state comprehensive emergency operations plan. It included new evacuation and shelter plans produced by the 12 parishes in the Southeast Louisiana Hurricane Task Force. Some parishes, such as Jefferson, updated their plans; some agencies, such as the New Orleans Fire Department, developed new strategies for a catastrophic storm.[31]

This period also exposed the fundamental weakness of the state's approach to pre-storm evacuation of residents without transportation. Under the state's plan, the National Guard was responsible for transportation, but the agency had no buses and intended to parcel out its inventory of troop transport trucks to individual parishes as it had always done.[32] The State's Comprehensive Emergency Management Plan, updated in 2000, left the responsibility for pre-storm evacuation with the parishes. "The primary means of hurricane evacuation will be personal vehicles," the plan said. "School and municipal buses, government-owned vehicles and vehicles provided by volunteer agencies may be used to provide transportation for individuals who lack transportation and require assistance in evacuating."[33]

Solving the problem involved more than assembling large numbers of buses, as the 1994 Hurricane Preparedness Study had emphasized. If no building in New Orleans could serve as a hurricane shelter, then all vehicles had a much longer drive to reach shelters, which influences clearance times.

A month before the start of the 2002 hurricane season, officials from the main state and federal agencies responsible for hurricane evacuations in Louisiana met to discuss the Bi-State Hurricane Evacuation Study – an event that underscored the challenges of arranging mass evacuations in a hurricane-prone region.[34] During the meeting, speakers noted that approximately 30 percent of Louisiana residents would evacuate to or through Mississippi in the event of a hurricane and that Louisiana wanted to begin using the contraflow land-reversal process to route residents eastward into Mississippi – an operation that could conflict with Mississippi's need to evacuate its own at-risk residents and tourists. [35]

By the 2002 hurricane season, the state's preparedness agency had moved into a new Emergency Operations Center in Baton Rouge that would serve as a command center during disasters for state and federal officials. In May 2002, the FEMA Region VI office produced its own "Hurricane Plan for Louisiana" that reflected the plans that the state and FEMA had developed.

When Katrina struck, Louisiana was in the process of bringing its emergency-management systems into conformance with the National Incident Management System (NIMS).[36] The NRP incorporates the NIMS. In its April 2005 revision to the State's EOP, Louisiana adopted a "State of Louisiana Incident Management System" (SLIMS), which is supposed to use the same flexible structure as NIMS "to manage all types of incidents, particularly those that require the establishment of Incident Command Posts at or near an incident site." However, in Katrina, a local incident-command post was not put into place until the second week of the response. In the first week, the state operated under its pre-SLIMS structure, with operations managed through the LOHSEP chain of command.

Colonel Smith and his operations division chief, Colonel William Doran, had different perspectives on the effectiveness of incident command at the local level. Colonel Doran believed that the differences between the incident-command structure envisioned under NIMS and Louisiana's actual practice were minor: "In our case, we still have a chain of command. It's just – it's set up just a little bit different, but I think in spirit we're doing incident command."[37]

Colonel Smith, on the other hand, saw a need for LOHSEP to educate parishes on incident command, and possibly even for legislation to address the issue:

> Some parishes do a better job of understanding the ICS system, the NIMS structures. Others don't do as good a job. … I will tell you that we have some that work together great and we have others that hardly speak to each other.[38]

LOHSEP's Chief of Operations testified to "holes" in the state plan in several areas, including state control of aviation; transportation and logistics; and prioritizing competing needs for emergency assistance. He saw a need for the state to incorporate the kinds of detail ("who, what, where, why, and how") found in military planning. The absence of that kind of detail made it necessary, in his opinion, to make plans "on the fly."[39]

However, the plan does show some awareness that people lacking vehicles or having mobility problems could require assistance in evacuating. Two annexes to the State's EOP, the Southeast Louisiana Hurricane Evacuation and Sheltering Plan, and the Louisiana Shelter Operations Plan, address that issue.

The former was the creation of the Southeast Louisiana Hurricane Task Force. The revised plan of January 2000 was published by the State's Office of Emergency Preparedness, and lists 12 parish presidents and the mayor of New Orleans as signatories.[40] (In accordance with the EOP, LOHSEP required the plan to be updated at least once every four years; however, the updating due in 2004 did not occur prior to Katrina due to short staffing of the LOHSEP planning division.)[41]

The "situations" which the plan is designed to address are described in terms very similar to the scenario that served as the basis for the Hurricane Pam exercise. They include the following:

> 1. The Greater New Orleans Metropolitan Area represents a difficult evacuation problem due to the large population and it's [sic] unique layout.
>
> 2. This area is located in a floodplain much of which lies below sea level …
>
> 3. Tidal surge, associated with a "worst case" Category 3, 4 or 5 Hurricane … could cause a maximum inundation of 20 feet above sea level in some parishes …
>
> 4. The area is protected by an extensive levee system, but above normal water levels and hurricane surge could cause levee overtopping or failures.[42]

The plan also set forth a list of assumptions, including one directed specifically at the need for buses and other conveyances to evacuate those that lacked personal vehicles, stating:

The primary means of hurricane evacuation will be personal vehicles. School and municipal buses, government-owned vehicles and vehicles provided by volunteer agencies may be used to provide transportation for individuals who lack transportation and require assistance in evacuating.[43]

While the operational sections of the plan lack detail, and place very little responsibility on state government, they clearly envision a role for parish governments in evacuating those who cannot self-evacuate. Those sections divide responsibilities between risk-area parishes (in the hurricane strike zone), host-area parishes (parishes outside the strike zone where evacuees may be sheltered), and the state. No transportation obligations are imposed on host-area parishes. The responsibilities on the other two are further grouped by phases, i.e., precautionary/voluntary evacuation; recommended evacuation; and mandatory evacuation.

In a precautionary/voluntary evacuation, the Plan states that in risk-area parishes, "Local transportation resources should be marshaled and public transportation plans implemented as needed." There are no requirements for the state to marshal transportation resources.

In a recommended evacuation, the Plan directs risk-area parishes to "Mobilize transportation to assist persons who lack transportation or who have mobility problems." The state is directed to "Mobilize State transportation resources to aid in the evacuation of people who have mobility and/or health problems."

In mandatory evacuations, the Plan only directs risk-area parishes to "Assist persons with mobility limitations to find last resort refuge [and to m]obilize all transportation resources and request assistance from the state as needed." The text is unclear whether the resources are to be mobilized solely to transport persons with mobility limitations to last-resort refuges, or for broader purposes. The obligations of the state are even more limited, and no clearer: The state is to "Direct the evacuation and shelter of persons having mobility limitations, including persons in nursing homes, hospitals, group homes and non-institutionalized persons."[44]

Part VI of the plan defines the role of staging areas and last resort refuges. It contemplates that staging areas will be designated, and transportation will be pre-positioned to transport people from those areas to shelters until evacuation routes are closed, at which point the staging areas "will become Last Resort Refuges." Once weather conditions permit, rescue teams are supposed to transport evacuees from last-resort refuges to designated shelters. The plan does not specify who has responsibility to transport people from staging areas to shelters, either before evacuation routes are closed or after they reopen.[45] However, state officials consistently took the position in staff interviews that transporting evacuees was the responsibility of parish or local government.[46]

The Shelter Operations Plan is the creation of the Louisiana Shelter Task Force, made up of in-land parishes, i.e., parishes likely to receive evacuees from low-lying or coastal parishes during a major hurricane.

The plan includes a statement regarding transportation that closely resembles language in the Southeast Louisiana Hurricane Evacuation and Shelter Plan:

> The primary means of hurricane evacuation will be personal vehicles. However, school and municipal buses and, where available, specialized vehicles will be used to transport those hurricane evacuees who do not have transportation.[47]

While this part of the plan is silent on the entity expected to provide the buses and vehicles to transport people lacking personal vehicles, Part III identifies local governments in the Southeast and Southwest Hurricane Task Forces as being responsible to transport evacuees to shelters. The language suggests that the risk-area parishes were already planning to provide that transportation (although they evidently failed to follow through on those plans). In a subsection labeled "Individual Evacuee" under Section III.B Reception and Care – Planning Considerations, it states:

> Most evacuees are expected to relocate using their personal vehicles. Local governments of the two Hurricane Task Forces (Southeast and Southwest) are expected to assist in evacuating those residents who do not own vehicles. Evacuating parishes plan to transport these people to reception areas in Sector C of the Shelter Area parishes using school and municipal buses, and special purpose vehicles.[48]

The Shelter Operations Plan also required nursing homes to maintain emergency plans that address evacuation and sheltering of their patients, and their patients are not allowed into special-needs shelters "unless the homes' prearrangements have utterly failed."[49] Nursing homes were to contract in advance with commercial carriers for patients, staff, and staff families; the plan cautions that ambulance companies may be overwhelmed with demands for service in emergencies; and it directs home health-care agencies to assist the patient or his caregivers in making transportation arrangements.[50]

All organizations that provide care to special-needs people, but do not have enough transportation in emergencies, were required to arrange for supplemental transportation. If those arrangements failed, they were to notify local OEPs, and the latter are to notify needs in excess of their community capacity to LOHSEP. In turn, LOHSEP was required to report these needs to the Louisiana National Guard, which in turn was supposed to meet them with its own assets or "arrange for supplemental transportation assistance from other state agencies, the Federal Government, private businesses, other organizations, and volunteer groups."[51]

Finally, Katrina revealed a weakness in LOHSEP's use of Standard Operating Procedures (SOP) in managing emergencies. LOHSEP's SOP describe the staffing of the EOC during non-emergency situations as well as progressive levels of threatened emergencies; EOC organization in emergencies; information handling procedures; responsibilities of the principal functional groups; and certain administrative matters. Attached to it are appendices listing the responsibilities of supporting agencies at each level of EOC activation, EOC checklists, and forms for recordkeeping and public notification.

The Shelter Operations Plan Checklists identify actions to be taken at each stage of EOC activation, and provide a place for a LOHSEP to initialize and note the date and time each action is completed. Some of the items are administrative, e.g., faxing forms to parishes and requesting kitchen support for the EOC, while others relate to key aspects of preparing for disaster response. Examples of the latter category are "LOHSEP Executes Evacuation Shelter Plan" and "Begin Mandatory Evacuation Procedures."[52]

While the checklist could have served as an important tool to identify shortcomings in preparedness, its effectiveness in Katrina was limited because LOHSEP had no means to verify the accuracy of input data and information. For example, the list included an important action item relating to whether nursing homes were prepared to evacuate their patients. Specifically, it required the "Louisiana Nursing Home Association EOC Liaison [to] call all nursing homes and other custodial care organizations in the risk area to insure that they are prepared to evacuate their residents." A LOHSEP official checked this item off as having been done even though, as it turned out, preparations for evacuation of nursing homes were far from adequate. As he subsequently acknowledged, the representation of the Nursing Home Association liaison that he had called nursing homes provided no assurance that the calls were effective.[53]

The Parishes

Parish governments, like the state government, often underfunded their emergency-management functions, although in degrees that varied between parishes. As Colonel Smith testified, the problem was primarily a matter of competing demands on finite resources:

> In most cases, not in all, the [parish] emergency-management function does take a back seat. I mean they're interested in roads, they're interested in bridges, they're interested in infrastructure and they don't have the final resources to deal with all of those things that they have to deal with on a day-to-day basis. So the emergency-support functions a lot of times take a back seat due to resourcing primarily.[54]

Local officials have also found it increasingly difficult to navigate the regulations associated with DHS grants for emergency preparedness and homeland security. "You have to be a Philadelphia lawyer and a CPA just to interpret the rules and to get the dollars," according to Colonel Smith.[55]

Orleans Parish

Funding emergency preparedness has clearly not been a priority in Orleans Parish. Terry Tullier, who served in the New Orleans Fire Department (NOFD) before becoming Director of the City's Office of Emergency Preparedness from 2001 through 2004, noted the dramatic difference in staffing of the two organizations. In the NOFD, he said, there were

> probably some 830-840 people who would be happy to say, yes sir, and do pretty much anything I needed for them to do. And suddenly I was confronted with an organization that had three people in it. ... And I very quickly found out that this was going to be a real challenge for me to operate within the confines of such a small structure.[56]

Tullier complained to the city administration about the understaffing of his office, noting that the OEP in neighboring Jefferson Parish (under Walter Maestri) was far higher. In response, Tullier was told "Well, you're never going to have a dozen people in your shop like Walter does over there and just try and do the best you can."[57] Turnover has also been a serious problem at the New Orleans' OEP: There have been five directors since 1993, and the position was vacant from December 2004, when Tullier retired, to March 2005, when Matthews was appointed.[58]

Orleans Parish maintains a Comprehensive Emergency Management Plan (CEMP) that stresses the importance of pre-disaster evacuation. The plan acknowledges that "Approximately 100,000 citizens of New Orleans do not have means of personal transportation."[59] It also says that "The safe evacuation of threatened populations when endangered by a major catastrophic event is one of the principle [sic] reasons for developing a Comprehensive Emergency Management Plan,"[60] and it lists identification of at-risk populations and of transportation resources as two of the "primary tasks of evacuation planning."[61] While the plan assumes that most people will self-evacuate, it appears to envision active government involvement in providing transportation when it says that "The City of New Orleans will utilize all available resources to quickly and safely evacuate threatened areas. ... Special arrangements will be made to evacuate persons unable to transport themselves or who require specific life saving assistance."[62] It also says that "Transportation will be provided to those persons requiring public transportation from the area."[63]

The plan also includes a list of assigned tasks for various city personnel and agencies including, among others, the mayor, the OEP, and the Regional Transit Authority (RTA). One of the RTA tasks is to "Supply transportation as needed in accordance with the current standard operating procedures and to position supervisors and dispatch evacuation buses."[64]

While the plan recognizes the mayor's authority to issue evacuation orders, and specifically refers to mandatory evacuation, it does not specify how (or whether) such orders will be enforced or whether anyone would be excluded from the orders.[65] However, the Louisiana Shelter Operations Plan, which is also an Appendix to the New Orleans CEMP, states that a mandatory evacuation order is "the final, most serious phase of evacuation. Authorities will put maximum emphasis on *encouraging* evacuation and limiting ingress."[66] This suggests that the city (and the state) may not have intended that mandatory orders would be legally enforced.

The NOFD maintains hurricane guidelines that include a provision for last areas of refuge. These refuges are facilities which are multi-level, with a center core stairwell and in strategic locations around the city.[67] Each of the NOFD's eight Districts are required to identify facilities which meet the pre-requisites for last areas of refuge, confirm with the facility that fire personnel can be housed there, and reconfirm that commitment during pre-season preparations.[68] The plan includes multiple last areas of refuge, with some including back-up locations, and notes the contact person and phone number for that facility. The descriptions of each location also note whether the facility includes adequate space to park department apparatus.[69] Personnel report to these refuges upon decision by the superintendent, which will generally occur when winds reach approximately 40 miles per hour prior to landfall.[70]

Jefferson Parish

As noted above, Jefferson Parish has committed far more resources to emergency management than Orleans Parish. It has a Director, Walter Maestri, who has served in that position for nine years, and 11 permanent staff.[71] During times of emergency, the staff swells to more than 100.[72] Prior to Katrina, the EOC had approximately 80 land lines into the building, with two high-capacity T-1 data-transmission lines that connected to all of the office's data systems.[73] The Parish had its own 800 megahertz system for first responders and public works, together with an 800 megahertz system provided by the state.[74] The Parish had a 911 call center, with the calls being routed to four operational units – police, fire, emergency medical, or public works.[75] The Jefferson Parish Emergency Operations Plan was one of only two EOPs in the State of Louisiana that had been officially approved by FEMA. The other was St. Tammany Parish.[76]

The Parish EOP includes detailed provisions addressing the use of municipal buses to transport residents without other means of transportation. [77] It also includes measures for establishment of a backup EOC in the event of a Category 4 or higher hurricane.[78]

Plaquemines Parish

The Plaquemines Parish Homeland Security Office of Emergency Preparedness has a full-time staff of two – a Director, Jesse St. Amant, and his secretary, who also serves as the 911 supervisor.[79] The office coordinates with the Parish EMS Department to manage the evacuation of the Parish's special needs population.[80] EMS monitors the Parish's special-needs population and arranges for their transportation by ambulance to a regional hospital during emergencies.[81]

The Plaquemines Parish Emergency Operations Plan's Basic Plan directly mirrors the State Basic Plan. It is augmented by 20 appendices setting forth organizational charts, government lines of succession, key facilities and workers.[82] A transportation annex notes that approximately 12 percent of the population could require public transportation for evacuation, and commits the Parish to provide buses and trucks for evacuation, as well as make sure that special-needs populations, including inmates, elderly, and the handicapped, all have transportation.[83]

St. Bernard Parish

The St. Bernard Parish Office of Homeland Security and Emergency Preparedness also has a staff of only two – a director, Larry Ingargiola, and his secretary.[84] The staff is supplemented with about 20 volunteers during emergencies.[85] Parish government has never allowed the emergency director to fully open or staff the EOC during a hurricane, including during Katrina.[86]

The St. Bernard Emergency Operations Plan (EOP) also mirrors the State's EOP and includes multiple appendices. The evacuation appendix notes the need to address transportation of people without personal vehicles, but fails to make provision for that transportation.[87]

St. Tammany Parish

The St. Tammany Parish Office of Emergency Management and Homeland Security is staffed with a director, Dexter Accordo, and two deputy directors.[88] The Parish EOC is unusual for southeast Louisiana in having a state-of-the-art communications system that includes a "reverse 911 [system] where you can dial up people by geographic area, and you can broadcast an audio message to them, giving them direction of what's going on."[89] The EOC also maintains an operations center staffed by support agencies such as the Louisiana National Guard, the Louisiana Department of Transportation and Development, the St. Tammany Sheriff's Department, the Fire Department, and EMS.[90] Requests for assistance that cannot be met by these agencies are routed to the state as E-Team requests.[91]

The Parish's Emergency Operations Plan is similar to St. Bernard Parish's plan in that it identifies evacuation of residents without personal vehicles as an issue, but lacks provisions to address it.[92]

Federal Involvement

As discussed elsewhere in the Report, the Federal Emergency Management Agency and the Army Corps of Engineers have statutory authorization – and appropriations – to assist the hurricane planning and response of state and local agencies.[93] Many other federal agencies, perhaps most notably the U.S. Coast Guard, can get involved early and intensely.

There is no question that effective and timely federal assistance in disaster planning and response is vital. Local, state, and federal agencies' response to Hurricane Andrew in 1992 was widely criticized as poorly coordinated and ineffective. The General Accounting Office (GAO, later renamed the Government Accountability Office) concluded later that future hurricanes on the scale of Andrew "will quickly outstrip the capacity of all but the federal government to respond in the critical first 12 to 24 hours with life-sustaining mass care."[94]

On May 18, 1993, nine months after Hurricane Andrew and with a new hurricane season only two weeks away, National Hurricane Center Director, Robert H. Sheets, Ph.D., testified in a U.S. Senate hearing, "Rebuilding FEMA: Preparing for the Next Disaster."[95]

Because of the time it took Andrew to reach the Louisiana coast, authorities had managed to evacuate approximately 1.25 million people from the New Orleans metropolitan area. The process took three days, but officials in New Orleans expected 60 to 80 hours warning to complete evacuation.[96] Sheets knew this was not nearly good enough to prevent mass casualties. "We don't have the skill, meteorologically speaking, to provide a sufficient warning for those long lead times," he explained.[97]

If Hurricane Andrew's track had shifted slightly and hit New Orleans directly, the projected storm surge into Lake Borgne on the eastern side of the city, and on into Lake Pontchartrain to the northwest would have overflowed the levees into New Orleans. "The city of New Orleans would have gone under 18 to 20 feet of water," he said.[98]

Several federal agencies played an important role in the task of improving protections for Louisiana.

The Army Corps of Engineers

The involvement of the Corps of Engineers reflected the agency's long history of dealing with the impact of major hurricanes, especially in Louisiana. When Hurricane Betsy flooded New Orleans in 1965, the Corps was one of the most important federal responders and handled the disaster-assistance missions later transferred to FEMA.[99] The Corps designed most of the levee system that protected the New Orleans area. By statute, the Corps is authorized to assist state and local agencies, upon their request, with disaster preparedness.[100] Under the Federal Response Plan, FEMA could assign the Corps to conduct search-and-rescue missions and supply water, ice, and fuel.[101] In the event of severe flooding from a hurricane, the Corps was responsible for assisting local levee boards in restoring damaged levees and in removing floodwaters trapped inside them.

The relationship between the Corps and local levee boards and agencies was complex and not without tension. But in carrying out the dewatering program, the Corps "assumed that any emergency response will be fully coordinated with the appropriate levee districts, parish drainage departments, and local and state officials."[102]

The National Weather Service

The National Hurricane Center (NHC) within the National Weather Service (NWS) monitors storms and provides broad-scope advisories on size, track, expected point of landfall, height of storm surge, and flooding. With its 1996 creation of the Hurricane Liaison Team, the NHC also came to serve as a source of situational awareness for emergency managers.[103] Phone calls and visits from NWS forecasters who worked in the agency's four offices in Louisiana supplement the warnings with specific local knowledge.[104]

The NWS was a critical partner with the Corps and FEMA in the Hurricane Evacuation Studies process. The agency's scientists provided the storm-surge projections that gave local emergency managers guidance on when to order an evacuation, what to evacuate, and where it was safe to open shelters. After Hurricane Camille in 1969, the NWS developed the Sea, Lake, and Overland Surges from Hurricanes (SLOSH) computer program to estimate the surge of an incoming hurricane. The SLOSH modeling software could model storm surges for hurricanes of many sizes, strengths, and tracks.[105] The evacuation studies conducted by FEMA and the Army Corps of Engineers use the simulated storm surges as a basis.[106]

The Federal Emergency Management Agency and Hurricane Evacuation Studies

While Louisiana's Disaster Act affirmed local and state officials' authority to compel evacuation, safely evacuating more than a million people from the New Orleans area involves a complex ballet that ranges over three states and requires the cooperation of dozens of local, state, and federal agencies, and the American Red Cross.[107]

In 1994 this collaboration produced the equivalent of a desk reference for hurricane evacuation decision makers, known as the Southeast Louisiana Hurricane Preparedness Study. It established evacuation zones for each parish and provided estimated "clearance times" to evacuate each zone based on hurricanes of different sizes, strengths, and forward speeds.[108]

The 1994 study assumed that the levee system "would be subject to overtopping" by storm surge from a Category 4 or 5 hurricane, and even by some slow-moving Category 3 hurricanes.[109] The study showed that no shelter in New Orleans south of Interstate 12 was safe from the potential reach of Category 4 or Category 5 storm surge and inundation.[110] The study took note that about 15 percent of New Orleans residents (roughly 75,000 by the 1994 estimate) had no means of personal transportation, and cautioned, "The large number of residents reliant on public transportation could create significant problems during an evacuation and should be accounted for in the planning process."[111]

The 1994 study offered another caution while explaining the limitations of the SLOSH models of potential hurricane impact:

> The performance of a levee or floodwall depends on many factors (design criteria, construction techniques, maintenance, severity of storm, etc.) and these factors cannot be accounted for by the SLOSH model. The SLOSH model runs performed for the Lake Pontchartrain basin assumed that the levees and floodwalls remained intact, even if overtopped. In past storms, such as Hurricane Betsy and Hurricane Juan, portions of levees have failed. The failure of a levee or floodwall could significantly increase the extent and degree of flooding. Emergency-management officials should be aware of the potential for a failure in the protection and the corresponding impacts.[112]

Final Warnings

Ten years later, on June 1, 2004, Wilson Shaffer, Ph.D., a SLOSH-model expert, traveled to Louisiana to provide an informal briefing to parish emergency managers on new SLOSH studies that showed a greater number of Category 3 hurricanes would overtop the levees in New Orleans.[113] In e-mail messages during this period, Brett Herr, the Corps official in charge of the Bi-State Hurricane Evacuation Study in New Orleans, said the "new surge inundation maps show significant portions of Orleans and Jefferson Parishes that are susceptible to flooding from slow-moving Category 2 and fast Category 3 hurricanes. We had previously thought that the city would…fare pretty well for these types of storms. The new maps will result in significantly longer [evacuation] clearance times for these scenarios."[114]

The new studies used in the Hurricane Pam exercise of July 2004 provided further pre-Katrina grounds for caution. FEMA and LOHSEP sponsored the exercise for more than 300 participants, including parish emergency managers, state officials, FEMA and NWS representatives, volunteer agencies, and others involved in emergency management. The hypothetical Hurricane Pam was posited to be a strong, slow-moving Category 3 storm preceded by 20 inches of rain. The exercise projected results including over 60,000 deaths, more than 1 million people evacuated, and 10 to 20 feet of water in New Orleans. Except for the deaths figure, the Hurricane Pam projections were generally close to the real-life experience of Katrina.[115] (See Chapter 8 of this Report for further discussion of the exercise and its results.)

On June 1, 2005, Shaffer returned to Louisiana to present a briefing of the latest storm-surge estimates for New Orleans. His slide presentation was titled "Hurricanes: Nature's Weapons of Mass Destruction." It included a 40-year-old photograph of the severe flooding that occurred during Hurricane Betsy and a color graphic of flooding by a composite of possible Category 3 hurricanes. It showed that more Category 3 storms could cause overtopping of the levee system than the Army Corps of Engineers had previously stated.[116]

Another reminder of the deadly potential of hurricanes was given shortly before Katrina's arrival by the Louisiana Water Resources Research Institute at LSU:

> If a hurricane approaches New Orleans from any number of tracks from the south or southeast, water will be pushed from the Gulf of Mexico into Mississippi Sound, Lake Borgne and Lake Pontchartrain. A FEMA storm surge model, NOAA's SLOSH model, and now … experimental storm surge models

Flooded New Orleans
U.S. Coast Guard photo

based on the most recent levee heights and detailed land elevation data for southern Louisiana, have verified that *a slow-moving Category 3 hurricane or greater of these tracks have the potential to flood the New Orleans "bowl."* …

Recent survey evidence (UNO [University of New Orleans], July 2005) indicates that while many people do feel threatened by Category 4 storms, and will evacuate oncoming storms such as Hurricane Ivan (2004), some still do not realize how dangerous even a Category 2 or 3 storm from the right direction can be. Because of this they are less likely to evacuate. If you are told by emergency officials to evacuate any incoming hurricane or even tropical storm, you should still go, as early as possible.[117] [Emphasis in original]

In August 2005, the NHC updated its chronicle of hurricane activity and highlighted the growing potential for catastrophic impact:

Records for the most intense U.S. hurricane in 1935, and the costliest, Andrew in 1992, occurred in years which had much below-average hurricane activity. A large death toll in a U.S. hurricane is still possible. … Continued coastal growth and inflation will almost certainly result in every future major landfalling hurricane (and even weaker hurricanes and tropical storms) replacing one of the current costliest hurricanes. … If warnings are heeded and preparedness plans developed, the death toll can be reduced. In the absence of a change of attitude, policy, or laws governing building practices (codes and location) near the ocean, however, large property losses are inevitable.[118]

Before the month was out, the soundness of that warning would be apparent.

What Were the Emergency-Management Implications of
Facts About Levees and Hurricanes?

Whether the New Orleans levees and floodwalls were in fact built to Category 3 standards – much less upgraded to account for sinking soil and rising seas – is an important question. But it has limited bearing on judging the reasonableness and adequacy of preparations for Katrina.

The professional literature on hurricane preparation contained evidence well before Hurricane Katrina that planners would do well to err on the side of caution. A 1990 Army Corps of Engineers and FEMA assessment of the relatively low toll of 40 deaths from Hurricane Hugo's strike on the coast of Georgia and the Carolinas in the previous year concluded that:

> Much of the success in minimizing loss of life during Hugo can be attributed to local directors taking the SLOSH values seriously and evacuating those areas that the SLOSH data and associated mapping said would need to be evacuated.

> The most difficult issue regarding Hugo's hazards characteristics revolved around the storms' reported change from a Category 2 to a Category 4 hurricane in such a short period of time immediately before landfall. Fortunately many local directors took action for a Category 3 hurricane and had completed evacuation of the coastal barrier islands several hours before landfall. … Some officials indicated it may be prudent in some situations to take action for one category above that of the threatening hurricane. This proved wise on the part of local officials in Hugo.[119]

FEMA's 1994 Southeast Louisiana Hurricane Preparedness Study seconded the advice, citing a Louisiana state agency as one of its sources:

> To account for inaccuracies in forecasting the behavior of approaching hurricanes, the National Hurricane Center and the Louisiana Office of Emergency Preparedness recommend that public officials faced with an eminent [sic] evacuation prepare for the evacuation as if the approaching hurricane will intensify one category above the strength forecast for landfall.[120]

Ten years later, in 2004, two Louisiana State University researchers, John Pine and Hassan Mashriqui, offered the same counsel in a FEMA training session, "Hurricane Storm Surge Modeling and Analysis." After pointing out that "there is always the uncertainty" about hurricane intensity at landfall, and uncertainty about its track before landfall, they said:

> This is why a rule of thumb for emergency managers is to plan for a storm one category higher than what is forecast. This is a reasonable precaution to help minimize the loss of life from hurricanes. … The path and direction of the storm can change at any point making the actual area impacted by the storm as it makes landfall difficult to predict.[121]

Recent years have given emergency planners more opportunities to prepare for the worst. It is generally accepted that an era of more intense Atlantic hurricane activity began in 1995. The National Oceanic and Atmospheric Administration (NOAA) attributes the activity to naturally occurring cycles in climate patterns near the equator, and says each cycle of "the tropical multi-decadal signal" that influences storm generation may last 20 to 30 years, or longer.[122]

During the below-normal hurricane cycle that ran 1970-1994, NOAA reports, "The Gulf Coast averaged less than one hurricane landfall per season, and the East Coast averaged one hurricane landfall every five years. This is in sharp contrast to the average of three U.S. hurricane landfalls during very active seasons." NOAA foresees "many more landfalling tropical storms, hurricanes and major hurricanes in the United States," with potential impacts multiplied by population growth and new construction in coastal areas.[123]

Whatever the current phase of multi-decadal hurricane variability may be, the NWS has pointed out that an element of unpredictability always remains:

> No outlook can give certainty as to whether or not a particular locality will be impacted by a hurricane in any given year. Residents and government agencies of coastal or near-coastal regions should always maintain hurricane preparedness efforts, regardless of the overall outlook for a given year. … hurricane-spawned disasters can occur even in years with normal (or below normal) levels of activity.[124]

Johns Hopkins University Professor Robert A. Dalrymple, an engineer who represented the American Society of Civil Engineers in post-Katrina assessments of the New Orleans levees, has recently made the point even more starkly:

> There is the possibility of a storm stronger than Katrina. Although a Category 5 hurricane is perhaps a 500-year event, no one knows when it might occur.[125]

Of course, Katrina did reach Category 5 status, though it moderated somewhat before landfall. The NHC's 4 p.m. Friday, August 26, Hurricane Discussion Number 14 warned:

> Katrina is expected to be moving over the Gulf Loop Current after 36 hours ... which when combined with decreasing vertical [wind] shear ... should allow the hurricane to reach Category Four status before landfall occurs. [Ellipses in original.][126]

At 10 a.m. Saturday, the NHC warned in Hurricane Advisory Number 17 that "It is not out of the question that Katrina could reach category 5 status at some point before landfall."[127] And in fact, by Sunday morning, Katrina's maximum wind speeds exceeded 170 miles per hour; Category 5 is 155 mph or higher. It was not quite as strong as Camille, but much bigger.[128] Katrina "made landfall, at the upper end of Category 3 intensity with estimated maximum sustained winds of 110 kt [knots, or about 127 miles per hour], near Buras, Louisiana at 1110 UTC [6:10 a.m. CT] 29 August."[129]

In other words, with reservations about the ruggedness of New Orleans' hurricane-protection system already long established, with a historical record of extreme storms, with recommendations already in print for a prudent one-category-higher standard for disaster planning, with knowledge that a new cycle of more intense hurricane activity was under way, with the limits of prediction and the variability of storms understood, and with Katrina in the Gulf of Mexico and tagged as early as Friday as a potential Category 4 hurricane, officials had multiple grounds for anticipating that the coming hurricane could exceed the nominal strength of the region's defenses.

The prudence of emergency-management response when an approaching storm threatens an area depending on levees is a matter of deep concern beyond Katrina, and beyond Louisiana. It is a national issue, as noted in a recent statement of professional opinion from the National Association of State Floodplain Managers:

> Levees are only built to a certain level of protection, which will be exceeded at some point in the future. Reliance on levees should be an option of last resort. Current levee design and construction standards are inadequate. Levees that protect critical facilities, such as hospitals, emergency operations centers,

police, emergency medical services and fire stations, major infrastructure and large and vulnerable urban centers such as New Orleans must be constructed to a higher level of protection than those protecting rural or sparsely populated areas. A comprehensive and adequate levee policy would recognize the need for these differences. Levees in rural areas can utilize the 100 year flood (1% chance flood) level of protection, but only if local land use requirements prevent the area from becoming a highly urbanized area. Existing urban areas and critical facilities need protection to at least the 500 year (0.2% chance flood, and in coastal areas a category 5 hurricane) standard to avoid the catastrophic consequences, such as those experienced in the New Orleans area. It is important to recognize that levee failures in the New Orleans area is [sic] simply the tip of the iceberg – we have thousands of miles of levees "protecting" large and critical urban communities in this nation.[130]

---

1 U.S. Library of Congress, Congressional Research Service, Protecting New Orleans: From Hurricane Barriers to Flood-walls," by Nicole T. Carter, Dec. 13, 2005, p. 1.

2 Virginia R. Burkett, David B. Zilkoski, and David A. Hart, "Sea-Level Rise and Subsidence: Implications for Flooding in New Orleans, Louisiana," U.S. Geological Survey Subsidence Interest Group Conference, Nov. 27-29, 2001, p. 63. http://www.nwrc.usgs.gov/hurricane/Sea-Level-Rise.pdf. Accessed on Apr. 4, 2006 [hereinafter Burkett, "Sea-Level Rise Subsidence"].

3 Burkett, "Sea-Level Rise Subsidence," p. 63.

4 Michael Grunwald and Susan Glasser, "The Slow Drowning of New Orleans," The Washington Post, Oct. 9, 2005, p. A01.

5 U.S. Library of Congress, Congressional Research Service, The Civil Works Program of the Army Corps of Engineers: A Primer, by Nicole T. Carter and Betsy A. Cody, Feb. 3, 2005, pp. 5-6.

6 Burkett, "Sea-Level Rise Subsidence," p. 67.

7 U.S. Army Corps of Engineers, New Orleans District, Hurricane Betsy, 8-11 September 1965, After Action Report, July 1966, p. 5.

8 Lyndon Baines Johnson Library and Museum, University of Texas, "Transcript of audio of President Johnson in New Orleans following landfall of Hurricane Betsy, September 10, 1965." http://www.lbjlib.utexas.edu/johnson/AV.hom/Hurricane/audio_transcript.htm. Accessed on Apr. 5, 2006.

9 Written Statement of Anu Mittal, Director, Natural Resources and Environment, Government Accountability Office, for the U.S. Senate, Committee on Environment and Public Works, hearing on Comprehensive and Integrated Approach to meet the Water Resources Needs in the Wake of Hurricanes Katrina and Rita, Nov. 9, 2005, pp. 1, 5. http://www.gao.gov/new.items/d06244t.pdf. Accessed on Apr. 5, 2006.

10 U.S. Army Corps of Engineers, New Orleans District, "Project Fact Sheet: Lake Pontchartrain, LA. and Vicinity Hurricane Protection Project, St. Bernard, Orleans, Jefferson, and St. Charles Parishes, LA," May 23, 2005. http://www.mvn.usace.army.mil/pao/visitor/lkpon1.asp. Accessed on Apr. 5, 2006.

11 National Oceanic and Atmospheric Administration (NOAA), Hurricane Research Division, "How Are Atlantic Hurricanes Ranked?" http://www.aoml.noaa.gov/hrd/tcfaq/D1.html. Accessed on Apr. 3, 2006 ("Category 3, 4, and 5 hurricanes are collectively referred to as major (or intense) hurricanes. These major hurricanes cause over 83% of the damage in the USA even though they account for only 21% of tropical cyclone landfalls.").

12 U.S. Army Corps of Engineers, "Frequently Asked Questions." http://www.mvn.usace.army.mil/IPET_13_Mar_FAQ_Public.pdf. Accessed on Apr. 26, 2006.

13 U.S. Army Corps of Engineers, "How Safe is New Orleans from Flooding?" fact sheet, Sept. 11, 2003. http://www.usace.army.mil/civilworks/hot_topics/ht_2003/11sep_msy.htm. Accessed on Apr. 5, 2006.

14 Dr. Marc Levitan, "Comparative Analysis of Hurricane Vulnerability in New Orleans and Baton Rouge," Louisiana State University Hurricane Center, Apr. 2003, p. 1. http://www.publichealth.hurricane.lsu.edu/Adobe%20files%20for%20webpage/LevitanHurrVulnBR&NO.pdf. Accessed on Apr. 5, 2006.

15 National Weather Service, National Hurricane Center, "The Most Intense Hurricanes in the United States 1851-2004," July 27, 2005. http://www.nhc.noaa.gov/pastint.shtml. Accessed on Apr. 5, 2006.

16 Louisiana Office of Homeland Security and Emergency Preparedness (LOHSEP), Emergency Operations Plan, Apr. 2005, Section IV.B, p. 8 [hereinafter Louisiana Emergency Operations Plan].

17 State of Louisiana, Executive Order KBB 05, Apr. 1, 2005.

18 LOHSEP, "About the Agency," Mar. 20, 2006. http://www.ohsep.louisiana.gov/agencyrelated/aboutagency.htm. Accessed on Apr. 9, 2006.

19 LOHSEP, "About the Agency," Mar. 20, 2006. http://www.ohsep.louisiana.gov/agencyrelated/aboutagency.htm. Accessed on Apr. 9, 2006.

20 *Louisiana Emergency Operations Plan*, Section I, p. 1.

21 *Louisiana Emergency Operations Plan*, Section I, p. 1.

22 *Louisiana Emergency Operations Plan*, Section II, B, pp. 5-6.

23 *Louisiana Emergency Operations Plan*, Attachment 3.

24 Committee staff interview of Col. Jeff Smith, Louisiana National Guard (Ret.), Acting Deputy Director, Emergency Management, LOHSEP, conducted on Jan. 13, 2006, transcript p. 13.

25 Col. Smith interview, Jan. 13, 2006, p. 26; Committee staff interview of Lt. Col. William Doran, Louisiana Air National Guard, Chief, Operations Division, LOHSEP, conducted on Dec. 2, 2005, transcript p. 164.

26 Committee staff interview of Sean Fontenot, former Chief, Preparedness Division, LOHSEP, conducted on Jan. 10, 2006, transcript p. 124; Committee staff interview of Maj. Gen. Bennett Landreneau, Adjutant General, Louisiana, conducted on Jan. 11, 2006, transcript pp. 124-125; Committee staff interview of Terry Ryder, Executive Counsel, Office of the Governor, LA, conducted on Jan. 10, 2006, transcript pp. 138-141; Lt. Col. Doran interview, Dec. 2, 2005, pp. 63, 163; Committee staff interview of Col. Steven Dabadie, former Chief of Staff, Louisiana National Guard, conducted on Jan. 12, 2006, transcript p. 45.

27 Lt. Col. Doran interview, Dec. 2, 2005, pp. 191-193.

28 Maj. Gen. Landreneau interview, Jan. 11, 2006, p. 124; Col. Smith interview, Jan. 13, 2006, pp. 23-24.

29 Ryder interview, Jan. 10, 2006, p. 143.

30 Lt. Col. Doran interview, Dec. 2, 2005, p. 196.

31 Committee staff interview of Capt. Paul Hellmers, Engine 18, Second Platoon, Fifth District, New Orleans Fire Department, LA, and Capt. Joe Fincher, Engine 18, Third Platoon, Fifth District, New Orleans Fire Department, LA, conducted on Nov. 7, 2005, transcript pp. 12-13. Each of the NOFD's eight Districts is required to identify facilities which meet the pre-requisites for a last area refuge, confirm with the facility that fire personnel can be housed there, and reconfirm that commitment during pre-season preparations. *Source*: New Orleans Fire Department, *2005 Hurricane Guidelines*, p. 2–1; Capt. Hellmers and Capt. Fincher joint interview, Nov. 7, 2005, p. 16. The plan includes multiple Last Areas of Refuge, with some including back-up locations, and notes the contact person and phone number for that facility. The descriptions of each location also note whether the facility includes adequate space to park department apparatus. *Source*: New Orleans Fire Department, *2005 Hurricane Guidelines*, pp. A2–1 through A6–2. Personnel report to these refuges upon decision by the superintendent, which will generally occur when winds reach approximately 40 miles per hour prior to landfall. *Source*: Committee staff interview of Charles Parent, Superintendent, New Orleans Fire Department, LA, and Bruce Martin, Deputy of Administration, New Orleans Fire Department, LA, conducted on Nov. 10, 2005, transcript p. 26. In addition to provision of refuges for fire personnel and equipment, the NOFD guidelines are specific as to the types of supplies personnel are to bring with them, including toiletries, clothing, a three-day supply of water, and three gallons of water. Personnel are also encouraged to bring life jackets and/or boats. *Source*: New Orleans Fire Department, *2005 Hurricane Guidelines*, pp. 2–3 through 2–4.

32 Louisiana National Guard, *Emergency Procedures Operations Plans for Military Support to Civil Authorities*, Oct. 24, 2001. Provided to Committee; filed as Bates no. 000153. During 2001, the Guard revised its own operating plans in such areas of law enforcement in ways that illustrate how its personnel were layered into the ranks of the region's law enforcement agencies. "The concept of this operation provides for a massive joint response 24 hours pre-landfall and 48 hours post-landfall of a major hurricane forecasted to strike the Greater New Orleans area," and outlined the planned distribution of soldiers, helicopters, high profile trucks, emergency generators, water trailers and other equipment to the Louisiana State Police and local agencies, assigning a total of 420 Guardsmen to the New Orleans Police Department, with 200 deployed initially at the Superdome, 100 at the Convention Center and 12 at each of eight police district stations.

33 *Louisiana Emergency Operations Plan*, Supplement 1A, "Southeast Louisiana Hurricane Evacuation and Sheltering Plan," Jan. 2000, p. II-2 [hereinafter "Southeast Louisiana Hurricane Evacuation and Sheltering Plan"].

34 FEMA, Bi-State Hurricane Evacuation Study, May 2, 2002. Provided to Committee; filed as Bates no. DHS-FEMA-0058-00001607.

35 FEMA, Bi-State Hurricane Evacuation Study, May 2, 2002, pp. 16-17.

36 Sean R. Fontenot, e-mail to Arthur W. Adelberg, Senate Committee staff member, Feb. 3, 2006, 11:21 a.m.

37 Lt. Col. Doran interview, Dec. 2, 2005, pp. 143-145.

38 Col. Smith interview, Jan. 13, 2006, pp. 17-19.

39 Lt. Col. Doran interview, Dec. 2, 2005, pp. 147-150.

40 "Southeast Louisiana Hurricane Evacuation and Sheltering Plan," pp. i-ii.

41 Fontenot interview, Jan. 10, 2006, pp. 115-122.

42 "Southeast Louisiana Hurricane Evacuation and Sheltering Plan," p. II-1.

43 "Southeast Louisiana Hurricane Evacuation and Sheltering Plan," p. II-2.

44 "Southeast Louisiana Hurricane Evacuation and Sheltering Plan," pp. III-1-6.

45 "Southeast Louisiana Hurricane Evacuation and Sheltering Plan," p. VI-1.

46 Col. Smith interview, Jan. 13, 2006, p. 185; Maj. Gen. Landreneau interview, Jan. 11, 2006, p. 142.

47 *Louisiana Emergency Operations Plan*, Supplement 1C, "Louisiana Shelter Operations Plan," July 2000, p. 9. [hereinafter "Louisiana Shelter Operations Plan"].

48 "Louisiana Shelter Operations Plan," p. 11-12 (emphasis added).

49 *Louisiana Emergency Operations Plan*, "Louisiana Shelter Operations Plan," Annex X, "Special Needs Plan," Apr. 2000, pp. 3-4 [hereinafter Annex X, "Special Needs Plan"].

50 Annex X, "Special Needs Plan," p. 8.

51 Annex X, "Special Needs Plan," pp. 7-8. Presumably the National Guard was assigned this responsibility because of its role as the primary responsible agency for transportation at the time the SN Plan was drafted. Had the plan been updated after Apr. 2005, when DOTD succeeded the Guard as the primary agency responsible for transportation, presumably the plan would have assigned the SN transportation responsibility to DOTD.

52 Louisiana Office of Emergency Preparedness (LOEP), Standard Operating Procedures, EOC Hurricane/Major Event Checklist. The version produced to the Committee bears the date 10/24/2005. The record is unclear as to whether the version includes updates through that date. Committee staff interview of James Ballows, Senior Operations Officer, LOHSEP, conducted on Jan. 4, 2006, transcript pp. 15-16.

53 Ballows interview, Jan. 4, 2006, pp. 13-14.

54 Col. Smith interview, Jan. 13, 2006, p. 19; Lt. Col. Doran interview, Dec. 2, 2005, p. 63 ("Some parishes do a great job, others don't. It's not standardized").

55 Col. Smith interview, Jan. 13, 2006, pp. 19-21.

56 Committee staff interview of Terry Tullier, former Deputy Director, New Orleans Fire Department and Director, New Orleans Office of Emergency Preparedness, LA, conducted on Nov. 22, 2005, transcript pp. 7-8.

57 Tullier interview, Nov. 22, 2005, pp. 10-11.

58 Tullier interview, Nov. 22, 2005, p. 2; Committee staff interview of Chief Joseph Matthews, Director, New Orleans Office of Emergency Preparedness, LA, conducted on Nov. 23, 2005, transcript p. 152. Directors prior to Terry Tullier and Chief Joseph Matthews were Brian Giddings, Robert Eichorn, and Frank Hijuelos. Committee staff interview of Saraya Flores-Arias, Executive Assistant to the Director, New Orleans Office of Emergency Preparedness, LA, conducted on Dec. 19, 2005, pp. 7-9, 14-15.

59 New Orleans Office of Emergency Preparedness, *Comprehensive Emergency Management Plan*, May 2005, p. 19 [hereinafter *New Orleans CEMP*].

60 *New Orleans CEMP*, p. 12.

61 *New Orleans CEMP*, p. 12.

62 *New Orleans CEMP*, p. 14.

63 *New Orleans CEMP*, p. 14. While the term "persons requiring public transportation" is broad enough to include those without personal vehicles, the quoted sentence is followed by the parenthetical "(See Special Needs Transportation, ESF 1)." Precisely what the parenthetical refers to is unclear, but it raises the question whether the sentence was meant only to apply to people with special needs.

64 *New Orleans CEMP*, p. 18. While the plan does not expressly define "Standard Operation Procedures" or "SOP," the term apparently refers to the provisions of the plan.

65 *New Orleans CEMP*, p. 13.

66 *New Orleans CEMP*; Annex X, "Special Needs Plan," p. 4 (emphasis added).

67 Capt. Hellmers and Capt. Fincher interview, Nov. 7, 2005, pp. 12-13.

68 Capt. Hellmers and Capt. Fincher interview, Nov. 7, 2005, p. 16.

69 New Orleans Fire Department, *2005 Hurricane Guidelines*, pp. A2–1 through A6–2.

70 Parent and Martin interview, Nov. 10, 2005, p. 26.

71 Committee staff interview of Walter Maestri, Ph.D., Director, Jefferson Parish Office of Emergency Management, LA, conducted on Oct. 25, 2005, transcript pp. 11-12.

72 Maestri interview, Oct. 25, 2005, p. 12.

73 Maestri interview, Oct. 25, 2005, p. 40.

74 Maestri interview, Oct. 25, 2005, p. 40.

75 Maestri interview, Oct. 25, 2005, p. 41.

76 Maestri interview, Oct. 25, 2005, pp. 25-27.

77 Jefferson Parish Office of Emergency Management, *Emergency Operations Plan*, Aug. 2002, Annex D, p. 13.

78 Jefferson Parish, *Catastrophic Weather Event ("Doomsday") Plan*. Provided to Committee.

79 Committee staff interview of Jesse St. Amant, Director, Homeland Security Office of Emergency Preparedness, Plaquemines Parish, LA, conducted on Nov. 9, 2005, transcript pp. 3, 20-21.

80 St. Amant interview, Nov. 9, 2005, p. 15.

81 St. Amant interview, Nov. 9, 2005, p. 15.

82 Plaquemines Parish, *Multi-Hazard Emergency Operations Plan*, 2003, Basic Plan Appendices.

83 Plaquemines Parish, *Multi-Hazard Emergency Operations Plan*, 2003, Annex D, p. 6–1.

84 Committee staff interview of Larry Ingargiola, Director, Department of Homeland Security and Emergency Preparedness, St. Bernard Parish, LA, conducted on Oct. 26, 2005, transcript p. 8.

85 Ingargiola interview, Oct. 26, 2005, p. 7.

86 Ingargiola interview, Oct. 26, 2005, pp. 13-14.

87 St. Bernard Parish, *Emergency Operations Plan*, June 2004, Annex D, p. D–2.

88 Committee staff interview of Dexter Accordo, Director, Emergency Management and Homeland Security, St. Tammany Parish, LA, conducted on Nov. 10, 2005, transcript p. 19.

89 Accordo interview, Nov. 10, 2005, p. 47.

90 Accordo interview, Nov. 10, 2005, pp. 64-66.

91 Accordo interview, Nov. 10, 2005, p. 71.

92 St. Tammany Parish, *Multi-Hazard Emergency Operation Plan*, 2004, Annex D, p. D–54.

93 *Southeast Louisiana Hurricane Preparedness Study*, prepared by the U.S. Army Corps of Engineers, for FEMA Region VI, Aug. 2004, p. 1-2 [hereinafter *Southeast Louisiana Hurricane Preparedness Study*, 1994] ("The study authority for the Federal Emergency Management Agency is the Disaster Relief Act of 1974 (Public Law 93-2881, and the study authority for the Corps of Engineers is Section 206 of the Flood Control Act of 1960 (Public Law 86-645). These laws authorize the allocation of resources for planning activities related to hurricane preparedness.").

94 Testimony of J. Dexter Peach, Assistant Comptroller, General Resources, Community, and Economics, before the U.S. Senate, Committee on Armed Services, Subcommittee on Nuclear Deterrence, Arms Control and Defense Intelligence, hearing on *Disaster Management: Recent Disasters Demonstrate the Need to Improve the Nation's Response Strategy*, May 25, 1993, p. 16.

95 Testimony of Robert Sheets, Ph.D., Director, National Hurricane Center, before the U.S. Senate, Committee on Governmental Affairs, hearing on *Rebuilding FEMA: Preparing for the Next Disaster*, May 18, 1993, p. 45.

96 Ed Rappaport, National Hurricane Center, "Preliminary Report Hurricane Andrew 16 - 28 August, 1992" Dec. 10, 1993, addendum Feb. 7, 2005 – category 5 upgrade ("It is estimated that 1,250,000 people evacuated from parishes in southeastern and south-central Louisiana.").

97 Sheets, Senate Committee on Governmental Affairs hearing, May 18, 1993, p. 45.

98 Sheets, Senate Committee on Governmental Affairs hearing, May 18, 1993, p. 45.

99 U.S. Army Corps of Engineers, New Orleans District, *Hurricane Betsy, 8-11 September 1965, After Action Report*, July 1966, p. 10.

100 Written Statement of Anu Mittal, Director, Natural Resources and Environment, Government Accountability Office, for the U.S. Senate, Committee on Homeland Security and Governmental Affairs, hearing on *Hurricane Katrina: Who's in Charge of the New Orleans Levees?*, Dec. 15, 2005, pp. 1-3.

101 U.S. Army Corps of Engineers, New Orleans District, *Catastrophic Disaster Response Plan*, pp. 12-14.

102 U.S. Army Corps of Engineers, New Orleans District, *Un-watering Plan, Greater Metropolitan Area, New Orleans, Louisiana*, Aug. 18, 2000, p. 1.

103 Written Statement of Max Mayfield, Ph.D., Director, Tropical Prediction Center and National Hurricane Center, National Weather Service, National Oceanic and Atmospheric Administration, for the U.S. House, Select Bipartisan Committee to Investigate the Preparation for and Response to Hurricane Katrina, hearing on *What Did Officials Know About Potential Impact of Katrina? When Did They Know It? And, How Was the Information Conveyed to the Public?*, Sept. 22, 2005, p. 3.

104 Written Statement of Brig. Gen. David L. Johnson, Assistant Administrator, Weather Services, National Oceanic and Atmospheric Administration, for the U.S. House, Committee on Science, hearing on *NOAA Hurricane Forecasting*, Oct. 7, 2005.

105 Written Statement of Mayfield, House Select Committee hearing, Sept. 22, 2005 pp. 2-3.

106 Written Statement of Mayfield, House Select Committee hearing, Sept. 22, 2005 p. 3.

107 U.S. Army Corps of Engineers, Information on Hurricane Evacuation Studies, p. 8. Provided to Committee.

108 *Southeast Louisiana Hurricane Preparedness Study*, 1994, pp. 1–2, 1–14.

109 *Southeast Louisiana Hurricane Preparedness Study*, 1994, p. 5–2.

110 *Southeast Louisiana Hurricane Preparedness Study*, 1994, p. 5–2.

111 *Southeast Louisiana Hurricane Preparedness Study*, 1994, p. 4–6.

112 *Southeast Louisiana Hurricane Preparedness Study*, 1994, p. 2–37.

113 Committee staff interview of Wilson Shaffer, Ph.D., Chief, Evaluations Branch, National Weather Service, National Oceanic and Atmospheric Administration, conducted on Feb. 24, 2006, transcript pp. 45-46.

114 Brett Herr, e-mail to Jay Baker, Mar. 15, 2006, 12:15 p.m. Provided to Committee; filed as Bates no. DHS-FEMA-0025-0002638.

115 Written Statement of Madhu Beriwal, President and Chief Executive Officer, IEM, Inc., for the U.S. Senate, Committee on Homeland Security and Governmental Affairs, hearing on *Preparing for a Catastrophe: The Hurricane Pam Exercise*, Jan. 24, 2006, p. 1. IEM was the main contractor that prepared the exercise for FEMA and LOHSEP.

116 Wilson Shaffer, National Weather Service, "Louisiana's Vulnerability to Hurricane Storm Surge," PowerPoint presentation, June 1, 2005. Provided to Committee.

117 Louisiana Water Resources Research Institute, Louisiana State University, "Would New Orleans Really Flood in a Major Hurricane? How is that possible?," 2005.
http://www.publichealth.hurricane.lsu.edu/convert%20to%20tables/Would%20New%20Orleans%20Really%20Floodtf.htm. Accessed on Apr. 6, 2006.

118 National Oceanic and Atmospheric Administration, Technical Memorandum, "The deadliest, costliest, and most intense United States tropical cyclones from 1851 to 2004 (and other frequently requested hurricane facts)," Aug. 2005, pp. 11-12. http://www.nhc.noaa.gov/pdf/NWS-TPC-4.pdf. Accessed on Apr. 9, 2006.

119 U.S. Army Corps of Engineers and FEMA, "Hurricane Hugo Assessment, Review of Hurricane Evacuation Studies Utilization and Information Dissemination," Jan. 1990, p. 2–2. http://www3.csc.noaa.gov/hes_docs/postStorm/H_HUGO_ASSESSMENT_REVIEW_UTILIZATION_INFO_DISSEMINATION.pdf Accessed Apr. 5, 2006.

120 *Southeast Louisiana Hurricane Preparedness Study*, 1994, p. 2–2.

121 John C. Pine, Hassan Mashriqui, LSU Hurricane Center, "Hurricane Storm Surge Modeling and Analysis," FEMA Course Title: Hazard Mapping and Modeling, Session 10, Nov. 18, 2004, p. 16-14. http://training.fema.gov/EMIWeb/downloads/Session%2010%20Hurricanes92004111804.doc. Accessed on Apr. 5, 2006.

122 National Oceanic and Atmospheric Administration, "NOAA attributes recent increase in hurricane activity to naturally occurring multi-decadal climate variability," NOAA Magazine Online, Nov. 29, 2005. http://www.magazine.noaa.gov/stories/mag184.htm. Accessed on Mar. 8, 2006.

123 National Oceanic and Atmospheric Administration, "NOAA attributes recent increase in hurricane activity to naturally occurring multi-decadal climate variability," NOAA Magazine Online, Nov. 29, 2005. http://www.magazine.noaa.gov/stories/mag184.htm. Accessed on Mar. 8, 2006.

124 National Weather Service, "Atlantic Hurricane Outlook," Jan. 28, 2003, p. 2. http://products.weather.gov/PDD/AHO.pdf. Accessed on Apr. 5, 2006.

125 Louisiana Coastal Wetlands Conservation and Restoration Task Force, "Interview with Robert A. Dalrymple," *WaterMarks*, Number 30, Mar. 2006, p. 14. http://www.lacoast.gov/watermarks/2006-03/watermarks-2006-03.pdf. Accessed on Apr. 5, 2006.

126 National Hurricane Center, Hurricane Katrina Forecast Timeline, 2006, p. 3. Provided to Committee [hereinafter NHC Timeline].

127 NHC Timeline.

128 National Oceanic and Atmospheric Administration, National Climatic Data Center, "Climate of 2005: Summary of Hurricane Katrina," Dec. 29, 2005. http://lwf.ncdc.noaa.gov/oa/climate/research/2005/katrina.html#rain. Accessed on Apr. 26, 2006.

129 Richard D. Knabb, Jamie R. Rhome, and Daniel P. Brown, National Hurricane Center, "Tropical Cyclone Report Hurricane Katrina 23-30 August 2005," Dec. 20, 2005, p. 1. http://www.nhc.noaa.gov/pdf/TCR-AL122005_Katrina.pdf#search='Tropical%20Cyclone%20Report%20Hurricane%20Katrina'. Accessed on Apr. 26, 2006.

130 Association of State Floodplain Managers, Inc., "Hurricanes Katrina & Rita: Using Mitigation to Rebuild a Safer Gulf Coast," Sept. 9, 2005, pp. 4-5. http://www.floods.org/PDF/ASFPM_HurricaneKatrina_WhitePaper_090905.pdf. Accessed on Apr. 4, 2006.

Grounded, Mississippi
U.S. Coast Guard photo

Emergency Management: Mississippi

Mississippi emergency-management law gives the Governor broad powers during disasters, and establishes the Mississippi Emergency Management Agency (MEMA) as the agency responsible for carrying out emergency management in the state. The system places significant, front-line responsibility for disaster preparedness and response on local governments.

State Powers and Responsibilities

Mississippi law provides that a state of emergency exists when a disaster is of a magnitude beyond the control of any municipality or county, and "requires combined forces of the state to combat."[1] The Governor is empowered to declare a state of emergency.[2]

During a disaster, the Governor serves as a bridge between federal and local governments. Mississippi law authorizes the Governor to direct the various state agencies, including the Mississippi National Guard, to take measures necessary to combat a disaster and to direct local law enforcement in order to keep good order.[3] The entity primarily responsible for emergency-management planning and direction is MEMA.[4] The Governor appoints the head of MEMA.[5]

Mississippi law authorizes the creation of mutual-aid pacts both within the state and between Mississippi and other states.[6] Mississippi is a signatory to the state-to-state Emergency Management Assistance Compact (EMAC); MEMA directs its participation.[7] An intrastate mutual-aid pact, established in 1995,[8] sets out the mechanism for counties and municipalities to contribute, via MEMA, emergency-management assets and personnel to disaster-hit areas.[9] All of the coastal counties are part of this agreement.[10]

Emergency Management: Hurricanes

The state hurricane plan details the four key hurricane hazards – storm surge, high winds, tornadoes, and flooding from rain – and notes the challenge facing emergency managers along the Gulf Coast: "The tremendous commercial and residential development along the coast due to the advent of dockside gambling has greatly increased the potential devastation of a major hurricane."[11]

The Mississippi Comprehensive Emergency Management Plan (the Hurricane Plan), created in 1999, correctly assumed that a major hurricane (category 3 or higher) would strike the Mississippi coast within the next 10 years.[12] It also assumed that residents, as well as local and state responders, would be on their own after landfall: "Due to multi-state infrastructure damage, assistance will not be available from the federal government or non-affected states for at least 72 hours after the hurricane."[13]

The plan places responsibility for pre- and post-landfall sheltering on local governments, encouraging cooperation agreements with local American Red Cross chapters.

A unique feature of the Hurricane Plan is its provision for pre-landfall deployment of small engineering units of the Mississippi National Guard to the coastal counties when a major

Ruined homes, Bay St. Louis, MS
Sun Herald news photo, Biloxi/Gulfport, MS

storm approaches. The engineer units' high-clearance equipment and vehicles allow them to operate in flooded areas, especially for search-and-rescue missions, when local first responders like fire departments cannot do so. Accordingly, MEMA and the Mississippi National Guard dispatched small engineering detachments and other National Guard personnel to the three coastal counties before Katrina hit.[14]

MEMA hosts an annual hurricane conference which focuses on the state's southernmost 12 counties, those most exposed to hurricanes. Officials from Louisiana and Alabama often attend.[15] State programs also include twice-yearly training on HURREVAC, the computer program used to forecast hurricanes, for emergency managers, first responders, staff from Mississippi's Keesler Air Force Base, and other federal personnel on the coast, as well as officials from Stennis Space Center, located in southwestern Mississippi.[16]

Counties and Cities

Under Mississippi's emergency-management system, local governments and their first responders form the first line of response. Localities must update their response plans at least every five years.[17] MEMA must review them for consistency with the state's own plan and legal requirements.[18]

During a disaster, the state activates an emergency operations center (EOC) to guide response, working in conjunction with EOCs operated by individual counties.[19] The state plan also allows local governments to proclaim local emergencies, establish their own emergency-management systems, and seek support from state and federal governments.[20] MEMA directs each locality to appoint an emergency-management coordinator and give that coordinator direct, personal responsibility for organizing, administering, and operating the local system.[21]

When Katrina hit, each of the Gulf Coast counties had its own EOC, an emergency-management director, and local responsibilities parceled out according to the 16 emergency-support functions (ESFs) in the state plan. In the coastal counties, local fire departments and law enforcement (both county sheriffs and municipal police) have lead roles in emergency response. For example, in Harrison County, personnel from the largest fire departments (Gulfport, Biloxi, and Long Beach) and police departments helped staff the county EOC, in addition to their responder duties.[22]

Mass Care

By Sunday evening, August 28, thousands of people displaced by Katrina were in shelters across the region.[23] At the peak, September 5, the state had 121 shelters open, with an additional 12 on standby. Over 15,000 people were registered in these shelters – about half of their total capacity.[24] The state was able to provide sufficient shelter for the special-needs population, although it often had to move these individuals further inland for appropriate accommodations.

Many residents found shelter conditions quite difficult because of shortages of food and water and sanitation problems. Some shelters were closed to consolidate operations, forcing residents to relocate. Though their challenges were formidable, state and local governments and the American Red Cross could have prepared better. Planning needed to be more detailed for such a catastrophic disaster, during which residents typically need longer-term shelter.

State and Locals Select and Manage Shelters

Federal, state, and local governments worked with the American Red Cross and other non-profit organizations and opened or placed on standby at least 133 shelters, with room for almost 31,000 people.[25] Many of these shelters had been approved by the Red Cross before the storm made landfall, which meant that, initially, the Red Cross would staff and manage them. Red Cross criteria include a building's location, at least 18 feet above sea level, and its capability to withstand high winds.[26] Local Red Cross chapters worked with emergency-management and state officials to identify and select shelters.[27] The Red Cross is responsible for providing food, water, and ice to its own shelters.

MEMA and the Mississippi Department of Human Service (MDHS), working with local governments and the Red Cross, first opened shelters north of Interstate 20, a major east-west highway that runs through Jackson.[28] This took evacuees out of the coastal area and accommodated evacuees from Louisiana.[29] The state preferred to open more and smaller shelters than fewer and larger ones because, as Jim Craig of the Mississippi Department of Health explained, it is more difficult to monitor and control illness with a large group of people in a single confined location.[30]

Local governments decided to open additional, non-Red Cross designated shelters to accommodate evacuees who preferred to stay close to home. As Gulfport Police Commander Alfred Sexton explained:

> Most citizens are of the mindset they're not going to go far from their homes. … We had officers actually stopping and picking up people on the side of the road and taking them to the closest shelters … a lot of people … historically … wait until they see rain or wind and then they want to move to a shelter.[31]

Local emergency-management shelters must have met MEMA or local standards. These shelters are initially under the direction of the local emergency-management agency and are staffed by county and MDHS personnel. MDHS is notified by MEMA or the county emergency-management agency that its assistance is needed to staff and/or operate a shelter.[32] Local governments are responsible for providing food, water, and ice to non-Red Cross designated shelters, though they can request help with operations and supplies from the Red Cross and MDHS.

Local organizations such as churches also operated independent shelters. These groups, according to state and local officials, were "pretty much on their own" for staffing, supplying, and managing the shelters.[33] Richard Dawkins of the MDHS estimated that about 60-70 percent of shelters opened for Hurricane Katrina were Red Cross designated; the remainder consisted of local emergency-management and independent shelters.[34] Residents were notified of shelter locations and capacity levels through the news media.

Coastal County Shelters Were Options of Last Resort

Shelters of last resort – places protecting from high winds, heavy rains, and storm surge, but with little food and water – were needed for those who could not, or chose not to, evacuate. On August 27, MEMA urged coastal counties not to open local shelters in order to encourage people to evacuate north. However, Tom McAllister, MEMA's Director for Response and Recovery, estimated that the coast ended up opening a lot of shelters:

> Granted, they don't meet the Red Cross standard … but it's better than being out on the highway. And we identified a lot of those, school buildings, churches, … large community buildings, so we could get people off the road at the last minute.[35]

In some cases, the Mississippi Department of Health (MDH) had to place nurses in shelters of last resort because they became special-needs shelters.[36]

Special-Needs Shelters Posed a Challenge for State and Local Governments

The special-needs population on the Gulf Coast includes older adults and individuals with disabilities. For example, in Biloxi, a city of about 50,000 people, 26 percent are residents with disabilities.[37]

A special-needs shelter is intended for individuals who have no other resources and who need assistance that cannot be guaranteed in a regular shelter (e.g., medication that requires refrigeration, oxygen equipment, etc.). It is not intended for patients who need substantial or constant medical care.[38]

Robert Latham, MEMA's Executive Director, described special-needs sheltering as a "tremendous problem."

> When I took this job in 2000 that was one of the biggest issues. … How do we take care of the special needs population, especially on the Gulf Coast where you have a lot of retirees and there are a lot of people with health needs?[39]

After the 2004 hurricane season, MEMA had asked local emergency managers to designate shelters in each county for citizens with special needs. According to MEMA, this would have ensured that a location had everything needed for special-needs citizens during an evacuation.[40] While local officials agreed that counties needed such shelters, some counties did not have adequate resources to purchase supplies and equipment, such as backup generators, beds, and medical equipment for these facilities.[41] Staffing was another challenge; special-needs shelters require MDH medical staff with appropriate training.[42]

Four special-needs shelters were open after the storm made landfall, in Lincoln and Jones Counties, at Biloxi High School, and at Pearl River Community College in Hattiesburg.[43] As needs grew, three others were opened on September 2.[44] Since many of the coastal counties did not have special-needs shelters, these vulnerable populations were forced to go as far as Jackson, about 150 miles from the coast.[45] Individuals and caregivers faced the difficult choice between the dangers of evacuation and attempting to ride out the storm.

Many of the coastal counties used hospitals or other facilities for their special-needs populations. For example, Butch Loper, Director of Jackson County's Emergency Management Agency, utilized the county's two hospitals for special-needs patients.[46]

Since Katrina, the state has developed a plan to provide an additional 1,500 beds for the special-needs population, on a more statewide basis. During the next disaster, it will utilize the state's 15 community colleges and their multiple campuses, as special-needs shelters. According to Craig, the Pearl River Community College, because of its ample facilities and personnel, including a cafeteria with an on-staff nutritionist, water and wastewater systems, and a police force, worked very well as a special needs shelter for Katrina victims.[47] He described it as a self-contained city.

Shelters Suffered From Overcrowding and Commodity Shortages

Many residents who took refuge in a public shelter found conditions extremely difficult. Shelters had shortages of food and drinking water, sanitation problems, lack of electricity, and no running water for bathing. Kristen Dellinger, a volunteer, described the shelter at Bay St. Louis High School, in Hancock County:

Wrecked bridges, Ocean Springs, MS
Sun Herald news photo, Biloxi/Gulfport, MS

> This "shelter" had no resemblance to the "neat cots-in-a-row" kind of place that often comes to mind. … Most people had staked out areas on the sidewalks outside under covered walkways. They had thin pieces of blue plastic to sleep on. … The school hallways were dark and filled with streaks of mud. The odor was horrendous. Raw sewage, I think.[48]

Shelters without running water gave doctors concerns about the use of portable toilets, and about the lack of equipment to test the safety of drinking water.[49] Officials in Biloxi suspected an outbreak of dysentery and closed a shelter. About 400 people had been staying there, and many ignored warnings to stay away from the water. Although no one developed dysentery, many shelter residents had developed the Norwalk virus, an intestinal illness also known as the "cruise ship virus."[50]

State and local officials acknowledged that conditions at many of the shelters were less than ideal. The state had problems obtaining some of the supplies and equipment, such as generators, that were desperately needed at the shelters given the extreme heat and crowded conditions.[51]

To make matters worse, the Red Cross failed to provide adequate supplies and services at both designated and local shelters. According to Gulfport Police officers who were providing security at the shelters, many of the shelters ran out of food and water. This was a chronic problem for the first two weeks after landfall.[52]

After food and water finally arrived in the county, Colonel Joe Spraggins, Harrison County's Emergency Manager, asked Oscar Barnes, the local Red Cross representative why the Red Cross was not delivering the items to the shelters and was told that Red Cross volunteers and staff were prohibited from driving at night during a disaster.[53] In order to get the supplies to the shelters, Gulfport Police took over distribution duties.[54]

Lack of communication and transportation infrastructure problems made it difficult for the Red Cross and other agencies to get needed supplies and services to the shelters. Due to the severity of Katrina, the larger shelters filled up fast, forcing the Red Cross to open up its additional shelters on a tiered basis, rather than open all sites simultaneously. Shelters were placed in tiers based on their location and were opened from first to fourth tiers consecutively. In some areas, the agency even had to do quick impromptu assessments, using a checklist, to validate compliance with criteria before opening up additional shelters. This is extremely unusual for the Red Cross.[55]

The magnitude of the disaster may have overwhelmed the Red Cross' ability to provide adequate shelter conditions for an extended period of time. According to Robert Latham, MEMA's Executive Director, the Red Cross was not prepared to handle such a large catastrophe. In Mississippi, organization was extremely short-staffed and as a result was not able to adequately serve all coastal counties. In addition, the Red Cross, like MEMA, suffered from commodity shortages due to logistical problems.[56] John McGuire, Red Cross's interim chief, while defending the organization's performance, said that with Hurricane Katrina, the Red Cross's biggest sin was reacting based on its response to previous hurricanes: "We had a failure of imagination. We didn't think big enough."[57]

---

1 Miss. Code Ann. § 33-15-5(f).

2 Miss. Code Ann. § 33-15-11(b)(17).

3 Miss. Code Ann. § 33-15-11.

4 Miss. Code Ann. § 33-15-7.

5 Among its responsibilities, Mississippi Emegency Management Agency (MEMA) is required to:

- Prepare a state comprehensive emergency plan to be coordinated with the plans of the federal government and other states. Source: Miss. Code Ann. § 33-15-14(2)(a).

- Assign lead and support roles to state agencies and personnel for emergency support functions and other activities. *Source:* Miss. Code Ann. § 33-15-14(2)(a)(viii)(1).

- Provide for the deployment of state resources in case of disaster, including specifically the deployment (and pre-disaster deployment in certain circumstances) of the Mississippi National Guard. Direct and support the preparation of emergency plans and organizations by local governments. *Source:* Miss. Code Ann. § 33-15-14 (2)(a)(v) and (b).

- Provide personnel, equipment, and other resources from state agencies and from other Mississippi localities to reinforce areas stricken by disaster. *Source:* Miss. Code Ann. § 33-15-15(a).

6 Miss. Code Ann. § 33-15-19.

7 Committee staff interview of Robert Latham, Executive Director, MEMA, conducted on Jan. 27, 2006, transcript p. 11.

8 MEMA, "Statewide Mutual Aid Compact." http://www.msema.org/SMAC. Accessed on Feb. 28, 2006.

9 MEMA, The State of Mississsissippi Statewide Mutual Aid Compact (SMAC), June, 2000. Provided to Committee; filed as Bates nos. MEMA-00023847 through 00023857.

10 MEMA, The State of Mississississippi Statewide Mutual Aid Compact (SMAC), County and City Members, p. II–B–1. Provided to Committee; filed as Bates no. MEMA-00028968.

11 MEMA, *Mississippi Emergency Operations Plan, Volume II: Mississippi Comprehensive Emergency Management Plan (CEMP)*, May 14, 1999, p. APP B–1. Provided to Committee [hereinafter *Mississippi CEMP*, May 14, 1999].

12 *Mississippi CEMP*, May, 14, 1999, p. APP B–2.

13 *Mississippi CEMP*, May, 14, 1999, p. APP B–3.

14 Latham interview, Jan. 27, 2006, p. 24; Committee staff interview of Lt. Col. Lee Smithson, Director of Military Support, Mississippi Army National Guard, conducted on Jan. 25, 2006, transcript pp. 15-16.

15 Committee staff interview of Brenda Rembert, Director, Planning, Training and Exercise Bureau, MEMA, conducted on Jan. 26, 2006, transcript pp. 27-28.

16 Rembert interview, Jan. 26, 2006, pp. 29-31.

17 *Mississippi CEMP*, May, 14, 1999, pp. Basic–21 through Basic–22.

18 Miss. Code Ann. § 33-15-14(2)(d); *Mississippi CEMP*, May, 14, 1999, p. Basic–21.

19 Miss. Code Ann. § 33-15-17(c)(3).

20 *Mississippi CEMP*, May, 14, 1999, p. Basic–22.

21 *Mississippi CEMP*, May, 14, 1999, p. Basic–21.

22 Committee staff interview of Pat Sullivan, Fire Chief, Gulfport Fire Department, MS, conducted on Dec. 7, 2005, transcript pp. 58-59.

23 MEMA, Hurricane Situation Report #8, Hurricane Katrina, Aug. 28, 2005, 9:30 p.m. CT, p. 7. Provided to Committee; filed as Bates no. MEMA-0010884.

24 MEMA, Hurricane Situation Report #40, Hurricane Katrina, Sept. 5, 2005, 2:35 a.m. CT, p. 8. Provided to Committee; filed as Bates no. MEMA-0011290.

25 MEMA, Hurricane Situation Report #40, Hurricane Katrina, Sept. 5, 2005, 2:35 a.m. CT, p. 8. Provided to Committee, filed as Bates no. MEMA-0011290.

26 Jenny Lee Allen, "Don't Bother Looking for a Red Cross Shelter in Charlotte," Sarasota *Herald-Tribune*, Aug. 13, 2004, p. A4.

27 Committee staff interview of Tom McAllister, Director of Response and Recovery, MEMA, conducted on Jan. 27, 2006, transcript pp. 49-50. The local American Red Cross will open the shelter and begin the management of it. Department of Human Services is called, in some cases, to help manage and/or staff the shelters. Committee staff interview of Richard Dawkins, Program Manager, Division of Economic Assistance, Mississippi Department of Human Services, conducted on Dec. 13, 2005, transcript pp. 19-20.

28 McAllister interview, Jan. 27, 2006, pp. 51-52. "The *Shelter Resource Directory* provides for shelter activation for Louisiana evacuees starting in the north end of the state and moving south as they fill up, thereby leaving the shelters nearest to the Mississippi Gulf Coast accessible to Mississippi residents should the need for coastal evacuation occur." *Mississippi CEMP*, May 14, 1999, p. ESF–6–2.

29 Latham interview, Jan. 27, 2006, p. 108.

30 Committee staff interview of Jim Craig, Director, Office of Health Protection, Mississippi Department of Health, conducted on Jan. 25, 2006, transcript p. 47.

31 Committee staff interview of Alfred C. Sexton, Commander of Administration, Gulfport Police Department, MS, conducted on Dec. 8, 2005, transcript pp. 58-60.

32 Emergency management agency designated or approved shelters are initially under the direction of the local EMA Director, who would be responsible for opening and staffing the shelter, most often using MDHS personnel. Dawkins interview, Dec. 13, 2005, pp. 5-6.

33 Dawkins interview, Dec. 13, 2005, p. 56.

34 Dawkins interview, Dec. 13, 2005, p. 58.

35 McAllister interview, Jan. 27, 2006, pp. 50-52.

36 Craig interview, Jan. 25, 2006, p. 18.

37 National Council on Disability, NCD Brief on Hurricane Katrina Affected Areas, Sept. 2, 2005. http://www.jfanow. org/jfanow/index.php?mode=A&id=2497. Accessed on Mar. 8, 2006.

38 *See e.g.*: Harrison County and Hancock County Emergency Medical Services Districts, "Guidelines for Evacuation and Management of Individuals with Disabilities and Special Needs During Disasters," May 28, 2001. Provided to Committee.

39 Latham interview, Jan. 27, 2006, p. 109.

40 MEMA, "Hurricane Awareness Week May 30 – June 3," news release, May 28, 2005, p. 3.

41 Committee staff interview of Butch Loper, Emergency Management Director, Jackson County, MS, conducted on Dec. 6, 2005, transcript p. 11.

42 Craig interview, Jan. 25, 2006, p. 14; Dawkins interview, Dec. 13, 2005, p. 14.

43 MEMA, Hurricane Situation Report #20, Hurricane Katrina, Aug. 31, 2005, 1:30 a.m. CT, p. 7. Provided to Committee; filed as Bates no. MEMA-0011000.

44 Special-needs shelters were opened in Newton, Attala, Clarke, Lauderdale, Lincoln, Harrison, and Forrest Counties. MEMA, Hurricane Situation Report #28, Hurricane Katrina, Sept. 2, 2005, 1 a.m. CT, p. 11. Provided to Committee; filed as Bates no. MEMA-0011104.

45 McAllister interview, Jan. 27, 2006, p. 71.

46 Loper interview, Dec. 6, 2005, p. 11.

47 Craig interview, Jan. 25, 2006, pp. 19-20.

48 Kirsten Dellinger, *Hurricane Katrina Kirsten Dellinger*, Society for the Study of Social Problems, Sept. 5, 2005. http://www.sssp1.org/index.cfm/pageId/540. Accessed on Apr. 8, 2006.

49 Kellogg Schwab, Ph.D., "Assessing the Aftermath of Hurricane Katrina," John Hopkins Bloomberg School of Public Health, Sept. 12, 2005, pp. 1-2. http://www.jhsph.edu/Katrina/schwab_aftermath.html. Accessed on Apr. 8, 2006.

50 Jerry Mitchell, "Biloxi Woman Feels Like Nomad in GA," *The Clarion-Ledger*, Sept. 23, 2005. http://www.clarion-ledger.com/apps/pbcs.dll/article?AID=/20050923/NEWS0110/509230373/1260. Accessed on Apr. 8, 2006; "Dysentery Fears Closes Shelter in Biloxi," My DNA, Sept. 4, 2005. http://www.mydna.com/health/digestive/news/resources/news/200509/news_20050904_dysen.html. Accessed on Apr. 10, 2006; The Norwalk virus is passed in the stool of infected persons. People get infected by swallowing stool-contaminated food or water and usually recover in 2 to 3 days without serious or long-term health effects. Directors of Health Promotion and Education, "Norwalk Virus Infection." www.dhpe.org/infect/norwalk.html. Accessed on Apr. 8, 2006.

51 McAllister interview, Jan. 27, 2006, pp. 53-55.

52 Sexton interview, Dec. 8, 2005, pp. 62-65.

53 Committee staff interview of Col. Joe Spraggins, Director, Emergency Management Agency, Harrison County, MS, conducted on Nov. 17, 2005, transcript pp. 119-121.

54 Sexton interview, Dec. 8, 2005, pp. 48-51.

55 Committee staff interview of Ellen Noble, Chapters Solution Manager, Southeast Service Area, American Red Cross, conducted on Dec. 13, 2005, transcript pp. 29-32.

56 Latham interview, Jan. 27, 2006, pp. 117-120.

57 Jacqueline L. Salmon, "The Clock's Ticking on Red Cross Overhaul," *The Washington Post*, Mar. 21, 2006, p. A04.

The Times-Picayune

50 CENTS 169th year No. 221 | TUESDAY, AUGUST 30, 2005 | **HURRICANE EDITION**

CATASTROPHIC

STORM SURGE SWAMPS 9TH WARD, ST. BERNARD

LAKEVIEW LEVEE BREACH THREATENS TO INUNDATE CITY

NINTH WARD: An elderly resident is rescued from chest-high floodwaters by two New Orleans police officers.

STAFF PHOTO BY ALEX BRANDON

By Bruce Nolan
Staff writer

Hurricane Katrina struck metropolitan New Orleans on Monday with a staggering blow, far surpassing Hurricane Betsy, the landmark disaster of an earlier generation. The storm flooded huge swaths of the city, as well as Slidell on the north shore of Lake Pontchartrain, in a process that appeared to be spreading even as night fell.

A powerful storm surge pushed huge waves ahead of the hurricane, flooding much of St. Bernard Parish and New Orleans' Lower 9th Ward, just as Betsy 40 years ago. But this time the flooding was more extensive, spreading upriver as well to cover parts of the Bywater, Marigny and Treme neighborhoods.

As with Betsy, people scrambled into their attics or atop their roofs, pleading for help from the few passers-by.

The powerful Category 4 storm crossed the coast near the mouth of the Pearl River shortly after daybreak with winds of 135 mph. Naval Air Station-Joint Reserve Base in Belle Chasse reported an early morning gust of 105 mph.

With the power out throughout the area and fierce winds raging throughout the day, officials barely began Monday to assess the full damage of the monstrous storm, which was expected to leave thousands homeless and many more coping with damage from the wind and water.

Meantime, 5 miles to the west, engineers worked to close a breach along the New Orleans side of the 17th Street Canal.

Huge drainage pumps ordinarily can drive millions of gallons of rainwater uphill through

See **KATRINA**, *A-4*

Flooding wipes out two communities

By Brian Thevenot and Manuel Torres
Staff writers

As Jerry Rayes piloted his boat down St. Claude Avenue, just past the Industrial Canal, the eerie screams that could barely be heard from the roadway grew louder as, one by one, faces of desperate families appeared on rooftops, on balconies and in windows, some of them waving white flags.

The scene wouldn't change for the next three hours, as Rayes and his son and nephew boated down St. Claude Avenue and deep into St. Bernard Parish, where water smothered two-story houses, people and animals. The men had to duck to miss streetlights that towered over Judge Perez Drive, the parish's main thoroughfare.

The people Rayes rescued all told the same story, already written on their stunned and shivering

See **FLOOD**, *A-6*

INSIDE

DOWNTOWN: The damage to the Hyatt Regency on Poydras Street shows that vertical evacuation is no solution to the dangers of a Category 4 hurricane. **See story, A-15**

PHOTO BY A.J. SISCO

After the mighty storm came the rising water

By Doug MacCash and James O'Byrne
Staff writers

A large section of the vital 17th Street Canal levee, where it connects to the brand new 'hurricane proof' Old Hammond Highway bridge, gave way late Monday morning in Bucktown after Katrina's fiercest winds were well north. The breach sent a churning sea of water from Lake Pontchartrain coursing across Lakeview and into Mid-City, Carrollton, Gentilly, City Park and neighborhoods farther south and east.

As night fell on a devastated region, the water was still rising in the city, and nobody was willing to predict when it would stop. After the destruction already apparent in the wake of Katrina, the American Red Cross was mobilizing for what regional officials were calling the largest recovery operation in the or-

ganization's history.

Police officers, firefighters and private citizens, hampered by a lack of even rudimentary communication capabilities, continued a desperate and impromptu boat-borne rescue operation across Lakeview well after dark. Coast Guard helicopters with searchlights criss-crossed the skies.

Officers working on the scene said virtually every home and business between the 17th Street Canal and the Marconi Canal, and between Robert E. Lee Boulevard and City Park Avenue, had water in it. Nobody had confirmed any fatalities as a result of the levee breach, but they conceded that hundreds of homes had not been checked.

As the sun set over a still-roiling Lake Pontchartrain, the smoldering ruins of the Southern Yacht Club were still burning, and smoke streamed out over

See **BREACH**, *A-2*

"Hurricane Pam": Warning Flag for Katrina

On the day after Hurricane Katrina made landfall, the New Orleans *Times-Picayune* front-page banner said it all: "KATRINA: THE STORM WE'VE ALWAYS FEARED."[1]

Hurricanes are a fixture of life on the Louisiana Coast. Years before Katrina, all levels of government knew that a large, slow-moving catastrophic hurricane was likely to hit New Orleans, flood the city, and claim thousands of lives, overwhelming state and local agencies' ability to respond effectively and requiring assistance from the federal government to respond to the disaster.[2]

This understanding prompted efforts in 1999 to secure federal support to develop a comprehensive plan to respond to a catastrophic hurricane in New Orleans. Following nearly five years of delays, in 2004 the Federal Emergency Management Agency (FEMA) provided funding to begin that development.[3] The project, "Southeast Louisiana Catastrophic Hurricane Plan," confirmed the limitations of the state and local agencies. It used an exercise scenario known as "Hurricane Pam" that incorporated well-founded assumptions about the impact of a slow-moving Category 3 hurricane on New Orleans. Based on scientific research and dozens of emergency-management studies, the Hurricane Pam scenario predicted:

- Widespread flooding throughout the city

- 67,000 dead

- 200,000 to 300,000 in need of evacuation after landfall

- Hundreds of thousands displaced

- Sheltering and evacuation needs exceeding state and local governments' capabilities

- Hospitals overcrowded with special-needs patients, with backup generators running out of fuel or failing before patients could be moved elsewhere

- Incapacitated first responders and parish resources

- Compromised situational awareness[4]

Despite the comprehensive foreknowledge of the consequences of a catastrophic hurricane hitting New Orleans, underscored and amplified by the Hurricane Pam exercise, emergency-management officials were not prepared when Katrina struck. They did, however, recognize that Katrina would have many of the consequences anticipated by the Pam exercise. As Katrina approached the Gulf Coast on August 27, two days before landfall, FEMA produced slides indicating that the impact of this storm could be worse than Pam's predictions. A 9 a.m. FEMA briefing document said, "Exercise projection [Pam] is exceeded by Hurricane Katrina real life impacts."[5]

Hurricane Pam was only the most recent study predicting consequences of a catastrophic hurricane. To varying degrees, federal, state, and local governments have long been sounding alarms about virtually every problem that became reality with Katrina – for example, evacuation, sheltering, law and order, search and rescue, and a need for leadership.

The exercise addressed their concerns and resulted in an improved response to Hurricane Katrina. However, the response could have been far better had Hurricane Pam been completed earlier.[6] This section details the significance of Pam and its influence on the Katrina response. Most important, though, it demonstrates that Katrina was not an unpredictable catastrophe, but in fact was predicted.

Hurricane Pam: In the Beginning

The threat of a catastrophic hurricane hitting New Orleans has long been contemplated by scientists, planners, emergency-management personnel, and managers. In what was often called the "New Orleans Scenario," the worst-case event was imagined as a Category 3 or higher hurricane hitting the New Orleans metropolitan area with catastrophic impact.[7] This would be "worst case," primarily because the storm surge would cause devastating flooding in an area that is below sea level and whose protective levees would trap the floodwater.[8] The flooding, coupled with an immobile population of 100,000 or more, would contribute to a situation that would quickly exceed the response capabilities of both local and state resources and would require the assistance of federal resources on a scale never before seen.[9]

In late September 1998, Hurricane Georges wreaked havoc in the Caribbean before heading across southern Florida on a direct path to Louisiana. At the last moment, the hurricane veered away, sparing New Orleans from what could have been a devastating blow.[10] The near miss prompted emergency planners to take stock again of how ill-prepared the region was for a major hurricane.[11]

Planners took their first steps in response to Hurricane Georges in the fall of 1999. Colonel Michael Brown – no relation to the Michael Brown who directed FEMA as Katrina struck – then Assistant Director of the Louisiana Office of Emergency Preparedness, organized a meeting with officials from FEMA Region VI (the region with emergency-management responsibilities over Louisiana), the Army Corps of Engineers, other state agencies, parishes, and his own office to explore the effect of Hurricane Georges had it not turned and gone north.[12]

To develop the planning scenario, the group sought input from experts from such institutions as Louisiana State University (LSU) and the Hurricane Prediction Center.[13] The group quickly realized that a slow-moving Category 3 hurricane was sufficient to cause catastrophic damage.[14]

Over the course of several meetings in the succeeding months, the planning committee put together a Statement of Work (SOW, also known as work plan), to be submitted to FEMA in support of a request to fund the development of a "working plan for the search and rescue, evacuation, sheltering, provisioning, and infrastructure restoration for the greater New Orleans area."[15] On August 14, 2000, Col. Brown requested funding from FEMA. FEMA did not respond to the funding request at that time.[16]

Shortly after taking office, President Bush appointed Joe Allbaugh to be the Director of FEMA. Allbaugh visited New Orleans in the spring of 2001 and expressed surprise that there was no federal plan to respond to a catastrophic hurricane in the region.[17] According to one report, Allbaugh pledged to support development of a plan and in August 2001, asked the Louisiana Office of Emergency Preparedness and FEMA Region VI officials to write up a proposal.[18]

That August, Region VI Director Ron Castleman reiterated to FEMA headquarters the urgent need for catastrophic planning, emphasizing that a catastrophic hurricane in the

New Orleans area "could affect a wide area of Louisiana and neighboring states and would present serious response and recovery problems that could exceed collective capabilities."[19] Castleman asserted that the planning proposal "could save many lives."[20]

The proposal anticipated massive impacts from a major hurricane, including over 1 million people evacuating New Orleans, 300,000 to 500,000 people trapped in flood areas, a storm surge of over 18 feet overflowing levees and leaving New Orleans under 14 to 17 feet of water, rescue operations impeded, hospitals overcrowded with special-needs patients and backup generators running out of fuel or failing before patients could be moved.[21]

Objectives for the work included: (1) plan for direction and control of the response; (2) plan for maximizing evacuation; (3) plan for transporting people, supplies, and equipment; and (4) plan for rescue and relocation of stranded citizens, hospital patients, and other special populations. The proposal foresaw the importance of having a plan that took into account the thousands that would be unable to leave the area on their own accord, thus it recommended that the future contractor assess existing evacuation plans; recommend changes; identify pick up points for people without transportation; identify resources, facilities, and services for pre-storm evacuation; and identify additional transportation assets needed.[22]

An updated SOW was developed in August 2001. Its stated purpose was to enhance "Federal Response Planning activities by focusing on specific catastrophic disasters: those disasters that by definition will immediately overwhelm the existing disaster response capabilities of local, state, and federal governments." It further stated that the "initial area of focus will be New Orleans, Louisiana . . . to improve federal, state, local-government, and private-sector ability to respond to a worst-case catastrophic hurricane in the Greater New Orleans Metropolitan Area in order to prevent loss of life; minimize the number of injuries; house, feed, and protect up to a million survivors and evacuees; and begin long-term recovery in the affected area."[23]

This work plan stipulated that the contractor's work should support eventual development of an introductory general plan and sub-plans that would constitute a comprehensive "New Orleans Metropolitan Area Catastrophic Hurricane Plan." The top-priority area of analysis was identifying the number and location of potential evacuees and assessing existing evacuation plans.[24]

URS Corporation, a large firm specializing in homeland security, was selected as contractor for the project in September 2001, and in October, FEMA paid URS $97,000 to gather information to build a thorough understanding of the nature and magnitude of the hurricane problem.[25] On December 18 and 19, 2001, the project leadership team of state and federal representatives held a kickoff meeting.[26] One of several issues discussed was the recognition that a hurricane could strand 250,000 to 350,000 people in the New Orleans area, 10 percent of whom would likely be people with special needs. The team also noted that hospitals would probably have difficulty getting people out of the city, and that the Louisiana Office of Emergency Preparedness (LOEP) had plans for stranded people to gather on dry stretches of levees or interstate highways where boats or barges could reach them.[27]

The team emphasized that "the final product should be a hurricane operations plan – not a mitigation plan." In essence, it should "[lay] out what the local government can do, what the state can do, what the state cannot do, and what the federal government needs to do" in response to a catastrophic hurricane.[28] This operations plan was distinguished from the routine response by the federal government in which the government comes in after-the-fact with a checkbook to pay for damage caused by the storm and the state and locals accept the check with the intent of using it to lessen the impact of future storms.[29]

The project moved in "starts and stops" for a year because of budget problems, reassignment of FEMA staff to homeland-security issues, difficulties in negotiating a subcontract with LSU and disagreements between LOEP and FEMA over the scope of work.[30] Meanwhile, FEMA collected information from other sources regarding the threat potentially facing New Orleans.

In May 2002, FEMA Region VI published a summary of a Bi-State Evacuation Study that unequivocally stated that the metropolitan New Orleans area had very limited evacuation routes, and that approximately 100,000 people were without transportation.[31] In slides dated June 19, 2003, FEMA recognized that a major hurricane striking the New Orleans area "would be a disaster of cataclysmic proportion," and that 250,000 to 350,000 people would be stranded. Minutes of a June 2003 meeting regarding the New Orleans scenario at FEMA headquarters with FEMA contractors state "that massive federal assistance would be expected for this type of event [catastrophic hurricane]. Louisiana won't be able to deal with this. Responders and their families may be the victims themselves."[32]

By late July 2003, URS Corporation had made progress on its catastrophic planning work for FEMA and the Louisiana Office of Homeland Security and Emergency Preparedness (LOHSEP), which was the successor agency to the Louisiana Office of Emergency Preparedness (LOEP). The Corporation finalized maps showing inundation, elevation and water depth. In the fall, URS drafted a white paper on long-term sheltering.[33] The premise of the paper was that 600,000 people would evacuate New Orleans in the event of a catastrophic hurricane, and that long-term shelter could be needed for perhaps 90 percent of the evacuees because de-watering of the city could take up to a year.[34] These documents completed URS Corporation's contractual obligation to FEMA and LOHSEP.[35]

In November 2003, the White House Deputy National Security Adviser, General John A. Gordon, went to New Orleans to receive a briefing on catastrophic hurricane planning efforts for the region. During the comprehensive, detailed briefing, he learned about the catastrophic consequences of a Category 3 hurricane hitting New Orleans.[36] General Gordon reported to the White House about this meeting.[37] About this same time, FEMA Headquarters informed officials of Region VI and LOHSEP's Chief Planner, Sean Fontenot, that an unspecified amount of funding had become available.[38] Fontenot was uncertain about how they received the funding, but recalled that the money was approved in March 2004 and had to be spent by September 30, 2004.[39]

The Work Begins

Working with staff from Region VI, Fontenot developed a proposal for an exercise that encompassed 14 elements ranging from pre-landfall evacuation, to emergency response, to post-response recovery, and rebuilding matters. While the customary practice in emergency planning was to develop a plan, then to test it with an exercise, the planners concluded that the six short weeks that they had been given were insufficient to proceed in a traditional manner. Thus, the sequence was reversed: they designed an exercise from which to create the plan.[40]

At a meeting in early April 2004, FEMA officials deemed the proposal too costly, causing LOHSEP officials to trim pre-landfall evacuation and five other issues. Witnesses stated that pre-landfall evacuation was deleted from the Hurricane Pam exercise because the issue had been examined by other studies, as well as state and local plans.[41] On the other hand, post-landfall response planning had received very little attention, so, according to FEMA witnesses, the limited FEMA funds would be best applied to post-landfall planning.[42]

In late May 2004, FEMA notified the state that it had selected Innovative Emergency Management, Inc. (IEM), as contractor for this newer phase of the project, which sought the actual development of a catastrophic hurricane plan for southeast Louisiana.[43] As distinct from the information-gathering process conducted by URS, this phase sought to develop the actual plan.[44]

Between late May and mid-July 2004, LOHSEP worked with FEMA Region VI staff, consultants from IEM, Mark Levitan, Ph.D., of the LSU Hurricane Center, and others to flesh out the details of the exercise. Concluding that it was unreasonable to expect to complete a plan in the initial series of workshops, they designed the exercise with the expectation that they would ask FEMA to support a series of follow-on meetings.[45]

The initial Hurricane Pam workshops took place from July 16 until July 23, 2004. Attendance included over 300 participants from 15 federal agencies, 20 state agencies, 13 parishes, five volunteer agencies, LOHSEP, FEMA Region VI, FEMA HQ and IEM.[46] The participants focused on issues relating to schools, search and rescue, sheltering, temporary housing, temporary medical care, and debris removal.[47] IEM compiled the notes from each workshop into a draft plan. On August 6, 2004, IEM produced a 120-page draft "Southeast Louisiana Catastrophic Hurricane Functional Plan."[48]

Shortly after the July sessions, LOHSEP asked FEMA for funding for additional workshops. Again, obtaining funding was difficult.[49] A follow-on session set for September 2004 had to be postponed when FEMA could not come up with $15,000 to pay travel expenses for participants.[50] FEMA officials frequently cited "DHS taxes" as the reason for funding challenges that delayed the planned additional exercise sessions.[51]

Eric Tolbert, FEMA's former Director of Response, recalled many difficulties in funding the scenario and follow-on sessions.[52] The turning point, he said, was when FEMA Director Brown returned from Asia after the disastrous, earthquake-driven tsunami of December 2004. Tolbert described Brown as being "obsessed with catastrophic events." Tolbert told Brown that a large hurricane hitting New Orleans might produce a higher death toll than the tsunami.[53] Brown expressed support for funding catastrophic planning. Meanwhile, IEM consolidated and published the draft plans from the July 2004 portions of the exercise in January 2005.[54]

Follow-up Sessions[55]

Two follow-up workshops were eventually held: "Transportation, Staging and Distribution" in late July 2005, and "Temporary Medical" just days before Katrina struck.[56] Notes from the transportation session reveal that while the workshop was supposed to deal with issues of commodity logistics, participants focused specifically on the need for buses to transport rescued people to shelters.[57] The notes also emphasized the importance of marshalling these buses before landfall so that, following the storm, they would be immediately available to evacuate those stranded in the area. Notably, the participants also reported that planning for distribution of commodities was complete, but was "less than 10% done with transportation planning when you consider the buses and the people."[58]

In the same transportation session, New Orleans Office of Emergency Preparedness Chief Joseph Matthews told the working group at Pam that the city could not execute a massive post-landfall evacuation for two main reasons: (1) they had reserved local transit buses and school buses, but lacked drivers qualified to participate in evacuations; and (2) city officials had not completed negotiations with other transportation companies.[59]

"Pam" come true, New Orleans
Clarence Williams/Iris Photocollective photo

Consequently, with recognition of the need to transport many tens of thousands of people after landfall, participants in the exercise developed a timeline that called on the agencies to "Pre-Stage buses and drivers" 50 hours before landfall by providing "600 buses (Local/State/Federal) and 1,200 drivers (Local/State/Federal/Volunteers)."[60]

The shelter chapter of the draft plan that arose from the Hurricane Pam exercise is slightly more detailed on the issue of transportation, and includes references to pre-landfall evacuation. It assumes that while the primary means of pre-landfall evacuation would be personal vehicles, "school and municipal buses and, where available, specialized vehicles will be used to transport those hurricane evacuees who do not have transportation."[61] Federal, state, and local government representatives were keenly aware of the critical need for buses and the corresponding need for sheltering, yet no level of government followed through with arranging for the buses and additional shelters to aid post-landfall evacuation.[62]

On August 23 and 24, 2005, the Southeast Louisiana Catastrophic Hurricane Temporary Medical Care Supplementary Planning Workshop was held. From this workshop, the Temporary Medical Care section was updated. Emergency planners refined some of the medical support techniques eventually used during Hurricane Katrina, such as the use of centralized, medical triage centers (known as TMOSAs or Temporary Medical Operations Staging Areas) to provide medical screening and care for Katrina survivors. However, as discussed in greater detail in Chapter 24: Medical Assistance, the Hurricane Pam exercise failed to identify solutions to key medical problems it had anticipated, including the need to evacuate patients from hospitals and nursing homes trapped by rising floodwaters.[63]

On August 27, 2005, two days before landfall, IEM hastily published and delivered to FEMA a draft transportation plan based on the "Transportation, Staging and Distribution" workshops held July 25 through 29, 2005.

Hurricane Pam in Action

Hurricane Pam 2004 was more than an exercise. It was a unique planning endeavor that resulted in functional plans that were considered for and actually put to use in real-life situations before, during, and after Hurricane Katrina. Most exercise participants agreed that many of the plans were useful even though they were not final. Though they needed some cleaning up, the resulting drafts were "fightable," that is, "detailed enough to be implemented and to guide response and recovery operations."[64]

IEM President and CEO Madhu Beriwal echoed this view, saying, "though the plan was not finished, many elements of Hurricane Pam still proved to be highly useful in response and recovery to Hurricane Katrina days, weeks, and months after the massive storm struck the Gulf Coast."[65] Senior FEMA officials requested, reviewed, or referred to Hurricane Pam materials to gauge the potential impact of Hurricane Katrina and to plan response actions. According to Brown, "The Hurricane Pam book was flying everywhere. It was all over FEMA; it was everywhere."[66]

Slides dated 9 a.m., August 27, 2005, at FEMA headquarters stated, "Current projected path takes storm directly over New Orleans." They also cited the Pam exercise prediction of 60,000 fatalities and 1 million-plus persons displaced, predicting that Pam's estimates would be "exceeded by Hurricane Katrina real life impacts."[67] Also on August 27, Patrick Rhode, FEMA's Acting Deputy Director, was seeking a copy of the Hurricane Pam plan; he learned that numerous copies of the plan were being made for distribution to FEMA employees.[68] The primary Federal Coordinating Officer in charge of response operations in Louisiana, William Lokey, actually embedded IEM employees in the National Response Coordination Center (NRCC) and the State's Emergency Operations Center (EOC) during the response to Hurricane Katrina to use their Hurricane Pam and emergency-management expertise.[69]

The night manager of the National Response Coordination Center (NRCC), the federal hub for situation information management, sent an e-mail to her director saying that she and others had scoured the Pam plan during their overnight shift on August 28 and found that the Hurricane Pam plan had identified a number of tasks for federal entities. It further revealed that a number of these assigned tasks had not been addressed thus far in the federal response.[70]

In particular, during Hurricane Katrina, a "lily-pad" type of search-and-rescue operation was implemented.[71] By using this methodology, victims were rescued and transported to a safe area of high ground. The idea was that from there another group would transport them to a Temporary Medical Operations Staging Area (TMOSA). There, the rescued would undergo a medical-triage screening process to determine individuals' medical-care needs.[72]

During Hurricane Katrina, search-and-rescue crews successfully retrieved thousands of people from harm's way and deposited them on dry land. In some cases, the rescued individuals were deposited at two of the three TMOSAs envisioned during the Hurricane Pam planning workshops.[73] Unfortunately, the Hurricane Pam concept was only half successful because many people rescued by the search-and-rescue teams were transported to dry ground where there was no system to support them and no ground transportation to take them to a better place for days. In other words, they were taken to veritable "islands," only to be left there without food, water, and other critical necessities.[74]

By late August 2005, FEMA had committed more than $1.5 million to developing the Hurricane Pam exercise.[75] Because some officials took the initiative to press for significant funding and overcome bureaucratic delays, some important lessons from Hurricane Pam were available and were put to good use in responding to Katrina – only a few of which were noted above. On the other hand, it is unfortunate that Louisiana allowed relatively small funding shortfalls – such as FEMA's inability to fund $15,000 in travel expenses in September 2004 – to delay progress in further plan development. Given the importance to the state of the exercise, Louisiana should have considered using its own funds to fill these gaps in federal funding.

In any event, far too many of the Hurricane Pam lessons were not applied. Despite this being "the storm we've always feared," despite awareness of the impact of such a storm on New Orleans, and despite the fact that federal, state, and local agencies came together in July 2004 to do a "live rehearsal" of a response in such a circumstance as Katrina – over a year before it made landfall – too little was done to act on the plans resulting from Hurricane Pam.

1 Bruce Nolan, "Katrina: The Storm We've Always Feared," New Orleans *Times-Picayune*, Aug. 30, 2005, p. A-1.

2 Committee staff interview of Eric Tolbert, former Director, Response Division, Federal Emergency Management Agency (FEMA), conducted on Dec. 1, 2005, transcript p. 70 ("In the hurricane business in emergency management, all of us have known for years and years about the New Orleans scenario. That's what we refer to it as, the New Orleans scenario, which was either the overwash or the failure of the dock system, the levee system. Literally, anybody in this business that studied hurricanes, if you flew into New Orleans all you were looking for was the levee system. You wanted to see it because you had heard so much about it. The risk was uniformly known by the emergency management professionals."). Ed Buikema, Acting Director of Response during Katrina, said that a large hurricane hitting New Orleans was considered by FEMA to be one of the worst catastrophes that could ever occur in the United States. Committee staff interview of Edward Buikema, Acting Director, Response Division, FEMA, conducted on Nov. 21, 2005, transcript p. 234.

3 Committee staff interview of Sean Fontenot, former Chief, Preparedness Division, Louisiana Office of Homeland Security and Emergency Preparedness (LOHSEP), conducted on Jan. 10, 2006, transcript pp. 42-43, 71.

4 LOHSEP, Hurricane Pam and Related Docs (18). Provided to Committee.

5 FEMA, Tropical Storm Katrina, briefing slides, Aug. 27, 2006, 9 a.m. Provided to Committee; filed as Bates no. DHS-FEMA-0055-0002140.

6 Testimony of Madhu Beriwal, President and CEO, IEM, Inc., before the U.S. Senate, Committee on Homeland Security and Governmental Affairs, hearing on Preparing for a Catastrophe: The Hurricane Pam Exercise, Jan. 24, 2006. Beriwal suggested that the response to Hurricane Katrina could have been greater had the exercise been completed earlier: "When Hurricane Katrina struck, the Hurricane Pam planning was not complete. No training or exercises had occurred using this planning document. The first test was Hurricane Katrina. … However […] even though the plans and planning were incomplete, Hurricane Pam helped save lives and reduce suffering after the massive catastrophe of Hurricane Katrina." Written Statement of Beriwal, Senate Committee hearing, Jan. 24, 2006, p. 8. According to Eric Tolbert, "The [Pam] exercise was just last year, and then they get hit this year. It takes time to continue developing plans and procedures. Thankfully, we had that exercise last year so that at least federal, state and local had gone through the process and had thought about the consequences and had begun drafting plans or it would not have even gone as well as it did." Tolbert interview, Dec. 1, 2005, p. 76.

7 Louisiana Office of Emergency Preparedness (LOEP), Southeast Louisiana Hurricane Evacuation and Sheltering Plan, Jan. 2000, Part I, A, Summary.

8 Tolbert interview, Dec. 1, 2005, p. 70.

9 FEMA, Task Order #125, Statement of Work: Catastrophic Hurricane Planning, New Orleans Metropolitan Area, Aug. 22, 2001. Provided to Committee; filed as Bates no. URS 0000053 [hereinafter FEMA, Statement of Work, Aug. 22, 2001].

10 Mark Fischetti, "Drowning New Orleans," Scientific American, Oct. 2001, pp. 78, 84 ("New Orleans is a disaster waiting to happen.").

11 Fontenot interview, Jan. 10, 2006, pp. 42-43.

12 Committee staff interview of Matt Farlow, Information Technology Division Chief, LOHSEP, conducted on Dec. 1, 2005, transcript p. 11.

13 Committee staff interview of Wayne Fairley, Response Operations Branch Chief, FEMA, conducted on Jan. 18, 2006, transcript p. 7.

14 Fairley interview, Jan. 18, 2006, p. 7.

15 *See generally*: LOHSEP, Hurricane Pam and Related Docs (18). Provided to Committee. The FEMA Statement of Work described a scenario of catastrophic consequences from a Category 3, 4, or 5 hurricane:

- The City of New Orleans is flooded with 14' to 17' of water

- The metro area is without power, food, water, medicine and transportation

- 250,000 to 350,000 people remain in stranded conditions with limited self rescue capability

- Up to 50,000 persons are stranded in the surrounding river parishes

- Possible 5,000 dead and 15,000 injured within the city

- Shelters are overcrowded and people stranded throughout the rest of the state

- Hazardous materials released throughout the city

- No or limited traditional access to all area

- All pumping stations inoperable
- Hospitals overcrowded with special needs patients and family members
- Hospitals have no or limited power

16 Farlow interview, Dec. 1, 2005, p. 11-16.

17 Fontenot interview, Jan. 10, 2006, p. 59.

18 Scott Wells, e-mail to Mark Wallace R6, Gary Jones, Chuck Gregg, Ron Castleman and Brenda Black, Mar. 18, 2004, 7:51 a.m. Provided to Committee; filed as Bates nos. DHS-FEMA-0058-0000025 through 0000027.

19 Ron Castleman, memorandum to Lacy Suiter, Aug. 8, 2001. Provided to Committee; filed as Bates no. DHS-FEMA-0074-0000025.

20 Castleman, memorandum to Suiter, Aug. 8, 2001; Mr. Fairley stated in his staff interview that a draft of the proposal was first sent to Region VI, which returned it with directions to eliminate items outside the scope of FEMA funding. Fairley interview, Jan. 18, 2006, pp. 49-50.

21 FEMA and LOEP, Proposal for Development of a New Orleans Metropolitan Area Catastrophic Hurricane Plan, Aug. 2001. Provided to Committee; filed as Bates nos. DHS-FEMA-0074-0000027 through 0000028.

22 FEMA, Statement of Work, Aug. 22, 2001, Bates no. URS 0000055.

23 FEMA, Statement of Work, Aug. 22, 2001, Bates no. URS 0000052.

24 FEMA, Statement of Work, Aug. 22, 2001, Bates no. URS 0000055.

25 Scott Wells, e-mail to Mark Wallace R6, Gary Jones, Chuck Gregg, Ron Castleman and Brenda J. Black, Mar. 18, 2004, 7:51 a.m. Provided to Committee; filed as Bates nos. DHS-FEMA-0058-0000025 through 0000027.

26 Fontenot interview, Jan. 10, 2006, p. 60. According to Fontenot, there was a short delay from the time of contract award to URS to the date of the kickoff meeting due to the 9/11 attack and resulting circumstances.

27 New Orleans Hurricane Preparedness Project, Meeting of Organizing Committee, Dec. 2001. Provided to Committee; filed as Bates nos. DHS-FEMA-0058-0001506 through 0001514.

28 New Orleans Hurricane Preparedness Project, Meeting of Organizing Committee, Dec. 2001. Provided to Committee; filed as Bates no. DHS-FEMA-0058-0001579.

29 Committee staff interview of Sandy Coachman, Federal Coordinating Officer, FEMA, conducted on Nov. 16, 2005, transcript p. 92.

30 Scott Wells, e-mail to Mark Wallace R6, Gary Jones, Chuck Gregg, Ron Castleman and Brenda J. Black, Mar.18, 2004, 7:51 a.m. Provided to Committee; filed as Bates nos. DHS-FEMA-0058-0000025 through 0000027.

31 FEMA, Bi-State Hurricane Evacuation Study, May 2, 2002. Provided to Committee; filed as Bates no. DHS-FEMA-0058-0001607.

32 Chuck Gregg, e-mail to John Gambel, Oct. 21, 2005, 3:22 p.m. Provided to Committee; filed as Bates nos. DHS-FEMA-0025-0002597 through 0002598 (the subject is a June 26, 2003 meeting at FEMA headquarters to discuss the Strawman Draft.).

33 FEMA, Task Order Number 125, Work Accomplished February 20, 2004 through March 5, 2004. Provided to Committee, filed as Bates nos. URS 0000115 through 0000116.

34 Long-Term Sheltering Following a Catastrophic Hurricane in Southeast Louisiana, prepared by URS Corporation for FEMA, Jan. 2004. Provided to Committee; filed as Bates nos. URS 0000232 through 0000244.

35 Dale Lehman, letter to Carrie Ouellettee, Mar. 5, 2004. Provided to Committee; filed as Bates no. URS 0000059.

36 Fontenot interview, Jan. 10, 2006, pp. 68-69.

37 Tony Robinson, e-mail to Wayne Fairley and Mark Wallace R6, May 17, 2004, 1:46 p.m. Provided to Committee; filed as Bates nos. DHS-FEMA-0058-0000077 through 0000078.

38 Fontenot interview, Jan. 10, 2006, pp. 71-72.

39 Fontenot interview, Jan. 10, 2006, pp. 71-72.

40 Fontenot interview, Jan. 10, 2006, pp. 72-73.

41 Fontenot interview, Jan. 10, 2006, pp. 88-90; Beriwal, Senate Committee hearing, Jan. 24, 2006.

42 Fontenot interview, Jan. 10, 2006, pp. 88-91; Fairley interview, Jan. 18, 2006, pp. 2, 57-58. During his interview with HSGAC staffers, Fairley explained why pre-landfall evacuation was not part of the Pam planning: "We, over the course a time, working with the state, discussed transportation for evacuation. That's always been something that was recognized as a need. The state, however, felt that they had that segment in hand. The state had a evacuation plan, evacuation routes, evacuation maps." Fairley interview, Jan. 18, 2006, p. 23.

43 Testimony of Sean Fontenot, former Chief, Preparedness Division, LOHSEP, before the U.S. Senate, Committee on Homeland Security and Governmental Affairs, hearing on Preparing for a Catastrophe: The Hurricane Pam Exercise, Jan. 24, 2006.

44 Fontenot interview, Jan. 10, 2006, pp. 87-88; Fontenot, Senate Committee hearing, Jan. 25, 2006.

45 Fontenot interview, Jan. 10, 2006, pp. 78-80.

46 FEMA, Louisiana Catastrophic Hurricane Planning Project, Matrix of Planning Topics and ESFs, Dec. 8, 2004. Provided to Committee; filed as Bates no. DHS-FEMA-0058-0000377; IEM, Inc., 2004 Louisiana Catastrophic Hurricane Planning Exercise, Executive Summary. Provided to Committee; filed as Bates no. IEM/TEC04-081.

47 FEMA and IEM, Inc., Hurricane Pam 2004, Breakout Room Topics. Provided to Committee; filed as Bates no. DHS 0001998.

48 IEM, Inc., Southeast Louisiana Catastrophic Hurricane Functional Plan, Draft, Aug. 6, 2004. Provided to Committee.

49 Tolbert interview, conducted on Dec. 1, 2005, transcript pp. 135-136 ("I think lack of funding contributed significantly. I was under no pressure to continue with it because I didn't have money anyway. … We had a set budget, all the money that we could scrape together out of my operating budget and that was the limit. … Had we had more money, we probably would have expanded it.").

50 Fontenot interview, Jan. 10, 2006, pp. 79-80.

51 Tolbert interview, Dec. 1, 2005, pp. 57-58.

52 Tolbert interview, Dec. 1, 2005, pp. 71-72, 80. Notes of a March 30, 2004 teleconference indicate a concern about moving forward quickly to avoid the hurricane season: "Tolbert: Can timeframe slip? To September 30? Sean Fontenot: Probably not. And unless Contractor for Exercise can be secured by April 12, Exercise likely not happen because of hurricane seasons." LOHSEP, Response No. 8, Mar. 30, 2004 Eric Tolbert Teleconference. Provided to Committee.

53 Tolbert interview, Dec. 1, 2005, pp. 85-86.

54 IEM, Inc., Memorandum, Re: Development of the Southeast Louisiana Catastrophic Hurricane Plan Documentation, Sept. 5, 2005. Provided to Committee.

55 IEM, Inc., Memorandum, Re: Development of the Southeast Louisiana Catastrophic Hurricane Plan Documentation, Sept. 5, 2005. Provided to Committee.

56 IEM, Inc., Memorandum, Re: Development of the Southeast Louisiana Catastrophic Hurricane Plan Documentation, Sept. 5, 2005. Provided to Committee.

57 IEM, Inc., Louisiana Catastrophic Planning Phase 1B: Unified Command Final Briefing Highlights, July 29, 2005. Provided to Committee.

58 IEM, Inc., Louisiana Catastrophic Planning Phase 1B: Unified Command Final Briefing Highlights, July 29, 2005. Provided to Committee. Director Joseph Matthews of the New Orleans Office of Emergency Preparedness also pointed out at this meeting that the City had a problem with the lack of qualified drivers for buses that could be used in an evacuation. Committee staff interview of Joseph Matthews, Director, Office of Emergency Preparedness, City of New Orleans, LA, conducted on Nov. 23, 2005, transcript pp. 67-68.

59 Matthews interview, Nov. 23, 2005, pp. 196-200.

60 A FEMA official at the workshop suggested to the other participants that 5,000 buses per day would needed. Committee staff interview of Jules Hurst, Transportation Supervisor, Logistics Branch, FEMA, conducted on Dec. 27, 2006, transcript p. 34 ("At first we were told that – I said you got to give me a number to work with here, and when they said how many buses do we need, they said, okay, 75,000 refugees a day – refugees? Evacuees a day for 10 days. And they said, What do you need? And I said 5,000 buses a day.").

61 Southeast Louisiana Catastrophic Hurricane Plan, prepared by IEM, Inc. for FEMA and LOHSEP, Aug. 6, 2005, p. 72 [hereinafter Southeast Louisiana Catastrophic Hurricane Plan, Aug. 6, 2005].

62 Transportation needs are also addressed in the Search and Rescue chapter, albeit in more cursory terms. The section describing the execution of the plan includes the notation that post-landfall operations will include "coordination and evacuation of the rescued persons." While there are general references to the possibility that parishes may be so severely damaged that they are incapable of even asking for support, the text does not specify whether state or federal support for transporting rescued victims will be relied on, stating merely that "ESF-1 [the emergency support function dealing with transportation] will provide transportation of rescued victims." Southeast Louisiana Catastrophic Hurricane Plan, Aug. 6, 2005, pp. 72, 75.

63 Committee staff interview of James Aiken, M.D., Medical Director for Emergency Preparedness, Medical Center of Louisiana, City of New Orleans, LA, conducted on Jan. 11, 2006, transcript pp. 66-68; EST_ESF08, e-mail to Robert Jevec, Jack Beall, and MST-1, Aug. 29, 2005, 5:30 a.m. Provided to Committee; filed as Bates nos. DHS-FEMA-0098-0003758 through 0003759 ("Advanced planning was never completed on how the patients left in the hospital will be evacuated after the event. The use of boats to support the other ESFs has been fairly comprehensive, and ESF #8 has yet to be completed.").

64 FEMA, Louisiana Project, Phase I-B Proposed Schedule, Jan. 25, 2005, p. 5. Provided to Committee; filed as Bates no. DHS-FEMA 0058-0002144. Madhu Beriwal, the president of IEM, told HSGAC staff during a briefing that the premise of the planning workshops was that the participants were developing actual plans and that IEM's role was to simply clean up the products from the workshop, compile and present them in a final formatted plan.

65 Written Statement of Madhu Beriwal, Senate Committee hearing, Jan. 24, 2006, p. 5.

66 Committee staff interview of Michael Brown, former Director, FEMA, conducted on Jan. 23, 2006, transcript p. 215.

67 FEMA, Tropical Storm Katrina, briefing slides, Aug. 27, 2005. Provided to Committee; filed as Bates no. DHS-FEMA-0055-0002140 ("Exercise projections exceeded by Hurricane Katrina real life impacts.").

68 William Lokey, e-mail to Patrick Rhode and David Garratt, Aug. 27, 2005, 9:07 a.m. Provided to Committee; filed as Bates no. DHS-FEMA-0085-0003860.

69 Committee staff interview of William Lokey, FEMA, Federal Coordinating Officer for Hurricane Katrina in Louisiana, conducted on Nov. 4, 2005, transcript p. 185 ("One of the things we did do, the contract planners from IEM-I'm not sure what IEM stands for, but our contractor we have for catastrophic planning-I got them activated on Saturday to embed them, [they] showed up Sunday to help remind people what people had agreed to in the planning process we had done in the Hurricane Pam scenarios.").

70 Richard Harmon, e-mail to EST-DIR [Mary Ann Lyle], Aug. 28, 2005, 4:07 a.m. Provided to Committee; filed as Bates no. DHS-FEMA-0132-0001814.

71 Beriwal, Senate Committee hearing, Jan. 24, 2005.

72 The Temporary Medical Care section detailed the concepts of search and rescue bases of operations (SARBOOs) and temporary medical and operations staging areas (TMOSAs). As stated in Chapter 24, Medical Assistance: "The plan called for search-and-rescue teams to drop people at Search-and-Rescue Bases of Operations (SARBOOs) near the flooded areas, where paramedics would perform initial triage. Rescuees would then be transported to Temporary Medical-and-Operations Staging Areas (TMOSAs), larger areas with temporary medical facilities, for care and triage." In response to Hurricane Katrina, the SARBOO/TMOSA approach proved crucial to being able to provide medical services when hospitals were filled.

73 Committee staff interview of Jimmy Guidry, M.D., Medical Director and State Health Officer, Louisiana Department of Health and Hospitals, conducted on Dec. 20, 2005, transcript pp. 21-22.

74 Committee staff interview of Lt. Col. Keith LaCaze, Assistant Administrator, Law Enforcement Division, Louisiana Department of Wildlife and Fisheries, conducted on Nov. 30, 3005, transcript pp. 55-63.

75 FEMA, Amendment of Solicitation of Contract, Sept. 21, 2004. Provided to Committee; filed as Bates nos. DHS-FEMA-0076-0000038 through 0000043.

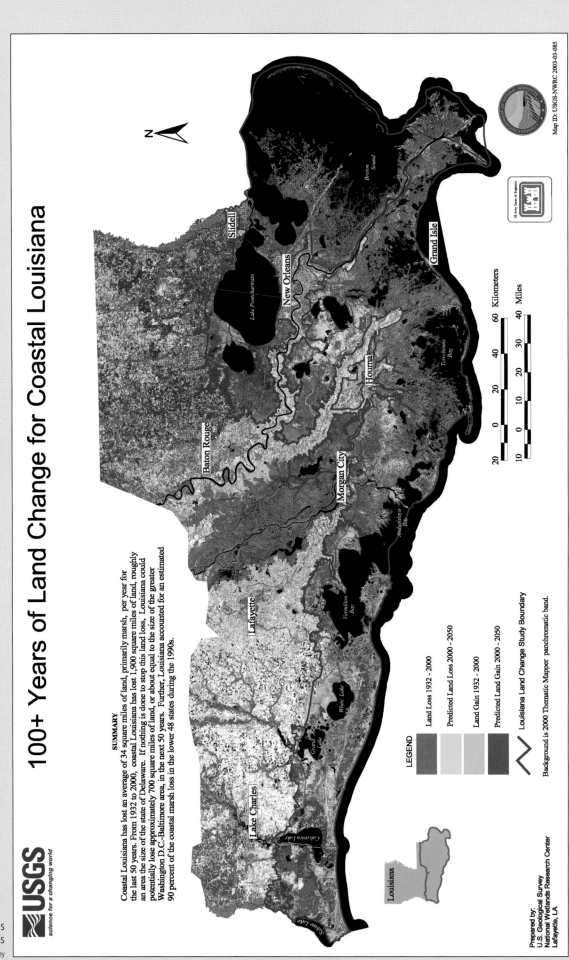

100+ Years of Land Change for Coastal Louisiana

≋USGS
science for a changing world

Coastal Louisiana's changing lands
U.S. Geological Survey

SUMMARY

Coastal Louisiana has lost an average of 34 square miles of land, primarily marsh, per year for the last 50 years. From 1932 to 2000, coastal Louisiana has lost 1,900 square miles of land, roughly an area the size of the state of Delaware. If nothing is done to stop this land loss, Louisiana could potentially lose approximately 700 square miles of land, or about equal to the size of the greater Washington D.C.-Baltimore area, in the next 50 years. Further, Louisiana accounted for an estimated 90 percent of the coastal marsh loss in the lower 48 states during the 1990s.

LEGEND

- Land Loss 1932 - 2000
- Predicted Land Loss 2000 - 2050
- Land Gain 1932 - 2000
- Predicted Land Gain 2000 - 2050
- Louisiana Land Change Study Boundary

Background is 2000 Thematic Mapper panchromatic band.

Louisiana

Slidell
New Orleans
Lake Pontchartrain
Breton Sound
Grand Isle
Baton Rouge
Houma
Terrebonne Bay
Morgan City
Atchafalaya Bay
Lafayette
Vermilion Bay
White Lake
Grand Lake
Lake Charles
Calcasieu Lake
Sabine Lake

20   0   20   40   60 Kilometers
10   0   10   20   30   40 Miles

Prepared by:
U.S. Geological Survey
National Wetlands Research Center
Lafayette, LA

Map ID: USGS-NWRC 2003-03-085

Effects of Environmental and Engineering Changes

A vital part of the Hurricane Katrina story lies in nearly two centuries of natural and man-made changes to the Louisiana coastline. When New Orleans was settled in 1718, the primary flood threat was from the Mississippi River, not the Gulf of Mexico. An expansive coastal landscape separated the city from the Gulf and served as a buffer from any storms moving ashore.[1]

That protective landscape no longer exists. The ever-changing and disappearing coastline has left New Orleans more susceptible to hurricanes and contributed to the damage inflicted by Katrina. Should this trend continue, New Orleans and the rest of coastal Louisiana will become even more vulnerable to damage from future storms, and efforts to protect the city with levees and floodwalls will be undermined.

While a comprehensive analysis of coastal Louisiana's environmental challenges and potential remedies is beyond the scope of this report, this chapter briefly examines some of the potential impacts of Louisiana's altered landscape on hurricane protection.

Louisiana's Changing Coastal Landscape is Increasing Hurricane Vulnerability

The Louisiana coastline is changing more rapidly than any other part of the country and, as a result, is becoming more vulnerable to hurricanes. Over the last 70 years, Louisiana has lost more than 1,900 square miles of coastal land – an area roughly the size of Delaware.[2] At the peak of the trend in the 1960s and 1970s, Louisiana was losing 40 square miles of coastal land per year.[3] This loss has slowed in recent years, primarily because the most vulnerable lands have already disappeared, but Louisiana is still losing 10 square miles of coastal land per year.[4] As a civil-engineering magazine put it, "in southeastern Louisiana a football field worth of wetlands sinks into the sea every 30 minutes."[5]

These coastal lands primarily consist of wetlands, including extensive cypress swamps and grass marshes. But Louisiana's barrier islands (an elongated chain of islands running parallel to the coast and serving as a barrier against waves) and even many higher ridges, which were formed by large amounts of sediment piling up along past banks of the Mississippi River, are also disappearing. The U.S. Geological Survey (USGS) projects that an additional 700 square miles could be lost by 2050 if no further actions are taken to halt or reverse current processes.[6]

The Mississippi River is the single most important factor in sustaining coastal Louisiana.[7] The river brings water, sediments, and nutrients from 41 percent of the land area of the contiguous U.S. to the coast of Louisiana. Prior to the extensive building of levees and dams along the Mississippi, the river carried nearly 400 million tons of sediment to the Louisiana Coast every year – enough to cover 250 square miles of land a foot deep in sediment.[8] The growing wetlands fed by the accumulating sediments, nutrients, and fresh water of the Mississippi have added 9,600 square miles of land to the Louisiana coastline over the last 6,000 years – a rate of 1.25 square miles per year.[9] At its peak, this land, known as the Mississippi deltaic plane, accounted for nearly 20 percent of the land area of present-day Louisiana, including New Orleans.

Major causes of land loss in Louisiana have been identified.[10] Dams and diversions along the Mississippi River and its tributaries have greatly reduced the amount of sediment that reaches coastal Louisiana, and levees force the remaining sediment so far offshore that it falls directly onto the outer continental shelf and beyond, where it no longer contributes to sustaining or building coastal lands.[11] By blocking natural flooding cycles, levees prevent fresh water and nutrients from the Mississippi River from nourishing and sustaining wetlands.[12] Ten major navigation canals and more than 9,000 miles of pipelines servicing approximately 50,000 oil-and-gas production facilities in coastal Louisiana result in a large direct loss of land and also contribute to wetland loss from saltwater intrusion and dredging.[13]

In addition, the Louisiana deltaic plane is essentially sinking, in a process known as subsidence, which occurs naturally as sediments deposited by the Mississippi are compacted over time.[14] Oil and gas production further contribute to subsidence, potentially causing local subsidence three times greater than the highest natural subsidence rates.[15] Finally, sea level is rising, primarily as a result of global warming.[16]

The deterioration of Louisiana's coastal landscape of barrier islands, wetlands, and higher ridges, and the effects of subsidence have made coastal communities more vulnerable to hurricane flooding.[17] New Orleans, in particular, is widely considered to be more vulnerable to hurricanes both because land in the city has subsided and because much of the barrier islands and wetlands that once surrounded the city has disappeared.[18]

Many of the mechanisms by which barrier islands, shoals, marshes, forested wetlands, and other features of the coastal landscape protect against hurricanes are well known. Geologic features such as barrier islands or the land mass associated with wetlands can block or channel flow, slow water velocities, and reduce the speed at which storm surge propagates. These effects can significantly restrict the volume of water available to inundate the mainland.[19]

Forested wetlands can greatly diminish wind penetration, reducing surface waves and storm surge. Shallow water depths weaken waves via bottom friction and breaking, while vegetation provides additional frictional drag and further limits wave buildup. Where wetlands and shallow waters lie in front of levees, they absorb wave energy and reduce the destructiveness of storm waves on the levees.[20]

Depending on the rate of relative sea-level rise, healthy coastal wetlands can maintain a near-sea-level landscape by trapping sediments or accumulating organic material, thus helping to counter subsidence and global sea-level rise. In contrast, when Louisiana's coastal wetlands deteriorate and disappear, the land held in place by the wetlands undergoes wave erosion, eventually washing away and leaving behind open water 10 to 12 feet deep.[21]

On the other hand, the quantitative impact of wetlands and other coastal features on hurricane protection is poorly known. Anecdotal data accumulated after Hurricane Andrew suggests a storm-surge reduction along the Louisiana coast of about three inches per mile of marsh.[22] During Hurricane Katrina, bottom friction and breaking reduced the average height of the highest one-third of waves from 55 feet in deep water (with peak waves above 80 feet), to 18 feet in shallower water outside of the barrier island east of New Orleans,[23] to a fraction of that height in protected areas.

Researchers at the Louisiana State University (LSU) Hurricane Center found that, during Hurricane Katrina, levees protected by wetlands had a much higher survival rate than those bordering open water. For example, large sections of the Mississippi River Gulf Outlet (MRGO) levees that had little or no wetland separating them from Lake Borgne disintegrated, while the nearby 20-Arpent Canal levee, protected by a buffer of marsh and wooded wetlands, remained standing. According to LSU researchers, an area about the size of a football field with the tree density equal to that found in most Louisiana swamps would reduce wave energy in a storm by 90 percent. These researchers further found that friction from marsh grasses and shrubs reduced water speed from Hurricane Katrina in some places from seven feet per second to three feet per second.[24]

Subsidence is also contributing substantially to hurricane vulnerability. Subsidence occurs across the entire region, and therefore impacts not only natural features such as wetlands and barrier islands, but also man-made structures such as buildings and levees. According to a recent report by the U.S. Army Corps of Engineers (Corps) Interagency Performance Evaluation Task Force (IPET), which examines the hurricane-protection levee system, the average rate of subsidence across the area is 0.6 feet over a decade.[25]

The rate of subsidence is frequently greater under cities and towns than under natural features: when areas are drained in order to prepare them for buildings, organic material in the soil decomposes and leads to further subsidence. In addition, the levees themselves further subside due to their own weight pressing down on the unstable soils of the New Orleans area. As a result, the effectiveness of the levee system deteriorates over time as both the levees and the region subside. The IPET report concluded that some portions of the hurricane protection system around New Orleans are almost two feet below their original elevations,[26] further increasing their own vulnerability, and that of the areas they are designed to protect, to the power of hurricanes.

The changes to Louisiana's coastline have serious implications for the long-term sustainability of the region. Land subsidence and predicted global sea-level rise during the next 100 years mean that areas of New Orleans and vicinity now 5 to 10 feet below mean sea level will likely be 8 to 13 feet or more below mean sea level by 2100.[27] At the same time, the loss of wetlands, barrier islands, and other natural features could eliminate protection from waves and allow for higher and faster moving storm surges.[28] According to the National Academy of Sciences, these trends will make much of Louisiana's southern delta uninhabitable without substantial new engineering projects.[29]

In the long term, New Orleans and other regions of the Louisiana deltaic plane cannot be protected without taking proper account of the tremendous change that is continuing to occur to Louisiana's coastal landscape.

The Mississippi River Gulf Outlet's Contribution to Damage from Hurricane Katrina

Congress authorized construction of the Mississippi River Gulf Outlet (MRGO) in 1956 to facilitate commercial shipping access to the Port of New Orleans from the Gulf of Mexico. Upon its completion in 1965, the MRGO provided a route 40 miles shorter than the alternative up the Mississippi River. The MRGO also provides a connection from the Gulf of Mexico to the Gulf Intracoastal Waterway (GIWW), which is a recreational and commercial waterway running east-west from Texas to Florida. Though the MRGO produced commercial benefits, those benefits came at a cost to the environment. The Corps estimates that the construction of the channel led to substantial loss of wetlands, which, as noted above, help slow and decrease the power of storms before they hit populated areas.

The MRGO also contributed to a potential "funnel" for storm surges emerging from Lake Borgne and the Gulf into the New Orleans area.[30] The "funnel" was created by the intersection of the MRGO from the southeast and the GIWW from the northeast into the confined channel, referred to as the GIWW/MRGO that separates New Orleans East and the Ninth Ward/St. Bernard Parish. The levees on the south side of the MRGO and the levees on the north side of the GIWW converge from being about 10 miles apart where they straddle Lake Borgne to a few hundred yards apart where the MRGO merges into the GIWW.[31] The western part of the "funnel" is a six-mile-long section of the combined GIWW/MRGO, which was enlarged by a factor of three when the MRGO was built in order to expand it from a barge channel to accommodate ocean-going vessels.[32]

Prior to Hurricane Katrina, many warned that the potential funnel would accelerate and intensify storm surges emerging from Lake Borgne and the Gulf into the downtown New Orleans area. The funnel had been described as a "superhighway" for storm surges or the "Crescent City's Trojan Horse" that had the potential to "amplify storm surges by 20 to 40 percent," according to some storm modeling.[33] Researchers at LSU believed that in creating this funnel, "the US Army Corps of Engineers had inadvertently designed an excellent storm surge delivery system – nothing less – to bring this mass of water with simply tremendous 'load' – potential energy – right into the middle of New Orleans." [34]

The extent to which MRGO, and the funnel it helped create actually contributed to the hurricane's damage is still being investigated, but there have been some preliminary findings. A recent report issued by the Corps' IPET concluded that the portion of MRGO running from the GIWW to the Gulf (called "Reach 2") did not significantly impact the height of Katrina's storm surge, not because the "funnel" effect was nonexistent, but because the storm was so great it nullified the impact of either the wetlands or the intersection of the MRGO and the GIWW – the funnel – at the height of the surge.[35]

While the IPET report concluded that the Reach 2 portion of MRGO had little impact on Katrina's storm surge, it did find that the six-mile combined section of the GIWW/MRGO (called "Reach 1") carried the storm surge from Lake Borgne into New Orleans. The combined GIWW/MRGO served as a link between Lake Borgne and Lake Pontchartrain, enabling the storm surge in one lake to affect the storm surge in the other. During Katrina, a 14 to 17-foot surge coming from Lake Borgne into the funnel between MRGO and the GIWW was as much as 10 feet above water levels in Lake Pontchartrain.[36] This large difference in the water levels between the two lakes increased the flow of water in the direction of the city and eventually into Lake Pontchartrain.

To address this problem, the IPET report recommended that flow through the combined channels "must be dramatically reduced or eliminated," either by a permanent closure or a structure that can be selectively used to block storm surges flowing between Lakes Pontchartrain and Borgne along the combined GIWW/MRGO.[37]

Researchers at the LSU Hurricane Center who have looked at models of Katrina have concluded that it is not just the volume of water that is important, but also the velocity. These researchers found that the funnel accelerated the speed of the water when the larger volume in the funnel, and especially the water in the MRGO, was forced into the single merged GIWW/MRGO channel.[38] The increased velocity of the water as it made its way through the channel pounded on the floodwalls lining the sides,[39] weakening them and making them more vulnerable to the overtopping and scouring that occurred during the storm. Maximum current velocities in the combined GIWW/MRGO channel were greater than eight feet per second, which is nearly three times the velocity necessary to cause serious potential for erosion in the soils of the adjacent levee.[40]

Investigations continue into MRGO's contribution to damage caused by Katrina, but there is general agreement that the presence of the MRGO destroyed wetlands that otherwise would have provided additional defenses. This happened because the MRGO served as a conduit for saltwater from the Gulf of Mexico to intrude into the freshwater wetlands. The saltwater damaged and destroyed wetlands, which resulted in the loss of land that had served as part of the city's defenses against hurricanes and other storms.[41] According to the National Academy of Sciences, MRGO has resulted in "tremendous environmental damage, including saltwater intrusion, land loss, and worsening the effects of wave damage during hurricanes and storms."[42]

Over the past 40 years, the erosion from the saltwater has contributed to the widening of the MRGO from 600 feet to 2,000 feet, an average of 35 feet per year, and the loss of more than 19,000 acres of land.[43] Had there been no wetlands at all east of the MRGO and the GIWW, preliminary storm modeling has shown, the Katrina storm surge may have been anywhere from three to six feet higher along St. Bernard Parish/Ninth Ward and New Orleans East.[44] Continued wetland loss will increase the vulnerability of the city, making overtopping by storm surges even more likely in the future.[45]

The building of MRGO and the combined GIWW/MRGO resulted in substantial environmental damage, including a significant loss of wetlands that had once formed a natural barrier against hurricanes threatening New Orleans from the east. MRGO and the GIWW/MRGO provided a connection between Lake Borgne and Lake Pontchartrain that allowed the much greater surge from Lake Borgne to flow into both New Orleans and Lake Pontchartrain. These channels further increased the speed and flow of the Katrina surge into New Orleans East and the Ninth Ward/St. Bernard Parishes, increasing the destructive force against adjacent levees and contributing to their failure. As a result, MRGO and the combined GIWW/MRGO resulted in increased flooding and greater damage from Hurricane Katrina.

1 Working Group for Post-Hurricane Planning for the Louisiana Coast, "A New Framework for Planning the Future of Coastal Louisiana after the Hurricanes of 2005," Jan. 26, 2006, p. 8 [hereinafter Working Group for Post-Hurricane Planning, "A New Framework"].

2 Working Group for Post-Hurricane Planning, "A New Framework," p. 8.

3 Working Group for Post-Hurricane Planning, "A New Framework," p. 8.

4 Working Group for Post-Hurricane Planning, "A New Framework," p. 9.

5 Greg Brouwer, "The Creeping Storm," *Civil Engineering Magazine*, June 2003, p. 10.

6 A study by the United States Geological Survey "forecasts that an additional 448,000 acres could be lost by 2050 if no further actions are taken to halt or reverse current processes." 448,000 acres is the equivalent of 700 square miles. *Source:* U.S. Library of Congress, Congressional Research Service, *Coastal Louisiana: Attempting to Restore an Ecosystem*, by Jeffrey Zinn, Oct. 25, 2004, p. 5 [hereinafter CRS, *Coastal Louisiana: Attempting to Restore an Ecosystem*].

7 National Academy of Sciences, *Drawing Louisiana's New Map: Addressing Land Loss in Coastal Louisiana*. Washington: National Academies Press, 2006, p. 11 [hereinafter NAS, *Drawing Louisiana's New Map*].

8 NAS, *Drawing Louisiana's New Map*, pp. 22-27. Tons converted to square miles using 1.5 tons per cubic yard. *Source:* Sherwood M. Gagliano, "The Life and Times of Mississippi River Sediment," presented at the Workshop on River Resources Management in the 21st-century, Feb. 20, 2003.

9 Working Group for Post-Hurricane Planning, "A New Framework," p. 1.

10 CRS, *Coastal Louisiana: Attempting to Restore an Ecosystem*, p. 5.

11 CRS, *Coastal Louisiana: Attempting to Restore an Ecosystem*, p. 5. *See also:* NAS, *Drawing Louisiana's New Map*, p. 31; Virginia Burkett, David B. Zilkoski, and David A. Hart, "Sea-Level Rise and Subsidence: Implications for Flooding in New Orleans, Louisiana," Subsidence Interest Group Conference, Proceedings of the Technical Meeting, Nov. 27-29, 2001, p. 64.

12 John W. Day, Jr., et al., "Pattern and Process of Land Loss in the Louisiana Coastal Zone: An Analysis of Spatial and Temporal Patterns of Wetland Habitat Change," Estuarine Research Federation, 1999, pp. 193-200.

13 NAS, *Drawing Louisiana's New Map*, p. 30.

14 CRS, *Coastal Louisiana: Attempting to Restore an Ecosystem*, p. 5.

15 Robert A. Morton and Noreen A. Purcell, U.S. Geological Survey, "Wetland Subsidence, Fault Reactivation, and Hydrocarbon Production in the U.S. Gulf Coast Region," Sept. 2001.

16 James G. Tituse and Vijay K. Narayanan, U.S. Environmental Protection Agency, "The Probability of Sea Level Rise," Sept. 1995, p. iii. According to the Environmental Protection Agency, "[t]here is new and stronger evidence that most of the warming over the last 50 years is attributable to human activities" and that the "warmer temperatures are expected to raise sea level by expanding ocean water, melting mountain glaciers, and melting parts of the Greenland Ice Sheet." U.S. Environmental Protection Agency, "Global Warming – Climate, Future Climate," Jan. 7, 2000. http://yosemite.epa.gov/

OAR/globalwarming.nsf/content/ClimateFutreClimate.html. Accessed on Apr. 17, 2006; U.S. Environmental Protection Agency, Global Warming – Climate, Climate, Jan. 7, 2000. http://Yosemite.epa.gov/OAR/globalwarming.nsf/content/climate.html. Accessed on Apr. 17, 2006.

17 Working Group for Post-Hurricane Planning, "A New Framework," p. 9; U.S. Library of Congress, Congressional Research Service, *Protecting New Orleans: From Hurricane Barriers to Floodwalls*, by Nicole T. Carter, Jan. 26, 2006, p. 10 [hereinafter CRS, *Protecting New Orleans: From Hurricane Barriers to Floodwalls*].

18 CRS, *Protecting New Orleans: From Hurricane Barriers to Floodwalls*, p. 10.

19 Working Group for Post-Hurricane Planning, "A New Framework," p. 15.

20 Working Group for Post-Hurricane Planning, "A New Framework," p. 15.

21 Working Group for Post-Hurricane Planning, "A New Framework," p. 16.

22 Working Group for Post-Hurricane Planning, "A New Framework," p. 15.

23 Abby Sallenger, e-mail to David Hunter, Senate Committee staff member, Mar. 14, 2006, 3:51 p.m.

24 Bob Marshall, "Studies Abound on Why the Levees Failed. But Researchers Point out that Some Levees Held Fast Because Wetlands Worked as Buffers During Katrina's Storm Surge," New Orleans *Times-Picayune*, Mar. 23, 2006, p 1.

25 U.S. Army Corps of Engineers, Interagency Performance Evaluation Task Force, Performance Evaluation Plan and Interim Status, *Report 2 of a Series*, Mar. 10, 2006, p. III–6 [hereinafter IPET, *Report 2 of a Series*].

26 IPET, *Report 2 of a Series*, p. I–2.

27 Virginia Burkett, David B. Zilkoski, and David A. Hart, "Sea-Level Rise and Subsidence: Implications for Flooding in New Orleans, Louisiana," Subsidence Interest Group Conference, Nov. 2001, p. 63.

28 Working Group for Post-Hurricane Planning, "A New Framework," pp. 15-18.

29 NAS, *Drawing Louisiana's New Map*, p. 38.

30 IPET, *Report 2 of a Series*, p. E–7.

31 Ivor L. van Heerden, G. Paul Kemp, Wes Shrum, Ezra Boyd and Hassan Mashriqui, Louisiana State University, Center for the Study of Public Health Impacts of Hurricanes, *Initial Assessment of the New Orleans' Flooding Event during the Passage of Hurricane Katrina*, p. 4 [hereinafter LSU, *Initial Assessment of New Orleans Flooding*].

32 LSU, *Initial Assessment of New Orleans Flooding*, p. 4.

33 Michael Grunwald, "Canal May Have Worsened City's Flooding; Disputed Project Was a 'Funnel' for Surge, Some Say," *The Washington Post*, Sept. 14, 2005, p. A21.

34 LSU, *Initial Assessment of New Orleans Flooding*, p. 4.

35 IPET, *Report 2 of a Series*, p. E–7.

36 LSU, *Initial Assessment of New Orleans Flooding*, p. 4.

37 IPET, *Report 2 of a Series*, p. E–7.

38 Hassan S. Mashriqui et al., "Experimental Storm Surge Simulations For Hurricane Katrina," *Coastal Hydrology and Processes* (publication pending) [hereinafter Mashriqui, "Experimental Storm Surge"].

39 Mashriqui, "Experimental Storm Surge"; Matthew Brown, "MRGO'ing, going, gone? Most everyone wants to close the shipping channel. But how closed is close?" New Orleans *Times-Picayune*, Nov. 27, 2005, p. 1.

40 Mashriqui, "Experimental Storm Surge."

41 NAS, *Drawing Louisiana's New Map*, p. 30.

42 NAS, *Drawing Louisiana's New Map*, p. 38.

43 NAS, *Drawing Louisiana's New Map*, pp. 38-39.

44 Working Group for Post-Hurricane Planning, "A New Framework," p. 16.

45 Working Group for Post-Hurricane Planning, "A New Framework," p. 16.

LAST LINE OF DEFENSE: HOPING THE LEVEES HOLD

Army Corps of Engineers officials say hurricane levees in the New Orleans area will protect residents from a Category 3 hurricane moving rapidly over the area. But computer models indicate even weaker storms could find chinks in that armor.

BARRIERS OF EARTH AND CONCRETE

Levees and floodwalls that protect against flooding from both the Mississippi River and hurricanes are built by the Army Corps of Engineers and are maintained by local levee districts. The corps and the local districts share the construction cost of hurricane levees, while the Mississippi River levees are a federal project. Local levee districts also build and maintain nonfederal, lower-elevation levees with construction money from each district's share of property taxes and state financing.

LEVEES AND FLOODWALLS
- Mississippi River
- Hurricane protection
- Interior parish

Notes: Levee and floodwall elevations are drawn with an extremely exaggerated vertical height but are in proportion to each other. Numbers on specific sections represent average heights in feet above sea level.

HEIGHT ISN'T EVERYTHING

Different factors permit Lake Pontchartrain levees of varying elevations to withstand an 11½-foot storm surge plus several feet of waves:

Levees on higher ground and separated from the water by 5 miles of marshland need be only 12½ feet tall

Levees fronted by boulders and concrete rubble breakers can be about 14 feet high

Levees without any breakers need to be about 17 feet tall or taller

Seawalls on the water must be 22 feet high

Note: The height and shape of a levee is based on the roughness of the area over which waves pass to reach the structure, and the slope of the structure.

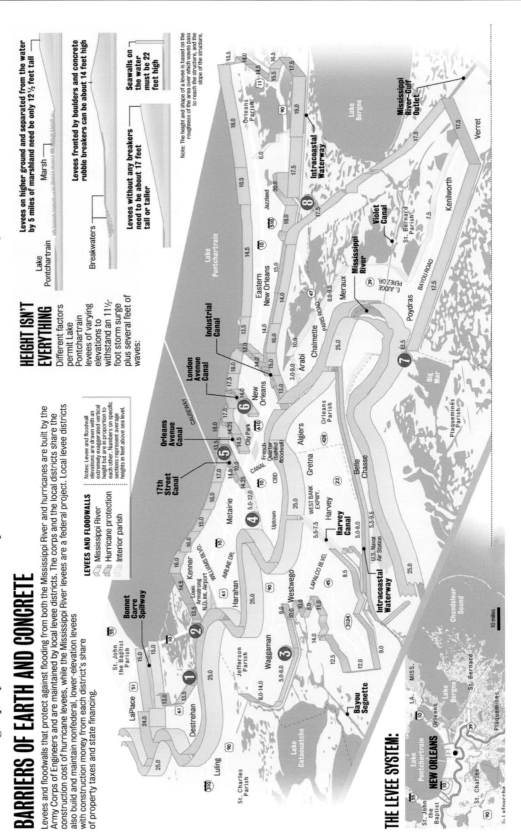

THE LEVEE SYSTEM:

Levees: Who's in Charge?

An Overview of Levees in Southeast Louisiana

Levees are large embankments, usually of earth or stone, that make up part of the flood-control system designed and built to protect New Orleans from hurricanes and floods. Levees line the Mississippi River, the shores of Lake Pontchartrain, and the Mississippi River Gulf Outlet (MRGO), and are part of the protective rings around New Orleans East and St. Bernard Parish.

Other structures may also be used to protect an area from flooding. The Army Corps of Engineers (the Corps), sometimes in concert with local and state government and sometimes on its own, built floodwalls, drainage canals, pumps, and floodgates to control the flow of excess water in and around the city.

- Floodwalls, which are high vertical walls built of concrete and steel, are used in more urban areas because they do not require as much space as earthen levees with their wide foundations.

- Because floodwater will find its way through any breaks in the levees, massive gates are located throughout the system wherever there are openings for streets or railroads. These gates are closed in anticipation of "high-water" events such as very high tides, floods, and hurricanes.

- Because many parts of the region are at or below sea level, many areas also have a system of pumps and canals to remove rain and floodwater from areas protected by the levee system.[1]

All of these systems – more than 200 gates and 125 miles of levees and floodwalls – worked together to form the flood-control system that was designed to protect metropolitan New Orleans from storms like Hurricane Katrina.[2]

The Roles and Responsibilities of the U.S. Army Corps of Engineers, the Orleans Levee District, and the Louisiana Department of Transportation and Development

The U.S. Army Corps of Engineers

Levee systems of the size needed to protect the New Orleans area are often collaborative efforts between federal and local governments.[3] The federal role in such projects is carried out by the Corps, an agency within the Department of Defense (DOD) charged with both military and civilian missions.[4] Military missions are assigned within the military command structure, while civilian flood-control projects are authorized by Congress in legislation.[5]

Flood-control projects usually begin when a community feels a need for protection and contacts the Corps. If the Corps does not already have the statutory authority to respond, then Congress may grant it. After initial studies, the Corps may enter into a project-cooperation or assurance agreement with a local sponsor acting on behalf of the community. The assurance agreements for projects generally set forth roles of the parties, including payment obligations, design and construction responsibilities, and operations-and-maintenance (O&M) duties before and after the project is complete.[6]

The levee system that protects most of New Orleans, including areas that experienced major breaches and flooding during Katrina – such as the 17th Street and London Avenue Canals, New Orleans East, and most of St. Bernard Parish – is a Corps project called the Lake Pontchartrain and Vicinity Hurricane Protection Project (Lake Pontchartrain Project). There are several other federal cost-shared projects that protect other parts of southeastern Louisiana.[7] The Corps' involvement in these projects was mostly through its New Orleans District, one of the Corps' largest with more than 1,200 employees, and part of the Corps' Mississippi Valley Division headquartered in Vicksburg, Mississippi.[8] When Katrina made landfall, the New Orleans District was under the command of Colonel Richard P. Wagenaar, who had assumed control only six weeks before.[9]

The assurance agreements for the Lake Pontchartrain Project made the Corps responsible for designing and constructing the project. Local sponsors provided the land for levee construction and rights-of-way, and agreed to share the cost. The Corps was to turn the completed project over to the local sponsors for O&M consistent with the Corps' standards, i.e., making sure the flood-control system actually works on a day-to-day basis and protects those living inside the system.[10] To help the local sponsor do this, the Corps is required by its rules and regulations to provide the local sponsor with an operations manual[11] and then conduct annual inspections to be sure the local sponsor is doing what it is supposed to do.[12]

In addition to its authority to build flood-control projects, the Corps also has statutory authority in federal cost-share flood-control projects like the Lake Pontchartrain Project to act in anticipation of, or response to, flood emergencies. In this role, the Corps may help the local sponsors deal with the flood threat to the levee system, and aid state and local governments trying to prevent flood damage. This "flood-fighting" authority is authorized by Public Law 84-99, also known as the "Flood Act."[13] In the days following Katrina, the Corps used its Flood Act authority to close off the levee breaches at the 17th Street and London Avenue Canals, which were filling the city with water, and to make other emergency repairs.[14]

The Orleans Levee District

One of the local sponsors for the Lake Pontchartrain Project was the Orleans Levee District, one of the first five levee districts created by the state in 1879. The levee districts, which were established to be a funding source for and to ensure local involvement in levee construction and operation,[15] all had the same general duty: to do what was necessary to "insure the thorough and adequate protection of the lands of the district from damage by flood … for the adequate drainage control of the district."[16]

Like the Corps under the Flood Act, the levee districts have broad statutory obligations in addition to their obligations under their assurance agreements on individual levee projects. For example, regardless whether a project was being designed and constructed by the Corps or had been turned over for O&M to the local sponsor, state law charged the levee districts with adopting rules and regulations for maintaining a "comprehensive levee system."[17] State law authorized them to obtain engineering assistance from the Louisiana Department of Transportation and Development (LA DOTD) in Baton Rouge if they needed additional technical expertise.[18] State law also required levee-district board members to attend once during their term in office an educational program on how to care for and inspect levees.[19]

To carry out their primary duty of flood control, state law not only authorized the levee districts to serve as local sponsors for federal cost-share projects, but also to raise money pursuant to taxing and bonding authorities. The Orleans Levee District, uniquely, was also authorized to engage in various business enterprises,[20] making it an entity with some governmental qualities (taxing and bonding authority) and some corporate qualities – the authority to engage in for-profit businesses like operating the Lakefront Airport, running two marinas along Lake Pontchartrain, and leasing dock space to a riverboat casino.[21]

The revenues the Orleans Levee District earned from the businesses and its taxing and bonding authority were substantial. The Orleans Levee District financial statements for the fiscal year ending June 30, 2005, show it collected more than $24 million from property taxes and $14 million from its business-type activities in the previous 12 months.[22] The same report said the district had $21 million in unallocated general funds and $13 million in a "special levee improvement fund."[23] The levee improvement fund, according to the levee district's former president, James Huey, could "only be used for flood protection projects and/or flood-related projects."[24]

Although the levee district's primary responsibility was flood protection, it spent large amounts on non-flood related activities (e.g., licensing a casino, or operating an airport and marinas, or leasing space to a karate club, beautician schools or restaurants) rather than applying the money to flood protection or emergency preparedness.[25] For example, the Orleans Levee District's Emergency Operations Center (EOC) sat outside the protection of the levee system at the Lakefront Airport, vulnerable to the very hurricanes the levee system was designed to protect against.[26] For years the district had studied moving its EOC inside the flood protection system, but never did.[27] The levee district's Chief Engineer, Stevan Spencer, described the situation as a "very bad joke" that dated back to at least 1998, when Hurricane Georges flooded the airport.[28] Spencer said "there was never funding" to move the EOC.[29] Yet in 2003, the Orleans Levee District spent $2.4 million to repair the "Mardi Gras Fountain" in a park near Lake Pontchartrain.[30] When Katrina made landfall, Orleans Levee District staff had to be rescued, mostly by boat, from the flooded EOC at the airport[31] before they could survey damage or assist with repair efforts at the 17th Street and London Avenue Canals.

The Orleans Levee District was also aware of a levee in New Orleans East that was considered to be three feet below its design height.[32] Levee-district board minutes and conversations with Corps personnel suggest that paying for repairs to this low levee was considered to be the Corps' responsibility.[33] Federal funding was unavailable, but instead of paying for the repairs itself and asking for reimbursement from the Corps, as it had with previous projects,[34] the levee district merely sent letters to its Congressional delegation asking for federal funding.[35]

Pressed to explain how the Orleans Levee District made spending decisions, Huey offered no direct explanation, but focused on the district's multiple obligations – not only was the district responsible for flood control, but it also had statutory requirements to maintain recreational space and was authorized by state law to engage in non-flood related business ventures.[36] A review of the levee-district board minutes of recent years revealed that the board and its various committees spent more time discussing its business operations than it did the flood-control system it was responsible for operating and maintaining.[37]

The Louisiana Department of Transportation and Development (LA DOTD)

Though not a party to the assurance agreements for the Lake Pontchartrain Project, LA DOTD and its Office of Public Works (OPW) have statutory responsibilities to assist and oversee certain levee district functions. State law tasks LA DOTD with approving any activity that might compromise the levees,[38] and with administering training sessions to levee-district board members and their inspectors on caring for and inspecting levees.[39]

To the extent training sessions were held, they were organized by the Association of Levee Boards of Louisiana, an organization that lists Edmund Preau as its Secretary-Treasurer.[40]

Preau is an Assistant Secretary in LA DOTD and leads the OPW within the Department, which is responsible for LA DOTD's levee-related activities.

When James Huey, who served on the levee district's board for more than 13 years (nine as president), was read the section of state law describing the training requirement, he said it was the first he had heard of it.[41] Huey explained: "You know what that is? That's going up to a workshop for a weekend and having a crawfish boil up here and hear a couple people talk about some things and they get a little piece of paper and they honored the law."[42] Huey was then asked whether the Association sessions addressed how to inspect levees. He responded, "No, nothing."[43]

LA DOTD also had the statutory responsibility to "review" each levee district's emergency-operations manual every two years.[44] According to Preau, this review entailed checking whether relevant contact information had been updated and whether the levee district had included any new flood-control systems within its jurisdiction in its planning.[45] The review entailed no assessment of whether the levee district had stockpiled materials or had the personnel necessary to assess an emergency and respond accordingly.[46] Preau said he assumed any more elaborate review would have been done by the Louisiana Office of Homeland Security and Emergency Preparedness (LOHSEP).[47]

Louisiana's Emergency Operations Plan (EOP) made the LA DOTD the primary state agency overseeing Emergency Support Function (ESF-3), Public Works and Engineering. ESF-3 encompassed critical infrastructure in the state, including the "construction, maintenance and repair of state flood control works."[48] ESF-3 also dictated that, "When an emergency is imminent, the ESF 3 Coordinator [who is to be designated by LA DOTD Secretary Johnny Bradberry] will assess the potential impact of the threat on the state's infrastructure and work with other authorities to ensure that any necessary immediate repairs or arrangements for critical structures and facilities are initiated."[49] ESF-3 also said, "As the emergency progresses, the coordinator will monitor the status of the infrastructure and effect emergency repairs where needed and feasible."[50]

The LA DOTD did not acknowledge or accept its responsibility under ESF-3. Preau told Committee investigators that he didn't think the provision applied to LA DOTD: "I'm not sure what that means, because we don't have any state flood control works. State doesn't own any flood control works."[51] By Preau's reading, a levee project was covered only if it was owned by the state, not simply if it was in the state. As Preau read it, LA DOTD had no responsibility to coordinate with levee districts on critical facilities like the Lake Pontchartrain Project. This response is problematic: the responsibilities articulated under ESF-3 are specifically delegated to the LA DOTD, and the plain language employed by the State's Emergency Operations Plan cannot be unilaterally dismissed as meaningless by the people it covers.

The result was that neither LA DOTD nor any state agency made sure that the state's levee districts were integrated into the state's emergency-planning process, much less genuinely prepared for an emergency. As a result, when Katrina made landfall, no Orleans Levee District personnel were located at, or in contact with, emergency managers in Baton Rouge; nor was any mechanism in place to request additional support from the state.

Notwithstanding Preau's insistence that the LA DOTD had no responsibilities under ESF-3 for the levee system, LA DOTD ultimately played an active role in efforts to close levee breaches in New Orleans in the aftermath of Katrina.

Design and Construction of the Lake Pontchartrain Project

During Katrina, levees and floodwalls were overwhelmed throughout the New Orleans area, and in several places were breached. Some of these failures occurred in parts of the Lake

Pontchartrain Project. Understanding the link between the breaches and the nature and organization of the Lake Pontchartrain Project requires some background.

Congress authorized the Lake Pontchartrain Project in the Flood Control Act of 1965 to provide hurricane protection to areas around Lake Pontchartrain in Orleans, Jefferson, St. Bernard, and St. Charles Parishes.[52] The project called for design and construction of about 125 miles of levees and floodwalls to be completed by 1978 at a cost of $85 million. The project was still not complete when Katrina hit, and its cost had grown to more than $750 million as of 2005.[53]

As authorized by Congress, the project was to protect the area from what the Corps called the "Standard Project Hurricane" (SPH), a model storm "based on the most severe combination of meteorological conditions considered reasonably characteristic of that region."[54] The SPH was developed in 1959 by what was then called the United States Weather Bureau, which updated the SPH after the devastating impact of Hurricane Betsy in 1965. The SPH was revised again in 1970, 1977, and 1979 by the Weather Bureau's successor, the National Oceanic and Atmospheric Administration (NOAA).[55] There is no evidence that design parameters of the Lake Pontchartrain Project were modified in light of NOAA's changes to the reference-model storm.[56]

Nevertheless, the Corps has repeatedly maintained that the SPH was the equivalent of a fast-moving Category 3 storm on the Saffir-Simpson scale – a measurement scale that rates the strength of hurricanes on a scale of Category 1 to Category 5, with Category 5 being the most intense. For example, at a press conferences immediately after the storm, Lieutenant General Carl Strock, the Commander of the Corps and its Chief of Engineers, explicitly said that the Corps "knew" that the levee system "would protect from a Category 3 hurricane,"[57] and the page on the Lake Pontchartrain Project on the Corps' website after Katrina said, "The SPH is equivalent to a fast-moving Category 3 hurricane."[58]

This claim is misleading: the Saffir-Simpson scale was not adopted until 1977, 12 years after the Lake Pontchartrain Project was authorized. Al Naomi, the Corps' Senior Project Manager for the project, acknowledged that the Corps never conducted a formal study comparing the SPH to the Saffir-Simpson scale, so the claim that the Lake Pontchartrain Project provided Category 3 protection was at best a rough estimate, and at worst, simply inaccurate:

> SPH has … wind speed, central pressure, and surge. You go in and say what is my wind speed for an SPH? You look at it. It's a very high Category 2 storm on the Saffir-Simpson Scale. I look at my central pressure for SPH. I go to the Saffir-Simpson Scale, it's a mid-range Cat 4. I say, what is my surge? SPH surge in the lake at 11 and a half [feet] on the Saffir-Simpson, that is a Category 3 range. What am I going to tell the Rotary Club? What do I have? Generally in talking to the hydrologist, you can say it's about equivalent to a fast-moving Cat 3. It's not really that, but for their understanding that is what you can say. That is what we say. What happens is the press gets this and it says we have Cat 3 protection. That is not really true. It's SPH protection which may be equivalent to a fast-moving Cat 3 storm.[59]

However, the view that the hurricane protection system could protect the greater New Orleans region from a moderate and/or fast-moving Category 3 storm was widely held within the Corps' New Orleans District. Prior to Hurricane Katrina, the New Orleans District issued numerous news releases to the general public (some of which are referenced below), stating that the hurricane-protection system provided some level of Category 3 protection:

• December 19, 2001, *N.O. hurricane bridge contract awarded, Corps, Levee Board will floodproof two bridges in Gentilly*: "The bridge floodproofing will protect neighborhoods along the London Avenue, Orleans Avenue and 17th Street Canals from storm surges from Lake Pontchartrain. The system of levees, floodwalls and bridges is designed to protect against fast-moving Category 3 hurricanes."[60]

• May 27, 2003, *Cross Bayou Drainage Structure to reduce flooding in St. Charles Parish*: "The structure is part of the Lake Pontchartrain Hurricane Protection Project and is the second of five such structures to be built in St. Charles Parish. ... These contracts, to be completed in 2004, will result in a levee system that provides protection from a Category 3 storm for St. Charles Parish."[61]

• August 21, 2003, *Filmore Bridge in Gentilly will reopen on Friday, Aug. 22. Mirabeau Bridge is closing Wednesday, Aug. 27 for hurricane floodproofing*: "The systems of levees, floodwalls and bridges is designed to protect against fast-moving Category 3 hurricanes."[62]

This view was also held by the Corps' New Orleans District Commander (Colonel Wagenaar[63]) and the District's Emergency Manager (Michael Lowe[64]). The same representations were made in more substantive Corps written materials.[65]

Moreover, the Lake Pontchartrain Project, as it stood in the path of Katrina, was still not complete as designed. Some portions were still under construction, and soil subsidence (sinking) had left portions of the project with less elevation above sea level than intended. In other words, some elements of the project were not even high enough to protect against the Standard Project Hurricane, let alone a genuine Category 3 hurricane.

The Corps was well aware of this fact. As Jerry Colletti, the New Orleans District's Manager for Completed Works explained, the Corps never tried "to provide full-level protection on an annual basis . . . we just can't raise everything to the design height for each storm that would come through."[66]

Meanwhile, the National Weather Service (NWS) concluded from a new model of projected storm surges that the Lake Pontchartrain Project would be more vulnerable to hurricanes than previously thought – that more Category 3 and even certain Category 2 hurricanes would overtop parts of the levee system and produce flooding.[67] Dr. Wilson Shaffer, who studies storm surges at NWS, said this discovery was shared with the Corps, perhaps as early as 2003, but certainly by 2004. The findings were also shared with LOHSEP and with state and local emergency managers at the Louisiana Emergency Preparedness Association's June conferences in 2004 and 2005.[68] At a minimum, this information should have prompted a fresh look at the adequacy of the Lake Pontchartrain Project, but like the NOAA updates to the Standard Project Hurricane in the 1970s, it does not appear that either the state or the Corps took any action to respond to the new information.

Effect of Subsidence on the Level of Protection

As noted earlier, the level of protection provided by the levee system was affected not only by its design, but also by geologic subsidence, or soil sinking. The entire coastal region of Louisiana had been subsiding for millions of years, as the enormous weight of the sediments continually deposited by the Mississippi River enters the Gulf of Mexico, pushing down on the earth's crust. Human activities like extracting oil and natural gas, pumping water, raising buildings, and even adding to levees and floodwalls all accelerate subsidence. (*See* Chapter 9.) As the entire region subsides, the effective height of the levees above sea level, and thus the level of protection they provide, decreases.[69] A recent report concluded that a section of levee that was overtopped and failed during Katrina was nearly three feet below its design height.[70]

All of these factors should have persuaded the Corps to reconsider its public claims that the Lake Pontchartrain Project provided Category 3-level protection.

Operation and Maintenance (O&M)

Maintaining a flood-control system is essential, but is complicated in southeast Louisiana by the recurring need to rebuild levees to compensate for subsidence. The Corps is not supposed to turn over a project until it is complete; until then, the Corps is responsible for O&M.[71] Once a project is turned over, the local sponsor must conduct O&M to Corps standards "to obtain maximum benefits."[72] This includes checking for "undue settlement" of the levee, water seeping through or under it, and growth of damaging brush, and taking immediate action to address potential emergencies.[73]

Because the Lake Pontchartrain Project was not complete, according to the Corps' Senior Project Manager for the project, Alfred Naomi, it had been formally turned over to the local sponsor, but remained in an "interim" status:

> There are still pieces that have to be done. We are not going to turn over a piece of the project until every piece in that ring of protection is completed. If there is one little thing left to do I think by regulation – I could be wrong. I think we have to have the entire system 100 percent complete so we turn over the entire segment that is protected, a certain area of the city.[74]

Nonetheless, the Corps did nominally turn over parts of the project to local sponsors to maintain when it determined that construction on that particular part or "reach" was complete.[75] The Corps sent letters to the Orleans Levee District and others to this effect, informing each district that it now had O&M responsibility for that unit.[76] Personnel within the Corps' New Orleans District referred to these letters as "turnover letters" even though they were not the "official total project completion turnover" letters.[77] The Orleans Levee District did not respond to these letters or even acknowledge their receipt.[78]

When the Committee asked for copies of the de-facto turnover letters, it received only a limited response. The letters submitted did not cover the entire project, and some were pre-1965, before the project was even authorized.[79] In short, the exact legal status of the project segments and the degree to which the Corps and local sponsors like the Orleans Levee District were truly responsible for maintenance is at best uncertain.

Other conflicting and irregular procedures in the turnover process went beyond the turnover letters. The Corps was supposed to require local sponsors to report semi-annually to its District Engineer on inspection and O&M for the flood-control system.[80] Colletti, the Corps' Operations Manager for Completed Works, explained that the Corps unilaterally decided not to require the Orleans Levee District to provide the report.[81] In addition, for each completed work, the Corps is required to give the local sponsor an operations manual.[82] Colletti said his office gave no such manual to the Orleans Levee District for levees and floodwalls, but merely provided a one-page set of guidelines similar to a part of the Code of Federal Regulations that detailed obligations of local sponsors.[83]

The Corps' observance of rules and regulations for completed projects took the form of a required annual inspection conducted around June 1 – the start of hurricane season – by representatives from the Corps, the Orleans Levee District, the LA DOTD, and other interested parties (e.g., the City and the Port of New Orleans).[84] These inspections appear to have taken about four hours, covered at least a hundred miles of levees and floodwalls,[85] and would usually involve a motorcade that would stop at pre-determined spots to allow the group to look over an area and discuss issues.[86] The purpose of the inspections, according to the Corps, was to ensure O&M compliance by the local sponsor, but not to test the system's actual structural integrity or measure whether it was at design height.[87] Perhaps the most colorful explanation of the annual inspection was offered by former Orleans Levee District president Huey, who suggested that the event was more of a social occasion than a genuine technical inspection:

> They normally meet and get some beignets [pastries] and coffee in the morning and get to the buses. And the colonel and the brass are all dressed up. You have commissioners, they have some news cameras following you around and you have your little beignets and then you have a nice lunch somewhere or whatever. And that's what the inspections are about.[88]

Ineffective Inspection Regime

The weaknesses of this inspection approach can be seen in the last pre-Katrina annual inspection of the Lake Pontchartrain Project in May 2005. It apparently did not address some known vulnerabilities. The W-30 Floodgate along the Inner Harbor Navigation Canal had been destroyed by a train accident in 2004 by the New Orleans Public Belt Railroad.[89] This gate was intended to close off the levee at a point where the railroad track passed through it. The railroad had provided money for repairs,[90] but the floodgate was still broken when Katrina struck, even though Huey, then board president, told an April 5, 2005, levee-district board meeting that he considered the broken gate to be an "emergency."[91] Under state law, Huey had the authority to address such emergencies without going through the standard contracting process.[92] Asked why he did not use his emergency authority to repair the gate before hurricane season, Huey simply said, "I do not know. My bottom-line, straightforward answer: I don't know."[93]

Another problem apparently not dealt with in the annual inspection was a levee in New Orleans East that was three feet short of its design height. Like the W-30 floodgate, the problem remained unaddressed when Katrina made landfall, even though Naomi, the Corps' Senior Project Manager, considered repair "vital" to protecting the city.[94] In addition, Corps rules and regulations for completed works require local sponsors, like the Orleans Levee District, to fix defects promptly.[95] Finally, the Corps' rules on levees require local sponsors to ensure that "No trees exist, the roots of which might extend under the wall and offer accelerated seepage paths."[96] However, one of the forensic teams investigating the levees' failure, and Corps officials, found trees growing along the 17th Street and London Avenue Canals.[97] In spite of the major defects requiring repairs, the Orleans Levee District's Chief Engineer said he expected the district to get "an outstanding review in regards to the maintenance of the levees" from the 2005 inspection.[98]

The Committee learned during its investigation that the 17th Street and London Avenue Canal floodwalls weren't part of the 2005 inspection because they were inaccessible by car. It appears likely that they were never inspected by the Corps after construction was finished in the early 1990s,[99] partially because the floodwalls abutted private property, which made them difficult, but certainly not impossible, to access.[100] It seems likely that the only physical inspections they received would have been conducted by Orleans Levee District personnel mowing the grass, making visual inspections, and identifying problems like holes dug by wild animals, significant erosion, etc. The personnel responsible for this work received no specialized training on care or inspection of levees and floodwalls,[101] and supporting documentation of these inspections comprised nothing more than worker timesheets indicating the work conducted, such as mowing the grass, the location of the work, and the hours spent doing the job.[102]

When asked who was responsible for fixing problems once they were identified, Orleans Levee District leadership explained that there was an undocumented understanding that "major" problems would be brought to the attention of the Corps and "minor" problems would remain the responsibility of levee district personnel.[103] However, and as noted by the Orleans Levee District Chief Engineer, Stevan Spencer, the district's total in-house, engineering expertise amounted to three engineers[104] – a level of expertise not on par with the challenges posed by the hurricane protection system within the jurisdiction of the Orleans Levee District.

The only other inspection the Orleans Levee District claims to have made of the levees was a field survey of floodwall heights every two to three years to check for subsidence.[105] If the Orleans Levee District did, in fact, conduct these surveys, it did not identify the severity of the subsidence along the 17th Street and London Avenue Canals documented by the Corps' forensic team.[106] The Orleans Levee District certainly did not conduct any structural analysis of the floodwalls; nevertheless, when asked by the Committee about the quality of the Orleans Levee District's operations and maintenance regime over the years, Colletti said that the Corps "felt that they've done an outstanding job."[107]

The Orleans Levee District's O&M practices and the passive oversight by the Corps did not meet what experts consider to be the standard of care for a flood control system like the Lake Pontchartrain Project. For example, in a letter to the Committee, Dr. Ernst G. Frankel of the Massachusetts Institute of Technology explained that visual surveys are not sufficient because potentially catastrophic voids can occur well below the surface of the levees. To expose internal degradation, holes must be drilled in the levees to retrieve core samples for analysis. Acoustic equipment can be used to scan the density of material layers at various depths.[108] No entity conducted such an analysis of the New Orleans flood-control structures,[109] nor were efforts made by the Levee District to obtain equipment to improve its inspection regime.[110] Professor Frankel added that inspection of levees below the waterline was also necessary to detect hidden threats to their integrity. The Orleans Levee District's simple visual inspections failed in this respect as well.

Lack of Coordination with the Sewerage and Water Board of New Orleans

Because New Orleans and surrounding parishes are below sea level and ringed by levees, rain and flood waters that enter must be pumped out. The Sewerage and Water Board of New Orleans (the Water Board) has the responsibility for maintaining a system of pumps and canals for this purpose. (The Water Board also runs the municipal water and sewer systems.) Floodwalls along two of these drainage, or outfall, canals sustained major breaches – the 17th Street and London Avenue Canals. However, the Orleans Levee District and the Corps, at least to the extent the Corps had not turned over the entire project to the local sponsor, are responsible for the floodwalls that line these canals.

In the aftermath of Katrina, the New Orleans *Times-Picayune* newspaper reported that six months before Katrina, several residents near the 17th Street Canal told the Water Board that they had found water in their yards.[111] (A similar story was carried by National Public Radio.)[112] Following the *Times Picayune* report, the Water Board conducted an inquiry into these allegations and concluded that the water reported by these property owners was coming from a water-service line and not from the canal. This conclusion was documented in a letter from the Water Board to the *Times-Picayune* and provided to the Committee.[113]

The 17th Street Canal floodwall broke within several hundred feet of where the water seepage was reported. The Committee was not able to independently confirm either the news reports or the Water Board's explanation. However, it is clear that the Water Board had no plan in place or arrangement with either the Corps or the Orleans Levee District to address this sort of situation. The Water Board's Executive Director, Marcia St. Martin, explained how her organization dealt with such situations:

> What we do is if a person says that there's water that's ponding in front of my house, we look to see whether or not a Board asset, which is the water meter, has a defect or a leak. If we determine it has a defect or a leak, we repair it. If we determine it's not coming from the Board's asset, we say to the customer, "It has to be a private property leak and you need to seek the services of a plumber."[114]

The Corps has relied on local residents to inform it about these types of problems, but had no public outreach program to urge residents to do so.[115] When the Corps did receive reports of seepage or other issues, it had no process to formally document and address the issues.[116] Likewise, the Orleans Levee District had no plan to reach out or communicate with residents to encourage the identification or the sharing of reports of leakage or other problems.[117]

Emergency Response

Louisiana law requires levee districts to have emergency plans. The Orleans Levee District had such a plan, but the plan did not contemplate repairing major breaches like those experienced along the 17th Street and London Avenue Canals.[118] Instead, the levee district assumed that, consistent with the informal distinction it used in classifying O&M problems – that minor problems were its responsibility and major problems were the Corps' responsibility – fixing any breach in the system would be the Corps' responsibility because it would be "major."[119] The Corps, meanwhile, was under the impression that the Lake Pontchartrain Project had been turned over to the levee district and so it was the levee district's responsibility to be the first responders for any emergency, regardless of the size.[120] The conflicting expectations resulted in a breakdown in the preparation for and response to Katrina among all involved – the Corps, the LA DOTD, and the Orleans Levee District.

At the Committee's December 15, 2005 hearing, "Hurricane Katrina: Who's in Charge of the New Orleans Levees?" the parties involved had no agreement on emergency responsibilities. Chairman Susan Collins asked the witnesses – Colonel Wagenaar, head of the Corps' New Orleans District; Preau, LA DOTD's Assistant Secretary for the Office of Public Works; and James Huey, former President of the Orleans Levee Board on August 29, 2005 – about their responsibilities. Chairman Collins received three different answers:

> **Colonel Wagenaar** (Corps of Engineers): Senator, my original thought was that it was the Orleans Levee District.[121]

> **Mr. Preau** (Louisiana Department of Transportation and Development): Originally, levee districts are supposed to be first responders on situations like this. If it is beyond their control, beyond their resources, then it would move up to the state level to take over. I think it was beyond the state's resources at that point. We looked towards the federal government, who had a lot more resources than we did, and who we've relied upon in the past to do major repairs. If you read the project agreements, most major repairs are to be undertaken by the Corps of Engineers on federal projects.[122]

> **Mr. Huey** (former President, Orleans Levee Board): First of all, it is unequivocally, I would say, the Corps of Engineers.[123]

U.S. Army Corps of Engineers Plans and Preparations

The Corps eventually assumed responsibility on September 1 – three days after the storm – for closing the 17th Street Canal and London Avenue Canal breaches, but institutional confusion over who was in charge and inadequate preparations delayed its taking the lead on repairs. On the morning of Katrina's landfall, August 29, as explained to the Committee, Colonel Wagenaar was under the impression that the Orleans Levee District was responsible for the Lake Pontchartrain Project and for responding to emergencies.[124] Consistent with this understanding, Colonel Wagenaar explained to the Committee that his command did not pre-position personnel to survey possible breaches or material to fill a possible breach beyond what was already available through the Corps' routine operations.[125] Moreover, the Corps did not have any standing contracts with contractors to respond to an emergency situation.[126]

The Corps' New Orleans District did not suffer from a lack of available emergency plans, though it is unclear whether any were complete, ready for implementation, or followed. For example, the New Orleans District had an Emergency Operations Plan and an accompanying letter of July 2005 from Colonel Wagenaar affirming that the plan was in effect should it be needed; but, when asked whether the Corps' New Orleans District followed the Emergency Operations Plan when it responded to Katrina, he responded, "Yeah. I mean, probably was. I don't know."[127]

The District had other plans as well. Versions of an "All Hazards Contingency Plan," a "Continuity of Operations Plan," a "Catastrophic Disaster Response Plan" and various versions of an unwatering plan[128] for removing floodwater from the city were all provided to the Committee in response to its document requests for any emergency plans in effect on August 23. The Corps' Emergency Manager in New Orleans explained that the Corps was considering combining the plans or perhaps shortening them. He said that the District was asking questions like, "Do we go from flood plan to hurricane plan to all hazards plan? Does it become too cumbersome? Should we have smaller plans so people actually read them? I think we were moving back to a specific hurricane plan."[129] It does not appear that any of the plans were complete, let alone followed.

In Colonel Wagenaar's defense, the Mississippi Valley Division's Hurricane Contingency Plan (Contingency Plan) contemplated a hurricane of Katrina's strength hitting the city and rendering the New Orleans District a victim, incapable of executing Corps missions or obligations under the assurance agreements for the Lake Pontchartrain Project, the National Response Plan (NRP) or the Flood Control Act.[130] The Contingency Plan called on other Corps districts within the Mississippi Valley Division like St. Louis, Vicksburg, and Memphis to carry out the New Orleans District's missions.[131] For example, the Contingency Plan stated that the Corps' St. Louis District would perform civil-works missions, which include project inspections, emergency repair of damaged facilities, and any Flood Act activities.[132] Despite the decision by Colonel Wagenaar to evacuate his personnel before landfall in accordance with the plan, there appears to have been confusion and delay in pre-positioning the resources of the other districts or reassigning the New Orleans district's responsibilities to the other districts within the Mississippi Valley Division. In fact, the commander of the Mississippi River Division did not issue the order implementing the Contingency Plan until September 3, nearly five days after the storm and two days after the Corps took control of the repair efforts along the 17th Street Canal and London Avenue Canal.[133]

Closing the Breaches – Conflict and Confusion

With Katrina approaching, and even though the Contingency Plan provided that his district be considered a victim of the storm, Colonel Wagenaar chose to personally wait out the hurricane with a small staff in the New Orleans District's hurricane bunker. On the morning of August 29, Colonel Wagenaar said he was notified about possible breaches as early as 5 a.m.[134] Around 2 or 3 p.m., after the weather calmed, he tried to make his way to the 17th Street Canal by four-wheel drive vehicle: no helicopters were immediately available, and no pre-storm efforts had been made to secure one.[135] Because of damage to the area, Colonel Wagenaar was only able to reach the intersection of I-10 and I-610, just north of Metairie Cemetery and just a few blocks east of the 17th Street Canal, where he was able to view the flooding first hand. He saw:

> people everywhere, and then we saw the water, and the water was – all you could see were the trees sticking out of the water, so I knew that – I mean, that's probably 10 or 15 feet of water. … I knew we had a problem. This water had to come from somewhere. I didn't know where, but I knew that we had a problem.[136]

Throughout the previous night and the following day, Colonel Wagenaar encountered difficulties with communications. His satellite phone worked sporadically and e-mail became inoperable when the servers shut down.[137] However, Colonel Wagenaar was able to send an e-mail later Monday evening after his failed attempt to reach the 17th Street

Canal to his commander at the Mississippi Valley Division. He informed Brigadier General Robert Crear that he had seen "15+ feet of water" and that there were unofficial reports that more than 40,000 homes were underwater in East Orleans and St. Bernard Parishes.[138] Colonel Wagenaar had no dedicated communications with the Orleans Levee District, the LA DOTD or even the Coast Guard. In fact, Colonel Wagenaar was unaware that the Coast Guard was flying missions over the city on August 29 – "The first time I knew they flew over the city was when I got back [to the District office] and was watching the news [video footage of the flooding] and going, 'Where the hell did that come from?'"[139]

At about 7:15 the next morning, August 30, Colonel Wagenaar sent two members of his staff to assess the breaches.[140] Though the Corps believed that the levee districts would be the first responders for any breaches,[141] Colonel Wagenaar proceeded to discuss ways to repair the floodwall breaches with the New Orleans District's Chief of Engineering. Any plans that were discussed were hampered by not having materials, personnel, or aircraft pre-positioned to survey the damage and make repairs.[142] Colonel Wagenaar was not able to carry out an air survey of the New Orleans area until late Tuesday morning.[143]

Also on Tuesday and carrying over to Wednesday, LA DOTD employees surveyed the breaches and began working with the West Jefferson Levee District – a neighboring levee district, not directly impacted by the flooding, that had volunteered material and personnel to help – and whatever Orleans Levee District personnel were available to devise a way to close the breaches. They generally agreed upon a plan to dump as much broken-up concrete as possible into the holes in the floodwalls.[144] The Corps' personnel who were able to make it to the scene believed it would be more efficient to drive sheet pile (long steel sheets) across the mouth of the canal itself to prevent more water from entering the canal and making its way through the breaches.[145] The levee districts, the LA DOTD, and the Water Board opposed closing off the canal and insisted on moving forward with their original plan, which included building a road to access the breaches to dump the concrete. Colonel Wagenaar was asked about the disagreement:

> Who was doing it, who was in charge, you know, and what parish was what and who could build what road and what trucks could be used and what equipment could be used, you know. … I mean, the issue was, is the. … [West Jefferson] Levee District had like five trucks, dump trucks and an excavator. And here we bring in a contractor that's ready to go that's got 20 trucks. … I mean, we're bringing federal contractors – we're bringing the federal government to bear on the problem. And they [the West Jefferson Levee District] were like, "Well, you can't do that, that's our road." They were working on building this

road back there. "Well, you can't" – you know, "We're building the road, you can't do that." … I mean, all – pretty much a turf war almost. … And it just got to the point where, you know, we were mobilizing contractors . . . and they wouldn't let us operate on the bridge [the Hammond Highway Bridge]. Mike Stack [with LA DOTD] and – you know, Giuseppe [with the West Jefferson Levee District] blocked some of our equipment from moving with his vehicles.[146]

This disagreement illustrated the overall confusion among federal, state, and local entities over who was responsible for the Lake Pontchartrain Project. As mentioned above, Colonel Wagenaar thought the levee districts were responsible for the repairs,[147] but the Orleans Levee District did not have the personnel or the material available to address the situation. The leadership vacuum was filled by LA DOTD personnel who assumed command of the initial repair efforts.[148] That effort, too, proved inadequate, at least according to Colonel Wagenaar, who thought it was best that the Corps take over[149] – "[W]e had a bunch of dysfunctional stuff going on out there, and we figured if we didn't do it and take over and marshal federal resources at this problem, that we'd be here for quite a while trying to fix this hole."[150]

The levee districts and the LA DOTD personnel on the scene did not agree with Colonel Wagenaar's decision, so ultimately, on Thursday, September 1, LA DOTD Secretary Johnny Bradberry, and the Corps' Director of Civil Works, Major General Don Riley, resolved the dispute, concluding that the repair effort would be a Corps-directed operation.[151] Colonel Wagenaar explained that, in pressing for control of the repair effort, he was relying on the Corps' authority under the Flood Act, an authority the Corps had regardless of who was in charge of the Lake Pontchartrain Project, to act independently of the assurance agreements and any action the Corps had taken to turn over the floodwalls to the Orleans Levee District for O&M.[152] When General Crear issued his order implementing the Mississippi Valley Division's Hurricane Contingency Plan on September 3, he, too, cited the Corps' Flood Act authority as the basis to "provide critical emergency support to the people of the affected areas."[153]

Conclusion

Resolving the dispute over who was in charge of the repair effort and the full-scale efforts to fill the breaches took three days. No such dispute should have occurred, and resolution should not have taken so long. Responsibilities among the levee districts, the LA DOTD, and the Corps should have been understood and documented. An interagency emergency response plan should have been in effect. The Corps should have pre-positioned personnel and material from either the New Orleans District, or the other districts within the Mississippi Valley Division and identified in the Division's Hurricane Contingency Plan, to assess and repair immediate problems. In the end, neither the Corps, the LA DOTD, nor the levee districts had any plan in place, nor had they determined or planned in advance who would be responsible for, and have the assets nearby, to address a major breach of the levees or floodwalls.

---

1 U.S. Army Corps of Engineers, Interagency Performance Evaluation Task Force, Performance Evaluation Plan and Interim Status, *Report 2 of a Series*, Mar. 10, 2006, pp. IV–1 through IV–39 [hereinafter IPET, *Report 2 of a Series*].

2 Testimony of Max Hearn, Director, Orleans Levee District, LA, before the U.S. Senate, Committee on Homeland Security and Governmental Affairs, hearing on *Hurricane Katrina: Who's in Charge of the New Orleans Levees?*, Dec. 15, 2005.

3 U.S. Library of Congress, Congressional Research Service, *The Civil Works Program of the Army Corps of Engineers: A Primer*, by Nicole T. Carter and Betsy A. Cody, Dec. 9, 2005, p. 3 [hereinafter CRS, *The Civil Works Program*].

4 CRS, *The Civil Works Program*, p. 1.

5 Congressional direction usually comes through authorization legislation like the Water Resources Development Act, which Congress tends to consider every two years, or as part of the annual appropriations process. U.S. Library of Congress. Congressional Research Service, *Water Resources Development Act (WRDA): Army Corps of Engineers Authorization Issues in the 109th Congress*, by Nicole T. Carter. Mar. 13, 2006, p. 2.

6 Supplemental Agreement Between the United States of America and the Orleans Levee District for Local Cooperation at Lake Pontchartrain and Vicinity High Level Plan, June 21, 1985. This agreement included a common O&M provision that could be found in other assurance agreements. It stated, in part, that the Orleans Levee District was required to "[m]aintain and operate all features of the project in accord with regulations prescribed by the Secretary of the Army, including levees, floodgates and approach channels, drainage structures, drainage ditches, or canals, floodwalls, and stoplog structures."

7 U.S. Army Corps of Engineers, New Orleans District, "Mississippi Valley Division Work Flood Control Act Project Maps," last updated on June 10, 1998. http://www.mvn.usace.army.mil/eng2/edsd/proj_maps/pmap_fcp2.htm. Accessed on Apr. 11, 2006.

8 U.S. Army Corps of Engineers, New Orleans District, "Who We Are." http://www.mvn.usace.mil/pao/whoweare/index/asp. Accessed on Apr. 21, 2006.

9 Committee staff interview of Col. Richard Wagenaar, District Commander, New Orleans District, U.S. Army Corps of Engineers, conducted on Nov. 15, 2005, transcript p. 16.

10 A common provision in the assurance agreements for the Lake Pontchartrain Project required the Orleans Levee District to "[m]aintain and operate all features of the project in accordance with regulations prescribed by the Secretary of the Army, including levees, floodgates and approach channels." Various Assurance Agreements for Lake Pontchartrain and Vicinity Protection Project, dates vary. Provided to Committee; Written Statement of Anu K. Mittal, Director, Natural Resources and Environment, Government Accountability Office, for the U.S. Senate, Committee on Homeland Security and Governmental Affairs, hearing on *Hurricane Katrina: Who's in Charge of the New Orleans Levees?*, Dec. 15, 2005, pp. 1-2.

11 33 C.F.R. § 208.10.

12 Committee staff interview of Jerry Colletti, U.S. Army, Operations Manager for Completed Works, New Orleans District, U.S. Army Corps of Engineers, conducted on Nov. 22, 2005, transcript, pp. 19-27.

13 33 U.S.C. § 701n.

14 Col. Wagenaar interview, Nov. 15, 2005, pp. 114-115; U.S. Army Corps of Engineers, Mississippi Valley Division, Operations Order 01-05 (Hurricane Katrina), *MVD Hurricane Contigency Plan 18 May 2005*, Sept. 3, 2005. Provided to Committee [hereinafter, Mississippi Valley Division, Operations Order 01-05, Sept. 3, 2005].

15 Edmond J. Preau, Jr., Association of Levee Boards of Louisiana, "The History and Function of Louisiana's Levee Boards," PowerPoint presentation. http://www.albl.org/workshops.php. Accessed on Mar. 22, 2005.

16 La. R.S. 38:306.

17 La. R.S. 38:306 (B).

18 La. R.S. 38:306 (B) and (C).

19 La. R.S. 38:301 (B).

20 La. Const. Art. VI, § 39; La. Const. Art. VI, § 41; La. R.S. 38:307; La. R.S. 38:335.

21 La. R.S. 38:306 (B). As of June 2005, there were estimates that the casino lease generated about 20 percent of the Orleans Levee District's revenue. Orleans Levee District, Basic Financial Statement, June 30, 2005, p. ix; Committee staff interview of Steven Spencer, U.S. Army, Chief Engineer, Orleans Levee District, U. S. Army Corps of Engineers, conducted on Nov. 14, 2005, transcript pp. 123-124.

22 Orleans Levee District, Basic Financial Statements, June 30, 2005, p. 14. Provided to Committee.

23 Orleans Levee District, Basic Financial Statements, June 30, 2005, p. 16. Provided to Committee.

24 Committee staff interview of James Huey, former President, Orleans Levee Board, LA, conducted on Nov. 29, 2005, transcript p. 19.

25 Orleans Levee District, Basic Financial Statements, June 30, 2005, p. 14. *See also:* Testimony of James Huey, former President, Orleans Levee Board, LA, before the U.S. Senate, Committee on Homeland Security and Governmental Affairs, hearing on *Hurricane Katrina: Who's in Charge of the New Orleans Levees?*, Dec. 15, 2005 ("[Senator Collins:] … And, in fact, when we reviewed the minutes of the board's meetings, we found that a majority of the meeting time was actually spent discussing these commercial enterprises, whether it was the licensing of the casino or the operations of the airport or the marinas or the commercial leases with the karate business and the beauty shop and the restaurants. Do you think it is appropriate for the board to be involved in these commercial activities? Do those business activities detract time and attention from what is truly the mission of the board, which is to ensure the safety, the maintenance, the operations of the levees?" "[Mr. Huey:] Yes and no.").

26 Spencer interview, Nov. 14, 2005, pp. 66-67; Committee staff interview of Max Hearn, Executive Director, Orleans Levee District, LA, conducted Nov. 14, 2005, transcript pp. 59-60.

27 Hearn interview, Nov. 14, 2005, pp. 59-60.

28 Spencer interview, Nov. 14, 2005, p. 67.

29 Spencer interview, Nov. 14, 2005, p. 67.

30 Money for the fountain came from the levee district's capital projects fund which was supported by funding from property taxes. Frank Donze, "Lakeside Legacy Lives," New Orleans *Times-Picayune*, July 12, 2004, Metro, p. 1.

31 Hearn interview, Nov. 14, 2005, pp. 31-32.

32 Orleans Levee District, Minutes of Joint Finance and Planning, Engineering and Construction Committee Meeting, July 5, 2005, p. 2. Provided to Committee [hereinafter Orleans Levee District, Minutes of Committee Meeting, July 5, 2005].

33 Orleans Levee District, Minutes of Committee Meeting, July 5, 2005, p. 2.

34 Hearn, Senate Committee hearing, Dec. 15, 2005.

35 Orleans Levee District, Minutes of Committee Meeting, July 5, 2005, p. 2.

36 Huey interview, Nov. 29, 2005, pp. 30-33.

37 La. R.S. 38:306.

38 La. R.S. 38:213; Committee staff interview of Edmund Preau, Assistant Secretary, Public Works and Inter-Modal Transportation, Louisiana Department of Transportation and Development, conducted on Nov. 17, 2005, transcript p. 38.

39 La. R.S. 38:301(B).

40 Huey interview, Nov. 29 2005, pp. 100-105; Association of Levee Boards of Louisiana, "About ALBL." http://www.albl.org/about_us.php. Accessed on Mar. 22, 2006.

41 Huey interview, Nov. 29, 2005, p. 101.

42 Huey interview, Nov. 29, 2005, p. 104.

43 Huey interview, Nov. 29, 2005, p. 105; Hearn interview, Nov. 14, 2005, pp. 44-45.

44 La. R.S. 38:319.

45 Preau interview, Nov. 17, 2005, pp. 41-42.

46 Preau interview, Nov. 17, 2005, pp. 41-42.

47 Preau interview, Nov. 17, 2005, pp. 44-45.

48 Louisiana Office of Homeland Security and Emergency Preparedness, *Emergency Operations Plan*, Apr. 2005, p. ESF-3-1 [hereinafter *Louisiana Emergency Operations Plan*, Apr. 2005].

49 *Louisiana Emergency Operations Plan*, Apr. 2005, p. ESF–3–2.

50 *Louisiana Emergency Operations Plan*, Apr. 2005, p. ESF–3–2.

51 Preau interview, Nov. 17, 2005, pp. 91-92.

52 Written Statement of Mittal, Senate Committee on Environment and Public Works hearing, Nov. 9, 2005, p. 2.

53 Written Statement of Mittal, Senate Committee on Environment and Public Works hearing, Nov. 9, 2005, "What GAO Found," and pp. 1-2.

54 Written Statement of Mittal, Senate Committee on Environment and Public Works hearing, Nov. 9, 2005, p. 4.

55 IPET, *Report 2 of a Series*, p. IV–13.

56 Though the level of protection that the Lake Pontchartrain Project was supposed to provide did not change once it was underway, the plan for building the project did. The initial design authorized in 1965 followed what was called the "Barrier Plan." This plan called for the construction of a barrier on the eastern edge of Lake Pontchartrain for the purpose of preventing storm surges from entering Lake Pontchartrain. This would have lowered the threat of storm surges rising in the lake and threatening the lake front levees and the communities they protected. However, in 1977, a federal district court issued a ruling enjoining the Crops from pursuing the Barrier Plan until the Corps addressed problems with the project's environmental impact statement. *Source:* Written Statement of Mittal, Senate Committee on Environment and Public Works hearing, Nov. 9, 2005, pp. 1-9.

In 1984, the Corps commissioned a reevaluation study to analyze the continued feasibility of the Barrier Plan and whether the Corps should opt for an alternative design called the "High-Level Plan." The High-Level Plan, which had been considered in 1965 and rejected, called for raising and strengthening the levees and floodwalls that would be affected by a storm surge from Lake Pontchartrain rather than building the barrier. The reevaluation study concluded that the High-Level Plan was more feasible and served as the impetus for changing the design of the project. *Source:* Written Statement of Mittal, Senate Committee hearing, Nov. 9, 2005, pp. 1-9.

During Katrina, there were several breaches along levees and floodwalls constructed as part of the High-Level Plan. In the aftermath of Katrina, there has been debate as to whether the Barrier Plan would have been more effective in fending off the storm surge. The position of the Corps of Engineers is that plans would have provided the same level of protection because they both would have been designed to the same standard – the Standard Project Hurricane – and would not have materially altered the outcome. As explained in recent Senate testimony by Daniel Hitchings, an official with the Mississippi Valley Division of the Corps:

   I would also like to correct one statement that was made earlier, I believe was related to the previously proposed Barrier Plan, in that it would not have made any difference. That statement I believe is accurate, but it is accurate not because it was an inadequate plan, and not because the storms would have gone up the MRGO [Mississippi River – Gulf Outlet – a shipping channel that connects to the Gulf of Mexico] anyway. It would not have made a difference because its authorized level was still the standard project hurricane.

Source: Testimony of Daniel Hitchings, Director, Task Force HOPE, U.S. Army Corps of Engineers, before the U.S. Senate, Committee on Environment and Public Works, hearing to "Evaluate the Degree to Which the Preliminary Findings on the Failure of the Levees are Being Incorporated Into the Restoration of Hurricane Protection," Nov. 17, 2005.

57 Lt. Gen. Carl Strock, Commander, U.S. Army Corps of Engineers, "Defense Department Special Briefing on Efforts to Mitigate Infrastructure Damage from Hurricane Katrina," press briefing, Sept. 2, 2005.

58 U.S. Army Corps of Engineers, New Orleans District, Project Fact Sheet, "Lake Pontchartrain, LA. and Vicinity Hurricane Protection Project, St. Bernard, Orleans, Jefferson, and St. Charles Parishes, LA." Last updated on May, 23, 2005. http://www.mvn.usace.army.mil/pao/response/HURPROJ.asp?prj=lkpon1. Accessed on Apr. 11, 2006.

59 Committee staff interview of Alfred Naomi, Senior Project Manager, Lake Pontchartrain and Vicinity Hurricane Protection Project, New Orleans District, U.S. Army Corps of Engineers, conducted on Nov. 16, 2005, transcript pp. 50-51.

60 Army Corps of Engineers, New Orleans District, "N.O. hurricane bridge contract awarded, Corps, Levee Board will floodproof two bridges in Gentilly," news release, Dec. 19, 2001.

61 Army Corps of Engineers, New Orleans District, "Cross Bayou Drainage Structure to reduce flooding in St. Charles Parish," news release, May 27, 2003.

62 Army Corps of Engineers, New Orleans District, "Filmore Bridge in Gentilly will reopen on Friday, Aug. 22. Mirabeau Bridge is closing Wednesday, Aug. 27 for hurricane floodproofing," news release, Aug. 21, 2003.

63 Col. Wagenaar interview, Nov. 15, 2005, p. 94 ("But, I mean, I knew that the city – I'd been briefed, you know, hurricane protection-wise, that generally the city could take a fast-moving Category 3, and anything else could be catastrophic. I mean, I was told that.").

64 Committee staff interview of Michael Lowe, Emergency Manager, New Orleans District, U.S. Army Corps of Engineers, conducted on Nov. 16, 2005, transcript p. 74 ("My understanding of the level of protection in the New Orleans area is a fast moving Category 3 hurricane on the Saffir-Simpson Scale. How I came about saying that, or my understanding of that, is mainly what I hear from the project manager who is deal – working on the hurricane systems."). See also: Lowe interview, Nov. 16, 2005, pp. 73-77, 81.

65 U.S. Army Corps of Engineers, New Orleans District, Un-Watering Plan, Greater Metropolitan Area, New Orleans, Louisiana, Aug. 18, 2000, p. 3. See also: U.S. Army Corps of Engineers, Hurricane Protection, Louisiana, June 28, 2002, p. 9.

66 Colletti interview, Nov. 22, 2005, transcript p. 22.

67 Committee staff interview of Wilson Shaffer, Ph.D., Chief, Evaluations Branch, National Weather Service, conducted on Feb. 24, 2005, transcript pp. 38-41.

68 Shaffer interview, Feb. 24, 2006, pp. 37, 61-67.

69 Written Statement of Roy K. Dokka, Ph.D., Director, Louisiana Spatial Reference Center and Center for GeoInformatics, Louisiana State University, for the U.S. House of Representatives, Committee on Transportation and Infrastructure, Subcommittee on Water Resources and Environment, hearing on Expert Views on Hurricane and Flood Protection and Water Resources Planning for a Rebuilt Gulf Coast, Oct. 20, 2005, pp. 2-6.

70 IPET, Report 2 of a Series, p. I–2

71 Mittal, Senate Committee hearing, Dec. 15, 2005; Naomi interview, Nov. 16, 2005, pp. 18-21.

72 33 C.F.R. § 208.10(a)(1).

73 33 C.F.R. § 208.10.

74 Naomi interview, Nov. 16, 2005, pp. 19-20. Mr. Hearn agreed that the Lake Pontchartrain Project had not been formally turned over to the Orleans Levee District. Hearn interview, Nov. 14, 2005, p. 76.

75 Colletti interview, Nov. 22, 2005, pp. 11-16.

76 Colletti interview, Nov. 22, 2005, pp. 11-16.

77 Colletti interview, Nov. 22, 2005, pp. 16-17.

78 Colletti interview, Nov. 22, 2005, p. 17.

79 In preparation for the Committee's December 15 hearing on the levee system, the Committee asked GAO to investigate whether parts or all of the Lake Pontchartrain Project had been turned over. The GAO report stated that, according to the Corps and the task force charged with rebuilding the levee system –Task Force Guardian, all but three sections of the Lake Pontchartrain Project in New Orleans had been turned over to the Orleans Levee District. The criteria used by the Corps and Task Force Guardian to make this determination were: (1) if the project unit was at its design height; (2) whether portions of the project was being operated and maintained by the Orleans Levee District; and (3) if the portion of the project had passed the annual inspection for completed works in accordance with Corps regulations. Neither the Corps nor Task Force Guardian relied on the turnover letters to make their determinations. Moreover, the assessment by the Corps and Task Force Guardian as to whether the Orleans Levee District was conducting daily O&M ignored the

fact that the levee district had obligations to look after flood control projects under state law separate and apart from the its role as a local sponsor under the assurance agreements. Source: Written Statement of Mittal, Senate Committee hearing, Dec. 15, 2005. Moreover, reliance on whether a part of the project passed the annual inspection is a canard. As discussed in more detail below, the Corps gave the Orleans Levee District passing grades for the annual inspections even though the inspections did not involve geotechnical studies assessing the strength of the system, analyses of whether the project was at its design height, or even stopping at the floodwalls along the 17th Street and London Avenue Canals because they were inaccessible by car, the mode of transportation generally used for the annual inspections. Moreover, the passing grades were given even though there were known vulnerabilities in direct contravention of the Corps' rules and regulations: vegetation was growing along the floodwalls, a railroad gate near the Inter Harbor Navigation Canal remained broken for more than a year, and there was a levee well below its design height in New Orleans East.

80 33 C.F.R. § 208.10(a)(6).

81 Colletti interview, Nov. 22, 2005, pp. 50-53.

82 33 C.F.R. § 208.10(a)(10).

83 Colletti interview, Nov. 22, 2005, p. 68.

84 Spencer interview, Nov. 17, 2005, pp. 10-12.

85 Hearn interview, Nov. 14, 2005, p. 43.

86 Spencer interview, Nov. 17, 2005, pp. 10-12.

87 Colletti interview, Nov. 22, 2005, pp. 20-28.

88 Huey interview, Nov. 29, 2005, pp. 108-109.

89 Orleans Levee District, Minutes of Joint Finance and Planning, Engineering and Construction Committee Meeting, Apr. 5, 2005, p. 6. Provided to Committee [hereinafter Orleans Levee District, Minutes of Committee Meeting, Apr. 5, 2005].

90 Huey interview, Nov. 29, 2005, p. 58.

91 Orleans Levee District, Minutes of Committee Meeting, Apr. 5, 2005, p. 6.

92 La. R.S. 38:2211.

93 Huey interview, Nov. 28, 2005, pp. 64-65.

94 Orleans Levee District, Minutes of Committee Meeting, Mar. 5, 2005, p. 7.

95 33 C.F.R. § 208.10(a)(8).

96 33 C.F.R. § 208.10(c)(1)(iii).

97 U.S. House, Select Bipartisan Committee to Investigate the Preparation for and Response to Hurricane Katrina, *A Failure of Initiative,* Washington: Government Printing Office, 2006, p. 92. *See also:* Ann Carrns, "Long Before Flood, New Orleans System was Prime for Leaks," *The Wall Street Journal*, Nov. 25, 2005, p. A1.

98 Orleans Levee Board, Minutes of Joint Finance and Planning, Engineering and Construction Committee, May 31, 2005, p. 6. Provided to Committee.

99 Colletti interview, Nov. 22, 2005, pp. 82-83; Hearn interview, Nov. 14, 2005, p. 48; Huey interview, Nov. 29, 2005, p. 107.

100 Colletti interview, Nov. 22, 2005, pp. 40-43.

101 Hearn interview, Nov. 14, 2005, pp. 45-48.

102 Hearn interview, Dec. 8, 2005, pp. 3-8.

103 Hearn interview, Nov. 14, 2005, pp. 11-12.

104 Spencer interview, Nov. 14, 2005, p. 45.

105 Hearn, Senate Committee hearing, Dec. 15, 2005.

106 Hearn, Senate Committee hearing, Dec. 15, 2005. *See also:* IPET, *Report 2 of a Series*, pp. I–2, III–6, III–26 through III–29, III–32 through III–40.

107 Testimony of Jerry Colletti, Manager for Completed Works, New Orleans District, U.S. Army Corps of Engineers, before the U.S. Senate, Committee on Homeland Security and Governmental Affairs, hearing on *Hurricane Katrina: Who's in Charge of the New Orleans Levees?*, Dec. 15, 2005.

108 Ernst G. Frankel, letter to the Honorable Senator Susan Collins, Dec. 14. 2005.

109 Committee staff interview of Jerry Colletti, Manager for Completed Works, New Orleans District, U.S. Army Corps of Engineers, conducted on Dec. 9, 2005, transcript p. 20.

110 Hearn, Senate Committee hearing, Dec. 15, 2005.

111 Bob Marshall, "Levee leaks reported to S&WB a year ago; Lakeview residents' complaints fell between the cracks," New Orleans *Times-Picayune*, Nov. 18, 2005, National, p. 1.

112 Frank Langfitt, "Residents Say Levee Leaked Months Before Katrina," National Public Radio, Nov. 22, 2005. http://www.npr.org/templates/story/story.php?storyId=5022074. Accessed on Apr. 10, 2006.

113 Marcia A. St. Martin, letter to the editor, New Orleans *Times-Picayune*, Dec. 5, 2005. Provided to Committee.

114 Committee staff interview of Marcia A. St. Martin, Executive Director, New Orleans Sewerage and Water Board, conducted on, Dec. 9, 2005, transcript p. 32.

115 Colletti interview, Nov. 22, 2005, pp. 59-60.

116 Colletti interview, Nov. 22, 2005, pp. 56-57.

117 Huey interview, Nov. 28, 2005, pp. 118-119.

118 Hearn interview, Nov. 14, 2005, pp. 54-55.

119 Spencer interview, Nov. 14, 2005, p. 56.

120 Testimony of Col. Richard Wagenaar, Chief Engineer, New Orleans District, Army Corps of Engineers, before the U.S. Senate, Committee on Homeland Security and Governmental Affairs, hearing on *Hurricane Katrina: Who's in Charge of the New Orleans Levees?*, Dec. 15, 2005.

121 Col. Wagenaar, Senate Committee hearing, Dec. 15, 2005.

122 Testimony of Edmond Preau, Assistant Secretary, Public Works and Intermodal Transportation, Louisiana Department of Transportation and Development, before the U.S. Senate, Committee on Homeland Security and Governmental Affairs, hearing on *Hurricane Katrina: Who's in Charge of the New Orleans Levees?*, Dec. 15, 2005.

123 Huey, Senate Committee hearing, Dec. 15, 2005.

124 Col. Wagenaar, Senate Committee hearing, Dec. 15, 2005.

125 Col. Wagenaar interview, Nov. 15, 2005 pp. 77-78; Lowe interview, Nov. 16, 2005, pp. 18-19.

126 Lowe interview, Nov. 16, 2005, p. 90.

127 Col. Wagenaar interview, Nov. 15, 2005, pp. 14-15.

128 Col. Richard P. Wagenaar, memorandum on the New Orleans District, Emergency Operations Plan, July, 2005; U.S. Army Corps of Engineers, *New Orleans District, All Hazards Contingency Plan*, August, 2005; U.S. Army Corps of Engineers, New Orleans District, *Continuity of Operations Plan* (Redacted); U.S. Army Corps of Engineers, New Orleans District, *Catastrophic Disaster Response Plan*. Since 2000, the New Orleans District has recognized that New Orleans would sustain extensive flooding in a major hurricane and has had a plan, known as the Un-watering Plan, to evacuate water from the city and surrounding parishes in such an event. U.S. Army Corps of Engineers, New Orleans District, *Un-Watering Plan, Greater Metropolitan Area, New Orleans, Louisiana*, Aug. 18, 2000.

129 Lowe interview, Nov. 16, 2005, p. 29.

130 U.S. Army Corps of Engineers, Mississippi Valley Division, *Hurricane Contingency Plan (CONPLAN)*, May 18, 2005, p. 1. Provided to Committee [hereinafter Mississippi Valley Division, *CONPLAN*].

131 Mississippi Valley Division, *CONPLAN*, pp. 3-4.

132 Mississippi Valley Division, *CONPLAN*, p. 4.

133 Mississippi Valley Division, Operations Order 01-05, Sept. 3, 2005.

134 Col. Wagenaar interview, Nov. 15, 2005, p. 52.

135 Col. Wagenaar interview, Nov. 15, 2005, pp. 54, 61-63.

136 Col. Wagenaar interview, Nov. 15, 2005, p. 57.

137 Col. Wagenaar interview, Nov. 15, 2005, p. 28.

138 Col. Richard P. Wagenaar, e-mail to Robert Crear, SITREP:29 August 2005, Aug. 29, 2005, 7:49 p.m. Provided to Committee.

139 Col. Wagenaar interview, Nov. 15, 2005, p. 69.

140 Col. Wagenaar interview, Nov. 15, 2005, pp. 62-63.

141 Col. Wagenaar interview, Nov. 15, 2005, p. 113; Lowe interview, Nov. 16, 2005, p. 5.

142 Col. Wagenaar interview, Nov. 15, 2005, pp. 77, 80-81.

143 Col. Wagenaar interview, Nov. 15, 2005, pp. 62-65.

144 Committee staff interview of Michael J. Stack, Engineer, New Orleans District Design Water Resources, Louisiana Department of Transportation and Development, conducted on Nov. 17, 2005; Hearn interview, Nov. 14, 2005, pp. 71-73.

145 Committee staff interview of Kenneth Crumholt, Resident Engineer, Construction Division, West Bank Hurricane Protection Project, New Orleans District, U.S. Army Corps of Engineers and Richard Pinner, Section Chief, Geotech Branch, Engineering Division, New Orleans District, U.S. Army Corps of Engineers, conducted on Nov. 16, 2005, transcript pp. 23-24.

146 Col. Wagenaar interview, Nov. 15, 2005, pp. 105-107. *See also:* Col. Wagenaar interview, Nov. 15, 2005, pp. 122-123

("I mean, so – I mean, just all these data points, and I'm relatively – I'm new, I mean, I don't – I mean, this whole Levee District/Sewer and Water Board concept was relatively new to me. But just these data points of: Who is in charge? I mean, where's the Parish President? Where is the Mayor? And then the State, 'Well they work for DOTD.' I'm like, 'Okay. Who is in charge?' That was my view. I still have that view. I mean, so at some point, I mean -- you know, there is an old local – there is an old saying in the Army: When in charge, take charge. And I know I was in charge of the Corps of Engineers, the district, so I mean, at some point, you know, you've got to make stuff happen. Because this was a bad situation.").

147 Col. Wagenaar interview, Nov. 15, 2005, pp. 111-113 ("I knew the levee districts were in charge, it was their project, that they had the responsibility to do the repair. … It's just a general operating principle here. I mean, we don't have O&M of these projects once we turn them over. … But no, I knew it was their job to fix these originally. We tended to want to let it go that way until – I mean, until it was obvious that it needed federal involvement.").

148 Hearn interview, Nov. 14, 2005, pp. 71-73.

149 Col. Wagenaar interview, Nov. 15, 2005, pp. 111-113.

150 Col. Wagenaar interview, Nov. 15, 2005, pp. 104-105.

151 Col. Wagenaar interview, Nov. 15, 2005, pp. 104-108.

152 Col. Wagenaar interview, Nov. 15, 2005, p. 114.

153 Mississippi Valley Division, Operations Order 01-05, Sept. 3, 2005.

Dry vs. wet: canal breach,
New Orleans
Commercial satellite imagery provided
by GeoEye, www.geoeye.com

"The New Orleans Scenario": State and Local Preparations

Preparations by Louisiana State Government

The seeds of Louisiana's failure to prepare were sown long before Hurricane Katrina approached the state. As detailed in other chapters,[1] Louisiana had been on notice of its vulnerability to catastrophic hurricanes for decades, but over the long term had never fully upgraded its emergency-response systems to the level necessary to protect its citizens from those events. Based on its own models and experience, it could have foreseen the inadequacy of many of its plans and resources, particularly its plans to evacuate people without personal transportation and the staffing of its state emergency-preparedness office.[2]

In short, when it received warnings of Katrina's approach, the state had reason to know that its emergency response systems were likely to fail, however diligently they were implemented. And fail they did.

The National Response Plan (NRP) makes clear that responsibility for seeing that state response systems function properly lies with the Governor. The plan states, "As a State's Chief Executive, the Governor is responsible for the safety and welfare of the people of that State. … [and] for coordinating State resources to address the full spectrum of actions … to prepare for [and] respond to … natural disasters."[3]

The days before Katrina struck showed a state striving to mount an effective response with stretched resources. State officials had monitored the storm since its birth as a tropical depression.[4] Terry Ryder, Governor Blanco's Executive Counsel, had standing instructions from the Governor to notify her whenever he learned of a tropical depression. Ryder informed Governor Blanco about Katrina sometime prior to August 26, before the storm even had an official name.[5] The State's Department of Wildlife and Fisheries (W&F), its lead agency for search and rescue, also started preparing early, reviewing emergency-preparedness manuals and "boarding up the hatches, bringing in the equipment that needed to be brought in and immovable equipment we tied down as best we could."[6]

The Louisiana Office of Homeland Security and Emergency Preparedness (LOHSEP) activated a team to coordinate emergency response at 2 p.m., Thursday, August 25.[7] Twenty minutes later, LOHSEP issued an electronic alert warning state agencies and parish emergency officials about the approach of Katrina.[8] The LOHSEP coordination team began working with state and local officials to organize evacuations and sheltering of special-needs patients.[9] The Louisiana National Guard also began preparations on Thursday afternoon, positioning fuel tankers at Hammond Airport, about 30 miles northwest of New Orleans.[10]

Preparations accelerated on Friday, August 26. At 11:30 that morning, a senior official of Louisiana Department of Transportation and Development (DOTD), the agency with primary responsibility for transportation out of a disaster area for people in need, instructed agency staff to prepare and be on standby for hurricane response.[11]

Shortly before 4 p.m. on Friday, Major General Bennett Landreneau's Chief of Staff, Colonel Steven Dabadie of the Louisiana National Guard, notified senior Guard officials of a conference call to take place at 6 p.m. to review support requirements and activate the Guard's response operations.[12] At 4 p.m., Governor Blanco declared a state of emergency, placing the National Guard and state agencies on full alert.[13] At 5 p.m., the first conference call of the southeast Louisiana Hurricane Task Force, which included emergency-management officials from all the southeastern parishes, took place.[14] The Louisiana State Police gave notice that it would open its Emergency Operations Center (EOC) the next morning.[15] LOHSEP said that it would activate its Emergency Operations Center (EOC) in Baton Rouge at "Level III," implying full staffing, by early Saturday morning.[16]

On Saturday, August 27, the Louisiana National Guard set up its Joint Operations Center (JOC) at Jackson Barracks, its permanent state headquarters in the Lower Ninth Ward of New Orleans; established backup JOCs at two other bases; and began coordinating the arrival of advance National Guard parties from Florida and Texas.[17] Governor Blanco, who had set up her base of operations at the LOHSEP EOC Saturday morning, spent the weekend commuting between the LOHSEP EOC and the Greater New Orleans EOC to meet with public officials and the press and survey the evacuations.[18]

On both Saturday and Sunday, Governor Blanco sent letters to President Bush requesting federal assistance under the Federal Stafford Act[19] and its implementing regulations.[20] Those authorities contain separate provisions for "emergencies" and "natural disasters;" the latter are considered more significant and justify higher levels of assistance. The letter sent on Saturday requested that the President issue an "emergency" declaration, specifying $9 million in anticipated support needs.[21] It also contained some notable errors, such as omitting Orleans Parish from the list of parishes wishing to receive federal assistance.[22]

With predictions of increasingly severe storm damage, the letter sent on Sunday sought an "expedited natural disaster" declaration, with a request of $130 million in aid; this letter corrected the previous letter and added Orleans Parish to the list of parishes needing assistance.[23]

Both letters included statements, required for funding under the Stafford Act, that the Governor anticipated an incident "of such severity and magnitude that effective response is beyond the capabilities of the state and affected local governments."[24] Neither letter asked for transportation assets to assist in the evacuation, or for any other assets that might be useful for emergency response. President Bush promptly issued both of the requested declarations.[25]

While Governor Blanco's letter sounded a note of urgency, she and other state officials missed other critical opportunities over the weekend to convey the extent to which the state's response capabilities were likely to be overwhelmed. Most important, in a video teleconference of federal, state, and local officials on Saturday, Colonel Jeff Smith, Acting Deputy Director of LOHSEP, answered a question from former FEMA Director Michael Brown of whether the state had "any unmet needs, anything that we're not getting to you that you need" in the negative:

> **Mike Brown:** Any questions? Colonel, do you have any unmet needs, anything that we're not getting to you that you need or —
>
> **Colonel Smith:** Mike, no. [Inaudible] resources that are en route, and it looks like those resources that are en route are going to – to be a good first shot. Naturally, once we get into this thing, you know, neck deep here, unfortunately, or deeper, I'm sure that things are going to come up that maybe some of even our best planners hadn't even thought about. So I think flexibility is going to be the key.[26]

Brown later testified that he was seeking information from the state on what it needed at that moment only,[27] and Colonel Smith later tried to downplay the significance of his response.[28] But his remarks reflect an underestimation of the state's level of unpreparedness. Given the frenzied efforts over the weekend to get hold of the incomplete drafts of plans under development from the Hurricane Pam exercise, it should not have taken Louisiana's "best planners" to identify shortfalls in ongoing preparations.

Throughout the weekend, LOHSEP invoked its standard operating procedures, which included a lengthy checklist for coordination of state agencies, non-governmental organizations (such as the American Red Cross), and parish authorities.[29] State Police, National Guard, and DOTD officials concentrated on evacuation efforts, which began in earnest on Saturday morning.[30] Evacuation using contraflow – a system that expedites evacuation by converting incoming highway lanes to outgoing – began at 4 p.m. on Saturday. New Orleans Mayor Ray Nagin issued his mandatory evacuation order, with the Governor's support, on Sunday morning. (See Chapter 16 for more about pre-storm evacuations.)

As Katrina approached the Gulf Coast, the National Guard had 5,700 troops in Louisiana, most of whom were reservists; by landfall all would be on alert. Additional members of the Louisiana Guard were due to return from Iraq shortly.[31] (Previously, the Louisiana National Guard's largest hurricane-related deployment – 2,500 troops – was prior to Hurricane Andrew in 1992.)[32]

Lining up at the Superdome
FEMA photo

By Sunday afternoon, General Landreneau, Adjutant General of Louisiana, established a command structure for the National Guard's response activities (Task Force Pelican) with General Gary Jones in charge. General Landreneau placed five separate task forces under General Jones' command to address each major responsibility: aviation, security, search and rescue, logistics, and engineering.[33]

The National Guard's emergency-response plan requires key troops to be positioned at key locations around the state. It can be amended as needed by fragmentary orders or "fragos."[34] As National Weather Service (NWS) reports provided updated guidance on Katrina's severity and direction, "constant order production FRAGO mode" kept refining the pre-positioning of Guard units.[35] The Guard also actively staged vehicles and aviation assets to be ready for search-and-rescue activities, movements of commodities, and evacuation assistance.[36]

Preparations by Local Government

Preparing the Superdome as a Special-Needs Shelter

The City of New Orleans has used the Superdome as a special-needs shelter since Hurricane Georges in 1998.[37] The Louisiana Department of Social Services has been responsible for running special-needs shelters in eight of nine defined regions in the state,[38] but the City of New Orleans Health Department has run the special-needs shelter in the Superdome[39] as part of its general municipal responsibilities. The city agreed to the special-needs eligibility criteria in the Region 1 plan for Orleans, Jefferson, St. Bernard, and Plaquemines Parishes.[40]

The Region 1 special-needs shelter plan defines special-needs people as those who are able to provide for their own basic care but have a medical condition requiring occasional assistance, intermittent access to electricity for medical treatments, or refrigeration of medications. The plan warns that "It is not appropriate to admit individuals to these shelters who require constant care or who require constant electricity to support machines necessary to maintain their life."[41]

Neither the Health Department nor any other city agency had compiled a comprehensive list of Orleans Parish (which has the same boundaries as the City of New Orleans) residents who qualified with special needs.[42] Planning at the special-needs shelter was determined by previous experience and Superdome capacity. The Region 1 plan called for preparations to receive 200 to 400 special-needs individuals.[43] Each was expected to bring a caregiver, meaning a total of 400 to 800 individuals.[44] Hurricanes Isidore and Ivan had each resulted in about 30 special-needs people, plus caregivers.[45] As a result of the plan, past experience, and the capacity of the Superdome, Dr. Kevin Stephens, Director of the City's Health Department, set up the shelter to accommodate approximately 1,200, comprising 600 special-needs people plus their caregivers.[46]

Preferring that special-needs patients leave the city entirely, the city issued a press release directing such individuals to two special-needs shelters outside New Orleans; toll-free telephone numbers were provided so citizens could call for information.[47] In a second release, Mayor Nagin added that the Superdome would not open for special-needs individuals until 8 a.m. on Sunday.[48] The release instructed special-needs citizens to call a special telephone number to confirm their eligibility.[49]

Both press releases added: "Anyone planning to spend time in a shelter should bring three to four days' worth of food, sleeping gear, and medical supplies including oxygen, medicine, and batteries for any necessary devices."[50] The releases also gave contact information for six ambulance services for non-emergency transportation.[51]

Pre-landfall preparations included staffing the shelter and checking inventory to determine what supplies would be needed.[52]

Throughout Saturday, City Health Department officials staged supplies – including cots, water, food, medications, phone lines, and generators – at the Superdome.[53] Provisions included ready-to-eat foods like peanut butter, crackers, water, juice, and cereal; the sheriff's department agreed to provide hot food as long as was feasible.[54]

Saturday evening, city and state personnel operated a 10-line telephone triage service for potential special-needs individuals,[55] guiding callers to the Superdome for evaluation, hospitals, or other destinations.[56] Callers with transportation were encouraged to leave the city.[57]

At about 6 p.m., Saturday, Stewart Simonson, Assistant Secretary for Public Health Emergency Preparedness, U.S. Department of Health and Human Services (HHS), called Dr. Stephens to see if he needed help. Dr. Stephens said he did not.[58]

At 8 a.m. on Sunday, the Superdome opened, as planned, for special-needs patients.[59]

Approximately 1,000 special-needs patients arrived throughout the day,[60] plus an undetermined number of caregivers. Colonel Pat Prechter, Deputy Commander of the National Guard's Louisiana Medical Command, noticed that some patients arriving in the shelter, following processing through registration and triage, required dialysis or constant oxygen, which would normally disqualify them as candidates for special-needs shelter admission.[61] Following this observation, and at the city's request, National Guard medical officials began assisting with triage.[62] Of the approximately 1,000 individuals who arrived at the special-needs shelter, 450 to 500 of the most critical were evacuated[63] to a special-needs shelter in Baton Rouge.[64]

Despite the pre-staging of substantial assets, officials realized on Sunday that additional supplies were necessary.[65] The city provided more medical oxygen[66] and large quantities of other supplies ranging from saline solution to adult diapers.[67] When Simonson called again on Sunday, Dr. Stephens accepted the help,[68] which included a FEMA Disaster Medical Assistance Team (DMAT) and material from the HHS's Strategic National Stockpile of emergency medical supplies.[69] While FEMA was able to get military-style rations, water, and ice to the Superdome, the DMAT had to stop in Baton Rouge because the Texas State Police had denied two requests for police escorts; once in Louisiana, the team met worsening weather conditions.[70] The team didn't make it to the Superdome before landfall.

Preparing the Superdome as a Refuge of Last Resort

In prior hurricanes, the Superdome had served as a refuge for those needing to ride out the storm for a few hours before returning home.[71] During Katrina, thousands would stay for days.

The Superdome with its storm-damaged roof
U.S. Coast Guard photo

Long-Term Planning for the Superdome as a Shelter of Refuge or Last Resort

For at least three years before Katrina hit, the city had initiated critical measures to prepare the Superdome for longer stays, but failed to follow through. Long-term planning began with an effort to get more people out of the city in the first place to ease eventual demands on the Superdome.[72] Soon after his inauguration in 2002, Mayor Nagin unsuccessfully urged New Orleans and Louisiana's Congressional delegation to find a way to develop a $200 million light-rail network to evacuate the 100,000 city residents without their own means to leave.[73] City officials also worked throughout 2004 and 2005 to develop memoranda of understanding (MOUs) between the city and transportation providers, but those initiatives were not completed before Katrina. (See Chapter 16.)

Limited shelter space outside the city placed additional pressure on the Superdome as well. The American Red Cross decided not to set up shelters south of I-10, the east-west interstate running north of two-thirds of New Orleans, because they would have been too close to what the Red Cross deemed a flood zone.[74]

In 2004, recognizing the need for greater shelter capacity, Mayor Nagin requested $850,000 from the New Orleans Congressional delegation for "a study … to determine the feasibility of upgrading the Louisiana Superdome, or any other facility, to serve as a refuge of last resort."[75] The city made similar requests to the Department of Homeland Security (DHS) and the Federal Emergency Management Agency (FEMA) in 2005.[76] These funding requests were denied, although the record does not indicate why. The city did not appeal to the state because of the perception that the state lacked the capability to help, and the city was planning on upgrading the Superdome under FEMA – not state – regulations.[77] The upgrade would have taken at least two more years (and cost $7 million to $17 million).[78]

The City Prepares and Opens the Superdome as a Refuge of Last Resort

Fearing that announcing the Superdome's availability too early might dissuade citizens from leaving the city,[79] the city waited until Saturday to announce that the Superdome would open on Sunday as a refuge of last resort.[80] Since 2004's Hurricane Ivan, the city's plan has been to use Regional Transit Authority (RTA) buses to deliver those without transportation to the Superdome.[81] Bus service began on Sunday at noon.[82] City officials believe that the majority of the population at the Superdome before landfall had come by bus.[83]

By late Sunday evening, about 10,000 people had shown up at the Superdome.[84] The Louisiana National Guard had pre-positioned 900,000 Meals Ready to Eat (MREs) rations and water for its staff's needs (though most were ultimately given to the storm victims).[85] Officials realized that even that cache would need augmenting, and rushed out requests for 350,000 additional MREs from the city and additional food and water from the state.[86] FEMA and the Louisiana National Guard were able to move in more rations and water before landfall.[87]

No one had made arrangements for portable toilets, however.[88] Dr. Stephens tried to contract directly with individual vendors on Saturday, August 27, but could not reach them.[89] Several Superdome witnesses interviewed considered this omission a central failure in pre-storm planning.[90]

The large number of people at the Superdome also required a significant security presence.[91] The New Orleans Police Department (NOPD) under Deputy Chief Lonnie Swain, was in charge, first with 40 officers and later with double that number.[92] In support of NOPD, the Louisiana National Guard pre-positioned considerable troops to assist with security, as well as other missions, such as engineering functions, communications, and food distribution.[93]

Pre-landfall security mainly entailed screening walk-ins and bus arrivals, searching for weapons.[94] When the downpour started around 6 p.m. Sunday, security screening moved inside the building.[95] This made it harder for city police to ensure that no one entered with a weapon.[96] The National Guard also pre-positioned about 10 high-water vehicles at the Superdome.[97] These trucks proved invaluable after many of the streets around the Superdome flooded.

When the Superdome opened to the general population, National Guard officers there asked the LOHSEP and the Texas and Florida National Guards for additional support. NOPD Deputy Chief Swain also requested additional police officers to assist at the Superdome.[98]

At Katrina's landfall on Monday morning, August 29, the Superdome's special-needs shelter and refuge of last resort housed over 10,000 people who would ride out the storm in its cavernous interior.[99]

---

1 *See:* Chapter 6: Emergency Management: Louisiana, and Chapter 16: Pre-Storm Evacuations.

2 *See:* Chapter 6: Emergency Management: Louisiana.

3 U.S. Department of Homeland Security, *National Response Plan.* Washington: Government Printing Office, Dec. 2004, p. 8 [hereinafter *NRP*].

4 Committee staff interview of Col. Henry Whitehorn, Superintendent, Louisiana State Police and Deputy Secretary, Department of Public Safety Services and Corrections, LA, conducted on Nov. 29, 2005, transcript p. 25.

5 Louisiana Office of the Governor, Response to the U.S. Senate Committee on Homeland Security and Governmental Affairs Document and Information Request Dated October 7, 2005 and to the U.S. House of Representatives Select

Committee to Investigate the Preparation for and Response to Hurricane Katrina, Overview of Gov. Kathleen Babineaux Blanco's Actions in Preparation for and Response to Hurricane Katrina, Dec. 2, 2005, p. 1 [hereinafter Louisiana Office of the Governor, Governor's Timeline].

6 Committee staff interview of Sec. Dwight Landreneau, Louisiana Department of Wildlife and Fisheries, conducted on Nov. 30, 2005, transcript pp. 17-20.

7 Louisiana's Preparation and Response to Hurricane Katrina Integrated Timeline, p. 5. *See also*: Committee staff interview of Lt. Col. William Doran, Louisiana Air National Guard, Chief, Operations Division, Louisiana Office of Homeland Security and Emergency Preparedness (LOHSEP), conducted on Dec. 2, 2005, transcript p. 32.

8 LOHSEP Chronology, p. 4. Provided to Committee.

9 Lt. Col. Doran interview, Dec. 2, 2006, p. 32.

10 Louisiana National Guard, Timeline of Significant Events for Hurricane Katrina, Dec. 7, 2005, p. 2. Provided to Committee.

11 Louisiana Integrated Timeline, p. 6; LOHSEP, *Emergency Operations Plan*, Apr. 2005, p. ESF–1–1.

12 Louisiana Integrated Timeline, p. 7; Committee staff interview of Col. David Aycock, Operations Officer, Louisiana Army National Guard, conducted on Jan. 4, 2006, transcript pp. 91-93.

13 Committee staff interview Andy Kopplin, former Chief of Staff, Office of the Governor, LA, conducted on Jan. 6, 2006, transcript p. 30; Louisiana Office of the Governor, Governor's Timeline, p. 2.

14 Louisiana Integrated Timeline, p. 7. *See also:* Committee staff interview of Sean Fontenot, former Chief, Preparedness Division, LOHSEP, conducted on Jan. 10, 2006, transcript p. 109.

15 Louisiana Integrated Timeline, p. 7.

16 Louisiana Integrated Timeline, p. 8. LOHSEP activation levels range from I to V, with levels of staffing for emergencies increasing as the activation level decreases. Level III staffing consists of a "Crisis Action Team" on 24-hour call augmented with additional staffing as required. Louisiana Office of Emergency Preparedness, EOC Standard Operating Procedures, May 28, 2002, p. 2 [hereinafter LOEP, Standard Operating Procedures].

17 Committee staff interview of Col. Glenn Curtis, Chief of Staff, Louisiana Army National Guard, conducted on Dec. 6, 2005, transcript pp. 62-63; Col. Aycock interview, Jan. 4, 2006, pp. 95, 100-102, 105; LANG Timeline, p. 4.

18 Louisiana Office of the Governor, Governor's Timeline, p. 3; Committee staff interview of Denise Bottcher, Press Secretary, Office of the Governor, LA, conducted on Jan. 9, 2005, transcript pp. 46-53.

19 "Robert T. Stafford Disaster Relief and Emergency Assistance Act," (P.L. 93-288), 42 U.S.C. § 5121 *et seq.* [hereinafter "Stafford Act," 42 U.S.C. § 5121]. The purpose of the Act is "to provide an orderly and continuing means of assistance by the Federal Government to State and local governments in carrying out their responsibilities to alleviate the suffering and damage which result from such disasters." – Stafford Act, 42 U.S.C. § 5121(b).

20 44 C.F.R. §§ 206.31-206.48.

21 Gov. Kathleen Blanco, letter to President George Bush, Aug. 27, 2005. Provided to Committee. Neither this letter nor a similar letter of August 28, 2005, from Governor Blanco to the President requesting declaration of an "expedited major disaster" for Louisiana and raising the requested Stafford Act aid total to $130 million, requested federal military assistance.

22 Gov. Kathleen Blanco, letter to President George Bush, Aug. 27, 2005. Provided to Committee.

23 Gov. Kathleen Blanco, letter to President George Bush, Aug. 27, 2005. Provided to Committee.

24 Gov. Kathleen Blanco, letter to President George Bush, Sept. 20, 2005. Provided to Committee.

25 70 Fed. Reg. 53238 (Sept. 7, 2005) (Louisiana; Emergency and Related Determinations); 70 Fed. Reg. 53803 (Sept. 7, 2005) (Louisiana; Major Disaster and Related Determinations).

26 Michael Brown, Federal Emergency Management Agency (FEMA) Daily Video Teleconference, Aug. 28, 2005, transcript pp. 18-19. Provided to Committee.

27 Committee staff interview of Michael Brown, former Director, FEMA, conducted on Feb. 23, 2006, transcript pp. 62-67.

28 Col. Perry Jeff Smith (Ret.), affidavit, Feb. 8, 2006, p. 8. Provide to Committee.

29 Committee staff interview of James Ballow, Senior Operations Officer, LOHSEP, conducted on Jan. 4, 2006, transcript p. 6; LOEP, Standard Operating Procedures, EOC Hurricane/Major Event Checklist, pp. 1-10.

30 Louisiana Office of the Governor, Governor's Timeline, p. 2; Lt. Col. Doran interview, Dec. 2, 2005, p. 38.

31 Col. Curtis interview, Dec. 6, 2005, p. 60. Roughly 40 to 50 percent of Louisiana's National Guard troops were in Iraq at that time. *Source:* Testimony of Gov. Kathleen Blanco, Louisiana, before the U.S. Senate, Committee on Homeland Security and Governmental Affairs, hearing on *Hurricane Katrina: The Role of the Governors in Managing the Catastrophe*, Feb. 2, 2006; Committee staff interview of Col. FG Dowden, U.S. Marine Corps (Ret.), Regional Liaison, New Orleans Department of Homeland Security and Public Safety, LA, conducted on Nov. 11, 2005, transcript p. 91. On Saturday morning, Governor Blanco approved the first call up of 2,000 Guardsmen; by landfall, all 5,700 would be called up. *Source:* Louisiana Office of the Governor, Overview of Governor Kathleen Babineaux Blanco's Actions in Preparation

for and Response to Hurricane Katrina, pp. 5-6 (Dec. 2, 2005). A National Guard summary dated Sept. 1, 2005, indicated that the then current committed forces included 5,176 Louisiana Guard troops. The reason for the discrepancy between that figure and the 5,700 troops reported by the Governor as having been called up by August 29 is unknown. *Source:* Louisiana Office of the Governor, Governor's Timeline, pp. 5-6.

32 Committee staff interview of Lt. Col. Jacques Thibodeaux, Joint Director of Military Support to Civilian Authorities and Branch Chief, Louisiana National Guard, conducted on Dec. 6, 2005, transcript p. 68.

33 Committee staff interview of Brig. Gen. Gary Jones, Assistant Joint Forces Commander, Louisiana Army National Guard, conducted on Dec. 7, 2005, transcript pp. 5-6, 61-62.

34 Col. Curtis interview, Dec. 6, 2005, pp. 14-15.

35 Col. Curtis interview, Dec. 6, 2005, pp. 79-80.

36 Col. Curtis interview, Dec. 6, 2006, pp. 152-54 (stating that the Guard pre-deployed high water vehicles, boats, and aviation assets, including helicopters). Col. Curtis explained the potential use for these assets: "They're pre-positioned for whatever the mission becomes. I mean, it can be search and rescue, it can be, you know, commodities, delivering food and water, that type thing. It can be not search and rescue, but it can be evacuation where people are caught behind, you know, in high water that they can't drive out of and et cetera. And we'll drive in, pick them up and bring them out, which a lot of that happened." Col. Curtis interview, Dec. 6, 2006, p. 154.

37 Col. Pat Prechter, Louisiana National Guard Medical Command, recalls responding to the Superdome to help staff the Special Needs Shelter for Hurricane Georges [in 1998]. Committee staff interview of Col. Pat Prechter, State Chief Nurse, Louisiana Army National Guard and Deputy Commander, Louisiana Medical Command, conducted on Jan. 6, 2006, transcript p. 8.

38 Committee staff interview of Kitty Lapeyrolerie, Regional Manager, Louisiana Rehabilitative Services and Emergency Preparedness Coordinator, Louisiana Department of Social Services, conducted on Dec. 20, 2005, transcript pp. 51-52.

39 Committee staff interview of Avis Gray, Regional Administrator, Region I, Office of Public Health, Louisiana Department of Health and Hospitals, conducted on Dec. 8, 2005, transcript p. 48.

40 Committee interview of Kevin Stephens, M.D., Director, New Orleans Health Department, LA, conducted on Nov. 9, 2005, transcript p. 16. *See also:* City of New Orleans, *City of New Orleans Special Needs Shelter Plan*, Mar. 2003, p. 2 [hereinafter *Region 1 Plan*, Mar. 2003]

41 It should be noted that the plan's definition of "special needs" differs at the margins with other city and state officials' interpretations of the definition. For example, Dr. Stephens defined special needs patients as those "who require electricity on an intermittent basis for sustaining life – not a continuous basis – patients who require additional special care to sustain their life." *Source:* Dr. Stephens interview, Nov. 9, 2005, p. 6. Louisiana Secretary of Health and Hospitals Dr. Fred Cerise said: "Those shelters are for individuals who basically have special health care needs and are not – would not be adequately taken care of in the general shelters…people with chronic medical conditions. We see people that are on medications that would need assistance with that. We have people who are on oxygen at home and who would need some special assistance. People that may be on dialysis and so they would need a place to go and coordinate that care. So people that can take care of themselves at home but require some assistance." *Source:* Committee staff interview of Sec. Fred Cerise, M.D., Louisiana Department of Health and Hospitals, conducted on Dec. 7, 2005, transcript p. 16. A Region 1 official, Avis Gray, offered this definition: "Special needs population are those individuals that are at home and are able to be cared [for] at home but they have health care issues that maybe they can't go in a regular shelter. This could be a diabetic who can't medicate themselves or people with some respiratory who don't need continuous O2." *Source:* Gray interview, Dec. 8, 2005, p. 24.

42 Dr. Stephens interview, Nov. 9, 2005, p. 32.

43 Dr. Stephens interview, Nov. 9, 2005, pp. 46-47.

44 Contemplation of a caretaker accompanying each patient is found in: Written Statement of Kevin Stephens, M.D., Director, New Orleans Health Department, LA, for the U.S. Senate, Committee on Homeland Security and Governmental Affairs, hearing on *Hurricane Katrina: Challenges in a Catastrophe: Evacuating New Orleans in Advance of Hurricane Katrina*, Jan. 31, 2006, p.3; Gray interview, Dec. 8, 2005, p. 25; *Region 1 Plan*, Mar. 2003, p. 3.

45 Dr. Stephens interview, Nov. 9, 2005, p. 48.

46 Dr. Stephens interview, Nov. 9, 2005, pp. 46-49 ("I don't want to plan for 30 and 40 … and have six hundred show up, and then you're totally overwhelmed.").

47 City of New Orleans, Mayor's Press Office, "Mayor Nagin Urges Citizens to Prepare for Hurricane Katrina," press release, Aug. 27, 2005. Provided to Committee [hereinafter Mayor's Press Office, "Mayor Nagin Urges Citizens to Prepare for Hurricane Katrina."]. On Saturday, August 27, the State of Louisiana opened two special-needs shelters outside of the City of New Orleans, in Alexandria and Monroe. Louisiana Department of Health and Hospitals, timeline. Provided to Committee.

48 City of New Orleans, Mayor's Press Office, "Mayor Nagin Urges Citizens to Evacuate If Possible," press release, Aug. 27, 2005. Provided to Committee [hereinafter Mayor's Press Office, "Mayor Nagin Urges Citizens to Evacuate If Possible."].

49 Mayor's Press Office, "Mayor Nagin Urges Citizens to Evacuate If Possible."

50 Mayor's Press Office, "Mayor Nagin Urges Citizens to Prepare for Hurricane Katrina"; Mayor's Press Office, "Mayor Nagin Urges Citizens to Evacuate If Possible."

51 Mayor's Press Office, "Mayor Nagin Urges Citizens to Prepare for Hurricane Katrina"; Mayor's Press Office, "Mayor Nagin Urges Citizens to Evacuate If Possible."

52 Ninety-six hours prior to landfall of Hurricane Katrina, Dr. Stephens convened a staff meeting to create a preparations time line for the special-needs shelter at the Superdome. The staff reviewed the updated Region 1 Hurricane Plan and began an inventory of supplies the Department needed to operate the shelter. *Source*: Dr. Stephens interview, Nov. 9, 2005, pp. 11, 13-14. Staffing plans for the SNS included 50 Health Department employees, 25 to 30 personnel from Region 1, and approximately 200 National Guard medics and armed personnel for security. *Source*: Dr. Stephens interview, Nov. 9, 2005, p. 48. Col. Pat Prechter, Deputy Commander of the Guard's Louisiana Medical Command, was ordered to provide 71 medical personnel to the SNS beginning at 8 a.m. on Sunday, August 28. Source: Col. Prechter interview, Jan. 6, 2006, pp. 29-30. Col. Prechter provided the following break-down of LANG personnel assigned to the SNS: 41-42 from Medical Command (MedCom), 18 from the 159th Air Guard (medical unit), and 11-12 from Company A1-11. Source: Col. Prechter interview, Jan. 6, 2006, p. 28.

53 Dr. Stephens interview, Nov. 9, 2005, p. 30.

54 Dr. Stephens interview, Nov. 9, 2005, pp. 61-62. Kitty Lapeyrolerie, the Emergency Preparedness Coordinator for the Louisiana Department of Social Services, also noted that the city's prison was supposed to provide food for the Superdome's special-needs shelter and did so before landfall. As a result, the Louisiana Department of Social Service officials said they did not ask for more food, even after the Superdome was opened to the general population on Sunday, because they expected the prison to continue to provide food for the special-needs shelter. But the prison was ultimately flooded and thus unable to provide any more food after landfall. Lapeyrolerie interview, Dec. 20, 2005, pp. 103, 137.

55 Written Statement of Dr. Stephens, Senate Committee hearing, Jan. 31, 2005, p. 5.

56 Gray interview, Dec. 8, 2005, p. 168.

57 Gray interview, Dec. 8, 2005, pp. 97-98.

58 Committee staff interview of Stewart Simonson, Assistant Secretary, Office of Public Health and Emergency Preparedness, U.S. Department of Health and Human Services, conducted on Feb. 16, 2006, transcript pp. 37-38.

59 Written Statement of Dr. Stephens, Senate Committee hearing, Jan. 31, 2005, p. 5 (photo of white board). *See also*: Dr. Stephens interview, Nov. 9, 2005, pp. 59, 72. City and state personnel registered, triaged, and evaluated arrivals and a floor plan was developed to designate SNS areas for certain patients, such as asthmatic or congestive heart failure patients.

60 Dr. Stephens, Nov. 9, 2005, p. 67. The SNS plan didn't include sheltering nursing-home residents, who were supposed to be handled through nursing homes' evacuation plans. One nursing home sent a busload of residents without a staff manager to the Superdome. While wondering why the bus hadn't headed out of the city instead, the SNS staff accepted the people in view of the worsening weather. Committee staff interview of Irby Hornsby, former Special-Needs Shelter Manager, New Orleans Region, Louisiana Department of Social Services, conducted on Jan. 5, 2006, transcript pp. 21-22, 86-88.

61 Col. Prechter interview, Jan. 6, 2006, pp. 42-43. There appears to be confusion regarding whether dialysis patients would be admitted. According to a transcript of Mayor Nagin's press conference on August 28, the Mayor stated, "This morning, the Superdome has already opened for people with special needs. If you have a medical condition, if you're on dialysis or some other condition, we want you to expeditiously move to the Superdome." *Source*: "New Orleans Mayor, Louisiana Governor Hold Press Conference," CNN Breaking News, Aug. 28, 2005, 10 a.m. ET. http://transcripts.cnn.com/TRANSCRIPTS/0508/28/bn.04.html. Accessed on Apr. 11, 2005 [hereinafter "Mayor Nagin and Gov. Blanco Hold Press Conference" Aug. 28, 2005.]

62 Col. Prechter interview, Jan. 6, 2006, p. 40.

63 Dr. Stephens interview, Nov. 9, 2005, p. 70.

64 Written Statement of Dr. Stephens, Senate Committee hearing, Jan. 31, 2006, p. 5.

65 Col. Prechter interview, Jan. 6, 2006, p. 45.

66 Both Dr. Stephens and Col. Prechter noted the need for oxygen. Dr. Stephens interview, Nov. 9, 2005, pp. 65-67; Col. Prechter interview, Jan. 6, 2006, p. 43.

67 Col. Prechter interview, Jan. 6, 2006, p. 45.

68 Simonson interview, Feb. 16, 2006, p. 39.

69 Simonson interview, Feb. 16, 2006, pp. 39-40.

70 Simonson interview, Feb. 16, 2006, p. 59. With regard to the DMAT, Ronald Martin with FEMA/NDMS-1, noted that the Oklahoma DMAT, which reported to Houston, was dispatched from Houston to the Superdome of Sunday, August 28, but did not reach the Superdome until Monday night for a number of reasons: (1) Two requests to the Texas State Police to provide a police escort for the caravan were denied; (2) the Houston City Police, which provided escort after the Texas State Police did not, could only get the team as far as the interstate; (3) the Louisiana State Police escort, which picked up the caravan at the Louisiana state line, and the DMAT had to stop in Baton Rouge due to deteriorating weather conditions, including high winds. Committee staff interview of Ronald Martin, Deputy Commander, Management Support Team, National Disaster Medical System, FEMA, conducted on Feb. 13, 2006, transcript pp. 35-42.

71 Committee staff interview of Col. Terry Ebbert, U.S. Marine Corps (Ret.), Director, New Orleans Office of Homeland

Security, LA, conducted on Jan. 10, 2006, transcript pp. 8-9 (defining refuge of last resort as follows: "The refuge of last resort is a concept that we instituted full well knowing that we were going to have – all the studies showed us that we were not going to get everybody out of this town in the number of hours that we had, and there were going to be naysayers who would wait, expecting a change, and the eleven hour when it didn't change, lives would be at risk. So the concept of refuge of last resort is a facility that will insure that when the eye of the hurricane passes and the storm goes away, you will be alive. That's the only integral important item that the refuge of last resort brings with it."); Col. Ebbert interview, Jan. 10, 2006, p. 9 (distinguishing the refuge of last resort from a shelter: "It was not a shelter, we weren't going to provide services. We knew we couldn't do that. But the refuge of last resort was set up to insure that those people were in a location where they would survive the water and the wind and the brunt of the hurricane. And we knew that if we had a bad hurricane, we were going to have a second phase of evacuation, that was a known fact.").

72 Evacuation needs to be the number one priority in advance of a catastrophic hurricane. Col. Ebbert interview, Jan. 10, 2006, pp. 41-43 ("evacuation is your number one priority and is where you need to concentrate your efforts because everybody that's out of here is a nonproblem for us.").

73 Mayor C. Ray Nagin, letter to the Honorable Sen. Mary Landrieu, Oct. 1, 2002, p. 2 (recognizing that as many as 100,000 people in New Orleans "have no means of transportation, rendering it impossible for them to evacuate the City" and requesting $200 million to develop a light rail system, which the Mayor deemed "necessary to facilitate the evacuation"); Garey Forster, e-mail to Julie Harris and others, "Landrieu Letter: Isidore," Sept. 29, 2002, 6:15 p.m. (urging staff to draft a letter on behalf of Mayor Nagin to Sen. Landrieu to reflect the points he made to her and Sen. Jim Jeffords, including the need for "Light Rail to exit 100k people."). The Committee does not know whether the city received responses to these letters.

74 Col. Ebbert interview, Jan. 10, 2006, p. 34 (stating that one of the "specific problems" with sheltering that hindered the city was "the abandonment at the federal and state level of sheltering south of I-10," which he described as "a pretty arbitrary decision."). Additional shelters inside New Orleans and just outside of it would have eased the strain at the Superdome, but it is not clear that those additional shelters would have fared much better in Katrina or some other catastrophic hurricane approaching New Orleans. On the one hand, Col. Ebbert claimed "there are buildings [south of I-10] that can sustain Cat 4 and Cat 5 hurricane hits." *Source:* Col. Ebbert interview, Jan. 10, 2006, p. 34 ("All you have to do is look around the city and know that the engineering is pretty sufficient in some of these."). On the other hand, Col. Ebbert could not say with confidence that the Mississippi River levees would hold in subsequent storms, thereby jeopardizing certain structures which the city might consider as potential shelters or refuges, such as the Morial Convention Center. *Source:* Col. Ebbert interview, Jan. 10, 2006, p. 41 ("Mother Nature could sink the Titanic, it can do away with most anything we can design."). *See also:* Committee staff interview of Kay Wilkins, Chief Executive Officer, Southeast Louisiana Chapter, American Red Cross, conducted on Dec. 20, 2005, transcript p. 14-18.

75 Col. Ebbert interview, Jan. 10, 2006, pp. 52-53 ("the lesson I took from Pam is that we had to have a way to shelter people, and we did."). In October 2004, the Mayor sent letters to the City's Congressional delegation: "New Orleans faces the reality that it is impossible to conduct a mandatory evacuation in advance of a Category 3, 4 or 5 hurricane. Even under the best conditions evacuation will leave at least 150,000 people in harm's way. Currently, no city shelters are designated for a major hurricane and neither the Red Cross nor any other agency provides shelters." *Source:* Mayor C. Ray Nagin, letters to Honorable Mary Landrieu, Honorable John Breaux, Honorable David Vitter, Honorable Richard Baker, Honorable Rodney M. Alexander, Honorable William J. Jefferson, Honorable Jim McCrery, Honorable Chris John, and Honorable W.J. "Billy" Tauzin, Oct. 27, 2004 [hereinafter Mayor Nagin, letters to Louisiana Congressional delegation, Oct. 27, 2004]. The City's Office of Homeland Security and Public Safety projected that the study would cost $850,000. *Source:* City of New Orleans, FY2006 Funding Request to Congress, Emergency Response Shelter/Plan Homeland Security Appropriations. Provided to Committee (requesting FY06 funding of $850,000 for "final feasibility and planning and design efforts for upgrading the Louisiana Superdome, or any other facility, to serve as a refuge of last resort for major hurricane and other natural and manmade disaster events"). *See also:* Col. Ebbert interview, Jan. 10, 2006, pp. 53-68 (stating that the city requested this funding from the federal government); Mayor Nagin, letters to Louisiana Congressional delegation, Oct. 27, 2004 ("The study should include, but not be limited to: upgrading and elevation of back up power systems with capacity to power all internal systems, structural hardening for Category 3 or higher winds, upgrade of elevated enclosed HVAC systems, upgrade of water and sewer systems to be able to function with loss of city water and power, expanded elevated parking to house larger city emergency vehicles, expanded storage areas to hold stockpiled emergency equipment and supplies, other security, pumping command and control requirements."); Brenda Hatfield, e-mail to Col. Terry Ebbert, Sept. 28, 2004, 9:42 a.m. (discussing effort to seek "funding to retrofit the Super Dome as a shelter of last resort").

76 City of New Orleans, FY2006 Funding Request to Congress, Emergency Response Shelter/Plan Homeland Security Appropriations. Provided to Committee; Col. Ebbert interview, Jan. 10, 2006, pp. 53-58, 65.

77 Col. Ebbert interview, Jan. 10, 2006, pp. 62-63 ("The state really doesn't have any – that's a commission. They barely live off of the maintenance that they make on the lease on that building, so the state didn't have any capability to do that, and they're not going to have any capability to do it in the future because we're going to rebuild it under FEMA regulations. Again, this is where you get caught up. Why do you have a system that hampers me from improving the capability and spending millions of dollars fixing the Superdome, but I can't bring it up one dollar better than it was before on the 28th of August? And that's what – you know, that still doesn't make any sense to me. And I can cite you fifteen examples of that. You want me to put my same old broken radio system in because I'm going to spend millions of dollars on an old radio system rather than putting millions of dollars into a new radio system.").

78 Col. Ebbert interview, Jan. 10, 2006, p. 66 (stating that implementation of the plan would have cost between $7 million and $17 million.). Since it would have taken at least two years to enact the appropriation for the $850,000 that would

have funded the plan, work on the implementation of the could not have begun until that time.

79 Col. Ebbert interview, Jan. 10, 2006, pp. 63, 79 ("if you opened that Dome up on Saturday, you'd have had 65,000 people in there and nobody would have gotten on the highways and left.").

80 Committee staff interview of Sally Forman, Communications Director, Office of the Mayor, City of New Orleans, LA, conducted on Jan. 10, 2006, transcript pp. 28-29, 31. According to the press releases that accompanied the 1 p.m. and 5 p.m. press conferences on Saturday, August 27, 2005, and the internal talking points for both press conferences, the only notations regarding the Superdome refer to it as a special needs shelter and do not mention that it might or will be opening at any point as a refuge of last resort. *Source:* Mayor's Press Office, "Mayor Nagin Urges Citizens to Prepare for Hurricane Katrina"; Mayor's Press Office, "Mayor Nagin urges Citizens to Evacuate if Possible"; City of New Orleans, Mayor's Press Office, "Event: Katrina Update, Talking Points Follow," Aug. 27, 2005, 1 p.m. Provided to Committee; City of New Orleans, Mayor's Press Office, "Event: Katrina Update, Talking Points Follow," Aug. 27, 2005, 5 p.m. Provided to Committee. During the press conference on Sunday morning, August 28, Mayor Nagin announced: "This morning, the Superdome has already opened for people with special needs. If you have a medical condition, if you're on dialysis or some other condition, we want you to expeditiously move to the Superdome. At noon today, the Superdome will then be opened up as a refuge of last resort, where we will start to take citizens that cannot evacuate." *Source:* "Mayor Nagin and Gov. Blanco Hold Press Conference" Aug. 28, 2005.

81 Col. Ebbert interview, Jan. 10, 2006, p. 81; Committee staff interview of Terry Tullier, former Deputy Director, New Orleans Fire Department and Director, New Orleans Office of Emergency Preparedness, LA, conducted on Nov. 22, 2005, transcript pp. 44-45 (stating that – dating back to Ivan – the city planned to stage buses "to move people to the Superdome and potentially even to the Convention Center, although I had some serious misgivings about whether or not that building would hold up.").

82 "Mayor Nagin and Gov. Blanco Hold Press Conference" Aug. 28, 2005.

83 Col. Ebbert interview, Jan. 10, 2006, pp. 81-82.

84 Committee staff interview of Lonnie Swain, Assistant Superintendent, New Orleans Police Department, LA, conducted on Nov. 9, 2005, transcript p. 39 ("Dome management was able to tell us that we now have everybody sitting in these seats, we don't have any more people standing outside, we don't have any more around the concourse, standing or whatever, we have about 10,000 people.").

85 The Louisiana National Guard had pre-positioned stock to be able to provide "some limited support to some special needs people. But the bulk of what [the National Guard] had there was for our troops. Brig. Gen. Jones interview, Dec. 7, 2005, pp. 86-87.

86 When NOPD Deputy Chief Lonnie Swain arrived at the Superdome on Sunday, he immediately called the City's Office of Emergency Preparedness and requested food and water, which Deputy Chief Swain said the Louisiana National Guard ultimately delivered before landfall. Swain interview, Nov. 9, 2005, pp. 44-47; Col. Ebbert interview, Jan. 10, 2006, p. 113 ("We made a request [for food and water], and the National Guard brought it in when they came and brought in both water and food into the Dome the night before the storm.").

87 Louisiana National Guard officials stated that their requests for additional food and water before landfall were met. *Source:* Committee staff interview of Col. Douglas Mouton, Commander, 225th Engineering Group, Louisiana National Guard, conducted on Dec. 1, 2005, transcript pp. 69-74 ("There was a quantity of food and water. I can't tell you exactly how much it was. … I believe it got there by 18-wheeler, and it was unloaded by the combination of guardsmen and Superdome management personnel."). Gen. Jones quickly put out a call for MREs and found enough from nearby National Guard contingency stocks to supply people with two servings a day until Tuesday afternoon. *Source:* Brig. Gen. Jones interview, Dec. 7, 2005, p. 88. LANG Col. Glenn Curtis recalled that on "Sunday we (LANG) delivered 9,792 MREs and 13,440 one-liter bottles of water of our contingency stock to the Superdome in support of shelter operations." *Source:* Col. Curtis interview, Dec. 6, 2005, pp. 128-130.

88 Dr. Stephens interview, Nov. 9. 2005, p. 94; Hornsby interview, Jan. 5, 2006, p. 31.

89 Dr. Stephens interview, Nov. 9, 2005, p. 94.

90 Swain interview, Nov. 9, 2005, pp. 112-113, 127; Testimony of Marty J. Bahamonde, Regional Director, External Affairs, Region I, FEMA, before the U.S. Senate, Committee on Homeland Security and Governmental Affairs, hearing on *Hurricane Katrina: How is FEMA Performing Its Mission at This Stage of Recovery?*, October 20, 2005 ("Imagine no toilet facilities for 25,000 confined people for five days. Women and children were forced to live outside in 95-degree heat because of the horrid smell and conditions inside. Hallways and corridors were used as toilets, trash was everywhere, and amongst it all children – thousands of them. It was sad, it was inhumane, it was heart-breaking, and it was so wrong.").

91 Col. Ebbert interview, Jan. 10, 2006, p. 114 ("Most of the security operation [at the Superdome] deal with the refuge of last resort.").

92 Swain interview, Nov. 9, 2005, p. 32; Col. Ebbert interview, Jan. 10, 2006, pp. 112-113. The officers commanding Louisiana National Guard (LANG) troops at the Superdome before and after landfall agreed that NOPD was the lead agency at the Superdome, and LANG was at the Superdome to support NOPD. Col. Mouton interview, Dec. 1, 2005, p. 64 ("I clearly saw our role to support the New Orleans Police Department, because this was a civil authority's shelter and we were augmenting their efforts."); Committee staff interview of Col. Thomas Beron, Commander, 61st Troop Command, Louisiana Army National Guard, conducted on Dec. 1, 2005, transcript, p. 65 ("That is the relationship … that we support the NOPD there.").

93 Committee staff interview of Col. Douglas Mouton, Commander, 225th Engineering Group, Louisiana National

Guard, and Col. Thomas Beron, Commander, 61st Troop Command, Louisiana National Guard, conducted on Dec. 1, 2005, transcript pp. 48, 64-65; Committee staff interview of Col. Steve Dabadie, former Chief of Staff, Louisiana National Guard, conducted on Jan.12, 2006, transcript pp. 67-68; Col. Ebbert interview, Jan. 10, 2006, pp. 113-117. Ultimately, the total LANG pre-landfall presence comprised 71 medical officers, 140 Army National Guard, 140 Air National Guard, and 46 Special Response Team members. *Source:* Col. Mouton interview, Dec. 1, 2005, p. 48-50 ("For the security missions, we have a requirement to provide soldiers to the Superdome, about 140, from the 527th engineering battalion … the most important place I felt I needed to be was in the Dome because that's where the most activity was because not only was it the 140 engineer soldiers, it was 140 air guardsmen, our 40- or 50-man SRT team was there … and about 90 from … the medical command); Col. Beron interview, Dec. 1, 2005, p. 50 (stating that LANG sent 46 Special Response Team members to the Superdome); Col. Prechter interview, Jan. 6, 2006, pp. 9-10 ("The plan calls for us to provide manpower, so like this year, we were to supply … 71 personnel to work alongside the City Health Department people to help man the Special Needs section, and that's what traditionally we have done. We have provided manpower to work alongside the City, and the State, I'm sure has been there, too, but the City is who I have known."). Col. Doug Mouton was in command of the National Guard security forces before landfall. *Source:* Swain interview, Nov. 9, 2005, pp. 40-41; Col. Mouton interview, Dec. 1, 2005, p. 61.

94 Col. Ebbert interview, Jan. 10, 2006, pp. 36, 114.

95 Swain interview, Nov. 9, 2005, pp. 35-39 ("Gotta get these people on the inside; can't leave 'em out here getting wet. You can't leave 'em out here in the wind. So we tried to speed up the process as much as possible, but it became apparent that we can't get these people into the Dome as quickly as we need to based on the conditions that are out here. … Once the weather really starts to deteriorate, we brought 'em in and looped 'em around on that concourse on the inside. They were not allowed to go into … the seating area of the Dome until they were actually checked for weapons.").

96 Swain interview, Nov. 9, 2005, pp. 35-39.

97 Col. Mouton interview, Dec. 1, 2005, p. 116.

98 Swain interview, Nov. 9, 2005, pp. 48-49 ("I had to request additional personnel, and once those individuals came in, determined who exactly they are, make sure that they are teamed up with supervisors and put everything in place and again coordinate that with the National Guard and to ensure that we were able to get all these evacuees into the Dome as quickly as possible and to make sure that we searched 'em and did all the necessary things to ensure their safety as well as ours.").

99 LOHSEP, Sitrep, Executive Summary, Hurricane Katrina, Aug. 29, 2005, 10 a.m. CT. Provided to Committee (stating that 10,342 were in the Superdome); Sally Forman, Communications Director, New Orleans Office of the Mayor, Timeline and Notes, Aug. 28, 2005. Provided to Committee ("Dome opens as shelter of last resort – 10,000 gather"); Forman interview, Jan. 10, 2006, p. 62 (stating that Col. Ebbert told her 15,000 to 20,000 people were at the Superdome before landfall.); Col. Ebbert interview, Jan. 10, 2006, pp. 52, 112 (estimating 12,000 to 15,000 were in the Superdome before landfall).

Sheltered and waiting
AP/Wide World Photos

Federal Preparations

The National Response Plan (NRP) was intended to form the basis of the federal government's response to disasters and for its interaction with state and local governments during such events. The response to the Hurricane Katrina disaster varied across the federal government.

The Department of Homeland Security (DHS), which is charged with preparing for and responding to domestic incidents, whether terrorist attacks or natural disasters, failed to lead an effective federal response to Hurricane Katrina. DHS did not fully adapt or adequately train to meet its obligations under the NRP before Hurricane Katrina. Nor did the Department address the known deficiencies of the Federal Emergency Management Agency (FEMA), such as staffing shortages, inadequate training, poor commodities tracking, and insufficient plans for post-disaster communications. In the critical days before landfall, DHS leadership mostly watched from the sidelines, allowed FEMA to take the lead, and missed critical opportunities to help prepare the entire federal government for the response.

The Coast Guard – like FEMA, a DHS component – prepared well, largely on its own initiative, due to its well-developed and well-exercised hurricane plans and a commitment to deploying assistance without waiting for requests.

Under the NRP, the Department of Defense has a supporting role for all Emergency Support Functions, and provides help as requested by FEMA. Traditionally, DOD's policy has been to step in only when local, state, and federal resources have been overwhelmed. DOD took modest steps to prepare before Katrina, deploying liaison personnel to coordinate the response and establishing administrative processes so that it was fully prepared to handle FEMA requests once they arrived.

The Department of Health and Human Services (HHS) began to mobilize U.S. Public Health Service officers days before the storm, but poor planning meant that some never arrived, while others got no further than Jackson, Mississippi. Though HHS ordered additional medical supplies from the Strategic National Stockpile the day before landfall so that they could arrive at the New Orleans Superdome before Katrina struck, they didn't arrive until the day of landfall.

Department of Homeland Security

DHS and its leaders failed to prepare the nation adequately for the unprecedented devastation of Hurricane Katrina. As discussed in Chapter 27, DHS failed to fully adapt and appropriately train to meet the requirements of the NRP in the nine months between its promulgation and Hurricane Katrina. Nor did the Department address FEMA's deficiencies such as staffing shortage, weaknesses in commodities tracking, and insufficient plans for post-disaster communications.

This chapter examines the steps DHS leaders took in the critical days before Katrina made landfall, and what they could have done differently to speed and coordinate the federal response and thereby reduce victims' suffering. As Katrina was bearing down on the Gulf Coast, they failed to take reasonable steps during that period to create a full awareness and a sense of urgency across the federal government about the impending catastrophe. DHS's actions and inactions during the days immediately prior to landfall had consequences in the days that followed.

Besides DHS's failure to organize, train, and equip its personnel under the NRP, poor preparation, and missed opportunities led to responders' improvising actions because they had no clear plan to guide them. The failures of the response flowed logically from these mistakes made before landfall.

DHS Leadership in the Days Before Landfall

The job of leading the federal response to a catastrophe rests with the Secretary of DHS.[1] In the days before Katrina made landfall, DHS Secretary Michael Chertoff's efforts in this regard fell short of what was reasonably expected of him.

Secretary Chertoff testified that he saw his role as "lead[ing] the entire Department, imparting strategic guidance and direction based upon the plan developed, priorities established, and information provided. I also work with the President and other Department heads and deal with governors, members of Congress and other officials."[2]

Secretary Chertoff testified that over the course of the weekend before landfall, he "followed planning activities closely" and "stayed in continual contact with senior DHS and FEMA officials and my experienced advisors."[3]

On the Saturday before landfall, Secretary Chertoff was at home working on unrelated matters, and his only apparent Katrina-related activity was to receive a briefing about that day's FEMA video teleconference (VTC).[4] These video teleconferences are a means by which key federal and state personnel involved in emergency management share information about their disaster preparations, including the latest weather forecasts, the progress of evacuations, and the pre-positioning of commodities.

On Sunday, Secretary Chertoff participated in the FEMA VTC. He heard assurances from then-FEMA Director Michael Brown and others that preparations were well in hand. For instance, Brown told attendees on the conference call "I want that supply chain jammed up as much as possible. ... Just keep jamming those lines full as much as you can with commodities" and "get to the edge of the envelope ... if you feel like you [missing] go ahead and do it. I'll figure out some way to justify it."[5]

Secretary Chertoff offered to assist Brown in enlisting aid from other DHS components: "If there's anything that you need from Coast Guard or any other components that you're not getting, please let us know."[6] Brown told Secretary Chertoff, "I appreciate it … the Coast Guard and ICE [Immigration and Customs Enforcement] and all of the others have been incredibly good to us." Secretary Chertoff also asked, "Are there any DOD assets that might be available? Have we reached out to them [DOD], and have we I guess made any kind of arrangement in case we need some additional help from them?" Brown responded that there were DOD assets at the State Emergency Operations Center (EOC) in Baton Rouge that were "fully engaged."[7]

Secretary Chertoff testified that he did not second-guess statements he heard on the Sunday VTC – including those by state emergency managers and state National Guard officials who, as he termed it, "express[ed] very clearly their satisfaction with the state of affairs."[8] During the August 28 conference call, Brown asked the Acting Deputy Director of the Louisiana Office of Homeland Security and Emergency Preparedness (LOHSEP), Colonel Jeff Smith, if there were "any unmet needs, anything that we're not getting to you that you need" to which Colonel Smith responded, "Mike, no . . . it looks like those resources that are en route are going to – to be a good first shot." Colonel Smith also cautioned that, "Naturally, once we get into this thing … I'm sure that things are going to come up that maybe some of even our best planners hadn't even thought about. So I think flexibility is going to be the key." He also stated that it would be important to "cut through any potential red tape when those things do arise."[9] The Mississippi representative on the call said "FEMA has been great. You're leaning forward, and we appreciate that." He later said, "We've got everything that we need from the federal government."[10] Secretary Chertoff thought the emergency-management officials on that call had hundreds of years of combined professional experience managing hurricanes.[11]

Secretary Chertoff also spoke with Governors Barbour of Mississippi, Blanco of Louisiana, and Riley of Alabama that day.[12]

The Secretary and other senior leaders did not take affirmative steps prior to landfall, beyond his statements on the Sunday VTC, to ensure that DHS components with operational responsibilities under the NRP were prepared to respond.[13] Instead, the evidence suggests that Secretary Chertoff and DHS responded to Katrina as if DHS headquarters had no special responsibilities outside the normal course of operations.

Despite assurances and lack of affirmative requests from the governors of the Gulf states, the Secretary still should have taken additional steps to better prepare his Department for the coming storm.

From all corners, the message throughout the weekend, especially at the Saturday and Sunday VTCs, was that a catastrophe was about to strike the Gulf Coast, and the greater New Orleans area in particular. The head of the National Hurricane Service, Max Mayfield, had been making calls to leaders in parishes, cities, states, and the federal government. The Hurricane Pam exercise in 2004 had predicted that flooding from a catastrophic storm – what had been known for years among meteorologists and government officials as the "New Orleans scenario" – might kill as many as 60,000. In the weekend conference call, Brown referred to the approaching storm as the "big one."[14] As Mayfield said, "I think the wisest thing to do here is plan on a Category 5 hurricane … no matter where it hits it's going to have an impact over a very, very large area. … I don't think any model can tell you with any confidence right now whether the levees will be topped or not, but that's obviously a very, very grave concern."[15]

During the weekend, as Katrina neared New Orleans, there was a need for initiative, for recognition of the unprecedented threat and the equally unprecedented response it required. Leadership – direction, encouragement, a sense of purpose and urgency – was needed. Secretary Chertoff did not provide it.

For example, he did not ask specifically what preparations were under way, how much material was being pre-positioned, and whether it would be enough.[16] And though the DHS Inspector General had issued a draft report in June 2005 stating that FEMA's logistics-management systems had performed poorly during the four Florida hurricanes in 2004,[17] Secretary Chertoff did not inquire whether the system could handle the expected impact of Katrina. The Committee has found no evidence to suggest that anyone, including Secretary Chertoff, attempted to determine if the system could handle the expected impact of Katrina. Similarly, a DHS study had concluded that FEMA's procurement office was understaffed.[18] Yet the Secretary did not ask whether this important office was up to the coming task.

Although he has stated repeatedly that he relied on Brown as his "battlefield commander,"[19] aside from on the Sunday VTC, according to Brown, Secretary Chertoff did not talk to his "commander" directly over the weekend, either while Brown was in Washington or after he left for the Gulf on Sunday afternoon.[20] In view of Secretary Chertoff's testimony that he stayed in contact with "senior DHS and FEMA officials and [his] experienced advisors,"[21] this omission is particularly inexplicable. Because Secretary Chertoff was placing so much faith in Brown to lead the preparations and response, it was incumbent on the Secretary to do more than just have a brief conversation with him in front of dozens of state, local, and federal officials – including the President of the United States – on a VTC. Secretary Chertoff should have called Brown privately to discuss in more detail the status of preparations and the level of cooperation Brown was getting from DHS and other government departments.

Conversely, Brown failed to inform the Secretary of the FEMA deficiencies that he has since claimed in testimony and media interviews to have known about at the time. These two key players' failure to communicate is evidence of the profound dysfunction then existing between DHS and FEMA leadership.

Additionally:

• There should have been a plan to maintain situational awareness at the Homeland Security Operations Center (HSOC). The Director of DHS' Operations Center, Matthew Broderick, testified "there was no plan."[22] The HSOC plans months in advance for events such as the Super Bowl, yet no effort was being made to identify sources of information specific to New Orleans and the Gulf Coast, such as local National Weather Service stations or local media outlets. Rather, the intention was to rely exclusively on FEMA officials and the very state and local entities that would be bearing the brunt of the storm's fury to provide situational awareness. Secretary Chertoff bears ultimate responsibility for ensuring that there is such a plan.[23] (See Chapter 19 for further information on situational awareness.)

• The National Communications System (NCS) never developed a plan to restore communications to emergency responders, such as the police and fire departments, after a catastrophic disaster. Instead, the NCS intended to rely solely on the private sector to restore communications capabilities.[24] Additionally, Peter Fonash, the Director of NCS, was not familiar with the "New Orleans scenario," until the day before landfall.[25] The Secretary bears ultimate responsibility for this lack of preparation.

• The investigation uncovered no evidence that anyone coordinated with the Department of Justice (DOJ) to determine which agency was going to take the lead under Emergency Support Function 13, Public Safety and Security.[26] (See Chapter 25, Public Safety and Security.) There was no DOJ representative at the Public Safety and Security desk at the FEMA National Response Coordination Center (NRCC),[27] FEMA's national operations center in charge of overall coordination of the response at the national level. Each of the Emergency Support Functions is represented there to coordinate activities in their area of expertise. Additionally DOJ did not have a response plan (either for itself or to coordinate with DHS) to execute Public Safety and Security responsibilities following a natural disaster.

• The investigation uncovered no evidence that senior DHS leadership contacted the leadership of Immigration and Custom Enforcement (ICE), Customs and Border Patrol (CBP), Federal Protective Service (FPS) or the Secret Service to assess their planning and preparation – or even to determine if they *were* planning and preparing. There was confusion over staffing the Public Safety and Security desk at the NRCC – FPS had attempted to send a representative to the desk, only to be rebuffed by FEMA.[28] Moreover, ICE was going forward with a previously scheduled conference in Baltimore for its Special Agents in Charge (SACs), and the New Orleans SAC was still planning to fly out Sunday

Inspecting: General Landreneau,
Mayor Nagin, Michael Brown,
Senator Landrieu (behind Brown),
President Bush, Senator Vitter
U.S. Coast Guard photo

morning to attend the conference rather than remain in the area to lead his office's response efforts after the storm had passed.[29]

In addition, the Secretary has broader responsibilities that reach across the federal government.[30] Yet, there is no evidence, nor any testimony by the Secretary, that he reached out to other Cabinet secretaries to assess their level of preparedness, to determine if they were coordinating efforts with DHS, or to ensure that they responded quickly and fully to any requests that might come from DHS or FEMA.[31]

Finally, it is reasonable to expect that the Secretary would be engaged with the President during critical times in a catastrophe. The Committee was unable to develop any record as to whether the Secretary was in fact keeping the President informed in the pre-storm period.

The lack of plans to maintain situational awareness, the lack of coordination in the deployment of federal law enforcement assets, and the communications problems at all levels of government all resulted in part from some of the pre-landfall inaction described above.

Much was expected of Secretary Chertoff, and there were things that only he, as a Cabinet secretary, could do. In his testimony before the Committee, U.S. Comptroller General David Walker (the head of the non-partisan Government Accountability Office, which is commonly referred to as the investigative arm of Congress) described the unique leverage of such a position: "No matter how capable the person [leading the response effort] might be, level matters in this town, unfortunately, especially with regard to certain departments and agencies like the Department of Defense. Hierarchy is real."[32]

What DHS Should Have Done

The evidence suggests that neither Secretary Chertoff nor DHS leaders fully understood the Department's responsibilities under the NRP. But he had at his disposal other mechanisms that could prompt greater coordination of response and recovery efforts, as well as to convey an increased sense of urgency. He did not take advantage of them. Three of these mechanisms warrant greater scrutiny.

What DHS Should Have Done: The Catastrophic Incident Annex

The NRP-Catastrophic Incident Annex (NRP-CIA) exists to create a "proactive national response to a catastrophic incident."[33] For a "typical" disaster, the standard practice is that the federal government does not extend aid until a state requests assistance. During a catastrophe, however, NRP-CIA activation prompts the government to help without waiting for requests.[34] Secretary Chertoff did not activate the NRP-CIA, as he had the authority to do.

None of the senior DHS officials interviewed recalled considering activating the NRP-CIA pre-landfall,[35] and it isn't clear from Secretary Chertoff's testimony whether he considered doing so.[36] Secretary Chertoff has since stated that he believed that Katrina "was not the type of event contemplated by the CIA"[37] because, in his view, the NRP-CIA was for "no-notice or short-notice incidents where anticipatory preparation and coordination with the state under the Stafford Act [which authorizes the federal government to play a role in emergency response] are not possible."[38] This interpretation is not imposed by the Stafford Act and is illogical. As Comptroller General Walker testified to the Committee, "The idea that we would be less proactive in dealing with a known natural disaster just defies common sense."[39]

The NRP-CIA refers to the Catastrophic Incident Supplement (NRP-CIS) for specific operational details such as what "incident-specific 'packages'" the various federal agencies will be expected to deploy once the NRP-CIA is activated.[40] The Supplement was still in draft when Katrina made landfall.[41] The draft Supplement provides that it should be used when the "Secretary determines that an incident has resulted or *will result* in a mass victim/mass evacuation situation."[42] The Committee believes that a major hurricane bearing down on a major American city lying below sea level qualifies as an event that is likely to result in "extraordinary levels of mass casualties, damage or disruption severely affecting the population, infrastructure, environment, economy, national morale, and/or government functions."[43]

It does appear that the issue was at least raised to a FEMA official. Janet Benini, a former Director for Response and Planning for the White House Homeland Security Council, worked on developing the Catastrophic Incident Supplement and a planning scenario that included a catastrophic hurricane striking Louisiana.[44] On Saturday, August 27, Benini e-mailed David Garratt, Deputy Director of FEMA's Recovery Division, to ask whether there was "any talk of implementing the Catastrophic Plan." Benini noted that "with a Cat 4 heading directly into New Orleans this might be the time." Garratt responded that he had heard no such discussion.[45]

Apart from any practical benefits, activating the NRP-CIA pre-landfall would have changed the tenor of federal preparation efforts, prompting federal agencies to anticipate state and local needs instead of waiting for requests from overwhelmed officials in Louisiana and Mississippi. Brown said: "[I]n every disaster we push, because we pre-positioned supplies and equipment, but in this case we should have started the push system that never stopped. You know, we pre-positioned and then tried to see what was going to happen and then started it back up again. We should have just kept pushing."[46]

Obviously, the precise effect of such an activation is difficult to quantify, and the NRP-CIA is not a panacea. As noted above, its operational component – the Catastrophic Incident Supplement – was not yet complete or in effect, nor had federal agencies trained or exercised its use. Nevertheless, the Committee believes that activating the NRP-CIA could have led to the mobilization and deployment of some additional assets before they were requested through normal NRP protocols.

Activating the NRP-CIA also could have accelerated the involvement of the Department of Defense. Under the NRP, DOD is a supporting agency to all 15 Emergency Support Functions. As discussed elsewhere in the report (see Chapter 26, Military Operations), the day after landfall, DOD took the initiative and activated forces, deploying troops and resources without waiting for requests for assistance from FEMA or the affected states. DOD eventually deployed over 20,000 active-duty military personnel and coordinated deployment of 50,000 National Guard troops, as well as hundreds of helicopters, and numerous ships.[47] Activating the NRP-CIA may have accelerated DOD planning even further, resulting in earlier pre-positioning of helicopters and deployment of ships, which did not sail from Norfolk, Virginia, until August 31, two days after landfall.[48]

While speculative, these examples illustrate how the disaster response may have proceeded more efficiently had DHS acted with a greater sense of urgency and activated the NRP-CIA before landfall.[49]

What DHS Should Have Done: Appointment of a PFO

Secretary Chertoff did not appoint a Principal Federal Officer (PFO) until the evening of Tuesday, August 30, approximately 36 hours after landfall.[50] The position is provided for in the NRP so that the Secretary will have an on-the-ground representative to oversee the federal response. It is designed to support the unified command structure and be the primary point of contact and situational awareness for the Secretary in a disaster area.[51] The Secretary appointed a PFO months in advance for events such as the Super Bowl.[52] Yet DHS waited until the day *after landfall* to appoint one for what many government officials – including Brown – feared was a potential catastrophe.

Secretary Chertoff testified that he did not appoint a PFO on Saturday, when the President issued the emergency declaration for Louisiana, because the PFO "doesn't exercise command authority; it is a coordinating authority." He also stated that he believed Brown had all the authority he needed to coordinate the federal effort by virtue of his rank within DHS. The Secretary elaborated:

> Given the fact that Michael Brown was an Under Secretary of the Department, so he was the third ranking member of the Department, at least in terms of level, and given the fact that he and the team working on this had been working together for a week, I frankly didn't think it was necessary at that point to add an additional title or additional measure of authority.[53]

The Committee disagrees that Brown's rank in DHS was a substitute for PFO designation. With other duties to perform, and with no way of knowing whether Katrina would be the only disaster in store, Brown was in no position to commit to the 100 percent on-scene focus required in a PFO. The Committee believes Secretary Chertoff should have appointed a PFO in conjunction with the President's declaration on Saturday, August 27.[54] Doing so could have laid the groundwork for a unified approach to preparation and signaled strongly that DHS and the federal government was stepping forward with all available assets. Appointment before landfall could have allowed the individual appointed to bring together state, local, and other federal officials in the region and to put in place coordinated plans for a response in advance of the storm rather than trying to establish control in the midst of the response. Deficiencies, such as the failure to evacuate special-needs individuals or the lack of planning for post-landfall evacuation of the general population, might have been identified earlier. None of this happened.[55]

That said, it's unclear that appointing Brown PFO prior to landfall would have improved the response. Brown has made it very clear that he did not want to be appointed PFO. In fact, he thought the entire concept "silly,"[56] as he felt it added an unnecessary layer of bureaucracy. The choice of Brown as PFO – whether before landfall or after – was poor, even if for no other reason than his animosity toward the PFO concept, the NRP, and DHS, not to mention his lack of emergency-management training and experience. Perhaps Secretary Chertoff, who was in his position for less than seven months, wasn't aware of Brown's attitudes or was poorly advised. Or perhaps he chose Brown in the hope that he would rise above policy differences in the face of catastrophe.

One of the PFO's main responsibilities is to keep DHS leadership informed of the situation on the ground,[57] but Brown, who has expressed disdain for this structure as inefficient, refused to communicate with the Secretary, circumventing the chain of command to communicate directly with the White House. His actions were inexcusable – not only insubordinate, but disruptive to DHS's awareness of the threats and problems that it was facing.

Brown was a poor choice for another reason. Even when appointed PFO, Brown remained the Director of FEMA, an apparent violation of the NRP's requirement that a PFO not be "'dual hatted' with any other roles or responsibilities that could detract from their overall incident-management responsibilities."[58] According to DHS Deputy Secretary Michael Jackson, "for the incident of a hurricane, PFO and Director of FEMA, '*macht Nichts*' [German: 'amounts to nothing']: they both have the same capacities, capabilities, performance capabilities in managing the events."[59] There is, however, a practical reason why a PFO should have no other responsibilities: the PFO has to be focused entirely on the catastrophe at hand. But just as DHS and Secretary Chertoff had responsibilities that were broader than Katrina, so, too, did FEMA and its Director. On Thursday, September 1, a minor earthquake occurred in California.[60] Had this earthquake been more severe – or had there been wildfires, flooding, or another disaster elsewhere – it remained FEMA's responsibility to respond, and the FEMA Director's job to see that it did so. Either Brown shouldn't have been appointed PFO, or someone else should have become Acting Director of FEMA. Neither happened.

What DHS Should Have Done: Activating the IIMG

The Interagency Incident Management Group (IIMG) brings together senior-level officials from multiple agencies, in theory to assist the Secretary of Homeland Security in managing national incidents. The IIMG was formally activated at 11:30 a.m., Tuesday, August 30.[61] Over the weekend, the Director of the IIMG, Robert Stephan, consulted twice with Matthew Broderick, who, as the Director of the Homeland Security Operations Center, the primary hub for domestic incident management, operational coordination and situational awareness, was charged with recommending activation to the Secretary. Stephan recalled asking Broderick whether there was "anything significant at this point in time that we need to be worried about and that would cause us to bring in the IMG [sic] this evening? And the answer was no."[62] Each time the two consulted, they decided that the FEMA and HSOC structures were "robust" enough without the IIMG.[63] Instead, prior to landfall, members of the IIMG were told to be ready to convene on 90 minutes' notice.[64]

It's unclear whether early activation of the IIMG might have resulted in a more effective federal response. Though the IIMG was designed to be a mechanism by which to share information, identify available resources, and coordinate government efforts, some witnesses criticized the IIMG as ineffective in practice. One witness derisively called it the "bright idea brigade."[65] The FEMA designee to the IIMG said that it actually hindered response efforts after its activation in Hurricane Katrina by meddling in operational details.[66] One emergency-preparedness officer said that "It became a huge animal you have to feed information to."[67]

Since the IIMG was not activated until recovery was under way, it's unclear whether response efforts would have improved if it had been activated pre-landfall. However, the decision not to activate the IIMG prior to landfall suggests that DHS leadership did not fully recognize the potential scope of the damage Katrina presented, or its obligation to lead the federal response in accordance with the NRP. While the performance of the IIMG appears to have been mixed after landfall, things might have gone more smoothly if it had been activated sooner and been allowed before the height of the crisis to work through issues associated with its first use since the implementation of the NRP.[68] Alternatively, if activating the IIMG before landfall was not called for in an incident the magnitude of Katrina, this calls into the question the utility of the organization itself and suggests that consideration should be given to abolishing it and distributing its functions to operating elements.

Conclusion

Despite knowledge that Katrina was a looming "nightmare scenario,"[69] DHS and Secretary Chertoff failed to adequately prepare the federal government for what became one of the most destructive natural disasters in the nation's history. As Katrina approached the Gulf Coast, those in the top ranks of DHS failed to understand the potential scope of the pending catastrophe and FEMA's limited capacity to address an event of this magnitude.

Equally important, DHS failed to carry out its own responsibilities under the NRP and associated Presidential Directives.[70] A November 2005 report by the DHS Inspector General regarding an April 2005 training exercise ("TOPOFF 3") found that "The exercise highlighted – at all levels of government – a fundamental lack of understanding for the principles and protocols set forth in the NRP."[71] Others in government – most notably then-FEMA Director Michael Brown – simply refused to accept the NRP, choosing instead to proceed as if the NRP did not exist.

Secretary Chertoff testified that he believed his role as chief executive of the Department was to impart strategic guidance and deal with senior officials, not be a "hurricane operator." But Secretary Chertoff came up short by his own yardstick. A chief executive should understand the responsibilities of the organization he runs. In the days before Katrina, Secretary Chertoff appeared not to have fully understood the broader role of DHS under the NRP. A strategic leader chooses capable subordinates and provides those subordinates with guidance, works effectively with other key government officials, and, in DHS's case, cooperates effectively with states. Even judging the Secretary by his own criteria, his performance in the nation's worst domestic disaster fell short of reasonable expectations.

The Federal Emergency Management Agency

FEMA Pre-Landfall

Before landfall, Scott Wells, Deputy Federal Coordinating Officer for Katrina in New Orleans, called Edward Buikema, FEMA's Acting Director of Response. "I don't think we're thinking big enough," he told Buikema. "[Katrina] is bigger than how we normally do things."[72]

Wells was exactly right. Despite knowing for years the catastrophic impact that a large hurricane could have on New Orleans, despite the predictions of the exercise known as Hurricane Pam, and despite FEMA's own internal slides showing projections that Katrina could be worse than Pam's predictions of 60,000 fatalities – FEMA just wasn't thinking big enough for Katrina.

DHS is the central federal entity for preparing for and responding to disasters. FEMA is one of the agencies within DHS charged with responsibilities under the NRP. FEMA is the lead agency for five of the 15 Emergency Support Functions under the NRP.[73] Despite these obligations, FEMA did not prepare adequately for Hurricane Katrina.

This section analyzes FEMA's preparations in the days during which Katrina was moving toward land.

FEMA officials knew the threat a large hurricane posed to New Orleans. Buikema testified that FEMA considered a large hurricane hitting New Orleans to be one of the worst catastrophes that could occur in the United States.[74] Eric Tolbert, FEMA's Director of Response until February 2005, testified that while at FEMA, the hurricane threat to New Orleans was his top priority and that FEMA knew a hurricane Category 3 or stronger could breach or overtop the levees.[75] (There is a more detailed discussion of FEMA's knowledge of the threat posed to New Orleans by a hurricane in Chapter 8.)

Despite this knowledge, FEMA's leadership failed to ensure that the federal government's preparations for the response were adequate. Its leaders didn't compel the federal government to think bigger than usual. They failed to ask the right questions to make sure FEMA's response was big enough. They did not utilize all available resources. FEMA seemed to be following pages from its regular playbook instead of a playbook made for "the big one."

Some of FEMA's pre-landfall failures had to do with FEMA's systematic weaknesses, discussed in Chapter 14. They included insufficient staff; limited ability to track commodities; unexercised, untrained, under-equipped emergency-response teams; unprepared disaster-assistance workforce; lack of operating procedures; and lack of necessary funding. FEMA Director Michael Brown sought additional funding to address many of these problems, but DHS did not provide sufficient additional funding. The failure to address or solve these many problems cast the die even before Katrina moved towards the Gulf Coast.

As early as Saturday morning, August 27, Michael Lowder, FEMA Deputy Director of Response, e-mailed several FEMA employees: "If [this] is the 'New Orleans' scenario, we are already way behind. Let's don't hold back. Let's make sure that all of our Emergency Support Functions are fully engaged and ramped up, everything turned on, etc. This may be IT!"[76] Because of the inadequate preparations, even before landfall, the federal government was already behind in fighting Katrina's terrible wrath.

Weather Warnings in the Days Before Landfall

In the days as Katrina moved through the Gulf of Mexico, FEMA was repeatedly warned that it was a potentially catastrophic hurricane headed toward the Gulf Coast. Despite these warnings, Brown has admitted that the federal government's level of preparedness wasn't adequate for the big one.[77] William Lokey, FEMA's Federal Coordinating Officer in Louisiana during Katrina, agreed: "Communications and coordination was lacking, preplanning was lacking. We were not prepared for this."[78]

The warnings began early. The 5 p.m. National Weather Service (NWS) report on Thursday, August 25, said some models showed Hurricane Katrina moving to the west, bringing it "inland between Mobile, Alabama, and Grand Isle, Louisiana [southeastern Louisiana]," although the National Hurricane Center (NHC) model did not show it moving that far west.[79] Six hours later a new NWS report predicted that Katrina was expected to strengthen and that "Katrina will be a dangerous hurricane in the northeastern Gulf of Mexico in about 3 days."[80]

By 11 a.m., Friday, August 26, the NWS report said that Katrina's track should "flatten out in a more westward direction." It reported some models showing the storm going west over Louisiana, but most showing Katrina going inland over the northeast Gulf Coast. The report warned, "Strengthening to a major hurricane is expected."[81] On a noon video teleconference between federal and state officials hosted by FEMA, Max Mayfield, NHC Director, warned: "Right now we're forecasting it to be a strong Category 3 hurricane. It's going to be stronger than that."[82] Another NHC official said that Katrina "has definitely shifted well to the west towards New Orleans … we've really got to pay attention all the way from Louisiana over into the Florida Gulf Coast."[83]

Thus, at least as early as Thursday evening, FEMA was aware of a dangerous hurricane forming in the Gulf of Mexico and by noon Friday was aware that Katrina was shifting west toward New Orleans. This awareness did not provoke action. On Friday, August 27, when asked, Brown permitted Acting Response Division Director Buikema to go to Alaska for a previously scheduled emergency-management conference even though "The predictions are now Katrina will turn into a Cat 4."[84] Buikema ultimately cut his trip short and returned from Alaska, arriving at FEMA headquarters on Sunday around 11 a.m.[85] As a result, however, he was unavailable until Sunday morning to oversee his division's preparations as the storm moved toward landfall.[86]

A Friday morning e-mail to Lokey from William Irwin of the U.S. Army Corps of Engineers, the lead agency for Emergency Support Function 3 (ESF-3) (which includes executing contracts for ice and water) under the NRP, expressed concern that FEMA was moving too slowly: "FEMA Region IV [covering Alabama and Mississippi, among other states] is reluctant to make a decision to provide mission assignments [the mechanism by which FEMA requests other federal agencies to provide support during a disaster response] for a possible Alabama hit. … The storm will speed up and rapidly strike on Monday and if FEMA/Alabama wants to have ESF#3 support … the trigger needed to be pulled already."[87]

On Friday, FEMA's national operations center and its Region IV operations center in Atlanta were operating at a moderate level of readiness.[88] The Texas-based Region VI operations center that covered Louisiana remained at its lowest state of readiness, for no known threat of disaster, on Friday.[89] Although by Friday morning the National Weather Service began predicting that Katrina was shifting towards the west, FEMA did not activate the national operations center to its highest readiness level until Saturday at 7 a.m.[90] The regional operations centers were activated to the highest level at noon Eastern Time on Saturday.[91]

By Saturday, warnings were growing even more grave. FEMA's 5:30 a.m. National Situation Report stated that Louisiana's Governor Kathleen Blanco had declared a state of emergency, noting that New Orleans was "of particular concern because much of that city lies below sea level. According to Governor Blanco, Lake Pontchartrain is a very large lake that sits next to the city of New Orleans and if the hurricane winds blow from a certain direction, there are dire predictions of what may happen in the city."[92] By early Saturday morning, the projected path of the storm was directly over New Orleans. FEMA briefing slides dated 9 a.m., August 27, 2005, at FEMA headquarters, stated: "Current projected path takes storm directly over New Orleans."[93] The briefing slides also noted that the Pam exercise predicted 60,000 fatalities and 1 million-plus persons displaced, and that Pam's estimates are "exceeded by Hurricane Katrina real life impacts."[94] (See Chapter 8.)

Also on Saturday morning, FEMA distributed copies of the Southeast Louisiana Catastrophic Hurricane Plan, also known as the Hurricane Pam plan, to its employees.[95]

On Saturday morning, the State of Louisiana requested an emergency declaration under the Stafford Act – the federal law that provides a framework for federal assistance and reimbursement to states struck by declared disasters – so that it could better prepare for the storm. President Bush granted Louisiana's request Saturday evening.[96] Mississippi and Alabama requested emergency declarations on Sunday; the President granted them the same day.[97] This unusual declaration of emergencies before landfall ensured that the federal government would finance many pre- and post-landfall actions taken by state and local officials.[98] This had only been done once in the previous 15 years, when President Clinton issued four pre-landfall declarations, all for Hurricane Floyd in 1999.[99]

By late Saturday and very early Sunday, the weather projections became even more severe, warning that Katrina could become a very intense and dangerous Category 5 hurricane, and that the storm surge could be as high as 25 feet in some areas.[100] Another Sunday weather report, from the Slidell, Louisiana, office of the National Weather Service, stated that "devastating damage expected ... a most powerful hurricane with unprecedented strength ... most of the area will be uninhabitable for weeks ... perhaps longer."[101]

FEMA's Sunday morning National Situation Report warned:

> Katrina could be especially devastating if it strikes New Orleans because the city sits below sea level and is dependent on levees and pumps to keep the water out. A direct hit could wind up submerging the city in several feel of water. Making matters worse, at least 100,000 people in the city lack the transportation to get out of town.[102]

Also on Sunday, DHS released a report, stating, "Any storm rated Category 4 or greater ... will likely lead to severe flooding and/or levee breaching. This could leave the New Orleans area being submerged for weeks or months. ... The magnitude of this storm is expected to cause massive flooding." This report was circulated to the White House's situation room, throughout DHS, and to all agencies in DHS's HSOC.[103]

Brown testified that he spoke to White House officials at least 30 times during the weekend prior to landfall, repeatedly warning them about Katrina.[104] Brown said he spoke directly to the President on Saturday, August 27, and warned that Katrina could be catastrophic.[105] Brown later called to ask that the President contact Governor Blanco and "do everything he could within his persuasive powers to convince [Louisiana officials] to do a mandatory evacuation."[106] Brown testified that he told both Chief of Staff Andy Card and Deputy Chief of Staff Joe Hagin prior to landfall that he was concerned about how bad Katrina could be, saying he thought Katrina could be the catastrophic "big one."[107]

On the Sunday before landfall, President Bush and Hagin both participated in FEMA's noon video teleconference (VTC), where Max Mayfield, Director of the National Hurricane Center, predicted Katrina would be a "very dangerous hurricane" and warned, "I don't think any model can tell you with any confidence right now whether the levees will be topped or not, but that's obviously a very, very grave concern."[108] Although the President appeared on the VTC, promised federal government assistance, and thanked Governor Blanco and Mississippi Governor Haley Barbour for heeding these warnings, and doing all they could possibly do to prepare for this storm, the President did not ask any substantive questions.[109] On that call Colonel William Doran, operations division chief for LOHSEP, noted that the State of Louisiana was "way ahead of the game there" with catastrophic planning "thanks to the help of FEMA, when we did the Hurricane Pam exercises."[110] Colonel Smith said Louisiana's evacuations were going "much better than it did during Ivan."[111]

After the Sunday noon VTC, Brown had another conversation with Hagin in which he said he again raised his concerns about the storm and complained that he had never been allowed to do the catastrophic planning that was necessary for FEMA to be prepared for a storm like Katrina that he had pushed to be able to do.[112] "I [was] just adamant that they understand my concern about New Orleans,"[113] Brown described the call.

FEMA'S Preparation for Katrina

FEMA's many failures in preparing for Katrina include: (1) multiple failures involving deployment of personnel; (2) not taking sufficient measures to deploy communications assets; (3) insufficient planning to be prepared to respond to catastrophic events, (4) not pre-staging enough commodities; (5) failures associated with deployment of disaster medical assistance teams and search and rescue teams; (6) failures involving evacuation; (7) failure to establish a joint field office quickly enough; and (8) failure to take measures prior to landfall to ensure proper security for emergency response teams. All of these contributed to FEMA's failed response, which will be discussed in later chapters.

FEMA's Deployment of Personnel for Katrina

FEMA went to war without enough troops. Unlike many other disasters, hurricanes provide emergency managers with advance warning. Thus, FEMA should also begin its preparations, such as personnel deployment, in advance of a storm. With each passing day, FEMA had more accurate information about the strength and path of the storm. FEMA's limited staff – it had only approximately 2,250 permanent, full-time employees in November 2005 and around a 17 percent vacancy rate when Katrina struck[114] – and resources require that its leadership be flexible and adaptable to changing predictions. As Katrina developed, FEMA was forced to choose how to allocate its limited staff across at least three states.

As early as Thursday, August 25, before landfall, FEMA was aware that Katrina would likely make a second landfall somewhere on the Gulf Coast. On Friday, FEMA decided to move an Advance Emergency Response Team (ERT-A) from the West Coast to Mississippi.[115] William Carwile was notified that he would be the Federal Coordinating Officer (FCO) in Mississippi. He arrived there on Saturday, August 27, to take charge of FEMA's response to what he later described as "the worst disaster to strike the United States in recent history from a response standpoint."[116]

By Friday afternoon, Katrina was shifting westward and was being projected to make landfall as a Category 4 hurricane. FEMA leadership discussed deploying the National Emergency Response Team (ERT-N), but deployed no teams to Louisiana until noon, Saturday, August 27.[117] ERT-N teams are emergency-response teams designed for high-impact events.[118] Shortly after September 11, 2001, ERT-N teams had about 125 to 175 members, but FEMA had gradually reduced their size to the current level of about 25 members.[119] While the NRP states that the Secretary of Homeland Security "determines the need for ERT-N deployment, coordinating the plans with the affected regions," Secretary Chertoff played no role in deploying the team.[120] The decision was made by FEMA senior leadership.[121] The team's Saturday deployment was simply too late, but it's unclear whether the Secretary's personal involvement would have sped it up. To make matters worse, once deployed, many team members were slow to reach the affected area, arriving only after landfall. Also, the deployed ERT-N went into service as a combination of the two national teams, rather than a pre-selected team, because of a shortage of FEMA employees and because some available team members were already deployed in the Gulf region.[122]

FCO Lokey arrived in Baton Rouge between 6 and 7 p.m. on Saturday, meeting Deputy FCO Scott Wells at the State EOC.[123] Lokey admitted that key positions on the ERT-N were not filled prior to landfall.[124] According to Lokey, by Saturday, only five ERT-N members had arrived, and by Sunday night only 12 to 15 ERT-N members were there.[125] Prior to landfall, then, only about half of the ERT-N members were in place.

According to Mike Hall, a leader of one of FEMA's ERT-N teams, team members are supposed to deploy immediately once activated.[126] Carwile said it is "very important" that an ERT-N arrive in a timely matter.[127] However, FEMA does not dictate how quickly those team members should arrive since they are coming from different parts of the country.[128] Carwile said that the ERT-N teams used to have procedures to speed their arrival, but that they had been discarded.[129]

FEMA deployed an ERT-A team from Region I, which is headquartered in Boston, to the Region VI center in Denton, Texas, on Sunday, August 28. Phil Parr, the leader of this team, arrived on Sunday late afternoon or early evening; his team arrived in staggered fashion, some arriving on Sunday, others on Monday, the day of landfall.[130] Of the 20 to 25 members assigned to his ERT-A team, about 10 eventually deployed.[131] On Saturday, Texas was not within the cone of the projected path of the hurricane.[132] According to a Parr e-mail, Parr agreed the storm was not headed to Texas.[133] On Monday, FEMA redirected Parr and some of his team members to Louisiana. Parr and his team members did not arrive in New Orleans until Tuesday, August 30.[134]

FEMA also did not have available the kind of first-responder teams it was supposed to have under the NRP. The First Incident Response Support Teams (FIRST teams) were not available when Katrina made landfall because FEMA had not yet hired staff for them.[135] FIRST teams are designed to arrive quickly to assess the situation and identify potential requirements for federal help, provide advice on protective actions, coordinate response activities, and assist with critical life saving measures. The teams are supposed to deploy with sophisticated communications equipment to support state and local first responders.[136] Several witnesses said these teams would likely have been a major asset in responding to Katrina.[137]

Prior to landfall, Marty Bahamonde, a FEMA public-affairs staffer, was the only FEMA employee deployed to New Orleans.[138] He arrived in New Orleans at 11 p.m. Saturday to prepare for VIP visits to the area. By chance, he rode out the storm in the New Orleans EOC, located near the Superdome.[139] On Sunday afternoon, there was a growing realization that more people were heading to the Superdome than officials had anticipated. Officials at the Orleans Parish EOC were becoming concerned. Bahamonde took pictures of the gathering crowds at the Superdome and sent them back to FEMA headquarters. Throughout Sunday, Bahamonde continued to provide information to FEMA headquarters about the growing numbers of people and the deteriorating conditions.[140]

Brown arrived in Baton Rouge on Sunday evening. He was accompanied by two FEMA press employees, a FEMA congressional-relations liaison, security detail, and his personal assistant, but no operations experts.[141] They traveled on military aircraft; FEMA's operational personnel took commercial flights.[142] Once in Baton Rouge, Brown went to dinner and to the hotel, but did not go to the state EOC.[143]

As discussed more fully in Chapter 14, FEMA suffered from staffing shortages, lack of training, and difficulties with its disaster-surge workforce. Moreover, the teams deployed were unprepared, unequipped, and (aside from many members participating in a simulated hurricane tabletop exercise the previous June) had not trained together as a team.[144] Carwile believed that his Mississippi team, though not an ERT-N, was actually more experienced and better-trained than the ERT-N team members sent to Louisiana.[145]

Staffing shortages and inadequacies contributed to FEMA's failure to prepare for Katrina.[146] Wells admitted that FEMA didn't have the staff to run a 24-hour operation in Katrina. People were working, he said, "50 hours over 2 days."[147] Carwile agreed:

> The inability to field experienced personnel in Mississippi had a major impact on our operations there. FEMA needs many more trained people who can deploy to disasters. Both career professionals and temporary disaster assistance employees (DAEs) [used by FEMA to quickly increase staffing during disasters] performed their jobs well in Mississippi, especially in the first chaotic days after landfall. However, there were not enough trained people to adequately staff all of the positions. Of all the shortfalls that I had to manage as FCO this was the most difficult. This paucity of qualified personnel hurt us in both the response and recovery phases of the operations.[148]

To make matters worse, FEMA had few personnel specifically devoted to response activities.[149] For instance, although there are generally pre-arranged rosters for emergency-response teams, often those members are in other jobs or working on other disasters and are not available when a new disaster hits. Therefore, the teams consist of individuals who have not necessarily previously served in these positions, who have not trained, worked, practiced, or planned together, and who are sometimes not qualified for the job. Wells referred to the way positions are filled on emergency response team as the "hey-you roster" and said that under this system "you get people that are not qualified for the job. It's secondary jobs for everybody. ... I can probably count on my hand the number of people that their primary job is go out in the field and do these things. This is not a team that goes out that is trained and worked and planned and operated together."[150]

In addition to full-time FEMA personnel, FEMA uses temporary employees, called Disaster Assistance Employees (DAEs), to surge up for disasters. According to Marie Sloan, director of the DAE program, fewer than half of the DAEs were available when Katrina made landfall – a typical availability rate.[151] Records show that FEMA was also slow to deploy available DAEs for Katrina. For instance, of the approximately 4,000 DAEs, only 25 were deployed on Friday, 116 on Saturday, and 53 on Sunday. FEMA spread these DAEs over four states to respond to Katrina's first landfall in Florida, and to its expected second-landfall states of Louisiana, Mississippi, and Alabama.[152]

DAEs and other FEMA personnel were also delayed in arriving at the actual disaster sites because of FEMA's policy that all personnel deployed to a disaster must first visit a "mobilizations center" in Florida or Georgia for things like badge issuance and briefings.[153] While some DAEs may have needed this check-in process in order to be better prepared, several FEMA leaders complained that this requirement delayed the deployment of workers to the disaster. For example, on the day after landfall, one FEMA employee complained that she had had "zero" DAE requests filled and that the DAE deployment process is "killing us. There has been no consistent guidance and not only are we unable to lean forward, we can't even stand up! ... this will bring us to our knees."[154] A few days after landfall, FEMA changed the policy to allow at least some personnel to deploy directly to the disaster.[155]

FEMA did not deploy operations personnel in or near the New Orleans metropolitan area prior to landfall. Central to FEMA's ability to provide assistance to state and local responders is to have trained personnel in the field prior to landfall. These individuals can provide invaluable situational awareness, serve as liaisons with the state and local officials, and help identify needs and coordinate the response. Yet, FEMA didn't deploy anyone to New Orleans, and in fact it actually evacuated qualified personnel out of New Orleans prior to landfall.[156]

In contrast, prior to landfall in Mississippi, FEMA deployed personnel to EOCs in several counties most likely to be impacted by the hurricane.[157] These liaisons provided valuable on-the-ground information and assistance to locals in the crucial hours immediately following landfall and were invaluable in helping to coordinate the response in Mississippi. FEMA has a longstanding policy of not putting its emergency responders in the path of a storm, so that they will not be in need of rescue themselves. Lokey, however, testified that he would have liked to put some individuals in local EOCs prior to landfall, just as Carwile did in Mississippi, but that he didn't have enough personnel to do so.[158] Instead, the only FEMA official in New Orleans was Bahamonde, the public affairs officer sent to prepare for eventual VIP visits. Ultimately, Bahamonde served in some operations capacities, such as providing critical situational awareness, including the notice of broken levees.[159] In Louisiana, FEMA's response was adversely impacted by the failure to put personnel in or near New Orleans in advance of the storm.

Communications

FEMA neglected to adequately pre-stage communication assets and sufficiently equip its personnel. In fact, Lokey said that he "still lose[s] sleep over" the fact that prior to landfall, more measures could have been taken to provide for communications.[160] "We obviously did not bring enough or plan enough satellite or cell phones or alternative technology," he said. "And once it all went bad, we scrambled to get it, but as I was the FCO, I should have, but … I obviously didn't." It was "a step I missed."[161]

Lokey found a safe place in Baton Rouge to park the "Red October," FEMA's large, mobile command center with significant communication assets and conference space, and on Saturday evening requested that Red October be placed there prior to landfall.[162] His request was denied,[163] because then-FEMA Director Michael Brown had reportedly reserved the center.[164] Lokey therefore had no communications vehicle available to him at the EOC on landfall, though one arrived the following day.[165]

FEMA did pre-stage communications vehicles, prior to landfall, at Barksdale Air Force Base in Shreveport, Louisiana, which offered a secured site out of the storm's immediate path and was a convenient place to stage.[166] This put the vehicles about 350 miles from New Orleans and about 250 miles from Baton Rouge, however. This distance, and the fact that FEMA did not request that the assets be deployed from Shreveport until over 24 hours after landfall, meant they took some time to reach their new locations for response work.[167] In at least some instances, this delay may have prevented the assets from being placed where most needed. For example, even though the area around the Superdome did not flood until around noon on Tuesday, FEMA was not able to get the Red October into the area because of flooding; Red October did not get to Baton Rouge until Wednesday.[168] Besides not placing communications vehicles at the EOC[169] and not adequately equipping its employees with communications assets, FEMA also did not place any communications assets in the Superdome prior to landfall. As discussed in Chapter 18, the failure to have communications assets in the Superdome cut the effectiveness of FEMA's on-site response team by 90 percent.[170]

As discussed below, there was vast devastation to the land-line and cellular communications networks after Hurricane Katrina, which made communications very difficult. Indeed, Wells said the lack of communications at the EOC made it like a "black hole."[171] Lokey referred to it as a "vacuum" and said it was "very difficult to have a good operational picture of all that was going on."[172] This hindered the response.

Catastrophic Planning

FEMA had long known it needed to do general catastrophic planning for responding to large disasters, but had problems getting necessary funding. Requests for $100 million for catastrophic planning and an additional $20 million for catastrophic housing planning in fiscal year 2004 and fiscal year 2005, respectively, were denied by DHS.[173]

Although catastrophic planning for southeast Louisiana was recognized as a priority by FEMA regional staff and the State of Louisiana in 1999, funding shortages, staffing changes, and competing priorities delayed the planning. Funding shortages also affected the scope of the planning. Some areas that the Louisiana Office of Homeland Security and Emergency Preparedness (LOHSEP) had identified as topics it wanted to address, such as pre-landfall evacuation, as well as other areas, were dropped.[174] Follow-up workshops were also postponed. Lack of funding also prevented implementation of the Hurricane Pam plan.[175]

Despite these setbacks, FEMA attempted to use the Pam plan in responding to Katrina. Copies of the Pam documents were circulated throughout FEMA on Saturday, August 27. Additionally, Lokey ordered the contractor for the Pam project to come to the EOC in Baton Rouge to assist FEMA employees in implementing Pam.[176] In responding to Katrina, however, FEMA failed to follow some aspects of Pam. For example, the draft Pam plan said Region VI would activate its regional coordination center when the NWS advised that a hurricane or tropical storm posed a threat to Louisiana.[177] It also said the FEMA headquarters would deploy an evacuation team.[178] However, Region VI did not activate the RRCC until Saturday morning and FEMA appears not to have sent an evacuation team to Louisiana.[179] It also appears that FEMA also failed to identify buses and drivers and pre-stage buses and drivers pre-landfall as suggested in Pam.[180]

While it is impossible to know whether completing the Southeast Louisiana Catastrophic Hurricane Plan sooner would have resulted in a better response to Katrina, it is clear that FEMA had failed to do enough catastrophic planning. FEMA wasn't prepared. This lack of planning inevitably led to mistakes in the response. As Secretary Chertoff said, Katrina "tested our planning, and our planning, I think, fell short."[181]

Commodities

At the beginning of the 2005 hurricane season, FEMA had pre-positioned commodities in the Gulf Coast region as a way to speed up the response to hurricanes.[182] The effort included 30 tractor-trailer loads of water, 17 trailer loads of ice, and 15 trailer loads of MRE military rations at Camp Beauregard, a federal staging area in central Louisiana.[183]

However, preparations for a hurricane should not have ended with that initial pre-positioning, and the supplies pre-positioned were not enough for a storm as strong as Katrina. Ken Burris, FEMA's Acting Chief Operating Officer, confirmed that the initial pre-positioning was only a start, and that the specifics of a storm dictate whether FEMA should move more supplies to the area or move commodities closer to the predicted landfall.[184] While some supplies already staged in the region were moved to Mississippi or Alabama, records indicate that relatively few additional truckloads arrived in FEMA's staging areas in the days before landfall.[185] Indeed, FEMA documents show that FEMA did not get any additional commodities to the Camp Beauregard, Louisiana, staging area as Katrina moved through the Gulf of Mexico.[186] The record is not clear whether additional supplies were moved into the region bypassing FEMA's staging areas. With Katrina bearing down on the Gulf Coast as a catastrophic storm, FEMA should have gotten additional supplies to its staging areas in Mississippi and Louisiana. Additionally, although FEMA tried to place some commodities in the Superdome prior to landfall, it was only able to get part of the quantities it intended there as its contractors stopped trucking due to weather conditions.[187]

Despite efforts to move some commodities into Mississippi, there were major deficiencies. Carwile wrote several e-mails on Sunday in which he expressed concern with commodities issues.[188] FEMA had ordered 400 trucks of ice, 400 trucks of water, and 250 trucks of MREs for the Meridian Naval Air Station in Mississippi before the storm made landfall. Although FEMA and state officials in Mississippi were never able to discover exactly how many truckloads actually arrived pre-landfall,[189] according to Tom McAllister, Director of Response and Recovery at MEMA the amount of supplies FEMA pre-positioned was "nowhere near what we asked for," leaving Mississippi "critically shorthanded" for the first few days.[190]

Some senior leadership at FEMA lacked a basic understanding of commodities. Patrick Rhode, then Acting Deputy Director of FEMA, received information on quantities of pre-staged supplies on Friday afternoon, two and a half days before landfall.[191] Rhode later told interviewers that he did not believe the amount was adequate, but admitted he did not know how much was in a truckload, and had no idea for the amount of commodities he believed should be pre-staged.[192] "I don't know if I would have said specifically that we needed to provide more," Rhode said. "I was concerned as to whether or not our experts believed that we were doing everything that we could."[193]

FEMA's poor planning for transportation was a key factor in the problems with commodities. Gary Moore, FEMA's Director of Logistics, said FEMA had difficulty moving commodities during Katrina.[194] For instance, on Saturday afternoon, FEMA realized it did not have enough truck drivers to deliver commodities and equipment and started reviewing resumes to hire additional drivers.[195] By Sunday afternoon, records show that FEMA was short 68 of the 94 drivers who would be needed to move commodities for a short response effort and short 162 drivers needed for a longer response.[196] To make matters worse, FEMA's transportation contractor, Landstar, does not own any vehicles. Instead, it locates independent drivers only after FEMA asks it to move commodities, which can also lead to delays.[197] FEMA had to compete against Landstar for drivers to hire[198] – a task made more difficult because it took place over a weekend.[199]

FEMA's failure to pre-stage more commodities prior to landfall contributed to the human misery caused by commodities shortages after landfall.

FEMA Deployment of Disaster Medical Assistance Teams

The National Disaster Medical System (NDMS) comprises specialized emergency-medical and response teams who are federal first responders in a medical emergency. FEMA activated the NDMS on the Thursday before landfall. Although a number of teams were mobilized and began moving into the Gulf region, this effort fell far short of needs. By the night before landfall, only four complete Disaster Medical Assistance Teams (DMATs), two partial teams, and a few small five person strike teams – a total of about 250 personnel – were staged in the entire Gulf region, and only one team was deployed in Louisiana.[200] Thus, fewer than 10 percent of FEMA's 52 DMAT teams were in the region. Moreover, though activating NDMS four days before Katrina's arrival was prescient, NDMS's decision to place teams far from Katrina's path meant the teams faced hundreds of miles and hours of travel to reach areas in need after landfall. The NDMS teams were plagued by other inadequacies, including that no deployed team possessed a full inventory of medical supplies.[201]

Search and Rescue

As more thoroughly discussed in Chapter 21, FEMA failed to take appropriate action pre-landfall to prepare for search and rescue operations. FEMA officials knew that a major hurricane striking New Orleans could cause widespread flooding throughout the metropolitan New Orleans area. Yet prior to landfall, FEMA pre-positioned only three of its 28 Urban

Search and Rescue (USAR) teams in Shreveport, Louisiana, and two others in Meridian, Mississippi.[202]

Despite the expectation of flooding, FEMA did not pre-position boats for its USAR teams.[203] One USAR team manager said later:

> I don't recall that, that we were thinking about, gee, we're going to need a lot of boats down here. Actually, when the hurricane went through there, the news was saying, it's not a big deal. It spared the city. That's kind of the impression we were getting from watching the news on there, so we were not thinking about massive amounts of boats and things like that at that time, that I can recall. I'm sure we had some discussions about it.[204]

Finally, FEMA pre-staged the teams in Shreveport[205] – approximately 340 miles from New Orleans. Lokey made this choice because he wanted to be sure they would be out of harm's way while the storm's path was uncertain.[206] However, this distance meant that FEMA USAR teams did not reach New Orleans until Monday night, and did not begin rescue missions until Tuesday morning[207] – 14 hours after the Coast Guard and state and local teams[208] began rescuing people. FEMA's teams were too few, too late, and boatless.

Evacuation

The evacuation of the Gulf Coast was one of the most critical and controversial issues addressed during the investigation. For a discussion of any role or responsibility FEMA may have had in planning for the pre- or post-landfall evacuation, see Chapters 16 and 22.

Establishing a Joint Field Office

A Joint Field Office (JFO) is a coordination center that FEMA sets up, where federal, state, and local organizations with primary responsibility for disaster response can work together and coordinate the response. FEMA did not take adequate steps to set up the JFO before landfall.[209] While the preparatory step toward a JFO – an Initial Operating Facility (IOF) – was opened pre-landfall,[210] the JFO was not fully operational until 12 days after landfall.[211]

In a disaster, FEMA's Mobile Emergency Response Systems employees are responsible for setting up the JFO. Lokey was told that the JFO would be operating within 72 hours.[212] The nine-day delay past that 72-hour period in completing JFO set-up was mostly due to difficulty in establishing Internet connectivity for the state's computer system.[213] The state could not move into the JFO until the technology issues were fixed.[214] Until the second week in September, members of the JFO coordination group in Louisiana were located at several different locations while lacking reliable communications and the many benefits of co-location. FEMA employees working at borrowed space at the state EOC shared limited communications equipment, had limited access to computers, and worked in cramped conditions.[215] FEMA employees held many meetings in hallways for lack of other space. These cramped conditions and delays in setting up the JFO made it very difficult for FEMA to coordinate and operate with the state officials, which impeded a unified response.[216] Coordination greatly improved once the JFO was fully functional.[217]

Some of the problems caused by delays in setting up the JFO might have been alleviated if Lokey had had regular access to a command vehicle in which he could hold meetings with state and local officials.[218] As noted, then-FEMA Director Michael Brown had reserved the Red October command center.[219] Lokey did not request another command vehicle because he was told the JFO would be operational in three days after landfall.[220]

Security

The Federal Protective Service (FPS) generally provides security for FEMA assets and personnel at FEMA's request. Even without the threat of violence, DMAT teams may require security because they arrive with a cache of prescription drugs. Similarly, FEMA's search-and-rescue teams come with substantial and valuable equipment. However, FEMA sent DMAT and USAR teams into the field without security and without coordinating with other agencies to provide for their security. Historically, the FPS "take[s] over the ESF-13 [public safety and security] in the event that FEMA does declare an emergency."[221]

It wasn't until the morning of August 30 that FEMA issued the first in a series of mission assignments to the FPS to provide security for its responders. Even then, FEMA's assignment did not mention the Superdome. The first request for support at the Superdome was not created until mid-afternoon on August 30.[222] The following day, FPS received an additional mission assignment to send 14 officers to the Superdome to provide crowd control for the evacuation.[223] By then, although it was reported to those in the Superdome complex that there were 14 FPS officers just a couple of blocks away on the overpasses, the officers "couldn't find a way into the Dome," probably because of the flooding. [224]

As early as Sunday, August 28, the Customs and Border Patrol (CBP) – federal law-enforcement assets at DHS's disposal – placed a 100-agent deployment element on full standby.[225] The availability of this unit was reported in the CBP's twice-daily situation reports to DHS, although it is not clear where they were located. It was not until Wednesday, August 31, that these federal law-enforcement personnel were called up for deployment, and another 18 hours passed before they arrived in Louisiana, "to assist National Guard with crowd control and evacuation of 25 to 30 thousand individuals from the New Orleans Superdome." [226]

FEMA issued each of these assignments too late to ensure a timely arrival of FPS personnel. By the time of the earliest FPS mission assignment[227] DMAT personnel and equipment had already staged at the Superdome complex with water quickly flooding all around them.

In the absence of FPS, or of any other dedicated security contingent, FEMA personnel in the Superdome found themselves forced to choose between their mission and their security.[228] The responders' concerns for their safety increasingly distracted them from delivering medical care. On Thursday morning, September 1, concerned for their own safety, FEMA's DMAT and ERT-A teams left the Superdome, leaving behind the team's "cache, equipment, and rental vehicles"[229] – not to mention patients and others taking shelter there. When these teams left, FEMA no longer had a presence at the Superdome, and the medical burden on remaining state and local health-care professionals increased.

Department of Defense

Perhaps one of the most obvious consequences of FEMA not "thinking big enough" was its delay in asking the Department of Defense to apply its resources. Brown conceded that he should have spoken with DOD Secretary Donald Rumsfeld prior to landfall to request assets.[230] So, too, should have Secretary Chertoff, as discussed above. As discussed in Chapter 26, DOD was surprised by the early silence from FEMA.[231]

The pre-landfall need for DOD assets such as helicopters, boats, and communications equipment, was considered but not acted upon by FEMA or DHS leadership. On the August 28 VTC, Secretary Chertoff inquired, "Are there any DOD assets that might be available? Have we reached out to them, and have we, I guess, made any kind of arrangement in case we need some additional help from them?"[232] Brown replied that "We have DOD assets over [here] at the EOC. They are fully engaged."[233] Apparently, Brown was referring to DOD liaisons to the EOC, known as Defense Coordinating Officers (DCOs); in this case, two individuals, rather than tangible resources that could be positioned or readied. Secretary Chertoff accepted this reply, telling Brown, "good job." Neither Brown nor Secretary Chertoff sought to ascertain or understand what specific capabilities DOD might bring to the response, nor did they seek to call upon those capabilities before landfall. [234]

Conclusion

FEMA's mistakes in preparing for Katrina were many, and, as we will see, contributed to its overall deficient response. Despite knowing for years the catastrophic impact a hurricane could have on New Orleans, FEMA's leadership failed to move far enough beyond its normal modes of operation as "the big one" moved to shore. Those ordinary operating protocols were inadequate for a catastrophic disaster, and did not make enough use of the assets at the agency's disposal. The words of one FEMA employee are telling: "We kind of assumed it was going to be just a regular, normal response to a disaster." FEMA's pre-landfall preparations fell far short of what the situation called for. FEMA was simply not "thinking big enough."

U.S. Coast Guard

As discussed in other sections, the Coast Guard performed well in the response to Hurricane Katrina. Any problems were due mostly to the poor preparation of other DHS components.

Unlike their counterparts in other DHS components, Coast Guard personnel were quite familiar with the NRP. They also had detailed plans for evacuation and continuity of government, had a clear mission statement, and were familiar with state and local officials and geography from their daily work as first responders and from their disaster planning. Although DHS failed to take advantage of the Coast Guard's intelligence-gathering capability in the critical hours after landfall, overall, the Coast Guard's advance moves were exemplary.

The Coast Guard is unique among federal agencies involved in emergency response in that it has military, law-enforcement, and first-response obligations.[235] Rigorous planning, training, and exercising are key elements in the Coast Guard's approach to disaster response.[236]

In the spring of 2005, as in every spring prior to the start of the hurricane season, the 8th Coast Guard District – which stretches from the Appalachians, to the Rockies, south of the Great Lakes, and to part of Florida – and all its subordinate units, including Sector New Orleans, exercised their hurricane plans.[237] Because personnel turnover in the New Orleans District runs about one-third each year, the exercise provides a good opportunity to bring new personnel into the Coast Guard's culture of operations on the Gulf Coast, including how to make hurricane plans for their own families.[238]

The exercise involved a simulation of a hurricane hitting New Orleans. As Rear Admiral Robert Duncan, the Commander of the 8th District, commented, "We take them through a timeline of the storm approaching, the storm getting close, the storm hitting, and the recovery piece."[239] During the exercise, Coast Guard officials visited state, municipal, and other EOCs, as well as their own pre-designated primary and secondary "safe havens" for pre-landfall evacuations.[240] They also confirmed critical phone numbers[241] and reviewed their Continuity of Operations Plan (COOP) to ensure they could maintain essential services without interruption:[242]

> Sector New Orleans will provide search and rescue support, restore essential aids to navigation, respond to hazardous material spills, manage waterways including traffic and safety or security zones, provide transportation of victims, provide essential waterborne and airborne logistics support, deliver vital supplies and materials, provide access to storm damaged areas to key response personnel, and perform any and all acts necessary to rescue and aid persons and protect and save property.[243]

Three days before the storm hit, Sector New Orleans sent out warnings to the port community, maritime industry, and the public at large urging them to take necessary precautions.[244] Staff established the Sector's alternative incident-command post in Alexandria, Louisiana, and evacuated their personnel and family members from New Orleans and nearby areas in the projected path of the storm.[245] Sector Mobile moved its command to Maxwell Air Force Base, Alabama.[246] Following its hurricane evacuation plan, the 8th District Command moved to St. Louis.[247]

The Coast Guard pre-positioned patrol boats, river tenders, and small boats and crews away from their exposed home ports.[248] They deployed the medium-endurance cutter USCGC *Spencer* from the East Coast to the Louisiana area so it could later act as a command-and-control platform.[249] They alerted a C-130 aircraft and crew in Clearwater, Florida, that they would be needed after landfall to assess damage to the off-shore oil facilities in the Gulf of Mexico.[250]

On August 27, the Coast Guard positioned its five search-and-rescue helicopters from Sector New Orleans in Houston, Texas, and Lake Charles, Louisiana, just out of the hurricane's path, so they could fly in behind the storm.[251] As they flew out of New Orleans that day, Captain Bruce Jones, the Commander of Coast Guard Air Station New Orleans, told his flight crews, "Take a last look folks, because when you come back, it will be under twenty feet of water."[252]

Coast Guard liaison officers were positioned at the State EOC in Baton Rouge and at the City EOC in New Orleans.[253] Admiral Duncan called Governors Blanco and Barbour and advised them of Coast Guard preparations for the storm.[254] At noon on Sunday, August 28, the Coast Guard closed the Mississippi River to all vessel movements, ceased cargo operations, and sent out final advisories to the maritime industries on necessary precautions to safeguard property.[255]

As it became clear that Katrina would make landfall in heavily populated areas, Coast Guard units in other stations around the country prepared to deploy following landfall,[256] though there were no orders to do so. As Coast Guard Vice Admiral Vivien Crea described Coast Guard culture, "There's just an understanding and a predisposition that … if something happens and you're in the way, you either hunker down or move out of the way so you can come in behind. If you're not in the target zone and it's bad enough, you better be prepared to go there and help out."[257]

At 2:50 p.m. on Monday, August 29, Coast Guard helicopters made their first rescue in the New Orleans area.[258]

As further discussed in Chapter 21, the Committee's investigation established that several factors contributed to the Coast Guard's success in preparing for Hurricane Katrina. First, rigorous planning, training, and exercising are key elements in the Coast Guard's approach to disaster response. Second, the Coast Guard's plans and exercises help personnel develop and maintain close ties to state and local officials, with whom they coordinated closely during the Katrina response effort. Third, the Coast Guard has a clearly articulated response mission understood by all personnel. Fourth, the Coast Guard notifies public- and private-sector partners of storm risks and of necessary safety precautions. Fifth, the Coast Guard aggressively moves personnel and assets out of the storm's path, but positions them to maximize their utility in the response effort. Finally, the Coast Guard plans for and rapidly deploys additional assets from outside the affected area without significant bureaucratic hurdles, owing to an institutional commitment to providing assistance whenever possible. The Coast Guard's efforts – including the rescue of over 33,000 people – demonstrate the effectiveness of proactive planning for disaster response.[259]

Unfortunately, DHS, which had extremely poor situational awareness of the storm's impact, failed to make use of the Coast Guard's early presence in the area. Coast Guard helicopter pilots were flying missions over the city as early as 3 p.m. on landfall day, Monday, August 29, and were probably the first federal officials to see the breach in the 17th Street Canal. Admiral Duncan was the highest-ranking federal official to see New Orleans on August 29, when he flew over the city at approximately 6 p.m. in a Coast Guard Falcon jet to perform a damage assessment, and saw widespread flooding. However, as discussed in Chapter 20, it does not appear that any effort was made to harness this information-gathering apparatus in service of the broader DHS mission.

U.S. Department of Health and Human Services and FEMA's National Disaster Medical System

On Thursday, August 25, four days prior to landfall, FEMA Response Division Chief Edward Buikema wrote a memo to his Operations Branch Chief, William Lokey, activating the National Disaster Medical System (NDMS) – a system of medical and specialty teams designed to respond to medical emergencies.[260] The basic unit of NDMS is the Disaster Medical Assistance Team (DMAT). FEMA "leaned forward" on the premise that Katrina presented a potentially catastrophic event, and began to mobilize and pre-position teams without state requests. (*See* Chapter 27 for a discussion of situations when the NRP empowers the federal government to offer help without waiting for requests.) They made these decisions based on senior leadership experience and the need to avoid delay, Beall said:

We front-loaded those resources, and then as the state would request ESF-8 – we need a team down at this hospital, that hospital – the resource was there. In the past, they would ask, and I would have to get a team rostered, get transportation, try to fly the resource, and get it. A lot of times it could get there, but you needed it yesterday, not two days from now.[261]

Mick Cote, the NDMS state representative in Region VI, which covers New Mexico, Oklahoma, Texas, Arkansas, and Louisiana, expressed the urgency felt by NDMS leadership in an e-mail to NDMS Director Jack Beall on August 27:

> 40+ medical facilities in the 11-Parish impact zone. Models predict up to 20 ft. of water in those 11 parishes with little hope of removing it in less than 2 months. The catastrophic plan predicts 7,500 casualties per day over a 5-day period and 60,000 fatalities. In addition, estimates place critical care patients, staff, families and refugees sheltered in hospital at 10,000+.[262]

Cote went on to inform Beall that the State of Louisiana had identified three medical staging areas to handle victims of the hurricane. These sites were expected to be outside of the storm path but close enough to send care quickly: Louisiana State University (LSU) in Baton Rouge (80 miles from New Orleans), Southeast Louisiana University in Hammond (58 miles), and Nichols State University in Thibodaux (67 miles). Cote communicated Louisiana's need to Beall: "Based on the casualty estimates, the plan calls for three full DMATs at each medical staging site and two medical strike teams[263] to be located at each of four Search and Rescue Bases of Operations."[264] Beall replied, "Mick, by 1800 hours tomorrow night, I will have 9 DMATS, 9 [five]-person strike teams, 2 MSTs [Management Support Teams]."[265]

Yet, by 6 p.m. on August 28, the night before Katrina's landfall, NDMS logs indicate that there were only four complete DMATs and two partial teams staged in the entire Gulf region, and only one of them deployed within Louisiana.[266] That team, Oklahoma-1 DMAT, had been directed to the Superdome not by NDMS, but at the request of U.S. Department of Health and Human Services (HHS) Assistant Secretary Stewart Simonson.[267] Under the

NRP, HHS is the federal agency responsible for coordinating federal medical care in an emergency.

After a Sunday-morning phone conversation with New Orleans's Health Director, Dr. Kevin Stephens, Assistant Secretary Simonson requested that two DMATs deploy to the Superdome before landfall.[268] FEMA sent only one team (Oklahoma-1), which did not manage to reach the Superdome before landfall.[269] It appears from the NDMS status reports that Oklahoma-1 was the only DMAT actually available to be deployed to the Superdome at that time.[270]

Aside from Oklahoma-1, which diverted to the Louisiana State University on Sunday night when it could not reach the Superdome, NDMS did not stage its DMATs at the Louisiana sites identified by Cote on August 27 or at any other locations in Louisiana or Mississippi. Instead it staged them outside these states: at the Hyatt Regency in Houston, Texas (350 miles from New Orleans); at the Noble Training Site in Anniston, Alabama (312 miles from Mobile, AL); and at the Marriot Hotel in Memphis, Tennessee (379 miles from Biloxi, Mississippi).[271]

It is not clear why NDMS chose these sites for the pre-staging of DMATs, especially after Louisiana apparently requested that the teams be brought closer. Under the NRP, ESF-8 (which is the interagency coordinating group for health care) is tasked with making decisions about the deployment of medical response assets.[272] On Sunday, August 28, Beall wrote an e-mail to Lokey asking "Bill, I am hearing the State of [Louisiana] is requesting DMATs be moved closer within the state. Can you advise?"[273] Lokey responded in ambiguous terms. "ESF 8 is working with state on a plan. No visibility on the outcome."[274] NDMS team status reports show that no NDMS teams were ever moved to Louisiana or Mississippi before landfall except for Oklahoma-1.[275]

In sum, while FEMA's Response Division deserves credit for activating the NDMS four days before Katrina's arrival, the NDMS decision to place teams so far away from Katrina's path meant they were hundreds of miles and hours of travel from areas in need. When HHS asked for two DMATs to go to the Superdome, FEMA apparently was unable to muster two teams to respond. The one team that actually arrived at one of Louisiana's three medical staging areas – Oklahoma-1 – was there by "mistake," because it couldn't reach the Superdome.

Assistant Secretary Simonson directed that HHS deploy its own assets to the Superdome as well. The morning of Sunday, August 28, Simonson directed the Office of Force Readiness and Deployment (OFRD) within HHS to assemble a team of 50 U.S. Public Health Service (USPHS) officers from Washington, D.C., and an additional team from the Atlanta area to provide medical support for the Superdome.[276] OFRD is the office that is responsible for deploying USPHS personnel.

OFRD had already begun to plan for Hurricane Katrina when it was still a tropical storm. On August 25, OFRD had been asked to roster a team of 100 USPHS officers for pre-deployment to the Gulf Coast. OFRD staff sent a mass e-mail to these 100 officers and then also tried to contact many via phone. Each time a USPHS team is needed, the team is created on an ad-hoc basis because USPHS officers are scattered across the nation and are not a part of pre-existing teams.[277]

By Saturday evening, Rear Admiral John Babb, the OFRD chief, reported that OFRD had been able to assemble 55 officers, who were waiting for travel orders.[278] (In such situations, officers reach their destinations by commercial flights; at this point, however, OFRD had not received the deployment destinations.[279]) When Assistant Secretary Simonson directed that a team be assembled to go to the Super-dome, this 55-person team could simply not get there before landfall.

As a result, on Sunday, Admiral Babb and his staff had to essentially start from scratch to assemble a new team that could be flown in by charter aircraft. They called hundreds of telephone numbers to reach USPHS officers in Washington, D.C., and Atlanta, but could only connect with 38 officers.[280] Eventually, 37 officers boarded the chartered flights arranged by Babb; a shortage of seats forced one officer to stay behind.[281]

Due to the late hour and deteriorating weather, the flights were routed to Jackson, Mississippi. The Health Service team got to Louisiana on the Tuesday after landfall, and was assigned to help staff the state's medical staging facility at Louisiana State University in Baton Rouge.[282]

Zephyr Field staging area, Louisiana
U.S. Coast Guard photo

Assistant Secretary Simonson also directed the HHS office that manages the Strategic National Stockpile (SNS) (a stockpile of medical supplies that can be provided to states in medical emergencies) in Atlanta, Georgia, to dispatch a shipment of supplies to the Super-dome.[283] Assistant Secretary Simonson based his request on an initial list dictated to him by Dr. Stephens, the New Orleans health director, on Sunday. Assistant Secretary Simonson e-mailed the director of the Strategic Stockpile around 1 p.m. that afternoon:

> I need to get the following to N[ew] O[rleans] before the H[urricane] strikes: Gloves, bandages, blanked [blanket], blood pressure cuffs, adult diapers, Ace wraps, slings, gauze, hot and cold packs, [glucometers] and sticks, oxygen and other basic medical supplies. They are expecting something like 50,000 people in the Super Dome. Any ideas about how to handle dialysis. What about oxygen, do we have any supplies? Please get this together asap and tell me how much we can send.[284]

Officials at the Strategic National Stockpile advised Assistant Secretary Simonson that they had located almost all of the materials and dispatched the shipment.[285] However, they were unable to transport the materials into New Orleans: "At this point, we believe cannot safely move to New Orleans prior to the hurricane so are making preparation to transport to Barksdale A[ir]F[orce]B[ase] [in northwest Louisiana] which FEMA indicates will be their logistics staging area."[286] These supplies did not reach Louisiana until mid-day on Monday, after landfall, and were turned over to the State of Louisiana late the same day.[287]

Department of Defense

Under the NRP, the Department of Defense (DOD) is assigned a supporting role for all Emergency Support Functions (ESFs), and can also be requested to provide assistance in support of those functions by FEMA.

At the headquarters level – the civilian Office of the Assistant Secretary of Defense for Homeland Defense (OASD-HD) and the uniformed Joint Directorate of Military Support (JDOMS) within the Pentagon's Joint Staff – officials took several actions in anticipation of receiving requests from FEMA, and monitored FEMA's teleconferences. When Hurricane Katrina appeared as a tropical depression on August 23, DOD officials took an inventory of available commodities, and identified medical facilities and potential staging bases for FEMA.[288] DOD officials at the Pentagon did not alter their usual asset-inventory process as Katrina strengthened and moved toward the Gulf Coast.[289] However, on the Sunday before landfall, JDOMS established a 24-hour "crisis action cell" to allow for rapid processing once they began to receive requests from FEMA.[290]

Military commanders have a limited authority to deploy assets without orders from their superior officers or authorization from the DOD – if commanders label the deployment an "exercise."

Within the Army, Lieutenant General Russel Honoré, Commander of the U.S. First Army based in Atlanta, Georgia, had provided assistance during the destructive 2004 hurricane season. As a Louisiana native, Lt. Gen. Honoré understood the potential damage Katrina could inflict on the Gulf Coast. In coordination with U.S. Northern Command (NORTH-COM) in Colorado Springs, Colorado, the headquarters for command and control of domestic military operations, he prepared to deploy himself and his staff on an "exercise mission" to Camp Shelby, an Army base in southern Mississippi. He also requested that assets he thought would be required in the immediate hours after landfall, including helicopters, small boats, and communications gear, be identified and alerted to speed their deployment in response to an eventual request.[291]

Within the Marine Corps, several generals began to assess the availability of helicopters and engineering equipment.[292] In the Navy, the Commander of the Second Fleet recognized that the USS *Bataan*, a helicopter-bearing ship in port in Texas, was well-positioned to provide assistance and ordered the ship to get underway on August 28 and steam in behind the hurricane.[293] The *Bataan* had been deployed to the area on an exercise, so the fleet commander was acting within his authority. As a result, once Katrina made landfall, the *Bataan*'s helicopters were among the first active-duty aircraft to conduct search-and-rescue missions beginning on Tuesday.[294] Nonetheless, DHS personnel questioned the admiral's forethought and authority, and were reportedly angered that the Navy had acted in advance of a request.[295]

At NORTHCOM, the Operations Directorate commenced daily teleconferences on August 24.[296] On August 19, as a general measure for the hurricane season, the Secretary of Defense had granted authority for NORTHCOM to take several specific measures prior to landfall.[297] Beginning on August 26, NORTHCOM used this authority to deploy coordinating personnel first to Florida, then to Alabama, Mississippi, and Louisiana. The Louisiana representatives arrived the night of August 27. Under this authority and in response to a request from FEMA, NORTHCOM designated two military bases in Mississippi and Louisiana as federal staging facilities.[298]

The preparations by the commanders were not always coordinated with DOD, and on at least one occasion, met with resistance from a DOD headquarters component. General Honoré's request on the eve of landfall that certain assets be identified for immediate use[299] was not answered by the Joint Staff,[300] despite the fact that the NORTHCOM Director of Operations made the same request by personally contacting the Director of JDOMS.[301] Several witnesses explained that, traditionally, the Pentagon will only take disaster-assistance action with a specific request from FEMA and once the actual requirement has been verified,[302] though as noted above, several commanders took the initiative to mobilize and alert assets in advance of FEMA requests.

Although DOD was prepared to receive and process requests, it received very few requests from FEMA prior to landfall. In addition to staging bases, FEMA requested that DOD provide helicopters for rapid needs assessment prior to landfall; JDOMS only approved this request 12 hours after landfall, a sign, according to some witnesses, of its initial reluctance to provide assistance without the conditions described above.[303] And although the Department's preparations for Katrina were consistent with its procedures and prior practices in civil-support missions, they were not sufficient for a storm of Katrina's magnitude. Additional preparations in advance of specific requests for support could have enabled a more rapid response.

1 Homeland Security Presidential Directive-5 clarifies the responsibilities given to DHS by the Homeland Security Act by formally designating the Secretary of Homeland Security as the "principal federal official for domestic incident management." The NRP further affirms the preeminent role of the DHS Secretary in coordinating the federal response to a disaster. Thus, the authority of the DHS Secretary is derived from the President in HSPD-5 within the framework of the NRP. The White House, Homeland Security Presidential Directive-5: Management of Domestic Incidents, Feb. 28, 2003.

2 Questions for the Record of Sec. Michael Chertoff, U.S. Department of Homeland Security, for the U.S. Senate, Committee on Homeland Security and Governmental Affairs, hearing on *Hurricane Katrina: The Homeland Security Department's Response*, Feb. 15, 2006, p. 15.

3 Questions for the Record of Sec. Chertoff, Senate Committee hearing, Feb. 15, 2005, p. 15.

4 Testimony of Sec. Michael Chertoff, U.S. Department of Homeland Security, before the U.S. House, Select Bipartisan Committee to Investigate the Preparation for and Response to Hurricane Katrina, hearing on *Hurricane Katrina: The Role of the Department of Homeland Security,* Oct. 19, 2005.

5 Michael Brown, FEMA Daily Video Teleconference, Aug. 28, 2005, transcript p. 37. Provided to Committee; filed as Bates no. DHS-FEMA-0105-0000102.

6 Sec. Michael Chertoff, FEMA Daily Video Teleconference, Aug. 28, 2005, transcript p. 38. Provided to Committee; filed as Bates no. DHS-FEMA-0105-0000103.

7 Sec. Chertoff, VTC, Aug. 28, 2005, p. 38.

8 Sec. Chertoff, Senate Committee Hearing, Feb. 15, 2006.

9 Col. Jeff Smith, FEMA Daily Video Teleconference, Aug. 28, 2005, transcript pp. 18-19. Provided to Committee; filed as Bates nos. DHS-FEMA-0105-0000083 through 0000084.

10 FEMA Daily Video Teleconference, Aug. 28, 2005, transcript p. 21. Provided to Committee; filed as Bates no. DHS-FEMA-0105-0000086. Brown testified that by his questions, he was seeking information from the state on what it needed at that moment only. Committee Staff interview of Michael Brown, former Director, FEMA, conducted on Feb. 23, 2006, transcript pp. 62-67.

11 Sec. Chertoff, Senate Committee hearing, Feb. 15, 2006. Sec. Chertoff also testified that he relied on FEMA's experience and expertise: "If there is nothing else that FEMA is an expert in, it is hurricanes." *Source:* Sec. Chertoff, Senate Committee hearing, Feb. 15, 2006. However at the time of Katrina, only one individual in FEMA's front office, Acting Chief Operating Officer Ken Burris, had emergency management experience before joining FEMA. Prior to joining FEMA, Brown had been working as a Commissioner for the International Arabian Horse Association for approximately 10 years. Acting Deputy Director and Chief of Staff Patrick Rhode, Policy Director Brooks Altshuler, Acting Deputy Chief of Staff Scott Morris, and Special Assistant Michael Heath all had no prior emergency management experience. *Source:* Committee staff interview of Michael Brown, former Director, FEMA, conducted on Jan. 23, 2006, transcript pp. 219-220.

12 Questions for the Record of Sec. Chertoff, Senate Committee hearing, Feb. 15, 2005, p. 15.

13 In his response to one of the Committee's post-hearing questions, Sec. Chertoff described his activities over the weekend as follows: "In the weekend before landfall, I followed planning activities closely and I stayed in continual contact with senior DHS and FEMA officials and my experienced advisers. I participated in the noontime FEMA VTC on Sunday, August 28, at which time I explicitly asked Mr. Brown if he required any additional assistance from other DHS components, and if he was getting everything he needed from DOD. Louisiana officials also noted at that time that they were satisfied with the level of pre-positioning of assets and cooperation that they were receiving from FEMA. I was also in direct personal contact with each of the governors of the affected states that day, and repeatedly thereafter." *Source:* Questions for the Record of Sec. Chertoff, Senate Committee hearing, Feb. 15, 2005, p. 15; Committee staff interview

of John Wood, Chief of Staff, U.S. Department of Homeland Security, conducted on Jan. 27, 2006, transcript pp. 59-60 ("I mean, I think that there was certainly informal communication in which he was, you know, briefed about the status of things and to which he may have given, you know, feedback, but I don't recall, you know, memos or specific, you know, orders and things like that; not to say there weren't any, but I don't recall."); Committee staff interview of Michael Jackson, Deputy Secretary, U.S. Department of Homeland Security, conducted on Jan. 27, 2006, transcript pp. 60-61; Committee staff interview of Matt A. Mayer, Counselor to Deputy Secretary, U.S. Department of Homeland Security, conducted on Jan. 26, 2006, transcript pp. 74-75; Committee staff interview of Robert Stephan, Assistant Secretary for Infrastructure Protection, U.S. Department of Homeland Security, conducted on Jan. 13, 2006, transcript pp. 50-51.

14 Brown, VTC, Aug. 28, 2005, p. 38.

15 Max Mayfield, FEMA Daily Video Teleconference, Aug. 28, 2005, transcript pp. 3-6. Provided to Committee; filed as Bates nos. DHS-FEMA-0105-0000068 through 0000071.

16 Although Sec. Chertoff has stated that over the course of the weekend before landfall he "followed planning activities closely" and "stayed in continual contact with senior DHS and FEMA officials and my experienced advisors," *Source:* Questions for the Record of Sec. Chertoff, Senate Committee hearing, Feb. 15, 2006, p. 15. The Secretary has provided no more detail about these discussions, so it is unclear what he learned or what questions he asked. Aside from the foregoing, the Committee's investigation has uncovered no other evidence regarding the specifics of such inquiries – no e-mails referring to Sec. Chertoff's inquiries and no communications with anyone outside his senior staff at DHS. UnderSecretary Brown testified that he did not recall speaking directly with Sec. Chertoff the weekend before landfall. *Source:* Brown interview, Jan. 23, 2006, p. 88. Deputy Sec. Jackson did speak with Brown over the weekend. Brown testified that he told Deputy Sec. Jackson that he was concerned that Katrina could be a catastrophic event, but did not ask Deputy Sec. Jackson for any additional assistance from DHS because he believed FEMA could and would make those requests through the Emergency Support Functions or directly to other DHS components. *Source:* Brown interview, Jan. 23, 2006, pp. 88, 96, 105.

17 U.S. Department of Homeland Security, Office of Inspector General, "Emergency Preparedness and Response Could Better Integrate Information Technology with Incident Response and Recovery," Sept. 2005. In an August rebuttal to the draft report, Brown disputed its findings and argued that FEMA had responded successfully to the hurricanes. The IG responded that Brown "incorrectly equate[d] the agency's ability to meet the disaster challenges to date with effective and efficient IT management. While we state in our report that [FEMA] was able to get through the 2004 hurricanes, we also recognize that FEMA's accomplishments were not necessarily because of its IT systems, but often in spite of them. Users across [FEMA] consistently told us that they did not use the headquarters-supplied systems, but instead relied upon alternative methods, such as creating ad hoc spreadsheets and databases or resorting to manual methods, to perform their jobs. Where IT systems were used, they often did not operate effectively." U.S. Department of Homeland Security, Office of Inspector General, "Emergency Preparedness and Response Could Better Integrate Information Technology with Incident Response and Recovery," Sept. 2005, pp. 23, 35.

18 Committee staff interview of Pat English, Chief Procurement Officer, FEMA, conducted on Jan. 5, 2006, transcript pp. 64, 81-84 ("I know he [DHS Chief Procurement Officer Greg Rothwell] briefed senior management in DHS, the Under Secretary, the DepSec, and on that scorecard, FEMA['s procurement office] was red, which indicated, you know, understaffed.").

19 Sec. Chertoff, House Select Committee hearing, Oct. 19, 2005; Questions for the Record of Sec. Chertoff, Senate Committee hearing, Feb. 15, 2006, pp. 44, 84.

20 Brown interview, Jan. 23, 2006, p. 88; Questions for the Record of Sec. Chertoff, Senate Committee hearing, Feb. 15, 2006, p. 15

21 Questions for the Record of Sec. Chertoff, Feb. 15, 2006, p. 15.

22 Committee staff interview of Brig. Gen. Matthew Broderick, U.S. Marine Corps (Ret.), former Director, Homeland Security Operations Center, U.S. Department of Homeland Security, conducted on Jan. 19, 2006, transcript pp. 81-82.

23 Broderick interview, Jan. 19, 2006, p. 82.

24 Committee staff interview of Peter Fonash, Ph.D., Director, National Communication System, U.S. Department of Homeland Security, conducted on Jan. 27, 2006, transcript pp. 49-52.

25 Fonash interview, Jan. 27, 2006, pp. 120-21.

26 Questions for the Record of Sec. Chertoff, Senate Committee hearing, Feb. 15, 2006, p. 15; Wood interview, Jan. 27, 2006, pp. 56-57; Mayer interview, Jan. 26, 2006, pp. 76-77; Brig. Gen. Broderick interview, Jan. 19, 2006, pp. 208-210; Jackson interview, Jan. 27, 2006, pp. 69-71.

27 An "ATF Summary of Significant Activity" produced by the ATF said that on Sept. 2, 2005, the "ATF established point of contact at the ESF 13 Desk and the NRCC and at the IIMG." Bureau of Alcohol, Tobacco and Firearms, Summary of Significant Activity. Provided to Committee; filed as Bates no. ATF 0000000009.

28 Committee staff interview of Wendell Shingler, Director, Federal Protective Service, U.S. Department of Homeland Security, conducted on Jan. 31, 2006, transcript pp. 54-55.

29 John Clark, e-mail to Gary Lang and others, Sept. 1, 2005, 5:58 p.m. Provided to Committee; filed as Bates no. DHS-ICE-1-0002-0000550.

30 The White House, Homeland Security Presidential Directive-8: National Preparedness, Dec. 17, 2003; U.S. Department of Homeland Security, *National Response Plan*. Washington: Government Printing Office, Dec. 2004, pp. 9, 15

[hereinafter *NRP*].

31 Questions for the Record of Sec. Chertoff, Senate Committee hearing, Feb. 15, 2006, p. 15.

32 Testimony of David Walker, U.S. Comptroller General, Government Accountability Office, before U.S. Senate, Committee on Homeland Security and Governmental Affairs, hearing on *Hurricane Katrina: Recommendations for Reform*, Mar. 8, 2006.

33 U.S. Department of Homeland Security, *National Response Plan, Catastrophic Incident Annex*. Washington: Government Printing Office, Dec. 2004, p. CAT–1 [hereinafter *NRP-CIA*].

34 *NRP-CIA*, p. CAT–5.

35 Stephan interview, Jan. 13, 2006, p. 35; Broderick interview, Jan. 19, 2006, p. 37.

36 Although the Secretary provides several reasons why it was not a mistake not to have activated the CIA, the Secretary never explicitly states that he considered and rejected this alternative. The NRP-CIA also was not activated for Hurricane Rita, but the federal government's preparation was more proactive pre-landfall than was the case for Hurricane Katrina.

37 Questions for the Record of Sec. Chertoff, Senate Committee hearing, Feb. 15, 2006, p. 3.

38 Questions for the Record of Sec. Chertoff, Senate Committee hearing, Feb. 15, 2006, p. 3.

39 Walker, Senate Committee hearing, Mar. 8, 2006. Secretary Chertoff argued that in the case of Katrina there was a great deal of coordination with the states, and the President's pre-landfall declarations had opened "the legal and strategic floodgates to allow as much information – as much resources and as many assets to be pushed into the theater of engagement as possible." He added that "If there is a different view of the Annex, I am always ready to consider clarifying the text." *Source:* Questions for the Record of Sec. Chertoff, Senate Committee hearing, Feb. 15, 2005, p. 4.

40 *NRP-CIA*, p. CAT–1 ("Accordingly, upon designation by the Secretary of Homeland Security of a catastrophic incident, Federal resources – organized into specific "packages" – deploy in accordance with the NRP-CIS and in coordination with the affect State and incident command structure.").

41 In his response to one of Committee's questions, the Secretary asserted that more assets than those that were called for under the CIS were in fact pre-positioned. *Source:* Questions for the Record of Sec. Chertoff, Senate Committee hearing, Feb. 15, 2005, pp. 3-4. Any suggestion that the CIS was followed de facto is not accurate, since two of the actions called for by the CIS pre-landfall – appointing a PFO pre-landfall and activating the IIMG – were not carried out in that timeframe. Committee staff interview of David Garratt, Acting Director of Recovery, FEMA, Jan. 9, 2006, pp. 8-13.

42 U.S. Department of Homeland Security, *National Response Plan, Catastrophic Incident Supplement*, Draft for Official Use Only, Sept. 2005, p. 10. Provided to Committee; filed as Bates no. DHS-FEMA-0109-0000010 [hereinafter *Catastrophic Incident Supplement*].

43 *NRP-CIA*, p. CAT–1.

44 Garrett interview, Jan. 9, 2006, pp. 36-37. Janet Benini, e-mail to Eric Tolbert and Ron Castleman, July 1, 2004, 4 p.m. Provided to Committee; filed as Bates no. DHS-FEMA-0058-0000261.

45 Janet Benini, e-mail to David Garret, Aug. 27, 2005, 12:30 p.m. Provided to Committee; filed as Bates no. DHS-FEMA-0096-0000395.

46 Brown interview, Feb. 23, 2006, p. 167.

47 Testimony of Paul McHale, Assistant Secretary of Defense for Homeland Defense, U.S. Department of Defense, before the U.S. Senate, Committee on Homeland Security and Governmental Affairs, hearing on *Hurricane Katrina and the Defense Department Response*, Feb. 9, 2006.

48 U.S. Northern Command, USNORTHCOM Hurricane Katrina Timeline (Draft), pp. 9-11. Provided to Committee; U.S. Fleet Forces Command, briefing slides, "Hurricane Katrina Nay Mission: Providing Rescue and Civil Support Relief from the Sea, Air and Land," Nov. 14, 2005, p. 8. Provided to Committee.

49 Two emergency management experts, Chuck Mills and John Harrald, both told committee staff that they believe that invoking the NRP-CIA would have made a difference by instilling a "sense of urgency" in the response. Committee staff interview of Chuck Mills, Vice President, Emergency Management Services International, Inc., and John Harrald, Ph.D., Co-Director, The George Washington University Institute for Crisis, Disaster, and Risk Management, conducted on Feb. 14, 2006 (untranscribed).

50 Sec. Michael Chertoff, memorandum to Deputy Secretary and others, Aug. 20, 2005. Provided to Committee; filed as Bates nos. DHS 0002822 through 0002824.

51 *NRP*, p. 33.

52 Committee staff interview of Ken Kaiser, Special Agent in Charge, Boston Field Office, Federal Bureau of Investigation, Jan. 25, 2006, transcript p. 46.

53 Sec. Chertoff, Senate Committee hearing, Feb. 15, 2006, p. 40.

54 Some witnesses saw the appointment of a PFO as important to a coordinated effort. For example, Admiral Thad Allen – who would ultimately be named to replace Mike Brown as PFO and was widely praised for his efforts in that role – sent an e-mail to Chief of Staff John Wood on the day of landfall suggesting that a PFO should be appointed. *Source:* Committee staff interview of Vice Adm. Thad Allen, Chief of Staff, U.S. Coast Guard, conducted on Feb. 3, 2006, transcript pp. 113-114. And, although it occurred after landfall, Assistant Secretary of Defense for Homeland Defense Paul McHale

told staff in an interview that he asked his Deputy Peter Verga to call DHS Tuesday morning, August 30, regarding the lack of a PFO. McHale stated that he thought that naming a PFO "would be an important initial step in triggering the capabilities available under the NRP." *Source:* Committee staff interview of Paul McHale, Assistant Secretary of Defense for Homeland Defense, U.S. Department of Defense, conducted on Jan. 4, 2006, transcript p. 131.

55 Hurricane Rita demonstrated the difference that early appointment of a qualified PFO can make. There, an early, massive and coordinated federal effort was led by a PFO appointed two days before landfall. The federal government provided over 650 buses for general evacuation and arranged for ambulances and aircraft to evacuate thousands of special needs individuals. While there is no doubt that much of the federal government's pre-Rita steps were a result of lessons learned from Katrina, and though the Rita evacuation as a whole was far from perfect, the federal effort was coordinated, in no small part because a PFO was in place to lead it at a very early point.

56 Brown interview, Jan. 23, 2006, p. 70.

57 *NRP*, p. 33 ("The PFO provides a primary point of contact and situational awareness locally for the Secretary of Homeland Security").

58 *NRP*, p. 33.

59 Jackson interview, Jan. 27, 2006, p. 41.

60 FEMA Operations Center, e-mail to Brooks Altshuler and others, Sept. 1, 2005, 10:07 p.m. Provided to Committee; filed as Bates no. DHS 0003138. The e-mail was also sent to Michael Brown and indicated that a "light" earthquake measuring 4.8 on the Richter Scale had occurred in California.

61 Under the NRP, the decision to activate the IIMG rests with the Secretary, but Stephan testified that he took the action because he knew the Secretary was traveling and was concerned that he would be difficult to reach. Stephan interview, Jan. 13, 2006, pp. 44-45.

62 Stephan interview, Jan. 13, 2006, p. 68.

63 Stephan interview, Jan. 13, 2006, p. 57.

64 Stephan interview, Jan. 13, 2006, p. 23.

65 Committee staff interview of Col. Don Harrington, National Guard, Liaison to National Response Coordination Center, U.S. Department of Defense, conducted on Jan. 6, 2006, transcript pp. 17-18.

66 Committee staff interview of Gil Jamieson, Acting Director, National Incident Management System Integration Center, FEMA, conducted on Dec. 20, 2005, transcript pp. 81-85.

67 Committee staff interview of Capt. Michael McDaniel, Navy Emergency Preparedness Liaison to FEMA, U.S. Navy Reserves, conducted on Dec. 2, 2005, transcript p. 112.

68 The IIMG was activated for Hurricane Isabel in September 2003 and several times when the government's alert level was raised to "orange." Broderick interview, Jan. 19, 2006, pp. 48, 99-100. Katrina, however, was the first major test of the IIMG since the NRP was completed.

69 In testimony before the U.S. House of Representatives Committee investigating the preparation for and response to Hurricane Katrina, Sec. Chertoff stated "We went into this situation the weekend before with an understanding and with warnings that this was potentially the nightmare scenario that I think people have talked about for years in terms of New Orleans." Sec. Chertoff, House Select Committee hearing, Oct. 19, 2005.

70 Homeland Security Presidential Directive-5 clarifies the responsibilities given to DHS by the Homeland Security Act by formally designating the Secretary of Homeland Security as the "principal federal official for domestic incident management." The NRP further affirms DHS's responsibilities: "During actual or potential Incidents of National Significance, the overall coordination of Federal incident management activities is executed through the Secretary of Homeland Security. Other Federal departments and agencies carry out their incident management and emergency response authorities and responsibilities within this overarching coordinating framework."

71 U.S. Department of Homeland Security, Office of Inspector General, "A Review of Top Officials 3 Exercise," Nov. 2005, p. 6.

72 Committee staff interview of Scott Wells, Deputy Federal Coordinating Officer for Hurricane Katrina in Louisiana, FEMA, conducted on Nov. 14, 2005, transcript p. 118, 129.

73 FEMA is the lead agency for ESF-3 (Public Works and Engineering), ESF-5 (Emergency Management), ESF-6 (Mass Care, Housing and Human Services), ESF-9 (Urban Search and Rescue) and ESF-14 (Long Term Community Recovery and Mitigation. *NRP*, p. ESF-v.

74 Committee staff interview of Edward Buikema, Acting Director of Response Division and Regional Director, Region V, FEMA, conducted on Nov. 21, 2005, transcript p. 234.

75 Committee staff interview of Eric Tolbert, former Director, Response Division, FEMA, conducted on Dec. 1, 2005, transcript pp. 137-38.

76 Michael Lowder, e-mail to EST-DIR and others, Aug. 27, 2005, 8:58 a.m. Provided to Committee; filed as Bates no. DHS-FEMA-0068-0000257.

77 Brown interview, Feb. 23, 2006, transcript p. 99.

78 Testimony of William Lokey, Federal Coordinating Officer for Hurricane Katrina in Louisiana, FEMA, before the

U.S. Senate, Committee on Homeland Security and Governmental Affairs, hearing on *Hurricane Katrina: Urban Search and Rescue in a Catastrophe*, Jan. 20, 2006.

79 National Hurricane Center, Hurricane Katrina Discussion #9, Aug. 25, 2005, 5 p.m. ET, http://www.nhc.noaa.gov/archive/2005/dis/al122005.discus.009.shtml?. Accessed on Sept. 5, 2005.

80 National Hurricane Center, Hurricane Katrina Discussion #10, Aug. 25, 2005, 11 p.m. ET. http://www.nhc.noaa.gov/archive/2005/dis/al122005.discus.010.shtml?. Accessed on Sept. 5, 2005.

81 National Hurricane Center, Hurricane Katrina Discussion #12, Aug. 26, 2005 11 a.m. ET. http://www.nhc.noaa.gov/archive/2005/KATRINA.shtml?. Accessed on Sept. 5, 2005. *See also*: FEMA, National Situation Report, Aug. 27, 2005, 5:30 a.m., p. 2. Provided to Committee; filed as Bates no. DHS-FEMA-0037-0000262.

82 Max Mayfield, FEMA Daily Video Teleconference, Aug. 26, 2005, p. 4. Provided to the Committee; filed as Bates no. DHS-FEMA-0105-0000025.

83 Bill Reed, FEMA Daily Video Teleconference, Aug. 26, 2005, p. 7. Provided to the Committee; filed as Bates no. DHS-FEMA-0105-0000028.

84 Michael Brown, e-mail to Edward Buikema, Aug. 26, 2005, 12:41 p.m. Provided to Committee; filed as Bates no. DHS-FEMA-0028-001396. Patrick Rhode recommended that Buikema return to headquarters "with anyone else who is needed – vs. fishing in Alaska." *Source:* Patrick Rhode, e-mail to Brooks Altshuler and Michael Health, Aug. 26, 2005, 9:26 a.m. Provided to Committee, filed as Bates no. DHS-FEMA-0085-0004035.

85 Buikema interview, Nov. 21, 2005, pp. 128-129.

86 Buikema interview, Nov. 21, 2005, pp. 128-129. Buikema admitted that most of the preparations for the storm were done by others, but he was in communication with both his deputy Michael Lowder and Undersecretary Michael Brown. *Source*: Buikema interview, Nov. 21, 2005, p. 238.

87 William Lokey, e-mail to Michael Lowder, Aug. 26, 2005, 3:03 p.m. Provided to Committee; filed as Bates no. DHS-FEMA-0028-0000245.

88 ESFs activated at the National Operations Center included Transportation (1), Public Works and Engineering (3), Firefighting (4), Emergency Management (5), Resource Support (7), External Affairs (15) and a military liaison. At the region IV level, ESFs activated included Transportation (1), Public Works and Engineering (3), Firefighting (4), Resource Support (7), Long-Term Recovery and Mitigation (14), External Affairs (15), and Department of Defense. *Source:* FEMA, National Situation Report, Aug. 26, 2005, 5:30 a.m., p. 2. Provided to Committee; filed as Bates no. DHS-FEMA-0037-0000191. Alabama's own activation of its EOC was also at its lowest level of activation on August 26 at noon and they did not plan to raise it to the highest level until 9 a.m. the following day. *Source:* FEMA Daily Video Teleconference, Aug. 26, 2005, p. 10. Provided to Committee; filed as Bates no. DHS-FEMA-0105-0000031.

89 FEMA, Shift Change Briefing, Aug. 27, 2005, 7 a.m. Provided to Committee; filed as Bates no. DHS-FEMA-0055-0000548.

90 National Hurricane Center, Hurricane Katrina Discussion #12, Aug. 26, 2005 11 a.m. ET. http://www.nhc.noaa.gov/archive/2005/KATRINA.shtml? Accessed on Apr. 25, 2006. *See also*: FEMA, National Situation Report, Aug. 27, 2005 5:30 a.m., p. 2. Provided to Committee; filed as Bates no. DHS-FEMA-0037-0000262.

91 FEMA, Region VI Regional Response Coordination Center, Situation Report 1, Aug. 27, 2005, p. 1. Provided to Committee; filed as Bates no. DHS-FEMA-0073-0000118; FEMA, Region VI Status Briefing, Aug. 27, 2005, p.1. Provided to Committee; filed as Bates no. DHS-FEMA-0073-0000197.

92 FEMA, National Situation Report, Aug. 27, 2005, 5:30 a.m., p. 2. Provided to Committee; filed as Bates no. DHS-FEMA-0037-0000262.

93 FEMA, "Tropical Storm Katrina," Aug. 27, 2005, 9 a.m. Provided to Committee; filed as Bates no. DHS-FEMA-0055-0002139.

94 FEMA, "Tropical Storm Katrina," Aug. 27, 2005, 9 a.m., pp. 1-3. Provided to Committee; filed as Bates nos. DHS-FEMA-0055-0002139 through 0002141.

95 Sharon Blades, e-mail to Michael Pawlowski and others, Aug. 27, 2005, 10:35 a.m. Provided to Committee; filed as Bates no. DHS-FEMA-0028-0000455.

96 70 Fed. Reg. 53238 (Sept. 7, 2005); Col. Jeff Smith, FEMA Daily Video Teleconference, Aug. 27, 2005, p. 10. Provided to Committee; filed as Bates no. DHS-FEMA-0105-0000049.

97 70 Fed. Reg. 54061-62 (Sept. 13, 2006); 70 Fed. Reg. 53239 (Sept. 7, 2005).

98 "Robert T. Stafford Disaster Relief and Emergency Assistance Act." (P.L. 93-288), 42 U.S.C. § 5191.

99 64 Fed. Reg. 51975-01; 64 Fed. Reg. 51976-02; 64 Fed. Reg. 52316-02; 64 Fed. Reg. 52318-01.

100 National Hurricane Center, Hurricane Katrina Advisory #19, Aug. 27, 2005, 10 p.m. CT. http://www.nhc.noaa.gov/archive/2005/pub/al122005.public.019.shtml? Accessed on Sept. 5, 2005; National Hurricane Center, Hurricane Katrina Special Discussion # 20, Aug. 28, 2005, 2 a.m. ET. http://www.nhc.noaa.gov/archive/2005/dis/al122005.discus.020.shtml?. Accessed on Sept. 5, 2005.

101 Michael Lowder, e-mail to Michael Brown and others, Aug. 28, 2005, 2:06 p.m. Provided to Committee; filed as Bates no. DHS 0002487.

102 FEMA, National Situation Report, Aug. 28, 2005, 5:30 a.m., p. 2. Provided to Committee; filed as Bates no. DHS-FEMA-0037-0000354.

103 Jon MacLaren, e-mail to William Flynn and others, Aug. 28, 2005, 2:49 p.m. Provided to Committee; filed as Bates nos. DHS-INFP-0003-0001949 through 0001950; William Flynn, e-mail to Bob Stephan and others, Aug. 28, 2005, 6:39 p.m. Provided to Committee; filed as Bates no. DHS-INFP-0003-0001850; Frank DiFalco, e-mail to HSOC.HSIN and others, Aug. 28, 2005, 8:31 p.m. Provided to Committee; filed as Bates nos. DHS-HSOC-0002-0000059 through 0000099; Lon Biasco, e-mail to HSOC-All-Desks, Aug. 28, 2005, 10:33, p.m. Provided to Committee; filed as Bates no. DHS-HSOC-0002-0000114; Andrew Akers, e-mail to HSOC SWO and others, Aug. 29, 2004, 1:47 a.m. Provided to Committee; filed as Bates no. WHK–15894.

104 Testimony of Michael Brown, former Director, FEMA, before the U.S. Senate, Committee on Homeland Security and Governmental Affairs, hearing on *Hurricane Katrina: The Roles of the DHS and FEMA Leadership*, Feb. 10, 2006.

105 Brown, Senate Committee hearing, Feb. 10, 2006.

106 Brown, Senate Committee hearing, Feb. 10, 2006; Brown interview, Feb. 23, 2006, pp. 33-34.

107 Brown interview, Jan. 23, 2006, p. 91.

108 Mayfield, VTC, Aug. 28, 2005, pp. 2, 6. On that same call, the National Hurricane Center discussed storm surges: "Well obviously where it's headed you're at the worst possible locations for storm surge. You remember Camille and its 26 feet. I would advise all the folks that are in the potential path of this storm to be looking at their maximum off the surge models, the meows and whatnot off of a Category 4 or 5 storm, and plan accordingly. *Source:* Bill Ryder, FEMA Daily Video Teleconference, Aug. 28, 2005, pp. 4-5. Provided to Committee; filed as Bates nos. DHS-FEMA-0105-0000044 through 0000045. Joe Hagin, White House Deputy Chief of Staff, was on the VTC, listening to these warnings. *Source:* Joe Hagin, FEMA Daily Video Teleconference, Aug. 27, 2005, p. 24. Provided to Committee; filed as Bates no. DHS-FEMA-0105-0000063.

109 FEMA Daily Video Teleconference, Aug. 28, 2005, pp. 13-15. Provided to Committee; filed as Bates nos. DHS-FEMA-0105-0000066 through 0000104.

110 Col. William Doran, FEMA Daily Video Teleconference, Aug. 28, 2005, p. 17. Provided to Committee; filed as Bates no. DHS-FEMA-0105-0000082.

111 Col. Smith, VTC, Aug. 28, 2005, p. 17.

112 Brown interview, Feb. 23, 2006, p. 34.

113 Brown interview, Feb. 23, 2006, p. 36.

114 FEMA, Employee Count as of Nov. 12, 2005. Provided to the Committee; filed as Bates no. DHS-FEMA-0082-0000208; Committee staff interview of Michael Hall, Acting Director, Human Resources, FEMA, conducted on Nov. 28 2005, transcript p. 61.

115 Written statement of William Carwile III, Federal Coordinating Officer for Hurricane Katrina in Mississippi, FEMA, for the U.S. Senate, Committee on Homeland Security and Governmental Affairs, hearing on *Hurricane Katrina: Perspectives of FEMA's Operations Professionals,* Dec. 8, 2005, pp. 1-2.

116 Written Statement of William Carwile III, Senate Committee Hearing, Dec. 8, 2005, pp. 1-2.

117 FEMA, National Situation Report, Aug. 28, 2005, 5:30 a.m., p. 2. Provided to Committee; filed as Bates no. DHS-FEMA-0037-0000355.

118 *NRP*, p. 40.

119 Committee staff interview of William Lokey, Federal Coordinating Officer for Hurricane Katrina in Louisiana, FEMA, Jan. 20, 2006, transcript pp. 197-198; Committee staff interview of William Carwile III, Federal Coordinating Officer for Hurricane Katrina in Mississippi, FEMA, conducted on Dec. 6, 2005, transcript p. 78.

120 *NRP*, p. 40.

121 Questions for the Record of Sec. Chertoff, Senate Committee hearing, Feb. 15, 2006, p. 61; Lokey interview, Nov. 4, 2005, pp. 32-33.

122 According to William Lokey, "When Mr. Brown decided to dispatch the ERT-N on Saturday morning, because we don't have a lot of people and a number of the ERT–N … were already deployed to Florida, Alabama, Mississippi, and in Louisiana, out of their respective regions, what I asked was that [we] activate both the Red and Blue team and fill the rosters with whoever called back first. So we in essence had a plaid response of people." Lokey interview, Nov. 4, 2005, pp. 32-33.

123 Lokey interview, Nov. 4, 2005 pp. 42-43.

124 Lokey interview, Jan. 20, 2006, p. 200.

125 Lokey interview, Nov. 4, 2005, p. 41.

126 Hall interview, Dec. 1, 2005, p. 218.

127 Carwile interview, Dec. 6, 2005, pp. 78-80.

128 Hall interview, Dec. 1, 2005, pp. 217-220.

129 Carwile interview, Dec. 6, 2005, p. 79.

130 Parr interview, Nov. 16, 2005, pp. 10-11, 102.

131 Parr interview, Nov. 16, 2005, p. 11.

132 Additionally during the Saturday video teleconference the National Weather Service official stated that although it couldn't "totally rule out the possibility" of the storm hitting Texas, "there's nothing we're looking at now . . . that would take it that far west." *Source:* Bill Reed, FEMA Daily Video Teleconference, Aug. 27, 2004, p. 8. Provided to Committee; filed as Bates no. DHS-FEMA-0105-0000047. *See also:* National Hurricane Center, Katrina Graphics Archive, Aug. 27, 2005, 4 p.m. CT and 10 p.m. CT, http://www.nhc.noaa.gov/archive/2005/KATRINA_graphics.shtml. Accessed on Apr. 25, 2006.

133 Philip Parr, e-mail to James Russo, Aug. 27, 2005, 2:57 p.m. Provided to Committee; filed as Bates no. DHS-FEMA 0073-0000174. Gary Jones, Director of FEMA Region VI said that a team was sent to Texas in case the hurricane took a turn towards Texas. *Source:* Committee staff interview of Gary Jones, Acting Regional Director, Region VI, FEMA, conducted on Jan. 11, 2006, transcript p. 44; Phil Parr, e-mail to James Russo, Aug. 27, 2005, 2:57 p.m. Provided to Committee; filed as Bates nos. DHS-FEMA-0073-0000430 through 0000432.

134 Parr interview, Nov. 16, 2005, pp. 28-29.

135 Buikema interview, Nov. 21, 2005, p. 110.

136 Buikema interview, Nov. 21, 2005, p. 109; Tolbert interview, Dec. 1, 2005, p. 54.

137 Buikema interview, Nov. 21, 2005, p. 113; Committee staff interview of Michael Lowder, Deputy Director of Response, FEMA, conducted on Nov. 10, 2005, transcript p. 79. *See also:* Tolbert interview, Dec. 1, 2005, p. 54 (discussing the response capabilities of FIRST teams).

138 Brown interview, Feb. 23, 2006, p. 19.

139 Committee staff interview of Marty Bahamonde, Director, External Affairs, Region I, FEMA, conducted on Oct. 7, 2005, transcript pp. 39-40.

140 Bahamonde interview, Oct. 7, 2005, pp. 45-47.

141 Committee staff interview of Tom Bossert, former Deputy Director of Legislative Affairs, FEMA, conducted on Dec. 20, 2005, transcript pp. 27-28

142 Marshall Sanders, e-mail to Michael Heath and others, Aug. 27, 2005, 7:55 p.m. Provided to Committee; filed as Bates nos. DHS-FEMA-0086-0002291 through 0002293.

143 Bossert interview, Dec. 20, 2005, pp. 60-61.

144 Committee staff interview of Bob Fenton, Response Branch Chief for Region IX and Operations Chief, FEMA, conducted on Dec. 22, 2005, transcript pp. 20-22; Lokey interview, Jan. 20, 2006, pp. 47-48, 197-198.

145 Carwile interview, Dec. 6, 2005, pp. 111-112.

146 FEMA exacerbated its lack of qualified personnel by deploying the trained staff it did have as late as Friday and Saturday before landfall on Monday.

147 Wells interview, Nov. 14, 2005, pp. 67-68. Wells also said "This was a catastrophic disaster. We don't have the structure; we don't have the people for a catastrophic disaster. It's that simple." *Source:* Wells interview, Nov. 14, 2005, p. 69.

148 Written Statement of Carwile, Senate Committee hearing, Dec. 8, 2005, pp. 6-7.

149 Wells interview, Nov. 15, 2005, p. 59.

150 Wells interview, Nov. 14, 2005, pp. 55-56, 70.

151 Committee staff interview of Marie Sloan, Section Chief, Disaster Workforce Response Division, FEMA, conducted on Mar. 1, 2006, transcript pp. 8-9; Hall interview, Nov. 28, 2005, pp. 24-25; FEMA, "Daily Disaster and Post Disaster and Other Travel Deployments (DAEs only)." Provided to Committee; filed as Bates nos. DHS-FEMA-0055-0000209 through 0000211.

152 FEMA, "Daily Disaster and Post Disaster and Other Travel Deployments (DAEs only)." Provided to Committee; filed as Bates nos. DHS-FEMA-0055-0000159 through 0000160.

153 Hall interview, Dec. 1, 2005, pp. 171-172.

154 Nancy Ward, e-mail to William Carwile, Aug. 30, 2005, 7:50 p.m. Provided to Committee; filed as Bates no. DHS-FEMA-0083-0000490.

155 Michael Hall, e-mail to Mary Lynne Miller, Gary Jones, and Teresa Gauger, Aug. 31, 2005, 6:11 p.m. Provided to Committee; filed as Bates no. DHS-FEMA-0069-0000490.

156 Sandy Coachman, FEMA FCO, was in New Orleans working a previous disaster. On Sunday, she was ordered to evacuate New Orleans prior to the storm's landfall. *Source:* Committee staff interview of Sandy Coachman, Federal Coordinating Officer, Region VI, FEMA, conducted on Nov. 15, 2005, transcript p. 7. Scott Wells testified that it was "contrary to our policy" and "doctrine" to have placed personnel in New Orleans prior to landfall. *Source:* Wells interview, Nov. 14, 2005, pp. 172-173.

157 Carwile interview, Dec. 6, 2005, transcript pp. 97-99. However, Scott Wells testified that there is general reluctance

by states to allow FEMA liaisons in the states. *Source*: Wells interview, Nov. 14, 2005, p. 131.

158 Lokey interview, Nov. 4, 2005, pp. 91-92.

159 Bahamonde interview, Oct. 7, 2005, pp. 126-129.

160 Lokey interview, Jan. 20, 2006 pp. 31-32.

161 Lokey interview, Jan. 20, 2006, pp. 21,18.

162 Lokey interview, Jan. 20, 2006, p. 23.

163 Lokey interview, Jan. 20, 2006, p. 23.

164 Lokey interview, Jan. 20, 2006, p. 23.

165 Committee staff interview of William Milani, Chief, Mobile Operations Section, Logistics Branch, FEMA, conducted on Jan. 12, 2006, transcript p. 59.

166 Committee staff interview of James Attaway, Telecommunications Specialist, Mobile Emergency Response System, Region VI, FEMA, conducted on Jan. 13, 2006, transcript pp. 97-99.

167 Milani interview, Jan. 12, 2006, pp. 59, 70

168 Milani interview, Jan. 12, 2006, p. 59.

169 FEMA did not ask MERS, FEMA's communications unit, to deploy to the EOC pre-landfall. *Source:* Milani interview, Jan. 12, 2006, pp. 54-55.

170 Committe staff interview of Philip Parr, Federal Coordinating Officer, Region I, FEMA, conducted on Nov. 16, 2005.

171 Wells interview, Nov. 15, 2005, p. 116

172 Lokey interview, Jan. 20, 2006, p. 173.

173 Tolbert interview, Dec. 1, 2005, pp. 28-29; Ron Castleman, e-mails to Patrick Rhode and Michael Brown, Dec. 29-30, 2003. Provided to Committee. Despite these denials, funding for catastrophic planning for New Orleans was found elsewhere in the Response Divisions budget. DHS authorized money for fiscal year 2006 for FEMA's catastrophic planning initiative. FEMA requested $20 million for this initiative, but as of February 2006, only $65,000 had been obligated. Questions for the Record of Sec. Chertoff, Senate Committee hearing, Feb. 15, 2006, p. 65.

174 Committee staff interview of Wayne Fairley, Branch Chief, Response Operations Region VI, FEMA, conducted on Jan. 18, 2006, transcript pp. 129-132; Committee staff interview of Sean Fontenot, Former Chief, Preparedness Division, Louisiana Office of Homeland Security and Emergency Management, conducted on Jan. 10, 2006, transcript pp. 52-58, 89-92. According to witnesses, with the need to narrow the project scope, pre-landfall evacuation was eliminated because, unlike other subjects, it had frequently been the subject of planning over the years. *Source:* Testimony of Madhu Beriwal, President and CEO, Innovative Emergency Management Inc., before the U.S. Senate, Committee on Homeland Security and Governmental Affairs, hearing on *Preparing for a Catastrophe: The Hurricane Pam Exercise,* Jan. 24, 2006; Fontenot interview, Jan. 10, 2006, pp. 57-58, 89-92.

175 Testimony of Michael Brown, former Director, FEMA, before the U.S. House, Select Bipartisan Committee to Investigate the Preparation for and Response to Hurricane Katrina, hearing on *The Role of the Federal Emergency Management Agency*, Sept. 27, 2005.

176 Lokey interview, Nov. 4, 2005, pp. 184-187. At 8:19 a.m. on Aug. 27, 2005, FEMA's Acting Deputy Director Patrick Rhode e-mailed the Acting Director of Response a request for a copy of the New Orleans Catastrophic Plan. *Source:* Patrick Rhode, e-mail to David Garratt and others, Aug. 27, 2005, 8:19 a.m. Provided to Committee; filed as Bates no. DHS-FEMA-0085-0003866. At 9:07 a.m. William Lokey replied to Rhode, Brown, and other that "Copies are being made as we speak." *Source:* William Lokey, e-mail to Patrick Rhode, David Garratt and others, Aug. 27, 2005, 9:07 a.m. Provided to Committee; filed as Bates no. DHS-FEMA-0085-0003860. At 10:35 a.m. Sharon Blades e-mailed 25 FEMA personnel including William Lokey, Tony Robinson, Gary Jones, and Wayne Fairley an electronic version of the plan, and told them that copies were being printed. *Source:* Sharon Blades, e-mail to Michel Pawlowski and others, Aug. 27, 2005, 10:35 a.m. Provided to Committee; filed as Bates no. DHS-FEMA-0085-0003570. Later that afternoon Deputy Chief of Staff Brooks Altshuler e-mailed twice asking for additional copies for the front office. *Source:* Brooks Altshuler, e-mail to Sharon Blades and others, Aug. 27, 2005, 3:36 p.m. Provided to Committee; filed as Bates no. DHS-FEMA-0085-0003325. A few minutes later he received a reply that 50 copies were being printed. *Source:* Michel Powlowski, e-mail to Brooks Altshuler and others, Aug. 27, 2005, 3:42 p.m. Provided to Committee; filed as Bates no. DHS-FEMA-0085-0003570. At 8:37 p.m. that night Sharon Blades again e-mails Altshuler: "We have printed up more plans and they are on the mezz in Area A. We are also printing copies of the latest drafts and a preface explaining the planning process and the various documents because they all have not been finalized and assembled into one document. This will, we hope, avoid confusion." *Source:* Sharon Blades, e-mail to Brooks Altshuler and others, Aug. 27, 2005, 8:37 p.m. Provided to Committee; filed as Bates no. DHS-FEMA-0085-0003325.

177 *Southeast Louisiana Catastrophic Hurricane Plan,* prepared by IEM, Inc. for LOHSEP and FEMA, Sept. 2005, p. 2 [hereinafter *Southeast Louisiana Catastrophic Hurricane Plan*, Sept. 2005].

178 *Southeast Louisiana Catastrophic Hurricane Plan,* Sept. 2005, p. 4.

179 Tony Robbins, FEMA Daily Video Teleconference, Aug. 27, 2005, p. 15. Provided to Committee; filed as Bates no. DHS-FEMA-0105-0000054; Wells interview, Nov. 15, 2005, p. 66.

180 Wells interview, Nov. 15, 2005, p. 66.

181 Sec. Michael Chertoff, *The Charlie Rose Show*, PBS, Jan. 9, 2006, 11 a.m. ET. Transcript accessed on LexisNexis.

182 Committee staff interview of Gary Moore, Director, Logistics, FEMA, conducted on Dec. 9, 2005, transcript p. 30.

183 Robbins, VTC, Aug. 27, 2005, pp. 16-17. *See also*: FEMA, Commodities Status as of Aug. 29, 2005. Provided to Committee; filed as Bates no. DHS-FEMA-0127-0010528.

184 Committee staff interview of Kenneth Burris, Acting Director of Operations, FEMA, Dec. 29, 2005, p. 16.

185 FEMA, FEMA LC's, PPS, TSS & Ice Storage, Commodity Status as of Aug. 26, 2005, 9:30 a.m. Provided to Committee; filed as Bates no. DHS-FEMA-0127-0014017. *See also*: FEMA, Commodities Status as of Aug. 29, 2005. Provided to Committee; filed as Bates no. DHS-FEMA-0127-0010528.

186 Federal Operational Staging Area Camp Beauregard, LA Situation Report as of 1900 28 Aug. 2005. Provided to Committee; filed as Bates no. DHS-FEMA-0080-0000005; FEMA, FEMA LC's, PPS, TSS, & Ice Storage, Aug. 26, 2005, Provided to Committee; filed as Bates no. DHS-FEMA-0127-0014017.

187 Ernest Hudson e-mail to Wayne Fairley et al., Aug. 29, 2005, 11:47. Provided to Committee; filed as Bates no. DHS-FEMA-0080-000003; Brooks Altshuler, e-mail to Patrick Rhode and others, Aug. 28, 2005, 5:56 p.m. Provided to Committee; filed as Bates no. DHS-FEMA-0085-0004937.

188 Michael Lowder, e-mail to Gary Moore and others, Aug. 28, 2005, 1:03 p.m. Provided to Committee; filed as Bates no. DHS-FEMA-0083-0000716; Michael Lowder, e-mail to William Carwile, Aug. 28, 2005, 12:37 p.m. Provided to Committee; filed as Bates no. DHS-FEMA-0083-0000718; Gary Moore, e-mail to Michael Lowder and others, Aug. 28, 2005, 1 p.m. Provided to Committee; filed as Bates nos. DHS-FEMA-0068-0001236 through 0001237; Michael Lowder, e-mail to William Carwile, Aug. 28, 2005, 12:31 p.m. Provided to Committee; filed as Bates no. DHS-FEMA-0083-0000722.

189 Committee staff interview of Tom McAllister, Director of Response and Recovery, MEMA, conducted on Jan. 25, 2006, transcript p. 8.

190 McAllister interview, Jan. 25, 2006, pp. 8-9.

191 Committee staff interview of Patrick Rhode, former Acting Deputy Director, FEMA, conducted on Dec. 22, 2005, transcript pp. 40-42.

192 Rhode interview, Dec. 22, 2005, pp. 42-47.

193 Rhode interview, Dec. 22, 2005, pp. 53.

194 Moore interview, Dec. 9, 2005, p. 37.

195 Teresa Gauger, e-mail to Lisa Williams, Marie Sloan, and Michael Hall, Aug. 27, 2005, 11:33 a.m. Provided to Committee; filed as Bates no. DHS-FEMA-0069-0001575. *See also*: Sloan interview, Mar. 1, 2006, pp. 31-33.

196 Kerry Young, e-mail to Jules Hurst and Mary Ann Veitch, Aug. 28, 2005, 3:08 p.m. Provided to Committee; filed as Bates no. DHS-FEMA-0127-0011518.

197 Moore interview, Dec. 9, 2005, p. 35.

198 Moore interview, Dec. 9, 2005, pp. 35-37. Moore testified that FEMA's transportations system "catastrophically… broke down" because of the disaster. *Source*: Moore interview, Dec. 9, 2005, p. 83.

199 Moore interview, Dec. 9, 2005, p. 36.

200 FEMA, NDMS Resource Status, Aug. 28, 2005, 8 p.m. ET. Provided to Committee.

201 Committee staff interview of Jack Beall, Chief, National Disaster Medical System, FEMA, conducted on Jan. 10, 2006, transcript pp. 10-13.

202 Lokey interview, Nov. 4, 2005, pp. 66-67, 72-83, 90.

203 Lokey interview, Nov. 4, 2005, pp. 67-68, 80.

204 Committee staff interview of James Strickland, Team Member, Urban Search and Rescue, FEMA, conducted on Jan. 25, 2006, transcript pp. 38-39.

205 Strickland interview, conducted on Jan. 25, 2006, pp. 33-34.

206 Lokey interview, Nov. 4, 2005, pp. 88-90.

207 Strickland interview, conducted on Jan. 25, 2006, pp. 44-45, 82-83.

208 Testimony of Capt. Bruce C. Jones, U.S. Coast Guard, Commanding Officer, Air Station New Orleans, before the U.S. Senate, Committee on Homeland Security and Governmental Affairs, hearing on *Always Ready: The Coast Guard's Response to Hurricane Katrina*, Nov. 9, 2005.

209 Attaway interview, Jan. 13, 2006, pp. 77-78. After he learned the city was flooding and it was a major catastrophe, MERS took steps to get additional resources and supplies. "I went about having our guys locate the local communications…and establishing accounts with them. We actually started ordering supplies. I got into the building next door and started doing a survey of the building to layout the facility that we wanted to put in there. We did quite a lot of work right quick." *Source*: Attaway interview, Jan. 13, 2006, pp. 77-78.

210 Lokey interview, Jan. 20, 2006, pp. 8-9. "A JFO does not exist until the facility is fully functional. Until that time, the people may be working in the building and it is called an Initial Operating Facility (IOF)." The IOF in Louisiana began operating pre-landfall and was rapidly ramped over the course of 12 days until a designation as JFO on September 9. "So as other Federal agencies started arriving, by a couple of days, there were several hundred people there. There were a thousand people there within a week." *Source:* Lokey interview, Jan. 20, 2006, p. 10. However, state employees could not move into the JFO until the technology issues were addressed, thus although federal agencies were at the IOF, because the state employees could not be there, it was harder to coordinate the response.

211 Lokey interview, Jan. 20, 2006, p. 101; Committee staff interview of Lucy Brooke, Emergency Management Program Specialist, FEMA, conducted on Jan. 24, 2006, transcript p. 16; Committee staff interview of Mark Misczak, Individual Assistance Branch Chief, Region VI, FEMA, conducted on Nov. 14, 2005, transcript p. 12.

212 Lokey interview, Nov. 4, 2005, p. 30.

213 Lokey interview, Jan. 20, 2006, pp. 9-10.

214 Lokey interview, Jan. 20, 2006, p. 30; Committee interview of William King, Branch Chief, Region V, Radiological Emergency Preparedness Program, Technical Services Branch, FEMA, conducted on Jan. 17, 2006, transcript p. 93.

215 For example, the FEMA Director of Planning in Louisiana, Bill King, said the EOC only had one computer dedicated to FEMA. *Source:* King interview, Jan. 17, 2006, p. 91. One FEMA employee who worked in EOC until the JFO opened explained: "You're limited. I mean, we had a – it was a little office. … [There was] one telephone in there that the Comm Center knew that number and knew that was a room where FEMA people were working, and so every call that came in got funneled in there, no matter who it was for or who was calling. And people would come in and use that phone – the search and rescue guys or whatever – come in and use that phone and leave that number for [them] to call, so it was kind of telephone central when it'd work." *Source:* Brooke interview, Jan. 24, 2006, p. 54.

216 Lokey interview, Jan. 20, 2006, p. 25.

217 Lokey interview, Jan. 20, 2006, p. 28.

218 Lokey interview, Jan. 20, 2006, pp. 24-25.

219 Lokey interview, Jan. 20, 2006, pp. 17, 23.

220 Lokey interview, Jan. 20, 2006, pp. 23-24.

221 Shingler interview, Jan. 31, 2006, p. 11.

222 "Need 10-12 FPS officers to escort NDMS teams assigned to Louisiana Super Dome in New Orleans. Twenty-four hour coverage required NDMS teams are comprised of 35 members." *Source:* FEMA, Mission Assignment, 1603DR-LA-FPS-02, Sept. 30, 2005, p. 1. Provided to Committee; filed as Bates no. DHS-FEMA-0035-0000023.

223 "Request (14) FPS [Federal Protective Service] officers to deploy to LA Superdome to assist in crowd control during Superdome evacuation. Must be equipped with crowd control weaponry." FEMA, Mission Assignment, 1603DR-LA-FPS-04, Sept. 31, 2005, p. 1. Provided to Committee; filed as Bates no. DHS-FEMA-0035-0000143.

224 Parr interview, Nov. 16, 2005, p. 93.

225 U.S. Customs and Border Protection, Commissioner's Situation Room, Aug. 29, 2005, 2:30 p.m. Provided to Committee; filed as Bates no. DHS-CBP1-0001-0000003.

226 U.S. Customs and Border Protection, Commissioner's Situation Room, Aug. 31, 2005, 3 p.m. Provided to Committee; filed as Bates no. DHS-CBP1-0001-0000029.

227 "Request (29) Federal Protective Service (FPS) personnel to provide physical security to assure the safety of personnel and equipment of NDMS teams (i.e., DMAT, DMORT, VMAT) deployed and staged in Region 6" to provide 24-hour coverage/escort for NDMS teams and equipment assigned to multiple locations affected by Hurricane Katrina. FEMA, Mission Assignment, 1603DR-LA-FPS-01, Sept. 30, 2005, p. 1. Provided to Committee; filed as Bates no. DHS-FEMA-0035-0000015.

228 But contrast with the National Guard testimony in the Superdome that there was no security problem. Committee staff interview of Col. Pat Prechter, State Chief Nurse, Louisiana Army National Guard and Deputy Commander, Louisiana Medical Command, conducted on Jan. 6, 2006, transcript pp. 63-68, 100-103; Committee staff interview of Brig. Gen. Gary Jones, Assistant Joint Forces Commander, Louisiana Army National Guard, conducted on Dec. 7, 2005, transcript pp. 81-82, 171-175, 222-223.

229 Gary Sirmons, e-mail to Gerald Gomes, Sept. 1, 2005 11:09 p.m. Provided to Committee; filed as Bates no. DHS-FEMA-0136-0000021. Later on CCN, DMAT personnel thought that they "saw looters … going through the [team] CA-6's personal belongings." *Source:* Gerald Gomes, e-mail to Gary Sirmons and others, Sept. 2, 2005, 3:53 p.m. Provided to Committee; filed as Bates no. DHS-FEMA-0136-0000021. "The team commanders were not comfortable moving into the arena [Thursday night]. We discussed the situation at length, but I was not able to assuage their fears. Further, the FPS Regional Director decided he wouldn't take the teams in until tomorrow morning." *Source:* William Lokey, e-mail to Steven Posner, Gary Simons, and Joan Harding, Sept. 1, 2005, 10:08 p.m. Provided to Committee; filed as Bates no. DHS-FEMA-0136-0000022.

230 Brown, Senate Committee hearing, Feb. 10, 2005.

231 Committee Staff interview of Gen. Richard Myers, U.S. Air Force (Ret.), former Chairman of the Joint Chiefs of Staff, conducted on Feb. 28, 2006, transcript p. 9.

232 Sec. Chertoff, VTC, Aug. 28, 2005, p. 38.

233 Brown, VTC, Aug. 28, 2005, pp. 38-39.

234 Sec. Chertoff, VTC, Aug. 28, 2005, pp. 38-39.

235 Written Statement of Rear Adm. Robert Duncan, U.S. Coast Guard, Commander, 8th Coast Guard District, for the U.S. Senate, Committee on Homeland Security and Governmental Affairs, hearing on *Always Ready: The Coast Guard's Response to Hurricane Katrina*, Nov. 9, 2005, p. 2. The Coast Guard is "a law enforcement authority as well as an armed force." Testimony of Rear Adm. Robert Duncan, Commander, 8th Coast Guard District, before the U.S. Senate, Committee on Homeland Security and Governmental Affairs, hearing on *Always Ready: The Coast Guard's Response to Hurricane Katrina*, Nov. 9, 2005.

236 U.S. Coast Guard, "U.S. Coast Guard: America's Maritime Guardian," Jan. 1, 2002, pp. 55-56 ("Successful mission execution begins with a thorough understanding of the environment in which we operate. Based on that understanding, we develop operational concepts, acquire appropriate equipment, and put our people through rigorous formal training. We build on that foundation by continuous training and drills, by improving our personal skills and by maintaining our equipment at the highest state of readiness. In short, consistently successful performance requires thorough preparation.").

237 Written Statement of Rear Adm. Duncan, Senate Committee hearing, Nov. 9, 2005, p. 2. In fact, Coast Guard Air Station New Orleans exercised its hurricane plan several times each season. Testimony of Capt. Bruce C. Jones, U.S. Coast Guard, Commanding Officer, Air Station New Orleans, before the U.S. Senate, Committee on Homeland Security and Governmental Affairs, hearing on *Always Ready: The Coast Guard's Response to Hurricane Katrina*, Nov. 9, 2005.

238 Rear Adm. Duncan, Senate Committee hearing, Nov. 9, 2005.

239 Scott R. Gourley, "The Coast Guard and Hurricane Katrina," *Homeland Security*, Jan. 2006.

240 Written Statement of Rear Adm. Duncan, Senate Committee hearing, Nov. 9, 2005, p. 2.

241 Written Statement of Rear Adm. Duncan, Senate Committee hearing, Nov. 9, 2005, p. 2.

242 Written Statement of Rear Adm. Duncan, Senate Committee hearing, Nov. 9, 2005, p. 2.

243 Testimony of Capt. Frank Paskewich, U.S. Coast Guard, Commander, Coast Guard Sector New Orleans, before the U.S. Senate, Committee on Homeland Security and Governmental Affairs, hearing on *Always Ready: The Coast Guard's Response to Hurricane Katrina*, Nov. 9, 2005.

244 Capt. Paskewich, Senate Committee hearing, Nov. 9, 2005.

245 Capt. Paskewich, Senate Committee hearing, Nov. 9, 2005; Committee staff interview of Capt. Frank Paskewich, Commander Coast, U.S. Coast Guard, Guard Sector New Orleans, conducted on Oct. 6, 2005 (Captain Paskewich told staff there were no Coast Guard dependents left in the city of New Orleans prior to landfall).

246 U.S. Coast Guard, Hurricane Katrina: Response and Recovery, Sept. 7, 2005, p. 4.

247 Written Statement of Rear Adm. Duncan, Senate Committee hearing, Nov. 9, 2005, p. 3; Committee staff interview of Capt. Bruce Jones, U.S. Coast Guard, Commanding Officer, Coast Guard Air Station New Orleans, conducted on Oct. 6, 2005.

248 Capt. Paskewich, Senate Committee hearing, Nov. 9, 2005. For example, the Seagoing Buoy Tender Coast Guard Cutter *Cypress*, home ported in Mobile, Alabama, was pre-staged in Houston, Texas and loaded with as many Aids to Navigation supplies as "she could physically carry." *Source*: Written Statement of Rear Adm. Duncan, Senate Committee hearing, Nov. 9, 2005, p. 3.

249 Written Statement of Rear Adm. Duncan, Senate Committee hearing, Nov. 9, 2005, p. 3. Vice Adm. Vivian Crea, the Coast Guard Atlantic Area Commander, authorized this movement. *Source*: Written Statement of Rear Adm. Duncan, Senate Committee hearing, Nov. 9, 2005, p. 3. The cutter *Spencer* arrived in New Orleans two days after landfall. *Source*: Written Statement of Rear Adm. Duncan, Senate Committee hearing, Nov. 9, 2005, p. 3.

250 Rear Adm. Duncan, Senate Committee hearing, Nov. 9, 2005; Capt. Jones interview, Oct. 6, 2005. In fact, this C-130 was later used by the Coast Guard as a communication platform relaying messages to and from the helicopter search and rescue crews operating over the city. *Source*: Captain Jones interview, Oct. 6, 2005.

251 Capt. Jones interview, Nov. 2, 2005.

252 Capt. Jones interview, Nov. 2, 2005.

253 Committee staff interview of Lt. Cmdr. Shari Ben-Iesau, U.S. Coast Guard, Public Affairs Officer, Coast Guard Sector New Orleans, Oct. 18, 2005, transcript pp. 2-3; Committee staff interview of Lt. Valerie Boyd, U.S. Coast Guard, Command Center Watch Officer, 8th District Office Headquarters, New Orleans, conducted on Nov. 7, transcript pp. 4-6.

254 Rear Adm. Duncan, Senate Committee hearing, Nov. 9, 2005.

255 Capt. Paskewich, Senate Committee hearing, Nov. 9, 2005.

256 Written Statement of Rear Adm. Duncan, Senate Committee hearing, Nov. 9, 2005, p. 3.

257 Committee staff interview of Vice Adm. Vivien Crea, U.S. Coast Guard, Commander, Coast Guard Atlantic Area, conducted on Jan. 3, 2006, transcript p. 16.

258 Capt. Jones, Senate Committee hearing, Nov. 9, 2005.

259 The Department of Defense deployed in support of the Coast Guard and rescued 2,911 people. FEMA also ran search and rescue missions, and saved over 6,000 people.

260 National Disaster Medical System, 2006. www.oep-ndms.dhhs.gov. Accessed on Apr. 24, 2006; U.S. Department of Homeland Security, Current NDMS Overview, Jan. 6, 2006.

261 Beall interview, Jan. 10, 2006, p. 29.

262 Mick Cote, e-mail to Jack Beall, Aug. 27, 2005, 6:24 p.m. Provided to Committee; filed as Bates nos. DHS-FEMA-0098-0004489 through 0004490.

263 Strike teams are small, four to five person medical treatment teams which are deployed where or when a full 35 person Disaster Medical Assistance Team is not needed.

264 Mick Cote, e-mail to Jack Beall, Aug. 27, 2005, 6:24 p.m. Provided to Committee; filed as Bates nos. DHS-FEMA-0098-0004489 through 0004490.

265 Jack Beall, e-mail to Mick Cote, Aug. 27, 2005, 5:29 p.m. Provided to Committee; filed as Bates no. DHS-FEMA-0098-0004489.

266 FEMA, NDMS Resource Status, Aug. 28, 2005, 10 p.m. ET. Provided to Committee.

267 Committee staff interview of Stewart Simonson, Assistant Secretary, Office of Public Health and Emergency Preparedness, U.S. Department of Health and Human Services, conducted on Feb. 16, 2006, transcript pp. 57-59.

268 Simonson interview, Feb. 16, 2006, pp. 37-39, 57-59.

269 Simonson interview, Feb. 16, 2006, pp. 58-59.

270 FEMA, NDMS Resource Status, Aug. 28, 2005, 4 p.m. ET. Provided to Committee.

271 FEMA, NDMS Resource Status, Aug. 28, 2005, 4 p.m. ET. Provided to Committee; Rand McNally, Maps & Directions, www.randmcnally.com. Accessed on Apr. 24, 2006.

272 *NRP,* pp. ESF #8-1 through ESF #8-13.

273 Jack Beall, e-mail to William Lokey, Aug. 28, 2005, 11:53 a.m. Provided to Committee; filed as Bates no. DHS-FEMA-0098-0003831.

274 William Lokey, e-mail to Jack Beall, Aug. 28, 2005. Provided to Committee; filed as Bates no. DHS-FEMA-0098-0003831.

275 FEMA, NDMS Resource Status, Aug. 29, 2005, 10 a.m. ET. Provided to Committee.

276 Committee staff interview of Rear Adm. John Babb, Director, Office of Force Readiness and Deployment, U.S. Department of Health and Human Services, conducted on Feb. 8, 2006, transcript pp. 5, 22-26.

277 Rear Adm. Babb interview, Feb. 8, 2006, pp. 14-15, 22-23.

278 John Babb, e-mail to Kenneth Moritsugu, Aug. 28, 2005, 6:06 p.m. Provided to Committee; filed as Bates no. OSG 186.

279 Rear Adm. Babb interview, Feb. 8, 2006, p. 23.

280 Rear Adm. Babb interview, Feb. 8, 2006, p. 24.

281 Rear Adm. Babb interview, Feb. 8, 2006, p. 24; U.S. Department of Health and Human Services, PHS Katrina Response: Baton Rouge Deployment Alpha Team, Oct. 16, 2005. Provided to Committee.

282 U.S. Public Health Service, briefing on Hurricane Katrina: PHS Response, Team Alpha, given to Senate Committee staff, Jan. 12, 2006.

283 SNS OPS Center Lead, e-mail to KC Decker, Aug. 28, 2005, 6:14 p.m. Provided to Committee; filed as Bates nos. OPHEP 471 through 472. These supplies were dispatched by truck from Atlanta and Tennessee on the afternoon of September 28 and arrived at Camp Beauregard, LA after landfall.

284 Stewart Simonson, e-mail to Steven Adams and others, Aug. 28, 2005, 1:07 p.m. Provided to Committee; filed as Bates no. OPHEP 27780.

285 SNS OPS Center, e-mail to Stewart Simonson and others, Aug. 28, 2005, 4:37 p.m. Provided to Committee; filed as Bates no. OPHEP 27150.

286 SNS OPS Center, e-mail to Stewart Simonson and others, Aug. 28, 2005, 4:37 p.m. Provided to Committee; filed as Bates no. OPHEP 27150.

287 U.S. Department of Health and Human Services, Flash Report #4 – Hurricane Katrina, Aug. 29, 2005, 8:30 a.m. ET. Provided to Committee; filed as Bates nos. OPHEP 28247 through 28248; U.S. Department of Health and Human Services, Flash Report #5 – Hurricane Katrina, Aug. 29, 2005, 3 p.m. ET. Provided to Committee; filed as Bates nos. OPHEP 28249 through 28251; U.S. Department of Health and Human Services Flash Report #6 – Hurricane Katrina, 3 a.m. ET, Aug. 30, 2005, p. 2. Provided to Committee; filed as Bates nos. OPHEP 28252 through 28254; SNS OPS Center Lead, e-mail to EOC Report and others, Aug. 29, 2005, 7:54 p.m. Provided to Committee; filed as Bates no. CDC 2899.

288 Committee staff interview of Col. Richard Chavez, U.S. Air Force, Senior Military Advisor for Civil Support, Office

of the Assistant Secretary of Defense for Homeland Defense, conducted on Nov. 9, 2005, transcript, pp. 36-37.

289 Col. Chavez interview, Nov. 9, 2005, p. 41.

290 Committee staff interview of Col. Darryl L. Roberson, U.S. Air Force, Assistant Deputy Director for Antiterrorism and Homeland Defense, Operations Directorate, Joint Staff, conducted on Nov. 10, 2005, transcript p. 31.

291 First U.S. Army, Message to U.S. Northern Command, "Request for Force Capabilities (Title X) ISO possible DSCA operations as a result of Hurricane Katrina," Aug. 5, 2005, 2816 Z.

292 Committee staff interview of Lt. Gen. James Amos, U.S. Marine Corps, Commander, Second Marine Expeditionary Force, conducted on Dec. 14, 2005, transcript, p. 9; Committee staff interview of Maj. Gen. Douglas O'Dell, U.S. Marine Corps, Commander, Fourth Marine Division, conducted on Dec. 14, 2005, transcript pp. 16-18.

293 Committee staff interview of Vice Adm. Mark Fitzgerald, U.S. Navy, Commander, U.S. Second Fleet, conducted on Nov. 15, 2005.

294 Committee staff interview of Capt. Rick Snyder, U.S. Navy, Executive Officer, USS *Bataan*, conducted on Nov. 14, 2005.

295 Michael Ritchie, e-mail to Anthony Capra, Aug. 29, 2005, 1:14 p.m. Provided to Committee; filed as no. MMTF 00418-05.

296 Committee staff interview of Col. Thomas Muir, U.S. Army, Deputy Chief of Current Operations, U.S. Northern Command, conducted on Dec. 6, 2005, transcript p. 14.

297 Chairman of the Joint Chiefs of Staff, Message to Commander, U.S. Northern Command, et al., "CJCS EXORD," Aug. 5, 2005, 1923 Z.

298 U.S. Northern Command, USNORTHCOM Hurricane Katrina Timeline (Draft), pp. 2-3. Provided to Committee.

299 First U.S. Army, Message to U.S. Northern Command, "Request for Force Capabilities (Title X) ISO possible DSCA operations as a result of Hurricane Katrina," Aug. 5, 2005, 2816 Z .

300 Committee staff interview of Maj. Gen. Richard Rowe, U.S. Army, Director of Operations, U.S. Northern Command, conducted on Jan. 20, 2006, transcript pp. 31-32.

301 Maj. Gen. Richard Rowe, e-mail to NC-JOC – Director – OMB and others, Aug. 28, 2005, 5:31 p.m. Provided to Committee; filed as MMTF00452-05.

302 Maj. Gen. Rowe interview, Jan. 20, 2006, p. 31; Committee staff interview of Capt. Michael McDaniel, U.S. Navy, Navy Emergency Preparedness Liaison Officer to FEMA, conducted on Dec. 2, 2005, transcript p. 156; Col. Harrington interview, Jan. 6, 2006, p. 89.

303 The Defense Department intends to broaden the actions it takes in advance of a hurricane's landfall. According to several witnesses, the Joint Staff is considering broadening the Severe Weather Order to allow NORTHCOM to designate or position helicopters, boats, and communications gear prior to landfall. *Source:* Committee staff interview of Maj. Gen. Terry Scherling, U.S. Air Force, Director of the Joint Staff, National Guard Bureau, conducted on Jan. 19, 2006, transcript p. 81; Maj. Gen. Rowe interview, Jan. 20, 2006, p. 29. Col. Richard Chavez, the Senior Military Advisor in the Office of the Secretary of Defense for Homeland Defense, explained that in the future he intends to include shallow-draft boats among the assets that he inventories prior to landfall. *Source:* Col. Chavez interview, Nov. 9, 2005, p. 27. In light of the lack of situational awareness experienced by almost all entities within the Department during the first 24 hours after landfall, many witnesses have attested to a need to deploy information-gathering assets – including National Technical Means – so as to gain timely and accurate information in the first critical hours after a disaster. *Source:* McHale interview, Jan. 4, 2006, p. 136. Because the issue raises questions of domestic intelligence-gathering and dissemination of potentially classified material, the Department has yet to determine an appropriate solution.

Secretary Chertoff, left, with President
and Lt. Gen. H. Steven Blum

National Guard photo

Department of Homeland Security: Roles and Responsibilities

General Authorities and Responsibilities

Both in design and in fact, the Department of Homeland Security (DHS) is the central federal entity for preparedness and response to disasters, including catastrophic events like Hurricane Katrina. The Homeland Security Act of 2002 established the Department and provides that one of DHS's missions is "acting as a focal point regarding natural and manmade crises and emergency planning."[1] DHS was created to bring together multiple, disparate agencies to create synergy and ensure a coordinated approach to preventing, preparing for, and responding to catastrophes, whether caused by terrorism or nature.[2]

Since DHS's creation, several executive actions have further articulated its role. Homeland Security Presidential Directive 5, issued by President Bush on February 28, 2003, formally designated the Secretary of Homeland Security as the "principal federal official for domestic incident management."[3] It also made the Secretary responsible for developing and administering the National Response Plan (NRP) and the National Incident Management System (NIMS), a system for enabling responders from different jurisdictions to work together.[4] Homeland Security Presidential Directive 8 (HSPD-8), issued on December 17, 2003, further designated the Secretary as "the principal Federal official for coordinating the implementation of all-hazards preparedness in the United States," and gave the Secretary, in cooperation with other Federal departments and agencies, responsibility for "coordinat[ing] the preparedness of federal response assets, and the support for, and assessment of, the preparedness of state and local first responders."[5]

In addition, DHS has assumed responsibilities under the Robert T. Stafford Relief and Emergency Assistance Act (Stafford Act).[6] Among other things, the Stafford Act authorizes and provides the administrative mechanisms for the federal government to assist state and local governments in disasters.[7] The President, or the Secretary of Homeland Security as his delegate, has the authority to provide "assistance essential to meeting immediate threats to life and property resulting from a major disaster."[8] This authority specifically allows the Secretary to do any work essential to saving lives or preserving public health and safety, including search and rescue, emergency medical care, emergency mass care, emergency shelter, and provision of food, water, medicine, and other essential needs, including movement of supplies or persons.[9] In addition, the Homeland Security Act gives the Secretary, through the Under Secretary for Emergency Management and Response, the responsibility for "providing the federal government's response to terrorist attacks and major disasters,"[10] and charges FEMA with conducting emergency operations to save lives and property "through positioning emergency equipment and supplies, through evacuating potential victims, through providing food, water, shelter, and medical care to those in need, and through restoring critical public services."[11]

On February 28, 2003, the day before the new Department began operating and FEMA became part of DHS, President Bush modified Executive Order 12148, delegating most Presidential responsibilities under the Stafford Act to the Secretary of Homeland Security, rather than to the Director of FEMA, as had previously been the case.[12]

New Orleans family

The NRP further confirms DHS's central role in disaster preparedness and response. The Plan, reviewed by the White House's Homeland Security Council and signed by the heads of 30 federal agencies, states that:

> During actual or potential Incidents of National Significance, the overall coordination of federal incident management activities is executed through the Secretary of Homeland Security. Other federal departments and agencies carry out their incident management and emergency response authorities and responsibilities within this overarching coordinating framework.[13]

Practically, these authorities invested DHS with at least four categories of responsibility:

1. *Leadership.* The Secretary of the Department of Homeland Security has clear duties to lead and manage the federal response to disasters such as Katrina. He carries ultimate responsibility for managing FEMA and other DHS components and is charged with coordinating overall federal operations.[14] Among his many responsibilities, the Secretary must marshal federal resources, decide whether to appoint a Principal Federal Official to lead the federal response on the ground,[15] and decide whether to implement the Catastrophic Incident Annex, which provides for an accelerated, proactive national response to a catastrophic incident.[16]

2. *Coordination and Support.* DHS can use various structures and resources to coordinate and support the overall response effort. Among these, the Homeland Security Operations Center (HSOC) is supposed to act as a hub for situational awareness and incident management in a disaster. Some 45 agencies staff the HSOC to facilitate information flow among agencies;[17] during Katrina, the HSOC distributed situation reports twice a day that were widely disseminated throughout the government. The Interagency Incident Management Group (IIMG) is also housed at DHS. Comprising senior-level representatives of a variety of agencies, the IIMG is supposed to coordinate federal resource and operational requirements and make strategic recommendations to the Secretary, who has the power to activate the IIMG based on the nature, severity, magnitude, and complexity of a threat or incident.[18]

3. *Operational Responsibilities.* DHS has significant, ground-level operational responsibilities in responding to disasters. DHS and its component agencies are primary or coordinating agencies for nine of the 15 Emergency Support Functions (ESFs) in the NRP – categories of federal capabilities that can be brought to bear to provide support in domestic incidents – including public safety and security, communications support, and emergency management.[19] DHS components such as the Coast Guard also have significant missions and statutory responsibilities independent of the NRP.[20] FEMA also controls the activation and movement of search and rescue and directs the National Disaster Medical Support System.

4. *Preparedness.* Besides its response roles, DHS has primary responsibility for strengthening national preparedness – including the planning, training, and equipment necessary to prevent, respond to, and recover from major domestic incidents – under HSPD-8 and the Homeland Security Act.[21] Section 502 of the Homeland Security Act gives the Secretary, acting through the FEMA Director, responsibility for "helping to ensure the effectiveness of emergency response providers to terrorist attacks, major disasters, and other emergencies."[22] The Department has authority over primary grants and training programs for state and local first responders and emergency managers.[23] Pursuant to HSPD-8, DHS has developed a National Preparedness Goal, establishing national emergency-management and preparedness priorities.[24] DHS ties its preparedness requirements to grant funding, requiring that all states submit emergency plans in order to get funding and that the money be used to meet the capabilities and priorities set forth by the National Preparedness Goal.[25]

Title VI of the Stafford Act also places significant responsibilities for national emergency preparedness on the FEMA Director and, through the Homeland Security Act, on DHS,[26] providing, among other things, that the federal government is to provide the necessary direction, guidance, and assistance "so that a comprehensive preparedness system exists for all hazards."[27]

The Role of the Federal Government

Our nation has a system of dual sovereignty. The federal government has limited, enumerated powers, and state governments retain primary responsibility to protect the public's health and safety, so-called "police powers."[28] This is commonly known as "federalism." Traditionally, state and local officials have managed the response to an incident in the first instance, and the federal government for the most part provides assistance only as requested. This approach makes sense: during an emergency, states typically have authority to exercise extraordinary powers to commandeer resources, control property, order evacuations, suspend laws, and take other extreme measures.[29] In addition, state and local authorities have large numbers of public-safety employees that are first responders to every emergency. The individuals closest to an emergency incident generally know the locality best, and are wholly accountable to the local electorate for their actions.

Congress established the Stafford Act to provide assistance "by the federal government to state and local governments in carrying out their responsibilities to alleviate the suffering and damage which result from . . . disasters."[30] The Stafford Act respects the state's role in determining when it is overwhelmed and the assistance that it wants from the federal government. The Stafford Act requires that the governor of a state request the President declare a major disaster for a portion or all of a state. Such requests include a description of how the state's resources are overwhelmed.[31] The President then can decide to declare a major disaster and determine the federal assistance that will be provided "in support of state and local assistance efforts."[32] Thus, the Stafford Act provides for consultation with state officials prior to the provision of federal assistance in the first instance. The subsequent federal government response is cognizant of underlying concerns for the state's continued authority over the direction of the response efforts and respects state autonomy under our federal system of government. Traditionally, FEMA has required that states make requests not only for the initial declaration of a disaster or emergency but also for specific types of assistance such as the provision of commodities or assistance with search and rescue efforts.

In a catastrophic situation, however, the traditional mode of operation under the Stafford Act may not serve the Act's purposes because state and local governments may become so overwhelmed that they can't effectively make specific requests for assistance. In such circumstances, the federal government may have to act without a request from a state.

The NRP explicitly provides for a proactive federal response in the Catastrophic Incident Annex (NRP-CIA).[33] The NRP defines a catastrophic event as "any natural or manmade incident, including terrorism, that results in extraordinary levels of mass casualties, damage, or disruption severely affecting the population, infrastructure, environment, economy, national morale, and/or government functions."[34] According to the NRP, only the Secretary of Homeland Security or the Secretary's designee may initiate implementation of the NRP-CIA.[35]

The NRP-CIA recognizes that, in a catastrophe, "federal and/or national resources are required to augment overwhelmed state, local, and tribal response efforts" and therefore provides for the identification and rapid deployment of essential resources expected to be urgently needed to save lives and contain incidents.[36] The NRP-CIA provides that standard procedures regarding requests for assistance "may be expedited or, under extreme circumstances, temporarily suspended" in the aftermath of a catastrophe.[37]

At the same time, the NRP-CIA is sensitive to concerns for state autonomy. Thus, notification and coordination with states are still to occur, though "the coordination process should not delay or impede the rapid mobilization and deployment of critical federal resources."[38] And federal resources are generally deployed to mobilization centers close to the incident scene "until requested by state/local incident command authorities,"[39] though in certain circumstances, they may be deployed directly to the incident scene to assist in responding to the incident.

1 "The Homeland Security Act of 2002." (P.L. 107-296), 6 U.S.C. § 111(b).

2 U.S. House, Homeland Security Act of 2002, S. Rept. 107-609, July 24, 2002, p. 63. Among the 22 pre-existing entities that were brought together as part of DHS were FEMA, the U.S. Coast Guard, the Transportation Security Administration, the National Communications System (which coordinates emergency communications), and law enforcement entities such as the U.S. Secret Service and the Federal Protective Service. Prior to becoming part of the Department of Homeland Security, FEMA was a stand-alone agency. Most of the other entities that were incorporated into DHS were transferred from other cabinet departments: for example, the Coast Guard had previously been part of the Department of Transportation and the Secret Service had been part of the Treasury Department.

3 The White House, Homeland Security Presidential Directive-5: Management of Domestic Incidents, Feb. 28, 2003, Section 4.

4 The White House, Homeland Security Presidential Directive-5: Management of Domestic Incidents, Feb. 28, 2003, Sections 15-16.

5 The White House, Homeland Security Presidential Directive-8: Domestic Preparedness, Dec. 17, 2003, Section 4. All-hazards preparedness is defined in the Directive as "preparedness for domestic terrorist attacks, major disasters, and other emergencies." *Source*: The White House, Homeland Security Presidential Directive-8: Domestic Preparedness, Dec. 17, 2003, Section 2(a). Preparedness is defined as "the existence of plans, procedures, policies, training, and equipment necessary at the Federal, State, and local level to maximize the ability prevent, respond to, and recover from major events." *Source*: The White House, Homeland Security Presidential Directive-8: Domestic Preparedness, Dec. 17, 2003, Section 2(h).

6 "Robert T. Stafford Disaster Relief and Emergency Assistance Act." (P.L. 93-288), 42 U.S.C. §§ 5121-5206. FEMA's responsibilities were delegated to the Department of Homeland Security by Executive Order 13286, Feb. 28, 2003, 68 Fed. Reg. 10619 (Mar. 3, 2003).

7 "Stafford Act," 42 U.S.C. § 5170a.

8 "Stafford Act," 42 U.S.C. § 5170b.

9 "Stafford Act," 42 U.S.C. § 5170b; 42 U.S.C. § 5170b(a)(3). This is the authority pursuant to a major disaster declaration. Under an emergency declaration, the authority is similar but phrased more generally, providing that "Whenever the federal assistance provided under subsection (a) of this section with respect to an emergency is inadequate, the President may also provide assistance with respect to efforts to save lives, protect property and public health and safety, and lessen or avert the threat of a catastrophe." "Stafford Act," 42 U.S.C. § 5192(b).

10 "Homeland Security Act," 6 U.S.C. § 312(3).

11 "Homeland Security Act," 6 U.S.C. § 317(a)(2)(c).

12 Executive Order 13286, 68 Fed. Reg. 10619 (Mar. 5, 2003), Section 52. Executive Order 12148, July 20, 1979, (Federal Emergency Management), as amended, is further amended by: (a) striking "the Federal Emergency Management Agency" whenever it appears and inserting "the Department of Homeland Security" in lieu thereof; and (b) striking "the Director of the Federal Emergency Management Agency" wherever it appears and inserting "the Secretary of Homeland Security" in lieu thereof. *See also*: Executive Order 12673, 54 Fed. Reg. 12573 (Mar. 28, 1989), Section 1 (amending Executive Order 12148).

13 U.S. Department of Homeland Security, *National Response Plan*. Washington: Government Printing Office, Dec. 2004, p. 15 [hereinafter *NRP*].

14 *NRP*, p. 9 ("Pursuant to HSPD-5, the Secretary of Homeland Security is responsible for coordinating Federal operations within the United States to prepare for, respond to and recover from terrorist attacks, major disasters, and other emergencies.").

15 *NRP*, p. 33.

16 *NRP*, Catastrophic Incident Annex, p. CAT–1.

17 *NRP*, p. 24.

18 *NRP*, p. 22.

19 *NRP*, ESF Annex, p. ESF–v.

20 As discussed in greater detail in subsequent sections, DHS itself shares the lead responsibility for supporting public safety and security (ESF-13) with the Department of Justice, and its component, the National Communications System (NCS), is supposed to take the lead in providing communications support (ESF-2) during a disaster. FEMA has the lead responsibility for emergency management under ESF-5, which includes central responsibilities for domestic incident management as well as management and administrative support for the National Response Coordination Center (NRCC), Regional Response Coordination Center (RRCC), and Joint Field Office (JFO), according the NRP. Also under the NRP, FEMA serves as the primary and/or coordinating agency for Public Works and Engineering (ESF-3); Mass Care, Housing and Human Services (ESF-6); Urban Search and Rescue (ESF-9); Long-Term Community Recovery and Mitigation (ESF-14); and, in conjunction with DHS, External Affairs (ESF-15). The Coast Guard, in addition to its responsibilities under the NRP for oil and hazardous material response (ESF-10), has the statutory authority to save lives and property imperiled by flood by performing any and all acts necessary to rescue and aid persons and protect and save property...at any time and any place at which the Coast Guard facilities and personnel are available and can be effectively utilized. 14 U.S.C. § 88(a)(1) and (b).

21 "Homeland Security Act," 6 U.S.C. 312(1); The White House, Homeland Security Presidential Directive-8: Domestic Preparedness, Dec. 17, 2003.

22 "Homeland Security Act," 42 U.S.C. § 502(1); 6 U.S.C. § 312(1).

23 *See e.g.*: "Homeland Security Act," 6 U.S.C. § 238; The White House, Homeland Security Presidential Directive-8: Domestic Preparedness, Dec. 17, 2003; U.S. Department of Homeland Security, Interim National Preparedness Goal, Mar. 31, 2005.

24 The White House, Homeland Security Presidential Directive-8: Domestic Preparedness, Dec. 17, 2003, Section 5.

25 U.S. Department of Homeland Security, Preparedness Directorate, Office of Grants and Training, Financial Management Guide, Jan. 2006, p. 11.

26 "Stafford Act," 42 U.S.C. §§ 5195-5197(g); "Homeland Security Act," 6 U.S.C. § 112(a)(3) (vesting all functions of all officers, employees, and organizational units of the Department of Homeland Security in the Secretary of Homeland Security). In fulfilling these responsibilities, the Director of FEMA may conduct or arrange training programs for emergency-preparedness officials, and may provide financial contributions to the states for emergency preparedness. "Stafford Act," 42 U.S.C. § 5131. Moreover, under Section 201 of the Stafford Act, the President is authorized to establish a program of disaster preparedness that includes: (1) preparation of disaster preparedness plans for mitigation, warning, emergency operations, rehabilitation, and recovery; (2) training and exercises; and (3) coordination of federal, state, and local preparedness programs. "Stafford Act," 42 U.S.C. § 5131(a).

27 "Stafford Act," 42 U.S.C. § 5195. Under the Act, the term "emergency preparedness" is defined to mean all those activities designed to minimize the effects of a hazard upon a civilian population. "Stafford Act," 42 U.S.C. § 5195. These activities include "the establishment of appropriate organizations, operational plans, and supporting agreements, the recruitment and training of personnel, the conduct of research, the procurement and stockpiling of necessary materials, and supplies, the provision of suitable warning systems, the construction or preparation of shelters, shelter areas, and control centers, and, when appropriate, the non-military evacuation of the civilian population." "Stafford Act," 42 U.S.C. § 5195(a)(3)(A).

28 *See e.g.*: Gregory v. Ashcroft, 501 U.S. 452, 457-60 (1991).

29 *See e.g.*: La R.S. 29:721 *et seq.* (Louisiana Emergency Assistance and Disaster Act).

30 "Stafford Act," 42 U.S.C. § 5121(b).

31 "Stafford Act," 42 U.S.C. § 5770.

32 "Stafford Act," 42 U.S.C. § 5170(a)(1).

33 *NRP*, Catastrophic Incident Annex, p. CAT–1.

34 *NRP*, p. 43; Catastrophic Incident Annex, p. CAT–1.

35 *NRP*, Catastrophic Incident Annex, p. CAT–1.

36 *NRP*, Catastrophic Incident Annex, p. CAT–1. *See also*: *NRP*, Catastrophic Incident Annex, p. CAT-3 ("The response capabilities and resources of the local jurisdiction … may be insufficient and quickly overwhelmed. Local emergency personnel who normally respond to incidents may be among those affected and unable to perform their duties.").

37 *NRP*, p. 44; Catastrophic Incident Annex, p. CAT–4.

38 *NRP*, Catastrophic Incident Annex, p. CAT–4.

39 *NRP*, Catastrophic Incident Annex, p. CAT–2.

Flooding, Louisiana

The Federal Emergency Management Agency (FEMA)

Assessing FEMA's status as Hurricane Katrina struck the Gulf Coast is fundamental to determining whether the federal government was prepared to respond to a catastrophic event.

The Committee's investigation found systemic and leadership failures, displayed in both the preparation for and response to Hurricane Katrina, at both the Department of Homeland Security (DHS) and FEMA. These failures contributed to human suffering and the loss of life. The causes of many of these failures were known long prior to Katrina and had been brought repeatedly to the attention of both DHS and FEMA leadership. Despite warnings, leadership failed to make vital changes.

In August 1992, Hurricane Andrew struck Florida as a Category 5 hurricane.[1] Its $43.7 billion bill of damages (in 2005 purchasing power) was the worst ever recorded in the U.S. until Hurricane Katrina.[2] A post-storm study by the National Academy of Public Administration (NAPA) revealed failures in the response to Andrew that would repeat themselves in the response to Katrina, such as the erroneous initial assumption that heavily populated areas were spared the brunt of the storm, which delayed response when those assumptions turned out to be wrong.[3] In evaluating the response, NAPA concluded that FEMA was "a patient in triage," adding that the "President and Congress must decide whether to treat it or let it die ... FEMA has been ill-served by congressional and White House neglect, a fragmented statutory charter, irregular funding, and uneven quality of its political executives ... the agency remains an institution not yet built."[4] The report found that FEMA had inadequate leadership.[5] It recommended a limit on the number of presidential appointees and filling leadership positions with the most qualified FEMA employees.[6] The report also found that FEMA needed to do far more to develop state and local emergency-management capacity.[7] If the key changes it recommended were beyond reach, the report added, more dramatic action – such as "abolishing FEMA" – should be taken.[8]

After President Clinton took office, he appointed James Lee Witt as FEMA Director. Witt had been the Director of Arkansas' Office of Emergency Services. In March 1994, NAPA reviewed FEMA's reforms in response to its post-Andrew recommendations. The new report opened, "The greatest plus for the emergency management function and for FEMA has been the appointment of James Lee Witt, an experienced emergency manager, as director of FEMA."[9]

Following Andrew, FEMA appeared to improve. A study by George Mason University's Mercatus Center found that, since its reorganization in 1993, "FEMA has significantly improved its ability to deal with disasters," highlighting several improvements to recovery and mitigation programs, as well as employee training.[10] The report concluded that FEMA had shown "major improvement in both performance and cost-effectiveness" achieved through "a collection of management actions that transformed a bureaucratic, process-driven organization into a responsive, results-driven organization."[11] Another study pointed to agency leadership: "An example of a best practice in agency transformation is the revitalization of … FEMA under the leadership of Director James Lee Witt. FEMA serves as an instructive case study of how to transform a troubled organization."[12] The report commended the selection of senior officials with emergency-management experience and found that the experience resulted in improvements.[13] That being said, the report noted that "the agency is still not free of problems."[14]

In 2001, Joe Allbaugh succeeded Witt as Director and took a different approach to restructuring FEMA. Shortly after he became Director, Allbaugh testified to House and Senate committees:

> Many are concerned that federal disaster assistance may have evolved into an oversized entitlement program. … Expectations of when the federal government should be involved and the degree of involvement may have ballooned beyond what is an appropriate level. We must restore the predominant role of state and local response to most disasters. Federal assistance needs to supplement, not supplant, state and local efforts.[15]

Allbaugh acknowledged FEMA's successful transformation, but offered a new vision when he explained FEMA's budget in Senate testimony: "Today, FEMA is being called a model of government success due to the hard work and dedication of the career employees, … however, FEMA is not free from problems."[16]

In March 2001, the United States Commission on National Security/21st Century, a congressionally mandated independent commission set up to study our nation's security challenges issued a report (the Hart-Rudman report) that recommended sweeping changes in our nation's approach to securing the homeland. It found that "the United States is today very poorly organized to design and implement any comprehensive strategy to protect the homeland."[17] Among other things, the Hart-Rudman report recommended that Congress create a new homeland-security agency with responsibility for planning, coordinating, and integrating various U.S. government activities involved in homeland security.[18]

The report saw a prominent role for FEMA within the new homeland-security agency, and in fact proposed building the new agency "upon the capabilities of. … FEMA."[19] The homeland-security agency "would be legislatively chartered to provide a focal point for all natural and manmade crisis and emergency planning scenarios. It would retain and strengthen FEMA's 10 existing regional offices as a core element of its organizational structure."[20] The report considered FEMA to be a "necessary core" of the proposed homeland security-agency.[21]

The Hart-Rudman report envisioned a homeland-security agency that would "employ FEMA's principle of working effectively with state and local governments, as well as with other federal organizations, stressing interagency coordination."[22] It said that "much of [the agency's] daily work will take place directly supporting state officials in its regional offices around the country."[23]

The largest terrorist attack on U.S. soil prompted Congress to take the Hart-Rudman report to heart: In the wake of the terrorist attacks on September 11, 2001, Congress passed the Homeland Security Act, which created the DHS in an effort to better organize and coordinate our nation to prevent and respond to terrorist attacks, while maintaining the varied responsibilities of the 22 agencies merged into the new Department. This was the largest reorganization of government since the creation of the Department of Defense in 1947. The main objective behind the creation of DHS was to consolidate our assets relevant to homeland security so that our homeland-security efforts could be more coordinated and efficient.

Consistent with the Hart-Rudman recommendations, the Homeland Security Act transferred FEMA, its responsibilities, assets, and liabilities to the Emergency Preparedness and Response Directorate of the new Department. FEMA retained its name and its director was named Under Secretary of Emergency Preparedness and Response. Though formed in the wake of 9/11, DHS's primary mission included carrying out all functions of entities transferred to the Department, "including by acting as a focal point regarding natural and manmade crisis and emergency planning."[24]

Among other things, the Act makes the Secretary of Homeland Security, acting through the Under Secretary for Emergency Preparedness and Response, responsible for

> helping to ensure the effectiveness of emergency response providers to terrorist attacks, major disasters, and other emergencies, providing the federal government's response to terrorist attacks and major disasters, … aiding in the recovery from terrorist attacks and major disasters, … building a comprehensive national incident management system with federal, state, and local government personnel, agencies, and authorities to respond to such attacks and disaster, … [and] developing comprehensive programs for developing interoperable communications technology, and helping to ensure that emergency response providers acquire such technology.[25]

FEMA, within DHS, was an important part of Congress's vision to making our nation safe. Consistent with the Hart-Rudman report, DHS was to build upon FEMA's strengths, and FEMA, the center of the Emergency Preparedness and Response Directorate, could better coordinate our nation's vast assets to be prepared to respond to any disaster, whether natural or manmade. One of the fundamental reasons for bringing together multiple agencies was to create synergy, molding individual capabilities into a stronger, more effective and more coordinated approach to preventing and responding to catastrophes, whether caused by terrorism or nature.

Not long after DHS was formed, DHS leadership started taking critical functions from FEMA and moving them to other places within DHS. In January 2004, then-Secretary Tom Ridge removed numerous preparedness-grant programs from FEMA and placed them in another office within DHS.[26] Secretary Chertoff later removed from FEMA all of its preparedness activities – essentially formalizing Ridge's January 2004 actions[27] – and consolidated preparedness activities into a single directorate led by an Undersecretary for Preparedness.[28] Prior to the January 2004 changes, preparedness was one of FEMA's essential roles.

FEMA Was Not Prepared to Respond to the Catastrophic Effects of Hurricane Katrina

Former FEMA Director Michael Brown has said that he knew the weekend before Katrina's landfall that neither the federal government nor New Orleans was prepared for the "big one."[29] DHS Secretary Chertoff conceded,

> Although FEMA pre-positioned significant numbers of personnel, assets and resources before the hurricane made landfall, … we now know that [FEMA's] capabilities were overwhelmed by the magnitude of the storm. … The people did what they could. It was a question of whether they had the tools and capabilities that they needed in order to do the job properly.[30]

Brown testified that he repeatedly told White House officials that FEMA was not prepared to handle a catastrophe. He gave the same warnings to DHS officials.[31]

The investigation explored several reasons for FEMA's lack of preparedness, including unqualified political leadership, budget shortages, inadequate workforce, FEMA's inclusion within DHS, and underdeveloped and inadequate response capabilities.

FEMA's Senior Leadership

Brown and most of his front-office staff had little or no emergency-management experience prior to joining FEMA.[32] While it is unclear that emergency-management experience alone is the single qualifier for senior leadership at FEMA, the leadership at the time of Katrina also lacked basic management experience and the leadership ability required to coordinate the entire federal government's response to a catastrophic event. Brown advocated to DHS and the White House to address FEMA's needs, but he was generally unsuccessful. He presided over the agency as morale plummeted. He refused to operate within the chain of command in which FEMA resided. He failed to work collaboratively with state officials in Louisiana during Hurricane Katrina, the most significant disaster during his tenure.

Brown became DHS Under Secretary for Emergency Preparedness and Response, and therefore FEMA Director, in early 2003.[33] Brown first joined FEMA as General Counsel[34] in February 2001, and from there progressed quickly to front-office duties. By the fall of 2001, then-Director Joseph Allbaugh named him Acting Deputy Director for FEMA.[35] Prior to joining FEMA, Brown had little to no prior relevant emergency-management experience.[36] Early in his career, he had some experience with municipal government, including municipal management,[37] and had been a Commissioner for the International Arabian Horse Association for about 10 years.

Patrick Rhode joined FEMA in 2003 as Chief of Staff for Brown.[38] Prior to coming to FEMA, Rhode had no experience in emergency management. After communications work in business and government, Rhode did advance work for George Bush's 2000 presidential campaign.[39] After the election, Rhode did advance work for the White House and then briefly worked as a White House liaison for the Department of Commerce.[40] Rhode then accepted a position as the Associate Administrator of the Small Business Administration, and remained there until his move to FEMA.[41] Brown named Rhode Acting Deputy Director of FEMA in the summer of 2005,[42] and Rhode was therefore in charge at headquarters as Brown traveled to the Gulf Coast just before Katrina struck.

Rhode and Brown were not the only FEMA officials lacking emergency-management experience. With the exception of a FEMA employee who joined Brown's front office staff as Acting Director of Operations about a year after Brown became Under Secretary, none of the other individuals in the front office during the entire time he served as Under Secretary had any prior emergency-management experience.[43] Indeed, several FEMA leaders came from campaign rather than emergency-management backgrounds.[44] Additionally, a review of the biographies by by Committee staff of FEMA regional directors since 2001 show that many of them had little or no emergency-management experience as well.

Eric Tolbert, Director of Response at FEMA until February 2005, said:

> The impact of having politicals [appointees] in the high ranks of FEMA … that's what killed us, was that in the senior ranks of FEMA there was nobody that even knew FEMA's history, much less understood the profession and the dynamics and the roles and responsibilities of the states and local governments.[45]

FEMA's senior managers did include some experienced emergency-management personnel. For example, Ed Buikema, Acting Director of the Response Division at the time Katrina struck, had 26 years of experience with the state police in Michigan, 15 of them in their emergency-management division.[46] Michael Lowder, Deputy Director for Response, spent over 31 years as a first responder or emergency manager.[47] Ken Burris, the Acting Director of Operations, was a firefighter for 23 years before joining FEMA in 1999.[48] Gary Moore, FEMA's Director of Logistics, was a police officer for 26 years, finishing as second-rank-

Porter Avenue, Biloxi, MS
Sun Herald news photo, Biloxi/Gulfport, MS

ing member of the Maryland State Police before assuming federal emergency-management positions in the Department of Health and Human Services and DHS in 1992.[49]

In January 2005, MITRE, a non-profit consulting firm, completed an assessment to identify problems preventing FEMA from dealing quickly with disasters. The assessment was based on confidential interviews of FEMA's 11 senior executives.[50] Key themes that emerged from the interviews included the number of, and lack of qualifications of, political appointees, the number of temporary and acting staff, and frequent lack of operational experience as reasons why FEMA was underperforming.[51] A few of the unattributed statements made during interviews included:

- "The void is in leadership. There's none. … It's reactions to politics and hot potatoes."[52]

- "None of the senior leadership understand the dynamics of how response and recovery actually works. … This administration doesn't understand the value and importance of emergency management."[53]

- "Patrick [Rhode] is purely political; he thinks White House."[54]

In evaluating the failures in Hurricane Andrew, NAPA had concluded that "FEMA has had insufficient leadership … necessary to create a high-performance, high-reliability institution."[55] History seemed to be repeating itself.

Budget Issues

Several witnesses testified that FEMA's capabilities were harmed by limited funding and resources. For instance, some expressed concern that FEMA's ability to respond to Hurricane Katrina was harmed by fees levied by DHS to cover costs associated with "membership" within the Department. These witnesses complained that DHS "taxed" FEMA – essentially redirecting funds Congress appropriated to FEMA to DHS. Director Brown testified that $77.9 million had been lost in this way between fiscal year 2003 and fiscal year 2005, a 14.8 percent decrease in FEMA's discretionary spending account since joining DHS.[56]

In interviews with Committee staff, DHS Deputy Secretary Michael Jackson and Chief Financial Officer Andrew Maner disputed the idea that a DHS tax harmed FEMA, though Maner conceded DHS had taken a total of $25 million from FEMA's base.[57] Jackson explained that the "taxes" are actually consolidated costs designed to procure services for all component agencies at a lower unit cost (e.g., maintenance contracts for copiers or overnight package delivery contracts).[58] However, Ken Burris, FEMA's Acting Chief Operating Officer, said that in order to pay DHS's contributions or "taxes," FEMA could no longer afford to refill personnel positions when they became vacant.[59]

Regardless of the reason for it, numerous FEMA witnesses testified that because of a lack of resources, FEMA simply could not completely perform its mission. Brown and other FEMA employees testified that FEMA sought additional funding on several occasions, but that generally, DHS or the Office of Management and Budget (OMB) denied his requests.

One area for which FEMA sought additional funding was catastrophic planning. In fiscal year 2004 FEMA sought $100 million for catastrophic planning, and in fiscal year 2005, sought $20 million to develop a catastrophic housing plan and $80 million to improve FEMA's national response teams. DHS, however, denied these requests.[60] Then-FEMA Director of Response Eric Tolbert believed that planning for New Orleans was important enough to set aside funding from other parts of the response budget, though the planning was delayed in part by funding shortages.[61] FEMA has not done enough planning to be prepared for a catastrophic disaster.

FEMA's budget shortages manifested themselves in several ways, thus hindering FEMA's ability to be adequately prepared for and respond to a catastrophe. Some of those ways will be further discussed below.

Personnel Shortages

FEMA is a small agency with approximately 2,500 permanent full-time employees. Over the last few years, FEMA has suffered numerous personnel problems, hindering its ability to prepare for and respond to a catastrophic event. While it had previously enjoyed a dedicated, Senior Executive Service level of experienced emergency managers, a "brain drain" sapped this core expertise.[62]

Over the last few years, FEMA has operated with a 15 to 20 percent vacancy rate; many positions cannot be filled because of budget shortages.[63] FEMA tried to get additional funding from DHS, but the requests were generally denied. The personnel shortages negatively impacted FEMA's ability to achieve its mission.[64] For example, due to staffing shortages, William Lokey, the Chief of Operations in the Response Division, said that FEMA had not completed a final Concept of Operations for its National Emergency Response Teams (ERT-N); the Incident Management Handbook, which would explain procedures for managing disasters to those working in disasters; or a final Concept of Operations for the 2005 hurricane season.[65]

Because of personnel needs, FEMA relies heavily on two types of temporary employees hired under the Stafford Act: Disaster Temporary Employees (DTEs), whose one-year appointments may be extended an unlimited number of times; and a Cadre of On-Call Response and Recovery Employees (CORE employees), whose four-year appointments may be extended an unlimited number of times, in two-year increments. DTEs are not eligible for certain employer-paid benefits.[66]

Initially, FEMA intended that these temporary appointments would provide it with the flexibility needed for readiness during disaster operations.[67] However, a July 2004 report by the U.S. Office of Personnel Management (OPM) found that under FEMA's staffing practices at the time of the report – which still reflected the agency's needs in 1996 – some DTE and CORE employees appeared to have worked for FEMA continuously for 10 years or longer with few, if any, breaks in service.[68] The report found that FEMA's extensive use of these two categories of temporary employees indicates that such employees are not being used for temporary purposes, but rather to fill critical needs and provide a stable, baseline workforce.[69] The report criticized FEMA for this practice because, although DTE and CORE employees are working side by side with permanent employees, doing the same work, the appointments are starkly different, including the provision of benefits.[70] OPM found that these practices had indirectly created a tier-based workforce and had hurt morale.[71] OPM made several recommendations to remedy these problems.[72] To date, FEMA has not implemented OPM's recommendations.[73]

Staffing shortages impeded FEMA's ability to prepare for a catastrophe. Additionally, as will be described in several other chapters, FEMA's inadequate numbers of trained staff also had a negative impact on the response to Katrina.

FEMA's Response Capabilities

FEMA has responsibilities in both disaster response and recovery. Response includes actions taken during or after an emergency. Recovery involves short-term activities to return life-support systems after an emergency – such as rebuilding and assisting victims in dealing with damage caused by a disaster.

Several FEMA Federal Coordinating Officers (FCOs) said that FEMA is capable of handling small and medium-size disasters, but is not organized for large response operations. As FCO Scott Wells said, "FEMA is not trained, FEMA is not equipped, FEMA is not organized to do very large response operations. … If you want big capability, you got to make a big investment. And there is no investment in response operations for a catastrophic disaster."[74] FCO Phil Parr said that FEMA focuses on recovery rather than response.[75]

FEMA officials identified problems with FEMA's performance during the 2004 hurricane season and went to DHS seeking funding to correct the problems. Because of these recognized problems, in January 2005 FEMA began initiatives in seven areas: (1) logistics; (2) enhancement of the disaster-workforce surge system; (3) enhancement of National Disaster Medical System; (4) enhanced catastrophic-disaster planning and exercises; (5) National Emergency Operations Center and Regional Operations Center upgrades; (6) enhanced individual-assistance and public-assistance programs to expedite services delivery; and (7) disaster-communication upgrades.[76] The approval process required FEMA to submit "business cases" to OMB to obtain funding to undertake the initiative. According to emails, revised business cases for four of the initiatives were due on August 26, 2005, but were extended a few days because of Hurricane Katrina's landfall.[77]

Inadequate Surge Workforce

FEMA must have the ability to quickly expand its staff in order to perform the many tasks required for an effective disaster response. To fill these vital jobs, the agency relies on a cadre of reservists called Disaster Assistance Employees (DAEs). The reliance on this temporary workforce also severely undermines response capabilities, as these frequently inexperienced and untrained individuals usually make up the bulk of FEMA's workforce in a disaster.

Since 1992, 12 studies have found problems with the DAE system.[78] An assessment in early 2004 found many problems, including a "lack of experienced and well-trained Reservists to answer the immediate call" during disasters."[79] It concluded that a need exists to redesign the disaster workforce and hire and recruit more people as the "increasing threat of terrorism and other man-made crises along with potential requirements of multiple deployments to major disasters necessitates a renewed focus on readiness capabilities."[80] DAEs undergo the majority of their training in the field during disaster response.[81] Because of funding shortages, none of the recommendations in the 2004 study has been implemented.[82] A May 15, 2005, FEMA report also confirmed the problems with the DAE workforce.[83]

Additionally, according to Wells, FEMA designates only 8 percent of the reservist cadre for response; the rest is devoted to recovery.[84] Wells added that most of the reservists were simply not cut out for response operations.[85] Because many are retirees, Wells said, most "don't belong in response operations where they have to work 18 to 24 hours a day and sleep … on concrete."[86] FEMA's reliance on this cadre once again during Katrina undermined its response.

When the storm struck, there were about 4,000 DAEs in FEMA's cadre.[87] As usual, only 40 to 50 percent were available.[88] Prior to Katrina, FEMA had put a hiring freeze on reservists and because of budget limits had capped the number of DAEs that could be on the rolls.[89] Days after Katrina, the hiring freeze was lifted, and FEMA has since added over 4,000 DAEs.[90] This isn't the first time FEMA has been caught in a big disaster without an adequate workforce. Because of the number of individuals needed to respond to 2004 hurricane season, when four hurricanes hit Florida, FEMA had to greatly ramp up its workforce and hired a lot of new people.[91] At the end of the season, FEMA released them.[92]

The DAEs let go after the 2004 hurricane season could have been valuable in the Katrina response. Wells testified there were not enough people in the reservist cadre to assist FEMA in responding to Hurricane Katrina, and those that were present did not have the specific training necessary for the type of response required on the Gulf Coast.[93] Michael Hall, Acting Director of Human Resources, agreed with Wells' assessment. Hall calls the DAE system "broken."[94]

Having enough qualified people to work in a disaster is a necessity for an effective response. FEMA's current surge-workforce system is plagued with problems that impeded the response.

Emergency Response Teams

FEMA uses emergency-response teams to respond to events. National Emergency Response Teams (ERT–Ns) are designed for high-impact events. The readiness and strength of these teams have declined dramatically since 9/11; at the time of Katrina they were inadequately trained, exercised, and equipped. Before 9/11, ERT–Ns had training and leadership meetings at least once a year;[95] after the attacks, they had three or four major training exercises.[96] But starting in 2004, there was no more money forthcoming for the teams and, according to a FEMA official in charge of one of the ERT–Ns, the teams could not meet for exercises.[97] Moreover, although the NRP calls for having three ERT–Ns and a fourth National Capitol Region Team to be able to respond to incidents, DHS currently has only two ERT–Ns.[98] The National Capitol Region Team does not exist.

Post-9/11, the ERT–N teams had about 125 to 175 members; now each has about 25.[99] The team deployed to New Orleans was newly formed, had not trained or exercised together as a team, and lacked equipment.[100] Because of these inadequacies, William Carwile, a FEMA FCO and former ERT–N leader, referred to the teams as "theoretical."[101] FEMA's draft concept of operations states that all ERT–N team members will be fully trained by June 1, 2006. Lokey described this goal as nothing more than "wishful thinking."[102]

A June 30, 2004, memo from FEMA's cadre of FCOs to Brown listed a series of the agency's problems, including inadequate funding for the ERT-Ns. The memo stated that FEMA's ERT–Ns were "unprepared" because they had "zero funding for training, exercises, or team equipment."[103] It also stated that there was a lack of training and policy guidance and standards for the operations section of the emergency response team.[104] It said that resources were needed "in order to rebuild the teams to levels appropriate for them to manage the next big one."[105] Brown did not respond, and no changes were made.[106] Brown said he could not obtain funding for the needed changes.[107] It was in this sub-par state that an ERT-N responded to Katrina.

According to the NRP, FEMA is also supposed to be able to deploy rapid-response Federal Incident Response Support Teams (FIRST) to establish an immediate federal presence at the scene of an Incident of National Significance.[108] But no FIRST teams existed at landfall.[109] Indeed, FEMA did not advertise to hire team members until the summer of 2005.[110] Witnesses testified that FIRST teams could have provided helpful assistance had they been deployable for Katrina.[111]

FEMA's other emergency-response teams are also unprepared. According to Wells, emergency-response teams generally have not planned and worked together.[112]

National Disaster Medical System

The National Disaster Medical System (NDMS) contains a number of specialized emergency medical and response teams, called Disaster Medical Assistance Teams (DMATs), who are the federal government's first responders in a medical emergency. Prior to Katrina, NDMS had significant problems. For example, when Katrina made landfall, the DMATs were not fully prepared. Of the 52 teams, FEMA considered only 27 fully operational at the time of Katrina and lacked criteria to determine levels of readiness for veterinary and mortuary teams.[113]

FEMA had no centrally managed and integrated NDMS training/exercise program for the teams.[114] NDMS lacked adequate management support at both the headquarters and field levels.[115] Funding issues limited FEMA's ability to bring the teams to full strength and to expand the number of teams despite geographic disparities in their availability; in fact, NDMS had no long-range strategic plan to develop new teams.[116] None of the teams had a fully supplied equipment cache when they deployed to Katrina.[117] One longstanding team member said that he believed that morale among NDMS teams had never been lower than it was at the time they mobilized for Katrina.[118] Recognizing many of these problems with NDMS, FEMA sought to make improvements in January 2005 by naming NDMS as one of its Disaster Support Initiatives.

Urban Search and Rescue Team

Urban Search and Rescue (USAR) teams are another type of team FEMA has available for response. USAR teams provide life-saving assistance. Before Katrina, FEMA's USAR teams lacked the plans, funds, personnel, and equipment to respond to a catastrophe. According to Eric Tolbert, former FEMA Director of Response, USAR funding was "grossly inadequate and the teams are held together on a shoestring budget."[119] Until 9/11, the USAR program operated disaster-to-disaster, using hand-me-down equipment and often purchasing equipment and supplies at the time of the disaster.[120] Until Congress appropriated funds in 2004, USAR had no vehicles and had to rent trucks in order to mobilize for emergencies.[121] The USAR teams also have no water-rescue capabilities, even though urban areas can flood. This translated to a serious lack of USAR capabilities in Hurricane Katrina.

Ruins of the 9th Ward,
New Orleans
GAO photo

Lack of Operational Doctrine

FEMA has not developed operational doctrine for responding to disasters in over four years. According to Carwile:

> There is no clear understanding of the responsibilities of each level (Washington, the Regions, deployed Emergency Response Teams) and how they are to interact. This lack of operational doctrine results in unacceptable levels of overlap, double, and triple ordering of resources, and interminably long video teleconferences and conference calls. While some of these are necessary, they can disrupt field operations.[122]

The MITRE study discussed above also found that standard operating procedures were nonexistent, outdated, or inconsistent, and recommended that FEMA develop a clear concept of operations and train employees on the procedures.[123] Despite the fact that one interviewee said, "Our biggest impediment is lack of command and control, not fully defining our standard operating procedures so everyone understands and adheres to them," FEMA had not completed a concept of operations by the time Hurricane Katrina struck the Gulf Coast.[124] MITRE also recommended that FEMA establish a full-time planning function.[125]

Poor Contracting and Procurement Practices

Long before Katrina even began to develop into a storm, FEMA's procurement capability was stressed beyond its limts. Though FEMA's procurement office was "authorized" to have 55 full-time employees, it had not been provided funding for that number for several years.[126] When Katrina hit, the staff was only 36.[127] For the six years before Katrina, FEMA's Chief

Procurement Officer, Patricia English, had split her time between two FEMA assignments, working as either Acting Chief Financial Officer or Deputy Chief Financial Officer, in addition to her procurement duties.[128] This level of staffing was inadequate – and known to be so. In early 2005, DHS conducted a study of the agency's procurement capabilities, and concluded that the condition of FEMA's procurement office was "red" – understaffed – and that a staff of somewhere between 95 and 125 was necessary for the workload in a normal year.[129]

The results of this understaffing were predictable. English testified that "There's not enough staffing to do the day-to-day activities required by the agency just through our normal appropriation. When disasters hit, it just expands the problem."[130] Major contracts – such as for delivering assistance directly to disaster victims – were slow to be finalized and were not complete as Katrina approached the Gulf Coast.[131] In the face of Katrina, FEMA cut short the planned procurement process and issued non-competitive contracts to the four primary companies it had been interviewing.[132] Tolbert testified, "That's the reason all these contracts are done as emergency contracts that are never complete because there's no capability in FEMA to do procurement. It is overwhelmed day to day, much less going into a disaster, and that's just the facts. … We could never get procurement done."[133] His assessment of FEMA's procurement capacity was stark: "The procurement capability in FEMA also is dead."[134]

English is emphatic that staffing has to be improved: "I cannot go through another hurricane season with the limited staff that I have."[135] FEMA's procurement office is now beginning to look for more staff, but is finding it difficult to find qualified individuals.[136]

FEMA in the Department of Homeland Security

Removing Functions from FEMA

After Congress merged FEMA into DHS, DHS leadership took actions that fundamentally changed FEMA's functions.

Kathleen Tierney, Director of the Natural Hazards Center at the University of Colorado, testified that post 9/11, DHS made some crucial, if understandable, mistakes in its efforts to meet the new threat of terrorism. These include rejecting the principle of "integrated emergency management," while simultaneously failing to implement an approach commonly referred to as "all-hazards" preparedness.[137]

The cycle of emergency management – called "integrated emergency management" – involves four basic phases:

> 1. Mitigation: activities taken to eliminate or reduce risks to life and property from natural and man-made hazards;
>
> 2. Preparation or preparedness: activities taken in advance of an emergency that develop capabilities for an effective response in the event of an emergency;
>
> 3. Response: actions taken during or after an emergency; and
>
> 4. Recovery: a short-term activity to return vital life-support systems after an emergency.

This cycle of integrated emergency management holds that preparedness, response, recovery, and mitigation require synergy and must be managed within the same basic structure.

Traditionally, FEMA has had the responsibility for performing each of these functions – responsibilities that were recognized in the Homeland Security Act.[138] However, in January

2004, then-Secretary Ridge removed numerous preparedness-grant programs from FEMA and placed them in another office within DHS, over Brown's objections. [139] In July 2005, Secretary Chertoff announced that he was stripping from FEMA all preparedness activities – essentially formalizing former Secretary Ridge's January 2004 action, which removed grant programs from FEMA as well as removing any of the other remaining preparedness responsibilities from FEMA.[140] These changes, part of Secretary Chertoff's "Second Stage Review," took effect in October 2005.

By removing preparedness functions from FEMA, DHS leadership departed from the concept of integrated emergency management described above. In support of its action, DHS argued that the establishment of a Preparedness Directorate was meant to "synthesize the functions of state and local liaisons, relationships, grants, training and the like. We expect to gain greater synergies through this integration."[141]

Several witnesses before the Committee opined that splitting preparedness from response was a serious mistake. Bruce Baughman, President of the National Emergency Management Association and Director of the Alabama State Emergency Management Agency, testified that the ability to make grants provided the mechanism for FEMA to be involved in the development of plans and the exercising of those plans. Otherwise, he added, "The only time we see the FEMA staff is when we have a disaster. They are not involved."[142] Tolbert agreed that preparedness should not be split from response.[143]

DHS gave the responsibility for FEMA's preparedness-grant programs to the Office of Domestic Preparedness (ODP) within the Office of State and Local Government Coordination and Preparedness, a law-enforcement, terrorism prevention-focused organization formerly part of DOJ.[144] Ed Buikema, the Acting Director of Response, said FEMA had little visibility into the state preparedness activities coordinated by ODP, and that there should have been much better communication and coordination between ODP and FEMA.[145] The Office of State and Local Government Coordination also assumed the primary liaison role with the states, diminishing the preparedness role of FEMA regions even further.[146] Professors Herman Leonard and Arnold Howitt of Harvard's John F. Kennedy School of Government, believe that this separation

> may hamper necessary alignment between the way in which preparedness has been designed and the way in which response needs to operate. At a minimum, it makes maintaining alignment difficult; at worst, it will result in serious mismatch between what has been prepared and the actions the responders want to take.[147]

Leonard testified that the most critical alignment for high performance is that between "the way you prepared to respond and your ability to execute that," and said it is "very hard to understand" why you would separate them.[148]

A consequence of this separation was that FEMA's role in preparing for disasters was eliminated. The separation also meant that FEMA ceased providing financial assistance to states for preparedness activities. Thus, FEMA was no longer able to influence activities tied to funding the states, including training, planning and exercising, or providing evaluation of such activities. This limitation of FEMA's role has hindered FEMA's relationship with the states. DHS's decision to separate preparedness from response was a mistake that hampered the alignment between the way preparedness is designed and the way response should operate.

FEMA's Placement in DHS

The Committee found no evidence that the placement of FEMA into DHS itself was a problem. Indeed, the Committee found that the placement of FEMA's functions within DHS can enhance our nation's emergency-management system.

As explained more thoroughly above, DHS was created to bring together federal assets relevant to defending our homeland. Preparing for and responding to disasters – either manmade or natural – is an important part of this function. Some of the assets brought into DHS included elements of Customs and Border Protection, Immigration and Customs Enforcement, Coast Guard, and substantial communications assets.[149] There is a synergy created by bringing together these assets within the Department that can be brought to bear under DHS leadership in the event of a disaster. The Committee agrees that if FEMA were moved out of the Department, we would lose that synergy.[150] Taking FEMA back out of DHS would move it further away from the substantial assets within DHS that can be brought to bear in responding to catastrophes.

The additional resources within DHS that can be applied to emergency management are a major advantage. What was formerly the responsibility of a small, 2,500-person independent agency is now the responsibility of a large department. DHS has more internal resources than FEMA had when it was an independent agency. With these additional resources, more responsibilities in a response to an emergency are housed under one department. For example, when FEMA was an individual agency, under the Federal Response Plan, the plan that existed before the NRP became effective in 2005, FEMA was the lead for only two of the 12 Emergency Support Functions (ESFs), the incident-specific response processes.[151] Under the NRP, DHS is either the coordinator or has lead responsibility for nine of the 15 ESFs.[152] DHS also houses the Homeland Security Operations Center (HSOC), which is designed to continually monitor potential emergencies and incidents.[153] Additionally, DHS's employees offer a pool of potential employees for deployment to disasters. Indeed, DHS employees were called to support some of FEMA's functions during Katrina.

Taking FEMA out of DHS would also "stovepipe" preparedness activities. It makes no sense to have one agency doing preparedness for terrorist attacks and another agency doing preparedness for natural disasters, as many of the required steps are the same.[154] This bifurcation would lead to inefficiencies and duplication of effort. Bifurcated, competing preparedness systems could also confuse state and local officials, who would have to hook into one system to prepare natural disasters and another system to prepare for terrorists. Frank Cilluffo, Associate Vice President for Homeland Security and Director of the Homeland Security Policy Institute at George Washington University, agreed and testified that moving FEMA out of DHS would simply obscure the real issues:

> In my opinion, to re-create FEMA as an independent agency further obfuscates and bifurcates an already too complex systems-to-systems approach. … To have state and local government and first responders plug into one system to respond to bad weather and another system to respond to bad people is unrealistic. There is no reason to have competing systems in an environment of limited resources. The problem is not really one of organizational design. The requisite policy in law exists. The challenge is one of management and leadership.[155]

While pulling FEMA out of DHS might be a politically expedient quick fix – a reshuffling of the boxes to suggest the problem is being fixed – this would simply not get to the core of problems of the federal government response in Katrina. Although FEMA certainly is an agency that has problems, DHS Inspector General Richard Skinner correctly observed that "transferring FEMA out of the department, in my opinion, would be a major mistake. We [would be] simply transferring the problem."[156]

Others agreed that FEMA's problem was not a rsult of its placement in DHS. For example, David Walker, Comptroller General of the United States, testified:

I would respectfully suggest that the quality of FEMA's leadership – and that is more than one person, I might add – as well as the adequacy of FEMA's resources will probably have more to do with their ultimate success than whether or not they are in the Department of Homeland Security. Let us keep in mind that the Coast Guard is part of the Department of Homeland Security. And so merely because one is or is not in the Department of Homeland Security is not, in and of itself, I would respectfully suggest, dispositive.[157]

Professors Leonard and Howitt also testified that preparedness and response need not be separated from DHS. In written testimony to the Committee, they state:

The task of preparation against disasters seems a natural fit with the overall mission of DHS. If the Department is to be held accountable for enhancing security for Americans and the American way of life, and takes seriously the broad array of possible threats, then preparing against natural disasters (and operating the response mechanisms in the event of a crisis) should fit as well as preparation against and response to other threats.[158]

Professors Leonard and Howitt contend that preparing for and responding to natural disasters like Katrina can be handled either well or poorly either inside or outside of DHS. They write: "Provide leadership that understands and assesses the full range of threats to security and that knows how to help its constituent organizations develop excellence, and there is no reason why preparation for and response to disasters needs to be in its own enclave (or in a different agency)."[159]

In short, the problems in DHS's response to Katrina must be fixed, not transferred. The benefits of the placement of FEMA's functions in DHS must be realized, not undermined. Our nation's emergency-management system will benefit the most if FEMA's functions remain within DHS.

Discussions Regarding FEMA's Capabilities

Brown testified that within the Administration, he repeatedly made his views known that FEMA had problems. Brown stated that he had alerted DHS officials that FEMA did not have the capability to respond to a catastrophe,[160] telling DHS officials that "FEMA's on the verge of failures; we're stretching personnel."[161] Brown said he discussed his concerns about FEMA's capabilities with various DHS officials: Deputy Secretary Michael Jackson, then-Secretary of Homeland Security Tom Ridge, then Deputy Secretary Admiral James Loy, Under Secretary for Management Janet Hale, and Chief Financial Officer Andy Maner. [162]

Brown testified that at the end of a meeting on another subject, he informed President Bush that FEMA did not have the ability to respond to a catastrophe like the Indian Ocean tsunami of December 2004 that hit Asia.[163] The conversation occurred at a "100,000-foot level," telling the President that we are not prepared, that we are not doing the kind of planning and exercises that we need to do for housing, response, and medical care in this country if we have that kind of natural disaster. In a subsequent media interview, Brown said the President responded "Well, go get ready."[164]

Brown also testified he repeatedly told Andy Card, White House Chief of Staff, Joe Hagin, Deputy Chief of Staff, and Josh Bolten, then Deputy Chief of Staff, that FEMA did not have the capabilities to respond adequately to a catastrophe, and sought additional resources.[165] Brown said that he told these officials several times that "DHS was not really following the Homeland Security Act and giving [FEMA] the muscle that it was supposed to have."[166] It is difficult to fully assess Brown's testimony: despite requests from the Committee, the White House has not provided information regarding Brown's allegations.

Conclusion

Prior to Katrina's landfall, FEMA suffered from a number of problems: unqualified senior political leadership, budget shortages, personnel shortages, and inadequate response capabilities. FEMA simply was not prepared. Although some have argued that FEMA's merger into the DHS weakened FEMA, there is no evidence that the merger itself was indeed the problem. Instead, decisions made by DHS leadership weakened FEMA and impeded its ability to respond to disasters.

These weaknesses notwithstanding, Brown testified on September 24, 2003, before a Senate Environmental and Public Works subcommittee, that FEMA was taking steps to reduce disaster- response times so that "disaster teams will be able to respond anywhere in the country within 12 hours and disaster logistics packages, commodities, and equipment can be delivered anywhere within 24 hours."[167] By any measure, FEMA's response capabilities fell short of this goal when Hurricane Katrina made landfall.

1 National Oceanic and Atmospheric Administration, National Climactic Data Center, "Hurricane Katrina, A Climatological Perspective," Oct. 2005, p. 21. http://www.ncdc.noaa.gov/oa/reports/tech-report-200501z.pdf. Accessed Mar. 20, 2006.

2 National Oceanic and Atmospheric Administration, National Climactic Data Center, "Hurricane Katrina, A Climatological Perspective," Oct. 2005, p. 21. http://www.ncdc.noaa.gov/oa/reports/tech-report-200501z.pdf. Accessed Mar. 20, 2006.

3 *Coping with Catastrophe: Building an Emergency Management System to Meet People's Needs in Natural and Manmade Disasters*, prepared by National Academy of Public Administration for U.S. Congress and the Federal Emergency Management Agency (FEMA), Feb. 1993, pp. vii, 1 [hereinafter *Coping with Catastrophe*].

4 *Coping with Catastrophe*, p. ix.

5 *Coping with Catastrophe*, pp. 50-51.

6 *Coping with Catastrophe*, pp. 64-66.

7 *Coping with Catastrophe*, p. 88.

8 *Coping with Catastrophe*, p. x.

9 *Review of Actions Taken To Strengthen the Nation's Emergency Management System*, prepared by National Academy of Public Administration for U.S. Congress and FEMA, Mar. 1994, p. 3.

10 Jerry Ellig, "Learning From the Leaders: Results-Based Management at the Federal Management Agency," Mar. 29, 2000, pp. 2, 5.

11 Jerry Ellig, "Learning From the Leaders: Results-Based Management at the Federal Management Agency," Mar. 29, 2000, p. 33.

12 R. Steven Daniels and Carolyn L. Clark-Daniels, "Transforming Government: The Renewal and Revitalization of the Federal Emergency Management Agency," Apr. 2000, p. 6 [hereinafter Daniels and Clark-Daniels, "Transforming Government"].

13 Daniels and Clark-Daniels, "Transforming Government," p. 7.

14 Daniels and Clark-Daniels, "Transforming Government," p. 18.

15 Written Statement of Joe M. Allbaugh, then Director, FEMA, for the U.S. House, Committee on Appropriations, Subcommittee on Veterans Affairs, Housing and Urban Development and Independent Agencies, hearing on *VA and HUD Appropriations*, May 17, 2001.

16 Written Statement of Allbaugh, House Committee on Appropriations, Subcommittee on Veterans Affairs, Housing and Urban Development and Independent Agencies hearing, May 17, 2001.

17 United States Commission on National Security/21st Century, "Road Map for National Security, Imperative for Change," Mar. 15, 2001, p. 10 [hereinafter "Road Map for National Security"].

18 "Road Map for National Security," pp. 14-15.

19 "Road Map for National Security," p. 14.

20 "Road Map for National Security," p. 14.

21 "Road Map for National Security," p. 14.

22 "Road Map for National Security," p. 17.

23 "Road Map for National Security," p. 17.

24 "The Homeland Security Act of 2002." (P.L. 107-296) 6 U.S.C. § 101.

25 "The Homeland Security Act of 2002." (P.L. 107-296) 6 U.S.C. § 502.

26 Ridge transferred the following programs in this action: Assistance to Firefighters program, Emergency Management Performance Grant program, first responder counter-terrorism training assistance, state and local all-hazards emergency operations planning, Citizens Corps, interoperable communications equipment, Community Emergency Response Teams, and Metropolitan Medical Response System (MMRS).

27 Besides formalizing what had already been transferred, Chertoff transferred the U.S. Fire Administration, hazardous material training, the chemical stockpile, the radiological emergency preparedness programs, and Bioshield.

28 U.S. Department of Homeland Security, "Secretary Michael Chertoff, U.S. Department of Homeland Security Second Stage Review Remarks," July 13, 2005, p. 7.

29 Committee staff interview of Michael Brown, former Director, FEMA, conducted on Feb. 23, 2006, transcript p. 99.

30 Written Statement of Sec. Michael Chertoff, U.S. Department of Homeland Security, for the U.S. House, Select Bipartisan Committee to Investigate the Preparation for and Response to Hurricane Katrina, hearing on *Hurricane Katrina: The Role of the Department of Homeland Security*, Oct. 19, 2005, p. 3. *See also*: Testimony of Sec. Michael Chertoff, U.S. Department of Homeland Security, before the U.S. House, Select Bipartisan Committee to Investigate the Preparation for and Response to Hurricane Katrina, hearing on *Hurricane Katrina: The Role of the Department of Homeland Security*, Oct. 19, 2005.

31 Brown interview, Feb. 23, 2006, pp. 137-138, 141, 143, 145.

32 Remarkably, two FEMA witnesses, Patrick Rhode and Brooks Altshuler, pointed to experience on a presidential advance team as relevant training to manage a disaster. Committee staff interview of Patrick Rhode, former Acting Deputy Director, FEMA, conducted on Dec. 22, 2005, transcript p. 74; Committee staff interview of Brooks Altshuler, former Acting Deputy Chief of Staff and Policy Director, FEMA, conducted on Dec. 15, 2005, transcript pp. 27-30.

33 Committee staff interview of Michael Brown, former Director, FEMA, conducted on Jan. 23, 2006, transcript p. 7. Since the fall of 2001, Brown had been serving as the Acting Deputy Director of FEMA. In Aug. 2002, President Bush appointed him to the Transition Planning Office for the newly established DHS, to serve as the transition leader for the Emergency Preparedness and Response (EP&R) Division. Brown resigned from FEMA on Sept. 12, 2005.

34 Brown interview, Jan. 23, 2006, p. 7. Brown received his JD from Oklahoma City University School of Law. *See also*: The White House, "President Bush Announced his Intention to Nominate," press release, Jan. 10, 2003. http://www.whitehouse.gov/news/releases/2003/01/20030110-6.html. Accessed on Oct. 15, 2005.

35 Brown interview, Jan. 23, 2006, p. 7.

36 On the biography provided to the Committee during his confirmation to be Deputy Director of FEMA, Brown listed that from 1975 to 1978 he was "Assistant City Manager, Police, Fire & Emergency Services for the City of Edmond, Oklahoma." *See*: U.S. Senate, Committee on Governmental Affairs, *Hearing to Consider the Nomination of Michael D. Brown to be Deputy Director of the Federal Emergency Management Agency*, June 19, 2002. Brown's attorney described this as a "distinction without a difference" and points to an affidavit from the former City attorney for the City of Edmond stating that Brown's job as Assistant to the City Manager included responsibility for several emergency management related activities. The White House never sent Brown's nomination to be Under Secretary for Emergency Preparedness and Response to the Senate. Instead, the White House simply elevated Brown from the Deputy Director to the Under Secretary position. The White House asserted it had the authority to do so under Section 1511 of the Homeland Security Act of 2002. The Committee disputes the appropriateness of this action.

37 Brown has a degree in public administration and political science from Central State University, now called University of Central Oklahoma. While still in college, in 1977 Brown began an internship with the planning department of the City of Edmond, a suburb of Oklahoma City. Upon completion of his internship, Brown became a full-time employee of the City of Edmond, serving as an assistant to the city manager. Late in his tenure with the City of Edmond, Brown assisted in the development of an emergency operations center for the city. Brown left the City of Edmond to join the Senate Finance Committee for the Oklahoma Legislature. Brown entered the private practice of law in which he represented municipalities in various matters. Brown interview, Jan. 23, 2006, pp. 5-6.

38 Rhode interview, Dec. 22, 2005, p. 7. Rhode left FEMA in Jan. 2006.

39 Rhode interview, Dec. 22, 2005, pp. 6-7.

40 Rhode interview, Dec. 22, 2005, pp. 6-7.

41 Rhode interview, Dec. 22, 2005, pp. 6-7.

42 Rhode interview, Dec. 22, 2005, pp. 10-11.

43 Brown interview, Jan. 23, 2006, pp. 119-220.

44 For example, Brooks Altshuler, former FEMA Policy Director and former Acting Deputy Chief of Staff, did not have any emergency-management experience prior to working at FEMA but had worked on the Bush-Cheney 2000 presidential campaign. *Source*: Altshuler interview, Dec. 15, 2005, pp. 6-7. Scott Morris, Director, Florida Long Term Recovery Office and Former Chief of Staff, had no known emergency-management experience prior to working at FEMA, but had worked for Maverick Media as a media strategist for the Bush-Cheney 2000 presidential campaign. *Source*: FEMA, "About FEMA, Scott R. Morris, Deputy Chief of Staff." http://www.fema.gov/txt/pao/impact/2004_july_Aug.txt (website no longer available).

45 Committee staff interview of Eric Tolbert, former Director of Response, FEMA, conducted on Dec. 1, 2005, transcript p. 33.

46 Committee staff interview of Edward Buikema, Acting Director of Response Division and Regional Director, Region V, FEMA, conducted on Nov. 21, 2005, transcript pp. 4-7.

47 Committee staff interview of Michael Lowder, Deputy Director of Response, FEMA, conducted on Nov. 10, 2005, transcript pp. 4-5.

48 Committee staff interview of Ken Burris, former Acting Director of Operations, FEMA, conducted on Dec. 29, 2005, transcript pp. 5-7.

49 Committee staff interview of Gary Moore, Director, Logistics Branch, FEMA, conducted on Dec. 9, 2005, transcript pp. 3-5.

50 The 11 executives interviewed were: Brooks Altshuler, Director of Policy; Michael Brown, Under Secretary; Ed Buikema, Regional Director/Acting Director of Response; Ken Burris, Director of Operations; William Carwile III, Federal Coordinating Officer; Dan Craig, Director of Recovery; Mike Lowder, Supervisory Program Specialist; Gary Moore, Logistics Branch Chief; Patrick Rhode, Chief of Staff; Eric Tolbert, Director of Response and Scott Morris, Deputy Chief of Staff. *Source*: MITRE Corp., Center for Enterprise Modernization, Initial Assessment of EP&R. Provided to Committee; filed as Bates no. 000194.

51 MITRE Corp., Center for Enterprise Modernization, Initial Assessment of EP&R. Provided to Committee; filed as Bates no. 000172.

52 MITRE Corp., Interviews conducted at EP&R/FEMA, Jan. 2005. Provided to Committee; filed as Bates no. 000246.

53 MITRE Corp., Interviews conducted at EP&R/FEMA, Jan. 2005. Provided to Committee; filed as Bates no. 000242.

54 MITRE Corp., Interviews conducted at EP&R/FEMA, Jan. 2005. Provided to Committee; filed as Bates no. 000220. Other statements made during interviews conducted for the MITRE study include: "OK to have political appointees but there should be criteria. They are well meaning but they are clueless." *Source*: MITRE Corp. Interviews conducted at EP&R/FEMA, Jan. 2005. Provided to Committee; filed as Bates no. 000193; "You've got a bunch of amateurs that don't understand the seriousness of their decisions. They're more into the politics and culture of FEMA than the outcome of the response capability. ... The entire senior management is political. Subject to the whims every four years. If FEMA is to survive, must do a better job of recruiting, supporting, developing and moving them, an investment in people." *Source*: MITRE Corp., Interviews conducted at EP&R/FEMA, Jan. 2005. Provided to Committee; filed as Bates no. 000243; "[Political appointees] don't have the skills, and haven't been trained [...] true also for career employees, they aren't trained." *Source*: MITRE Corp., Interviews conducted at EP&R/FEMA, Jan. 2005. Provided to Committee; filed as Bates no. 000216.

55 *Coping with Catastrophe*, p. 48.

56 Testimony of Michael Brown, former Director, FEMA, before the U.S. House, Select Bipartisan Committee to Investigate the Preparation for and Response to Hurricane Katrina, hearing on *Hurricane Katrina: The Role of the Federal Emergency Management Agency*, Sept. 27, 2005.

57 Brown produced some documents related to FEMA budget issues that DHS did not produce. To the extent DHS did not provide all documents requested by the Committee, the Committee does not have a complete picture on budget issues. Committee staff interview of Michael Jackson, Deputy Secretary, U.S. Department of Homeland Security, conducted on Jan. 27, 2006, transcript pp. 109-110. Committee staff interview of Andrew Maner, Acting Chief Financial Officer, U.S. Department of Homeland Security, conducted on Feb. 2, 2006, transcript p. 46.

58 Jackson interview, Jan. 27, 2006, pp. 109-110.

59 Burris interview, Dec. 29, 2005, pp. 195-196.

60 Ron Castleman, e-mail to Patrick Rhode, Michael Brown and others, Dec. 30, 2003, 11:07 a.m. Provided to Committee.

61 Ron Castleman, e-mail to Patrick Rhode, Michael Brown and others, Dec. 30, 2003, 11:07 a.m. Provided to Committee.

62 MITRE Corp., Center for Enterprise Modernization, Initial Assessment of EP&R. Provided to Committee; filed as Bates no. 000146. *See also*: Brown interview, Feb. 23, 2006, p. 96 (mentioning the brain drain).

63 Brown interview, Jan. 23, 2006, pp. 125-127 (stating that at one time, FEMA had 500 positions that could not be filled because of funding shortages); Committee staff interview of Michael Hall, Acting Director of Human Resources, FEMA, conducted on Nov. 28, 2005, transcript pp. 71-78. This vacancy rate is compounded by the fact that 50 percent

of FEMA's current workforce is eligible for retirement within the next five years. *See also*: FEMA, Administration and Regional Operations, Fiscal Year 2007, Congressional Justification, p. 9.

64 Hall interview, Nov. 28, 2005, pp. 71-78. Hall testified that for the last 1½ years, FEMA had run a 17 percent vacancy rate: "You know, now when you run a 15% vacancy rate and every person you detail means one more against that talent pool that you've got there, so a 2,300 person staff, when you slice that, that's already sliced pretty thin. It obviously has an impact . . . instead of doing the top seven things, you're only going to get to do the top four things or five things right now." Region VI was also greatly in need of staff. The investigation revealed memos written by Region VI Acting Director Gary Jones seeking to fill vacancy positions. In each of those memos, Jones wrote: "Region VI is one of the busiest Regions in the country with regard to disaster activity and has the potential for a number of catastrophic events including catastrophic hurricane along the Louisiana and Texas Coast, with southeast Louisiana being our biggest concern." Several of these positions were for the response division. Gary Jones, memorandum to Ron Castleman, May 7, 2003. Provided to Committee; filed as Bates nos. DHS-FEMA-0074-0000007 through 0000008; Gary Jones, memorandum to Ron Castleman, May 8, 2003. Provided to Committee; filed as Bates nos. DHS-FEMA-0074-0000009 through 0000010.

65 Committee staff interview of William Lokey, Federal Coordinating Officer for Hurricane Katrina in Louisiana, FEMA, conducted on Jan. 20, 2006, transcript pp. 58-59, 188-190.

66 U.S. Office of Personnel Management (OPM), Report of the 2004 Disaster Temporary Employees Review, July 2004, p. 1.

67 OPM, Report of the 2004 Disaster Temporary Employees Review, July 2004, p. 2.

68 OPM, Report of the 2004 Disaster Temporary Employees Review, July 2004, p. 2.

69 OPM, Report of the 2004 Disaster Temporary Employees Review, July 2004, p. 2.

70 OPM, Report of the 2004 Disaster Temporary Employees Review, July 2004, p. 2.

71 OPM, Report of the 2004 Disaster Temporary Employees Review, July 2004, p. 2.

72 OPM, Report of the 2004 Disaster Temporary Employees Review, July 2004, p. 3.

73 Hall interview, Nov. 28, 2005, pp. 70-71. Indeed, it is unclear if FEMA is working to implement such recommendations as Michael Hall, Acting Director of Human Resources suggested that implementation was not being handled by his office, but instead through some disaster support initiatives, which are being led by Marie Sloan. Marie Sloan, however, said that the Human Resources Division was handling the recommendations. *See also*: Committee staff interview of Marie Sloan, Section Chief, Disaster Workforce, Response Division, FEMA, conducted on Mar. 1, 2006, transcript, p. 65.

74 Committee staff interview of Scott Wells, Deputy Federal Coordinating Officer for Hurricane Katrina in Louisiana, conducted on Nov. 15, 2005, transcript p. 58.

75 Committee staff interview of Phil Parr, Federal Coordinating Officer, Region I, FEMA, conducted on Nov. 16, 2005, transcript pp. 145-146.

76 Michael Brown, memorandum to various FEMA officials, Jan. 3, 2005. Provided to Committee; filed as Bates nos. DHS-FEMA-0079-0000093 through 0000094.

77 Patricia Stahlschmidt, e-mail to Edward Buikema and others, Aug. 29, 2005, 4:49 p.m. Provided to Committee; filed as Bates nos. DHS-FEMA-0068-0000009 through 0000010.

78 Sloan interview, Mar. 1, 2006, p. 56. Some of the problems found in a 2002 assessment included: (1) the means to keep DAE's informed on general information, training opportunities, policy and procedure updates is "spotty at best and nonexistent at worst"; (2) problems with the capabilities of the technology for the deployment system; and (3) issues with the training of the DAE's. *See also*: Maj. Gen. John R. D'Araujo, Jr., "Disaster Workforce Assessment, 7 Jan 02 through 8 Feb 02." Provided to Committee; filed as Bates nos. DHS-FEMA-0095-0000287 through 0000291.

79 FEMA, Response Division/Recovery Division, "Disaster Workforce Redesign," Apr. 10, 2004, p. 31. Provided to Committee; filed as Bates no. DHS-FEMA-0095-0000063.

80 FEMA, Response Division/Recovery Division, "Disaster Workforce Redesign," Apr. 10, 2004, pp. 3, 31. Provided to Committee; filed as Bates nos. DHS-FEMA-0095-0000035, 0000063.

81 Hall interview, Nov. 28, 2005, pp. 44-45.

82 Sloan interview, Mar. 1, 2006, pp. 65-66.

83 FEMA, "Monthly RAMP Report: Remedial Action Management Program," May 15, 2005. Provided to Committee; filed as Bates no. DHS-FEMA-0095-0000590.

84 Wells interview, Nov. 15, 2005, p. 59.

85 Wells interview, Nov. 15, 2005, p. 59.

86 Wells interview, Nov. 15, 2005, p. 59.

87 Sloan interview, Mar. 1, 2006, p. 51.

88 FEMA, DAE Availability Report. Provided to Committee; filed as Bates no. DHS-FEMA-0055-0000210. *See also*: Sloan interview, Mar. 1, 2006, p. 9; Hall interview, Nov. 28, 2005, p. 22; Hall interview, Dec. 1, 2005, p. 173.

89 Sloan interview, Mar. 1, 2006, pp. 57-58; Hall interview, Nov. 28, 2005, pp. 24-25.

90 Sloan interview, Mar. 1, 2006, pp. 8, 25, 61.

91 Sloan interview, Mar. 1, 2006, pp. 60-61.

92 Sloan interview, Mar. 1, 2006, pp. 60-61.

93 Wells interview, Nov. 15, 2005, pp. 60-63 (explaining that response operations were a "different animal . . . [T]hat takes special training. That takes teamwork … [DAEs] only come on for actual disasters. I can't bring them on just to do training and stuff; or if they can, it's hard to get them.").

94 In an e-mail message to Michael Hall, Acting Director of Human Resources, on Aug. 31, 2005, Justin DeMello, FEMA FCO, writes, "The whole DAE system is broken … we need to abandon it and move to something better . . . Hall responds "You are preaching to the choir my friend!!" Michael Hall, e-mail to Justin DeMello, Aug. 31, 2005, 10:50 a.m. Provided to Committee; filed as Bates no. DHS-FEMA-0069-0001283.

95 Committee staff interview of William Carwile III, Federal Coordinating Officer for Hurricane Katrina in Mississippi, FEMA, conducted on Dec. 6, 2005, transcript p. 59.

96 Carwile interview, Dec. 6, 2005, p. 46.

97 Carwile interview, Dec. 6, 2005, p. 59.

98 U.S. Department of Homeland Security, *National Response Plan*. Washington: Government Printing Office, Dec. 2004, p. 40 [hereinafter *NRP*]. *See also*: Lokey interview, Nov. 4, 2005, p. 11.

99 Carwile interview, Dec. 6, 2005, p. 77; Lokey interview, Nov. 4, 2005, p. 11.

100 Carwile interview, Dec. 6, 2005, pp. 47-48, 111-112; Lokey interview, Jan. 20, 2006, pp. 197-198.

101 Carwile interview, Dec. 6, 2005, pp. 22-23.

102 Lokey interview, Jan. 20, 2006, pp. 191-192.

103 Federal Coordinating Officers, memorandum to Michael Brown, Jun. 30, 2004, p. 3. Provided to Committee.

104 Federal Coordinating Officers, memorandum to Michael Brown, Jun. 30, 2004, p. 3. Provided to Committee.

105 Federal Coordinating Officers, memorandum to Michael Brown, Jun. 30, 2004, p. 3. Provided to Committee.

106 Brown interview, Jan. 23, 2006, pp. 151-152. Testimony of William Carwile III, Federal Coordinating Officer for Hurricane Katrina in Mississippi, FEMA, before the U.S. Senate, Committee on Homeland Security and Governmental Affairs, hearing on *Hurricane Katrina: Perspectives of FEMA's Operations Professionals,* Dec. 8, 2005.

107 Brown interview, Jan. 23, 2006, p. 150.

108 *NRP,* p. 41.

109 Hall interview, Nov. 28, 2005, p. 76.

110 Hall interview, Nov. 28, 2005, p. 76.

111 Buikema interview, p. 113. Committee staff interview of Eric Tolbert, former Director, Response Division, FEMA, conducted on Dec. 1, 2006, pp. 53-54, 115.

112 Wells interview, Nov. 15, 2005, pp. 55-56.

113 FEMA, "Business Case, NDMS Section/Operations Branch/Response Division." Provided to Committee; filed as Bates no. DHS-FEMA-0098-0004751.

114 FEMA. "Business Case, NDMS Section/Operations Branch Response Division." Provided to Committee; filed as Bates no. DHS-FEMA-0098-0004751.

115 FEMA. "Business Case, NDMS Section/Operations Branch/Response Division." Provided to Committee, filed as Bates no. DHS-FEMA-0098-0004768. Committee staff interview of Jack Beall, Chief, National Disaster Medical System, FEMA, conducted on Jan. 10, 2006, transcript p. 7.

116 FEMA, "Business Case, NDMS Section/Operations Branch/Response Division." Provided to Committee, filed as Bates no. DHS-FEMA-0098-0004759.

117 Beall interview, Jan. 10, 2006, p. 11.

118 Committee staff interview of Capt. Art French, Deputy Chief Medical Officer, Disaster Medical Assistance Team PHS-1, National Disaster Medical System, FEMA, conducted on Mar. 2, 2006, p. 104.

119 Tolbert interview, Dec. 1, 2005, pp. 40-41.

120 Tolbert interview, Dec. 1, 2005, p. 40.

121 Tolbert interview, Dec. 1, 2005, pp. 40-41.

122 Written Statement of William Carwile III, Federal Coordinating Officer for Hurricane Katrina in Mississippi, FEMA, for the U.S. Senate, Committee on Homeland Security and Governmental Affairs, hearing on *Hurricane Katrina: Perspectives of FEMA's Operations Professionals,* Dec. 8, 2005, p. 9.

123 MITRE Corp., Center for Enterprise Modernization, Initial Assessment of EP&R, Mar. 7, 2005, p. 3. Provided to Committee. The assessment stated "When the next terrorist events happen, ER&R will be called on operationally. The

[concept of operations] would be designed for this realize and put the elements in place for EP&R to be better positioned to carry the day."

124 MITRE Corp., Center for Enterprise Modernization, Initial Assessment of EP&R, Mar. 7, 2005, p. 9. Provided to Committee; Lokey interview, Jan. 20, 2006, pp. 189-90.

125 MITRE Corp., Center for Enterprise Modernization, Initial Assessment of EP&R, Mar. 7, 2005, p. 12. Provided to Committee.

126 Committee staff interview of Pat English, Chief of Procurement and former Acting CFO, FEMA, conducted on Jan. 5, 2006, transcript pp. 17-18.

127 English interview, Jan. 5, 2006, pp. 17-18.

128 English interview, Jan. 5, 2006, p. 75.

129 English interview, Jan. 5, 2006, pp. 64, 81-84. Senior DHS leaders were briefed about this. "I know he [DHS Chief Procurement Officer Greg Rothwell] briefed senior management in DHS, the Under Secretary, the DepSec, and on that scorecard."

130 English interview, Jan. 5, 2006, p. 18.

131 English interview, Jan. 5, 2006, pp. 31-33, 44-46.

132 English interview, Jan. 5, 2006, pp. 34-39, 43-44.

133 Tolbert interview, Dec. 1, 2005, p. 130.

134 Tolbert interview, Dec. 1, 2005, p. 130.

135 English interview, Jan. 5, 2006, p. 29.

136 English interview, Jan. 5, 2006, pp. 86-87.

137 Written Statement of Kathleen J. Tierney, Director, Natural Hazards Center, for the U.S. Senate, Committee on Homeland Security and Governmental Affairs, hearing on *Hurricane Katrina: Recommendations for Reform*, Mar. 8, 2006, p. 5.

138 6 U.S.C. § 317.

139 Brown argued that the removal of preparedness functions from FEMA was a mistake and wrote then-DHS Secretary Tom Ridge in September 2003 that the shift left the agency without first-responder or emergency-management funding to distribute – a factor Brown believes hurt FEMA's ability to fulfill its responsibilities to help state and locals prepare for disasters. Brown interview, Feb. 23, 2006, pp. 80-81.

140 Sec. Chertoff, letter to Congress, July 8, 2005 (as required by Section 872 of the Homeland Security Act).

141 Questions for the Record of Sec. Michael Chertoff, U.S. Department of Homeland Security, for the U.S. Senate, Committee on Homeland Security and Governmental Affairs, hearing on *Hurricane Katrina: The Homeland Security Department's Response*, Feb. 15, 2006, p. 14.

142 Testimony of Bruce P. Baughman, President, National Emergency Management Association and Director, Alabama State Emergency Management Agency, before the U.S. Senate, Committee on Homeland Security and Governmental Affairs, hearing on *Hurricane Katrina: Recommendations for Reform*, Mar. 8, 2006.

143 Baughman, Senate Committee hearing Mar. 8, 2006. Eric Tolbert, Former Director of Response, agreed that splitting preparedness from response was a mistake. Tolbert interview, Dec. 1, 2005, pp. 49-50 (People observed that FEMA should have been better prepared, should have had a higher level of readiness, but then you strip the very people out who were responsible for conducting and planning exercises and establishing national standards. You strip them out and put them in another directorate that doesn't even have accountability to the FEMA director or the undersecretary. In my opinion, it's a huge mistake. You have to define preparedness. That's the problem. In my mind, preparedness is readiness, could be better defined as readiness. That's investment in capability that's going to respond to an event. The department's definition of preparedness includes that but it's also prevention. So a lot of the money in the homeland security funding programs, the grant funding, has shifted from the initial two years of being almost exclusively the consequence capability over to preventing. So now there are huge investments in the prevention and the readiness posture funding has gone significantly down.).

144 Dr. John Harrald, e-mail to Michael Alexander, Senate Committee staff member, Mar. 28, 2006.

145 Buikema interview, pp. 61, 68.

146 Dr. John Harrald, e-mail to Michael Alexander, Senate Committee staff member, Mar. 28, 2006.

147 Questions for the Record of Herman B. Leonard, Ph.D., Professor of Public Management, John F. Kennedy School of Government and Professor of Business Administration, Harvard Business School, Harvard University and Arnold M. Howitt, Ph.D., Executive Director, Taubman Center for State and Local Government, John F. Kennedy School of Government, Harvard University, for the U.S. Senate, Committee on Homeland Security and Governmental Affairs, hearing on *Hurricane Katrina: Recommendations for Reform*, Mar. 8, 2006, p. 2.

148 Testimony of Herman B. Leonard, Ph.D., Professor of Public Management, John F. Kennedy School of Government and Professor of Business Administration, Harvard Business School, Harvard University, before the U.S. Senate, Committee on Homeland Security and Governmental Affairs, hearing on *Hurricane Katrina: Recommendations for Reform*,

Mar. 8, 2006.

149 "The Homeland Security Act of 2002." (P.L. 107-296).

150 Testimony of Richard Skinner, Inspector General, U.S. Department of Homeland Security, before the U.S. Senate, Committee on Homeland Security and Governmental Affairs, hearing on *Hurricane Katrina: Recommendations for Reform*, Mar. 8, 2006.

151 FEMA, *Federal Response Plan*, Apr. 1999, p. 14.

152 *NRP*, ESF Annexes, ESF–v through ESF–vi.

153 *NRP*, p. 24.

154 Skinner, Senate Committee hearing, Mar. 8, 2006.

155 Testimony of Frank J. Cilluffo, Associate Vice President for Homeland Security and Director of the Homeland Security Policy Institute, George Washington University, before the U.S. Senate, Committee on Homeland Security and Governmental Affairs, hearing on *Hurricane Katrina: Recommendations for Reform*, Mar. 8, 2006.

156 Skinner, Senate Committee hearing, Mar. 8, 2006.

157 Testimony of David Walker, Comptroller General of the United States, before the U.S. Senate, Committee on Homeland Security and Governmental Affairs, hearing on *Hurricane Katrina: Recommendations for Reform*, Mar. 8, 2006.

158 Written Statement of Herman B. Leonard, Ph.D., Professor of Public Management, John F. Kennedy School of Government and Professor of Business Administration, Harvard Business School, Harvard University, before the U.S. Senate, Committee on Homeland Security and Governmental Affairs, hearing on *Hurricane Katrina: Recommendations for Reform*, Mar. 8, 2006.

159 Written Statement of Leonard, Senate Committee hearing, Mar. 8, 2006.

160 Brown interview, Feb. 23, 2006, p. 137.

161 Brown interview, Feb. 23, 2006, p. 145.

162 Brown interview, Feb. 23, 2006, pp. 144-146. For example, Former Under Secretary Brown produced a Mar. 16, 2004 letter to DHS Deputy Secretary Admiral Loy where he stated that FEMA was struggling because of serious budget shortages. Brown wrote that "preparations for the future are being mortgaged or deferred indefinitely." The letter explained that OMB had designated two-thirds of FEMA's budget as "non-homeland security" funds and that "non-homeland security funds" would be held to zero budget growth beginning in FY 2006. This paints a grim picture for FEMA's future. Although solid targets have not yet been released by CFO's shop, we have been told to expect to reprogram our FY 2006 budget plans to absorb a cut of $100 million. … It is quite clear that many if not most of our current un-funded requirements and shortfalls will have to be deferred in favor of more Homeland Security (terrorism) priorities.

163 Brown interview, Feb. 23, 2006, p. 141.

164 Paul Singer, "Brown's Flood of Criticism," *National Journal*, Mar. 10, 2006.

165 Brown interview, Feb. 23, 2006, p. 143.

166 Brown interview, Feb. 23, 2006, p. 138. Brown testified that he had so many conversations with White House officials telling them that FEMA was not prepared for a catastrophe that it reached a point that his staff had to tell him to back off.

167 Written Statement of Michael Brown, former Director, FEMA, for the U.S. Senate, Committee on Environment and Public Works, Subcommittee on Clean Air, Climate Change and Nuclear Safety, hearing on *FEMA Oversight*, Sept. 24, 2003, p. 4.

Grounded, Louisiana
U.S. Coast Guard photo

Government Response:
The Role of the White House

A catastrophic event requires decisive leadership at all levels – from the affected locality, to the state government, to federal agencies, and to the White House. Hurricane Katrina was a test in leadership. There were warnings. But there was not enough done to prepare. There was the catastrophe. But on the day it struck, there was uncertainty and a lack of awareness as to the extent of the damage. There was a response. But it was, initially, halting and not up to a disaster of such consequence.

There was leadership, but not the measure Americans expected as they witnessed the devastation and human suffering Katrina left in her wake. Though it was not alone, the White House failed to meet these expectations in at least three respects:

> • Actual or Constructive Knowledge: The White House knew or should have known that Katrina could turn into the long-feared "New Orleans Scenario," and could wreak devastation throughout the Gulf Coast region. The White House also may have been aware that FEMA was not prepared for such a catastrophe;

> • Lack of Situational Awareness: Despite receiving information from multiple sources on the extent of the damage in New Orleans, the White House does not appear to have been aware that levees had broken and the city was flooding on the day of the storm and, indeed, appears to have remained for some time under the misimpression that the levees did not break until the day after Katrina made landfall; and,

> • Inadequate Initial Response: The initial response to Katrina was halting and inadequate, in part due to poor situational awareness. Ultimately, the President and his team brought the full resources of the federal government to bear on the catastrophe.

Advance Knowledge of a Catastrophic Scenario, FEMA's Shortcomings, and the Approach of the Storm

Katrina's devastation should not have been a surprise to the White House.

In early 2004, the White House Deputy National Security Advisor, General John A. Gordon, went to New Orleans to receive a briefing on catastrophic-hurricane planning efforts for the region. The detailed briefing covered the catastrophic consequences of a Category 3 hurricane hitting New Orleans. General Gordon reported this to the White House, which may have influenced the funding that resulted in the Hurricane Pam exercise.[1] In addition, another White House aide, Janet Benini,[2] attended the Hurricane Pam exercise. Benini also chaired the group that developed the National Planning Scenarios, a set of 15 plausible, high-consequence events used by the federal government to come up with preparedness goals and lists of emergency response capabilities that federal, state, and local responders should have. One event included among the scenarios is modeled on a hurricane hitting New Orleans.

There were also ample warnings specific to Hurricane Katrina. The National Weather Service, FEMA, other Department of Homeland Security components such as the National Infrastructure Simulation and Analysis Center, and state officials warned the White House repeatedly over the weekend before landfall that Katrina was likely to be a catastrophe.[3] The documents the White House provided to this Committee show that prior to and after landfall, the White House Homeland Security Council (HSC)[4] received large amounts of information from DHS's Homeland Security Operations Center (HSOC), as well as other federal agencies and departments, including the National Guard Bureau, the Department of Energy, and the National Oceanic and Atmospheric Administration concerning the situation that could develop. The American Red Cross and other organizations were also briefed. Moreover, as Secretary of Homeland Security Michael Chertoff said, the President was "acutely aware of Katrina and the risk it posed" during the weekend before landfall.[5] "We went into the weekend before," Chertoff said, "with an understanding and with warnings that this was potentially the nightmare scenario that I think people have talked about for years in terms of New Orleans."[6]

On the Saturday before the storm made landfall, FEMA Director Michael Brown relayed to state, local, and federal officials – including the White House – his fears of the devastation Katrina could cause. During FEMA's August 27[7] noon video-conference call, Brown voiced the following concerns:

> I know I'm preaching to the choir on this one, but I've learned over the past four and a half, five years, to go with my gut on a lot of things, and I've got to tell you my gut hurts on this one. It hurts. I've got cramps. So, we need to take this one very, very seriously.[8]

Joe Hagin, White House Deputy Chief of Staff, participated on the same conference call while in Crawford, Texas, and listened to the warnings presented by Brown and others. He asked no questions and offered only the following statement: "We're here, and anything we can do, obviously, to support you, but it sounds like the planning, as usual, is in good shape, and good luck to the states and just know that we're watching, and we'll do the right thing as fast as we can."[9]

The warnings continued through the night: At 11:24 p.m., the White House received a National Hurricane Center report stating: "The bottom line is that Katrina is expected to be an intense and dangerous hurricane heading towards the North Central Gulf Coast and this has to be taken very seriously."[10]

At noon on Sunday, August 28, President Bush participated from his ranch in Crawford, Texas, with FEMA, Department of Homeland Security, and state officials in a video-conference call in which Max Mayfield, Director of the National Hurricane Center, predicted Katrina would be a "very dangerous hurricane":

> The problem that we're going to have here — remember, the winds go counterclockwise around the center of the hurricane. So if the really strong winds clip Lake Pontchartrain, that's going to pile some of that water from Lake Pontchartrain over on the south side of the lake. I don't think any model can tell you with any confidence right now whether the levies will be topped or not, but that's obviously a very, very grave concern. ... And, quite frankly, for the folks in Louisiana, if you can't get people out, you know, if you're ever going to, you know, talk about vertical refuge [sheltering in the upper stories of tall buildings], this is the time to do it.[11]

During the same call, Brown stated: "My gut tells me — I told you guys my gut was that this (missing) is a bad one and a big one," and that Katrina could be "a catastrophe within a catastrophe."[12] The State of Louisiana Office of Homeland Security and Emergency Preparedness' Chief of Operations, Bill Doran, also informed the President on the same call that the state was doing "catastrophic planning" for Katrina.[13] The President asked no questions, but made the following statement:

> I want to assure the folks at the state level that we are fully prepared to not only help you during the storm, but we will move in whatever resources and assets we have at our disposal after the storm to help you deal with the loss of property. And we pray for no loss of life, of course.
>
> Unfortunately, we've had experience at this in recent years, and I — the FEMA folks have done great work in the past, and I'm confident, Mike, that you and your team will do all you can to help the good folks in these affected states.
>
> Again, I want to thank Governor Blanco and Governor Riley and Governor [Barbour], Governor Bush of Florida, for heeding these warnings, and doing all you can possibly do with your state folks and local folks to prepare the citizenry for this storm.
>
> In the meantime, I know the nation will be praying for the good folks in the affected areas, and we just hope for the very best.[14]

In addition to the conference call, the White House continued to receive additional warnings of the storm's projected force and fury throughout the day.

The White House also may have received warnings that FEMA lacked the support and capability to prepare for and respond to a Katrina-like catastrophe. Brown claims to have warned President Bush, White House Chief of Staff Andrew Card, and White House Deputy Chief of Staff Joe Hagin as early as January 2005 that "We [FEMA] weren't getting the money we needed [and] we weren't getting the personnel that we needed," and that, consequently, FEMA was not ready to handle a disaster like a tsunami.[15]

It is not clear what, if anything, the White House did to address these concerns and to help ensure that FEMA was ready when disaster struck. But the concerns appear to have gone unheeded by the White House and DHS in the period prior to Katrina.

On the other hand, the President did take significant steps in preparation for the storm. On Saturday evening, in response to Governor Blanco's request earlier that day, President Bush took the unusual step of issuing an emergency declaration for the State of Louisiana, which the White House described as being "indicative of the recognition that Katrina had the potential to be particularly devastating."[16] The declaration effectively assured the state that the federal government would pay for costs associated with evacuating residents prior to the storm.

In addition to authorizing funds to help with the pre-storm evacuation, President Bush urged that an evacuation take place. On Sunday, August 28, President Bush spoke with Governor Blanco to encourage her to order a mandatory evacuation of New Orleans.

While these steps were important and commendable, the White House could have marshaled federal resources more proactively in advance of the storm. Katrina was a hurricane that the White House knew or should have known could cause massive devastation in and around New Orleans. The preparations simply were not proportionate to the likely imminent catastrophe.

President Bush greeting Mayor Nagin, Secretary Chertoff

Lack of Situational Awareness

The record indicates that as early as 11:13 a.m. ET, on Monday, August 29, the White House Homeland Security Council circulated to, among others, Homeland Security Advisor Frances Townsend, Deputy White House Chief of Staff Joe Hagin, Deputy Homeland Security Advisor Ken Rapuano, and White House Counsel Harriet Miers, a report indicating the following:

- A levee in New Orleans had broken;

- Through a report from the Homeland Security Operations Center, water was rising in the city's Lower Ninth Ward;

- Through a report from the State of Louisiana, water was rising at one foot per hour; and

- Through a report from Mayor C. Ray Nagin of New Orleans, problems with a pumping station were causing flooding in New Orleans.[17]

Brown claims that, also on Monday, he reported to Deputy Chief of Staff Hagin on the developing catastrophe in New Orleans.[18] Brown told the Committee that, by no later than 6 p.m. CT on the day of landfall, Hagin knew the 17th Street levee in New Orleans had broken, and that the city was flooding.[19]

Still, the White House does not appear to have been cognizant that Katrina was flooding the streets, homes, and hospitals of New Orleans on Monday, the day of the storm's landfall. President Bush later characterized the mindset on Monday, August 29, after learning that

Katrina did not hit New Orleans directly: "a sense of relaxation."[20] In addition, as late as Friday, September 2, the President expressed the belief that the levees broke on Tuesday, the day after landfall, even though they had broken on Monday.

On Tuesday, August 30, the White House received confirmation that Katrina was an undeniable catastrophe. At 12:02 a.m. ET, the White House received a report from the Homeland Security Operations Center that included the following statement by FEMA's lone official in New Orleans that day, Marty Bahamonde: "There is a quarter-mile [breach] in the levee near the 17th Street Canal about 200 yards from Lake Pontchartrain allowing water to flow into the City – an estimated 2/3 to 75% of the city is under water."[21]

At 6:33 a.m. ET, Tuesday morning, the White House received a Department of Homeland Security situation report confirming the extent of damage and flooding in New Orleans:

> Widespread and significant flooding has occurred throughout the city of New Orleans, extending eastward, across the Mississippi gulf coast into coastal Alabama. The following flood reports have been received for the city of New Orleans:
>
> • Industrial Canal at Tennessee St.: levee has been breached with water to a depth of 5 feet at Jackson Barracks;
>
> • 17th St. at Canal Blvd.: levee has been breached – breach extends several 100 meters in length;
>
> • Much of downtown and east New Orleans is underwater, depth unknown at this time.

The U.S. Army Corps of Engineers estimates are in progress and project that it could take months to dewater the City of New Orleans.[22]

A report at 10:23 a.m. ET on Tuesday, from the Homeland Security Operations Center detailed the location of the breached levees and noted specific concerns about the 17th Street Canal and Tennessee Street levees.[23]

Brown also told the Committee of a secure telephone call he said was held on Tuesday afternoon with President Bush, Vice President Cheney, Secretary Chertoff, and Deputy Chief of Staff Karl Rove. Brown claims to have told them that at least 90 percent of the city's population had been displaced and he "needed military assets [because] this was the big one."[24] Brown also told them that he "needed the help of the entire cabinet … DOD and HHS and everybody else," and that there was a "discussion about convening the cabinet."[25] Brown opined that, up until that conversation took place, he believed that the White House had failed to comprehend fully the catastrophic nature of Hurricane Katrina.[26]

A Hesitant Response

Despite these reports of a catastrophe, the White House failed to grasp the gravity of the situation as it unfolded. As a result, the White House's initial response appeared halting and inadequate. Throughout Monday, the day of the storm, the President maintained his regular schedule. In the morning, he celebrated Senator John McCain's birthday at Luke Air Force Base near Phoenix, Arizona.[27] Later that morning, the President had a "Conversation on Medicare" at the Pueblo El Mirage RV Resort and Country Club in nearby El Mirage, Arizona.[28] He also spoke to the people in the Gulf Coast region, offering that, "When the storm passes, the federal government has got assets and resources that we'll be deploying to help you."[29]

Likewise, on Monday afternoon, the President flew to California and gave a speech in Rancho Cucamonga on Medicare and the new prescription-drug benefit. There, he reassured his audience that the government was prepared to respond to Katrina.[30] But this did not turn out to be the case.

The hesitancy continued into the following day. Despite mounting reports on the extent of the catastrophe, no one from the White House participated in FEMA's intergovernmental conference call on Tuesday at noon.

At noon ET that day, the President stood at a naval base in San Diego and offered a picture of a fully prepared federal government that was ready to respond to Katrina: "Our teams and equipment are in place and we're beginning to move in the help that people need."[31]

On the same day, White House Press Secretary Scott McClellan announced the President would return to Washington, D.C., the following day in order to "oversee the response efforts from there."[32]

Thereafter, the White House began to chart a more aggressive course of response to Katrina. At a 5:11 p.m. briefing Wednesday evening, President Bush, surrounded by his Cabinet, addressed the nation from the Rose Garden and announced that he had called the Cabinet together, and had "directed Secretary of Homeland Security Mike Chertoff to chair a Cabinet-level task force to coordinate all our assistance from Washington."[33]

The task force demanded a list of available resources from each federal agency assigned responsibility under the National Response Plan.[34] For example, the White House asked FEMA on Wednesday for "the inventory of all department agency operations/activity … are there any Federal powers or other processes that could be implemented to expedite the response or make it more efficient … [w]hat are the plans for providing housing to … displaced people?"[35] Had these questions been asked and this sense of urgency imparted earlier, vital federal help might have arrived sooner.

The more vigorous response continued throughout the week. For example, despite reports of lawlessness in New Orleans and the need for federal assistance, there were only a handful of FBI and other Department of Justice law-enforcement officers in the New Orleans area as of Thursday morning. As DOJ continued to formulate a response plan, President Bush discussed with the Attorney General the situation in New Orleans, and DOJ officers began to deploy that day. Likewise, on Saturday, the President ordered thousands of active-duty military forces to deploy to the region to assist in what he saw was an unacceptable response to the suffering of thousands of Katrina victims in various locations around the city.

---

1 Committee staff interview of Gary Jones, Acting Regional Director, Region VI, Federal Emergency Management Agency (FEMA), conducted on Jan. 11, 2006, transcript pp. 48-49, 149-152; Committee staff interview of Wayne Fairley, Response Operations Branch Chief, Region VI, FEMA, conducted on Jan. 18, 2006, pp. 2, 57-58; Ron Castleman, e-mail to Patricia English, May 17, 2004, 10:11 a.m. Provided to Committee; filed as Bates no. DHS-FEMA 0058-0000097.

2 Janet Benini was Director of Response and Planning for the White House Homeland Security Council prior to Hurricane Katrina's landfall. She did not work at the White House during the Katrina response.

3 The White House does not dispute that the President received these warnings and communications before landfall: "The President received regular briefings, had countless conversations with Federal, State, and local officials, and took extraordinary steps prior to landfall." U.S. Assistant to the President for Homeland Security and Counterterrorism, *The*

Federal Response to Hurricane Katrina: Lessons Learned. Washington: Government Printing Office, Feb. 2006, pp. 28-29 [hereinafter The White House, *Hurricane Katrina Lessons Learned*]. But the White House did not detail in either its report, The Federal Response to Hurricane Katrina Lessons Learned, Frances Fragos Townsend's February 13, 2006 speech at the NEMA's mid-year conference, or elsewhere, any specific details about the briefings or conversations. The White House, *Hurricane Katrina Lessons Learned*, pp. 28-29, 174.

4 The White House, Homeland Security President Directive-1: Organization and Operation of the Homeland Security Council, October 29, 2001. HSPD-1 states that the White House Homeland Security Council (HSC), is a unit within the White House responsible for coordination of homeland security activities between all federal departments and agencies. The HSC also is responsible for circulating information throughout the White House during a catastrophe. As stated during a Committee briefing conducted by the White House on February 3, 2006, the HSC handles preparedness issues and immediate response issues. It also serves as a gate-keeper to mitigate duplicative information requests to other agencies.

5 Testimony of Sec. Michael Chertoff, U.S. Department of Homeland Security, before the U.S. Senate, Committee on Homeland Security and Governmental Affairs, hearing on *Hurricane Katrina: The Homeland Security Department's Preparation and Response*, Feb. 15, 2006.

6 Testimony of Sec. Michael Chertoff, U.S. Department of Homeland Security, before the U.S. House, Select Bipartisan Committee to Investigate the Preparation for and Response to Hurricane Katrina, hearing on *Hurricane Katrina: The Role of the Department of Homeland Security*, Oct. 19, 2005.

7 White House Briefing given to Committee, conducted by Kenneth Rapuano, Deputy Assistant to the President for Homeland Security, Dec. 13, 2005.

8 Michael Brown, FEMA Daily Video Teleconference, Aug. 27, 2005, transcript p. 22. Provided to Committee.

9 Joseph Hagin, FEMA Daily Video Teleconference, Aug. 27, 2005, transcript p. 24. Provided to Committee.

10 Andrew Akers, e-mail to Homeland Security Operations Center Senior Watch Officer and others, Aug. 27, 2005, 11:24 p.m. Provided to Committee; filed as Bates nos. WHK 0005865 through 0005867. The other addressees for the e-mail are DC-NSC-WHSR, Bethany Nichols, Elliot Langer, Kirstjen Nielsen, Joel Bagnal, Elizabeth Farrell, Julie Bentz, Daniel Kaniewski and copied to Matthew Broderick, Frank DiFalco, Bob Stephan, John Chase, Tom Dinanno, Edward McDonald, Gail Kulish, Tom Paar, Michael Jackson, John Wood, National Interagency Coordination Center, Secretary Briefing Staff, HSOC.HSIN.

11 Max Mayfield, Ph.D., FEMA Daily Video Teleconference, Aug. 28, 2005, transcript pp. 6, 10. Provided to Committee.

12 Michael Brown, FEMA Daily Video Teleconference, Aug. 28, 2005, transcript p. 37. Provided to the Committee. During his staff interview on February 23, 2006, Brown discussed a telephone call with Joe Hagin after the Noon VTC. He described the conversation as follows: "And Hagin and I were having a conversation just about how bad this one was going to be and, you know, dad-gamut all the – I mean, I was really bitching at Hagin about all of the planning I'd been asking for and you know, the catastrophic planning we'd been wanting to do, you know, now – and now here we are, and, you know, saying to him, you know, dad-gamut, why didn't I quit earlier – then, you know, you guys knew I wanted to quit. I mean, we're having this sparring match about all of this stuff that I was really mad about because I knew I was walking into this hornets' nest, I'm really ticked off, because I know how bad this thing's going to be." Brown further described the conversation: "I'm just adamant that they understand my concern about New Orleans. I mean, I don't know how to get this across to people that I have pushed and pushed for catastrophic disaster planning; we had chosen New Orleans as the first place to do catastrophic disaster planning; and now, damn it, here was a, you know, a Cat 5 bearing down on – on New Orleans." Committee staff interview of Michael Brown, former Director, FEMA, conducted on Feb. 23, 2006, transcript pp. 34, 36-37.

13 Bill Doran, FEMA Daily Video Teleconference, Aug. 28, 2005, transcript pp. 16-17. Provided to Committee.

14 President George Bush, FEMA Daily Video Teleconference, Aug. 28, 2005, transcript pp. 14-15. Provided to Committee. *The Federal Response to Hurricane Katrina Lessons Learned* describes the President as actively engaged the weekend prior to landfall, communicating with state and local officials and offering federal resources.

15 Brown interview, Feb. 23, 2006, pp. 137-139, 141. Brown testified that he had put the White House on notice of FEMA's lack of capabilities to respond adequately to a catastrophe before Katrina approached the Gulf. Brown interview, Feb. 23, 2006, p. 143. In addition, Brown suggested that he spoke with the White House earlier than January, 2005 regarding his concerns for FEMA. Specifically, when Brown was asked whether it was fair to say he was communicating with the White House during his tenure as Undersecretary and "expressing to them that FEMA was not ready; FEMA needed more resources." Brown replied and discussed a letter sent to Sec. Tom Ridge in Sept. 2003, regarding FEMA's integration in the Department of Homeland Sec. Although he said he raised this letter with Clay Johnson and Joe Hagin, and the fact that FEMA would fail if many of the proposed changes occurred, he also suggested that he spoke to Clay Johnson generally about the problems with FEMA. When asked what he expressed to Johnson, and whether they were the same kinds of concerns previously described, Brown stated: "The same kind of concerns but probably in more detail with Clay at times because Clay was heading up the transition team for DHS, and so he really understood kind of what we should be doing and shouldn't be doing. And I would have a lot of conversations with Clay about it." Brown interview, Feb. 23, 2006, pp. 139-141. Brown did not address these concerns publicly or in writing with Congress. However, during his appearance before the U.S. House Select Bipartisan Committee to Investigate Preparation for and Response to Hurricane Katrina hearing on Sept. 27, 2005, Brown alluded to having had some conversations with members of Congress, though not with any members of this Committee regarding the state of FEMA. When asked about the emaciation of FEMA, Brown suggested that for several years, he privately discussed how FEMA would become extremely limited in both personnel and financial resources hindering its capacity to handle a disaster. In response to a question

about Brown expressing his concerns about FEMA privately, but not publicly, Brown stated: "I can go to bed at night and sleep because I know I fought that battle." In addition, later in the hearing when asked why he expressed his views about FEMA's problems privately versus publicly, Brown testified that he wanted to work within the system to make the needed changes. Brown, House Select Committee hearing, Sept. 27, 2005. Apparently, those efforts failed.

16 The White House, *Hurricane Katrina Lessons Learned*, p. 27.

17 Daniel Kaniewski, e-mail to Dan Bartlett and others, Aug. 29, 2005, 11:13 a.m. Provided to Committee; filed as Bates no. OVP 004795. The other addressees are Todd Beyer, Bill Burck, Trent Duffy, Joseph Hagin, Brian Hook, Brett Kavanaugh, Emily Kropp, William McGurn, Stephen McMillin, Harriet Miers, Bruce Miller, Susan Ralston, Kenneth Rapuano, Scott Sforza, Kristen Silverberg, Heidi Smith, Frances Townsend, and copied to Steven Atkiss, Jessica Bennett, Stephen Black, Jamie Brown, John Burke, Shannon Burkhart, John Currin, Robert DeServi, DL-HSC-BTS, DL-HSC-CHEM-BIO, DL-HSCEXECSEC, DL-HSC-Front, DL-HSC-PPR, DL-NSC-WHSR, Lindsey Drouin, Debbie Fiddelke, Erin Healy, Taylor Hughes, Lauren Kane, Karyn Richman Kendall, Matthew Kirk, Ross Kyle, Jeannie Mamo, Christopher Michel, Alexander Mistri, John Mitnick, Derrick Morgan, Erin Nagle, Neil Patel, Dana Perino, Douglas Pitkin, Heather Roebke, Daniel Wilmot, Candace Wysocki, DeWitt Zemp ("Flooding significant throughout the region and a levee in New Orleans has reportedly been breached sending 6 to 8 feet of water throughout the 9th Ward area of the city. Per the Governor, water is rising at 1 foot per hour and the New Orleans mayor reports problems with a pumping station, causing flooding. HSOC reports that due to the rising water in the 9th Ward, residents are in their attics and on their roofs."). The President's knowledge of when New Orleans' levees breached has been the subject of much media attention. In the week after landfall, the President himself made statements regarding the levee breaches. For instance, on Friday, September 2, 2005, during a press conference in Biloxi, Mississippi, the President stated: "The levees broke on Tuesday in New Orleans. On Wednesday, we – and Thursday we started evacuating people. A lot of people have left that city. A lot of people have been pulled out on buses. It's – I am satisfied with the response. I'm not satisfied with all the results. They started pulling people off roofs immediately. They started rallying – we started rallying choppers to get people off rooftops, started savings lives. I mean, thousands of peoples' lives have been saved immediately, and that's good news. This is one of the worst storms in our nation's history. New Orleans got hit by two storms, one the hurricane, and then the flood. And it's going to take a monumental effort to continue moving forward, but we will." The White House, "President Tours Biloxi, Mississippi Hurricane Damaged Neighborhoods," press release, Sept. 2, 2005. Provided to Committee; filed as Bates nos. WHK 01656, 01658. As set forth herein, several pieces of evidence show the levees breached on Monday.

18 On the noon video teleconference, Brown said he spoke with President Bush at least twice on the day of landfall, likely prior to noon. Brown stated: "I talked to the President twice today, once in Crawford and then again on Air Force One." Michael Brown, FEMA Daily Video Teleconference, Aug. 29, 2005, p. 14. Provided to Committee. Brown also testified that he spoke to Hagin on at least two occasions on the day of landfall. Testimony of Brown, Senate Committee hearing, Feb. 10, 2005. *See also*: Andy Card, e-mail to Michael Brown, Aug. 29, 2005, 9:51 p.m. Provided to Committee (showing that Brown spoke with Hagin on August 29 to provide updates of the situation in New Orleans). When asked whether he spoke directly to the President on the night of landfall concerning Bahamonde's over flight, Brown said he could not recall if he spoke to the President then. Brown stated: "I really don't recall if the President got – normally during my conversations with Deputy Chief of Staff [Hagin], sometimes the President would get on the phone for a few minutes, sometimes he wouldn't, and I don't recall specifically that night whether he did or not." Brown, Senate Committee hearing, Feb. 10, 2006.

19 Brown interview, Feb. 23, 2006, pp. 24-25 ("Question: Is there any reason for us to doubt that after you talked to Joe Hagin 5 or 6 o'clock on Monday evening, August 29, that he then knew from you that the 17th Street Canal levee had broke and the city was flooding? Answer: I don't think there is any reason for any of us to doubt that they knew that. Question: Okay. And that they knew that at least in part from your phone conversation with Joe Hagin, correct? Answer: That's correct."). Brown said he spoke with Hagin on Monday evening to discuss Bahamonde's report of his New Orleans flyover over New Orleans, but could not recall whether he specifically told Hagin in that call that the levees had broken. *Source*: Brown interview, Feb. 23, 2006, p. 21 ("I think I used the phrase to Joe that, you know, our – the worst nightmare is occurring. I can't recall all of the words I used other than, this is, you know, our worst – this is the worst scenario; this is, you know my worst fears are coming true. You know, I used the phrase, you know we have breaches of the canals"); Brown, Senate Committee hearing, Feb. 10, 2006, ("I think I told him that we were realizing our worst nightmare, that everything we had planned about, worried about, that FEMA, frankly, had worried about for 10 years, was coming true.") Brown said he told Hagin or White House Chief of Staff Andrew Card about the levee breaches late in the afternoon on Monday because he recalled they were "debating" at the state Emergency Operations Center whether the levees were breached or overtopped. *Source*: Brown, Senate Committee hearing, Feb. 10, 2006; Deposition of Michael Brown, before the House Katrina Select Committee staff, Feb. 11, 2006, pp. 113-114. Brown also received an e-mail from Card at 9:51 p.m., Monday, in which Card acknowledged Brown's continued contact with Hagin and said: "Joe Hagin has kept me well-informed of your reports." *Source*: Andy Card, e-mail to Michael Brown, Aug. 29, 2005, 9:51 p.m. Provided to Committee. Brown responded and stated: "Thanks for writing, Andy. This is a bad one." *Source*: Michael Brown, e-mail to Andy Card, Aug. 29, 2005, 10 p.m. Provided to Committee.

20 The White House, "President, Lieutenant General Honoré Discuss Hurricane Relief in Louisiana," press release, Sept. 12, 2005. Provided to Committee; filed as Bates nos. WHK 01723, 01725.

21 U.S. Department of Homeland Security, HSOC Spot Report #13, Aug. 29, 2005, 10:30 p.m. Provided to Committee; filed as Bates no. WHK-07159. The Report further stated: "Only one of the main pumps is reported to still be working but cannot keep up with the demand and its longevity is doubtful." The White House received this report at 12:02 a.m., Tuesday, Aug. 30, 2005. Michael Izner, e-mail to HSOC.HSIN and others, Aug. 30, 2005, 12:02 a.m. Provided to Committee; filed as Bates nos. WHK 07158 through WHK 07160. The other addressees for the e-mail are DL-NSC-WHSR, the National Interagency Coordination Center, as well as the following officials, Bethany Nichol, Elliott Langer, Kirstjen

Nielsen, Joel Bagnal, Elizabeth Farrell, Julie Bentz, Daniel Kaniewski, Richard Davis, Michael Barton and copied to Matthew Broderick, Frank DiFalco, Bob Stephan, John Chase, Tom Dinanno, Edward McDonald, Gail Kulish, Tom Parr, Michael Jackson, and John Wood.

22 Michael Izner, e-mail to DL-NSC-WHSR, Aug. 30, 2005, 6:33 a.m. Provided to Committee; filed as Bates no. WHK 06264. The other addressees of the e-mail are Bethany Nichols, Elliott Langer, Kirstjen Nielsen, Joel Bagnal, Elizabeth Farrell, Julie Bentz, Daniel Kaniewski, Richard Davis, Michael Barton, and copied to Matthew Broderick, Frank DiFalco, Bob Stephan, John Chase, Tom Dinanno, Edward McDonald,

Gail Kulisch, Tom Paar, Michael Jackson, (DepSec), John Wood, (COS), National Interagency Coordination Center Secretary Briefing Staff, HSOC.HSIN, HSOC.SWO.

23 Insung Lee, e-mail to DL-NSC-WHSR and others, Aug. 30, 2005, 10:23 a.m. Provided to Committee; filed as Bates nos. WHK 07910 through WHK 07913. The other addressees of the e-mail are Bethany Nichols, Elliott Langer, Kirstjen Nielsen, Joel Bagnal, Elizabeth Farrell, Julie Bentz, Daniel Kaniewski, Richard Davis, Michael Barton, Matthew Broderick, Frank DiFalco, Bob Stephan, John Chase, Tom Dinanno, Edward McDonald, Gail Kulisch, Tom Paar, Michael Jackson, John Wood, (COS), National Interagency Coordination Center, Secretary Briefing Staff; HSOC.HSIN, HSOC.SWO, HSOC.FEMA, HSOC.DOD, HSOC.State&Local

24 Brown interview, Feb. 23, 2006, pp. 89-90. Brown also testified about this conversation before a closed-session with the House. On pages 111-112, when asked what he said in the secure call, he responds: "That probably 90 percent of the population of New Orleans had been displaced, that we had a true catastrophic disaster on our hands, that this was probably one of the most serious things that the country had faced; that it was. We needed to be doing everything possible." Deposition of Michael Brown before the House Katrina Select Committee, Feb. 11, 2006, pp. 111-112.

25 Brown interview, Feb. 23, 2006, p. 90.

26 Brown interview, Feb. 23, 2006, pp. 97-98.

27 The White House, Photo Gallery, Aug. 29, 2005. http://www.whitehouse.gov/news/releases/2005/08/images/20050829-5_p082905pm-0125-515h.html. Accessed on Mar. 2, 2006.

28 The White House, "President Participates in Conversation on Medicare," press release, Aug. 29, 2005. http://www.whitehouse.gov/news/releases/2005/08/20050829-5.html. Accessed on Mar. 7, 2006.

29 The White House, "President Participates in Conversation on Medicare," press release, Aug. 29, 2005. http://www.whitehouse.gov/news/releases/2005/08/20050829-5.html. Accessed on Mar. 7, 2006.

30 The White House, "President Discusses Medicare, New Prescription Drug Benefits," press release, Aug. 29, 2005. http://www.whitehouse.gov/news/releases/2005/08/20050829-11.html. Accessed on Mar. 7, 2006.

31 The White House, "President Commemorates 60th Anniversary of V-J Day," press release, Aug. 30, 2005. http://www.whitehouse.gov/news/releases/2005/08/20050830-1.html. Accessed on Mar. 11, 2006.

32 The White House, "Press Gaggle by Scott McClellan, Naval Air Station North Island, San Diego, California," Aug. 30, 2005. Provided to Committee; filed as Bates nos. WHK 01632 through 01633 (QUESTION: This is more - this is more symbolic. Cutting short his vacation is more symbolic because he can do all this from the ranch, right? McCLELLAN: No, I think – no, I disagree. Like I said, this is one of the most devastating storms in our nation's history, and the President, after receiving a further update this morning, made the decision that he wanted to get back to D.C. and oversee the response efforts from there.").

33 The White House, "President Outlines Hurricane Katrina Relief Efforts," press release, Aug. 31, 2005. Provided to Committee; filed as Bates nos. WHK 01636 through 01637.

34 Committee staff interview of Laurence Broun, Departmental Emergency Coordinator, U.S. Department of Interior, conducted on Mar. 21, 2006, transcript pp. 15-16.

35 Insung Lee, e-mail to Homeland Security Operations Center, Senior Watch Officer and others, Aug. 31, 2005, 12:41 p.m. Provided to Committee; filed as Bates nos. WHK 12588 through 12598. The other addressees of the e-mail are DL-NSC-WHSR, Bethany Nichols, Elliott Langer, Kirstjen Nielsen, Joel Bagnal, Elizabeth Farrell, Julie Bentz, Daniel Kaniewski, Richard Davis, Michael Barton, Matthew Broderick, Frank DiFalco, Bob Stephan, John Chase, Tom Dinanno, Edward McDonald, Gail Kulisch, Tom Paar, Michael Jackson, (DepSec), John Wood, (COS); National Interagency Coordination Center; Secretary Briefing Staff; HSOC.HSIN; IMD.

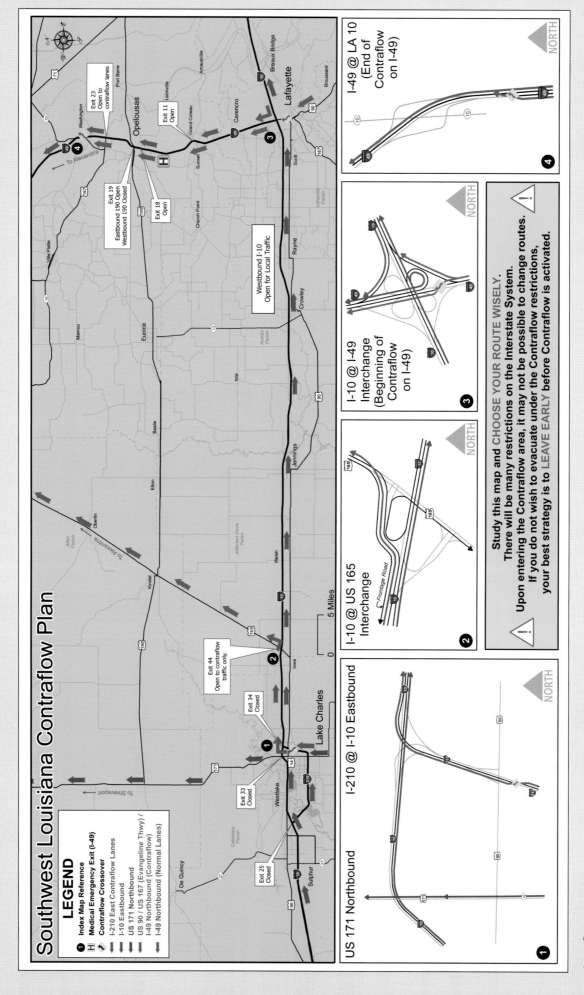

Southwest Louisiana Contraflow Plan

LEGEND

- 1 Index Map Reference
- H Medical Emergency Exit (I-49)
- Contraflow Crossover
- I-210 East Contraflow Lanes
- I-10 Eastbound
- US 171 Northbound
- US 90 / US 167 (Evangeline Thwy) / I-49 Northbound (Contraflow)
- I-49 Northbound (Normal Lanes)

Exit 23 Open to contraflow lanes

Exit 19 Eastbound 190 Open Westbound 190 Closed

Exit 18 Open

Exit 11 Open

Westbound I-10 Open for Local Traffic

Exit 44 Open to contraflow traffic only.

Exit 34 Closed

Exit 33 Closed

Exit 25 Closed

To Alexandria

To Shreveport

0   5 Miles

1 US 171 Northbound
I-210 @ I-10 Eastbound

2 I-10 @ US 165 Interchange

3 I-10 @ I-49 Interchange (Beginning of Contraflow on I-49)

4 I-49 @ LA 10 (End of Contraflow on I-49)

Study this map and CHOOSE YOUR ROUTE WISELY.
There will be many restrictions on the Interstate System.
Upon entering the Contraflow area, it may not be possible to change routes.
If you do not wish to evacuate under the Contraflow restrictions,
your best strategy is to LEAVE EARLY before Contraflow is activated.

Contraflow evacuation map
Louisiana Office of Homeland Security and
Emergency Preparedness

Pre-Storm Evacuations

Louisiana

Louisiana's successful evacuation of about one million people from greater New Orleans through phased movements and the one-way "contraflow" use of highways was a great improvement over the Hurricane Ivan evacuation a year earlier. Still, officials expected that 100,000 to 150,000[1] persons would be unable or unwilling to evacuate the region before Hurricane Katrina struck.

This included those with special needs, such as the elderly and infirm; the poor, those lacking means to leave; and those simply refusing to evacuate, regardless of reason or means, and choosing to take their chances in "hurricane roulette."[2]

Some of those responsible for the evacuation argue that those who wished to leave the city prior to landfall did so. The Director of Homeland Security for the City of New Orleans, Terry Ebbert, stated that of the "100,000 left behind, most of that 100,000 chose to stay behind. That's a big difference."[3] This view seems to depend on an expansive definition of "evacuation." As Joseph Matthews, Director of the New Orleans Office of Emergency Preparedness (OEP) noted, officials may have considered "transporting [people] to the Superdome" evacuation as well.[4]

In any case, there was long-standing recognition that 100,000 to 150,000 people would remain in the city following an evacuation order, and that some of them would remain only because they could not move themselves. Officials explored means of moving people out of the city, but the issue took a back seat to plans to use the Superdome as a special-needs shelter and a refuge of last resort.

> **Before Landfall, Louisiana, Mississippi, and the Affected Southeast Louisiana Parishes Agreed to and Successfully Executed Louisiana's Contraflow Plan**

Even before catastrophe strikes, evacuations are not simple.

Careful planning is essential to a successful pre-landfall evacuation because of the problems that traffic congestion and timing pose for the evacuees. Evacuation from the greater New Orleans area faces unique challenges for at least four reasons. First, evacuating the area requires at least a 45 to 80-mile trip (as compared to the 10 to 15-mile trip out of the affected areas in Mississippi). Second, there are only two or three ways out of the area. Third, one of those ways out of the area runs into Mississippi, requiring that state's cooperation. And fourth, because of the limited number of ways to exit the metropolitan area, the northern-most parishes within the area (Orleans and Jefferson) must wait patiently for the southern-most parishes within the area (St. Bernard and Plaquemines) to evacuate first; otherwise, the northern parishes will choke off the southern parishes' ability to evacuate. When these problems go unaddressed, thousands of people might be precluded from evacuating or delayed in Hurricane Ivan- or Rita-like traffic jams extending for hundreds of miles.

After the pre-landfall evacuation for Hurricane Georges first exposed these problems in September 1998, the 13-parish Southeast Louisiana Hurricane Task Force asked the Louisiana Office of Emergency Preparedness[5] (LOEP) to solve these problems by creating a "contraflow" plan.[6]

Generally speaking, contraflow turns all highway lanes in one direction, creating additional roadways for the execution of evacuation. Louisiana's contraflow plan applied to Interstates 10, 12, 55, and 59, so that all lanes of those highways would be heading out of New Orleans either upstate or east to Mississippi.

Louisiana did not use its contraflow plan until the pre-storm evacuation for Hurricane Ivan in September 2004. In that initial experiment, the state and the parishes encountered serious problems with the execution of the contraflow plan, including disagreements among parishes as to which parishes should evacuate first and the emergence of traffic choke points in Baton Rouge and Slidell, Louisiana.[7] These problems resulted in delays of 12-15 hours for people evacuating from the New Orleans metropolitan area,[8] as well as the deaths of nursing-home residents who died on the road in the heat and chaos of evacuating for Hurricane Ivan.[9]

To address the problems with contraflow that arose before Hurricane Ivan made landfall, the Governor ordered the Louisiana State Police (LSP) and the Department of Transportation and Development (DOTD) to develop a better evacuation plan.[10] Those agencies assembled a task force and worked with private consultants, traffic engineers, parish leaders, and local law-enforcement organizations in the relevant communities and conducted focus groups with residents to revise the plan.[11]

What resulted from this effort was the state's 2005 contraflow plan, known as the Southeast Louisiana Emergency Evacuation Plan (LEEP). The plan resulted from cooperation between the governors and state police forces of Louisiana and Mississippi, as well as the state's successful brokering of an agreement signed in April 2005 by the 13 parishes of the Southeast Louisiana Hurricane Task Force.

The LEEP addressed the problems identified during Hurricane Ivan by (1) directing as much traffic as possible away from what had been chokepoints at Baton Rouge and Slidell,[12] (2) creating special procedures for coordination between Louisiana and Mississippi,[13] and (3) requiring Jefferson and Orleans Parishes to wait to evacuate their residents until after their neighboring parishes announced the evacuation of their residents.[14]

As to the last point, the LEEP seeks to manage the order in which parishes evacuate by establishing three phases for the pre-storm evacuation, based on geographic location and the time in which tropical storm force winds are forecasted to reach the affected area. Under the plan, Phase 1 of the evacuation begins at the 50-hour mark before landfall of a Category 3 or higher hurricane, but contraflow only begins in Phase 3, once Jefferson and Orleans Parishes have ordered evacuations, at around the 30-hour mark before landfall and after.[15]

Once the Governor finalized the plan in the spring of 2005, the state initiated a media blitz and public education campaign, with media outlets, the American Red Cross, and businesses like Wal-Mart, Home Depot, and Lowe's all helping to distribute more than 1.5 million copies of the "Louisiana Citizen Awareness & Disaster Evacuation Guide."[16]

Governor Blanco initiated contraflow at 4 p.m. on Saturday, August 27, and ended it at 5 p.m. on Sunday, August 28, with no vehicles waiting in queues to leave the potential impact area.[17]

By all accounts, Louisiana, Mississippi, and the Southeast Louisiana parishes successfully executed the 2005 LEEP, before Hurricane Katrina made landfall. With that plan, Louisiana evacuated approximately 1 million people before landfall.[18]

The post-Ivan revisions to the plan also contributed to the success of the pre-landfall evacuation, as traffic jams exceeded two to three hours at most before Katrina made landfall, compared to the 12 to 15-hour traffic jams evacuees experienced before Ivan made landfall.[19]

There was also close consultation between Louisiana and Mississippi officials, including conversations between Governor Blanco and Governor Barbour, which resulted in coordination between the two states on the execution of the pre-landfall evacuation.[20]

Despite the success of the revamped contraflow plan, some officials saw opportunities for more improvement. Major John Miller, from the Mississippi Department of Public Safety, said that he would have state troopers stand farther back from the road next time: "[E]very third or fourth car has to stop and ask him a question,"[21] snarling traffic. Other suggestions included diverting some traffic to avoid the bottlenecks at the northern ends of I-55 and I-59,[22] and working for better state-to-state communications interoperability.[23]

St. Bernard, Plaquemines, St. Tammany, and Jefferson Parishes successfully followed and executed the LEEP.

In St. Bernard Parish, Larry Ingargiola, the Director of Homeland Security and Emergency Preparedness for St. Bernard Parish, stated that he called for an evacuation of St. Bernard Parish – albeit something short of an actual mandatory evacuation – during the late evening of Friday, August 26.[24] He recalled mentioning on the news that "We strongly recommend that you leave now because I don't believe I have enough body bags to cover the people that stay."[25] The following evening, Saturday, August 27, the parish "called for mandatory evacuation, strongly recommended evacuation."[26] Between Friday and Saturday, he said, all television channels in Orleans, Jefferson, Plaquemines, and St. Bernard Parishes ran scrolling news "zippers" noting the type of evacuation called for at the time.[27] Moreover, Ingargiola described some of his parish's concern about issuing a mandatory evacuation as follows:

> The big decision on mandatory evacuation is monetary, the businesses themselves. When you do a mandatory evacuation, the businesses are required to close down. The refineries are required to close down. We have three very large refineries down [here]. … It takes them roughly 8 to 12 hours to close down the refinery. Every time they close it down, it's over a million dollars to close it down and another million to bring it up. … It's not something you do easy.[28]

Furthermore, when asked whether St. Bernard's evacuation of Saturday night was coordinated with other parishes, Ingargiola responded that it was not, because of concern that other parishes would act unilaterally:

> No. We had a problem with Ivan because Jefferson Parish pulled the plug before everybody else for mandatory evacuation and contraflow was in [effect] … If the other parishes, Orleans and Jefferson, pull the plug and we get contraflow, we are stuck. We can't exit because we have one exit, Parish Road. You can't go. You are not going to send your people through New Orleans because they are doing the same thing you're doing. They are going to sit in another parking lot.[29]

Despite these challenges, Ingargiola noted that St. Bernard Parish was able to successfully evacuate 92 percent of its population[30] of approximately 66,000.[31] When asked whether he felt his Friday night call for evacuation was early enough, Ingargiola said it might have been wiser to do so on Thursday.[32] But Thursday, he noted, was a sunny day – had he called for an evacuation then, "The people would have thought I was crying wolf. That is your biggest fear, believe me. Somebody in my position, you will call it and somebody will just not believe what you call."[33]

In Plaquemines Parish, Jesse St. Amant, Director of the Plaquemines Parish Homeland Security Office of Emergency Preparedness, described its pre-storm evacuation policy and results:

People like myself, as emergency managers, should not be thinking, if I make a mandatory declaration and I make that recommendation to the governor, that he hesitates to do that because it might cost too much, you're putting a dollar value on [a life].

And in my business, if you ask how much it costs to do something, you're in the wrong business cause you could in fact cost someone their life.

You have to do what you must do to save life, and promise, and I take it very seriously. I'll give you an example. By declaring a mandatory evacuation, it cost Philips Conoco millions of dollars to safely shut down a petrochemical facility, and then it cost millions of dollars to start it up. The two most dangerous kinds of petrochemical facilities is the shutdown and the start-up of that facility. Very dangerous; very costly. Yet I don't hesitate to advise parish presidents. He does not hesitate to support me. I have his ear. He has – since I've been here, he has – he hired me. And let me suggest this to you … I will relate success. We had a 93 percent evacuation rate, one [of] the highest in the area, probably in the whole state. But we know we're also the most vulnerable. So the options aren't that great. You have to be out of this high-risk area.

The other issue that we do is we do – we're probably the first jurisdiction in the State of Louisiana to [start the evacuation process] that because we extend in the Gulf of Mexico.[34]

Plaquemines Parish issued a mandatory evacuation on Saturday, August 27.[35]

In St. Tammany Parish, Dexter Accordo has been the Director of Emergency Management and Homeland Security since July 18, 2004.[36] He said St. Tammany used the *EarthCall* notification system – a "reverse 911 [system] where you can dial up people by geographic area, and you can broadcast an audio message to them, giving them directions of what's going on"[37] – to warn residents to leave. When you order a mandatory evacuation, Accordo said, "At no point for the most part is it logistically feasible to go and knock on everybody's door, reach in and grab that person and yank them out of their house."[38] So a broader program of education is called for:

We reinforce it with the brochure [of evacuation maps], we reinforce it with the phone calls, we reinforce it with the outreach program training, we reinforce it with other forms of media … If I tell you, you need to do this, you're going to probably hesitate, but if you know why because we educate you why you need to do it, then there's a stronger probability you're going to do it.[39]

Accordo also spoke to the unique geography of St. Tammany Parish. He stated that the parish "represent[s] about two-thirds of the evacuation routes" for the metropolitan area, specifically the twin spans (I-10), the Causeway, and the "old highway" (highway 90) on the east side of St. Tammany and Orleans Parishes.[40] These plans have a large impact on St. Tammany Parish:

We get the biggest push probably through our area. We have to be cognizant of that because long before that 30-hour moment [i.e., the third phase of the State's evacuation plan], we're starting to feel the impacts of all this traffic.[41]

The number of evacuees from St. Tammany parish is uncertain. Accordo estimated that several hundred people were evacuated to a large special-needs shelter at Covington High School,[42] that 4,000 to 6,000 more were housed in other parishes' shelters,[43] and that about

127,000 were evacuated from the parish entirely, subject to check against a University of New Orleans post-storm study.[44]

In Jefferson Parish, Walter Maestri, Ph.D., is the Director of Emergency Management and Homeland Security.[45] Maestri recalls that Jefferson Parish President Aaron Broussard announced to the parish residents on late Friday afternoon, August 26, "that they should be ready to go [i.e., evacuate] Saturday morning."[46] He believes that about 70 to 80 percent of the residents of Jefferson Parish evacuated prior to the storm,[47] a "successful evacuation."[48] Maestri noted that Broussard's call for a parish evacuation on Friday afternoon to take effect the following Saturday morning was not a call for a mandatory evacuation:

> None of the Southeast Louisiana parishes, the larger ones, Orleans, Jefferson, St. Tammany, make mandatory evacuations. The reason for it, guys, is it's unenforceable. You can't do it. … Now as you know, Mayor Nagin later changed that. He went to mandatory, after first going to recommended. But the bottom line is that we did not and never will in Jefferson call mandatory because you can't do it.[49]

With respect to the 20 to 30 percent of persons who did not evacuate the parish, Maestri thinks "they got extremely lucky," because the parish only got a "glancing blow."[50] He notes that what hit Jefferson parish was primarily a "wind event … and that's why the fatalities are as low as they are. But the water is the killer. And we didn't get the water in Jefferson."[51] Moreover, Maestri said about half of the residents that did not evacuate before the storm moved to refuges of last resort within the parish, and the other half stayed in their homes.[52] Lastly, Maestri indicated that the parish's refuges of last resort were stocked with food, water, and first-aid supplies.[53] Maestri noted that he has a professional level, full-time person on his staff – the Shelter Coordinator – who has the responsibility to oversee and operate all of the parish shelters and refuges.[54]

The City of New Orleans Failed to Prepare a Draft Mandatory Evacuation Order Before Katrina Approached the Gulf Coast

Although it can never be known what impact earlier issuance of a mandatory-evacuation order would have had on the pre-landfall evacuation of New Orleans, it is clear that the city did not resolve all issues incident to a mandatory-evacuation order and did not have one prepared before Katrina approached the Gulf Coast.

On Friday, August 26, Mayor Nagin held a press conference at City Hall to announce that city officials were monitoring Hurricane Katrina.

On Saturday, August 27, Mayor Nagin joined Governor Blanco, and other officials for a press briefing at 1 p.m., during which the Mayor advised, according to talking points prepared for that briefing, that citizens should prepare for the storm, to include checking on neighbors and particularly the elderly, and announced the city would be calling for a voluntary evacuation later that afternoon or the morning of August 28 to coincide with the initiation of contraflow.[55]

According to a press report, Mayor Nagin said, "This is not a test. This is the real deal. Things could change, but as of right now, New Orleans is definitely the target for this hurricane," later adding, "We want you to take this a little more seriously and start moving – right now, as a matter of fact."[56] The Mayor also recommended that residents of Algiers, the Lower Ninth Ward, and low-lying areas begin evacuating. Citizens were also advised that there were two special-needs shelters open in the state in Alexandria and Monroe.

When Mayor Nagin issued a mandatory-evacuation order on Sunday, August 28, at approximately 9:30 a.m. CT,[57] it was the first time the City of New Orleans had ever issued a mandatory-evacuation order,[58] even though state law authorizes any parish to issue one.[59] He had ordered his staff to begin working on the order at noon on Saturday, August 27. According to witnesses, the city took nearly 24 hours to issue the order because it first needed to resolve legal and logistical questions.[60]

Chief among the issues to resolve was the determination of which classes of individuals would be exempted from the order. As initially drafted, there were four categories of exceptions: essential personnel of the city, regulated utilities, hospitals (including patients), and operating hotels (including guests).[61] After this draft was circulated to senior staff for review and comment, the list of exceptions was expanded to include the media and essential personnel of nursing homes (including residents). But then Colonel Terry Ebbert, New Orleans' Director of Homeland Security and Public Safety, recommended that the city not except nursing homes.[62]

The final order included the following exceptions: essential personnel of the United States of America, State of Louisiana and City of New Orleans; essential personnel of regulated utilities and mass-transportation services; essential personnel of hospitals and their patients; essential personnel of the media; essential personnel of the Orleans Parish Criminal Sheriff's Office and its inmates; and essential personnel of operating hotels and their patrons.[63]

In addition to these issues, the city was also concerned about how it would enforce the mandatory-evacuation order, and what transportation resources it had at its disposal to facilitate execution of the order.[64]

Long-term planning and preparation by the city before Katrina approached the Gulf Coast could have obviated this nearly 24-hour effort to resolve these issues.

Nevertheless, Governor Blanco insisted that Mayor Nagin's planning had been adequate, pointing out that evacuation was well underway before the mandatory-evacuation order was issued.[65]

> **The New Orleans Health Director, Who Initiated Draft Agreements to Provide Transportation for New Orleanians Without the Means to Evacuate, Deserves Credit for His Ingenuity and Effort, but the City's Director of Homeland Security and Public Safety Should Have Finalized These Agreements Before and During the 2005 Hurricane Season**

Although the city's emergency plans anticipated at least 100,000 people without the means to evacuate after a catastrophic natural disaster,[66] the city's top officials failed to plan and prepare adequately for the pre-landfall evacuation of this less-mobile segment of the population.

When Terry Tullier, the former Director of the New Orleans Office of Emergency Preparedness, who served in that position from May 2001 to his retirement in 2004, realized "that the city did not have the resources and at the time … perhaps not even the political will"[67] to move this segment of the population, he began exploring other transportation options. One was a volunteer program called Operation Brother's Keeper, which would enlist private citizens to help those who lacked transportation to evacuate.[68] A second involved informal discussions with the Regional Transportation Authority (RTA), the Orleans Parish School Board, and Amtrak to determine whether they would agree to provide transportation for a pre-landfall evacuation of New Orleans.[69]

Operation Brother's Keeper (OBK) was a faith-based initiative developed in collaboration with Kay Wilkins, the area's local Chapter Director of the American Red Cross. Through the program, churches would identify those within their congregations who did not have the means or ability to leave the city and match them with those who could help. Tullier recalled briefing Mayor Nagin and Col. Ebbert, with Wilkins, about the initiative: "Mayor Nagin said in no uncertain terms, anything that the city can do to support you, I'm all for this initiative."[70] There was apparent financial support for OBK, including a grant of $216,000 from a private organization.[71]

Although Operation Brother's Keeper was in place before landfall, it was not fully developed as logistical issues such as rally points and destinations had not been determined.[72]

The second of these initiatives, seeking alternative transportation from a variety of providers, was developed in late 2004, when Dr. Kevin Stephens, Director of the New Orleans Health Department, resumed Tullier's work after he stepped down as the City's Director of Emergency Preparedness (OEP), leaving the post vacant for almost six months.[73] Between Tullier's retirement in December 2004 and the appointment of Chief Matthews in March 2005, the OEP director's position was vacant. During this time, Dr. Stephens entered the breach and went to work on securing transportation for an evacuation of the city. Dr. Stephens explained why he saw the need to contract for transportation and shelters:

> All of our plans had primarily been [to] evacuate [to] the Superdome. And so I just thought that maybe as a general shelter, refuge of last resort, we should probably try to get some places outside the city and not at the Superdome because of the limitations of the Superdome. ... So I called Amtrak and I called the school board and RTA and other guys ... and asked them would they be willing to transport people out of the city, and they said sure, we'd be happy to.[74]

Dr. Stephens prepared draft memoranda of understanding (MOUs) among the City of New Orleans and Amtrak, the RTA, the Orleans Parish School Board, and the Cities of Baton Rouge and Hammond, Louisiana, contemplating use of various transportation resources to evacuate people from New Orleans prior to a hurricane. These drafts, with the exception of the Amtrak MOU, were internal documents, not shared with the other named entities.[75]

Responsibility for the MOUs returned to the City's OEP shortly after the Mayor appointed Chief Matthews to replace Tullier as Director in March 2005.[76]

Throughout the spring and summer of 2005, logistical obstacles dogged planning for the MOUs. Once people were evacuated from the city, was there enough shelter space to accommodate them? Once Amtrak delivered them to the Hammond train station, how would they be moved to state shelters? Most importantly, in the view of Chief Matthews, there was a shortage of drivers qualified to participate in an evacuation.[77]

However, the City's OEP, part of the City's Office of Homeland Security and Public Safety, did not follow through sufficiently to ensure execution of a single one of those agreements.[78] Shortly thereafter in June 2005 – three months before Katrina made landfall – the City's Director of Homeland Security and Public Safety, Colonel Ebbert, effectively decided to halt the negotiations on these MOUs, based on the following rationale: "June starts the hurricane season. You can't go to war still drafting you[r] plan, so you have to make decisions of what you're going to do this season."[79] With that decision, Colonel Ebbert lost opportunities to push his subordinate, Chief Matthews, to close these deals, and to ask the Mayor, the state, and the federal government for assistance in brokering these agreements.[80] The Committee disagrees with Colonel Ebbert that the city would be incapable of continuing work on long-term preparations for a catastrophic storm in the midst of hurricane season, as was evidenced by the city's participation in a July 2005 workshop on transportation staging and distribution of commodities.

The Director of the City of New Orleans Office of Emergency Preparedness Turned Down Offers of Assistance With the Pre-landfall Evacuation From the Regional Transit Authority (RTA)

Using federal funding granted in 2004,[81] the New Orleans Office of Emergency Preparedness composed a Comprehensive Emergency Management Plan (the plan) to establish procedures to prepare the city for an emergency such as a hurricane. The plan divided emergency response into the standard Emergency Support Functions (ESFs), designating the Regional Transit Authority (RTA) as the primary agency[82] for transportation during an evacuation.[83]

Specifically, the plan required the RTA to: "Supply transportation as needed in accordance with the current Standard Operating Procedures; place special vehicles on alert to be utilized if needed; position supervisors and dispatch evacuation buses; and if warranted by scope of evacuation, implement additional service."[84] The plan listed the following entities as supporting agencies under ESF-1: Orleans Parish School Board (OPSB), Louisiana Department of Transportation, Louisiana National Guard, and Amtrak.[85]

It was the understanding of James Tillie, RTA's Chief Operating Officer, that the city would direct the RTA "to transport the citizens of the city from one location to safe harbor," although for Katrina that meant the Superdome and not shelters outside of New Orleans.[86]

The city's plan required the New Orleans OEP to coordinate and facilitate preparedness and planning for the plan's designated response agencies, such as the RTA.[87] The plan also required the OEP to direct and control those agencies with ESF responsibilities, such as the RTA, during emergency response operations.[88] Although RTA is not a city agency, the Director of the Office of Emergency Preparedness, Chief Matthews, acknowledged that the RTA, as the primary agency for ESF-1, would answer to and receive direction from the City's OEP.[89]

Before Katrina made landfall, the RTA owned 372 buses and employed 650 drivers.[90] RTA officials estimated that each bus could transport 40 people and their luggage out of the city during an evacuation.[91] Of the drivers, approximately 100 volunteered for evacuation duty. (The number who remained in the city post-landfall was slightly lower, because some were prevented from returning to the city after driving special-needs evacuees to Baton Rouge because, consistent with the contraflow plan, the roads were closed a few hours before landfall.)[92]

Notwithstanding the RTA's role under the City's Emergency Operations Plan, RTA assets were not fully utilized in the pre-landfall evacuation because the Director of the New Orleans OEP, Chief Matthews, turned down the RTA's offers of assistance on the Saturday and Sunday before landfall, citing a lack of identifiable shelters as the reason.[93]

The City of New Orleans, the State of Louisiana, and the Federal Government Failed to Retain Drivers for the Pre-landfall Evacuation, After City Officials Informed State and Federal Officials of This Need Over a Month Before Landfall

Although the New Orleans OEP Director, Chief Matthews, informed state and federal officials – over a month before Katrina hit – that New Orleans lacked bus drivers for a pre-landfall evacuation,[94] that need went unaddressed before landfall.

The city had apparently designated buses from the RTA and the Orleans Parish School Board (the School Board), but the City's Office of Emergency Preparedness was having difficulty getting them to agree to provide the city with bus drivers for the evacuation.[95] Both the RTA and the School Board are independent creatures of state law and do not report directly to the city, although the city – through its majority representation on the School Board – has the opportunity to exert control over it.[96]

At the July 2005 transportation, staging, and commodities distribution workshop (which was part of the Hurricane Pam planning project), Chief Matthews alerted state and federal officials of this hole in the city's planning for the pre-landfall evacuation.[97] Although he did not request assistance from the state and federal officials for buses or drivers,[98] the federal officials who participated in the workshop understood that the city needed drivers: FEMA representative Jules Hurst recalled the local officials reporting that "they didn't know if they could get the drivers to report."[99] A U.S. Department of Transportation representative, Dan Prevo, also recalled, based on the Pam discussions, that there was "no certainty that the drivers – if the buses would be made available, that the drivers would be available . . . a whole lot of research had to be done with regard to how many drivers would be available, or the liability issues that might be faced for the buses and for the drivers."[100]

Informed of this need for drivers for over a month before Katrina hit, state and federal officials failed to explain why they did not take steps to recruit and retain drivers to participate in the pre-landfall evacuation. This inertia on the part of the state and federal government, which had been on notice of the city's inability to muster drivers on their own, added to the city's failures and resulted in a paucity of drivers available to participate in the pre-landfall evacuation – indeed, only 100 RTA drivers volunteered for duty.[101]

The State's Lead Agency for Transportation, the Louisiana Department of Transportation and Development, Failed to Meet its Responsibility Under the State's Emergency Operations Plan for Identifying, Mobilizing, and Coordinating Transportation to Assist With a Pre-Landfall Evacuation

The state failed to provide any transportation to New Orleans for the pre-landfall evacuation mainly because the Secretary of the Louisiana Department of Transportation and Development (LA DOTD) chose to ignore the Department's responsibility under ESF-1 (transportation) of the April 2005 Louisiana Emergency Operations Plan to take the lead for coordinating transportation for the evacuation of at-risk populations.[102]

In January 2005, Louisiana Office of Homeland Security and Emergency Preparedness (LOHSEP) officials explicitly told Gordon Nelson, LA DOTD Assistant Secretary for Operations, and Joseph Modicut, the Department's emergency services coordinator, that primary responsibility for Emergency Support Function 1 (ESF-1) would likely be shifted from the Louisiana National Guard to the LA DOTD to make the state's plan consistent with the National Response Plan, which in December 2004 assigned the U.S. Department of Transportation to be the lead agency for ESF-1.[103] They also told the LA DOTD officials that their role in an emergency would be to coordinate obtaining buses from other sources, recognizing that LA DOTD did not maintain a fleet of its own.[104] Despite this notice and despite having signed the state plan in April, thereby binding the Department to assigned responsibilities within it, LA DOTD Secretary Johnny Bradberry and his Department took no steps to fulfill that responsibility. Bradberry said he assumed, albeit incorrectly, that the National Guard would handle mass bus transportation.[105]

Testifying before the Committee, Secretary Bradberry attempted to defend his agency by saying that the plan was "in transition," and that he signed the plan to "keep things moving," meaning he did not want to hold up the state's overall emergency-operations planning process because of this issue. Nevertheless, he didn't "necessarily agree with the idea that the Department of Transportation needs to have this transportation function."[106]

Because he felt that the city was addressing the evacuation of its citizens,[107] Secretary Bradberry said that he had never had a conversation with Mayor Nagin, Colonel Ebbert, or Chief Matthews, about the evacuation of New Orleans residents without their own means to do so. Secretary Bradberry said: "We have done nothing to fulfill this responsibility … we put no plans in place to do any of this."[108]

Despite the January meeting with LOHSEP officials and the April signing of the plan by Secretary Bradberry, Nelson claimed he did not learn about the Department's new responsibility until a July 2005 workshop, and Modicut said he did not learn about the new duty until the weekend before Katrina made landfall.[109] Nelson disagreed with the assignment because the Department did not have an in-house stable of transportation resources, but he said nothing at the time.[110] The Committee finds no reasonable explanation of why, for more than four months, the Department's Assistant Secretary for Operations and Chief of Emergency Services were unfamiliar with a fundamental shift in the Department's operational responsibilities under the state's revised plan. These officials, like Secretary Bradberry, did not advise state officials that DOTD signed a plan that it did not intend to follow, choosing to remain silent.

In a letter to the U.S. Senate Homeland Security and Governmental Affairs Committee, Secretary Bradberry commented on his Department's lack of ESF–1 planning:

> To criticize the Louisiana Department of Transportation for failure to have a plan in place for transportation assets which were never requested is wholly unfair and unjust. Yes, DOTD should have acted sooner transitioning into the new responsibilities under the 2005 State Emergency Operations Plan, but the fact remains that DOTD did not receive any requests for transportation prior to Hurricane Katrina.[111]

Secretary Bradberry's defense that there were no requests for transportation prior to Katrina rings hollow. The city discussed their lack of buses and drivers needed for a successful evacuation with state and federal officials at the July 2005 transportation, staging and commodities distribution workshop. Had LA DOTD taken meaningful steps to develop a plan, they would quickly have seen the inability of local government to manage its evacuation needs as a potentially catastrophic hurricane approached. Moreover, the state was not required to wait – and should not have waited – for a request from the city before offering assistance, particularly when a catastrophe was imminent.

As Katrina approached, some state officials were "leaning forward in the foxhole with [their] finger on the trigger."[112] Secretary Bradberry was not one of those officials.

The Louisiana Office of Homeland Security and Emergency Preparedness Did Not Exercise Sufficient Oversight to Ensure that Louisiana Department of Transportation and Development Would Fulfill its Responsibilities Under the State's April 2005 Plan

The Louisiana Emergency Operations Plan assigned LOHSEP primary responsibility for "all emergency activities conducted by state, local and parish governments … before, during and after natural and technological disasters."[113] Included within the scope of this charge is "planning and preparations before emergencies."[114] This imposed the duty on LOHSEP to ensure that other agencies carry out their assigned responsibilities under the plan.[115] LOHSEP failed to discharge this duty in the case of LA DOTD's ESF–1 responsibilities for transportation under the state plan.

As noted earlier, LA DOTD officials Modicut and Nelson met with senior LOHSEP and Louisiana National Guard officials in January 2005 to discuss a possible shift of assigned responsibility for ESF–1 from the Louisiana National Guard to LA DOTD.[116] At this meeting and in subsequent correspondence, LOHSEP's Chief of Planning, Sean Fontenot, said that LA DOTD understood the responsibilities it would be accepting, and he attempted to provide some initial guidance regarding expectations for planning:

Flooded school buses, New Orleans
AP/Wide World Photo

> DOTD, the biggest concern … was they had no resources. They didn't own buses. They didn't own [trucks], but the Guard owns trucks. … You go to the Guard and say, "We need trucks," the Guard will give you trucks if they have them to give you. The buses, I mean, DOTD has relationships with organizations and agencies like Louisiana Motor Transit Authority Association. Use some of your – this is what I told them, use some of your contacts, use some of your relationships to build these databases, and things of that nature, and they agreed and they understood that, and we moved on.[117]

Based on Fontenot's statement that Modicut and Nelson were at the meeting, both should have been aware of the issue and, presumably, aware that the state was going to be looking to DOTD to meet this need.[118]

Despite this meeting and subsequent correspondence, once the plan was signed in April 2005, there was no substantive follow-up by LOHSEP officials to ensure that DOTD was undertaking planning to fulfill the new responsibilities assigned to it under the plan. As

Louisiana National Guard commander Major General Bennett Landreneau acknowledged, the need for LOHSEP to ensure that DOTD met its planning responsibilities "slipped through the cracks."[119]

Governor Blanco Did Not Request Transportation Resources From the Federal Government for Pre-landfall Evacuation

Although it is unclear precisely what transportation assets the state could have mobilized over the weekend to assist the city with the pre-landfall evacuation, neither the Governor nor any other state official offered to provide transportation to assist with the pre-landfall evacuation or requested federal assistance.

On August 27, the Governor sent President Bush a letter, requesting $9 million for assistance for emergency protective measures under the Stafford Act, the federal law that coordinates federal disaster assistance to states.[120] Although the Governor, in this letter, requested that $2.5 million be directed to evacuation needs, she did not specify a need for transportation.[121] The President issued an emergency declaration the same day, effectively granting the Governor's request.

During video teleconferences with local, state, and federal officials on Saturday, August 27, and on Sunday, August 28, state officials discussed the success of contraflow,[122] but did not raise the issue of additional transportation assets, despite the long-standing realization that 100,000 people in New Orleans lacked transportation. Although LOHSEP Acting Deputy Director Colonel Jeff Smith noted on that call that the Governor "is very appreciative of the federal resources that have come into the state and the willingness to give us everything you've got because, again, we're very concerned with this," neither he nor the Governor made a specific request of the federal government for transportation resources before landfall.[123]

This lamentable failure by the Governor to request transportation resources shows not only a lack of initiative, but also a failure of leadership.

Mississippi

Before Katrina reached the Gulf Coast, thousands of Louisiana and Mississippi residents evacuated to other states, including Texas and Oklahoma. In Mississippi, localities declared mandatory evacuations as the hurricane approached. These were carried out relatively well, but some residents chose to disregard the orders. Many had already complied with two false-alarm evacuations over the last year.[124] Others had disagreeable evacuation experiences. Still others, approaching the end of the month, no longer had enough money to support themselves and their families on the road. State and local governments performed their roles well in evacuating those who agreed to leave, but must do better by those without the means.

Evacuations of General Population Went Relatively Well

The Mississippi Emergency Management Agency (MEMA) and the Mississippi Department of Transportation (MDOT) worked together to develop a hurricane evacuation guide that provides residents with a hurricane disaster checklist, information on evacuation routes, contraflow plans,[125] traffic control information, and emergency contact information.[126]

Though local governments must ultimately decide whether to order an evacuation,[127] the state participates in the decision making process.[128] This coordination is critical because once the city or county declares an emergency evacuation, the state becomes responsible for managing traffic flow and maintaining shelters.[129] In preparing for Katrina, state officials worked with: the liaisons MEMA dispatched to the lower six counties along the Mississippi Gulf Coast; the Forrest County Emergency Operations Center in Hattiesburg; and the Louisiana Emergency Operations Center (because of contraflow agreements between Mississippi and Louisiana that provide for evacuations out of Southeast Louisiana to Mississippi).[130]

The Mississippi Emergency Management Agency began monitoring the storm's path and strength on August 24 – five days before landfall – and issued its first hurricane situation report that day.[131] Two days later, another MEMA report notified state and local agencies that the storm was now projected to make landfall near the Alabama/Mississippi border on Monday morning as a Category 4 hurricane.[132] As a result, Governor Barbour declared a state of emergency which, according to Darryl Neely, the Governor's Policy Advisor, prompted locals to begin evacuating coastal residents. State agencies met that afternoon at the state Emergency Operations Center (EOC) in Jackson, Mississippi,[133] and MEMA informed the three coastal counties of the storm's path and projected landfall.[134]

When Robert Latham, the Executive Director of MEMA, which is located in Jackson, headed to the coast on August 27 to meet with county emergency managers to discuss storm preparations, he was worried that many would ignore evacuation orders.[135]

Latham and other state officials, who had reports of low traffic counts on many evacuation routes and of residents having hurricane parties on the beach,[136] encouraged local officials to begin issuing mandatory, coordinated evacuation orders.[137] Though many local governments had already issued strongly recommended,[138] or mandatory evacuations,[139] and were beginning to evacuate areas threatened by Hurricane Katrina throughout Friday evening and Saturday, some cities and counties were "slow to get them to come around,"[140] according to the MEMA's Response and Recovery Director:

> We were trying to make them understand that this was a bad storm and they didn't want to move aggressively enough with the evacuation orders … they should have called for a mandatory evacuation much earlier … based on the information … they had … we felt that they should have called for mandatory evacuations of a larger area earlier and gotten the people out of there.[141]

According to Latham, emergency managers had a tough call to make in terms of evacuating residents:

> They did understand how serious [the storm] could be … after you'd already been through two or three evacuations, … you go to your mayor or your supervisor and say, we've got to do this evacuation, … then it falls back on the mayor or the board to … stand up to public scrutiny when … nothing happens. … They have to get reelected … that's just an unfortunate part of it.[142]

Because Katrina continued to intensify, National Hurricane Center Director Max Mayfield personally began calling state and local officials in the evening of August 27 to emphasize the threat.[143] Mayfield also briefed Governor Barbour,[144] comparing Katrina to Camille, the Category 5 storm that struck Mississippi in 1969. Governor Barbour and Latham felt the comparison to Camille would resonate, and asked Mayfield to convey the gravity of Katrina to the public.[145] According to state and local officials, Mayfield and the Governors' press and public announcements had the desired effect. Traffic counts on evacuation routes began increasing.[146]

Mandatory Evacuations Declared

Five Mississippi counties – Hancock, Jackson, Harrison, Stone, and Pearl River[147] – issued mandatory-evacuation orders on or before August 28 for specific areas[148] or zones in their counties and/or those living in mobile homes.[149] Residents were told to travel north or northeast to avoid incoming traffic from Louisiana and to use public shelters north of I-10.[150]

Many Residents Disregarded the Mandatory Evacuation Orders Due to Complacency, Poor Evacuation Experiences, and Insufficient Financial Resources to Support Themselves and Their Families on the Road

State and local officials issued news releases, made appearances on local television and radio stations, used public address systems and, in certain neighborhoods, even went door-to-door to inform coastal residents about evacuation orders. Major Wayne Payne, Harrison County's Deputy Sheriff, said that officers were particularly concerned about residents in the Henderson Point and D'Iberville areas, where the houses are built on stilts or are near water:[151]

> Henderson Point here, we went door to door. We said, this is a bad one, you all need to get out. … These are houses on stilts. I mean, they're 10, 15 feet off the ground and they're gone. They're wiped out.[152]

Because officers did not have the authority to "drag people out of their homes" in places like Gulfport,[153] they were forced to resort to more psychological forms of persuasion. If a resident refused to evacuate in Harrison County, an officer asked him to fill out a form indicating next of kin, which seemed to have the intended effect.[154] In Waveland and Bay St. Louis, first responders asked holdouts to make sure to have Social Security numbers on their body in permanent marker for easy identification after the storm. Police compiled lists of locals who were determined to stay in their homes, recording names, birth dates, Social Security numbers, and next of kin.[155] These tactics proved effective in persuading residents to leave their homes.

Several factors contributed to resistance to evacuation. Evacuations earlier in the summer preceding a tropical storm and Hurricane Dennis, which largely turned out to have been false alarms, fostered skepticism.[156] Others who had made it through 1969's Hurricane Camille, the Category 5 storm that was the region's benchmark for catastrophic storms until Katrina hit, thought they would see no worse. Harrison County's Deputy Sheriff, Major Payne, explained:

> I had a cousin that stayed in his house, and he said, Well, Camille only put a foot of water in my house. He stayed … and had to climb in the attic to survive. Water got within six inches of his attic … During Hurricane Camille, the tracks [railroad embankments] pretty well stopped the water. [With Katrina] we had storm surge on the Interstate.[157]

More than two-thirds of Katrina's casualties in Mississippi were of retirement age, complicating evacuation. Others feared that looters would strike if they abandoned their homes.[158] As the end of August neared, some residents had insufficient resources to support their families on the road. Latham explained:

> People on fixed income had … paid their rent, they paid the utilities, bought their food for the month. … I mean, a lot of people live check to check. And this is the 29th. And people … said, look I don't have money to evacuate.[159]

The average cost of evacuation for three days for a family of four, including lodging, food and transportation, could easily exceed a thousand dollars. Many county residents had already evacuated several times that summer and simply could not afford it. Colonel Joe Spraggins, Director of Harrison County's Emergency Management Agency recalled the explanation of one resident:

> I'm single and have two children. … I already evacuated … twice when you all called before. And I had a choice. Because I am behind on everything now because I had to pay to go do that, and I have low income, and I had a choice, do I feed my children next month and pay the house rent or do I evacuate?[160]

State and local officials say that negative evacuation experiences in the past also contributed to residents' reluctance to leave. The evacuation before Hurricane Ivan had stalled in and around Hattiesburg, where major evacuation routes converge, tripling the three-hour drive from the Gulf Coast to Jackson.[161] As a result, Governor Barbour had asked Mississippi Public Safety Commissioner George Phillips to develop a plan that would provide additional law-enforcement officers to expedite evacuations, especially in the Hattiesburg area.[162] According to state officials, the plan,[163] completed prior to the 2005 hurricane season, was executed flawlessly when residents evacuated during Katrina.[164]

By late Saturday and early Sunday – the day before landfall – Mississippi Department of Transportation officials reported "consistently high" traffic counts and a "continuous increase in traffic" in contraflow areas (I-55 and I-59)."[165] By late Sunday evening, traffic along the evacuation routes had decreased substantially.[166] MDOT and MEMA officials stated that the evacuations went relatively well. According to MDOT's Law Enforcement Coordinator, the biggest problem was residents' waiting until the last minute to evacuate and then expecting traffic to be minimal.[167]

Residents who, for a variety of reasons, ignored evacuation orders faced a greater set of problems than those evacuating. State and local governments performed efficiently and effectively in evacuating those residents who agreed to leave, and persuading those who were undecided. Nevertheless, these agencies could have done better by the many residents of their communities who didn't make it out not because of intransigence, but because they didn't have the means. State and local officials have an obligation to help evacuate those who need assistance and should have specific plans to do so.

The Federal Government

The Federal Government Did Not Reach Out to State or Local Authorities About Transportation Alternatives for Those Lacking Means for Pre-Landfall Evacuation

In public-hearing testimony, Department of Homeland Security (DHS) Secretary Michael Chertoff acknowledged the critical importance of pre-landfall evacuation: "In a situation like a flood in Katrina or an earthquake, the critical, the number-one most important thing is to get people out of the area in advance. Once the event has occurred, it's going to be very difficult to rescue people."[168]

As noted earlier, while Governor Blanco asked President Bush for and received the government's help in paying the costs of contraflow, among other pre-storm needs, she did not ask for transportation from the federal government to assist the state with the pre-landfall evacuation. Thus, in an effort to obtain transportation assistance, the Governor did not initiate the longstanding practice of making a formal request of the federal government for assistance.

The federal government played no role in providing transportation for pre-landfall evacuation. Both in the run-up to Katrina and subsequent interviews, federal officials provided the same explanation: they were accustomed to the longstanding practice of generally deferring to the primary emergency response to state and local governments.[169] Although the National Response Plan (NRP) does not specifically address evacuations, a "basic premise of the NRP is that incidents are generally handled at the lowest jurisdictional level possible," and that in "some instances, a Federal agency in the local area … may provide direction or assistance consistent with its specific statutory authorities and responsibilities."[170] (*See* Chapter 12 and 27 for a fuller discussion of the NRP and the specific statutory authorities.)

Throughout the weekend of August 27 and 28 it had become increasingly clear to federal, state, and local officials that Hurricane Katrina would be a catastrophe. Mayor Nagin took the unprecedented step (albeit with some hesitation) of calling for a mandatory evacuation of New Orleans. Both President Bush and Governor Blanco actively encouraged that step. There was no question that evacuation before landfall was the highest priority.

While the widespread support for mandatory evacuation is laudable, it is unfortunate that the federal government did not take a greater interest in the practicality of that evacuation in a city widely known to have made no arrangements for evacuation of the thousands of its citizens lacking personal transportation. Federal officials had participated actively in the Hurricane Pam exercise (*See* Chapter 8), which predicted that some 100,000 New Orleanians would lack means of evacuation.[171] Federal officials did not need to wait for a request before offering help.

Although time would not have been on their side in the last two days before landfall, the DHS had a window – however slim – within which to act. But it does not appear that DHS leaders asked about what the state and the city were doing to evacuate the 100,000 people without transportation. Nor did they ask whether it would be useful for the federal government to mobilize and deploy buses or drivers to Southeast Louisiana.[172] Nor did they ask whether it would be helpful to use the weight of the federal government to urge railroads, airlines, transit systems, or cruiselines to become engaged in the pre-landfall evacuation.

Further, as the Committee found in Chapters 12 and 27, Secretary Chertoff failed to activate the Catastrophic Incident Annex (CIA) to the National Response Plan before landfall. Had Secretary Chertoff activated the CIA, it would have sent a clear message to federal agencies that they should be pushing assets, including transportation assets, forward to mobilization centers close to the disaster or in certain circumstances directly to the incident scene.

During the Hurricane Pam exercise, and follow-up July 2005 workshop, federal officials had heard state and local officials openly discuss their shortage of buses and other resources to evacuate that population.[173] While there is some disagreement as to the firmness of federal commitment, federal officials evidently discussed at least the possibility of providing the buses that the state lacked.[174] Participants in the July 2005 Pam workshop on transportation, staging, and commodities distribution even agreed on a timetable to pre-stage buses ahead of landfall, to be prepared for post-landfall evacuation needs.[175] Even though this planning wasn't complete by the time Katrina struck, federal officials were aware of evacuation challenges for state and local governments.

With no plans to supplement state and local transportation resources, federal options were limited. Getting buses from distant sources to New Orleans, as it did after landfall, may not have been realistic, depending on when the effort was initiated over the weekend. On the other hand, there were many transportation assets either in the area (such as municipal buses, riverboats and cruise ships) or accessible (such as trains and airplanes) that the federal government could have helped to make available. The post-landfall resourcefulness of many officials who arranged for transportation alternatives suggests what could have been easily attempted before landfall.

There is other evidence that the federal government can mobilize transportation resources for evacuation when it chooses to do so. Pursuant to a request from the State of Louisiana, the U.S. Department of Transportation (DOT) contracted for 1,100 buses and two drivers per bus for post-landfall evacuation during Katrina. Federal officials also staged a major air evacuation.[176] Later, in preparation for Hurricane Rita, DOT reached out to transit agencies from Texas to Georgia to Florida.[177] Four days before Hurricane Rita made landfall, FEMA, through DOT, ordered immediate staging outside of New Orleans of 650 buses "for use in evacuation of New Orleans and Southern parishes."[178] Also before Hurricane Rita made landfall, the U.S. Department of Defense (DOD) evacuated 1,204 patients and people with special needs before landfall, between 7 a.m. on September 21, when they received the mission assignment and noon on September 23.[179]

The DOT's Federal Transit Administration (FTA) is in a uniquely strong position to coordinate privately and publicly owned buses. The FTA has close relationships with regional transit authorities through emergency preparedness operations. For instance, New Orleans' RTA is a 92 percent federally funded agency and has extensive relationships with the regional office of DOT.[180] Also, DOT situation reports show that the FTA was keeping close tabs before landfall on the Baton Rouge transit system buses.[181] Although the state was late asking the Baton Rouge transit system to participate in the post-landfall evacuation of New Orleans, it appears that the DOT did not ask the Baton Rouge transit system to participate at all.

Federal officials were both aware of state and local shortfalls, and had both the capacity and opportunities to help. But in the absence of adequate plans and policies, federal officials were paralyzed to act.

At 10:15 a.m. Sunday, August 28, the day before landfall, FEMA's Acting Deputy Director Patrick Rhode, sent an e-mail to other FEMA officials, conceding that time had run out to help New Orleans with pre-landfall evacuation.[182] Contraflow ended at 5 p.m. that day.[183] Whether that seven-hour interval offered any opportunity for useful federal action is unclear, but federal officials did not engage state and locals on the issue.

During a noon video-teleconference call the same day, then-FEMA Director Michael Brown asked Colonel Smith if there were "any unmet needs, anything that we're not getting to you that you need" to which Colonel Smith responded, "Mike, no." Brown testified that he was seeking information from the state on what it needed at that moment only.[184] As with Rhode's e-mail, by noon on Sunday, time was limited for the federal government to help New Orleans with its pre-landfall evacuation.

Secretary Chertoff was right when he said that evacuation was the primary mission before landfall.[185] A concentrated effort by the federal, state, and local governments to effect a more complete evacuation of New Orleans before landfall would have likely reduced the number of people to care for at the Superdome, the Convention Center, and other collection sites; eased the burden of the search-and-rescue effort; lessened the challenge of the post-landfall evacuation; and reduced the number of critical supplies, medical support, and law enforcement that were needed in New Orleans after landfall.

The Federal Government Had the Authority to Assist With Pre-Landfall Evacuation, Even in the Absence of a Request for Assistance from State and Local Governments

Due to disagreement among officials as to whether, when, and to what extent the federal government could assist with a pre-landfall evacuation, it is helpful to examine the law and policy directing the way in which federal officials could have assisted with the pre-landfall evacuation.

Federal law imposes no requirement for the federal government to aid pre-landfall evacuations. Such a requirement would be inconsistent with the principle that local and state authorities have primary responsibility for emergencies, receiving federal assistance only when their own resources are overwhelmed. However, federal law does not prohibit the federal government from extending assistance, even without a request from the state, when preparing for or responding to an imminent catastrophe such as Hurricane Katrina.

The Robert T. Stafford Disaster Relief and Emergency Assistance Act (the Stafford Act) gives the federal government the authority to assist the state and local governments with an evacuation. Congress made clear in the Stafford Act that its purpose was to "vest responsibility for emergency preparedness jointly in the Federal government and the states and their political subdivisions."[186] Included within the Stafford Act's definition of "emergency preparedness" is any measure "undertaken in preparation for anticipated hazards," such as "the non-military evacuation of the civilian population."[187]

The Stafford Act also authorizes the President – and, through Executive Orders, the Secretary of Homeland Security[188] – to direct federal agencies to "provide assistance essential to meeting immediate threats to life and property resulting from a major disaster," including but not limited to the "movement of supplies or persons" and the "reduction of immediate threats to life, property, and public health and safety."[189] A common-sense reading of this language would indicate that the Stafford Act authorized the President to direct a federal agency to help state and local governments move people out of New Orleans both before and after landfall to meet the "immediate threat" of Katrina.

The Homeland Security Act of 2002 enumerates FEMA's functions which include assistance with evacuations. Under the Act, FEMA's mission is "to reduce the loss of life and property and protect the Nation from all hazards by leading and supporting the Nation in a comprehensive, risk-based emergency management program," including the responsibility for mitigation of risk to people and property, planning, and responding "to save lives … through evacuating potential victims."[190]

FEMA's mission under the Homeland Security Act was to take steps to mitigate the risks to people that could arise from Katrina; plan to help officials prepare for Katrina and similar catastrophic storms; plan for an evacuation in the event of a catastrophic storm; respond to Katrina by "evacuating potential victims"; and coordinate efforts by other officials.[191]

The Catastrophic Incident Annex (CIA) to the NRP delineates federal policy on a more proactive response to catastrophes. These issues are discussed in Chapters 12 and 27.

Provisions for Household Pets

Hurricane Katrina revealed that consideration of the needs of those with pets should be a factor in emergency planning for evacuations and sheltering.

The City of New Orleans' plans do not refer to pets, but the State of Louisiana's EOP includes an appendix entitled, "Animal Management in Disasters," which directs veterinarians, animal control personnel, and humane society volunteers to, among other things, "coordinate with the Louisiana Shelter Task Force on the sheltering of companion animals."[192] The NRP does not address the implications of evacuation and sheltering for pets, but has scattered references to animals. Most of these references relate to preventing outbreaks of disease through animals.[193]

More than 50 percent of U.S. households have pets.[194] In the aftermath of Katrina, the media brought to light many stories of individuals who refused to evacuate without their animals.[195] One study revealed that childless households with pets were twice as likely to fail to evacuate as households with children. In other words, in childless households, owners "were apparently willing to jeopardize their lives to stay with their pets."[196] In his after-action report on Hurricane Katrina, Captain Mark Willow of the Homeland Security Division of the New Orleans Police Department wrote that "Some of the fatalities in New Orleans and surrounding areas may be attributable to the fact victims would not leave their pets at home or would not consider leaving without them."[197]

Evacuation with pets before the storm was difficult for many since emergency shelters usually prohibit animals. The American Red Cross did not allow animals in its shelters.[198] Animals can cause allergic reactions for some residents of the shelter, increase hygiene problems, and may become dangerous or unruly in the stressful setting of a shelter.[199] Even after the storm passed, the media reported on many individuals unwilling to leave their homes despite dangerous conditions unless rescuers agreed to rescue their pets as well.[200]

The national organization of the American Red Cross works cooperatively with animal welfare organizations to develop procedures for stationing animal shelters close to its own shelters.[201] In this way, owners are able to evacuate with their pets and maintain contact after arrival at the shelter. The American Red Cross implements this policy by encouraging local chapters to work with animal organizations to establish local agreements.[202] However, Gulf Coast victims did not have pet accommodations inside or in close proximity to many of the available shelters.[203] In particular, the New Orleans Superdome, the city's refuge of last resort, had no pet shelter facilities inside or close by, and the Committee has seen no evidence of formal arrangements for Superdome refugees' pets.[204]

During Katrina, the Lamar-Dixon Expo Center in Gonzales, Louisiana, (approximately 30 miles from Baton Rouge) was designated as an animal shelter. Typically used for 4-H events and rodeos, it has almost 1,000 horse stalls and thus was able to serve both large and small animals.[205] During Katrina, the Center handled approximately 8,500 rescued animals.[206]

For Katrina, FEMA activated all four of its Veterinary Medical Assistance Teams ("VMAT") to the Gulf Coast.[207] This involved more than 200 veterinarians and was FEMA's largest simultaneous deployment of veterinary relief.[208] The National Guard and Louisiana State Police assisted in collecting stray dogs.[209] On September 2, 2005, the American Society for the Prevention of Cruelty to Animals (ASPCA) and the Humane Society of the United States (HSUS) began a coordinated campaign with a dozen local organizations and volunteers from across the country to rescue animals from the aftermath of Katrina.

For Katrina, no standardized system for tracking rescued animals was in place. The website Petfinder.com came to play an important role in allowing owners to find rescued pets.[210]

1 The number 100,000 is cited during numerous interviews including: Committee staff interview of Terry Tullier, then Director, New Orleans Office of Emergency Preparedness, LA, conducted on Nov. 22, 2005, transcript p. 18. *See also*: City of New Orleans, Emergency Response Shelter/Plan appropriations request, FY2006, p. 1 (Col. Terry Ebbert is the point of contact, "The city of New Orleans faces the reality that it is impossible to conduct a mandatory evacuation in advance of a Category 3, 4, or 5 hurricane, as well as respond to other disasters including terrorism. Even under the best conditions that currently exist in terms of emergency response in the New Orleans region, evacuation would leave 150,000 people in harm's way.").

2 Some attribute the reason for choosing not to leave as cultural. Both Col. Terry Ebbert and former Office of Emergency Preparedness Director Terry Tullier expressed this sentiment in interviews. Col. Ebbert noted: "But these people hadn't seen a Cat 3 since Betsy, 1965. So you're talking about people who don't think it's going to hit them. Ivan last year bored down on us until it got to the mouth of the Mississippi and it turned. … And I think it's a cultural thing that's been brought along." *Source*: Committee staff interview of Col. Terry Ebbert, Director, New Orleans Office of Homeland Security, LA, conducted on Oct. 13, 2005, transcript p. 97. Tullier said, "The first thing is a public official has to convince this cultural masses [sic] that have accumulated this cultural philosophical viewpoint over 40 years, has to convince them it is in their best interests [inaudible] to leave." *Source*: Tullier interview, Nov. 22, 2005, p. 216.

3 Col. Ebbert interview, Jan. 12, 2006, p. 44.

4 Committee staff interview of Joseph Matthews, Director, New Orleans Office of Emergency Preparedness, LA, conducted on Nov. 23, 2005, transcript p. 193.

5 In 2003, the state renamed this office the Louisiana Office of Homeland Security and Emergency Preparedness.

6 Committee staff interview of Sean Fontenot, former Chief, Preparedness Division, Louisiana Office of Homeland Security and Emergency Preparedness (LOHSEP), conducted on Jan. 10, 2006, transcript pp. 108-109 ("After Hurricane Georges in '98, local government in Southeast Louisiana Hurricane Task Force, which is comprised of the thirteen parishes in the southeast corner of the state … went to the state and said, 'we need help with this. We need Contraflow. We need you to do this.'").

7 During the Hurricane Ivan evacuation, traffic ground to a halt in Baton Rouge as I-10 and 1-12 converged. Sheila Grissett, "Evacuation decision expected today for metropolitan area," New Orleans *Times-Picayune*, July 8, 2005. http://www.nola.com/news/t-p/frontpage/index.ssf?/base/news-3/1120800310204660.xml. Accessed on May 15, 2006.

8 Committee staff interview of Sec. Johnny Bradberry, Louisiana Department of Transportation and Development, conducted on Nov. 17, 2005, transcript pp. 38-39.

9 Committee staff interview of Joseph Donchess, Executive Director, Louisiana Nursing Home Association, conducted on Jan. 9, 2006, transcript pp. 64-65.

10 Committee staff interview of Henry Whitehorn, Superintendent, Louisiana State Police, conducted on Nov. 29, 2005, transcript p. 19.

11 Whitehorn interview, Nov. 29, 2005, pp. 20-21.

12 The plan established three corridors out of New Orleans on I-55 North, I-10 West, and I-10 East and excluded I-12 as a route to Baton Rouge, with hopes of directing as many people away from Baton Rouge as possible. *Source*: Committee staff interview of Bob Chapman, Emergency Services Manager, Mississippi Department of Transportation, and William Huff, Director, Enforcement, Mississippi Department of Transportation, conducted on Dec. 14, 2005, transcript pp. 28-30**.** Starting contraflow requires stopping traffic in the lanes heading into the evacuation area. This process takes about 30 minutes. Once contraflow is initiated, the routes leading out of the area are limited to help alleviate congestion caused by people who might otherwise try to turn or change routes. At a specific point, on I-10 West, I-10 East, and I-55 North, traffic must follow designated routes which end up either west of Baton Rouge or in Mississippi. As depicted on the Louisiana Citizens Awareness & Disaster Evacuation Guide, I-10 West will have eight lanes of traffic leading out of New Orleans, but at mile marker 209, those traveling on the eastbound lanes will be diverted onto the westbound lanes of I-10 and will continue west on I-10 toward Baton Rouge; those on the westbound lanes will be forced to go on to I-55 North to travel to Mississippi. If evacuees take I-10 East, they will also eventually wind up on I-51 traveling to Mississippi passing through Slidell. To alleviate congestion caused by entering or exiting traffic, traffic is "laned," meaning that once on the route the evacuee is dedicated for some extended period of time. *Source*: Louisiana State Police, Louisiana Department of Transportation and Development, and LOHSEP, *Overview of the Louisiana Emergency Evacuation Plan*, 2005 [hereinafter *Overview of the Louisiana Emergency Evacuation Plan*].

13 Under the plan, if contraflow into Mississippi is needed, the Louisiana governor will contact the Mississippi governor, who will make the decision whether to implement contraflow. *Source*: Chapman and Huff interview, Dec. 14, 2005, pp. 69-71**.** The improved LEEP has two possible contraflow route operations: Option 1, Louisiana contraflow to state line, which is full-lane reversal only within the borders of Louisiana; and Option 2, Mississippi contraflow to I-59 mile marker and to I-55 mile marker 31. Mississippi requests four hours advance notice for contraflow to the state line, three additional hours advance notice to start I-55 and I-59 contraflow operations if the state line operation is already in place, and seven hours notice to go straight into I-55 and I-59 contraflow operations. These points were chosen to end contraflow because of concerns about manpower and the desire to get traffic flowing normally prior to arrival at a major metropolitan area, particularly Hattiesburg. *Source*: Mississippi Department of Transportation, *Contraflow Plan for Interstate Hurricane Evacuation Traffic Control*, Aug. 2005, pp. 7, 20, 22, 37, 39; Chapman and Huff interview, Dec. 14, 2005, p. 50.

14 Committee staff interview of Lt. Col. Mark Oxley, Chief of Staff, Louisiana State Police and Lt. Col. Joseph Booth, Special Projects Deputy Superintendent, Louisiana State Police, conducted on Dec. 9, 2005, transcript pp. 33-34. Phase

three of LEEP includes areas on the East Bank of the Mississippi River in the New Orleans metropolitan area, which are within the levee protection system but remain vulnerable to a slow moving Category 3 or any Category 4 or 5 storm. *Source: Overview of the Louisiana Emergency Evacuation Plan.* Following Hurricane Dennis, during which Jefferson Parish evacuated out of plan order, Jefferson Parish President Aaron Broussard sent a letter in July 2005 to Governor Blanco criticizing part of the state's evacuation plan. According to the Jefferson Parish Director of Emergency Management, Dr. Walter Maestri, the plan put a tremendous burden on local law enforcement to get people through parish neighborhoods and onto the Interstates. Further, because of Jefferson Parish's geographic boundaries, citizens of the parish, depending on what part of the parish they reside, fall in Phase 1, Phase 2, and Phase 3 zones. So, "If we follow the State plan perfectly one of our three groups has got to leave at night in the dark." *Source:* Committee staff interview of Walter Maestri, Ph.D., Director, Jefferson Parish Office of Emergency Management, LA, conducted on Oct. 25, 2005, transcript pp. 90-92. It should be noted that Jefferson Parish followed the State Plan for the Katrina evacuation, although it helped matters for Jefferson Parish that the state operated the evacuation on a "compressed time line." While a "compressed time line" was in place for Hurricane Katrina, Jefferson Parish was criticized in Hurricane Dennis for compressing the time line of their evacuation. *Source:* Maestri interview, Oct. 27, 2005, pp. 20-21.

15 The LEEP is based on a phased evacuation process which calls for specific action by specified location at certain designated times before the scheduled landfall of a Category 2 or greater hurricane: (1) Phase 1 – at 50 hours before the onset of tropical storm winds, areas south of the intracoastal waterway may evacuate; (2) Phase 2 – at 40 hours before the onset of tropical storm force winds, areas south of the Mississippi River which are levee protected but remain vulnerable to Category 2 or higher storms may evacuate; (3) Phase 3 – at 30 hours before the onset of tropical storm force winds, areas along the East Bank of the Mississippi River in the New Orleans metropolitan area which are within the levee protection system but remain vulnerable to a slow moving Category 3 or any Category 4 or 5 storm may evacuate. The contraflow plan, reversing highway lanes so that all traffic can flow away from the potential impact area, is implemented during Phase 3. *Overview of the Louisiana Emergency Evacuation Plan.*

16 Whitehorn interview, Nov. 29, 2005, pp. 18-22.

17 Oxley and Booth interview, Dec. 9, 2005, pp. 167, 203.

18 Mayor Nagin, in testimony before the Committee on Feb. 1, 2006 stated, "Our region had one of the most successful mass evacuations in the history of the United States. Over 90% of our residents evacuated. Over one million people left the region within 24 hours." *Source:* Testimony of Mayor C. Ray Nagin, City of New Orleans, LA, before the U.S. Senate, Committee on Homeland Security and Governmental Affairs, hearing on *Hurricane Katrina: Managing the Crisis and Evacuating New Orleans* Feb. 1, 2006. In testimony before the Committee on Feb. 2, 2006, Governor Blanco stated that "1.3 million people" were moved to safety "through our contraflow plan." *Source:* Written Statement of Gov. Kathleen Blanco, Louisiana, for the U.S. Senate, Committee on Homeland Security and Governmental Affairs, hearing on *Hurricane Katrina: The Role of Governors in Managing the Catastrophe*, Feb. 2, 2006, p. 1.

19 Bradberry interview, Nov. 17, 2005, pp. 38-39.

20 Testimony of Gov. Haley Barbour, Mississippi, before the U.S. House, Select Bipartisan Committee to Investigate the Preparation for and Response to Hurricane Katrina, hearing on *Hurricane Katrina Preparedness and Response by the State of Mississippi*, Dec. 7, 2005.

21 Committee staff interview of Maj. John Miller, Highway Safety Patrol, Public Safety Department, MS, conducted on Dec. 14, 2005, transcript p. 18.

22 Maj. Miller interview, Dec. 12, 2005, p. 19.

23 Maj. Miller interview, Dec. 12, 2005, p. 31.

24 Committee staff interview of Larry Ingargiola, Emergency Manager, St. Bernard Parish, LA, conducted on Oct. 26, 2005, transcript p. 69-70.

25 Ingargiola interview, Oct. 26, 2005, p. 69.

26 Ingargiola interview, Oct. 26, 2005, p. 64.

27 Ingargiola interview, Oct. 26, 2005, p. 79.

28 Ingargiola interview, Oct. 26, 2005, p. 65.

29 Ingargiola interview, Oct. 26, 2005, p. 68.

30 Ingargiola interview, Oct. 26, 2005, p. 66. Mr. Ingargiola noted that it is his belief that it takes between 36 to 48 hours to evacuate that percentage of people from St. Bernard Parish. *Source:* Ingargiola interview, Oct. 26, 2005, p. 73. Additionally, Mr. Ingargiola stated that he was happy with this percentage, noting that, "I would have loved to see more people get out, but I don't think we would have been able to get more people out than what we did." *Source:* Ingargiola interview, Oct. 26, 2005, p. 100. "The ones that were left that we had to evacuate wouldn't have left no matter what. I don't think. We would have had to personally drag them out." *Source:* Ingargiola interview, Oct. 26, 2005, p. 153.

31 U.S. Census Bureau, "QuickFacts: St. Bernard Parish, Louisiana," 2004. http://quickfacts.census.gov/qfd/states/22/22087.html. Accessed on Mar. 27, 2006.

32 Ingargiola interview, Oct. 26, 2005, p. 75.

33 Ingargiola interview, Oct. 26, 2005, p. 75.

34 Committee staff interview of Jesse St. Amant, Director, Plaquemines Parish Office of Emergency Preparedness, con-

ducted on Nov. 9, 2005, transcript p. 23-25.

35 Louisiana, Preparation and Response to Hurricane Katrina Integrated Timeline, p. 13. Provided to Committee.

36 Committee staff interview of Dexter Accordo, Emergency Manager, St. Tammany Parish, LA, conducted on Nov. 10, 2005, transcript pp. 3-4.

37 Accordo interview, Nov. 10, 2005, p. 47.

38 Accordo interview, Nov. 10, 2005, p. 50.

39 Accordo interview, Nov. 10, 2005, p. 50.

40 Accordo interview, Nov. 10, 2005, pp. 94-95.

41 Accordo interview, Nov. 10, 2005, p. 95.

42 Accordo interview, Nov. 10, 2005, pp. 96-97.

43 Accordo interview, Nov. 10, 2005, p. 97.

44 Accordo interview, Nov. 10, 2005, pp. 108-109.

45 Maestri interview, Oct. 25, 2005, p. 7.

46 Maestri interview, Oct. 25, 2005, p. 102.

47 Maestri interview, Oct. 25, 2005, pp. 75-76; Committee staff interview of Walter Maestri, Ph.D., Director, Jefferson Parish Office of Emergency Management, LA, conducted on Oct. 27, 2005, transcript p. 37. Maestri stated that this estimation is based on the analysis conducted by the Survey Research Center of the University of New Orleans. Maestri interview, Oct. 27, 2005, p. 37.

48 Maestri interview, Oct. 25, 2005, pp. 98-99. Moreover, Maestri stated, "We define that as everybody who wanted to go had the opportunity to go in Jefferson [parish]. So from my perspective that was a success." Maestri interview, Oct. 25, 2005, p. 99.

49 Maestri interview, Oct. 25, 2005, pp. 102-103.

50 Maestri interview, Oct. 25, 2005, p. 76.

51 Maestri interview, Oct. 25, 2005, p. 76.

52 Maestri interview, Oct. 25, 2005, p. 166.

53 Maestri interview, Oct. 27, 2005, pp. 49-51.

54 Maestri interview, Oct. 25, 2005, p. 20.

55 City of New Orleans, Mayor's Press Room, Katrina Update, Talking Points, Aug. 27, 2005, 1 p.m. Provided to Committee.

56 "Mayor Urges Storm Preparations," New Orleans *Times-Picayune*, Aug. 27, 2005. http://www.nola.com/newslogs/breakingtp/index.ssf?/mtlogs/nola_Times-Picayune/archives/2005_08.html. Accessed on Mar. 21, 2006.

57 Gordon Russell, "Nagin orders first-ever mandatory evacuation of New Orleans," New Orleans *Times-Picayune*, Aug. 28, 2005. www.nola.com/newslogs/breakingtp/index.ssf?/mtlogs/nola_Times-Picayune/archives/2005_08.html. Accessed on Apr. 15, 2006. When announcing the mandatory evacuation, the Mayor said, "I am this morning, declaring that we will be doing a mandatory evacuation," and "I wish I had better news for you. But we are facing a storm that most of us have feared. I do not want to create panic. But I want the citizens to understand that this is very serious. … We sent out a fax to all the churches that we could this morning, basically alerting them to exactly what we're doing, and asking them to buddy up, to find members in their congregations, to check on the senior citizens or a citizen who may not … have the means and is totally reliant upon public transportation to get around." The Mayor noted that the Superdome would open to the general public as a refuge of last resort at 12 p.m. There were 12 locations identified by the Regional Transit Authority (RTA) and announced by the Mayor as designated pick-up points for individuals in need of transport to the Superdome. The locations were: (1) E.J. Morris Senior Center, 1616 Caffin Ave.; (2) Frantz, 9th Ward, 3811 N. Galvez St.; (3) Warren Easton, Mid-City, 3019 Canal St.; (4) Augustine, Mid-City, 425 S. Broad St.; (5) S. Williams, Uptown, 5712 S. Claiborne Ave.; (6) Rabouin, CBD, 727 Carrondelet St.; (7) Arthur Monday Center, 1111 Newton St.; (8) O. Perry Walker H.S., West Bank, 2832 General Meyers; (9) Abramson, New Orleans East, 5552 Read Blvd.; (10) N.O. Mission, 1130 Oretha Castle Halley Blvd.; (11) McMain Uptown, 5712 South Claiborne; (12) Sarah T. Reid High School, New Orleans East, 5316 Michoud Blvd. Mayor C. Ray Nagin, "New Orleans Mayor, Louisiana Governor Hold Press Conference," Aug. 28, 2005. http://transcripts.cnn.com/TRANSCRIPTS/0508/28/bn.04.html. Accessed on Mar. 27, 2006.

58 Mayor Nagin, Senate Committee hearing, Feb. 1, 2006.

59 Louisiana Statute 29:724D(5) authorizes the Governor to direct and compel the evacuation of all or part of the population from any stricken or threatened area within the state if he deems this action necessary for the preservation of life or other disaster mitigation, response, or recovery. Louisiana Statute 29:727F(5) authorizes parish presidents to direct and compel the evacuation of all or part of the population from any stricken or threatened area within the boundaries of the parish if he deems this action necessary for mitigation, response, or recovery measures.

60 The policy of the city's previous mayoral administration was to shun mandatory evacuation orders because they would be "difficult to enforce" in a city the size of New Orleans. *Source*: Tullier interview, Nov. 22, 2005, p. 16. But Mayor Nagin testified that his main concern with issuing a mandatory evacuation order was whether the city would have

adequate legal authority to do so. *Source*: Mayor Nagin, Senate Committee hearing, Feb. 1, 2006. According to Sally Forman, communications Director for Mayor Nagin, the Mayor made a decision on Saturday morning, Aug. 27, to call for a mandatory evacuation: "The Mayor said it in the Saturday morning meeting, make it happen. Saturday morning. He said if there is any way to make this happen, make it happen. I don't care what you have to do, make it happen." *Source*: Committee staff interview of Sally Forman, Communications Director, Office of the Mayor, City of New Orleans, LA, conducted on Jan. 10, 2006, transcript p. 18.

61 Sherry Landry, e-mail to Mayor Nagin and others, Aug. 27, 2005, 11:31 p.m. CT. Provided to Committee. The subject line is: Mandatory Evacuation Order and the text reads, "This is just a draft of a mandatory evac order. Please review. Are there any other exceptions that should be made?" The text of the draft follows this question. Another copy of the e-mail, a response from Col. Terry Ebbert to Sherry Landry and others, dated Aug. 27, 2005, shows the time of the Landry e-mail as 22:30:32 hours (or 10:30 p.m.). The reason for this time stamp discrepancy is not clear.

62 About an hour after the nursing-home exception was added to the draft order, Col. Terry Ebbert sent an e-mail to the city attorney to warn, "Many of the facilities are in single level buildings with marginal electrical back up. I recommend we not give them a opportunity to stay." Terry Ebbert, e-mail to Sherry Landry, Aug. 28, 2005, 12 a.m. CT. Provided to Committee.

63 Civil District Court for the Parish of Orleans, Promulgation of Emergency Orders, Aug. 28, 2005. Provided to Committee.

64 Testimony of Col. Terry Ebbert, Director, New Orleans Office of Homeland Security, LA, before the U.S. Senate, Committee on Homeland Security and Governmental Affairs, hearing on *Hurricane Katrina: Challenges in a Catastrophe: Evacuating New Orleans in Advance of Hurricane Katrina*, Jan. 31, 2006 ("The delay was basically designed in and occurred because of the difficulties with doing something that [we had not] done before. And that is one of the challenges that we face this year is we have to, ahead of time, one, decide, what mandatory evacuation means. Two, what measures, legal measures, are we going to utilize to carry it out? Are we going to force people with police out of their particular homes? And then, three, ensure that when we issue that, that we have the capability to move these people.").

65 Testimony of Gov. Kathleen Blanco, Louisiana, before the U.S. House, Select Bipartisan Committee to Investigate the Preparation for and Response to Hurricane Katrina, hearing on *Hurricane Katrina: Preparedness and Response by the State of Louisiana*, Dec. 14, 2005; Maestri interview, Oct. 25, 2005, p. 109 ("[The Mayor of New Orleans] has a large population that doesn't have the resources to evacuate on their own. They either don't have vehicles or their vehicles are not roadworthy. And that's a real problem, if you take non-roadworthy vehicles onto the interstate and onto the evacuation plan you stop it, you halt it. Nobody is going to be able to get out if these cars all start breaking down. So you have got to have this plan to deal with that.").

66 Mayor Ray Nagin, letter to the Honorable Mary Landrieu, Oct. 1, 2002 ("As many as 100,000 residents of New Orleans have no means of transportation, rendering it impossible for them to evacuate the City."); City of New Orleans, FY2006, Funding Request to Congress, Emergency Response Shelter/Plan Homeland Security Appropriations, Attachment: "The Louisiana Superdome: Refuge of Last Resort." Provided to Committee.

67 Tullier interview, Nov. 22, 2005, p. 18. Tullier served as Interim Director beginning in May 2001 and became Director shortly after Mayor Nagin was elected to office. Tullier interview, Nov. 22, 2005, pp. 5-6.

68 Our Brother's Keeper (OBK) was a faith-based initiative developed in collaboration with Kay Wilkins, local chapter director of the American Red Cross. Tullier interview, Nov. 22, 2005, pp. 18-20, 78-80.

69 In addition to OBK, Tullier had informal conversations with representatives from the Regional Transportation Authority, the Orleans Parish School Board, and Amtrak about using their transportation assets to move people out of high-risk areas. *Source*: Tullier interview, Nov. 22, 2005, p. 22. No formal agreements emerged, but in preparation for Hurricane Ivan, RTA buses had been staged to deliver citizens to the Superdome from assembly points throughout the city. *Source*: Tullier interview, Nov. 22, 2005, p. 20.

70 Tullier interview, Nov. 22, 2005, p. 81.

71 Committee staff interview of Kay Wilkins, Chief Executive Officer, Southeast Louisiana Chapter, American Red Cross, conducted on Dec. 20, 2005, transcript p. 27.

72 Wilkins interview, Dec. 20, 2005, p. 92 ("You had to first identify a lot of other intricacies. How are we going to meet, where are we going to go, how are we going to be sure who picks them up at the right time, bring them back at the right time? What about food, sitting in traffic? All of that takes a very simple solution and makes it extremely complex and challenging.").

73 Committee staff interview of Kevin Stephens, M.D., Director, New Orleans Health Department, conducted on Nov. 9, 2005, transcript p. 25.

74 Dr. Stephens interview, Nov. 9, 2005, pp. 21-22. In addition to Amtrak, RTA, and the Orleans School Board, also made contact with the Delta Queen river boat.

75 Dr. Stephens interview, Nov. 9, 2005, pp. 26-28.

76 Recognizing that the city would need to make contact with other parishes regarding the MOUs, in April or May 2005, Dr. Stephens provided the drafts to the Director of the Office of Emergency Preparedness, Joseph Matthews. *Source*: Dr. Stephens interview, Nov. 9, 2005, pp. 23-24. The draft MOUs became part of the discussion on a larger, comprehensive evacuation plan for the city. Matthews said he started conversations with various agencies, including Amtrak, RTA, and the school board, sometime between March and May 2005, adding, "It was basically my office taking the lead." *Source*:

Matthews interview, Jan. 10, 2005, pp. 14, 30. Matthews did not know whether conversations with these entities had begun before his tenure. *Source*: Matthews interview, Jan. 10, 2005, p. 13.

77 Matthews interview, Jan. 10, 2006, pp. 43-44.

78 Col. Ebbert interview, Jan. 10, 2006, p. 44

79 Col. Ebbert interview, Jan. 10, 2006, p. 44

80 Matthews interview, Jan. 10, 2006, p. 36 ("We brought the state in on the end. … The state – we were planning on bringing other entities in as we went along. First we were going to try locally, then reaching out, getting the MOUs, and then moving forward."). Also, the record is not clear as to the level of contact Dr. Stephens made with the state government to help the city execute these MOUs. Once the Louisiana Office of Homeland Security and Emergency Preparedness (LOHSEP) became aware in late May 2005 that the city was working on a plan to obtain outside transportation, LOHSEP officials sought to meet with the City's Office of Emergency Preparedness. *Source*: Fontenot interview, Jan. 10, 2006, pp. 133-135 (indicating that Dr. Stephens had discussed these MOUs with Dr. Jimmy Guidry, Medical Director, Louisiana Department of Health and Hospitals, and the State Health Officer for Louisiana). According to the then-Chief of Planning for LOHSEP, Sean Fontenot, the newly appointed New Orleans Office of Emergency Preparedness Director, Matthews, told LOHSEP officials in late May that he was not aware of what Dr. Stephens was doing. *Source*: Fontenot interview, Jan. 10, 2006, pp. 133-135.

81 U.S. Department of Homeland Security, Detailed Project Report by Project Type, Aug. 22, 2005, pp. 3, 13.

82 New Orleans Office of Emergency Preparedness, *Comprehensive Emergency Management Plan*, May 2005 [hereinafter *New Orleans* CEMP]. The Plan defines the role of the primary agency as follows:

> An ESF primary agency is responsible for:
>
> 1. Coordinating response efforts within the functional area in order to achieve the specified desired outcome;
>
> 2. Providing an appropriate level of staffing for effective operation;
>
> 3. Activating and subtasking support agencies;
>
> 4. Managing mission assignments and coordinating tasks with support agencies;
>
> 5. Supporting and keeping other ESF primary agencies and organizational elements informed of ESF operational priorities and activities;
>
> 6. Obtaining equipment, supplies, and services as required following established regulations, policies, and procedures;
>
> 7. Coordinating response efforts with appropriate regional, state, and federal responders and support agencies, and volunteer support organizations;
>
> 8. Supporting planning for short and long term emergency and disaster operations.
>
> *New Orleans* CEMP, Appendix: Emergency Support Functions.

83 *New Orleans* CEMP, Appendix: Emergency Support Functions, p. 3.

84 *New Orleans* CEMP, Annex I: Hurricanes, p. 18.

85 The Plan defines the role of a supporting agency as:

> An ESF support agency is responsible for:
>
> 1. Supporting the ESF primary agency by conducting operation using its authority, capabilities, and resources;
>
> 2. Supporting the ESF primary agency mission assignments;
>
> 3. Providing status and resource information to the primary agency;
>
> 4. Supporting planning for short and long term emergency and disaster operations.
>
> *New Orleans* CEMP, Appendix: Emergency Support Functions, p. 3.

86 Committee staff interview of James Tillie, Safety Director, Regional Transit Authority, City of New Orleans, LA, conducted on Dec. 19, 2005, transcript p. 18. As a political sub-division of the State of Louisiana, the RTA does not report directly to the Mayor. As a quasi-governmental agency, it is funded by local taxes, fares collected on the buses and federal funding sources. Committee staff interview of William Deville, General Manager and Chief Executive Officer, Regional Transit Authority, City of New Orleans, LA, conducted on Nov. 22, 2005, transcript pp. 5-6.

87 *New Orleans* CEMP, pp. 2-3.

88 *New Orleans* CEMP, pp. 9-10.

89 Matthews interview, Jan. 10, 2006, pp. 9-10.

90 Deville interview, Nov. 22, 2005, pp. 40, 42.

91 Tillie interview, Dec. 19, 2005, p. 11.

92 Deville interview, Nov. 22, 2005, p. 64.

93 James Tillie, e-mail to William Deville, Oct. 23, 2005, 11:29 a.m. Provided to Committee. The e-mail had a cc to Pat Judge and was in regard to RTA Activities for Hurricane Katrina. ("Nothing significant occurred on Saturday, August 27, 2005 as it relates to the RTA. I asked Chief Matthews, Director of the OEP if RTA would be required to evacuate citizens from the CITY OF NEW ORLEANS. Chief Matthews stated that shelters had not been identified. Therefore, RTA was not needed on Saturday, August 27, 2005. On Sunday, August 28, 2005 at about 9:00 a.m. I had another conversation with Chief Matthews relative to evacuating citizens from the CITY OF NEW ORLEANS. I advised him that RTA had approximately 100 operators and buses at Canal Station available to evacuate citizens out of town. Chief Matthews advised me that they still had not identified shelters to receive evacuees."). The Orleans Parish School Board (the School Board) designee to the EOC reported that he left a voice-mail message for the Director of the Office of Emergency Preparedness on Friday, August 26, to ask if the School Board's buses and drivers would be needed to evacuate the city, but said he never heard back and assumed the School Board's buses weren't needed. *Source:* Committee staff interview of Ed Johnson, Safety and Training Manager, New Orleans Public Schools, LA, conducted on Nov. 29, 2005, transcript pp. 10-11, 20-21. It is unclear how useful the School Board's offer on Friday would have been since that same School Board employee reported that the school buses were not moved to high ground because there were too few bus drivers working on a pay-day Friday afternoon. *Source:* Johnson interview, Nov. 29, 2005, pp. 33-34.

94 Matthews interview, Jan. 10, 2006, pp. 20-21, 44 ("It was a well known fact that drivers were the impediment."); Col. Ebbert interview, Jan. 10, 2006, p. 50 (stating that the city's need for evacuation drivers "was always a constant discussion").

95 Matthews interview, Jan. 10, 2006, pp. 43-44 ("Q: Did you have buses? A: Well, yes, that's what we were told by RTA and the New Orleans public school system that there were busses. They had identified a number of buses, but as always, drivers were the problem. I think it was like 350 buses or something like that that were identified."). Despite this assertion, as noted in above endnote, RTA and OPSB officials assert that they offered buses and drivers.

96 Under Louisiana law, the Orleans Parish School Board (the School Board) is a constituted corporate body, and is funded by local taxes and state and federal funding sources. *Source:* La. R.S. 15:51. The School Board had 324 functional buses and approximately 250 drivers, available at least on a part-time basis. *Source:* Committee staff interview of Marva White, Director, Transportation Department, Orleans Parish School Board, LA, conducted on Nov. 23, 2005, transcript p. 12. Approximately 260 buses were lost to flooding. *Source:* White interview, Nov. 23, 2005, p. 14. These resources presumably could have been utilized if emergency planners had arranged for drivers, fuel, and destinations for evacuees, and resolved liability issues, employment contract concerns, and logistical issues.

97 Matthews interview, Jan. 10, 2006, pp. 22-25 ("We have buses, we have everything but drivers."). However, other state and federal officials, who participated in that workshop, recalled the city informing them of a need for buses, as well: According to the notes from the July 2005 workshop, Don Day of the U.S. Department of Transportation said, "We're less than 10% done with this trans[portation] planning when you consider the buses and the people," and Col. William Doran of the Louisiana Office of Homeland Security and Emergency Preparedness said, "buses we are tapping will be from the Parish. Might not be able to get a driver. Orleans Parish might be RTA buses. Drivers not provided." *Source:* IEM, Inc., notes from Unified Command Final Briefing, July 29, 2005, p. 4.

98 Matthews interview, Jan. 10, 2006, pp. 22-25 (Interview question: "At any time prior to Hurricane Katrina did you make a request for assistance from the state or federal government for drivers?" Matthews answer: "No.").

99 Committee staff interview of Jules Hurst, Transportation Supervisor, Logistics Branch, FEMA, conducted on Jan. 27, 2006, transcript p. 37.

100 Committee staff interview of Dan Prevo, former Region VI Regional Emergency Transportation Representative, U.S. Department of Transportation, conducted on Jan. 17, 2006, transcript pp. 12-14.

101 Deville interview, Nov. 22, 2005, p. 50.

102 Under the state's plan, LA DOTD was responsible for "identifying," "mobilizing," and "coordinating" transportation for the evacuation of at risk populations. Under the LA EOP ESF #1, DOTD is charged with the following:

Under ESF #1, I. Purpose: ESF 1 provides transportation out of a disaster area for people in need, and provides transportation essential to support emergency response in the event of a disaster.

Under ESF #1, II. Scope: The State services provided under this ESF will include the identification, mobilization and coordination of available state owned, private industry and volunteer transportation equipment, manpower and technical expertise to meet the requirements of providing essential emergency response in the event of an emergency or disaster.

Under ESF #1, III.A. Concept of Operations, Mitigation: The Secretary of [DOTD] will designate an ESF 1 Emergency Transportation Coordinator to organize and coordinate transportation services.

Under ESF #1, III.B.1. Concept of Operations, Preparedness: The Coordinator will develop plans and procedures to mobilize transportation to support emergency evacuation for at risk populations and to support other operations of State Agencies.

Under ESF #1, III.B.2. Concept of Operations, Preparedness: The Coordinator will maintain information about transportation resources, with particular emphasis on resources in or near state risk areas.

Under ESF #1, III.C.1. Concept of Operations, Response: The Coordinator will process requests for transportation and arrange for National Guard, state agency, private industry and volunteer resources to be allocated to the highest priority missions.

Under ESF #1, III.C.2. Concept of Operations, Response: The Coordinator will continue to acquire, allocate and monitor transportation resources as the emergency continues.

Under ESF #1, IV.A. Organization and Responsibilities: The [DOTD] has the Primary Responsibility for Emergency Transportation. That responsibility includes coordinating with support agencies to make sure that they develop and maintain plans and procedures.

Under ESF #1, VIII. Plan Maintenance: This ESF 1 Transportation Coordinator is responsible for developing, maintaining and coordinating plans, procedures, arrangements and agreements in support of this ESF. Louisiana Office of Homeland Security and Emergency Preparedness, *Emergency Operations Plan*, Apr. 2005, ESF-1 [hereinafter *Louisiana Emergency Operations Plan*].

It should also be noted that DOTD is listed as a supporting agency under the New Orleans OEP Comprehensive Emergency Management Plan. *New Orleans* CEMP, Emergency Support Functions Appendix, p. 3.

103 Fontenot interview, Jan. 10, 2006, pp. 22-23.

104 Fontenot interview, Jan. 10, 2006, pp. 25-26.

105 Sec. Bradberry interview, Dec. 21, 2005, p. 68.

106 U.S. Senate, Committee on Homeland Security and Governmental Affairs, hearing on *Challenges in a Catastrophe: Evacuating New Orleans in Advance of Hurricane Katrina*, Jan. 31, 2006.

107 Sec. Bradberry interview, Nov. 17, 2005, pp. 47-48 ("I had a confidence level that the city was addressing that issue.").

108 Sec. Bradberry interview, Dec. 21, 2005, pp. 84-85.

109 LA DOTD's Assistant Secretary for Operations, Gordon Nelson, said he first became aware that the State was expecting LA DOTD to be responsible for ESF-1 Transportation, specifically, buses for an evacuation, at a July 2005 meeting of the Southeast Louisiana Task Force in St. Charles Parish. Committee staff interview of Gordon Nelson, Assistant Secretary for Operations, Louisiana Department of Transportation and Development, conducted on Jan. 6, 2006, transcript pp. 52-55. Committee staff interview of Joseph Modicut, Emergency Services Coordinator, Louisiana Department of Transportation and Development, conducted on Jan. 5, 2006, transcript pp. 38-39.

110 Nelson interview, Jan. 6, 2006, pp. 58-59.

111 Sec. Johnny Bradberry, letter to the Honorable Susan Collins and the Honorable Joseph Lieberman, Re: Supplemental Testimony, Feb. 14, 2006. Provided to Committee.

112 Committee staff interview of James Ballow, Senior Operations Officer, LOHSEP, conducted on Jan. 4, 2006, transcript p. 151.

113 *Louisiana Emergency Operations Plan*, p. ESF-5–1.

114 *Louisiana Emergency Operations Plan*, p. ESF-5–1.

115 Ballow interview, Jan. 4, 2006, p. 154.

116 Fontenot interview, Jan. 10, 2006, pp. 22-23 (Discussing Jan. 2005 meeting, attended by Modicut, Nelson, LOHSEP Acting Deputy Director Col. Jeff Smith, and LOHSEP Chief of Planning Sean Fontenot, regarding LOHSEP's intention to reassign ESF-1 responsibilities to LA DOTD.).

117 Fontenot interview, Jan. 10, 2006, pp. 24-25.

118 As Col. Jeff Smith stated, "Well, they [DOTD] signed off on the plan, so you know, the assumption has to be that they understood that that was the role or I would assume they wouldn't have signed off on the plan." Committee staff interview of Col. Jeff Smith, Acting Deputy Director, LOHSEP, conducted on Jan. 13, 2006, transcript pp. 171-172.

119 Committee staff interview of Maj. Gen. Bennett Landreneau, Adjutant General, Louisiana, conducted on Jan. 11, 2006, transcript p. 154 (Responding affirmatively to a question whether LOHSEP's discharge of its duty to ensure that LA DOTD met its responsibilities under ESF-1 "slipped through the cracks.").

120 Gov. Kathleen Blanco, letter to President George Bush, Aug. 27, 2005, pp. 2 and Enclosure.

121 In the letter to President Bush, Governor Blanco sought the following distribution of funds to assist the state with the coordination of the evacuation, but she did not specify a request for transportation resources:

> Louisiana State Police (LSP): Costs to support evacuations (Providing support for the phased evacuation of the coastal areas) – $300,000 for a non-direct landfall.

> Louisiana Department of Wildlife and Fisheries (WLF): Costs to support evacuations (Supporting the evacuation of the affected population and preparing for search and rescue missions) – $200,000 for a non-direct landfall.

> Louisiana Department of Transportation and Development (DOTD): Costs to support evacuations (Coordinating traffic flow and management of the evacuation routes with local officials and the state of Mississippi) – $2,000,000 for a non-direct landfall.

Letter from Governor Blanco to President George Bush, Aug. 27, 2005, pp. 2 and Enclosure.

122 Col. Jeff Smith, FEMA Daily Video Teleconference, Aug. 28, 2005, p. 17. Provided to Committee ("I'll just tell you that the evacuation process is going much better than it did during Hurricane Ivan. Nobody anticipated that it would be easy. Nobody anticipated that there wouldn't be traffic jams. But by and large, it has gone much better than it did with Ivan.").

123 Col. Jeff Smith, FEMA Daily Video Teleconference, Aug. 28, 2005, p. 16. Provided to Committee.

124 Committee staff interview of Darryl Neely, Policy Advisor, Office of the Governor, Mississippi, conducted on Jan. 21, 2006, transcript p. 12-14.

125 Contraflow is a program designed for quick emergency evacuation of an area. Some incoming highway lanes to a city are changed to outbound lanes.

126 Mississippi Department of Transportation, Mississippi Hurricane Evacuation Guide, 2006. http://www.mdot.state. ms.us/cetrp/ms_coastal_hurricane_05_01_06.pdf. Accessed on May 5, 2006.

127 Harrison County, Standard Operating Procedures for Hurricane Evacuation, May 2003, p. 1. Harrison County's Standard Operating Procedures for Hurricane Evacuation state that a number of factors must be considered in deciding whether to order an evacuation. Among them are "the characteristics of the hurricane itself. Magnitude, intensity, spread of onset, and duration are all significant elements to be considered. These will determine the number of people to be evacuated and the time and distance of travel necessary to insure safety. Another important facet is the availability of evacuation routes, their capacities, and their vulnerability to hurricanes. Mode of transport is also very significant and provisions must be made for those persons unable to supply their own transportation."

128 Committee staff interview of Robert Latham, Executive Director, Mississippi Emergency Management Agency (MEMA), conducted on Jan. 27, 2006, transcript pp. 51-52, 56.

129 Committee staff interview of Robert Chapman, State Transportation Emergency Coordinator, Mississippi Department of Transportation, conducted on Dec. 13, 2005, transcript p. 32. Testimony of Robert Latham, Executive Director, MEMA, before the U.S. House, Select Bipartisan Committee to Investigate the Preparation for and Response to Hurricane Katrina, hearing on Hurricane Katrina: Preparedness and Response by the State of Mississippi, Dec. 7, 2005.

130 Latham interview, Jan. 27, 2006, p. 25. Latham, House Select Committee hearing, Dec. 7, 2005.

131 MEMA, Hurricane Situation Report, Aug. 24, 2005, 10 a.m. Provided to Committee; filed as Bates no. MEMA-0010808.

132 MEMA, Hurricane Situation Report, Aug. 26, 2005, 4:30 p.m. Provided to Committee; filed as Bates no. MEMA-0010828.

133 MEMA, Hurricane Situation Report, Aug. 27, 2005, 12 noon. Provided to Committee; filed as Bates no. MEMA-0010834. State agencies also began preparing for the evacuation of Louisiana residents. On Saturday, Louisiana's Department of Transportation informed Mississippi's Department of Transportation that it would begin implementing contraflow (which reverses the flow of traffic on some inbound highway lanes) later that afternoon. State law enforcement officers were deployed along the routes and in communities to assist evacuation operations. Mississippi had revised its evacuation plan after encountering traffic problems during Hurricane Ivan in 2004. Chapman and Huff interview, Dec. 14, 2005, pp. 12-20; Neely interview, Jan. 21, 2006, pp. 5-7.

134 Robert Latham, e-mail to various Mississippi officials, Aug. 26, 2005, 3:46 p.m. Provided to Committee.

135 Robert Latham, e-mail to various Mississippi officials, Aug. 26, 2005, 3:46 p.m. Provided to Committee ("The big question now is will our citizens evacuate if they are asked to do so? I plan to go to the coast tomorrow.").

136 Latham interview, Jan. 27, 2006, pp. 37-39.

137 MEMA's emergency operations plan emphasizes the importance of coordinating evacuations within and among counties. Source: MEMA, Mississippi Comprehensive Emergency Management Plan, 1999, Section ESF-1–4. MEMA's Executive Director, Robert Latham, told committee staff that after Hurricane Dennis, he was concerned about lack of clarity in evacuation orders. Officials, particularly in Harrison County, had considered evacuating by flood zone, whereas many coastal residents didn't know in which zone they lived. Latham met with coastal emergency management officials to streamline the process. "If you are doing a mandatory in one area and the county next to you or the city next to you is only doing a recommended … it gets confusing." Source: Latham interview, Jan. 27, 2006, pp. 32-33.

138 Local governments currently make evacuation decisions without criteria on the conditions that need to be in place for a "recommended" evacuation, "strongly recommended" evacuation and "mandatory" evacuation.

139 MEMA, Hurricane Katrina Situation Report, Aug. 28, 2005, 4 p.m.

140 Committee staff interview of Tom McAllister, Director, Response and Recovery, MEMA, conducted on Jan. 27, 2006, transcript p. 37.

141 McAllister interview, Jan. 27, 2006, pp. 36-40.

142 Latham interview, Jan. 27, 2006, p. 43.

143 Committee staff interview of Max Mayfield, Ph.D., Director, National Hurricane Center, conducted on Jan. 27, 2006, transcript p. 56.

144 Mayfield said that he had only made such a call to warn a governor once before in his career. He stated that "I just wanted to be able to go to sleep that night knowing I had done everything I could do." John Pain, "Federal Forecasters Got Hurricane Right," Associated Press Online, Sept. 16, 2005.

145 Latham interview, Jan. 27, 2006, pp. 36. 54.

146 Latham interview, Jan. 27, 2006, pp. 36-37. Committee staff interview of Maj. Wayne Payne, Deputy Sheriff, Harrison County, MS, conducted on Dec. 6, 2005, transcript p. 25.

147 The three Mississippi coastal counties are Hancock, Harrison, and Jackson, commonly referred to as the "Mississippi Gulf Coast." Pearl River, Stone, and George lie directly to the north.

148 Since many residents weren't sure in what zone they lived, Jackson County decided to call for evacuation by topographical area. Committee staff interview of Butch Loper, Emergency Management Director, Jackson County, MS, conducted on Dec. 6, 2005, transcript pp. 39-40.

149 MEMA, Director's Brief, Aug. 29, 2005, 5:02 p.m. Provided to Committee; filed as Bates no. 0010700.

150 See Chapter 24, Medical Assistance, for a discussion of nursing home evacuations.

151 Maj. Payne interview, Dec. 6, 2005, pp. 5, 25.

152 Maj. Payne interview, Dec. 6, 2005, p. 25.

153 Committee staff interview of Paul Bennett, Deputy Chief of Police, City of Gulfport, MS, conducted on Dec. 8. 2005, transcript p. 8.

154 Ryan LaFontaine, "Police Issued Life-or-Death Directive," *Sun Herald*, Feb. 18, 2006; Joshua Norman, "Why Did They Stay," *Sun Herald*, Feb. 18, 2006.

155 Ryan LaFontaine, "Police Issued Life-or-Death Directive," *Sun Herald*, Feb. 18, 2006; Joshua Norman, "Why Did They Stay," *Sun Herald*, Feb. 18, 2006.

156 Neely interview, Jan. 21, 2006, pp. 13-14.

157 Maj. Payne interview, Dec. 6, 2005, p. 23-27.

158 Ryan LaFontaine, "Police Issued Life-or-Death Directive," *Sun Herald*, Feb. 18, 2006; Joshua Norman, "Why Did They Stay," *Sun Herald*, Feb. 18, 2006.

159 Latham interview, Jan. 27, 2006, p. 39.

160 Committee staff interview of Col. Joseph Spraggins, Director, Harrison County Emergency Management Agency, MS, conducted on Nov. 17, 2005, transcript, pp. 65-66.

161 Chapman interview, Dec. 13, 2005, pp. 39-40.

162 Latham, House Select Committee hearing, Dec. 7, 2005.

163 In addition, MDOT now publicizes alternative routes, coordinates the traffic signals on Highway 49, and has published a brochure on evacuation guidelines. Chapman interview, Dec. 13, 2005, pp. 38-40.

164 Chapman interview, Dec. 14, 2005, p. 34. Chapman interview, Dec. 13, 2005, p. 33. Latham, House Select Committee hearing, Dec. 7, 2005.

165 MEMA, Director's Brief, Aug. 28, 2005, 7 p.m.

166 MEMA, Director's Brief, Aug. 29, 2005, 4:30 p.m..

167 Committee staff interview of Willie Huff, Law Enforcement Coordinator, Mississippi Department of Transportation, conducted on Dec. 14, 2005, transcript pp. 34-35.

168 Testimony of Sec. Michael Chertoff, U.S. Department of Homeland Security, before U.S. House, Select Bipartisan Committee to Investigate the Preparation for and Response to Hurricane Katrina, hearing on *Hurricane Katrina: The Role of the Department of Homeland Security,* Oct. 19, 2005.

169 During an interview with HSGAC staff, the Federal Commanding Officer for Baton Rouge affirmatively responded that the federal government did not begin evacuations until the state made the request. Committee staff interview of William Lokey, Federal Coordinating Officer for Hurricane Katrina in Louisiana, FEMA, conducted on Jan. 20, 2006, transcript p. 124. At the Orleans Parish level, Col. Terry Ebbert noted, "Pre-landfall evacuation was a city, state, region function." Col. Ebbert interview, Jan. 10, 2006, p. 109.

170 U.S. Department of Homeland Security, *National Response Plan.* Washington: Government Printing Office, Dec. 2004, p. 15 [hereinafter *NRP*].

171 IEM Inc., 2004 Louisiana Catastrophic Hurricane Planning Exercise, Executive Summary. Provided to Committee.

172 Lokey interview, Jan. 20, 2006, p. 62.

173 U.S. Department of Transportation, Regional Transportation Representative, Region 6, Don Day, transcript of Unified Command Final Briefing, July 29, 2005, p. 4 ("600 buses needed just to move people from collection points. … We need to pre-identify the sources for these buses and have them lined up and ready. There are plans to evacuate buses and operators out before the storm. Requires forethought, prior action. We have never looked into what it takes to make a bus staging/dispatch area. … We're at less than 10% done with this trans planning."). It also became known to DOT officials that the city lacked drivers for the buses. *Source*: Prevo interview, Jan. 17, 2006, pp. 12-14. (Stating that based on the Pam discussions, there was "no certainty that the drivers — if the buses would be made available, that the drivers would be available … a whole lot of research had to be done with regard to how many drivers would be available, or the liability issues that might be faced for the buses and for the drivers."); Hurst interview, Jan. 27, 2006, p. 37 (Recalling that local officials in the Pam follow up workshops reported "they didn't know if they could get the drivers to report."). From discussions at the transportation working group, state and local officials expected that the federal government would help the state and locals with the evacuation. *Source*: Committee staff interview of Dolph Diemont, Region X, Regional Emergency Transportation Representative, U.S. Department of Transportation, conducted on Jan. 6, 2006, transcript pp. 30-31 ("The

people that were involved in that work group must have sensed the same thing that I did, that there was a large reliance on the federal team coming in and fixing everything. … The state and locals had some plan in place for evacuation with buses, school buses and other buses, and they knew that FEMA would have to augment that in some way.").

174 Diemont interview, Jan. 6, 2006, pp. 30-31.

175 In September 2005, after Katrina had made landfall, IEM (FEMA's contractor for the Hurricane Pam exercise) published and distributed a transportation annex to the Southeast Louisiana Catastrophic Hurricane Plan, and this transportation annex reflected the upshot of conversations had during the Hurricane Pam July 2005 transportation working group meetings. *Southeast Louisiana Catastrophic Hurricane Plan*, prepared by IEM, Inc. for LOHSEP and FEMA, Sept. 2005, Appendix 1, p. 1(Noting that "local/state/federal" officials "pre-landfall" should "identify/validate … 600 buses [and] 1,200 drivers").

176 U.S. Department of Transportation, Hurricane Katrina-Situation Report, Sept. 3, 2005, 5 p.m., p. 2. Provided to Committee; U.S. Department of Transportation, Actions for Hurricane Katrina, Annotated Chronology of Significant Events, Oct. 6, 2005, p. 8.

177 Committee staff interview of Vincent Pearce, Manager, National Response Program, Department of Transportation, conducted on Jan. 6, 2006, transcript p. 46 ("We looked at Atlanta. We actually – they actually called and talked to transit fleets, the phrase I remember was "all the way East to Jacksonville," and I know all the way West to El Paso, to determine what those fleets had, what their plans were, how they might be able to participate in an evacuation if it were to be needed.").

178 FEMA, MA Task Order Form, Sept. 20, 2005, p. 1. Provided to Committee.

179 Air Mobility Command, Aeromedical Evacuation Inputs NDMS Patient Movement AAR, briefing slides, Dec. 12-13, 2005. http://www1.va.gov/emshg/page.cfm?pg=111. Accessed on Mar. 15, 2006.

180 Deville interview, Nov. 22, 2005, pp. 136, 143 ("They're responsible for oversight on all of our grants and our projects. They meet with us quarterly to review all of our projects and the way we – plus they're also responsible, doing procurement reviews and financial reviews, triennial reviews. I mean, they're really reviewing the books. We see 'em quite often. So I got to know Bob [USDOT] pretty well in that regard.").

181 U.S. Department of Transportation, Hurricane Katrina-Situation Report, Aug. 29, 2005, 5 p.m., pp. 5-6. Provided to Committee.

182 Patrick Rhode, e-mail to Edward Buikema, Michael Lowder and Ken Burris, Aug. 28, 10:16 a.m. Provided to Committee ("Have we asked all eoc's via emac or esf (transportation) to make transportation assets available to assist New Orleans today with evacuations? I know we need 72 hours to do this – we don't have it – not sure what state is applying if someone can get some granularity on this issue.").

183 Oxley and Booth interview, Dec. 9, 2005, p. 203.

184 Committee staff interview of Michael Brown, former Director, FEMA, conducted on Feb. 23, 2006, transcript pp. 62-67.

185 Sec. Chertoff, House Select Committee hearing, Oct. 19, 2005. Others agreed: FEMA's logistic branch transportation supervisor Jules Hurst, who recalled having a discussion about pre-landfall evacuation during the Pam planning sessions, testified: "Pre-landfall is definitely desirable to post-landfall, because the population being evacuated obviously doesn't suffer the effects of the storm, at least hopefully." *Source:* Hurst interview, Jan. 27, 2006, p. 54. The city's Director of Homeland Security and Public Safety similarly testified that in a catastrophe, "evacuation is the number one priority." *Source:* Col. Ebbert interview, Jan. 10, 2006, p. 41.

186 42 U.S.C. § 5195 ("The Congress recognizes that the organizational structure established jointly by the Federal government and the States and their political subdivisions for emergency preparedness purposes can be effectively utilized to provide relief and assistance to people in areas of the Untied States struck by a hazard. The Federal government shall provide necessary direction, and guidance, and shall provide necessary assistance, as authorized in this title so that a comprehensive emergency preparedness system exists for all hazards.").

187 42 U.S.C. § 5195a(3)(A).

188 On February 28, 2003, President Bush modified Executive Order 12148, delegating most presidential responsibilities under the Stafford Act to DHS (rather than to FEMA, as had previously been the case). 68 Fed. Reg. 10619 (Feb. 28, 2003), Sec. 52. ("Executive Order 12148 of July 20, 1979 ('Federal Emergency Management'), as amended, is further amended by: (a) striking 'the Federal Emergency Management Agency' whenever it appears and inserting 'the Department of Homeland Security' in lieu thereof; and (b) striking 'the Director of the Federal Emergency Management Agency' wherever it appears and inserting 'the Secretary of Homeland Security' in lieu thereof."). *See also:* Executive Order 12673, 54 Fed. Reg. 12573 (Mar. 28, 1989), Sec. 1 (amending Executive Order 12148).

189 42 U.S.C. § 5170b(a)(3).

190 6 U.S.C. § 317(a).

191 6 U.S.C. § 317(a).

192 *Louisiana Emergency Operations Plan*, Apr. 2005, Appendix 3, Animal Management in Disasters.

193 *NRP*, pp. 14, 41, ESF-11. Neither the Hurricane Pam exercise nor the resultant Southeast Louisiana Catastrophic Hurricane Plan contemplated the shelter and transportation of pets.

194 Sebastian E. Heath, Phillip H. Kass, Alan M. Beck, and Larry T. Glickman, "Human and Pet-related Risk Factors for Household Evacuation Failure During a Natural Disaster," *American Journal of Epidemiology*, 153:7, p. 659.

195 *See e.g.*: Stephen Nohlgren, "Without Fido, some won't flee," *St. Petersburg Times*, Aug. 26, 2005. http://www.sptimes.com/2005/08/26/news_pf/Weather/Without_Fido_some_wo.shtml; *See also*: "Katrina survivors face dilemma over pets," Reuters, Sept. 8, 2005. http://www.msnbc.msn.com/id/9260578/did/9260578/print/1/displaymode/1098/; Maryann Mott, "Katrina Pet Rescue Efforts Offer Lessons for the Future," National Geographic News, Sept. 21, 2005. (http://news.nationalgreographic.com/news/2005/09/0921_050921_disaster_pet_tips.html. Accessed on Apr. 24, 2006.

196 Sebastian E. Heath, Phillip H. Kass, Alan M. Beck, and Larry T. Glickman, "Human and Pet-related Risk Factors for Household Evacuation Failure During a Natural Disaster," *American Journal of Epidemiology*, 153:7, pp. 662-663.

197 New Orleans Police Department, Initial (30-day) After Action Report-Summary. Provided to Committee. *See also*: Matthews interview, Oct. 14, 2005, pp. 37-38 ("A lot of people would not evacuate because a pet is part of their family. If their pet can't go with them, then they chose not to leave.").

198 American Humane Association, *Summary Report of the National Emergency Animal Management Summit*, Jan. 8-9, 2006, p. 11.

199 Maryann Mott, "Katrina Pet Rescue Efforts Offer Lessons for the Future," National Geographic News, Sept. 21, 2005. http://news.nationalgeographic.com/news/2005/09/0921_050921_disaster_pet_tips_2.html. Accessed on Apr. 24, 2006. Quoting Red Cross spokesman Nick Shapiro, "The Red Cross shelters must be designed to accommodate everybody. ... We can't add the risk of animal bites, fleas, other insects, and hygiene issues to an already stressful environment like a mass care shelter." *See also*: American Humane Association, *Summary Report of the National Emergency Animal Management Summit*, Jan. 8-9, 2006, p. 6 (Discussing the risk of disease and contamination for volunteers at animal shelters and the need to periodically assess the likelihood that particular animal will bite.).

200 "Katrina Survivors Face Dilemma over Pets," Reuters, Sept. 8, 2005. http://www.msnbc.msn.com/id/9260578/did/9260578/print/1/displaymode/1098/. Accessed on Apr. 24, 2006; Maryann Mott, "Katrina Pet Rescue Efforts Offer Lessons For the Future" National Geographic News, Sept. 21, 2005. http://news.nationalgeographic.com/news/2005/09/0921_050921_disaster_pet_tips_2.html. Accessed on Apr. 24, 2006.

201 American Humane Association, *Summary Report of the National Emergency Animal Management Summit*, Jan. 8-9, 2006, p. 11.

202 American Humane Association, *Summary Report of the National Emergency Animal Management Summit*, Jan. 8-9, 2006, p. 11.

203 "Katrina Survivors Face Dilemma over Pets," Reuters, Sept. 8, 2005. http://www.msnbc.msn.com/id/9260578/did/9260578/print/1/displaymode/1098/. Accessed on Apr. 24, 2006.

204 Matthews interview, Oct. 14, 2005, pp. 37-38.

205 Stu Hudson, "Katrina's Stranded Pets Spur Massive Aid Effort," *National Geographic News*, Sept. 9, 2005. http://news.nationalgeographic.com/news/2005/09/0909_050909_katrina_petrescue.html. Accessed on Apr. 24, 2006.

206 William Wan, "A Lesson from Katrina: Pets Matter; Disaster Plans Include First Aid, Evacuation Options for Four-Legged Victims," *The Washington Post*, Jan. 2, 2006, p. B01.

207 VMAT is part of the National Disaster Medical System (NDMS) and "will supplement the relief efforts already underway by local veterinarians and emergency responders." American Veterinary Medical Association, "Animal Health." http://www.avma.org/disaster/vmat/default.asp. Accessed on May 8, 2006.

208 William Wan, "A Lesson from Katrina: Pets Matter; Disaster Plans Include First Aid, Evacuation Options for Four-Legged Victims," *The Washington Post*, Jan. 2, 2006, p. B01.

209 Carl Sullivan, "Pets in Peril," *Newsweek*, Sept. 15, 2005. www.msnbc.msn.com/id/9326408/site/newsweek/print/1/displaymode/1098/. Accessed on May 8, 2006.

210 American Humane Association, *Summary Report of the National Emergency Animal Management Summit*, Jan. 8-9, 2006, p. 5.

Hauling sandbags,
New Orleans
U.S. Army photo

Why the New Orleans Levees Failed

What makes the New Orleans levees unusual is the high stakes involved in terms of the population being protected. ... In a system with several hundred miles of levees, it is very difficult to do suitable investigation and basically to nail all the details. ... If you leave one detail unnailed, you leave a vulnerability which may in the end bring the whole system down.[1]

— Raymond Seed, Ph.D., National Science Foundation-sponsored
Independent Levee Inspection Team (ILIT), University of California, Berkeley

The flooding of the metropolitan New Orleans area challenged emergency response at all levels. This flooding was largely caused by failures of the levees and floodwalls in and around New Orleans. An examination of why the levees failed to protect New Orleans is critical,[2] and several teams of scientists of varied affiliation are presently conducting massive studies of the mechanisms responsible for the flooding. Topics of forensic analysis include:

- Levee breaches along the 17th Street, London Avenue, and the Inner Harbor Navigation Canals

- Overtopping of various levees and floodwalls

- Design and construction issues

- Proper levee/floodwall oversight

- Subsidence in the metropolitan New Orleans area

- The impact of the Mississippi River Gulf Outlet (MRGO)

The Levee Breaches Along the 17th Street and London Avenue Canals

Three levee breaches along the major stormwater drainage, or "outfall," canals of central New Orleans – one breach on the east side of the 17th Street Canal and two others along the London Avenue Canal (on the east and west) – caused catastrophic flooding in the heart of the city. These canals are part of the city's drainage system and allow rain and flood waters to be pumped out of the city into Lake Pontchartrain.

Breaches in the floodwalls along these canals caused water from Lake Pontchartrain to flood into, among other areas, the Central Business District, the blocks surrounding the Superdome, Lakeview, Mid City, the area around Tulane University, and Lakewood.[3] It was this flooding that made the humanitarian and rescue efforts at the Superdome and Convention Center so difficult.

Scientists have confirmed that these levee and floodwall breaches were unlike the failures of levees and floodwalls in other areas of the metropolitan New Orleans region, which were overtopped by Katrina's storm surge. There is scientific consensus that the floodwalls along the 17th Street Canal (and the London Avenue Canal) were not, prior to failure, overtopped by the storm surge from Lake Pontchartrain.[4] A report by the U.S. Army Corps of Engineers' Interagency Performance Evaluation Task Force (IPET) – an academically diverse group of scientists examining, among numerous other issues, the type of failure in the 17th Street Canal breach – gave two causes for the breach.

Breached floodwall, New Orleans
Marty Bahamonde photo

First, the concrete floodwall, which stood erect at the crest of the earthen levee and was supported by steel sheetpiles driven into, and below, the earthen levee, was pushed away from the canal by waters rising toward the protected land side. As it was pushed away, a gap was created between the floodwall (along with the sheetpile upon which it was supported) and the adjacent levee embankment soils. This allowed flood waters to rush into the gap, apply pressure against the lower sheetpiles supporting the floodwall underground, and push the embankment section aside. Once the embankment began to be pushed aside, a second failure mechanism combined to produce a catastrophic failure of the wall. This second mechanism was the failure of an unusually weak layer of clay at the foundation or "toe" of the levee. Under pressure from floodwaters pressing on the wall, this layer gave way and allowed the "lateral translation," or movement, of the earthen levee supporting the floodwall along the "failure plain" in the weak clay layer. These combined mechanisms resulted in the violent sideways heave of the entire embankment section.[5]

While the forensic teams generally agree that the 17th Street Canal breach was the result of structural failure, they disagree whether the original design anticipated this problem. The IPET report said that it did not.[6] However, in the National Science Foundation-sponsored Independent Levee Inspection Team's (ILIT) *Initial Comments on Interim (70%) IPET Study Report*, Raymond B. Seed, Ph.D., and Robert G. Bea, Ph.D., took issue with the IPET's assertion – a concern also raised by the American Society of Civil Engineers External Review Panel.[7] The ILIT stated that the Corps of Engineers had a "masterful knowledge and understanding of the complex and challenging geology of this region in the 1950's,"[8] and "should not claim that the weak foundation soil strata at the 17th Street Canal breach site were unexpected, and that no prior publications would have disclosed this possibility."[9]

The ILIT scientists also referenced a test conducted prior to the construction of the 17th Street Canal, which, according to Seed and Bea, foreshadowed the catastrophic failure at the breach site. They say a Corps field test of a levee and sheetpile-supported floodwall in 1985, just south of Morgan City, LA, predicted exactly the sort of failure that occurred at the 17th Street Canal. The model levee embankment and the sheetpile-supported concrete floodwall were sized and built to simulate conditions expected for the 17th Street, Orleans, and London Avenue Canals, as well as major portions of the Inner Harbor Navigational Canal. "Thus," the NSF team concluded, "there would seem to be little justification for the contention that the sheetpile failure mode disclosed by the IPET analyses had not previously been seen, or published, and that it could not have been anticipated."[10]

The two breach sites along the London Avenue Canal appear to have been the result of foundational instability near the fine sand and clay substratum layers at the site.[11]

Overtopping of Various Levees and Floodwalls

As noted, the flooding in the heart of the city was caused by the breaches along the 17th Street and London Avenue Canals. But most of the levee and floodwall failures in the metropolitan New Orleans area – including New Orleans East, the Lower 9th Ward, St. Bernard

Parish, and Plaquemines Parish – "were caused by overtopping, as the storm surge rose over the tops of the levees and/or their floodwalls and produced erosion that subsequently led to failures and breaches."[12] One report described the overtopping as follows:

> Overtopping was most severe on the east side of the flood protection system, as the waters of Lake Borgne were driven west towards New Orleans, and also farther to the south, along the lower reaches of the Mississippi River. Significant overtopping and erosion produced numerous breaches in these areas. The magnitude of overtopping was less severe along the Inner Harbor Navigation Canal (IHNC) and along the western portion of the Mississippi River Gulf Outlet (MRGO) channel, but this overtopping again produced erosion and caused additional levee failures.[13]

Finally, as described more fully in the design and construction subsection below, one report notes that, "it appears that many of the levees and floodwalls that failed due to overtopping might have performed better if relatively inexpensive details had been added and/or altered during their original design and construction."[14]

Design and Construction Issues

Understanding the design and/or construction shortcomings of protective structures is critical as the Corps of Engineers proceeds with the rebuilding of the New Orleans region's hurricane protection system.

As one report observes, the protective system is a "piecemeal" assemblage of elements that "evolved over a long period of time."[15] By contrast, a proper system "would integrate components and … would contain a level of redundancy sufficient that, if a levee failed, all would not be lost."[16]

For the most part, the reports reviewed by the Committee have revealed the following critical design and construction issues: (1) I-wall vs. T-wall design; (2) vulnerable "transition points" within the protective system; (3) accessibility to breach sites; and (4) enhanced protection.

Ripped-out sheetpile with chunks of floodwall attached, New Orleans
Louisiana National Guard photo

I-wall vs. T-wall Design

"I-wall" floodwalls run along the top of earthen levees and are supported by metal sheetpiles driven into, and below, the earthen levees to various depths. As noted above, the erosion of soils on the protected land side of these floodwalls was caused by water cascading over the tops of the structures themselves, reducing the walls' resistance to pressure from the water side.[17] This type of failure was "most dramatic" along the Inner Harbor Navigation Canal next to the Lower Ninth Ward."[18]

This type of failure mechanism was not a problem at most T-wall floodwalls, which look like an inverted "T" and are constructed with concrete bases with more substantial, armored foundations.[19] Their horizontal platforms provide more stability for the vertical wall and give the levee soil some protection from water pouring over the top of the wall.

Transition Points

The Lake Pontchartrain and Vicinity Hurricane Protection Project (Lake Pontchartrain Project) was authorized in the Flood Control Act of 1965 to provide hurricane protection to areas around Lake Pontchartrain in Orleans, Jefferson, St. Bernard, and St. Charles Parishes.[20] The total project called for the design and construction of approximately 125 miles of levees and floodwalls.[21] Parts of the system were built at different times and involved the review and co-operation of different local levee districts. Quite often, this resulted in non-uniform junctions. Scientists examining these "transition points" found inconsistencies in crest heights, types of protective structures, and materials used.[22] In some places, floodwalls stood at a higher elevation than adjoining earthen levees, which concentrated the flow of water to the non-uniform intersection, "causing turbulence that resulted in erosion of the weaker levee soil."[23]

One report noted that the key to the transition-points problem is that "infrastructure elements [were being] designed and maintained by multiple authorities."[24] The report said the result is that "the weakest (or lowest) segment or element controls the overall performance" of the hurricane protection system.[25] One engineering recommendation was that crest heights – the highest elevations of the structure being used, regardless whether it is just a levee or a floodwall standing upon a levee – should be planned to guide overtopping waters "preferentially" toward locations that would minimize damage.[26]

Accessibility to Breach Sites

Scientists also found that the design of the levees and floodwalls along the major outfall canals (the 17th Street and London Avenue Canals) hampered emergency operations at the breach sites, despite a Corps of Engineers regulation[27] about the importance of access roads to levees for inspection, maintenance, and flood-fighting. These narrow access roads usually run along the crown of the earthen levee itself. However, the report noted that adding I-walls to levees in highly built-up areas of New Orleans had sacrificed road access to the tops of the levees. These decisions resulted in very significant increases in time and cost when it became necessary to close breaches along these canals.[28] Emergency roads needed to be constructed to get access to the breached areas so that construction equipment and fill materials could be brought in.

Enhanced Protection

Hurricane Katrina was a catastrophic storm that exceeded the design limits of parts of the levee system. Nevertheless, some portion of the flooding that occurred could have been lessened had the levees themselves not been eroded – and ultimately breached – by overtopping. The scientific community has determined that the hurricane protection system designed to protect the people living within the metropolitan New Orleans area could have (and should have) been constructed with enhanced protective features. As noted in one report:

> A fundamental flaw in the floodwalls and levees is that they include no means of accommodating overtopping that does not inflict major damage or destruction. … Most of the 350 miles of levees in New Orleans are unprotected from devastating damage and potentially total destruction if overtopped.
>
> The question is not whether the levees will again be overtopped but when and by how much they will be overtopped.[29]

Another report found that the performance of many levees and floodwalls could have been greatly improved "and some of the failures likely prevented, with relatively inexpensive modifications" of the system, such as riprap (a loose assemblage of broken stones and concrete), concrete splash slabs, or pavement on the protected side of the levees to guard against anticipated overtopping.[30]

The failure of the system's design to adequately address the impact of significant overtopping likely resulted in a system more prone to failure in a major hurricane and should have raised greater concern about the effects of overtopping.

Proper Hurricane Protection System Oversight

As alluded to in the "transition points" subsection above, scientists have noted that there are design/technical problems with the hurricane protection system that they attribute to numerous "infrastructure elements [being] designed and maintained by multiple authorities."[31]

As Seed testified before the Committee during a public hearing:

> No one is in charge. You have got multiple agencies, multiple organizations, some of whom aren't on speaking terms with each other, sharing responsibilities for public safety. The Corps of Engineers had asked to put flood gates into the three canals [structures that would, upon activation, block the waters of Lake Pontchartrain from entering the drainage canals], which nominally might have mitigated and prevented the three main breaches that did so much destruction downtown. But they weren't able to do that because, unique to New Orleans, the Reclamation Districts who were responsible for maintaining the levees are separate from the Water and Sewage District, which does the pumping. Ordinarily, the Reclamation District does the dewatering pumping, which is separate from the water system. These guys don't get along. The Sewage District was so concerned they wouldn't be able to pump through gates which had to be opened and closed that in the end, the Corps, against its desires, was forced instead to line the canals [with the floodwalls], which they did with some umbrage, and the locals bore a higher than typical fraction of the shared cost as a result of that …
>
> Levees in the New Orleans area are at different heights. You can stand – we have a photograph in our report at one section where you can clearly see five different elevations, all within 100 yards of each other. If you have got five different elevations within 100 yards, the person who built the lowest section wins because they become the public hazard. There is a need to coordinate these things.[32]

As a report by the ASCE's External Review Panel (ERP) notes:

> The ERP sees clearly that organizational complexities and the ways in which decisions are made are among the most important factors that influenced the performance of the hurricane protection system. Organizational effectiveness has been and will continue to be questioned, with justification. It is impossible for the ERP to conceive a mechanism through which the levee system can be rebuilt and operated effectively and efficiently with such organizational discontinuity and chaos.[33]

Subsidence in the Metropolitan New Orleans Area

In addition to design and construction issues, soil subsidence – "the lowering or sinking of [the] earth's surface"[34] – has impaired the protection offered by the New Orleans levee system. In the New Orleans area, subsidence is caused primarily by the cumulative weight of millions of years of soil and silt deposits left by the Mississippi River as it enters the Gulf of Mexico. The sediment literally presses down on the earth's crust, causing the land to sink. As a result, the water level rises, gradually increasing vulnerability to tides and storms. The levees themselves can also subside because of their own weight pressing down on the swampy soils upon which they are built.

As a result, it appears that the level of protection actually provided by the New Orleans region's levee system at the time of Katrina was significantly lower than intended:

> Many sections of the levees and floodwalls were substantially below their original design elevations, an effective loss of protection. For example, the

Plugging a breached floodwall,
New Orleans

structures associated with the Inner Harbor Navigation Canal were originally constructed to an elevation of 15 feet (relative to mean sea level) but are now just over 12 feet, a typical loss of approximately 2.7 feet in elevation over the lifetime of the project.[35]

The report noted that "subsidence is occurring at a rate of up to one inch every three years" in the New Orleans region.[36]

Subsidence routinely creates problems for those trying to construct levees and other structures at known heights above sea level. As stated in one IPET report, due to the complex and variable subsidence in southeast Louisiana, "establishing an accurate vertical reference for measurements has been a constant challenge."[37] Unfortunately, until the October 2005 release by the U.S. Department of Commerce's National Geodetic Survey of 85 benchmarks located in southern Louisiana, which showed heights (elevations) accurate to between 2 and 5 centimeters (roughly 1 to 2 inches), surveyors, engineers, and the U.S. Army Corps of Engineers in New Orleans evaluated the levees and structures built and in use against vertical heights that had not been calibrated nor checked for several years.[38]

As a result, it appears that the levees were not built and maintained at the proper level above sea level. Since the level of protection that the levees provide is so closely related to their height above sea level, which affects their ability to block increased water levels driven by hurricanes, the failure to build and maintain the levees at the proper elevation diminished the level of protection they provided.

1 Testimony of Raymond Seed, Ph.D., National Science Foundation, before the U.S. Senate, Committee on Homeland Security and Governmental Affairs, hearing on *Hurricane Katrina: Why Did the Levees Fail?*, Nov. 2, 2005.

2 This section analyzes and summarizes the following scientific reports: The November 2, 2005, American Society of Civil Engineers (ASCE) and National Science Foundation (NSF) *Preliminary Report on the Performance of the New Orleans Levee System in Hurricane Katrina on August 29, 2005*, [hereinafter, "ASCE/NSF *Preliminary Report*"]; The December 5, 2005, *Summary of Field Observations Relevant to Flood Protection in New Orleans, LA: Interim Report to Task Force Guardian* by the Interagency Performance Evaluation Task Force [hereinafter, "IPET *Summary of Field Observations*"]; The January 10, 2006, Interagency Performance Evaluation Task Force *Performance Evaluation Plan and Interim Status, Report 1 of a Series: Performance Evaluation of the New Orleans and Southeast Louisiana Hurricane Protection System* [hereinafter, "IPET *Report 1 of a Series*"]; The February 20, 2006, American Society of Civil Engineers *External Review Panel Progress: Report Number 1* [hereinafter, "ASCE *ERP Progress Report Number 1*"]; The March 10, 2006, Interagency Performance Evaluation Task Force *Performance Evaluation, Status and Interim Results, Report 2 of a Series: Performance Evaluation of the New Orleans and Southeast Louisiana Hurricane Protection System* [hereinafter, "IPET *Report 2 of a Series*"]; and various other ASCE and NSF preliminary evaluations of the IPET *Report 2 of a Series*.

For background, it should be understood that the U.S. Army Corps of Engineers (USACE) responded to Hurricane Katrina with, among other things, the activation of Task Force Guardian (TFG), with the crucial responsibility of repairing the damages to the hurricane protective system by the storm. *Source:* U.S. Army Corps of Engineers, Interagency Performance Evaluation Task Force, *Summary of Field Observations Relevant to Flood Protection in New Orleans, LA,"* Dec. 5, 2005, p. 2 [hereinafter IPET, *Summary of Field Operations*]. In addition, the Interagency Performance Evaluation Task Force (IPET) was established on October 10, 2005, by the Chief of Engineers of the USACE, and sanctioned by the Secretary of Defense in a directive to the Secretary of the Army on October 19, 2005. *Source:* U.S. Army Corps of Engineers, Interagency Performance Evaluation Task Force, Performance Evaluation Plan and Interim Status, *Report 1 of a Series*, Jan. 10, 2006, p. 3 [hereinafter IPET, *Report 1 of a Series*]. The IPET, "comprised of leading experts in a comprehensive array of science and engineering disciplines [is] charged with studying the response of the hurricane protection system during Katrina for lessons learned." *Source:* IPET, *Summary of Field Observations*, p. 2. Moreover, the IPET is to "provide credible and objective scientific and engineering answers to fundamental questions about the performance of the hurricane protection and flood damage reduction system in the New Orleans metropolitan area." *Source:* IPET, *Report 1 of a Series*, p. 3. The American Society of Civil Engineers (ASCE) External Review Panel (ERP) then "provide[s] for an external, expert, and constructive technical review of the activities and products of the [IPET]." *Source:* IPET, *Report 1 of a Series*, Appendix D, p. D–7. While this review is to be comprehensive, and done on a periodic basis, it is clear that the "ERP has no approval authority on the findings of the [IPET], nor are the ERP's recommendations to the [IPET] binding, but the [IPET] will give serious consideration to each." *Source:* IPET, *Report 1 of a Series*, Appendix D, p. D–8.

On Nov. 2, 2005, the Committee held a public hearing entitled, "Hurricane Katrina: Why Did the Levees Fail?" [hereinafter, "HSGAC Levee 1 Hearing"]. The witnesses for this hearing were representatives and/or heads of several different forensic data gathering teams investigating why the levees in and around New Orleans failed. Testifying before the Committee were Raymond B. Seed, Ph.D., on behalf of the National Science Foundation (NSF), Peter Nicholson, Ph.D., P.E., on behalf of the ASCE, Ivor van Heerden, Ph.D., of the LSU Hurricane Center and on behalf of the State of Louisiana Forensic Data Gathering Team, and Paul F. Mlakar, Ph.D., P.E., on behalf of the USACE. The bulk of Seed and Nicholson's formal written testimony provided for the HSGAC Levee 1 Hearing summarized the ASCE/NSF *Preliminary Report*.

During the HSGAC Levee 1 Hearing, Mlakar specifically noted the IPET objective: "The final results will include conclusions as to the causes of the failures and recommendations for the future design and construction of such infrastructure nationwide. These results will be independently reviewed by an external panel of the [ASCE]. At the request of the Secretary of Defense, the National Academies will also independently assess the results and report to the Assistant Secretary of the Army for Civil Works." *Source:* Testimony of Paul Mlakar, Senior Research Scientist, Army Engineer Research and Development Center, before the U.S. Senate, Committee on Homeland Security and Governmental Affairs, hearing on *Hurricane Katrina: Why did the Levees Fail?*, Nov. 2, 2005.

On Nov. 2, 2005 – the day of the HSGAC Levee 1 Hearing – the ASCE and NSF teams jointly released the ASCE/NSF *Preliminary Report*. As noted in the report itself, the "ASCE/NSF *Preliminary Report*" present[ed] the results of field investigations performed by collaborating teams of scientists and engineers in the wake of the passage of Hurricane Katrina, to study performance of the regional flood protection systems and the resulting flooding that occurred in the New Orleans area." *Source:* American Society of Civil Engineers and National Science Foundation, *Preliminary Report on the Performance of the New Orleans Levee System in Hurricane Katrina on Aug. 29, 2005*, Nov. 2, 2005, p. 1–1 [hereinafter, ASCE/NSF, *Preliminary Report*]. The initial field investigations conducted in preparation for the report took place from Sept. 28, through Oct. 15, 2005. *Source:* ASCE/NSF, *Preliminary Report*, p. iv. Following the ASCE/NSF *Preliminary Report*, on Dec. 5, 2005, the IPET *Summary of Field Observations* was issued, which consisted of an "IPET review provided [to] Task Force Guardian with a simple statement of concurrence or nonoccurrence from the IPET floodwall and levee sub team and additional relevant discussion for each of the major findings of the ASCE/NSF "*Preliminary Report*." *Source:* IPET, *Report 1 of a Series*, Appendix F, p. F–2.

Consistent with IPET's mission, it produced its first evaluation of the metropolitan New Orleans area hurricane protection system on Jan. 10, 2006. The IPET *Report 1 of a Series* is a massive document. Moreover, as noted in its "Purpose" section, "IPET, *Report 1 of a Series* provides a strategic overview of the IPET, the final IPET Scopes of Work on a task-by-task basis, including changes resulting from the review of the [ASCE ERP], and a status report on the work accomplished to date." *Source:* IPET, *Report 1 of a Series*, p. 4. However, and as noted by the Feb. 20, 2006, ASCE ERP *Progress Report Number 1*, "the IPET [*Report 1 of a Series*] presented no specific findings and conclusions, which is not surprising in view of the many questions that as yet are unanswered." *Source:* American Society of Civil Engineers, letter to Lt. Gen. Carl Strock, "ERP Progress Report Number 1," Feb. 20, 2006, p. 2. Provided to the Committee [hereinafter ASCE, "ERP Progress Report Number 1"]. The IPET Final Report "will include the completed analyses for consequences and risk and reliability," and is scheduled for release on June 1, 2006. *Source:* IPET, *Report 1 of a Series*, viii.

According to the IPET *Report 1 of a Series*, Objectives section, the IPET's overall review is focused on answering the following critical questions:

   a. **The Flood Protection System:** What were the design criteria for the pre-Katrina hurricane protection system, and did the design, as-built construction, and maintained condition meet these criteria? (1) What were the design assumptions and as-built characteristics of the primary components of the flood protection system? (2) What records of inspection and maintenance of original construction and post-Katrina repairs are available that documents their conditions? (3) What subsurface exploration and geotechnical laboratory testing information was available as the basis of design, and were these conditions verified during construction? (4) Were the subsurface conditions at the locations of levee failures unique, or are these same conditions found elsewhere?

b. The Storm: What were the storm surges and waves used as the basis of design, and how do these compare to the storm surges and waves generated by Hurricane Katrina? (1) What forces, as a function of location and time, were exerted against the hurricane protection system by Katrina?

c. The Performance: How did the floodwalls, levees, pumping stations, and drainage canals, individually and acting as an integrated system, perform in response to Hurricane Katrina, and why? (1) What were the primary failure mechanisms and factors leading to failure for those structures suffering catastrophic failure during the storm? (2) What characteristics allowed components of the system to perform well under exceptional loads and forces? (3) What was the contribution of the pumping stations and drainage system in the unwatering of flooded areas? (4) What areas or components of the flood protection system have sustained damages that reduce their protection capacity and may need some reconstitution of capacity?

d. The Consequences: What have been the societal-related consequences of the Katrina-related damage? (1) How are local consequences related to the performance of individual components of the flood protection system? (2) What would the consequences have been if the system would not have suffered catastrophic failure? (3) What are the consequences of Katrina that extend beyond New Orleans and vicinity?

e. The Risk: Following the immediate repairs, what will be the quantifiable risk to New Orleans and vicinity from future hurricanes and tropical storms? (1) What was the risk to New Orleans and vicinity from hurricanes prior to Katrina? (2) On June 1, 2006, what will be the condition and engineering integrity of the New Orleans hurricane protection system, including structural repairs? *Source:* IPET, *Report 1 of a Series*, p. 6–7.

While all of these questions are important ones – many of which are addressed throughout the balance of this Committee's Report, the following have a direct bearing upon this section of the Committee's Report: questions (a) and (a)(1)-(4); (b) and (b)(1); and (c) and (c)(1)-(2). In any event, given the state of the IPET's review at the time of this Committee's Report, the IPET *Report 1 of a Series* can best be used to demonstrate what the DOD sanctioned team of scientists is doing (or plans to do), while also taking note of what it is not doing (as referenced in the ASCE *ERP Progress Report Number 1*).

As noted above, the IPET Final Report is scheduled for release on June 1, 2006. Overall, and as largely recognized by the ASCE ERP, the IPET's goal (and its approach to meeting this goal) is a critical and comprehensive one. The IPET Final Report has the makings to be – if conducted as planned, including the duo-layered review process – the definitive work on the lingering scientific/forensic questions related to Hurricane Katrina. However, and as referenced elsewhere in this Committee's Report, the organizational problems referenced in the ASCE ERP *Progress Report Number 1*, and also by the scientists who testified before the Committee at the HSGAC Levee 1 Hearing, are significant issues that must be properly addressed before residents of the greater New Orleans area are to exude confidence in the hurricane protection system charged with protecting their lives and livelihoods.

3 Ivor L. van Heerden, G. Paul Kemp, Wes Shrum, Ezra Boyd and Hassan Mashriqui, Louisiana State University, Center for the Study of Public Health Impacts of Hurricanes, *Initial Assessment of the New Orleans' Flooding Event during the Passage of Hurricane Katrina*, pp. 7-10. [hereinafter LSU, *Initial Assessment of New Orleans Flooding*]. The LSU professors also noted that, "[w]ater poured through the three deep breaches of the drainage canals into the New Orleans Metro bowl for more than 60 hours, until early Thursday morning, when the level inside reached equilibrium with the water in the lake at about 3 feet above sea level, and with the 'average' home in the flooded neighborhoods standing in six to nine feet of water." LSU, *Initial Assessment of New Orleans Flooding*, p. 10.

4 ASCE/NSF *Preliminary Report*, pp. iv-v, 2–3, 8–2; IPET, *Summary of Field Observations*, p. 8; and IPET, *Report 1 of a Series*, pp. 113-114; U.S. Army Corps of Engineers, Interagency Performance Evaluation Task Force, Performance Evaluation Plan and Interim Status, *Report 2 of a Series*, Mar. 10, 2006, p. vi-3 [hereinafter IPET, *Report 2 of a Series*].

5 IPET, *Report 2 of a Series*, p. I–4. *See also:* Raymond B. Seed and Robert G. Bea, National Science Foundation-Sponsored Independent Levee Inspection Team (ILIT), Univ. of Calif. at Berkeley, *Initial Comments on Interim (70%) IPET Study Report*, Mar. 12, 2006, p. 1 [hereinafter, ILIT, *Initial Comments on Interim (70%) IPET Study Report*]. It should be noted that the ASCE ERP, noted above, seems to be satisfied with the IPET's assessment: "In its initial review of the U.S. Army Corps of Engineers' [IPET] second report, *Status and Interim Results*, the [ASCE] External Review Panel (ERP) members are generally satisfied with the group's analysis and progress. More specifically, we have been impressed with the IPET's investigation of the 17th Street failure mechanism." American Society of Civil Engineers, "Statement attributable to David Daniel, Ph.D., P.E., president of the University of Texas, Dallas, Chair, American Society of Civil Engineers (ASCE) External Review Panel (ERP)," news release, Mar. 10, 2006, p. 1.

6 IPET, *Report 2 of a Series*, p. I–4 (emphasis added).

7 American Society of Civil Engineers, letter to Lt. Gen. Carl Strock, Mar. 23, 2006, pp. 1-2. Provided to the Committee. Wherein the ASCE ERP also noted the Corps' knowledge regarding soil/foundational issues in the area of the major outfall canals, and the floodwall field test demonstrating similar failure mechanisms as that actually realized at the site of the 17th Street Canal and referenced in the IPET *Report 2 of a Series*.

8 ILIT, *Initial Comments on Interim (70%) IPET Study Report*, p. 1.

9 ILIT, *Initial Comments on Interim (70%) IPET Study Report*, p. 1.

10 ILIT, *Initial Comments on Interim (70%) IPET Study Report*, p. 3. *See also:* American Society of Civil Engineers, Letter to Lt. Gen. Carl Strock, Mar. 23, 2006.

11 IPET, *Report 1 of a Series*, p. 106.

12 At this point, it should be noted that the IPET team undertook an analysis to determine the effects of the Mississippi River Gulf Outlet (MRGO) upon the storm surge generated by Hurricane Katrina. The note, which examined "the impact of the MRGO on large scale catastrophic storm surge development and propagation," found as follows:

> The MRGO is a dredged channel that extends southeast to northwest from the Gulf of Mexico to a point where it first merges with the Gulf Intracoastal Waterway (GIWW), and then continues westward until it intersects the Inner Harbor Navigation Canal (IHNC). ... The first 9 miles, the bar channel, are in the open Gulf. The next 23 miles of the channel lie in the shallow open waters of Breton Sound. From there, the inland cut extends 14 miles to the northwest with open marsh on the northeast and a 4,000-ft wide dredged material placement bank on the southwest side. At this point the channel cuts across the ridge of a relict distributary of the Mississippi River, Bayou La Loutre. For nearly the next 24 miles, there is a hurricane protection levee atop a dredged material placement bank on the southwest side of the channel and Lake Borgne and open marsh lie to the northeast. A portion of the levee protecting St. Bernard Parish/ Chalmette and the portion of the hurricane protection levee along the south side of Orleans East Parish, north of the GIWW, form the "funnel" that is often referenced. The point where the MRGO and GIWW channels merge is just to the east of the Paris Road Bridge. ... From this point, the merged GIWW/ MRGO channel continues west for about 6 miles to the point where it intersects the IHNC; this portion has hurricane protection levees on both banks. The IHNC extends from Lake Pontchartrain, to the north, to the Mississippi River to the south. The IHNC has levees or floodwalls along both banks. ... The MRGO bar channel authorized depth is 38 ft; the authorized bottom width is 600 ft. The remainder of the channel has an authorized depth of 36 ft and an authorized bottom width of 400 or 450 ft, depending on location.

> It is important to distinguish between two sections of the MRGO and the role each plays in tide and storm surge propagation. One is the east-west oriented section that runs between the IHNC and the confluence of the GIWW/MRGO near the Paris Road Bridge ... and hereinafter referred to as Reach 1. The other is the much longer southeast-northwest section ... hereinafter referred to as the Reach 2. IPET, *Report 2 of a Series*, Appendix E, p. E–2.

Citing past studies, and analyses of their own, the IPET report noted the following regarding MRGO/Reach 2:

> The change in storm surge induced by MRGO/Reach 2 (computed as a percentage of the peak surge magnitude) is greatest when the amplitude of the storm surge is low, on the order of a few feet or less. In these situations, changes induced by the MRGO are rather small, 0.5 ft or less, but this amount is as much as 25% of the peak surge amplitude. When the long wave amplitude is very low, the surge is more limited to propagation via the channels. Once the surge amplitude increases to the point where the wetlands become inundated, this section of the MRGO plays a diminished role in influencing the amplitude of storm surge that reaches the vicinity of metropolitan New Orleans. For storm surges of the magnitude produced by Hurricane Betsy and Katrina, which overwhelmed the wetland system, the influence of MRGO/Reach 2 on storm surge propagation is rather small. When the expansive wetland is inundated, the storm surge propagates primarily through the water column over this much larger flooded area, and the channels become a much smaller contributor to water conveyance. *Source:* IPET, *Report 2 of a Series*, Appendix E, p. E–4. ... The reasons for the very limited influence of the MRGO/ Reach 2 in the vicinity of New Orleans for strong storm events are clear. First, the MRGO does not influence the important preliminary east-west movement of water that drives the significant build up of surge in the early parts of the storm. Second, the northerly propagation of surge during the later stages of the storm are only minimally influenced by the MRGO because the increased hydraulic conveyance associated with the channel is very limited for large storms due to the large surge magnitude and especially due to the very large lateral extent of the high waters on the Mississippi-Alabama shelf that build up early on from the east. In addition, the propagation direction of this surge wave does not typically align with the MRGO and furthermore the southeasterly winds which align with the MRGO occur only very briefly. *Source:* IPET, *Report 2 of a Series*, Appendix E, p. E–6.

Finally, the report said of MRGO/Reach 1:

> While the simulations clearly show that Reach 2 of the MRGO does not significantly influence the development of storm surge in the region for large storm events, Reach 1 (the combined GIWW/ MRGO section) and the IHNC, together, provide a hydraulic connection between Lake Borgne and Lake Pontchartrain. As a result of this connection, the storm surge experienced within the IHNC and Reach 1 (GIWW/MRGO) is a function of storm surge in both Lakes; a water level gradient is established within the IHNC and Reach 1 that is dictated by the surge levels in the two lakes. This is true for both low and high storm surge conditions. To prevent storm surge in Lake Borgne from reaching the IHNC or GIWW/MRGO sections of waterway, flow through the Reach 1 channel must be dramatically reduced or eliminated, either by a permanent closure or some type of structure that temporarily serves to eliminate this hydraulic connectivity. The presence of an open channel is the key factor.

> The hurricane protection levees along the south side of Orleans Parish [Orleans East] and the eastern side of St. Bernard Parish along the MRGO, which together are referred to as a funnel, can locally collect and focus storm surge in this vicinity depending on wind speed and direction. This localized focusing effect can lead to a small local increase in surge amplitude. Strong winds from the east tend to maximize the local funneling effect. *Source:* IPET, *Report 2 of a Series*, Appendix E, p. E–7.

A team of scientists from LSU, however, seem to take a different position on the MRGO channel. In a report entitled, LSU, *Initial Assessment of New Orleans Flooding*, Ivor L. van Heerden, G. Paul Kemp, Wes Shrum, Ezra Boyd and Hassan Mashriqui state the following:

> As the eye of the storm approached the latitude of New Orleans, a 14-17 foot surge was pushed into the western apex of a triangle known as the "Funnel", so called because the hurricane protection levees that form the south bank of the MRGO and the north bank of the GIWW converge from being about 10 miles apart to a few hundred yards at the banks of the GIWW where it separates the East Orleans and St. Bernard basins. The Funnel is a 6-mile long section of the GIWW where the cross-section was enlarged by a factor of three when the MRGO was built to expand it from a barge channel to accommodate ocean-going vessels. At the western end, the Funnel focused a jet into the IHNC. The US Army Corps of Engineers had inadvertently designed an excellent storm surge delivery system – nothing less – to bring this mass of water with simply tremendous "load" – potential energy – right into the middle of New Orleans. *Source*: LSU, Initial Assessment of New Orleans Flooding, p. 4.

13 ASCE/NSF, *Preliminary Report*, pp. iv-v.

14 ASCE/NSF, *Preliminary Report*, pp. iv-v.

15 ASCE, "ERP Progress Report Number 1," p. 3.

16 ASCE, "ERP Progress Report Number 1," p. 3.

17 ASCE/NSF, *Preliminary Report*, p. 8–1. See also: IPET, *Summary of Field Observations*, p. 6.

18 IPET, *Summary of Field Observations*, p. 6.

19 ASCE/NSF, *Preliminary Report*, p. 8–1. However, it should be noted that while the IPET report concurred with the ASCE/NSF *Preliminary Report* finding regarding the T-walls, noting that, "if overtopping of T-walls did occur, it did not lead to extensive scour and erosion," the IPET team also stated that there were some T-wall structures "that had significant scour, but none showed evidence of distress or movement" IPET, *Summary of Field Observations*, p. 6.

20 Written Statement of Anu Mittal, Director, Natural Resources and Environment, U.S. General Accountability Office, for the U.S. Senate on Environment and Public Works, hearing on *Comprehensive and Integrated Approach to Meet the Water Resources Needs in the Wake of Hurricanes Katrina and Rita*, Nov. 9, 2005, p. 2.

21 Written Statement of Mittal, Senate Committee on Environment and Public Works hearing, Nov. 9, 2005, p. i.

22 ASCE/NSF, *Preliminary Report*, pp. 8–1 through 8–2; *see also* IPET, *Summary of Field Observations*, pp. 6-7; IPET, *Report 1 of a Series*, p. 114.

23 IPET, *Summary of Field Observations*, pp. 6-7.

24 ASCE/NSF, *Preliminary Report*, pp. 8–1 through 8–2.

25 ASCE/NSF *Preliminary Report*, pp. 8–1 through 8–2.

26 ASCE/NSF *Preliminary Report*, p. 8–3. It should be noted that the IPET team generally agreed with these ASCE/NSF comments, however, while the IPET recognized that planning for overtopping by adjusting crest heights "should be considered," the team stated that there are a number of uncertainties regarding the location and size of these planned "spillways." IPET, *Summary of Field Observations*, p. 11.

27 U.S. Army Corps of Engineers, *Engineering and Design, Design and Construction of Levees*, Apr. 30, 2000, Section 8–9.

28 ASCE/NSF, *Preliminary Report*, pp. 8–3 through 8–4. It should also be noted that the IPET team concurred, specifically noting that, "Given the logistical difficulties in accessing and sealing the breaches to unwater flooded areas, [TFG] should carefully reconsider the guidance of EM 1110-2-1913, Section 8-9 [the Army Corps regulation on point]." IPET, *Summary of Field Observations*, p. 11.

29 ASCE, "ERP Progress Report Number 1," p. 3.

30 ASCE/NSF, *Preliminary Report*, p. 8–3. *See also*: IPET, *Summary of Field Observations*, p. 10.

31 ASCE/NSF, *Preliminary Report*, pp. 8–1 through 8–2. The IPET team, however, has left "the issues of organizational and jurisdictional complexities that can impact the effectiveness of the physical system" to be treated separately. IPET, *Report 2 of a Series*, p. I–1.

32 Testimony of Raymond Seed, Ph.D., Team Leader, National Science Foundation, before the U.S. Senate, Committee on Homeland Security and Governmental Affairs, hearing on *Hurricane Katrina: Why Did the Levees Fail?*, Nov. 2, 2005.

33 ASCE, "ERP Progress Report Number 1," p. 2.

34 IPET, *Report 2 of a Series*, p. III–6.

35 IPET, *Report 2 of a Series*, p. I–2.

36 IPET, *Report 2 of a Series*, p. III–6.

37 IPET, *Report 2 of a Series*, p. I–2.

38 IPET, Report 2 of a Series, p. III-6. Significantly, the report found that geodetic elevations are very time-dependant in the New Orleans area "and must be periodically adjusted to account for apparent sea level changes." It also recommended annual reviews to measure subsidence. IPET, Report 2 of a Series, p. III–53.

Communication Voids

T he inability of government officials and first responders to communicate during a response to an emergency – whether terrorist attacks, natural disasters, or everyday operations – results in the loss of lives. Problems with communications operability and interoperability constituted one of the main reasons for governments' failures in response to Katrina. *Operability* refers to the basic functionality of any device ("Is it working?"). *Interoperability* refers to the device's ability to connect with other devices and share voice or data communications ("Can the police talk to firemen?" or "Can hospitals electronically share patient medical records with emergency health-care providers?")

While there can be no interoperable communications where no communications exists at all – the situation confronting many first responders in Louisiana and across the Gulf Coast immediately after Katrina – an interoperable communications system may be more resilient than "stove- piped" systems. For example, systems can be built with tower sites that have overlapping coverage so that if a single tower goes down, total coverage is not lost in a particular area.[1]

Katrina inflicted widespread destruction on communications and electrical infrastructure. With cellular towers down, land lines submerged, and no power, telephone and wireless communications were largely impossible in the areas most heavily affected by the hurricane.

Mississippi Governor Haley Barbour summed up the lack of communications: "My head of the National Guard might as well have been a Civil War general for the first two or three days because he could only find out what is going on by sending somebody. He did have helicopters instead of horses, so it was a little faster, but the same sort of thing."[2] Emergency personnel from across the Gulf Coast have described how the communications breakdown complicated the coordination of federal, state, and local response. For example:

• In New Orleans, Mayor Nagin's command center at the Hyatt Regency Hotel lost all communications.[3] After landfall – though before flooding – Mayor Nagin had to walk across the street to City Hall in order to speak to city emergency managers.[4] One phone line in the Mayor's room in the Hyatt would sometimes connect a call out, but could not receive incoming calls.[5] It was not until Thursday, September 1, three days after landfall, that the Mayor's command center began to receive e-mails. On Friday, September 2, the White House provided the Mayor with a mobile phone but he had to lean out of storm-damaged rooms at the hotel to get a signal.[6]

• Larry Ingargiola, Director of the Office of Emergency Preparedness for St. Bernard Parish, Louisiana, lost phone and cellular communications on Monday afternoon following landfall. Later that night, the emergency radio system went down; he was left without any communications until August 31. Ingargiola, who went up to the roof of his building with his family when the water started to rise, received word of the levees' breaching from Louisiana Wildlife and Fisheries (W&F) officials who rode by in boats.[7]

• The Louisiana officials in charge of evacuating the Tulane Medical Center received oral authorization from the State Emergency Operations Center (EOC) to use buses in the possession of the National Guard to evacuate the patients. When the National Guard asked for proof of authorization, the head of the rescue team could not get through to the State EOC on his cell phone. Without

(Left Page)
Ruins in Gulfport, MS
(U.S. Coast Guard photo)

the use of the buses, the rescue team resorted to evacuating the patients in the backs of pick-up trucks, with wheelchairs, stretchers, and other equipment loaded into boats pulled behind the trucks.[8]

• Phil Parr, who was part of the Federal Emergency Management Agency (FEMA) Advance Emergency Response Team at the Superdome, estimated that the lack of effective communications at the Superdome reduced FEMA's effectiveness by 90 percent.[9]

• With the loss of phone and computer capabilities, the only way FEMA officials in Harrison County, Mississippi could track water, food, and other requested relief supplies was to send a police car to the distribution center at Stennis Space Center, located in Hancock County, near Louisiana, so that they could communicate using the police car's radio.[10]

• Scott Wells, the Federal Coordinating Officer at the State EOC in Baton Rouge, said that communication with both New Orleans and the FEMA regional office in Denton, Texas, after landfall was so poor that it was like being in a "black hole."[11]

• Health-care providers' inability to share data complicated the task of caring for thousands of patients and others injured during the storm. Injured citizens from the Gulf Coast were being treated at many different locations, often far from their homes, sometimes in other states. The lack of an interoperable data system often prevented medical personnel from obtaining information about patients, even if their facility had suffered no hurricane damage. To complicate matters further, no continuous records were kept to identify and track patients or the treatment they received. Often the identification-and-tracking system consisted of paper stapled to victims' bed sheets or taped to their bodies.[12] One hospital official found that the only reliable way to confirm that planeloads of new evacuee patients were en route was to check with local air-traffic controllers.[13]

Some private-sector entities, however, were much more successful in dealing with communications problems. The Senate Homeland Security and Governmental Affairs Committee's private-sector hearing featured testimony from companies about the communications challenges they faced, how they overcame them, and how any success they achieved after landfall depended on successful communications, including communications between the field and the company's headquarters, within headquarters, and with state and local emergency operations centers.

In its testimony before the Committee, the Starwood hotel company discussed how it managed events on the ground in New Orleans, backed up by its corporate headquarters, which enabled the company to help approximately 2,100 guests, employees, and their families weather the storm in safety at two hotels.[14] Through effective planning and pre-positioning of phones, Starwood never lost contact with areas outside the affected region. Satellite phones were deployed to the hotels, and Starwood maintained its Internet connection, which permitted employees and guests to communicate with the outside world.[15] (One of its New Orleans hotels had two information-technology employees on-site and battery backups for their computer systems, which enabled the Internet connection.) Through media reports received via the Internet, managers on the ground knew what was going on around them when all other forms of communications had failed. Local responders and journalists sometimes relied on Starwood's communications capabilities since the city's communications system was largely lost.[16]

The Wal-Mart retail-merchandise chain stressed the importance of "efficient" communication, and described it as "absolutely the key to success at a higher level."[17] Wal-Mart
developed situational awareness at the local level and passed it quickly to its emergency
operations center, which compiled a big picture for the company. The business-unit representatives in the emergency operations center made decisions on tactics and strategies based
upon the "big picture" information and then moved aggressively to disseminate objectives
back to company response teams and field teams for further dissemination.[18] Wal-Mart determined that the "face-to-face communication at the Emergency Operations Center level,
where the decision makers congregate, is the most efficient method of communication."[19]

The Mississippi Power public utility recognized the importance of communications to an
effective response, particularly the ability to communicate with thousands of additional
workers brought in from outside the region to help with restoration and repairs. Mississippi
Power relied on its only viable form of communication – its internal system Southern Linc
Wireless.[20] This system was designed with considerable redundancy and proved reliable despite suffering catastrophic damage. Within three days, the system was functioning at nearly
100 percent. Mississippi Power told the Committee that it "also installed its own microwave
capability to 12 remote staging areas in order to transmit material inventory data into our
automated procurement process."[21] The company said, "When communication circuits
of another company were down, our information technology group would find a way to
bypass those circuits and restore critical communications."[22]

The storm and flooding severely damaged both the commercial and public safety communications infrastructure.[23] This created chaos for every aspect of governments' response
– search and rescue, medical care, law enforcement, and provision of commodities. This
section addresses each type of infrastructure and then considers the local, state, and federal
governments' efforts to provide emergency and interoperable communications capabilities.

Commercial Communications Infrastructure

BellSouth, the largest local phone company in the region, lost service at 33 of the central
offices that route calls.[24] This was the first time that water damage had put switching centers
out of service on their network.[25] Almost 3 million customers were without phone service
in the days after landfall and over 20 million calls attempted on Tuesday, August 30, the day
after landfall, could not be completed.[26] Of the 545 central offices that remained in service,
over 180 had to run on generators due to the loss of commercial power.[27]

Commercial wireless communications also suffered. Over 1,000 of some 7,000 cellular towers in the affected area were knocked out of service.[28] Some of the switching centers that
connected to cellular towers were flooded, while others were damaged by high winds.[29] To
restore cellular coverage, cellular providers brought in over 100 portable cellular towers,
called cellular on wheels or cellular on light truck, to the Gulf Coast. Each portable tower
provided cellular coverage over a limited area on a temporary basis.[30]

The generators supplying power to the central offices had limited fuel supply,[31] and needed
to be replenished about every three days. BellSouth obtained fuel trucks to top off its generators, proceeding into New Orleans with an armed convoy.[32] Other companies had problems obtaining fuel for their generators. For example, Cox Louisiana Telecom LLC, which
serves 85,000 customers, had fuel trucks that were destined for switch facilities intercepted
by FEMA and turned away. FEMA also took fuel away from technicians with service trucks
in the field.[33] In addition, FEMA commandeered a fuel tanker from BellSouth in order to
refuel helicopters.[34]

The commercial sector also had to negotiate security concerns. At BellSouth's main central office on Poydras Street in New Orleans, which serves as a regional hub for multiple telecommunications carriers, reports of violence and looting caused the New Orleans Police Department (NOPD) and Louisiana State Police (LSP) to advise employees to evacuate the building.[35] Two days after the evacuation, the FBI and the U.S. Marshals Service provided security so that BellSouth workers could return to the Poydras Street building to fuel the generators, which were running low but never went out of service.[36] In an effort to obtain security for all telecommunications providers, the National Communications System (NCS), the federal government's lead agency for the response to communications problems, sought assistance from the Department of Defense (DOD), which forwarded the request to the Louisiana National Guard.[37] In the end, however, security arrangements with the Louisiana National Guard fell through.[38] Ultimately, telecommunications providers hired private security to protect their workers and supplies.[39]

Repair workers also had difficulty gaining access to their equipment and facilities in the field because police and National Guard in some cases refused to let them enter the disaster area. MCI sought a letter from Louisiana Governor Kathleen Blanco to access parts of New Orleans based on a requirement from the LSP, and Verizon Wireless wanted access and security for technicians restoring cellular service in New Orleans.[40] Industry representatives said that their technicians would benefit from having uniform credentialing that is recognized by the multiple law-enforcement agencies operating in a disaster area.[41]

Damage to First Responders' Communications Infrastructure

Besides destroying commercial lines, Katrina decimated the towers and electronic equipment that support land mobile-radio systems, the primary means of communication for first responders. This made it difficult for officials at all levels of government to communicate. Officials from NOPD, the Louisiana Department of Wildlife and Fisheries, and the Louisiana National Guard testified that their law-enforcement and search-and-rescue efforts were hindered by the lack of communications.[42]

Government officials at the Louisiana State EOC in Baton Rouge had trouble communicating with those in the disaster area.[43] State and local emergency operations centers were left in a "communications void," often unable to communicate with first responders or to relay requests for assistance up the chain of command.[44] Part of the problem was serious call congestion on surviving land lines.[45] BellSouth said that it tried to reroute calls around damaged infrastructure, and the State EOC eventually had more lines installed to provide additional capacity.

In New Orleans, only one tower that was at the airport remained operational: One tower was inundated by the storm surge, while two others had equipment damaged or lost power because of flood waters.[46] Many police, fire, EMS dispatch centers, and 911 centers were rendered unusable by flood waters.[47] The ACU-1000 interoperability devices, which provided limited interoperability by patching together different radio systems and were located within the Rosedale Fire Station, had to be abandoned because of flood waters.[48] Katrina's devastating impact on communications infrastructure around New Orleans forced first responders to rely on five or fewer mutual-aid channels – recognized by multiple agencies as channels to use when the coordinating electronics of the radio system fails – for voice-radio communications.[49] But around 4,000 people were competing to use that constricted capacity.[50] The heavy congestion resulted in delays before communications could be established.[51]

In St. Bernard Parish, extreme winds damaged communications towers and antennas, while flood waters inundated the 911 call center and forced the evacuation of buildings housing

communications for the Fire and Sheriff's Departments. All voice-radio communications were lost except for very limited radio-to-radio communications.[52] Plaquemines Parish lost the parish government communications tower and communications center. The Plaquemines Sheriff lost the 911 communications and dispatch center, and all towers. It would be three weeks before Plaquemines Parish had any means of communications. The Jefferson Parish Sheriff's Office lost the main tower supporting its communications system. As a result of this destruction, antennas supporting its communications center were relocated to the boom of a 400-foot crane for months.[53]

The Louisiana State Police Department worked with FEMA to provide support to local departments whose communications capacity had been devastated by the storm. FEMA agreed to pay $15.9 million to Motorola to repair and augment the regional system and to purchase 600 portable radios. The contract for these repairs was signed approximately two weeks after landfall.[54]

911 Communications

Along with first responder communications, Katrina wreaked havoc on the 911 systems on which the public relies to contact first responders. During the Katrina crisis, 911 was unavailable for untold numbers of victims. At least 38 of the 911 centers in the region lost their ability to function during Katrina.[55]

When 911 systems go down, some call centers still re-route calls to other centers. However, telecommunicators on the receiving end did not have access to maps, data, and other information necessary to direct first responders to callers in need of help.[56] Also, only the voice is rerouted, while critical data (e.g., electronic information about a call's point of origin) is not. However, in many cases, due to the widespread destruction in Louisiana, even voice signals could not be rerouted. As a result, when citizens dialed 911, they got a busy signal. [57]

Meanwhile, the influx of thousands of first responders into the region greatly increased the workload for 911 call-center operators who were victims of the storm themselves. Some left when their families evacuated. Those remaining operated under tremendous stress.[58] A North Carolina 911 official helping the response effort in St. Tammany Parish, Louisiana, observed that no plan existed to bring additional, credentialed telecommunicators into the region, and that early Emergency Management Assistance Compact (EMAC) requests for inter-state assistance did not include 911 operators.[59]

Role of the National Communications System

Under the National Response Plan (NRP), Emergency Support Function-2 (ESF-2, Communications) ensures the provision of federal communications support to federal, state, local, tribal, and private-sector response efforts during an Incident of National Significance. The coordinator for ESF-2 activities is the National Communications System (NCS), an interagency consortium managed within the Department of Homeland Security (DHS).[60] The Deputy Manager and Director of NCS is Peter Fonash, Ph.D. [61]

Before Hurricane Katrina, NCS never had to repair the land mobile radio (LMR) systems that are operated by local governments and used by first responders.[62] In fact, the organization did not have an operational plan to systematically assess an incident's impact on the LMR systems and respond to local governments' communications needs for operability, or interoperability, during emergencies.[63] Fonash did not know what communications assets were available across the federal government, nor what communications assets DHS, DOD, or other agencies may have been deploying. "Even the federal agencies themselves, DOD, for example … didn't even have the control within DOD of all the assets being deployed by DOD because different parts of DOD were deploying assets and there was no central control," he said.[64] Without knowledge of what communications assets federal agencies were bringing into the area, NCS could not effectively prioritize the use of those assets.[65]

Fonash acknowledged that NCS had inadequate information about the communication situation in the New Orleans area. According to NCS protocol, its headquarters receives such information only when its personnel on the ground have run into "problems [they] can't fix."[66] The magnitude of the damage in Louisiana proved this system inadequate. Fonash said that NCS staff was "so busy handling the crisis that they were probably not giving us the situational awareness that we should have been getting. . . . We just didn't have enough people down there."[67] Eventually, Fonash sent additional staff to the region and placed a contact at the Louisiana state EOC.

Several communications assets were not deployed at all, or could have been deployed sooner:

> • The U.S. Forest Service maintains over 5,000 radios, the largest civilian cache of radios in the United States, but many remained unused.[68]

> • FEMA Mobile Emergency Response Support (MERS) units, which include trucks with satellite capabilities, were at Barksdale Air Force Base in Shreveport, LA, outside the disaster area, during landfall, and did not travel to the State EOC in Baton Rouge until the day after landfall.[69]

> • DOD had communications assets, including radio systems, which could have been deployed sooner.[70]

> • DHS's Prepositioned Equipment Program (PEP) pods containing communications equipment did not start deploying until a week after landfall.[71]

The NCS did identify and provide satellite communications vans to New Orleans City Hall, LSP in Baton Rouge, the Mobile Army Surgical Hospital at the New Orleans Airport, and to the National Guard in Jefferson Parish.[72] NCS also provided a cellular unit on a truck to the Louisiana State EOC.[73] In addition, NCS identified the need to provide a temporary LMR communications solution to the eight-parish area around New Orleans, working with FEMA to initiate the contract.[74] But most of these NCS assets were not provided until days after the storm struck or were only provided to select locations. Indeed, satellite vans were not en route to the LSP in Baton Rouge until September 1, and high water kept one satellite van from reaching New Orleans City Hall until three days after landfall.[75]

It appears that some requests for the NCS to provide communications capabilities to local governments were not made until a few days after landfall. For example, Colonel Jeff Smith, Louisiana's Acting Deputy Director for Emergency Preparedness, did not submit a form requesting "communications with the affected parish EOCs" until 5 p.m. on September 1 – more than three days after landfall.[76] Fonash said that he wasn't aware that the state EOC had communications problems until the state made its request on September 1.[77] An e-mail indicates that Governor Blanco did not ask for assistance with communications until the evening of August 31, two days after landfall; in that case, the federal ESF-2 representative in Baton Rouge met with a state official the next day.[78] Under the NRP, though, the NCS could have offered assistance even before the state made an official request for help.

Mobile Emergency Response Systems

FEMA's Mobile Emergency Response Support (MERS) division maintains roughly 300 mobile vehicles, most of which provide logistics support to FEMA. MERS units are dispersed throughout the country at five MERS stations. The MERS vehicles range from small sport-utility vehicles to large tractor trailers with expandable conference room space. The deployments are self-sustaining and include fuel, water, and power.[79]

The primary responsibility of MERS is to provide communications capabilities to FEMA, including the Joint Field Office (JFO), the Emergency Response Team A (ERTA), and the Rapid Needs Assessment Team. During a disaster, MERS units may provide some communications support to the state EOC, if requested by the state.[80] However, MERS does not view this type of assistance to first responders as part of its mission.[81]

The MERS Thomasville, GA, detachment (serving FEMA Region IV) and Denton, TX, detachment (serving FEMA Region VI) deployed the weekend before landfall.[82] Recognizing the power of the storm, over the weekend MERS sent personnel, vehicles, and assets to the disaster area from its other detachments across the country as well as from the MERS National Capital Region team.[83] After landfall, MERS equipment also was used to support National Disaster Medical System (NDMS) and Urban Search and Rescue (USAR) efforts and, approximately one week after landfall, helped to build the office for Coast Guard Admiral Thad Allen's command center.[84]

Despite the level of MERS equipment deployed to the Gulf Coast, MERS was overwhelmed by the extent of communications needs, and experienced difficulties in supporting FEMA personnel.

The MERS team assigned to the JFO in Baton Rouge on Saturday, August 27, was in place on Sunday, August 28, although not at the level needed to support the JFO, which eventually grew to more than 2,000 people. After landfall, MERS had to provide additional communications support, including a high-capacity T-1 cable capable of providing hundreds of phone lines.[85] FEMA employees experienced difficulties calling out of the JFO because

MERS relies largely on local landlines and cellular systems that had failed or were heavily congested.[86] One MERS technician estimated that eight of every 10 calls failed, noting that FEMA employees relying on landlines "have no higher priority than anybody else, [such as] the guy using the pay phone down at the corner of the street trying to make an outgoing call, and most of the facilities are dead or down or under water."[87] MERS therefore had to bring in satellite capabilities to provide a reliable means of getting calls in and out.[88]

Before landfall, FEMA Region IV requested that MERS deploy a detachment to the state EOC in Jackson, MS.[89] In FEMA Region IV, the MERS unit from Denton, TX, sent support to Baton Rouge pre-landfall for FEMA's Rapid Needs Assessment teams and the FEMA JFO, but otherwise staged its vehicles and equipment at Barksdale Air Force Base in Louisiana.[90] These vehicles included the so-called "Red October," a large tractor-trailer vehicle.[91]

Post-landfall, the vehicles staged at Barksdale could not move until the high winds had subsided along the coast. On Tuesday, August 30, the day after landfall, the Barksdale equipment mobilized. A communications vehicle was sent to the Louisiana state EOC.[92] Red October started out for New Orleans but had to be held in Lafayette, Louisiana on the night of August 30 due to difficulties navigating around debris.[93] In the end, Red October did not go to New Orleans because flood levels were too high for it to reach the Superdome.[94] It eventually went to Baton Rouge, where it served as FEMA Director Michael Brown's command center.[95]

No MERS vehicles ever reached the Superdome because of flooding, exacerbating problems there. Sandy Coachman, who was part of the FEMA team at the Superdome, said that at one point she could see a MERS vehicle on an overpass on I-10. She could see the driver, and they waved their phones in the air to signal each other, but that was the extent of their ability to communicate.[96] The failure of a MERS communications vehicle to reach the Superdome cut off any meaningful communications with the EOC in Baton Rouge. Coachman said her satellite phone, cell phone, and Blackberry handheld wireless device all failed to work.[97] The only way the FEMA team could communicate was by using National Guard phones, which often could not get through to the EOC because of congestion on the system.[98] It is unclear why FEMA did not instruct MERS to deploy a smaller communications vehicle to the Superdome when the Red October experienced difficulties moving there, or why FEMA did not attempt to airlift smaller MERS equipment (satellite phones in particular) into the Superdome once New Orleans flooded.

The response to Katrina stretched MERS's resources and exposed the difficulty that MERS would encounter in responding to simultaneous catastrophes in different parts of the country. When Hurricane Rita hit, MERS Chief William Milani had to negotiate with the Federal Coordinating Officers directing the federal response in the Katrina region to get MERS assets released from areas devastated by Katrina, and also had to contract out for additional assets. Given that the response to Katrina essentially stripped bare all five MERS detachments, Chief Milani was uncertain how MERS could have responded if another major disaster occurred during the response to Katrina.[99]

Satellite Communications

Satellite phones don't rely on the ground-based infrastructure necessary for land mobile radio, land-line, and cellular communications. But there is anecdotal evidence that satellite communications experienced their own problems: New Orleans Mayor Ray Nagin said that he had "a huge box of satellite phones that did not work."[100] In Mississippi, a FEMA employee, Mike Beeman, said that satellite phone connections were "sporadic."[101] And while wireless Blackberry devices worked, batteries were hard to recharge because of the lack of commercial electricity.[102]

The problems with satellite phones do not appear to have been caused by the phones themselves or the satellite networks; rather, a combination of user error and buildings or other objects obstructing satellite signals are the more likely culprits. In fact, NCS was not aware of any problems with the satellite phone networks.[103] And Walt Gorman, a vice-president at Globalstar, which supplied many satellite phones to the federal government, Louisiana, and Mississippi, said that users with difficulty operating satellite phones probably did not know how to use them properly because they had not received training. Therefore, users may have had problems putting them in the correct mode, directing the antennae, or dialing the correct numbers.[104]

Louisiana supplied satellite phones to New Orleans parishes a few years ago, but after the state stopped paying for the satellite monthly service fee, all but three parishes discontinued the service and returned the phones to the state.[105] These satellite phones might have been useful if they had been available during Katrina. To fill the communications gap, Louisiana tried to bring in communications trailers with transmitters to restore cellular communications, but those efforts were hampered by the flooding.[106]

In Mississippi, all Mississippi Emergency Management Agency (MEMA) personnel had mobile satellite radios for communications; satellite radios permanently mounted in the three coastal counties were available as well. After Katrina struck, this was often the only functional form of communications in the state.[107] Satellite worked so well that MEMA purchased additional portable satellite phones for state emergency response teams.[108] Even though coastal county EOCs had satellite capability, the strong winds of Katrina shifted their antennas, resulting in failed communications.[109] In addition, MEMA deployed a mobile communications unit and Pearl River County had a mobile communications trailer that it purchased with DHS grants, which allowed it to communicate after Katrina.[110]

Pre-Landfall Attempts to Improve Louisiana's Public-Safety Communications Infrastructure

The problem of interoperable communications was brought to the nation's attention on September 11, 2001, when police and firefighters at the World Trade Center had difficulty communicating with each other. However, it is a long-standing problem. According to David Boyd, head of project SAFECOM, an "umbrella" DHS program designed to coordinate federal efforts to promote interoperability, the inability to communicate effectively across jurisdictions and disciplines was a problem in the Air Florida crash in Washington, D.C., in 1982; in New York City when the World Trade Center was first attacked in 1993 and again on September 11, 2001; and when the Murrah Federal Building was destroyed in Okalahoma City in 1995. Sixty thousand individual local jurisdictions – including police, fire, and emergency medical services – finance, own, operate, and maintain over 90 percent of the nation's public safety wireless infrastructure.[111]

As in most states, parishes in the New Orleans area and state agencies maintain different communication systems, which make it difficult for public safety agencies to communicate during everyday emergencies, let alone disasters on the scale of Katrina.

The State of Louisiana operates on a statewide analog wireless system installed in 1996. It supports voice communication only. This system is presently used by approximately 70 agencies with 10,000 subscribers. This system consists of 46 tower sites and 28 dispatch consoles. The LSP operate an aging data network that cannot support additional users. The Louisiana Totally Interoperable Environmental (LATIE) Strategic Plan says that while "this system was quite sophisticated for its time, advances in technology have rendered it virtually obsolete."[112]

Large parts of the communications systems in southeastern Louisiana are outdated and have been in various stages of disrepair for several years. In Orleans Parish the communications system is an 800 MHz system, which supports police, fire, EMS and the Office of Emergency Preparedness. (MHz (Megahertz) denotes the frequency on which the equipment operates and public safety radio equipment often can only operate on a specific frequency.) The age of the equipment created problems in getting technical support.[113]

In St. Bernard Parish, the 400 MHz communications system is so old that it must be maintained by purchasing repair parts through the eBay auction site on the Internet.[114] Various volunteer fire departments have other types of communications systems. Jefferson Parish has an 800 MHz "Motorola Digital Smart Zone System" for the Sheriff's Office, but the rest of the parish agencies use an analog system, which makes it nearly impossible to communicate with the Sheriff's Office. In Plaquemines Parish, the Sheriff's Department uses an 800 MHz analog system that cannot communicate with digital systems.[115]

According to FG Dowden, who works on interoperable communications and other issues for the New Orleans Office of Homeland Security, the only interoperable system in use in southeastern Louisiana prior to the storm was between the NOPD and the Jefferson Parish Sheriff's Office; it used "console patches" to connect their 800 MHz controllers, which provided a degree of interoperability.[116]

ACU-1000 units also provided limited interoperability. The ACU-1000, which is manufactured by JPS Raytheon, acts as a converter between radios from each system. But it can support only a limited number of channels for communications, and it requires a person to manually configure the connections with the radios.[117]

Well before Katrina struck, Louisiana agencies encountered funding problems as they sought to enhance communications interoperability. In 2004 and again in January 2005, the Louisiana State Police attempted to secure $105 million to upgrade its communications infrastructure from an outdated, 800 MHz analog system which is no longer supported by the vendor to a modern 700 MHz digital interoperable network. That amount was considered an "inexpensive" way to connect existing operating systems in the state to a common, statewide network. The State Police sought funding from Congress, via earmark requests to Louisiana's Congressional delegation, as well as through Louisiana's state budget process and grant opportunities with DHS' Office of Domestic Preparedness, but was not successful.[118]

The greater New Orleans area also analyzed options for creating a region-wide, modern 800 MHz system, well before Katrina struck. However, estimates ranged as high as $45 million, which local officials considered "cost prohibitive."[119] Just buying compatible radios for New Orleans Parish alone would cost almost $20 million.[120] Therefore, the region developed a plan for a region-wide system involving all four parishes in the region, which would be phased in over time.[121]

According to Dowden, New Orleans applied for and received a grant through the Community Oriented Policing Services (COPS) program at the Department of Justice (DOJ) that would have provided interoperability for the four-parish region by upgrading St. Bernard Parish and Plaquemines Parish to 800 MHz trunk radio systems and providing bridging technology between two or more of the 800 MHz systems (which Orleans and Jefferson Parishes already had).[122] This grant also would have allowed some of the systems to have P-25 compliant technology (an interoperability standard designed by the government and private industry). However, the project was 18 months from completion when Katrina struck.[123] If the project had been completed by the initial time table, the loss of communication towers might not have been quite as significant because there probably would have been at least two towers fully operational from the new system.[124]

New Orleans has a "tactical interoperability plan" developed pursuant to DHS grant guidance, but this plan was developed around an improvised-explosive-device scenario, not for an event of widespread destruction like that caused by a hurricane. According to Col. Dowden, a catastrophic hurricane plan "takes into account all of the assets within the region, and then pre-scripts what you would do in the event you lose specific towers or capabilities."[125] Even though the risk of major hurricanes striking New Orleans was well known, that kind of communications plan had never been developed.

In addition to funding, interoperability also always raises technical and policy issues. As Colonel Joseph Booth of the LSP put it, "there's always issues about who's going to control it, who's making decisions, what technology to go with, what capabilities, what kind of local control there is."[126]

1 Committee staff interview of FG Dowden, U.S. Marine Corps (Ret.), Regional Liaison, New Orleans Department of Homeland Security and Public Safety, LA, conducted on Nov. 11, 2005, transcript p. 50.

2 Testimony of Gov. Haley Barbour, Mississippi, before the U.S. Senate, Committee on Homeland Security and Governmental Affairs, hearing on *The Role of the Governors in Managing the Catastrophe*, Feb. 2, 2006.

3 Committee staff interview of Sally Forman, Communications Director, City of New Orleans, LA, conducted on Jan. 10, 2006, transcript pp.120-121.

4 Forman interview, Jan. 10, 2006, p. 68.

5 Forman interview, Jan. 10, 2006, p. 101.

6 Forman interview, Jan. 10, 2006, p. 121.

7 Committee staff interview of Larry Ingargiola, Director, Homeland Security and Emergency Preparedness, St. Bernard Parish, LA, Oct. 26, 2005, transcript pp. 91-93, 103-104.

8 Testimony of Lt. Col. Keith LaCaze, Assistant Administrator, Law Enforcement Division, Louisiana Department of Wildlife and Fisheries, before the U.S. Senate, Committee on Homeland Security and Governmental Affairs, hearing on *Hurricane Katrina: Urban Search and Rescue in a Catastrophe*, Jan. 30, 2006.

9 Committee staff interview of Phil Parr, Federal Coordinating Officer, Region I, Federal Emergency Management Association (FEMA), conducted on Nov. 15, 2005, transcript p. 28.

10 Committee staff interview of Michael Beeman, Director, Preparedness Division, Region II, FEMA, conducted on Jan. 20, 2006, transcript p. 71.

11 Committee staff interview of Scott Wells, Deputy Federal Coordinating Officer for Hurricane Katrina in Louisiana, FEMA, conducted on Nov. 14, 2005, transcript p. 116.

12 Committee staff interview of Knox Andress, RN, Christus Schumpert Health System, Shreveport, LA, conducted on, Mar. 10, 2006 (untranscribed).

13 Andress interview, Mar. 10, 2006.

14 Written Statement of Kevin T. Regan, Regional Vice President of Operations, Starwood Hotels & Resorts Worldwide, Inc., for the U.S. Senate, Committee on Homeland Security and Governmental Affairs, hearing on *Hurricane Katrina: What Can Government Learn From Private Sector's Response?*, Nov. 16, 2005, p. 5.

15 Written Statement of Regan, Senate Committee hearing, Nov. 16, 2006, p. 6.

16 Committee staff interview of Kevin Regan, Regional Vice President of Operations, Starwood Hotels & Resorts Worldwide, Inc., conducted on Nov. 3, 2006 (untranscribed).

17 Written Statement of Jason Jackson, Wal-Mart Stores, Inc., for the U.S. Senate, Committee on Homeland Security and Governmental Affairs, hearing on *Hurricane Katrina: What Can Government Learn From Private Sector's Response?*, Nov. 16, 2005.

18 Written Statement of Jackson, Senate Committee hearing, Nov. 16, 2005.

19 Written Statement of David Ratcliffe, Southern Company, for the U.S. Senate, Committee on Homeland Security and

Governmental Affairs, hearing on *Hurricane Katrina: What Can Government Learn From the Private Sector's Response?*, Nov. 16, 2005.

20 Written Statement of Radcliffe, Senate Committee hearing, Nov. 16, 2005, pp. 4-5.

21 Written Statement of Radcliffe, Senate Committee hearing, Nov. 16, 2005, p. 5.

22 Written Statement of Radcliffe, Senate Committee hearing, Nov. 16, 2005, p. 5.

23 The White House report on Katrina aptly concluded, "The complete devastation of the communications infrastructure left emergency responders and citizens without a reliable network across which they could coordinate." U.S. Assistant to the President for Homeland Security and Counterterrorism, *The Federal Response to Hurricane Katrina Lessons Learned*. Washington: Government Printing Office, Feb. 2006, p. 55.

24 Written Statement of William Smith, Chief Technology Officer, BellSouth, for the U.S. Senate, Committee on Homeland Security and Governmental Affairs, hearing on *Managing Law Enforcement and Communications in a Catastrophe*, Feb. 6, 2006, p. 4.

25 Written Statement of Peter M. Fonash, Ph.D., Deputy Manager, National Communications System, U.S. Department of Homeland Security, for the U.S. Senate, Committee on Homeland Security and Governmental Affairs, hearing on *Managing Law Enforcement and Communications in a Catastrophe*, Feb. 6, 2006, p. 6.

26 Written Statement of Fonash, Senate Committee hearing, Feb. 6, 2006, p. 1; Federal Communications Commission, *Consumers Out of Service*. Provided to Committee.

27 Written Statement of Fonash, Senate Committee hearing, Feb. 6, 2006, p.1; Written statement of Smith, Senate Committee hearing, Feb. 6, 2006, p. 4.

28 Committee staff interview of Christopher Guttman-McCabe, Vice President, Regulatory Affairs, CTIA, conducted on Jan. 24, 2006, transcript p. 20.

29 Guttman-McCabe interview, Jan. 24, 2006, p. 21.

30 Guttman-McCabe interview, Jan. 24, 2006, pp. 11-12.

31 Committee staff interview of William Smith, Chief Technology Officer, BellSouth, Inc., conducted on Jan. 25, 2006 (untranscribed).

32 Smith interview, Jan. 25, 2006.

33 Kay Jackson, e-mail to La Public Service Commission, Sept. 20, 2005, 6:08 p.m. Provided to Committee.

34 Smith interview, Jan. 25, 2006.

35 Written Statement of Smith, Senate Committee hearing, Feb. 6, 2006, p. 8.

36 Written Statement of Smith, Senate Committee hearing, Feb. 6, 2006, p. 8; Written statement of Fonash, Senate Committee hearing, Feb. 6, 2006, p. 7.

37 Tom Wetherald, e-mail to Peter Fonash, Sept. 3, 2005, 9:37 p.m. Provided to Committee; filed as Bates nos. DHS-INFP-0002-0000737 through 0000738. *See also*: Committee staff interview of Jeffrey Glick, Chief of Critical Infrastructure Protection, National Communications System, conducted on Feb. 3, 2006, transcript p. 60 (explaining NCS's efforts to work through the NRCC and ESF-13 process as well as with the National Guard).

38 Glick interview, Feb. 3, 2006, p. 60

39 Guttman-McCabe interview, Jan. 24, 2006, p. 25.

40 Kim Hunter Reed, e-mail to Jeanne Wright and others, Aug. 30, 2005, 1:57 p.m. Provided to Committee; Brian Eddington, e-mail to LA Public Service Commission, Sept. 2, 2005, 7:20 p.m. Provided to Committee; Michael Vitenas, e-mail to LA Public Service Commission, Sept. 2, 2005, 5:10 p.m. Provided to Committee.

41 Guttman-McCabe interview, Jan 24, 2006, p. 28.

42 Testimony of Warren Riley, Superintendent, New Orleans Police Department, LA, before the U.S. Senate, Committee on Homeland Security and Governmental Affairs, hearing on *Managing Law Enforcement and Communications in a Catastrophe*, Feb. 6, 2006; Testimony of Capt. Timothy Bayard, Commander, Vice and Narcotics Squad, New Orleans Police Department, LA, before the U.S. Senate, Committee on Homeland Security and Governmental Affairs, hearing on *Managing Law Enforcement and Communications in a Catastrophe*, Feb. 6, 2006; Testimony of Lt. Col. Keith LaCaze, Assistant Administrator, Law Enforcement Division, Louisiana Department of Wildlife and Fisheries, before the U.S. Senate, Committee on Homeland Security and Governmental Affairs hearing on *Managing Law Enforcement and Communications in a Catastrophe*, Feb. 6, 2006; Testimony of Brig. Gen. Brod Veillon, Assistant Adjutant General, Louisiana National Guard, before the U.S. Senate, Committee on Homeland Security and Governmental Affairs, hearing on *Managing Law Enforcement and Communications in a Catastrophe*, Feb. 6, 2006.

43 FEMA's Federal Coordinating Officer for Louisiana, William Lokey, said there were problems making calls in and out of the State EOC. Committee staff interview of William Lokey, Federal Coordinating Officer for Hurricane Katrina in Louisiana, FEMA, conducted on Jan. 20, 2006, transcript p. 6.

44 Wells interview, Nov. 14, 2006, p. 116

45 Glick interview, Feb. 3, 2006, pp. 29-20.

46 Testimony of FG Dowden, Regional Liason, New Orleans Department of Homeland Security, LA, before the U.S. Senate, Committee on Homeland Security and Governmental Affairs, hearing on *Managing Law Enforcement and Communications in a Catastrophe,* Feb. 6, 2006; Col. Dowden interview, Jan. 26, 2006.

47 Dowden, Senate Committee hearing, Feb. 6, 2006.

48 Dowden, Senate Committee hearing, Feb. 6, 2006; Dowden interview, Nov. 11, 2005, pp. 33-34.

49 Dowden, Senate Committee hearing, Feb. 6, 2006.

50 Dowden interview, Jan. 26, 2006.

51 Dowden interview, Nov. 11, 2005, pp. 33-34.

52 Dowden, Senate Committee hearing, Feb. 6, 2006.

53 Dowden, Senate Committee hearing, Feb. 6, 2006.

54 Committee staff interview of Lt. Col. Mark Oxley, Chief of Staff, Louisiana State Police, and Lt. Col. Joseph Booth, Deputy Superintendent, Crisis Response and Special Operations, Louisiana State Police, conducted on Dec. 9, 2005, transcript pp. 78-79.

55 Written Statement of Kevin J. Martin, Chairman, Federal Communications Commission, for the U.S. House, Committee on Energy and Commerce, Subcommittee on Telecommunications and the Internet, hearing on *Public Safety Communications from 9/11 to Katrina: Critical Public Policy Lessons,* Sept. 29, 2005, p. 2.

56 Committee staff interview of Craig Whittington, 911 Coordinator for Guilford Metro 911, Greensboro, NC, Mar. 13, 2006 (untranscribed).

57 Whittington interview, Mar. 13, 2006.

58 Whittington interview, Mar. 13, 2006.

59 Whittington interview, Mar. 13, 2006.

60 U.S. Department of Homeland Security, *National Response Plan.* Washington: Government Printing Office, Dec. 2004, pp. ESF #2–1 through 2–3.

61 Fonash interview, Jan. 27, 2006, p. 4.

62 Fonash interview, Jan. 27, 2006, p. 37.

63 Fonash interview, Jan. 27, 2006, pp. 50-51.

64 Fonash interview, Jan. 27, 2006, p. 60.

65 Fonash interview, Jan. 27, 2006, p. 62.

66 Fonash interview, Jan. 27, 2006, p. 116.

67 Fonash interview, Jan. 27, 2006, pp. 118-120.

68 Written Statement of Mark Rey, Under Secretary, Natural Resources and Environment, U.S. Department of Agriculture, for the U.S. House, Committee on Homeland Security, Subcommittee on Emergency Preparedness, Science, and Technology, hearing on *Ensuring Operability During Catastrophic Events,* Oct. 26, 2005, p. 3.

69 Committee staff interview of William Milani, Chief, Mobile Operations Section, Logistics Branch, FEMA, conducted on Jan. 12, 2006, transcript p. 59.

70 U.S. Department of Defense, "DOD Support to Hurricane Katrina," Executive Summary. Provided to Committee; filed as Bates no. 00614 ("DOD provided 1500 mobile radios . . . ; radios arrived September 6 and given to the 82nd Airborne at the New Orleans Airport."). When the DOD troops returned to their home stations, they provided 1500 of their radios to the National Guard troops. Committee staff interview of Col. James Kohlman, U.S. Army, U.S. Northern Command, U.S. Department of Defense, conducted on Dec. 6, 2005, transcript pp. 20, 39.

71 Marc Short, e-mail to Matt Mayer, Sept. 5, 2005, 10:51 a.m. Provided to Committee, filed as Bates no. DHS-FRNT-0010-0000386.

72 Written Statement of Fonash, Senate Committee hearing, Feb. 6, 2006, p. 6.

73 Written Statement of Fonash, Senate Committee hearing, Feb. 6, 2006, p. 6.

74 Written Statement of Fonash, Senate Committee hearing, Feb. 6, 2006, p. 7.

75 National Communications System, "National Communications System Response to Hurricane Katrina." Provided to Committee; filed as Bates no. DHS-INFP-0001-0000672.

76 FEMA, Action Request Form, Sept. 1, 2005. Provided to Committee.

77 Fonash interview, Jan. 27, 2006, p. 114.

78 Thomas Falvey, e-mail to Peter Fonash, Sept. 1, 2005, 2:25 p.m. Provided to Committee; filed as Bates nos. DHS-INFP-0002-0000026 through 0000027.

79 Milani interview, Jan. 12, 2006, pp. 7-9, 23-25.

80 Milani interview, Jan. 12, 2006, pp. 19-23.

81 Milani interview, Jan. 12, 2006, pp. 28, 129.

82 Milani interview, Jan. 12, 2006, p. 49.

83 Milani interview, Jan. 12, 2006, pp. 24, 53-54.

84 Milani interview, Jan. 12, 2006, pp. 96, 99, 103-04.

85 Committee staff interview of James Attaway, Telecommunications Specialist, Mobile Emeregency Response System, Region VI, FEMA, conducted on Jan. 13, 2006, transcript p. 27; Milani interview, Jan. 12, 2006, pp. 56-57.

86 Attaway interview, Jan. 13, 2006, pp. 9, 12-13; Milani interview, Jan. 12, 2006, p. 60.

87 Attaway interview, Jan. 13, 2006, p. 29.

88 Attaway interview, Jan. 13, 2006, pp. 28-29.

89 Milani interview, Jan. 12, 2006, pp. 52-53.

90 Attaway interview, Jan. 13, 2006, pp. 19, 79; Milani interview, Jan. 12, 2006, pp. 53-54.

91 Milani interview, Jan. 12, 2006, p. 59.

92 Milani interview, Jan. 12, 2006, p. 59.

93 Milani interview, Jan. 12, 2006, pp. 59, 70.

94 Milani interview, Jan. 12, 2006, p. 70.

95 Milani interview, Jan. 12, 2006, pp. 95-96.

96 Committee staff interview of Sandy Coachman, Federal Coordinating Officer, Region VI, FEMA, conducted on Nov. 16, 2005, transcript pp. 16-18.

97 Coachman interview, Nov. 16, 2005, pp. 16-18.

98 Coachman interview, Nov. 16, 2005, p. 18.

99 Milani interview, Jan. 12, 2006, pp. 78-79.

100 Testimony of Mayor C. Ray Nagin, City of New Orleans, LA, before the U.S. Senate, Committee on Homeland Security and Governmental Affairs, hearing on *Managing the Crisis and Evacuating New Orleans*, Feb. 1, 2006.

101 Beeman interview, Jan. 20, 2006, p. 85.

102 Dowden interview, Nov. 11, 2005, p. 194.

103 Fonash interview, Jan. 27, 2006, p. 152.

104 Walt Gorman, Vice President, Globalstar, e-mail to Rob Strayer, Senate Committee staff member, Mar. 8, 2006, 1:23 p.m.

105 U.S. House, Select Bipartisan Committee to Investigate the Preparation for and Response to Hurricane Katrina, *A Failure of Initiative*. Washington: Government Printing Office, 2006, pp. 172-173 [hereinafter U.S. House, *A Failure of Initiative*].

106 Col. Dowden Interview, Nov. 11, 2005, p. 195.

107 U.S. House, *A Failure of Initiative*, p. 172; Testimony of Robert R. Latham, Jr., Executive Director, Mississippi Emergency Management Agency (MEMA), before the U.S. House, Select Bipartisan Committee to Investigate the Preparation for and Response to Hurricane Katrina, hearing on *Hurricane Katrina: Preparedness and Response by the State of Mississippi*, Dec. 7, 2005.

108 U.S. House, *A Failure of Initiative*, p. 173; Latham, House Select Committee hearing, Dec. 7, 2005; Committee staff interview of William Brown, Operations Chief, MEMA, conducted on Jan. 26, 2006.

109 Written Statement of Robert R. Latham Jr., Executive Director, MEMA, for the U.S. House, Select Bipartisan Committee to Investigate the Preparation for and Response to Hurricane Katrina, hearing on *Hurricane Katrina: Preparedness and Response by the State of Mississippi*, Dec. 7, 2005, pp. 3-4.

110 U.S. House, *A Failure of Initiative*, p. 172; Committee staff interview of Michael Brown, former Director, FEMA, conducted on Jan. 26, 2006, pp. 16-17.

111 Testimony of David Boyd, Director, SAFECOM, Office of Interoperability and Compatibility, U.S. Department of Homeland Security, before the U.S. House, Committee on Homeland Security, Subcommittee on Emergency Preparedness, Science and Technology, hearing on *Ensuring Operability During Catastrophic Events*, Oct. 26, 2005.

112 Louisiana Totally Interoperable Environment Strategic Plan (LATIE), Executive Summary, p. 3. Provided to Committee.

113 Dowden interview, Nov. 11, 2005, pp. 11-12.

114 Dowden interview, Nov. 11, 2005, p. 15.

115 Dowden interview, Nov. 11, 2005, pp. 12-13.

116 Dowden interview, Nov. 11, 2005, p. 13

117 Dowden interview, Nov. 11, 2005, pp. 32-34.

118 Lt. Col. Oxley and Lt. Col. Booth interview, Dec. 9, 2005, pp. 48, 51, 54.

119 Written Statement of Dowden, Senate Committee hearing, Feb. 6, 2006, p. 3.

120 Dowden interview, Nov. 11, 2005, p. 41.

121 Written Statement of Dowden, Senate Committee hearing, Feb. 6, 2006, p. 3.

122 Written Statement of Dowden, Senate Committee hearing, Feb. 6, 2006, p. 2.

123 Dowden interview, Nov. 11, 2005, p. 211.

124 Dowden interview, Nov. 11, 2005, p. 49.

125 Dowden interview, Nov. 11, 2005, p. 201.

126 Booth interview, Dec. 9, 2005, p. 68.

Wrecked marina,
Ocean Springs, MS
Sun Herald photo

Lack of Situational Awareness

Federal Situational Awareness

Having an ability to "connect the dots" was a main goal during the creation of the Department of Homeland Security (DHS). The Homeland Security Operations Center (HSOC) is a key element, designed to be "the nation's nerve center for information sharing and domestic incident management."[1] Hurricane Katrina was the HSOC's first major, public test, and it failed. At the federal level, there was a startling lack of situational awareness as Katrina came ashore. On the day of landfall, DHS ignored, disregarded, or simply failed to obtain readily available reports that would have – and should have – led to an understanding of the increasingly dire situation in New Orleans and the remainder of the Gulf Coast.

DHS witnesses have offered essentially two explanations for the lack of situational awareness on Monday, August 29. First, they fault Federal Emergency Management Agency's (FEMA) former Director Michael Brown and his agency for failing to provide the HSOC with crucial information. Second, they invoke the "fog of war" metaphor and assert that conflicting reports rendered the HSOC unable to develop any sense of the "ground truth."

These are at best only partial explanations for the HSOC's failure to understand the scope of the unfolding disaster. Brown did fail to forward critical information in his possession, which is inexcusable. However, the HSOC's failure to obtain reports of breaches and massive flooding issued by the National Weather Service (NWS), the Army Corps of Engineers, and the media, was unrelated to anything Brown or FEMA did or did not do. Indeed, throughout the day of landfall the HSOC received reports – including from two DHS Protective Security Advisors (PSAs)[2] stationed in the region – that uniformly reflected a growing catastrophe. To the extent these reports "conflicted," it was only about the scope of the catastrophe described, not the existence of the catastrophe itself.

The failure to "connect the dots" is best captured by the situation report ("sitrep") issued by the HSOC at 5 p.m. Central Time (all subsequent times Central) on Monday, August 29. During hurricanes and other significant incidents, the HSOC issues sitreps at 5 a.m. and 5 p.m. to many customers, including DHS leadership and the White House.[3] In crucial areas this sitrep was both incorrect and incomplete. It was incorrect in stating that "preliminary reports indicate the levees in New Orleans have not been breached; however, an assessment is still pending."[4] In fact, most preliminary reports stated just the opposite. It was incomplete in stating generically that "flooding is reported in New Orleans,"[5] but failing to provide any detail about the widely reported scope of the flooding or the devastating results – for example, that residents were seeking refuge from rising water in their attics and on rooftops.

In a dynamic situation such as Katrina, time was of the essence, as people were in desperate circumstances. It may never be known for certain how the lack of awareness contributed to the overall failure of the federal government to respond adequately in a timely manner. It is known, however, that the 5 p.m. sitrep was the last report DHS Secretary Michael Chertoff received on the day of landfall,[6] and he went to bed Monday night with the incorrect belief that the levees had not been breached and that Katrina had not done the worst that had been predicted.[7] This incorrect sitrep was also forwarded to the White House. Several days later President Bush later remarked that "I myself, thought we had dodged a bullet."[8]

Analysis of the Failure

The HSOC's failure to maintain situational awareness during Katrina grew out of a lack of planning and flawed analysis. Though plans for obtaining situational awareness are developed for events like the Superbowl and national political conventions, HSOC Director Matthew Broderick acknowledged that "there was no plan developed" for maintaining situational awareness during Katrina.[9]

This lack of planning led to numerous failings. Neither HSOC Director Broderick nor HSOC Deputy Director Frank DiFalco knew that DHS had a representative in New Orleans and another in the Louisiana State Police Emergency Operations Center in Baton Rouge sending reports to the HSOC. Indeed, on the day of landfall, the HSOC failed to recognize, or disregarded as unconfirmed, many of the reports that it did receive. The HSOC similarly failed to obtain reports and information that it should have obtained. As the week progressed, situational awareness improved little if at all, evidenced most pointedly by DHS's belated awareness of the thousands of people gathering at the Convention Center.

There were also structural flaws in the way the HSOC obtained information from other federal agencies and other sources. The twice-a-day HSOC sitreps contained information that, in most cases, was at least three and, often, five or more hours old. During Katrina, FEMA input to the HSOC sitrep was due three hours before a sitrep was issued.[10] FEMA's internal deadline for submissions to the HSOC was, in turn, two hours earlier.[11] Thus, by design a 5 p.m. sitrep reflected information that was at least five hours old.

Between sitreps, HSOC issued "Spot Reports" on breaking news. Starting at approximately 6:35 p.m., the HSOC generated numerous Spot Reports accurately detailing the devastation in New Orleans. However, many of those who were on the e-mail distribution list for these Spot Reports, issued late into the night on Monday, appear not to have read them when they were received. Witnesses also explained that, as a general matter, they viewed the sitreps as more authoritative than the Spot Reports. They testified almost universally that they were not aware of the inundation of New Orleans until after the 5 a.m. sitrep Tuesday morning – 12 or more hours after the HSOC began issuing the grave Spot Reports detailed below.

During the Day of Landfall, a Litany of Reports Stated that Levees Had Failed, and Detailed the Increasingly Severe Flooding

Prior to issuing the flawed 5 p.m. sitrep, the HSOC issued two Spot Reports during the morning of landfall. One, at 8:25 a.m., was based on a press conference by New Orleans Mayor Ray Nagin and stated in part that water was coming over the levees in the Ninth Ward. Almost two hours later, at 10:22 a.m., the HSOC issued another Spot Report, including reports that water was rising at the National Guard's Jackson Barracks in the Ninth Ward, adding that it was unknown whether this was the result of breaching or overtopping. It also stated that the 911 call centers in St. Bernard and Orleans Parishes had been shut down and evacuated. Ten minutes later, the information in this second Spot Report was also distributed in an e-mail to, among others, DHS Chief of Staff John Wood and Deputy Secretary Michael Jackson.

The Committee has discovered no other communications out of the HSOC prior to the 5 p.m. sitrep. Both before and after the two morning Spot Reports, however, the HSOC received reports of levee breaches, levee overtopping, flooding, and people trapped on roofs. Equally troubling are the reports the HSOC apparently never received. As discussed below, some of this information was received by FEMA, but not forwarded in a timely way to the HSOC. However, the majority of this information was available from other sources, including government agencies that have desks within the HSOC, and major media outlets. These reports are described below, with the ones that the HSOC received highlighted in **bold**:[12]

- At 8:14 a.m., the New Orleans National Weather Service office reported a levee breach along the Industrial Canal.[13]

- **At 9 a.m. on the morning of landfall, the HSOC received an e-mail from Louis Dabdoub, the PSA on the ground in New Orleans. Dabdoub's report stated in part: "It is getting bad. Major flooding in some parts of the city. People are calling in for rescue saying they are trapped in attics, etc. That means water is 10 feet high there already. Trees are blowing down. Flooding is worsening every minute. ... The bad part has not hit here yet."**[14]

- At 9 a.m., the New Orleans NWS office reported overtopping in Orleans and St. Bernard Parishes and "Extensive and life threatening storm surge flooding occurring along the Louisiana and Mississippi coast."[15]

- **At 9:36 a.m., Dabdoub sent another e-mail to the HSOC, reporting that "The lower parishes of La [Louisiana], Plaq[uemines] and St Bernard parish's [sic] are under water."**[16]

- At 10:13 a.m., the White House Homeland Security Council issued a spot report – which appears not to have been sent to the HSOC – reporting that "flooding is significant throughout the region and a levee in New Orleans has reportedly been breached sending 6-8 feet of water throughout the 9th Ward area of the city. Per the Governor, water is rising at 1 foot per hour and the New Orleans Mayor reports problems with a pumping station, causing flooding."[17]

- **At 10:17 a.m., PSA David Hunter, who was in the Louisiana State Police Emergency Operations Center (EOC), reported "continued heavy flooding in area of New Orleans just east of the Industrial Canal (9th Ward). ... Calls coming into state EOC from citizens trapped in their houses, some in the attics or on the roof. State National Guard HQs at Jackson Barracks has 5 feet of water in some of its buildings."**[18]

- **At 10:41 a.m., the HSOC received a copy of an 8 a.m. "Katrina Brief" created by the Transportation Security Administration (TSA), which stated, in part, that "the National Weather Service has reported that a levee broke on the Industrial Canal near the St. Bernard-Orleans Parish line, and 3 to 8 feet of flooding was possible. ... In the uptown area of New Orleans on the south shore of Lake Pontchartrain, floodwaters by [sic] have already intruded on the first stories of some houses and some roads are impassable. ... There is heavy street flooding throughout Orleans, St. Bernard, and Jefferson parishes."**[19]

- At 11 a.m., the Louisiana State Police Emergency Operations Center issued a situation report which reported a breach of the levee on 17th Street Canal.[20]

- At 11:40 a.m., the New Orleans NWS office issued one of the most stark warnings of the day: "Widespread flooding will continue across the parishes along the south shore of Lake Pontchartrain in the greater New Orleans area. ... This continues to be an extremely life threatening situation. ... Those seeking refuge in attics and roof-tops are strongly urged to take the necessary tools for survival. For example ... *those going into attics should try to take an axe or hatchet with them so they can cut their way onto the roof to avoid drowning should rising flood waters continue to rise into the attic.*" (emphasis added).[21]

• At 12:51 p.m., the HSOC received a Coast Guard "Status Update" which reported a "levee in New Orleans has been breached sending 3 to 8 feet of water into the 9th Ward area of the city."[22]

• At 1:14 p.m., a PSA reported a "levee breach on the 17th St. Canal (the border between Orleans and Jefferson Parishes) reported by the New Orleans Fire Dept."[23]

• At 3:05 p.m., and then again at 3:10, 4:20, and 8:13, the New Orleans NWS office issued a report stating that "extensive and life threatening storm surge flooding remains in progress at this time … especially in the New Orleans area. … Widespread flooding has occurred and storm water runoff will exacerbate the problem."[24]

• A 4 p.m. Situation Report issued by the NWS Southern Region Headquarters stating that "Very widespread and significant flooding has occurred throughout the city of New Orleans … Industrial Canal at Tennessee Street: levee has been breached … 17th Street at Canal Blvd: levee has been breached – breach extends several 100 meters in length[;] Much of downtown and east Orleans is underwater; depth unknown at this time."[25]

• At 4 p.m., LOHSEP issued a situation report detailing three levee breaches: "St. Bernard & 9th Ward Levee breach (reported by Sewage & Water Board). … Haynes Blvd Pump Station Levee Breach (reported by Jackson Barracks) … 17th Street Canal levee breach, flooding Lakeview area."[26]

• During the 4 p.m. hour, Fox News interviewed Ivor van Heerden, Director, Louisiana State University's Center For the Study of Public Health Impacts of Hurricanes, who said that "the National Weather Service [is] reporting that one of the levees was breached, and obviously, as the reporters have said, there's very, very significant areas of New Orleans that did flood from the levee overtopping. In some areas we have about 11 feet of standing water. People have been forced out onto the roofs of their homes."[27]

In addition to these reports, at 11 a.m., Brown, FEMA's Acting Deputy Director Patrick Rhode, Secretary Chertoff, Deputy Secretary Jackson, White House Deputy Chief of Staff Joe Hagin, representatives of the affected states, and individuals from numerous federal agencies attended the video teleconference (VTC) that FEMA hosted daily during Katrina. During this call, which was monitored by a Senior Watch Officer at the HSOC, a National Hurricane Center hydrologist said "We have significant flooding occurring right now, beyond the storm surge flooding."[28] "We are truly experiencing some devastation here," Colonel Jeff Smith, Acting Deputy Director of the Louisiana Office of Homeland Security and Emergency Preparedness, said. William Lokey, FEMA's Federal Coordinating Officer (FCO), then the lead federal official in Louisiana, echoed this:

> To give you an idea of what's going on down there, there is eight to ten feet of water in St. Bernard Parish. In New Orleans Parish, we have got water in the eastern part. And down in the Ninth Ward that borders St. Bernard Parish, we're going to have serious search and rescue efforts that are going to need to take place once we can get back in. … We are pretty much inundated right now, and our next priorities are going to be search and rescue and saving lives.[29]

During the call, Hagin asked about the status of the levees. Louisiana Governor Kathleen Blanco responded:

We keep getting reports in some places that maybe water is coming over the levees. We heard a report unconfirmed. I think we have not breached the levee. We have not breached the levee at this point in time. That could change, but in some places we have floodwaters coming in New Orleans East and the line St. Bernard parish where we have waters that are eight to ten feet deep, and we have people swimming in there, that's got a considerable amount of water itself.[30]

Governor Blanco also reported "maybe as many as 30 or more calls from people who are trapped."[31] It appears that neither Mayor Nagin nor anyone else in New Orleans was on this call.

It is difficult to understand why the 5 p.m. sitrep reflected few of the facts – and none of the urgency – conveyed by these reports. It is inexcusable that it included no mention of the reports of levee breaches that the HSOC received. On the contrary, the sitrep conveyed a false impression that there were multiple and uncontradicted reports that the levees had held. In fact, extensive investigation has uncovered nothing beyond Governor Blanco's qualified statement on the noon VTC stating that the levees had held. All other reports received by the HSOC pointed to the contrary.

The HSOC Failed Either to Obtain or to Recognize Crucial Reports

The apparent failure to obtain the NWS reports issued by the local offices is a particularly troubling example of how the HSOC's failure to plan for Katrina manifested itself. These reports contained some of the earliest indications of levee breaches and catastrophic flooding and were readily available – NWS's parent agency, the National Oceanic and Atmospheric Administration (NOAA), maintains a desk in the HSOC.[32] When asked about these reports, Broderick suggested that they may not have been obtained because they were issued by local

NWS stations. He did not know whether anyone at the HSOC was responsible for monitoring local weather stations during a major weather event. Common-sense steps such as identifying and monitoring local sources of information – particularly ones run by the federal government – would seem an obvious course of action for the HSOC in the days before landfall. And yet, no one within the HSOC appears to have given this any thought.

It is equally troubling that both Broderick and the HSOC Deputy Director DiFalco did not know of the reports of breaches and massive flooding that did come in during the day. Neither knew that two PSAs were on the ground submitting reports, nor were they aware of the Transportation Security Administration and the Coast Guard reports received. The 4 p.m. sitrep issued by the NWS Southern Region Headquarters, which included details of two major breaches, is similarly noteworthy. Though it was received in the HSOC – and forwarded from the Department of Defense desk in HSOC to senior Pentagon officials at 5:25 p.m. on the day of landfall[33] – it apparently went unnoticed by HSOC leadership that night. Both the importance and the perceived reliability of this report are underscored by the fact that the HSOC's Tuesday morning (5 a.m.) sitrep included verbatim reports of levee breaches and flooding from this then-13-hour-old 4 p.m. report. This NWS sitrep makes all the more inexplicable the HSOC's inaccurate 5 p.m. sitrep.

The attitude of the HSOC and DHS leadership toward media reports was, at best, contradictory. On one hand, HSOC witnesses expressed an understandable reluctance to rely on media reports, which often carry outdated or preliminary information during an evolving event.[34] On the other hand, Broderick relied on media reports in concluding that the situation in New Orleans was not catastrophic on Monday night: "The only one data point that I really had, personally, visually, was the celebration in the streets of New Orleans of people drinking beer and partying."[35] It is difficult to understand why DHS officials would find the credibility of alarming news reports suspect, but have no such hesitation taking comfort in media stories that, superficially at least, suggested that the situation was stable.

After the 5 p.m. Sitrep, the HSOC Issued Three Reports Reflecting the Growing Catastrophe, But DHS Leadership Did Not Read or Did Not Understand Them

After the 5 p.m. sitrep, reports of the increasingly dire situation in New Orleans continued. Many were received by the HSOC, and, indeed, the HSOC issued three Spot Reports that detailed levee breaches and extensive flooding. These reports included:

> • At 5:08 p.m., an American Red Cross Situation Report received by the HSOC stated in part, "Reports of flooding vary based on region with some levees in new Orleans reportedly breeched [sic]. Extensive flooding in the Lower 9th Board [sic] and St. Bernard Parish may be a result of water going over the tops of the levees."[36]

> • At 6 p.m., CNN's Jeanne Meserve reported "a scene of utter devastation. In an entire neighborhood, water has come up to the eaves of the houses and [I] am told this is not the worst of it. That beyond this, part of the upper Ninth Ward, I'm told the main part of the ward further down is even worse. The water is over the houses. This is a life and death situation. I think by the end of the night we're going to find a lot more death than we ever imagined."[37]

> • A 6:35 p.m. Spot Report issued by the HSOC was based on information received at some earlier time from the Corps of Engineers. It stated, in part, "A small breach reported at 17 Street Canal by local firemen. … Report that Dun-

can Pumping Station and Bonnebelle Pumping Station suffered roof damage, inundation of pumps, and are not operating at this time. Reported overtoppings of levee near Arabi and Inner Harbor Navigation Canal. Some level of widespread flooding has occurred. Report there has been a breach of the levee in the east of Harvey Canal, west bank area."[38]

• A Situation Report issued at 7:34 p.m. by the Corps of Engineers described major flooding in New Orleans and stated, "All Jefferson and Orleans Parish Pumping Stations are inoperable as of 29 Aug."[39]

• At 8 p.m. on CNN's *Larry King Live*, Brown said, "This is a catastrophic disaster. I've just started getting reconnaissance reports from my folks in the field and I'm anticipating now that I'm going to have to prepare for housing at least tens of thousands of victims that are going to be without homes for literally months on end. … FEMA folks who have been with the agency for, you know, 15 or 20 years, … call in and talk about how this is the worst flooding they've ever seen in their entire lives and talking about just neighborhoods after neighborhoods gone."[40]

• At 8:30 p.m., PSA Hunter reported "widespread flooding, and some suspected fatalities (bodies spotted floating in water) in an area of town near the Industrial Canal. The flooding cannot be alleviated due to the large water pumps which normally keep the city dry being out of service."[41]

• A 9:30 p.m. Spot Report based on two overflights of New Orleans by Marty Bahamonde, the only FEMA official in the city, said in part, "There is a quarter-mile breech [sic] in the levee near the 17th Street Canal about 200 yards from Lake Pontchartrain allowing water to flow into the City. … Only one of the main pumps is reported to still be working but cannot keep up with the demand and its longevity is doubtful … an estimated 2/3 to 75% of the city is under water. … Hundreds of people were observed on the balconies and roofs of a major apartment complex in the city. … A few bodies were seen floating in the water and Coast Guard pilots also reported seeing bodies but there are no details on locations or numbers."[42]

• At 10 p.m., MSNBC interviewed Lieutenant Kevin Cowan, Louisiana Office of Emergency Preparedness, who said, "There's a lot of heavy rain. There was some breaching of the levee system that pushed the water into St. Bernard Parish and into New Orleans proper itself, flooding neighborhoods. Streets are completely flooded. … There were some breaches where water was pushed over the top. I am sure there were areas that the levee did fail. We haven't gotten complete reports."[43]

• At 10:47 p.m., a Spot Report reporting that "According to Remote Sensing Imagery and available Census data, approximately 136,000 housing units in New Orleans have been impacted by flooding."[44]

Though the three Spot Reports listed above were widely distributed by e-mail,[45] few DHS witnesses recalled seeing them. Despite the fact that it was late at night and that Secretary Chertoff did not use e-mail, the HSOC made no effort to ensure that DHS leadership or the White House actually reviewed and understood the messages, or that they received this critical information in another form.[46]

The Superdome, cut off
AP/Wide World photo

Nearly all DHS witnesses, including those who were on the distribution list for the Spot Reports, testified that they did not know that the levees failed or that New Orleans was suffering catastrophic flooding until Tuesday morning. Many still did not know that the levees had breached and the city flooded on Monday as Katrina came ashore.[47] When shown these three Spot Reports, DHS witnesses consistently attempted to minimize their import, claiming that they were unconfirmed, conflicting, or unreliable.[48]

The attitude of DHS witnesses toward reports of flooding was also surprising. From the time Friday afternoon when forecasts put New Orleans in the bull's-eye of the storm, every indication was that Katrina could cause horrific devastation.[49] Yet time and again, DHS witnesses suggested that the reports of flooding received during the day were "typical," "expected," "standard," and the "normal, typical hurricane background stuff."[50] While such a reaction might be understandable in a "typical" hurricane, in light of all that was known about Katrina's power and the risks peculiar to New Orleans, these reports warranted a greater level of concern.

Moreover, in addition to these widely distributed reports, on Monday evening, FEMA Acting Deputy Director Patrick Rhode spoke with Deputy Secretary Michael Jackson to update him on the deteriorating situation.[51] Later that night, both Wood and Jackson received e-mails about Bahamonde's overflight of New Orleans. At 8:29 p.m., Wood received an e-mail from a DHS public-affairs official, which related that "the first (unconfirmed) reports they are getting from aerial surveys in New Orleans are far more serious than media reports are currently reflecting. Finding extensive flooding and more stranded people than they had originally thought – also a number of fires."[52]

At 10:05 p.m., Jackson received an e-mail from Rhode summarizing many of the same observations from Bahamonde's overflight that had already been reported to the HSOC, including that there was a 200-yard-long failure of one levee and that most of the city was flooded. Neither recalled seeing the e-mails that night. In sum, there is no evidence that overnight Monday into Tuesday any senior DHS official saw the reports that would have informed them that Katrina was a catastrophe of unprecedented dimensions.

Continued Failure of Situational Awareness – the Convention Center

In many regards, DHS's situational awareness did not improve as the week went on. The situation at the Convention Center in New Orleans provided the most striking illustration of this. Despite media reports on Wednesday night and video Thursday morning of thousands of people at the Convention Center[53] – and no later than shortly after noon, images of two dead bodies[54] – HSOC reports do not even mention the situation until *Friday* morning. Secretary Chertoff himself learned about the Convention Center from an NPR reporter at 1 p.m. on Thursday.[55] During that interview, the Secretary initially tried to dismiss the reporter's questions about the Convention Center as "a rumor or you get someone's anecdotal version of something."[56]

Witnesses have offered no satisfactory explanation of how this breakdown occurred. Broderick testified first hearing reports of thousands at the Convention Center on Wednesday evening. However, "We actually and initially were confusing the Superdome with the Convention Center. We didn't realize that it was a separate entity. Even on Thursday, we were sorting it out."[57] On Thursday, he dispatched Wendell Shingler, the Director of the Federal Protective Services (FPS), to investigate. Broderick testified that Shingler arrived that evening and reported that there were approximately a thousand people gathered at the Convention Center, that food and water was available, and that New Orleans police were present. Broderick believes that Shingler failed to appreciate the true size of the Convention Center. Because media reports persisted, Broderick sent Shingler back Friday morning, at which point the accurate report of thousands stranded came back.[58]

The failure of DHS, and the HSOC in particular, to take note of ubiquitous media reports of the situation at the Convention Center is disturbing. Skepticism toward media reports in a crisis situation makes sense, but these were backed up by video, and media-based reports to DHS leadership and the White House could have included appropriate caveats. Instead, DHS and the HSOC did not forward media reports, which left the country's leadership woefully uninformed.

FEMA Failed to Forward Information to the HSOC on a Timely Basis

DHS witnesses were uniform in their criticism of FEMA, and Brown in particular, for failing to provide crucial information to DHS and the HSOC on a timely basis. This criticism, while warranted, does not completely account for HSOC's inadequate situational awareness. While Brown and FEMA should have kept the HSOC better informed of developments on the ground, the HSOC never should have depended exclusively on FEMA for information. Moreover, as detailed above, it did not. Reports were actually arriving, and others were available, from plenty of other credible sources.

Nevertheless, the FEMA leadership appears to have failed to send critical information to DHS and the HSOC. Though Brown testified that he provided reports to the White House at several points during the day of landfall, he did not call Secretary Chertoff because in his view, "It would have wasted my time."[59] He appears not to have communicated with the HSOC at all about conditions on the ground. It appears also that several significant e-mails were not forwarded to the HSOC.[60] These included a series of e-mails between 8:36 and 9:19 a.m. containing reports: from a member of FEMA's liaison team at the National Hurricane Center, that the Industrial Canal levee had failed; a summary of a report from Marty Bahamonde, the FEMA official, that detailed severe flooding, people trapped in attics, and failing pumps;[61] and a 10:51 a.m. e-mail to FEMA's Deputy Director of Response with Bahamonde's news that the New Orleans Fire Department was reporting a 20-foot-wide breach in the 17th Street levee.[62]

Brown's testimony made clear that he purposely refused to provide updates to the HSOC and to Secretary Chertoff. Though Broderick testified that he believed that FEMA intentionally limited its reports,[63] investigation found no independent evidence to support this, and it does not appear that Lokey, Rhode, or others in FEMA did so. To the contrary, Lokey testified that "Michael Brown did not tell me to [in] any way, shape, or form stop any flow of information" and that he was not aware of any other limitation on the transmission of information to the HSOC.[64] Rhode sent several e-mails to, and had at least one phone conversation with, Jackson on Monday. Finally, nine of the Spot Reports issued by the HSOC on Monday were ascribed to FEMA, a clear indication that there was a steady information flow from FEMA's National Response Coordination Center into the HSOC.

Conclusion

The HSOC did not devise and implement a system to ensure access to all significant, relevant information that became available as Katrina neared and then landed on the Gulf Coast. Compounding the problem, even though the HSOC had enough information by late Monday afternoon to conclude that the levees had failed, it issued a key situation report that reflected and propagated incorrectly optimistic information about conditions in New Orleans.

Situational Awareness of Louisiana State Officials

Louisiana should have had a much easier time maintaining situational awareness than the federal government. In contrast to DHS, which was operating out of Washington, D.C., Louisiana's Emergency Operations Center (EOC) was in Baton Rouge, close to the primary hurricane impact area, and there were thousands of National Guard troops and other state and local officials on the ground in southeast Louisiana before, during, and after landfall to feed information. Nonetheless, while Louisiana avoided some of the obvious failures of the federal government, its record of maintaining situational awareness was mixed, at best.

The Louisiana Office of Homeland Security and Emergency Preparedness (LOHSEP) addressed situational awareness in its Standard Operating Procedures (SOP). The SOP identified guiding principles for information handling, including, "The prompt capture, assessment and rapid dissemination of information within the EOC contributes markedly to quick response and effective decision making during an emergency."[65] It also required "all personnel involved in the emergency" to "aggressively seek the status of these items as quickly as possible … before, during and after an event" and to report it to the EOC.[66]

In fact, first responders and others in the area affected by Katrina needed little encouragement to pass on information to the state EOC, since they relied heavily on the EOC to process their requests for assistance. But information came from numerous other sources as well, including National Guard on-the ground and fly-over reports,[67] Louisiana State Police reports,[68] and media coverage.[69] Some information even came from callers in other states.

LOHSEP compiled the data flow into situation reports that were updated several times a day.[70] Topics included weather, status and staffing of the emergency operations center, data on injuries and fatalities, shelter populations, status of nursing homes and hospitals, road closures, utility and communications outages, and status of response missions. Naturally, the length of these sitreps grew dramatically as the response progressed. For example, a LOHSEP sitrep at 10 a.m. on Sunday, the day before landfall, ran just nine pages; by Wednesday evening, the report was 75 pages.[71] Senior officials at LOHSEP did not have to rely solely on sitreps, as they also received a steady stream of information from emergency-management officials on the ground.[72]

LOHSEP was not alone in having an information-gathering strategy in the state. The Louisiana National Guard, which supplied information to LOHSEP, also had an information network to meet its own needs. The senior Guard official in Louisiana, Major General Bennett Landreneau, was stationed with the Governor in the LOHSEP command room.[73] As the hurricane approached, the command staff directed 10 air-squadron operations-support teams and troops on the ground to report to the Joint Operations Command at the Superdome every two hours.[74] In addition, they stationed liaison officers with radio equipment at local parish offices, and held their own series of conference calls with parish emergency-support officials throughout the night before landfall to monitor the hurricane's effects.[75]

However, these elaborate information-gathering systems did not prevent serious breakdowns in the state's situational awareness. One notable example was Governor Blanco herself, who evidently was unaware of earlier reports of levee breaches when she made her statement to state and federal officials in the noon video teleconference on the day before landfall that "We have not breached the levee at this point in time."[76] This was a particularly unfortunate misstatement, as it may have contributed to the federal government's confusion about the status of the levees. The record does not indicate when she learned her statement was inaccurate, or whether she made any attempt to inform the state and federal officials on the video teleconference, including the White House deputy chief of staff, of her mistake.

The state's response was also hampered by a lack of information about the locations of people in distress. For example, the state was slow to learn about people brought by search-and-rescue teams to the major highway intersection in west New Orleans known as the Cloverleaf.[77] Similarly, LOHSEP did not learn about people assembling at the Convention Center until well after crowds amassed there. Mayor Nagin bears some of the blame for the delay, as he apparently failed to inform other officials when he decided, on Tuesday, August 30, to open the Convention Center as a shelter when the Superdome became overcrowded.[78] Just the same, it was striking to hear the LOHSEP operations manager, Colonel William Doran, testify that his information on that situation was limited to what he saw on TV and occasional reports from security officers.[79]

The National Guard, which took charge of the Convention Center on Friday, September 2, learned about the situation there inadvertently. Brigadier General Gary Jones of Louisiana, Joint Force Commander of all National Guard troops involved in the Katrina operation, said, "We had no knowledge of [the people there] until we sent out reconnaissance patrols [on August 31], and those reconnaissance patrols came back and said, 'Oh, by the way, it looks like you've got another group of about 15,000 sitting over there.'"[80]

Lack of situational awareness contributed to problems in Louisiana in distributing food, water, and other commodities. In particular, logistics managers expressed frustration at not knowing when commodities were shipped or when they arrived.[81] (See Chapter 23, Logistics.)

While lack of incoming information left LOHSEP unaware of important developments, in some cases the fault lay with LOHSEP's inability to process the information it did receive. As Lt. Col. Doran testified, LOHSEP was simply not equipped for the volume of information it needed to assess:

> It may have been just for the fact that we were, again, rapidly overwhelmed to be able to target what information is good, what is not, the amount of information coming in. It's just like in intelligence, you get an amount of information and then you have to sift through to find out what's good information, what's bad, and what is factual, what's not. Then you have to prioritize.[82]

The state also lacked systems to organize incoming information in a manner that was useful for emergency response, making it necessary in some cases to improvise those systems on the fly. A notable example was information about the location of the large numbers of people calling in on 911 lines. Assuming the many 911 calls it received were requests for rescue, LOHSEP, with no plans for managing the callers' information, transferred them to the Louisiana Department of Wildlife & Fisheries (W&F) representative on staff. With help from the Louisiana Geological Survey, a research institution within Louisiana State University, a W&F representative named Robbie Duthu developed a system to plot incoming calls on a map that was forwarded to search-and-rescue personnel daily.[83]

---

1 On its Web site, DHS says the HSOC "serves as the nation's nerve center for information sharing and domestic incident management. ... The HSOC is in constant communication with the White House, acting as the situational awareness conduit for the White House Situation Room by providing information needed to make decisions and define courses of action." U.S. Department of Homeland Security, "Fact Sheet: Homeland Security Operations Center (HSOC)," press release, July 8, 2004. http://www.dhs.gov/dhspublic/interapp/press_release/press_release_0456.xml. Accessed on Mar. 8, 2006.

2 PSAs are within the Infrastructure Protection Office at DHS, and there are approximately 68 spread around the country. DHS's Web site describes PSAs as "Homeland security experts identified in major metropolitan communities across the country to serve as liaisons between the Department and other partners on issues of critical infrastructure protection." U.S. Department of Homeland Security, "Fact Sheet: Key Priorities Update March 1, 2004 – March 1, 2005," press release, Mar. 2004. http://www.dhs.gov/dhspublic/display?theme=43&content=4279&pring=true. Accessed on Apr. 12, 2006.

3 The morning sitreps are included in the DHS Secretary's briefing book.

4 Federal Emergency Management Agency (FEMA), National Situation Report, Aug. 29, 2005, 6 p.m., p. 1. Provided to Committee; filed as Bates no. DHS 0001181.

5 FEMA, National Situation Report, Aug. 29, 2005, 6 p.m., p. 13. Provided to Committee; filed as Bates no. DHS 0001193.

6 In his answer to one of Senator Lieberman's Questions for the Record submitted after Secretary Chertoff's appearance before the Committee on Feb. 15, 2006, the Secretary wrote, "The last report I received on Monday evening from the HSOC stated that preliminary reports had indicated the levees had not been breached, and that the situation was still being assessed." This is almost a direct quote from the 6 p.m. sitrep. Questions for the Record of Sec. Michael Chertoff, U.S. Department of Homeland Security, for the U.S. Senate, Committee on Homeland Security and Governmental Affairs, hearing on *Hurricane Katrina: The Homeland Security Department's Preparation and Response,* Feb. 15, 2006, p. 51.

7 Testimony of Sec. Michael Chertoff, U.S. Department of Homeland Security, before the U.S. Senate, Committee on Homeland Security and Governmental Affairs, hearing on *Hurricane Katrina: The Homeland Security Department's Preparation and Response,* Feb. 15, 2006.

8 President George W. Bush, "President, Lieutenant General Honoré Discuss Hurricane Relief in Louisiana," press

release, Sept. 12, 2005. http://www.whitehouse.gov/news/releases/2005/09/20050912.html. Accessed on Mar. 8, 2006.

9 Committee staff interview of Brig. Gen. Matthew Broderick, Director, Homeland Security Operations Center, U.S. Department of Homeland Security, conducted on Jan. 19, 2006, transcript pp. 81-82.

10 Brig. Gen. Broderick interview, Jan. 19, 2006, p. 37.

11 Committee staff interview of Richard Gray, Team Leader, Information and Assessment Team and Team Leader, National Response Coordination Center, FEMA, conducted on Jan. 20, 2006, transcript p. 85.

12 DHS produced to the Committee documents from the Senior Watch Officer (SWO) at the HSOC on the day of landfall but did not produce documents from the individual desk officers at the HSOC. Because of this refusal – and because all but one of the bolded reports listed below was found somewhere other than in the SWO e-mails – the Committee does not, and cannot, represent that these bolded reports are the entirety of those received by the HSOC on the day of landfall. There are numerous other reports that the Committee believes may have reached the HSOC, but absent complete production, there was no way to determine if in fact they were received.

13 National Weather Service, New Orleans-Baton Rouge, LA Office, Flash Flood Warning, Aug. 29, 2005, 8:14 a.m. CT. Provided to Committee.

14 Louis Dabdoub, e-mail to Michael Waters and others, Aug. 29, 2005, 9 a.m. Provided to Committee; filed as Bates no. DHS-INFP-0003-0001768.

15 National Weather Service, New Orleans-Baton Rouge, LA Office, Hurricane Katrina Local Statement, Aug. 29, 2005, 9 a.m. CT. Provided to Committee.

16 Louis Dabdoub, e-mail to Michael Waters and others, Aug. 29, 2005, 9:36 a.m. Provided to Committee; filed as Bates no. DHS-INFP-0003-0001768.

17 Daniel Kaniewski, e-mail to Dan Bartlett and others, Aug. 29, 2005, 11:13 a.m. Provided to Committee; filed as Bates no. 004795. Elsewhere this document cites the HSOC as reporting that "due to the rising water in the 9th Ward, residents are in their attics and on their roofs."

18 Francis Patno, e-mail to Ira Stern and others, Sept. 1, 2005, 9:54 p.m. Provided to Committee; filed as Bates nos. DHS-INFP-0003-0001497, 0001499.

19 Darryl Mahoney, e-mail to HSOC.HSIN and others, Aug. 29, 2005, 11:41 a.m. Provided to Committee; filed as Bates no. DHS-HSOC-0002-0000186.

20 Louisiana State Police, Emergency Operations Center, Hurricane Katrina Situation Report, Aug. 29, 2005, 11 a.m. Provided to Committee; filed as Bates nos. 000001 through 000004.

21 National Weather Service, New Orleans-Baton Rouge, LA Office, issued by Mobile, AL Office, Flash Flood Warning, Aug. 29, 2005, 11:40 a.m. CT. Provided to Committee.

22 Lt. Robert Walls, e-mail to LANTHMHLS Watch and others, Aug. 29, 2005, 1:51 p.m. Provided to Committee.

23 Francis Patno, e-mail to Ira Stern and others, Sept. 1, 2005, 9:54 p.m. Provided to Committee; filed as Bates nos. DHS-INFP-0003-0001497, 0001500.

24 National Weather Service, New Orleans-Baton Rouge, LA Office, Hurricane Katrina Local Statement, Aug. 29, 2005, 3:05 p.m. CT. Provided to Committee; National Weather Service, New Orleans – Baton Rouge, LA Office, Hurricane Katrina Local Statement, Aug. 29, 2005, 3:10 p.m. CT. Provided to Committee; National Weather Service, New Orleans – Baton Rouge, LA Office, issued by Mobile, AL Office, Hurricane Katrina Local Statement, Aug. 29, 2005, 4:20 p.m. CT. Provided to Committee; National Weather Service, New Orleans – Baton Rouge, LA Office, issued by Mobile, AL Office, Hurricane Katrina Local Statement, Aug. 29, 2005, 8:13 p.m. CT. Provided to Committee.

25 Anthony Capra, e-mail to DoD.DomesticIncidentManagement, Aug. 29, 2005, 5:25 p.m. Provided to Committee; filed as MMTF 00418-05. The receiver of this e-mail was redacted. In an e-mail to investigators, Col. Dave Rhodes states that the prior e-mail was sent to the above e-mail distribution list. Col. Dave Rhodes, e-mail to Tom Eldridge, Dan Berkovitz, and Eric Andersen, Senate Committee staff members, Apr. 19, 2006, 10:36 a.m.

26 Louisiana Office of Homeland Security and Emergency Preparedness (LOHSEP), Sitrep, Executive Summary, Hurricane Katrina, Aug. 29, 2005, 4 p.m. CT. Provided to Committee; filed as Bates nos. DHS-FEMA-0028-0001109, 0001138

27 Ivor van Heerden, Live Event, Fox News Network, "Special Coverage: Hurricane Katrina Pounds New Orleans," Aug. 29, 2005, 5 p.m. ET. Transcript accessed on LexisNexis.

28 John Schmidt, FEMA Daily Video Teleconference, Aug. 29, 2005, transcript pp. 9-10. Provided to Committee.

29 William Lokey, FEMA Daily Video Teleconference, Aug. 29, 2005, transcript pp. 17-18. Provided to Committee.

30 Gov. Kathleen Babineaux Blanco, FEMA Daily Video Teleconference, Aug. 29, 2006, transcript pp. 20-21. Provided to Committee. In his responses to the Committee's Questions for the Record, Secretary Chertoff repeatedly references Governor Blanco's statement regarding the levees. Questions for the Record of Sec. Chertoff, Senate Committee hearing, Feb. 15, 2006, pp. 9, 15, 47, 48, 51, 81. As we now know, this statement was incorrect when it was made – reports coming into both the Louisiana State Emergency Operations Center and the HSOC detailed that the levees had breached. Moreover, this noon statement does not somehow contradict the many later reports of breaches that came in from varied sources.

31 Robert Latham, FEMA Daily Video Teleconference, Aug. 29, 2005, transcript. 22. Provided to Committee. Reports from Mississippi during the VTC were no less ominous. Max Mayfield accurately stated that the storm surge in the

Biloxi area would be "very, very devastating." *Source:* Mayfield, FEMA Daily Video Teleconference, Aug. 29, 2005, transcript p. 5. Latham, Director of the Mississippi Emergency Management Agency, stated "It certainly looks like it is a catastrophic event that we all expected" and reported that the Hancock County Emergency Operations Center collapsed while the Jackson County Emergency Operations Center was flooded. *Source:* Latham, VTC, Aug. 29, 2005, pp. 22-23. He also reported calls from "citizens who are trapped in the second floor of their homes, in the attics of their homes and roofs, and we cannot get to them." *Source*: Latham, VTC, Aug. 29, 2005, pp. 22-23. The historic scope of the unfolding disaster was clear to him: "I suspect that the history books, that this event will replace Camille as far as Mississippi is concerned." *Source*: Latham, VTC, Aug. 29, 2005, p. 24.

32 Brig. Gen. Broderick interview, Jan. 19, 2006, p. 84. Though this investigation uncovered no evidence of anyone at the HSOC or DHS being aware of these NWS reports, it is possible that these reports were received or reviewed by the NOAA desk at the HSOC. However, because DHS refused to produce e-mails from this desk we were unable to determine if in fact this happened. Thus, we consider these to be reports that HSOC failed to obtain. However, if in fact the HSOC did obtain these reports, they would simply be added to the long list of reports that the HSOC received but failed to understand or appreciate.

33 Anthony Capra, e-mail to DoD.DomesticIncidentManagement distribution list, Aug. 29, 2005, 5:25 p.m. Provided to Committee; filed as MMTF00418-05. The receiver of this e-mail was redacted. In an e-mail to investigators, Col. Dave Rhodes states that the prior e-mail was sent to the above e-mail distribution list. Source: Col. Dave Rhodes, e-mail to Tom Eldridge, Senate Committee staff member, and others, Apr. 19, 2006, 10:36 a.m.; Anthony Capra, e-mail to Paul McHale, Aug. 29, 2005, 5:25 p.m. ET. Provided to Committee.

34 While media reports are often not the most reliable, during interviews some witnesses went to illogical lengths in trying to explain why the media was not to be trusted. For instance, when shown the front page of the August 30, 2005, New Orleans *Times-Picayune* (posted online at 2:43 a.m. CT) – which showed an elderly man being rescued from his home in chest-deep water – Broderick said, "You know, this could be one house flooded, and the houses around it aren't even touched." Brig. Gen. Broderick interview, Jan. 19, 2006, pp. 166-167.

35 Brig. Gen. Broderick interview, Jan. 19, 2006, pp. 130-131.

36 Eric Jones, e-mail to Eric Jones and others, Aug. 29, 2005, 6:08 p.m. Provided to Committee; filed as Bates nos. WHK-06494 through 06499.

37 Jean Meserve, *Anderson Cooper 360 Degrees*, CNN, "Hurricane Katrina Slams Gulf Coast," Aug. 29, 2005, 7 p.m. ET. Transcript accessed on LexisNexis.

38 U.S. Department of Homeland Security, HSOC Spot Report #7, Aug. 29, 2005, 7:35 p.m. Provided to Committee; filed as Bates no. DHS-FEMA-0055-0007575.

39 U.S. Army Corps of Engineers, Situation Report #3, Aug. 30, 2006, 0034 Z. Provided to Committee.

40 Michael Brown, *Larry King Live*, CNN, "Tracking Hurricane Katrina," Aug. 29, 2005, 9 p.m. ET. Transcript accessed on LexisNexis.

41 Francis Patno, e-mail to Ira Stern and others, Sept. 1, 2005, 9:54 p.m. Provided to Committee; filed as Bates nos. DHS-INFP-0003-0001497, 0001502.

42 U.S. Department of Homeland Security, HSOC Spot Report #13, Aug. 29, 2005, 10:30 p.m. Provided to Committee; filed as Bates nos. DHS-HSOC-0004-0005521 through 0005522.

43 Lt. Kevin Cowen, *The Situation with Tucker Carlson*, MSNBC, "The Situation for August 29, 2005," Aug. 29, 2005, 11 p.m. ET. Transcript accessed on LexisNexis.

44 U.S. Department of Homeland Security, HSOC Spot Report #12, Aug. 29, 2005, 11:47 p.m. Provided to Committee; filed as Bates no. DHS-FEMA-0055-0007581.

45 All reports appear to have gone to multiple desks in the HSOC as well as to Secretary Chertoff's briefing staff. Beyond this group, distribution lists for reports added different officials. For example, the Spot Report detailing Marty Bahamonde's overflight went to, among others, Deputy Secretary Jackson, Chief of Staff Wood, Secretary Chertoff's military aide, Broderick, Stephan, and the White House Situation Room and individuals within the White House Homeland Security Council.

46 In response to one of Senator Collins' Questions for the Record submitted after Secretary Chertoff's appearance before the Committee on February 15, 2006, the Secretary was critical of just such a reliance on e-mails to communicate important information. Specifically, he criticized FEMA Acting Deputy Director Patrick Rhode for using e-mail to provide a report of the Bahamonde overflight to Deputy Secretary Jackson: "E-mails are not the most appropriate way of conveying urgent or important information, especially late at night. Instead, the right course would have been to notify the HSOC, which reaches both the Deputy Secretary and me by telephone at any time of day or night." *Source:* Questions for the Record of Sec. Chertoff, Senate Committee hearing, Feb. 15, 2006, p. 10; *See also:* Questions for the Record of Sec. Chertoff, Senate Committee hearing, Feb. 15, 2006, p. 50 ("The best means of communicating important information with high-ranking officials was by telephone call to the HSOC, who could reach me any time of the day or night, not via e-mail."). In fact, in the case of the Rhode e-mail, the HSOC had already been informed of the Bahamonde overflight, evidenced by the HSOC Spot Report detailing the report that is time-stamped 10:30 p.m., 35 minutes before the Rhode e-mail. *Source:* U.S. Department of Homeland Security, HSOC Spot Report #13, Aug. 29, 2005, 10:30 p.m. Provided to Committee; filed as Bates no. DHS-HSOC-0004-0005521 through 0005522. However, the same is not true of the three Spot Reports (Spot Report numbers 7, 13, and 12 issued at 6:35, 9:30, and 10:47 CT respectively.) – no efforts were made by HSOC officials to call or otherwise ensure that senior officials received these critical reports. *Source:* Brig. Gen. Brod-

erick interview, Jan. 19, 2006, pp. 168-169.

47 Committee staff interview of Robert Stephan, Assistant Secretary of Homeland Security for Infrastructure Protection, U.S. Department of Homeland Security, conducted on Jan. 13, 2006, transcript pp. 115-116 ("I still am not convinced that it was a known fact that there were widespread levee breaches or gaps or massive flooding happening some time on Monday."); Brig. Gen. Broderick interview, Jan. 19, 2006, pp. 129-130 ("But the doomsday scenario of New Orleans, the levees breaking and tons of water going in and washing people away did not happen, and the people of New Orleans and the State and everyone else kind of breathed a sigh of relief. That later on, those failures started occurring at greater lengths on that levee system, and that's when the preponderance of water, as I understand it, started coming in was in the middle of the night."); Committee staff interview of Frank DiFalco, then-Deputy Director, Homeland Security Operations Center, U.S. Department of Homeland Security, conducted on Jan. 13, 2006, transcript p. 121 ("Q: Do you know now that the levees breached on Monday? A: I don't know if they breached Monday.").

48 Brig. Gen. Broderick interview, Jan. 19, 2006, p. 163 (Describing the spot report of the Bahamonde overflight as "not an excitable report to me. It's of interest, and if I had received it, I'd go back and drill down and ask for some more clarity."); Brig. Gen. Broderick interview, Jan. 19, 2006, pp. 159-160 (stating that because the 6 p.m. sitrep reported no breaches, the 7:35 p.m. Spot Report "wouldn't have gotten me excited"); Brig. Gen. Broderick interview, Jan. 19, 2006, pp. 165-166 (questioning the 11:47 spot report which stated that 136,000 homes had been affected by flooding: "I mean, who says 136,000 houses. Did someone count all of them, or is that someone's wild guess?"); Stephan interview, Jan. 13, 2006, p. 35 (stating, after reviewing the spot report of the Bahamonde overflight, "[I did] not know what a breach on this particular section of New Orleans means to the overall, you know, picture"); Stephan interview, Jan. 13, 2006, p. 39 (even after the spot report of the Bahamonde overflight was issued, there was still no "confirmed information that we had massive breaching and flooding occurring"); DiFalco interview, Jan. 13, 2006, p. 107 (saying that the Bahamonde overflight did not merit a call to the Secretary or other senior staff to ensure that it was received, and stating "It says it's from Public Affairs. So, again, we're back to the issue of, okay, that's fine, Public Affairs is saying this is what's going on, what's the engineers saying?"); Question for the Record of Sec. Chertoff, Senate Committee hearing, Feb. 15, 2006, p. 51 (the Secretary dismissed the 7:35 p.m. spot report as "uncontrovertibly tentative, and giv[ing] no indication that the 'small breach' could not be repaired."). It is difficult to understand how the report of a breach of the crucial levee on the 17th Street Canal could be minimized because it did not state that the breach could *not* be repaired. Indeed, in the face of the dire predictions before landfall and the myriad reports of flooding after landfall, the presumption should have been to take the report any breach seriously absent some statement to contrary. Finally, this spot report, which reflected an earlier Army Corps of Engineers report, also described a second levee breach, failing pumps, widespread flooding, and overtopping.

49 In response to one of Senator Collins' Questions for the Record submitted after Secretary Chertoff's appearance before the Committee on February 15, 2006, the Secretary said, "We knew that this storm had the potential to wreak havoc on the Gulf Coast and could cause enormous damage to entire region." Questions for the Record of Sec. Chertoff, Senate Committee hearing, Feb. 15, 2006, p. 6.

50 Stephan interview, Jan. 13, 2006, p. 59 ("typical" and "expected"); Committee staff interview of John Wood, Chief of Staff, U.S. Department of Homeland Security, conducted on Jan. 27, 2006, transcript p. 64 ("expected"); Brig. Gen. Broderick interview, Jan. 19, 2006, p. 164 ("standard"); Brig. Gen. Broderick interview, Jan. 19, 2006, p. 105 ("normal, typical hurricane background stuff"); Brig. Gen. Broderick interview, Jan. 19, 2006, p. 131 ("There's always flooding after a hurricane"); Brig. Gen. Broderick interview, Jan. 19, 2006, p. 146 ("Every time there's a hurricane, there's a flood. So, you know, to say there is flooding in a particular part of town is a normal expectation of what's happening in a hurricane."). In addition, in response to one of Senator Akaka's Questions for the Record submitted after Secretary Chertoff's appearance before the Committee on February 15, 2006, the Secretary said, "Flooding is an incident of almost all hurricanes." Questions for the Record of Sec. Chertoff, Senate Committee hearing, Feb. 15, 2006, p. 74.

51 Committee staff interview of Patrick Rhode, Acting Deputy Director, FEMA, conducted on Jan. 4, 2006, transcript p. 50.

52 When shown this e-mail during a staff interview, Wood minimized its importance: "I do not equate extensive flooding necessarily with the type of flooding that we had due to the levee breach." *Source:* Wood interview, Jan. 27, 2006, p. 74. In response to one of Senator Akaka's Questions for the Record submitted after Secretary Chertoff's appearance before the Committee on February 15, 2006, the Secretary said "The e-mail to my chief of staff does not mention levee breaches. There is a critical distinction between flooding and breach of a levee. Flooding is an incident of almost all hurricanes. Levee breach is extraordinary." *Source:* Questions for the Record of Sec. Chertoff, Senate Committee hearing, Feb. 15, 2006, p. 74.

53 During the 8 o'clock hour on Wednesday, August 31, reporter Chris Lawrence told Paula Zahn on CNN that "There are literally thousands of people lined up at this convention center wandering aimlessly, I mean, mothers with their babies, little kids, walking through this putrid water. And there's this dead body that is just sitting there. And I asked one of police officers and he said, we can't – we can barely control the situation as it is. We can't even worry about dead right now." *Source:* Chris Lawrence, *Paula Zahn Show*, CNN, "President Bush Promises Massive Hurricane Relief Effort; Thousands Feared Dead in New Orleans," Aug. 31, 2005, 8 p.m. ET. Transcript accessed on LexisNexis. During the 10 p.m. broadcast of *Scarborough Country* on MSNBC, Michelle Hofland reported that "We are hearing some really frightening stories tonight down at the convention center. … Well, we are told that down there, at that convention center, it is absolute chaos. We haven't been down there, Joe, because we are told that it's just not a safe place to be. So, you have families with children and everything down at that convention center. Cars are being carjacked. And there's no one there, we are told, to take care of the thousands of people who are there." *Source:* Michelle Hofland, *Scarborough Country*, MSNBC, "Scarborough Country For August 31, 2005," Aug. 31, 2005, 10 p.m. ET. Transcript accessed on

LexisNexis. The next morning, in the 7 a.m. ET hour, Chris Lawrence reported "I mean right here at the convention center, which is just a couple of blocks away from us, as we were driving in, there were thousands, thousands of people just sleeping on the streets of New Orleans. I mean mothers with their children, entire families have nowhere to go. You walk by and people don't have water. They're running out of food." *Source:* Chris Lawrence, *American Morning*, CNN, "Massive Evacuation from New Orleans Coming to Sudden Halt; Looting and Lawlessness Continue to Escalate," Sept. 1, 2005, 7 a.m. ET. Transcript accessed on LexisNexis. In the 10 a.m. hour, CNN Producer Jim Spellman reported that "The convention center was the secondary place where people were to go. The first being the Superdome. And thousands of people are there. They slept outside. The inside of the convention center is just crammed." *Source:* Jim Spellman, *CNN Live Today*, CNN, "Chaos and Catastrophe in New Orleans; FEMA Briefing," Sept. 1, 2005, 10 a.m. ET. Transcript accessed on LexisNexis.

54 Video shown on CNN's 1 p.m. ET "Live From … " broadcast showed at least two bodies next to the convention center. Chris Lawrence, *Live From …* , CNN, "Rescue Operations Suspended Due to Security Issues; Stranded Hurricane Victims Dying in New Orleans; Officials Face Chaos, Lack of Communication," Sept. 1, 2005, 1 p.m. ET. Transcript accessed on LexisNexis.

55 Evan Thomas, "Michael Chertoff: 'What the Hell is Going on?'" *Newsweek*, Jan. 2, 2006. http://www.msnbc.msn.com/id/10511927/site/newsweek/. Accessed on Mar. 10, 2006.

56 Sec. Michael Chertoff, *All Things Considered*, NPR, "Michael Chertoff discusses US aid effort being criticized in New Orleans," Sept. 1, 2005, 8 a.m. ET. Transcript accessed on LexisNexis.

57 Brig. Gen. Broderick interview, Jan. 19, 2006, pp. 171-172.

58 Brig. Gen. Broderick interview, Jan. 19, 2006, pp. 173-174. Committee staff interviewed Federal Protective Service Director Shingler, but his recollection was inconsistent with that of other witnesses and with the documents obtained. Committee staff interview of Wendell Shingler, Director, Office of Federal Protective Service, Border and Transportation Security, U.S. Department of Homeland Security, conducted on Feb. 14, 2006, transcript pp. 15-17.

59 Testimony of Michael Brown, former Director, FEMA, before the U.S. Senate, Committee on Homeland Security and Governmental Affairs, hearing on *Hurricane Katrina, The Roles of DHS and FEMA Leadership*, Feb. 10, 2006. Brown testified that he believed that he could accomplish things more quickly by calling the White House directly.

60 The Committee cannot be certain that these e-mails were not sent to DHS, because DHS never produced e-mails from the FEMA desk in the HSOC that would have been the most likely recipient of these reports.

61 Patrick Rhode, e-mail to Michael Health, Aug. 29, 2005, 10:19 a.m. Provided to Committee; filed as Bates nos. DHS 0005684 through 0005685.

62 Michael Heath, e-mail to Michael Lowder, Aug. 29, 2005, 11:51 a.m., pp. 1-2. Provided to Committee; filed as Bates nos. DHS-FEMA-0029-0002959 through 0002960.

63 Testimony of Brig. Gen. Matthew Broderick, former Director, Homeland Security Operations Center, U.S. Department of Homeland Security, before the U.S. Senate, Committee on Homeland Security and Governmental Affairs, hearing on *Hurricane Katrina: The Roles of DHS and FEMA Leadership*, Feb. 10, 2006.

64 Committee staff interview of William Lokey, Federal Coordinating Officer for Hurricane Katrina in Louisiana, FEMA, conducted on Jan. 20, 2006, transcript p. 175.

65 LOHSEP, Standard Operation Procedures, Section 5.a.(1). Provided to Committee; filed as Bates nos. 000008 through 000009.

66 LOHSEP, SOP Level I Activation, Sec. KK. Provided to Committee; filed as Bates no. 000055.

67 Committee staff interview of Col. David Aycock, Operations Officer, Louisiana National Guard, conducted on Jan. 4, 2006, transcript p. 212; Committee staff interview of Col. Jeff Smith, Jr., Louisiana National Guard (Ret.), Acting Deputy Director, Emergency Management, Louisiana Office of Homeland Security and Emergency Preparedness, conducted on Jan. 13, 2005, transcript p. 141; Committee staff interview of Brig. Gen. Gary Jones, Commander, Joint Force Pelican, Louisiana Army National Guard, conducted on Dec. 7, 2005, transcript p. 96.

68 Committee staff interview of Lt. Col. William Doran, Louisiana Air National Guard, Chief, Operations Division, Louisiana Office of Homeland Security and Emergency Preparedness, conducted on Dec. 2, 2005, transcript p. 73.

69 Lt. Col. Doran interview, Dec. 2, 2005, p. 115.

70 Col. Smith interview, Jan. 13, 2006, pp. 144-145.

71 Compare LOHSEP, Sitrep, Aug. 28, 2005, 11 a.m. Provided to Committee; filed as Bates nos. 000001 through 000009, with LOHSEP, Sitrep, Aug. 31, 2005, 10 p.m. Provided to Committee; filed as Bates nos. 000001 through 0000075.

72 Col. Smith interview, Jan. 13, 2006, pp. 232-233.

73 Col. Aycock interview, Jan. 4, 2006, p. 212.

74 Committee staff interview of Lt. Col. Thibodeaux, Joint Director of Military Support to Civilian Authorities, Louisiana National Guard, conducted on Dec. 6, 2005, transcript pp. 146-147.

75 Lt. Col. Thibodeaux interview, Dec. 6, 2005, p. 149.

76 Gov. Kathleen Babineaux Blanco, FEMA Daily Video Teleconference, Aug. 29, 2005, transcript pp. 20-21. Provided to Committee.

77 Lt. Col. Doran interview, Dec. 2, 2005, p. 146; Committee staff interview of Brig. Gen. Brod Veillon, Assistant Adjutant General, Louisiana National Guard, conducted on Nov. 29, 2005, transcript p. 45.

78 See Chapter 23, p. 11.

79 Lt. Col. Doran interview, Dec. 2, 2005, pp. 133-134.

80 Brig. Gen. Jones interview, Dec. 7, 2005, p. 96.

81 Committee staff interview of Col. Jadwin Mayeaux, Deputy Director, Homeland Security, Louisiana Office of Homeland Security and Emergency Preparedness, conducted on Nov. 29, 2005, transcript pp. 34-35.

82 Lt. Col. Doran interview, Dec. 2, 2005, p. 160.

83 Committee staff interview of Robert Duthu, Liaison to Louisiana State Emergency Operations Center, Louisiana Department of Wildlife and Fisheries, conducted on Dec. 8, 2005, transcript pp. 271-276.

Facing the media
U.S. Coast Guard photo

Protecting Infrastructure;
Public Communication;
Role of the Media

Critical Infrastructure

Hurricane Katrina had a devastating impact on many types of critical infrastructure – "Systems and assets," according to the National Response Plan, "whether physical or virtual, so vital to the United States that the incapacity or destruction of such systems and assets would have a debilitating impact on security, national economic security, national public health or safety, or any combination of those matters."[1]

The New Orleans levee system naturally received the most attention, but Katrina also placed the nation's energy supply, chemical-production capacity, and fuel pipelines in serious jeopardy. The disaster highlighted the need for industry and government coordination to assess the implications of the damage to such infrastructure, to prioritize the restoration of specific infrastructure, and to have mechanisms in place to facilitate restoration.

Because of the lack of coordinated restoration plans, significant infrastructure problems were left to be addressed in ad-hoc manner:

> • Immediately after landfall, the Colonial Pipeline, a 5,519-mile system that transports fuel from Texas, Louisiana, Mississippi, and Alabama to distribution points throughout 12 states and the District of Columbia,[2] reported that two major lines were shut down due to power outages. The company dispatched generation equipment, but FEMA regional representatives – understandably – diverted the generators to hospitals.[3] However, additional planning would have readied enough generators for both purposes. It was not until a full week after the storm that the Colonial Pipeline was restored to full capacity.[4] The Colonial pipeline is one of two key pipelines that carries up to 100 million gallons of gas, heating oil, and other petroleum products to the Southeast and the East Coast.[5] A sustained shut-down could have a serious impact on the nation's energy supply.

> • A flooded chemical plant that manufactured liquid hydrogen used by NASA and the Air Force and in the finishing process of some steel parts did not receive dewatering assistance from the Army Corps of Engineers until September 5.[6] This plant alone was responsible for 31 percent of North America's industrial-hydrogen production, and consequently NASA agreed to share its stored supply of hydrogen with the Department of Defense to compensate for this lost production.[7]

> • The restoration and maintenance of critical telecommunications infrastructure was beset by a variety of security challenges, including the need to provide security for facilities and equipment, for repair crews, and for convoys bringing in fuel and other supplies.[8] BellSouth's struggles provide one example of this, and the company's security issues wound up being addressed through a patchwork of means. The Louisiana State Police escorted employees out of the build-

ing when BellSouth had to evacuate its New Orleans Main Central Office on the afternoon of Tuesday, August 30 (the day after landfall) because of reports of violence.[9] The following day, BellSouth sought help from the U.S. Marshals Service to protect their facility.[10] The Department of Justice, after coordinating through FEMA pursuant to Emergency Support Function-13 (ESF-13) of the National Response Plan (NRP),[11] agreed to send in U.S. Marshals to secure the facility, and sent in FBI agents by helicopter until the marshals could arrive.[12] In addition, state police provided security for convoys of fuel and water.[13] BellSouth also needed assistance to provide security for their repair crews. The National Communications System (NCS),[14] after going through the ordinary ESF process, and with the consent of FEMA, sought this further assistance from DOD, which forwarded the request to the Louisiana National Guard.[15] In the end, however, security arrangements with the Louisiana National Guard fell through and BellSouth ended up arranging for private security protection for its workers.[16] Pre-existing arrangements concerning security for such critical infrastructure could have eased these challenges and helped to facilitate the speedy restoration of the telecommunications infrastructure.

The federal, state, and local governments, and the private sector all are responsible for planning to protect and restore critical infrastructure. Within the federal government, Congress has assigned the Department of Homeland Security (DHS) a leadership role on critical infrastructure, including the task of developing a national plan for protecting it.[17] Unfortunately, DHS has lagged in its responsibility to develop this plan and to create a meaningful inventory with prioritization for securing the nation's key assets. Although DHS issued an interim National Infrastructure Protection Plan (NIPP) in February 2005 and a draft version of the final plan in November 2005 that proposes to assess vulnerabilities of critical infrastructure and prioritize protective measures, it still has not implemented the final plan.[18] If the prioritization of vulnerable critical infrastructure had been completed prior to Katrina, it may have been helpful for coordinating restoration of that infrastructure.

Currently, the NRP, the comprehensive federal framework for managing major domestic incidents, divides responsibility for restoring critical infrastructure among several Emergency Support Functions, each of which has different lead agencies.[19] No cross-cutting entity under the NRP takes a comprehensive approach to setting critical-infrastructure restoration priorities – or attempts to address the many infrastructure interdependencies that exist. Nor does the NRP address the way in which federal agencies should work with state and local governments to respond to emergencies that affect critical infrastructure in their jurisdictions. It is important that the NRP address the roles of federal, state, and local governments and the private sector in restoring critical infrastructure. To this end, the NRP should be amended to have an Emergency Support Function that is responsible for assessing the damage to critical infrastructure, taking measures to mitigate the impact on the economy and national security, and restoring critical infrastructure. The Department of Homeland Security should be responsible for leading this Emergency Support Function, but it should have the involvement of the private sector, other federal agencies, and state and local governments, as appropriate.

Because approximately 85 percent of critical infrastructure in the United States is privately owned and operated,[20] and because private industry has vital information about its infrastructure, it is critical that industry actively work with the federal government in order to establish priorities for restoration. A model for private-sector involvement can be found in the DHS's draft NIPP that will establish 17 sector-specific coordination groups and a cross-sector council that can consider infrastructure interdependencies.[21] According to DHS's draft plan, these sector-specific groups will include industry representatives and representatives from all levels of government (federal, state, and local) when appropriate that will develop sector-specific plans for sharing information, assessing the vulnerability of critical infrastructure, and implementing protection measures. These sector-specific groups would be a useful mechanism for acquiring the necessary stakeholder information to set priorities for the restoration of critical infrastructure and coordinating private sector and government efforts to achieve prioritization goals.

Media and Public Affairs – ESF-15

Rumors proliferate in times of war, civil unrest, and natural disaster. If widespread and sensational, they can become disruptive – and become news events in themselves. The public suffers when federal, state, and local governments tasked with disseminating public health, safety, and security information fail to do their jobs as envisioned by emergency-response planning.

Media and Government's Role

It is essential that the news media receive accurate disaster information to circulate to the public. News media can also help inform the public by reporting on rumors and soliciting evidence and comment on their plausibility, if any. They may inadvertently do damage by reporting on rumors without seeking context or confirmation, or by presenting them as established facts. The *Evening Sun* newspaper of New York City announced this news atop its front page on April 15, 1912:

> ALL SAVED FROM TITANIC AFTER COLLISION
> RESCUE BY CARPATHIA AND PARISIAN; LINER IS BEING
> TOWED TO HALIFAX AFTER SMASHING INTO A ICEBERG.[22]

The factual deficiencies of those headlines – based, if readers dove deeply enough into the article's text, on a passing reference to an unquoted report by parents of a ship's unnamed telegrapher – are now apparent, but they remind us that there is nothing new about the phenomenon of news media reporting rumor.

Nearly a century later, the proliferation of news outlets, the competition to be first with a powerful story, the technologies that make broad reach and rapid reporting possible, and the 24-hour cycle of Web and broadcast news can increase the chance that rumors will creep unlabelled or unchallenged into news stories. And when public officials fail to provide timely, accurate, and credible public information – or stand before microphones and cameras to spread rumors themselves – rumor can become a serious threat to civil order and to relief efforts.

For example, on August 29, the day of landfall, ABC's "World News Tonight" reported: "In New Orleans, entire neighborhoods are underwater, but the levees held. The nightmare scenario of an entire city underwater did not happen." Other broadcasters said: "New Orleans dodged the big bullet" (NBC's "Today" show, August 29) and "They dodged the bullet, but they still got a sound bruising" (National Public Radio's "Talk of the Nation," August 29).[23] As the public learned later, on-the-scene reports by emergency officials, residents, and the press had already described flooding from levee breaches and overtopping several hours earlier. For example, Ivor van Heerden, the Director of Louisiana State University's Center for the Study of Public Health Impacts of Hurricanes, relayed that "the National Weather Service [is] reporting that one of the levees was breached ... as the reporters have said, there's very, very significant areas of New Orleans that did flood from the levee overtopping. In some areas we have about 11 feet of standing water. People have been forced out onto the roofs of their homes."[24] Yet as late as the next morning, August 30, there were still news items like this *Washington Post* report:

> Some experts predicted the storm could become one of the worst catastrophes in U.S. history. But the city managed to avoid the worst of the worst. The Mississippi River did not breach New Orleans's famed levees to any serious degree.[25]

Others issued conflicting reports, even within their own stories.[26] Accurate reporting was at a premium, not only concerning the damage to the levees, but also with respect to security and law-enforcement issues, as discussed below.

Getting news from the field, through the editing process, and to the public, all under time pressure, is a challenge. While modern technology makes correction of mistaken reports easier and faster than in the days of the *Titanic*, thanks to the same technology, news travels that much more quickly in the first place, magnifying the potential damage of erroneous reports.

Government's Public-Affairs Responsibilities in the Event of a Disaster

Accurate information is never as critical as during an emergency. It's also never more difficult to obtain. Emergency-response planning – in this case, the NRP and the State of Louisiana's Emergency Operations Plan (LA EOP) – tasks federal and state agencies with delivering reliable information to the public and the media in the event of a disaster.[27] During Hurricane Katrina, however, officials at all levels of government either failed to comprehend these roles or ignored these obligations, though there were times when officials understood and carried out their duties.

The NRP's Public Affairs Support Annex directs DHS, in coordination with its component FEMA, to "mobilize" federal assets to deliver information to the public regarding emergencies as well as "use media monitoring … and other techniques to identify rumors, misinformation, inaccurate reports …" and rapidly correct them.[28] The NRP also calls for establishing a federal Joint Information Center (JIC) to support the Joint Field Office (JFO) with public-affairs matters and information dissemination during an emergency, at the location of the disaster, depending on the incident's requirements.[29] However, the DHS reported that its federal JIC was not established until September 6 – over a week after Hurricane Katrina made landfall.[30]

State emergency agencies coordinate with the federal effort. The Louisiana Office of Homeland Security and Emergency Preparedness (LOHSEP) has primary responsibility for "initiating, organizing and coordinating all aspects of Emergency Public Information,"[31] including the activation of a state Joint Information Center which would incorporate federal communications activity.[32] Yet it is not clear whether during the response to Hurricane Katrina a state JIC was established, although state officials maintained an information center in a trailer behind the Office of Emergency Preparedness in Baton Rouge, which provided briefings from this location every four hours.[33]

Both federal and state agencies have mutual obligations to formulate a coordinated message. The NRP envisions the JFO, or federal JIC, to work "in close coordination with other JICs to integrate into a Joint Information System (JIS) providing consistent, coordinated, and timely information during an incident,"[34] and as stated above, the LA EOP envisions integrating federal communications activities into the state JIC. However, it appears this goal was not immediately carried out, or even understood, during the response to Hurricane Katrina.

A DHS/FEMA after-action report attributed some of the difficulty and, ultimately, the failure of federal and state officials to ensure a flow of accurate, timely information to factors including the overwhelming damage to communication infrastructure, the early lack of co-location between federal (DHS/FEMA) and state public-information centers, reliance on field staff to relay information on sporadically functional equipment, and the pressure on public-information staff to react to media queries as opposed to pushing out new information.[35] Specifically, DHS Inspector General Richard Skinner testified before the Committee that his department found there should have been more cooperation between federal and state public-affairs officials.[36]

Media Performance During Katrina

As for the media, some of the rumor traffic in Katrina derived from the reliance of reporters on dubious sources. A New Orleans *Times-Picayune* reporter later chastised himself for passing along unconfirmed a National Guardsman's comment that a freezer at the city's Convention Center held "30 or 40" bodies, and another soldier's comment that the dead included a "7-year-old with her throat cut." As Brian Thevenot, the *Times-Picayune* reporter, went on to note, "Neither the mass of bodies nor the allegedly expired child would ever be found," but the rumor was eventually traced to gossip in the food line at a nearby casino where military and police personnel were staging.[37]

The impact of rumors – sharks swimming in downtown New Orleans, dead babies in trash cans, and stacks of bodies at the Superdome and the Convention Center – was compounded by misinformation from officials. New Orleans Mayor Ray Nagin told a nationwide TV audience about people "in that frickin' Superdome for five days watching dead bodies, watching hooligans killing people, raping people."[38] New Orleans Police Superintendent Eddie Compass reported that babies were being raped there.[39] Both statements were unfounded.

Inaccurate rumors reported without caveats, particularly with respect to law enforcement, included: "Violent gangs are roaming the streets at night, hidden by the cover of darkness" (Fox News), troops on rooftops looking for snipers as "gunfire crackled in the distance" (Los Angeles *Times*), "a young man run down and then shot by a New Orleans police officer" (Ottawa *Sun*), and "Girls and boys were raped in the dark and had their throats cut and bodies were stuffed in the kitchens while looters and madmen exchanged fire with weapons they had looted" (*Financial Times* of London).[40]

The frequency and apparent authority of rumor-based reporting during Hurricane Katrina added to public confusion about events along the Gulf Coast. As two *Washington Post* investigators concluded:

> The sensational accounts delayed rescue and evacuation efforts already hampered by poor planning and a lack of coordination among local, state, and federal agencies. People rushing to the Gulf Coast to fly rescue helicopters or to distribute food, water, and other aid steeled themselves for battle.[41]

Impact of Misinformation on Response Efforts

At 9:15 p.m. CT on Thursday, September 1, DHS issued a report that FEMA's search-and-rescue forces "ceased operations until National Guard can assist TF's [Urban Search and Rescue Task Forces] with security."[42] James Strickland, a member of FEMA's Urban Search and Rescue team, explained that throughout the day there had been reports of shootings and rioting in the streets.[43]

And at that point, we said, okay, we're not sending out any of our teams unless they have some type of force protection with them, which at the time was kind of scarce. ... So that day, by the time we got force protection kegged up with everybody, we had really lost most of the day, the daylight gone…If any went out, it was very limited as to what went out because we didn't have a sufficient protection plan.[44]

Louisiana Wildlife & Fisheries
team making a rescue
FEMA photo

Search and Rescue

We would put two officers in a boat, one guy to operate the boat and another guy with a flashlight to give him direction. … Most of our communication at this point is by voice. And they would go out and like I said, it wasn't any problem to find people, there were people everywhere, people were everywhere, every house, people on the porches, people on the roofs, people shouting from windows and you would just go to it and load up the people that you could take and tell them, We'll be back for the rest of you. …

We encountered every kind of medical condition that you can just about imagine, we had diabetics, we had bedridden patients, we had some security issues. … And it was constant, I mean it was limitless, you never got a break in the number of people you were bringing out.[1]

— Lt. Col. Keith LaCaze
Louisiana Department of Wildlife and Fisheries

Search and Rescue

On the day of Hurricane Katrina's landfall, rescuers from Louisiana's Department of Wildlife and Fisheries (W&F) didn't need their standard grid system for searches. From every direction, thousands of people on rooftops were calling for help in the dark – that evening, lights from the search-and-rescue boats and helicopters were the city's only source of illumination.[2]

W&F would bring the rescuees back to one of three staging areas on highway overpasses. By 1 a.m. Tuesday, hundreds were massed at these locations, reaching capacity. By Tuesday afternoon, W&F alone had rescued 1,500 people.[3]

Federal, State, and Local Rescuers Saved Thousands of Lives

Federal, state, and local officials combined to rescue over 60,000 people after landfall.[4]

Federal

FEMA is the federal government's lead agency for Emergency Support Function 9 (ESF-9, Search and Rescue) under the National Response Plan (NRP),[5] but during Katrina, some perceived the Coast Guard to have been the lead federal agency for search and rescue (SAR).[6] The Coast Guard rescued over 33,000 people.[7] The U.S. Department of Defense (DOD), which deployed in support of the Coast Guard, rescued 2,911 people.[8] FEMA rescued over 6,000 people.[9]

FEMA's Urban Search and Rescue (USAR) teams comprise state and local teams that FEMA contracted to assist the federal government during an emergency. In exchange for funding from FEMA for training and equipment, state and local search-and-rescue teams agree to be deployed by FEMA when needed. There are 28 such teams around the country, many associated with local fire departments. The men and women on these teams are themselves the first responders for disasters in their own communities. When FEMA deploys them, they become federal assets and, therefore, no longer state or local first responders.[10]

State

The Louisiana W&F is the state's lead agency for ESF-9.[11] W&F and out-of-state agencies rescued about 21,000 people trapped in the greater New Orleans area after landfall.[12] The Louisiana National Guard, which supported W&F under ESF-9, rescued another 9,313 people.[13]

Local

The New Orleans Fire Department (NOFD) and New Orleans Police Department (NOPD) officers – the exact number is unknown – worked with little rest in the first week after land-fall, even as their own families remained trapped or were evacuated.[14] NOFD is the City of New Orleans' lead agency for SAR; the NOPD supported NOFD.[15]

Hurricane Katrina Confirmed What Hurricane Pam Had Predicted: Decimated Local Responders

Hurricane Katrina confirmed what Hurricane Pam predicted: many local first respond-ers had been incapacitated and thrown into disarray by the severe hurricane. The section on SAR in the plan that grew out of Hurricane Pam stated: "Parish resources in the most severely impacted areas will not be available for several weeks or even months, as they were not removed from the area prior to the storm."[16] But even if Hurricane Pam predicted that Parish resources would not be available, William Lokey, FEMA's Federal Coordinat-ing Officer (FCO), the organization's lead officer in Louisiana, who was stationed in Baton Rouge before landfall, pointed out that Hurricane Pam "did not envision the number of first responders in New Orleans that would become disaster victims and would not be available to take part in that plan."[17]

Pam's conclusion that parish resources wouldn't be available for weeks, if not months, may have derived from the city's inadequate preparedness for search and rescue. For example, the NOFD owned no boats;[18] the NOPD owned only five.[19] Although the NOFD was well trained in USAR and incident command, it had no training in water SAR.[20] The NOFD had applied in 2005 to DHS for water USAR training, even lining up an instructor, but DHS denied its application.[21] In the absence of boats and water SAR training, NOFD and NOPD officers had to commandeer and hot-wire boats to improvise rescue missions.[22]

Finally, the Hurricane Pam exercise predicted that a similar hurricane in real life would "result in flooding of many roads, limiting access into many areas until flood waters sub-side."[23] Such a warning required readiness for air and water rescue; specifically, Hurricane Pam called for 20,000 boat-based rescues and about 1,000 helicopter rescues.[24] Emergency planners at all levels of government should have realized that large-scale search-and-rescue operations would be likely if a major hurricane struck New Orleans.[25]

Responders Prepare for the Storm

Although the search-and-rescue teams who deployed after landfall performed heroically, two agencies stand out, the U.S. Coast Guard and the Louisiana W&F.

U.S. Coast Guard

In general, the Coast Guard performed exemplary work in its search-and-rescue missions. Several factors may explain why: (1) pre-positioning of assets close enough to be useful on Monday, August 29, the day of landfall, but still out of harm's way;[26] (2) training and equipment for water missions; (3) an organizational culture that encourages personnel to respond proactively;[27] (4) a familiarity with incident response generally and the Incident Command System specifically throughout the entire organization;[28] and (5) a long-term presence in the affected areas, promoting familiarity with the region and working relationships with state and local agencies.[29]

The Coast Guard's Eighth District, which covers 26 states, is headquartered in New Orleans.[30] The Coast Guard Air Station in New Orleans, like all the Coast Guard units along the Gulf Coast, exercises its hurricane plans several times each season.[31] In New Orleans, the Coast Guard exercises regularly with other state and local agencies and in particular has worked closely with the boat forces of the Louisiana W&F.[32] Pre-landfall, the Coast Guard placed liaisons at both the state Emergency Operations Center (EOC) in Baton Rouge and at the New Orleans Office of Emergency Preparedness.[33]

A key factor in the Coast Guard's rapid reaction is that, unlike FEMA, the Coast Guard sees itself as a first responder.[34] Prior to landfall, based on the forecasted intensity of the storm, the Coast Guard decided to move its headquarters to its alternate site in St. Louis, Missouri,[35] and to use its alternate incident-command post in Alexandria, Louisiana,[36] approximately 200 miles away. The Coast Guard evacuated personnel and their family members[37] from the direct path of the storm and pre-positioned personnel and assets north, east, and west of the predicted track, but close enough to maintain its ability to return them to the affected area.[38]

As a result, the Coast Guard was able to begin search-and-rescue missions by 2:50 p.m. on the day of landfall. The winds were still consistently 45-50 knots (about 52 to 58 m.p.h.) strong[39] when a rescue swimmer named Laurence Nettles was lowered by helicopter and navigated his way through tree limbs to rescue a four-month-old infant, her mother and grandmother, and their pet dog in Plaquemines Parish.[40] Of the more than 33,000 rescues the Coast Guard completed, 12,500 made use of helicopters.[41] This was far more than the Hurricane Pam prediction of 21,000 total rescues, of which 1,000 would be helicopter rescues.[42] Within the first few days, about 40 percent of the Coast Guard's national helicopter fleet converged on the Gulf Coast to assist in search and rescue and air delivery of food and water.[43]

Louisiana Department of Wildlife and Fisheries

While the Coast Guard served as the primary source of air SAR, the Louisiana W&F was the primary source of water SAR, and performed equally admirably. Like the Coast Guard, W&F officers, trained for water-rescue missions, were adequately equipped, had pre-positioned search-and-rescue assets close enough to be useful on the day of landfall, and were composed of men and women familiar with the affected area and other federal, state, and local agencies involved.

On Monday, W&F transported 60 boats to New Orleans from their pre-staged areas, and by 4 p.m. that day launched the boats from one of three staging areas strategically located on high ground throughout the city.[44] W&F also received assistance from the Louisiana National Guard, which had pre-deployed boats and helicopters in and outside of New Orleans.[45]

Shortcomings in the Preparation and Support for the SAR Missions

All levels of government could have provided far better support for these heroes and the people they rescued. Inadequate planning, preparation, and support compromised the SAR missions, and should be drastically improved for future catastrophes.

Prior to Katrina, the NRP considered SAR to focus primarily, if not entirely, on SAR in collapsed structures.[46] The NRP reflects this belief by titling the mission as Urban Search and Rescue (USAR) and by requiring FEMA, rather than some other agency, to act as the lead agency for ESF-9. However, Katrina required search-and-rescue efforts not only in urban collapsed structures but also in a water environment. U.S. Coast Guard Vice Admiral Vivean Crea acknowledged that the federal response plan should be capable of covering more than one type of search and rescue.[47]

Pre-positioning of Search-and-Rescue Assets: Local and State

Despite the success of the U.S. Coast Guard and the W&F in pre-positioning search-and-rescue assets, similar efforts by other agencies at the state and local levels failed in very basic ways.

Because New Orleans lacked enough boats, complying with the NOFD Emergency Operations Plan required many NOFD officers to pre-position their personal boats.[48]

Although W&F pre-positioned search-and-rescue assets both within and on the outskirts of the affected areas, the Louisiana National Guard pre-positioned its boats and high water vehicles primarily at Jackson Barracks, which flooded when the Industrial Canal levee broke and flooded the Lower Ninth Ward. The floodwaters rendered many of the boats and high water vehicles unusable on the day of landfall.[49] As many witnesses said, a hurricane's precise landfall and impact are difficult to predict.[50] Nonetheless, placing a key element of local first response at Jackson Barracks, one of the lowest points in the city, was not an exercise in prudent planning.

Pre-positioning of Search-and-Rescue Assets: Federal

Although the Coast Guard successfully pre-staged search-and-rescue assets, FEMA did not.[51] FEMA pre-staged only three search-and-rescue teams in Shreveport, LA, and only two in Meridian, MS.[52]

FEMA officials point out that FEMA is not a first responder for disasters,[53] but its modest pre-landfall deployment is still hard to understand, considering that the Pam exercise had revealed a critical need for immediate search-and-rescue capability. FEMA did activate 16 additional search-and-rescue teams, but not until Tuesday, August 30, the day after landfall. (It activated 10 more the following day.)[54] FEMA Federal Coordinating Officer (FCO) William Lokey told the Committee that FEMA did not pre-stage more search-and-rescue teams because the state did not request additional teams before landfall.[55] But Lokey reasonably should have known, from FEMA's participation in the Hurricane Pam exercise, that the state and locals' search-and-rescue capabilities would need to be supplemented in the event of a catastrophic storm – which Lokey recognized Katrina to be.[56] The state did not request additional search-and-rescue teams, and FEMA failed to offer them.

That FEMA pre-staged three teams in Shreveport, approximately 340 miles away from New Orleans, contributed to the delay.[57] The teams left Shreveport for Baton Rouge on Monday, August 29, moving to the greater New Orleans area only late that night.[58] As a result, they were not able to begin rescuing people until Tuesday morning,[59] whereas the other federal, state, and local operations began search and rescue Monday afternoon, as soon as the storm died down.[60]

FEMA Lacked Water-Rescue Capabilities

"Water rescue is not part of the USAR mission," Lokey testified before the Committee.[61] Indeed, when FEMA search-and-rescue teams arrived in New Orleans, they did not have boats.[62] Instead, the FEMA teams joined boats operated by volunteers or other agencies.[63]

Although most of the 28 teams FEMA could tap for search and rescue lacked a water-rescue capability,[64] FEMA was able to acquire eight teams in California that did possess that training.[65] FEMA should have pre-staged teams trained in water rescue given that catastrophic post-storm flooding was anticipated. Some have argued that FEMA should have search-

and-rescue teams designed for a water environment, as drowning accounts for 90 percent of deaths in hurricanes.[66] However, Lokey said that FEMA teams do not arrive on the scene quickly enough for it to make sense to equip and train them for those kinds of searches,[67] even though long-term planning and training for water rescue would have obviated the need for on-the-scene equipping and training. Some have suggested that it might be worthwhile for FEMA teams to have some basic training and equipment for working in a flooded environment (e.g., life jackets), while more serious water rescue should be left to the states and the Coast Guard.[68] Some have said FEMA cannot support water rescue under the current budget and would require additional funding.[69] FEMA was ill-equipped to carry out its ESF-9 obligation in a setting that was anything but a surprise.

Beyond an initial training course in 2000, FEMA's Red, White, and Blue Incident Support Teams (ISTs), which coordinate and manage the search-and-rescue missions, received no training.[70]

Communications Failures

Almost immediately after landfall, communications for the SAR personnel at all levels of government failed to one degree or another. Storm damage rendered many communications systems inoperable while heavy traffic stalled others. Each agency had unique challenges, suffering from communications that were neither operable nor interoperable. Indeed, these widespread communications failures contributed mightily to the failures of coordination among search-and-rescue agencies, which we address below.[71]

Communications Failures: Local

The fire and police departments' communications suffered from both inoperability and lack of interoperability.

The NOFD and NOPD were supposed to operate on an 800 megahertz system, but storm damage forced them to switch to their contingency plan: the mutual-aid channel, used by all first responders in the area. The mutual-aid channel required each officer to wait his or her turn, sometimes for 20 minutes, before speaking. NOFD used the mutual-aid channel until Thursday, September 1. NOPD used it until Saturday, September 3.[72]

Although the mutual-aid channel was operational, NOFD officers could not transmit to certain parts of the city because of its limited range. As a result, NOFD officers essentially had to play the children's game "Operator": An NOFD officer would hear officer A trying to talk to officer B, and would relay A's message to B, if B was within the eavesdropper's range.[73]

Communications Failures: State

The Department of Wildlife and Fisheries also suffered from unique communications failures. W&F set up three operations centers strategically located around New Orleans. However, its officers could not communicate by radio with the boats carrying out SAR missions, requiring the operations centers to dispatch "runners" to deliver messages.[74] (The boats, in turn, had trouble communicating with National Guard and Coast Guard helicopters.) Ultimately, the operations centers were able to make contact using walkie-talkies purchased from a local sporting-goods store.[75]

After years of research, a Deputy Superintendent of Louisiana State Police in 2004, and again in January 2005, presented to the state and federal governments a detailed, $105 million proposal for interoperability infrastructure.[76] According to W&F witnesses, the plan might well have avoided the communications failures between officials in Baton Rouge and New Orleans, as well as the communications among agencies, by bringing all state and local officials' radio communications onto the same network.[77]

Communications Failures: Federal

Communication capabilities for the Coast Guard varied, both by time and by unit. Although the UHF radio frequency used by Coast Guard helicopters to communicate at a local and unit level continued to work well after Katrina, VHF frequencies typically used to communicate with the Coast Guard and other emergency responders by outside entities (boaters, hospitals, etc.) were cluttered, and frequently overloaded.[78]

Coast Guard pilots also reported difficulty communicating with their bases, including the Coast Guard Air Station in New Orleans, which returned to limited operational status on Monday afternoon, August 29. They estimated that only 40 percent of their communication attempts with bases were successful.[79] They were attempting to reach the Coast Guard Air Station in New Orleans, Baton Rouge, and other bases by using other aircraft, including a Coast Guard C-130 surveying oil rigs in the Gulf of Mexico and a Customs and Border Protection P-3 AWACS (Airborne Warning and Control System), as mobile communications-relay platforms. These planes would patch calls through to Coast Guard bases, since most ground infrastructure was not operational.

Some Coast Guard personnel were able to use personal cell phones to relay information to other Coast Guard offices, at least initially. But as the infrastructure for cell phone service began failing, this means of communication had to be abandoned.[80]

The Coast Guard should have been better prepared for an anticipated breakdown in communications infrastructure. While not initially deployed for that purpose, aircraft such as the C-130 and P-3 AWACS proved useful in relaying communications. More thought should be given to determining whether this or other temporary means of communication should be used in other large-scale incidents like Katrina.

Unified Command – Coordination of Search-and-Rescue Missions

While many individuals went to heroic lengths to rescue victims, their efforts would have been far more effective if agency efforts were better coordinated. Officials from nearly every search-and-rescue agency told Committee staff that they lacked basic maps of the area.[81] At one point, state and local officials tore maps out of telephone books, so that out-of-state search-and-rescue teams could have some sense of where they were going.[82] However, high floodwaters in New Orleans hid street signs from view,[83] complicating their efforts.

Efforts by DOD and the National Guard to coordinate the airborne search-and-rescue mission by dividing up the city[84] are discussed below.

The lack of coordination had several significant consequences. Agencies searched areas without knowing whether those areas already had been searched by others.[85] The agencies in boats were mostly unable to coordinate with the National Guard or the Coast Guard to request helicopters if victims needed to be airlifted.[86] Finally, the lack of coordination prevented food, water, and other critical needs from reaching the rescuees gathered at the search-and-rescue collection sites.[87]

According to Captain Tim Bayard, the lack of coordination at the local level, resulted from a lack of planning, direction, and leadership from the City of New Orleans' Office of Emergency Preparedness (OEP) and inoperable communications.[88] For example, the NOPD decided the day before landfall to set up a command post from the trunk of a car and at picnic tables outside of Harrah's Casino, but Captain Bayard did not know where the mobile command center for the city's OEP was.[89]

Although W&F was the lead state agency for the search-and-rescue mission, it failed to establish itself as a leader for other state and local agencies involved in search and rescue.[90]

Rescue boats, New Orleans
U.S. Coast Guard photo

This is likely due in part to the lack of communications capability and how overwhelmed W&F officials were.

At the federal level, FEMA did not establish a local command site for search and rescue either before or on the day of landfall.[91] On Monday, the FEMA teams had no plan for a base of operations in the greater New Orleans area. They ultimately settled on the parking lot at a Sam's Club in Jefferson Parish.[92] On Tuesday, FEMA moved its command to Zephyr Field, the New Orleans Saints' practice field in Jefferson Parish,[93] but by this time both W&F and the Louisiana National Guard had already established their own local command posts elsewhere.[94] Under the NRP, federal and state governments were supposed to establish a unified command for search and rescue,[95] but both levels of government failed to achieve that objective.[96] Poor communications capabilities after landfall exacerbated the challenge of coordination between state and federal agencies. W&F and FEMA did not establish a unified command for search and rescue until Wednesday, two days after landfall, at Zephyr Field.[97]

Although there was no unified command for search and rescue in New Orleans, there is some evidence of a stronger coordination effort made for federal, state, and local search-

and-rescue resources at the EOC in Baton Rouge, according to the U.S. Coast Guard Search and Rescue Controller Valerie Boyd assigned to Baton Rouge. She said that the Coast Guard, FEMA, W&F, the Louisiana National Guard and others formed a joint search-and-rescue task force at the state EOC on Sunday, August 28.[98] The task force met twice a day over the next two weeks, to try to coordinate the joint search-and-rescue response. Agencies there would update surface and aviation asset spreadsheets on a daily basis, and the Louisiana State Police would provide search-and-rescue case information coming into the EOC via the 911 system to the Coast Guard, who would triage cases to the extent practicable, and convert street addresses to latitude and longitude coordinates.[99] The Coast Guard would then pass along the triaged cases and coordinate, but not direct, any other search-and-rescue assets.[100]

No Plan for Ground Transportation to Evacuate People from USAR Collection Points

As noted earlier, ground transportation arrived in the greater New Orleans area unnecessarily late. The absence of planning for ground transportation by the federal and state governments contributed to the appalling conditions at the Superdome, the Convention Center, the I-10 overpasses, and other search-and-rescue collection sites.

Inadequate Resources

Louisiana National Guard Brigadier General Brod Veillon testified: "We are a force of 11,000 people, and so … you can't handle this size of a catastrophe. … [The Emergency Mutual Assistance Compact (EMAC)] is designed to compensate for that,"[101] and "parallel to [her use of EMAC] the Governor made the call to the President for DOD assets."[102]

As described earlier, the NOFD and NOPD lacked critical watercraft. For nearly a decade, successive New Orleans mayors have imprudently denied NOFD funding requests for watercraft.[103]

After landfall, bureaucracy continued to impede essential relief.[104]

W&F pre-staged the roughly 200 boats at its disposal and deployed them in staggered phases throughout the storm. But many of those boats were small; FEMA denied requests for larger rubber rafts[105] because, according to FEMA's lead official in Louisiana, the rubber rafts would not have been strong enough to maneuver in water filled with debris.[106] Lieutenant Colonel Keith LaCaze with W&F disagreed, claiming that the rafts would have been valuable – particularly in the early days – either for maneuvering in very shallow water near doors and windows or in saving additional trips to collection sites by collecting rescuees in rubber rafts that could be towed behind regular boats.[107] At a minimum, FEMA's denial of the request is an example of the organization's failure to follow its own principle of letting those closest to the situation determine how best to meet needs.

DHS was slow to deploy equipment pods that contained standardized equipment to sustain or replenish up to 150 first responders. DHS pre-positions these pods at strategic locations nationwide in order that they can arrive at a disaster site within 4 to 12 hours.[108] However, DHS waited until at least two days after landfall to advise either Mississippi or Louisiana of their availability.[109] Thus, nearly a week after landfall, the equipment pods were still en route.[110] DHS official Matt Mayer, who was in charge of these pods,[111] acknowledged that DHS "made a mistake" and should have deployed these pods earlier.[112] Captain Fincher of the NOFD bemoaned the fact that he and other first responders did not have these equipment pods earlier since they contained assets that would have been very useful to the NOFD officers: an 18-wheeler full of "turn-out clothes, breathing apparatus, search and rescue cameras, … hazardous material equipment, … communications system, [and] … decontamination set-ups."[113]

On the day before landfall, the U.S. Department of the Interior (DOI) offered two teams of law-enforcement officers to FEMA. These officers would have proved highly valuable, when security concerns later in the week undermined FEMA's search-and-rescue effort. But FEMA did not make use of those teams,[114] and Lokey, FEMA's FCO in Louisiana, testified that he was unaware of the offer.[115]

In its response to the Committee's interrogatories, DOI stated that "In the immediate aftermath of the hurricane, DOI delivered to FEMA a comprehensive list of its deployable assets that were immediately available for humanitarian and emergency assistance," including 300 boats and 400 law-enforcement officers.[116] However, DOI's Emergency Coordinator, Laurence Broun, later told the Committee that DOI, in fact, did not send the list to FEMA and instead sent the list to the White House Homeland Security Council, not "in the immediate aftermath of the hurricane," but on Saturday, September 3, five days after landfall. Broun does not know if the White House ever sent the list to FEMA,[117] and Lokey was unaware of the offer.[118]

Emergency Mutual Assistance Compact

In addition to designating the W&F as the lead state agency for search and rescue, the Louisiana Emergency Operations Plan specifies that W&F is to seek assistance through EMAC, if W&F's capabilities are overwhelmed.[119] W&F witnesses testified that the agency would have benefited from a request for additional SAR resources from other state governments through the EMAC process before, rather than after, landfall. Lokey specifically advised Colonel Jeff Smith, the Acting Deputy Director for Emergency Preparedness at LOHSEP, to use EMAC to get swift-water rescue teams from California because Lokey knew that California had robust water-rescue capabilities.[120] Neither Lokey nor Col. Smith realized until the day of landfall or just the day before that California was not a signatory to EMAC.[121] Ultimately, FEMA and W&F operated outside the EMAC channels to request this assistance. FEMA was able to bring in eight California swift-water teams on August 30, because they happened to be embedded in an organization with which FEMA had contracts for its USAR program.[122]

In contrast to W&F, the Louisiana National Guard placed EMAC requests pre-landfall. The National Guard asked for helicopters from Arkansas, which approved the request before landfall.[123] Moreover, Bennett Landreneau, the Adjutant General of Louisiana, testified before the House Select Bipartisan Katrina Committee that the Louisiana National Guard knew "immediately" that its resources would be overwhelmed and consequently sought other assistance through EMAC.[124] Forty-eight states and four territories provided requested assistance.

W&F also encountered bureaucratic difficulties in making EMAC requests. Some states could not comply immediately because they were uncertain whether they had proper authorization.[125] W&F Secretary Dwight Landreneau testified that it would be helpful to have a list of all assets available from each state so that states in need could call on that help more efficiently.[126] Notably, it was by chance that Lokey was able to advise Louisiana about which states had water rescue teams that it could request through EMAC. Lokey, due to his prior experience with the National Urban Search and Rescue Program,[127] advised Col. Smith to reach out to California and a few other states that he knew had water–rescue capabilities.[128] No standardized list of such teams exists for state emergency managers.

Managing and Utilizing Volunteers

Volunteers, who started to arrive as early as Monday evening, proved a great benefit to the search-and-rescue mission in its first days. Many provided boats to transport FEMA and other personnel to conduct search-and-rescue missions[129] when only other agencies' boats were available.

At the same time, some volunteers were not well-prepared for water search and rescue. For instance, some of the boats were too big to navigate flooded streets in New Orleans. Moreover, the Louisiana W&F required volunteers to have food, water, fuel, and life jackets; many didn't and were turned away.[130] Several volunteers – as well as some out of state officers – were unfamiliar with the city.[131] Finally, the Department could not handle the numbers of volunteers: one day as many as 200 volunteers showed up but could not be effectively used because "about half of them did not have the equipment that was necessary to help."[132]

Security Risks

On Monday evening, after W&F officers reported sounds of gunfire, one NOFD team aborted its SAR mission, though it eventually returned to its post.[133] Tensions continued to run high in the area, but did not escalate until Thursday, when media – at times incorrectly – reported widespread looting and violence.[134]

On Thursday, FEMA ordered its search-and-rescue missions in New Orleans to stop for the entire day and pull back to Zephyr Field until more security arrived.[135] Captain Patrick Lampard of the NOFD recalled that as these teams began to pull back, they recommended that the NOFD also withdraw due to the security concerns. Based on this recommendation, Capt. Lampard decided to pull back his NOFD teams that day as well,[136] although some NOFD officers ignored the command.[137]

Although no other search-and-rescue witnesses have said that conditions on Thursday were such that they would have stopped their mission,[138] the need for security might very well have been legitimate,[139] and the rapid deployment of additional law-enforcement officers would have been helpful, as shown in Chapter 25 on Public Safety and Security. Also, at least one FEMA search-and-rescue team member has recommended that FEMA search-and-rescue teams might have been able to continue their work if they deployed with force protection.[140]

Also, in some cases, search-and-rescue teams met resistance from residents who refused to leave their homes, despite the devastation.[141] It was only on September 10 that the Department of Justice gave federal agents permission to use force to enter buildings to rescue remaining victims.[142]

Mississippi

Pre-Storm Planning

In Mississippi, the state emergency plan puts SAR operations in the hands of the Mississippi Emergency Management Agency (MEMA), with support from other state agencies.[143] Hurricane Katrina SAR operations were conducted along the Mississippi Gulf Coast by local first responders, state-sourced SAR personnel, the Coast Guard, rescue teams provided by FEMA, and teams from other states. Jim Brinson of the State Office of Homeland Security directed SAR operations from the State Emergency Operations Center in Jackson and, later, from the Gulf Coast.[144]

Mississippi planning provides that local first responders – especially fire-department personnel and sheriffs (who are the presumptive incident commanders for their respective counties under the state plan) – have initial responsibility for SAR operations.[145] For large-scale disasters requiring outside resources, the plan points to four sources: (1) Mississippi personnel and equipment secured by MEMA from other areas of the state; (2) federal assets sourced by FEMA; (3) resources from other states via the EMAC; and (4) Mississippi National Guard support.[146] Brinson did not consult the state emergency plan to review these options, but the SAR response to Katrina involved significant aid from each source, and appeared consistent with the plan.

The identification and staging of SAR assets began on August 27, before landfall. Within two days, MEMA had identified 19 teams consisting of rescue personnel from throughout the state.[147] In addition, FEMA pre-deployed USAR teams on August 27 to the Meridian Naval Air Station in east-central Mississippi, near the Alabama border, approximately 140 miles from the Gulf Coast; first to arrive were task forces from Ohio and Indiana, later augmented by teams from other states and additional FEMA USAR teams.[148] Meanwhile, local first responders had pre-positioned equipment like fire trucks and rescue vehicles in anticipation of the storm.

On August 28 and 29, SAR teams and equipment continued to arrive. These included FEMA teams, which were staged in Meridian, Mississippi, and in Florida before landfall.[149] Fire fighters and first responders from other Mississippi counties awaited the storm at the State Fire Academy in Pearl, near the state capital of Jackson.[150] EMAC teams from Florida formed up and awaited direction from MEMA.[151] In addition, Mississippi National Guard elements staged at Camp Shelby, near Hattiesburg, approximately 65 miles north of Gulfport and, to a lesser degree, along the three coastal counties.

Search-and-Rescue Operations Post-Landfall

Hurricane Katrina overwhelmed local SAR responders, who faced flooding, impassable debris fields, obliterated roads, and vast areas requiring searches.[152] Personnel and equipment converged on the Gulf Coast late Monday, August 29, and early Tuesday. Coast Guard teams began air and water SAR missions on August 29.

The level of devastation Katrina inflicted on the Gulf Coast posed a huge challenge for rescuers. Often, roads were impassable and had to be cleared before rescuers were able to start SAR operations. Rescuers sometimes could not wait for the roads to be cleared. For example, the White Cypress subdivision in northern Hancock County, the westernmost county on the Mississippi Gulf Coast, and its 200 residents were completely cut off by fallen trees. Rescuers had to be airlifted into the area while forestry teams were still working to reopen roads.[153]

Rescuers faced debris piles that were often two to three stories high and as many as four blocks wide. The debris extended all along the Mississippi Gulf Coast and stretched inland several hundred yards in some places, to four miles in others. The debris field itself was extraordinarily hazardous. It contained not only the remains of houses, buildings, and automobiles, but also hazards such as chemical spills and gas leaks. In Gulfport, the hurricane had destroyed a number of containers at the port holding chicken carcasses and pork bellies intended for export, and scattered the contents along the coast. This put thousands of decomposing chickens where SAR operations were later to take place. As Pat Sullivan, Gulfport's Fire Chief, aptly summarized, it was "an impossible situation."[154]

In part because communication was so difficult along the Gulf Coast, MEMA decided to headquarter state, federal, and EMAC search-and-rescue operations in Harrison County, the geographically central and most populous coastal county, while local responders remained deployed along the coast.[155] For SAR purposes, the Mississippi Gulf Coast was divided into three areas: Jackson/George Counties, with Jackson County easternmost on the coast and George to its north; Harrison/Stone Counties, with Harrison central on the coast and Stone to its north; and Hancock/Pearl River Counties, with Hancock County westernmost on the coast and Pearl River to its north. Maps and grids helped ensure that areas were searched in a coordinated, methodical manner.[156]

Various officials in Mississippi reported good coordination among local, state, federal, and EMAC resources.[157]

Rescue teams combined Mississippi and out-of-state personnel to mix local knowledge with the specialized equipment and training available to federal and state teams, as Jim Brinson, the SAR coordinator, described:

> You know, somebody from New York isn't real sure what water moccasins and alligators do in a severe storm. They get very nasty. My [Mississippi] guys understand this, they live here, they hunt here. And on the flip side USAR teams are trained to do specific things and have specific equipment to do search and rescue in that type of urban environment that many guys don't have: robots, acoustic mics, fiber-optic cameras, things like that.[158]

Officials estimate that the teams assisting local first responders consisted of approximately 550 SAR personnel[159] including Mississippi first responders sent by MEMA, 17 FEMA rescue and incident-management teams,[160] and rescuers from Florida and other states sent though the EMAC. These figures do not include personnel from the Coast Guard and Mississippi National Guard, who figured importantly in search-and-rescue operations. For example, the Coast Guard rescued and airlifted 1,700 stranded residents.[161] The Mississippi National Guard provided manpower and engineering support along the Gulf Coast,[162] and conducted SAR in devastated Hancock County on Mississippi's western Gulf Coast.[163]

Search-and-rescue operations continued for about a week before moving into recovery phase.[164]

Despite the many challenges SAR teams faced, Mississippi officials were generally pleased with search-and-rescue efforts. They praised the hard work and professionalism of the FEMA and EMAC teams, and of Mississippi first responders.[165]

Gulfport Fire Chief Pat Sullivan was effusive in his praise:

> If everything went like the FEMA USAR teams, FEMA would get the academy award. … [The] FEMA USAR [urban search and rescue] teams, you can't say enough about what they did and how they did it and [the] equipment they brought in and the way that they were here to help you.[166]

Department of Defense and National Guard Air Search and Rescue

Accumulation of Aircraft

Despite the increased number of military helicopters in the Gulf Coast by the end of the first week, the number of helicopters capable of performing search and rescue – the most critical of all missions – was still inadequate for the number of victims in need of rescue, leading to delays in saving lives and reducing suffering.

On Saturday, August 27, two days before Hurricane Katrina made landfall, the Louisiana National Guard began to supplement its state inventory of helicopters, requesting four CH-47 and two UH-60 helicopters from the National Guard Bureau. The helicopters were sent from neighboring states through the EMAC system, beginning with two UH-60s from Oklahoma, which arrived on Monday.[167] By Monday, Army National Guard helicopters totaled 15 in Louisiana and 13 in Mississippi.[168] As soon as gale-force winds subsided below flight-restriction levels, on Monday afternoon, the helicopters commenced SAR missions, continuing through the evening.[169] Louisiana and Mississippi had 60 helicopters available for this initial response. The aircraft and crew flew around-the-clock due to the overwhelming number of emergency missions facing them. Additional National Guard aircraft did not begin to arrive in numbers until five days after landfall.[170] By September 8, however, 150 Army National Guard aircraft were operating in the Joint Operating Area.[171]

The active-duty (Title 10) military involvement in Air SAR began Tuesday evening, with the arrival of the amphibious-warfare helicopter carrier USS *Bataan* (see Chapter 26, Military Operations) carrying three MH-60s and two MH-53s, and continuing with a steady buildup of assets through September 8, when the total number of active-duty helicopters peaked at 143.[172] The *Bataan* had been positioned in the Gulf of Mexico at the conclusion of an exercise and, on the orders of the Second Fleet commander, had steamed northward toward New Orleans following the storm's passage. The first helicopters launched at 5 p.m. CT, once the *Bataan* was in range of the coast.[173] Upon landing in New Orleans Tuesday evening, the pilots reported to the Coast Guard Air Station commander, who as the designated On-Scene Commander, coordinated all air assets then engaged in search-and-rescue missions.[174]

Aircraft began arriving in greater numbers on Wednesday, August 31, when six Army helicopters – three UH-60s and three CH-47s – reported to the Louisiana National Guard at the Superdome. Six additional Army helicopters arrived in Baton Rouge from Fort Benning, GA, on Thursday, September 1, and performed medical evacuation missions in New Orleans.[175] Five Air Force helicopters from Patrick and Moody Air Force Bases deployed on their own authority to Mississippi on Wednesday, performing SAR missions in Hawkins, and Gulfport-Biloxi.[176] By Friday, 21 Air Force HH-60 helicopters were operating from Jackson, MS.[177]

By the latter half of the week, helicopters from all services had joined the efforts, including Marine utility and heavy lift aircraft from New River, NC; Air Force UH-60s from various locations; and Navy SH-60 helicopters from Jacksonville, FL. Many of the Jacksonville-based aircraft were delayed for several days, however, as the Navy planned to transport them aboard ships which would pick them up in Florida on Friday and arrive in the region on Sunday. Friday, however, they were ordered to fly over land to the region, and operate from one of the military bases ashore,[178] and were joined by 13 additional Navy aircraft flown in from Naval Air Station North Island in San Diego, CA.[179]

Though FEMA requested at least 45 helicopters from DOD between the day before landfall[180] – two on Sunday,[181] five just past midnight Monday,[182] and 38 on Tuesday[183] – DOD deployed far more, exceeding 45 by Wednesday. Still, according to Army personnel, there were no superfluous aircraft in the field.[184] Vice Admiral Vivien Crea, Commander of the Coast Guard Atlantic Area, described her visit on "Saturday talking to the rescue swimmers, who were talking to me with tears in their eyes and the frustration and the fear that they weren't going to get to everybody on time." As late as Saturday, she said, there were "absolutely not enough assets."[185]

And although the total number of military helicopters – active-duty and National Guard – reached 293 on September 8, the number does not accurately reflect the number of assets devoted to SAR. Many of the helicopters in the region were not equipped with the hoist necessary for SAR, and many were light utility helicopters, without the necessary lift capacity. Others, such as the MH-53s from USS *Bataan*, are so large that the down-wash from their rotors would push a victim underwater, and thus cannot be used for SAR. While these aircraft served essential roles in medical evacuation, personnel transport, and logistical missions, hoist-equipped aircraft were a highly valuable asset, and far less numerous. Furthermore, the available SAR-capable aircraft were, at times, tasked with support missions more appropriate to the utility aircraft, detracting from the more urgent life-saving mission.[186]

Lack of Search-and-Rescue Coordination

Although the National Search and Rescue Plan (1999) covers conduct and interagency coordination in small-scale SAR operations, no plan exists for large-scale SAR operations during a declared disaster.

Agencies and individuals performed heroically under exhausting, hazardous, and unprecedented circumstances. Yet the lack of an interagency plan to address search strategy, planning, and organization, communications, a centralized command structure, air-traffic control, and reception of victims led to hazardous flight conditions, inefficient employment of resources, and protracted waits by victims in need of rescue.

The hundreds of aircraft that arrived on the Gulf Coast faced an overwhelming task. From throughout the miles upon miles of destruction, the number of distress calls mounted by the day, and as SAR crews would fly to respond to calls, they would often pass over many more victims in need of rescue.[187] The aircraft and crews flew long and difficult hours to the point of exhaustion, and at the same time, flew in extraordinarily dangerous and confusing conditions in congested skies, rescuing thousands of victims from rooftops, attics, apartments, and overpasses. The participants included not just the DOD, National Guard, and Coast Guard, but numerous civilian elements such as the DOI, state and local law-enforcement agencies, and commercial entities. Yet in the chaos of Katrina's aftermath, no network of coordination linked these resources; even the DOD assets remained under separate and changing commands for many days. No common strategy to a thorough and expeditious search existed, and no unified air-traffic control system ensured safety of flight. At the root of these problems is the fact that the United States lacks an appropriate national plan for SAR in large-scale disasters.

The National Search and Rescue Plan is a multi-agency plan, agreed to by the DOD, DOI, and the Department of Transportation, among other federal agencies, providing guidance "for coordinating civil search-and-rescue (SAR) services to meet domestic needs and international commitments."[188] It outlines the roles and responsibilities of various agencies in establishing an integrated structure for SAR missions. Although the plan reflects a consensus rather than doctrine, its intent is to achieve "the effective use of all available facilities in all types of SAR missions."[189] Perplexingly, however, it expressly does not apply during declared emergencies and disasters:

> Civil SAR does *not* include operations such as … overall response to natural or man-made disasters or terrorist incidents; and typical disaster response operations, such as: locating and rescuing victims trapped in collapsed structures or other assistance provided under the scope of the Federal Response Plan.[190]

In a catastrophic disaster, then, there is currently *no* mechanism for planning SAR operations over extensive areas in both maritime and overland environments, or establishing a sufficiently broad command and control structure to encompass all agencies and assets involved.

Although ESF-9 under the NRP covers USAR – "locating, extricating, and providing onsite medical treatment to victims trapped in collapsed structures"[191] – it does not address such massive efforts as Katrina, involving the combination of air, surface, and ground efforts. According to Admiral Crea:

> I was surprised by the nebulous nature of the National SAR Plan once I started looking at it from the post-Katrina perspective, because as a Coast Guard aviator and operator, I had always … assumed that I could do any search and rescue, and certainly in the maritime environment, and I would do it in any inland environment if somebody asked me to do it. … I was surprised when I read that it's more of a not-to-interfere type of a basis. … I think the maritime piece is pretty clear, but I think the inland piece needs a little more structure, perhaps.[192]

The lack of an adequate plan for large-scale SAR led to two major shortcomings in DOD's air search-and-rescue missions: inadequate air-traffic control and poor coordination of deployed aircraft.

Rear Admiral Joseph Kilkenny, who reported to Joint Task Force Katrina as the commander of maritime forces, agreed. Considering that an easily imaginable attack with a weapon of mass destruction would require a similarly complex SAR response, standardization of SAR procedures must become a priority, he said.[193] As Second Fleet's "Lessons Learned" Report observed, "An ad hoc grid reference system was established due to lack of awareness of the common grid reference system already designed by the U.S. National Search and Rescue Supplement."[194] Some regions were missed while others remained unsearched for long periods of time,[195] and stranded citizens were still being rescued on September 8, 11 days after landfall.[196]

Safe on an Interstate island

Because the storm had incapacitated military and civilian air-traffic control radar systems throughout the Gulf Coast, much of the airspace was uncontrolled,[197] creating a hazardous and inefficient situation, with pilots relying simply on a "see-and-avoid" system, without the essential tracking or separation normally provided by an Air Traffic Controller.[198] "I am amazed at the volume of traffic that was in that [Area of Responsibility] and there was not a mid-air collision," Rear Admiral Dan Lloyd, a Coast Guard representative at U.S. Northern Command (NORTHCOM) said. [199]

Coordination was poor because no overarching command existed to assign search sectors, communicate with all assets, or direct aircraft to respond to distress calls. Second Fleet recommended, "Centralized Command and Control, with subordinate sector command and control of air, land, and water-borne assets, in place as soon as possible, will maximize safety and capabilities."[200] The different services each directed their own aircraft, with the structure changing continuously due to the rapid buildup of assets in the operating area throughout the first week.

From Tuesday, August 30, to Wednesday, August 31, DOD air assets operated with Coast Guard aircraft under the coordination of Coast Guard District Eight.[201] Beginning Wednesday, August 31, all DOD air assets were controlled by Admiral Kilkenny, based on USS *Bataan*.[202] Beginning Wednesday, August 31, Army SAR assets reported to the Louisiana National Guard, stationed at Eagle Base at the Superdome.[203] Beginning late in the week, Air Force and other shore-based SAR assets reported to the Joint Force Air Component Commander, who arrived at Camp Shelby, Mississippi, on Thursday, September 1.[204] On Saturday, September 3, Air Force Brigadier General Harold Moulton arrived from NORTHCOM to consolidate command and control of all Title 10 SAR units from a mobile headquarters unit at Naval Air Station Joint Reserve Base in Belle Chasse.[205] Meanwhile, the National Guard established their SAR coordination headquarters at Zephyr Field, the New Orleans Saints' practice field in Jefferson Parish.[206]

According to the Lessons Learned Report from USS *Bataan*, the lack of a unified communications system among these numerous authorities further complicated the SAR mission. While aircraft communicated with their respective commanders while on the ground, "once airborne … aircraft from all services and the local authorities took tasking via radio calls from one another," rather than from their operating bases.[207] This ad-hoc tasking system led to a lack of an overall strategy, in which victims were often deposited at intermediary locations, requiring further transport. Admiral Crea elaborated:

> We would take somebody for a Medevac to the airport where they were supposed to be triaged and further evacuated, and that place got saturated. So my helicopter would come in … with a medical patient and be told to hold for a half-hour until they could fit them in. Or in some cases, they were told to fly to Baton Rouge, which is like a 2-hour flight. So there we were wasting one helicopter taking one patient all the way to Baton Rouge to drop them off before he'd get back. So I think, clearly, with better organization and planning, that things could have been divided up into missions and sectors and so forth. That was just understandably due to the terrible communications and the chaos and trying to figure out who's in charge initially, and so forth.[208]

General Moulton, tasked with instituting a centralized SAR plan, described the "crisis mode" of operations he found upon his arrival:

> If you had a helicopter, you flew it in, you found somebody on the top of the roof, you grabbed them, and you took them to safety. And it appeared from our perspective that the procedures for doing that were not developed, were not organized. … And I think sort of by – by routine they started ending up dropping people off at certain places.[209]

With his headquarters at NORTHCOM, and with leaders and representatives of the forces already engaged in SAR, he developed a plan to integrate the numerous agencies and their hundreds of assets, operating across the air, ground, littoral, and urban environments. The team assembled on September 5, and the overall intent was to achieve a thorough search of the disaster area with all agencies operating on a common strategy and using a common communications network. As described in Chapter 26, large numbers of active-duty military ground troops had then arrived, and together with the thousands of National Guard troops, were able to conduct the thorough door-to-door searches to ensure that all areas had been covered.

Katrina exposed a significant gap in our nation's plans for SAR in a catastrophe. Thousands of lives were saved by the heroic efforts of the pilots, aircrew, and swimmers, together with the thousands of personnel operating in boats and on land. From the moment Katrina cleared the Gulf Coast, SAR was the primary mission, as decreed by leaders of the response, and as reflected by the actions of the Coast Guard and the National Guard as soon as the winds would permit safe flight. But it is necessary to harness these efforts and this heroism in a single cohesive plan that would provide all agencies a centralized coordination structure, a unified communications network, restorable air-traffic control system, and a common search-and-evacuation strategy in order to ensure that in the next large disaster, which may occur in an entirely different environment, this primary mission is a collaborative and efficient success.

1 Committee staff interview of Lt. Col. Keith LaCaze, Assistant Administrator, Law Enforcement Division, Louisiana Department of Wildlife and Fisheries, conducted on Nov. 30, 2005, transcript pp. 51-53.

2 Committee staff interview of Sec. Dwight Landreneau, Louisiana Department of Wildlife and Fisheries, conducted on Nov. 30, 2005, transcript pp. 44-45.

3 Testimony of Lt. Col. Keith LaCaze, Assistant Administrator, Law Enforcement Division, Louisiana Department of Wildlife and Fisheries, before the U.S. Senate, Committee on Homeland Security and Governmental Affairs, hearing on *Hurricane Katrina: Urban Search and Rescue in a Catastrophe*, Jan. 30, 2006 ("The number of people evacuated during that 36 hour period, in my estimate, would be approximately 1,500 people at the three sites we performed evacuations.").

4 Testimony of Jeff Smith, Acting Deputy Director, Louisiana Office of Homeland Security and Emergency Preparedness (LOHSEP), before the U.S. House, Select Bipartisan Committee to Investigate the Preparation for and Response to Hurricane Katrina, hearing on *Hurricane Katrina: Preparedness and Response by the State of Louisiana*, Dec. 14, 2005 (estimating 60,000 people were rescued); Lt. Col. LaCaze, Senate Committee hearing, Jan. 30, 2006 (estimating 60,000 people were rescued); Testimony of Madhu Beriwal, President and Chief Executive Officer, IEM, Inc., before the U.S. Senate, Committee on Homeland Security and Governmental Affairs, hearing on *Preparing for a Catastrophe: The Hurricane Pam Exercise*, Jan. 24, 2006 (estimating between 60,000 and 100,000 people were rescued.).

5 U.S. Department of Homeland Security, *National Response Plan*. Washington: Government Printing Office, Dec. 2004, Emergency Support Function Annex, p. ESF #9–1 [hereinafter *NRP*].

6 *See e.g.*: Committee staff interview of James Strickland, Team Member, Urban Search and Rescue, Federal Emergency Management Agency (FEMA), conducted on Jan. 25, 2006, transcript p. 42 (stating that the Southeast Louisiana Hurricane Plan listed the U.S. Coast Guard as the lead federal agency for search and rescue and then relied on that information).

7 Written Statement of Madhu Beriwal, President and Chief Executive Officer, IEM, Inc., for the U.S. Senate, Committee on Homeland Security and Governmental Affairs, hearing on *Preparing for a Catastrophe: The Hurricane Pam Exercise*, Jan. 24, 2006, p. 6. In all, the Coast Guard completed over 12,500 air rescues, 11,500 surface (boat) rescues and 9,400 hospital evacuations during Katrina. While its air missions garnered much media coverage, it conducted almost half its rescues and evacuations by boats. U.S. Coast Guard, Factcard, "Coast Guard Response to Hurricane Katrina." http://www.uscg.mil/hq/g-cp/comrel/factfile/index.htm. Accessed on Apr. 6, 2006.

8 Written Statement of Beriwal, Senate Committee hearing, Jan. 24, 2006, p. 6.

9 Testimony of William Lokey, Federal Coordinating Officer for Hurricane Katrina in Louisiana, FEMA, before the U.S. Senate, Committee on Homeland Security and Governmental Affairs, hearing on *Hurricane Katrina: Urban Search and Rescue in a Catastrophe*, Jan. 30, 2006 (stating that FEMA rescued 6,582 people); Strickland, interview, Jan. 25, 2006, pp. 86-87 (stating that FEMA rescued around 6,000 people). *See also:* U.S. Department of Homeland Security, Emergencies & Disasters, "Hurricane Katrina: What Is Government Doing." http://www.dhs.gov/interweb/assetlibrary/Katrina.htm. Accessed on Apr. 11, 2006.

10 Written Statement of William Lokey, Federal Coordinating Officer for Hurricane Katrina in Louisiana, FEMA, for the U.S. Senate, Committee on Homeland Security and Governmental Affairs, hearing on *Hurricane Katrina: Urban Search and Rescue in a Catastrophe*, Jan. 30, 2006, pp. 2-3.

11 LOHSEP, *Emergency Operations Plan*, Apr. 2005, p. ESF-9-2 [hereinafter *Louisiana Emergency Operations Plan*, Apr. 2005]; Committee staff interview of Maj. Jeff Mayne, Supervisor, Special Investigator Section, and Legislative Liaison, Louisiana Department of Wildlife and Fisheries, conducted on Nov. 30, 2005, transcript p. 10.

12 Lt. Col. LaCaze interview, Nov. 30, 2005, pp. 134-136; Lt. Col. LaCaze, Senate Committee hearing, Jan. 30, 2006.

13 Written Statement of Beriwal, Senate Committee hearing, Jan. 24, 2006, p. 6 .

14 Committee staff interview of Capt. Paul Hellmers, Engine 18, Second Platoon, Fifth District, New Orleans Fire Department, LA, conducted on Nov. 7, 2005, transcript p. 137 ("from our perspective, we were going to stay there for weeks or as long as it took, you know? We had no intention of leaving until we were told it's time to go."); Capt. Hellmers interview, Nov. 7, 2005, p. 220 ("And by Saturday evening it was painfully clear that this was not going to be like one [these] small storms. So, me, I wasn't the only one. There were other people who were pretty much sure it was going to flood. I moved as much of my belongings to my second floor as I could, tried to save what I could before I went to work. Obviously, had I not gone to work, well, I could have saved a lot more of my belongings, but me and most other firemen went to work."); Testimony of Capt. Timothy Bayard, Commander, Vice Crimes and Narcotics Section, New Orleans Police Department, LA, before the U.S. Senate, Committee on Homeland Security and Governmental Affairs, hearing on *Hurricane Katrina: Urban Search and Rescue in a Catastrophe*, Jan. 30, 2006.

15 New Orleans Office of Emergency Preparedness, *Comprehensive Emergency Management Plan*, May 2005, Appendix – Emergency Support Functions, p. 7 (assigning the primary responsibility for Emergency Support Function 9 – search and rescue – to the New Orleans Fire Department, and assigning the New Orleans Police Department as a supporting agency for search and rescue).

16 *Southeast Louisiana Catastrophic Hurricane Plan*, prepared by IEM, Inc. for LOHSEP and FEMA, Jan. 2005, p. 65 [hereinafter, *Southeast Louisiana Catastrophic Hurricane Plan*, Jan. 2005].

17 Committee staff interview of William Lokey, Federal Coordinating Officer for Hurricane Katrina in Louisiana, FEMA, conducted on Nov. 4, 2005, transcript p. 113.

18 Committee staff interview of Charles Parent, Superintendent, New Orleans Fire Department, LA, conducted on Nov. 10, 2005, transcript pp. 9-10, 33-38; Capt. Hellmers interview, Nov. 7, 2005, p. 18-19 (stating that the NOFD "does not own any boats other than a … deep-water boat"); Capt. Hellmers interview, Nov. 7, 2005, pp. 192-193 (preferring "one boat for every two rescuers").

19 Capt. Bayard, Senate Committee hearing, Jan. 30, 2006.

20 Parent interview, Nov. 10, 2005, pp. 39-40; Capt. Bayard, Senate Committee hearing, Jan. 30, 2006 (stating that NOPD and NOFD are working on "cross-training police officers and firemen in water and urban rescue procedures").

21 Mike Joseph, the New Orleans Fire Department Liaison to the New Orleans Office of Homeland Security and Public Safety who was responsible for that office's applications to the U.S. Department of Homeland Security's Office for Domestic Preparedness (ODP) grants, said that ODP denied his request for water rescue training that would have been held just days before Katrina hit. *Source:* Committee staff interview of Michael Joseph, Liaison to New Orleans Office of Homeland Security, New Orleans Fire Department, LA, conducted on Nov. 8, 2005, transcript pp. 18-20.

> I mean just Friday before the hurricane I was denied – I had written a proposal about two months before or a month and a half before. We wanted to have awareness and operational level training to water rescue. The Friday before the storm, request denied, does not meet the parameters of ODP. … Just the irony is just unbelievable, because this training was scheduled for that Saturday and Sunday before landfall of Katrina. … And that's just total coincidence because we had been trying to get this water training for over a year as part of our new USAR Team, Urban Search and Rescue, which we formed over a year ago. The committee was formed probably in April or May of '04, which I serve on that committee, and that's always something that we wanted to have as part of our USAR was some type of water capability. And we probably found the appropriate and affordable instructor, and you know, as I said, I wrote a little proposal and sent it out through the process to ODP, and it was denied.

The record does not indicate why DHS denied the application.

22 Committee staff interview of Capt. Joseph Fincher, Engine 18, Third Platoon, Fifth District, New Orleans Fire Department, LA, conducted on Nov. 11, 2005, transcript p. 97.

23 *Southeast Louisiana Catastrophic Hurricane Plan*, Jan. 2005, p. 65.

24 Written Statement of Beriwal, Senate Committee hearing, Jan. 24, 2006, p. 6. Additionally, the January 2005 plan that came out of the Hurricane Pam exercise predicted that hundreds of thousands would need to be evacuated after landfall of a catastrophic storm in New Orleans. *Southeast Louisiana Catastrophic Hurricane Plan*, Jan. 2005, p. 30.

25 Two days before landfall, many FEMA officials, including the FCO, received via e-mail, the plan that came out of the Hurricane Pam exercise, including the section on search and rescue. *Source:* Sharon Blades, e-mail to Michel Pawlowski, Linda Hammett Morgan, Pete Jensen, Robert Jevec, Cassandra Ward, Debra Clark, William Lokey, Michael Lowder, Rick Tinker, Pleasant Mann, Richard Brown, Jr., Richard Gray, Vanessa Quinn, Ronald Goins, Bill Zellars, Ted Lifty, Shauna M. Blanchard-Mbangah, Gerilee Bennett, Pat Bowman, Tony Robinson, Gary Jones, Joe Bearden, Wayne Fairley, Chris Riley, and Kara Satra, "Sela Plan," Aug. 27, 2005, 10:35 a.m. Provided to Committee; filed as Bates no. DHS-FEMA-0028-0000455. However, FEMA search and rescue Incident Support Team member James Strickland said he did not receive the plan, and that it would have been very helpful to have been briefed on the Southeast Louisiana Catastrophic Hurricane Plan and the Hurricane Pam exercise before Katrina made landfall. *Source:* Strickland interview, Jan. 25, 2006, pp. 70-71.

26 Written Statement of Rear Adm. Robert F. Duncan, U.S. Coast Guard, Commander, Eighth Coast Guard District, for the U.S. Senate, Committee on Homeland Security and Governmental Affairs, hearing on *Always Ready: The Coast Guard's Response to Hurricane Katrina*, Nov. 9, 2005, p. 1.

27 Testimony of Capt. Frank M. Paskewich, U.S. Coast Guard, Commander, U.S. Coast Guard Sector New Orleans, before the U.S. Senate, Committee on Homeland Security and Governmental Affairs, hearing on *Always Ready: The Coast Guard's Response to Hurricane Katrina*, Nov. 9, 2005 ("We simply would not dream of not responding. If there is a possibility to use a Coast Guard asset or Coast Guard people to help out when people need assistance, we are going to find a way to do it. We are not going to wonder whether we have the authority to do it, we are just going to take action.").

28 Testimony of Rear Adm. Robert F. Duncan, U.S. Coast Guard, Commander, Eighth Coast Guard District, before the U.S. Senate, Committee on Homeland Security and Governmental Affairs, hearing on *Always Ready: The Coast Guard's Response to Hurricane Katrina*, Nov. 9, 2005; Capt. Paskewich, Senate Committee hearing, Nov. 9, 2005 ("I am not sure I can recall in the last two years actually making it through a night without getting a phone call about responding to a particular incident. We are trained to do that, and I think that is our strength. We respond, and it is ingrained in our culture.").

29 Written Statement of Rear Adm. Duncan, Senate Committee hearing, Nov. 9, 2005, p. 2.

30 Committee staff interview of Rear Adm. Robert F. Duncan, U.S. Coast Guard, Commander, Eighth Coast Guard District, conducted on Oct. 18, 2005, transcript pp. 7-8.

31 Testimony of Capt. Bruce C. Jones, U.S. Coast Guard, Commanding Officer, Air Station New Orleans, LA, before the U.S. Senate, Committee on Homeland Security and Governmental Affairs, hearing on *Always Ready: The Coast Guard's Response to Hurricane Katrina*, Nov. 9, 2005.

32 Rear Adm. Duncan, Senate Committee hearing, Nov. 9, 2005.

33 Capt. Paskewich, Senate Committee hearing, Nov. 9, 2005.

34 "The Coast Guard success in completing all of our assigned missions after one of the most devastating storms in the Nation's history was a result of well-honed first responder skills, our ability to pre-plan and our multi-mission nature." Capt. Paskewich, Senate Committee hearing, Nov. 9, 2005. The Coast Guard also executed its other missions – containing or remediating hundreds of oil spills; clearing the waterways for navigation; delivering critical supplies by air – in addition to search and rescue in the aftermath of Katrina.

35 Rear Adm. Duncan interview, Oct. 18, 2005, pp. 9-10.

36 Capt. Paskewich, Senate Committee hearing, Nov. 9, 2005.

37 To minimize the direct impact on Coast Guard personnel, which would have adversely affected response efforts, the Coast Guard evacuated (non-essential) personnel and their family members from the Gulf Coast region. "We exercise before every hurricane season. … It is a good opportunity for us to bring people into the culture, to understand what the threats are in the Gulf Coast, how we would deal with that, make sure they have their own plans for their families, to talk about those things. … We did that this time. We actually left the area." Rear Adm. Duncan, Senate Committee hearing, Nov. 9, 2005.

38 Capt. Paskewich, Senate Committee hearing, Nov. 9, 2005.

39 Committee staff interview of Lt. Cmdr. Tom Cooper, U.S. Coast Guard, Helicopter Pilot and Engineering Officer, Air Station New Orleans, LA, conducted on Oct. 18, 2005, transcript pp. 11-12.

40 Capt. Jones, Senate Committee hearing, Nov. 9, 2005 ("Laurence Nettles was lowered from an H65 and threaded his way between tree limbs to reach a four-month old infant, her mother and grandmother stranded in deep flood waters in lower Plaquemines Parish at 2:50 that day.").

41 U.S. Coast Guard, Factcard, "Coast Guard Response to Hurricane Katrina." http://www.uscg.mil/hq/g-cp/comrel/factfile/index.htm. Accessed on Apr. 11, 2006.

42 Written Statement of Beriwal, Senate Committee hearing, Jan. 24, 2006, p. 6. However, a FEMA PowerPoint presentation dated Aug. 27, 2005, two days before Katrina made landfall in the Gulf, noted that there were likely to be "incredible search and rescue needs (60,000+)." FEMA, "Tropical Storm Katrina: 0900 August 27, 2005," PowerPoint presentation. Provided to Committee; filed as Bates no. DHS-FEMA-0055-0002142.

43 Rear Adm. Duncan, Senate Committee hearing, Nov. 9, 2005.

44 Lt. Col. LaCaze interview, Nov. 30, 2005, p. 46.

45 Testimony of Brig. Gen. Brod Veillon, Assistant Adjutant General, Louisiana Air National Guard, before the U.S. Senate Committee on Homeland Security and Governmental Affairs, hearing on *Hurricane Katrina: Urban Search and Rescue in a Catastrophe,* Jan. 30, 2006; Committee staff interview of Col. Thomas Beron, Commander, 61st Troop Command, Louisiana Army National Guard, conducted on Dec. 9, 2005, transcript pp. 104-105; Committee staff interview of Lt. Col. Jacques Thibodeaux, Joint Director of Military Support to Civilian Authorities, Louisiana National Guard, conducted on December 9, 2005, transcript pp. 151-153, 157-161.

46 "See, Urban Search and Rescue Teams, this was the first time they'd ever actively done water rescues. They carry water equipment to work around in a water environment, but FEMA policy had been that we don't do water rescue. We do structural collapse rescue assets. … Well, in hindsight, what I would have done, since Urban Search and Rescue Teams aren't water rescue teams, I would have worked more with the State through EMAC and whatnot." Lokey interview, Nov. 4, 2005, pp. 66-67.

47 Committee staff interview of Vice Adm. Vivean Crea, U.S. Coast Guard, Commander, Coast Guard Atlantic Area and Commander, Maritime Defense Zone Atlantic, conducted on Jan. 3, 2006, transcript p. 76 ("Q: Do you think that's a change that needs to be made to the National SAR Plan, or does there need to be something in the National Response Plan which addresses – A: It would be nice to think that that was an all-hazards, all-encompassing plan, at least a reference to a relevant document that would go into more depth.").

48 New Orleans Fire Department, *2005 Hurricane Guidelines,* 2005, p. 2–4; Committee staff interview of Capt. Fincher, Engine 18, Third Platoon, Fifth District, New Orleans Fire Department, LA, and Capt. Hellmers, Engine 18, Second Platoon, Fifth District, New Orleans Fire Department, LA, interview, conducted on Nov. 7, 2005, transcript pp. 171-173.

49 The National Guard's decision to keep its assets at Jackson Barracks is particularly puzzling given that it could have stationed at least some of the assets at New Orleans police stations throughout the city instead. According to New Orleans Police Department (NOPD) Superintendent Warren Riley (then Deputy Chief) the NOPD had asked the Louisiana National Guard to station some of its high-water vehicles (that can drive through flooded areas) and boats at eight police stations pre-landfall. However, the Guard told him that they would supply vehicles to only three or four NOPD stations, but would not be able to supply them with boats at that time. *Source:* Committee staff interview of Warren Riley, Superintendent of Police, New Orleans Police Department, LA, conducted on Jan. 12, 2006, transcript pp. 121-122. But LANG Brig. Gen. Veillon was not aware of the NOPD request. *Source:* Brig. Gen. Veillon, Senate Committee hearing, Jan. 30, 2006.

50 The officer in command of the Louisiana National Guard forces in New Orleans before and after landfall, General Gary Jones said that deciding whether to pre-position equipment at Jackson Barracks in the future would be a "tough call." Committee staff interview of Brig. Gen. Gary Jones, Assistant Joint Forces Commander, Louisiana Army National Guard, conducted on Dec. 7, 2005, transcript pp. 79-80 ("We pre-position as much of the stuff as we can. For example, the aviation support; we typically move out, get it right on the edge. The engineer teams, we do that, so forth. But if you're going to be missioned at Jackson Barracks – which, obviously, that's some of the most vulnerable part of the area – you have to take some risk. And, you know – I guess the question is, it kind of becomes a damned if you do, damned if you don't. If

we had not positioned some of the trucks and stuff there that ultimately got lost, and the water had not gotten up as high as it was, then we would have faced criticism for the slowness of response for doing that. Historically we've always pre-positioned things there. This storm was of a magnitude that far surpassed anything that we previously had to deal with."); Col. Beron interview, Dec. 1, 2005, pp. 29-30 ("[I]f the industrial canal had broken on the west side instead of the east side, Jackson Barracks would have been high and dry and those vehicles would have been fine. As to places to move to higher ground, overpasses, bridges, they have inherent problems with vulnerability to wind and other things. So you maybe take them out of the water risk and put them in another risk. I'll tell you that nowhere really comes to mind. You think of an elevated parking garage maybe would be good. You can't exactly drive an 18-wheeler into something like that. I'll tell you that I've thought and nothing comes immediately to mind that would lead me to believe that's a better place because it offers this. Everything that I've thought of so far has pros and cons, frankly."); Committee staff interview of Col. Glenn Curtis, Chief of Staff, Louisiana Army National Guard and Col. Jacques Thibodeaux, Joint Director of Military Support to Civilian Authorities, Louisiana National Guard, conducted on Dec. 6, 2005, transcript pp. 46-57.

51 Lokey, Senate Committee hearing, Jan. 30, 2006 (stating that in retrospect, he would have activated more search and rescue teams before landfall).

52 Lokey, Senate Committee hearing, Jan. 30, 2006; Strickland interview, Jan. 25, 2006, pp. 31-32.

53 Committee staff interview of William Lokey, Federal Coordinating Officer for Hurricane Katrina in Louisiana, FEMA, conducted on Jan. 20, 2006, transcript p. 184. Moreover, Lokey stated that he made a conscious decision to station the USAR teams in Shreveport rather than Baton Rouge. At the time, he explained, Baton Rouge was expected to be in the path of the storm and he wanted the USAR teams out of harm's way. *Source:* Lokey interview, Jan. 20, 2006, pp. 88-90. According to Lokey, FEMA is now considering a five-year plan that would revise its practices and budget to ensure that its search–and–rescue teams arrive within 12 hours after landfall. *Source:* Lokey interview, Nov. 4, 2005, p. 153.

54 Lokey, Senate Committee hearing, Jan. 30, 2006.

55 Lokey interview, Nov. 4, 2005, pp. 81-82.

56 Lokey interview, Nov. 4, 2005, p. 82.

57 Strickland interview, Jan. 25, 2006, pp. 33-34 ("I would have preferred being slightly closer.").

58 Strickland interview, Jan. 25, 2006, pp. 35-37, 42-48.

59 Strickland interview, Jan. 25, 2006, pp. 82-83.

60 Although it is generally not advisable for even first responders to begin search–and–rescue missions when the winds are above 40 mph, some of the NOFD officers literally threw caution to the wind. Fincher interview, Nov. 7, 2005, p. 93 ("Personally, I guess I didn't have good communications with me because I wasn't aware and I really didn't give a damn about what anybody else wanted. I knew there were people dying. I was pretty sure I could get out safely and get the boat back so we could get our rescue operations underway.").

61 Lokey, Senate Committee hearing, Jan 30, 2006; Strickland interview, Jan. 25, 2006, p. 15 ("I don't deem we were in the water rescue business.").

62 Committee staff interview of Eric Tolbert, former Director, Response Division, FEMA, conducted on Dec. 1, 2005, transcript, p. 40 (stating that FEMA lacks any water rescue capability); Strickland interview, Jan. 25, 2006, p. 21 ("We don't own boats.").

63 Strickland interview, Jan. 25, 2006, pp. 15, 83, 21-22 (stating that the FEMA search–and–rescue teams "were at the mercy of the people who showed up with the boats.").

64 The teams are trained and equipped to rescue people from collapsed structures, as after an earthquake. The team members are not trained or equipped for a flooded environment. Lokey interview, Nov. 4, 2005, pp. 66, 70.

65 Strickland interview, Jan. 25, 2006, pp. 29-30; Lokey, Senate Committee hearing, Jan 30, 2006.

66 Beriwal, Senate Committee hearing, Jan. 24, 2006 ("As you might know, nine of ten deaths that occur in a hurricane are due to storm surge and due to drowning from rain and storm surge. So we wanted to create ten to 20 feet of water in the City of New Orleans, which would constitute a catastrophic scenario for Southeast Louisiana.").

67 Lokey interview, Nov. 4, 2005, p. 79.

68 Strickland interview, Jan. 25, 2006, p. 17 ("FEMA Urban Search and Rescue does not need to get into the water rescue business….But in any event, yeah, there is probably a little bit higher level of training that the USAR system needs to have in order to safely operate in a water environment."); Strickland interview, Jan. 25, 2006, p. 18 (stating that the mission to do water rescue is that of the "Coast Guard and the federal, local and state."); Lokey, Senate Committee hearing, Jan. 30, 2006.

69 Strickland interview, Jan. 25, 2006, p. 19 (explaining that FEMA lacks boats and does not have the funding to support water rescue); Strickland interview, Jan. 25, 2006, p. 27 ("But that's not to say that if they plan this out, and they fund it correctly, and they hit every step, and they connected all their dots, maybe we could get into the water rescue business."); Lokey, Senate Committee hearing, Jan. 30, 2006.

70 Strickland interview, Jan. 25, 2006, pp. 12-13 ("It's kind of irritating to me, but they don't [provide additional training for IST teams]. They haven't in five years."); Strickland interview, Jan. 25, 2006, p. 14 (stating that with additional training, the IST teams "would have had a little bit smoother response … when you only see people [when] … we go out on a disaster … it's kind of hard; that's not the optimum time to do training, when you're up to your elbows in some kind of

an incident."); Strickland interview, Jan. 25, 2006, p. 20 (explaining that "when you show up for something like Katrina … there's no time to be trying to get our act together then."); Strickland interview, Jan. 25, 2006, p. 22 ("When you're in and around polluted, contaminated water like that, there's a health and safety issue that we would have to prepare for. There's that higher level of training that they need to have.").

71 Capt. Bayard, Senate Committee hearing, Jan. 30, 2006; Lt. Col. LaCaze, Senate Committee hearing, Jan. 30, 2006.

72 Capt. Fincher and Capt. Hellmers interview, Nov. 7, 2005, pp. 105-110, 113, 115-116 (stating that the "Fire Alarm," the NOFD main communications center, flooded and went down around 6:20p or 7:20p on Monday, August 29, 2005, forcing prompting NOFD to follow its contingency plan and use the National Mutual Aid Channel); New Orleans Fire Department, *2005 Hurricane Guidelines*, 2005, pp. 3–2 through 3–7.

73 Capt. Hellmers interview, Nov. 7, 2005, pp. 111-112 (stating "that happened many times with not just me, but other people doing the same thing, relaying messages between people when it was clear they couldn't hear each other.").

74 Lt. Col. LaCaze interview, Nov. 30, 2005, pp. 62-63.

75 Sec. Landreneau interview, Nov. 30, 2005, p. 16.

76 Committee staff interview of Lt. Col. Joseph Booth, Deputy Superintendent, Crisis Response and Special Operations, Louisiana State Police, conducted on Dec. 9, 2005, transcript pp. 47-49. The record does not reveal why the proposal was not accepted.

77 Sec. Landreneau, Louisiana Department of Wildlife and Fisheries, explained that he would have difficulty communicating from Baton Rouge at the state's Emergency Operations Center to his officers operating in New Orleans, such as Lt. Col. Keith LaCaze. Sec. Landreneau interview, Nov. 30, 2005, p. 1. *See also:* Lt. Col. LaCaze interview, Nov. 30, 2005, pp. 15-17 ("If we were in Baton Rouge and Keith was on Clearview Avenue in Metairie, [Department of Wildlife & Fisheries Major] Jeff [Mayne] would get a call and sometimes when we were lucky we could communicate from Baton Rouge to New Orleans, but then the next link is to be able to communicate from our operations center to the boats, that was virtually impossible and some of it because [we were] overwhelmed by traffic, you're in between big buildings. So we tried regular cell phones, we tried satellite phones, we ended up going to the local Academy Sports stores and we bought the little hand-held walkie-talkies. At least people in the boats could talk but it still didn't assist us in getting communications from New Orleans to Baton Rouge and back. … Is your communications with other agencies good or bad, and we would say we can't communicate with them. Well, it wasn't that we had a misunderstanding between the agencies, we just couldn't talk to them."); Brig. Gen. Veillon, Senate Committee hearing, Jan. 30, 2006; Strickland interview, Jan. 25, 2006, pp. 123-124.

78 Capt. Jones, Senate Committee hearing, Nov. 9, 2005; Lt. Cmdr. Cooper interview, Oct. 18, 2005, pp. 19-20; Committee staff interview of Lt. Cmdr. Mark Vislay, U.S. Coast Guard, HH-60J Instructor Pilot, Training Division, Aviation Training Center Mobile, AL, conducted on Oct. 26, 2005, transcript pp. 18-19.

79 Lt. Cmdr. Vislay interview, Oct. 26, 2005, p. 17.

80 Lt. Cmdr. Cooper interview, Oct. 18, 2005, pp. 50-52.

81 Strickland interview, Jan. 25, 2006, p. 124; Lt. Col. LaCaze interview, Nov. 30, 2005, p. 189.

82 Sec. Landreneau interview, Nov. 30, 2005, pp. 189-190.

83 Lt. Col. LaCaze interview, Nov. 30, 2005, p. 49 ("As the water began to rise too it would have been extremely difficult for us to identify streets and addresses, so once the address on the side of the house or that little mark is under water, it's kind of hard to go to a certain physical address. The same thing with street signs. Already some of the guys were not familiar with the city of New Orleans and then I guess even an added difficulty with the street signs being covered by water, so it was difficult.").

84 Committee staff interview of Brig. Gen. Brod Veillon, Assistant Adjutant General, Louisiana Air National Guard, conducted on Nov. 29, 2005, transcript pp. 101-103.

85 Committee staff interview of Capt. Timothy Bayard, Commander, Vice Crimes and Narcotics Section, New Orleans Police Department, LA, conducted on Nov. 21, 2005, transcript p. 165.

86 Strickland interview, Jan. 25, 2006, p. 95 ("We couldn't buy a ride on a DoD helicopter.").

87 According to Sheriff Harris Lee for Jefferson Parish, it is only by chance that he learned that thousands of people were sitting on I-10 in need of food and water. As a result, the people lacked food and water for as long as a full day. Committee staff interview of Harry Lee, Sheriff, Jefferson Parish, LA, conducted on Jan. 9, 2006, transcript pp. 34-37.

88 Capt. Bayard, Senate Committee hearing, Jan. 30, 2006. *See also:* New Orleans Police Department, Initial (30-day) After Action Report, Report of Captain Timothy Bayard, Oct. 16, 2005, p. 1. Provided to Committee ("The Office of Emergency Preparedness needs to be revamped. If their role is to have us prepared to handle a disaster such as this they FAILED. [emphasis in original] They lacked a plan, did not provide the necessary equipment, provided no direction or leadership, did not coordinate or attempt to have commanders of field operations coordinate with any state, or federal agency etc.").

89 Capt. Bayard interview, Nov. 21, 2005, p. 33; Capt. Bayard, Senate Committee hearing, Jan. 30, 2006.

90 Capt. Bayard interview, Nov. 21, 2005, pp. 83-84.

91 Strickland interview, Jan. 25, 2006, p. 56.

92 Strickland interview, Jan. 25, 2006, pp. 42-48.

93 Strickland interview, Jan. 25, 2006, p. 60.

94 Maj. Sandy Dares, Enforcement Division, Louisiana Department of Wildlife and Fisheries, Hurricane Katrina Activity Report (discussing Wildlife and Fisheries command post at Causeway and I-10 on Aug. 30, 2005); Brig. Gen. Veillon interview, Nov. 29, 2005, pp. 30-31.

95 Strickland interview, Jan. 25, 2006, pp. 54-55; *NRP*, p. 39.

96 For example, one FEMA search and rescue team member testified that W&F failed to keep a representative at Zephyr Field, where FEMA and the Coast Guard had set up "on the fly" a local unified command for search and rescue on Wednesday, August 31, 2005. Strickland interview, Jan. 25, 2006, p. 58; Capt. Fincher interview, Nov. 7, 2005, p. 226 ("We kind of stumbled into FEMA. It wasn't planned.").

97 Strickland interview, Jan. 25, 2006, p. 56 ("the first time we got all of the unified commanders … was 48 hours after the hurricane made landfall, and that's not good.").

98 Committee staff interview of Lt. Valerie Boyd, U.S. Coast Guard, Command Center Watch Officer, Eighth District Office Headquarters, New Orleans, LA, conducted on Nov. 7, 2005, transcript p. 20.

99 Lt. Boyd interview, Nov. 7, 2005, pp. 15-16.

100 Lt. Boyd interview, Nov. 7, 2005, p. 23.

101 Brig. Gen. Veillon interview, Nov. 29, 2005, p. 188.

102 Brig. Gen. Veillon interview, Nov. 29, 2005, p. 153.

103 Parent interview, Nov. 10, 2005, p. 9. With such a significant need for water search and rescue, it is inexcusable that no level of government provided New Orleans' first responders with more boats. Fincher interview, Nov. 7, 2005, pp. 120-121 (requesting assistance for search and rescue at 3 p.m., on Monday, August 29, 2005); Capt. Hellmers interview, Nov. 7, 2005, p. 121 ("I assume when I tell people that the water is up to the roofs of houses that the people above me are going to do everything within their power to send help. I mean, it's pretty clear there's [sic] people drowning.").

104 Capt. Hellmers interview, Nov. 7, 2005, pp. 205-207 ("If you call and say your house is on fire, you don't have to do any more. The fire department is coming. You don't have to sign a piece of paper to let them in you door, you know, they come.").

105 Louisiana Department of Wildlife and Fisheries, E-Resource Request, Res-113736-911082805, Aug. 29, 2005, 11:39 p.m. CT. Provided to Committee (including a handwritten remark above the request for rubber rafts that reads "Request Denied.").

106 Lokey, Senate Committee hearing, Jan. 30, 2006.

107 Lt. Col. LaCaze, Senate Committee hearing, Jan. 30, 2006.

108 Jeffrey Hall, e-mail to Marc Short, Sept. 2, 2005, 10:04 p.m. Provided to Committee; filed as Bates no. DHS-FRNT-0010-0000294. *See also*: Committee staff interview of Matt Mayer, former Chief of Staff and Senior Policy Advisor, Office of Domestic Preparedness Security, U.S. Department of Homeland Security, conducted on Jan. 26, 2006, transcript pp. 24-25. It appears that FEMA officials were unaware of, or forgot about, the pods that DHS held. Currently, DHS is reevaluating whether this program should come under FEMA control. Mayer interview, Jan. 26, 2006, pp. 26-27.

109 Mayer interview, Jan. 26, 2006, pp. 26-27; Jeffrey Hall, e-mail to Marc Short, Sept. 2, 2005, 10:04 p.m. Provided to Committee; filed as Bates no. DHS-FRNT-0010-0000294.

110 Capt. Fincher interview, Nov. 7, 2005, pp. 193-196.

111 Mayer interview, Jan. 26, 2006, p. 37.

112 Mayer interview, Jan. 26, 2006, pp. 37, 143 ("[B]ottom line is, hindsight, we would have deployed the PODS much sooner than when we did. We didn't. We made a mistake.").

113 Fincher interview, Nov. 7, 2005, pp. 193-196.

114 Committee staff interview of Laurence Broun, Emergency Coordinator, U.S. Department of the Interior, conducted on Mar. 21, 2006, transcript pp. 9-12. Broun stated that although a DOI representative had conversations with some FEMA personnel about the law enforcement personnel, but ultimately, FEMA did not follow through on the DOI offer.

115 Lokey, Senate Committee hearing, Jan. 30, 2006; Lokey interview, Jan. 20, 2006, pp. 50-51.

116 U.S. Department of the Interior, Office of the Assistant Secretary, Police, Management and Budget, Response to the U.S. Senate, Committee on Homeland Security and Governmental Affairs, Document and Information Request Dated Oct. 7, 2005, Nov. 7, 2005, p. 20.

117 Broun interview, Mar. 21, 2006, pp. 15-19.

118 Lokey, Senate Committee hearing, Jan. 30, 2006; Lokey interview, Jan. 20, 2006, pp. 50-51.

119 *Louisiana Emergency Operations Plan*, Apr. l, 2005, pp. 14-15 ("The State of Louisiana is a signatory to the Emergency Management Assistance Compact (EMAC), as stated in the Louisiana Homeland Security and Emergency Assistance and Disaster Act of 1993 as amended. If an emergency becomes too widespread or serious for parish and state resources, the Director LOHSEP will process a request for assistance through EMAC.").

120 Lokey interview, Nov. 4, 2005, p. 73. *See also:* Lokey interview, Jan. 20, 2006, pp. 152-153.

121 Lokey interview, Nov. 4, 2005, p. 74.

122 Lokey interview, Jan. 20, 2006, pp. 152-153. On Saturday, Aug. 27, 2005, Gov. Blanco also facilitated the request by calling Gov. Schwarzenegger. California officially became a signatory to EMAC on September 13, 2005. California, Office of the Governor, "Governor Schwarzenegger Signs Emergency Management Assistance Compact Legislation," press release, Sept. 13, 2005.

123 Brig. Gen. Veillon interview, Nov. 29, 2005, p. 152; Brig. Gen. Veillon, Senate Committee hearing, Jan. 30, 2006.

124 Testimony of Maj. Gen. Bennett C. Landreneau, Adjutant General, Louisiana, before the U.S. House, Select Bipartisan Committee to Investigate the Preparation for and Response to Hurricane Katrina, hearing on *Hurricane Katrina: Preparedness and Response by the Department of Defense, the Coast Guard, and the National Guard of Louisiana, Mississippi, and Alabama*, Oct. 7, 2005.

125 Lt. Col. LaCaze, Senate Committee hearing, Jan. 30, 2006 ("requests were bogged down in the process, in the pipe, so to speak"); Lokey, Senate Committee hearing, Jan. 30, 2006 (recalling "delays of people not wanting to respon[d] because they didn't have the right signature to assure they were covered under the EMAC compact").

126 Sec. Landreneau interview, Nov. 30, 2005, pp. 116-117 ("South Carolina couldn't leave the state until they could call a FEMA number. And we talked about this as a way to improve this, if FEMA or whoever is in charge of this would give us a list of approved department agencies. … It would have been great because South Carolina took us basically a day from the time they got word that they … were packed up and ready to come, they were stationed up in a convoy ready to go but they couldn't move. And I don't blame them, they couldn't leave because the proper paperwork wasn't done.").

127 Lokey interview, Nov. 4, 2005, p. 8.

128 Lokey interview, Jan. 20, 2006, p. 152.

129 Strickland interview, Jan. 25, 2006, pp. 117-118.

130 Sec. Landreneau interview, Nov. 30, 2005, pp. 169-174.

131 Capt. Fincher interview, Nov. 7, 2005, pp. 153-154; Sec. Landreneau interview, Nov. 30, 2005, pp. 189-190.

132 Sec. Landreneau interview, Nov. 30, 2005, p. 70; Strickland interview, Jan. 25, 2006, pp. 169-170.

133 Lt. Col. LaCaze interview, Nov. 30, 2005, pp. 48-49, 66-69.

134 Strickland interview, Jan. 25, 2006, p. 66 (recalling that "Thursday … is when it seemed like the whole thing, New Orleans, was imploding"); Strickland interview, Jan. 25, 2006, pp. 91-93 (stating that "on the 1st, … there were all these reports … that there was shooting, … that they were rioting in the streets and all this.").

135 FEMA-NRCC, e-mail to Clair Blong and others, "HSOC SPOT REP #53," Sept. 1, 2005, 8:31 p.m. Provided to Committee; filed as Bates no. DHS-FEMA-0051-0000193 ("Status of US&R Task Force in LA. … All assets have ceased operations until National Guard can assist TF's with security."); Strickland interview, Jan. 25, 2005, pp. 66, 91; Lokey interview, Jan. 20, 2005, pp. 148-149.

136 Committee staff interview of Capt. Patrick Lampard, Fifth District, New Orleans Fire Department, LA, conducted on Jan. 11, 2006, transcript pp. 76-78.

137 Capt. Hellmers interview, Nov. 7, 2005, p. 170 (stating that some NOFD officers "said no, we're not stopping" and turned their radios off).

138 Capt. Hellmers interview, Nov. 7, 2005, pp. 162-163 ("And our area wasn't really that dangerous.…for one thing, we were armed, but there was the potential of criminals getting into our area, but I didn't see it as a big problem. We go into burning buildings for a living, and I'm not really that worried about running into a criminal. Not that I don't value my own life, I do, … I'm not particularly afraid of some possible danger.").

139 Strickland interview, Jan. 25, 2006, pp. 91-92.

140 Strickland interview, Jan. 25, 2006, pp. 94-95.

141 Lokey interview, Jan. 20, 2006, pp. 209-211.

142 On September 10, 2005, the Department of Justice ruled: "Federal agents may pursue house-to-house forced entry rescue attempts where deemed appropriate." The ruling was interpreted as allowing federal agents to force entry into a house to rescue someone trapped or injured in a building, but not to take part in a forced evacuation. Linda Bizzarro, e-mail to James A. McAtamney and others, "Legal Opinion on entry into homes," Sept. 13, 2005, 3:26 p.m. Provided to Committee; filed as Bates no. DAG 000000107.

143 Mississippi Emergency Management Agency (MEMA), *Mississippi Emergency Operations Plan, Volume II: Mississippi Comprehensive Emergency Management Plan (CEMP)*, May 14, 1999, section ESF-9, p. 9-1 [hereinafter *Mississippi CEMP*, May 14, 1999].

144 Committee staff interview of Jim Brinson, Response Coordinator, Office of Homeland Security, Mississippi Department of Public Safety, conducted on Dec. 14, 2005, transcript p. 12.

145 *Mississippi CEMP* May, 14, 1999, section ESF-9, pp. 2-3.

146 *Mississippi CEMP*, May, 14, 1999, section ESF-9, pp. 9-5, 9-8 through 9-9.

147 MEMA, Hurricane Situation Report #11, Hurricane Katrina. Aug. 29, 2005, 9 a.m., p. 8. Provided to Committee; filed at Bates no. MEMA-0010905.

148 FEMA, Urban Search and Rescue National Response System, Incident Support Team (White) Transition Team, Executive Summary, Sept. 11, 2005. Provided to Committee [hereinafter USAR, Executive Summary].

149 Brinson interview, Dec. 14, 2005, p. 18. After the storm, additional FEMA teams were staged in Texas and sent to Mississippi. USAR, Executive Summary.

150 Brinson interview, Dec. 14, 2005, pp. 24-26.

151 Brinson interview, Dec. 14, 2005, pp. 23-24.

152 For example, Paul Bennett of the Gulfport Police Department recounted what search-and-rescue responders encountered in Harrison County immediately after the storm:

> And in some of the areas that we could not get to – and I very distinctly remember one of the first units that had gone out, he had gotten as close as he could to a particular neighborhood and he couldn't get in because you couldn't find the road. And residents were actually swimming out to the vehicle trying to get – because they saw the vehicle. They saw the flashing blue lights. But they were swimming out to the vehicle trying to get to it. And that's when it really started – we started getting our feedback from the field, Hey, this is very, very bad.

Committee staff interview of Paul Bennett, Deputy Chief of Police, Gulfport Police Department, MS, conducted on Dec. 7, 2005, pp. 33-34.

153 Brinson interview, Dec. 14, 2005, pp. 63-64.

154 Committee staff interview of Pat Sullivan, Fire Chief, Gulfport Fire Department, MS, conducted on Dec. 7, 2005, pp. 127-144.

155 Brinson interview, Dec. 14, 2005, pp. 16-17.

156 Brinson interview, Dec. 14, 2005, pp. 39-69.

157 See e.g., Committee staff interview of Michael Beeman, Director, National Preparedness Division, Region II, FEMA, conducted on Jan. 20, 2006, transcript p. 161-162.

158 Brinson interview, Dec. 14, 2005, p. 40.

159 Brinson interview, Dec. 14, 2005, p. 50.

160 USAR, Executive Summary. The FEMA teams deployed were a mix of larger, approximately 80 person "Type I" teams and smaller "Type III" teams consisting of 20-30 people.

161 Written statement of Gov. Haley Barbour, Mississippi, for the U.S. Senate, Committee on Homeland Security and Governmental Affairs, hearing on Hurricane Katrina: The Role of Governors in Managing Catastrophe, Feb. 2, 2006, p. 3.

162 Committee staff interview of Lt. Col. Lee Smithson, Director of Military Support, Mississippi Army National Guard, conducted on Jan. 25, 2006, transcript pp. 30-31.

163 Lt. Col. Smithson interview, Jan. 25, 2006, pp. 28, 42.

164 Brinson interview, Dec. 14, 2005, p. 36. A FEMA report on search and rescue in Mississippi indicates that field operations for FEMA teams ended a couple of days later, on September 10, 2005. USAR, Executive Summary.

165 Brinson interview, Dec. 14, 2005, p. 62. Mississippi Governor Haley Barbour, among others, has noted the efforts of Coast Guard personnel in particular in conducting rescue efforts. Written statement of Gov. Barbour, Senate Committee hearing, Feb. 2, 2006, p. 3.

166 Sullivan interview, Dec. 7, 2005, pp. 104-105.

167 National Guard Bureau, National Guard After Action Review: Hurricane Response, "National Guard Timeline," Dec. 21, 2005, pp. 10-12. Provided to Committee.

168 National Guard Bureau, "Current Intelligence," briefing slide, Aug. 29, 2005, 2 a.m. Provided to Committee.

169 Written Statement of Maj. Gen. Bennett C. Landreneau, Adjutant General, Louisiana, for the U.S. Senate, Committee on Homeland Security and Governmental Affairs, hearing on Hurricane: Katrina: The Defense Department's Role in the Response, Feb. 9, 2006, p. 4.

170 National Guard Bureau, National Guard After Action Review: Hurricane Response, "Army National Guard." Dec. 21, 2005, p. 72.

171 Office of the Assistant Secretary of Defense for Homeland Defense, "Katrina Helicopter Flow into JOA." Provided to Committee.

172 Office of the Assistant Secretary of Defense for Homeland Defense, "Katrina Helicopter Flow into JOA." Provided to Committee.

173 Committee staff interview of Capt. Rick Snyder, U.S. Navy, Executive Officer, USS Bataan, conducted on Nov. 14, 2005 (untranscribed). The "Lessons Learned" inputs from USS Bataan state that although the three MH-60 aircraft were employed in SAR missions, the two heavy-lift MH-53 helicopters could not be used for Search and Rescue "due to their inability to provide direct support of hoisting survivors from rooftops or out of the water." USS Bataan, Combined

Bataan Lessons Learned Form, "Airborne Communications." Provided to Committee.

174 Committee staff interview of Capt. Bruce Jones, U.S. Coast Guard, Commanding Officer, Air Station New Orleans, LA conducted on Nov. 9, 2005 (untranscribed).

175 Committee staff interview of Col. Daniel Shanahan, U.S. Army, Commander, 1st Air Cavalry Brigade, 1st Cavalry Division, U.S. Department of Defense, conducted on Feb. 23, 2006 (untranscribed).

176 Insung Lee, e-mail to HSOC.SWO and others, "HSOC #4317-05 HC Katrina – DoD Update 311145 Aug 05m," Aug. 31, 2005, 11:50 a.m. Provided to Committee; filed as Bates no. WHK-12712.

177 JTF-Katrina, Commander's Assessment, Sept. 2, 2005. Provided to Committee.

178 Committee staff interview of Cmdr. Thomas Quinn, U.S. Navy, Director of Operations, Commander Naval Air Forces, Atlantic, conducted Nov. 15, 2005 (untranscribed).

179 U.S. Northern Command, "USNORTHCOM Hurricane Katrina Timeline," draft, p. 16; JTF-Katrina, Commander's Assessment, Sept. 3, 2005. Provided to Committee.

180 Office of the Assistant Secretary of Defense for Homeland Defense, "Hurricane Katrina Mission Assignments (MA's) Recap," Dec. 2, 2005. Provided to Committee.

181 FEMA, Mission Assignment, 3212EM-LA-DOD-01, Aug. 28, 2005. Provided to Committee.

182 FEMA, Mission Assignment, 1604DR-MS-DOD-01, Aug. 30, 2005, 12:16 a.m.; FEMA, Mission Assignment, 1604-DR-MS-DOD-02, Aug. 30, 2005, 12:43 a.m. Provided to Committee; filed as Bates no. DHS 0000803.

183 FEMA, Mission Assignment, 1604DR-MS-DOD-07, Aug. 30, 2005, 10:03 p.m. Provided to Committee; filed as Bates no. DHS 0000848.

184 Col. Shanahan interview, Feb. 3, 2006.

185 Vice Adm. Crea interview, Jan. 3, 2006, p. 52.

186 USS *Bataan*, Combined Bataan Lessons Learned Form, "Aircraft Support Effectiveness." Provided to Committee ("BATAAN's MH-60Ss were tasked with providing direct support for the transportation of Task Force Officials under-utilizing the capability of a SAR capable aircraft complete with rescue swimmers. … The New Orleans area contained many land based helicopter assets with no hoist capability that could have carried out this tasking thus freeing up BATAAN's hoist capable H-60s to provide rescue assistance when the need was at its greatest."). National Guard Bureau, *National Guard After Action Review: Hurricane Response,* pp. 67-68 (elaborates on the importance of the availability and readiness of hoist-equipped aircraft.).

187 USS *Bataan*, Combined Bataan Lessons Learned Form, "Coordination of Rescue Aircraft." Provided to Committee.

188 National Search and Rescue Committee, *United States National Search and Rescue Plan,* 1999, Nov. 2, 2000. http://www.uscg.mil/hq/g-o/g-opr/nsarc/nsp.htm. Accessed on Feb. 27, 2006 [hereinafter *United States National Search and Rescue Plan,* 1999].

189 *United States National Search and Rescue Plan,* 1999.

190 *United States National Search and Rescue Plan,* 1999 (emphasis added).

191 *NRP*, Urban Search and Rescue Annex, p. ESF #9–1.

192 Vice Adm. Crea interview, Jan. 3, 2006, pp. 75-76. "Theoretically, you'd want to have different sectors or search areas, but the magnitude of the people popping up, my guys would say they would fly in – they'd see one person on a roof, they'd fly in to get them, and the noise of the helicopter, all of a sudden other people would start poking their heads out, you know? So instead of having one person, now they had 50 people, or they'd, you know, break a hole through the roof, get that one guy out, and he'd say, 'I've got ten more people inside the house,' which, you know, would clearly exceed the capability of that – you know, particularly if it was one of our smaller helicopters. So then you'd have to draw in more." Vice Adm. Crea interview, Jan. 3, 2006, p. 57.

193 Committee staff interview of Rear Adm. Joseph Kilkenny, U.S. Navy, former Joint Force Maritime Component Commander, Joint Task Force Katrina, conducted on Nov. 30, 2005 (untranscribed).

194 U.S. Second Fleet, Fleet-14, *Katrina Lessons Learned*, "JTF Katrina Search and Rescue," p. 27. Provided to Committee.

195 U.S. Second Fleet, Fleet-05, *Katrina Lessons Learned*, "JTF Katrina Air Command and Control," p. 13. Provided to Committee. ("Inadequate Command and control allowed some search areas to be missed while others were searched multiple times.").

196 Col. Shanahan interview, Feb. 23, 2006.

197 National Guard Bureau, *National Guard After Action Review: Hurricane Response*, "Army National Guard," Dec. 21, 2005, p. 90 ("All FAA and Military air traffic control and air command and control systems were rendered inoperable as Katrina passed. … There was no known preplanning for the Command and Control of … diversified participants each having different radios, frequencies and some with little or no … rescue training.").

198 National Guard Bureau, *National Guard After Action Review: Hurricane Response*, "Army National Guard," Dec. 21, 2005, p. 73 ("There was no overall control, flight following, or separation of the many agency aircraft engaged around New Orleans, LA and Gulfport, MS creating potentially unsafe condition. A plan is required to facilitate the employment of military ATC assets in such cases.").

199 Committee staff interview of Rear Adm. Dan Lloyd, U.S. Coast Guard, former Chief, Interagency Coordination Group, U.S. Northern Command, conducted on Dec. 8, 2005, transcript pp. 116-117.

200 U.S. Second Fleet, Fleet-05, *Katrina Lessons Learned*, "JTF Katrina Air Command and Control," p. 13. Provided to Committee.

201 Vice Adm. Crea interview, Jan. 3, 2006, pp. 43-44.

202 Joint Task Force Katrina, Message to *USS Bataan*, "JTF Katrina FRAGO-2 to Hurricane Katrina EXORD," Aug. 31, 2005, 1634Z. Provided to Committee.

203 Col. Shanahan interview, Feb. 23, 2006.

204 Capt. Robert Reininger, e-mail to Maj. Gen. Richard Rowe, "Re: Bataan," Sept. 1, 2005, 10:54 a.m. Provided to Committee.

205 Committee staff interview of Brig. Gen. Harold Moulton, Director, Standing Joint Headquarters-North, U.S. Northern Command, conducted on Dec. 5, 2005, transcript pp. 25-26, 55-56.

206 Brig. Gen. Moulton, Dec. 5, 2005, p. 58.

207 USS *Bataan*, Combined Bataan Lessons Learned Form, "Airborne Communications." Provided to Committee.

208 Vice Adm. Crea, Jan. 3, 2006, pp. 54-55.

209 Brig. Gen. Moulton, Dec. 5, 2005, p. 56.

High and dry in Houma, LA
National Guard photo

Post-Landfall Evacuation

For several days after landfall, evacuation of New Orleans proceeded slowly, compounding the misery of residents stranded by the storm. The National Response Plan (NRP), the Louisiana Emergency Operations Plan, and the New Orleans Comprehensive Emergency Plan stipulate that, typically, emergency response is locally initiated and coordinated.

Federal, state, and local authorities knew long before the storm that at least 100,000 residents of New Orleans would lack the means to evacuate.[1] Nonetheless, the city failed to pre-stage buses and drivers outside the flood zone. Meanwhile, the state's lead agency for transportation during an evacuation ignored its responsibilities.

The plans mentioned above stipulate that local and state governments may call on federal support if their own resources become overwhelmed. For catastrophic events, the NRP, the federal government's blueprint for its preparation and response to national emergencies, adds that the federal government does not need to wait for requests from state or local government before offering assistance. Although details of this policy were still under development when Hurricane Katrina – an undisputedly catastrophic storm – struck, this should not have prevented federal officials from preparing before landfall to assist with post-landfall evacuation. Unfortunately, federal officials, including those working out of Louisiana's Emergency Operations Center in Baton Rouge, did little to prepare and were forced to scramble to provide assistance after Katrina struck.

As the Department of Homeland Security (DHS) and the Federal Emergency Management Agency (FEMA) stated in their own after-action report: "Hurricane Katrina has presented the need for a national focus on evacuation and sheltering."[2]

An Incomplete Pre-Landfall Evacuation Likely Compounded the Post-Landfall Evacuation

Some 10,000 to 15,000 New Orleans residents took shelter at the Superdome, the "refuge of last resort" for those without the means to evacuate,[3] suggesting many may have preferred to leave the city altogether as part of a pre-landfall evacuation had they been offered the means. Their staying behind placed their lives in jeopardy and increased the strain on responders.[4]

Before Landfall, the City Failed to Designate Buses and Drivers for a Post-Landfall Evacuation

Before landfall, the city failed to designate buses or drivers for post-landfall evacuations. Although the Regional Transit Authority (RTA), the local municipal bus agency in New Orleans, did stage a fleet of buses at the Poland Street Wharf,[5] a high-ground location inside the city that remained unflooded, no level of government attempted to move drivers to those buses until Thursday, three days after landfall,[6] even though the route to the wharf remained open throughout the crisis.

Before Landfall, the Louisiana Secretary of Transportation and Development Ignored His Department's Responsibility to Prepare for the Post-Landfall Evacuation

The Louisiana Department of Transportation and Development (LA DOTD) failed in its duty, under the state's emergency plan, to arrange transportation for post-landfall evacuation. As discussed in Chapter 16, in April 2005, the State of Louisiana transferred responsibility for transportation during an evacuation from the Louisiana Office of Homeland Security and Emergency Preparedness (LOHSEP) to the LA DOTD. Despite signing the agreement, LA DOTD Secretary Johnny Bradberry believed his organization was not suited to the task because it did not have an in-house stable of transportation and drivers like the state Department of Tourism or the Louisiana National Guard.[7] The record shows no evidence that he raised these concerns outside his department between April 2005 and landfall.[8] Before and after Katrina, Secretary Bradberry's agency provided no transportation for evacuation, except for five ferries to evacuate 6,000 people from St. Bernard and Plaquemines Parishes.[9]

Ultimately, thousands of buses were mobilized for evacuation through contracts with transportation providers, which LA DOTD – like any other state agency – could have arranged both before and after landfall. Secretary Bradberry conceded as much, admitting that his agency was best positioned in the state to contract with railroads and that it makes sense for the state's lead agency for transportation to be responsible for negotiating agreements with other transportation providers.[10] The Committee concludes that LA DOTD's failure to carry out its duties under the state's emergency plan delayed the efforts to locate in-state buses.

LOHSEP, which was responsible under the state's emergency plan for making sure Secretary Bradberry's agency carried out its duties, did not urge him to take steps to prepare before the storm for post-landfall evacuation.[11] But the Committee finds Secretary Bradberry primarily responsible for his department's inertia after landfall to coordinate transportation resources.

Inadequate Planning Hamstrung the Federal Government's Assistance With the Post-Landfall Evacuation

As discussed elsewhere in this report, federal officials knew that (1) a catastrophic hurricane could leave hundreds of thousands of New Orleans residents stranded, as 2004's Hurricane Pam catastrophic-storm exercise had predicted (see Chapter 8, Hurricane Pam), (2) that such a storm would incapacitate state and local resources, and (3) that the NRP authorized federal officials to offer help without requests from state and local governments (see Chapter 27, Failures in Implementation of the NRP). Therefore, failures by the federal government to prepare before landfall for post-landfall evacuation were not failures of law, but, at least in part, of leadership.[12] Federal officials at the highest levels failed to make full use of existing authority and resources that were available despite the incompleteness of planning for catastrophic storms.

At a Hurricane Pam transportation workshop in late July 2005, federal, state, and local officials had discussed New Orleans' need, before landfall, for at least 600 buses and 1,200 drivers for post-landfall evacuation.[13] A FEMA official suggested that, in fact, 5,000 buses a day would be necessary.[14] However, unified federal, state, and local planning for evacuation after a catastrophic New Orleans storm was "less than 10 percent done" by the day before landfall and a written draft of the plan was not ready until September 9, 2005.[15]

One U.S. Department of Transportation (DOT) official testified that "the people that were involved in that work group must have sensed the same thing that I did, that there was a large reliance [by state and local participants] on the federal team coming in and fix[ing] everything."[16] Likewise, the head of Louisiana's National Guard, who was briefed about the workshop, testified that FEMA officials there agreed that they "would have the responsibility for the evacuation" of New Orleans.[17] A FEMA official testified that, while at the work-

Louisiana National Guard official in charge, that they were trying to obtain buses.[50] But they had trouble reaching their superiors in Baton Rouge,[51] which may have slowed the procurement. As DHS and FEMA noted in their after-action report: "During Hurricane Katrina, catastrophic communications failures caused confusion during the post-landfall evacuation operation."[52]

FEMA's delays are regrettable, because buses arrived quickly after FEMA finally tasked the DOT with the mission. DOT officials immediately began contracting for buses,[53] the first of which arrived at a staging area at Mile Marker 209 (La Place, Louisiana) around 6:30 a.m. on Wednesday.[54] By midnight Thursday, less than 24 hours after DOT received the tasking order, approximately 200 buses were participating in evacuations.[55]

Evacuee buses, Louisiana

The Governor also turned to state resources,[56] asking Leonard Kleinpeter, a special assistant to the Governor and the head of the Office of Community Programs, an agency with contacts in all the parishes, on Tuesday to locate buses,[57] though without authority to commandeer those buses. Kleinpeter and his staff began to line up buses from local school districts and churches on Tuesday,[58] and lined up school buses that LOHSEP commandeered on Thursday, after the Governor issued an Executive Order on Wednesday.[59] The Governor's staff did not perceive a need for an Executive Order before Wednesday because the bus owners, including school superintendents, contacted by staff were highly cooperative to that point. On Wednesday, however, the need for an Executive Order emerged when some school systems began to oppose the state's request for buses and media reports of lawlessness became pervasive.[60]

In all, the state and federal government obtained and sent 2,000 buses to New Orleans, which began heading there Wednesday, but did not arrive until Thursday.[61]

Conditions in New Orleans Deteriorated Throughout the Week

Highway Overpasses

During the Hurricane Pam working group, government officials planned to collect rescuees on highway overpasses, which they referred to as "lily pads."[62] The state's Department of Wildlife and Fisheries staged at least three highway-overpass collection points: the Elysian Fields exit (near the city's Ninth Ward), the St. Bernard exit (the next exit some 2,000 feet away), and the Interstate 10 – Interstate 610 split (near the border of Orleans and Jefferson Parishes).[63] The Louisiana National Guard and Coast Guard also collected rescuees from the Lower Ninth Ward and brought them to the third floor of Jackson Barracks and a highway overpass.[64]

The overpass at the I-10 Causeway intersection (less than a mile into Jefferson Parish from the I-10 and I-610 split), which became known as the "Cloverleaf," became one of the biggest collection points in New Orleans, as well as an ad-hoc triage point. The presence of medical assistance drew others, and soon the resources there (food, water, and medicine) were overwhelmed.[65]

Dr. Scott Delacroix, who was treating patients at the Cloverleaf, reported severe shortages of medical supplies and other necessities to Dr. Jimmy Guidry, the Secretary of the Louisiana

Department of Health and Hospitals. At one point, Dr. Delacroix was forced to drive to Baton Rouge and raid the stockpiles of supplies languishing in the parking lot of the state emergency-operations center.[66]

When government-sponsored buses began trickling into New Orleans on Wednesday evening, they picked up rescuees on highway overpasses like the Cloverleaf (which was not cut off by flood waters) in addition to heading to the Superdome or the Convention Center.[67]

The Superdome

The Superdome lost electricity on Monday morning and plumbing on Tuesday, resulting in a sanitation crisis. The population doubled by Wednesday, as citizens who had stayed in their homes during the storm sought refuge. As a result, health officials were forced to move the special-needs population to the New Orleans Arena, across the walkway from the Superdome.[68]

Security opened the doors of the Superdome for the first time late on Tuesday, so that people could see for themselves that the surrounding area was flooded and evacuation would be difficult. Even outside, the temperature and humidity were so brutal that the National Guard had helicopters hover over the concourse to function like massive fans.[69]

Some 20,000 to 30,000 people languished under these conditions until Thursday at the earliest and as late as Saturday.

The Convention Center

Although the city had not planned before landfall to open the Morial Convention Center to the public as a shelter or refuge, Mayor Nagin opened the facility on Tuesday, August 30.[70] No officials had planned for the food, water, medical support, and security needs of the people who took shelter there.

Unlike the Superdome (rumors to the contrary notwithstanding), the Convention Center, where evacuees from the city's hotels may have become attractive targets for theft,[71] experienced some crime, and the New Orleans Police Department (NOPD) became overwhelmed there.[72]

Although the record is inconclusive about when the federal government became aware that the city had opened the Convention Center to the public,[73] the state learned about it on Wednesday.[74] However, Adjutant General Landreneau instructed the Louisiana National Guard officers who were evacuating the Superdome to stick to their mission.[75]

Late on Thursday night or early on Friday morning, however, the city's Director of Homeland Security and Public Safety asked General Landreneau to take control of the Convention Center, provide relief, and evacuate the 19,000 people who had gathered there.[76]

The U.S. Army Located a Staging Area and Coordinated the Buses' Trip to New Orleans

At 5 p.m. Wednesday evening, as buses finally began arriving in LaPlace, Louisiana, Governor Blanco asked Lieutenant General Russel L. Honoré, Commander, First Army, and Commander of Joint Task Force Katrina, to coordinate the evacuation of New Orleans.[77] General Honoré delegated that responsibility to Brigadier General Mark Graham, who had arrived in Baton Rouge that day. General Graham established a staging area at Mile Marker 209 near LaPlace, Louisiana (up to this point the buses were staging on I-10 a few miles away by default), and informed DOT, which was responsible for procuring the buses and drivers.[78]

On Thursday morning, General Graham learned that Governor Blanco wanted those buses heading to the Superdome to pick up 5,000 rescuees at the Cloverleaf first.[79] General Graham sent two liaison officers there, where they coordinated the convoys of buses arriving from Mile Marker 209.[80] The two evacuation operations ran simultaneously. General Graham estimated that the Superdome evacuation was set back only an hour by this diversion.[81]

The Louisiana National Guard Planned and Executed the Movement of Buses from Off-Ramps to the Superdome and Convention Center

The Louisiana National Guard (LANG) at the Superdome routed buses from the O'Keefe Avenue off-ramp (a few blocks to the southwest of the Superdome) to the Superdome.[82]

First, National Guard officers designated a pick-up spot for buses to meet Superdome evacuees, as the area immediately adjacent to the Superdome was flooded. The National Guard designated the Loyola Street entrance to the Hyatt Regency Hotel as the pick-up spot because the road only had a foot-and-a-half of water.[83]

Second, National Guard officers identified a path to the Hyatt Regency Hotel pick-up point for evacuees, from the outdoor concourse surrounding the Superdome to the adjacent mall, which connected indoors to the Hyatt. Guardsmen and NOPD officers lined the path, ensuring that only Superdome evacuees would be entering buses, and that they would not be harassed by other people who had not sought refuge at the Superdome, but who wanted to sneak onto buses designated for the Superdome evacuees.[84]

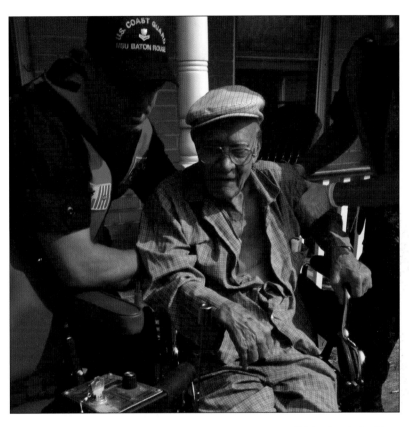

Helping hands, Louisiana
U.S. Coast Guard photo

Third, National Guard officers identified and secured a route for buses from the I-10 off-ramp to the Loyola Street entrance of the Hyatt, locating checkpoints strategically along the way.[85]

Evacuation of the Superdome Swung into Full Gear on Thursday

Buses finally arrived in large numbers in front of the Hyatt on Thursday morning, September 1. The DOT also expended considerable energy trying to arrange for rail cars, but without much luck.[86] In the end, just 97 people were evacuated, in a single trip, by rail.[87]

The Evacuation of the Convention Center Began and Ended on Saturday

On Friday morning, at 8 a.m., the National Guard's General Jones ordered Colonel Jacques Thibodeaux to plan and execute a "rescue mission," in coordination with the NOPD, at the Convention Center by noon that day.[88] Colonel Thibodeaux designed a plan to bring law and order to the Convention Center within the first 30 minutes, provide food, water, and medicine within five hours, and evacuate the premises within 48 hours.[89] Supported by National Guard units from five other states, Colonel Thibodeaux carried out the plan at noon, and National Guard troops secured the entire complex in under 15 minutes without incident. The 19,000 people taking refuge were evacuated the next day within eight hours, in buses sent by General Graham, helicopters, and the Canal Street Ferry.[90]

Every Level of Government Failed to Identify an Adequate Number of Shelters Before Landfall

Before landfall, neither the city, state, nor federal government identified adequate sheltering space outside the area that would become the flood zone. Adequate sheltering space was not identified until Wednesday, August 31, two days after landfall.

Small evacuee secured,
New Orleans

U.S. Coast Guard photo

Sheltering options within the State of Louisiana are limited in part because the American Red Cross, the entity primarily responsible for sheltering under the NRP, will not certify any shelters below the I-10 and I-12 split outside of Baton Rouge because the risk of flooding is too great.[91]

A FEMA situation report published at 10 p.m. on Tuesday, August 30 stated: "The State requested assistance in relocating all remaining victims of Hurricane Katrina out of the Superdome shelter. Limiting factors include identifying where they are to be relocated to and identifying the transportation required."[92] A Department of Homeland Security document published a few hours later noted, under the heading "Decisions needed," that the state was "expected to identify location[s] of alternate shelter locations this morning."[93]

On Tuesday night, Governor Blanco had instructed Ann Williamson, the state's Secretary of Social Services, to find a shelter for 25,000 people by 6 a.m. on Wednesday.[94] At 1:30 a.m. on Wednesday, Secretary Williamson called Texas to request the use of the Astrodome.[95] Secretary Williamson explained that she had to ask for the Astrodome because demand for shelter space exceeded what was available in Louisiana.[96] Between 8:30 and 9:30 a.m. on Wednesday morning, Governor Blanco called Governor Perry of Texas, who agreed to open the Astrodome to receive Katrina evacuees.[97] According to General Honoré, "the destination was Houston ... because Baton Rouge is full. Shreveport is full. Jackson, Mississippi is full. There's no more capacity in the state."[98]

Family Reunification and Prevention of Missing Children and Adult Scenarios

A total of 13,502 adults were reported to the National Center for Missing Adults (NCMA) as a result of Katrina,[99] and a total of 5,088 children were reported to the National Center for Missing and Exploited Children (NCMEC).[100] Many shelters did not have intake forms or release forms to track individuals, or they did not use these forms. Additionally, FEMA did not fully cooperate with NCMA or NCMEC to help reunite families, citing privacy concerns (which could have been addressed). Finally, due to the lack of coordinated reporting or tracking of missing persons, family members often had to repeatedly call several organizations to seek help with finding family members.

1 Committee staff interview of Terry Tullier, Director, New Orleans Office of Emergency Preparedness, LA, conducted on Nov. 22, 2005, transcript p. 18. FEMA sent the Committee a 2003 document from the state that recognized that "250,000 to 350,000 people [would] remain in stranded conditions with limited self rescue capability" after landfall of a major hurricane in the greater New Orleans area. *Source:* Sean Fontenot, memorandum to FEMA, Aug. 22, 2003, p. 2. Provided to Committee; filed as Bates nos. DHS-FEMA-0079-0000004 through 0000005 (indicating the document was also sent on Aug. 25, 2004 to the U.S. Department of Health and Human Services.); Ron Castleman, memorandum to Lacy Suiter, "Catastrophic Planning for New Orleans," Aug. 8, 2001. Provided to Committee; filed as Bates no. DHS-FEMA-074-0000027 (stating a need to evacuate 300,000 to 350,000 after landfall of a catastrophic hurricane in New Orleans.). According to a 2006 Emergency Response/Shelter Plan appropriations request document for which Col. Terry Ebbert is the point of contact, "The city of New Orleans faces the reality that it is impossible to conduct a mandatory evacuation in advance of a Category 3, 4, or 5 hurricane, as well as respond to other…disasters including terrorism. Even under the best conditions that currently exist in terms of emergency response in the New Orleans region, evacuation would leave 150,000 people in harm's way." *Source:* City of New Orleans, FY2006 Funding Request to Congress, Emergency Response Shelter/Plan Homeland Security Appropriations. Provided to Committee.

2 FEMA, *DHS/FEMA Initial Response Hotwash: Hurricane Katrina in Louisiana*, Feb. 13, 2006, p. 45 [hereinafter *DHS/FEMA Initial Response Hotwash*, Feb. 13, 2006].

3 City officials interviewed did not know exactly how many people the RTA buses brought to the Superdome on Sunday, but the City's Director of Homeland Security and Public Safety said that the majority of the total population at the Superdome before landfall arrived there by bus. *Source:* Committee staff interview of Col. Terry Ebbert, U.S. Marine Corps, (Ret.), Director, New Orleans Office of Homeland Security, LA, conducted on Jan. 10, 2006, transcript pp. 81-82. The total population of the Superdome before landfall is not known with certainty, but evidence in the record indicates that a range of 10,000 to 15,000 people were there before landfall. *Source:* Louisiana Office of Homeland Security and Emergency Preparedness (LOHSEP), Situation Report, Executive Summary, Hurricane Katrina, Aug. 29, 2005, 10 a.m. CT. Provided to Committee (stating that 10,342 were in the Superdome); Sally Forman, Communications Director, New Orleans Office of the Mayor, Timeline and Notes, Aug. 28, 2005. Provided to Committee ("Dome opens as shelter of last resort – 10,000 gather"); Col. Ebbert interview, Jan. 10, 2006, pp. 52, 112 (estimating 12,000 to 15,000 were in the Superdome before landfall).

4 *DHS/FEMA Initial Response Hotwash*, Feb. 13, 2006, p. iii (stating that with Katrina's "mass evacuation to locations throughout the country and other spillover effects nationwide, human resources were stretched particularly thin.").

5 U.S. Department of Transportation, Hurricane Katrina-Situation Report, Aug. 28, 2005, 3 p.m., p. 3 ("All buses and large support vehicles not in use are being moved to the Poland St. Wharves, the highest place in New Orleans."); Committee staff interview of Dwight Brashear, Chief Executive Officer and General Manager, Capital Area Transit System, Baton Rouge, LA, conducted on Jan. 5, 2006, transcript pp. 56-57 (recalling conversation RTA Director William DeVille telling Mr. Brashear that the RTA "parked 180 buses up there"). U.S. Department of Transportation official circulated an e-mail, reporting that buses would be moved to "docks" before the storm hit, to a number of federal officials, including the Administrator for the Federal Transit Administration, Robert Jamison and the Homeland Security Operations Center. *Source:* Robert Patrick, e-mail to Anthony Tisdale, Aug. 28, 2005, 11:52 a.m. Provided to Committee; filed as Bates no. DHS-HSOC-0002-0000055 ("Buses not being used are being moved to docks. Oddly enough the high ground in new Orleans [sic]. Houma does not have high ground but are securing facilities. … Please forward to all interestd [sic] paries [sic]. Ps. I've spoken with bill deville. Rta gm and he will keep us updated."). Tisdale forwarded this e-mail ten minutes later to a number of U.S. Department of Transportation (USDOT) officials, including Robert Jamison, the Administrator of the Federal Transit Authority, Department of Homeland Security (DHS) officials, including one at DHS headquarters and one at the Homeland Security Operations Center. *Source:* Anthony Tisdale, e-mail to Roger Bohnert and others, Aug. 28, 2005, 12:02 p.m. Provided to Committee; filed as Bates no. DHS-HSOC-0002-0000055.

6 On Thursday, a Capital Area Transit Systems official, Dwight Brashear, learned of these buses from RTA Director William DeVille and immediately took steps to move drivers to those buses, so that they could participate in the evacuation of New Orleans. Brashear interview, Jan. 5, 2006, pp. 56-59.

7 Committee staff interview of Sec. Johnny Bradberry, Louisiana Department of Transportation and Development, conducted on Dec. 21, 2005, transcript p. 80 ("So it makes sense to me what would be an agency that would be more closely tied to a function that could provide both, drivers and buses and we needed to iron that out. Could it be – could it be tourism. They know, they have all the buses, companies in the State, et cetera, et cetera, et cetera. So I had a real issue with resources as it relates to this. Not only in terms of drivers and buses, but in terms of in my opinion not having the resources that National Guard had. They obviously have access to a lot more people, resources than DOTD people do."). Although he signed the state's April 2005 Emergency Operations Plan along with the Governor and every other state official, Sec. Bradberry testified that he "had serious issues" with LA DOTD's responsibility under that plan because "we didn't feel like we were the best quote agency or group to coordinate that." *Source:* Sec. Bradberry interview, Dec. 21, 2005, pp. 78-79. Sec. Bradberry testified that he disagreed with the assignment of his department to lead the state's ESF-1 effort because "My main issue is that it's a resource issue. We don't feel like, first of all, we're not in the transit business, we have the title of Department of Transportation but we're not in the transit business. We have no buses, we have no drivers." *Source:* Sec. Bradberry interview, Dec. 21, 2005, p. 80.

8 Secretary Bradberry said that between April 2005 and landfall, he was not personally involved in any conversations with any Louisiana Office of Homeland Security and Emergency Preparedness officials about his department's new transportation responsibilities under the April 2005 plan. *Source:* Sec. Bradberry interview, Dec. 21, 2005, pp. 84-85. Sec. Bradberry's chief subordinates, LA DOTD Assistant Secretary of Operations Gordon Nelson and LA DOTD Chief

of Emergency Services Joe Modicut learned about the assignment of this responsibility to LA DOTD in July 2005, after which Asst. Sec. Nelson tried to schedule a meeting with LOHSEP Acting Deputy Director Col. Jeff Smith, but the meeting did not take place before Katrina made landfall, even though Modicut does not recall becoming aware of the department's responsibility until the weekend before landfall. *Source:* Committee staff interview of Gordon Nelson, Assistant Secretary of Operations, Louisiana Department of Transportation and Development, conducted on Jan. 6, 2006, transcript pp. 52-59; IEM, Inc., notes from Unified Command Final Briefing, July 29, 2005, p. 3. Provided to Committee (placing Joe Modicut at the July 2005 transportation working group meeting); Committee staff interview of Joe Modicut, Emergency Services Coordinator, Louisiana Department of Transportation and Development, conducted on Jan. 5, 2006, transcript p. 38 (stating he did not know LA DOTD was responsible for transportation under the state plan until the weekend before landfall).

9 On Tuesday and Wednesday, the state's Department of Transportation and Development used five ferries to evacuate 6,000 people from those parishes. Sec. Bradberry interview, Dec. 21, 2005, pp. 108, 113-114; Nelson interview, Jan. 6, 2006, pp. 79-83.

10 Sec. Bradberry interview, Dec. 21, 2005, pp. 172-183, 192-193.

11 Sec. Bradberry interview, Dec. 21, 2005, p. 86; Louisiana Office of Homeland Security and Emergency Preparedness, *Emergency Operations Plan*, Apr. 2005, p. BASIC-4–A–1 [hereinafter *Louisiana Emergency Operations Plan*, Apr. 2005] (stating that the Louisiana Office of Homeland Security and Emergency Preparedness would be the lead agency for Emergency Support Function 5 – Emergency Management – which required LOHSEP to "[p]repare detailed implementing procedures for all primary functions, to include the procedures by which the office will be alerted and activated for 24-hour operations when needed.").

12 *DHS/FEMA Initial Response Hotwash*, Feb. 13, 2006, p. 45 ("The Federal government has neither generic nor specific evacuation plans."). The Department of Homeland Security and FEMA recognized their failure to train personnel for an evacuation, before Katrina approached the Gulf Coast. *DHS/FEMA Initial Response Hotwash*, Feb. 13, 2006, p. v ("Hurricane Katrina highlighted the need to train operations personnel for evacuation.").

13 Don Day, Region VI Regional Emergency Transportation Representative, Office of Intelligence, Security and Emergency Response, U.S. Department of Transportation, cited in notes from Unified Command Final Briefing, July 29, 2005, p. 4. Provided to Committee (reporting to other federal, state, and local officials: "600 buses needed just to move people from collection points. … We need to pre-identify the sources for these buses and have them lined up and ready. There are plans to evacuate buses and operators out before the storm. Requires forethought, prior action. We have never looked into what it takes to make a bus staging/dispatch area."); *Southeast Louisiana Catastrophic Hurricane Plan*, prepared by IEM, Inc. for LOHSEP and FEMA, Sept. 2005, Appendix 1, p. 1 [hereinafter *Southeast Louisiana Catastrophic Hurricane Plan*, Sept. 2005] (Noting that "local/state/federal" officials "pre-landfall" should "identify/validate … 600 buses [and] 1,200 drivers"); Committee staff interview of Don Day, Region VI Regional Emergency Transportation Representative, Office of Intelligence, Security and Emergency Response, U.S. Department of Transportation, conducted on Jan. 17, 2006, transcript p. 57 (stating that the need for 1,000 buses "came out of the forethought, a little bit of the thought process of Pam.").

Day briefed another DOT official on what Day learned at Pam: "Don Day was the U.S. DOT rep in that [Pam] work group and I was mainly talking to him. I remember being debriefed as needing hundreds of buses, hundreds of buses to augment the hundreds of buses they already had there in New Orleans. … " *Source:* Committee staff interview of Dolph Diemont, Region X Regional Emergency Transportation Representative, Office of Intelligence, Security and Emergency Response, U.S. Department of Transportation, conducted on Jan. 6, 2006, transcript p. 26 ("I remember Don Day agonizing over that. We were working long hours in there, trying to come up with a plan, a way, some way to move all those people. And we said oh, this is so huge, we're going to need so many buses, we're going to need all of this planning and communications and cooperation, coordination, all of this to come together. It's really a massive effort."). DOT official, Dan Prevo, who participated in that working group, recalled the needed number of buses discussed without prompting. *Source:* Committee staff interview of Dan Prevo, Region VI Regional Emergency Transportation Representative, Office of Intelligence, Security and Emergency Response, U.S. Department of Transportation, conducted on Jan. 17, 2006, transcript p. 14 ("They talked in terms of 600 buses. And the reason I remember that is that once we got into Katrina where we didn't have the number of evacuees or number of injured that were estimated in this Pam exercise. But we ended up calling up about 1,100 buses. So even that, that 600 estimate had we gotten the number of evacuees and casualties that were estimated during Pam, we would have needed considerably more than the 600 than first estimated.").

14 A FEMA official at the workshop suggested to the other participants that 5,000 buses per day would be needed. Committee staff interview of Jules Hurst, Transportation Supervisor, Logistics Branch, FEMA, conducted on Dec. 27, 2005, transcript p. 34 ("At first we were told that – I said you got to give me a number to work with here, and when they said how many buses do we need, they said, okay, 75,000 refugees a day – refugees? Evacuees a day for 10 days. And they said, What do you need? And I said 5,000 buses a day.").

15 Don Day, Region VI Regional Emergency Transportation Representative, Office of Intelligence, Security and Emergency Response, U.S. Department of Transportation, cited in notes from Unified Command Final Briefing, July 29, 2005, p. 4. Provided to Committee ("We're at less than 10% done with this trans planning when you consider the buses and the people."). The inadequacy of local resources to evacuate New Orleans had been a longstanding concern. *Source:* Brian Wolshon, Elba Urbina, and Marc Levitan, Louisiana State University Hurricane Center, *National Review of Hurricane Evacuation Plans and Policies*, 2001, p. 18 ("The total number of busses in all of New Orleans would provide only a fraction of the capacity needed to transport all of these people."). It also became known to DOT officials that city lacked drivers for the buses. *Source:* Prevo interview, Jan. 17, 2006, pp. 12-14 (stating that based on the Pam discussions, there was "no certainty that the drivers – if the buses would be made available, that the drivers would be available … a whole

lot of research had to be done with regard to how many drivers would be available, or the liability issues that might be faced for the buses and for the drivers"); Hurst interview, Jan. 27, 2006, p. 37 (recalling that local officials in the Pam follow-up workshops reported "they didn't know if they could get the drivers to report.").

16 Diemont interview, Jan. 6, 2006, pp. 30-31; *Southeast Louisiana Catastrophic Hurricane Plan*, Sept. 2005, Appendix 1, p. 1 (noting that "local/state/*federal*" officials "pre-landfall" should "identify/validate ... 600 buses [and] 1,200 drivers") (emphasis added).

17 Testimony of Maj. Gen. Bennett Landreneau, Adjutant General, Louisiana, before the U.S. Senate Committee on Homeland Security and Governmental Affairs, hearing on *Hurricane Katrina: The Defense Department's Role in the Response*, Feb. 9, 2006; Committee staff interview of Maj. Gen. Bennett Landreneau, Adjutant General, Louisiana, conducted on Jan. 11, 2006, transcript pp. 68, 133.

The Secretary of Transportation and Development of the State of Louisiana also expected federal involvement in the pre-storm preparation for the post-landfall evacuation. Sec. Bradberry interview, Dec. 21, 2005, p. 87 ("My assumption was that once the Federal Government was informed that a disaster or a potential disaster was to strike that appropriate assets would be deployed accordingly, that included buses, that included National Guard from other areas, that included FEMA and their other assets besides buses, it included the whole gamut.").

18 Hurst interview, Dec. 27, 2005, p. 36. However Scott Wells, the Federal Coordinating Officer during Katrina and a Hurricane Pam participant testified the state officials at Pam told him not to worry about evacuation because the state did not need help with that aspect. Committee staff interview of Scott Wells, Deputy Federal Coordinating Officer for Hurricane Katrina in Louisiana, FEMA, conducted on Nov. 14, 2005, transcript pp. 86-87.

19 Patrick Rhode, e-mail to Edward Buikema, Michael Lowder and Ken Burris, Aug. 28, 2005 10:16 a.m. Provided to Committee; filed as Bates no. HS-FEMA-0091-0000320 ("I know we need 72 hours to do this – we don't have it."); Committee staff interview of Vincent Pearce, Manager, National Response Program, Office of Intelligence, Security, and Emergency Response, U.S. Department of Transportation, Jan. 6, 2006, p. 72 (stating that DOT worked with the Metropolitan Transit Authority for the City of New York to get buses to New Orleans after landfall, but that "it wasn't an instantaneous thing" in part because "you have to put different tires and wheels on inner-city buses to move them interstate," and then "once they were ready to move, it was going to take ... about 24 hours just to get the buses ready to move downrange.").

20 By contrast, in the run up to Hurricane Rita, FEMA deployed over 300 people to prepare for the evacuation. *DHS/FEMA Initial Response Hotwash*, Feb. 13, 2006, p. 5 ("When it came time to prepare for evacuation when Hurricane Rita threatened, over 300 people were reporting to the various teams.").

21 Compare Hurst interview, Jan. 27, 2006, pp. 8, 44 (stating the heads-up would have occurred "about 48 to 72 hours prior" to the time when the task order was ultimately placed on Wednesday, at 1:45 a.m.) with Committee staff interview of Reggie Jones, ESF-1 Program Manager, Office of Intelligence, Security and Emergency Response, U.S. Department of Transportation, conducted on Jan. 17, 2006, pp. 23, 31 (stating that the heads up was made as early as "Friday night ... or Saturday morning"); *See also:* Committee staff interview of Mike Foran, Region IV Regional Emergency Transportation Representative, Office of Intelligence, Security and Emergency Response, U.S. Department of Transportation, conducted on Jan. 17, 2006, transcript p. 38 (recalling that he proposed 500 buses, and Hurst said, "you might have to double it"). Although Hurst recalled giving a handwritten note with this request to Reggie Jones, a DOT representative staffing the ESF-1 desk at the NRCC during Katrina, the DOT has not produced the note in response to the Committee's document requests. Hurst's request made its way into a DOT document published at 3p.m. on Sunday, Aug. 28, 2005, which reported that "coordination is underway... with the DOT national transportation contractor for possible provision of buses." U.S. Department of Transportation, Hurricane Katrina – Situation Report #4, Aug. 27, 2005, 3 p.m., p. 4. Provided to Committee.

22 Landstar Express America Inc., Hurricane Katrina Response Research, Aug. 28, 2005. Provided to Committee; Foran interview, Jan. 17, 2006, p. 38.

23 Patrick Rhode, e-mail Edward Buikema, Michael Lowder and Ken Burris, Aug. 28, 2005, 10:16 a.m. Provided to Committee; filed as Bates no. DHS-FEMA-0091-0000320 ("Have we asked all eoc's via emac or esf (transportation) to make transportation assets available to assist New Orleans today with evacuations? I know we need 72 hours to do this – we don't have it – not sure what state is applying if someone can get some granularity on this issue.").

24 Patrick Rhode, e-mail to Edward Buikema, Michael Lowder and Ken Burris, Aug. 28, 2005, 10:16 a.m. Provided to Committee; filed as Bates no. DHS-FEMA-0091-0000320.

25 It should be noted, however, that on Saturday, Aug. 27, 2005, the Governor did ask the President for funds to assist with the state's coordination of the evacuation. Gov. Kathleen Blanco, letter to President George Bush, Aug. 27, 2005, pp. 2 and Enclosure A. Provided to Committee (requesting $2.5 million for evacuation-related funds for the Louisiana State Police, Louisiana Department of Wildlife and Fisheries, and the Louisiana Department of Transportation and Development, but no request for transportation.).

26 Testimony of Sec. Michael Chertoff, U.S. Department of Homeland Security, before the U.S. Senate, Committee on Homeland Security and Governmental Affairs, hearing on *Hurricane Katrina: The Homeland Security Department's Preparation and Response*, Feb. 15, 2006.

27 Sec. Chertoff, Senate Committee hearing, Feb. 15, 2006.

28 President George Bush, FEMA Daily Video Teleconference, Aug. 28, 2005. Provided to Committee; filed as Bates nos. DHS-FEMA-0105-0000079 through 0000080, 0000103 through 0000104;

29 Sec. Chertoff, Senate Committee hearing, Feb. 15, 2006 (stating that after the video teleconference call of Sunday, Aug. 28, 2005, he "did not call the Department of Transportation and say, I want to see the plan.").

30 Maj. Gen. Landreneau, Senate Committee hearing, Feb. 9, 2006 ("We had procedures in place. We had contingencies to be able to get the personnel to the buses because the water was rising. In every case, from Monday through Thursday, there were – we had plans in place and we had contingencies to be able to get all of the personnel onto the buses."); Col. Ebbert interview, Oct. 13, 2005, p. 121 (stating that "there was no reason not to move people … out of the Superdome").

31 *Southeast Louisiana Catastrophic Hurricane Plan*, Sept. 2005 ("Parish resources in the most severely impacted areas will not be available for several weeks or even months, as they were not removed from the area prior to the storm.")

32 Testimony of Mayor C. Ray Nagin, City of New Orleans, LA, before the U.S. Senate Committee on Homeland Security and Governmental Affairs, hearing on *Hurricane Katrina: Managing the Crisis and Evacuating New Orleans*, Feb. 1, 2006; Col. Ebbert interview, Oct. 13, 2005, p. 121; Committee staff interview of Sally Forman, Communications Director, Office of the Mayor, City of New Orleans, LA, conducted on Jan. 10, 2006, transcript pp. 70-76; Mayor C. Ray Nagin, City of New Orleans, "Post-Hurricane Katrina Critical Needs Assessment," Aug. 29, 2005, p. 1. Provided to Committee [hereinafter Mayor Nagin, "Post-Hurricane Katrina Critical Needs Assessment"]

33 The list did not list evacuation as a critical need, but it did state that "vehicles and drivers to coordinate the transport from the Dome to the Convention Center would also be required," if and when the city were to open the Convention Center as a refuge of last resort "in lieu of the Superdome." Mayor Nagin, "Post-Hurricane Katrina Critical Needs Assessment," p. 1; Forman interview, Jan. 10, 2006, pp. 75-76 (noting that transportation needs were not listed).

34 The mayor's communications director provided the Committee with transcribed notes for each day's activities immediately preceding and following landfall. For Tuesday, Aug. 30, 2005, her notes stated: "Call to [Chief of Staff to the Governor] Andy Kopplin for No. 1 priority from state for buses." Sally Forman, Communications Director, New Orleans Office of the Mayor, Timeline and Notes, Aug. 30, 2005. Provided to Committee; Forman interview, Jan. 10, 2006, pp. 99-100 (noting that the city may have also made earlier requests for buses).

35 Forman interview, Jan. 10, 2006, pp. 100-104.

36 Brashear interview, Jan. 5, 2006, p. 57; Committee staff interview of James Tillie, Safety Director, Regional Transit Authority, New Orleans, LA, conducted on Dec. 19, 2005, transcript p. 46.

37 Forman interview, Jan. 10, 2006, pp. 92-93, 99.

38 Louisiana Office of the Governor, Response to the U.S. Senate Committee on Homeland Security and Governmental Affairs, Document and Information Request Dated Oct. 7, 2005 and to the U.S. House of Representatives Select Committee to Investigate the Preparation for and Response to Hurricane Katrina, Overview of Governor Kathleen Babineaux Blanco's Actions in Preparation for and Response to Hurricane Katrina, Dec. 2, 2005, p. 7 [hereinafter Louisiana Office of the Governor, Governor's Timeline] (Governor Blanco told the President on Monday, "We need your help. We need everything you've got." Brown told Governor Blanco that FEMA had "500 buses on standby, ready to be deployed," and that Governor Blanco recommended to him that FEMA put two drivers in each bus, so they can alternate shifts and rest without losing time.); Maj. Gen. Landreneau, Senate Committee hearing, Feb. 9, 2006.

39 Louisiana Office of the Governor, Governor's Timeline, p. 9 (stating that Governor Blanco asked Maj. Gen. Landreneau on Tuesday to check on the status of the FEMA buses); Maj. Gen. Landreneau, Senate Committee hearing, Feb. 9, 2006; Louisiana Office of Emergency Planning, Louisiana Department of Transportation and Development, and Louisiana State Police, "OEP, DOTD, LSP Timeline," p. 18. Provided to Committee ("OEP, 8/31/05, 1:30:00, Verbal request to FEMA ESF-1 for 455 buses."); Testimony of Michael Brown, former Director, FEMA, before the U.S. Senate, Committee on Homeland Security and Governmental Affairs, hearing on *Hurricane Katrina: The Role of U.S. Department of Homeland Security and FEMA Leadership*, Feb. 10, 2006 (stating that Brown requested 500 buses from other FEMA officials, but that FEMA did not task the U.S. Department of Transportation for buses until Wednesday, August 31, 2005, two days after landfall).

40 Brown, Senate Committee hearing, Feb. 10, 2006; Louisiana Office of the Governor, Governor's Timeline, p. 9 ("the expected and promised federal resources still have not arrived on Wednesday.").

41 Louisiana Office of the Governor, Governor's Timeline, p. 9.

42 Louisiana Office of the Governor, Governor's Timeline, pp. 9-10.

43 Louisiana Office of the Governor, Governor's Timeline, p. 10.

44 FEMA, Tasking Request and Assignment Form, Aug. 31, 2005, 1:45 a.m. Provided to Committee (tasking "Transportation" to send 455 buses to New Orleans).

45 Brown, Senate Committee hearing, Feb. 10, 2006 (unable to explain why the buses did not arrive when expected, and why FEMA did not task the U.S. Department of Transportation for buses until Wednesday, Aug. 31, 2005); Sec. Chertoff, Senate Committee hearing, Feb. 15, 2006 (incorrectly understood that 450 FEMA buses were on their way to New Orleans on Tuesday night, before any FEMA tasking order went out to DOT.); Sec. Chertoff, Senate Committee hearing, Feb. 15, 2006 (stating that "the biggest failure was not getting buses in.").

46 FEMA, Tasking Request and Assignment Form, Aug. 31, 2005, 1:45 a.m. Provided to Committee (tasking "Transportation" to send 455 buses to New Orleans).

47 Committee staff interview of Col. Jeff Smith, Louisiana National Guard (Ret.), Acting Deputy Director, Emergency Management, LOHSEP, conducted on Jan. 13, 2006, pp. 113-114 (stating that a FEMA official "at the headquarters

decided based on the number of people and everything that 455 would be enough.").

48 Col. Smith interview, Jan. 13, 2006, p. 116.

49 The Governor's efforts were also set back by a miscommunication from FEMA. Phil Parr, a FEMA official on the ground at the Superdome, developed a plan (which ultimately proved impracticable) to use Chinook helicopters to evacuate the Superdome. Testimony of Phil Parr, Federal Coordinating Officer, Region I, FEMA, before the U.S. Senate, Committee on Homeland Security and Governmental Affairs, hearing on *Hurricane Katrina: Perspectives of FEMA's Operations Professionals*, Dec. 8, 2005. At one point on Wednesday, that plan was communicated by FEMA to Ty Bromell of the state's Office of Rural Development. *Source:* Louisiana Office of the Governor, Governor's Timeline, p. 11; Committee staff interview of Ty Brommel, Executive Director, Louisiana Governor's Office of Rural Development, conducted on Jan. 10, 2006, transcript p. 19. Reacting to that information, Bromell then sent out a statewide e-mail at 10:30 a.m., which read, in part, "NO MORE CALLS FOR BUSES!" *Source:* Ty Bromell, e-mail to Rochelle Michaud Dugas and others, Aug. 31, 2005, 10:30 a.m. Provided to committe. Brommel interview, Jan. 10, 2006, p. 19. It is unclear from the record whether FEMA told Brommel to stop the buses, or whether he ordered the staff to stop getting buses on his own, communications between FEMA. Later in the day, the same staffer learned that the effort to obtain buses should continue and sent out an e-mail to that effect. *Source:* Brommel interview, Jan. 10, 2006, pp. 28-29.

50 Committee staff interview of Brig. Gen. Gary Jones, Assistant Joint Forces Commander, Louisiana Army National Guard, conducted Dec. 7, 2005, transcript pp. 89, 90-91.

51 Parr, Senate Committee hearing, Dec. 18, 2005; *DHS/FEMA Initial Response Hotwash*, Feb. 13, 2006, p. 46 ("An example of a problem associated with the lack of communications was during the Superdome evacuation coordination. The liaison team at the Superdome attempted to coordinate with the Federal and State elements at the State Emergency Operations Center (EOC) in Baton Rouge. Communications to Baton Rouge failed, so the liaisons coordinated with the [FEMA Region VI Regional Response Coordination Center (RRCC) in Denton, TX] and [the National Response Coordination Center (NRCC) in Washington, D.C.]. Consequently, the EOC in Baton Rouge had no visibility on this operation."). Although this communications failure limited FEMA officials' visibility on the evacuation of the Superdome, it should not have eliminated their visibility, assuming they could share information with state officials at Baton Rouge.

52 *DHS/FEMA Initial Response Hotwash*, Feb. 13, 2006, p. 46.

53 At 3:47 a.m., DOT dispatched the first 50 buses with 200-250 more buses anticipated in the next 12-18 hours. U.S. Department of Transportation, Actions for Hurricane Katrina, Annotated Chronology of Significant Events, Oct. 6, 2005, p. 4. [hereinafter DOT, Timeline, Oct. 6, 2005].

54 DOT, Timeline, Oct. 6, 2005, p. 4.

55 DOT, Timeline, Oct. 6, 2005, p. 4.

56 It is not clear whether the Governor delegated the post-storm evacuation responsibilities outside of LA DOTD because she knew LA DOTD was supposed to be responsible for the post-storm evacuation. Committee staff interview of James Ballow, Senior Operating Officer, LOHSEP, conducted on Jan. 4, 2006, pp. 81-84 (stating that the likely conclusion from the Governor's assignment of the post-storm evacuation to Leonard Kleinpeter was that she determined the LA DOTD was not able to fulfill its post-storm evacuation functions under the plan, but "maybe there is a possibility that maybe she wasn't familiar with the plan itself enough to know who to call either. I am not sure. I really can't say how she arrived at that decision.").

57 Louisiana Office of the Governor, Governor's Timeline, p. 8; Committee staff interview of Leonard Kleinpeter, Special Assistant to the Governor and Director, Louisiana Office of Community Programs, conducted on Jan. 10, 2006, transcript pp. 6-9, 18 ("And I called my – remember the part about being director of [the Office of Community Programs] and rural areas and in charge of all of that. And my folks knew those people on a first named basis. I knew some as well. And I picked the phone up and said, "We need the school buses." And we started calling for school buses. And we called for school buses and we put some in motion as fast as we could.").

58 Louisiana Office of the Governor, Governor's Timeline, p. 8; Kleinpeter interview, Jan. 10, 2006, p. 18.

59 Executive Order No. KBB 2005-31, "Emergency Evacuation by Buses," Aug. 31, 2005; Louisiana Office of the Governor, Governor's Timeline, p. 11.

60 Kleinpeter interview, Jan. 10, 2006, pp. 28-30, 98-101; Brommel interview, Jan. 10, 2006, pp. 43-47.

61 The evacuation was also assisted by Dwight Brashear with the Capital Area Transit System (CATS), whom the state enlisted on Wednesday night to follow up on the Governor's Executive Order and procure school buses. *Source:* Brashear interview, Jan. 5, 2006, pp. 5-6. To that point, the state had been operating without a professional transportation logistics expert, and when Mr. Brashear arrived at the state's EOC, he found not only a lack of planning for the use of buses in evacuation, but also little useful information to assist him in his task: "This was major … but it was almost like they weren't – like they were being hit with a hurricane for the first time. Maybe nobody thought it would ever happen, I guess." *Source:* Brashear interview, Jan. 5, 2006, p. 85.

62 Committee staff interview of Maj. Jeff Mayne, Supervisor, Special Investigator Section, Louisiana Department of Wildlife and Fisheries, conducted on Nov. 30, 2005, transcript pp. 72-73, 156; Sec. Landreneau interview, Nov. 30, 2005, pp. 191-192; Committee staff interview of Avis Gray, Regional Administrator, Region I, Office of Public Health, Louisiana Department of Health and Hospitals, conducted on Dec. 8, 2005, transcript pp. 157-161.

63 Committee staff interview of Lt. Col. Keith LaCaze, Assistant Administrator, Law Enforcement Division, Louisiana Department of Wildlife and Fisheries, conducted on Nov. 30, 2005, transcript pp. 70-71.

64 Committee staff interview of Brig. Gen. Brod Veillon, Assistant Adjutant General, Louisiana National Guard, conducted on Nov. 29, 2005, transcript pp. 31, 41-42.

65 According to Sheriff Harris Lee of Jefferson Parish, it is only by chance that he learned that thousands of people were sitting on I-10 in need of food and water. As a result, the people lacked food and water for as long as a full day. Committee staff interview of Harry Lee, Sheriff, Jefferson Parish, Louisiana, conducted on Jan. 9, 2006, transcript pp. 34-37.

66 Committee staff interview of Scott Delacroix, M.D., resident, LSU, conducted on Feb. 20, 2006 (untranscribed).

67 Lt. Col. LaCaze interview, Nov. 30, 2005, pp. 143-144; Committee staff interview of Col. Glenn Curtis, Chief of Staff, Louisiana National Guard, conducted on Dec. 6, 2005, transcript pp. 264-265; Committee staff interview of Lonnie Swain, Assistant Superintendent, New Orleans Police Department, LA, conducted on Nov. 9, 2005, transcript pp. 101-102.

68 Louisiana National Guard (LANG) officials on the ground at the Superdome began talking about evacuation planning to some extent on Monday night, but those conversations intensified on Tuesday, when the area around the Superdome flooded. On Tuesday, Maj. Gen. Landreneau ordered Gen. Gary Jones, who was in command of the LANG officers on the ground in New Orleans during Katrina, to take control of the evacuation, even though LANG usually served in a supporting role. Gen. Jones assumed his job would be to provide security for the people at the Superdome and get people to the buses, when they arrived. *Source:* Brig. Gen. Jones interview, Dec. 7, 2005, p. 93 ("FEMA was saying we'll get you the buses, and I was responsible for the security of the people until the buses came."). Nevertheless, Gen. Jones had his soldiers experiment with high water vehicles to see if they could be used to evacuate people, but the vehicles had limited capacity, and there were concerns about whether they could handle the volume of passengers give the depth of water on the ground. *Source:* Brig. Gen. Jones interview, Dec. 7, 2005, pp. 106-107.

69 Swain interview, Nov. 9, 2005, p. 102.

70 Mayor Nagin, Senate Committee hearing, Feb. 1, 2006.

71 Col. Ebbert interview, Jan. 10, 2006, pp. 115-116, 137-138; Mayor Nagin, Senate Committee hearing, Feb. 1, 2006 (stating that people from the hotels evacuated to the Convention Center).

72 Maj. Gen. Landreneau interview, Jan. 11, 2006, p. 265 ("New Orleans Police Department was becoming overwhelmed at the Convention Center.").

73 Mayor Nagin, Senate Committee hearing, Feb. 1, 2006 ("With all due respect to Secretary Chertoff and Mr. Brown, I don't understand how anyone in authority, with this type of crisis, can say that they were not aware that we had a crisis in New Orleans, and we had people that were stranded on roofs, on highways, and at the Convention Center, and they didn't know about it. That is just next to impossible. The entire Nation was enthralled on this disaster, so I categorically reject their claims."). Key DOD officials did not learn of the need until Thursday, Sept 1. Committee staff interview of Brig. Gen. Mark Graham, U.S. Army, Deputy Commanding General, Fifth U.S. Army, conducted on Jan. 12, 2006, transcript p. 105.

74 Brig. Gen. Jones interview, Dec. 7, 2005, pp. 96, 190-191.

75 Brig. Gen. Jones interview, Dec. 7, 2005, p. 196.

76 Maj. Gen. Landreneau interview, Jan. 11, 2006, pp. 265-266 (stating that Col. Ebbert called him late on Thursday night); Col. Ebbert interview, Jan. 10, 2006, pp. 151-155 (stating that he called Maj. Gen. Landreneau late on Thursday night); Lt. Col. Jacques Thibodeaux, memorandum on the events surrounding the Louisiana National Guard rescue mission of the Morial Convention Center, Dec. 2, 2005, p. 1 [hereinafter Lt. Col. Thibodeaux, memorandum on the Convention Center, Dec. 2, 2005] ("Early Morning Hours (Approximate 0200), 2 Sep 05–MG Landreneau receives a verbal request from NO Emergency Operations Manager, COL(R) Terry Ebbert to conduct a rescue mission at the MCC. COL(R) Ebbert requests the mission be conducted in coordination with the New Orleans Police Department and that it commence the same day.").

77 Louisiana Office of the Governor, Governor's Timeline, p. 10; Brig. Gen. Graham interview, Jan. 12, 2006, pp. 26-28.

78 Brig. Gen. Graham interview, Jan. 12, 2006, pp. 54-55. By Wednesday evening, a sufficient numbers of buses had amassed at Mile Marker 209. *Source:* Brig. Gen. Graham interview, Jan. 12, 2006, p. 81. He developed a plan: 10 buses at a time would leave mile marker 209, escorted by two State Troopers; they would travel to the Hyatt Regency (adjacent to the Superdome complex) where evacuees would board. *Source:* Brig. Gen. Graham interview, Jan. 12, 2006, pp. 78-79. The convoys (or "serials") would be appropriately spaced – when buses arrived at the Hyatt, the liaison officers on site would call back to Mile Marker 209, at which point another serial would leave. By the time the first serial was loaded, the next serial had already arrived. *Source:* Brig. Gen. Graham interview, Jan. 12, 2006, p. 55.

79 Brig. Gen. Graham interview, Jan. 12, 2006, pp. 95-96.

80 Brig. Gen. Graham interview, Jan. 12, 2006, p. 57.

81 Brig. Gen. Graham interview, Jan. 12, 2006, p. 96.

82 Committee staff interview of Lt. Col. Jacques Thibodeaux, Joint Director of Military Support to Civilian Authorities, Louisiana National Guard, conducted on Jan. 12, 2006, transcript pp. 44-49.

83 Committee staff interview of Lt. Col. Jacques Thibodeaux, Joint Director of Military Support to Civilian Authorities, Louisiana National Guard, conducted on Dec. 16, 2005, transcript p. 261; Lt. Col. Thibodeaux interview, Jan. 12, 2006, pp. 44-49, 64; Brig. Gen. Graham interview, Jan. 12, 2006, pp. 53, 64, 69.

84 Lt. Col. Thibodeaux interview, Jan. 12, 2006, p. 64; Brig. Gen. Graham interview, Jan. 12, 2006, p. 83.

85 Lt. Col. Thibodeaux interview, Jan. 12, 2006, pp. 39-65 (discussing story of LANG officials catching U.S. Navy officers in the act of posing as hotel contractors and stealing buses headed to the Superdome, so that the officers could use them to evacuate the stranded families of Naval officers in New Orleans); Lt. Col. Thibodeaux, memorandum on the Convention Center, Dec. 2, 2005, p. 3.

86 Diemont interview, Jan. 6, 2006, pp. 99-100.

87 U.S. DOT, Timeline, Oct. 6, 2005, p. 6.

88 Lt. Col. Thibodeaux, memorandum on the Convention Center, Dec. 2, 2005, p. 1 ("BG Jones further advises LTC Thibodeaux that … the mission must start not later than 1200 hours.").

89 Lt. Col. Thibodeaux, memorandum on the Convention Center, Dec. 2, 2005, pp. 1, 3 ("LTC Thibodeaux establishes goals for each phase: Law & Order: 30 Minutes, Relief: 5 Hours and Evacuation: 48 Hours."); Lt. Col. Thibodeaux interview, Jan. 12, 2006, pp. 31-32, 132-133.

90 Lt. Col. Thibodeaux interview, Jan. 12, 2006, p. 35. DOD assets on the ground at the Convention Center created some confusion for the LANG officers at times. For example, LANG Lt. Col. Thibodeaux, in charge of the Convention Center missions for the Guard, discussed the unannounced landing of a limited number of DOD helicopters on Friday, which if used at that time to evacuate people, would have forced the Guard and DOD to decide who would get on the helicopters, thereby potentially enraging the rest of the crowd. Source: Lt. Col. Thibodeaux interview, Jan. 12, 2006, pp. 147-149. Lt. Col. Thibodeaux explained that he made arrangements with the DOD helicopter pilots to have the helicopters return to the Convention Center on Saturday to participate in the coordinated evacuation at that time. Source: Lt. Col. Thibodeaux interview, Jan. 12, 2006, pp. 147-149. Although Lt. Col. Thibodeaux initially thought 20,000 to 22,000 people were at the Convention Center, he later determined that 19,000 people were there, and they were evacuated by Saturday, September 3, 2005, at 6:30 p.m. CT. Source: Lt. Col. Thibodeaux, memorandum on the Convention Center, Dec. 2, 2005, p. 9 ("1830 hours, 3 Sep 05-LTC Thibodeaux reports evacuation complete to JOC. LTC Thibodeaux estimates the total numbers evacuated: 2000 via the Canal Street Ferry, 14000 via 269 buses and 3000 (mostly elderly and medical) via helicopters.").

91 Committee staff interview of Kay Wilkins, Chief Executive Officer, Southeast Louisiana Chapter, American Red Cross, conducted on Dec. 20, 2005, transcript pp. 14-18. See also: Col. Ebbert interview, Jan. 10, 2006, pp. 34-35 (characterizing the Red Cross's ban on sheltering South of I-10 as "arbitrary").

92 U.S. Department of Homeland Security, Region VI RRCC Spot Report #26, Aug. 20, 2005, 10 p.m. CT. Provided to Committee; filed as Bates no. DHS-HSPC-0003-0001157.

93 U.S. Department of Homeland Security, HSOC Spot Report #30, Aug. 31, 2005, 2 a.m. ET, p. 2. Provided to Committee; filed as Bates nos. DHS-FEMA-0061-0000575 through 0000576 ("New, alternate shelter locations have not been determined but sites have been considered and the State is making a decision early today.").

94 Louisiana Office of the Governor, Governor's Timeline, p. 9; Committee staff interview of Sec. Ann Williamson, Louisiana Department of Social Services, conducted on Dec. 7, 2005, transcript pp. 98-99. Sec. Williamson and her team analyzed the shelter capacity in Louisiana and determined that the demand outstripped the supply. At around 10 or 10:30 that evening, they arrived at the final plan – use the Astrodome in Houston, TX. Sec. Williamson immediately conveyed this plan to the TAG and the Governor's executive staff. Sec. Williamson and her team reached out to officials in Texas that night. Sec. Williamson interview, Dec. 7, 2005, pp. 98-99, 102-106.

95 Sec. Williamson interview, Dec. 7, 2005, p. 105.

96 Sec. Williamson interview, Dec. 7, 2005, p. 102.

97 Louisiana Office of the Governor, Governor's Timeline, p. 10; Sec. Williamson interview, Dec. 7, 2005, pp. 105-106. According to Gen. Russell Honoré, " … the destination was Houston … because Baton Rouge is full. Shreveport is full. Jackson, Mississippi is full. There's no more capacity in the state." Committee staff interview of Lt. Gen. Russell Honoré, U.S. Army, Commanding General, First U.S. Army, conducted on Jan. 9, 2006, transcript p. 93.

98 The Committee's investigation has revealed that the insufficiency of in-state sheltering options was also an obstacle to pre-landfall evacuation, and even to pre-storm planning in the months leading up to Katrina. When RTA representative James Tillie called Chief Matthews over the weekend to offer their services, he was told that city planners had not yet identified destinations for potential evacuees. Source: James Tillie, e-mail to William Deville, "RTA Actives for Hurricane Katrina," Oct. 23, 2005, 11:29 a.m., p. 1. Provided to Committee. Similarly, the lack of available in-state sheltering options was an obstacle to efforts to conduct advance planning for evacuation; for example, one of the obstacles to the finalization of draft MOUs between the City and Amtrak to procure emergency means of evacuation was that the city planners could not provide destinations for the evacuees. Source: Committee staff interview of William Crosbie, Senior Vice-President of Operations, The National Railroad Passenger Corporation (Amtrak), conducted on Feb. 17, 2006, transcript p. 77.

99 Kym I. Pasqualini, National Center for Missing Adults, e-mail to Patricia Rojas, Senate Committee staff member, Mar. 29, 2006, 10:53 p.m. See also: National Center for Missing Adults. http://www.missingadults.org.

100 National Center for Missing and Exploited Children, "National Center for Missing and Exploited Children Reunites Last Missing Child Separated by Hurricane Katrina and Rita," press release, Mar. 17, 2006. http://www.missingkids.com/missingkids/servlet/NewsEventServlet?LanguageCountry=en_US&PageId=2317. Accessed on Mar. 30, 2006.

Offloading drinking water
Army National Guard photo

Logistics

Although some FEMA witnesses testified that FEMA had pre-positioned more commodities before Hurricane Katrina made landfall than before any other previous storm, it was not enough to sustain the tens of thousands of people left stranded by the hurricane. FEMA's logistics system became critical to providing additional food, water, ice, portable toilets, fuel, generators, and other necessary supplies to the impacted areas. However, as Secretary of Homeland Security Michael Chertoff testified: "FEMA's logistics systems simply were not up to the task."[1] Former FEMA Director Michael Brown agreed: "FEMA has a logistics problem."[2]

In some cases, state and local officials faced such overwhelming circumstances that they could not assess or communicate their needs accurately to FEMA. At other times, the system itself revealed flaws, as red tape prevented the prompt and complete acquisition and distribution of assets. To some degree, each level of government shares some of the responsibility for the failure of the FEMA commodities system after landfall.

Ordinary people forced to endure inhuman circumstances were the victims of these failures. Without generators, plumbing, or portable toilets, the Superdome became a stadium of human waste rotting in extreme heat. In Mississippi, victims who took refuge in public shelters found shortages of food and water, sanitation problems, and lack of electricity.

FEMA

The failed response to fulfill basic critical needs following Hurricane Katrina highlighted long-standing problems with FEMA logistics. With state and local authorities overwhelmed, the unprecedented demand for commodities fell – as the Hurricane Pam exercise predicted – on the federal government.

FEMA's logistics failure during the Katrina crisis was no surprise. FEMA already knew it lacked staff and systems needed to respond to a large disaster.[3] William Lokey, Federal Coordinating Officer (FCO) in Louisiana, told Committee investigators that FEMA regularly fails to track supplies: "It has been a problem at every disaster I'm aware of."[4]

In 2004, Ken Burris, the FEMA Acting Director of Operations, initially requested $60 million for modified logistical requirements that included logistical tracking systems.[5] In January 2005, FEMA submitted an initiative to the Department of Homeland Security (DHS) to improve its logistics system.[6] Documentation for the request reveals the burdens on FEMA's antiquated logistics systems. For example, warehouse-space requirements in some areas have grown as much as 10 times and the transportation mission had grown over 300 percent in three years, while staff support for these functions had been unchanged for seven years.[7] The request concluded the logistics system was not functional, resulting in the "total inability to accomplish the FEMA mission in accordance with the performance goals."[8] The status quo would also "negatively impact the ability to rapidly respond to both no-notice incidents and notice disasters and incidents."[9]

FEMA's poor planning for transportation was a key factor in the problems with commodities. Gary Moore, FEMA Director of Logistics, said FEMA had difficulty moving commodities during Katrina.[10] For instance, on Saturday afternoon, FEMA realized it did not have enough truck drivers to deliver commodities and equipment and started reviewing résumés to hire additional drivers.[11] By Sunday afternoon, August 28, records show that FEMA was short 68 of the 94 drivers who would be needed to move commodities for a short response effort and 162 drivers for a longer response.[12] To make matters worse, FEMA's transportation contractor, Landstar, does not own any vehicles. Instead, it locates independent drivers only after FEMA asks it to move commodities, which can also lead to delays.[13] FEMA then had to compete against Landstar for drivers to hire.[14] Drivers were also hard to come by because the commodities needed to be moved over a weekend.[15]

Staffing shortages hindered FEMA's logistics response to Katrina. In addition to the shortage of drivers, FEMA did not have enough people in Louisiana to staff a 24-hour operations center after the storm hit, which required many people to work more than 50 hours straight.[16] FEMA's own evaluation of its response in Louisiana admitted that, "Lack of sufficient trained logistics staff significantly detracted from our response to Hurricane Katrina in Louisiana and jeopardized the overall logistics mission."[17]

Unlike many large private shippers, FEMA could not track assets en route to destinations. As Moore explained: "I can tell you today when they leave someplace and I can tell you when they arrive someplace because they're manually counted when they got through the gate. In the middle of that, I don't know where they are."[18]

FEMA's decision to wait to determine whether pre-positioned assets were sufficient – instead of maintaining a constant stream of supplies – compounded the problem, as admitted by FEMA Director Brown: "We pre-positioned and then tried to see what was going to happen and then started it back up again. We should have just kept pushing."[19]

The logistics plan used in Katrina grew out of the Hurricane Pam catastrophic-storm exercise begun in 2004, and was still in development when Katrina struck. It envisioned a sequence of commodity deliveries from Federal Operational Staging Areas (FOSAs) to regional staging areas (RSAs), and then to local points of delivery (PODs). The plan assumed that as many as 160,000 people would require supplies.[20] Local officials viewed the commodities distribution plan as one of the most valuable products of the Hurricane Pam exercise,[21] and FEMA officials scrambled to find, read, and use the Pam documents in the days before Katrina's landfall.[22]

The Hurricane Pam plan guidelines for commodity distribution are internally inconsistent.[23] The power, water, and ice distribution section states that FEMA will direct the U.S. Army Corps of Engineers to have "approximately one-day's supply of water and ice – 1,530,000 gallons of water [322 truckloads] and 5.5 million pounds of ice [137.5 truckloads] – at Camp Beauregard, a federal staging area, in Pineville, LA, before the hurricane makes landfall."[24] Camp Beauregard was chosen because it was far enough inland to be safe from hurricanes, yet close enough to quickly deliver supplies.[25] Later in the document, pre-landfall planning charts specify that one day's supply of ice and water would be 32 to 40 truckloads each. The same sections identify one day's supply of Meals Ready to Eat (MREs) and tarps to be 15 to 20 truckloads and 36 to 34 truckloads respectively.[26]

FEMA had 30 truckloads of water, 17 truckloads of ice, 15 trailer loads of MREs, and 6 trailer loads of tarps at Camp Beauregard before the storm.[27] These commodities had been positioned at the beginning of the 2005 hurricane season as part of a new way to speed up the response to hurricanes, but FEMA did not get any additional commodities to Beauregard as Katrina moved through the Gulf of Mexico.[28]

Despite some efforts to move some commodities into Mississippi, there were major deficiencies in commodities prestaging there. FEMA's FCO for Mississippi, William Carwile, wrote several e-mails throughout Sunday to his superiors in which he expressed concern with commodities issues. Despite the fact that FEMA had ordered 400 trucks of ice, 400 trucks of water, and 250 trucks of MREs for the Meridian Naval Air Station in Mississippi, by the evening of August 29 only 30 trucks of water, 15 of MREs, two of tarps, and 30 of ice were at the base.[29]

FEMA's action of staging supplies early in the season throughout the Gulf Coast no doubt helped the response to Katrina.[30] But these supplies were not enough for a storm as strong as Katrina. The preparations for the hurricane should not have ended with the initial pre-positioning of supplies. Burris confirmed that the initial pre-positioning was only a start, and the specifics of a storm would dictate whether FEMA should move more supplies to the area.[31] While some supplies already staged in the Gulf region were moved to Mississippi or Alabama, records indicate that relatively few additional truckloads arrived in the primary FEMA staging areas in the days before landfall.[32] The record is not clear whether additional supplies were moved into the region, bypassing the primary FEMA staging areas. In any event, the Committee believes that with Katrina bearing down on the Gulf Coast as a catastrophic storm, FEMA should have moved additional supplies to its primary staging areas in Mississippi and Louisiana.

Commodities such as water, ice, food, tarps, and generators were delivered inefficiently and ineffectively to Mississippi and Louisiana both before and after landfall. In Mississippi, Carwile expressed concerns in a September 1 e-mail to some senior FEMA officials, including Director Brown, that the "System appears broken. … Will now attempt to get product in alternate ways."[33]

A week after landfall, Carwile wrote that the food deliveries were "totally unacceptable."[34] Robert Latham, Director of Mississippi's Emergency Management Agency, testified that he received only 10 to 20 percent of the food and water he requested during the days he described as critical, and did not receive adequate supplies until September 9, 12 days after landfall.[35]

FEMA's logistics also failed to meet demands in Louisiana. Colonel Terry Ebbert, Director of Homeland Security for the City of New Orleans, told the Committee that he had difficulty getting food and water the week after the storm;[36] Lokey confirmed that requests were not being met.[37] In particular, FEMA was unable to fill the number of requests for MREs.[38] However, as noted by Colonel Al Jones, the Department of Defense (DOD) liaison officer who started working on logistics issues with Director Brown on September 2, local emergency managers had difficulty articulating an accurate level of demand for commodities given the catastrophic conditions and lack of communications.[39]

FEMA recognized that it had failed.[40] Perceiving an overwhelmed logistics system, FEMA Director Brown "reached back to headquarters and had discussions about [how he] wanted all logistics turned over to DOD."[41] On September 1, FEMA headquarters contacted the Department of Defense, requesting that DOD take over full logistics operations in Louisiana and Mississippi,[42] thus proposing the transfer of one of its most important functions to another entity. (See Chapter 26 for additional information on this mission assignment and DOD's resulting actions).

Considerable attention has been paid to this attempt to turn over FEMA's troubled logistical efforts to the Department of Defense. After discussions among FEMA and DOD officials, on September 2 FEMA issued a $1 billion mission assignment to DOD to plan and execute the procurement, transportation, and distribution of commodities in Louisiana and Mississippi. FEMA officials authorized spending up to $1 billion on this mission, an estimate, as one FEMA official said, that was large enough to give DOD the authority to "cover the eventualities" that might arise in accomplishing this mission.[43]

Assistant Secretary of Defense Paul McHale testified of this mission that DOD "got the largest request for assistance in the history of the United States. And it wasn't anything other than … 'full logistics support throughout the entire area of responsibility.'" McHale continued that he felt that this was a "very broad, fairly loosely defined mission requirement" but since it was a "crisis circumstance, we felt that we should take that on, and we did."[44]

DOD's performance under this mission assignment was ultimately considerably less than full logistical support. DOD appears to have identified certain areas of FEMA's logistics system that required immediate attention – namely sourcing, tracking, and transportation – and restored the flow and distribution of commodities to both Louisiana and Mississippi. Hence, FEMA retained control over many of its traditional tasks.[45]

Of the billion dollars authorized, DOD has sought reimbursement from FEMA for approximately $100 million of work.[46] Billing records compiled by FEMA indicate DOD has sought reimbursement from FEMA partly for substantial costs for ship leases, fuel, airlift support, personnel travel, and some food.[47]

The day before the mission assignment to DOD, despite FEMA leaders' acknowledgement of the logistics problems, DHS Secretary Chertoff was publicly claiming otherwise:

> The limiting factor here has not been that we don't have enough supplies. …
> We not only had a hurricane; we had a second catastrophe, which was a flood.
> That flood made parts of the city very difficult to get through. If you can't get
> through the city you can't deliver supplies. … I'm telling you that we are get-
> ting food and water to areas where people are staging. … The limitation here
> on getting food and water to people is the condition on the ground.[48]

Other factors contributed to the logistics struggle. For example, communications between officials within Louisiana and with FEMA headquarters were almost nonexistent. As Scott Wells, the Deputy FCO in Louisiana said, "There was just a big communications void" in Baton Rouge.[49] FEMA had done little before landfall to ensure communications capabilities after landfall. (*See* Chapter 18, Communication Voids) The FEMA team leader at the Superdome had very limited communication capabilities with superiors in Baton Rouge and elsewhere, and estimated that this lowered his operational effectiveness by 90 percent.[50]

Additionally, as discussed in Chapter 25, both FEMA and state officials cited security issues as a principal reason for delayed delivery of commodities.[51]

Problems with Request for Assistance Systems

Louisiana's Staff and E-Team Server Were Overwhelmed

The Louisiana Office of Homeland Security and Emergency Preparedness (LOHSEP), the agency in charge of the Louisiana Emergency Operations Center (EOC) under the Louisiana Emergency Plan, uses a computerized request system called E-Team to log requests from state or local emergency officials. Louisiana officials said that the number of incoming requests overwhelmed their E-Team server.[52] LOHSEP ordered a replacement server for overnight delivery, but it was not installed until August 31.[53]

Parishes that lacked Internet access transmitted their requests to LOHSEP by telephone, fax, and ham radio,[54] though the loss of key communications infrastructure between New Orleans and Baton Rouge undermined these efforts.[55] Although the E-Team system was at times interminably slow, it never completely stopped working.[56]

When the state receives requests for assistance, the state is supposed to validate the requests before passing them to FEMA. A validation process eliminates frivolous or low-priority requests or those requests best handled by other states through the EMAC system. In Louisiana, officials lacked understanding of what assistance FEMA could appropriately provide. That lack of understanding led to submission of requests that wasted FEMA's time and resources. As Wells put it:

> When the state gets all these requests, they're supposed to consolidate them and see if they can meet those [requests] and they pass them to us. That mechanism of the state consolidating and screening requests was nonexistent [in Louisiana]. Everything was passed to us.
>
> People wanting pens, paper – and this was back in October – an air-conditioner, a bus for the Mayor to go to Atlanta; all that stuff comes straight to us, … there's no validation at the state level. We were just – we were getting actually thousands of requests.[57]

At the Committee's December 8 hearing, Wells further elaborated that requests for ammunition, golf carts, bus rides for Mayor Nagin and his staff, and portable air conditioners were intermingled with legitimate, high-priority requests.[58] Wells told the Committee that the "hundreds and hundreds" of invalid requests "clogg[ed] down the system for the legitimate requests."[59] Wells' testimony is uncontroverted. Louisiana's failure to adequately prioritize its requests to FEMA wasted FEMA's time and limited resources..

The Systems That FEMA and the States Used to Process Requests for Aid Were Incompatible, Delaying Fulfillment

Requests to FEMA, on the other hand, must be submitted on an Action Request Form (ARF). The ARFs and the state's E-Team system are not compatible, so state officials had to fill out both E-Team requests and FEMA ARFs. While Lokey did not think the incompatibility slowed the response to requests, it certainly complicated the tracking of requests, as will be discussed below.[60]

After a standard hurricane, FEMA has 72 hours to establish a Joint Field Office (JFO), which uses Mission Assignments – broad orders based on the ARFs – to task various government agencies to provide needed assets. After Katrina, however, the JFO in Louisiana did not become fully operational for 12 days after landfall, forcing state and FEMA officials to send important functions over to the FEMA Regional Operations Center in Denton, Texas.[61] Instead of coordinating with an on-site JFO, state and FEMA officials had to spend time reaching regional officials[62] who were often unacquainted with the situation in Louisiana.[63]

FEMA also didn't have enough staff.[64] The FEMA team in Louisiana had a single individual who worked 18 to 20-hour shifts to fill out and submit ARFs. Despite repeated requests for additional staff, Wells was still trying to get more staff as late as September 9. Wells called the shortage of people to process assistance requests "our biggest problem."[65]

FEMA Could Not Track Requests

Once FEMA submitted requests for assistance to the agencies expected to complete them, it had no efficient way to track progress by those agencies. FEMA's review of the Katrina response in Louisiana found that tracking difficulties led to duplication of requests, orders, and efforts.[66] The inability to track left some orders "unfilled, unchecked, or misdirected."[67]

Sometimes, state officials had a hard time following up on state E-Team requests they had transferred to FEMA's ARFs, as FEMA often failed to record on the ARFs their corresponding E-Team request. LOHSEP designated staffers to manually match up E-Team requests with ARFs, but that cumbersome process proved inadequate for the magnitude of the task.[68] Eventually FEMA started logging the state numbers, which made tracking request easier, though the system was still far from perfect.[69]

Judgment Errors Within the System Also Hampered the Response

The Louisiana Nursing Home Association (LNHA), which represents 80 percent of the nursing homes in the State of Louisiana, had a desk at the state EOC in Baton Rouge[70] because it had primary responsibility for helping nursing homes coordinate evacuations. LNHA submitted E-Team requests during the first days of the crisis, but then LOHSEP revoked its privilege[71] because LNHA was not a government agency.[72] Meanwhile, hundreds of nursing-home patients were stranded by rising water. LNHA was forced to set up and privately coordinate nursing-home rescue efforts.[73] As a result, rescues were delayed.

FEMA personnel admitted that there was a chance that an approved request would be denied at FEMA's Regional or National Headquarters. For example, FEMA denied a state request for 1,000 small rubber rafts because the boats would not be useful for rescues in debris-filled water. A state official disagreed and testified that the boats would have been valuable for towing behind motorboats and picking up victims in shallow water.[74] LOHSEP's Colonel Jeff Smith felt that reasonable requests were being "filtered," probably because not all levels of authority recognized the severity of the situation.[75]

Emergency Management Assistance Compacts

As noted elsewhere, the Emergency Management Assistance Compact (EMAC) is an inter-state agreement[76] to provide mutual aid when disaster strikes.[77] Forty-nine states, along with the District of Columbia, Puerto Rico, and the Virgin Islands have all enacted legislation to become part of the Compact,[78] and Congress has given its consent.[79] Upon declaration of an emergency, states can pre-position assets and wait for a request for assistance from the affected state.[80]

Both Louisiana and Mississippi asked for assistance through the EMAC system during the Hurricane Katrina disaster. Every member state as well as the District of Columbia and Puerto Rico responded, providing a wide range of equipment, medical aid and supplies.[81] Hurricane Katrina resulted in the largest EMAC response in U.S. history.[82]

The EMAC system demonstrated both its value and limitations during Katrina. Carwile testified that the resources made available through EMAC – almost 25,000 personnel who performed close to 900 missions, were crucial.[83] Mississippi Governor Haley Barbour agreed, singling out Florida's search-and-rescue teams and law-enforcement officials.[84] The Louisiana National Guard described EMAC as "the most successful feature of our response."[85]

Louisiana Commodities

The Louisiana Emergency Operations Plan designates LOHSEP as the lead state agency for coordinating the distribution of commodities. In Katrina's aftermath, emergency managers in Louisiana faced two distinct logistical challenges after landfall: (1) providing massive quantities of commodities to the enormous numbers of victims in the Superdome and Convention Center, and (2) disbursing relatively smaller amounts to the thousands of victims scattered across southeast Louisiana and the greater New Orleans metropolitan area – chiefly, the collection sites for rescuees along highway overpasses. Not surprisingly, they performed best in delivering to locations where the need was rapidly identified and supply lines could be established. But LOHSEP failed to coordinate and establish supply lines to the ad-hoc, unplanned distribution points.

Katrina revealed what the Hurricane Pam exercise and resulting plans assumed: the catastrophic storm would severely limit the capabilities of local authorities,[86] thereby requiring FEMA and the state to lead the distribution of commodities to the affected areas after landfall. Wells said that FEMA's responsibility was to get commodities to the federal staging areas, and then, according to the planning done during the Hurricane Pam exercise, the state and FEMA would decide how they would deliver the commodities the "last mile" to the public distribution points.[87]

Before landfall, FEMA and the state pre-positioned more commodities at FEMA's Operations Staging Area at Camp Beauregard (in Pineville, Louisiana – 220 miles from New Orleans) than any previous storm (although less than the amount discussed at Hurricane Pam).[88]

Consistent with the assumptions in the Hurricane Pam exercise, the flooding that resulted from Katrina left some parish governments' resources incapacitated,[89] making it necessary for FEMA and LOHSEP to push commodities to them without waiting for requests.[90] Before and after landfall, LOHSEP's operating principle for moving commodities was "if you can't get it yourself, then you turn to FEMA."[91]

Some parishes, however, asked for more commodities than the state or FEMA could provide.[92] LOHSEP and the National Guard also experienced difficulties in coordinating the delivery of commodities and the equipment needed by parishes.[93] In some cases a commodity delivery would be made by the National Guard to a parish distribution point, but the parish did not have access to a forklift, thus making unloading the delivery unnecessarily problematic.[94] Although the magnitude of the operation overwhelmed the manpower and equipment of Louisiana National Guard, making it necessary to rely on support from other states,[95] those needs should have been anticipated and planned for accordingly.

Some of the parishes' needs could have been met through better long-term planning and preparation. First, had FEMA and the state had executed more contracts with vendors before the storm for critical supplies, that would have saved time during the post-storm crisis.[96] Second, key commodities were not sent until two days after landfall from Zephyr Field, FEMA's post-landfall operational staging area in Jefferson Parish, to the Superdome.[97] Third, high-water vehicles were needed to deliver commodities to flooded areas like the Superdome. The Louisiana National Guard failed to anticipate needing to use its high-water vehicles to distribute commodities and failed to anticipate the manpower and equipment needs of a large-scale commodities distribution.[98] Fourth, planners failed to ensure that all supply PODs in affected areas would be set up on high ground. Many parish-designated PODs were flooded.[99] LOHSEP and the parishes had to establish alternative drop points.[100] Fifth, although Hurricane Pam working groups had discussed establishing Search and Rescue Bases of Operations (SARBOOs), temporary collection sites for rescuees on highway overpasses, neither FEMA nor the state had planned or prepared for a coordinated system of commodities distribution to the SARBOOs, where the situation became critical as transportation to evacuate the rescuees was delayed.[101]

Sanitation

Masses of people gathered at the Superdome, Convention Center, and various search-and-rescue drop points around town without basic sanitation. Superdome plumbing ceased to operate shortly after a levee breached and the pumps that maintained water pressure failed.[102] FEMA public-affairs official Marty Bahamonde characterized the Superdome as

> a shelter of last resort that cascaded into a cesspool of human waste and filth. Imagine no toilet facilities for 25,000 people for five days. Women and children were forced to live outside in 95-degree heat because of the horrid smell and conditions inside. Hallways and corridors were used as toilets, trash was

everywhere, and amongst it all children – thousands of them. It was sad, it was inhumane, it was heart-breaking, and it was so wrong.[103]

Sanitary conditions at the Convention Center were little better, although the relatively smaller crowd did have more open area available.[104]

On Tuesday, the New Orleans Police Department and the Louisiana National Guard requested portable toilets for the Superdome.[105] A FEMA representative at the Superdome promised to have toilets delivered the next day, Wednesday.[106] But law-enforcement agencies had checkpoints set up on major highways and prevented individuals without credentials from getting past some checkpoints. According to one portable-toilets vendor, he was turned away twice at security checkpoints in Plaquemines Parish (where his supply yard was located) when he tried to fulfill the order. Eventually, the National Guard provided an armed escort that enabled him to make the delivery on Saturday. By that time, the Superdome evacuation was nearly complete.[107]

Superdome

As the storm approached, city, state, and federal officials raced on the day before landfall to stock the Superdome with the additional food and water that would be needed for the refuge of last resort's massive incoming population.[108]

While FEMA and the National Guard were able to provide additional MREs and water before landfall,[109] officials were able to locate enough food for Sunday and Monday only. Despite some "touch and go" moments as deliveries lagged behind the arrival of more people seeking shelter,[110] officials were able to feed the Superdome population twice a day.

On Monday and Tuesday, however, federal and state officials described the situation at the Superdome as "desperate"[111] and "beyond critical,"[112] as an estimated 25,000 to 30,000 people gathered there.[113]

While Superdome residents never experienced an outright food and water shortage (as Bahamonde predicted to Brown),[114] other essential commodities – portable generators, lights, and batteries – did not arrive before the evacuation.[115] Better long-term planning would have avoided these pitfalls.

On Tuesday, Mayor Nagin asked Brown for many of these commodities, which FEMA officials knew were staged at Zephyr field, 10 miles west of the Superdome.[116] Lack of security and usable roadways did not interfere with the delivery of those commodities to the Superdome. At any time after the storm abated on Monday, officials at the Superdome could receive commodities at nearby highway overpasses, where they would be loaded onto high-water vehicles for delivery to the Superdome.[117] It remains unclear which entity bears responsibility for the failure to deliver commodities to the Superdome.

Convention Center

Unlike the Superdome, which emergency planners at all levels of government expected to become a refuge of last resort, Mayor Nagin's opening of the Convention Center as a refuge two days after landfall was largely unplanned. As a result, over the weekend, no food or water was pre-positioned there, and no commodities arrived there until Friday, September 2. Lokey said, "The state and the locals did not preplan or preposition anything, and so there was obviously a problem there."[118]

Although the City made no pre-landfall preparations to use the Convention Center as a refuge, Mayor Nagin included the possibility of using the Convention Center in lieu of the Superdome on a list he presented to FEMA Director Brown on Tuesday, the same day on which Mayor Nagin opened the Convention Center. The document stated, under the heading "Refuge of Last Resort–Superdome":

> (Alternative Need) Access to the Convention Center to use it as the refuge of last resort in lieu of the Superdome; *if this option is exercised*, each of the above-listed needs [generators, lights, video equipment, security and food and water] would be required for the Convention Center and, additionally, vehicles and drivers to coordinate the transport from the Superdome to the Convention Center would be required.[119] [Emphasis added.]

Unfortunately, when Mayor Nagin opened the Convention Center as a refuge, the city did not provide food and water to those it would house, and did not tell federal officials that the Convention Center had been opened.[120]

When questioned about opening the Convention Center, Mayor Nagin testified that he asked FEMA two or three times a day to deliver supplies there.[121] But when pressed to provide specific examples of requests, Mayor Nagin suggested that the Committee speak to Colonel Terry Ebbert, Director of the New Orleans Office of Homeland Security and Public Safety, as the person who would have told FEMA about the city's opening of the Convention Center as a shelter.[122] When the Committee asked Colonel Ebbert whether he told FEMA of the city's decision to open the Convention Center, he stated that the city never made an official decision to open the Convention Center.[123] When pressed further on whether he made a request for food and water to be delivered to the Convention Center, Colonel Ebbert said, "I did not make that request."[124] The first written request for food and water at the Convention Center came on Friday.[125]

Nevertheless, Lokey said that Colonel Jeff Smith, the Acting Deputy Director for the Louisiana Office of Homeland Security and Emergency Preparedness, made him aware on Tuesday or Wednesday that thousands of people were beginning to congregate at the Convention Center.[126] The state asked FEMA to send food and water to the Convention Center, but security concerns delayed their delivery until Thursday, according to Lokey.[127] Lokey also said that he was depending on requests from the state before sending any other commodities to the Convention Center.[128]

Further complicating the response to the developing situation at the Convention Center was confusion among Department of Homeland Security HSOC officials, who were tasked

Sorting through donations
U.S. Coast Guard photo

with gathering and disseminating critical information, and who erroneously believed the Convention Center and the Superdome were the same location.[129]

The result of Mayor Nagin and Colonel Ebbert's lack of planning, preparation, action, and coordination, combined with security concerns and DHS's lack of situational awareness, was that food and water for the 19,000 people at the Convention Center began to arrive on Thursday, but did not arrive in meaningful quantities until Friday, when the National Guard arrived with food and water provided by FEMA.[130]

Mississippi Commodities

The Federal Logistics System Failed to Provide an Adequate Supply of Commodities in the Aftermath of Hurricane Katrina in Mississippi

Hurricane Katrina disrupted the state's economic and physical infrastructure, complicating the ability of authorities and citizens to acquire commodities such as food, water, ice, and fuel.[131]

The federal logistics system could not adequately respond. FEMA's Federal Coordinating Officer in Mississippi, William Carwile, said that only about 25 percent of requested water and ice, and a short supply of MREs arrived in Mississippi in the first week and a half after landfall.[132] Robert Latham, Executive Director of the Mississippi Emergency Management Agency (MEMA), estimated that Mississippi had to make do with even less – 10 percent to 20 percent of requests during the critical days after landfall.[133]

Positioning Supplies Prior to Landfall

Prior to landfall, state authorities realized that the massiveness of the storm required pre-landfall preparations. Tom McAllister, MEMA's Response and Recovery Director, said that MEMA requested that FEMA pre-position supplies at Meridian Naval Air Station in east-central Mississippi near the Alabama border.[134] Bob Fenton, a FEMA Region IX (covering the western United States) official, who served as Director of Operations for Mississippi during Katrina, upped the request.[135] Unfortunately, FEMA was unable to provide the requested supplies. In fact, McAllister, and apparently Fenton, were never able to discover how much had been pre-staged.[136] McAllister said the initial failure to pre-position adequate supplies left Mississippi "critically shorthanded."[137]

Post-landfall State and Federal Supply "Pipelines"

Both the federal and state governments supplied commodities. Because the FEMA logistical system fell short, the State of Florida and the National Guard maintained the "pipeline" until FEMA recovered.[138] Valuable help also came from Voluntary Organizations Active in Disaster (VOADs), such as the Red Cross and the Salvation Army.

Supplies from FEMA

Local authorities transferred requests they couldn't fulfill to MEMA,[139] which conveyed them to FEMA in cases when it couldn't help. MEMA and FEMA officials in Mississippi alike complained that requests disappeared as if into a "black hole."[140] As Carwile said, "During Hurricane Katrina we seldom had visibility of critical resources, i.e., body bags, refrigerated trucks for temporary morgues, etc., because FEMA does not have a reliable system for tracking commodities, equipment, and personnel."[141] As a result, local and state authorities were often "totally in the dark," causing friction.[142] The ice, food, and water that *were* delivered went to "staging areas" serving regions within the state,[143] and then to smaller Points of Distribution (PODs)[144] operated by the Mississippi National Guard.

The Florida "Pipeline"

Before entering the Gulf of Mexico, Hurricane Katrina had passed over south Florida, appearing to pose a risk to the Florida Panhandle, as Hurricane Ivan had done in 2004. Florida readied emergency-management assets, which were thus readily available when the storm finally struck further west.[145] Using the Stennis Space Center, located near the Gulf Coast and close to the Louisiana border, as a staging area, "Task Force Florida" brought food, water, and ice, as well as law-enforcement personnel, search-and-rescue assets, and other assistance.[146] The Florida teams "basically circumvented" FEMA's logistical system, as MEMA's McAllister said.[147]

Florida's contributions raised Mississippi to 40 to 50 percent of requested amounts, which proved crucial to the distribution of commodities.[148] "Robert [Latham] and I continue to rely on you all (FL),"[149] Carwile wrote in a September 3 e-mail to Craig Fugate, the Director of Florida's emergency-management agency. Florida's operation in Mississippi lasted for approximately six weeks, with most personnel and assets returned to Florida by October 1.[150]

The National Guard "Pipeline"

On Wednesday, August 31, the National Guard realized that not only were an insufficient number of MREs being delivered to south Mississippi, but massive debris fields were preventing individuals in need from reaching distribution points.[151] In response, Major General Harold Cross, the head of Mississippi's National Guard, requested that Northern Command (NORTHCOM), the federal military command responsible for North America, send MREs from military stocks.

Within seven or eight hours, aircraft were arriving at the Gulfport Combined Regional Training Center (CRTC), the National Guard airbase near the Gulfport airport, with MREs and water.[152] All vehicles leaving the CRTC were required to take along at least 10 cases of water and 10 cases of MREs, to be handed out whenever National Guardsmen encountered survivors.[153]

Starting August 30, the National Guard also delivered commodities by air after advance helicopters scouted for support needs, often by landing and talking with survivors.[154] Commissioner of Public Safety George Phillips, whose agency also had helicopters assessing the situation, recalled the desperation: "It was horrible … the minute people heard helicopters, … they came, people came running out, holding up signs SOS and need help and food and water."[155] If supply helicopters couldn't touch down, they would drop the supplies.[156] Approximately 1.2 million MREs and over 1 million gallons of water were distributed in this way, mostly in the September 1 through September 9 period.[157]

Difficulties Arise in the Distribution System

While all three of the supply "pipelines" were operational soon after landfall, the distribution system did not work smoothly. Michael Beeman, FEMA Division Director for Harrison County, the central county on Mississippi's Gulf Coast, noted that the first trucks with water and ice arrived without notice on August 30.[158] Often supplies would be discovered only when an official happened to spot a truck and approached the driver.[159] In an e-mail sent on September 4, a FEMA official in Mississippi informed Carwile and Fenton that a priority commodity shipment to Pearl River County, a county on the Louisiana border approximately 20 miles north of the coast, was a "no show," leaving lines of people waiting in vain for food and water.[160]

Many trucks arrived at the Meridian staging area mislabeled. Others bypassed staging areas and traveled directly to the coast, with no specific destination.[161] Stennis Space Center, in essence, became a large terminal where supply trucks were loaded and unloaded, but without

C-130 transport unloading
U.S. Air Force photo

expert truck management. This problem was also reflected in numerous reports of trucks standing idle at Stennis. As one official said, Stennis did not have "real terminal operations going on out there."[162]

An apparent shortage of trucks aggravated the problem.[163] Many truck drivers refused to leave staging areas without armed escorts.[164] Others, as McAllister explained, did not grasp the urgency of their tasks.[165]

McAllister estimated that much of the reported confusion at Stennis began ten days after landfall. He attributed this confusion to difficulties in determining the rate at which the PODs were distributing supplies. Immediately following landfall, the tremendous need for supplies ensured that the supplies were sent out of Stennis to the PODs right after they arrived. Beginning around day ten, more supplies were flowing into Stennis than were being distributed to the PODs; this resulted in a backlog of trucks. It took four to five days for officials at Stennis to balance the supply of commodities being delivered to Stennis with the demand for commodities at the PODs Stennis supported. By this point, the PODs were also becoming increasingly useful because road-clearing work was enabling more people to get to them.[166]

Difficulties with Fuel

Fuel shortages created another problem.[167] The fuel shortage had a number of causes, including damage to Mississippi's refining capacity; fuel suppliers no longer keeping a large quantity of fuel in stock due to price fluctuations; the loss of electricity crippling service stations' ability to pump fuel; and incompatibility between many tankers and vehicles requiring fuel.[168]

The emergency manager for Jones County, located approximately 70 miles north of the coast, noted that following Hurricane Katrina, "Fuel turned out to be as important as food, water, and ice."[169] The loss of electricity in Mississippi forced parts of the state's infrastructure to rely on fuel for power. Because of this, the fuel shortage had the potential to cause significant problems.[170] When the City of Gulfport, located on the central part of the coast, loses electricity, as it did following Katrina, its water wells rely on a back-up fuel supply. The generators contain enough diesel fuel to operate independent of the electric grid for 24 hours. If this back-up fuel runs out, Gulfport loses its water supply and depends on bottled water. Following Katrina, Gulfport came perilously close to running out of fuel.[171] Fuel shortages were also a problem for hospitals, many of which had no more than a three-day supply.[172]

While state and local officials were able to make do with what fuel they had and with what was brought into the state through FEMA, the shortage came perilously close to causing a crisis. Given the importance of fuel to first responders and private citizens, as well as its importance to infrastructure, emergency managers must place a higher priority on ensuring an adequate supply in the aftermath of a disaster.

Private-Sector Logistics

The companies that testified at the Committee's private-sector hearing all had in place deliberate plans for deploying and tracking material and personnel. From batteries, fuel, and generators to food and water, Wal-Mart, Starwood, IBM, and Mississippi Power knew what they would need, had those commodities either in place or at staging areas outside the storm's path, and had a plan for moving them in immediately after the storm.[173] These companies also had employees from unaffected regions at the ready, to assist in the region once the storm passed, and they responded proactively.[174]

Within seven days of Katrina's making landfall, Mississippi Power had 11,000 workers on the ground from 23 states and Canada.[175] They utilized mutual-assistance agreements, in place prior to the storm, to "borrow" employees from other utility companies.[176] IBM knew their services would be needed after the storm and deployed a Crisis Response Team to Baton Rouge to immediately begin working with government and non-governmental organizations to address critical needs.[177] Starwood also had a corporate-response team staged at a safe distance, but ready to move in once the storm had passed.[178]

Wal-Mart managed logistics effectively and delivered commodities quickly when responding to Katrina.[179] Wal-Mart has its own fleet of trucks, 100 distribution centers, and stores located all over the country.[180] Of the 100 distribution centers, eight have reserved "disaster merchandise" square footage, with approximately $4.7 million in "disaster merchandise" stockpiled for emergencies, including more than 250,000 gallons of drinking water.[181] Wal-Mart also has relationships with vendors that help with surge requests during times of emergency.[182] The company has a specific protocol for responding to disasters, and operates an emergency operations center year-round to coordinate crises around the country.[183]

With Hurricane Katrina, Wal-Mart used its expertise to move in supplies and operate effectively.[184] In the first three weeks after landfall, the company "delivered approximately 2,500 trailers of emergency supplies … including trucks of water and supplies that flowed into the New Orleans metropolitan area beginning on Saturday, September 3, for emergency service workers, shelters, and hospitals. A total of three temporary mobile pharmacies [were] provided to support communities, and a 16,000-square foot 'tent store' was erected to serve a community where the store had been all but demolished."[185] Based on past experience with major storms and hurricanes, Wal-Mart knew what supplies would be sought prior to the hurricane making landfall and what would be needed for the recovery phase after the storm.[186]

1 Written statement of Sec. Michael Chertoff, U.S. Department of Homeland Security, for the U.S. Senate, Committee on Homeland Security and Governmental Affairs, hearing on *Hurricane Katrina: The Homeland Security Department's Preparation and Response*, Feb. 15, 2006, p. 5.

2 Testimony of Michael Brown, former Director, Federal Emergency Management Agency (FEMA), before the U.S. House, Select Bipartisan Committee to Investigate the Preparation for and Response to Hurricane Katrina, hearing on *Hurricane Katrina: The Role of the Federal Emergency Management Agency*, Sept. 27, 2005.

3 In January 2005, FEMA leaders acknowledged in the internal review called the "MITRE Report" the weakness of FEMA logistics with comments such as "We are not good at tracking assets," "If the White House asks, 'Where are the water trucks?' I can't tell them" and "We've had 3 or 4 people ordering water for the same people." The MITRE Report was a report commissioned by FEMA Director Brown to review FEMA's "policies, plans, organization and systems to increase consistency, effectiveness, timeliness, and effectiveness in carrying out its core mission." Participants were members of FEMA's senior leadership. MITRE Corp., Draft Statement of Work, Planning Support for Emergency Preparedness and Response Directorate, U.S. Department of Homeland Security, Jan. 2005. Provided to Committee.

4 Committee staff interview of William Lokey, Federal Coordinating Officer for Hurricane Katrina in Louisiana, FEMA, conducted on Nov. 4, 2005, transcript p. 151.

5 Ken Burris, e-mail to Matt Jadacki, Sept. 18, 2004, 11:52 a.m. Provided to Committee; filed as Bates nos. DHS-FEMA-0079-0000120 through 0000121 ("I have broken the request from response and recovery into the following strategic areas and the following amounts. Let me know what you think and I will have it put in a formalized document.").

6 Michael Brown, memorandum to various FEMA officials, "Disaster Support Initiatives," Jan. 3, 2005. Provided to Committee; filed as Bates nos. DHS-FEMA-0079-0000093 through 0000095.

7 Ken Burris, e-mail to Matt Jadacki, Sept. 18, 2004, 11:52 a.m. Provided to Committee; filed as Bates nos. DHS-FEMA-0079-0000120 through 0000121. *See also*: FEMA, Under Sec. Disaster Support Initiatives #1, Reinvent Logistics Business Case (First DRAFT), Jan. 31, 2005. Provided to Committee; filed as Bates no. DHS-FEMA-0079-0000130 ("The staffing level of the DSIC, Logistics Centers and transportation support staff has remained at the same level as commissioned over seven years ago.").

8 FEMA, Under Sec. Disaster Support Initiatives #1, Reinvent Logistics Business Case (First DRAFT), Jan. 31, 2005. Provided to Committee; filed as Bates no. DHS-FEMA-0079-0000133.

9 FEMA, Under Sec. Disaster Support Initiatives #1, Reinvent Logistics Business Case (First DRAFT), Jan. 31, 2005. Provided to Committee; filed as Bates no. DHS-FEMA-0079-0000130.

10 Committee staff interview of Gary Moore, Director, Logistics Branch, FEMA, conducted on Dec. 9, 2005, transcript p. 37.

11 Theresa Gauger, e-mail to Lisa Williams, Aug. 27, 2005, 11:33 a.m. Provided to Committee; filed as Bates no. DHS-FEMA-0069-0000772. *See also*: Committee staff interview of Marie Sloan, Chief, Disaster Workforce Section, Response Division, FEMA, conducted on Mar. 1, 2006, transcript p. 31.

12 Kerry Young, e-mail to Jules Hurst, II, Aug. 28, 2005, 3:08 p.m. Provided to Committee; filed as Bates no. DHS-FEMA-0127-0011518.

13 Moore interview, Dec. 9, 2005, p. 35.

14 Moore interview, Dec. 9, 2005, pp. 35-37.

15 Moore interview, Dec. 9, 2005, p. 56.

16 Committee staff interview of Scott Wells, Deputy Federal Coordinating Officer for Hurricane Katrina in Louisiana, FEMA, conducted on Nov. 15, 2005, transcript p. 68.

17 FEMA, *DHS/FEMA Initial Response Hotwash: Hurricane Katrina in Louisiana*, Feb. 13, 2006, p. 10 [hereinafter *DHS/FEMA Initial Response Hotwash*, Feb. 13, 2006].

18 Moore interview, Dec. 9, 2005, pp. 59-61 ("I have no idea. I have no way to contact them. … The problem with the system is it's a bit like … the bombing of Pearl Harbor. …We don't know. We mark these things in when it goes through the gate. They pass it to another individual, who passes it to another individual, and they get distorted numbers by the time it get back to us. It is a nightmare trying to get the right information. … Not only is it with my shop, it's also then on the other side with the FCO's log people when they're trying to get accurate numbers on what they have, and they call, they pick the phone up and they got one person and they are also busy and they say, well, you've got ten, and they find out they've got 20, or it's even more ridiculous. Someone might tell them you've got 100 out there and you've got 500 out there.").

19 Committee staff interview of Michael Brown, former Director, FEMA, conducted on Feb. 23, 2006, transcript p. 167.

20 *Southeast Louisiana Catastrophic Hurricane Plan*, prepared by IEM, Inc. for Louisiana Office of Homeland Security (LOHSEP) and FEMA, Sept. 2005, Appendix 6 [hereinafter *Southeast Louisiana Catastrophic Hurricane Plan*, Sept. 2005].

21 Committee staff interview of Col. Jadwin Mayeaux, Louisiana Army National Guard (Ret.), Deputy Director, Homeland Security, LOHSEP, conducted on Nov. 29, 2005, transcript pp. 16-17; Committee staff interview of Lt. Col. William Doran, Louisiana Air National Guard, Chief, Operations Division, LOHSEP, Dec. 8, 2005, transcript pp. 163-164; Com-

mittee staff interview of Lt. Col. Jacques Thibodeaux, Joint Director, Military Support to Civilian Authorities, Louisiana National Guard, conducted on Dec. 6, 2005, transcript p. 1.

22 At 8:19 a.m. on Aug. 27, 2005 FEMA's Acting Deputy Director Patrick Rhode e-mailed the Acting Director of Response a request for a copy of the New Orleans Catastrophic Plan. *Source*: Patrick Rhode, e-mail to David Garratt, Aug. 27, 2005, 8:19 a.m. Provided to Committee; filed as Bates no. DHS-FEMA-0085-0003866. At 9:07 a.m. Lokey replied to Rhode, Brown, and others that "Copies are being made as we speak." *Source*: William Lokey, e-mail to Patrick Rhode and David Garratt, Aug. 27, 2005, 9:07 a.m. Provided to Committee; filed as Bates no. DHS-FEMA-0085-0003860. At 10:35 a.m. Sharon Blades e-mailed 25 FEMA personnel including William Lokey, Tony Robinson, Gary Jones, and Wayne Fairley an electronic version of the plan, and told them that copies were being printed. *Source*: Sharon Blades, e-mail to Michel Pawlowski, Aug. 27, 2005, 10:35 a.m. Provided to Committee; filed as Bates no. DHS-FEMA-0085-0003570. Later that afternoon Deputy Chief of Staff Brooks Altshuler e-mailed twice asking for additional copies for the front office. *Source*: Brooks Altshuler, e-mail to Sharon Blades, Aug. 27, 2005, 3:36 p.m. Provided to Committee; filed as Bates no. DHS-FEMA-0085-0003325. A few minutes later he received a reply that 50 copies were being printed. *Source*: Michel Powlowski, e-mail to Brooks Altshuler, Aug. 27, 2005, 3:42 p.m. Provided to Committee; filed as Bates no. DHS-FEMA-0085-0003570. At 8:37 p.m. that night Blades again e-mails Altshuler: "We have printed up more plans and they are on the mezz in Area A. We are also printing copies of the latest drafts and a preface explaining the planning process and the various documents because they all have not been finalized and assembled into one document. This will, we hope, avoid confusion." *Source*: Sharon Blades, e-mail to Brooks Altshuler, Aug. 27, 2005, 8:37 p.m. Provided to Committee; filed as Bates no. DHS-FEMA-0085-0003325.

23 *Southeast Louisiana Catastrophic Hurricane Plan*, Sept. 2005, Appendix 5, p. 10.

24 *Southeast Louisiana Catastrophic Hurricane Plan*, Sept. 2005, p. 24. The Southeast Louisiana Catastrophic Hurricane Plan (Hurricane Pam) includes charts to convert individual servings of commodities into truckloads. Example: one truckload of water = 4,750 gallons. *Southeast Louisiana Catastrophic Hurricane Plan*, Sept. 2005, Appendix 4, p. 8.

25 Committee staff interview of Wayne Fairley, Response Operations Branch Chief, Region VI, FEMA, conducted on Jan. 18, 2005, transcript pp. 18-19.

26 *Southeast Louisiana Catastrophic Hurricane Plan*, Sept. 2005, Appendix 4, Appendix 5, p. 10.

27 FEMA Video Teleconference, Aug. 27, 2005, pp. 16-17; FEMA, Commodities Status as of Aug. 29, 2005. Provided to Committee; filed as Bates no. DHS-FEMA-0127-0010528.

28 Committee staff interview of Ken Burris, former Acting Director of Operations, FEMA, conducted on Dec. 29, 2005, transcript p. 14; FEMA, Federal Operational Staging Area, Situation Report, Aug. 28, 2005, 7 p.m. Provided to Committee; filed as Bates nos. DHS-FEMA-0080-0000005 through 0000006; FEMA, FEMA LC's, PPS, TSS & Ice Storage, Commodity Status as of Aug. 26, 2005, 9:30 a.m. Provided to Committee; filed as Bates no. DHS-FEMA-0127-0014017.

29 FEMA, Commodities Status as of Aug. 29, 2005. Provided to Committee; filed as Bates no. DHS-FEMA-0127-0010528.

30 Fairley interview, Jan. 18, 2006, pp. 18-19.

31 Burris interview, Dec. 29, 2005, p. 14.

32 FEMA, FEMA LC's, PPS, TSS & Ice Storage, Commodity Status as of Aug. 26, 2005, 9:30 a.m. Provided to Committee; filed as Bates no. DHS-FEMA-0127-0014017; FEMA, Commodities Status as of Aug. 29, 2005. Provided to Committee; filed as Bates no. DHS-FEMA-0127-0010528.

33 Michael Brown, e-mail to William Carwile, Michael Lowder, Edward Buikema, and Gary Moore, Sept. 2, 2005, 8:35 a.m. Provided to Committee; filed as Bates no. DHS-FEMA-0083-0000329.

34 William Carwile, e-mail to Mary Lynne Miller, Michael Lowder, and Edward Buikema, Sept. 6, 2005, 4:47 p.m. Provided to Committee; filed as Bates no. DHS-FEMA-0028-0000742.

35 Written Statement of Robert Latham, Executive Director, Mississippi Emergency Management Agency (MEMA), for the U.S. House, Select Bipartisan Committee to Investigate the Preparation for and Response to Hurricane Katrina, hearing on *Hurricane Katrina: Preparedness and Response by the State of Mississippi*, Dec. 7, 2005.

36 Committee staff interview of Col. Terry Ebbert, U.S. Marine Corps (Ret.), Director, New Orleans Office of Homeland Security, City of New Orleans, Louisiana, conducted on Jan. 10, 2006, transcript p. 140.

37 Lokey interview, Nov. 4, 2005, p. 150.

38 *DHS/FEMA Initial Response Hotwash*, Feb. 13, 2006, p. 16.

39 Committee staff interview of Col. Al Jones, U.S. Army, Senior Army Advisor, Georgia Army National Guard, conducted on Mar. 2, 2006, transcript p. 31.

40 Committee staff interview of Michael Brown, former Director, FEMA, conducted on Jan. 23, 2006, transcript p. 158 ("Our logistics just sucked. It was awful."); Committee staff interview of William Lokey, Federal Coordinating Officer for Hurricane Katrina in Louisiana, FEMA, conducted on Jan. 20, 2005, transcript p. 71.

41 Brown interview, Jan. 23, 2006, p. 185.

42 Patrick Rhode, e-mail to Michael Lowder, Sept. 1, 2005, 8:33 a.m. Provided to Committee; filed as Bates no. DHS 0000927. The mission assignment was later cut to 500 million on Sept. 7.

43 Lokey interview, Jan. 20, 2006, p. 134. *See also*: Committee staff interview of Col. Roberta Woods, U.S. Army, Chief of Plans and Operations Division, Logistics Directorate, U.S. Northern Command, U.S. Department of Defense, conducted on Dec. 7, 2005, transcript pp. 82-83 (the $1 billion was an estimate).

44 Testimony of Paul McHale, Assistant Secretary of Defense for Homeland Defense, U.S. Department of Defense, before the U.S. Senate, Committee on Homeland Security and Governmental Affairs, hearing on *Hurricane Katrina: The Defense Department's Role in the Response*, Feb. 9, 2006.

45 Lokey interview, Jan. 20, 2005, p. 137 ("I'm not sure they ever took over that. . . . This, to me, was a broad, encompassing statement to cover any eventuality, and the military may have assisted in moving ice and water, but I'm not aware of that. As far as I'm concerned, all the requests came through my logistics train to our people supporting this out of Camp Beauregard."). Committee staff interview of Brig. Gen. Matthew Broderick, U.S. Marine Corps (Ret.), former Director, Homeland Security Operations Center, U.S. Department of Homeland Security, conducted on Jan. 19, 2006, transcript p. 64 ("Q: Do you know whether DOD actually did end up taking over the procurement, transportation, and distribution of ice, water, food, fuel, and medical supplies? A: They did not. They augmented and supplemented … no, not the full logistical.").

46 FEMA, Hurricane Katrina billing spreadsheet. Provided to Committee.

47 Department of the Army, "1604DR-MS-DOD-19 – Uses of Funds." Provided to Committee (indicating $51,122,526.05 designated for "Lunch meals w/ drinks; meals tailored operational; commercial meals; meals individual; DLA MRSs; freight charges"); FEMA, Hurricane Katrina billing spreadsheet. Provided to Committee (indicating $2,981,123.90 expended for "ship lease, port /canal charges, & prop fuel for Algol, Altair, Bellatrix, Pollux, Pillilaau"; $1,084,587.24 for Diesel fuel; $39.56 for "unleaded gasoline").

48 Sec. Michael Chertoff, All Things Considered, NPR, "Michael Chertoff discussed US aid effort being criticized in New Orleans," Sept. 1, 2005, 8 a.m.

49 Wells interview, Nov. 15, 2005, p. 116.

50 Committee staff interview of Phil Parr, Federal Coordinating Officer, Region I, FEMA, conducted on Nov. 16, 2005, transcript p. 28.

51 Committee staff interview of Brig. Gen. Brod Veillon, Assistant Adjutant General – Air, Louisiana National Guard, conducted on Nov. 29, 2005, transcript pp. 65-66; Lokey interview, Jan. 20, 2006, pp. 116-117.

52 Committee staff interview of Terry Vallarautto, Interoperability Coordinator, LOHSEP, conducted on Dec. 1, 2006, transcript pp. 39-40; Committee staff interview of Matt Farlow, Information Technology Division Chief, LOHSEP, conducted on Dec. 1, 2005, transcript p. 53;

53 Vallarautto interview, Dec. 1, 2005, pp. 39-40; Farlow interview, Dec. 1, 2005, p. 53.

54 Vallarautto interview, Dec. 1, 2005, p. 42.

55 Committee staff interview of William Smith, Chief Technology Officer, BellSouth Corp., conducted on Jan. 25, 2006 (untranscribed).

56 Farlow interview, Dec. 1, 2005, p. 56.

57 Wells interview, Nov. 11, 2004, pp. 205-206.

58 Testimony of Scott Wells, Deputy Federal Coordinating Officer for Hurricane Katrina in Louisiana, FEMA, before the U.S. Senate, Committee on Homeland Security and Governmental Affairs, hearing on *Hurricane Katrina: Perspectives of FEMA's Operations Professionals*, Dec. 8, 2005.

59 Wells, Senate Committee hearing, Dec. 8, 2005.

60 Lokey interview, Nov. 4, 2005, p. 128.

61 Committee staff interview of Lucy Brooke, Emergency Management Program Specialist, FEMA, conducted on Jan. 24, 2006, transcript p. 16.

62 Brooke interview, Jan. 24, 2005, p. 53.

63 Committee staff interview of Col. Jeff Smith, Louisiana National Guard (Ret.), Acting Deputy Director, Emergency Management, LOHSEP, conducted on Jan. 13, 2006, transcript pp. 108-113.

64 Brooke interview, Jan. 24, 2005, p. 51; *DHS/FEMA Initial Response Hotwash*, Feb. 13, 2006, p. 32 ("It is estimated that the ERT had 25% of the staff that were needed." "DHS/FEMA needs to have 24/7 staffing capability for each section. The agency needs to be willing and able to provide heavy staffing at the start of a disaster, and establish minimum staffing requirements based on responsibilities of the sections. Failure to do so causes fatigue, mistakes and errors in judgments in the units.").

65 Scott Wells, e-mail to Michael Hall, Sept. 9, 2005, 5:42 p.m. Provided to Committee; filed as Bates no. DHS-FEMA-0040-0003030.

66 *DHS/FEMA Initial Response Hotwash*, Feb. 13, 2006, p. 38

67 *DHS/FEMA Initial Response Hotwash*, Feb. 13, 2006, p. 38

68 Louisiana Office of Homeland Security and Emergency Preparedness, *Emergency Operations Plan*, Apr. 2005, p. 10 [hereinafter *Louisiana Emergency Operations Plan*]; Col. Smith interview, Jan. 13, 2006, p. 32.

69 Brooke interview, Jan. 24, 2005, p. 35.

70 Committee staff interview of Joseph Donchess, Executive Director, Louisiana Nursing Home Service Corporation, conducted on Jan. 9, 2006, transcript pp. 6, 12-13.

71 Donchess interview, Jan. 9, 2006, pp. 35-38.

72 Donchess interview, Jan. 9, 2006, p. 36.

73 Donchess interview, Jan. 9, 2006, p. 38.

74 Testimony of Lt. Col. Keith LaCaze, Assistant Administrator, Law Enforcement Division, Louisiana Department of Wildlife and Fisheries, before the U.S. Senate, Committee on Homeland Security and Governmental Affairs, hearing on *Hurricane Katrina: Urban Search and Rescue in a Catastrophe*, Jan. 30, 2006.

75 Col. Smith interview, Jan. 13, 2006, pp. 108-113.

76 EMAC was established by Congress through Joint Resolution in 1996 (P.L 104-321), 110 Stat. § 3877.

77 For information on EMAC, see http://www.emacweb.org.

78 California joined on Sept. 21, 2005, after Hurricane Katrina made landfall. California, Office of the Governor, "Governor Schwarzenegger Signs Emergency Management Compact Legislation," press release, Sept. 13, 2005. Provided to Committee.

79 P.L. 104-321 (Oct. 19, 1996).

80 Once a state requests EMAC support, a team is deployed to the disaster area and works with the state to determine requirements and match those needs to available resources. *Source*: National Emergency Management Association (NEMA), "How does EMAC work?" http://www.emacweb.org. Accessed on Apr. 15, 2006. EMAC representatives are located within the NRCC as well, to help facilitate requests and ensure there is no duplication of effort at the federal level. *Source*: Committee staff interview of Richard Gray, Team Leader, Information and Assessment Team and Team Leader, National Response Coordination Center, FEMA, conducted on Jan. 20, 2006, transcript pp. 31-33.

81 Louisiana National Guard, Task Force Pelican, "Hurricane Katrina: Overview of Significant Events," Nov. 28, 2005, pp. 5-6. Provided to Committee.

82 Committee staff interview of Maj. Gen. Bennett Landreneau, Adjutant General, Louisiana, conducted on Jan. 11, 2006. transcript pp. 63-64.

83 Written Statement of William Carwile, Federal Coordinating Officer for Hurricane Katrina in Mississippi, for the U.S. Senate, Committee on Homeland Security and Governmental Affairs, hearing on H*urricane Katrina: Perspectives of FEMA's Operations Professionals*, Dec. 8, 2005, p. 5.

84 Testimony of Gov. Haley Barbour, Mississippi, before the U.S. Senate, Committee on Homeland Security and Governmental Affairs, hearing on *Hurricane Katrina: The Role of the Governors in Managing the Catastrophe*, Feb. 2, 2006.

85 Louisiana National Guard, Task Force Pelican, "Hurricane Katrina: Overview of Significant Events," Nov. 28, 2005, pp. 5-6. Provided to Committee.

86 *Southeast Louisiana Catastrophic Hurricane Plan,* prepared by IEM, Inc. for the LOHSEP and FEMA, Sept. 2005, Transportation, Staging and Distribution of Critical Resources: Draft Functional Plan, p. 1.

87 Wells interview, Nov. 15, 2005, pp. 88-89; Fairley interview, Jan. 18, 2006, pp. 19-20.

88 To help push these commodities closer to the disaster area, FEMA and the Louisiana Office of Homeland Security and Emergency Preparedness worked together at the Emergency Operations Center in Baton Rouge before landfall to bring more commodities to the staging area and, therefore, into the "pipeline." *Source*: Col. Mayeaux interview, Nov. 29, 2005, pp. 20-21, 64-65 (acknowledging that Pineville was FEMA's main operational staging area for commodities). Both before and after landfall, FEMA sent commodities from Pineville to Regional Staging Areas in Hammond (a city 60 miles northwest of New Orleans) and Harrahan (a suburb just to the west of New Orleans). *Source*: Col. Mayeaux interview, Nov. 29, 2005, pp. 64-65. FEMA also drew on supplies stockpiled at Barksdale Air Force Base in northwest Louisiana and elsewhere in the country. *Source*: Col. Mayeaux interview, Nov. 29, 2005, pp. 21, 64-65, 98.

89 *Southeast Louisiana Catastrophic Hurricane Plan,* prepared by IEM, Inc. for LOHSEP and FEMA, Sept. 2005, Transportation, Staging and Distribution of Critical Resources: Draft Functional Plan, p. 1.

90 Col. Mayeaux interview, Nov. 29, 2005, pp. 25-26; Lt. Col. Doran interview, Dec. 8, 2005, p. 157 ("We thought about … we've got to push commodities down regardless, because we know people are going to need food and water. And we weren't – you know, we didn't wait for a request for that. We said, we know we're going to need to move food and water down to the area.").

91 Col. Mayeaux interview, Nov. 29, 2005, pp. 20-21.

92 Col. Mayeaux interview, Nov. 29, 2005, pp. 56-57. *See also*: Col. Mayeaux interview, Nov. 29, 2005, pp. 68-69 ("MR. ADELBERG: It was areas that you weren't staffing. It was just places where people were asking for commodities to be supplied? COL MAYEAUX: Yes, sir. MR. ADELBERG: And for one reason or another, the word wasn't getting to you that they needed more than you were able to provide? COL MAYEAUX: That is correct, more than I could provide. I didn't know there were people there.").

93 Col. Mayeaux interview, Nov. 29, 2005, pp. 34-35.

94 Col. Mayeaux interview, Nov. 29, 2005, pp. 34-35.

95 Committee staff interview Col. Steven Dabadie, former Chief of Staff, Louisiana National Guard, conducted on Jan. 12, 2006, transcript pp. 138-39 ("We were simply out of capabilities and resources because we got overwhelmed with the flood, and we needed to get those EMAC forces in. For example, you know, commodity distribution almost took an entire brigade. They struck a brigade out of – Pennsylvania National Guard, they were the ones doing the commodity distribution when they came in.").

96 The Department of Homeland Security recommended this year that FEMA "establish contracts for priority resources prior to the onset of disasters." *Source*: *DHS/FEMA Initial Response Hotwash*, Feb. 13, 2006, pp. 10-11 (stating that the "lack of pre-negotiated contracts for large recurring services impacted the overall response"). The National Guard acknowledged in its After Action Report that "last minute scrambling to locate & contract required equipment and services to support commodity distribution (e.g., forklifts, Port-a-Lets, tents, meal contractors, etc.) created delays in supporting Parish requests." *Source*: Louisiana National Guard, After Action Report, Task Force Griffin, Commodities Distribution, Jan. 4, 2006 (recommending that LOHSEP, FEMA, and local authorities execute such contracts in advance of future storms). Nevertheless, LOHSEP's Col. Mayeaux claimed that the state did not run out of bulk commodities. *Source*: Col. Mayeaux interview, Nov. 29, 2005, p. 64.

97 Testimony of Mayor C. Ray Nagin, City of New Orleans, LA, before the U.S. Senate, Committee on Homeland Security and Governmental Affairs, hearing on *Hurricane Katrina: Managing the Crisis and Evacuating New Orleans*, Feb. 1, 2006.

98 Louisiana National Guard, After Action Report, Task Force Griffin, Commodities Distribution, Jan. 4, 2006; Col. Mayeaux interview, Nov. 29, 2005, pp. 34-35.

99 Lt. Col. Doran interview, Dec. 8, 2005, pp. 158-59.

100 Col. Mayeaux interview, Nov. 29, 2005, pp. 33-34.

101 While it is difficult to quantify the problem, there is anecdotal evidence of people clamoring for food and water wherever they could find authorities who might be able to help. For example, Louisiana Department of Wildlife & Fisheries Lt. Col. Keith LaCaze had difficulty establishing a medical evacuation point on Wednesday morning because "we had a lot of evacuees who were assembling there and asking for water and food, which was interfering with the medical staff who were trying to attend to the patients on the ground." Lt. Col. Keith LaCaze, Activity Report on Hurricane Katrina, pp. 3-4.

102 Committee staff interview of Brig. Gen. Gary Jones, Assistant Joint Forces Commander, Louisiana Army National Guard, conducted on Dec. 7, 2005, transcript p. 90.

103 Testimony of Marty J. Bahamonde, Director, External Affairs, Region I, FEMA, before the U.S. Senate, Committee on Homeland Security and Governmental Affairs, hearing on *Hurricane Katrina in New Orleans: A Flooded City, A Chaotic Response*, Oct. 20, 2005.

104 Committee staff interview of Lt. Col. Jacques Thibodeaux, Joint Director of Military Support to Civilian Authorities and Branch Chief, Louisiana National Guard, conducted on Jan. 12, 2006, transcript p. 131.

105 Brig. Brig. Gen. Jones interview, Dec. 7, 2005, p. 91; Committee staff interview of Lonnie Swain, Assistant Superintendent, New Orleans Police Department, LA, conducted on Nov. 9, 2005, transcript p. 63.

106 Brig. Gen. Jones interview, Dec. 7, 2005, pp. 89-91, 162-163.

107 Committee staff interview of Chris Villar, Owner, Go-Cans, LLC, conducted on Jan. 26, 2006 (untranscribed).

108 Swain interview, Nov. 9, 2005, p. 66. When NOPD Deputy Chief Lonnie Swain arrived at the Superdome on Sunday, he immediately called the city's Office of Emergency Preparedness and requested food and water, which Deputy Chief Swain said the Louisiana National Guard ultimately delivered before landfall. *Source*: Swain interview, Nov. 9, 2005, pp. 44-47. The National Guard had pre-positioned stock to be able to provide "some limited support to some special needs people. But the bulk of what [the National Guard] had there was for our troops. *Source*: Brig. Gen. Jones interview, Dec. 7, 2005, pp. 86-87. Gen. Jones quickly put out a call for MREs and found enough from nearby National Guard contingency stocks to supply people with two servings a day until Tuesday afternoon. *Source*: Swain interview, Nov. 9, 2005, p. 66. LANG Col. Glenn Curtis also ordered trucks to move food and water from Camp Beauregard to the Superdome on Sunday, Aug. 28, 2005. *Source*: Committee staff interview of Col. Glenn Curtis, Chief of Staff, Louisiana National Guard, conducted on Dec. 6, 2005, transcript pp. 129-130. As the Louisiana National Guard's Deputy Commander for Katrina, Col. Glenn Curtis, said: "Once it became a shelter of last resort we just knew we would need food and water there." *Source*: Col. Curtis interview, Dec. 6, 2005, p. 134.

109 Louisiana National Guard officials stated that their requests for additional food and water before landfall were met. Committee staff interview of Lt. Col. Douglas Mouton, Commander, 225th Engineering Group, Louisiana Army National Guard, conducted on Dec. 1, 2005, transcript pp. 69-74.

110 NOPD Deputy Chief Lonnie Swain testified that officials were able to feed the population at the Superdome twice a day, but that the flow of food and water was at times "touch and go" and resulted in periodic frustration. Swain interview, Nov. 9, 2005, pp. 65-68.

111 Brig. Gen. Jones interview, Dec. 7, 2005, pp. 86-87 (The National Guard had pre-positioned stock to be able to provide "some limited support to some special needs people. But the bulk of what [the National Guard] had there was for our troops.").

112 Committee staff interview of Marty Bahamonde, Director, External Affairs, Region I, FEMA, conducted on Oct. 7, 2005, transcript p. 191 ("There was not enough food in the Superdome, there was not enough water in the Superdome to properly provide meals and water for the continued growing number of people that were constantly coming to the Superdome. It never really stopped. They kept coming. Estimates now were up to 25,000, 30,000 people at the Superdome.").

113 Bahamonde interview, Oct. 7, 2005, p. 191.

114 Although Bahamonde recalled being "once again consumed with finding food" on Wednesday, it does not appear that food or water ever ran out at the Superdome. *Source*: Bahamonde interview, Oct. 7, 2005, p. 195; Brig. Gen. Jones interview, Dec. 7, 2005, p. 88. The fact that an MRE is designed to feed a person for up to two days helped: "You can actually survive for two days on one MRE. So had it gotten really desperate, we would have come up with a plan to bust them open and split them up." *Source*: Brig. Gen. Jones interview, Dec. 7, 2005, p. 87. *See also*: Col. Curtis interview, Dec. 6, 2005, pp. 127-28; Committee staff interview of Lt. Col. William Doran, Chief, Operations Division, LOHSEP, conducted on Dec. 2, 2005, transcript p. 132.

115 Swain interview, Nov. 9, 2005, p. 65 ("We never received flashlights or batteries. We never received generators. Period.").

116 Mayor C. Ray Nagin, City of New Orleans, LA, "Post-Hurricane Katrina Critical Needs Assessment," Aug. 29, 2005; Mayor Nagin, Senate Committee hearing, Feb. 1, 2006.

117 Swain interview, Nov. 9, 2005, p. 93 ("I don't think they were able to come in – well, on Monday, they would have been able to; yes. Tuesday morning is when the water came in. After that, supply trucks were not able to drive into the Dome. They were driven up on to the up ramp or down ramp of the interstate, the I-10, and from there I think they were unloaded or whatever on to, I guess, the high-water vehicles, and supplies were brought in.").

118 Lokey interview, Jan. 20, 2006, p. 116.

119 Mayor C. Ray Nagin, City of New Orleans, LA, "Post-Hurricane Katrina Critical Needs Assessment," Aug. 29, 2005, p. 1.

120 Penya Moses-Fields, letter to The Honorable Susan M. Collins and The Honorable Joseph I. Lieberman, Jan. 30, 2006, "Attachment A: Timeline of Mayor Nagin's Activities, Aug. 26, 2005 – Sept. 6, 2005." Timeline entries include: Wed., Aug. 31 – "Convention Center – numbers growing, no food or water Still no food and water"; Thurs., Sept. 1 – "Center – numbers growing, no food or water."

121 Mayor Nagin, Senate Committee hearing, Feb. 1, 2006.

122 Mayor Nagin, Senate Committee hearing, Feb. 1, 2006.

123 Col. Ebbert interview, Jan. 10, 2006, p. 131.

124 Col. Ebbert interview, Jan. 10, 2006, p. 139.

125 FEMA, Action Request Form, Sept. 2, 2005. Provided to Committee.

126 Lokey interview, Jan. 20, 2006, p. 116 ("Q: When did you become aware of any problems or issues at the convention center? A: Sometime Tuesday or Wednesday, when we got word from Jeff Smith that people were showing up at the convention center. The first thing we heard, there were 5,000 people there. Then we heard there were 25,000 people there. … But early in the game, we heard that people were congregating there, too, mainly probably late Tuesday, because Tuesday was when the flooding really--when people started leaving their homes and wading and swimming and everything toward the Dome and the convention center.").

127 Lokey interview, Jan. 20, 2006, pp. 116-117:

Mainly what I did was respond to the State's request to get food and water to them, because again, the States and the locals did not preplan or preposition anything, and so there was obviously a problem there. And I remember sending, and again, I don't know how many, but trucks of food and water. And after they were dispatched from Camp Beauregard, I remember hearing all the things about loss of control and law and order and things like that and I got worried about my truck drivers driving into a situation like that and getting mobbed. Then I heard that the local officials, whoever that is, the National Guard was holding the trucks and were going to go in the next morning, whatever morning that was, probably Wednesday or Thursday morning, when they went in with security to establish order. And they would have to speak to that, exactly what they did, but again, we got a lot of the rumors about the law and order breakdown and what not. But I do remember that my trucks didn't go down there without appropriate protection when they went in on the morning, so I'm guessing that might have been Thursday morning with just all the things that were going on, but I do not know for sure.

Lokey interview, Jan. 20, 2006, pp. 116-117.

128 Lokey interview, Jan. 20, 2006, pp. 117-118 ("Well, again, some of our medical assets may have been sent [to the Convention Center], but again, we respond to requests from the State as a result of requests from the local governments, and other than getting the people out of there and getting food into them, I don't have a recollection of another specific request from Jeff Smith at the time relative specific to the [Convention Center], other than the evacuation and the life-sustaining food and water.").

129 Brig. Gen. Broderick interview, Jan. 19, 2006, pp. 171-172.

130 Louisiana National Guard, Timeline of Significant Events for Hurricane Katrina, Dec. 7, 2005. Provided to Com-

mittee. The National Guard did not move to the Convention Center until noon on Friday. When the Guard did arrive at the Convention Center on Friday, they saw people barbecuing food outside the Convention Center. *Source*: Lt. Col. Thibodeaux interview, Jan. 12, 2006, pp. 122-123, 126-127. It is not clear from the record where the people at the Convention Center obtained the means to grill food outside, but the Guard who approached the Convention Center for the first time on Friday correctly saw the outdoor cooking as a sign that their missions to establish law and order and to provide relief there would be executed without incident. *Source*: Lt. Col. Thibodeaux interview, Jan. 12, 2006, pp. 126-127 ("It was an extremely heart moving thing to see these people that needed help come to you and say 'thanks, I appreciate you guys are here.'"); Brig. Gen. Jones interview, Dec. 7, 2005, pp. 194-195 ("In fact, quite the contrary to what we thought, or what our intelligence had told us the situation was, and what the Mayor and some of the other folks told us, the people actually cheered us, you know, as we came in. And we had absolutely no problem getting control of the Convention Center, setting up the food distribution point. They were very orderly."). In contrast to the optimism engendered from seeing a working barbecue outside the Convention Center, LANG officials became pessimistic when they first entered the structure because they saw what seemed to be about 100 people lying dead all over the floor of the building. But when those officials returned to the inside of the structure, hours after they had provided food, water, and medical relief to the crowd, not one of the people they had presumed to be dead were there: they were never dead; they were asleep, passed out from exhaustion, dehydration and malnourishment. This turn of events came as a great relief to the LANG officials at the Convention Center. *Source*: Lt. Col. Thibodeaux interview, Jan. 12, 2006, pp. 159-60. Within five hours of their noon arrival, the Guard had brought in food and drink for the people there. *Source*: Brig. Gen. Veillon interview, Nov. 9, 2005, pp. 66-67 ("The crowd did that in a very orderly manner. We had no problems. We fed them. We gave them all they wanted and told them that we would be shortly evacuating them."); Lt. Col. Thibodeaux interview, Jan. 12, 2006, pp. 127, 141-142 ("We drove down in there and immediately began to interact with the crowd. The questions that – the comments they made to us is 'we need help.' 'We need food, water. How are we going to get out of here. Please just help us. What is going on. Thank you. Thank you so much for coming here.'"). Troops patrolled throughout the night, encouraging people to eat as much as they wanted and informing them of the following day's evacuation. *Source*: Lt. Col. Thibodeaux interview, Jan. 12, 2006, p. 157.

131 While there is a consensus that food and water are vital, lifesaving commodities, some dispute exists as to whether ice belongs in that same category.

132 Written Statement of Carwile, Senate Committee hearing, Dec. 8, 2005, p. 6.

133 Written Statement of Latham, House Select Committee hearing, Dec. 7, 2005, p. 3.

134 Committee staff interview of Tom McAllister, Director of Response and Recovery, MEMA, conducted on Jan. 25, 2006, transcript pp. 5-7.

135 McAllister interview, Jan. 25, 2006, pp. 5-7.

136 In an interview with Committee staff, McAllister explained: "I never saw them. And the problem we had on my side as far as stateside, I never had visibility of those. I never knew how many we actually had. And I kept trying to find out, you know, how many do we have staged? How much is there? … I never got an answer of any kind. … It was in the pipeline, it's en route or it's – you know, it was those type of answers we were getting out of Nashville in logistics. I mean, Bob [Fenton] was even frustrated … because he couldn't get any visibility on them either. You know, he couldn't – he wanted to be able to tell me I've got 250 ice sitting in Meridian. Well, we never did know that. We never knew what was actually there at Meridian, or I didn't." McAllister interview, Jan. 25, 2006, pp. 7-8.

137 McAllister interview, Jan. 25, 2006, pp. 8-9.

138 Committee staff interview of Mike Beeman, Director, National Preparedness Division, Region II, FEMA, conducted on Jan. 20, 2006, transcript p. 168.

139 McAllister interview, Jan. 25, 2006, pp. 32-34.

140 McAllister interview, Jan. 25, 2006, pp. 27-30.

141 William L. Carwile III, White Paper, "The Response and Initial Recovery to Hurricane Katrina in Mississippi: A Field Perspective," Feb. 22, 2006, p. 25. Provided to Committee.

142 McAllister interview, Jan. 25, 2006, pp. 27-30.

143 U.S. Department of Homeland Security, *National Incident Management System*, Mar. 1, 2004, p. 136.

144 In Harrison County, the county operated an LSA within the county that would receive supplies from Stennis and then distribute them to the PODs. Beeman interview, Jan. 20, 2006, pp. 74-76.

145 Florida had prepositioned supplies off of I-10 near Jacksonville, Florida and was prepared to move into Mississippi to respond to the storm's impact. Committee staff interview of Mike DeLorenzo, Bureau Chief, Bureau of Preparedness and Response, Florida Division of Emergency Management, conducted on Feb. 9, 2006 (untranscribed).

146 DeLorenzo interview, Feb. 9, 2006.

147 McAllister interview, Jan. 25, 2006, pp. 8-9.

148 McAllister interview, Jan. 25, 2006, pp. 32-34.

149 William Carwile, e-mail to Craig Fugate and others, Sept. 3, 2005, 3:21 p.m. Provided to Committee; filed as Bates no. DHS 0003582.

150 DeLorenzo interview, Feb. 9, 2006.

151 In an interview with Committee staff, Lieutenant Colonel Lee Smithson, Director of Military Support for the Mississippi Army National Guard, stated that: "Getting on into the 31st of Aug., 1st of Sept. we were getting some commodities in and we realized really on the 31st of Aug. that there was no way given what we thought the number of people who did not evacuate was, which my rough estimates was about 100,000 people along. . . the six coastal counties. . . . we knew that there was no way that with central distribution points, with the debris fields that were out there, that people could come in and get water, ice and MREs." Committee staff interview of Lt. Col. Lee Smithson, Director of Military Support, Mississippi Army National Guard, conducted on Jan. 25, 2006, transcript pp. 43-45.

152 Committee staff interview of Maj. Gen. Harold A. Cross, Adjutant General, Mississippi Military Department, conducted on Jan. 26, 2006, transcript pp. 21-22, 28.

153 Mississippi National Guard, Joint Force Headquarters, Adjutant General's Office, "Hurricane Katrina Narrative," Oct. 20, 2005, p. 2.

154 Mississippi National Guard, Joint Force Headquarters, Adjutant General's Office, "Hurricane Katrina Narrative," Oct. 20, 2005, p. 3.

155 Committee staff interview of George Phillips, Commissioner, Mississippi Department of Public Safety, conducted on Jan. 26, 2006, transcript p. 41.

156 Lt. Col. Smithson explained this process during an interview with Committee staff: "[W]e would send our small helicopters out and they would find pockets of displaced Americans or whatever you want to call them, and it was really easy to find them because they'd hear the helicopters coming and they'd make signs and hold them up. So they would radio back and that's where we would go in and drop things." Lt. Col. Smithson interview, Jan. 25, 2006, p. 44.

157 Mississippi National Guard, Joint Force Headquarters, Adjutant General's Office, "Hurricane Katrina Narrative," Oct. 20, 2005, p. 3.

158 Beeman interview, Jan. 20, 2006, p. 61.

159 Mike Beeman related the following anecdote in an interview with Committee staff:

> There were times when the trucks would just pull off the highway. We'd find them parked along [U.S.] 49. …One of the requirements for the sheriff's department and the local police departments was whenever they saw a diesel truck sitting somewhere that might be idling the engine and all that, the truck driver was asleep, go over and find out who he was, what he had in the back end, because we many times [we] knew items were sent to us, but we didn't know where they were because the system, once [Stennis] sent it out, we had no idea what was sent. … We knew that we were expecting ice, water, and food, but if something else were sent, we wouldn't know it, because again, we had no notification process and information process that it was coming to us. … We'd finally find maybe five or six truckloads of water or ice that were sitting off the roadway in some apron at a supermarket or whatever and we'd just send them on down to this site, get them back on track. Some of them sat sometimes two or three days. I found 25 trucks one day, all with blue tarps on them, that were sitting down at the Wal-Mart [on U.S. 49]. … But they were sitting there. Somebody told me all these trucks were down there, so I drove down there and started knocking on the truckers' doors and I said, 'What do you have in the back end?' And they said, 'Tarps.' And I said, 'Tarps?' Well, ultimately it turned out to be blue roof, the stretch material, but they were just sitting, and sitting there for three or four days. They were just sitting there, waiting for somebody to tell them where to go with the loads of blue tarp, blue stretch material. … I have no idea where they came from. … They just appeared.

Beeman interview, Jan. 20, 2006, pp. 80-82.

160 James Russo, e-mail to William Carwile and Robert Fenton, Sept. 4, 2005, 10:01 a.m. Provided to Committee; filed as Bates no. DHS-FEMA-0094-0002227.

161 Lt. Col. Smithson interview, Jan. 25, 2006, pp. 55-57.

162 He described management of the trucks as amounting to: "Guys in golf carts going up and waking up a truck driver saying, what have you got in the truck, that kind of thing. And then, okay, take this truck and go over two roads because there's just – I mean, there were literally – the road network out at the ammunition plant looks like this calendar, you know, you've got a lot of east-west, north-south roads that just go nowhere, they're just a road with trees on either side of them. So there were at times hundreds of trucks just parked out there. And, you know, that took them a while to get it under control." Lt. Col. Smithson interview, Jan. 25, 2006, pp. 103-104.

163 McAllister interview, Jan. 25, 2006, p. 34.

164 Lt. Col. Smithson interview, Jan. 25, 2006, pp. 105-106. This was confirmed in an interview with officers of the Gulfport Police Department. Committee staff interview of Cmdr. Alan Weatherford, Gulfport Police Department, MS, conducted on Dec. 8, 2005, transcript p. 90.

165 As he explained during an interview with Committee staff: "Truck drivers are not emergency [personnel]. They may load up and go to the house for two days. They may park it. They're going to take their days off. And that load that you loaded out on Friday, you may not see it until Tuesday. And that caused us frustrations, you know. Some days we had big loads – you know, you can always count on Monday, Tuesday and Wednesday you had a bunch of trucks because everybody that loaded out at the end of the week can take a couple days off. Now, Monday, they're ready to roll." McAllister interview, Jan. 25, 2006, pp. 34-35.

166 McAllister interview, Jan. 25, 2006, pp. 40-45.

167 Latham testified before the House that, "The fuel issue was something that, to be honest with you, just caught us out of left field." Testimony of Robert Latham, Executive Director, MEMA, before the U.S. House, Select Bipartisan Committee to Investigate the Preparation for and Response to Hurricane Katrina, hearing on *Hurricane Katrina: Preparedness and Response by the State of Mississippi*, Dec. 7, 2005.

168 McAllister interview, Jan. 25, 2006, pp. 75-77.

169 Don McKinnon, e-mail to James McKay, Senate Committee staff member, Feb. 16, 2006, 5:53 p.m.

170 These problems were often made worse because of the apparent difficulties with FEMA even acquiring generators. In a questionnaire submitted for an after action report, Gulfport Public Works Director Kris Riemann wrote that: "FEMA support for items such as generators often took 2-4 days to get. In many cases we already had a generator from another source by the time FEMA went through their long process. I would think there would be a faster way to get generators in place especially for the water and sewer system when every day counts so much to our residents." Kris Riemann, Director of Public Works, City of Gulfport, MS, "Hurricane Katrina Post-Incident Survey," sent to Crystal Johnson, Nov. 3, 2005.

171 Committee staff interview of Kris Riemann, Director of Public Works, City of Gulfport, MS, conducted on Dec. 7, 2005, transcript pp. 60-62.

172 Committee staff interview of Jim Craig, Director of Health Protection, Mississippi Department of Health, conducted on Jan. 25, 2006, transcript p. 44.

173 Written Statement of Jason Jackson, Director of Business Continuity, Global Security Division, Wal-Mart Stores, Inc. for the U.S. Senate, Committee on Homeland Security and Governmental Affairs, hearing on *Hurricane Katrina: What Can Government Learn from the Private Sector's Response?*, Nov. 16, 2005, p. 6; Written Statement of David M. Ratcliffe, President and CEO, Southern Company, for the U.S. Senate, Committee on Homeland Security and Governmental Affairs, hearing on *Hurricane Katrina: What Can Government Learn from the Private Sector's Response?*, Nov. 16, 2005, p. 2; Written Statement of Kevin T. Regan, Regional Vice President, Hotel Operations, Starwood Hotels and Resorts Worldwide, Inc., for the U.S. Senate, Committee on Homeland Security and Governmental Affairs, hearing on *Hurricane Katrina: What Can Government Learn from the Private Sector's Response?*, Nov. 16, 2005, p. 4.

174 Written Statement of Jackson, Senate Committee hearing, Nov. 16, 2005, p. 7; Written Statement of Ratcliffe, Senate Committee hearing, Nov. 16, 2005, p. 2; Written Statement of Regan, Senate Committee hearing, Nov. 16, 2005, p. 4.

175 Written Statement of Ratcliffe, Senate Committee hearing, Nov. 16, 2005, p. 2.

176 Written Statement of Ratcliffe, Senate Committee hearing, Nov. 16, 2005, p. 2

177 Written Statement of Stanley S. Litow, Vice President, Corporate Community Relations, IBM Corporation, for the U.S. Senate, Committee on Homeland Security and Governmental Affairs, hearing on *Hurricane Katrina: What Can Government Learn from the Private Sector's Response?*, Nov. 16, 2005, p. 2.

178 Written Statement of Regan, Senate Committee hearing, Nov. 16, 2005, p. 4.

179 Written Statement of Jackson, Senate Committee hearing, Nov. 16, 2005, p. 6.

180 Testimony of Jason Jackson, Director of Business Continuity, Global Security Division, Wal-Mart Stores, Inc. for the U.S. Senate, Committee on Homeland Security and Governmental Affairs, hearing on *Hurricane Katrina: What Can Government Learn from the Private Sector's Response?*, Nov. 16, 2005.

181 Written Statement of Jackson, Senate Committee hearing, Nov. 16, 2005, p. 6.

182 Written Statement of Jackson, Senate Committee hearing, Nov. 16, 2005, p. 6.

183 Jackson, Senate Committee hearing, Nov. 16, 2005.

184 Jackson, Senate Committee hearing, Nov. 16, 2005.

185 Written Statement of Jackson, Senate Committee hearing, Nov. 16, 2005, p. 9.

186 Jackson, Senate Committee hearing, Nov. 16, 2005.

Storm victims waiting at the airfield

Medical Assistance

Introduction to the Health Impacts of Hurricane Katrina

In both Mississippi and Louisiana, the onset of Hurricane Katrina found significant populations of acutely ill patients in hospitals and patients in nursing homes who were not evacuated.[1] In the case of acutely ill hospital patients, most hospitals decided that the medical risk of moving these patients outweighed the benefit, and chose to shelter-in-place. Unfortunately, the majority of the hospitals were not adequately equipped to carry out this function in the face of a storm the magnitude of Katrina.[2] Some nursing homes made similar decisions based on difficulties they encountered in previous evacuations or for other reasons. All told, some 235 deaths occurred in 28 of Louisiana's hospitals and nursing homes.[3] Special-needs patients transported themselves or were evacuated to the Superdome and to other shelters.[4] Although an estimated 450 special-needs patients were evacuated from the Superdome prior to landfall and transferred to a state-supported shelter in Baton Rouge, many more remained in the city.[5]

So on the eve of Katrina's landfall, federal, state, and local medical emergency managers found themselves confronted with the need to evacuate and care for thousands of medically compromised individuals – a circumstance forewarned in the Hurricane Pam exercise a year before Katrina.[6] Even more telling is the fact that these officials were apparently well aware of the situation that they would face. For example, a U.S. Department of Health and Human Services (HHS) e-mail describes information communicated on a FEMA-arranged conference call on Sunday night, August 28, just hours before landfall. The e-mail stated that 40 to 50 patients at the Superdome special-needs shelter were critical-care medical patients and that there were approximately 2,500 hospital patients still in New Orleans. The e-mail goes on to say, "Advanced planning was never completed on how the patients left in the hospitals will be evacuated after the event," and later noted, "it is assumed that many of the hospital generators will lose power given the expected height of the water."[7]

Similar circumstances were reported in Mississippi. A report from HHS Region IV emergency representatives in Atlanta, also on Sunday evening, reported that in Mississippi there were "no hospital evacuations other than 8 critical patients from VA [Veterans Affairs]" and "out of 29 Skilled Nursing Facilities only 2 reported evacuations."[8]

After the storm, federal, state, and local officials, and health-care workers in Mississippi and Louisiana faced extraordinary demands for health services, including evacuation of thousands of hospital and nursing-home patients. In addition, the health-care response system was taxed to its limits dealing with care of survivors and tens of thousands of people who had fled from the coastal regions and required medical care for pre-existing illnesses and chronic diseases, as well as preventing the spread of disease among these evacuees, many of whom were now living in crowded shelters.[9]

All of this had to be done in areas where major portions of the health-care system had been damaged or destroyed. All but three hospitals in the New Orleans area were incapacitated[10] and essentially all hospitals in the Mississippi Gulf Coast area sustained some level of physical damage and operational disruption (from loss of power, evacuation of staff, disruption of their supply systems, etc.). Charity Hospital in New Orleans, rendered inoperable by flood water, was one of only two major trauma centers in the entire state.[11]

Medical Assistance: Louisiana

As Hurricane Katrina approached Louisiana, hospitals and nursing homes had to decide which of their thousands of patients and residents could be safely evacuated, and to where. Once Katrina struck, hospitals and nursing homes had to care for those left behind, as well as new arrivals – all while dealing with flooding, power outages, supply shortages, security problems, and other issues.

Medical Evacuations

Temporary triage and medical-care facilities, developed as part of the Hurricane Pam exercise, provided triage for tens of thousands of evacuees and victims. The plan called for search-and-rescue teams to drop people at Search-and-Rescue Bases of Operations (SARBOOs) near the flooded areas, where paramedics would perform initial triage. Rescuees would then be transported to Temporary Medical-and-Operations Staging Areas (TMOSAs), larger areas with temporary medical facilities, for care and triage. Using this system, the state successfully triaged approximately 60,000 people.[12] With a capacity of 800 beds to provide medical care, the TMOSA at the Pete Maravich Center on the Louisiana State University (LSU) campus in Baton Rouge was the largest temporary emergency facility ever built, according to Dr. Jimmy Guidry, the Medical Director for the Louisiana Department of Health and Hospitals (DHH).[13] However, while the SARBOO/TMOSA structure was critical to handling the large volume of people needing attention, the plan did not work exactly as intended. For example, the New Orleans airport became a major triage center, especially for critically ill patients evacuated from hospitals, even though it was not part of the state plan. And as stated by Dr. Guidry, the state also lacked adequate transportation resources to evacuate all of the victims:

> Most of the hospitals did not have helipads, so they either had to go to the Superdome helipad or to another hospital's helipad. The helicopters that we did have were not willing to make a flight beyond picking them up there and bringing them to the airport, because they had to go back and pick up some more folks. So they weren't going to take them to anywhere [else] in the state by helicopter if they could avoid it because that would be loss of time. So most of the helicopter pick ups were from a helipad next to a hospital, to the airport or to the Causeway, depending on the critical [condition] of the patient. From the airport and from the Causeway, then it was buses or planes.[14]

Many victims did eventually arrive at the TMOSAs, although this created a significant transportation problem because of the large number of evacuees in New Orleans. Eventually buses were organized to carry out this function, as further described by Dr. Guidry, the buses were used

> when we started evacuating the large numbers at Causeway and the large numbers at the Superdome. Those buses would then bring the patients by the TMOSA and at the TMOSA, then we would triage them to see whether they could continue on the trip that the buses was taking them to, either a general shelter in Louisiana or a general shelter outside of Louisiana.[15]

Some of the difficulties experienced in moving victims into the state's medical-triage system were compounded by the fact that the evacuation of hospitals was simply not addressed in Hurricane Pam, despite the presumption that New Orleans would flood and that the hospitals would become inoperable. In fact, the Hurricane Pam exercise assumed that some 2,000 patients would be sheltered in place in area hospitals that would cease to operate as functional medical facilities due to flooding – a prediction that came strikingly close to reality during Katrina.[16] Little action was taken to address this daunting scenario prior to Katrina.

As explained by Dr. James Aiken, Medical Director for Emergency Preparedness for the Medical Center of Louisiana in New Orleans (a.k.a. Charity and University Hospitals):

> Well, to start with my own hospital, it [Pam] did not change our planning at all. I don't think it changed anyone else's planning that I am aware of … The focus of the health care planning that I participated in [during the exercise] had to do with not what happens within what we call the affected areas [that] have flooding but what happened on dry land. And most of the activities that happened in the health care breakout sessions had to do with standing up the temporary medical support sites.
>
> [M]any of my colleagues registered our concerns that we were literally writing off any serious planning above and beyond what we had then, which was to tell the hospitals they were going to have to be self-sufficient for three to five and now seven days. …
>
> So the Hurricane Pam, again, exercises and planning efforts, as far as I know, never addressed the issue of pre-threat evacuation or actually serious detailed planning for the affected area. [17]

Notwithstanding the failure of emergency planners during the Hurricane Pam exercise to address the need to evacuate hospitals, the hospitals were required to have emergency and evacuation plans. For example, DHH regulations required hospitals to have such plans, and for those plans to be made available to regional emergency officials upon request.[18] Nonetheless, these requirements proved woefully inadequate. As Dr. Guidry explained:

> It is not a requirement for licensure [for hospitals] to have generators at a certain level, at a certain place. It is not a requirement for licensure that [the hospital] show proof that your plan is operational.
>
> It was not a requirement prior to this event [Hurricane Katrina] that they would turn in plans defining what their evacuations plans [are].
>
> When I had discussions with a number of these hospitals in this area over the years, the questions was, "How are you going to evacuate?" And their response was always, "We do not plan to evacuate. Our evacuation plan will be to get those people out that can travel, elective surgeries. But we will remain here with the people that are not able to get out and the people that are going to need our care so that we can be here after the event."
>
> I can tell you that next hurricane season, there are going to be a lot more people leaving and the plan is going to change drastically. Those that do stay will be the hospitals that have the capability of hardening their structures and putting their generators higher because it does not make sense to stay in a bowl, if you will.[19]

In the end, hospitals in southeastern Louisiana were simply reluctant to follow their plans and evacuate the critically ill because of the danger, expense, and uncertainty of the hurricane path itself. As LSU's Dr. Aiken put it:

> Hurricanes have a remarkable capability of changing directions quickly. And so when you say, "In the line of the path of a storm," you know, for us, that path actually gets realized after the fact. So when you talk about evacuating patients from the number of hospitals that now exist, and we have to expand this conversation beyond New Orleans, because, quite frankly, a lot of the destination

hospitals that some of the areas use would be the same ones that we [LSU] would want to use. …

How do you decide which hospitals should evacuate and where should they go? I mean, do we evacuate the entire coastline? …

And again, remember 24 hours [prior to landfall of the hurricane], we do not want anybody on the road. So the risk benefit [issue arises], and also remember every single patient who is critically ill requires almost their own means of transportation, whether it's an ambulance or helicopter. We certainly could put a couple in. But for our critical care patients, school buses [are] not usually the answer.[20]

In addition, evacuation would have required New Orleans area hospitals to confront the difficult problem of finding other hospitals that could take their patients. As Dr. Guidry explained, in Louisiana under normal situations, sick or emergency patients with pressing needs are sent to the New Orleans region, which hosts a large number of medical facilities, the state's "medical Mecca." However, Katrina reversed that burden, causing 25 hospitals in the area to try to find places for their patients outside of New Orleans, and "the rest of the state can't absorb it."[21]

However successful it had been in prior hurricanes, the strategy of hospitals to stay open for critically ill patients and storm victims proved untenable in Katrina. After a few days, most hospitals that had stayed open were running out of fuel for their backup generators, making it impossible to operate effectively or, in some cases, at all, due to flooding. In desperation, they appealed to DHH to help them evacuate. Dr. Guidry found that helicopters and other transportation assets were tied up in search-and-rescue efforts:

And so their plan was stock up, be prepared to stay in place a few days. Most hurricanes, three days, five days out, you're done with it and be ready to take care of people after. The calls started coming in saying we're about to lose power, we're going to have to bag [manually ventilate] patients. We got to get them out of here. We got to get them out of here. We got to get them out of here. And I was asking for the resources to move them. Search and rescue is going to have to move them. I got to have the helicopters, I got to have the planes to move them out. … So it then becomes where do I send them, how do I get them there, how do I get them out of there. So the Hospital Association is coming to me in tears, the folks there are in tears trying to help their folks and I'm beating my head to try to get the help. And you've got the search and rescue that's trying to get people out of water and rooftops and out of hospitals. And that's all the competing needs for the limited assets.[22]

First responders attempting to answer hospital-evacuation calls faced chaotic conditions, particularly in the early days after landfall. Security concerns, including rumors of snipers, thwarted rescue efforts.[23] Communications were poor, making it difficult to coordinate with ambulances and helicopters. Flooded streets thwarted attempts to drive through New Orleans. Dr. Fred Cerise, Secretary of DHH, who participated in evacuation missions in New Orleans, described the challenge of attempting to take seven patients by truck from Charity Hospital to the Superdome special-needs shelter:

And we picked up seven people, some that needed dialysis, to take back to the Superdome. By this time it was dark; it was late, probably midnight. And there were people … outside of the Superdome that were sleeping all around the outer concourse. And so the truck had to – made its way up the external ramp to get to the helipad. And the guard was trying to clear the path, and by this time it's … late, late Wednesday night. … It's very tense in the Superdome by this point. People are belligerent, not wanting to get – they're getting woken up to move. …

I'm in the back of the truck and I hear this loud, "Move it, move, move, move." And I look back and there's like 30 Guardsmen running at the crowd with their rifles drawn. I – my initial thought was they were just trying to scatter the crowd, which they did. But then they turned into the Superdome and I saw a medic team come running against traffic at me, and this is when they had a Guardsman that was shot in the Superdome. These guys were going in to get their guy out that had gotten shot.[24]

Evacuating special-needs patients from the Superdome presented its own set of challenges, partly because they were next to the general-population shelter. As noted elsewhere, evacuation of the general public didn't get under way until late Wednesday, due to the delayed arrival of buses. Meanwhile, state officials had begun evacuating special-needs patients from the site by helicopter and boat. Seeing the special-needs evacuation proceeding, some members of the general public "figured out that if they were sick they might get out earlier. And so they started having chest pains and they started getting sick so they could get out earlier."[25] Officials were also concerned that the general population, angry at having to stay behind, would become violent. [26]

Flooding around the Superdome also interfered with medical evacuations. Officials had staged ambulances before landfall on the upper and outer concourses, expecting to use them for evacuation once the storm passed. Unfortunately, rising water on Monday evening prevented their use.[27] Thereafter, patients who could tolerate the ride were transported in high-water trucks to ambulances at other locations; others had to wait for helicopters.[28] Patients were loaded in ambulances, boats, high-water vehicles, aircraft, and even 18-wheeler trucks.[29] Many patients required continuous, individual medical care while in transit.[30] The logistics were nearly overwhelming, as described by Dr. Cerise:

It's not a simple ordeal. Put them on manual bagging for people off the ventilator; put them on a spine board. The interior of the hospital was dark, and so they would carry them down 12 flights of stairs on the external stairwell over their heads on a spine board making tight turns to get these people down onto the boat.

Got them to boat and we took them over to the hospital. I can tell you we had a policeman on the boat, because I remember the people throwing stuff at us from the Interstate, Claiborne overpass. And there was a shouting match that went on with the police and the guys that were throwing boxes and stuff down at the boats.[31]

Overall, Aiken described the process of evacuating patients as "one of the issues that I feel less than satisfied, most unsatisfied about. I think it sort of overwhelmed us, and I think we had a fingers-crossed attitude."[32]

Aiken also felt that the State Emergency Operations Center (EOC) did not always appreciate the urgency of his requests for assistance. While acknowledging that his demands were competing with those of other responders, he believed he would have fared better if EOC officials involved in handling requests had been at the scene of the crisis:

I don't know if it was because the right decision maker wasn't at the desk at the time, like with ESF-8 or whatever. But there was always this, "I will see what I can do." And then they would come back and say, "I think we need – we got the information, but I got a feeling we better start looking at other options."

If we could just work out a system. Either bring in distant EOC personnel down to the scene, whether it's FEMA or whoever else the lead agents are, and work side by side. Conditions are horrible, but they are not impossible. That to me could be the optimal eyes and ears. But if you don't have that, I felt like I was negotiating a lot. And I know I had competing of interest, and I understood that.[33]

Nursing Home Evacuations

Nursing homes in the metropolitan New Orleans area had their own Emergency Operations Plans (EOPs) that incorporated evacuations. In addition, Louisiana law required nursing homes to maintain EOPs and provide them to their parish emergency managers to "review and approve" the plans.[34] In reality, the Committee staff found that few parishes followed through on this guidance. One parish emergency manager from the metropolitan area thought he only had to review the plan.[35] The emergency manager for the City of New Orleans felt that the law did not provide parish emergency managers with the means to enforce the regulations.[36]

The Committee also found that there was no process to vet the plans for consistency and practicability. For example, many nursing homes rely on ambulance services to evacuate their populations. During a crisis, however, ambulance services may be in use by other nursing homes or hospitals. Furthermore, nursing homes and hospitals are not required to evacuate.[37] The facility's plan could simply be to weather the storm – even if the nursing home is in a flood-prone area. In short, nursing homes are only required to have their emergency plans *on the books*, which is a far cry from ensuring that they will actually work during a time of crisis.

The results were predictable. As Katrina approached, nursing homes found themselves without evacuation resources. In some cases, they turned to hospitals to take their patients, even though hospitals couldn't guarantee patient safety. Aiken described the situation after nursing-home officials discovered that their memoranda of understanding (MOUs) with government agencies or other entities for transportation or other resources had been overtaken by events:

We get a panic call 24 to 36 hours out. They have exhausted their MOUs. They have been told "No" on their level, we don't have what we said we would have for you in terms of buses or ambulances or even helicopters. And they call us …

We are not saying no. We are saying, "We may go under water. Our patients may die. You putting them with us [has] not increased their likeliness or likelihood to survive necessarily."

We do everything we can to assist them in getting out. If somebody does show up, we take them in, which is what we do. Again, it's a very awkward. It's very frustrating and, quite frankly, very scary, and I will even say a deadly situation.[38]

Medical Supply and Preparations

Medical institutions also struggled in obtaining adequate supplies, such as fuel. Dr. Aiken described Charity Hospital generators as "running on fumes for the first day or two."[39] For many hospitals, lack of fuel became the decisive factor, forcing them to shut down and evacuate. As there was no statutory or regulatory requirement that generators be located above levels exposed to flooding,[40] many generators flooded. Hospitals lost power abruptly, making rapid evacuation essential. The LSU computer system was also heavily damaged, seriously impairing access to patient records.[41]

On the other hand, pre-stocked food and medical supplies at Charity Hospital were adequate to carry the facility through until the National Guard could re-supply.[42] Dr. Kevin Stephens, Director of the New Orleans Department of Health, who oversaw medical care for special-needs patients at the Superdome, also said that he had "no problems with supplies," although medical oxygen ran low at one point.[43]

DHH managed to keep supplies flowing, but only through extraordinary measures. On Sunday, August 28, DHH put the Centers for Disease Control (CDC) on notice that it might need supplies from the Strategic National Stockpile, which CDC would deliver within 12 hours of the request. However, when DHH did make the request shortly after Katrina passed, CDC did not come through promptly, and Guidry was forced to obtain needed supplies elsewhere: "I personally signed for an order of five million dollars' worth of medical equipment from a private vendor because I didn't know where else to go, who was ready to deliver to me when I needed it. And so I did not have the funding for that, but I signed for it and got the Governor's backing to make that happen."[44]

Support from Federal Medical Teams

Apart from supplies, the state depended heavily on a steady flow of outside medical personnel, including Federal Emergency Management Agency (FEMA) Disaster Medical Assistance Teams (DMATs), which are nominally 35-member self-contained emergency medical teams, to stay on top of health-care needs.[45] DHH opened seven special-needs shelters around the state[46], and every one of them wanted to have a DMAT with its medical personnel and supplies to assist them.[47] According to Dr. Guidry, "we couldn't get enough teams here quick enough to meet those demands, so we went for quite some time before we got enough teams to meet the demand."[48] A team of U.S. Public Health Service (USPHS) officers also arrived in Louisiana on Tuesday night, August 30, and USPHS helped staff the state's triage facility at LSU for the duration of the event.[49]

State and local health officials described two occasions when DMATs redeployed from the special-needs facility at the Superdome, leaving an increased burden for medical professionals still on site. According to these officials, the first instance occurred either late on Monday or Tuesday, shortly after the special-needs operations were relocated from the inner concourse of the Superdome to the neighboring basketball arena. At that point, state and local health officials stated that two DMAT teams assigned to the facility left, apparently concerned about their equipment getting wet.[50] It should be noted, however, that according to the National Disaster Medical Systems (NDMS) Management Support Team Commander on site, Ronald Martin, the teams did leave the arena floor, but that he redeployed the DMAT teams to avoid the rising water. He stated that he moved one team to the mezzanine area and one team out of the Superdome to the adjacent elevated highway. Martin explained that he was concerned about keeping all of his assets within the Superdome if further flooding were to occur[51]. At least one local official was concerned about this change, and it did have the practical effect of reducing available resources inside the Superdome. According to Dr. Stephens, those teams were needed to help relieve his medical staff in their third straight day of caring for special needs patients and facing burnout.[52]

The second occasion occurred on Thursday when all of the DMAT teams at the Superdome (as well as city health department and Emergency Medical Services (EMS) personnel) pulled out due to security concerns.[53] General Gary Jones of the Louisiana National Guard, and Incident Commander at the Superdome, claimed that he was surprised by their abrupt departure, leaving behind at least 500 critical-care patients with no provisions for the transition:

> Dr. Lupin came up to me and he said, "Sir" – and he was pretty irate – he said, "You know, how do you expect me to deal with all of these critical care patients here?" And I said, "What are you talking about?" … And he said, "All the pa-

tients over there on that ramp." And I said, "Why are you dealing with them?" … He said, "FEMA left." He said, "They left"; and he said, "They didn't leave any supplies, I don't have charts, I don't know what's wrong with these people, I don't know – they got IVs in their arms, I don't even know really what's supposed to happen, what the plan is or anything else."[54]

General Jones said he made no secret of his displeasure to FEMA officials:

> [The FEMA team leader] came back and she said we're back, and this is so-and-so, and he's going to be the lead guy. And I said, "Are you going to stay this time?" And they said, "Oh, yeah, we're going to stay." And I said, "Well, good, because I would hate to have to shoot somebody." And they laughed and they said, "You're joking." And I said, "Think so?" You know, and I – and I was joking. Obviously, I mean, I wasn't going to shoot anybody. But I kind of voiced my displeasure with the fact that they had left me unsupported.[55]

Hundreds of special-needs patients were cared for at the Superdome and eventually evacuated. In the end, 19 nursing homes evacuated pre-landfall, and leaving 34 to do so after the hurricane.[56] Moreover, a total of 12,000 patients and caregivers were evacuated from hospitals before and after Katrina with 25 hospitals evacuating in the first five days post-landfall.[57]

Many of these patients endured terrible suffering. Of the 400 patients at Charity Hospital, nine died, including some directly as a result of the prolonged evacuation process.[58] Dr. Stephens described rushing special-needs cases out of the Superdome before they started "to decompensate" [lose their vital functions]. He said, "I knew that I had to get people from the Dome to somewhere else … another day or two, [and] these fragile elderly people were going to start dropping out on me [dying]."[59] Similarly, Dr. Cerise, Secretary of DHH, said that many special-needs patients in the Superdome were elderly people who couldn't take care of themselves, and that it was clear some had not received necessary attention when they were moved from the Superdome to the neighboring arena.[60]

The severity of these patients' problems was made even more clear as this investigation developed more information on pre-storm planning and emergency coordination during the response. Some of the more troubling information came from the Executive Director of the Louisiana Nursing Home Association (LNHA), Joseph Donchess, who has been with the LNHA for nearly 20 years. Although the LNHA had an established seat at the state EOC, and was initially allowed access to E-Team, the state's electronic emergency request tracking system, these practices were interrupted during the response to Katrina. Donchess said:

> It's my personal opinion that nursing homes and hospitals are just too low of a priority and I'm very disappointed in that because here you're talking about the most frail population there is and they're relying on two non-profit associations to pretty much get this work done and it was never intended for us to be that kind of life saver organizations. … And that's what we had to act as during this last storm.[61]

> For the first two days, LNHA was on its own to improvise and find ways to rescue the elderly in nursing homes. We helped members and nonmembers alike. At first, LNHA could submit E-Team missions, but by the fourth day our E-Team missions were denied because we were not a governmental agency.[62]

Once the LNHA was denied access to the E-Team system, Donchess and other LNHA personnel sought Dr. Guidry and DHH's authorization for LNHA's needs. However, this practice also proved ineffective, as Dr. Guidry "had 100 different things" he had to do himself, so it was still very difficult for the LNHA to get its requests approved for the benefit of the many nursing home residents counting on assistance.[63]

Another troubling aspect of the state's emergency-preparedness structure was a gaping hole in the state's planning and coordination as it related to hospitals and nursing homes under the State's Emergency Operations Plan (EOP). Under the State's EOP, Emergency Support Function 8 (ESF-8, Public Health and Medical Services), responsibilities were divided between two state agencies. DHH was responsible for public health, sanitation, medical, and health assistance to special-needs shelter operations, mental health, and crisis counseling. The LSU Health Sciences Center, which runs the state's public hospital system, was responsible for providing and coordinating hospital care and shelter for nursing-home and home-health patients with acute care requirements, as well as casualties of emergencies and disasters. LSU also had the lead role in coordinating hospital planning and actions with private hospitals and other facilities.[64]

Unfortunately, the emergency-preparedness and response system laid out in the Louisiana EOP did not reflect reality for nursing homes and hospitals in Louisiana. LSU did not, and was not equipped to provide and coordinate hospital care and shelter for nursing-home, special-needs, or home-health patients as called for in the plan. Nor did LSU coordinate the overall planning and actions of private hospitals during emergencies as it was required to do.[65] To the extent any agency met these responsibilities, it was DHH, which did so through a program to prepare hospitals to respond to bioterrorist attacks. This program was funded through the U.S. Health Resources and Services Administration (HRSA), an agency of the U.S. Department of Health and Human Services (HHS), and was not intended to deal with issues such as hurricane preparations.[66]

However, some aspects of the HRSA program did come into play. For example, under the HRSA program, DHH had previously worked with hospitals to establish a hospital emergency network to track available hospital beds and communicate information among hospitals which was used during Katrina.[67] However, while the HRSA program did provide some level of preparedness among the hospital community, this safety net for the charges and responsibilities that were supposed to have been shouldered by LSU under the state plan did not fully replace the work that LSU was supposed to do either before or during the response to Katrina.

The investigation sought to determine why this aspect of the state emergency plan was not followed. For one, LSU simply did not accept its responsibilities under the State's EOP, though it appears to have been understood that these responsibilities existed. As explained by Aiken:

> Oh, I understand the confusion because we are not doing it the way – exactly the way – the Emergency Operations Plan. … The way it realistically and the way it has operated, not only during Hurricane Katrina but for some of the other instances where hurricanes have come very close to us over the last couple of years, that LSU actually does not coordinate the overall hospital response. They tend to focus – and, obviously, since I don't sit there, I can't say exactly what they do minute to minute. … But I have a feeling that people … who sat in that chair [at the state EOC and have] been assigned that responsibility, they tend to focus on LSU hospitals and the HRSA, the people who have been employed through the HRSA grant and have traditionally been present to help coordinate the overall network, which certainly includes us, but also includes all the private hospitals. What you see in the plan is not what actually happens. It's certainly a job deserving of many more people than the plan calls for. And, again, these are all comments that I made public during the revision

process earlier this year. In my opinion, the plan is not realistic. It should be more reflective of how we really do it, and I certainly hope that changes.[68]

LSU's responsibilities under the State's 2005 EOP were not new. Prior iterations, specifically the 2001 plan, made LSU's responsibilities for planning and coordinating hospital care and shelter for nursing-home and home-health patients even more explicit.[69]

As a result of LSU's failure, there was inadequate attention to emergency planning for important components of the health-care system in Louisiana. Dr. Aiken said he was not aware of any planning by LSU or other involved agencies at the state level for nursing-home and home-health patients under the State's EOP:

> I don't know of any substantial act of involvement that LSU has on nursing-home and home-health patients, truly across the board on an emergency basis, planning, preparation, or the actual response itself. Nursing homes in this state have always been a huge concern for us. ... We over the years through the local emergency-preparedness committees, through every level of emergency planning that I have been involved with, we have always been concerned over their involvement, what they do during storms, that kind of thing. And I am not aware of any instance where LSU has had a – again, on Baton Rouge, on a State Office of Emergency Preparedness or Emergency Operation Center level – has had any real impact or influence on [them].[70]

Dr. Aiken also noted that he was "99 percent sure" that his boss, Don Smithburg, Chief Executive Officer of LSU Health Care Services Division (HCSD) and Executive Vice President for the LSU system, "didn't spend much time in providing or coordinating care for nursing home or home health placement, except for those patients that may have arrived at our hospital, which they did, the night before at Charity."[71] Smithburg admitted to LSU's shortcomings, stating that the individual charged with the overall planning and coordination for emergency preparedness and management for the Charity and University Hospitals, the Chief Operating Officer "was weak and not engaged and not communicative with the rest of our staff in that responsibility."[72] (Smithburg terminated this employee in February 2005.)[73] Furthermore, when asked by Committee staff if LSU had the resources or manpower to meet its charges under the State's EOP, regardless of whether the Chief Operating Officer for the system was competent in his/her position or not, Smithburg said, "There's no way."[74]

Dr. Aiken spoke of his concerns about the flaws in the state EOP to superiors in the LSU HCSD, to Colonel Jadwin W. "Jay" Mayeaux, Louisiana's Deputy Director of Homeland Security, and to the State Medical Officer, Dr. Guidry.[75] But the responsibilities stayed with LSU.[76]

Despite this notable vacuum in the State's EOP, Dr. Aiken was reasonably certain that the HRSA network acted as a surrogate for LSU in meeting the hospital-related responsibilities under ESF-8.[77] However, the Committee's investigation revealed that this safety net did not work as well as some would have hoped. Erin Downey, the HRSA Program's Director of Emergency Preparedness at the time, on contract with the DHH, was at the State EOC in Baton Rouge for the Katrina response, and had a different view:

> So you had emergency preparedness people calling and asking for resources, expressing their concerns, calling the command center or ... they would call their coordinator, and then their coordinator would call ... When requests were coming in to us, ... our marching orders were to put everything in E-Team, okay, because what that was, was a way of facilitating that or standardizing all of the requests, funneling them through one main decision point, and

that was the total breakdown. Now, I would love to say something different about that, but that was a total breakdown.[78]

Medical Assistance: Mississippi

Hurricane Katrina devastated the medical infrastructure of south Mississippi, destroying or severely damaging 14 of the 16 hospitals in the region's six counties.[79] Three hospitals were damaged so severely that they were forced to close, including the only acute-care hospital in Hancock County.[80] One hospital, Select Specialty Hospital in Gulfport, was destroyed in the storm.[81]

The storm also damaged or destroyed other medical facilities in the southernmost six counties. More than a third of primary-care clinics were closed or destroyed.[82] In addition, the damage done to the local physical infrastructure has resulted in longer response time for ambulances and a greater reliance on airlifting patients for care.[83] Seventy-three nursing homes were affected, including 16 in the southernmost six counties; two were destroyed.[84]

As the lead state agency under the Mississippi Comprehensive Emergency Management Plan's ESF-8 for health and medical services, the Mississippi Department of Health (MDH) played the lead state role in response to this catastrophe. Under that plan, MDH is charged with providing state assistance to local governments in response to public-health and medical-care needs following a disaster.[85] While the MDH does not provide primary care, once the Governor declares an emergency, all health and medical considerations fall within the purview of MDH.[86]

Dr. Brian Amy, Mississippi's State Health Officer and the top health official in the state, explained that although MDH was prepared and had recently increased its capacity to respond, it did not have the capacity to deal with disasters of Katrina's magnitude.[87] MDH activated its EOC at the MDH central office in Jackson on August 27, two days before landfall. The department pre-positioned response personnel, such as public-health nurses in special-needs shelters throughout South Mississippi and emergency-response coordinators in coastal county EOCs. It also worked with representatives from FEMA's National Disaster Medical System and HHS that arrived before landfall to request that additional federal help be readied, including DMATs, medical personnel capable of providing medical care following disaster.[88] These teams were eventually positioned at every affected hospital, treating 15,500 patients (out of 17,649 reported injuries), in the first days after landfall.[89]

MDH also supports pre-landfall evacuation. In these efforts, MDH assists in evacuating nursing-home, special-needs, and sometimes hospital patients.[90] These facilities are generally evacuated well prior to the general evacuation so that ambulances do not have to fight traffic congestion.[91] MDH also has a "decompression plan," to assist in discharging patients who can safely leave the hospital early.[92]

MDH regulates nursing homes in Mississippi. Jim Craig, MDH's incident commander during Katrina, reported that nursing homes asked to evacuate prior to Katrina did so.[93]

This hasn't always been the case. According to Governor Haley Barbour, one nursing home resisted evacuation prior to Hurricane Ivan. In response, Governor Barbour had the director of the state-run, low-income Medicaid program call them:

> We had to make one of the nursing homes evacuate, and that's where Medicaid comes in because that is who pays them. And if they get sort of uncertain of

Flooded reception area, Hancock
Medical Center, Mississippi
Provided to Committee

whether they need to evacuate, I get the Director of Medicaid to call them, and they get a better attitude.[94]

Ultimately, MDH responded to Katrina with over 1,400 personnel.[95] Immediately following landfall, MDH began to assess and support local medical facilities. In addition, MDH's state epidemiologist led a team to the coast to assess damage to hospitals. The largest immediate problem was a severe fuel shortage. With power out in the area, many health-care facilities were forced to rely on generators. As a result, MDH officials began procuring and delivering fuel. The other major post-landfall challenge was maintaining security at health-care facilities, as they generally had power, drawing local residents displaced by the storm.[96]

In addition to federal help, Mississippi received considerable help from other states under the Emergency Management Assistance Compact (EMAC). Dr. Amy has stated that Mississippi "owe[s] a special debt of gratitude to our friends from other state public health agencies, particularly Florida, Kentucky, Indiana, Illinois, and North Carolina." He singled out for special praise the Florida Department of Health, which dispatched more than 300 personnel to Mississippi, and Kentucky, which sent more than 100 personnel.[97]

One of the most significant resources deployed to Mississippi under EMAC was Carolina-1.[98] Carolina-1 is a portable hospital unit that includes a surgical suite, x-rays, a laboratory, a pharmacy, and 100 beds.[99] According to Craig, when Mississippi first contacted Carolina-1, it was bound for Louisiana. Due to legal-liability issues it re-deployed to Mississippi.[100] Ultimately, Carolina-1 deployed to the Bay St. Louis area in Hancock County, where it became the central health-care provider in the county, replacing the Hancock County Medical Center devastated by Katrina.[101]

Mississippi also became the first state to receive, stage, store, and distribute the Strategic National Stockpile (SNS) Push Pack. Within 12 hours of Dr. Amy's official request, the CDC delivered eight truckloads of SNS medical supplies for Mississippi medical facilities. Supplies continued to flow into Mississippi for two weeks until Mississippi's facilities were able to reestablish their regular supply channels.[102]

Federal Health Response

Use of the National Disaster Medical System

The National Disaster Medical System (NDMS) is the nation's primary federal response capability to meet medical needs in times of disaster when state and local systems are overwhelmed. Part of FEMA's Response Division, the NDMS has two basic components.[103] The first is a collection of special medical and response teams that are on call to provide medical care during national emergencies.[104] The second component is a partnership of FEMA, the Veterans Affairs (VA), the Defense Department (DOD) and HHS that maintains a network of hospitals and coordination centers throughout the United States to transport and care for large numbers of patients in an emergency.[105] This network was originally established to provide medical care within the United States for military casualties, but was used essentially for the first time on a large scale during Katrina to evacuate medical patients from New Orleans.[106]

NDMS teams comprise some 9,000 volunteers.[107] These volunteers organize, train, and deploy as part of geographically dispersed teams supported by local sponsors. When they deploy, the team members become temporary federal employees, which provides them a salary, reimbursement for expenses, and liability coverage.[108] The basic unit of the NDMS is the DMAT. NDMS also contains specialty teams which can deliver logistical support, mortuary, veterinary, burn- and crush-injury care, and other services. Ideally, a DMAT consists of 35 health professionals who are deployable within six hours with a well maintained supply and equipment cache, and have the capability to treat 250 casualties and sustain themselves over a 72-hour period.[109] A full DMAT typically has three to four physicians and a mix of nurses, pharmacists, paramedics, and physician assistants. Hurricane Katrina led to activation of 98 percent of the NDMS teams.[110]

Notwithstanding this extensive deployment, the NDMS teams were hampered by numerous problems. Beall described DMAT medical supply cache shortfalls as a common condition

> At last year's conference in Orlando, I asked every team there, if you have your complete federal cache, raise your hand. Not one team raised their hand because we've never been able to finish out buying the cache. … We had ordered all the stuff to finish these teams 100 percent, and as I had been advised, the million dollars had been pulled back for some reason. Some people talk about [a "tax"] or whatever DHS may have applied [to FEMA's budget]. I cannot testify that was the reason, but know that that order was cut by $1 million, and that these teams did not have 100 percent cache when we deployed them for Katrina, so we went into a response with a shortfall.[111]

FEMA was also limited in its ability to make all of the teams fully operational and to expand the number of NDMS teams due to lack of resources.[112] Of the 52 DMATs, only 25 are considered fully operational.[113]

NDMS also lacked sufficient administrative resources to sustain NDMS operations, let alone improve them. NDMS was transferred from HHS in 2003 pursuant to the Homeland Security Act,[114] but some administrative-support positions did not transfer from HHS. Other support positions were moved out of NDMS to FEMA's own logistics section.[115] To compound the situation, when activated, NDMS routinely sends its administrators to be part of field operations. Beall said, "At the initial launch of Katrina, I was really the only operations person in NDMS left in the section, and the other people that were there were operational specialists, which I had to send to the field … I never went home. I slept on the floor in my office."[116]

NDMS Team Deployment Problems

As described more fully in Chapter 12, on Thursday, August 25, four days prior to Katrina's landfall, FEMA Response Division Chief Ed Buikema activated the NDMS system and began to mobilize and pre-position its medical and mortuary teams. Although FEMA understood that states were relying on these resources to help them cope with the expected aftermath of the storm, FEMA had delays in mobilizing, deploying and staging its teams. For example, although the NDMS regional representative for Louisiana told NDMS leadership on Saturday, August 27, that Louisiana would need nine DMATs to staff its medical triage centers, these teams were not available before landfall.[117] FEMA also selected team staging areas that were hundreds of miles away from the coastal areas where they ultimately expected to be deployed and efforts by Louisiana to get FEMA to bring them closer were apparently unsuccessful.[118]

Some delays in deployment were the result of the logistics and travel system that FEMA uses for NDMS. For example, a DMAT from San Diego was mobilized on Sunday, August 28, the day before landfall. (The team would ultimately be deployed to the New Orleans Airport to assist in the medical evacuation there.) By the time NDMS headquarters approved the team roster late on Sunday night, there were no flights remaining to transport the team. The team's after-action report said, "We could have been to Houston [one of the NDMS staging areas] half a day earlier, and to Baton Rouge a day earlier" if there had been a more efficient travel-approval process.[119] NDMS also relies on team supply trucks to transport medical supplies. In this case, the San Diego team's medical-supply trucks were to drive all the way from San Diego to Louisiana.[120] Finally, because team drivers are also "essential key team members," the San Diego team found itself short "six more team members, when we became engaged at the airport."[121]

Inadequate DMAT Team Support

By all accounts, NDMS teams delivered excellent care given the constraints of the environment in which they were working and living.[122] NDMS team members worked tirelessly and heroically in difficult and sometimes desperate conditions. Three NDMS DMATs were also deployed on August 30 to the New Orleans airport to support the medical evacuation effort being established there.[123] The DMATs provided care to more than 4,000 patients in what would become one of the largest contemporary mass-casualty triage and evacuations in the United States.[124] For the first two-and-a-half days, the three DMATs provided care to patients without relief in what one NDMS doctor called the "hospital from Hell."[125]

The NDMS teams could not operate without rest. It is unclear why more medical teams did not arrive at the airport until Friday, September 2, when the NDMS log indicates the presence of two additional DMATs, MA-2 and FL-3.[126] Their help was still desperately needed, but additional medical support should have deployed sooner. As described by the commander of a logistical support team sponsored by the U.S. Forest Service – an Incident Management Team (IMT) – that arrived at the airport on September 1, the situation demanded more medical and support assets, and sooner:

> Upon arrival at the Louis Armstrong New Orleans International Airport on September 1, the scene the IMT encountered could best be described as surreal. DMAT's had hundreds of patients scattered about the main terminal and ticketing area. Over 300 of these were confined to stretchers. Most were elderly and infirmed, but many had encountered injuries due to the accidents related to the hurricane. Medical personnel were stretched to the breaking point.[127]

The shortage of personnel also meant it was more difficult to provide adequate triage. The NDMS teams operated from the perspective that the best care was simply to put patients on planes and get them out of the facility. DOD and private-sector planes were used to transport patients to hospitals wherever possible.[128] When asked how patients were tracked, Captain Art French, one of the NDMS doctors who tried to manage the DMATs at the airport, replied, "We wrote down their names, where they were going, and with whom on a piece of paper. Those pieces of paper I hope are still there."[129] In between was an "expectant area" where failing patients were provided comfort care. In the end, 26 patients died at the airport, mostly in this area. Capt. French said that despite conditions at the airport the care of these patients was fully adequate and that these patients would have probably died in any medical setting.[130]

Although DMATs are supposed to deploy with management support from Management Support Teams (MSTs), no organized MST deployed to the airport.[131] Instead, an ad-hoc MST was created from NDMS personnel on-site. In fact, neither of the two men who would eventually co-direct the NDMS medical operations of the New Orleans Airport was formally assigned that duty.[132] They had traveled on their own to the airport to help out when their other assignments were canceled. When they arrived Wednesday, they were confronted with three medical teams, CA-4, TX-4, and WA-1, without any management support, facing growing numbers of patients, and increasingly difficult conditions, so they assumed leadership roles.[133] This ad-hoc management team did its best to manage the situation, but had no ability to communicate even with NDMS leadership in Baton Rouge.[134] When asked why he thought an MST was not deployed to the airport given the difficulty and complexity of the mission, Capt. French observed that there were no MST staff left to send.[135]

The lack of experienced MST members led to other problems. At one point, Beall e-mailed that his field operators were not supporting the DMATs sufficiently: "I need a plan put together on how the teams will be supported. Many of the leaders in the field are not well versed on NDMS field ops."[136] The response: "Then they shouldn't be leaders, nor should they be in the field without supervision."[137] One team complained, "We all know what disasters are, we would not be here if we did not want to help. But when the situation is compounded by mismanagement it makes our jobs much more difficult to do. We have asked for items and heard nothing as to the status of the request."[138]

Medical evacuation
U.S. Air Force photo

Many teams had difficulty communicating. The DMATs at the Superdome had satellite phones, but had difficulty utilizing them because they were initially not programmed properly and the truck-mounted units would not work inside the building.[139] The NDMS MST commander on-scene deployed with only his personal cell phone.[140] Management was aware of the problem, but seemed unable to resolve it. On September 1, Beall complained, "Communication has been the worst I have seen."[141] Eight days after Katrina's landfall, he was still desperately trying to obtain communications capability. He e-mailed, "Where are the sat[ellite] phones for the NDMS teams? Teams do not have communications."[142]

Beall attributes some of these problems to the way in which DHS absorbed NDMS from HHS. The NDMS logistics personnel were transferred to the FEMA logistics branch rather than remaining with their agency. Beall remarked, "So all the logistic shortfalls and all the things that we're starting to see in the after action, it's because the person working the logistics side of the house did not have any background in NDMS. ... we need a lot of supplies, and what I don't need is somebody to tell me, 'Why do you need this, why are you asking for that?' I don't need someone to slow up that request, and that's what you'll see"[14]

NDMS Patient Movement

On the night of Tuesday, August 30, federal emergency managers authorized the medical evacuation of hospital and other acute-care patients from New Orleans.[144] This was the first time a full-scale operation using the NDMS patient-movement capability had ever been initiated.[145] The plan called for DMATs to establish a triage center at the New Orleans airport and to utilize assigned Air Force aircraft to move the patients to hospitals around the country.[146] As described above and in the after-action reports of the agencies that participated, more than 4,000 patients were evacuated through the airport although less than half (approximately 1,800) were actually placed on Air Force aircraft.[147] The remainder were placed on National Guard and private aircraft. The distinction is important because only those patients who were placed on the Air Force aircraft were logged into the NDMS patient movement-tracking system. The tracking system was not accessible for all patients and as a result, there was no systematic way of knowing what had become of everyone.[148]

As noted above, medical teams on site were overwhelmed by the volume of patients. There was essentially no overall command structure governing the medical evacuation, especially during the first three or four critical days.[149] Operations at the airport were also plagued by a lack of effective management of the airport complex and the simultaneous civilian evacuation, a shortage of security, and a lack of logistical support. Although a U.S. Forest Service-sponsored Incident Management Team arrived at the airport on Thursday, September 1, and began to provide badly needed logistical support to the NDMS teams and other federal personnel, their deployment to the airport was essentially accidental.[150] While the evacuation was a success in that it succeeded in moving thousands of patients, and the NDMS network operated largely as intended, it clearly did not work as well as it should have.

Medical Surge

HHS is the coordinating federal agency for federal public-health and medical-assistance activities under the National Response Plan (NRP) (ESF-8, Public Health and Medical Services).[151] Within HHS, the Office of Public Health and Emergency Preparedness (OPHEP) leads the Department's preparedness and response activities and is tasked with coordinating activities within HHS and with other federal agencies. During Hurricane Katrina, one of OPHEP's primary responsibilities was to meet medical-surge needs, which involved increasing capacity to provide medical care by providing more healthcare personnel, more health-care facilities, and more health-care supplies across the affected region.

Personnel

HHS drew from four primary sources to meet emergency health-personnel needs. First, the U.S. Public Health Service (USPHS) is the principal personnel surge resource for HHS. There were approximately 6,000 officers in the USPHS under the command of the U.S. Surgeon General in 800 locations around the country at the time of Hurricane Katrina.[152] In the immediate aftermath of Katrina, from August 30–September 16, HHS deployed 2,132 USPHS officers. Second, the Medical Reserve Corps (MRC), comprising 62,000 local volunteer healthcare workers in state-sponsored teams across the country, deployed approximately 6,900 volunteers during Katrina.[153] The third source of federal health personnel was a federal volunteer database created in the immediate aftermath of Katrina that had approximately 34,000 volunteers. Of this total, only 1,400 eventually deployed.[154] The fourth source was turning to other federal agencies such as the Department of Defense (DOD) or Veterans Affairs for assistance.

U.S. Public Health Service

Under the Public Health Service Act, the Secretary of HHS has broad authority to mobilize and direct the USPHS in times of a public health emergency. USPHS officers work in many parts of the federal government around the country.[155] They include physicians, nurses, pharmacists, engineers, environmental health officers, dentists, mental-health providers, scientists, therapists, epidemiologists, and other public-health professionals.[156] They are a uniformed service, and can be directed to leave their normal jobs to deploy under the direction of the Secretary of HHS in an emergency.

As described more fully in Chapter 12, the HHS Office of Force Readiness and Deployment (OFRD), which is responsible for overseeing USPHS officers deployed in an emergency, began identifying personnel for deployment (known as "rostering") well before landfall, starting August 25. HHS's original goal was to create a 100-person team to deploy to the area prior to landfall.[157] However, only 37 officers arrived – in Jackson, Mississippi, mere hours before landfall, late Sunday night. They were far from their original destination of the Superdome in New Orleans.

Once in Jackson, the team had limited capability. USPHS officers are not issued medical equipment or supplies nor are there pre-arranged teams or equipment caches.[158] These officers did not have any capacity to provide care by themselves without additional logistical support, especially to support special-needs patients such as individuals with heart conditions, diabetes, or oxygen requirements. The team remained in Jackson, Mississippi, until Tuesday due to high winds, lack of electricity, and lack of communications.[159] When they were finally able to leave, they traveled to Baton Rouge to staff the state-run medical triage center at the athletic center of LSU.[160]

There are several reasons why HHS, with 6,000 USPHS officers theoretically available, could not send a complete team to the affected parts prior to landfall. Each time a USPHS team is needed, it is formed ad-hoc: officers are not assigned to pre-existing teams, so teams must be assembled from lists of available officers matching both needed skills and the numbers of officers. They must then fly in from multiple locations using commercial transport. Because the 100 team members originally identified to deploy were spread across the country, there was no practical way to move them into New Orleans at the last moment.[161]

In addition to these early efforts, on Monday, August 29, rostering continued in an effort to identify USPHS officers to deploy to the New Orleans area.[162] According to Rear Admiral John Babb, the USPHS officer who heads OFRD, teams were identified for deployment by Tuesday, August 30, but mission assignments were not made.[163] For instance, many of the officers were slated to staff mobile field hospitals, known as Federal Medical Shelters or FMSs. During the course of that week, Admiral Babb fulfilled staffing requests for ten 250-bed FMS units,[164] but the units were not ready. Consequently, there was initially no place to send the teams.[165] Furthermore, once placed on a team roster, USPHS officers were then sent to a travel contractor to arrange commercial travel.[166] However, the travel contractors did not deploy the teams as OFRD had them structured due to commercial flight limitations and disruptions.[167] Admiral Babb said deployment of the USPHS teams "would have been much more successful had we had geographically connected teams so that we could have deployed people from a given location instead of from all over the place."[168] The reliance on an outside travel contractor without the capacity to deploy and rotate approximately 3,000 personnel from around the country did not result in a uniform and predictable deployment process and adversely impacted HHS's response.

As a result of these factors, and despite its efforts to begin to roster personnel before landfall, no significant USPHS deployments, other than the initial team of 37, occurred until the end of the first week following Katrina.[169]

USPHS deployment difficulties also relate to a number of organizational factors. USPHS teams do not have their own medical and support supplies, pharmaceuticals, food, housing, and other logistical capabilities that allow them to be self-sustaining.[170] Admiral Babb specifically cited a lack of medical and supply resources as contributing to deployment delays.[171] USPHS also relies upon commercial travel services. Robert Lavender, Deputy Director of Information Technology and Communications within OPHEP, cited problems with closed airports, ground-transportation problems, and lack of hotels and other housing options as impeding deployment.[172] In essence, HHS personnel depend on the local economy, infrastructure, and commercial transportation for deployment and ongoing support – a requirement that could not be easily met in the wake of a catastrophic hurricane or likely in other emergency situations. Deployment logistics were further strained by the fact that USPHS officers were rotated out of the field every two weeks, significantly adding to the logistical workload.[173]

USPHS deployments were also compromised by the daily professional commitments of USPHS officers.[174] Many USPHS officers were also federal employees playing essential roles in their agencies, such as the Indian Health Service and the Bureau of Prisons, making them unavailable for deployment. USPHS officers were also supposed to notify the Medical Affairs Branch in the USPHS about any changes in their deployment availability.[175] However, status updates did not systematically occur.[176] Numerous e-mails were sent to OFRD from USPHS officers stating that they could not leave their agencies because of employment obligations or other reasons such as illnesses or pregnancies.[177] In other cases, USPHS personnel were members of other emergency teams, such as the NDMS teams managed by FEMA. If they had already deployed as part of those teams, they were no longer available to deploy as part of USPHS.[178]

Hurricane Katrina was not the first time these problems with USPHS deployment have been identified. An after-action report published by the CNA Corporation, a non-profit research firm, following Hurricanes Frances and Ivan, documented many of the same issues.[179] A key criticism in the CNA report was that USPHS rotational rosters were not "ready-go" personnel assets, which means they did not have supplies and equipment to provide clinical services.[180] Again, this continued to be a problem for deployments pre-landfall and afterwards for Hurricane Katrina. CNA also cited limited travel and logistics support for officers as problematic.[181] Travel-logistics problems continued into Hurricane Katrina, as OPHEP relied again on an outside contractor with insufficient capacity to effectively deploy a significant number of people. OFRD also had no mechanism in place for tracking the movement and placement of USPHS personnel in the field at the time of Hurricanes Frances and Ivan,[182] and again did not have the capacity to do so during Katrina. As a result, Admiral Babb stated that OFRD "didn't have visibility necessarily about where people were. Were they still at home? Were they in flight status? Were they there and gainfully employed?"[183] Problems with the USPHS team identification and notification process were not resolved for the 2005 hurricane season despite the difficulties during the Frances and Ivan deployments. The prior year's difficulties were compounded, because Katrina required significantly more personnel than Frances and Ivan.[184]

It is clear that the USPHS, in its current form, cannot respond to public-health and medical emergencies quickly. When the local economy, and physical and health infrastructure are compromised, the USPHS deployment process is crippled because they require supplies, facilities, and transportation to be individually arranged for each USPHS officer and/or team. All of these issues raise questions as to what the USPHS's emergency-deployment capabilities truly are, what should be expected of it, and what its future role should be.

If USPHS is truly going to be a first responder for medical emergencies, significant changes must be made. As Assistant Secretary Stewart Simonson said, "I think it's clear that one of the things we need is a quick-response force within the Public Health Service and the ability to move people pre-identified into emergencies in a much faster way than we can now."[185]

Credentialing and the Medical Volunteers

Any significant medical or public health response will require that health-care personnel move across localities and states to assist in meeting personnel surge needs, as illustrated by Hurricane Katrina. The Public Health Service and Bioterrorism Preparedness and Response Act of 2002 (P.L. 107-188) mandated a national credentialing system for all health professionals to ensure that health-personnel surge needs are quickly and efficiently met.[186] In response, HRSA[187] created the Emergency System for Advance Registration of Volunteer Health Professionals (ESAR-VHP) to provide a credentialing system to move health professionals within and across states in the event of an emergency. Each state individually joins the ESAR-VHP system in order to provide advance registration of their volunteer health professionals. At the time of Hurricane Katrina, only 12 states were part of the credentialing system.[188] Credentialing criteria for health-care workers were not standardized across states.[189] And even for those 12 states, HHS had no oversight of the states' credentialing systems in order to determine which volunteers might be available or whether volunteers were registered in multiple systems.[190]

In the immediate aftermath of Katrina, HHS began receiving numerous calls from health professionals wanting to volunteer their time and services to the affected region. In response, HHS created an entirely new federal volunteer-signup website.[191] For lack of a national credentialing system, HHS decided to rely on a private contractor to individually verify the credentials of the 34,000 individuals who volunteered in the weeks after Katrina.[192]

The volunteering and deploying process was time- and resource-consuming at best. After registering on the website, volunteers were contacted by the private contractor to verify their credentials. Volunteers were sent to the HHS Human Resources Office to be hired as temporary employees, then to OPHEP for deployment. Credentialing became a significant bottleneck in the process, and there seemed to be no consistent plan as the weeks went on.[193] Numerous documents indicate credentialing delays by the private contractor, who was hired and started work only after landfall.[194] Because different organizations were handling credentialing, hiring, and deployment, HHS had limited information on volunteers in the system and where they were being deployed.[195] The volunteers also posed a host of difficulties for the HHS logistics department because volunteers were not familiar with travel regulations, procedures, and reimbursement protocols, among other issues.[196] Creating this massive federal volunteer effort during the crisis took a significant amount of effort and resources at the federal and the local level and impaired HHS's ability to function as efficiently as possible.

Once created, the new volunteer system experienced many problems. Numerous documents indicate constant additions and changes to the website,[197] underscoring the unplanned nature of this project in the midst of a significant national catastrophe. This was also singularly a federal effort. Staff to the Secretary of HHS made clear in an e-mail to those administering the database that there was a lack of coordination with states around volunteer recruitment.[198] States felt that the HHS volunteer-recruitment effort conflicted with their own efforts to recruit and organize volunteers, who they would dispatch themselves, and the HRSA-sponsored credentialing programs they had been encouraged to establish.[199] It also failed to directly include state emergency-management agencies which were trying to fill requests for medical assistance from the Gulf Coast to ensure the efforts were coordinated and not duplicative.[200]

Eventually, approximately 1,400 out of 34,000 volunteers in HHS's volunteer system actually deployed, or only 3.5 percent of those that signed up on the volunteer website. The costs of HHS's constructing and maintaining this database, and of contracting with a private credentialing entity, are not known. In the end, it was unable to efficiently process volunteers.

The federal volunteer-deployment effort was a haphazard attempt to respond to undoubtedly well-intentioned people offering help in the immediate aftermath of Katrina. While it is human nature to want to volunteer and assist in the face of a major disaster, the significant effort made to attempt to accommodate individual volunteers may not have been the best use of resources.[201]

To date, HHS has failed to meet its statutory mandate to create a national credentialing system to allow health professionals to work across localities and states to meet healthcare personnel surge needs. Had a national credentialing system been in place for Katrina, volunteer health professionals would likely have been utilized more quickly and effectively, obviating the need to create an entirely new federal volunteer database and deployment effort in the midst of a national crisis.

Facilities

Katrina devastated much of the medical infrastructure in Louisiana and Mississippi, leaving some 2,500 hospital patients in New Orleans alone in need of relocation. Thousands of elderly nursing-home and assisted-living patients, and others with chronic medical conditions, such as heart disease, diabetes, and mental illness, required medical care. However, surviving local capacity to meet their needs was limited. Anticipating these medical needs, HHS launched a major effort to deploy mobile hospitals units even though the concept was still in development and HHS's capability was very limited.

Federal Medical Shelters (FMS)

OPHEP's Office of Mass Casualty Planning had started to develop a Federal Medical Shelter (FMS) capability to establish field hospitals for a mass-casualty event. HHS hoped to expand its response capability and avoid relying on DOD medical units, which historically can take some time to deploy.[202] The FMSs would act as all-hazards medical facilities with the capacity to treat patients with basic medical needs. An FMS unit would include hospital cots and medical supplies. Healthcare personnel would also be needed to staff the unit. However, at the time of Hurricane Katrina, the FMSs were still under development and not ready for field units to be established.[203] Assistant Secretary Simonson said, "They were not an operational asset, really. They were still at a concept asset."[204] Assistant Secretary Simonson nonetheless ordered HHS to supply and staff mobile units.[205]

Supply Procurement for FMS

The Strategic National Stockpile (SNS) at the Centers for Disease Control and Prevention played a key role in acquiring supplies to staff the mobile FMS units. Assistant Secretary Simonson tasked the stockpile program with procuring a total of 10,000 hospital beds' worth of equipment and supplies for the FMSs and asked HHS staff "to lean forward and be very aggressive" in making the acquisitions.[206] He sent an e-mail on Wednesday, August 31, to his staff and to the CDC Director that HHS needed "to get the first 2,500 beds for the Federal medical shelters staged by midnight on Friday. … I must tell you there is no margin for error. I implore you – please go all out on this."[207] The entire FMS program was only at the conceptual stage: HHS had two of their own FMS units they were developing with a capacity of approximately 500 beds, with a "fairly modest pharmaceutical cache," and with approximately three days' worth of material support for non-acute patients for their mobile units.[208]

Procuring the FMS units was the "first foray into a broader all-hazards support function"[209] for the stockpile program and it placed an enormous burden on it. So significant was the impact, that on Saturday, September 3, less than a week into the event, Assistant Secretary Simonson himself e-mailed the director of the office overseeing the SNS and the Acting Director of the SNS, and asked them to place less effort on FMS acquisition and refocus their efforts on medical resupply for Mississippi.[210] At the time, Mississippi was experiencing great difficulty in getting needed medical supplies, and as explained below, required HHS to ship them a 50-ton emergency Push Pack to tide the state over until other supplies could reach them.

FMS Location

Deployment of the FMS units was further hampered by a lack of coordination with states on where or how the mobile units should be placed to maximize their utility; negotiations initially only occurred with DOD in advance of any state requests for the facilities.[211] An e-mail stated, "HHS is completing the delivery of the 1st Wave – 2,500 beds etc. Now working the 2nd Wave of 2,500 and early working of the 3rd Wave of 5,000 (total 10K beds). However, this has – for the most part – [been] accomplished without feedback from the States."[212] To its credit, OPHEP attempted to anticipate health needs and worked with HHS partners to develop estimates of personnel required to operate FMSs, but they did not have adequate intelligence from states, FEMA, or their own personnel to generate concrete estimates of the need for the 10,000 beds or the locations at which to deploy them. As late as September 2, days after procurement for additional beds had been aggressively undertaken by the SNS,[213] OPHEP was still trying to develop relationships with the DOD medical facilities at which they hoped to place the units[214] and some locations proved impractical. At Eglin Air Force Base in Florida and Ft. Polk, Louisiana, FMSs were deployed but never used, requiring these units to be redeployed. In short, initial placement decisions were not made in consultation with state emergency managers or with adequate situational awareness of medical needs, so resources had to be redirected and reprioritized.[215]

Blu-Med and USNS *Comfort*

HHS spent a considerable effort acquiring the use of two Blu-Med hospital surge units – mobile medical facilities – one from Nevada and one from North Carolina. These are commercially available medical units manufactured by Blu-Med Response Systems in Kirkland, Washington. Like the FMS units, they were a means to increase medical-facility surge capacity. Deployment of these units became the subject of protracted negotiations among sponsors, host states, and emergency managers.

In the end, the Nevada unit was the subject of conflict about need between NDMS and HHS. NDMS argued it was not needed, while HHS wanted it deployed. By the time the Nevada unit was to finally arrive at the New Orleans airport, NDMS concluded that there was no need for it, saying, that "Stu Simonson did not want to turn off Blu-Med, saying that PHS staff would staff it if needed."[216] Confirming NDMS's assessment, the Blu-Med hospital unit shipped from Nevada to the New Orleans airport was never used there. It was shipped several days later to Gulfport, Mississippi[217], but took an extended period of time to set up.[218] The Carolina unit was shipped directly to Mississippi, where it was used extensively,[219] suggesting that the deployment of the units was a mixed success.

The hospital ship USNS *Comfort* was another asset made available to meet medical surge needs after Katrina. It is a DOD asset with a significant hospital-bed capacity and its own personnel and supplies. However, it is not quickly deployable. On September 2, Assistant Secretary Simonson sent a letter to Assistant Secretary of Defense for Homeland Security Paul McHale requesting that the *Comfort* be deployed with personnel and supplies to treat 1,000 patients;[220] however, it did not arrive at its location in Pascagoula, MS, until Friday, September 9. By that time, an e-mail within the Secretary's office reported, "Nobody could think of a mission for [the *Comfort*]. State Health Department was clear that they had nothing at this time."[221] The *Comfort* was eventually redeployed to Louisiana. The FMS and Blu-Med units and the *Comfort* took a significant amount of time to deploy and, in some cases, became available only after the greatest need for medical care had passed.

Medical Supply Capacity

One of the major challenges in preparing for and responding to medical emergencies is acquiring and delivering medical supplies, including pharmaceuticals, to address a broad range of health conditions and threats. During Katrina, medical supplies were needed for a range of situations: (1) hospitals and other health care facilities cut off from their normal sources of supply by the storm, (2) large evacuee populations, (3) medical responders, including medical teams from HHS and other agencies, and (4) unique medical problems caused by the storm, such as the need for tetanus vaccines. Despite its role as the coordinator of ESF-8, HHS has limited medical assets.[222] During the event, HHS relied primarily on the CDC, as an HHS operating division, to provide medical supplies, equipment, and pharmaceuticals through their SNS division.

Supplying HHS Personnel and HHS Assets

USPHS officers are not normally issued basic supplies or equipment. Consequently, during Katrina HHS had to procure supplies to equip its personnel. For instance, the OPHEP logistics official reported purchasing 1,200 "primary medical bags."[223] Budgetary considerations were the primary reasons why purchases such as these were not made previously, though concerns about shelf life of products and logistics considerations were also factors.[224]

Strategic National Stockpile

HHS maintains a stockpile of medicine and medical supplies for use in public health emergencies through its SNS program. These materials are supplied from both regional government warehouses and from vendor-managed inventories (VMI), which are private medical-supply companies that fill orders as needed during emergencies. However, the primary assets in the SNS are "Push Packs." These pre-packaged units contain about 50 tons of pharmaceutical and medical supplies, and are intended to arrive anywhere in the United States within 12 hours of a deployment decision. States are expected to formally request supplies from the SNS and are periodically evaluated by CDC on their ability to accept and distribute supplies from the stockpile. Once a state's request is approved by HHS, SNS dispatches the Push Pack with a security escort and a special assistance team to help state and local health agencies receive and distribute the supplies. If an emergency requires additional or different medical supplies, the SNS turns to their private vendors, who are expected to ship supplies to arrive within 24 to 36 hours of a request.[225]

Supply Requests

Normal procedures for deploying SNS supplies were overtaken by events from the outset. On Sunday, August 28, the day before landfall, Assistant Secretary Simonson directed SNS to dispatch a select set of medical supplies to the Superdome.[226] Although these supplies were shipped on Sunday, they did not reach Louisiana until Monday, when they were turned over to the state.[227] While the vast majority of medical supplies provided by HHS came from vendors, the State of Mississippi formally requested deployment of a Push Pack because no other supply requests were being filled quickly.[228] Although a Push Pack can be delivered quickly, it is not the first choice when general medical supplies and pharmaceuticals to treat chronic conditions are requested, because its contents are tailored to terrorist attacks and other medical countermeasures. When Mississippi's Push Pack arrived, HHS had to separate general medical supplies and pharmaceuticals out of the 50-ton shipment.[229] A Push Pack request from Louisiana was apparently discussed, but there was no formal request for deployment.[230]

Mississippi's letter requesting a Push Pack was sent to HHS on Thursday, September 1.[231] However, there was uncertainty and tension between HHS headquarters and CDC as to who was responsible for authorizing its release.[232] OPHEP noted that it had no direct control over assets provided by the SNS.[233] An SNS official stated, "I think, probably this is one of the areas where we've not really practiced around the optimal way to go through command and control around a protracted natural disaster. ... I think that there could be value in formalizing some of the processes around release of the stockpile."[234] The movement of requests and approvals through multiple channels created confusion at senior OPHEP and CDC levels, though there is no evidence that this confusion delayed deployment.

Medical Supply Problems

The SNS was never designed to serve as sustained operation delivering medical supplies directly to health-care providers. Informal reports from USPHS officers deployed to the LSU triage center stated that the medical-supply packages sent by SNS did not arrive labeled and lacked basic items, such as bandages and alcohol.[235] Generally, SNS supplies were tailored for use by an acute-care facility for people with life-threatening injuries or illnesses. However, many of the patients passing through the triage center suffered from long-term, chronic diseases such as diabetes. As a result, the triage center ran out of key pharmaceuticals needed for chronic care within one day of initiating operations.[236] There was no organized method for resupply and USPHS officers reported calling multiple sources – the HHS Secretary's Operations Center (SOC), the SNS, and private vendors – to try to meet resupply needs.[237]

The USPHS officers reported that most of the medical problems encountered were acute exacerbation of chronic diseases, such as hypertension, diabetes, congestive heart failure, and psychiatric conditions,[238] which usually require daily medications. They also reported numerous patients in need of kidney dialysis and of oxygen, both of which were in short supply.[239] However, the SNS has historically focused on bioterrorist attacks and not routine health problems, even in large evacuations such as that which occurred in Katrina.[240] Thus, they did not anticipate and were not prepared to meet the medical needs of a general population that had been displaced by a disaster, despite the key preparedness role HHS plays under the NRP.

As one HHS headquarters official stated, "I don't believe the Stockpile is as comprehensive as everyone believes it is."[241] Katrina highlighted the need for broader medical preparation and planning that includes chronic-disease groups,[244] as states and localities turned to the federal government to fill gaps in its medical-supply chains. The SNS was also not designed to be an on-going medical supply operation. [242] However, the CDC acknowledges that there must be a national capacity to tailor medical-supply delivery for different types of disasters when normal chains of delivery are disrupted.[243] Katrina has highlighted the need to ensure a national capacity to move supplies and pharmaceuticals to areas in need when local health infrastructure is compromised.

Conclusions

According to HHS, between August 30 and September 16, the SNS acquired or distributed some $38 million worth of medical supplies, including 14 FMS units accounting for some 3,500 patient beds, 440,000 doses of various vaccines valued at $9 million, and hundreds of thousands of doses of antibiotics and maintenance medications for chronic diseases such as diabetes, heart disease, high blood pressure, and other conditions.[245] HHS adapted the SNS system, which was not designed or prepared to provide basic medical supplies and pharmaceuticals, to become a *de facto* medical-supply chain for a devastated region. However, the ad-hoc system created in the wake of Katrina is not geared to handle a broad range of emergency health needs, especially ones related to the day-to-day health problems of the U.S. population. One HHS official summarized it best when he stated, "From a medical supply standpoint, we were ill prepared. We didn't have and we don't have today, the assets, the medical assets, to support this kind of an incident."[246]

Emergency Support Function 8: Coordination Issues

The NRP designates the HHS as the coordinator and primary response agency for ESF-8, Public Health and Medical Services. ESF-8 provides both public-health and medical-care support ranging from deployment of medical-care personnel, to the provision of medical equipment and supplies, to patient evacuation.[247] In this role, HHS theoretically becomes the lead agency for federal medical response in a federally declared emergency, working with and coordinating the deployment of assets from other federal agencies.[248] Within HHS, this function is carried out primarily by the Assistant Secretary for Public Health Emergency Preparedness.[249]

Conflicts with FEMA and NDMS

During Katrina, HHS had mixed success in carrying out its role as the lead agency for ESF-8. Some agencies, notably DOD, appear to have accepted HHS as the ESF-8 lead. Others, notably FEMA, did not. Although an effort was made to establish a unified incident command for ESF-8 at the agency-headquarters level to resolve conflicts and improve coordination, this did not occur until September 5, a week after landfall.[250] It is unclear whether establishing such a structure would have substantially aided the initial response efforts or fully resolved ESF-8 coordination issues, but it is clear that there were interagency-coordination problems during the event. These occurred principally between HHS and FEMA, and ranged from a failure to share basic operational information, to more complex tasks such as making asset-deployment decisions.

NDMS teams were staged and deployed with minimal, if any, coordination with HHS. When asked about coordination between FEMA and HHS in the deployment and pre-staging of NDMS teams and his efforts to get a DMAT to the Superdome before landfall, Assistant Secretary Simonson explained that even though he was able to convince the acting head of FEMA's Response Division, Ed Buikema, to send a DMAT to the Superdome, this was the exception, not the rule:

> Now I should say, contrary to what has been reported in other places, the NDMS was not overly concerned with our views on where particular assets should go. And so it's not clear to me that we have – we had then much say in where they would go. I think the Superdome situation revealed to Ed [Buikema] how weak the pre-deployment was and I think it was very difficult for them to resist that it was a logical deployment at that point. But that was between me and Ed. That wasn't part of a structure.[251]

Another example of this deployment issue is documented in an e-mail exchange between Simonson and Beall, the NDMS chief, on Saturday, September 3. At the time, efforts were still under way to evacuate the Superdome and the Convention Center. The medical teams handling the medical evacuation at the airport were being overwhelmed. Beall and Simonson exchanged a series of e-mails about replacing DMATs providing medical care at evacuation centers in Texas.[252] Beall later reported that there were five NDMS teams in Texas.[253] This exchange raises questions such as why these capable NDMS teams were staffing evacuee centers when there was a critical need for them in New Orleans, and how these deployment decisions were made.

 ESF-8 also included oversight of mortuary affairs and deployment of the NDMS Disaster Mortuary Operational Response Teams (DMORT).[254] Operational insight by ESF-8 was no better in deployment of these teams. When asked about HHS's participation in a plan for addressing the large number of expected fatalities in the Gulf, the Deputy Assistant Secretary at HHS charged with this responsibility said:

> It didn't come for approval. FEMA runs its own operations so they didn't ask if we approve or not. But, as I said, we had a liaison. We had a DMORT person working upstairs. So he, he writes this up and shares it with us and it served as an, it served as an important thing for us to work with. This is, this was not developed with our input.[255]

These examples raise basic questions not only about whether the right medical assets were being deployed to the right locations during the response, but also, more fundamentally, about who was in charge of those decisions. It clearly was not HHS, the lead for ESF-8 in the NRP. HHS/NDMS coordination problems are unfortunately not a new issue and were identified as a problem in responding to the 2004 hurricanes.[256] The causes were not addressed then and obviously remain.

HHS Coordination Resources

The reasons for these ESF-8 coordination problems are perhaps best articulated by an analysis prepared by one HHS OPHEP staff member at the height of the crisis on September 3. This analysis locates the problem in a lack of situational awareness by HHS and a lack of direct cooperation from NDMS: "Given NDMS's: superior situational awareness; no mandate to share their Intel [intelligence]; and clear and forceful decision to NOT allow us to be a part of their operational planning, OPHEP lacks the ability to properly lead ESF#8."[257] Implicit in the analysis is that HHS lacks sufficient emergency-response and coordination assets in the field.

Whether the ESF-8 command-and-control problems can be attributed solely to the factors identified in the HHS analysis, there does appear to be an inadequate level of HHS emergency planning and coordination capability both in the field and headquarters. As the staff analysis points out, HHS has only recently established 10 regional emergency coordinators – one for each federal region.[258] The Region VI coordinator who was responsible for covering Louisiana did not assume that position until April 2005, and so was not familiar with the situation in Louisiana.[259] In addition, she was responsible for a large, five-state area covering Arkansas, New Mexico, Oklahoma, and Texas, as well as Louisiana.[260] At the time Katrina made landfall, the Region VI coordinator had not yet visited Louisiana, nor had she met or communicated with Louisiana's ESF-8 officials.[261]

This lack of awareness of Louisiana's hurricane or health preparations was further exacerbated by the fact that no one from OPHEP participated in the Hurricane Pam exercise – which shaped much of the state's medical-response plan used for Katrina – or follow-up medical workshops, including one held the week before Katrina. As a result, the Region VI coordinator had to often depend on the NDMS regional staff for information and insight into the crisis in Louisiana as it unfolded.[262] In addition, virtually all of the HHS regional emergency coordinators were deployed to Mississippi and Louisiana response operations.[263] This left a gap in their own regions in the event of another crisis, or even, in this event, when Katrina evacuees began to flow to other regions and required health and medical coordination services.

Lack of Emergency Preparedness Program and Response Integration

Although HHS has several medical-emergency preparedness programs to help state and local public-health officials and health-care facilities prepare for emergencies, these programs are not carried out by OPHEP. HRSA[264] carries out a bioterrorism hospital-preparedness program and a medical-volunteer credentialing program. CDC carries out a public-health bioterrorism cooperative-grant program and a program to deliver emergency medical supplies from the SNS. Although OPHEP has general oversight of these programs within HHS,[265] as do the emergency coordinators at the regional level, they do not administer these programs. HRSA and CDC personnel administer the programs and have the primary interactions with state and local health officials.[266]

Although these HHS preparedness programs are primarily focused on the threat of bioterrorism, several of them did provide demonstrable "all-hazards" benefits which were utilized during Katrina (The exception is the HRSA credentialing program). For example, the HRSA hospital-preparedness program was used to procure satellite phones for hospitals in Mississippi, which allowed the state to establish and maintain communications throughout the hospital system during Katrina despite the loss of most other communications alternatives.[267] In Louisiana, the HRSA hospital program was used to establish a statewide hospital network before Katrina that was used to track available hospital beds during the event and provide information about the status and emergency needs of the hospital system.[268] The CDC stockpile program was used extensively both to provide medical supplies through vendor managed inventories and through the deployment of a Push Pack in Mississippi. These programs and the relationships that are established between HHS and state and local personnel are not integrated into OPHEP emergency-preparedness and response efforts.

A similar situation occurred between health-care delivery facilities – both hospitals and community clinics – and the HHS operating divisions that provide reimbursement and financial support to those facilities and maintain close day-to-day relationships. During Katrina, HRSA became a conduit for status reports and requests for emergency assistance from community-health clinics to HHS emergency-operations center, and the administrator of HRSA provided facility-specific needs from HRSA funded programs, primarily health centers and rural hospitals.[269] The Centers for Medicare and Medicaid Services played a similar role for hospitals.[270]

It is clear that HHS and its operating divisions provided significant medical-preparedness capabilities before the event and response capabilities during it. However, as witnesses and interview subjects repeatedly said during this investigation, joint planning, exercises, and relationships among emergency responders are essential to effective, coordinated operations in a crisis. OPHEP, as the lead HHS organization for emergency preparedness and response, had very limited interaction with state and local officials. It also had limited ability to ensure that the Department's own agencies were truly providing effective preparedness programs and emergency-response capability.

SERT Deployment

Although HHS deployed emergency response coordinators to staff the Louisiana and Mississippi EOCs prior to landfall, HHS did not send the Secretary's Emergency Response Team (SERT) to those states until several days into the event.[271] These teams are supposed to be the Secretary's direct, on-scene representative and the local command-and-control organization for health resources. The Louisiana SERT team leader, Admiral Craig Vanderwagen, USPHS, did not arrive in Baton Rouge until Friday afternoon, September 2. The Mississippi SERT team leader, Admiral Brenda Holman, USPHS, did not arrive in Jackson until Sunday afternoon, September 4. It then took additional time for them to fully constitute their SERT teams. As explained in an e-mail from the deputy commander for the Mississippi SERT, on Monday, September 5, a week after landfall, "We are a little behind with this response. ... Members of the MST [management support team] and added SERT members are arriving slowly."[272]

The impact on response effectiveness of HHS's not having additional "boots on the ground" more quickly is hard to evaluate. However, there is evidence that a greater HHS presence was needed earlier. For example, HHS began to acquire and deploy mobile field-hospital-type facilities to the region early in the event. HHS identified several military bases to host these facilities, including Eglin Air Force Base in Florida and Fort Polk in Louisiana. Although this deployment plan allowed HHS to begin bringing significant amounts of medical supplies into the region, the Louisiana SERT team quickly recommended abandoning the Fort Polk operation and redistributing its supplies to other locations in Louisiana.[273] Similar adjustments had to be made in Florida, where they were never used, and Mississippi, inviting the question whether quicker, better deployment decisions could have been made with the benefit of a greater SERT presence earlier in the event.

Another example where greater SERT presence appears to have been needed was in the difficult, chaotic, first-of-a-kind evacuation of patients from the New Orleans airport, where there was little command and control, and insufficient medical personnel, supplies, communications, and security.[274] Despite the importance of this mission and the extraordinarily difficult circumstances, it appears there was little if any HHS presence. As reported by a NDMS representative at the airport to the NDMS Director, Beall, as operations were winding down on Sunday, September 4: "Just a heads-up. There has not been any HHS/ESF-8 representation at the airport operation site during any portion of this evolution."[275]

Advance Deployment and Procurement

Early in the event, HHS enlisted DOD's help to deploy resources in advance of state assistance requests. HHS began to request DOD assistance in staffing mobile medical facilities shortly after landfall on Monday, August 29.[276] Although no formal state request had been made for these resources, HHS took the initiative to acquire and deploy some 2,250 beds initially, in anticipation of large numbers of patients. In the absence of an actual mission assignment, HHS formalized the request in a letter from Assistant Secretary Simonson to Paul McHale, Assistant Secretary of Defense for Homeland Security, on August 31.[277] The letter justified the request as follows: "In light of the grave situation in the southern coastal regions, and consistent with the National Response Plan's Catastrophic Incident Annex, Secretary Leavitt has directed the deployment of multiple Federal Medical Shelters. I am therefore writing to request assistance from the Department of Defense (DOD), as outlined below in completing this deployment in a timely fashion."[278] DOD accepted the request even though the Catastrophic Incident Annex had not yet been formally invoked, and promptly tasked its field elements to respond that day.[279] Later the same week, Simonson made an additional written request to McHale, again invoking the Catastrophic Incident Annex, for deployment of the hospital ship USNS *Comfort* and outlining expected future requests.[280] Again, DOD accepted the request and the *Comfort* embarked from Baltimore the same day.[281]

While not unique to ESF-8, the procedure for deploying and requesting federal assets in advance of state requests is unclear. Although the Catastrophic Incident Annex was invoked here to enable the federal government to "lean forward" and to begin to deploy significant medical assets in anticipation of Mississippi's and Louisiana's needs, this Annex was not formally in effect at the time, nor is it clear how such decisions should be made in the future. In the cases cited here, circumstances required these decisions to be made at a senior political level in the absence of a formal process, as Assistant Secretary Simonson explained:

> What I should have written was in the spirit of the Catastrophic Incident [Annex]. … But there was substantive agreement on these procedural legalistic issues that we were trying to work with. What I was trying to do was to get out on the ice so that if we were needed I wouldn't have to start from a standing stop. I wanted to be there. I wanted to be out there so that we could advance in two places where we were needed with as little lead time as possible. And so no, there were no ARFs or MAs or anything else issued. This was coming right from us. And thank God much of this wasn't needed, as it turned out. But in the end I think it was the right thing to do. What authority? The authority is a general one. We have fairly general authority under the Public Service Health Act to assist the states.[282]

HHS also relied upon its own limited funds to begin advance procurements of FMS units and take other actions in advance of formal mission assignments. For example, it used some $5 million in surplus funds available in its Public Health and Social Service Emergency Fund appropriation to begin these purchases. As Assistant Secretary Simonson explained, "There's no money in the Public Health Service's emergency fund, other than the monies that are being channeled through the CDC and to HRSA for their grant programs. It's not like there's a big contingency fund there."[283] He also explained that although Section 319 of the Public Health Service Act provides for the creation of a special emergency fund, "There's just nothing in the fund and I don't think there ever has been."[284] HHS also deferred other purchases for the SNS, such as a planned purchase of antibiotics, to free additional funds to buy medical supplies for Katrina.[285] It is not clear that this approach to incurring costs in the absence of a formal Stafford Act request from a state provides HHS with sufficient capability to "lean forward" in catastrophic public health emergency.

Mortuary Responsibilities

Although it is clear that ESF-8 is responsible for victim identification and mortuary functions, a serious problem developed during Katrina in collecting and transporting deceased victims. The usual capabilities of local coroners and first responders were limited or nonexistent in affected parts of Louisiana. Although FEMA initially accepted responsibility for collecting bodies of victims and tried to hire a contractor to recover bodies, FEMA was unsuccessful in negotiating a contract. NDMS DMORT teams were pressed into service to perform this function[286] and federal-level resolution of the problem became the responsibility of ESF-8, although this responsibility had not previously been assigned to ESF-8, or any other ESF. This made an already difficult task more so. As the Deputy Assistant Secretary with responsibility for this function at OPHEP explained,

> [Given] the number of bodies and the complexity that came with the hurricane, there wasn't any coordinated way to go ahead and figure how we're going to do the recovery. And … that's not an ESF 8 function, that is recovering bodies is not a health and medical thing. Processing them in terms of identifying them through the pathologic and mortuary affairs part, that is in ESF-8. So one of the gaps that existed is . . . what kind of national coordination policy do we have for recovery of remains?[287]

1 The remaining patient population in southeast Louisiana was estimated at between 2,000 and 2,500 at the time of landfall, and more than 625 in Mississippi. New Orleans planned to shelter some 400 special- needs patients at the Superdome, but there has been no precise number established for the special-needs population in New Orleans expected or treated. U.S. Department of Health and Human Services (HHS), Secretary's Operations Center, Flash Report #4 – Hurricane Katrina, Aug. 29, 2005, 8:30 a.m. ET. Provided to Committee; filed as Bates no. OPHEP 28247; HHS, Secretary's Operations Center, Flash Report #5 – Hurricane Katrina, Aug. 29, 2005, 3 p.m. ET. Provided to Committee; filed as Bates no. OPHEP 28249; Mississippi Emergency Management Agency (MEMA), Hurricane Katrina Situation Report #19, Aug. 30, 2005, 6:30 p.m. ET, p. 8. Provided to Committee; filed as Bates no. MEMA-0010984.

2 Hospitals in the New Orleans area, for example, had not relocated their emergency generators and electric switch gear above flood level. In the case of the LSU hospitals in New Orleans, Charity and University, the hospital system had been unable to obtain funding from the legislature to accomplish this goal. Committee staff interview of James Aiken, M.D., Medical Director, Office of Emergency Preparedness, Medical Center of Louisiana in New Orleans, conducted on Jan. 11, 2006, transcript pp. 73-75; Committee staff interview of Don Smithburg, Executive Vice President and Chief Executive Officer, Health Care Services Division, Louisiana State University, conducted on Feb. 7, 2006, transcript pp. 15-17.

3 The Attorney General of Louisiana, Charles Foti, is investigating these deaths. Criminal charges have already been brought in the case of one nursing home and eight cases, involving five nursing homes and three hospitals are active and open at this time. Kris Wartelle, e-mail to David Berick, Senate Committee staff member, Mar. 21, 2006, 3:02 p.m.

4 Committee staff interview of Avis Gray, Regional Administrator, Region I, Office of Public Health, Louisiana Department of Health and Hospitals, conducted on Dec. 8, 2005, transcript pp. 99-100, 108-109.

5 Gray interview, Dec. 8, 2005, pp. 179-180. *See also*: HHS, Secretary's Operations Center, Flash Report #6 – Hurricane Katrina, Aug. 30, 2005, 3 a.m. ET. Provided to Committee; filed as Bates no. OPHEP 28252.

6 *Southeast Louisiana Catastrophic Hurricane Plan*, prepared by IEM, Inc. for LOHSEP and FEMA, Sept. 2005, pp. 99-111 [hereinafter *Southeast Louisiana Catastrophic Hurricane Plan*, Sept. 2005]. Section 14.0 "Temporary Medical Care," includes the following planning assumption "All 40 medical treatment facilities in the impacted area are affected by the high-water levels, loss of electricity, loss of communications, and storm-force winds, rendering them isolated and useless. At best, they will shelter-in-place whatever patients they were not able to discharge prior to landfall. In addition, refugees (non-injured or ill individuals) will come to those treatment facilities for sheltering. All patients, staff, family members, and

refugees will require evacuation from nonfunctional facilities. These treatment facilities may require restoration of power, as well as medical, water, and food re-supply, until evacuation is complete." The planners also estimated that there would be more than 2,000 hospital and a minimum of 900 special needs patients needing evacuation after landfall along with hospital and nursing home staff. *See also: Southeast Louisiana Catastrophic Hurricane Plan*, Sept. 2005, Appendix A.

7 Philip Navin, e-mail to EOC Report, Aug. 29, 2005, 6:58 a.m. Provided to Committee; filed as Bates nos. CDC 747 through 749.

8 EOC Report, e-mail to Donald Benken and others, Aug. 28, 2005, 1 p.m. Provided to Committee; filed as Bates nos. CDC 725 through 726.

9 The low incidence of infectious-disease outbreaks among survivor and evacuee populations appears to be the result of successful public health surveillance of shelters and public-health intervention. During August 29-October 30, 2005 a total of 81 reports were investigated by Louisiana infectious-disease epidemiologists. MMWR Morbidity and Mortality Weekly Report, *Surveillance in Hurricane Evacuation Centers – Louisiana, September – October 2005*, Jan. 20, 2006, Vol. 55, No. 2, pp. 31-35.

10 Suzan Dunaway, e-mail to Monica Giovachino, Sept. 3, 2005, 12:45 p.m. Provided to Committee; filed as Bates no. OPHEP 932.

11 Committee staff interview of Erin Downey, Louisiana Hospital Association, Director of Emergency Preparedness (Liaison to Health and Resources and Services Administration), conducted on Jan. 20, 2006, transcript pp. 43-44.

12 Committee staff interview of Jimmy Guidry, M.D., Medical Director and State Health Officer, Louisiana Department of Health and Hospitals, conducted on Dec. 20, 2005, transcript p. 116.

13 Testimony of Jimmy Guidry, M.D., Medical Director and State Health Officer, Louisiana Department of Health and Hospitals, before the U.S. Senate, Committee on Homeland Security and Governmental Affairs, hearing on *Challenges in a Catastrophe: Evacuating New Orleans in Advance of Hurricane Katrina*, Jan. 31, 2006.

14 Dr. Guidry interview, Dec. 20, 2005, pp. 42-45.

15 Dr. Guidry interview, Dec. 20, 2005, pp. 44-45.

16 *Southeast Louisiana Catastrophic Hurricane Plan*, Sept. 2005, pp. 99-111.

17 Dr. Aiken interview, Jan. 11, 2006, pp. 66-68. *See also*: Keith Holtermann, e-mail to Robert Blitzer and others, Aug. 29, 2005, 1:38 a.m. Provided to Committee; filed as Bates nos. CDC 747 through 749 ("Advanced planning was never completed on how the patients left in the hospitals will be evacuated after the event. The use of boats to support the other ESFs has been fairly comprehensive, and ESF #8 has yet to be completed.").

18 La. Admin. Code 48:1, Chapter 93, § 9335 (Nov. 2003). Moreover, the regulations state that "as a minimum," the plan shall include the following: Emergency procedures for evacuation of the hospital; Comprehensive measures for receiving and managing care for a large influx of emergency patients; Comprehensive plans for receiving patients who are being relocated from another facility due to a disaster; and the system or procedure to ensure that medical charts accompany patients in the event of a patient evacuation and that supplies, equipment, records and medications would be transported as part of an evacuation. Furthermore, and as noted by the Feb. 16, 2006, U.S. Senate Committee on Health, Education, Labor and Pensions, *Chairman's Report on Elder Evacuations During the 2005 Gulf Coast Hurricane Disasters*, issued by Senator Michael B. Enzi, p. 2, the Centers for Medicare and Medicaid Services mandate that nursing homes and hospitals maintain EOPs as a prerequisite to receiving Medicare and Medicaid payments. The Joint Commission on Accreditation of Healthcare Organizations has a similar requirement as a prerequisite to accreditation. U.S. Senate, Committee on Health, Education, Labor and Pensions, *Chairman's Report on Elder Evacuations During the 2005 Gulf Coast Hurricane Disasters*, Feb. 16, 2006.

19 Dr. Guidry, Senate Committee hearing, Jan. 31, 2006.

20 Dr. Aiken interview, Jan. 11, 2006, pp. 62-63.

21 Dr. Guidry interview, Dec. 20, 2005, p. 87.

22 Dr. Guidry interview, Dec. 20, 2005, pp. 86-87.

23 Dr. Aiken interview, Jan. 11, 2006, pp. 91-92; Dr. Guidry interview, Dec. 20, 2005, p. 71.

24 Committee staff interview of Sec. Fred Cerise, M.D., Louisiana Department of Health and Hospitals, conducted on Dec. 2, 2005, transcript pp. 164-166. Ironically, on Sunday evening, before it was known that the hospitals would flood, some special-needs patients who were too ill to be treated at the Superdome had been moved to one of the hospitals. *See also:* Committee staff interview of Col. Pat Prechter, State Chief Nurse, Louisiana Army National Guard and Deputy Commander, Louisiana Medical Command, conducted on Jan. 6, 2006, transcript pp. 41-42.

25 Dr. Guidry interview, Dec. 20, 2005, p. 68.

26 Dr. Guidry interview, Dec. 20, 2005, pp. 70-71 ("And so you had those large numbers of people in the Dome without power, without sewerage, waiting for buses, waiting for transportation. And you had the special-needs patients getting flown out by helicopter or taken out by boat. And our intent was to get the sick out first. And that's real difficult to do when there's 20,000 people right next door. And there was a lot of discussion and I hear this from my boss as well who was there, that they were afraid that the people were going to get violent. That time was taking too long, that they were all in each others' faces and they were afraid that violence was going to break out and everybody was afraid for their life.").

27 Dr. Cerise interview, Dec. 2, 2005, pp. 229-230.

28 Dr. Cerise interview, Dec. 2, 2005, pp. 212, 230-231.

29 Dr. Aiken interview, Jan. 11, 2006, pp. 100-101.

30 Dr. Aiken interview, Jan. 11, 2006, pp. 90-91, 94.

31 Dr. Cerise interview, Dec. 2, 2005, pp. 156-157.

32 Dr. Aiken interview, Jan. 11, 2006, pp. 134.

33 Dr. Aiken interview, Jan. 11, 2006, pp 143.

34 La. Admin. Code 48:1, Chapter 97, § 9729 (January 1998). The law also states that each plan "shall be activated at least annually, either in response to an emergency or in a planned drill," and that "the nursing home's performance during the activation of the plan shall be evaluated and documented." Moreover, "[a]s a minimum," the written plans must describe: the evacuation of residents to a safe place, either within the nursing home or to another location; the delivery of essential care and services to nursing home residents; the provisions for the management of staff, including distribution and assignment of responsibilities and functions; a plan for coordinating transportation services required for evacuating residents to another location; and assurance that the resident's family or sponsor is notified if the resident is evacuated to another location.

35 Walter Maestri, emergency manager for Jefferson Parish, said "Nursing homes are required by state law and by licensing statutes to have in place an emergency operations plan. … The enforcement is in the hands of the State of Louisiana and the parishes through the emergency management office. Each nursing home that functions in Jefferson Parish is mandated by State law to send to me once a year a copy of their emergency plan. We peruse that plan, we have no requirement, the State does not require us to approve or disapprove the plan. But we must peruse it and affirm to the State that there is a plan." Committee staff interview of Walter Maestri, Ph.D., Director, Jefferson Parish Office of Emergency Management, conducted on Oct. 27, 2005, transcript p. 218.

36 Joseph Mathews, emergency manager for Orleans Parish said, "Hospitals, nursing homes, special care – yeah, they should have an adequate plan. It's required by the State that they have an adequate plan. [I review e]ach one of them individually, page by page – I look at it and basically [inaudible]. They are supposed to submit a plan to my office, yes. … An adequate plan includes a plan of evacuating and moving those persons. … Basically they're governed by the State, and all I can do at my office is ask that they comply. As far as any punitive measures or anything like that, I don't have the authority to do anything. I can – the best I can do is report it to the State, send them correspondence [inaudible] it's basically up to the State." Committee staff interview of Joseph Matthews, Director, New Orleans Office of Emergency Preparedness, LA, conducted on Nov. 23, 2005, transcript pp. 130-131, 133.

37 Dr. Guidry interview, Dec. 20, 2005, pp. 107-108; Dr. Aiken interview, Jan. 11, 2006, pp. 49-51.

38 Dr. Aiken interview, Jan. 11, 2006, pp. 49-52.

39 Dr. Aiken interview, Jan. 11, 2006, pp. 85, 118. It should be noted, however, that while Dr. Aiken did say that Charity Hospital generators were "running on fumes for the first day or so," he also noted that "[a]nd then I think maybe Wednesday or Thursday, we had more [generator fuel] than we needed."

40 Dr. Guidry, Senate Committee hearing, Jan. 31, 2005. In a special session after Katrina, the Louisiana legislature enacted legislation calling for a re-examination of hospital building codes. *Source*: 2005 La. Acts 41 (1st Extraordinary Session).

41 Dr. Aiken interview, Jan. 11, 2006, pp. 127-128.

42 Dr. Aiken interview, Jan. 11, 2006, p. 118.

43 Committee staff interview of Kevin Stephens, M.D., Director, New Orleans Health Department, LA, conducted on Nov. 19, 2005, transcript pp. 65-66.

44 Dr. Guidry interview, Dec. 20, 2005, pp. 32-33, 105.

45 Committee staff interview of Roseanne Pratts, Director, Emergency Preparedness, Louisiana Department of Health and Hospitals, conducted on Jan. 31, 2006, transcript p. 18.

46 Dr. Guidry, Senate Committee hearing, Jan. 31, 2006.

47 Dr. Guidry interview, Dec. 20, 2005, p.65.

48 Dr. Guidry interview, Dec. 20, 2005, p. 65.

49 U.S. Public Health Service, PHS Katrina Response: Baton Rouge Deployment Alpha Team, briefing slides, Oct. 16, 2005. Provided to Committee.

50 Dr. Stephens interview, Nov. 10, 2005, pp. 25-26; Dr. Guidry interview, Dec. 20, 2005, pp. 58-59, 61-63; Pratts interview, Jan. 31, 2006, pp. 18-19; Col. Prechter interview, Jan. 6, 2006, p. 55.

51 Committee staff interview of Ronald Martin, Deputy Commander, Management Support Team, National Disaster Medical System, FEMA, conducted on Jan. 13, 2006, transcript pp. 53, 63-68.

52 Dr. Stephens interview, Nov. 10, 2005, pp. 25-26.

53 Col. Prechter interview, Jan. 6, 2006, pp. 100, 102, 109, 115.

54 Committee staff interview of Brig. Gen. Gary Jones, Louisiana National Guard, conducted on Dec. 7, 2005, transcript p. 180; Col. Prechter interview, Jan. 6, 2006, p. 115.

55 Jones interview, Dec. 7, 2005, p. 189.

56 Dr. Guidry interview, Dec. 20, 2005, p. 75. However, it should be noted that Joseph Donchess, Executive Director of the Louisiana Nursing Home Association, stated that 21 nursing homes were evacuated pre-storm and 36 were evacuated post-storm, amounting to a total of about 5,500 to 6,000 nursing home residents evacuated pre- and post-storm. Testimony of Joseph Donchess, Executive Director, Louisiana Nursing Home Service Corporation, before the U.S. Senate, Committee on Homeland Security and Governmental Affairs, hearing on *Challenges in a Catastrophe: Evacuating New Orleans in Advance of Hurricane Katrina*, Jan. 31, 2006.

57 Dr. Guidry, Senate Committee hearing, Jan. 31, 2006.

58 Dr. Aiken interview, Jan. 11, 2006, pp. 106-107.

59 Dr. Stephens interview, Nov. 10, 2005, pp. 26-27.

60 Dr. Cerise interview, Dec. 2, 2005, p. 177.

61 Committee staff interview of Joseph Donchess, Executive Director, Louisiana Nursing Home Service Corporation, conducted on Jan. 9, 2006, transcript p. 128.

62 Donchess, Senate Committee hearing, Jan. 31, 2006.

63 Donchess, Senate Committee hearing, Jan. 31, 2006.

64 Louisiana Office of Homeland Security and Emergency Preparedness (LOHSEP), *Emergency Operations Plan*, Apr. 2005, p. ESF–8–1 (emphasis added). Provided to Committee.

65 Dr. Aiken interview, Jan. 11, 2006, pp. 20-21, 32-33, 34; Smithburg interview, Feb. 7, 2006, pp. 55, 60-61.

66 Downey interview, Jan. 20, 2006, pp. 17-21.

67 Downey interview, Jan. 20, 2006, pp. 50-54.

68 Dr. Aiken interview, Jan. 11, 2007, pp. 20-21 (emphasis added).

69 Under the 2001 EOP, LSU was responsible for the following: "The [CEO] of the [LSU] Health Sciences Center (HSC) Health Care Services Division (HCSD) shall be primarily responsible for participating in state, regional and parish planning to coordinate the provision of hospital care and shelter for nursing home and home health care patients with acute care requirements, and casualties of emergencies and disasters. The LSU-HSC-HCSD will have the lead role among state agencies in such planning." *Source:* LOHSEP, *Emergency Operations Plan*, March 2001, pp. M–1 through M–2. Furthermore, as explained by James Aiken, M.D., Medical Director for Emergency Preparedness for the Medical Center of Louisiana in New Orleans (a.k.a. Charity and University Hospitals), these sorts of responsibilities were held by LSU dating back to 1992. *Source:* Dr. Aiken interview, Jan. 11, 2006, pp. 18-21.

70 Dr. Aiken interview, Jan. 11, 2006, pp. 32-33 (emphasis added).

71 Dr. Aiken interview, Jan. 11, 2006, p. 34.

72 Smithberg interview, Feb. 7, 2006, p. 55.

73 Smithberg interview, Feb. 7, 2006, p. 55.

74 Smithberg interview, Feb. 7, 2006, pp. 60-61.

75 Dr. Aiken interview, Jan. 11, 2006, pp. 24-25.

76 Dr. Aiken interview, Jan. 11, 2006, p. 28.

77 Dr. Aiken interview, Jan. 11, 2006 pp. 21-22.

78 Downey Interview, Jan. 20, 2006, pp. 67-68, 69.

79 The six counties are Hancock, Harrison, Jackson, Pearl River, Stone, and George. Committee staff interview of Jim Craig, Director, Office of Health Protection, Mississippi Department of Health, conducted on Jan. 25, 2006, transcript p. 28.

80 The three hospitals were Hancock Medical Center in Bay St. Louis, Gulf Coast Medical Center in Gulfport, and L.O. Crosby in Picayune. U.S. Department of Health and Human Services and the Mississippi Department of Health, *Hurricane Katrina: Medical Support/Demobilization/Transition Plan for the State of Mississippi*, Jan. 2006, p. 3 [hereinafter *Mississippi Medical Support/Demobilization/Transition Plan*].

81 *Mississippi Medical Support/Demobilization/Transition Plan*, p. 3.

82 *Mississippi Medical Support/Demobilization/Transition Plan*, p. 3.

83 *Mississippi Medical Support/Demobilization/Transition Plan*, p. 7.

84 *Mississippi Medical Support/Demobilization/Transition Plan*, p. 3.

85 The plan provides that MDH is responsible for "the overall public health response, the triage, treatment and transportation of victims of a disaster, immediate support to hospitals and nursing homes, the provision of emergency mental health crisis counseling for individuals and the community, and the re-establishment of all health, medical and social service systems." MEMA, *Mississippi Emergency Operations Plan, Volume II: Mississippi Comprehensive Emergency Management Plan (CEMP)*, May 14, 1999, pp. ESF 8–1 through ESF 8–16. Provided to Committee.

86 Craig interview, Jan. 25, 2006, pp. 11-12.

87 Written Statement of Brian Amy, M.D., State Health Office, Mississippi Department of Health, for the U.S. House, Select Bipartisan Committee to Investigate the Preparation for and Response to Hurricane Katrina, hearing on *Hurricane Katrina: Preparedness and Response by the State of Mississippi*, Dec. 7, 2005, p. 3.

88 Written Statement of Dr. Amy, House Select Committee hearing, Dec. 7, 2005, pp. 9-10.

89 Written Statement of Dr. Amy, House Select Committee hearing, Dec. 7, 2005, p. 6.

90 Craig interview, Jan. 25, 2006, pp. 12-13.

91 Craig interview, Jan. 25, 2006, p. 36.

92 Craig interview, Jan. 25, 2006, pp. 12-13.

93 There is a potentially contrary report from HHS Region IV on the evening of August 28, 2005 stating that not all, in fact only two of 29 skilled-nursing facilities reported evacuations. EOC Report, e-mail to Donald Benken and others, Aug. 28, 2005, 10:04 p.m. Provided to Committee, filed as Bates no. CDC 725; Craig interview, Jan. 25, 2006, pp. 37-38.

94 Testimony of Gov. Haley Barbour, Mississippi, before the U.S. Senate, Committee on Homeland Security and Governmental Affairs, hearing on *Hurricane Katrina: The Role of the Governors in Managing the Catastrophe*, Feb. 2, 2006.

95 Craig interview, Jan. 25, 2006, p. 8.

96 Written Statement of Dr. Amy, House Select Committee hearing, Dec. 7, 2005, pp. 10-11.

97 Written Statement of Dr. Amy, House Select Committee hearing, Dec. 7, 2005, p. 15.

98 Craig interview, Jan. 25, 2006, pp. 28-29. In his testimony before the House Committee investigating Katrina, Dr. Amy recalled Carolina-1 being deployed by HHS. Written Statement of Dr. Amy, House Select Committee hearing, Dec. 7, 2005, p. 6.

99 Craig interview, Jan. 25, 2006, p. 24.

100 Craig interview, Jan. 25, 2006, pp. 30-31.

101 Craig interview, Jan. 25, 2006, pp. 28-29.

102 Written Statement of Dr. Amy, House Select Committee hearing, Dec. 7, 2005, pp. 16-17.

103 The National Disaster Medical System (NDMS) was formerly within the Department of Health and Human Services (HHS), Office of Emergency Preparedness (OEP). The Homeland Security Act transferred NDMS to DHS in 2003. "Homeland Security Act of 2002." (P.L. 107-296), 6 U.S.C. § 201.

104 U.S. Department of Homeland Security, National Disaster Medical System. http://www.oep-ndms.dhhs.gov/index.html. Accessed on Mar. 6, 2006.

105 U.S. Department of Veterans Affairs, National Disaster Medical System. http://www1.va.gov/EMSHG/page.cfm?pg=45. Accessed on Apr. 21, 2006.

106 U.S. Department of Veterans Affairs, "National Disaster Medical System (NDMS), Patient Movement After Action Review Meeting, December 12-13, 2005." http://www1.va.gov/emshg/page.cfm?pg=111. Accessed on Apr.21, 2006 [hereinafter NDMS Patient Movement AAR, Dec. 2005].

107 FEMA, *Current NDMS Overview*, Jan. 6, 2006. Provided to Committee.

108 FEMA, *Current NDMS Overview*, Jan. 6, 2006. Provided to Committee.

109 FEMA, *Current NDMS Overview*, Jan. 6, 2006. Provided to Committee.

110 Deployments included 40 DMAT's, 16 strike teams, 8 DMORTs, 4 VMATs and 3 MSTs. In the Louisiana and Mississippi this meant 1,265 and 667 personnel, respectively, for a total of 1,932 NDMS team members. FEMA, Hurricane Katrina NDMS Resource Status Report, Sept. 5, 2005, 11 p.m. Provided to Committee.

111 Committee staff interview of Jack Beall, Chief, National Disaster Medical System, FEMA, conducted on Jan. 10, 2006, transcript p. 11.

112 Committee staff interview of Capt. Art French, M.D., U.S. Public Health Service, Deputy Chief Medical Officer, Disaster Medical Assistance Team PHS-1, National Disaster Medical System, FEMA, conducted on Mar. 2, 2006, transcript p. 98.

113 National Disaster Medical System, Team Ratings 12-20-05.xls, Jan. 6, 2006. Provided to Committee.

114 "Homeland Security Act of 2002," (P.L. 107-296), 6 U.S.C. §§ 313, 503.

115 "I know there were 144 positions that were in OEP. I've been given that number, and I was led to believe, when were transferred to FEMA, that HHS kept 40 of these positions – I think that's a number – and then the rest, I think it was 17 moved into logistics. Those personnel would have come out of that operations division." Beall interview, Jan. 10, 2006, p. 16.

116 Beall interview, Jan. 10, 2006, p. 7.

117 Mick Cote, e-mail to Jack Beall, Aug. 27, 2005, 3:24 p.m. Provided to Committee; filed as Bates no. DHS-FEMA-0098-0004489.

118 William Lokey, e-mail to Jack Beall, Aug. 28, 2005, 1:13 p.m. Provided to Committee; filed as Bates no. DHS-FEMA-0098-0003831.

119 FEMA, NDMS After-Action Report, Disaster Medical Assistance Team San Diego CA-4, Mission: Hurricane Ka-

trina, Dec. 29, 2005. Provided to Committee.

120 Additional delays resulted when one truck had a mechanical problem an hour outside of San Diego resulting in an additional seven to eight hour delay. The cause of the mechanical failure was a part that had been the subject of a manufacturer's recall, but had not yet been repaired because of instructions from FEMA to delay the repair. FEMA, NDMS After-Action Report, Disaster Medical Assistance Team San Diego CA-4, Mission: Hurricane Katrina, Dec. 29, 2005. Provided to Committee.

121 FEMA, NDMS After-Action Report, Disaster Medical Assistance Team San Diego CA-4, Mission: Hurricane Katrina, Dec. 29, 2005. Provided to Committee.

122 Craig Interview, Jan. 25, 2006, pp. 24-26.

123 FEMA, Hurricane Katrina NDMS Resource Status Report, Aug. 30, 2005, 10 p.m. Provided to Committee.

124 Capt. Art French, M.D., After-Action Presentation, "New Orleans Airport Evacuation: The MST Perspective on the Hospital from Hell," briefing slides, Feb. 2006.

125 Capt. Art French, M.D., After-Action Presentation, "New Orleans Airport Evacuation: The MST Perspective on the Hospital from Hell," briefing slides, Feb. 2006.

126 FEMA, Hurricane Katrina NDMS Resource Status Report, Sept. 2, 2005. Provided to Committee.

127 George Custer, After Action Report – FEMA Hurricane Katrina, Southern Area Incident Management Team, p. 1. Provided to Committee.

128 Capt. French interview, Mar. 2, 2006, pp. 14, 17-18, 25-26, 36.

129 Capt. French interview, Mar. 2, 2006, p. 55.

130 Capt. French interview, Mar. 2, 2006, pp. 22-26.

131 Capt. Art French, M.D., After-Action Presentation, "New Orleans Airport Evacuation: The MST Perspective on the Hospital from Hell," briefing slides, Feb. 2006; Capt. French interview, Mar. 2, 2006, pp. 10, 15

132 Capt. French interview, Mar. 2, 2006, pp. 6-11.

133 Capt. French interview, Mar. 2, 2006, pp. 10, 16.

134 Capt. French interview, Mar. 2, 2006, p. 16.

135 Capt. French interview, Mar. 2, 2006, p. 15.

136 Jack Beall, e-mail to EC William Piggot, Sept. 1, 2005, 4:11 p.m. Provided to Committee; filed as Bates no. DHS-FEMA-0098-0002099.

137 William Piggot, e-mail to Jack Beall, Sept. 1, 2005, 4:51 p.m. Provided to Committee; filed as Bates no. DHS-FEMA-0098-0002099.

138 Chris Turner, e-mail to Jack Beall, Sept. 2, 2005, 8:48 a.m. Provided to Committee; filed as Bates no. DHS-FEMA-0098-0001737.

139 Martin interview, Jan. 13, 2006, pp. 54-58, 146-148.

140 Martin interview, Jan. 13, 2006, p. 32.

141 Jack Beall, e-mail to Thomas Bowman, Sept. 1, 2005, 7:27 a.m. Provided to Committee; filed as Bates no. DHS-FEMA-0098-0002216.

142 Jack Beall, e-mail to Chris Turner, Sept. 6, 2005, 10:21 p.m. Provided to Committee; filed as Bates no. DHS-FEMA-0098-004204.

143 Beall interview, Jan. 10, 2006, p. 48.

144 FEMA, Mission Assignment, 1603DR-LA-HHS-02, Aug. 31, 2005. Provided to Committee; filed as Bates no. OPHEP-28877; FEMA, Mission Assignment, 1603DR-LA-HHS-02, Aug. 31, 2005. Provided to Committee; filed as Bates nos. OPHEP 28878 through 28879.

145 Beall interview, Jan. 10, 2006, pp. 43-44; Capt. Art French, M.D., After-Action Presentation, "New Orleans Airport Evacuation: The MST Perspective on the Hospital from Hell," briefing slides, Feb. 2006.

146 Robert Jevec, e-mail to Gary Kleinman and others, Aug. 31, 2005, 10:41 a.m. Provided to Committee; filed as Bates nos. DHS-FEMA-0098-0004357 through 0004358.

147 NDMS Patient Movement AAR, Dec. 2005.

148 Capt. French interview, Mar. 2, 2006, pp. 13-14, 54-56.

149 Capt. French interview, Mar. 2, 2006, pp. 64-65; *See also*: FEMA, NDMS After-Action Report, Disaster Medical Assistance Team San Diego CA-4, Mission: Hurricane Katrina, Dec. 29, 2005. Provided to Committee; *See also*: OR-2 DMAT, Hurricane Katrina – After Action Report, Sept. 25, 2005. Provided to Committee.

150 The Incident Management Team was designed to provide food, showers, and other logistical support for emergency teams working in the field. Upon arriving in Louisiana, the Team literally sent out "scouting parties" to determine where their logistical support could be used after they determined that their original mission assignment to establish a base camp

in Port Allen, Louisiana was already being met by another agency. One of the scout teams identified the airport as a critical need and the team got permission from its regional coordinator to relocate there. George Custer, After Action Report – FEMA Hurricane Katrina, Southern Area Incident Management Team, TX=FEM-05004, Provided to Committee.

151 U.S. Department of Homeland Security, *National Response Plan*. Washington: Government Printing Office, Dec. 2004, p. 12.

152 Committee staff interview of Rear Adm. John Babb, Director, Office of Force Readiness and Deployment, U.S. Public Health Service, U.S. Department of Health and Human Services, conducted on Feb. 8, 2006, transcript, pp. 5, 24.

153 Rear Adm. Babb interview, Feb. 8, 2006, pp. 5.

154 Rear Adm. Babb interview, Feb. 8, 2006, pp. 41-45.

155 U.S. Department of Health and Human Services, Concept of Operations Plan (CONOPS) for Public Health and Medical Emergencies, Jan. 2005, p. 4, Appendix A.

156 U.S. Public Health Service, "History of the Commissioned Corps." http://www.usphs.gov/html/history.html. Accessed on Apr. 21, 2006.

157 Rear Adm. Babb interview, Feb. 8, 2006, p. 22; Committee staff interview of U.S. Public Health Service, Alpha Team members, Jan. 12, 2006 (untranscribed).

158 Rear Adm. Babb interview, Feb. 8, 2006, pp. 14-15.

159 Rear Adm. Babb interview, Feb. 8, 2006, p. 33; U.S. Public Health Service, Alpha Team members interview, Jan. 12, 2006; U.S. Public Health Service, briefing on Hurricane Katrina: PHS Response, Team Alpha, given to Senate Committee staff, Jan. 12, 2006.

160 U.S. Public Health Service, briefing on Hurricane Katrina: PHS Response, Team Alpha, given to Senate Committee staff, Jan. 12, 2006; U.S. Public Health Service, briefing on PHS Katrina Response: Baton Rouge Deployment Alpha Team, Oct. 16, 2005. Provided to Committee. The USPHS team at the PMAC worked with a team of volunteers from Illinois obtained through an EMAC agreement and a DMAT team that was stationed there for approximately one week.

161 Rear Adm. Babb interview, Feb. 8, 2006, pp. 22-24.

162 Officers were identified to support NDMS and the Strategic National Stockpile (SNS), a LA hospital, and to staff the FMSs which were part of OPHEP's strategy to increase facility surge capacity. *See also*: John T. Babb, e-mail to William C. Vanderwagen and others, Aug. 29, 2005, 2:12 p.m. Provided to Committee; filed as Bates no. OSG170.

163 Rear Adm. Babb interview, Feb. 8, 2006, p. 62.

164 Rear Adm. Babb interview, Feb. 8, 2006, pp. 69-70.

165 It was explained that since USPHS personnel do not have pharmaceuticals, medical supplies and equipment, and other supports, it would be best to couple their deployments to the FMS shelters. Rear Adm. Babb interview, Feb. 8, 2006, pp. 61-63, 66-67.

166 Rear Adm. Babb interview, Feb. 8, 2006, p. 72.

167 Rear Adm. Babb interview, Feb. 8, 2006, pp. 69-71 ("Basically, we had been told to put together people that would staff ten 250-bed federal medical shelters, which we did. But when they began to deploy them, they didn't necessarily deploy the teams the way we had them structured. … When the travel contractor deployed people, well, parts of teams arrived in different places. … New Orleans airport was almost non-functional. It was accepting very few flights. Baton Rouge had – every seat was full. Every time we turned around, we were trying to get flights in there and couldn't get people there.").

168 Rear Adm. Babb interview, Feb. 8, 2006, pp. 71-72.

169 Rear Adm. Babb interview, Feb. 8, 2006, p. 62.

170 Rear Adm. Babb interview, Feb. 8, 2006, pp. 14-15, 35-37.

171 Rear Adm. Babb interview, Feb. 8, 2006, p. 67: "So to look at the delay in the deployment as thought it was because officers didn't get down field is assuming that the resource was there and waiting on them or that they were taking it with them, and that was not the case. They had to wait until the resource got there."

172 Committee staff interview of Robert E. Lavender, Jr., Deputy Director of Information Technology Communications, U.S. Department of Health and Human Services, conducted on Feb. 3, 2006, transcript p. 10 ("In this year's hurricane season, you couldn't get into airports, so we had to find the closest airport and find a way to transport our people from that remote airport into the area in which we were asking them to provide services. So it was – this year was different from anything I've ever experienced in that it required a lot of creativity. There were no hotels, so one of the things that I did was – we call them rock star buses. We had sleeper buses sent in that slept 12 people. And so we did the best we could to provide as reasonable an accommodation as we could for the people that we were deploying.").

173 Lavender interview, Feb. 3, 2006, pp. 74-75. Two week deployments have traditionally been used because of the dual federal role of many USPHS officers and the nature of the typical disaster deployment.

174 Rear Adm. Babb interview, Feb. 8, 2006, p. 16. Despite Secretary of HHS Michael Leavitt activating the USPHS on Sunday, August 28, which made all USPHS deployments mandatory, many USPHS officers were still unable to deploy due to professional commitments at their daily positions. Committee staff interview of Rear Adm. Craig Vanderwagen, Acting Chief Medical Officer, Indian Health Service, and Officer, U.S. Public Health Service, U.S. Department of Health

and Human Service, conducted on Feb. 7, 2006, transcript pp. 2, 62-64; Lavender interview, Feb. 3, 2006, pp. 74-75.

175 Rear Adm. Babb interview, Feb. 8, 2006, pp. 79-80. USPHS officers are required to update their status and obtain medical waivers when necessary as they come on-call and they receive e-mail reminders each time they are on-call to update their availability status. However, there are no sanctions for not reporting changes in deployment status or for not deploying.

176 Rear Adm. Babb interview, Feb. 8, 2006, pp. 79-80.

177 Noreen Hynes, e-mail to John Babb, Aug. 30, 2005, 3:55 a.m. Provided to Committee; filed as Bates no. OSG162.

178 Capt. French interview, Mar. 2, 2006, p. 67.

179 Monica Giovachino, et al., *Hurricanes Frances and Ivan: Improving the Delivery of HHS and ESF#8 Support*, The CNA Corporation, IPR 11208, Feb. 2005, pp. 42-43 [hereinafter, *Hurricanes Frances and Ivan: Improving the Delivery of HHS and ESF#8 Support*]. The report focused on improving the HHS ESF-8 response and focused a section on the USPHS. Prior to Hurricane Katrina, Hurricanes Frances and Ivan involved the largest deployment of personnel from HHS and its ESF-8 partners. The report stated that officers were deployed from each region of the country and each USPHS rotational roster was "tapped for personnel." The CNA report concluded, "This examination reveals a fractured system that does not have the manpower or administrative infrastructure necessary to support a major deployment." The report concluded that OFRD does not have the capacity to coordinate major personnel deployments, as evidenced by the fact that senior level staff spent the weekend to identify and contact officers individually by phone for deployment.

180 *Hurricanes Frances and Ivan: Improving the Delivery of HHS and ESF#8 Support*, p. 45 ("Each roster is *not* set up to be a 'ready-go' asset for OASPHEP. Instead it is a pool of personnel that may be available in a time of need.").

181 *Hurricanes Frances and Ivan: Improving the Delivery of HHS and ESF#8 Support*, p. 46.

182 *Hurricanes Frances and Ivan: Improving the Delivery of HHS and ESF#8 Support*, p. 43.

183 Rear Adm. Babb interview, Feb. 8, 2006, p. 78.

184 PHS deployed 138 officers for Frances and 263 for Ivan. *Source*: *Hurricanes Frances and Ivan: Improving the Delivery of HHS and ESF#8 Support*, pp. 39-40. A total of 1,885 were deployed to affected areas and 247 to other locations for Katrina. *Source*: U.S. Department of Health and Human Services, Response to the U.S. Senate, Committee on Homeland Security and Governmental Affairs, Feb. 28, 2006, p. 42.

185 Committee staff interview of Stewart Simonson, Assistant Secretary for Public Health Emergency Preparedness, U.S. Department of Health and Human Services, conducted on Feb. 16, 2006, transcript p. 107.

186 "Public Health Security and Bioterrorism Preparedness and Response Act of 2002." (P.L. 107-188), 42 U.S.C. § 201 ("The Secretary shall, directly or though an award of a grant, contract, or cooperative agreement, establish and maintain a system for the advance registration of health professionals for the purpose of verifying the credentials, licenses, accreditations, and hospital privileges of such professionals when, during public health emergencies, the professionals volunteer to provide public health services. … In carrying out the preceding sentence, the Secretary shall provide for an electronic database for the verification system.").

187 HRSA's mission is to provide national leadership, program resources and services needed to improve access to culturally competent, quality health care. They support healthcare systems that are culturally competent, comprehensive, and provide quality care for the goal of optimal health for all.

188 Simonson interview, Feb. 16, 2006, p. 112.

189 Rear Adm. Babb interview, Feb. 8, 2006, p. 39.

190 Rear Adm. Babb interview, Feb. 8, 2006, pp. 54, 39; Simonson interview, Feb. 16, 2006, p. 112. In FY2005, HHS asked for funding for a portal that would have pooled the data across all states to create a national credentialing mechanism; however, the request was not funded.

191 Norman Coleman, e-mail to Norman Coleman and others, Sept. 2, 2005, 12:06 a.m. Provided to Committee; filed as Bates no. OPHEP 9408. On Saturday September 3, the Web site was opened to the public.

192 Rear Adm. Babb interview, pp. 19, 44.

193 Clara Witt, e-mail to Thomas Christl and others, September 7, 2005, 1:20 p.m. Provided to Committee; filed as Bates no. OPHEP 9779. Even after the private contractor was hired and work was under way, there were talks within HHS to use states to assist in credentialing in the process after the federal contractor had already initiated the process

194 Clara Witt, e-mail to Ann Knebel, Sept. 7, 2005, 8:31 p.m. Provided to Committee; filed as Bates no. OPHEP 9990.

195 John Babb, e-mail to Ann Knebel, Sept. 5, 2005, 9:02 a.m. Provided to Committee; filed as Bates no. OPHEP 9660. Rear Admiral Babb stated, the volunteers, "are going straight to OPHEP and we don't have any visibility. At this point, that's fine. But I would like to know what kinds of personnel are being deployed."

196 Lavender interview, Feb. 3, 2006, pp. 66-67.

197 For instance, numerous changes were made to the website to include specialties of healthcare workers left off the original list. Lynn May, e-mail to Norman Coleman, Sept. 3, 2005, 5:37 p.m. Provided to Committee; filed as Bates no. OPHEP 8636; Mary Couig, e-mail to Ann Knebel, Sept. 4, 2005, 8:42 a.m. Provided to Committee; filed as Bates no. OPHEP 8635.

198 Teresa Brown-Jesus, e-mail to Ann Knebel, Sept. 6, 2005, 5:26 p.m. Provided to Committee; filed as Bates no. OPHEP 9805 ("States … have continued to express their concerns about the way that federal volunteer recruitment ef-

forts have been implemented.").

199 The Federal volunteer database also created conflict with the purpose and mission of the Medical Reserve Corps (MRC). The MRC is comprised of health professionals who voluntarily join locally-sponsored medical units that can be called upon to provide additional medical personnel in an emergency. The Director of the MRC expressed concerns almost one week after the hurricane about the confusion surrounding the deployment process and how the MRC units would be integrated into the federal volunteer database that HHS had established. Because there was no clear connection between the MRC and the Federal volunteer database efforts, HHS created conflicting and overlapping volunteer systems. Ann Knebel, e-mail to Norman Coleman and others, Sept. 7, 2005, 5:55 a.m. Provided to Committee; filed as Bates no. OPHEP 9755; Robert Tosatto, e-mail to Ann Norwood, Sept. 7, 2005, 3:39 p.m. Provided to Committee; filed as Bates no. OPHEP 9670.

200 Ann Knebel, e-mail to Norman Coleman and others, Sept. 7, 2005, 5:55 a.m. Provided to Committee; filed as Bates no. OPHEP 9755; Robert Tosatto, e-mail to Ann Norwood, Sept. 7, 2005, 3:39 p.m. Provided to Committee; filed as Bates no. OPHEP 9670.

201 Dr. Guidry interview, Dec. 20, 2005, pp. 53, 56 ("To try to match up the resources with where they were needed became a full-time job…(t)he teams that worked the best, were like Illinois had a medical team. They came and you could hand them off a shift and they could pretty much handle it because they came trained and working together. They were organized. Other professionals who showed up as volunteers really have not trained in such events and really makes it difficult to perform when it's not well organized.").

202 Simonson interview, Feb. 16, 2006, p. 31. The FMS capacity for OPHEP has not been funded to date, but all development occurred using year-end money.

203 Lavender interview, Feb. 3, 2006, p. 57.

204 Simonson interview, Feb. 16, 2006, p. 66.

205 The Logistics section of OPHEP bore much of the burden for acquiring and coordinating movement of the FMSs, such as personnel and supplies. Given the growing list of demands for the mobile medical units, personnel, and supplies, OPHEP logistics had to exponentially increase their staff of four full-time employees; thus, many new staff did not have experience with procedures of the Logistics office. The lack of experience in the Logistics office, with the added burden of coordinating the establishment of unproven and never utilized FMS units prototype, compounded the logistical difficulties in Washington and on the ground. Lavender interview, Feb. 3, 2006, pp. 6-9, 31-32, 89-90. See also: Stewart Simonson, letter to Paul McHale, Aug. 31, 2005. Provided to Committee; filed as Bates no. OPHEP 27874. OPHEP requested assistance to support the following FMS unit deployments: 500 beds at Eglin Air Force Base in Pensacola, FL; 750 beds at Fort Polk, LA; 500 beds at Naval Air Station in Meridian, MS; and 500 beds at Mississippi Air National Guard Base in Jackson, MS.

206 Committee staff interview of Robert E. Blitzer, Deputy Assistant Secretary, Operations Security Program, U.S. Department of Health and Human Services, conducted on Feb. 2, 2006, transcript p. 96.

207 Stewart Simonson, e-mail to William Gimson and others, Aug. 31, 2005, 6:33 p.m. Provided to Committee; filed as Bates no. OPHEP 27771.

208 Committee staff interview of Richard Besser, Director of Coordinating Office for Terrorism Preparedness and Emergency Response, Centers for Disease Control and Prevention, and Steve Adams, Acting Director of the Strategic National Stockpile, Centers for Disease Control and Prevention, conducted on Feb. 14, 2006, transcript p. 14.

209 Besser and Adams interview, Feb. 14, 2006, p. 12.

210 Stewart Simonson, e-mail to William Gimson and others, Sept. 3, 2005, 7:22 a.m. Provided to Committee; filed as Bates no. OPHEP 27077 ("We are struggling right now with a Miss hospital resupply mission. The Push Pack may tide them over for a little while, but I need to pick-up the pace on this order. Please tell me if we cannot do both (FMS and Miss Hosp) resupply at once – if this is the case, we may have to back-off for a bit on the FMS ordering. I cannot have Miss run out of provisions." To which, SNS staff eventually replied "…we are doing this right now, SNS is focusing in the MS re-supply right now and will see if they can move back to the FMCS ordering this afternoon."). See also: Galen P. Carver, e-mail to Stewart Simonson, Sept. 3, 2005, 9:13 a.m. Provided to Committee; filed as Bates no. OPHEP 27076.

211 Simonson interview, Feb. 16, 2006, pp. 71-72.

212 Tom Sizemore, e-mail to Michael L. Vineyard, Sept. 3, 2005, 8:45 a.m. Provided to Committee, filed as Bates no. OPHEP 24464.

213 Centers for Disease Control and Prevention, Division of the Strategic National Stockpile, "Hurricane Katrina Update," Aug. 31, 2005. Provided to Committee; filed as Bates no. OPHEP 27774.

214 Robert Claypool, e-mail to William "Contact" Vanderwagen, Sept. 2, 2005, 7:49 a.m. Provided to Committee; filed as Bates no. OPHEP 24227.

215 Stewart Simonson, e-mail to Richard Chavez, Sept. 2, 2005, 5:29 p.m. Provided to Committee; filed as Bates no. OPHEP 27839 ("We have been turned away from the gate at the Mississippi Air National Guard Base in Jackson. We are diverting the beds scheduled for that facility to Meridian. Can you confirm with the base commander there that they will accept them. This is urgent."). For instance, MS could not transport their residents to Eglin Air Force Base in Pensacola, FL; therefore, two FMS units were moved to MS. Source: Sandy Bogucki, e-mail to Stewart Simonson, Sept. 4, 2005, 3:24 p.m. Provided to Committee; filed as Bates no. OPHEP 27584. In Louisiana, Mike Milner was assisting Adm. Vanderwagen in redeploying the FMSs that OPHEP had mapped out. He stated that at Ft. Polk there had been *no* patients and that the mission was redefined to support special needs shelters based on the state requests; this was only one of several FMS staffing and placement decisions that had to be interrupted by the SERT in Louisiana alone. Source: Mike Milner, e-mail

to William C. Vanderwagen, Sept. 5, 2005, 11:35 p.m. Provided to Committee; filed as Bates no. OPHEP 8198.

216 Stewart Simonson, letter to Paul McHale, Sept. 2, 2005. Provided to Committee; filed as Bates no. OPHEP 27877.

217 Shayne Brannman, e-mail to Gregory Davis, Sept. 8, 2005, 11:05 a.m. Provided to Committee; filed as Bates no: OPHEP 8745.

218 Craig interview, Jan. 25, 2006, pp. 72, 75.

219 Craig interview, Jan. 25, 2006, pp. 24-25; 28-29.

220 Paul McHale, letter to Stewart Simonson, Sept. 2. 2005. Provided to Committee; filed as Bates no. OPHEP 27880.

221 Gregory Banner, e-mail to KC Decker, Sept. 9, 2005, 10:39 p.m. Provided to Committee; filed as Bates no. OPHEP 8196.

222 Lavender interview, Feb. 3, 2006, pp. 35-49.

223 Lavender interview, Feb. 3, 2006, p. 35. Lavender acquired "primary medical bags … so that … when our people arrived on the ground, they could provide primary treatment, whether it be bandaging or removing a splinter, whatever it happened to be. But I procured those early in the event because we didn't have them," unfortunately, USPHS teams were not equipped with these materials and supplies prior to the event or as a matter of procedure because it was not "perceived to be a requirement."

224 Lavender interview, Feb. 3, 2006, pp. 45-46.

225 Centers for Disease Control and Prevention, "Strategic National Stockpile (SNS)," Apr. 14, 2005. http://www.bt.cdc.gov/stockpile/. Accessed on Apr. 21, 2006.

226 These supplies were dispatched by truck from Atlanta and Tennessee on the afternoon of September 28 and arrived at Camp Beauregard, LA after landfall.

227 HHS, Secretary's Operation Center Flash Report #6 – Hurricane Katrina, Aug. 30, 2005, 3 p.m., p. 2. Provided to Committee; filed as Bates no. OPHEP 28253.

228 Gregory Banner, e-mail to Keith Holtermann, Sept. 2, 2005, 2:39 a.m. Provided to Committee; filed as Bates nos. OPHEP 27869 through 27870 "My understanding of the situation is that hospitals and medical facilities along the coast are in desperate need of resupply for a variety of expendables. Supply requests have been submitted but the planned delivery times are still more than 24 hours away. The SNS push packages contain a number of needed items and so in the interest of speeding up the delivery of supplies to the hospitals, a push package was requested. This appeared to be the quickest way to obtain at least part of the needed supplies.").

229 Sandy Bogucki, e-mail to SNS OPS Center Lead, Sept. 2, 2005, 8:27 a.m. Provided to Committee; filed as Bates no. OPHEP 27642.

230 Besser interview, Feb. 14, 2006, pp. 53-55 ("I don't think that there was a complete understanding of what it meant to request a push pack and what that provided … we were trying to make sure the people on the ground specified clearly what it was that they wanted. And in Louisiana, a lot of what … people wanted was a restoration of their supply chains and their facilities, and a lot of chronic medications that weren't in push packs … sending out a push pack is an extremely expensive endeavor which is justifiable when the parties receiving it need what's in it. But it's, in my mind not justifiable for expense, plus a waste of people's time if they're getting, you know, 50 tons of material that isn't what they're looking for.").

231 Brian W. Amy, letter to Phil Naven, Sept. 1, 2005. Provided to Committee; filed as Bates no. OPHEP 27639 ("Mississippi's hospitals are in dire need of supplies from the Strategic National Stockpile's Push Packages … Sixteen hospitals located south of Interstate 20 are totally out of basic supplies, such as IV solutions and oral doses of broad spectrum antibiotics … as well as saline solutions, sterile water … syringes, etc. and all other related supplies. Thus far, supply requests have not been fulfilled for a variety of reasons. … Please note that the longer we are delayed in distributing supplies to hospitals, the more likely it will be that emerging infections will compound our all-ready overwhelming situation.").

232 Evidenced by an internal OPHEP e-mail "FYI, just got pinged by the DEOC [CDC's emergency operations center]. Gerberding [the Director of CDC] wanting to know who gave the permission to move SNS assets." Keith Holterman, e-mail to Stewart Simonson, Sept. 2, 2005, 6:33 a.m. Provided to Committee; filed as Bates no. OPHEP 28195.

233 Lavender interview, Feb. 3, 2006, p. 43.

234 Besser and Adams interview, Feb. 14, 2006, pp. 46-47.

235 U.S. Public Health Service, briefing on Hurricane Katrina: PHS Response, Team Alpha, given to Senate Committee staff, Jan. 12, 2006. These materials arrived on Tuesday, August 30 and the PHS team reported that the packages were not very manageable and were not well-suited to meet the needs of a 200-bed special needs shelter.

236 U.S. Public Health Service, briefing on Hurricane Katrina: PHS Response, Team Alpha, given to Senate Committee staff, Jan. 12, 2006.

237 U.S. Public Health Service, briefing on Hurricane Katrina: PHS Response, Team Alpha, given to Senate Committee staff, Jan. 12, 2006. They reported that there was no organized method for obtaining supplies – they often went to the SNS who reported that it would take 1-2 days after ordering for delivery, they would then speak with the SOC to push the SNS orders, and would also speak with private vendors and pharmacies.

238 U.S. Public Health Service, briefing on Hurricane Katrina: PHS Response, Team Alpha, given to Senate Committee

staff, Jan. 12, 2006.

239 U.S. Public Health Service, briefing on Hurricane Katrina: PHS Response, Team Alpha, given to Senate Committee staff, Jan. 12, 2006.

240 Besser interview, Feb. 14, 2006, pp. 9-10, 60-61 ("it's [the SNS] an asset that was developed around the bioterrorism, and has morphed to pandemics, but [it's] not been constructed in the same all-hazards approach as CDC as an agency is for public health events. For what it's worth, with all the hurricanes that have occurred since the program's inception in 1999, to my recollection, we've never deployed anything to a hurricane before, so it doesn't mean that we shouldn't have been thinking more broadly or – but in a environment of fixed resources, you know, we focus on missions that are clearly defined.").

241 Lavender interview, Feb. 3, 2006, p. 41.

242 Besser interview, Feb. 14, 2006, p. 10 ("I think, one of the things we saw with Katrina, here we had an organization that was designed for moving material, moving material very efficiently and effectively. It very quickly adapted to a situation where it was moving products that it hadn't been designed for. … What we saw in Louisiana was a complete loss of the supply chain for quite a large are in terms of medical supplies, and the stockpile was able to step up and become that chain – that delivery chain."). *See also*: Besser and Adams interview, Feb. 14, 2006, pp. 24-32.

243 Besser interview, Feb. 14, 2006, pp. 10-11 ("As we look at the [mission] for the stockpile … what we are looking at is, should the mission be broader, and if so … means developing logistical plans that are very different from a model where you are taking a large push pack delivering it and turning it over to the States … it's developing a logistical chain so that you're dealing with a wider array of products; you're dealing with ongoing consumption of products and replacement; you're putting in place systems for being able to look at what kind of patients are being seen so you can tailor your supplies in a very unique way. And I think, what Katrina demonstrates for us is a capacity that as country we need to have.").

244 Besser interview, Feb. 14, 2006, p. 76 ("I think that, I mean, Hurricane Katrina clearly identified chronic disease as an area that has to be addressed as part of response to major natural disasters. And if the SNS is the body that's going to do that, we need to put the systems in place to make that work.").

245 U.S. Department of Health and Human Services, Response to the U.S. Senate, Committee on Homeland Security and Governmental Affairs information request, Feb. 28, 2006, p. 41.

246 Lavender interview, Feb. 3, 2006, p. 50.

247 "As the primary agency for ESF #8, HHS coordinates the provision of Federal health and medical assistance to fulfill the requirements identified by the affected State, local and tribal authorities. ESF #8 uses resources primarily available from: HHS, including the Operating Divisions and Regional Office; the Department off Homeland Security (DHS); and other ESF #8 support agencies and organizations." *NRP*, p. ESF #8–4.

248 HHS possesses additional statutorily assigned health responsibilities under the Public Health Service Act, the Social Security Act, and the Federal Food, Drug, and Cosmetic Act. In fact, the Secretary of HHS declared public health emergencies for Louisiana, Mississippi and surrounding states pursuant to this independent authority beginning on Wednesday, August 31, 2005. U.S. Department of Health and Human Services, Concept of Operations Plan (CONOPS) for Public Health and Medical Emergencies, Jan. 2005, pp. 4-5, Appendix A.

249 *NRP*, p. 5

250 An initial planning meeting to establish "an interagency incident management system to address the ESF 8 public health and medical response" to Katrina was formally established held on Monday, September 5, 2005. A Unified Incident Management Team was established at the HHS headquarters in the Humphrey Building on that day. Secretary's Operations Center, e-mail to Allen Dobbs and others, Sept. 5, 2005, 2:44 p.m. Provided to Committee; filed as Bates nos. DHS-FEMA-0098-0000635 through 0000640.

251 Simonson interview, Feb. 16, 2006, pp. 64-65.

252 Jack Beall, e-mail to Stewart Simonson, Sept. 3, 2005, 10:56 a.m. Provided to Committee; filed as Bates no. OPHEP 27922.

253 Stewart Simonson, e-mail to Gerald Parker, Sept. 3, 2005, 2:55 p.m. Provided to Committee, filed as Bates nos. OPHEP 27922 through 27924.

254 *NRP*, pp. ESF 8–6, ESF 8–10.

255 Committee staff interview of Robert Claypool, M.D., former Deputy Assistant Secretary, Director of Mass Casualty Planning, Office of Public Health Emergency Preparedness, U.S. Department of Health and Human Services, conducted on Feb. 14, 2006, transcript p. 67.

256 The after-action report for HHS concerning the response to Hurricane Frances and Ivan recommended that the HHS Office of the Assistant Secretary for Public Health Emergency Preparedness work with the National Disaster Medical System (NDMS) "… to (i)mprove coordination between HHS and NDMS during response operations (the separation of NDMS from HHS has fractured ESF #8)." *Hurricanes Frances and Ivan: Improving the Delivery of HHS and ESF #8 Support*, p. 2.

257 Keith Holtermann, e-mail to Robert Love, Sept. 3, 2005, 1:27 a.m. Provided to Committee; filed as Bates nos. OPHEP 19978 through 19979.

258 NDMS and the Office of Emergency Preparedness at HHS were transferred to the Department of Homeland Security

when the Homeland Security Act was enacted in November, 2002, effective March, 2003 (P.L. 107-296 §503). Although the existing Office of Public Health Emergency Preparedness (OPHEP) was created by statute on June 12, 2002, and pre-dates the transfer, the resulting changes created a vacuum in HHS' emergency response capability which it is still trying to fill. *See also* P.L. 107-488 § 102.

259 Committee staff interview of Jean Bennett, Regional Emergency Coordinator, Region VI, Office of Public Health and Emergency Preparedness, U.S. Department of Health and Human Services, conducted on Mar. 1, 2006, transcript p. 5.

260 Bennett interview, Mar. 1, 2006, p. 5.

261 Bennett interview, Mar. 1, 2006, pp. 15-17.

262 HHS/OPHEP provided three reasons why it did not participate in any of the 2004 or 2005 Hurricane Pam medical discussions – (1) the exercise was sponsored by FEMA and they were not specifically invited, (2) a Region VI REC was not yet in place when the bulk of the exercise took place in 2004, and (3) the Region VI REC was unable to take part in the final ESF-8 Hurricane Pam follow-up workshop (which occurred just days before Katrina hit) due to a scheduling conflict.

263 Robert Blitzer, e-mail to Robert Claypool, Sept. 5, 2005, 11:37 a.m. Provided to Committee; filed as Bates no. OPHEP 28178.

264 HRSA is the agency within HHS that provides funding and training programs to health care providers, such as health clinics, to provide care to the uninsured, people with HIV/AIDS, and pregnant women, mothers, and children.

265 Dr. Claypool interview, Feb. 14, 2006, p. 38.

266 Bennett interview, Mar. 1, 2006, p. 20.

267 Craig interview, Jan. 25, 2006, p. 25.

268 Downey interview, Jan. 20, 2006, pp. 46-48; Dr. Guidry interview, Dec. 20, 2006, pp. 78-79.

269 Betty Duke, e-mail to Richard Carmona, Sept. 7, 2005, 6:02 p.m. Provided to Committee; filed as Bates nos. OPHEP 27217 through 27220.

270 Dianne Whittington, e-mail to Brian Kamoie, Sept. 4, 2005, 2:30 pm. Provided to Committee; filed as Bates nos. OPHEP 22014 through 022017; Committee staff interview of Gerald Parker, M.D., D.V.M., Ph.D., Principal Deputy Assistant Secretary, Office of Public Health Emergency Preparedness, U.S. Department of Health and Human Services, conducted on Feb. 10, 2006, pp. 52-54.

271 Vanderwagen interview, Feb. 7, 2006, pp. 46-47; Brian Kamoie, e-mail to Stewart Simonson, Sept. 3, 2005, 2:33 p.m. Provided to Committee; filed as Bates no. OPHEP 27072.

272 Clara Cobb, e-mail to Robert Love, Sept. 5, 2005, 11:19 a.m. Provided to Committee; filed as Bates no. OPHEP 8344.

273 Mike Milner, e-mail to William C. Vanderwagen, Sept. 5, 2005, 11:35 p.m. Provided to Committee; filed as Bates nos. OPHEP 8198 through 8199.

274 Capt. Art French, M.D., USPHS, After-Action Presentation, "New Orleans Airport Evacuation: The MST Perspective on the Hospital from Hell," briefing slides, Feb. 2006.; Capt. French interview, Mar. 2, 2006.

275 George Havens, e-mail to Jack Beall, Sept. 4, 2005, 10:47 a.m. Provided to Committee; filed as Bates no. DHS-FEMA-0098-0001413.

276 Mark Roupas, e-mail to Paul McHale, Aug. 29, 2005, 5:54 p.m. Provided to Committee; filed as MMTF 00418-05.

277 Stewart Simonson, letter to Paul McHale, Aug. 31, 2005. Provided to Committee; filed as Bates nos. OPHEP 27874 through 27875.

278 Stewart Simonson, letter to Paul McHale, Aug. 31, 2005. Provided to Committee; filed as Bates nos. OPHEP 27874 through 27875.

279 Office of the Assistant Secretary of Defense (Homeland Defense), Hurricane Katrina/Rita/Ophelia Interim Time-line, Nov. 2, 2005, p. 7. Provided to Committee ("Oral approval of SecDef and Draft MOD$ to SecDef EXORD tasks SECARMY to provide Ft. Polk deployment site, SECNAV to provide Naval Air Station Meridian site, SECAF to provide Eglin AFB site, and CNGB to coordinate use of MS Army National Guard Base.").

280 Stewart Simonson, letter to Paul McHale, Sept. 2, 2005. Provided to Committee; filed as Bates nos. OPHEP 27884 through 27885.

281 U.S. Joint Forces Command, Hurricane Katrina Comprehensive Timeline, Nov. 15, 2005, p. 8. Provided to Committee, filed as Bates no. MMTF 00500-05.

282 Simonson interview, Feb. 16, 2006, pp. 97-98.

283 Simonson interview, Feb. 16, 2006, p. 74

284 Simonson interview, Feb. 16, 2006, p. 75

285 Simonson interview, Feb. 16, 2006, p. 76

286 Stewart Simonson, e-mail to Jack Beall, Sept. 2, 2005, 9:18, p.m. Provided to Committee; filed as Bates no. OPHEP 27927.

287 Dr. Claypool interview, Feb. 15, 2006, pp. 63-64.

Louisiana State Police in New Orleans

Public Safety and Security

Among the many enduring images Katrina bequeathed to us was this: rampaging crowds wading through flooded streets and climbing through broken store windows, gleefully carrying off impossible loads of electronics and other goods they could not possibly use in the storm-ravaged city, all while New Orleans police were said to be standing by or even in some cases participating.[1] Footage of these events was played over and over again on network and cable news outlets during the initial days after the storm. Stories suggesting a near-total breakdown of law and order in key parts of the city of New Orleans soon saturated the media. But as the world watched aghast, many of the stories reported and repeated – including some by city leaders – were wrong.

The world saw the full range of events which can occur when law and order break down. A September 1, 2005, press report observed, for example, that "At flood-swamped Charity Hospital, looters with handguns forced doctors to give up stores of narcotics. Wal-Mart gun racks and ammunition supplies were stripped. … Thieves commandeered a forklift to smash the security glass window of one pharmacy, fleeing with so much ice, water, and food that they left a trail behind them. Brazen gangs chased down a state police truck filled with food, and even city officials were accused of commandeering equipment from a looted Office Depot.[2] New Orleans Police were said to be abandoning their posts in droves. On September 3, the *Los Angeles Times* reported seeing "dozens of Chinook helicopters dart[ing] overhead, transporting desperately ill patients from hospitals that were being evacuated by doctors and nurses under sporadic gunfire."[3] Charity Hospital reportedly had to suspend airlifting patients to a field hospital set up by the National Guard at Louis Armstrong New Orleans International Airport due to sniper fire.[4] A September 4, 2005, article in the *New York Times* reported that, "at least 200 police officers have walked away from their jobs and two have committed suicide."[5] And as late as September 6, then-Police Superintendent Eddie Compass expressed frustration about the police's inability to do anything about the "little babies getting raped" in the Superdome.[6] Some of these stories were true; some were false; some, partially true; others, inflated.

While the city was far from peaceful, its occupants were safer and more disciplined than it first appeared; some 90 percent of the New Orleans police force stayed on duty;[7] and there was only one confirmed incident of an attempted violent crime at the Superdome.[8] Nevertheless, both the perception of extreme threats of violence and the reality of a lesser, but still serious, level of disorder had a significant detrimental impact on Katrina's victims and on those who were trying to help them. During the first days after the storm, safety fears prompted FEMA's emergency-response team and a medical team to pull out of the Superdome, some search-and-rescue crews to suspend their efforts, and utility workers to forestall starting the critical task of repairing downed communications.[9]

While the magnitude of the storm's immediate impact on New Orleans, its infrastructure and its police force made some disruption of public order inevitable – and while individual local, state, and federal public-safety officers performed heroically throughout the disaster – the Committee's investigation has found several preventable causes that contributed to the real and perceived breakdown in public order. For example, Hurricane Pam, the principal planning exercise for a catastrophic hurricane event in New Orleans, did not include any public-safety or law-enforcement components, other than security at shelters.[10]

At the local level, New Orleans and its police department worked under the most challenging of circumstances. Given Katrina's impact on the city and its force, given the incredible need for assistance that inevitably resulted, and given the tens of thousands of public-safety officers and troops that ultimately were required to assist the city's efforts at maintaining order, it is apparent that the New Orleans Police Department (NOPD) would have been overwhelmed under these circumstances.

Unfortunately, its difficulties were exacerbated by several factors that better planning could have avoided. The city and the NOPD had only vaguely worded emergency plans and those plans didn't, for example, direct officers to refuges of last resort or provide for specific high-ground locations to shelter the emergency vehicles police would need to do their job after the storm passed. Both failures led to significant losses of resources that impeded the ability of individual officers to do their jobs. Except for ad hoc arrangements with neighboring Jefferson Parish to detain violent criminals in their jail, the city also lacked a backup site to detain those it arrested once the city jail flooded; as a result, the police department was compelled to release anyone arrested for a non-violent crime. Also importantly, city officials often compounded the public's fears – and thereby deterred professional and volunteer responders from doing their jobs – by repeating sensational rumors as fact.[11] On September 2, for example, Mayor Nagin opined, "What you are seeing is drug-starving, crazy addicts, drug addicts, that are wreaking havoc."[12] City officials failed to follow their own plans for responding to the news media's rumor reporting and for making sure that no city spokesman repeated a rumor before confirming it.

So, the NOPD, suffering from the destruction of its equipment and uniforms, the failure of a tenth of its forces to report for duty, the indecisiveness and unpreparedness of its leadership, blinded by lack of situational awareness and deafened by the lack of communications, was truly overwhelmed by the catastrophe besetting the city it was supposed to protect and serve.

At the state level, the record was mixed. The Louisiana State Police (LSP) poured its personnel and equipment into the New Orleans area to reinforce and re-equip the beleaguered NOPD. However, at the administrative level, the state struggled with the massive deputization burdens caused by the huge number of officers and agents responding to the area. It also did not have effective control over the Emergency Management Assistance Compact (EMAC) process for more than five days after landfall, and only then with the organizational aid of federal agencies. Governor Blanco and her senior staff may also have contributed to the delays in receiving outside assistance by the manner of their initial requests to the federal government and the timing of their requests to other states. However, as discussed later in this section, the Committee would find it very troubling if in fact the federal government failed to respond to a request from a state, even though the wrong officers signed the request, in a triumph of form over intent and urgent need.

At the federal level, the government's initial response fell far short of what the Gulf Coast's citizens could reasonably have expected. The National Response Plan's (NRP) Emergency Support Function-13 (ESF-13) gives the Department of Justice (DOJ) and the Department of Homeland Security (DHS) joint responsibility for, among other things, leading and coordinating federal efforts "in situations requiring extensive assistance to provide public safety and security and where State and local government resources are overwhelmed or are inadequate."[13] New Orleans' desperate need for extensive assistance in ensuring public safety was apparent – and requested by Colonel Henry Whitehorn of the State Police – within a day of landfall. Yet the federal response to requests for assistance there and elsewhere in the region was too slow to ramp up under the circumstances, having been severely hampered even before Katrina's landfall by a seemingly complete absence of planning – indeed a lack of a basic understanding of the Departments' roles and obligations – on the part of DOJ and DHS. In fact, DOJ did not assign anyone to coordinate the DOJ function until September 2. When federal assistance did begin to arrive in force, on Saturday, September 3, and Sunday, September 4, it acquitted itself well and provided immeasurable help to the response efforts.

But the failure to anticipate, plan for, and then provide adequate assistance in Katrina's initial days had a lasting impact on the response efforts.

I. The Local Response

A. Hurricane Katrina Delivered a Powerful Blow Against the Poorly Prepared New Orleans Police Department

As anywhere in the United States, the job of ensuring public safety and order in New Orleans falls in the first instance to the local police department. At the time Hurricane Katrina made landfall, the NOPD had a force of 1,668 sworn officers.[14] By the time the storm had passed, at least 147 failed to report for duty,[15] while 90 percent of the force remained on duty. But their ability to carry out their life-saving and law-enforcement missions was gravely compromised by material losses and communications blackouts they suffered in the storm.

The lack of uniforms, cars, weapons, and ammunition impacted the officers' ability to perform law-enforcement activities.[16] The lack of watercraft and training in water search and rescue limited their ability to rescue and move people from the affected area.[17] The loss of communications resulted in significantly diminished overall command and control and an inability to coordinate law-enforcement activities around the city among NOPD officers.[18] The lack of interoperable communications resulted in an inability to coordinate search-and-rescue operations and difficulty in coordinating law-enforcement operations with the military and with other law-enforcement agencies.[19]

As one officer noted, "Communications failed at the most critical time. Backup systems did not work at all. The radio system crashed and was not operational. This was critical to the operations and seriously hampered rescue operations. Lack of communication placed officers in extreme danger without an avenue for assistance. … 'Mutual aid' channels were hardly usable."[20]

FBI Special Agent in Charge Kenneth Kaiser graphically described the status of the NOPD force:

> They were running out of ammunition. They were running out of food and water. We were bringing them food and water. And we brought in our medical personnel … to look at the people. Some of these people had been on duty since the hurricane, hadn't heard from their wife and kids, hadn't left their post. Some of them were very ill. They had fevers. … A lot of them were wearing the same clothes they'd worn for seven, eight days.[21]

Even when officers were deployed, the fact that many had lost their uniforms decreased their effectiveness. As then-Chief of Operations Warren Riley noted in discussing NOPD presence at the Convention Center:

> So we had some officers that still had uniforms, but a lot of them were wearing blue jeans and t-shirts and khaki pants and Wal-Mart things that were given to us. … So a lot of people may have said, "The police, they aren't there," but we just weren't in uniform.[22]

These losses were the result not only of the storm, but also of the failure of planning and preparedness. Good planning should anticipate the full range of likely problems and breakdowns. It should reasonably have been anticipated that communications would have been lost in a major hurricane, while the effects could have been mitigated had a good plan been in place.

Unlike the New Orleans Fire Department's (NOFD) Hurricane Guidelines, the NOPD's plan does not include provision for last areas of refuge for hurricanes.[23] These refuges are multi-level facilities, with a center core stairwell, in strategic locations around the city. Each facility's availability to house personnel and/or equipment is reconfirmed during preseason preparations.[24] In addition to providing refuge for fire personnel, some of the locations in the NOFD's plan are also high-ground staging areas for equipment.[25] The NOPD's plan calls for all vehicles not being utilized to be relocated to safe locations but does not specify where, resulting in responsibility for unit assets being left up to individual commanders.[26] Unfortunately, many vehicles were parked in low-lying areas to avoid exposure to high-velocity winds and ended up submerged.[27]

The NOPD was unprepared to protect its assets or to provide for acquiring replacement equipment, precautions which would seem reasonable in a city built mostly below sea level.

Two issues identified by NOPD Command Staff in the After Action Reports (AAR) concern this lack of adequate resources to conduct law-enforcement and search-and-rescue operations under emergency conditions. The first, "Vehicles appropriate to operate in high water conditions," included a notation that, "Although some units had Expeditions [Ford SUVs], pick-up trucks, or other SUV-type vehicles, the majority of the department did not have access to a high profile vehicle which would allow for movement on streets filled with some water."[28] The second, "Watercraft to conduct rescue operations," noted, "Once the storm had passed, and the levees breached, many officers made use of commandeered modes of transportation. Boats of all types were put into use as methods of transportation for both officers and rescuees."[29]

Riley was Chief of Operations during preparations before Hurricane Ivan and Hurricane Katrina. Prior to Hurricane Ivan, Riley requested and received from the Louisiana National Guard (LANG) high-water vehicles which were staged at each of the police districts prior to the storm.[30] Before Hurricane Katrina, Riley said he asked for five high-water vehicles and five boats to be pre-staged at each of the Department's eight stations. Some vehicles were provided to three or four districts, but no boats were provided.[31] Major General Landreneau, head of the Louisiana National Guard, disputed the assertion regarding high-water vehicles, but documents he provided the Committee do not show that any boats were sent to district stations.[32]

The NOPD's own AARs provide evidence of the pervasive lack of preparedness. The AARs noted that the NOPD did not adequately supply its officers with basic provisions, nor did it have logistics in place to handle supplies. While some bottled water was distributed to officers, "There did not appear to be any pre-planning for food, water, weapons, and medical care."[33] As one officer noted, "The lack of provisions and a quartermaster system forced Officers to procure needed items from abandoned business locations."[34]

Despite challenges facing NOPD officers, maintaining and restoring public safety was of pre-eminent importance, for without it, those trying to help Katrina's victims could not do their jobs. While media reports may have exaggerated the extent of lawlessness, the fact remains that looting and other criminal acts were occurring around the city. There are no reliable statistics available due to the flooding of NOPD headquarters and the jail, but there is significant anecdotal evidence regarding such activity.

Captain Timothy Bayard described an example of looting observed when SAR teams were taking people to the Convention Center:

> We pulled four or five guys out of an apartment two blocks from the Convention Center. But at the time we didn't have any jails, didn't have anyplace to bring them, you know? So we pulled them out of burglarizing a guy's apartment above the store. They had already broken into the store.[35]

Riley described "three hours of mayhem" on Canal Street to which 60 officers responded:

> Well, there were some points where, for instance, Brooks Brothers was being looted. Our officers had some confrontations there. Saks Fifth Avenue was being looted. Some other stores along the block, I believe for the most part, like places that had athletic wear and tennis shoes, things like that.[36]

At the Superdome, despite media reports, including comments made by the NOPD's Compass, the number of violent acts appeared limited. There was an attempted assault on a young woman in one of the rest rooms.[37] Another incident involved the shooting of a National Guardsman which appeared to be an accidental shooting by a fellow Guardsman.[38] There was one suicide, but no homicides.[39]

Despite the absence of significant violent crime, there were nonetheless problems at the Superdome. FEMA Disaster Medical Assistance Teams (DMATs) and Emergency Response Teams (ERTs) and New Orleans Health Department (NOHD) personnel, decided to withdraw from the Superdome complex because they perceived the situation there as unsettled or unsafe.[40] Urban Search and Rescue (USAR) personnel curtailed operations until security was provided.[41] The NOPD feared carjackings by those seeking to flee New Orleans.[42] And the delivery of utility repair services apparently suffered delay until proper security for the workers and sites themselves existed.[43] Only when a secure environment was restored could basic needs truly be addressed.

Lack of readiness and loss of personnel and equipment were major contributing causes to the inability of the NOPD to maintain law and order in the devastated city. But they were not the only ones.

B. The Effectiveness of the NOPD Was Further Diminished by Command Confusion and Lack of Familiarity with Emergency-Operation Plans

Although the NOPD had an emergency-operations manual that included hurricane procedures, the Committee's investigation has not revealed any systematic training administered on a department-wide basis on its own plan, let alone the city's plan or the NRP. Riley surmised, based on the comments in some of the after-action reports done within the department, that some of the commanders had not read their operations manuals.[44] When asked what actions he took during his tenure as chief to ensure that officers were familiar with their responsibilities under the disaster-operations manual, Compass responded only that he "encouraged [his] commanders to make sure that people were very familiar with the hurricane plan."[45] Riley said that every commander (but not every officer) receives a version of the plan and that the plan is "probably reviewed as we have a hurricane approaching."[46] Not all information about procedures to be used during a storm is included within the text of the manuals. Alternative reporting locations, for instance, are not included other than a general instruction to "report to the nearest District Station or police facility."[47] Instead, the Department appears to rely on oral communication among and by commanders immediately before an event to inform the rank and file about rally locations.[48]

Compass recalled that members of specialized units underwent emergency-preparedness training conducted by Terry Ebbert, but that not every officer did.[49] For instance, many officers did not know what the OEP was.[50] The lack of familiarity by the department's rank and file with the OEP and other hurricane emergency procedures must be attributed in part to the department's leadership, including Compass and then-Chief Danny Lawless, the Department's designee at the EOC and Chief of Policy, Planning and Training. After the hurricane, Compass resigned[51] and Lawless was demoted because of his performance.[52] Riley explained that Lawless did not make an adequate effort to communicate information and that his successor would be someone trained in the Incident Command System (ICS).[53]

Deficiencies in the NOPD's manual, lack of training on this manual, lack of familiarity with it, or a combination of the three resulted in inadequate protection of department resources. One officer noted that he had not received training on the hurricane procedures in the NOPD's manual: "In 2004, the police department produced an elaborate hurricane plan and issued it to all its commanders. But it stayed on their bookshelves. The department didn't run exercises to familiarize officers with the plan."[54]

The After Action Report addressed another area critical to a department's command and control structure – leadership. This was the apparent lack of a clearly identified, unified command structure, an issue raised by members of the Command Staff:

> Unified Command: Although the police department normally has the entire command structure in place for normal, everyday operations, the scale of this event required the implementation of an ICS, where a unified command for all departments was a necessity. Who was the Incident Commander and how did we receive instructions from him or her? Where was the Unified Command position?[55]

One captain noted that, "Unified command was never established. This, in my mind, was the major problem with the response during Katrina" and the "Training in Incident/Unified Command for the department is critical."[56] Another noted that, "There did not appear to be an established incident Command, EOC, TOC [Tactical Operations Center] after the impact of the storm."[57]

A related critique was made by eight of the responding Command Staff officers of the City's Office of Emergency Preparedness (OEP), who noted:

> Total failure of OEP: Although identified as the point of command for the emergency, the OEP was out of communication with a large percentage of the department several times during the storm.[58]

C. The Loss of Detention Facilities to Hold Looters and Lawbreakers Contributed to the Public Safety Problem

Shortly after Katrina made landfall, flooding rendered the Orleans Parish Jail, the detention facility used by the city, uninhabitable, and the Criminal Sheriff was forced to evacuate it.[59] As a result, there was nowhere to detain most of those caught in criminal acts in Katrina's aftermath, so police had to release all but those caught committing violent acts.[60]

The breakdown of the detention system, while unavoidable given the extent of flooding, could have been anticipated. With proper contingency plans, existing prisoners could have been evacuated earlier and more easily to detention facilities identified before the storm, and new arrests could have proceeded with fewer processing and housing concerns.

The task of planning for managing prisoners in New Orleans is complicated by an unusual government structure. The jail is operated as a separate entity from the NOPD and the city. It is part of Orleans Parish operations, under the direction of an elected sheriff. Primary responsibility for planning and coordination of the jail's evacuation rests with the Criminal Sheriff.[61] Riley had a general understanding of the jail evacuation planning:

> Over the past many years, the prison has always been self-sufficient as it relates to [evacuation of the prison population]. They normally prepared to do two types of evacuations. One is to take their most violent offenders and have them relocated to another state facility, evacuating them before the storm. The other was a vertical evacuation … [for] less violent offenders.[62]

There was no pre-landfall coordination between the NOPD and the Orleans Parish. Yet, on the day following landfall, the prison – like much of the rest of the city – was surrounded by water estimated at five to six feet deep. At this time, the sheriff sought manpower assistance from the NOPD but was told that none could be spared.[63] On possibly Tuesday or Wednesday, the NOPD did agree to lend a few boats to allow the sheriff to move his prisoners to a nearby Interstate overpass that was above the water line.[64] In pictures seen around the country and the world, prisoners sat on the overpass under the watchful eye of deputy sheriffs supported by National Guard troops until arrangements could be made to move them to detention facilities outside the city.

With the parish jail closed, the NOPD found itself without the use of the jail's booking and intake-processing center.[65] During the first week after landfall, the City of New Orleans was not able to detain most of those caught in criminal acts in Katrina's aftermath. Police could only catch and release persons arrested for anything other than violent acts.[66] The NOPD's disaster-planning document does not address the possibility of the detention facility's being unavailable. The NOPD's After Action Report highlights the impact on law enforcement of the loss of the jail and the lack of a backup facility: "The repeated announcements from the city relative to its intention to, 'vigorously go after looters and prosecute them to the fullest extent of the law' appeared overly ambitious and unenforceable due to the evacuation of the jail. Once the facility to intake arrested subjects was made unavailable, arresting subjects was not an option,"[67] except to the limited extent an ad hoc arrangement with neighboring Jefferson Parish for detaining violent felons was made.[68]

The lack of a detention center and its impact on law enforcement were not lost on the state Attorney General and the United States Attorney for Eastern Louisiana.[69] By the first weekend after landfall, efforts were underway to identify an alternative location within the city.[70]

Flooding of the jail and its impact on both the prisoners held there and the detention of new arrestees clearly should have been anticipated. Given the NOPD's dependence on the Criminal Sheriff's office to provide critical support, the NOPD leadership should have taken steps as it developed its disaster plan to ensure that the plans of other relevant agencies addressed the NOPD's needs. It is not sufficient for agencies who are interdependent to develop their own plans; they must ensure that other agencies' plans synchronize with their own to meet mutual needs. The NOPD's and Orleans Parish's planning did not appropriately account for foreseeable contingencies.

D. Unsubstantiated Rumors of Lawlessness by City Officials and the Failure to Have a Plan for Verifying and Controlling Such Rumors Contributed to the Perceived Lack of Safety in New Orleans

The city apparently did not effectively plan or manage rumors of unrest, and some of its leaders unfortunately repeated them as fact while they were still rumor. This had the result of fueling unsubstantiated media reports that the city was out of control. NOPD Superintendent Compass, for example, made this comment about the Superdome as late as September 6: "We had little babies in there, little babies getting raped. You know how frustrating it is to be Chief of Police knowing inside these things are being done and you don't have enough manpower to go in there?"[71] On the same day, Mayor Nagin said: "They have people standing out there, have been in that frickin' Superdome for five days watching hooligans killing people, raping people."[72] Fortunately, neither statement turned out to be true; there were no confirmed rapes or murders at the Superdome.[73] But these statements, coming as they did from those the public would have reason to believe knew what they were talking about, created a sense of societal breakdown, and likely added to the sense of danger that deterred some first responders from quickly and effectively doing their jobs.

Among the responsibilities assigned to the NOPD's Public Information Officer (PIO) in the Emergency Operations Manual are: (1) release information authorized by the Incident Commander, (2) disseminate media-alert announcements as instructed by the Incident Commander, (3) be responsible for establishing rumor control, (4) schedule media briefings as necessary, and (5) be responsible for establishing a system to monitor incident rumor control.[74] Superintendent Riley noted that the standard policy in the department is to refer media inquiries to the PIO.[75]

While that was the policy, the practice was far different. Despite the department's standard policy of referring media inquiries to the PIO and concern expressed by officials about the impact of unsubstantiated rumors being reported by the media that the city was out of control, Compass fueled such reporting by speaking directly to the media, making sensationalized statements, such as the one noted above, about conditions in the Superdome.[76]

II. The State Response

A. The Louisiana State Police Substantially Supported NOPD with Personnel and Assets

Despite having a force of only 1,050 troopers,[77] the LSP carried out a variety of emergency-support functions during Katrina, not only by orchestrating the state's contraflow plan,[78] but by providing law-enforcement support to the embattled NOPD. As Brigadier General Mark Graham testified, LSP played an important role escorting buses during the evacuations of the Superdome and Convention Center.[79] LSP troopers conducted 1,300 escort missions within the first few days of Katrina.[80] In addition to security escorts for buses, troopers were dispatched to provide perimeter security, including a mission to secure the perimeter around City Hall, where the EOC was located.[81] They helped to secure the Superdome. As the population in Baton Rouge grew with the exodus from New Orleans, LSP troopers deployed to provide security at field hospitals and evacuee shelters.[82]

Among the LSP deployments were Special Weapons and Tactics (SWAT) Teams. The LSP's initial SWAT presence was in New Orleans prior to the storm.[83] Additional LSP SWAT teams arrived on Tuesday, August 30, with the remainder scheduled to arrive Wednesday, August 31.[84] While the LSP sent significant numbers of officers, Lieutenant Colonel Joseph Booth noted that there were some early problems getting officers into the city because of high water. "I've requested watercraft off and on for some eight to 10 years," Colonel Booth said, but those requests had been "Unsuccessful, unsuccessful."[85]

Eight hundred troopers were sent to New Orleans during the first few days after Katrina.[86] The small LSP force, like their NOPD counterparts, quickly became overwhelmed by the scope of the catastrophe and the many services expected of them. Meanwhile, their reassignment to New Orleans left a law-enforcement void in other parts of the state.[87] Still, more officers were needed, and on August 30, Colonel Whitehorn wrote to FBI Director Robert Mueller for help:

> As you are aware, the city of New Orleans, Louisiana has suffered massive damage caused by Hurricane Katrina. We are currently utilizing all State assets to stabilize the situation; however, looting continues to be a significant problem. As the head of Louisiana State Police, I am requesting any assistance you can provide to this agency to assist with the issue to include deployment of available tactical teams.[88]

The letter was faxed from the FBI on August 31 to Principal Associate Deputy Attorney General William Mercer.[89]

Another contribution of the LSP, which had published an 800 number before the storm, was fielding 911 calls from New Orleans residents trapped in their homes, as the 911 system in New Orleans failed in the first few days post-landfall. The LSP emergency operations center received 22,000 emergency calls over a period of approximately one month post-land-fall.[90] EOC staff e-mailed and hand delivered the messages to search-and-rescue agencies.[91]

The LSP, from their own supplies, helped to re-equip the NOPD by substantial resources including 137 vehicles which the LSP marked with the NOPD insignia, uniforms, ammunition, 300 pairs of boots, and other provisions as basic as socks and underwear, toothbrushes, and deodorant.[92]

B. The State of Louisiana Did Not Ask for Federal Law-Enforcement Assistance as Quickly as It Should Have

Consistent with emergency-management and constitutional principles generally, Louisiana state government also had a vital role to play in securing law-enforcement help from outside the state. As with local and federal governments, Hurricane Katrina exposed distinct short-comings and significant oversights in the state's planning and execution of its response.

As with other kinds of assistance, Louisiana's recourse when its own resources are over-whelmed with respect to law enforcement is through the Emergency Management Assistance Compact (EMAC). The state is a signatory to EMAC, as provided in the Louisiana Homeland Security and Emergency Assistance and Disaster Act of 1993,[93] as amended. According to the Louisiana Office of Homeland Security and Emergency Preparedness (LOHSEP) Emergency Operations Plan, if an emergency becomes too widespread or serious for parish or state resources, the Director of LOHSEP is supposed to request assistance through EMAC.[94]

EMAC establishes a process by which states receive mutual aid. Impacted states can request assistance over a wide range of services from those other signatory states without having to negotiate many of the legalities, which have been worked out through the compact. EMAC provided a valuable tool that supported many phases of disaster response, including law enforcement.

Such capabilities involved lending states' police forces, and, through Memoranda of Under-standing arranged by the National Guard Bureau, National Guard forces including military police.[95] According to Colonel Steven Dabadie, Chief of Staff of the Louisiana National Guard, "a large amount of those National Guardsmen that we had in New Orleans were performing security missions,"[96] including at shelters and commodities-distribution sites.[97]

During the first week after landfall, outside law-enforcement agencies were "showing up"[98] in New Orleans, without prior coordination. "It was pitch black in New Orleans," which resulted in "a couple situations" where one law enforcement agency ran into members of another when neither agency knew the other was in the area.[99] This could be attributed to the first responder self-deployment phenomenon identified after the September 11, 2001, terrorist attacks, and could be a recurring problem in future disasters.[100] It could also be the result of an EMAC process where both the local sheriffs association and LSP separately made EMAC requests. Colonel Whitehorn thought that "one EMAC request rather than the sheriffs doing EMAC and then State Police do[ing] another EMAC" made more sense.[101]

It was not until "around day five [that New Orleans] began to coordinate better."[102] Sub-stantial numbers of military personnel were on the ground, tens of thousands of people had been evacuated from the city, and, most importantly, the immediate search-and-rescue crisis was winding down. Additionally, substantial numbers of federal law-enforcement personnel were flowing into the state. Organization, largely absent in the first week, was established through a single check-in at the State Police facility in Baton Rouge operated in conjunction with a federal Law Enforcement Coordination Center (LECC) set up on September 5. Under the auspices of the lead federal law-enforcement officials, the LECC brought together representatives from LSP and local law enforcement, among others.

Thereafter, many out-of-state responders came with their own command structures in place, including clear lines of authority. This made the integration process work even more smoothly and allowed out-of-state responders to meet local needs even in areas where they were not familiar with the surroundings.[103]

The LSP ultimately oversaw the deputization of more than 400 law-enforcement officers from other states and more than 3,000 from the federal government.[104]

At the same time, the State of Louisiana did not request assistance in a form that the Department of Justice found acceptable until days after the storm. Governor Blanco sent a specific request on September 4, stating in part that "the request is made under the Justice Assistance Act of 1984 ('the Act'), 42 U.S.C. §§ 10501-10503, which authorizes the U.S. Department of Justice to provide law enforcement assistance to a State."[105] The State Attorney General's office has not provided the Committee with any information which has shed light on the timing and preparation of this letter, or Colonel Whitehorn's earlier request for assistance.

Moreover, it is not clear that Louisiana requested law-enforcement assistance from FEMA, which, in the first week, assigned hundreds of law-enforcement officials to New Orleans.[106]

Thus, the State waited several days after landfall before getting a request for law-enforcement assistance to the other states through EMAC, in a formal request, to the federal government for help in a form DOJ found acceptable.

III. The Federal Response

A. Neither DHS Nor DOJ Took Any Significant Steps Prior to Landfall to Understand, Plan For or Coordinate Their Joint ESF-13 Responsibilities Relating to a Natural Disaster

The National Response Plan's ESF-13 assigns the DHS and DOJ jointly to lead the federal government's public-safety and security efforts.[107] This is the only ESF for which two agencies are designated as both Coordinators and Primary Agencies, and the results of that joint assignment in Katrina show the wisdom of the unitary assignments for the other ESFs. By assigning this responsibility to more than one entity, the NRP effectively ensured that no one took charge. Because the NRP is silent on resolving leadership issues, DHS and DOJ neither coordinated with each other prior to Katrina, nor independently planned for carrying out their ESF-13 functions. As a result, the days immediately prior to and after landfall were spent figuring out precisely how to implement the ESF-13 responsibilities, rather than actually implementing them in full.

Even the simplest of questions were unresolved prior to Katrina. In the days after landfall, for example, officials at both DOJ and DHS expressed confusion over how the two agencies were supposed to coordinate and which of the two was supposed to take the lead. A September 1 memo among several senior DOJ officials suggested that "DHS is in the lead,"[108] and showing the extent of the confusion, the version of the September 1 DOJ memo produced to the Committee had a handwritten note from the Principal Associate Deputy Attorney General next to the caption "Responsibilities, ESF Coordinators/Primary Agencies" asking "How are these designated? By Whom?"[109] Meanwhile, a September 4 DHS e-mail expressed concern that "DOJ is looking to run this whole effort."[110] On the same day, another DHS e-mail noted that "We have several hundred DHS LEOs [Law Enforcement

Officials] already there and can mobilize several thousand more if our department can make a decision to seriously commit to this effort."[111]

Matthew Broderick, Director of the DHS's Homeland Security Operations Center, offered this candid testimony on the extent to which the ESF-13 responsibilities in a Katrina-like situation were neither contemplated nor understood: "In most cases in the NRP, the FBI has got the lead because it's a terrorist-related action, and they have to do the criminal investigation. No one had thought about a natural disaster."[112] Broderick described the confusion about who would be the lead as part of the "growing pains of working through the NRP,"[113] saying:

> In a natural disaster, there really is no reason for the FBI, there was no investi-
> gative part of it to be involved, particularly when the preponderance of the law
> enforcement – Federal law enforcement was all [Immigration and Customs
> Enforcement and Customs and Border Protection] owned by us anyway. So,
> if we had – if FEMA was overseeing it as a component, why not let our law
> enforcement component take the lead in doing that? … I think it was just a
> matter of no one thinking it through. … I don't think anybody had thought
> about the natural disaster scenario.[114]

In addition, neither DHS nor DOJ seems to have resolved which component within each agency was responsible for the Departments' ESF-13 responsibilities.[115] To this day, no witness interviewed by or document provided to the Committee has definitively identified the agency or component in charge of ESF-13 at DHS, or who made the decision to activate the support function. Senior Department officials couldn't tell the Committee who within the Department was in charge.[116] DHS Deputy Secretary Michael Jackson, for example, had no idea even when the Committee interviewed him which component of his agency was in charge of ESF-13, and he was unable to offer any insight into what DHS did as co-lead.[117] Instead, he repeatedly suggested pursuing this issue with FEMA, notwithstanding the fact that DHS, not FEMA, includes law-enforcement components.[118] His answer did not change after he was informed during this interview that the NRP assigns responsibility for ESF-13 to DHS as a whole, not to FEMA.[119]

The DHS official who ultimately served as the Department's lead law-enforcement person in Louisiana spoke candidly about his lack of familiarity with the NRP, and the lack of clarity in the guidance given him concerning the roles of DHS, ICE, or himself at the time of his deployment. Assistant Director of Immigration and Customs Enforcement's (ICE's) Office of Investigations Michael Vanacore told the Committee that, with respect to the NRP, "I … had a fleeting familiarity with it. To be honest, it wasn't something that was high on my radar screen with my particular responsibilities."[120] When he was first put on "standby" on September 2, he was told "that I would probably be going down in some capacity for ICE, but nobody was sure what that capacity would be."[121] Prior to his arrival on September 4, he said there was "nobody who's stepping up to say 'I'm in charge,' and I don't think any of us had the authority to step up and say, 'I'm in charge.' Hence, . . . the need for some sort of designation."[122] Upon his arrival, he recalled that processes were not in place for coor-dinating the chains of command among state, local, federal, regular military, and National Guard personnel.[123] Even as of September 6, two days after his arrival, he still did not know whether he was there "to coordinate ICE . . . or to coordinate all of DHS."[124]

Vanacore admitted that the role ICE played during the Katrina response had not been envisioned previously. "While the National Response Plan may call on DHS, it didn't call on ICE. And I think ICE stepped up and took on a role that nobody defined for us up until that point. Nobody told ICE, 'This is your role.'"[125] Vanacore questioned the wisdom of ICE's role as the ESF-13 lead for DHS: "I think we're primarily a law enforcement investiga-tive agency, and that's where our focus is. We do investigations. We really did not, up until

Patrolling a flooded city
Army National Guard photo

that point, have, I think, a focused role in a natural disaster response."[126] He also opined that uniformed officers within DHS might be better suited to respond than ICE investigators.[127]

In the days after Katrina, DOJ leadership seemed as confused as the leadership at DHS about how ESF-13 was supposed to work. The previously referenced memorandum among top DOJ officials includes a marginal notation on the third page that asks "who activates" ESF-13,[128] and a September 1 e-mail from Senior Counsel James McAtamney notes that requests from state and local officials should be directed to the Joint Field Office (JFO),[129] even though the JFO didn't exist until well into the next week. It also reports that a representative from the Bureau of Alcohol, Tobacco and Firearms (ATF) had deployed to DHS's Homeland Security Operations Center,[130] even though the NRP calls for such designees to report to an entirely different entity, the National Response Coordination Center.[131]

B. The Departments' Failure to Understand, Plan for and Implement Their ESF-13 Responsibilities in Natural Disasters Prior to Katrina Led to Delays in Providing Law-Enforcement Assistance

The confusion over the meaning of and responsibility for implementing ESF-13 had real-world consequences, because it prevented the federal government from hitting the ground running when the magnitude of Katrina's likely catastrophic consequences became apparent. If ever there were a case for the activation of ESF-13, Katrina was it. All indicators prior to landfall – from the President's call to Governor Blanco urging a mandatory evacuation, to FEMA Director Brown's comments on the Sunday, August 28, video teleconference in which DHS officials participated, that Katrina could be "a catastrophe within a catastrophe" [132]– left little doubt that Katrina would create, in the words of the ESF, "a situation requiring extensive assistance to provide public safety and security and where State and local government resources are overwhelmed or are inadequate."[133] Events immediately after landfall –most importantly the devastation of NOPD's capabilities – confirmed the need for a federal law enforcement cadre prepared, trained and ready to deploy to assist.

Yet the lack of advanced planning meant that it took several days after landfall – days in which the city and those helping it suffered from a lack of order and protection – for DOJ to move into the New Orleans area in force. On September 1 – three days after landfall – only 45 agents from 4 DOJ components were reportedly in the city, while as many as 215 were on hand in Baton Rouge.[134] Notably, 188 of the 214 FBI personnel assigned to the New Orleans office were on administrative leave as late as September 8,[135] presumably not participating in the response effort.[136] Nonetheless, starting on September 2, significant federal law-enforcement contingents began arriving in Louisiana. On September 6, there were reportedly 2,326 federal law-enforcement officers in the disaster relief area[137] – including 694 from DOJ. The combined federal law enforcement deployment was nearly equal to the total of LSP and NOPD officers in the State of Louisiana before landfall.[138]

In the midst of this time-sensitive need, federal law-enforcement agencies found themselves grappling with issues they had not resolved previously, including how their newly assigned public-safety and security functions would mesh with military assistance provided for civil disturbances.[139] DOJ, at least, envisioned its law-enforcement role in Katrina's aftermath as secondary to that of military troops sent to the affected states for these purposes.[140] In fact, Louisiana officials had requested such troops and thousands of military police and Guardsmen available and intended to reinforce the NOPD deployed to the city from August 31 through September 3.[141] The deployment of active-duty troops for such purposes, pursuant to an invocation of the Insurrection Act, also remained a real possibility.[142] The extent to which DOJ and DHS coordinated the deployment of their personnel and assets with any DOD entity remains unclear.

Similarly, it does not appear that DHS law-enforcement personnel, with the exception of the Federal Protective Service[143] and Customs and Border Patrol,[144] were preparing to assist with their ESF-13 response with much urgency. Senior Immigration, Customs and Enforcement (ICE) leadership, were at an ICE conference in Baltimore from August 29-31 at which Katrina merited only "some mention," and that was regarding plans for recovery of ICE assets, not a larger emergency response.[145] Among those attending was Mike Holt, the ICE Special Agent in charge in New Orleans, who was unable to get back to the city until the following Friday.[146]

There's another twist to the timing of the deployment of DOJ resources: although ESF-13 contemplates a broad role for federal law enforcement,[147] DOJ appears to take the position that it could only deploy resources to provide law-enforcement assistance to a state pursuant to 42 U.S.C. § 10501.[148] This statute provides a process for federal law-enforcement assistance to be provided to a state in the event of a "law enforcement emergency."[149] The process requires a written application[150] from a governor before DOJ can push its personnel into a state to provide "law enforcement assistance."[151] Although DOJ appears never to have responded to Col. Whitehorn's letter, it follows from the position it took in its responses to HSGAC's questions in its November 23, 2005, response concerning the applicability of 42 U.S.C. § 10501 that it found his August 30 request insufficient to allow for the dispatch of DOJ assistance to Louisiana, because it came from the superintendent of the State Police rather than the Governor herself.[152] As noted earlier, Colonel Whitehorn wrote asking for any assistance the FBI could provide, including deployment of available tactical teams.[153]

Although Colonel Whitehorn's letter does not comply with the terms of 42 U.S.C. § 10501, the lack of a compliant letter need not have prevented DOJ from deploying law-enforcement officers and resources to Louisiana. In the first place, the NRP, to which DOJ is a signatory, contemplates the deployment of federal law enforcement personnel and does not reference 42 U.S.C. § 10501.[154] In the second place, DOJ ended up deploying personnel to Louisiana before *receiving a compliant request under the statute*. Indeed, the bulk[155] of DOJ's responding personnel were in the state before Governor Blanco personally requested assistance on September 4.[156]

Another example of DOJ reliance on the absence of a formal 42 U.S.C. § 10501 request from the Governor is an exchange of e-mails between DOJ's Principal Associate Deputy Attorney General William Mercer, Senior Counsel McAtamney and Principal Deputy Assistant Attorney General Steve Bradbury, concerning a State request for ATF help with crowd control.[157] Bradbury wrote on September 1, "There is not currently a written request from the Governor to the AG to provide DOJ assistance to State and local law enforcement. We would not approve this State law enforcement activity until there is such a request and the AG has issued an order approving the request. ATF could move forward with preparations and pre-positioning but should not actually begin state law enforcement without such an order."[158]

Again, there is no record DOJ ever advised the Governor of its view of the prerequisite conditions for providing law-enforcement assistance.

On September 1, the Attorney General's deputy chief of staff, Kyle Sampson, sent an e-mail to the directors of the FBI, ATF, U.S. Marshals Service, and others, noting that "The AG intends to issue a directive to each of you later today to move additional resources into [Louisiana] in response to Hurricane Katrina and its aftermath."[159] Sampson also wrote that "the President has said publicly that looting and violence and lawlessness will not be tolerated and that he has spoken to his AG about it, so we want to ensure that we are bringing all of our [law enforcement] assets to bear on this." Each of the subordinate agencies was directed to "provide … in the next several hours, a rack-up of additional personnel, assets, and other resources … available to be applied directly to this problem."[160] The Attorney General issued a directive on Friday, September 2, designating DOJ assets to deploy to the affected region.[161]

Despite repeated requests, DOJ has not provided the Committee with sufficient information to determine the cause of the delay between receipt of Colonel Whitehorn's August 30 letter and issuance of the September 2 order directing the deployment of federal law-enforcement personnel to Louisiana. However, the Committee would find it unacceptable if the delay was caused by the fact that the request from Colonel Whitehorn did not technically meet the formula set forth 42 U.S.C. § 10501. This is particularly so given that DOJ has provided the Committee with no documentation or testimony indicating that it told Louisiana officials that Colonel Whitehorn's letter was insufficient. At a minimum, the letter should have been treated by DOJ with a greater sense of urgency than was disclosed to the Committee given the crisis that was still unfolding in Louisiana. It would be equally unacceptable if the reason was simply failure to plan for or anticipate the need for federal law-enforcement assistance under ESF-13.

It is also clear that other legal issues that should have been resolved long prior to landfall caused confusion and limited what DOJ would allow its personnel to do in the first week following Katrina. In the days before landfall, the ATF took the initiative to contact the Deputy Attorney General's office to seek "any guidance that would come from the Attorney General to all the Justice components about what authorities we'd be acting under and what our response would be."[162]

As the law-enforcement situation in New Orleans worsened with the storm's passing, DOJ law-enforcement agencies continued their quest for guidance as to the Department's plans to coordinate and implement a departmental response.[163] On the evening of August 31, DOJ advised its component agencies that it was still in the process of developing such guidance.[164] DOJ lawyers were still reviewing "a number of very sensitive legal/perhaps constitutional issues" with providing assistance on non-federal law-enforcement matters to state and local officials.[165]

On September 4, following receipt of Governor Blanco's official, written request for law-enforcement assistance, U.S. Attorney General Alberto Gonzales issued an order to DOJ law-enforcement officers authorizing them to assist law-enforcement officials in the State of Louisiana to enforce the laws of that state.[166] Even after the order was issued, the deputization process which was a state responsibility, proved to be "difficult." [167] ICE Assistant Director Vanacore described helping coordinate a deputization process for all federal agents with the Louisiana Attorney General's Office in which agents had to take an oath in the personal presence of a state assistant attorney general.[168] The numerous, rapid deployments of agents each day, combined with the limited number of assistant attorney generals available to conduct live deputization ceremonies, made it hard to get people together at the same time and place. Accordingly, they were forced to dispatch non-deputized agents with deputized agents, NOPD officers, or LSP troopers.[169] This increased the complexity of taking coordinated action.[170]

Similar issues arose regarding agents' powers to rescue residents trapped in their homes, or to conduct street patrols. For example, according to e-mails submitted by DOJ, a message – including an opinion from the office of the U.S. Attorney for the Eastern District of Louisiana – addressing FBI agents' authority regarding forced entries, forced evacuations, and rescues appeared on a password-protected website no earlier than September 10. On September 13, DOJ officials sought broader distribution of this message. As FBI Agent Kenneth Kaiser said, these kinds of issues "frustrated a lot of the agents,"[171] and he felt like he "was holding back the reins on a horse."[172]

Even today, it is unclear what sort of law-enforcement role DOJ envisions for federal law-enforcement officers in a natural-disaster scenario. In answers to the Committee's questions, the DOJ stated that ESF-13 "does not extend to providing federal law enforcement personnel to … enforce federal, state or local laws."[173] DOJ offers as an example to illustrate the type of support it could provide under ESF-13 that if a state or local law-enforcement agency had suffered the loss of communications equipment, it could submit a request for federal law-enforcement assets to the ESF-13 staff, who would evaluate it and then pass it on to the senior federal official. In contrast, Michael Bouchard, ATF's Assistant Director in Charge of Operations, believed that the requests would be passed from the NRCC to the IIMG.[174] Special Agent in Charge of the Boston Field Office Kenneth Kaiser, who has had substantial training on the NRP, including appointment as a PFO, expressed another view of the type of assistance contemplated by ESF-13, stating, "There's nothing in the ESF-13 that says that the FBI or any DOJ or any law enforcement agency is responsible for supplying food and clothing for these people. … ESF-13 does not address that at all. ESF-13 is a law-enforcement function and that's what we did. The other functions, resupplying and stuff like that, that is not a law enforcement function."[175]

According to DOJ, conferring the authority to enforce state and local laws on federal law-enforcement officers requires two steps. First, there must be a 42 U.S.C. § 10501 request for such assistance from a governor, and second, they must be deputized in accordance with the laws of the requesting state. Of course, federal law-enforcement officers could be deployed to a state without a gubernatorial request,[176] in any event, and could undertake federal missions and provide support to local law enforcement, while their mere presence would go a long way towards preserving order and security in a panic-stricken city. In addition, they could have performed search and rescue, thus permitting the NOPD and the LSP to focus more on traditional law-enforcement tasks such as crowd control. Between September 1 and September 3, DOJ law-enforcement components were in fact engaged in law-enforcement and search-and-rescue operations, including saving lives.[177]

The DHS and DOJ's confusion about their roles and authorities prevented the Departments from bringing the full weight of their resources to bear until roughly a week after landfall. It was not until the beginning of the second week that the federal agencies took action to establish a law-enforcement coordination center to track and coordinate arriving officers; designate officials to be in charge of that process; and arrange for deputization of federal officers by the states.

C. The Departments' Failure to Designate Senior Federal Law-Enforcement Coordinators Until Nearly a Week After Landfall, If They Ever Did, Further Hindered Response Efforts

Further adding to the confusion created by the NRP's joint delegation to DHS and DOJ of its ESF-13 responsibilities is another part of the NRP, which creates the position of Senior Federal Law Enforcement Official (SFLEO). According to the NRP, the SFLEO "is the senior law enforcement official from the agency with primary jurisdictional responsibility as directed by statute, Presidential directive, existing Federal policies, and/or the Attorney General."[178] The SFLEO directs intelligence/investigative law-enforcement operations in a national incident, such as terrorism, a national-security special event, or disaster. The NRP states that "In the event of a terrorist incident, this official will normally be the FBI SAC,"[179] but it doesn't specify who takes the post after a natural disaster. The jockeying for a law-enforcement position reflects the failure to engage in pre-incident planning for a federal law-enforcement role, at least in response to a national disaster, and played a role in this delay.

The NRP offers no insight into how the SFLEO is supposed to interact or coordinate with the ESF-13 agencies, or why two agencies are charged with primary and coordinating responsibility under ESF-13.[180] These ambiguities, as well as delay by both DHS and DOJ in designating a SFLEO, further contributed to the untimeliness of the federal public safety response and impeded the strategic coordination of incoming federal law-enforcement resources.[181] It further reflects the failure to engage in adequate, if any, pre-event planning for a federal law-enforcement role in response to a natural disaster.

Although FEMA and DHS appear to have considered the ESF-13 function activated two days prior to landfall, the eventual putative co-SFLEOs –Vanacore and FBI Special Agent Michael Wolf – were not identified until September 5, almost a week after landfall. While the reasons for this delay remain unclear, the shared responsibility for ESF-13 between DOJ and DHS, and in-fighting within DHS,[182] initially played a role.

The process by which DHS selected its prospective co-SFLEO is instructive as to the lack of definition. On September 2, ICE leadership told Vanacore that he would deploy to Louisiana to serve in a liaison capacity, though his exact duties remained unclear.[183] In this capacity, any information he provided was sent to ICE, not to senior DHS leadership.[184] He arrived in Baton Rouge late in the afternoon on September 4.[185] After he arrived in Baton Rouge he learned that he was made co-SFLEO, although without written designation.[186] Though an experienced leader, he had no specific training on the NRP and no natural-disaster response experience.[187] Vanacore determined that he could best contribute by assuming a coordination role.[188]

DOJ has been unclear in its statements to the Committee on the subject of SFLEO designation. According to Wolf, he assumed co-SFLEO responsibilities on September 4, but never received a formal designation; instead, he received his orders by telephone from the Bureau's Executive Assistant Director for Criminal Investigations.[189] Yet, William Mercer, DOJ's Principal Associate Deputy Attorney General, stated in his Committee interview that the SFLEOs were self-selected.[190] During a follow-up interview, he amplified on his earlier statements, stating that SFLEOs were not designated during the response, and that the U.S. Attorney for the Eastern District of Louisiana retained coordinating control over law-enforcement assets and personnel in New Orleans pursuant to a memorandum signed by the Attorney General dated September 4.[191]

With the arrival of the co-SFLEOs, the law-enforcement management situation in Louisiana, especially New Orleans, improved significantly, and local authorities were ultimately pleased with federal help, once it arrived.[192]

Vanacore and Wolf fulfilled their duties ably, in part because they could establish a productive working relationship,[193] but both noted that a single chain of command would have been more effective. Vanacore concluded, "You need one general in command. … We managed this because everybody agreed to be managed. But that's not the way to do things. … You don't run a war with co-generals."[194]

D. Conclusion

While federal law-enforcement officers eventually provided enormous assistance to state and local governments in the Gulf Coast region, more forethought and planning would have allowed them to provide greater and critically needed help when it was most needed – during the storm's immediate aftermath.

Perhaps testimony from Kenneth Kaiser, a former FBI Special Agent in Charge of the New Orleans Field Office who volunteered to deploy to New Orleans on August 31, and who assumed responsibilities as the Bureau's on-scene tactical commander, best summed up the lack of forethought by federal law enforcement planners. Kaiser had received Principal Federal Officer training under the NRP, and described himself as having received "as much training and crisis management exercis[ing] that probably anybody in the Bureau has ever [received]."[195] According to this experienced official, "I would have told you that prior to Katrina that there would be no way that the FBI would be as heavily involved in a natural disaster as we were down there. … Post-Katrina, I would say there definitely is a law enforcement aspect to these natural disasters, in the worst-case scenario."[196]

The Committee expects that this experience will prompt DOJ and DHS to engage in far better planning and coordination in anticipation of the next disaster.

---

1 Allen G. Breed, "Opportunists Help Themselves, Sometimes in Front of Police," *BC Cycle*, Aug. 30, 2005; "New Orleans probes police role in looting," The Associated Press, Sept. 29, 2005, 8:43 p.m. ET. http:// www.msnbc.msn.com/id/9535751/. Accessed on May 9, 2006.

2 Scott Gold, Lianne Hart, and Stephen Braun, "Katrina's Rising Toll," *Los Angeles Times*, Sept. 1, 2005, Part A, p. 1.

3 Scott Gold, Alan Zarembo, and Stephen Braun, "Katrina's Aftermath; Guardsmen Arrive in New Orleans; Pace of Evacuations Is Stepped Up," *Los Angeles Times*, Sept. 3, 2005, part A, p. 1.

4 Gold, Zarembo, and Braun, "Katrina's Aftermath," part A, p. 1.

5 Joseph B. Treaster, "Police Quitting, Overwhelmed by Chaos," *The New York Times*, Sept. 4, 2005, Section 1, p. 1.

6 Eddie Compass, *The Oprah Winfrey Show*, "Inside the Katrina Catastrophe," Sept. 6, 2005. http://www.oprah.com/tows/pastshows/200509/tows_past_20050906.jhtml. Accessed on Mar. 30, 2006.

7 Written Statement of Warren Riley, Superintendent, New Orleans Police Department, LA, for the U.S. Senate, Committee on Homeland Security and Governmental Affairs, hearing on *Hurricane Katrina: Managing Law Enforcement and Communications in a Catastrophe*, Feb. 6, 2006, p. 8.

8 Committee staff interview of Lonnie Swain, Assistant Superintendent, New Orleans Police Department, LA, conducted on Nov. 9, 2005, transcript pp. 75-76; Committee staff interview of Warren Riley, Superintendent, New Orleans Police Department, LA, conducted on Jan. 12, 2006, transcript p. 34.

9 Committee staff interview of Jeff Glick, Chief, Critical Infrastructure Protection Division, National Communications System, U.S. Department of Homeland Security, conducted on Feb. 3, 2006, transcript p. 59. *See also:* Committee staff interview of Christopher Guttman-McCabe, Vice President for Regulatory Affairs, Cellular Telecommunications and Internet Association, conducted on Jan. 24, 2006, transcript p. 25.

10 *See*: Chapter 8: Hurricane Pam: Warning Flag for Katrina.

11 *The Oprah Winfrey Show*, "Inside the Katrina Catastrophe," Sept. 6, 2005. http://www.oprah.com/tows/past-shows/200509/tows_past_20050906.jhtml. Accessed on Mar. 30, 2006.

12 Mayor C. Ray Nagin, "Transcript of WWL-AM Radio with New Orleans' Nagin," Sept. 2, 2005. http://www.cnn.com/2005/US/09/02/nagin.transcript/. Accessed on Mar. 20, 2006.

13 U.S. Department of Homeland Security, *National Response Plan*. Washington: Government Printing Office, Dec. 2004, p. ESF #13–1 [hereinafter *NRP*].

14 Written Statement of Riley, Senate Committee hearing, Feb. 6, 2006, p. 2.

15 Written Statement of Riley, Senate Committee hearing, Feb. 6, 2006, p. 8. According to NOPD officials, approximately 65 have been terminated, 60 have resigned, 12 have been suspended, and 37 others were still subject to disciplinary proceedings at the time of interview. Swain interview, Nov. 9, 2005, p. 122; Riley interview, Jan. 12, 2006, p. 148.

16 FBI Special Agent in Charge Kenneth Kaiser provided a vivid picture of the status of the NOPD force:

> They were running out of ammunition. They were running out of food and water. We were bringing them food and water. And we brought in our medical personnel to look at the people. Some of these people had been on duty since the hurricane, hadn't heard from their wife and kids, hadn't left their

post. Some of them were very ill. They had fevers. … A lot of them were wearing the same clothes they'd worn for seven, eight days.

Committee staff interview of Kenneth Kaiser, Special Agent in Charge, Boston Field Office, Federal Bureau of Investigation (FBI), conducted on Jan. 25, 2006, transcript p. 29. *See also:* Riley interview, Jan. 12, 2006, p. 75; Committee staff interview of Col. Mark Oxley, Chief of Staff, Louisiana State Police, conducted on Dec. 9, 2005, transcript p. 253.

17 New Orleans Police Department, Initial (30-day) After Action Report-Summary, p. 6. Provided to Committee [hereinafter NOPD, Initial After Action Report-Summary].

18 New Orleans Police Department Initial (30-day) After Action Report, Report of Capt. Jeffrey J. Winn, Oct. 10, 2005, p. 2; Written Statement of Capt. Timothy Bayard, Commander, Vice Crimes and Narcotics Section, New Orleans Police Department, LA, for the U.S. Senate, Committee on Homeland Security and Governmental Affairs, hearing on *Hurricane Katrina: Urban Search and Rescue in a Catastrophe*, Jan. 30, 2006, p. 2. Captain Bayard described the problem in his after action report: "our biggest flaw is the fact that we failed to communicate. … The instructions and plans that are formed at the top are not clearly communicated to the rank and file. … This causes confusion and misdirection. In the time of crisis our leaders need to be SEEN and HEARD." New Orleans Police Department, Initial (30-day) After Action Report, Report of Capt. Timothy Bayard, Oct. 16, 2005, p. 4. Provided to Committee [hereinafter Capt. Bayard, Initial After Action Report, Oct. 16, 2005].

19 New Orleans Police Department, Initial (30-day) After Action Report, Report of Capt. Jeffrey J. Winn, Oct. 10, 2005, p. 2. Provided to Committee [hereinafter Capt. Winn, Initial After Action Report, Oct. 10, 2005]; NOPD, Initial After Action Report-Summary, pp. 4, 6.

20 Capt. Winn, Initial After Action Report, Oct. 10, 2005, p. 2.

21 Kaiser interview, Jan. 25, 2006, p. 29.

22 Riley interview, Jan. 12, 2006, p. 75.

23 New Orleans Police Department, *Emergency Operations Manual*, 2005, p. 13–3. Provided to Committee [hereinafter NOPD, *Emergency Operations Manual*, 2005].

24 Committee staff interview of Capt. Paul Hellmers, Captain, Engine 18, Second Platoon, Fifth District, New Orleans Fire Department, LA and Capt. Joe Fincher, Engine 18, Third Platoon, Fifth District, New Orleans Fire Department, LA, conducted on Nov. 7, 2005, transcript pp. 12-13, 16; New Orleans Fire Department, *2005 Hurricane Guidelines*, p. 2–1. Provided to Committee [hereinafter NOFD, *2005 Hurricane Guidelines*].

25 NOFD, *2005 Hurricane Guidelines*, pp. A2–1 through A5–2, A7–1.

26 NOPD, *Emergency Operations Manual*, 2005, p. 13–3.

27 Committee staff interview of Lt. Col. Mark Oxley, Chief of Staff, Louisiana State Police, and Lt. Col. Joseph Booth, Deputy Superintendent, Crisis Response and Special Operations, Louisiana State Police, conducted on Dec. 9, 2005, transcript pp. 251-253.

28 NOPD, Initial After Action Report-Summary, p. 6 (This was noted by 12 officers, or 46.1% of respondents.).

29 NOPD, Initial After Action Report-Summary, p. 6 (This was noted by 10 officers, or 38.4% of respondents.).

30 Committee staff interview of Warren Riley, Superintendent, New Orleans Police Department, LA, conducted on Dec. 20, 2005, transcript p. 49.

31 Testimony of Warren Riley, Superintendent, New Orleans Police Department, LA, before the U.S. Senate, Committee on Homeland Security and Governmental Affairs, hearing on *Hurricane Katrina: Managing Law Enforcement and Communications in a Catastrophe*, Feb. 6, 2006; Riley interview, Dec. 20, 2006, pp. 45-51.

32 Maj. Damian K. Waddell, memorandum for Joint Force Headquarters Louisiana, Feb. 7, 2006. Provided to Committee. *See also:* Chad Michael Lynch, Louisiana Army National Guard, sworn statement, Feb. 8, 2006. Provided to Committee; Robert John Threeton, Louisiana Army National Guard, sworn statement, Feb. 8, 2006. Provided to Committee; David S. Silva, Louisiana Army National Guard, sworn statement, Feb. 8, 2006. Provided to Committee; Edward M. Knight, Louisiana Army National Guard, sworn statement, Feb. 9, 2006; Louisiana Army National Guard, high water vehicle list with assigned drivers. Provided to Committee; Col. Jonathan T. Ball, memorandum for the record, "Request for 'High Water' Trucks," Feb. 8, 2006. Provided to Committee.

33 Capt. Winn, Initial After Action Report, Oct. 10, 2005, p. 2; Riley interview, Jan. 12, 2006, p. 119 ("As it relates to food, food has never, ever been an issue. Most officers pack their own lunch, bring their own food, and prepare for the storm. … If you talk about a flood of this proportion for 14 days, then absolutely food and water was a definite issue."); Capt. Bayard, Initial After Action Report, Oct. 16, 2005, p. 2.

34 New Orleans Police Department, Initial (30-day) After Action Report, Report of Capt. Juan Quinton, p. 3. Provided to Committee.

35 Committee staff interview of Capt. Timothy Bayard, Commander, Vice Crimes and Narcotics Section, New Orleans Police Department, LA, conducted on Nov. 21, 2005, transcript pp. 93-94.

36 Riley interview, Jan. 12, 2006, p. 25.

37 Riley interview, Jan. 12, 2006, p. 34.

38 Swain interview, Nov. 9, 2005, pp. 77-78 (Mr. Swain related the incident in detail during his committee interview: There was a man in one of the locker rooms who was apparently looking for a place to use the rest room. "I think he may have had a stick or something in his hand, or whatever. I think the Guardsman went to approach him to determine what [he was] doing. … The floors were extremely slippery from the water and the much and everything else. … Apparently when the Guardsman approached, there was two Guardsmen, the one in the front, as they approached the guy, I don't know if this guy stood up from a squatting position or whatever. But the Guardsman in the front stepped back. When he stepped back , the Guardsman behind him apparently attempted to step back and slipped. As he was slipping, he had his gun apparently, his finger on the trigger, and his weapon discharged, hitting him in the leg.").

39 Riley interview, Jan. 12, 2006, p. 35.

40 Committee staff interview of Ronald L. Martin, Deputy Commander, Management Support Team, National Disaster Medical System, Federal Emergency Management Agency (FEMA), conducted on Jan. 13, 2006, transcript pp. 92-97; Committee staff interview of Marty Bahamonde, Regional Director, External Affairs, Region I, FEMA, conducted on Oct. 7, 2005, transcript pp. 200-201; Committee staff interview of Kevin Stephens, MD., Director, New Orleans Health Department, LA, conducted on Nov. 10, 2005, transcript pp. 50-63.

41 Committee staff interview of David Webb, Program Specialist, Program Office, National Search and Rescue, Urban Search and Rescue Response System, FEMA, conducted on Feb. 7, 2006, transcript pp. 58-61; Committee staff interview of James Strickland, Team Member, Urban Search and Rescue, FEMA, conducted on Jan. 25, 2006, transcript p. 91.

42 Douglas Crow, e-mail to Matthew Friedrich, Sept. 1, 2005, 6:58 p.m. Provided to Committee (discussing in part alleged carjackings on the road from New Orleans to Baton Rouge. FBI Special Agent in Charge Kenneth Kaiser also spoke of such fears in the context of power company trucks sustaining gunfire; the police also chased one truck involved in a highjacking.).

43 Kaiser interview, Jan. 25, 2006, p. 59; U.S. Department of Homeland Security, Hurricane Katrina DHS SitRep #23, Sept. 6, 2005, 6 p.m., pp. 9, 12, 14, 20. Provided to Committee; filed as Bates nos. DHS 0001487, 0001490, 0001492, 0001498.

44 Riley interview, Jan. 12, 2006, p. 125.

45 Committee staff interview of Eddie Compass, then-Superintendent, New Orleans Police Department, LA, conducted on Jan. 12, 2006, transcript p. 31.

46 Riley interview, Jan. 12, 2006, p. 31.

47 NOPD, *Emergency Operations Manual*, 2005, pp. 2-3, 13-12.

48 Riley interview, Dec. 20, 2005, p. 33.

49 Compass interview, Jan. 12, 2006, pp. 9-12.

50 Riley interview, Jan. 12, 2006, pp. 127-128.

51 Compass interview, Jan. 12, 2006, p. 128. Compass officially resigned from the NOPD on Oct. 31, 2005.

52 Riley interview, Jan. 12, 2006, p. 127.

53 Riley interview, Jan. 12, 2006, pp. 127-129.

54 Dan Baum, "Deluged," *The New Yorker*, Jan. 9, 2006, p. 54; Bayard interview, Nov. 21, 2005, pp. 46, 50.

55 NOPD, Initial After Action Report-Summary, p. 14.

56 New Orleans Police Department, Initial (30-day) After Action Report, Report of Capt. Robert Norton, Oct. 10, 2005, pp. 2-3.

57 Capt. Winn, Initial After Action Report, Oct. 10, 2005.

58 Capt. Winn, Initial After Action Report, Oct. 10, 2005.

59 Capt. Winn, Initial After Action Report, Oct. 10, 2005.

60 Capt. Winn, Initial After Action Report, Oct. 10, 2005.

61 Riley interview, Jan. 12, 2006, pp. 39-40.

62 Riley interview, Jan. 12, 2006, pp. 39-40.

63 Riley interview, Jan. 12, 2006, p. 40.

64 Compass interview, Jan. 12, 2006, p. 126.

65 Riley interview, Jan. 12, 2006, p. 44.

66 Riley interview, Jan. 12, 2006, p. 38.

67 NOPD, Initial After Action Report-Summary, p. 11.

68 Riley interview, Jan. 12, 2006, p. 38.

69 Committee staff interview of James Bernazzani, Special Agent in Charge, New Orleans Division, FBI, conducted on Jan. 25, 2006, transcript p. 88.

70 FBI, New Orleans Command Post, Baton Rouge, LA., Daily SitRep, Sept. 4, 2005. Provided to Committee; filed as Bates nos. FBI 000000127 through 000000130.

71 Eddie Compass, The Oprah Winfrey Show, "Inside the Katrina Catastrophe," Sept. 6, 2005. http://www.oprah.com/tows/pastshows/200509/tows_past_20050906.jhtml. Accessed on Mar. 30, 2006.

72 Mayor C. Ray Nagin, The Oprah Winfrey Show, "Inside the Katrina Catastrophe," Sept. 6, 2005. http://www.oprah.com/tows/pastshows/200509/tows_past_20050906.jhtml. Accessed on Mar. 30, 2006.

73 There was one attempted rape. *Source:* Riley interview, Jan. 12, 2006, pp. 34-35. There were 11 deaths at the Superdome, one was determined to have been a suicide. None were determined to be homicides. There was one gunshot injury involving a National Guardsman inside the Superdome which was determined to have been an accidental shooting. *Source*: Swain interview, Nov. 9, 2005, pp. 77-78.

74 NOPD, *Emergency Operations Manual*, 2005, p. 1–6.

75 Riley interview, Jan. 12, 2006, p. 133.

76 The NOPD's plan regarding press conferences and the release of information to the public required two levels of approval. While the PIO, as noted above, is tasked with responsibilities including release of information on authority of the Incident Commander and scheduling of media briefings as necessary, the plan also states that, "A media press room … *shall issue statements only with the permission from the Mayor's Public Information Office. Statements and decisions relating to the emergency shall emanate only from the Mayor and may be released only through the Public Information Officer."* NOPD, *Emergency Operations Manual*, 2005, p. 15–1 (emphasis in original).

77 Lt. Col. Oxley and Lt. Col. Booth interview, Dec. 9, 2005, p. 7.

78 Lt. Col. Oxley and Lt. Col. Booth interview, Dec. 9, 2005, pp. 14-24; The LSP is also the primary agency responsible under the State's plan for hazardous materials, and took steps before landfall to coordinate the removal or protection of dangerous materials. Troopers supported search-and-rescue missions, including rescuing 500 victims on their own. Lt. Col. Oxley interview, Dec. 9, 2005, p. 233.

79 Written Statement of Brig. Gen. Mark Graham, U.S. Army, Deputy Commanding General, Fifth U.S. Army, for the U.S. Senate, Committee on Homeland Security and Governmental Affairs, hearing on *Hurricane Katrina: Managing the Crisis and Evacuating New Orleans*, Feb. 1, 2006, pp. 2-4.

80 Committee staff interview of Col. Henry Whitehorn, Superintendent, Louisiana State Police and Deputy Secretary, Public Safety Services and Corrections, LA, conducted on Nov. 29, 2005, transcript p. 106.

81 Lt. Col. Oxley and Lt. Col. Booth interview, Dec. 9, 2005, p. 240.

82 Lt. Col. Oxley and Lt. Col. Booth interview, Dec. 9, 2005, pp. 287-288.

83 Lt. Col. Oxley and Lt. Col. Booth interview, Dec. 9, 2005, pp. 201-202.

84 Lt. Col. Oxley and Lt. Col. Booth interview, Dec. 9, 2005, p. 243; Louisiana State Police, LSP Hurricane Katrina Timeline of Events. Provided to Committee.

85 Lt. Col. Booth interview, Dec. 9, 2005, pp. 245-246.

86 Lt. Col. Oxley and Lt. Col. Booth interview, Dec. 9, 2005, pp. 250, 287.

87 Lt. Col. Oxley and Lt. Col. Booth interview, Dec. 9, 2005, pp. 287-98.

88 Col. Henry Whitehorn, letter to Robert Mueller, Aug. 30, 2005. Provided to Committee; filed as Bates nos. DAG 000000001 through 000000002.

89 The Whitehorn letter was faxed to Bill Mercer by Jon Solomon, FBI, on Aug. 31, 2005, at 7:12 p.m. Jon Solomon, facsimile to Bill Mercer, Aug. 21, 2005, 7:21 p.m. Provided to Committee; filed as Bates nos. DAG 000000001 through 000000002. *See also:* James McAtamney, e-mail to Bill Mercer and others, Aug. 31, 2005, 8:18 a.m. Provided to Committee; filed as Bates nos. 000000019 through 0000000020 (enclosing an attached file describing the impact on Hurricane Katrina on DOJ component agencies. The FBI section reports that the "Louisiana State Police (LSP) has indicated a formal request for FBI assistance is forthcoming. LSP is assisting the New Orleans PD, which has been significantly impacted. Looting is the major problem. Reporting indicates that the National Guard is predominately engaged in search and rescue. We will coordinate our response with the Department."). In an e-mail to McAtamney on Aug. 31, 2005, in which at 8:32 a.m., Edgar Domenech, ATF wrote: "I assume the department will be looking to implement a departmental response, let me know what you need." *Source:* Edgar Domenech, e-mail to James A. McAtamney, Aug. 31, 2005, 8:32 a.m. Provided to Committee; filed as Bates. no. DAG 000000014. McAtamney then wrote to Mercer and others, "Deputy Director Domenech from ATF raises a good point. Is a plan in place to coordinate the departmental effort in support of these offices? I think it would be helpful to add any information on our plans going forward to the update paper for the AG." *Source:* James A. McAtamney, e-mail to Paul Corts and others, Aug. 31, 2005, 8:44 a.m. Provided to Committee; filed as Bates no. DAG 000000014.

90 Lt. Col. Oxley and Lt. Col. Booth interview, Dec. 9, 2005, pp. 237-38.

91 Lt. Col. Booth interview, Dec. 9, 2005, p. 239.

92 Lt. Col. Oxley and Lt. Col. Booth interview, Dec. 9, 2005, pp. 253, 257, 291.

93 "Louisiana Homeland Security and Emergency Assistance and Disaster Act," LA R.S. 29:733.

94 Louisiana Office of Homeland Security and Emergency Preparedness (LOHSEP), *Emergency Operations Plan*, Apr. 2005, pp. 14-15.

95 Gov. Kathleen Babineaux Blanco, letter to Gov. Jeb Bush, Sept. 1, 2005, attachment "Memorandum of Understanding Between The State of Louisiana and The State of Florida." As discussed in Chapter 26: Military Operations, other states

began sending Military Police on Wednesday, Aug. 31, 2005, at Maj. Gen. Landreneau's request to the National Guard Bureau.

96 Committee staff interview of Col. Steven Dabadie, Chief of Staff, Louisiana National Guard, conducted on Jan. 12, 2006, transcript p. 146.

97 Committee staff interview of Col. Earl Santos, Joint Director of Military Support, Louisiana National Guard, conducted on Dec. 21, 2005, transcript pp. 34, 54, 93.

98 Riley interview, Jan. 12, 2006, p. 90.

99 Kaiser interview, Jan. 25, 2006, p. 66.

100 As the 9/11 Commission Report noted:

> Yet the Pentagon response encountered difficulties that echo those experienced in New York. As the "Arlington County: After Action Report" notes, there were significant problems with both self-dispatching and communications: "Organizations, response units, and individuals proceeding on their own initiative directly to an incident site, without the knowledge and permission of the host jurisdiction and the Incident Commander, complicate the exercise of command, increase the risk faced by bonafide responders, and exacerbate the challenge of accountability. …

> It is a fair inference, given the differing situations in New York City and Northern Virginia, that the problems in command, control and communications that occurred at both sites will likely recur in any emergency of similar scale. The task looking forward is to enable first responders to respond in a coordinated manner with the greatest possible awareness of the situation.

National Commission on Terrorist Attacks upon the United States, *The 9/11 Commission Report*. Washington: Government Printing Office, 2004, p. 315.

101 Col. Whitehorn interview, Nov. 29, 2005, pp. 111-112.

102 Riley interview, Jan. 12, 2006, p. 90.

103 Riley interview, Jan. 12, 2006, pp. 91-92 ("Everyone who came and worked under the command of NOPD, ranking officers, all SR team members worked under Captain Wynn, Captain Norton. We basically divided everyone up. … But the State Police, New York State Police, everyone who came in – for instance, some of the officers when they came in from around the state, they were assigned to districts. And they worked under our district commanders. And their commanders fully understood that if there was ever an issue, then, obviously, their commander would deal with ours. But everyone worked at the direction of NOPD commanders, even the National Guard.").

104 Col. Whitehorn interview, Nov. 29, 2005, p. 96. Lt. Col. Booth noted that in the State Police EOC, "We had other jurisdictions at our request. … California had, I would say, 24-hour presence … with us. New Orleans Police Department or the City of New Orleans requested assistance from various other agencies, I think through the EMAC process. We had the port authority from New York/New Jersey." Lt. Col. Booth interview, Dec. 9, 2005, p. 100.

105 Although Governor's Blanco's request letter is dated Sept. 3, it was not faxed to DOJ until Sept. 4. Gov. Kathleen Babineaux Blanco, letter to Alberto R. Gonzales, Sept. 3, 2005. Provided to Committee; filed as Bates nos. DAG 000000081 through 000000082.

106 *See e.g.*: FEMA, Mission Assignment, 1603DR-LA-FPS-05, Sept. 2, 2005. Provided to Committee; filed as Bates no. DHS-FEMA-0035-0000147; FEMA, Mission Assignment, 1603DR-LA-FPS-05, Aug. 31, 2005. Provided to Committee; filed as Bates no. DHS-FEMA-0035-0000148; FEMA, Mission Assignment, 1603DR-LA-CBP-01, Sept. 2, 2005. Provided to Committee; filed as Bates no. DHS-FEMA-0000551.

107 *NRP*, p. ESF#13–1.

108 McAtamney's memorandum said, "there have been no additional requests for federal law enforcement assistance from state or local officials, to my knowledge." *Source*: James A. McAtamney, memorandum to Ted Ullyot and Bill Mercer, Sept. 1, 2005, routing and transmittal slip. Provided to Committee; filed as Bates no. DAG 0000000101. At the time he wrote this, DOJ had already received the LSP Superintendent's letter to FBI Director Robert Mueller. That letter reported "massive damage" caused by the Hurricane, that "all state assets" were being used, but that "looting continue[d] to be a significant problem," and it requested "any assistance you can provide." *Source*: Col. Henry Whitehorn, letter to Robert Mueller, Aug. 30, 2005. Provided to Committee; filed as Bates nos. DAG 000000001 through 000000002. It is also unclear what position DOJ took regarding this request in light of 42 U.S.C. § 10501, which requires that an application for law enforcement assistance in an emergency "shall be submitted in writing by the chief executive office of a state to the Attorney General." *Source*: 43 U.S.C. § 10501(b). Governor Blanco sent such a letter to the Attorney General (dated September 3, 2005), via facsimile on September 4, 2005, but the Superintendent's letter clearly made a similar request four days earlier. *Source*: Gov. Kathleen Blanco, letter to Alberto R. Gonzales, Sept. 3, 2005. Provided to Committee; filed as Bates nos. DAG 000000081 through 000000083.

109 James A. McAtamney, memorandum to Ted Ullyot and Bill Mercer, Sept. 1, 2005. Provided to Committee; filed as Bates nos. DAG 000000101 through 000000106. Mercer included a question in the margin of the attached excerpt. McAtamney sent a memorandum in response to the question on September 12. James A. MacAtamney, memorandum to Bill Mercer, Sept. 12, 2005. Provided to Committee; filed as Bates no. DAG 000000100. Thus, Mercer first made note of these questions about ESF-13 at some time between September 1 and September 12.

110 Michael Vanacore, e-mail to John Clark and others, Sept. 4, 2005, 7:38 p.m. Provided to Committee; filed as Bates no.

DHS-ICE1-0001-0000026. *See also:* John Clark, e-mail to Matthew Broderick, Sept. 4, 2005, 10:34 p.m. Provided to Committee; filed as Bates no. DHS-HSOC-0004-0003339 ("Having failed in many aspects on preparation, emergency assistance and recovery, if we now turn our homeland security responsibility over to the FBI/DOJ, we might as well all await 3SR."). "3SR" is an apparent sarcastic reference to the "Second Stage Review (2SR)," through which Secretary Chertoff made substantial changes to DHS's structure and staffing.

111 John Clark, e-mail to Matthew Broderick, Sept. 4, 2005, 10:34 p.m. Provided to Committee; filed as Bates no. DHS-HSOC-0004-0003339.

112 Committee staff interview of Matthew Broderick, Director, Homeland Security Operations Center, U.S. Department of Homeland Security, conducted on Jan. 19, 2006, transcript pp. 208-209.

113 Broderick interview, Jan. 19, 2006, p. 208.

114 Broderick interview, Jan. 19, 2006, pp. 209.

115 The White House report recommends that the NRP be revised to designate DOJ as the sole primary agency responsible for ESF-13. U.S. Assistant to the President for Homeland Security and Counterterrorism, *The Federal Response to Hurricane Katrina: Lessons Learned.* Washington: Government Printing Office, Feb. 2006, p. 102.

116 Secretary Chertoff's Chief of Staff, John Wood, did not recall any discussions by or with the Secretary on pre-landfall ESF-13 action by DHS and did not know who within DHS was tasked with this responsibility. He only recalled that, at some point, apparently post-landfall, there were discussions about how best to utilize DHS law-enforcement assets. *Source:* Committee staff interview of John Wood, Chief of Staff, U.S. Department of Homeland Security, conducted on Jan. 27, 2006, transcript pp. 56-57. A DHS twice daily Sit Rep from the morning of August 30 contains a "Law Enforcement Issues" section broken into local, regional, and federal boxes. All list "Nothing to report" *Source:* U.S. Department of Homeland Security, Hurricane Katrina DHS SitRep #8, Aug. 30, 2005, 6 a.m., p. 7. Provided to Committee; filed as Bates no. DHS 00001209. The section entitled ESF-13 merely noted the availability of five FEMA "safety officers" and the drafting of a document regarding "Dangerous Critters & Plants in the Gulf Coast." *Source:* U.S. Department of Homeland Security, Hurricane Katrina DHS SitRep #8, Aug. 30, 2005, 6 a.m., p. 21. Provided to Committee; filed as Bates no. DHS 0001222 (This same Situation Report includes extensive details of activities undertaken pursuant to other ESFs.). When asked about this document, Wood said that he "strongly" suspected that more was being done than was listed, but could not identify anything. *Source:* Wood interview, Jan. 27, 2006, pp. 101-102.

117 Committee staff interview of Michael Jackson, Deputy Secretary, U.S. Department of Homeland Security, conducted on Jan. 27, 2006, transcript pp. 69-71.

118 Jackson interview, Jan. 27, 2006, pp. 69-71.

119 Jackson interview, Jan. 27, 2006, pp. 69-70.

120 Committee staff interview of Michael Vanacore, Director, Office of International Affairs, U.S. Department of Homeland Security, conducted on Jan. 27, 2006, transcript p. 8. During his first three days in Baton Rouge, "a lot of it seemed to be in a foreign language there because that whole National Response Plan had a language all its own, which I had never heard up until that point." Vanacore interview, Jan. 27, 2006, p. 35.

121 Vanacore interview, Jan. 27, 2006, pp. 13-14.

122 Vanacore interview, Jan. 27, 2006, p. 34.

123 Vanacore interview, Jan. 27, 2006, p. 50.

124 Vanacore interview, Jan. 27, 2006, p. 89.

125 Vanacore interview, Jan. 27, 2006, p. 108.

126 Vanacore interview, Jan. 27, 2006, p. 8.

127 Vanacore interview, Jan. 27, 2006, p. 108.

128 James A. McAtamney, memorandum to Ted Ullyot and Bill Mercer, Sept. 1, 2005. Provided to Committee; filed as Bates no. DAG 000000103.

129 James McAtamney, e-mail to Bill Mercer, Sept. 1, 2005, 2:06 p.m. Provided to Committee; filed as Bates no. DAG 00000065.

130 James McAtamney, e-mail to Bill Mercer, Sept. 1, 2005, 2:06 p.m. Provided to Committee; filed as Bates no. DAG 00000065. DOJ previously designated ATF to serve as the Department's ESF-13 coordinator in the event of a natural disaster. *Source:* Committee staff interview of Michael R. Bouchard, Assistant Director for Field Operations, Bureau of Alcohol, Tobacco, Firearms and Explosives, conducted on Jan. 24, 2006, transcript pp. 8-9. While the FBI took the lead in the field, this is not necessarily an internal inconsistency, but rather may be an administrative decision about how best to allocate the available leadership.

131 *NRP*, p. ESF #13–3; Committee staff interview of Lt. Cmdr. Brian Penoyer, U.S. Coast Guard, Operations Integration Staff, U.S. Department of Homeland Security, conducted on Mar. 2, 2006, transcript p. 68.

132 Michael Brown, FEMA Daily Video Teleconference, Aug. 28, 2005, transcript p. 36. Provided to Committee.

133 *NRP*, p. ESF #13–1.

134 Kyle Sampson, e-mail to Kimberly Smith, Brian Roehrkasse, William Mercer and Ted Ullyot, Sept. 1, 2005, 6:24 p.m. Provided to Committee; filed as Bates no. DAG 000000185 (noted eleven FBI agents, zero DEA agents, twenty-five ATF

agents, and nine USMS personnel available.). While there were federal law enforcement personnel in Baton Rouge, within an hour's drive or otherwise en route to the area, their readiness and availability for operational missions was severely compromised by the same kind of limitations faced by others in the city. *See, e.g.*: Bernazzani interview, Jan. 25, 2006, pp. 25-28, 34. Consistent with an evacuation plan, Agent Bernazzani evacuated all of his agents except for himself and three volunteers to protect the field office's classified information, communications systems, weapons and ammunition. *Source:* Bernazzani interview, Jan. 25, 2006, pp. 19-21. However, as of September 1, fifty-one employees of the New Orleans-based Field Office could not be located. *Source:* Bernazzani interview, Jan. 25, 2006, pp. 25-28. Reconstitution efforts were further hampered by local evacuation and continuity of operations plans that relied upon cell phone coordination amongst agents and the Field Office's own telecommunications hub, which was decimated. *Source:* Bernazzani interview, Jan. 25, 2006, p. 25.

135 Office of the Attorney General, OAG Request Hurricane Katrina FBI personnel, Nov. 16, 2005. Provided to Committee; filed as Bates no. SEPS 0000000045.

136 While it was prudent for the agents working in the field office to evacuate in the teeth of the storm in accordance with their pre-arranged plan, discussions within the agency that reviewed the FBI's response after the fact focused at least in part on the inadequacy of the FBI's ability to locate its forces in the aftermath of a catastrophe in the absence of local telephone communications. *Source:* Kaiser interview, Jan. 25, 2006, pp. 90-91, 97-98. Agents Kaiser and Bernazzani both participated in discussions with the Crisis Incident Response Group (CIRG) that evaluated the agency's response. *Source:* Kaiser interview, Jan. 25, 2006, p. 97; Bernazzani interview, Jan. 25, 2006, p. 67 (discussing "two or three meetings down at CIRG."). However, the DOJ never provided any after action report or similar document to the Committee.

137 Bureau of Alcohol, Tobacco, Firearms and Explosives, Situation Report for ESF-13, Sept. 6, 2005, 10:08 a.m. Provided to Committee; filed as Bates no. ATF000000002.

138 The NOPD had a strength of approximately 1,600 police officers. *Source:* Written Statement of Riley, Senate Committee hearing, Feb. 6, 2006, p. 2. The LSP has approximately 1,050 troopers. *Source:* Lt. Col. Oxley interview, Dec. 9, 2005, p. 7.

139 *See:* Chapter 26: Military Operations and Chapter 27: Failures in the National Response Plan.

140 For example, when ATF sought guidance on September 1 regarding requests from local officials for assistance with crowd control and other missions, a senior DOJ leader cautioned the ATF not to act without PFO coordination specifically because of reported deployment by the National Guard of 4,200 military police for civil duty. James McAtamney, e-mail to William Mercer, Theodore Ullyot, and Jeffrey Taylor, "Requests for Federal Law Enforcement Support," Sept. 1, 2005, 11:39 a.m. Provided to Committee; filed as Bates no. DAG000000290.

141 Committee staff interview of Lt. Gen. Steven Blum, U.S. Army, Chief, National Guard Bureau, U.S. Department of Defense, conducted on Jan. 19, 2006, transcript pp. 52-53. According to Lt. Gen. Blum, these deployments restored a significant degree of order by September 1, and that things were basically under control by September 2. Lt. Gen. Blum interview, Jan. 19, 2006, p. 81.

142 *See:* Chapter 26: Military Operations; Maj. Gen. Richard Rowe, e-mail to Maj. Gen. Thomas Miller and others, Aug. 31, 2005, 7:46 a.m. Provided to Committee, filed as Bates no. MMTF 00088-06 (recommending that Department look at "'what if' MAC DIS [Military Assistance for Civil Disturbances] required."). For more discussion of MACDIS and the Insurrection Act, see Chapter 26: Military Operations. ESF#13, in fact, includes a provision for "the event that State and local police forces (including the National Guard operating under State control) are unable to adequately respond to a civil disturbance or other serious law enforcement emergency," the state may request assistance under the Insurrection Act. *NRP*, p. ESF #13–2.

143 As of landfall, the Federal Protective Service (FPS), a small force within DHS had deployed 40 officers into New Orleans to protect federal buildings. FPS's mission to secure federal buildings and infrastructure and to provide security to FEMA during disasters may have prompted the Service to move directly into the city more rapidly than any other federal law-enforcement entity. Committee staff interview of Wendell Shingler, Director, Office of Federal Protective Service, U.S. Department of Homeland Security, conducted on Jan. 31, 2006, transcript pp. 17-19, 29.

144 As early as Sunday, August 28, 2005, the Customs and Border Patrol placed a contingent of 100 agents, drawn from its Border Patrol Search, Trauma, and Rescue (BORSTAR) teams and other specialized units, on standby. *Source:* Customs and Border Protection, Commissioner's Situation Room Report, Aug. 29, 2005, 2:30 p.m. Provided to Committee; filed as Bates nos. DHS-CBP1-0001-0000002 through 00000003. BORSTAR teams are "highly specialized units capable of responding to emergency search and rescue situations. … These teams … undergo a highly specialized regimen consisting of training in physical fitness and training in various other disciplines, including medial skills, technical rescue, navigation, communications, swiftwater rescue and air operations." *Source:* U.S. Customs and Border Protection, "BORSTAR," June 9, 2003. http://www.cbp.gov/xp/cgov/border_security/border_patrol/borstar/borstar.xml. Accessed on May 5, 2006.

145 Vanacore interview, Jan. 27, 2006, pp. 9-12.

146 Marcy Forman, e-mail to John P. Clark, Aug. 28, 2005, 12:50 p.m. Provided to Committee; filed as Bates no. DHS-ICE1-0002-0000650 (advising him that she has heard from New Orleans SAC Mike Holt and he is "on his way to Baltimore."). *See also:* George Forman, e-mail to John P. Clark and others, Sept. 1, 2005, 3:45 p.m. Provided to Committee; filed as Bates no. DHS-ICE1-0002-0000551 (discussing SAC Holt's travel plans to return to the New Orleans region on Friday, September 2, 2005.); John P. Clark, e-mail to Gary Lang, Matthew Broderick, Bob Stephan and others, Sept. 3, 2005, 4:38 p.m. Provided to Committee; filed as Bates nos. DHS-HSOC-0004-0003933 through 0003934 ("SAC Mike Holt had been out of the area but got back into New Orleans on Friday [September 2, 2005] and has been designated by DHS as the DHS law enforcement coordinator, assigned to specifically work with the New Orleans Mayor and Police Chief to assist with establishing law and order in the city area.").

147 *NRP*, p. ESF #13–1 (ESF-13 "integrates Federal public safety and security capabilities and resources to support the

full range of incident management activities associated with potential or actual Incidents of National Significance." It "provides a mechanism for coordinating Federal-to-Federal or Federal support to State and local authorities to include non-investigative/non-criminal law enforcement, public safety, and security capabilities during potential or actual Incidents of National Significance." It "generally is activated in situations requiring extensive assistance to provide public safety and security and where State and local government resources are overwhelmed or inadequate, or in pre-incident or post-incident situations that require . . . capabilities unique to the Federal Government.").

148 42 U.S.C. § 10501 provides that a state "may submit an application under this section for Federal law enforcement assistance," and that "an application for assistance under this section shall be submitted in writing by the chief executive officer of a State to the Attorney General, in a form prescribed by rules issued by the Attorney General." "The Comprehensive Crime Control Act of 1984." (P.L. 98-473), 42 U.S.C. § 10501. The Attorney General may consult as necessary with Department officials and has 10 days to respond. Despite DOJ's belief that this statute governed its response to Hurricane Katrina, the legislative history suggests that this section is an alternative to the Stafford Act, to be used in situations that do not satisfy the criteria of a "major disaster" under the Stafford Act:

> For decades, the Federal government has provided emergency assistance in response to natural disasters to units of State and local government. Communities devastated by hurricanes, tornadoes, floods and other similar calamities have benefited from coordinated federal response to these emergencies. 42 U.S.C. § 5152 et. seq. [Stafford Act]. There is, however, no coordinated Federal response to the existence of a man-made disaster. Similarly, Federal law enforcement officers are authorized to intervene in riots, but there is not [sic] organized mechanism for responding in a less blunt way.

Rep. William J. Hughes, U.S. House Committee on the Judiciary, Report on the "Justice Assistance Act of 1983," Report No. 98-68, 98th Cong. 1st Sess., p. 8.

149 42 U.S.C. § 10501. The term "law enforcement emergency" is defined as "an uncommon situation which requires law enforcement, which is or threatens to become of serious or epidemic proportions, and with respect to which State and local resources are inadequate to protect the lives and property of citizens or to enforce the criminal law." 42 U.S.C. § 10502(3).

150 The first indication in DOJ documents that a governor's letter was required occurred on Thursday, September 1, 2005. Shortly before noon, James McAtamney sent an e-mail to Bill Mercer and others to advise them that the ATF was "getting requests for agents for crowd control, etc." Mercer, in turn, forwarded this e-mail to Steve Bradbury, commenting that he was "not sure how Steve [Bradbury] will view our legal authority to accommodate this request. From an operations standpoint, I'd rather have ATF redeploy to other areas to enforce the firearms laws." *Source:* James A. McAtamney, e-mail to Bill Mercer, Theodore Ullyot, and Jeffrey Taylor, Sept. 1, 2005, 12:39 a.m. Provided to Committee; filed as Bates no. DAG000000290. Bradbury replied:

> There is not currently a written request from the governor to the AG to provide DOJ assistance to state and local law enforcement. We would not approve this state law enforcement activity until there is such a request and the AG has issued an order approving the request. ATF could move forward with preparations and pre-positioning but should not actually begin state law enforcement without such an order.

Steve Bradbury, e-mail to Bill Mercer, Theodore Ullyot, Jeffrey Taylor, Sept. 1, 2005, 12:03 p.m. Provided to Committee; filed as Bates no. DAG 000000290.

151 42 U.S.C. § 10501. *See also:* Committee staff interview of William Mercer, Principal Associate Deputy Attorney General, Office of the Attorney General, U.S. Department of Justice, conducted on Jan. 26, 2006, transcript pp. 29-30 ("But I guess if the question is how did the requests come in, let me turn to those. Because that's a very significant part of the Federal statute here. In Title 42 – and I think the provision is 42 USC 10501 – a governor, not a state attorney general, not a mayor – a governor can ask the Attorney General of the United States to deploy Federal law enforcement resources if the governor makes a proffer saying, 'We can't meet the responsibilities that we need to carry out for public safety, and I request that you deploy Federal resources to assist.' And we got a letter from Governor Barbour on Saturday the 3rd. And we responded that same day. It was faxed in on the 3rd, we met with the Attorney General on Saturday. He issued the order on Saturday. … And Governor Blanco faxed us a letter the next day.").

152 Col. Henry Whitehorn, letter to Robert Mueller, Aug. 30, 2005. Provided to Committee; filed as Bates nos. DAG 000000001 through 000000002.

153 Col. Henry Whitehorn, letter to Robert Mueller, Aug. 30, 2005. Provided to Committee; filed as Bates nos. DAG 000000001 through 000000002.

154 *See: NRP*, p. ESF #13–1.

155 Internal documents show on the morning of September 6, two days after DOJ received, and the Attorney General approved, Governor Blanco's letter requesting law enforcement assistance, a total of 694 DOJ personnel were in the "disaster area." *Source:* Situation Report for ESF-13, Sept. 6, 2005, 10:08 a.m., produced by the Bureau of Alcohol, Tobacco, Firearms and Explosives. Provided to Committee; filed as Bates no. ATF000000002. Based on other documents produced by DOJ, the committee identified approximately 520 DOJ law enforcement personnel who were deployed to Louisiana as of September 3, 2005, the day before DOJ received Governor Blanco's letter. The number of DOJ personnel deployed on September 3 represents 75% of the number available on September 6. *Source:* William E. Moschella, letter to the Honorable Susan M. Collins and the Honorable Joseph I. Lieberman, Response to Request for Information Dated Oct. 7, 2005, Dec. 21, 2005; Edgar Domenech, e-mail to Bill Mercer, Sept. 2, 2005, 4:51 p.m. Provided to Committee; filed as Bates nos. DAG 000000322 through 000000323; FBI, New Orleans Command Post, Baton Rouge, LA., Daily SitRep, Sept. 3, 2005. Provided to Committee; filed as Bates no. FBI 000000133,

156 Even without 42 U.S.C. § 10501 request letter from a governor, the Attorney General has the authority to re-deploy federal agents through the states to execute federal missions. In addition, the Stafford Act authorizes federal agencies, upon direction of the President following a major disaster declaration, to "provide assistance," including "any work or services essential to saving lives and protecting or preserving property and public health and safety," without a request from a governor (Sec. 7170(c)). *Source:* "Robert T. Stafford Disaster Relief and Emergency Assistance Act." (P.L. 93-288), 42 U.S.C. § 5170(b). The DOJ acknowledged in its interrogatory responses that it had authority to provide public safety support under this provision. *Source:* William E. Moschella, letter to the Honorable Susan M. Collins and the Honorable Joseph I. Lieberman, Response to Request for Information Dated Oct. 7, 2005, Nov. 23, 2005, p. 3. However, it is unclear whether the President contemplated or directed the Attorney General pursuant to this provision to deploy federal law enforcement to the region.

157 James A. McAtamney, e-mail to Bill Mercer, Theodore Ullyot, and Jeffrey Taylor, Sept. 1, 2005, 11:39 a.m. Provided to Committee; filed as Bates no. DAG 000000290.

158 Steve Bradbury, e-mail to Bill Mercer, Theodore Ullyot, Jeffrey Taylor, Sept. 1, 2005, 12:03 p.m. Provided to Committee; filed as Bates no. DAG 000000290.

159 Kyle Sampson, e-mail to Robert Mueller and others, Sept. 1, 2005, 11:56 a.m. Provided to Committee; filed as Bates no. DAG00000165.

160 Kyle Sampson, e-mail to Robert Mueller and others, Sept. 1, 2005, 11:56 a.m. Provided to Committee; filed as Bates no. DAG00000165.

161 Alberto Gonzales, memorandum for the heads of federal law-enforcement agencies, "Law Enforcement Response to Hurricane Katrina," Sept. 2, 2005. Provided to Committee; filed as Bates no. DAG 000000001.

162 Bouchard interview, Jan. 24, 2006, pp. 61-63 ("The discussions before the hurricane hit was myself and Mr. Dhillon, ... who works in the DAG's office. He's our contact person for ATF. And he was communicating with Mr. McAtamney, who also works in that office, about what the overall Justice coordinated effort would be. What, any guidance that would come from the attorney general to all the Justice components about what authorities we'd be acting under and what our response would be. Would there be one Justice agency in charge so that we could all say, almost like your mini ESF 13, let's all decide – and these are things that we talked about – we know this big thing is coming. We've been through it on smaller scales. Let's pre-identify all the assets that I've got all these emergency vehicles from every agency. Let's get them all located in one place so that we know, so when time comes and we ask for them, we know who the point of contact is. We're not scrambling to find out what do you have, who can do it, and how soon can you get there? ... I believe my first conversation with Mr. Dhillon on that – I have it in the log here. It was two or three days before it hit. Beginning August 28th."). *See also:* Bureau of Alcohol, Tobacco, Firearms and Explosives, ATF Summary of Significant Activity, Aug. 28-30, 2005. Provided to Committee; filed as Bates no. ATF 000000008 (documenting "contact with DAG office on preparing DOJ response to hurricane.").

163 Edgar Domenech, e-mail to James A. McAtamney, Aug. 31, 2005, 8:32 a.m. Provided to Committee; filed as Bates no. DAG 000000003 ("I assume the department will be looking to implement a departmental response [to Hurricane Katrina], let me know what you need.").

164 On August 31, 2005, at 4:07 p.m., Mercer and others at DOJ received an e-mail which said that Bell South's New Orleans' "office is critical communications infrastructure node that, if damaged by looters or others, would result in loss of comms in the area. They've asked for USMS assistance in protecting the facility, as the state/local police are overwhelmed. Advised USMS to notify FEMA of the request: DHS has the lead for protection of critical infrastructure. More important, DHS/FEMA is responsible for coordinating requests for support and directing capable [federal government] assets within the overall context of the NRP and Stafford Act." *Source:* James A. McAtamney, e-mail to Bill Mercer and others, Aug. 31, 2005, 4:07 p.m. Provided to Committee; filed as Bates nos. DAG 000000035 through 000000038. The internal DOJ approval process would last over four hours. Once the mission was approved, Arthur Roderick, Assistant Director, USMS, Operations Support Division, wrote an e-mail to DOJ saying, "I know all component [law enforcement agencies] are looking for this authority." *Source:* Art Roderick Jr., e-mail to James McAtamney and others, Aug. 31, 2005, 8:28 p.m. Provided to Committee; filed as Bates nos. DAG 000000060 through 000000061

165 Paul R. Corts, e-mail to Bill Mercer and others, including representatives of DOJ's law enforcement agencies, Aug. 31, 2005, 6:42 p.m. Provided to Committee; filed as DAG 000000042 ("Thanks for your attendance at the meeting today at noon. I appreciate the good response, especially given the very short notice. Thanks for the info sharing and thanks too for the good spirit that prevailed as we dealt with this horrific situation... Here is a quick bit of info following up on some of the points discussed today ... Requests from State and Locals to our Law Enforcement (LE) components for assistance with non-federal LE matters – OLC is reviewing this. There are a number of very sensitive legal/perhaps constitutional issues with this. We are trying to get guidance as quickly as possible. More tomorrow.").

166 Office of the Attorney General, Order No. 2779-2005, Sept. 4, 2005. Provided to Committee; filed as Bates no. DAG 000000091 ("Department of Justice law enforcement personnel who are engaged in this mission shall have the authority to enforce the laws of the United States and to assist law enforcement officials in the State of Louisiana to enforce the laws of that State. All such officers engaged in this mission shall coordinate with their state and local counterparts to make appropriate arrangements as necessary to ensure the most effective law enforcement assistance efforts in the State of Louisiana. In addition, all such officers shall be subject to the supervision of the United States Attorney for the Eastern District of Louisiana, who may delegate operational authority to appropriate Department of Justice officials.").

167 Vanacore interview, Jan. 27, 2006, pp. 77-78 ("Well, it was difficult. Louisiana was trying their best. The Attorney General's Office was doing a great job. But the problem was our people that needed to be deputized were moving targets. So we would send – they would send an Assistant Attorney General down to do a swearing-in. We'd fly her in, get a helicopter, and get her down to New Orleans. And by the time she got there, maybe the SRT team she was going to swear in had been

deployed. So we were having a little difficulty getting everybody in one place at one time. So efficient – I mean, they tried. It's a good process. But I don't think personal swearing-ins are the process in an event like that.").

168 Vanacore interview, Jan. 27, 2006, pp. 77-78.

169 Vanacore interview, Jan. 27, 2006, pp. 79-80.

170 Deputization took even longer in Mississippi, despite a simpler procedure, where the appropriate documents were not issued until September 9.

171 Kaiser interview, Jan. 25, 2006, p. 84.

172 Kaiser interview, Jan. 25, 2006, p. 84.

173 William E. Moschella, letter to the Honorable Susan M. Collins and the Honorable Joseph I. Lieberman, Response to Request for Information Dated Oct. 7, 2005, Nov. 23, 2005, p. 2 ("In other words, the support provided via the ESF-13 process does not extend to providing federal law enforcement personnel to engage in actual operational investigative activities to enforce federal, state or local laws. Instead, law enforcement support is provided within the overall umbrella of the Department of Homeland Security's coordination function under the authority of the Stafford Act or pursuant to inherent authority of the individual law enforcement agencies.").

174 Bouchard interview, Jan. 24, 2006, pp. 23-24 ("Any assets that would be needed on the ground in the affected areas would be calling up to Washington, asking for them. They would funnel them through the IIMG and to the ESF 13. At the same, people who say I may have these assets that are available in case they're needed are coming in from the other side through the ESF 13 to the IIMG, with the IIMG being the focal point that decides here is what the needs are, here's what the offer is, here's how we marry those up.").

175 Kaiser interview, Jan. 25, 2006, p. 53 ("The other functions, resupplying and stuff like that, that is not a law enforcement function. We did it because they needed it and we were trying to help out, but that's not a DOJ function whatsoever. We don't do that. We are not a consequence management. We are law enforcement, okay, and consequence management, which is what you're talking about, is strictly by FEMA and those other groups, and they did do it eventually, but in the meantime, we did that because, you know, what are we going to do, let them stay in the precincts without ammunition?").

176 Committee staff interview of William Mercer, Principal Associate Deputy Attorney General, U.S. Department of Justice, conducted on Feb. 23, 2006, transcript p. 44 ("And so I know that there were a whole lot of conversations that were going on…the ground. And what we had independent authority to do was to add a bunch of Federal resources to the affected area, which is what we did. We had independent authority to do that, and we did that."); Mercer interview, Feb. 23, 2006, p. 46 ("[C]ertainly it is very clear from the record that by the time [Governor Blanco's September 4, 2005] letter was submitted, we already had put a substantial number of Federal agents there.").

177 The DEA's "Hurricane Katrina Events Log" documents federal agents involved in a broad range of traditional and non-traditional law enforcement activities throughout the metropolitan New Orleans area. DEA reported that as of September 1, "DEA [New Orleans Field Division] agents departed with NOPD officers to assist them in their enforcement mission." That same day, "DEA agents provided security to Lt. Col. Leblanc, [LSP] Troop B, in his inspection of the New Orleans Superdome," and other sites within the city. On Sept. 3, Special Agents teamed with NOPD and Rapides Parish Sheriff's Office SWAT to clear buildings of snipers, conducted proactive patrols and provided security to firefighters putting out fires. Others built a boat launch in Plaquemines Parish for use in rescue operations; coordinated relief mission planning in St. Bernard Parish, and provided law enforcement and relief supplies in Gonzales. That same day, ASAC Kevin Harrison, New Orleans Field Division, and a team of 9 Special Agents rescued and evacuated over 70 senior citizens who were abandoned at a retirement home in New Orleans near the St. Bernard Parish line. Many residents of the home had already died as a result of dehydration and a lack of medical care. Water and food was provided to sustain them. They were transported to a shelter outside of the City of New Orleans on the West Bank of the Mississippi River to safety. Drug Enforcement Administration, New Orleans Field Division, Hurricane Katrina Events Log, Aug. 31- Sept. 7, 2005. Provided to Committee; filed as Bates nos. 000000141 through 000000142.

178 *NRP*, p. 35.

179 *NRP*, p. 35.

180 When ESF-13 is activated, the primary agencies assume responsibility for a series of actions and activities. Significant actions at the headquarters, regional and field levels include staffing the National and Regional Response Coordination Centers, Joint Field Office, and possibly the Emergency Response Team- Advance Element; coordinating with analogous regional and field ESF elements; and coordinating all federal activities with the local FBI field office, Joint Terrorism Task Force and other DOJ-led law enforcement and investigations and intelligence assessments. Incident management coordination may include: (1) supporting operational and tactical planning activities to prevent or mitigate potential incidents or threats to public safety, (2) the deployment of federal resources in response to such incidents or threats, (3) providing technical assistance in planning and assessment efforts, (4) establishing badging and credentialing processes, (5) helping control access to the incident site or critical facilities, (6) conducting traffic and crowd control, (7) protecting emergency responders and other relief workers, (8) protecting the people, facilities and supplies during distribution efforts; 9) providing surveillance support; and 10) supplying specialized equipment, clothing, and gear as needed. *NRP*, pp. ESF #13–3 through 13–4.

181 For these purposes, strategic coordination entails the macro-level planning and direction of operational missions or resources to achieve broad objectives while aiming to minimize redundancy and overlap and maximize efficiency, effectiveness and safety. By comparison, tactical coordination suggests lower level commanders of on-scene, operational units efforts to achieve micro-level ends via communication and cooperation with other, similarly situated commanders on the ground.

182 Michael Vanacore, e-mail John Clark and others, Sept. 4, 2005, 7:38 p.m. Provided to Committee; filed as Bates no. DHS-ICE1-0001-0000026 ("DOJ is looking to run this whole effort."); Marc Raimondi, e-mail to William Knocke, Sept. 4, 2005, 10:33 a.m. Provided to Committee; filed as Bates no. DHS-HSOC-0004-0003339 (e-mail entitled "FBI to take over?" reports "They [FBI] showed up here last night with a command center on wheels, a bunch of black Suburbans, and held a press conference."); Samuel Neglia, e-mail to Matthew Broderick, Sept. 4, 2005, 8:30 p.m. Provided to Committee; filed as Bates no. DHS-HSOC-0004-0003258 ("Need HEAVY Secretary Office Level push quickly w/ FBI to ensure the co-lead is DHS per NRP ESF-13."); Sigal Mandelker, e-mail to Matt Mayer, Sept. 2, 2005, 1:18 a.m. Provided to Committee, filed as Bates no. DHS-FRNT-0010-0000161 ("We're constantly trying to take the lead with State and locals on the Homeland Security mission and now we're giving DOJ the lead."). David M. Wulf, e-mail to James A. McAtamney and Carson W. Carroll, Sept. 4, 2005, 6:13 p.m. Provided to Committee ("We understand the FBI SAC Kiser [sic] will soon assume command of Federal law-enforcement activity at the Joint Field Office that will be set up in Louisiana. We feel it would make sense to install an ATF SAC as Deputy law-enforcement commander at the JFO (I suppose, in NRP parlance, he would serve as Deputy Senior Federal Law Enforcement Official). This would provide seamless coordination on ESF-13 related matters with our folks who are staffing the NRCC and IIMG 24/7. Also might make sense in view of the large number ATF agents (100+, I believe) on hand to be deployed for Katrina-related missions.") At approximately the same time, Wulf forwarded the e-mail to Samuel Neglia, Robert Shea and others at DHS, asking "Is this something you guys could push from DHS side?" David Wulf, e-mail to Samuel Neglia and others, Sept. 4, 2005, 6:15 p.m. Provided to Committee; filed as Bates nos. DHS-ICE1-0001-000000026 through 000000027.

183 Vanacore interview, Jan. 27, 2006, pp. 13-14.

184 Vanacore interview, Jan. 27, 2006, pp. 91-95.

185 Vanacore interview, Jan. 27, 2006, pp. 14, 17-18, 24.

186 Vanacore said in his interview that Brian Pennoyer, of PFO Brown's support staff, called him around midnight between September 4-5. Vanacore interview, Jan. 27, 2006, pp. 32-33.

187 Vanacore interview, Jan. 27, 2006, pp. 6, 8, 35.

188 Vanacore interview, Jan. 27, 2006, pp. 37-39.

189 FBI briefing to Committee, conducted by Michael J. Wolf, Critical Incident Response Special Agent in Charge, FBI, Dec. 20, 2005.

190 Mercer interview, Jan. 26, 2006, pp. 52-53 ("I think the people on the ground determine[d] that it would be useful to have an SFLEO and sort of a centralized process, and then that was created.").

191 Office of the Attorney General, Order No. 2779-2005, Sept. 4, 2005. Provided to Committee; filed as Bates no. DAG 000000091 (Authorizing the Deputy Attorney General to Take Certain Actions Related To Hurricane Katrina); Mercer interview, Feb. 23, 2006, pp. 63-67. Vanacore said that initially the U.S. Attorney had been designated the law enforcement lead, but that this changed when DOJ recognized that as a prosecutor, rather than a law-enforcement agent, he should deal "with the legal issues … and the little higher level things," because he was not going to "tell the cops what to do." Vanacore interview, Jan. 27, 2006, p. 55.

192 The then-Deputy Superintendent of the New Orleans Police Department offered this praise:

> The [Immigrations and Customs Enforcement] agents … stayed far longer than anyone else, working as a patrolman, riding around answering calls for service from our people. They were absolutely outstanding. … The FBI [Special Response] team was great. The [Drug Enforcement Agency] SR team was great. The [Alcohol Tobacco and Firearms] SR team was great.

Source: Riley interview, Jan. 12, 2006, pp. 88-89. NOPD Captain Bayard also praised counterparts at DEA, ATF, the United States Marshal's Service, and the FBI, especially FBI Agent Todd Cox, who helped address a continuing lack of coordination weeks later by further establishing a Command Center at the Royal Sonesta Hotel. *Source:* Capt. Bayard interview, Nov. 21, 2005, pp. 81-82, 119-120. The LSP's Col. Whitehorn cited the United States Secret Service for establishing a key credentialing process, while Jefferson Parish's Sheriff Harry Lee generally thought he received good support from federal agencies. *Source:* Col. Whitehorn interview, Nov. 29, 2005, pp. 116-117; Committee staff interview of Harry Lee, Sheriff, Jefferson Parish, LA, conducted on Jan. 9, 2006, transcript p. 108. New Orleans Director of Homeland Security Col. Ebbert had this to say:

> I want to go on record as thanking the federal agencies. By later in the week we had tremendous response with hundreds of federal agents from all the federal agencies. … The federal agents from all those agencies, both Justice and Homeland Security, worked together to help manage those resources throughout the city.

Source: Committee staff interview of Col. Terry Ebbert, U.S. Marine Corps (Ret.), Director, New Orleans Department of Homeland Security, conducted on Jan. 10, 2006, transcript p. 167.

193 Vanacore interview, Jan. 27, 2006, pp. 126-127; FBI briefing given to Committee, conducted by Michael J. Wolf, Critical Incident Response Special Agent in Charge, FBI, Dec. 20, 2005.

194 Vanacore interview, Jan. 27, 2006, pp. 128-129; FBI briefing given to Committee, conducted by Michael J. Wolf, Critical Incident Response Special Agent in Charge, FBI, Dec. 20, 2005.

195 Kaiser interview, Jan. 25, 2006, p. 54.

196 Kaiser interview, Jan. 25, 2006, pp. 94-95.

Guardsmen on the Gulf Coast
Clarence Williams/Iris Photocollective photo

Military Operations

Background: Military Support to Civil Authorities

The National Guard generally constitutes the first military support provided to civil authorities for domestic disaster relief. If civilian first responders and the National Guard cannot adequately respond, the Department of Defense (DOD) may be asked to deploy active-duty forces.

The Statutes and Role of the National Guard in Emergency Response

National Guard units conduct operations in one of three modes: (1) under control of their governor as commander-in-chief, on state active-duty status, with the state paying salaries and expenses; (2) under gubernatorial control, but operating under Title 32 of the U.S. Code, with the federal government paying mission costs;[1] or (3) under control of the President, having been federalized under provisions of Title 10 of the U.S. Code.[2] While governor-controlled, National Guard units may perform law-enforcement missions.[3] When federalized under Title 10, however, National Guard units, like regular federal forces, are generally prohibited from enforcing laws.[4]

National Guard missions performed in state active-duty status include assisting in response to natural disasters such as hurricanes and other storms, and fires and floods which have not been declared federal disasters. Governors routinely use their states' National Guards for disaster-relief missions when local first responders are overwhelmed.[5]

The DOD Strategy for Homeland Defense and Civil Support, dated June 2005, says local National Guard units are particularly well-suited for civil-support missions: They (1) are "forward deployed" in about 3,200 communities across the United States, (2) are readily available for use in either state active-duty status or Title 32 status, (3) routinely exercise with state and local first responders, and (4) have experience mobilizing for local disaster-relief missions.[6]

The National Response Plan (NRP) guides federal-agency emergency response and recognizes the role of governors in a federal system for the public safety and welfare of their states' people by coordinating state resources to prevent, prepare for, respond to, and recover from a variety of man-made or natural disasters. Moreover, the Plan recognizes the governor's constitutional role as the commander-in-chief of the state's military forces – the National Guard – when in state active-duty or Title 32 status.[7]

Emergency Management Assistance Compact Provides a Framework for Interstate Mutual Aid

The Emergency Management Assistance Compact (EMAC) is an interstate agreement that provides a framework for interstate mutual aid using the National Guard. The National Emergency Management Association, an association of state emergency managers, administers EMAC[8] and has developed a nine-step process for mutual aid.[9] In addition to the EMAC process, some state-to-state mutual-aid agreements also exist for providing law-enforcement and other assistance in a crisis.[10] States that receive assistance requests under EMAC are not obligated to send their National Guard units to affected states. In addition to the emergency managers' and state-to-state processes, the National Guard Bureau developed a 20-step process to deploy National Guard units in response to Hurricane Katrina under EMAC.[11]

DOD Has a Supporting Role Under a Key Presidential Directive and the National Response Plan

DOD has a key supporting role under Homeland Security Presidential Directive-5 (HSPD-5) dated February 28, 2003,[12] and the NRP.[13] The Presidential Directive specifies that DOD will provide military assistance to civil authorities for domestic incidents as directed by the President or when consistent with military readiness and appropriate under the circumstances and the law. The Directive also clearly states that the Secretary of Defense shall retain command of military forces when such forces are providing civil support. Finally, the Directive also requires DOD and the Department of Homeland Security (DHS) to establish "appropriate" relationships and mechanisms for cooperation and coordination between the two Departments.[14]

DOD responds to a domestic disaster within the National Incident Management System (NIMS), which provides a framework to integrate disaster response at all levels of government and the private sector. To coordinate its participation in the system, DOD has provided certain specialized training to military officers, known as Emergency Preparedness Liaison Officers, usually at the rank equivalent of Army colonel or Navy captain.[15] The Emergency Preparedness Liaison Officers deploy to national or regional incident-command centers such as the Homeland Security Operations Center to coordinate the DOD response to the event. To manage DOD's assistance as directed by HSPD-5, DOD has also provided specialized training to another cadre of colonels known as Defense Coordinating Officers (DCO).[16] These officers generally deploy to the Joint Field Office (JFO) or other incident-command centers to process urgent requests for DOD assistance needed to assist civil authorities in responding to the immediate needs of the situation.[17] DOD also provides a deployable support staff to the DCO, known as the Defense Coordinating Element, consisting of three to 30 service members or DOD civilians, depending on the nature and scope of the incident.[18] DOD may also provide military officers to augment the staff of the Principal Federal Officer (PFO), the designee of the Secretary of Homeland Security in executing the federal disaster response.[19] Finally, DOD has permitted FEMA, the Coast Guard, and other agencies to maintain a permanent presence at U.S. Northern Command (NORTHCOM), the DOD Combatant Command for the North American area of operations.[20] DOD may also provide augmentation to the FEMA office at NORTHCOM in a large-scale disaster.[21]

The NRP establishes a key support role for DOD in assisting the federal agency that leads the federal disaster response. The NRP points out that the Secretary of Defense authorizes defense support to civil authorities for domestic incidents as directed by the President, or when consistent with military readiness and appropriate under the circumstances and the law – virtually the same language as that used in HSPD-5. Similarly, as with the Directive, the NRP specifies that the Secretary of Defense retains control over military forces at all times during its assistance to civil authorities, as specified in Title 10 of the U.S. Code.[22]

In addition to assigning DOD a general role to support civil authorities, the NRP identifies DOD as a supporting agency to the lead agency in all 15 of the NRP's Emergency Support Functions (ESF), reflecting the fact that DOD has unique resources and capabilities to provide humanitarian relief in a catastrophe. It also identifies DOD's Army Corps of Engineers as a co-primary agency for ESF-3, Public Works and Engineering.[23] The table below provides additional information on DOD's assigned roles under the ESFs.

Emergency Support Function	DOD's Specific Role
1. Transportation	Provides military liaison to ESF-1 desk and military transportation to move resources, and assists in contracting for civilian aircraft.[24]
2. Communications	Uses own resources to provide own communications and coordinates numerous other communication issues with the Federal Emergency Communications Coordinator.[25]
3. Public Works and Engineering	Army Corps of Engineers provides technical assistance, engineering, and construction management.[26]
4. Firefighting	Conducts firefighting on DOD installations and assists other lead agencies for fire-fighting on non-DOD land.[27]
5. Emergency Management Annex	No specific role identified.[28]
6. Mass Care, Housing, and Human Services	Army Corps of Engineers provides ice and water; inspects shelter sites for suitability; and assists in construction of temporary shelters and temporary housing repair.[29]
7. Resource Support	No specific role identified.[30]
8. Public Health and Medical Services	Transports patients to medical care facilities; assists with mortuary services; procures and transports medical supplies; and provides DOD medical supplies, blood products, medical personnel, laboratory services, and logistics support.[31]
9. Urban Search and Rescue	When requested, serves as a primary source for rotary and fixed-wing aircraft to support urban search-and-rescue operations; and Army Corps of Engineers provides (1) certain training and structural integrity analysis, (2) assessments of whether buildings are safe to enter, (3) building stability monitoring, and (4) other services.[32]
10. Oil and Hazardous Materials Response	Provides the federal on-scene coordinator and directs response actions for releases of hazardous materials from its vessels, facilities, vehicles, munitions, and weapons; and Army Corps of Engineers provides response and recovery assistance involving radiological dispersion devices and improvised nuclear devices.[33]
11. Agriculture and Natural Resources	Assesses (1) the availability of DOD food supplies and storage facilities, (2) transportation equipment at posts near the affected area, and (3) laboratory, diagnostic, and technical assistance; and assists in animal emergency response; develops appropriate plans; and the Army Corps of Engineers provides expertise and resources to assist in removal and disposal of debris and animal carcasses.[34]
12. Energy	Coordinates emergency power team missions with power restoration activities and provides appropriate support.[35]
13. Public Safety and Security	If directed by the President, quells insurrection and provides physical and electronic security-systems assistance and expertise.[36]
14. Long Term Community Recovery and Mitigation	Provides technical assistance in community planning, civil engineering, and natural hazard risk assessment and supports national strategy development for housing, debris removal, and restoration of public facilities and infrastructure.[37]
15. External Affairs	No specific role identified other than to provide support as required.[38]

Applicable Statutes Provide DOD the Authorities to Deploy Forces

Various statutes govern DOD participation in emergency management. These statutes establish pre-disaster and disaster-response reimbursement procedures, authorize the use of military forces to put down insurrection, and generally prohibit the use of military forces for law-enforcement purposes except to put down insurrection and in certain other limited circumstances.

Economy Act

The Economy Act permits federal agencies to provide goods or services to another federal agency when such support is requested. Such assistance will not necessarily be related to disaster response.[39]

Stafford Act

The Stafford Act is the primary statute governing DOD and other federal agency disaster assistance under the NRP. Stafford Act reimbursements are authorized once a governor has asserted that state capabilities are overwhelmed and federal assistance is needed, and the President has declared an emergency.[40]

Insurrection Act

The Insurrection Act authorizes the President to use military force to suppress an insurrection or end other domestic violence. Specifically, the President may employ military forces to restore order, prevent looting, and engage in other law-enforcement activities.[41]

Posse Comitatus Act

The federal Posse Comitatus Act of 1878 prohibits the use of the Army and the Air Force (originally part of the Army) to execute the laws of the United States except where authorized by the Constitution or Acts of Congress. Congress enacted the law to restrict the use of federal troops in the conduct of law enforcement in the South during Reconstruction.[42] Federal courts have interpreted the Act to prohibit the use of troops in an active role of direct civilian law enforcement including search, seizure, and arrest. DOD has issued policy guidance extending the Posse Comitatus Act's restrictions to the Navy and Marine Corps. The Act does not apply to the National Guard when under the direct command of a state's governor.[43]

Congress has created a number of specific exceptions to the general restrictions in the Posse Comitatus Act to authorize DOD to use its personnel and equipment in a number of circumstances to

- assist with drug interdiction and other law-enforcement functions,
- protect civil rights or property, or suppress insurrection,
- assist the U.S. Secret Service,
- protect nuclear materials and assist in solving crimes involving nuclear material,
- assist with some terrorist incidents involving weapons of mass destruction, and
- assist with the execution of quarantine and certain health laws.[44]

Title 10

Title 10 of the U.S. Code establishes the armed services; defines their organization, missions, and general military powers; specifies personnel limits; defines training and education requirements and organizations; and specifies service, supply, and procurement roles. Generally, under Title 10, the military departments define training requirements, and design and implement the training.[45] Certain military commanders have interpreted this to mean that such training can include the deployment of forces from their home installation to another installation, which, coincidentally, also may position them for use in an upcoming mission in the same area.[46] In effect, this positions these commanders and forces closer to a disaster area before receiving a request for assistance, thus making them more immediately available to address immediate disaster relief needs.

Other Authorities

Under DOD doctrine, local commanders have the authority to unilaterally act to prevent immediate threats to life and property if it is not feasible to obtain prior approval from higher military authorities. At the same time, DOD directives require an oral civilian request before exercising this authority, except during a civil disturbance. DOD would be unlikely to obtain reimbursements for assistance rendered under the immediate-response authority.[47]

The Assistant Secretary of Defense (Homeland Defense) Prepares for and Guides DOD's Domestic Missions

The Assistant Secretary of Defense (Homeland Defense) is principally responsible for the overall supervision of Homeland Defense activities in DOD. The Assistant Secretary is to develop policies, conduct analyses, provide advice, make recommendations on homeland defense, and provide support to civil authorities, emergency preparedness, and domestic crisis management in DOD. The Assistant Secretary is also to assist the Secretary of Defense in providing policy direction to NORTHCOM, and other combatant commands, when appropriate, to guide development and execution of these commands' plans and activities. Lastly, the Assistant Secretary is also the DOD domestic crisis manager and represents the Department on Homeland Defense and support to civil authorities matters with the lead federal agency,[48] often DHS.[49]

DOD's Guidance and Key Strategy Documents Lay Out the Department's Views of Its Mission

DOD's guidance and Quadrennial Defense Review make clear that domestic natural-disaster response is not within the Department's primary mission set and will only be undertaken when forces are available, or if directed by the President or Secretary of Defense. Moreover, under the NRP, and consistent with departmental guidance, DOD provides support to the lead federal agency in responding to domestic natural disasters, but is not considered, and does not consider itself, to be a lead responder.[50]

DOD Directives Guide the Department's Domestic Disaster Response

DOD has issued a set of directives and related documents that together establish DOD policy for military assistance to civilian authorities. The first is DOD Directive 3025.1, Military Support to Civil Authorities (MSCA), which requires DOD components to provide support requested by civil authorities once properly approved by the designated DOD approval authorities. The Directive is premised on the notion that DOD support is only to be provided if civil response capabilities are overwhelmed, as determined by FEMA. It also states that DOD's military operations other than military assistance to civil authorities have priority unless otherwise directed by the Secretary of Defense. The Directive states that DOD components may not procure or maintain any supplies, material, or equipment exclusively for civil emergencies unless directed by the Secretary of Defense. Lastly, it also states that military forces will remain under the control of DOD at all times.[51]

Ordinarily, FEMA tasks DOD to perform a mission by sending DOD a "mission assignment." However, DOD takes the view that among federal agencies, it is unique in that under the Constitution and under the Goldwater-Nichols Act, there is a military chain of command from the President to the Secretary of Defense to the Combatant Commander. The NRP specifies that the Secretary of Defense retains control over military forces at all times during its assistance to civil authorities, as specified by Title 10 of the U.S. Code.[52] Under "existing authorities and as a matter of policy," DOD takes the position that "placing a FEMA official or a DHS official in command outside the Department of Defense within the military chain of command violates Goldwater-Nichols and is a bad idea."[53] DOD therefore interprets a "mission assignment" as a "request for assistance."

DOD Directive 3025.15, Military Assistance to Civil Authorities, was issued on February 18, 1997, and specifies the mechanisms that DOD's designated approval authorities will use to evaluate whether or not support should be provided to civil authorities. The Directive establishes the following six criteria against which requests are to be evaluated, usually by DOD's Office of the Joint Director of Military Support (JDOMS), which also determines what capability DOD has available to meet the request:[54]

- legality (compliance with laws),
- lethality (potential use of lethal force by or against DOD forces),
- risk (safety of DOD forces),
- cost (who pays, impact on the DOD budget),
- appropriateness (if it is in DOD's interest to conduct the requested mission), and
- readiness (DOD's ability to perform its mission).[55]

The JDOMS makes a recommendation to the Chairman of the Joint Chiefs of Staff whether to approve the request.[56] The Office of the Assistant Secretary of Defense (Homeland Defense) reviews the request for consistency with policy.[57]

DOD Directive 3025.12, Military Assistance for Civil Disturbances (MACDIS), governs DOD's response to requests from federal, state, or local governments' law enforcement agencies to assist with civil disturbances. The Directive requires a specific Presidential order before the military can deploy on such a mission, except that DOD commanders may act unilaterally in the case of unexpected disasters including an earthquake, fire, or flood; if life is endangered; or if local authorities are unable to control the situation and circumstances preclude obtaining prior authorization by the President.[58]

All three Directives are actually out of date, as the mentioned DOD components no longer have the responsibilities identified in the Directives or no longer even exist. For example, they specify that the Department of the Army is the DOD's executive agent for military support to civil authorities.[59] In fact, the JDOMS performed that function at the time of the Committee's investigation.[60] Directive 3025.1 designates the Commander-in-Chief of U.S. Atlantic Command as the planning agent for military support missions,[61] although that command was re-designated in October 1999.[62] Conversely, the Directives make no mention of U.S. Northern Command, even though that command began operations on October 1, 2002, to carry out the types of domestic missions contemplated in the Directives.[63]

DOD Differs Critically From Other Agencies

DOD's mission is to deter foreign aggression against the United States and to fight and win the nation's wars if deterrence fails. The Quadrennial Defense Review released in February 2006 addressed the use of military forces in domestic disaster-relief efforts. It pointed out that the ability of military forces to mitigate the effects of an attack on the homeland may also be useful for disaster-relief operations.[64]

While DOD's mission is clearly focused on overseas operations as documented in the defense strategy, the June 2005 Quadrennial Defense Review identifies five key strategic objectives to support civil authorities:

- achieve maximum awareness of potential threats,
- deter, intercept, and defeat threats at a safe distance,
- achieve mission assurance to ensure that DOD can continue to operate after an attack,

- support civil authorities in minimizing the damage and recovering from domestic chemical, biological, radiological, nuclear, or high-yield explosive mass-casualty attacks, and

- improve national and international capabilities for homeland defense and homeland security.[65]

While some active-duty and National Guard units are designed and structured to deploy rapidly as part of their military missions, the Department of Defense is not organized, funded or structured to act as a first responder for all domestic catastrophic disasters.[66]

The Military Departments Prepare the Forces but the Joint Community Generally Employs Them

In accordance with Title 10 of the U.S. Code, the Departments of the Army, Air Force, and Navy organize, train, and equip the force, among other things.[67] To organize the force, the military Departments establish such organizational structures as brigades, divisions, air wings, battle groups, air/ground task forces, and other configurations needed to facilitate accomplishment of the mission. In addition, the Departments identify, develop, and deliver training deemed appropriate to prepare the forces for their mission. Lastly, the Departments develop and acquire the weapons systems, equipment, and supplies needed by the forces to successfully carry out their missions.[68]

While the military departments organize, train, and equip the force, the combatant commands generally execute the missions.[69] DOD's unified-command plan establishes five geographically based combatant commands that are responsible for conducting operations in their individual areas of operations.[70] NORTHCOM is based in Colorado Springs, Colorado, and is responsible for conducting military operations in the United States, Canada, Mexico, Cuba, certain Caribbean islands, and in the sea and air approaches to the United States.[71]

NORTHCOM's specific mission is to conduct operations to deter, prevent, and defeat threats and aggression aimed at the United States within assigned areas of operations and, when directed by the President or Secretary of Defense, to provide defense support for civil authorities.[72] NORTHCOM's mission statement clearly indicates that the command only provides support to civil authorities if directed to do so, or the proposed mission is consistent with DOD's directives and other documents that specify the circumstances under which DOD conducts civil support.[73]

NORTHCOM consists of the command headquarters, certain small deployable headquarters units, and certain non-deployable headquarters organizations that would coordinate operations within defined geographic locations, such as the National Capital Region and Alaska.[74] NORTHCOM generally executes its assigned missions through Joint Task Forces which are established to carry out specific missions. NORTHCOM has a small number of forces assigned to its headquarters and subsidiary units.[75]

Status of Plans for Support to Civil Authorities

The Committee not know how effectively NORTHCOM planned for its role in Defense Support to Civil Authorities in a disaster response, nor is it clear if that planning is finished. At the Committee's hearing on February 9, 2006, the Commander of NORTHCOM, Admiral Timothy Keating, testified that Concept Plan 2501 (CONPLAN 2501) was "a comprehensive approach to providing Defense Support to Civil Authorities" and was "ready to be approved by the Secretary and it is on our shelf."[76] DOD defines a CONPLAN as "An operation plan in an abbreviated format that would require considerable expansion or alteration to convert it into an [operation plan] or [operation order]. A CONPLAN contains the combatant commander's strategic concept and those annexes and appendixes deemed necessary by the combatant commander to complete planning. Generally, detailed support requirements are not calculated."[77] Although DOD states, "The fact that CONPLAN 2501 was still in draft had no impact on the speed and efficiency of NORTHCOM's response," the Committee has been unable to evaluate this assertion because, despite repeated requests, DOD has not provided the CONPLAN to the Committee. DOD has stated, "We cannot release the Draft USNORTHCOM CONPLAN 2501. It is still deliberative and pre-decisional.[78]

DOD Issues Execute Orders to Direct Missions and Augments Northern Command With Additional Forces When Needed

DOD directs that assigned commands undertake missions when ordered to do so via certain mission orders including "Execute Orders." The Execute Order will be sent to commands assigned to missions and may include a variety of relevant information, including the provision of (1) intelligence or situational reports, (2) concepts of operations to be implemented, (3) procedures to be followed if assisting another lead federal agency, such as FEMA, (4) instructions in reporting on mission progress, and (5) mission-reimbursement information if appropriate.[79]

When given a mission via such an order, NORTHCOM submits a "request for forces" to the Secretary of Defense who, in turn, will assign appropriate forces for the duration of the mission. Forces temporarily assigned to Northern Command can be pulled from anywhere in the force structure, but generally consist of forces based in the United States which are not already deployed on another mission. DOD's Joint Forces Command issues an order transferring operational control of those forces from their current command to NORTHCOM for the duration of the mission.[80]

Defense Coordinating Officers and Elements Are Often DOD's First Deployers for Civil Support

Once DOD approves a request to provide defense support to civil authorities, it usually deploys the Defense Coordinating Office (DCO) and Defense Coordinating Element to the Joint Field Office (JFO) used to manage the federal response. The DCO serves as the single point of contact for requests to DOD originating at the JFO. (Other requests for DOD assistance may originate at such national response locations as the Homeland Security Operations Center.) The NRP identifies the DCO's position and describes its responsibilities.[81]

The officer may also assign liaison officers to the JFO-based ESFs and refer contentious issues to the Assistant Secretary of Defense (Homeland Defense) for resolution.[82]

U.S. Department of Defense Response

Introduction

> [The] movement of 72,000 men and women in military uniform within the United States is the largest deployment of military capability within our country since the Civil War. The scope and speed of … our DOD Katrina response, was the largest, fastest civil support mission in our nation's history.[83]
>
> *– Paul McHale, Assistant Secretary of Defense for Homeland Defense*

> When we got off the airplane, General [Russel] Honoré [Commander, Joint Task Force Katrina] picked me up about 30 minutes later. He flew in by his helicopter, grabbed me and said, okay, I'm going to go orient you to your mission … your job is to fix the airport and fix New Orleans.[84]
>
> *– Major General William Caldwell, U.S. Army, Commander, 82nd Airborne Division*

In general, DOD's response to Hurricane Katrina can be divided into three phases. In the first two phases – before landfall and immediately after landfall – DOD responded in accordance within its traditional posture under the NRP to provide assistance to civil authorities only after requested. However, as the DOD leadership recognized the potentially catastrophic nature of the disaster on Tuesday morning, August 30, 2005, DOD's approach shifted from this reactive approach to a forward-looking posture, including the mobilization of significant assets that DOD commanders anticipated might be needed for the response. This third phase represented a departure from DOD's traditional practice and enabled DOD to respond to requests for assistance in a timely manner.

During the first phase of DOD's response, in the week prior to landfall, DOD began to plan and prepare for the deployment of forces to provide support that might be requested by FEMA. DOD identified commodities that could be provided to FEMA, and led and participated in interagency teleconferences.[85] In addition, DOD deployed DCOs to Louisiana and Mississippi and identified military installations that would be available for FEMA use as staging bases. Although individual commanders exercised their own initiative to prepare, identify, and alert troops as a result of the forecasted magnitude of Katrina, and had expedited certain procedures, these actions were not coordinated by senior leaders of the Department. For the most part, DOD's actions were consistent with the type of pre-hurricane activities it had undertaken in the past. One of the lessons from Katrina is that these procedures are inadequate for a catastrophic incident.

The second phase occurred during and immediately after landfall. In this phase, DOD lacked any significant information regarding the extent of the storm's devastation. DOD officials relied primarily on media reports for their information. Many senior DOD officials did not learn that the levees had breached until Tuesday; some did not learn until Wednesday. As DOD waited for DHS to provide information about the scope of the damage, it also waited for the lead federal agency, FEMA, to identify the support needed from DOD. Although DOD continued to identify and prepare assets for potential deployments, for the most part DOD's actions during this phase were again consistent with its traditional posture under the NRP to be prepared to respond to requests, rather than actually begin responding on its own initiative. DOD's approach during this phase continued to be deliberative. The lack of situational awareness during this phase appears to have been a major reason for DOD's belated adoption of the forward-looking posture necessary in a catastrophic incident.

By Tuesday morning, however, DOD leadership began to recognize that the scope of the disaster may have been catastrophic, and that an expedited DOD response likely would be necessary. In addition, there was a growing frustration within DOD over the lack of requests for assistance from FEMA. On Tuesday morning the Deputy Secretary of Defense informed the commander of NORTHCOM that he had a "blank check" for any DOD resources that he believed were reasonably necessary for the Katrina response. The Chairman of the Joint Chiefs of Staff directed the chiefs of the various services to begin deploying forces they believed might be needed for the response. This third phase of the response represented the type of approach that may be necessary in a catastrophic incident: anticipating requests and deploying assets in advance of requests.

DOD's shift in approach during this third phase enabled DOD to quickly respond to FEMA's mission requests; in a number of instances DOD "response" began before FEMA submitted the request. FEMA officials stated that although in the past they had found DOD's process cumbersome, during Katrina they felt DOD responded quickly and effectively to FEMA's requests. In a number of critical instances, DOD offered its assets and support to FEMA and DHS; in these instances, too, DOD support was deemed effective.

The third phase, however, revealed a critical need for improvement in military planning and preparation for catastrophic incidents, as well as the need to better integrate the military response into the overall response. In addition to DOD's being tasked by FEMA to provide support, the State of Louisiana asked both the National Guard and DOD to provide large numbers of ground troops. The resulting movement of 50,000 National Guard and 22,000 active-duty troops in response to Katrina was the largest deployment of military capability within the United States since the Civil War. The National Guard and active-duty military response provided critical humanitarian relief that saved lives and eased the suffering of thousands.

Many of the state and federal requests for military support, however, lacked adequate specificity. The responses to the requests for military support often were poorly coordinated with each other, if at all. The deployments of the National Guard troops were not well coordinated with the active-duty forces. One result was that local, state, and federal officials had differing perceptions of the numbers of federal troops that would be arriving, the missions they would be performing, who was in command of the military forces, and who should be in command.

Discussion

Severe Weather Execute Order

On August 19, one week prior to Hurricane Katrina's initial landfall on the Atlantic coast of Florida, the Secretary of Defense delegated to NORTHCOM the authority to deploy certain DOD assets as necessary to prepare for a hurricane. NORTHCOM holds responsibility for command and control over military operations conducted in defense of the continental United States, and in support of civil authorities, responding directly to the Secretary of Defense. Previously, all authority to deploy any such DOD assets had rested exclusively with the Office of the Secretary of Defense and the Joint Staff, who serve as the uniformed advisors to the Secretary. However, recognizing that 2005 was forecast to be "a well above-average hurricane season" with "an above-average probability of a major hurricane landfall in the United States," the Secretary and the Joint Staff wanted to provide additional flexibility in advance of the hurricane season, and on Friday, August 19, issued the "Severe Weather Execute Order."[86]

The order authorized the commander of NORTHCOM to "provide support to FEMA for planning and conducting disaster response operations in affected areas" for the duration of the 2005 hurricane season. This order granted approval for NORTHCOM to take two actions prior to a hurricane's landfall:

> 1. NORTHCOM was able to deploy DCOs and their staffs. Under the NRP, DCOs serve as DOD representatives to the JFO – the locally established operations center where federal, state, and local officials coordinate response activities. The DCO processes requests for military assistance, and ordinarily serves as the local commander of supporting military forces.[87]

> 2. NORTHCOM was able to designate military installations for other uses, such as operational staging areas where FEMA could store commodities in preparation for distribution, or for ports.

Colonel Darryl Roberson, the Assistant Deputy Director of the Joint Staff for Antiterrorism and Homeland Defense, told the Committee: "It was unprecedented to allow NORTHCOM commander to move those kinds of assets in the [continental United States] without the [Secretary of Defense] being specifically notified on each occasion. So it was a big deal, and it proved to be very helpful, and allowed us to respond in a much quicker fashion than would normally have been the case last year."[88]

Colonel Don Harrington, the permanent National Guard/DOD Liaison to FEMA, who helped develop the order after serving in that capacity through the hurricane season of 2004, reported that it resulted in a much earlier deployment of DCOs. "It takes a while … to track down the SecDef [Secretary of Defense], get him to sign off on it, whether he's in China or wherever."[89]

NORTHCOM ordered DCOs to deploy to Mississippi and Louisiana on Sunday, August 28, one day prior to Katrina's second landfall.[90] However, in anticipation of formal orders, both officers deployed on Saturday and began to coordinate with FEMA personnel.[91] Additionally, NORTHCOM designated Naval Air Station Meridian, Mississippi (85 miles east of Jackson, Mississippi), and Barksdale Air Force Base, Louisiana (200 miles northwest of Baton Rouge, Louisiana), as staging areas in response to FEMA requests.[92]

The Pentagon: Office of the Secretary of Defense and the Joint Staff

In the civilian leadership at the Pentagon, the Assistant Secretary of Defense for Homeland Defense, Paul McHale, has responsibility for domestic operations and disaster assistance.[93] Colonel Richard Chavez was his Senior Military Advisor for Civil Support. On August 23, Colonel Chavez learned of what would become Hurricane Katrina when the National Hurricane Center began tracking Tropical Depression 12. In consultation with Assistant Secretary McHale, he began standard hurricane preparations by assessing the availability of three key assets: Meals Ready to Eat (MREs), emergency medical capabilities, and FEMA staging bases.[94] Colonel Chavez presented his findings to the Secretary of Defense on August 28, the day before landfall. Although Tropical Depression 12 had become Hurricane Katrina, and had swelled from Category 1 to Category 5 status by that time, DOD did not alter the scope of the inventory.[95]

The Office of the Assistant Secretary has not developed or implemented formal policies and procedures regarding that office's role in preparing the Department for a civil-support mission, let alone one of catastrophic magnitude. For example, Colonel Chavez conducted these preparations on his own initiative, having derived these criteria from experience rather than from codified DOD guidance. Indeed, he said his office had intended to formalize these anticipatory actions into a pre-storm checklist, and now plans, as a result of Katrina, to expand the scope of the inventory to include other foreseeable needs such as shallow-draft boats.[96] As Katrina demonstrated, DOD needs to have procedures and plans to more fully prepare for catastrophic events.

Within the Joint Staff, the office dedicated to supporting civil authorities is the Office of the Joint Director of Military Support (JDOMS), then led by Brigadier General Terry Scherling.[97] The JDOMS began "24-7" monitoring of the situation in the Gulf of Mexico on Sunday, August 28, also activating a Crisis Action Team to process requests from FEMA.[98] Because DOD reports solely to the President, DOD treats FEMA mission assignments as Requests for Assistance, then considers whether the request may be supported, examining such issues as legality, possible harm to civilians, and the effect on readiness for overseas missions. JDOMS received relatively few requests prior to landfall. FEMA requested two staging bases, and that DCOs and their staffs be deployed to Louisiana and Mississippi. These requests were granted by NORTHCOM on the authority delegated by the Severe Weather Execute Order.[99] FEMA's single request requiring JDOMS approval was received by DOD on Sunday at 5 p.m., requesting air and ground transportation "to support life saving and life sustaining missions."[100] As will be discussed below, JDOMS processed the request the following day, 12 hours after landfall.

U.S. Northern Command (NORTHCOM)

Having begun tracking Katrina as Tropical Depression 12 on August 23,[101] NORTHCOM issued a Warning Order on August 25, directing the Army, Navy, and Air Force to prepare to "provide the necessary resources to conduct disaster relief operations consistent with defense priorities."[102]

The NORTHCOM Operations Directorate began conducting teleconferences – which included FEMA, First and Fifth Armies, and supporting commands of the Navy, Marine Corps, and Air Force[103] – on August 24 in preparation for the initial landfall in Florida, continuing the teleconferences daily as the storm progressed into the Gulf. Before landfall, the conversations focused on evacuation plans for military bases, protection of military infrastructure, and the initial requests received from FEMA for staging bases and Defense Coordinating Officers and Elements.[104]

Prior to landfall, logistics experts at NORTHCOM were aware of FEMA's activities in positioning commodities. As in previous hurricanes, the planners listened in on daily video-teleconferences during which FEMA described its preparations in pre-positioning food, water, and ice.[105] They anticipated that they might be called upon to provide strategic airlift.[106] In addition, NORTHCOM planners had participated in the Hurricane Pam exercise in July 2004, and so were aware of the possible need for a "large-scale evacuation of personnel out of the city."[107] But because DOD had not been asked by FEMA to take on any responsibilities in the preparations, the Army planners, under the NRP, had no "direct relationship" with FEMA.[108] They were in "listen only mode."[109]

Army Commanders: First Army

Lieutenant General Russel L. Honoré, Commanding General of First U.S. Army, was responsible for Army forces east of the Mississippi River. He had served in that position through the destructive hurricane season of 2004, and was aware of the likely requests for DOD assistance post-landfall. According to General Honoré, First Army had begun tracking the tropical wave that would become Katrina on August 8,[110] well before it appeared as a tropical depression on the Pentagon's screen. On August 24, as Tropical Depression 12 became Tropical Storm Katrina, First Army issued a Warning Order, followed on August 25 by a Planning Order, deploying the DCO and his staff to Florida and ordering equivalent elements to prepare to deploy to Alabama, Georgia, and Mississippi.[111]

General Honoré recognized early response as essential to saving lives, and from experience knew that equipment such as helicopters, boats, and communications equipment would be required. He wanted the necessary equipment and personnel identified and alerted in advance so as to expedite their eventual deployment. The process would involve multiple entities: NORTHCOM as the commander of military operations, Joint Forces Command as the provider of resources to NORTHCOM, and the Joint Staff in the Pentagon to ultimately authorize the deployment.

To initiate this process, General Honoré sent a message to NORTHCOM at about 1 p.m. on Sunday, August 28, requesting by 7 p.m. an assessment of the resources it considered necessary.[112] His immediate superior, Army Forces Command, sent an identical request to Joint Forces Command requesting a response by 2 a.m. Monday.[113] After receiving General Honoré's request, NORTHCOM forwarded an identical message to the Joint Staff at the Pentagon.

In addition to forwarding the formal message, Major General Richard Rowe, Operations Director at NORTHCOM, recognized the urgency of the request and informally directed his staff to anticipate the need for military support: "[First Army] has forwarded request for capabilities. …We need to get [the Joint Staff and Joint Forces Command] thinking about types of support that may be needed – joint solutions."[114] General Scherling, the Director of Military Support on the Joint Staff, responded to his e-mail. "Good plan, Sir," she wrote. "This sounds VERY catastrophic."[115]

Nonetheless, according to General Rowe, "Joint Forces Command and the Joint Staff did not do anything." The Joint Staff did not even want to receive this message prior to landfall, he said, because a specific requirement had not yet been identified, and under DOD's role in the NRP, DOD was not to respond until a request had been processed through FEMA: "They believe perhaps the likelihood of having to provide this kind of … joint capabilities is not likely."[116] He reported to General Honoré that he was unable to provide the requested information, even 12 hours after Katrina's landfall in Louisiana: "Somewhat hamstrung by JDOMS desire to wait" for requests for assistance, he wrote.[117]

Army Commanders: Fifth Army

Fifth Army held responsibility over Army forces west of the Mississippi River, which included Louisiana. Colonel Tony Daskevich deployed from Fifth Army as DCO to Louisiana, departing at noon on Saturday prior to the official NORTHCOM orders. The order, however, instructed him to deploy without the full complement of staff, or Defense Coordinating Element, that would normally have accompanied him, and instead to deploy two planners. He explained that the decision to deploy only two planners was based on uncertainty as to Katrina's path and limited lodging space in Baton Rouge.[118] To give his staff the flexibility to join him once the storm had passed and he had established his role in Baton Rouge, he sent the Element staff to Houston.[119] Although he was concerned that they would not be available to assist him in the immediate aftermath, his Mississippi counterpart, Colonel Damon Penn, reassured him that "it takes a full 48 hours of assessment before they even start discussing DOD participation. I think you're in good shape."[120]

Upon arriving in Baton Rouge Saturday night, August 27, Colonel Daskevich met with the senior FEMA officials in Louisiana, William Lokey and Scott Wells. They discussed the weather predictions and the potential severity of Katrina's impact. There was no discussion of specific mission assignments to DOD, although there was a general discussion of what assets DOD might be able to provide.[121] At the time of his arrival, Colonel Daskevich, who had recently taken part in training on the NRP, understood that DOD planned to operate on a "pull" system, following its established role wherein DOD is to respond to requests rather than to provide assets prior to identification of a specific need.[122] Sunday morning, Colonel Daskevich met with Major General Bennett Landreneau, the head of Louisiana's National Guard, and again, received no specific requests for DOD assistance.[123]

Navy Commanders

As Katrina approached the Gulf Coast on Sunday, August 28, the helicopter landing ship USS *Bataan* lay in port in Ingleside, Texas, following an exercise in the Caribbean Sea. The *Bataan* offers a large flat deck, refueling capacity, vast hanger space for cargo transport, and substantial medical facilities. Vice Admiral Mark Fitzgerald, Commander of the Second Fleet, based in Norfolk, Virginia, placed the *Bataan* on alert, and offered it as an asset to NORTHCOM.[124] USS *Bataan* left port by midday, and, after re-embarking the helicopters – two medium-lift utility MH-60s and three heavy-lift MH-53s – moved to position herself behind Katrina as it came ashore.

Additionally, the Navy followed standard pre-landfall procedure by moving ships in the storm's path out to sea. Five supply and logistics vessels left New Orleans for the Gulf of Mexico, remaining close enough to provide assistance as soon as Katrina passed. Aircraft departed from the Gulf Coast for protection, but Construction Battalion engineers ("Seabees") in Gulfport, Mississippi, equipped with heavy-lifting vehicles and trained to build or rebuild structures quickly, sheltered from the storm locally in order to respond quickly if required.[125] In Baltimore, Maryland, the hospital ship USNS *Comfort* began preparations for deployment on Sunday.[126]

Marine Corps Commanders

New Orleans is home to the headquarters of the Marine Corps Reserve Forces and its warfighting component, the Fourth Marine Division, commanded by Major General Douglas O'Dell. General O'Dell evacuated his headquarters on Friday, August 26, to avoid the approaching storm.[127] Beginning Saturday, August 27, he began examining what Marine forces might be required for the response.

Realizing that transportation assets were the most difficult to move quickly and would be the linchpin if a fast response were required, he conducted assessments of the most important of these "enablers": amphibious vehicles; motor transport in the event that infantry were deployed or a large evacuation were required; and a command-and-control element to receive and direct forces. The assessment was complete by mid-day Monday, shortly after landfall.[128]

Realizing that his logistics and engineering equipment might also be required, Lieutenant General James Amos, Commander of the II Marine Expeditionary Force – a total of almost 50,000 troops – directed an assessment of resources such as bulldozers, trucks, road graders, mobile hospitals, and associated personnel.[129] "This is 35 years of being a Marine and it's what we call anticipating a mission,"[130] he stated, explaining his recognition that Katrina would be of devastating severity and that the Marines' assistance would assuredly be required.

General Honoré arriving on
USS *Bataan*
U.S. Navy photo

U.S. Transportation Command

U.S. Transportation Command (TRANSCOM) holds responsibility for ground, air, and sea logistical and transportation support to military operations, and is assigned a supporting role to U.S. Department of Health and Human Services (HHS) in patient evacuation operations. As is standard practice in advance of a hurricane, TRANSCOM alerted numerous heavy-transport aircraft at bases throughout the country in the event that mass transportation of supplies, personnel, or evacuees would be required. The aircraft were alerted on Sunday, August 28, and included C-5s and C-17s at Dover, Travis, Charleston, and McCord Air Force Bases.[131] Additionally, TRANSCOM alerted two Contingency Response Wings,[132] whose mission is to deploy to a damaged airfield, and rapidly repair the runway, lighting, navigation, and communications systems to restore aircraft operations.

Immediate Response After Landfall

Situational Awareness

Like the rest of the federal government, for at least 24 hours after landfall, DOD had poor awareness of the extent of devastation in Louisiana and Mississippi. Throughout Monday, the day of landfall, DOD personnel remained in "wait-and-see mode." In Katrina, this period of damage assessment took much longer than usual. Many of the first responders were immobilized by damage or flooding, and communications systems were incapacitated. As a result, DOD personnel relied on media reports; nearly all interviewed by the Committee said that by Monday evening they had concluded from various media reports that New Orleans had "dodged a bullet."[133] They were not aware either of the levee breaches and overtopping, or the extensive flooding that followed.

The challenge of obtaining rapid and reliable information about hurricane damage is not new. According to what was then known as the General Accounting Office (GAO), "In the case of [1992's] Hurricane Andrew, it was several days before the local authorities realized how bad the situation was and how much assistance was needed." The GAO recommended "supporting state and federal agencies should not waste time waiting for accurate assessments but use their experience to push obviously needed assistance toward devastated communities before citizens begin to die for lack of it."[134]

Initial Request for Assistance: Two Helicopters

At 7 p.m. Monday, the Joint Directorate of Military Support (JDOMS) issued the first official order for military support to the response, directing the deployment of two helicopters to meet FEMA's request for two helicopters to support initial surveys of the storm damage and the most urgent requirements by Rapid Needs Assessment teams. The order also provided general guidance to the armed services: "Be prepared to provide additional personnel, units, equipment, airlift, and/or other support as requested by FEMA and approved by SecDef."[135] Colonel Roberta Woods, Deputy Director of Logistics at NORTHCOM, interpreted this order on Monday evening to mean that beyond the two helicopters, NORTHCOM and the services were to think ahead as to what they might provide: "At that time, again, we still had…no specific requirements to meet, no mission assignments, or word of mission assignments at that time."[136]

The First Air Cavalry Brigade in Fort Hood, TX, received orders to provide the two helicopters early Tuesday morning, and the aircraft were in Baton Rouge by 1 p.m.[137] They had launched within hours of receiving orders, but the JDOMS sent its orders 12 hours after landfall, and 24 hours after having received the request.[138] However, FEMA had requested that these two helicopters begin operations "8/30/2005 Tuesday," so they arrived on the day FEMA requested.[139] The lack of situational awareness early in the response may have contributed to a delay; other witnesses have attributed the time of response to Department bureaucracy and a "cultural reluctance" to commit Department assets to civil support missions unless absolutely necessary.

DOD Culture and Bureaucracy May Have Impeded the Process Initially

Assistant Secretary McHale disputed that idea, saying that although, prior to the 21st century, DOD's traditional role placed a primary focus on overseas missions, "September 11 made it very clear that homeland defense and civil support missions were … equal to or of even greater importance than other more traditional missions." He maintained that "if [resistance within the Department] ever had existed, [it] had ceased to exist in terms of the recognition of the importance of homeland defense and civil support missions."[140]

Some DHS officials have asserted that they were frustrated by how long it took DOD to approve requests for assistance,[141] and have suggested that a delay in processing the large requests for assistance from DOD – the logistics request approved September 2, and a second set of requests approved September 5 – slowed the response effort. Some FEMA witnesses also said that they would have liked "things to happen faster" in terms of DOD's bringing in assets for the response.[142]

In its own analysis, the White House asserted that DOD's "21-step" approval process – which included converting a mission assignment into a Request for Assistance and reviewing the request for legality and appropriateness, among other things – was "overly bureaucratic" and "resulted in critical needs not being met."[143] FEMA Deputy Federal Coordinating Officer (FCO) in Louisiana Scott Wells and other witnesses[144] described the process of gaining assistance from DOD as a "negotiation" in which DOD, along with the other government entities, collaborates in dividing up what needs to be done and by whom.[145]

Colonel Chavez testified that FEMA officials did not always have a good understanding of what assets and resources DOD could provide to best accomplish a mission and of DOD's processes for responding to FEMA's requests for assistance.[146]

Top DOD officials vigorously disputed the assertion that their approval process slowed the arrival of DOD assets. General Richard Myers, Chairman of the Joint Chiefs of Staff during the Katrina response, said, "I don't know if we have a 21-step process or not. If we do, it's one that takes 21 seconds to complete."[147] General Myers said DOD would "never" wait to start planning to execute a mission until formal orders were signed, saying such an approach would be "incongruous" with DOD culture.[148] Assistant Secretary McHale concurred, saying, "I can tell you, in a crisis, there are no 21 steps for approval."[149]

But some military officers reported encountering difficulties in responding to FEMA's early requests. Captain Michael McDaniel, the lead Navy liaison to FEMA, described his experience in processing the helicopter request: "JDOMS is notorious or has been notorious, 'Well, you can't ask for it that way. You need to do it like this.' Well, tell me how I need to ask for it, you know? I just need some helicopter support down there."[150] Colonel Harrington, the lead DOD and National Guard Liaison to FEMA, agreed that "Yes, there were some delays over there for different reasons, and that created some angst,"[151] adding:

> I think it's just a cultural thing, all the way up. From last year, it was both JDOMS, [Office of the Assistant Secretary of Defense for Homeland Defense], and the SecDef. It was the entire – and even Northern Command to a degree, even though Northern Command was a little more proactive. Just a cultural reluctance that they want to make sure that mission analysis is done and all the options are explored before you come to DOD.[152]

Prior to landfall, General Honoré had asked General Rowe, NORTHCOM Director of Operations, to identify certain assets for the response, including helicopters, boats, and communications equipment, but 12 hours after landfall General Rowe replied that he was "somewhat hamstrung by JDOMS desire to wait for [Requests for Assistance]"[153] and could not provide these critical assets to General Honoré. To the Committee, General Rowe explained: "I think the primary resistance is the organizational resistance and absence of a detailed, approved plan."[154]

"It's hard to get them to do anything where there is a chance of failure," Wells said, adding that DOD wants "to know 80 to 90 percent of the information before they will commit an asset to work with you."[155] Wells asserted that DOD "could have played a bigger role. They could have played a faster and a bigger role."[156]

While FEMA and DHS officials have complained that DOD did not do enough, and was slow to process requests, this investigation has found that, in fact, FEMA originated very few requests in this early period. In one instance, DOD received complaints from DHS about actions it did take. As discussed above, the Navy had ordered the helicopter carrier USS *Bataan* to sail towards New Orleans behind the storm, and to prepare to provide assistance. However, on Monday afternoon, a senior DOD representative to DHS reported to Assistant Secretary McHale's staff that "folks over here [are] hopping mad about the news of the Navy ship that announced their deployment without evident legal authority."[157] The USS *Bataan*, the military's most significant pre-landfall deployment, with helicopters prepared to assist with search and rescue, was challenged by DHS. The Office of the Assistant Secretary of Defense for Homeland Defense had to reassure DHS that USS *Bataan* was simply pre-position-ing, and in fact would not engage in the response without the proper request and authoriza-tion.[158] *Bataan*'s helicopters launched on Tuesday, becoming the first active-duty aircraft to assist with search and rescue.

The Committee has found that the JDOMS was slow in approving the initial request for he-licopter support in Louisiana. The record shows that the time required to process this initial request was not consistent with the scale of the disaster. This timeline and the testimony of witnesses both within and outside of DOD indicates that, while the extent of the damage may not have been known, both a traditional treatment of civil support as a secondary mission and a bureaucratic process slowed the response within the Department. The expeditious response by the helicopters themselves demonstrates that the Army was ready to mobilize, but that in this case, orders slowed the response. As will be seen, however, any reluctance and bureaucracy gave way beginning Tuesday, as top DOD officials took steps to expedite the responsiveness and bypass the ordinary approval process in moving assets forward.

The Pentagon: Office of the Secretary of Defense and the Joint Staff

During the first two days after landfall, then-Acting Deputy Secretary of Defense Gordon England exercised primary authority over the Department's response because the Secretary was traveling with the President.[159] Deputy Secretary England described the level of ac-curate information in the Pentagon for the first 24 hours as "no input except what was on the news;"[160] his primary source of information was the television. He said he attempted to contact FEMA Director Michael Brown and other DHS officials early Monday morning, but was unsuccessful.[161]

Assistant Secretary McHale's office received a situation report at 5 p.m. Monday which in-cluded information indicating that the Industrial Canal and the 17th Street Canal levees had breached and that "much of downtown and east New Orleans is underwater."[162] Assistant Secretary McHale's office attempted to contact the Army Corps of Engineers that eve-ning and in the early hours of the next morning regarding these and other reports of levee breaches, but even into Tuesday morning, the Corps was unable to confirm whether the levees had been breached or overtopped, and whether any such damage could be repaired.[163] At 1:47 p.m. on Tuesday afternoon, DHS transmitted to DOD a report that the Army Corps had confirmed the breach at the 17th Street levee[164] and at 3:15 p.m., Assistant Secretary McHale's office received an e-mail detailing the Army Corps's intentions for repairing the breach.[165]

Assistant Secretary McHale acknowledged that damage assessment was one area of the mili-tary response that should be improved, particularly after reviewing the lessons of Hurricane Andrew: "One of the fundamental lessons learned … from Katrina is the need to have avail-able immediate wide-area surveillance capabilities in order to more accurately and rapidly determine how much damage has been experienced."[166]

On Tuesday morning, Assistant Secretary McHale instructed his Principal Deputy, Peter Verga, to encourage DHS to appoint a Principal Federal Official (PFO). The NRP dictates that in catastrophic incidents, the Secretary of Homeland Security is to designate a PFO to coordinate the overall federal response,[167] and given the now-apparent scale of the disaster, a PFO would be critical to managing the necessary response efforts. Assistant Secretary McHale said:

It was becoming increasingly clear that the damage was so severe that we would likely have a declaration of a major disaster and that a principal federal official ... was going to be a central element of leadership in terms of the federal response. ... I, therefore, thought that having a named PFO would be an important initial step in triggering the capabilities available under the National Response Plan. So I directed Peter Verga to call DHS and ... serve as a catalyst for the consideration to urge the appointment of a principal federal official ... because the PFO, once appointed, would become a critical enabler of follow-on DOD capabilities. By the end of that day, Mike Brown was appointed the PFO.[168]

Furthermore, General Honoré had deployed to the Gulf Coast from Georgia, and NORTHCOM was preparing to designate him as the commander of active-duty military forces committed to the response. Another motivation underlying DOD's suggestion to DHS that it name a PFO appears to be concern within the Pentagon over the potential interpretation of the presence of a three-star general that the military was assuming control over the disaster response. An internal DOD e-mail indicates concern over a uniformed officer "being senior person on the ground." The message also indicates a preference that General Honoré report to a civilian official, and DOD maintain the appropriate posture of the military playing a supporting role.[169]

It is not clear what role Verga's phone call played in Secretary of Homeland Security Michael Chertoff's decision to appoint a PFO; Assistant Secretary McHale stated in testimony, "All I know for sure is we did make that recommendation and that, by the end of the day, a PFO ... had been appointed."[170]

U.S. Northern Command (NORTHCOM)

As discussed in Chapter 12 (Federal Preparations), NORTHCOM Operations Directorate had been conducting daily interagency teleconferences since August 24 to coordinate the military response.[171] By 1:30 p.m. Mountain Time Monday, damage assessments were beginning, but were not conclusive.[172] NORTHCOM's Deputy Director of Intelligence, Captain Brett Markham, told the Committee that "we relied heavily, on the 29th, on our National Technical Means"[173] (sensory equipment managed by national intelligence agencies to collect information for the benefit of the entire federal government). He said that some information – including a graphic representation of flooding received from the National Geospatial Agency[174] – was collected on August 29,[175] but that it didn't present a sufficiently clear picture.[176] Colonel Wesley McClellan, a senior member of NORTHCOM's Interagency Coordination Group, which comprises numerous interagency representatives, said that it also lacked damage assessment information, and was unable to specify the types of support needed from DOD.[177] Like his counterparts at the Pentagon, Admiral Keating, the NORTHCOM Commander, also woke up on Tuesday believing that "New Orleans dodged a bullet."[178] However, as the extent of the damage became clear on Tuesday, NORTHCOM staff clearly saw the need for military assistance, but was frustrated by the paucity of requests for assistance. Brigadier General Harold Moulton, who later in the week deployed from NORTHCOM to establish a command-and-control headquarters in New Orleans, described the growing frustration that developed as the damage became apparent:

The National Response Plan process establishes a sequence which goes from local asking for help from the state, state asking for help from the federal government, the federal looking around and choosing which appropriate spot through the mission assignment process to eventually get into. ... That whole concept seemed to be, for lack of a better term, frustrating for this staff and for

Admiral Keating as they were trying to figure out how to respond to this compelling human tragedy that they could see unfolding on TV.[179]

Colonel Daskevich, who had deployed from Oklahoma on Saturday to serve as the DCO – NORTHCOM's direct representative – in Baton Rouge, reported to the State Emergency Operations Center at 4:30 a.m. Monday.[180] He also spent most of Monday struggling to gain an accurate picture of the situation, and acknowledged that from Baton Rouge, he in fact had very little awareness of the developments in New Orleans. Colonel Daskevich appears to have received a report of levee failure on Monday.[181] However, because he was unfamiliar with the significance of the levees, he did not recognize the potential implications of this limited information.[182] "The hunt for information in the first 24, 48 hours after the storm was a challenge," he said.[183] Having deployed with only one additional staff member, as ordered by NORTHCOM, Colonel Daskevich acknowledged that a lack of manpower, communications equipment, and operating space within the State Emergency Operations Center rendered it "extraordinarily demanding to try to keep up with all of the information flow and, or course, to actually do business" during the first several days.[184]

The "Blank Check"

Whatever you can think of and get it moving *yesterday*, carriers, helos, trucks, amphibs, LCACs [Landing Craft Air Cushion], C-17s, C-130s, hospital ships, medical teams – whatever. Overkill is better than undershoot. POTUS [President of the Untied States] is coming back to D.C. tonight just for this.[185]

–Admiral Ed Giambastiani, Vice Chairman of the Joint Chiefs of Staff, to Admiral Keating, Commander of U.S. Northern Command, August 30, 2005.

Though officials had begun to learn more about the extent of the damage, through Tuesday morning the Department remained in a posture as dictated by the NRP, to allow FEMA to coordinate the response.[186] At the same time, senior officials within the Department responsible for homeland defense were becoming concerned that they were not receiving requests from FEMA, and that awaiting such requests could further delay the movement of military assets. Assistant Secretary McHale, who that morning met with Deputy Secretary England, and Chairman of the Joint Chiefs of Staff Gen. Myers to discuss the hurricane and the Department's response during the daily morning briefing, said that notwithstanding media reports "that were less sobering than the scope of the actual damage," the leadership recognized that the Department needed to mobilize its assets for the support requests they anticipated:

We were much more focused and concerned than the published reports of the damage might have justified. In part that was because certain key individuals expressed a deep concern that the damage was more severe than was being reported and so there was a collective sense that Hurricane Katrina was likely to be equal to or greater in damage than that of Hurricane Andrew in 1992.[187]

Yet officials within the Pentagon were surprised at the silence from FEMA. First thing in the morning, General Myers inquired from his Operations Directorate how many requests the Joint Staff had received, "and the answer was, We hadn't got any." A resulting discussion with the Deputy Secretary, then, led to the conclusion that "We need to start leaning forward – they're going to need some Department of Defense assets."[188]

During a meeting at 7:30 a.m. Central Time, Deputy Secretary England informed senior Pentagon officials, including representatives of the military services and the Chairman of the Joint Chiefs of Staff, of the Department's commitment to quickly provide to the

NORTHCOM Commander whatever assets were needed to support the overall hurricane response, and urged all commanders to "lean forward" to be able to quickly meet requests for assistance.[189] In a subsequent call that morning to Admiral Keating, Deputy Secretary England made clear that NORTHCOM would be provided any asset Admiral Keating deemed necessary.

Deputy Secretary England reported to Secretary of Defense Donald Rumsfeld:

> We are leaning forward on all fronts. I have authorized all local commanders to provide their assistance and have authorized NORTHCOM and the Chairman to take all appropriate measures to push forward available DOD assets that could be useful to FEMA.[190]

In a meeting at 3:40 p.m.,[191] General Myers then instructed his service chiefs to work together with NORTHCOM in determining necessary assets, telling them to pre-position resources in anticipation of a request for assistance from FEMA, if they thought it prudent.[192] To expedite the deployment process, he instructed the services to proceed on the authority of this vocal command – Secretary England's direct instruction to Admiral Keating, and his own guidance to the service chiefs – and that the necessary paperwork would follow later.[193] "Think large," he told them.[194]

A vocal command of this magnitude is extremely rare in DOD. For the purpose of ensuring legality, availability of resources, and documentation of the chain of command, all deployments are normally processed rigorously through specific written orders and electronic tracking systems. Deputy Secretary England's command represented an extraordinary delegation of military judgment, on the assurance that Admiral Keating would keep the Department informed. It was a "blank check,"[195] Deputy Secretary England said. Assistant Secretary McHale elaborated: "What was communicated … was what we in the military call 'commander's intent.' The message from the Deputy Secretary of Defense, consistent with the counsel provided by the Chairman of the Joint Chiefs, was to act with a sense of urgency and to minimize paperwork and bureaucracy to the greatest extent possible."[196] As Admiral Keating understood the direction, "We're moving anything we think FEMA will need. No obstacles from DOD or Joint Staff."[197] While DOD's inherent authorities to respond had not changed, and it was understood that all the necessary paperwork would follow, the decision reflected an extraordinary delegation to the military commanders. Assistant Secretary McHale said, "The climate in the decision-making process in this department could not have been more proactive than it was."[198]

Although individual commanders had already begun moving assets and conducting pre-deployment preparations, many witnesses have credited these actions with fundamentally shifting the overall response of DOD, particularly at the departmental level, into a proactive mode. Captain McDaniel, who represented the Navy to FEMA, said:

> The pendulum swung from one extreme to the other through this. I mean, it went from having to pry Secretary Rumsfeld's fingers off of a helicopter package … and this 100-pound [sic] gorilla just goes, "Okay, we've got it." Boom, and then the floodgates open.[199]

Colonel Harrington agreed that the "cultural reluctance" had now been overcome, and that attitudes within the Department "dramatically shifted" as "things got a little crazy."[200]

On Wednesday morning, the Chairman of the Joint Chiefs issued guidance to Joint Forces Command (which maintains control of most military assets within the United States until they are assigned to Combatant Commanders such as NORTHCOM), consistent with his guidance to the service chiefs on Tuesday: "(1) Continue to lean forward; (2) Remind services to work through Joint Task Force components; and (3) Be aggressive but don't get in FEMA's way."[201] Forces had begun to deploy in large numbers to the region, some requested by NORTHCOM, and many others volunteering on their own initiative. The initial result was a "wide open barn door," according to General Rowe, with NORTHCOM having difficulty tracking self-deployed assets.[202]

"Our primary concern for Wednesday will be search and rescue" Admiral Keating informed his staff. "Temperature index likely to exceed 100F in New Orleans. Folks that survived certain to need water, then food, then shelter."[203] However, officials at the Pentagon were surprised to have so few requests from DHS in the first few days after landfall.[204] (See Chapter 23 for information on the assistance-request system.)

Colonel Darryl Roberson, Assistant Deputy Director for Antiterrorism and Homeland Defense in the Joint Staff, described his frustration at not being asked to do more sooner:

> I will tell you that I personally felt very frustrated that we had not been called in earlier. We had assets available. We were all leaning forward. We knew we were going to receive them. We responded, in my opinion, in an unprecedented manner to everything that we got. I am absolutely convinced in my heart that it is a good-news story that DOD came to the rescue. That may sound strong. Obviously I'm biased. But in my mind, DOD saved the day to a large extent, and it was because of what we did. My frustration comes from the fact that I think we could have done it earlier if we had been asked.[205]

Assistant Secretary McHale expressed a similar frustration, stating that throughout the first week, he believed that FEMA's requests for assistance were still not commensurate with the scale of the catastrophe and the types of efforts that would be required of DOD, and that even "by Saturday it was clear that the [requests] we had received, reviewed, and approved were pretty narrow in scope."[206] Yet on the message conveyed by Deputy Secretary England, military forces converged upon the Gulf Coast.

Mobilization of Military Forces

Despite an overall lack of awareness within the Department about conditions in Louisiana and Mississippi, a number of military commanders within the services took action, pursuant to their own command authority, to prepare assets for potential requests for assistance. In general, it is possible to characterize commanders' actions throughout the first week as one of three types: (1) preparation and mobilization into the Joint Operating Area in coordination with NORTHCOM; (2) mobilization into the Joint Operating Area, but without full coordination with NORTHCOM; and (3) individual preparations conducted within the services, without specific orders to do so. To characterize the response most broadly, commanders took action consistent with the guidance of Deputy Secretary England and General Myers, making all reasonable efforts to pre-position assets or prepare for their deployment. And indeed, the overwhelming majority of deployments occurred prior to a request by DHS or FEMA. As will be discussed below, the lack of expected requests in fact led the Department to draft requests *for* FEMA, in recognition that such military assistance was required, but that FEMA had either failed to ascertain the requirements, or had inadequately expressed the requirements to DOD.

However, the original intent of the Secretary's vocal order was that despite the lack of paperwork, all deployments and preparations were to be undertaken in coordination with NORTHCOM to ensure that Admiral Keating had knowledge of all forces operating in the region, and to maximize the efficiency and effectiveness of the military response. The Committee has found that preparations in the early stages led to a faster response when the requests and orders finally came, and the pre-positioning of assets was essential to responding to immediate needs. Yet not all deployments were coordinated with NORTHCOM, possibly detracting from the unified effort as intended by officials, and ultimately causing NORTH-COM to deploy a headquarters "to get our arms around this Title 10 force structure that's now just basically all merging on the same local area,"[207] as described by the headquarters commander, General Moulton.

A NORTHCOM execute order at 10 p.m. Central Time expanded the geographic reach of commanders' ability to provide assistance under the Immediate Response Authority. Whereas this authority was previously limited to a commander's immediate vicinity, it now granted commanders located anywhere within the Joint Operating Area authority to provide assistance anywhere in the region, provided they coordinated with NORTHCOM through Joint Task Force Katrina.[208] The combination of this order with the vocal direction from Deputy Secretary England and General Myers broadened the authority of military commanders to operate domestically, and was an extraordinary departure from the Department's ordinary procedures. Because the Deputy Secretary and the Chairman of the Joint Chiefs had encouraged commanders to use their inherent authority to pre-position assets into the disaster area (while coordinating with NORTHCOM), this order now permitted any pre-positioned unit to provide assistance using the expanded immediate response authority.

Navy

The Committee found that, overall, the Navy showed a strong willingness to push assets into response efforts, ultimately sending more than 20 ships and 100 aircraft into the Gulf of Mexico, often in advance of a request or an order. The Navy provided a wide variety of mobile platforms for landing and servicing aircraft, treating patients, transporting enormous quantities of cargo and commodities, in addition to land-based assets which included engineering battalions of Seabees and logistics support.[209] But more than other services' assets, which may often arrive by air in a matter of hours, the mobility of the Navy's primary assets is limited by the "time-distance" problem: An immutable factor in a ship's ability to arrive on scene is the distance it must travel and its maximum steaming speed. In this case, the presence of the helicopter carrier USS *Bataan* in the Gulf of Mexico prior to Katrina proved extremely fortunate, for many of the ships had to steam from Norfolk, Virginia, and with the combined preparation and steaming time, did not arrive in the Gulf until Saturday and Sunday.[210] But preparations for the ships' deployment began shortly after landfall, even as the initial lack of damage assessments created an information vacuum.

In accordance with standard practice for hurricanes, Second Fleet Commander Vice Admiral Mark Fitzgerald placed a group of three amphibious-warfare ships in port in Norfolk, VA, on 24-hour alert for possible deployment.[211] These three ships – the USS *Iwo Jima,* USS *Shreveport,* and USS *Tortuga* – had been previously designated as the Expeditionary Strike Group (ESG) to respond to contingencies on the East Coast or in the Atlantic Ocean.[212] The ESG has large-deck vessels for landing helicopters, "well-decks" for retrieving amphibious landing craft, significant hangar and deck space for supplies, refueling capacity for helicopters, and facilities to provide showers, food, and water for both victims and response personnel. Admiral Fitzgerald also contacted Coast Guard Vice Admiral Vivien Crea, on Tuesday morning, and "offered help" from the Navy. He credits this channel of coordination as essential to the events of the first week; he had difficulty communicating with General Honoré and with NORTH-COM because of the initial focus on National Guard and Army land-based missions.[213] Admiral Crea confirmed that, "The Navy was very proactive in sending things down. We didn't have to ask them. … They started diverting ships and aircraft that direction."[214]

Meanwhile, having been stationed in the Gulf of Mexico at the conclusion of a previously scheduled exercise held prior to Katrina, the USS *Bataan* followed Katrina, and by Tuesday morning was within 150 to 200 miles of New Orleans.[215] Watching the news, the vessel's commanders began identifying ways to help. At 3 p.m. CT, the *Bataan* received orders from Second Fleet to send helicopters into New Orleans to conduct search and rescue missions in coordination with Coast Guard District Eight.[216] The Navy and Marine Corps helicopters were in the air by 5 p.m., and reported to the Coast Guard Air Station commander,[217] that, as the designated On-Scene Commander, held responsibility for coordinating all air search-and-rescue assets. They were joined by two Navy SH-3 helicopters from Pensacola that arrived unannounced at the Coast Guard station, offering their services.[218] In all, USS *Bataan*'s aircraft rescued, evacuated, or transported over 2,000 persons.[219]

Fleet Forces Command and Second Fleet identified Rear Admiral Joseph Kilkenny, Commander of the USS *Harry S. Truman* Carrier Strike Group, to represent the Navy on the proposed Joint Task Force Katrina under General Honoré.[220] The Task Force was formally established late Tuesday night; Admiral Kilkenny flew to Naval Air Station Pensacola Wednesday morning,[221] where he began coordinating the deployment of Navy helicopters to the region.[222] Admiral Kilkenny echoed Admiral Fitzgerald's statement that General Honoré was difficult to reach during the first few days, but that he was able to report back on his actions through Second Fleet;[223] Admiral Kilkenny said that he knew General Honoré's general intentions to focus on the immediate saving of lives through search and rescue, and could proceed by simply coordinating with Second Fleet.[224]

At 3 p.m. CT Tuesday, Fleet Forces Command had directed Second Fleet to launch the ESG. USS *Iwo Jima,* USS *Shreveport, and* USS *Tortuga* left Norfolk, Virginia, on Wednesday, scheduled to arrive off the Louisiana coast on Sunday afternoon.[225] They carried a standard load of equipment called the Disaster Relief Kit. The kit included supplies such as bulldozers, medical supplies, water purification, and other equipment.[226] Fleet Forces Command then deployed the aircraft carrier *Truman* (without orders from NORTHCOM) in order to provide fuel and deck space for the rapidly increasing fleet of helicopters. The aircraft carrier departed Norfolk on Thursday. On Friday NORTHCOM submitted a Request For Forces to the Joint Staff asking that *Truman* be committed to the response.[227] The *Truman* was tasked with supporting the Joint Task Force upon its arrival off the coast of Biloxi, MS, on Sunday, September 4.[228]

On Thursday, Admiral Crea requested that Second Fleet assist with clearing channels in order to reopen shipping lanes into New Orleans and the Mississippi River, one of the nation's most critical commercial routes, as quickly as possible.[229] USS *Grapple* deployed the same day, assisting with salvage operations in Pascagoula, MS, on September 6. The mine-countermeasures ship USNS *Altair* deployed from Ingleside, TX, on Friday, September 2, and commenced port clearance operations on Saturday, September 3, arriving alongside the pier in New Orleans the same day.[230] With the channel clear, the *Tortuga* was able to proceed up the river on Sunday, followed by the *Iwo Jima* on Monday, September 5.

In addition to serving as General Honoré's headquarters for the Joint Task Force in New Orleans, USS *Iwo Jima* provided showers, food, and rest for the first responders who had operated in the devastated city for a week. As the ship's captain described in an e-mail on September 6:

> We are one [of] the few full service airports in the area and have been operating aircraft … for almost 15 hours each day. We are also one of the only air

conditioned facilities within a 10 mile radius and … we are also the only hot shower within miles. All day long we have been accommodating local policemen, firemen, state troopers, National Guard, 82nd Airborne division personnel with hot showers and hot food.[231]

Numerous other ships and forces deployed, including the High Speed Vessel USS *Swift*, to replenish USS *Bataan* with disaster relief supplies, three Logistics Support vessels, and four amphibious hover-landing craft to transport supplies into New Orleans.[232] The hospital ship USNS *Comfort* had begun its preparations on Sunday before landfall; because its specialized personnel and equipment required additional preparation time, it deployed from Baltimore, MD, on Friday, September 2, arriving in Pascagoula, MS, on September 9.[233]

The Navy also deployed medium-lift and heavy-lift helicopters from 15 squadrons throughout the country. In addition to those already operating from the USS *Bataan*, a total of 50 rotary- wing aircraft deployed from Jacksonville, Norfolk, Corpus Christi, and San Diego,[234] to assist with search and rescue, evacuation, and logistical operations. (See Chapter 21, Search and Rescue) The heavy-lift H-53 aircraft assisted the levee-repair operations, dropping sandbags into the breaches.[235]

Army

General Honoré, based at Fort Gillem, GA, as Commanding General of First Army, planned to deploy to the Gulf Coast as soon as the storm had cleared. Although he had not been ordered to do so, he wanted to establish himself in the area to be positioned advantageously as the response progressed: "My thought was 'get there,' because the first rule of war is you've got to get there," he said.[236] His authority as an Army commander permitted him to move from one military installation to another provided that such a movement could be considered training. Thus, he created an "Exercise Katrina," and in coordination with NORTHCOM and his superior officer at Army Forces Command, planned his move to Camp Shelby, an Army facility in southern Mississippi.

General Honoré explained that it was not in his nature to wait for a Request for Assistance or deployment orders prior to moving: "That is a response, sometimes, by folks to say, 'Let's wait until they ask for something.' But in this case, we've got a case where we need to save life and limb. We can't wait for a [Request for Assistance] or shouldn't be waiting for one. If there's capability, we need to start moving."[237]

General Honoré informed NORTHCOM and Admiral Keating of his plan to deploy to Camp Shelby on Monday afternoon,[238] but because Katrina continued to track northward from the Gulf Coast, he could not move until Tuesday morning.[239] He arrived at 11 a.m. CT[240] and surveyed the base and the surrounding region of Gulfport and Biloxi, which looked to him like they "had been hit by a nuclear weapon."[241] General Honoré had previously received NORTHCOM's warning order to "be prepared to establish [Joint Task Force] Katrina covering the states of LA, MS, AL, FL, KY, TN, and GA for command and control of consequence management operations resulting from the severe weather caused by Hurricane Katrina."[242] (A *Warning Order* instructs a commander to take all necessary preparations so as to be able to react immediately to a likely forthcoming *Deployment Order* or *Execute Order*). A NORTHCOM Execute Order, sent at 4 p.m. CT, alerted him to establish the Joint Task Force "on order."[243] At 10 p.m. CT, he received that order, officially converting his training mission into an operational mission.[244] General Honoré assumed control over all active-duty forces then and subsequently involved in the response within the above states, now designated as the Joint Operating Area; he would report to NORTHCOM.

With General Honoré now in command of an area which bridged the areas of responsibility of First Army and Fifth Army, Fifth Army wanted to provide assistance to him. Colonel Daskevich, the DCO for Louisiana, lacked the necessary personnel and equipment to effectively cope with the constant flow of information and demands for his assistance from numerous levels and organizations. Fifth Army Deputy Commander Brigadier General Mark Graham deployed from Fort Hood on Wednesday to provide more senior DOD representation in Baton Rouge, and to handle the requests from higher levels. Bringing a small headquarters planning staff, he arrived at the Louisiana Emergency Operations Center at 5 p.m. CT and in a meeting with Governor Blanco, Louisiana Adjutant General Bennett Landreneau, and General Honoré was soon assigned the task of planning and coordinating the evacuation of New Orleans. [245]

Preparing for Deployment of Federal Troops

Of the vast quantity and range of military forces which deployed to the Katrina response, from ships and aircraft to medical teams and amphibious-assault craft, one deployment is distinguished from all others – one for which no FEMA mission assignment was issued, and which did not originate from a decision within DOD. On Saturday, September 3, the President ordered 7,200 troops from the high-alert units of the Army and the Marine Corps to deploy to Louisiana and Mississippi for the general purpose of humanitarian assistance. Although the Committee has not been provided access to documents and individuals explaining the reason for this deployment, the next section in this chapter will further discuss the events leading up to the deployment, beginning with Governor Blanco's plea to President Bush on the night of August 29 for "everything you have got" and continuing through further requests and discussions between Louisiana, NORTHCOM, and Washington, D.C. The following will present the preparations conducted by the Army and the Marine Corps, which began, as might be expected of prudent commanders, with planning for assistance that might be required, despite lack of specific guidance. Although the preparations within the Army and the Marine Corps proceeded on very similar timetables, the Committee has been unable to establish whether these preparations were conducted in coordination with or based on guidance from NORTH-COM, the Joint Staff, or the Office of the Assistant Secretary of Defense, or whether the services were preparing individually to react to the growing crisis in New Orleans.

82nd Airborne Division

The 82nd Airborne Division, commanded by Major General William Caldwell and based at Fort Bragg, NC, includes a combat unit known as the Division Ready Brigade, which consists of about 3,700 soldiers, is maintained on a high state of readiness, and has an advance element prepared to deploy anywhere in the world within 18 hours of receiving orders.[246] Beginning Tuesday, the Division's planning cell identified the assets that might be required to assist in the hurricane response, reviewed standing procedures for hurricane preparation, and consulted with an experienced DCO on the NRP and the standard procedures for providing assistance to civil authorities. Wednesday evening, Forces Command ordered that the Army "be prepared to provide a brigade-size force to operate distribution centers, and/or if appropriate authorization were received, conduct crowd control and security in the vicinity of New Orleans."[247]

General Caldwell considered this guidance to be vague, and merely a codification of the general guidance provided by Forces Command in preparation for hurricane season, but issued an internal warning order to the Division Ready Brigade, increasing the state of readiness. Although the Division usually keeps an advance team of only 120 soldiers on two-hour recall, General Caldwell ordered all 5,000 soldiers to stand by in two-hour response mode.[248]

After receiving a call Friday morning from the Commander of Forces Command, which to him signaled a high likelihood of involvement, General Caldwell directed his staff to commence an exercise simulating a rapid deployment, combining all elements of the brigade – aviation, infantry, logistics, communications, and certain types of support. He also coordinated with Lieutenant General Robert Dale of U.S. Transportation Command (TRANSCOM), based at Scott Air Force Base in St. Louis, MO, to pre-position four C-17 transport aircraft at Pope Air Force Base in North Carolina, in preparation for the deployment.[249]

Soldiers heading for the
Gulf Coast
Army National Guard photo

Friday evening, Forces Command issued warning orders indicating that a deployment was likely, the first specific indication to General Caldwell that the Division Ready Brigade would, on short notice, be required to assist with the distribution of commodities, crowd control, and security in New Orleans.[250]

On Saturday morning the President announced the deployment in an address to the nation:

Today I ordered the Department of Defense to deploy additional active-duty forces to the region. Over the next 24 to 72 hours, more than 7,000 additional troops from the 82nd Airborne, from the 1st Cavalry, the 1st Marine Expeditionary Force, and the 2nd Marine Expeditionary Force will arrive in the affected areas. These forces will be on the ground and operating under the direct command of General Russ Honoré.[251]

This public announcement was the first word that General Caldwell received that his brigade would deploy, although official orders from Forces Command arrived early in the afternoon.[252] General Caldwell contacted General Honoré, who told him: "[G]et here as fast as you can." General Honoré also asked General Caldwell to bring a substantial command-and-control capability, by which he meant the appropriate personnel, equipment, and communications assets to plan, direct, and coordinate the numerous missions required of them. General Caldwell adjusted his deployment package correspondingly, adding several headquarters elements to enable the coordination and integration of ground forces, aviation units, and support personnel.[253]

The deployment began within hours; General Caldwell arrived in New Orleans seven hours after the President's announcement. "Fix the airport, and fix New Orleans" was General Honoré's guidance. Over the next two days, the 82nd Airborne presence swelled to more than 3,000 soldiers, many of whom arrived in a convoy of nearly 1,400 vehicles from Fort Bragg, North Carolina.[254]

General Caldwell then learned further from General Honoré that his mission was, first, to conduct search and rescue, then to provide humanitarian assistance, and third to provide presence. In its initial days, the 82nd Airborne assisted in restoring order at New Orleans International Airport and at the Convention Center, which continued to be a focal point for evacuees throughout the city, simply through their presence, and established connections with the New Orleans Police Department. "I think the biggest, I'll be honest, [thing] we probably did was to give them a sense of assurance that everybody is there to help you," As General Caldwell said.[255] Beginning Sunday, the 82nd Airborne worked with the National Guard in dividing the city into search sectors, and on Monday amplified FEMA's search efforts by providing helicopters, boats, trucks, and additional troops to the Urban Search and Rescue (USAR) teams.[256]

First Cavalry Division

The First Air Cavalry Brigade of the 1st Cavalry Division in Fort Hood, TX, which consists of an aviation unit of UH-60 utility helicopters and CH-47 heavy-lift helicopters and a battalion of 1,500 troops, had begun "prudent planning" prior to landfall. The first order for two UH-60s arrived on Tuesday morning as a result of FEMA's request to support the Rapid Needs Assessment teams in Louisiana. Later that day, the brigade received orders for six additional aircraft, which departed for New Orleans on Wednesday and joined the Louisiana National Guard search-and-rescue efforts based at the Superdome.[257] (See Chapter 21.)

On Wednesday, the brigade received a warning order to prepare a command-and-control headquarters element for Title 10 (federalized National Guard) forces,[258] a conduit for communications and planning consisting of 50 soldiers. Accordingly, the brigade commander, Colonel Dan Shanahan, departed to Naval Air Station Belle Chasse in New Orleans on Thursday evening, reporting to Joint Task Force Katrina as an aviation task force in command of Army aviation units, and coordinating with the Coast Guard.[259] A medical evacuation unit of nine helicopters arrived from Fort Benning, GA, joining search-and-rescue efforts, evacuation, and distribution of food and water. By September 11, 50 aircraft were operating in Colonel Shanahan's task force, although there was "always a need for more aircraft."[260]

The Second Brigade Combat Team of the 1st Cavalry Division also received warning orders from Forces Command.[261] Like General Caldwell, Brigade Commander Colonel Bryan Roberts described the message's guidance as very general, but he ordered his staff to begin preparing approximately 300 light and heavy vehicles for deployment. Their vehicles were undergoing maintenance following their recent return from Iraq, and so needed a 72-hour period to ready for deployment. Colonel Roberts understood that the mission would likely involve search and rescue, evacuation, debris removal, traffic control, and distribution of commodities. Colonel Roberts believed the soldiers were well-versed in these tasks because they had performed similar missions in their overseas commitments.[262]

Colonel Roberts flew to New Orleans International Airport on Friday in order to survey the area where he expected the team to stage.[263] He returned to Fort Hood Saturday morning; by the time he arrived, the President had announced that the 1st Cavalry Division would deploy that day along with the 82nd Airborne.[264] He arrived with his advance element on Sunday and reported to General Caldwell. Colonel Roberts's unit began to arrive on Monday, with 1,638 troops on-site by Tuesday.

The 1st Cavalry operated primarily in Algiers Parish, on the south bank of the Mississippi River, conducting door-to-door search-and-rescue operations. Evacuation was to be voluntary only. Soldiers received guidance to knock on doors, and offer food, water, and assistance, and were all briefed on the Rules on the Use of Force,[265] which explained the implications of the Posse Comitatus Act, which prohibits federal military forces from engaging in law-enforcement duties. The rules stated, "Force will be used only as last resort. If you must use force to fulfill your duties, use the minimum force required."[266] The 133rd Field Artillery Regiment of the Texas National Guard was embedded within the brigade in order to provide law-enforcement capability to the brigade as it patrolled the parish.[267]

Marine Corps

II Marine Expeditionary Force and 4th Marine Division

Much like the Army commands described above, commands within the Marine Corps planned, beginning mid-week, for the deployment of troops that were the most prepared and set at the highest level of alert posture. Unlike the Army, however, the Marines took additional preparatory actions for a major troop deployment, including positioning a headquarters command element in New Orleans, and sending engineering equipment via Navy ships. Indeed, evidence before the Committee suggests that the Marines may have ordered a significant portion of their troops and assets to deploy prior to the President's order on Saturday.

Lieutenant General James Amos, Commander of the II Marine Expeditionary Force based at Camp Lejeune, NC, called together his Planning Team immediately after landfall on Monday. Having begun to identify engineering equipment and aircraft in the preceding days, he now instructed his staff to plan for a major deployment of air and ground forces.[268] As with the Norfolk-based naval units, there were initially no orders from NORTHCOM or the Joint Staff directing these Marine units to deploy. But mid-day Tuesday, after the Chairman of the Joint Chiefs had urged the services to be proactive in moving forces forward, General Amos received a Warning Order from his superior officer, the Commander of Marine Forces Atlantic, directing him to prepare to deploy the helicopters his staff had already identified.[269]

On Thursday, General Amos deployed helicopters and transport aircraft to Naval Air Station Pensacola in preparation for a variety of support missions.[270] Expecting that tasking would soon be forthcoming for "lots of Marines," he loaded his engineering equipment onto the USS *Iwo Jima* Strike Group on Thursday[271] and sent an advance party to establish a command-and-control headquarters at Naval Air Station Belle Chasse.[272] In anticipation of a deployment order he "put them [the 24th Marine Expeditionary Unit (24 MEU), an infantry battalion of 1,200 Marines] on their packs" in preparation to deploy as early as Friday.[273] At the time, the 24 MEU was the Marine equivalent of the Army's Division Ready Brigade, postured at the highest state of readiness and prepared to deploy anywhere in the world.

Evidence and testimony received by the Committee suggest that the Marine deployments were not fully coordinated within DOD, and that NORTHCOM was not fully aware of Marine Corps efforts in the Gulf. General Amos e-mailed General Honoré on Thursday morning, writing that he was sending helicopters and engineering equipment. "What can I do for you?" he asked.[274] General Honoré responded, "HELLO BROTHER GET HERE AS FAST AS YOU CAN."[275] Friday morning, when General Amos told General Honoré of his intentions to send a command-and-control suite to New Orleans, General Honoré replied: "[It's] hitting fan get here fast as you can."[276] That day General Amos flew five aircraft to Belle Chasse carrying 150 Marines – the majority of the battalion's command element – along with a mobile communications suite, capable of establishing a command-and-control headquarters anywhere in the world.[277] An e-mail to General Rowe of NORTHCOM from one of his planners shows that the Marines' preparatory movements were not coordinated with NORTHCOM: "They do not have orders to move out yet but they are inside our [Joint Operating Area] w/out [Joint Task Force Katrina] or [NORTHCOM visibility]."[278]

General O'Dell stated that a plan was already in place for the full deployment of Marines: "I knew it was General Amos's intention to deploy 24 MEU."[279] As General Amos confirmed, "I anticipated them leaving on Friday. I figured the [deployment] order was going to be signed on Friday."[280] The Committee received evidence that at least a preliminary or partial deployment order was signed on Friday.[281] On that date, Marine Forces Atlantic directed that a Marine task force, to consist of a broad range of air and ground amphibious assault assets from the 24 MEU and the Marine Reserve Forces, begin deploying on Friday, September 2, and fully deploy no later than Saturday, September 3.[282] The troops were to deploy to Naval Air Station Belle Chasse, using their authority to reposition from one military base to another (as General Honoré had done in his initial movement to Camp Shelby) and to prepare to support General Honoré. Once established at Belle Chasse, they would be able to provide support on the expanded Immediate Response Authority granted by NORTHCOM.

Under these authorities, the deployment order appears to have been given in the spirit of General Myers's guidance encouraging the services to pre-position assets to enable their rapid employment when requested by FEMA. However, the deployment does not appear to have been fully coordinated within DOD. In particular, unlike all other troop deployments into the area under NORTHCOM's command, there had been no corresponding request for forces from NORTHCOM. General Rowe stated that although he knew General Amos and General Honoré were communicating, he was unaware of the specific exchanges leading up to the order: "That's one part of the help that I will have to give you that we did not ask for. However, I am aware that General Amos and General Honoré corresponded. General Honoré shared that with me, that General Honoré at that point said the help would be appreciated."[283]

Furthermore, this urgent need for the deployment of Marine troops does not appear to have been fully communicated to other DOD officials considering whether there was a need to deploy active-duty troops.

The next day, Saturday, September 3, the President issued a broad order for the deployment of active-duty ground troops. Because General Amos had anticipated the deployment for several days, with his Marines "sitting on their packs," they were "ready to go. … I was determined that when we got the Execute Order, we were going to darken the skies with C-130s and get them down there as quickly as we can."[284] Over the next 28 hours, aircraft ferried 1,250 troops, now reporting to General O'Dell,[285] who had been appointed as Marine Component Commander for the Joint Task Force, reporting directly to General Honoré.

General O'Dell confirmed that the Friday order from Marine Forces Atlantic was subsumed into the President's order on Saturday: "Prior to the President's order, for planning, I knew that we would have elements of my division as I've described and 24 MEU from Camp Lejeune … available." Most significantly, he added that the only thing that the President's order changed about the Marines' plans was that an element from the West Coast joined the 24 MEU.[286]

The forces initially operated in southwestern Mississippi, and then moved to St. Bernard Parish and the Lower Ninth Ward in New Orleans to perform door-to-door search and rescue missions. The West Coast-based Marines of the 11 MEU, however, were an unexpected capability. General O'Dell explained that he had not incorporated them into his plans, and that it was a challenge for him to provide them appropriate tasking and operating space: "We had to find work for them. We really had to look to find work for them."[287] Ultimately, he said, the 11 MEU was tasked with debris removal in Slidell, Louisiana, where their efforts were initially welcomed, "but toward the end of the ten-day period, they were picking up sticks in granny's yard."[288]

U.S. Air Force and U.S. Transportation Command

Transportation Command (TRANSCOM) holds responsibility for ground, air, and sea logistical and transportation support to military operations, and is assigned a supporting role to the Department of Health and Human Services in patient evacuation operations. The command had alerted C-17 and C-5 transport aircraft on August 28; the crews were in three-hour standby status. According to Brigadier General Paul Selva, Director of Operations, TRANSCOM again followed its standard practice 12 hours after landfall, alerting eight additional aircraft.[289]

The first mission received was to transport eight Swift Water rescue teams from Travis and March Air Force Bases in California to Louisiana for surface search and rescue.[290] Although Deputy Secretary England approved the request by 11 a.m. on Tuesday, TRANSCOM still had to locate a suitable airfield to receive these heavy-lift aircraft. Colonel Glen Joerger was assigned on Monday as the TRANSCOM liaison to FEMA in Washington, D.C., and arranged for Contingency Response Groups – on alert since Sunday – to deploy to re-open the New Orleans and Gulfport airports; both had been flooded, and their lighting and communications systems had suffered damage.[291] As a result, it was determined that the aircraft would land at Lafayette Regional Airport while the larger fields were reopened. The Response Groups evaluated the condition, restoring lighting, communications, and navigation systems, and performing maintenance on departing planes. By Tuesday evening, the airports were reopened, and the TRANSCOM aircraft were able to land with the Swift Water teams.[292]

Some witnesses attributed the timeline of this mission to a delay within DOD in approving the mission assignment for the aircraft. And although the request was initiated during the period in which DOD's culture of reluctance is said to have slowed the approval process, the record shows that DOD personnel began work on this assignment on Monday, August 29, and that any delay was introduced by the difficulty in finding a suitable landing field rather than by the approval process itself.

On Thursday evening, September 1, DOD received a mission assignment to airlift evacuees from New Orleans to Houston.[293] The Joint Staff processed the request on Friday, but the first evacuation airlift from the New Orleans International Airport had already occurred by 8 a.m. Thursday morning.[294] The TRANSCOM operations at the airport actually involved three separate missions, according to Colonel Joerger: patient evacuation, citizen evacuation, and cargo delivery.[295] TRANSCOM provided 15 transport aircraft – five C-17s, C-5s, and C-130s each – for the evacuation of patients as part of the National Disaster Medical System[296] (National Disaster Medical System is an interagency system to evacuate patients and individuals with critical needs from hospitals in the event of an emergency). (See Chapter 22.) TRANSCOM evacuated 21,000 people from New Orleans by air between Thursday and Saturday.[297]

TRANSCOM also played a major role in the deployment of the 82nd Airborne Division. Once the deployment appeared likely to the division commander, TRANSCOM pre-positioned four C-17s at Pope Air Force Base in North Carolina on Friday afternoon.[298] When the President ordered the troops to deploy on Saturday morning, TRANSCOM diverted additional aircraft to Pope, enabling the movement of personnel, vehicles, helicopters, and supplies, to New Orleans International Airport within hours of the President's order.[299]

Standing Joint Force Headquarters-North

Though General Honoré initially deployed as commander of the First Army, with only a small staff, his command eventually grew to more than 22,000 personnel from all branches of the armed services.[300] The Joint Task Force Katrina command structure grew more complex by the day, incorporating additional command elements as additional assets from the different services were absorbed into the Task Force. Admiral Kilkenny arrived on Wednesday as the Commander of the Navy component and General O'Dell took command of the Marine component on Saturday; additionally Major General M. Scott Mayes, Commander of the First Air Force, based at Tyndall Air Force Base in Florida, arrived late in the week to take command of the Air Force assets and to coordinate control of the airspace with the Federal Aviation Association.[301]

It became apparent to NORTHCOM that additional measures were necessary to maintain command and control over the many active-duty assets and to coordinate with the ever-growing number of National Guard forces. Admiral Keating, for instance, reported that he had little sense of National Guard capabilities beyond simply the numbers of troops being deployed.[302] As for active-duty troops, he reported that after the President ordered 7,200 troops to mobilize, 8,800 actually deployed,[303] many of whom were included based on personal requests from General Honoré to his fellow generals. As a result, NORTHCOM had difficulty maintaining an operational picture of the total military involvement. General Rowe complained in an e-mail to General Honoré, that he was "getting killed by the 'good ideas flowing.' … Right now I have an unexplained 13th Corps support command flowing – about a thousand more 82nd Abn division than we asked for, odd Navy comms pieces. Unexplained marines. Services are killing me off of buddy deals."[304]

Once NORTHCOM had assumed control of the active-duty military response on Tuesday, headquarters deployed planning and coordination elements. But on Friday, NORTHCOM decided to deploy Standing Joint Force Headquarters-North, a NORTHCOM entity designed to rapidly deploy a command and control element, led by General Moulton. [305]

General Moulton arrived with a staff of 38 in New Orleans Saturday morning, just prior to the deployment of the 7,200 active-duty troops. He established his headquarters at the Naval Air Station. His first task was to integrate National Guard forces with active-duty ground troops to take advantage of the National Guard's law enforcement capabilities because the Posse Comitatus Act prohibits active-duty troops from engaging in law enforcement.[306] They also had to coordinate the numerous assets devoted to the search-and-rescue mission, which was currently operating under different commands and following different procedures. The Standing Joint Force Headquarters established a common search-and-rescue grid and assigned responsibilities to the various entities involved.

Finally, General Moulton transitioned from search-and-rescue coordination to broader planning of the federal response for Coast Guard Vice Admiral Thad Allen, the Deputy Principal Federal Official, who later replaced Michael Brown as Principal Federal Official (PFO). General Honoré assigned General Moulton, together with General Graham from Fifth Army, to provide the PFO with operational planning assistance in incorporating DOD resources into the overall effort.[307]

Logistics

In disaster response, commodities flow into an area called the Federal Operational Staging Area. Often, this is a DOD facility.[308] Under the NRP, the Army Corps of Engineers is responsible for procuring water and ice. The Army Corps contracts with vendors to purchase these goods, directing these vendors to deliver the commodities to the Operational Staging Area.

As for food, the other major commodity, FEMA typically requests military Meals Ready to Eat (MREs), which are ultimately supplied by the Defense Logistics Agency (DLA). FEMA assigns the General Services Administration (GSA) to arrange to have the MREs delivered to the Operational Staging Areas.[309]

A FEMA representative, usually from the affected FEMA region, manages these Operational Staging Areas. Based on priorities established by the state, the FEMA representative directs the movement of commodities from the staging area to locations in the state called Points of Distribution (PODs).[310] State and local personnel, often supervised by the National Guard, distribute goods at the PODs to the people who need them.

NORTHCOM had begun planning for large-scale logistics missions prior to Katrina's landfall. After landfall, NORTHCOM's logisticians were involved in the evacuation of patients, and were "heavily involved" in the evacuation of people from the Superdome.[311] However, prior to Friday, September 2, NORTHCOM was aware of, but not heavily involved with, FEMA's actions in moving commodities into the Gulf Coast.

Although DOD had been called upon to assist in the movement of commodities in past hurricanes, including Hurricane Ivan along the Gulf Coast in 2004, NORTHCOM's planners did not know before Friday that there was a need for them to become more involved in that issue in the Katrina response.[312] Nor did the planners, a subset of the NORTHCOM organization, believe they could become more actively involved without a request to do so from FEMA.[313] Said a senior NORTHCOM planner, "We didn't have details at that point in time, or real authority to gather those details."[314]

On Thursday, September 1, FEMA began asking DOD to take on responsibilities beyond those it had been called upon to fulfill in past disasters. For example, FEMA requested that DOD "provide airlift capability to transport" people being evacuated from New Orleans to Houston, Texas, with a cost estimate of $20 million.[315] On that same day, FEMA also asked DOD to assist in the logistics of moving food and water to New Orleans and elsewhere on the Gulf Coast.[316]

As the magnitude of the disaster was becoming clearer, there was growing concern among FEMA officials that Gulf Coast residents' basic needs for food and water were not being met, and that FEMA's logistics operation was becoming overwhelmed and would be unable to meet them.

Late Tuesday night or early Wednesday morning,[317] FEMA Director Michael Brown discussed with FEMA's Federal Coordinating Officer (FCO) in Louisiana, William Lokey, the need to expand DOD's role in the response, including logistics.[318] Brown said he raised this issue with personnel in the White House and urged them to declare an insurrection and federalize the entire response effort.[319] However, the Committee found no evidence that Brown's desire to have DOD play a larger role in logistics was communicated by FEMA officials to DOD officials until Thursday, September 1.[320]

On Thursday, Ed Buikema, the Acting Director of the Response Division at FEMA, approached Ken Burris, the Acting Director of Operations, and said that FEMA needed DOD's help with commodities, supplies, and logistics[321] because the high water made it "very difficult delivering supplies and commodities,"[322] because of DOD's human and material resources,[323] and because of the reports of civil disturbance "playing out on television."[324] Buikema's view was that "DOD is very well equipped to not only deliver things in difficult situations, but also to provide the security that is commensurate to delivering that kind of service."[325] Burris agreed.[326] Although FEMA moved more truckloads of commodities in the days following landfall than they did for all four major hurricanes that hit Florida in 2004,[327] Burris thought that it still wasn't enough to "keep up with the consumption rate."[328]

Lokey thought the request was necessary, less as a response to a specific set of challenging circumstances, than as a catch-all to cover all aspects of a rapidly changing and generally overwhelming situation.[329] According to him, this request was to "cover the eventualities … because … what we were faced with was well beyond anything I felt our system could handle."[330] Although Lokey's view was that DOD did not need to take over all logistics,[331] then-FEMA Director Brown says that was exactly what he wanted DOD to do.[332]

After speaking with Buikema on Thursday morning,[333] Burris called Colonel Chavez in the Office of the Assistant Secretary of Defense for Homeland Defense.[334] Burris told Colonel Chavez that "The FEMA logistics capability has been overwhelmed," and that he "wants DOD to take over logistics operations in Louisiana and Mississippi."[335] Colonel Chavez viewed this request as extraordinary because it appeared FEMA was asking DOD to take over its job.[336] Colonel Chavez says he asked Burris, "is this really what you want us to do, take over the function? He indicated that that is indeed what they wanted to do."[337] Colonel Chavez told Burris that the request "would require a Secretary DHS to Secretary DOD call to initiate and significant General Counsel input."[338]

The NRP stipulates that DOD is a supporting agency to all 15 ESFs. Thus, they are on notice that they may be called upon to assist civilian authorities in a variety of ways. However, in this instance, the civilian agency – FEMA – was asking DOD to take over a role it had not traditionally played in disaster response, and which is not listed as one of DOD's support functions in any of the listed ESFs.[339] Thus, Colonel Chavez's surprise is understandable.

After conferring with Colonel Chavez, Burris modified his request to state that FEMA wanted DOD to "provide the support and planning and execution of the full logistical support to the Katrina disaster in all declared states in coordination with FEMA."[340] Burris also conveyed the information to DHS Secretary Chertoff so he could make the request to Secretary Rumsfeld.[341]

Meanwhile, DOD sought clarification from officials at FEMA and from the Homeland Security Operations Center at DHS about the meaning of "full logistics support."[342] As details of the potential mission were being collected, Secretary Rumsfeld and Assistant Secretary McHale conferred with General Duncan McNabb, the Logistics Director for the Joint Chiefs of Staff.[343] In the Secretary's office, Assistant Secretary McHale asked General McNabb whether DOD could perform this mission. "We can," General McNabb told him.[344]

On Friday, September 2, FEMA sent the mission assignment to DOD. It stated:

> Assistance Requested: FEMA request[s] that DOD provide planning and execution for the procurement, transportation and distribution of ice, water, food, fuel and medical supplies in support of the Katrina [disaster] in Louisiana and Mississippi.[345]

When DOD performs work pursuant to an approved FEMA mission assignment, DOD is reimbursed for the amount it costs DOD to perform that work up to the total amount "obligated" or authorized by FEMA. FEMA authorized spending $1 billion for this assignment.[346] Both FEMA and DOD viewed the billion-dollar total as an estimate, but one large enough to give DOD authority "to do what needed to be done" to get commodities moving into the Gulf Coast.[347]

In the words of Assistant Secretary McHale, it "may well have been the single most complex civil support mission in the history of the U.S. military."[348] Ultimately, for reasons discussed below, DOD did not take over all logistics operations from FEMA, although they did provide significant assistance. DOD plans to or has sought reimbursement from FEMA for only $118 million of the $1 billion dollars obligated under this mission assignment.[349]

The Secretary of Defense approved the request orally on Friday, September 2,[350] and Assistant Secretary McHale notified DHS Deputy Secretary Jackson of the approval on Friday in an e-mail.[351]

On Saturday, September 3, the paperwork was approved, and DOD issued its order directing the commander of NORTHCOM, Admiral Keating, to "plan and develop a concept of operations to execute logistical support operations in affected states of Louisiana and Mississippi."[352]

On Friday, September 2, before the mission assignment was officially approved,[353] NORTHCOM's planning staff began gathering information in "excruciating detail" about what orders FEMA had already placed with the Defense Logistics Agency (DLA), "how many trucks are lined up, how many trucks have left, how many trucks have been loaded."[354] They started calling the operational staging areas and collecting detailed information from the FEMA representatives on the ground there.[355]

They learned that, unlike DOD, FEMA did not have "detailed supply accountability and the in-transit visibility of assets."[356] There was no tracking methodology, and no one within FEMA "owned" the complete commodities-movement process.[357] They also learned that the DLA was sourcing the MREs from only two facilities,[358] where loading was additionally constrained by space limitations and material-handling equipment.[359]

Commodities Crisis in Mississippi

NORTHCOM planners had little time to study FEMA's logistics system in Louisiana because of a developing crisis in Mississippi. "We have got to get food and water [there]," Colonel Damon Penn, the DCO in Mississippi told Colonel Roberta Woods, Chief of Plans and Operations in NORTHCOM's Logistics Division on Friday, September 2.[360]

Although the logistics mission assignment was broad, DOD's logisticians knew from experience that they had to prioritize, and quickly.[361] Colonel Woods described how she and her staff, using their knowledge of the DLA distribution system, worked to speed food to Mississippi:

> I know the food's been ordered [from DLA]. I know precisely how many thousands of cases have been ordered … and I know how many have left the warehouse.
>
> We discover that trucks that were inbound to Mississippi have not arrived in Mississippi but have been diverted to Louisiana. So … using that [billion dollar] mission assignment… [we] make the call … to use airlift to get some of those MREs into Mississippi. … We coordinate airlift of about 50,000 cases of MREs into Mississippi.
>
> We put in the requirement to TRANSCOM to airlift. We put in the requirement to DLA to prepare the stocks for airlift. And on Saturday afternoon, evening, the 3rd, I think about 10,000 cases are flown into Gulfport, and on Sunday, the 4th, 40,000 cases are flown in.
>
> Simultaneously now DLA is gathering more trucks to pick up MREs and have trucks begin delivering and – and that's the shot in the arm. That surge of assets got Mississippi out of crisis mode and got routine flow into both Mississippi and Louisiana.[362]

NORTHCOM planners also retooled the way FEMA procured and transported commodities. Previously, the DLA, which supplied MREs, loaded them onto trucks that had to be arranged by the U.S. Department of Transportation (DOT).[363] The new structure gave DLA authority to contract for those trucks on its own, improving the flow of commodities to Mississippi.[364]

Distribution of Commodities in Louisiana and Mississippi

As they gathered data on how FEMA's logistics system worked, the DOD planners were still unsure how much of the system DOD was being asked to assume and whether FEMA was going to back out of logistics completely.[365] Although DOD planners believed the last stage of commodities distribution would remain in the hands of the National Guard, they were not sure whether FEMA would remain in control of the operating staging areas[366] – Camp Beauregard, Louisiana, and the three Mississippi locations – all of which stand between the warehouse and the state-controlled points of distribution in the supply chain. By Saturday,

September 3, DOD developed a plan for how DOD would run operations at those staging areas traditionally run by FEMA.[367]

As part of developing the plan, a DOD official was tasked to "map" the commodities distribution system in Louisiana and Mississippi. This is how he described the process in Louisiana as of Tuesday, September 6:

> In LA, trucks arriving at the FOSA are redirected to one of 20 State Receiving Points and from there, redirected to local Distribution Sites where the MREs, water, and ice are provided to the people of Louisiana. The Beauregard FOSA keeps records of how many trucks are directed to each State Receiving point. … FEMA management at the FOSA provides C2 [command and control, in this case over the movement of commodities into and out of the site] of the supplies and equitably distributes based on the requirements at each State Receiving Point.[368]

The DOD official explained why he saw no need for federal active-duty troops to take over handing out commodities at the end of the distribution chain: "Unloading capabilities vary significantly at final distribution sites but at that point in the supply chain it doesn't make much difference. MREs could be issued from the back of the trailer if required."[369]

DOD never had to take over for FEMA at the Operational Staging areas. The commodities situation was stabilized in Mississippi by the large movement of food by air, and commodities distribution never turned into a crisis in Louisiana.[370] NORTHCOM's Colonel Woods described DOD's role as "very much a cooperative effort. FEMA stayed in – in the chain and in the processes, and we – we put shots in the arm, is what we did."[371]

Thus, although DOD provided an important contribution to improving FEMA's logistics operations, they did not – as was originally requested – "take over" those operations from FEMA. DOD's contribution was to quickly bring to bear its expertise in planning and executing commodities movements. It was not to deploy large numbers of active duty troops to run the supply chain. In fact, large numbers of National Guard troops already deployed performed the bulk of the distribution work.

Katrina demonstrated that DOD has well-developed expertise in logistics management, but there is no reason that FEMA could not develop a similar level of proficiency.

The Second Large Group of Requests For Assistance

An extraordinary number of military assets were deployed by DOD, including assets deployed by Presidential order and by the individual services, with the expectation their capabilities would be required. When Assistant Secretary McHale notified DHS Deputy Secretary Jackson that the Secretary of Defense had approved the logistics mission assignment, he added that DOD possibly would be able to do even more.[372] Given the level of devastation on the Gulf Coast, it was clear to Assistant Secretary McHale that "a much greater level of DOD activity was going to be required."[373] On the morning of Saturday, September 3, shortly before the President announced his decision to deploy 7,200 active duty troops to Louisiana, Assistant Secretary McHale and Deputy Secretary Jackson met at the White House. According to Deputy Secretary Jackson, the President wanted "to get these troops on the ground as fast as possible, and we were determined to get the additional support missions defined with clarity and the assets that might be needed to be brought along with them to move them as quickly as possible."[374]

Meanwhile, the President had announced the deployment, and the Army and Marine forces had begun to mobilize. Deputy Secretary Jackson and Assistant Secretary McHale met later that day with Deputy Secretary England at the Pentagon to begin "aggregating and classifying and categorizing what types of mission assignment activities we thought were needed by DOD.[375] Assistant Secretary McHale reported that they then "drew up a list of approximately 10 mission areas" in which DOD help had not yet been, but was likely to be, requested.[376]

The intent, according to Deputy Secretary Jackson, was to formulate "what are we trying to accomplish, what do we need to get done, how are we going to do it?"[377] On Saturday, September 3, and the following day, DOD and DHS officials "at very senior levels"[378] drafted a group of new DOD mission assignments:[379]

- conduct search-and-rescue operations,

- perform security-capabilities assessment and provide security-capabilities advice and technical assistance,

- collect and evacuate live persons to temporary processing centers,

- collect and remove bodies of deceased persons,

- restore flood-control systems,

- transport and distribute ice, water, food and medical supplies,[380]

- disease prevention and control,

- planning for the quarantine of areas within New Orleans,

- quartering and sustaining of FEMA headquarters support element and relief workers,

- health and medical support,

- debris removal,

- restoration of basic utilities and key transportation routes (land and water),

- geospatial-surveillance products and evaluations,

- logistical support at key air and sea distribution nodes,

- temporary housing, and

- long-range communications between headquarters nodes and firefighting.[381]

Between Saturday, September 3, and Monday, September 5, as the Army and Marine troops converged upon Louisiana by air and land from Texas, North Carolina, and California, DHS and DOD officials drafted and refined seven separate Requests For Assistance derived from the broader aggregated request.[382] These seven requests, totaling an estimated cost of $805 million,[383] were approved by the Secretary of Defense the evening of September 5.[384] The next morning, Tuesday, September 6, as the convoys of troops from the 82nd Airborne Division closed on New Orleans,[385] DHS Deputy Secretary Jackson sent an e-mail to Assistant Secretary McHale thanking him "for your help with the RFAs and all other things. Very grateful."[386]

As Assistant Secretary McHale and Admiral Keating both said, many of the requests in the second DHS set "already were in active execution" on September 5, when they were officially approved by the Secretary of Defense.[387] Deputy Secretary Jackson described the process as "one of the best examples of cutting through bureaucratic red tape and getting on with the job that I participated in during the course of these first several weeks."[388]

This investigation has shown that DOD was moving assets in many respects before they were either requested by FEMA or approved by the Secretary of Defense. The record indicates that DOD logisticians were gathering information and developing a plan to execute the logistics mission assignment on Friday, September 2, prior to its oral approval by the Secretary of Defense later that same day, and prior to its formal approval on Saturday, September 3. In addition, DOD was already involved in search-and-rescue operations,[389] evacuation operations,[390] health and medical support,[391] geospatial surveillance,[392] and logistical support at key air and sea transportation nodes,[393] restoring flood control systems,[394] and transporting commodities.[395]

FEMA witnesses corroborated DOD's claim that DOD was working on the requests for assistance in advance of formal approval.[396] FEMA, DHS, and state witnesses also praised DOD for its work in response to requests from FEMA.[397] Even Deputy Federal Coordinating Officer in Louisiana, Scott Wells, who criticized DOD for taking too long to approve mission assignments, said that DOD never failed to complete a mission assignment in timely fashion.[398] Wells' superior in Louisiana, Lokey, went further, stating "I do not think any military people I was working with were delaying doing anything but leaning extremely far forward."[399] Mississippi Governor Haley Barbour described the MREs flown in with the assistance of Department of Defense personnel as a "godsend."[400]

Mississippi

On August 26, in advance of Hurricane Katrina, Mississippi Governor Haley Barbour issued Executive Order 939, activating the National Guard under the command of Major General Harold A. Cross."[401] The Mississippi National Guard has five primary missions in hurricane response: (1) search and rescue; (2) law-enforcement operations; (3) commodity distribution; (4) casualty evacuation; and (5) debris removal from roads and along major power grids.[402]

General Cross called up several National Guard units, including engineering and military-police units, which deployed to Camp Shelby, 70 miles north of the Mississippi Gulf Coast, and Camp McCain, in north central Mississippi, by Sunday, August 28, the day before landfall. About 175 other soldiers were positioned in Mississippi's three coastal counties of Hancock, Harrison, and Jackson to assist in preparation for and immediate response to the storm. That day General Cross began to order 10 more units into action. By landfall the next day, 3,088 Mississippi service members had been activated, remaining units had been placed on alert, and requests for assistance from other states had been identified.[403]

Though search-and-rescue and evacuation operations continued during and immediately after landfall, the bulk of the forces were ordered to the coast once the winds died down early Monday evening. When the level of devastation became apparent, General Cross ordered all remaining Mississippi National Guard troops into action and executed pre-planned assistance agreements from other states. General Cross also requested assistance from other states under Emergency Mutual Assistance Compact (EMAC) agreements.[404]

Through EMAC, the National Guard was able to pull together a division-size force of over 14,000 soldiers and airmen from 40 states, including Mississippi, by September 4.[405] Total out-of-state force numbers peaked at nearly 12,000 by September 12, resulting in a combined force of over 16,000.[406]

Governor Barbour "emphatically" said that he never saw a need for federal troops and was never directly asked to federalize the Mississippi National Guard.[407] General Cross also stated that he never requested federal troops.[408] However, U.S. military personnel stationed at bases in Mississippi participated in the federal response to Katrina.[409]

By Wednesday evening, August 31, the National Guard began assisting with commodity distribution and began airlifting supplies to stranded residents.[410] Colonel Benjamin "Joe" Spraggins, Director of the Harrison County Emergency Management Agency, singled out this aspect of the National Guard's response for praise.[411]

In the storm's aftermath, the National Guard also had to contend with false alarms, which diverted crucial forces, as General Cross explained:

> But the first couple of days. … I had a need to get patrols out in communities and towns where there was looting reports. By the way, a lot of this was paranoia. People would call in saying they're looting this town, they're breaking into the hospital and la, la, la. And I would send MPs up there and no such thing was happening. And then we got a couple of reports of trucks being hijacked and we would send helicopter reconnaissance and MPs to that location and you'd see trucks stopped but they weren't being hijacked, they were just refusing to drive without a military escort.[412]

General Cross said his forces also supported local law enforcement:

> We didn't go in and take charge anywhere. We would go in and report to the sheriff or the police chief or the mayor and say, "Where do you need us?" And my standing orders were that you were to have at least one sworn officer with each squad of MPs so that they actually do the arrest.[413]

In an after-action report, the Mississippi National Guard said it had:

- cleared over 3,900 miles of roadway;

- directly or indirectly assisted in over 600 rescues;

- airlifted 1.2 million MREs, 1 million gallons of water and critical medicines;

- conducted over 3,000 presence patrols, assisting in 65 arrests for crimes ranging from looting to domestic-abuse violations; and

- distributed by ground and distribution points over 39 million pounds of ice, 5.4 million gallons of water, and 2.7 million MREs in 37 counties.[414]

Deployments of National Guard and Active-Duty Military Troops

> The obligations and duties of the Guard in time of war should be carefully defined, and a system established by law under which the method of procedure of raising volunteer forces should be prescribed in advance. It is utterly impossible in the excitement and haste of impending war to do this satisfactorily if the arrangements have not been made long beforehand.
>
> *–Theodore Roosevelt, First Annual Message to Congress, Dec. 3, 1901.*[415]

Summary

In the afternoon of Monday, August 29, several hours after Katrina's landfall, Governor Blanco telephoned President Bush. "We need your help," the Governor told the President. "We need everything you've got."[416] Based on their conversation, the Governor believed the President had "every intention to send all of the resources and assistance within the power of the federal government."[417] Yet although over the next several days Governor Blanco made at least two more personal pleas to the President, by phone and in person aboard Air Force One, asking for a total of 40,000 federal troops, it was not until Saturday,

September 3, five full days after landfall, that the President ordered 7,200 Army and Marine ground forces to Louisiana.

One of the key questions about the response to Katrina is, "Why did it take so long for the President to respond to the Governor's requests for federal troops?"[418]

Unfortunately, much of the story of the President's decisions remains opaque. The White House refused to permit the Committee to interview White House personnel about the President's decision or the actions of the White House staff. DOD instructed its personnel not to discuss communications with the White House. Because the Committee has been unable to develop a complete and accurate record regarding these decisions, it is unable to make any findings regarding the President's decision to order deployment of federal active-duty troops on Saturday, September 3, including the reasons why the President did not order that deployment sooner.

Nevertheless, the Committee has extensively interviewed Louisiana, DOD, and National Guard officials about their own decisions and actions. From their recollections, the Committee has been able to assemble a picture of a rapid but uncoordinated military response to the various requests for assistance.

Two more specific findings also have emerged. First, the large numbers of National Guard troops deploying into Louisiana were a major factor in DOD's decision not to deploy additional active-duty troops into Louisiana prior to the President's deployment order.

Second, the difference in opinion between state and federal officials about whether more active-duty military ground troops should have been deployed sooner appears to stem, in part, from the lack of coordination in the formulation and consideration of the various state and federal requests for military support. Requests for troops were made to the EMAC and the National Guard Bureau within DOD. Requests for troops also were made directly to the President, White House officials, and the commander of the military forces in Louisiana, General Honoré. Other requests for military assistance were made through FEMA according to the process set forth in the NRP for requesting DOD support. Many of the state and federal requests for military support lacked adequate specificity as to the missions to be performed or the capabilities being requested. The responses to the requests for military support often were poorly coordinated with each other. One result from this lack of specificity and coordination at all levels was that local, state, and federal officials had differing perceptions of the numbers of federal troops that would be arriving, the missions they would be performing, who was in command of the military forces, and who should be in command of those forces.

Discussion

The Constitution of the United States provides for two distinct chains of command for military forces within the United States: state governors command and control the state militias; and the President is Commander-in-Chief of the armed forces of the United States. The NRP recognizes that either of these two military forces may be called upon for support in the event of a disaster or emergency: the National Guard, under the command of the governor; federal active-duty forces, under the command of DOD; and, ultimately, the President. The NRP provides for two distinct avenues for requesting these two types of military assistance.

Under the NRP, a state may request federal military support through FEMA, the agency responsible for coordinating requests for federal disaster support. Although FEMA may direct other federal agencies to perform a "mission assignment," because the Secretary of Defense is the only federal official, other than the President, who may issue an order deploying U.S. military forces, DOD considers a FEMA mission assignment to be a "request for assistance." DOD evaluates each FEMA request for assistance to determine if the request is appropriately tasked to DOD and whether DOD has the ability and assets to perform the request. If DOD approves the request, the Secretary of Defense, or his designee, issues an order to the military to provide the requested assistance to FEMA.

Within FEMA, the Federal Coordinating Officer (FCO) is responsible for coordinating the requests for support made to the various federal agencies, including DOD.[419] The FCO is stationed at the Joint Field Office (JFO), which is the temporary federal facility established after a disaster for the coordination of federal, state, and local response activities.[420] The FCO, among others, works with the DOD Defense Coordinating Officer (DCO), who is also stationed at the JFO and is responsible for coordinating and processing all requests for assistance to DOD.[421] Unless DOD establishes a different command structure for a particular disaster – which it will usually do for a major event like Katrina – the DCO will also be the on-site commander in charge of the DOD response.

FEMA issued 93 requests for specific federal military assets and capabilities to DOD; in general, DOD quickly and effectively responded to these requests.[422] None of these requests, however, involved large numbers of ground troops.[423] The DCO in Louisiana "did not ever receive any specific request for large-scale federal forces that came from the state."[424] Rather, requests for large numbers of military troops were made directly to the President, other high-ranking Administration officials, and the military commander in the field.

The lack of specificity in these requests for federal military support, and the failure to coordinate their consideration through the coordination mechanisms used for the other requests for military assistance, was one of the sources of ongoing confusion and uncertainty regarding the scope and timing of the military response. The proliferation of processes used to request National Guard troops was yet another source of confusion.

In most circumstances – unless they are "federalized" for a specific purpose – National Guard forces will be operating under the command of the governors of the states. Typically, in a disaster, state National Guard troops will be called up or activated to full-time duty by a governor into "state active-duty" status, meaning they are under the command of the governor, performing state missions, such as humanitarian relief or law enforcement, and are paid for by state funds.

National Guard troops may also be under the control of a governor when activated under 32 U.S.C. § 502(f) ("Title 32" status). This provision allows the National Guard troops to be activated by DOD to perform training or "other duty," with federal pay and benefits, yet remain under the control of the governor. Such "other duty" may include disaster-relief work or law enforcement. For example, Title 32 was used to provide federal pay and benefits to the National Guard troops who temporarily provided additional security to a number of airports after the terrorist attacks on September 11, 2001.[425]

National Guard troops under the command of a governor, either in state active duty or Title 32 status, are not subject to the prohibitions in the Posse Comitatus Act against the use of any part of the military for law enforcement.[426] In Katrina, the flexibility to use the National Guard to perform law enforcement was a significant motive for the primary reliance on the National Guard rather than active-duty military troops. The retention of this flexibility was also one of the major reasons Governor Blanco resisted attempts to "federalize" her National Guard troops – i.e., place those troops into active-duty status and under the President's command.

The President may directly activate the National Guard, or "federalize" National Guard troops already in state active duty or Title 32 status, under a variety of circumstances. Under the Insurrection Act, the President may place the National Guard into federal service to suppress an insurrection against a state government, at the request of the state; enforce federal laws in the event of "unlawful obstructions, combinations, or assemblages, or rebellion against the authority of the United States"; or to prevent an interference within the state of a constitutional right.[427] Similarly, 10 U.S.C. §12406 provides the President the authority to call into federal service the members of the National Guard in the event of an invasion by a foreign nation, a rebellion, or if the President is "unable with the regular forces to execute the laws of the United States."[428] The Insurrection Act was recently invoked in 1992, at the request of the Governor of California, to quell the Los Angeles riots, and in 1989, in response to reports of looting in St. Croix, U.S. Virgin Islands, in the wake of Hurricane Hugo.[429]

The President may also employ active-duty troops under the Insurrection Act. DOD has prepared guidance for the use of active-duty troops to perform law enforcement missions, entitled "Military Assistance for Civil Disturbances (MACDIS)." The MACDIS guidance governs "planning and response by the DOD Components for military assistance to federal, state, and local government … and their law enforcement agencies for … civil disturbance operations, including response to terrorist incidents."[430]

National Guard troops called into federal service under these authorities operate under the command of the President, receive federal pay or benefits, and are not subject to the prohibitions in the Posse Comitatus Act against the use of federal troops to perform law-enforcement activities. National Guard troops called into federal active duty under other authorities, however, are subject to the Posse Comitatus Act restrictions. These other authorities permit the President to call up the National Guard in time of war, a declared national emergency, or when otherwise authorized by law.

National Guard helicopters
flying medical evacuations
U.S. Air Force photo

The NRP states that National Guard forces under the command of the governor, either under state active duty or Title 32 status, "are providing support to the Governor of their state and are not part of federal military response efforts."[431] Accordingly, unlike requests for military assets under the control of DOD, requests for National Guard troops not under the control of the governor are not coordinated and processed through either the FCO or the DCO.[432]

In those instances in which National Guard troops from outside an affected state are needed for disaster response, a governor may use the EMAC to obtain those troops from other states. The EMAC is a congressionally approved interstate compact that permits a state to request and receive whatever type of assistance it might need from another state, including state National Guard forces, to respond to a domestic emergency.[433]

During Katrina, Louisiana began requesting National Guard assets through the EMAC process on Friday, August 26, three days before landfall. The first EMAC support – National Guard helicopters from Oklahoma – arrived in Louisiana on Monday, August 29, the day of landfall. On Tuesday, August 30, more helicopters from Texas and Oklahoma and about 230 ground troops from Florida, Georgia, and Texas arrived through the EMAC process.[434]

In Katrina, the EMAC process proved neither suitable nor capable to handle the type of large-scale deployments of troops needed in the Gulf region. The EMAC was never intended or designed to coordinate large military troop deployments. As a result, both Louisiana and Mississippi turned to the National Guard Bureau to "expedite" the deployment of National Guard troops from other states. The National Guard Bureau is the DOD entity responsible for advising the Army and Air Force on National Guard matters and communicating with state governments including state National Guards.[435] Although the National Guard Bureau successfully expedited these troop deployments, they were not well coordinated with the other military responses, thereby contributing to the confusion as to the scope and effectiveness of the overall military response.

The National Guard Bureau's application for Title 32 status for these troops recognized the unsuitability of the state-to-state EMAC process for this type of large-scale military deployment. On September 5, the Bureau requested DOD to grant Title 32 status for all of "the National Guard forces currently responding to Hurricane Katrina" under the EMAC compact, retroactive to August 29, the day of landfall.[436] "The escalation from what was a local and regional response to one of national scope, and international attention, risks exceeding the capability and intent of the EMAC," the Bureau wrote.[437] "This development compels the transition of National Guard forces from State Active Duty (SAD) status under the EMAC to a federally funded status. Title 32 maintains DOD's flexibility to utilize federally funded National Guard troops in a federal response and support-to-law enforcement role without Posse Comitatus raising issues." The Bureau stated this change was imperative, as the EMAC arrangement was not "sustainable" or a "practical solution" for the maintenance of a military force this size.[438] On September 7, DOD granted the request for Title 32 status and funding.[439]

Prior to and shortly after Katrina's landfall, federal officials also recognized the possibility that military forces may be required for law enforcement. On August 28, the Vice President's Counsel, David Addington, wrote to William Haynes, the DOD General Counsel: "Given the potential massive size of the problem there could be civil unrest during the aftermath ... you might want to have an [Insurrection Act] proclamation ... in the can in case it is needed."[440] On the morning of Wednesday, August 31, as the media reported a deterioration in civil order in New Orleans, Northern Command's Operations Director, General Rowe, advised Pentagon officials, "recommend looking at 'what if' MACDIS required."[441] Later that morning, the Joint Director of Military Support described to General Rowe the statutory and Constitutional authorities governing the use of armed forces for law enforcement. She told General Rowe that she planned to advise "senior leadership" that such action could be taken by the President invoking the Insurrection Act following either a state request through the Department of Justice, or a unilateral decision by the President.[442]

The following discussion presents the record developed by the Committee regarding the State of Louisiana's requests for large-scale deployments of troops and the responses to those requests.

Tuesday, August 30: Governor Blanco asks General Landreneau, Adjutant General of the Louisiana National Guard, to request federal military assistance

As Governor Blanco toured New Orleans by helicopter and visited the Superdome Tuesday afternoon, the need for massive federal assistance became clear and urgent. Floodwaters were spreading and rising throughout the city. The crowd of people at the Superdome was growing by the thousands, as residents flooded out of their homes flocked to dry ground and people "plucked off the roofs" from around the city were deposited there as well.[443] Tensions rose too, due to concerns over food, water, security, and the fate of separated family members. The Governor determined that the people stranded there had to be evacuated "as soon as possible." She asked Major General Bennett Landreneau, the Adjutant General of the Louisiana National Guard, for information about the location of the buses to be used for the evacuation, and instructed him to "ask for all available assistance from the National Guard and the United States Government, specifically federal military assistance."[444]

Tuesday, August 30: General Landreneau speaks to General Honoré and to General Steven Blum, Chief of the National Guard Bureau

According to General Landreneau, he quickly relayed Governor Blanco's request for military troops to General Steven Blum, Chief of the National Guard Bureau, and then to General Honoré, who later that day was appointed Commander of Joint Task Force Katrina, consisting of all the active-duty military forces in the Gulf Coast region responding to Katrina.[445] Both General Honoré and General Blum, however, stated that General Landreneau first asked them for troops on Wednesday, August 31.[446]

Although the Governor's timeline indicates that she spoke with General Landreneau regarding the need for troops following her afternoon visit to the Superdome, General Landreneau stated that in a telephone conversation with General Honoré on Tuesday morning he "conveyed the Governor's desire for federal troops, in particular an Army division headquarters to plan, coordinate, and execute the evacuation of New Orleans."[447] General Landreneau stated that on that same day he asked General Blum to help obtain thousands of National Guard troops for relief efforts in Louisiana.[448]

General Honoré recalled that he first spoke with General Landreneau sometime Tuesday evening. Although General Landreneau mentioned the need to evacuate the Superdome, his main concern was the search and rescue efforts, which required helicopters, not ground troops.[449] According to General Honoré, General Landreneau said he had already spoken to General Blum, who had assured him that "a lot of ground capacity was on the way."[450] General Honoré stated that General Landreneau did not make any "particular request" for a large deployment of federal active-duty troops.[451]

Although General Blum recalled that he spoke with General Landreneau on Tuesday evening, he was unable to recall whether General Landreneau made a specific request for troops at that time.[452]

Although recollections differ as to whether General Landreneau specifically requested military assistance during either of these conversations on Tuesday, it is nonetheless clear that as of this date the state had established two new avenues, in addition to the traditional processes through the EMAC and the DCO, for requesting military support: (1) through General Blum and the National Guard Bureau, and (2) through General Honoré, the Commander of Joint Task Force Katrina. There were now four separate avenues for requests for military support; there would be little coordination among them.

Early hours, Wednesday, August 31: Louisiana National Guard Officers discuss with General Landreneau the need for more troops

Prior to and during landfall, Louisiana National Guard Brigadier General Gary Jones and the rest of his contingent had been stationed at Jackson Barracks, the headquarters of the

Louisiana National Guard in New Orleans, but by late Monday rising floodwaters forced him and his contingent to relocate to dry ground at the Superdome.

By late Tuesday, as it became apparent the Superdome would need to be evacuated, the senior Louisiana National Guard officers at the Superdome became concerned whether they had sufficient manpower to undertake this additional responsibility.[453] Sometime between 2 a.m. and 4 a.m. on Wednesday,[454] General Jones, his deputy Brigadier General Brod Veillon, and Colonel Steve Dabadie, Chief of Staff of the Louisiana National Guard, consulted with General Landreneau in Baton Rouge. General Jones recalled the conversation:

> And I told General Landreneau that I felt like taking on the mission of evacu-
> ating all those people, in addition to the security missions and the engineer
> missions, and so forth, I had, was probably beyond the capability, not of my
> troops, but of my planning staff to execute, the people I had on the ground.
> And I asked for some support. And what he told me was they planned on
> asking for an active-duty division headquarters to come in and take over the
> evacuation. But he also gave me a key piece of information in that. And that
> was, there ain't going to be nobody get there until they get there. Until you get
> relieved of that mission, that is your mission. So from that point on I took that
> mission, and that's how we got it. And we never did give it up, because no one
> else ever stepped up to the plate to pick that thing up.[455]

Colonel Dabadie similarly remembered that General Landreneau agreed with the need for an active "division headquarters" unit – meaning a team of one or two dozen active duty personnel with expertise in planning, command, and logistics – for coordination and execution of evacuation. [456]

According to General Veillon, General Landreneau had also said, "I am ahead of you. I have already called General Blum and we have additional assets that will be arriving in the morning."[457]

7:21 a.m., Wednesday, August 31: General Landreneau asks the National Guard Bureau to expedite the deployment process for National Guard troops from other states

By Wednesday morning, Louisiana officials recognized that the EMAC process was inadequate for this catastrophe. General Landreneau telephoned General Blum and asked for his help in expediting the EMAC process to send 5,000 National Guard soldiers to Louisiana. General Blum related the conversation:

> He said that he needed 5,000 soldiers more to help, and I'm going to tell you
> at this point, it was clear in his voice that it was pretty imminent need … [H]e
> communicated some emotion over the phone that he needed it, and he needed
> it now and that he reiterated that the armory at Jackson Barracks had flooded
> and that the Louisiana National Guard command and control had been relo-
> cated to the Superdome parking lot and that the Superdome is being cut off by
> rising water, it's becoming an island.[458]

Within minutes of General Landreneau's phone call, the Army National Guard began calling and e-mailing the Adjutant Generals of the National Guards across the country to alert them of the urgent need for National Guard military police, engineers, and high-water trucks.[459] On a noon video-teleconference with the Adjutant Generals from all of the states, General Blum reiterated the immediate need for these National Guard capabilities.

The National Guard Bureau's improvised process proved extremely effective in mobilizing tens of thousands of National Guard troops and assets. The process that began Wednesday

510

morning resulted in the deployment of over 30,000 National Guard troops within approximately 96 hours.[460] Partially as a result of their rapid deployment, however, most of the National Guard troops dispatched to Louisiana through this process did not know what their mission would be or where it would be performed until they arrived in Louisiana. The deployment process was "P for plenty," according to General Vaughn. "There was not a lot of preciseness."[461]

Table 1: Activated National Guard Personnel Serving in Louisiana and Mississippi [462]

Date	Number Serving in Louisiana			Number Serving in Mississippi		
	Louisiana National Guard Personnel	National Guard Personnel from Other States	Total	Mississippi National Guard Personnel	National Guard Personnel from Other States	Total
Aug. 30	5,804	178	5,982	3,822	16	3,838
Aug. 31	5,804	663	6,467	3,822	1,149	4,971
Sept. 1	5,804	2,555	8,359	3,823	2,861	6,684
Sept. 2	6,779	5,445	12,224	3,823	3,719	7,542
Sept. 3	6,779	10,635	17,414	3,823	6,314	10,137
Sept. 4	6,779	12,404	19,183	4,017	9,399	13,416
Sept. 5	6,779	16,162	22,941	4,017	10,999	15,016
Sept. 6	6,779	20,510	27,289	4,023	11,095	15,118
Sept. 7	6,779	22,589	29,368	4,023	11,388	15,411
Sept. 8	6,779	23,476	30,255	4,023	11,506	15,529

Source: Congressional Research Service, Hurricane Katrina: DOD Disaster Response, January 24, 2006, p. 12.

Although the National Guard Bureau's mission was to expedite the EMAC process, the deployments initiated from the Bureau were not well coordinated with the EMAC process. As the National Guard Bureau's Draft After Action Review found, National Guard forces were deployed "piece meal" into and out of Louisiana and Mississippi, and in many cases the Bureau's process overlapped the EMAC process, "causing confusion and duplicated efforts."[463] The review concluded, "the large-scale and sustained operations required for this disaster requires a more systematic approach."[464]

Even at the outset of the deployment process, the National Guard Bureau recognized the need for the National Guard to deploy a robust command and control capability along with the large number of troops that would be flowing into the state. General Blum immediately determined that additional command and control capability was needed in both Louisiana and Mississippi because National Guard combat brigades from each of those states were in Iraq.[465] Headquarters elements from the 35th Infantry Division in Kansas deployed into Louisiana and from the 38th Infantry Division in Indiana deployed into Mississippi.[466] "Both of these divisions had served in Bosnia and Kosovo and knew how to do Ph.D. level command and control elements," Lt. Gen Blum explained.[467] They began arriving in theater on Friday, September 2.[468] General Blum stated that command and control improved immediately afterwards.

Once they were on the ground, the command and control improved 100 percent in less than 24 hours. I mean, it started coming together. That's the only place where I wish I had been a little faster on the trigger shooting those guys downrange, because they brought a great capability that was very well needed, because frankly, the guys that were there were getting tired. It was like bringing in, you know, the relief team.[469]

The National Guard deployment process was not well coordinated with the command of the active-duty military forces either. Assistant Secretary McHale testified to the Congress, "Military command and control was workable, but not unified. National Guard planning, though superbly executed, was not well integrated with the Joint Staff in NORTHCOM."[470]

Senior DOD officers also expressed concern that the rapid, poorly coordinated state-to-state EMAC deployments, in effect "preempted" a large part of DOD's role to coordinate the overall military response in the event of a domestic catastrophe. General Rowe, Director of Operations at NORTHCOM, observed that although this process provided "incredible amounts of manpower," there was no integration or tasking of these forces until they arrived in the state. "It's a heck of a way to do military business," General Rowe commented.[471] Admiral Keating, Commander of NORTHCOM, stated that in a catastrophic event NORTHCOM, on behalf of DOD, should have a greater control over the deployment process.[472] Former Joint Chiefs of Staff Chairman General Myers agreed with both of these observations.[473]

9:30 a.m., Wednesday, August 31: General Honoré meets with General Landreneau and General Jones at the Superdome

General Honoré arrived at the Superdome at around 9:30 a.m. on Wednesday to assess the deteriorating conditions.[474] "When I got there Wednesday morning," General Honoré recalled, "it was hell."[475]

General Honoré informed General Landreneau about some of the military assets that were en route, including U.S. Navy ships, but there was no discussion of ground troops at this meeting.[476] General Honoré then met with New Orleans Mayor Ray Nagin, and Scott Wells, the FEMA Deputy FCO in Louisiana. Wells was the senior FEMA representative at the Superdome, reporting to William Lokey. They discussed how to evacuate the Superdome. Wells asked General Honoré if he could take the lead for the evacuation. According to Wells, General Honoré replied, "Whoa, wait a minute, I need to get my people here and then we'll talk later."[477]

As this exchange between Wells and General Honoré reflects, neither FEMA nor Louisiana officials had a clear understanding of General Honoré's role and capabilities. Phil Parr, the head of one of FEMA's emergency-response teams that was sent into Louisiana, was under the incorrect impression that General Honoré had been placed in charge of the Superdome evacuation.[478] He also was disappointed that General Honoré had not brought more troops: "He had no troops on the ground to do what needed to be done early on."[479]

State officials also did not have a clear understanding of the capabilities under General Honoré's command. General Landreneau stated, "I was expecting troops to arrive."[480] Other Louisiana National Guard officers echoed this expectation.[481]

General Honoré acknowledged that others may have misinterpreted his initial presence as the vanguard of a much larger military deployment of ground troops. General Honoré explained, however, that this was not a classic military operation, where a commanding general appears at the battlefront only in the presence of a large number of troops:

> In a classic military operation, I would have sat here in Atlanta and put a brigadier or a major general in Camp Shelby and maybe send a brigadier to New Orleans and to Biloxi. That's the classic. The general will sit back, get the feeds in from the troops. … So in this case, I reversed a paradigm. I left my staff at home and went forward on the battlefield, which may have given a perception to people when they saw me that all the federal troops were there, which was not the case. And I never [pretended] that that was the fact when I got there, but people come up with their own assumptions. Well, damn, if the general is here, his troops must be outside the city. … This is a humanitarian operation, not an attack on a foreign country where it gets secured and then the general comes in.[482]

Immediately after he found out that General Landreneau had made a direct request to General Honoré for federal military troops, Wells explained to Colonel Jeff Smith, General Landreneau's deputy at the Louisiana Office of Homeland Security and Emergency Preparedness, how this direct request to General Honoré disrupted the "unified command" the state and FEMA were trying to achieve – i.e., a coordinated process for requesting assistance and directing response activities:

> And I said, the state does not go to DOD directly, you're supposed to come to [FEMA], we will go to DOD to get whatever support you need. … That breaks – that not only violates protocol, but it breaks the whole unified-command approach, when you go out to another agency and then this three-star general just shows up.[483]

Morning, Wednesday, August 31: Governor Blanco calls the White House to ask for "significant resources"

According to the Governor's timeline:

> Governor Blanco places an urgent morning call to the White House in an effort to reach President Bush and express the need for significant resources. She is unable to reach President Bush or his Chief of Staff, Andrew Card. A later phone call reaches Maggie Grant in the White House Office of Intergovernmental Affairs. The Governor receives a call from Homeland Security Advisor Frances Townsend. Andrew Card returns her call too, and she requests his help in getting the promised FEMA buses into the New Orleans area.[484]

As the following events demonstrate, the transmission of the state's request for resources directly to the White House does not appear to have expedited the response to the state, at least with respect to federal military resources. White House officials did not understand what the Governor was requesting. There also appears to have been poor coordination between the White House and FEMA. Even after the Governor clarified the nature of her request directly with the President – that she wanted federal troops but not "federalization" – Brown continued to advocate to the White House that the response be "federalized." Additionally, Brown does not appear to have consulted with DOD regarding the need for federalization, either prior to or after advocating that position to the White House.

12:43 p.m., Wednesday, August 31: U.S. Senator David Vitter of Louisiana informs Terry Ryder, Executive Counsel to Governor Blanco, of a conversation with Karl Rove, White House Deputy Chief of Staff, regarding Rove's comments on "federalization"

In addition to former White House Chief of Staff Andrew Card, it appears that Governor Blanco's request to White House Homeland Security Advisor Townsend was passed along to Deputy Chief of Staff Karl Rove. Senator Vitter relayed to Ryder that Rove "understands that the Governor is asking to federalize the evacuation piece."[485] The Committee has been unable to determine what Rove's understanding at this time may have been regarding the Governor's request – whether he believed the Governor was seeking federal assistance in evacuating the Superdome, or seeking federal control of the evacuation.

2:30 p.m., Wednesday, August 31: Governor Blanco tells President Bush she does not want "federalization"

According to Ryder, immediately after he relayed Sen. Vitter's conversation with Rove to Governor Blanco, the Governor telephoned President Bush to clarify her request – she wanted federal assistance, but did not want to give up her command of the National Guard troops within the state. [486]

According to Ryder's notes, the Governor made it clear she did not want to "federalize" the evacuation. "I'm not asking for federalization," the Governor told the President. "It's not a federalization request."[487] Rather, the Governor told the President she wanted "to be a partner in a unified command."[488] Under a "unified command," the Governor would remain in command of the National Guard troops, and the President would be in command of the active-duty forces. Ryder also reported that the Governor also told the President, "We have a communication problem and [it] needs improvement."[489] The Governor repeated her request for federal military assistance.[490] At the Committee's hearing, when asked whether she was seeking National Guard or active-duty troops, Governor Blanco replied, "It was both. We needed troops."[491]

Mid-afternoon, Wednesday, August 31: FEMA officials consider federalization

At about the same time that the Governor informed the President that she did not want federalization, senior FEMA officials began discussing it. Lokey recalled a conversation with Brown:

> I remember going to Michael Brown and saying, this is beyond me, this is beyond FEMA, this is beyond the state. We need to, and I used the term, we need to federalize this or get a massive military invasion in here to get some help. And Mike said, "I'll talk to headquarters. I'll talk to DHS about that and I'll talk to the attorneys."[492]

Lokey told the Committee staff he did not understand what he meant when he used the term "federalization":

> I don't exactly know what I meant. What I meant was that – what I was talking about was turning this over to somebody that can manage something this size. I've never done something like this. I was trying my best. I wasn't doing very good at it. So that was just a term I used.[493]

Brown confirmed Lokey's account. [494] On Wednesday, Brown concluded that FEMA, state, and local capabilities were inadequate. He stated that Louisiana, "for whatever reason – culture, their system, their lack of resources," was "dysfunctional."[495] In Brown's view, the inability to establish a unified command was evidence of this dysfunction:

> There was not a unified command yet. The Governor was overwhelmed, and the Governor didn't have a good decision-making process set up around her where she could make decisions; bless her heart. I mean, it really bugged me. She had too many people coming in telling her what she needed to do, from

U.S. Senators all the way down to, I mean, I don't know who they were, just showing up in her little room coming in just hodgepodge saying, you need to be doing this and that and everything else.

And you just can't have that. You need to have a unified command where that stuff comes in and gets sorted out, and then [LOHSEP Acting Deputy Director] Jeff Smith or somebody comes in and says, Governor, here are your decision points, you need to go to X, or Y, or Z and make those.[496]

Brown stated that he recommended the entire response be "federalized," meaning that the President invoke the Insurrection Act and place the National Guard under the control of the active-duty forces:

Because at that time, we're looking at these stories of shootings and looting and everything else going on, and I'm fearful that's spiraling out of control, and I want active-duty troops that are ready, willing and able to kill in that area, because we can't do search and rescue with that kind of stuff going on.[497]

Brown stated that he telephoned either White House Chief of Staff Andrew Card or Deputy Chief of Staff Joe Hagin to recommend federalization of the response in Louisiana. "I had conversations that said, Andy, we need to federalize this thing."[498]

Although Brown told the Committee that for the next 72 hours he was a "strong advocate" of this position[499] – i.e., that a "massive military" involvement was necessary, including active-duty ground troops that were "ready, willing and able to kill" – there is scant evidence that he or anyone else in FEMA discussed this view with DOD. It appears that he did not discuss this issue with General Honoré, who told the Committee that nobody had ever expressed to him any need for active-duty ground troops.[500] Furthermore, it apparently was not until the next day, Thursday, September 1, that FEMA began discussing with DOD the need for DOD to take over the logistics mission.[501]

Assistant Secretary McHale stated that possibly as early as Wednesday, officials in the Pentagon began considering what role the military should play in restoring order, and whether active-duty troops should be used for law enforcement activities in addition to the 4,200 National Guard military police who were already deploying to the region.[502] On Saturday, September 3, the President ordered the deployment of 7,200 active-duty troops from the Army and the Marine Corps to Louisiana. Assistant Secretary McHale explained that they were sent "not for the purposes of law enforcement, but for … humanitarian relief. It was clear, however, that … they would be available and readily deployable for law enforcement-related missions if the President, under the Insurrection Act, were to use his statutory and Constitutional authority, to reassign those units for purposes of enforcing constitutional rights or other provisions of federal law."[503]

Mid-afternoon, Wednesday, August 31: Governor Blanco tells FEMA Director Brown and Louisiana Federal Coordinating Officer Lokey she does not want federalization

According to Lokey, "within an hour" of his conversation with Brown about federalization, Governor Blanco requested to see him. "What's this about you taking over my disaster?" she asked Lokey.[504] Governor Blanco later explained that she objected to federalization because it could have subjected the state's National Guard troops to the Posse Comitatus Act prohibition against federal troops conducting law enforcement activities.[505] "I did not want the Guard federalized," Governor Blanco testified. "It's very important for a governor to be able to retain control of the National Guard precisely for its law enforcement capabilities."[506]

Louisiana officials also believed there was no need to federalize the Guard. "Let me remind you the state is still sovereign," a member of the Governor's staff told Lokey and Brown. "We can handle it," General Landreneau added. [507] "Fine, good," Brown said.[508]

6 p.m., Wednesday, August 31: Governor Blanco asks General Honoré to coordinate the evacuation of New Orleans.

Late Wednesday afternoon, General Honoré arrived at the State Emergency Operation Center (EOC) in Baton Rouge, and met with Governor Blanco and General Landreneau. They discussed the state's priority missions, particularly search and rescue and the evacuation of New Orleans and the surrounding area. FEMA Director Brown was also present.[509] "Federalization" was not discussed. Governor Blanco asked General Honoré "to coordinate the evacuation efforts in New Orleans, so that General Landreneau can concentrate on saving lives, search and rescue, and law and order issues."[510]

In the midst of this discussion, General Graham, Deputy Commander of Fifth U.S. Army, arrived at the EOC, after driving seven hours from his headquarters in San Antonio, TX. General Graham brought with him 24 other personnel from Fifth Army headquarters for the purpose of providing support to the DCO in Baton Rouge. [511] Shortly after General Graham joined the discussion about the state's priorities, General Honoré turned to him and said, "Mark, evacuate the City of New Orleans and the Greater New Orleans area." "Yes, sir," General Graham replied.[512]

Again, the principal participants in these conversations expressed differing perceptions and expectations as to the numbers and types of military troops that would be following. Governor Blanco and General Landreneau appear to have been under the impression that General Honoré would use a large number of federal troops to conduct the evacuation; General Honoré believed large numbers of additional active-duty troops were not needed for this mission. At the very least, the persistence of these differing expectations and perceptions amongst these principals appears to indicate a failure in communication among the principals and among the various organizations they represented.

According to the Governor's timeline, the Governor asked General Honoré "if he brought a large number of soldiers, and learns that he arrived with only a small support staff. The evacuation must be conducted by National Guard troops, as the federal contingent has not arrived."[513]

General Landreneau told the Committee, "The Governor was very clear that she needed troops on the ground, that she needed a federal assistance. … She said she needed – she was using the number 40,000 and she was saying she needed soldiers, she needed boots on the ground."[514] General Landreneau added, however, that the Governor never specified which type of troops she was seeking. "I don't recall her ever defining or differentiating between active or National Guard. She wanted the help."[515]

General Landreneau recalled General Honoré "stating that he was aware that the National Guard EMAC forces were going to be flowing into the state."[516] "I don't recall the Governor ever saying that's not good enough," General Landreneau stated.[517]

Similarly, General Honoré did not recall the Governor's making any specific request for more federal ground troops.[518] Nor did General Honoré believe additional federal ground troops were necessary to meet the state's priorities. "The National Guard was flowing a lot of troops in there. And at the point in time, the priority mission was search and rescue."[519] General Honoré believed that for the search-and-rescue mission he needed "thousands of helicopters, not troops," and that for the Superdome evacuation mission he needed buses.

Based on this assessment of the resources needed to accomplish these missions, General Honoré did not request additional federal ground troops.[520]

Likewise, General Graham did not believe he needed additional troops. "I needed buses," General Graham said.[521] Shortly after enough buses were located, General Graham and his team coordinated the efforts of the Louisiana National Guard, Louisiana State Police, and other supporting agencies – whose personnel were already present – to actually conduct evacuations of the Superdome, the I-10 overpass, and the Convention Center.

6:05 p.m., Wednesday, August 31: General Richard Rowe, NORTHCOM, informs General Honoré that Governor Blanco is asking for federal active-duty troops

In an e-mail sent at 6:05 p.m., Major General Richard Rowe, Director of Operations at NORTHCOM, sought General Honoré's views on the Governor's requests for "federal troops":

> There should be calls coming your way. There is a desire to concentrate National Guardsmen into [New Orleans] for [law-enforcement]/security tasks. Governor has asked that federal troops pick up rest of the tasks being uncovered by Guard in state. Thoughts? What does this mean in terms of scale? Type capabilities?[522]

6:23 p.m., Wednesday, August 31: General Honoré's staff informs General Rowe there are enough National Guard troops

Replying to General Rowe, Colonel James Hickey, General Honoré's Executive Officer, wrote that "[We] think there are enough ARNG [Army National Guard] Soldiers and volunteers to perform all these missions," but that General Honoré would try to obtain more information about the state's request while in Baton Rouge that evening.[523]

8:40 p.m., Wednesday, August 31: DOD puts ground troops on alert

At 8:40 p.m., Army Forces Command put several of its forces with rapid-deployment ability on high alert ("Be Prepared to Deploy" status):[524] the 82nd Airborne Division of XVIII Airborne Corps, which describes its mission as, "Within 18 hours of notification, the 82nd Airborne Division strategically deploys, conducts forcible entry parachute assault and secures key objectives for follow-on military operations in support of U.S. national interests;"[525] and the 1st Cavalry Division of III Corps, which describes itself as the "Army's largest division and only armored contingency force, ready to deploy anywhere in the world on a moment's notice."[526]

Thursday, September 1: President Bush meets with Secretary of Defense Rumsfeld and General Blum to discuss the military response [527]

The Committee has been unable to obtain any details about this meeting.

11:46 a.m., Thursday, September 1: General Honoré tells General Rowe National Guard troops are sufficient

After meeting with Governor Blanco and General Landreneau the previous evening, General Honoré again informed General Rowe that he did not believe additional federal ground troops were necessary. Personally responding to General Rowe, General Honoré wrote:

> PUSH BACK. I WILL SEE GOV TODAY. WILL SHOW HER FLOW OF NG TROOPS. NG HAS GROUND FIGHT IN HAND WITH [24,000] IN NEXT R6 HOURS.[528]

General Blum confirmed that he and General Honoré were in agreement that the number of National Guard troops in the state and on the way was adequate:

> When I went down there on one of my trips, and we actually sat down on two buckets under a tree and we had a conversation, I mean, between the two of us saying hey, this is what I got coming down here, Russ, and he's going, It sounds right; it sounds good.[529]

1:46 p.m., Thursday, September 1: General Honoré urges Marines to "GET HERE AS FAST AS YOU CAN"

Early Thursday afternoon, General Honoré exchanged e-mail messages with General James Amos, Commander, II Marine Expeditionary Force, urging him to get to the New Orleans area as quickly as possible, along with the various assets he had placed aboard Navy amphibious ships that were steaming toward the Gulf Coast region. "HELLO BROTHER. GET HERE AS FAST AS YOU CAN," General Honoré wrote.[530] General Honoré explained to the Committee that he desired the capability that the Marines were bringing which included search-and-rescue helicopters, airspace command and control, and ground troops to assist with search and rescue and delivery of food and water. [531]

At the Committee's hearing, Senator Levin asked whether General Honoré's request for the Marines to deploy into New Orleans was inconsistent with the "push back" to the Governor's request for more active-duty troops. Admiral Keating, Commander of NORTH-COM, responded that it was his understanding the Governor was seeking military police, for which active-duty troops would have been unsuitable due to the restrictions in the Posse Comitatus Act, whereas General Honoré was seeking the particular capabilities the Marines could bring, such as helicopters and troops to conduct search and rescue.[532] However, General Rowe's e-mail of the previous day indicated that the Governor was seeking federal active-duty troops to perform non-law-enforcement activities so the National Guard troops could concentrate on law-enforcement activities.

General Honoré stated that there "wasn't a big cry for federal ground troops" at the time he wrote the e-mail,[533] but that on Friday, he believed additional active-duty ground forces would be helpful.[534] The record therefore remains unclear why the Marines were preparing to deploy ground troops at the same time that DOD officers were stating there was a sufficient number of National Guard troops on the ground.

1:50 p.m., Thursday, September 1: General Rowe tells General Honoré the official DOD guidance is to use National Guard forces to the fullest extent possible

Continuing the e-mail chain regarding the Governor's general desire for federal troops, General Rowe reports back to General Honoré:

> Guidance is "guard" in NO and "guard" to fullest extent possible for tasks in LA and MS. NGB [National Guard Bureau] supports. EMAC working. OSD [Office of Secretary of Defense] and CJCS [Chairman Joint Chiefs of Staff] agree with this.[535]

This DOD position is reflected in the DOD Strategy for Homeland Defense and Civil Support, which in the first instance relies upon the National Guard and military reserves for civil-support missions.[536] "The National Guard has more than three centuries of experience in dealing with domestic response," Assistant Secretary McHale explained. "It makes sense to use active-duty military forces primarily for overseas missions, war fighting missions, and to rely on Reserve component capabilities, most especially the National Guard, for homeland defense and civil support."[537]

The Chairman of the Joint Chiefs of Staff, General Myers, confirmed that this e-mail accurately reflected DOD's view, at the time, that in light of the large numbers of National Guard troops flowing into the region, there was not a need for additional active-duty troops.[538]

3:30 p.m., Thursday, September 1: Governor Blanco meets with General Honoré

The Governor's timeline does not mention this meeting;[539] General Honoré does not recall any request for federal troops at this meeting.[540]

7:45 p.m., Thursday, September 1: Rear Admiral Robert F. Duncan, U.S. Coast Guard, urges Governor Blanco to federalize the response

Early Thursday evening, Rear Admiral Robert F. Duncan, Commander, Eighth Coast Guard District, recommended to the Governor that she "federalize" the response. Terry Ryder, Executive Counsel to Governor Blanco, described Admiral Duncan's advice:

> He had been in the field with his folks on helicopters. He had one change of clothes. Many of the people – his house was under water. … He was having to use a Coast Guard credit card to buy water. He was mad at Mike Brown. That is why he was there. He ran into the Governor. While he is talking to the Governor, he does tell her … we need to get armed people on the street. He advised her to federalize, which that time was kind of clear he wanted to bring in the Department of Defense people forces.[541]

The record is not clear whether Admiral Duncan was recommending that additional DOD forces be brought in or, in addition, that the state National Guard troops be placed under federal command, as is suggested by the term "federalize."

9:20 p.m., Thursday, September 1: General Blum urges Governor Blanco not to federalize the response

On Thursday evening Governor Blanco met with General Blum. They discussed troop levels and the appropriate command-and-control structure for the military forces in the state. The Governor told General Blum that although she was "very happy" with the response of the National Guard, she was still not satisfied because she needed an additional 30,000 troops – to make a total of 40,000 troops within the state – and very few active-duty forces had arrived.[542] General Blum committed to work with General Landreneau to get the capabilities that the state needed, although General Blum did not believe that would necessarily entail 30,000 more ground troops.[543]

General Blum also recommended against placing the state National Guard forces under federal control. General Blum told the Governor and her staff that federalization was "not necessary to receive more federal assets," and "would have significantly limited [the state's] capacity to conduct law-enforcement missions."[544] He recommended the continuation of the joint command structure, whereby General Landreneau would continue to command the National Guard forces, and General Honoré would continue to command the active-duty forces.

Early mid-morning, Friday, September 2: Department of Defense officials discuss how to obtain greater federal control over the response in Louisiana

The Administration spent much of Friday, September 2, searching for ways to assert greater federal control over the response in Louisiana.[545] These efforts began with a series of meetings at the Pentagon involving Secretary of Defense Rumsfeld, Chairman of the Joint Chiefs of Staff General Myers, Assistant Secretary McHale, and Lieutenant General James Conway,

Director of Operations for the Joint Staff. According to DOD documents, the discussions concerned various options for gaining greater federal control over the military forces in Louisiana, including the National Guard forces. These options included use of the Insurrection Act and the designation of a single military officer to be in command of both the National Guard and active duty forces – a so-called "dual hat" commander.[546]

On several recent occasions prior to Katrina, DOD and several states had used a dual-hat commander to integrate the operations of the National Guard and active-duty forces.

The single dual-hat officer reported to the Governor when exercising command and control over the National Guard forces, and to the President when exercising command and control over the active-duty forces. This structure was employed at the 2004 Democratic and Republican National Conventions, and the 2004 G-8 Summit, where both active-duty and National Guard forces worked together to provide security.

Although the Committee was not able to interview White House officials about the President's actions or decisions, the military advantages of the dual-hat command structure – an integrated command structure for all of the military forces in the region – appear to have been a significant motivation underlying DOD's support for the proposal. Both General Myers and Assistant Secretary McHale advocated the dual-hat approach. For General Myers, establishing a single chain of command for all military forces was "a basic tenet of how we like to do our business."[547] At the time, Assistant Secretary McHale also supported the proposal because it would provide a more integrated command structure. According to Assistant Secretary McHale, he recommended the dual-hat command to the Secretary of Defense, who "reviewed that recommendation, concurred in that recommendation, and took it to the President for the President's consideration."[548]

Late morning, Friday, September 2: President Bush and Governor Blanco discuss the deployment of federal troops

President Bush arrived aboard Air Force One at the New Orleans Louis Armstrong Airport late Friday morning. Mayor Nagin, FEMA Director Brown, General Blum, White House Chief of Staff Card, White House Deputy Chief of Staff Hagin, Louisiana Senators Landrieu and Vitter, and several Louisiana congressmen were present for an initial meeting with the President and Governor Blanco. After the initial meeting, President Bush and Governor Blanco met privately.[549]

Aboard Air Force One, late Friday morning, September 2: Mayor Nagin recommends the federal government assume control

During the initial meeting aboard Air Force One, Mayor Nagin recommended that General Honoré be placed in charge.[550] Mayor Nagin testified:

> I probably was a bit pushy at that meeting, because in the midst of all the rhetoric that was going on around the table, I stopped everyone and basically said, "Mr. President, Madame Governor, if the two of you don't get together on this issue, more people are going to die in this city, and you need to resolve this immediately." And they said yes. And I said, "Well, everybody else in this room, let's leave and let them work this out right now."[551]

Aboard Air Force One, late Friday morning, September 2: Governor Blanco asks President Bush for more troops and rejects federalization

Still aboard Air Force One, Governor Blanco, President Bush, and Deputy White House Chief of Staff Hagen met privately for about 30 to 45 minutes. Governor Blanco again pressed the President for federal troops, as only about 13,000 of the 40,000 troops that she had requested had arrived. "I needed people," the Governor testified.[552] The President raised the issue whether the National Guard forces should be placed under federal command; the Governor made her position "very clear" that she did not want to give up her authority over the National Guard. "I told the President that the proper way to do business would be for me as governor to retain control of the National Guard and for him to simply send troops in."[553] The Governor told the President that if she changed her mind, she'd let him know within 24 hours.[554]

Approximately a week later, the New Orleans *Times-Picayune* reported what happened at that meeting as follows:

> After the session with Blanco, the President invited Nagin into his office and told the mayor that he was "ready to move today" on the troop deployments and had offered two command options to Blanco, Nagin said. The mayor did not identify the options. However, the President said Blanco wanted 24 hours to make a decision, according to Nagin, who later roasted the governor in national TV interviews for the delay: "It would have been great if we could have left Air Force One, walked outside, and told the world that we had this all worked out," Nagin told an interviewer. "It didn't happen, and more people died."[555]

The Committee has attempted to determine whether the deployment of federal troops was delayed in order to give the Governor time to reconsider her position on the Administration's proposal. On Friday, September 2, active-duty ground forces were prepared to deploy,[556] but the President did not issue the deployment order until late Saturday morning.

Both the White House[557] and the Governor's office[558] deny that this decision to deploy these or other active-duty ground troops was delayed by the President's request or the Governor's refusal to accede. General Blum, who was aboard Air Force One Friday morning as well, has said that this was also his impression.[559]

General Myers told the Committee that from a military perspective, it was necessary to establish the command-and-control structure before a sizeable number of troops would be deployed.[560] Then-FEMA Director Brown told the Committee that he and other Administration officials told the Governor that troops could be deployed more quickly if there were a more unified military command – i.e. all under federal control – but the President's request for greater authority over the military forces within the state was not part of any type of "carrot and stick" approach toward the Governor.[561] Because the White House has refused to permit White House officials to be interviewed by the Committee, and DOD officials have refused to discuss their conversations with White House officials, the Committee's record on this issue is incomplete.

Late afternoon, Friday, September 2: Pentagon officials continue to discuss options for assuming greater command of the response.

Throughout Friday, DOD officials continued to analyze various options for strengthening the federal response. These options included (1) invoking the Insurrection Act as a basis for asserting federal control over all of the military forces in the region, (2) appointing an active-duty officer to be "dual-hat" commander of both the National Guard and active duty forces, and (3) "Beef up FEMA," presumably meaning provide additional support to FEMA.[562]

11:32 p.m., Friday, September 2: White House faxes "dual-hat" proposal to Governor Blanco

Late Friday night, the White House faxed to the Governor a proposal, accompanied by a draft letter prepared for the Governor to transmit to the President, that would have established General Honoré as a dual-hat officer, providing him with command and control over the Louisiana National Guard, reporting to the Governor, while retaining command and control over active-duty forces in Louisiana, reporting through the DOD chain of command to the President.

The White House dual-hat proposal faxed to the Governor differed from the dual-hat commands used for the G-8 Summit and the 2004 political conventions in that in those previous instances, the dual-hat commander was a state National Guard officer who was placed into active-duty (Title 10) status for the purpose of also exercising command and control over the active-duty forces. The President's dual-hat proposal to Governor Blanco would have placed an active-duty officer rather than a National Guard federal officer in the dual-hat position. This active-duty officer would have exercised command and control over both the active-duty forces, acting under a chain of command that reported to the President, and command and control of the National Guard forces, reporting to Governor Blanco. The proposal also provided that in the event of a conflict, the federal chain of command would prevail.

Terry Ryder, the Governor's Executive Counsel, received the fax when it arrived at the Executive Mansion in Baton Rouge, near midnight:

> What happens is that fax comes in and I looked at it and realized it was an arrangement which was in the direction of so called federalization. … I immediately called the Governor. … I believe I told her I wanted to pull all of her senior advisors together immediately, and this is probably about midnight, to have them all look at it and to get back to her after we read that in the MOU. … I woke them all up and brought them back to the OEP and we all read it, brainstormed for a while, and at some point …we called the Governor back and said, "Governor, this is the so called federalization and this is what it does," and in that conversation with Landreneau, with [former FEMA Director James Lee]Witt, we refreshed our recollection on Gen. Blum's conversation on the night before.[563]

Andy Kopplin, Governor Blanco's Chief of Staff, told the Committee the Governor's immediate reaction:

> The Governor said, I'm not signing anything in the middle of the night. You guys do a thorough review of the issues surrounding it. … If it could save lives and deliver more resources, that's something that I would want to do.[564]

Later that night, Kopplin spoke to White House Chief of Staff Card. According to Kopplin, Card said, "They'd like the Governor to sign this letter asking for this [agreement]." Kopplin also said, "He indicated that it would improve coordination and speed the delivery of federal assets."[565]

Card and General Blum also spoke to Governor Blanco.[566] Governor Blanco told General Blum that she "certainly didn't want to make midnight decisions, even though I happened to be very wide awake."[567] When asked whether she felt "under pressure at that point, as compared to the conversation with the President earlier in the day," Governor Blanco answered, "Well, it was a very different kind of pressure, but I still told him no. … I was very definitive, sir. There was never a question in my mind as to the lines of authority."[568]

General Blum related that Governor Blanco never wavered from the position that she remained in charge of the National Guard forces in Louisiana:

The bottom line of it is there were many offers and overtures made to the Governor on command and control, but they all centered on a Federal officer being in charge of the Governor's National Guard, and that was rejected. It was offered by several messengers, and it was sent in various forms or variations. But the option was always – the bottom part of the option, the overriding piece of the option never deviated from it will be a federal officer that will be in charge of your National Guard and the federal troops that are there, and the Governor rejected the offer.[569]

8:56 a.m., Saturday, September 3: Governor Blanco telephones White House Chief of Staff Card to reject the dual-hat proposal

"In retrospect," Assistant Secretary McHale testified, "I'm glad that we did not invoke either a dual-hatted commander or the statutory authority under the Insurrection Act." He explained that "in a crisis environment, I think it's almost inevitable that a president and a governor will have differences of opinion. To put an officer in the crossfire between the two of them I think is untenable."[570]

11 a.m., Saturday, September 3: The President announces the deployment of 7,200 active-duty forces from the 82nd Airborne, 1st Cavalry, and II Marine Expeditionary Force[571]

These active-duty forces were placed under the command of General Honoré, and the National Guard forces remained under the command of Governor Blanco and General Landreneau.

Governor Blanco testified that she never needed these federal troops for law enforcement: "I had the National Guard for that."[572] Assistant Secretary McHale stated that DOD considered that these troops would be a contingency if additional forces were required to supplement the National Guard Military Police for law enforcement. But the President did not invoke the Insurrection Act, and the active-duty troops were never called to perform law enforcement. Rather they performed numerous other humanitarian missions, including door-to-door search and rescue, debris removal, and logistics support. Moreover, their mere presence had a reassuring effect, according to many witnesses. "That was a recognition by people that the administration and the nation was responding," said Colonel Terry Ebbert, the Director of Homeland Security for the City of New Orleans.[573]

Two days later, Admiral Keating expressed his confidence in the dual-command structure for the National Guard and active-duty forces. In response to a question about "what advantage or disadvantage federalizing the operation would have meant," Admiral Keating stated:

> From our perspective it would not have provided an advantage over our current situation. I think this is a topic of, I know it's a topic of discussion between the President, the Attorney General, the Secretary of Defense, and Secretary Chertoff, but from this headquarters through General Honoré. … We're satisfied with the current command and control arrangement where the Governors of Mississippi and Louisiana exercised their constitutional prerogative of control of the National Guard, and Russ Honoré as Joint Task Force Katrina's commander has command of the active-duty forces.[574]

Conclusion

To a large degree, the divergence of opinion between state and federal officials on the federal military response to troop-deployment requests appears to be the result of the ad-hoc processes by which the large-scale requests for troops were made and evaluated. The process envisioned by the NRP for requesting DOD assistance was not used for the large-scale requests for military troops. Instead, these requests were made through a variety of other channels, both state and federal. The requests were not specific; the responses were not coordinated. Communication among all of the entities involved in this issue ranged from poor to non-existent. It therefore is no surprise that there has never been a "meeting of the minds" on DOD's responsiveness to the state requests.

The Katrina response, as detailed in this section, indicates the need for better coordination between the states and the principal federal agencies involved in coordinating the military response – DOD, DHS, and FEMA. This response also indicates the need to better coordinate the responses of the military forces under the different state and federal commands – the National Guard and the active duty forces – especially in a catastrophic event.

Recommendations:

　• The Department of Defense (DOD) and the state governors should develop an integrated plan for the employment of National Guard units and personnel in state status when large-scale military support is requested by a state to respond to a catastrophic incident or disaster. The plan should include a process for identification of National Guard units with the capabilities required to respond to the incident or disaster, and should take into account the availability of National Guard units for mobilization for national-defense missions. The plan should include expedited procedures for requesting and approving federal funding under Title 32, United States Code, for National Guard forces employed in accordance with the plan, and procedures for DOD and governors, during a catastrophe, to coordinate the process of matching units and capabilities of National Guard forces with the requirements of governors.

　• All DOD support activities should be coordinated with the other federal support activities provided under the framework of the National Response Plan in the event of an emergency or disaster. The entire spectrum of potential DOD support activities should be integrated into the overall planning and preparedness activities led by the Department of Homeland Security at the federal, state, and local levels.

Department of Defense Conclusion

The Department's contributions to the Katrina response flow directly from its professional, sustained emphasis on education, training, retention, and rigorous adherence to standards, coupled with a budget and resources unparalleled across the government. Military culture also played a role, as many officials reported to the Committee that their efforts in response to Katrina were the most rewarding and satisfying missions of their often extensive careers. Lieutenant Colonel Gordon Ellis of the Ohio National Guard commanded a battalion that deployed to the Superdome during the first week, and reported:

> Like all commanders, my soldiers were there about seven days before they had their first shower. They never once complained while they were there, and to see the professionalism and the dedication that those young soldiers displayed

throughout that difficult time makes me immensely proud to have been a part of that.[575]

However, as with all agencies and all levels of government, Katrina exposed weaknesses of, and raised questions about, the military's mechanisms for responding to disasters. Given DOD's unmatched power and size, and its unique Constitutional status, these questions merit careful consideration.

To what extent should the nation rely upon the Department of Defense in disaster response? The Department of Homeland Security was created, in part, to respond to domestic emergencies, but Katrina revealed that in critical missions, particularly in logistics, search and rescue, and command and control, it was unprepared to address a catastrophe of Katrina's magnitude. At the same time, Department of Defense, since September 11, 2001, and since establishing U.S. Northern Command, has revised its mission to reflect a greater focus on homeland defense. Its capabilities in this arena have therefore grown more robust. But Assistant Secretary McHale cautioned against placing too much reliance upon the military's capabilities:

> I would urge you to think simultaneously about speed and the fundamental public policy missions, public policy questions associated with the role of the military within domestic American society and constitutional government. … We have to balance not only what the military is capable of doing, questions of speed and resources, but what the military ought to be doing consistent with the historically constrained role of the military within domestic American society.[576]

Is it wiser to further develop these capabilities in DHS? If DOD's resources were already engaged in an overseas mission, military support might not be available to the extent that it was during Katrina. In that case, a more capable DHS would be preferable, especially since many of the missions DOD performed were not uniquely military. DHS could adopt military models of logistics, training, career development, and centralized incident management to improve its ability to function independently.

At the same time, when military assistance is required, to what degree should we rely on a system in which specific assets are requested? After-action reviews stressed, just as they had following Hurricane Andrew, that DOD must not wait for requests to push assets forward. But Katrina revealed a tension between a system of planned, coordinated movement, and the value of commanders' initiative in moving in advance of orders. Initiative, in this case, proved essential to the swift deployment of resources, but it also contributed to an uncoordinated response, in which strategic commanders lacked clear visibility over the force structure.

Katrina also revealed tension between gubernatorial and Presidential executive powers, underlying a delicate federalist balance: should governors retain full control of their National Guard forces after catastrophic events? The governors of the two most seriously affected states here answered "yes" unequivocally.[577] Yet at the height of the crisis, the President and senior military and civilian DOD leaders grew concerned that the scale of the military response – both the size of the National Guard force and the addition of federal active-duty ground troops – required a single commander. Governor Blanco's rejection of their proposed solution, however, has led DOD officials to realize that unity of command, long a staple of military operations, can also prove inconsistent with states' Constitutional powers.

The final resolution was to achieve unity of effort through the close coordination of federal and state-controlled military forces. But as has been widely documented, numerous factors challenged this coordination. While the Committee has not determined that a lack of coordination impaired the effectiveness of the military response to Katrina, many leaders agree that we must establish mechanisms now to ensure unity of effort between the Guard and active-duty forces the next time they are called for such a common cause. Only through forethought, planning, and consensus among the agencies and levels of government can we ensure that we do not encounter a political or leadership crisis in a catastrophe that may be even more destructive, and provide less warning, than Katrina.

1 U.S. Department of Homeland Security, *National Response Plan.* Washington: Government Printing Office, Dec. 2004, p. 8 [hereinafter *NRP*].

2 Committee staff interview of Paul McHale, Assistant Secretary of Defense for Homeland Defense, U.S. Department of Defense, conducted on Jan. 4, 2006, transcript p. 85.

3 *NRP*, p. 43.

4 McHale interview, Jan. 4, 2006, p. 88.

5 National Academy of Public Administration, *The Role of the National Guard in Emergency Preparedness and Response*, Jan. 1997, pp. 18, 123-126.

6 U.S. Department of Defense, *Strategy for Homeland Defense and Civil Support*, June 2005, p. 35.

7 *NRP*, p. 8.

8 National Emergency Managers Association, "What is EMAC?" http://www.emacweb.org/?9. Accessed on Apr. 19, 2006.

9 National Emergency Managers Association, "How does EMAC Work?" http://www.emacweb.org/?142. Accessed on Apr. 19, 2006.

10 P.L. 104-321, 110 Stat. 3877, and 3879-3880.

11 National Guard Bureau, *National Guard After Action Review: Hurricane Response*, Dec. 21, 2005, p. 63.

12 The White House, Homeland Security Presidential Directive-5: Management of Domestic Incidents, Feb. 28, 2003.

13 *See*: *NRP*.

14 The White House, Homeland Security Presidential Directive-5: Management of Domestic Incidents, Feb. 28, 2003.

15 Committee staff interview of Col. Don Harrington, U.S. Army, Military Liaison to FEMA, conducted on Jan. 6, 2006, transcript pp. 6-8.

16 Committee staff interview of Col. Anthony F. Daskevich II, U.S. Army, Louisiana Defense Coordinating Officer, conducted on Jan. 10, 2006, transcript p. 10.

17 *NRP*, p. 42.

18 Col. Daskevich interview, Jan. 10, 2006, p. 15.

19 McHale interview, Jan. 4, 2006, p. 134.

20 Committee staff interview of Clair Blong, Liaison to U.S. Northern Command, FEMA, conducted on Dec. 8, 2005, transcript p. 9.

21 Blong interview, Dec. 8, 2005, p. 93.

22 *NRP*, p. 10; 10 U.S.C. § 162.

23 *NRP*, p. ESF–v.

24 *NRP*, p. ESF #1–4.

25 *NRP*, p. ESF #2–12.

26 *NRP*, pp. ESF #3–5 through 3–8.

27 *NRP*, p. ESF #4–4.

28 *NRP*, pp. ESF #5–1 through 5–6.

29 *NRP*, p. ESF #6–6.

30 *NRP*, pp. ESF #7–1 through 7–6.

31 *NRP*, p. ESF #8–9.

32 *NRP*, p. ESF #9–6.

33 *NRP*, p. ESF #10–10.

34 *NRP*, p. ESF #11–10.

35 *NRP*, p. ESF #12–4.

36 *NRP*, p. ESF #13–6.

37 *NRP*, p. ESF #14–5.

38 *NRP*, p. ESF #15–5.

39 31 U.S.C. § 1535.

40 42 U.S.C. §§ 5121-5206.

41 10 U.S.C. §§ 331-335.

42 U.S. General Accounting Office, *DOD Can Combat Fraud Better by Strengthening Its Investigative Agencies,* Mar. 21, 1983, p. 15.

43 18 U.S.C. § 1385.

44 U.S. General Accounting Office, *Homeland Defense: DOD Needs to Assess the Structure of U.S. Forces for Domestic Military Missions,* July 11, 2003, p. 11.

45 10 U.S.C. §§ 111, 3013, 3062, 3203-3207, 4301, 5013, 5062, 8013, 8062, 8201.

46 Committee staff interview of Lt. Gen. Russel L. Honoré, U.S. Army, Commanding General, First U.S. Army, conducted on Jan. 9, 2006, transcript p. 14.

47 Paul Wolfowitz, Memorandum for Secretaries of the Military Departments and others, "Reporting 'Immediate Response' Requests from Civil Authorities," Apr. 25, 2005. Provided to Committee; U.S. Department of Defense, Directive Number 3025.1, "Military Support to Civil Authorities (MSCA)," Jan. 15, 1993, pp. 7-8 [hereinafter DOD Directive 3025.1, MSCA].

48 Paul Wolfowitz, Memorandum for Secretaries of the Military Departments and others, "Implementation Guidance Regarding the Office of the Assistant Secretary of Defense for Homeland Defense," May 25, 2003. Provided to Committee.

49 *NRP*, p. 9.

50 McHale interview, Jan. 4, 2006, pp. 90, 109.

51 DOD Directive 3025.1, MSCA, pp. 5-7.

52 *NRP*, p. 10; 10 U.S.C. § 162.

53 Testimony of Paul McHale, Assistant Secretary of Defense for Homeland Defense, U.S. Department of Defense, before the U.S. Senate, Committee on Homeland Security and Governmental Affairs, hearing on *Hurricane Katrina: The Defense Department's Role in the Response*, Feb. 9, 2006.

54 Office of Management and Budget, *A Review of Existing Authorities and Procedures for Using Military Assets in Fighting Wildfires,* May 17, 2004, p. 7.

55 Committee staff interview of Col. Darryl Roberson, U.S. Air Force, Assistant Deputy Director, Antiterrorism and Homeland Defense, U.S. Department of Defense, conducted on Nov. 10, 2005, transcript p. 4

56 Committee staff interview of Maj. Gen. Terry Scherling, U.S. Air Force, Director of the Joint Staff, National Guard Bureau, U.S. Department of Defense, conducted on Jan. 19, 2006, transcript p. 8.

57 DOD Memorandum, *Implementation Guidance Regarding the Office of the Assistant Secretary of Defense for Homeland Defense,* Mar. 25, 2003, p. 1.

58 U.S. Department of Defense, Directive Number 3025.12, "Military Assistance for Civil Disturbances (MACDIS)," Feb. 4, 1994, pp. 3-5 and 8 [hereinafter DOD Directive 3025.12, MACDIS].

59 DOD Directive 3025.1, MSCA, p. 2; U.S. Department of Defense, Directive Number 3025.15, "Military Assistance to Civil Authorities," Feb. 18, 1997, p. 5; DOD Directive 3025.12, MACDIS, p. 6.

60 Joint Staff Washington, Message, "Transfer of the Army Director of Military Support Mission to the Joint Staff," May 2003. Provided to Committee.

61 DOD Directive 3025.1, MSCA, p. 4.

62 U.S. Joint Forces Command, "11: New Name, Future, Focus." http://www.jfcom.mil/about/History/abthist6.htm. Accessed on Apr. 20, 2006.

63 U.S. Northern Command, "U.S. Northern Command: History." http://www.northcom.mil/about_us/history.htm. Accessed on April 20, 2006.

64 U.S. Northern Command, "U.S. Northern Command: History." http://www.northcom.mil/about_us/history.htm. Accessed on April 20, 2006.

 U.S. Department of Defense, *Quadrennial Defense Review Report*, Feb. 6, 2006.

65 U.S. Department of Defense, *Strategy for Homeland Defense and Civil Support,* June 2005, pp. 2-3

66 Committee staff interview of Maj. Gen. William Caldwell, U.S. Army, Commander, 82nd Airborne Division, U.S. Department of Defense, conducted on Feb. 28, 2006, transcript p. 8; Committee staff interview of Lt. Gen. Steven Blum, Chief, National Guard Bureau, U.S. Department of Defense, conducted on Jan. 19, 2006, transcript pp. 110-111.

67 10 U.S.C. § 111.

68 10 U.S.C. §§ 3013, 5013, 8013.

69 10 U.S.C. §§ 162, 164.

70 U.S. Department of Defense, "Unified Command Plan: The World with Commanders' Areas of Responsibility." http://www.defenselink.mil/specials/unifiedcommand/. Accessed on Feb. 28, 2006.

71 U.S. General Accounting Office, *Homeland Defense: DOD Needs to Assess the Structure of U.S. Forces for Domestic Military Missions*, July 11, 2003, p. 5; U.S. Department of Defense, *Strategy for Homeland Defense and Civil Support*, June 2005, p. 8.

72 U.S. General Accounting Office, *Homeland Defense: DOD Needs to Assess the Structure of U.S. Forces for Domestic Military Missions*, July 11, 2003, p. 11.

73 U.S. Northern Command, "About Us." http://www.northcom.mil/about_us/about_us.htm. Accessed on Feb. 28, 2006.

74 U.S. Northern Command, "Joint Task Force Alaska." http://northcom.mil/about_us/JTF_Alaska.htm. Accessed on Feb. 28, 2006; U.S. Northern Command, "Joint Force Headquarters National Capital Region." http://www.northcom.mil/about_us/JFHQ_NCR.htm. Accessed on Feb. 28, 2006; U.S. Northern Command, "Standing Joint Force Headquarters North." http://www.northcom.mil/about_us/SJFHQN.htm. Accessed on Feb. 28, 2006.

75 U.S. Northern Command, "About Us." http://www.northcom.mil/about_us/about_us.htm. Accessed on Feb. 28, 2006.

76 Testimony of Adm. Timothy Keating, U.S. Navy, Commander, North American Aerospace Defense Command and U.S. Northern Command, U.S. Department of Defense, before the U.S. Senate, Committee on Homeland Security and Governmental Affairs, hearing on *Hurricane Katrina: The Defense Department's Role in the Response*, Feb. 9, 2006.

77 U.S. Department of Defense, DOD Dictionary of Military Terms, 2005. http://www.dtic.mil/jel.doddict/data/o/03883.html. Accessed on May 4, 2006.

78 Col. David Rhodes, e-mail to Tom Eldridge, Dan Berkovitz, Brian Lepore and Eric Andersen, Senate Committee staff members, Feb. 16, 2006, 6:33 p.m.

79 U.S. Department of Defense, "EXORD for DOD Support to FEMA for Hurricane Katrina," Aug. 29, 2005.

80 McHale interview, Jan. 4, 2006, transcript p. 118; U.S. Northern Command, message to Joint Staff Washington, "Request for Forces," Aug. 30, 2005, 1745 Z, p. 1-4. Provided to Committee (Z corresponds to Zulu time, the military designation for Greenwich Mean Time. It refers to the time at the prime meridian.); 10 U.S.C. § 162; Committee staff interview of Margaret Kruse, Joint Forces Command, U.S. Department of Defense, conducted on Nov. 16, 2005, record of interview pp. 1-2.

81 *NRP*, p. 42.

82 *NRP*, p. 42.

83 McHale interview, Jan. 4, 2006, p. 49 (Between Aug. 29 and Sept. 10, 2005, 72,000 military personnel were deployed to the Gulf Coast area: 50,000 National Guardsmen from every state and territory as well as the District of Columbia and 22,000 active-duty troops.).

84 Maj. Gen. Caldwell interview, Feb. 28, 2006, pp. 40-41.

85 Office of the Assistant Secretary of Defense (Homeland Defense), Hurricane Katrina/Rita/Ophelia Interim Timeline, Nov. 2, 2005, pp. 1-2. Provided to Committee.

86 Chairman of the Joint Chiefs of Staff, Message to Commander, U.S. Northern Command and others, "Severe Weather Execute Order (EXORD) for DOD Support to FEMA (FEMA)," Aug. 19, 2005, 2300 Z. Provided to Committee.

87 *NRP*, p. 37. Also, Chairman of the Joint Chiefs of Staff, *Homeland Security*, Joint Publication 3-26, Aug. 2, 2005, p. GL-7. ("A military or civilian official who has been designated by the Department of Defense to exercise some delegated authority of the Department of Defense executive agent to coordinate military support to civil authorities activities.").

88 Col. Roberson interview, Nov. 10, 2005, p. 29.

89 Col. Harrington interview, Jan. 6, 2006, p. 8.

90 U.S. Northern Command, Message to Chairman of the Joint Chiefs of Staff and others, "Mod 3 to EXORD Katrina," Aug. 28, 2005, 1200 Z. Provided to Committee.

91 Col. Daskevich interview, Jan. 10, 2005, p. 27; Col. Damon C. Penn, e-mail to Col. Mark Fields and Col. Anthony Daskevich, Aug. 27, 2005, 3:07 p.m. Col. Anthony Daskevich deployed the day before from the Fifth U.S. Army in Fort Sill, Oklahoma, to Baton Rouge, Louisiana, arriving at the temporary FEMA office by 6:30 p.m. Saturday, August 27. On the same day, Col. Damon Penn deployed from First Army and arrived in Jackson, Mississippi by 10 p.m.

92 U.S. Northern Command, Message to Chairman of the Joint Chiefs of Staff and others, "Mod 2 to EXORD Katrina," Aug. 27, 2005, 2230 Z; U.S. Northern Command, Message to Chairman of the Joint Chiefs of Staff and others, "Mod 3 to EXORD Katrina," Aug. 28, 2005, 1200 Z. Provided to Committee.

93 U.S. Department of Defense, "Office of the Assistant Secretary of Defense for Homeland Defense OASD(HD) DCIP." http://www.dod-ap.msiac.dmso.mil/oasd.htm. Accessed on Mar. 1, 2006 ("The Assistant Secretary of Defense for Homeland Defense (ASD(HD)) is the overall supervisor of homeland defense (HD) activities for the Department of Defense. The ASD(HD) will oversee HD activities, develop policies, conduct analysis, provide advice, and make recommendations on HD, support to civil authorities, emergency preparedness and domestic crisis management matters within the Department.").

94 Committee staff interview of Col. Richard Chavez, U.S. Air Force, Senior Military Advisor for Civil Support, Office of

the Assistant Secretary of Defense for Homeland Defense, U.S. Department of Defense, conducted on Nov. 9, 2005, transcript p. 36.

95 Col. Chavez interview, Nov. 9, 2005, p. 41. However, Col. Chavez did state in his interview that Katrina demonstrated the value of examining the availability of other assets; for example, having learned the value of an immediate employment of watercraft for the purpose of performing water rescues, Chavez stated that he intends to include low-draft and shallow-draft boats among his pre-landfall assessments during the coming year's hurricane season. Col. Chavez interview, Nov. 9, 2005, p. 27.

96 Col. Chavez interview, Nov. 9, 2005, p. 27.

97 U.S. Department of Defense, Joint Publication 3-26, "Homeland Security," Aug. 2, 2005, p. IV–10.

98 Col. Roberson interview, Nov. 10, 2005, pp. 31-32.

99 U.S. Northern Command, Message to Chairman of the Joint Chiefs of Staff and others, "NORTHCOM Mod 2 to EX-ORD Katrina," Aug. 27, 2005, 2230 Z; U.S. Northern Command, Message to Chairman of the Joint Chiefs of Staff and others, "NORTHCOM Mod 3 to EXORD Katrina," Aug. 28, 2005, 1200 Z. Provided to Committee. Brig. Gen. Scherling said that Katrina showed that additional assets might have been useful had they been deployed earlier, and that consideration was being given to broadening the Order for next year's season:

> There are certain types of capabilities that certainly should be considered, and the first thing that we want to do is gain situational awareness, so we want to have the ability to go in and assess a situation. We want to be able to save lives. And so, you want the capability to have search and rescue. And then, you want to be able to go in and stabilize the situation where you probably need potentially the Corps of Engineers and many of the things that are somewhat outlined broadly in the emergency support functions of the National Response Plan.

Maj. Gen. Scherling interview, Jan. 19, 2006, p. 81.

100 FEMA, Mission Assignment, 3212EM-LA-DOD-01, Aug. 28, 2005. Provided to Committee.

101 U.S. Northern Command, USNORTHCOM Hurricane Katrina Timeline (Draft), p. 1. Provided to Committee.

102 U.S. Northern Command, Message to U.S. Joint Forces Command and others, "WARNORD FOUR/Tropical Storm Katrina," Aug. 25, 2005, 0014 Z. Provided to Committee.

103 Committee staff interview of Col. Thomas Muir, U.S. Army, Deputy Chief, Current Operations, J33, U.S. Northern Command, U.S. Department of Defense, conducted on Dec. 6, 2005, transcript pp. 11-12.

104 Col. Muir interview, Dec. 6, 2005, p. 14.

105 Committee staff interview of Col. Roberta Woods, U.S. Army, Chief, Plans and Operations Division, U.S. Northern Command, U.S. Department of Defense, conducted on Dec. 7, 2005, transcript pp. 14, 37-38.

106 Col. Woods interview, Dec. 7, 2005, p. 12.

107 Col. Woods interview, Dec. 7, 2005, p. 14.

108 Col. Woods interview, Dec. 7, 2005, pp. 38, 12 ("Pre-incident we don't have any set actions that we take because we must respond to an approved mission assignment. So it's monitoring, trying to anticipate where there might be shortfalls and advise as – as appropriate if we see indications of shortfalls.").

109 Col. Woods interview, Dec. 7, 2005, p. 38.

110 Lt. Gen. Honoré interview, Jan. 9, 2006, p. 10.

111 U.S. Department of Defense, First U.S. Army, Joint Task Force Katrina, Hurricane Katrina Chronology. Provided to Committee.

112 First U.S. Army, Message to U.S. Northern Command, "Request for Force Capabilities (Title X) ISO possible DSCA operations as a result of Hurricane Katrina," Aug. 28, 2005, 1656 Z. Lt. Gen. Honoré requested assets as follows: 24 hours after landfall: satellite phones, light or utility helicopters for reconnaissance, damage assessment, and command/control shallow-draft boats for Search and Rescue and supply transportation. 48 hours after landfall: medium lift aviation for transportation of supplies and personnel medical units for Search and Rescue and evacuation, engineer units for construction, utility and transportation, power generators, military police units, high-water trucks.

113 U.S. Army Forces Command, Message to U.S. Joint Forces Command, "Request for Force Capabilities (Title X) is possible DSCA operations as a result of Hurricane Katrina," Aug. 28, 2005.

114 Maj. Gen. Richard Rowe, e-mail to NC-JOC – Director – OMB, Aug. 28, 2005, 5:31 p.m. Provided to Committee.

115 Maj. Gen. Terry Scherling, e-mail to Maj. Gen. Rowe, Aug. 28, 2005, 3:41 p.m. Provided to Committee.

116 Committee staff interview of Maj. Gen. Richard Rowe, Director of Operations, J3, U.S. Northern Command, U.S. Department of Defense, conducted on Jan. 20, 2006, transcript p. 31.

117 Maj. Gen. Richard Rowe, e-mail to Lt. Gen. Russel Honoré and Lt. Gen. Joseph Inge, Aug. 29, 2005, 6:46 p.m. Provided to Committee.

118 Col. Daskevich interview, Jan. 10, 2005, p. 28.

119 Col. Daskevich interview, Jan. 10, 2005, p. 30.

120 Col. Damon Penn, e-mail to Col. Anthony Daskevich, Aug. 28, 2005, 8:16 a.m. Provided to Committee.

121 Col. Daskevich interview, Jan. 10, 2005, pp. 24-25; Committee staff interview of William Lokey, Federal Coordinating Officer for Hurricane Katrina in Louisiana, FEMA, conducted on Nov. 4, 2005, transcript pp. 81-84.

122 Col. Daskevich interview, Jan. 10, 2005, pp. 39-40.

123 Col. Daskevich interview, Jan. 10, 2005, pp. 46-47. He and the leadership of Fifth Army decided to deploy the rest of his staff Sunday morning, but as the storm's path was still unclear, they sent the staff to Houston to await further direction. Col. Daskevich interview, Jan. 10, 2005, p. 30.

124 Committee staff interview of Vice Adm. Mark Fitzgerald, U.S. Navy, Commander, U.S. Second Fleet, U.S. Department of Defense, conducted on Nov. 15, 2005 (untranscribed). It is important to note that as a Fleet Commander, he did not possess the authority to command an operational mission; as directed by the Goldwater-Nichols Act, all Fleet-commanded missions must be classified as either training or equipping. Because NORTHCOM had not yet designated the Gulf as a Joint Operational Area, and because FEMA had not requested Navy assistance, *Bataan*'s movement on Aug. 28 was classified as training. But she proved to be one of the earliest, and therefore, most essential assets available in the critical first days after landfall.

125 U.S. Fleet Forces Command, briefing slides, "Hurricane Katrina Navy Mission: Providing Rescue and Civil Support Relief from the Sea, Air and Land," Nov. 14, 2005, p. 7. Provided to Committee.

126 U.S. Fleet Forces Command, briefing slides, "Hurricane Katrina Navy Mission: Providing Rescue and Civil Support Relief from the Sea, Air and Land," Nov. 14, 2005, p. 7. Provided to Committee.

127 Committee staff interview of Maj. Gen. Douglas O'Dell, U.S. Marine Corps, Commanding General, 4th Marine Division, U.S. Department of Defense, conducted on Dec. 14, 2005, transcript p. 12.

128 Maj. Gen. O'Dell interview, Dec. 14, 2005, pp. 16-18. It is important to note that he did not activate or move units into the gulf region prior to landfall or prior to receiving an order from NORTHCOM, but merely assessed availabilities and placed units on alert within the Marine Corps, similar to the process Lt. Gen. Honoré sought to achieve with his request message to NORTHCOM.

129 Committee staff interview of Lt. Gen. James Amos, U.S. Marine Corps, Commander, Second Marine Expeditionary Force, conducted on Dec. 14, 2005, transcript, p. 9.

130 Lt. Gen. Amos interview, Dec. 14, 2005, p. 11.

131 Committee staff interview of Brig. Gen. Paul Selva, U.S. Air Force, Director of Operations, U.S. Transportation Command, U.S. Department of Defense, conducted on Feb. 16, 2006, transcript p. 13.

132 U.S. Northern Command, USNORTHCOM Hurricane Katrina Timeline (Draft), p. 4. Provided to Committee.

133 Committee staff interview of Adm. Timothy Keating, U.S. Navy, Commander, North American Aerospace Defense Command and U.S. Northern Command, U.S. Department of Defense, conducted by Senator Susan Collins, Feb. 3, 2006, (untranscribed). Admiral Keating "woke up Tuesday morning saying New Orleans dodged a bullet." McHale interview, Jan. 4, 2006, p. 34. "At that point, the magnitude of the disaster was still unknown, Hurricane Katrina made landfall on Monday, August 29. The news reports that we had all read on the following morning prior to the meeting that is the subject of my testimony were consistently inaccurate. If you take a look at The Washington Post or other publications, it's clear that for reasons that I think we understand a little better now but have not yet fully explained, initial media reports were more optimistic than warranted. There were references in news stories to having dodged the bullet. This is not a criticism of the media coverage. This was a huge storm, the scope of the damage was vast, and situational awareness was not yet clear. In any event, we went into the meeting on Tuesday morning with media reports that were less sobering than the scope of the actual damage."

134 1A JOC Watch Battle Captain, e-mail to 5th Bde, 87th Div, S-3 Ops and others, Sept. 1, 2005, 4:03 p.m. Lt. Gen. Honoré was among the recipients and "DoD Force Protection Lessons Learned: Hurricane Andrew, 24 August 1992, South Florida" was attached. Provided to Committee.

135 Joint Staff, Message to U.S. Northern Command, "DOD Support to FEMA," Aug. 29, 2005, 2300 Z. Provided to Committee. (Authorized by Brig. Gen. Scherling.).

136 Col. Woods interview, Dec. 7, 2005, p. 28.

137 Committee staff interview of Col. Dan Shanahan, U.S. Army, Commander, 1st Air Cavalry Brigade, 1st Cavalry Division, U.S. Department of Defense, conducted on Feb. 23, 2006 (not yet transcribed).

138 FEMA, Mission Assignment, 3212EM-LA-DOD-01, Aug. 28, 2005. Provided to Committee.

139 FEMA, Mission Assignment Task Order Form, Aug. 28, 2005.

140 McHale interview, Jan. 4, 2006, p. 12.

141 *See e.g.*: Committee staff interview of Edward Buikema, Acting Director, Response Division, FEMA, conducted on Nov. 21, 2005, transcript p. 168. *See also*: Buikema interview, Nov. 21, 2005, p. 183 ("I think the process from beginning to end probably takes longer than it should."). However, Mr. Buikema was basing his statement that he was frustrated on a false premise, i.e., that the billion dollar logistics request was not "done" until Sept. 5. In fact, as discussed above, it was approved on Sept. 2. Buikema admitted that he "lost visibility" of this particular request and so had difficulty accounting for what he perceived caused a delay in its approval, but he still had an "instinct" that DOD was the cause for the delay. Buikema interview, Nov. 21, 2005, p. 171.

142 Buikema interview, Nov. 21, 2005, p. 213.

143 U.S. Assistant to the President for Homeland Security and Counterterrorism, *The Federal Response to Hurricane Katrina: Lessons Learned*. Washington: Government Printing Office, Feb. 2006, p. 54 [hereinafter, The White House, *Hurricane Katrina Lessons Learned*] ("From the time a request is initiated until the military force or capability is delivered to the disaster site requires a 21-step process."). The source for this statement is the U.S. Department of Defense, Joint Center for Operational Analysis, "Incident Command Request Briefing," Nov. 1, 2005. That PowerPoint briefing includes a slide depicting the DOD approval process, and includes the statement "21 steps to get a truck." The White House, *Hurricane Katrina Lessons Learned*, p. 54. The report then states that DOD's processes resulted in "critical needs not being met" citing a written statement by Mayor-President Melvin "Kip" Holden submitted for a hearing before the Senate Homeland Security and Governmental Affairs Committee on Sept. 28, 2005. Upon review, the statement by Mayor-President Holden does not support the factual assertion made by the Townsend Report because it does not relate to DOD.

144 Committee staff interview of William Lokey, Federal Coordinating Officer for Hurricane Katrina in Louisiana, FEMA, conducted on Jan. 20, 2006, transcript pp. 130-134. (One-billion dollar request was "negotiated with DOD")

145 Committee staff interview of Scott Wells, Deputy Federal Coordinating Officer for Hurricane Katrina in Louisiana, FEMA, conducted on Nov. 15, 2005, transcript p. 124.

146 Committee staff interview of Col. Richard Chavez, U.S. Air Force, Senior Military Advisor for Civil Support, Office of the Assistant Secretary of Defense for Homeland Defense, U.S. Department of Defense, conducted on Nov. 22, 2005, pp. 147-150; Col. Chavez interview, Nov. 9, 2005, p. 30 (DOD liaison officers helped FEMA officials "with the verbiage of the mission assignment.").

147 Committee staff interview of Gen. Richard Myers, U.S. Air Force (Ret.), former Chairman, Joint Chiefs of Staff, U.S. Department of Defense, conducted on Feb. 28, 2006, transcript p. 77.

148 Gen. Myers interview, Feb. 28, 2006, p. 79.

149 McHale, Senate Committee Hearing, Feb. 9, 2006.

150 Committee staff interview of Capt. Michael McDaniel, U.S. Navy, Navy Emergency Preparedness Liaison Officer to FEMA, conducted on Dec. 2, 2005, transcript p. 156.

151 Col. Harrington interview, Jan. 6, 2006, pp. 27-28.

152 Col. Harrington interview, Jan. 6, 2006.

153 Maj. Gen. Richard Rowe, e-mail to Lt. Gen. Russel Honoré and Lt. Gen. Joseph Inge, Aug. 29, 2005, 6:46 p.m. Provided to Committee.

154 Maj. Gen. Rowe interview, Jan. 20, 2006, p. 31.

155 Wells interview, Nov. 15, 2005, p. 123.

156 Wells interview, Nov. 15, 2005, p. 124.

157 Michael Ritchie, e-mail to Anthony Capra, Aug. 29, 2005, 1:14 p.m. Provided to Committee.

158 Col. Richard Chavez, e-mail to Anthony Capra and Michael Ritchie, Aug. 29, 2005, 2:35 p.m. Provided to Committee ("Does not fit policy for Immediate Response.").

159 McHale interview, Jan. 4, 2006, p. 29.

160 Committee staff interview of Gordon England, Deputy Secretary of Defense, conducted by Senator Susan Collins on Feb. 3, 2006 (untranscribed).

161 England interview, Feb. 3, 2006.

162 Anthony Capra, e-mail to Paul McHale, Aug. 29, 2005, 5:25 p.m. Provided to Committee.

163 Col. David Rhodes, e-mail to Tom Eldridge and Dan Berkovitz, Senate Committee staff members, May 3, 2006, 5:28 p.m.

164 Anthony Capra, e-mail to POL DoD HD Coordination Group and others, Aug. 30, 2005, 1:47 p.m. Provided to Committee.

165 Mark Roupas, e-mail to Paul McHale, Aug. 30, 2005, 3:15 p.m. Provided to Committee. It is unclear what constituted confirmation of the breach to Assistant Secretary McHale's office. Col. Chavez stated that Assistant Secretary McHale's office received confirmation from the Corps at sunrise Wednesday morning. Col. Chavez interview, Nov. 9, 2005, p. 85.

166 McHale interview, Jan. 4, 2006, p. 97.

167 *NRP*, p. 33.

168 McHale interview, Jan. 4, 2006, pp. 131-132.

169 Capt. Frank Thorp, e-mail to Lt. Gen. Walter Sharp, Aug. 30, 2005, 8:15 p.m. Provided to Committee.

170 Testimony of Paul McHale, Assistant Secretary of Defense for Homeland Defense, U.S. Department of Defense, before the U.S. House, Select Bipartisan Committee to Investigate the Preparation for and Response to Hurricane Katrina, hearing on *Hurricane Katrina: Preparedness and Response by the Department of Defense, the Coast Guard, and the National Guard of Louisiana, Mississippi and Alabama*, Oct. 27, 2005.

171 U.S. Northern Command, USNORTHCOM Hurricane Katrina Timeline (Draft), p. 1.

172 NC JOC-Director-OMB, e-mail to Maj. Gen. Richard Rowe and Rear Adm. Gene Brooks, Aug. 29, 2005, 4 p.m. Provided to Committee.

173 Committee staff interview of Capt. Brett Markham, U.S. Navy, Deputy Director of Intelligence, U.S. Northern Command and North American Aerospace Defense Command, U.S. Department of Defense, conducted on Dec. 7, 2005, transcript pp. 61-62.

174 Committee staff interview of Capt. Brett Markham, U.S. Navy, Deputy Director of Intelligence, U.S. Northern Command and North American Aerospace Defense Command, U.S. Department of Defense, conducted on Dec. 8, 2005, transcript p. 5.

175 Capt. Markham interview, Dec. 8, 2005, pp. 4-5.

176 Capt. Markham interview, Dec. 8, 2005, pp. 7-8.

177 Committee staff interview of Col. Wesley McClellan, U.S. Navy, Navy Emergency Preparedness Liaison to FEMA, U.S. Department of Defense, conducted on Jan. 23, 2006, transcript p. 18.

178 Adm. Keating interview, Feb. 3, 2006.

179 Committee staff interview of Brig. Gen. Moulton, U.S. Air Force, Director, Standing Joint Headquarters-North, U.S. Northern Command, U.S. Department of Defense, conducted on Dec. 5, 2005, transcript pp. 69-70.

180 Col. Daskevich interview, Jan. 10, 2005, p. 69.

181 Col. Daskevich interview, Jan. 10, 2005, p. 79.

182 Col. Daskevich interview, Jan. 10, 2005, pp. 78-80.

183 Col. Daskevich interview, Jan. 10, 2005, p. 85.

184 Col. Daskevich interview, Jan. 10, 2005, pp. 68-69.

185 Adm. Edmund Giambastiani, e-mail to Adm. Timothy Keating, Aug. 30, 2005, 4:59 p.m. Provided to Committee.

186 Col. Richard Chavez, e-mail to Tony Capra, Aug. 30, 2005, 8:25 a.m. Provided to Committee ("We need to keep these actions in the proper lane to avoid confusion and duplication of effort. FEMA is the lead and is the conduit for all Federal response coordination, planning and execution.").

187 McHale interview, Jan. 4, 2006, pp. 34-35.

188 Gen. Myers interview, Feb. 28, 2006, p. 9.

189 Col. David Rhodes, e-mail to Eric Andersen and Brian Lepore, Senate Committee staff members, Mar. 28, 2006, 4:25 p.m.; McHale interview, Jan. 4, 2006, p. 30.

190 Gordon England, memorandum to SECDEF [Donald Rumsfeld], Aug. 30, 2005. Provided to Committee.

191 Office of the Chairman of the Joint Chiefs of Staff, "Meetings Regarding Hurricane Katrina," Sept. 7, 2005. Provided to Committee.

192 Gen. Myers interview, Feb. 28, 2006, pp. 9-10 ("And so with a verbal order from the Deputy Secretary of Defense, I called all the service chiefs, and I ask them…what we've got to do is…we gotta lean forward. We know we're going to get asked to do things, so you services know what you provide and these kind of things, so work with Northern Command; make sure what you're doing is smart, but start to lean forward. And if you need to preposition or move stuff, start to move and preposition stuff, because you know we're going to get…the requests.").

193 Adm. Keating interview, Feb. 3, 2006.

194 Office of the Chairman of the Joint Chiefs of Staff, "Meetings Regarding Hurricane Katrina," Sept. 7, 2005. Provided to Committee.

195 England interview, Feb. 3, 2006.

196 McHale interview, Jan. 4, 2006, p. 37.

197 Adm. Timothy Keating, e-mail to Gen. Richard B. Myers and others, Aug. 30, 2005, 12:24 p.m. Provided to Committee.

198 McHale interview, Jan. 4, 2006, pp. 30-31.

199 Capt. McDaniel interview, Dec. 2, 2005, p. 69.

200 Col. Harrington interview, Jan. 6, 2006, p. 81.

201 U.S. Joint Forces Command, Hurricane Katrina Comprehensive Timeline, Nov. 15, 2006, p. 5. Provided to Committee.

202 Maj. Gen. Rowe interview, Jan. 20, 2006, p. 42.

203 Adm. Timothy Keating, e-mail to Brig. Gen. Frank Helmick and others, Aug. 30, 2005, 9:18 p.m. Provided to Committee.

204 McHale interview, Jan. 4, 2006, pp. 14-15 ("During that week, before …we had received a modest number of requests for assistance from the Department of Homeland Security. During that period of time, when the Department of Defense were prepared to review and approve a greater number of RFAs covering a wider range of missions than those we actually

received – in short, we were leaning forward in anticipation of RFAs from Department of Homeland Security, but because of the magnitude of the event and the complexity of some of the mission requirements, the RFAs had not yet begun to appear in large numbers…during that first week, the RFAs we had received were fairly specific and modest in scope.").

205 Col. Roberson interview, Nov. 10, 2005, p. 114.

206 McHale interview, Jan. 4, 2006, pp. 14-15, 39.

207 Brig. Gen. Moulton interview, Dec. 5, 2005, p. 43.

208 U.S. Northern Command, Message to Chairman of the Joint Chiefs of Staff and others, "NORTHCOM Mod 6 to EXORD Katrina," Aug. 31, 2005, 0300 Z. Provided to Committee.

209 U.S. Fleet Forces Command, Hurricane Katrina, Navy Mission: Providing Rescue & Civil Support Relief from the Sea, Air and Land, Aftermath. Provided to Committee; JTF-Katrina, Commander's Assessment, Sept. 3, 2005. Provided to Committee.

210 U.S. Northern Command, USNORTHCOM Hurricane Katrina Timeline (Draft), p. 1.

211 Vice Adm. Fitzgerald interview, Nov. 15, 2005.

212 Vice Adm. Fitzgerald interview, Nov. 15, 2005.

213 Vice Adm. Fitzgerald interview, Nov. 15, 2005.

214 Committee staff interview of Vice Adm. Vivien Crea, U.S. Coast Guard, Commander, Coast Guard Atlantic Area and Commander, Maritime Defense Zone Atlantic, conducted on Jan. 3, 2006, transcript p. 40.

215 Committee staff interview of Capt. Richard Snyder, U.S. Navy, Executive Officer, USS *Bataan*, conducted on Nov. 14, 2005 (untranscribed); JTF-Katrina, Commander's Assessment, Sept. 3, 2005. Provided to Committee.

216 Capt. Snyder interview, Nov. 14, 2005.

217 Capt. Snyder interview, Nov. 14, 2005.

218 Committee staff interview of Capt. Bruce Jones, U.S. Coast Guard, Commanding Officer, Coast Guard Air Station New Orleans, conducted on Nov. 9, 2005 (untranscribed). Evidence suggests that DOD had debated whether USS *Bataan* was authorized to provide assistance with its helicopters prior to being requested or ordered. Col. Chavez wrote in an e-mail to a DOD liaison at DHS that although Vice Adm. Fitzgerald had publicly announced the availability of USS *Bataan* and her helicopters, the ship's captain does not have the authority to assist unless specifically ordered: "Does not fit policy for Immediate Response." Col. Richard Chavez, e-mail to Tony Capra, Aug. 29, 2005, 2:35 p.m. Provided to Committee.

219 Capt. Snyder interview, Nov. 14, 2005.

220 Committee staff interview of Rear Adm. Joseph Kilkenny, U.S. Navy, former Joint Forces Maritime Component Commander, JTF Katrina, conducted on Nov. 30, 2005 (untranscribed).

221 U.S. Northern Command, USNORTHCOM Hurricane Katrina Timeline (Draft), p. 11. Provided to Committee.

222 Rear Adm. Kilkenny interview, Nov. 30, 2005.

223 Rear Adm. Kilkenny interview, Nov. 30, 2005; Vice Adm. Fitzgerald interview, Nov. 15, 2005.

224 Rear Adm. Kilkenny interview, Nov. 30, 2005.

225 JTF-Katrina, Commander's Assessment, Sept. 3, 2005. Provided to Committee.

226 Committee staff interview of Rear Adm. Reuben Bookert, U.S. Navy, Joint Force Maritime Component Commander, U.S. Second Fleet, conducted on Nov. 16, 2005 (untranscribed).

227 U.S. Northern Command, message to Joint Staff, "Request for Forces," Sept. 2, 2005, 0530 Z. Provided to Committee. The message also requested the USS *Whidbey Island* and four logistics ships from Military Sealift Command.

228 JTF-Katrina, Commander's Assessment, Sept. 4, 2005. Provided to Committee.

229 Vice Adm. Crea interview, Jan. 3, 2006, p. 41.

230 U.S. Fleet Forces Command, "Hurricane Katrina, Navy Mission: Providing Rescue and Civil Support Relief from the Sea, Air and Land," p. 9. Provided to Committee.

231 Rear Adm. Anthony Winns, e-mail to Lt. Gen. James Conway, Sept. 15, 2005, 1:20 p.m. Provided to Committee.

232 Insung Lee, e-mail to HSOC.SWO and others, Aug. 31, 2005, 11:50 a.m. Provided to Committee.

233 U.S. Fleet Forces Command, "Hurricane Katrina, Navy Mission: Providing Rescue and Civil Support Relief from the Sea, Air and Land," p. 9. Provided to Committee.

234 Committee staff interview of Cmdr. Thomas Quinn, U.S. Navy, Director of Operations, Naval Air Forces, Atlantic, conducted on Nov. 15, 2005 (untranscribed).

235 Vice Adm. Mark Fitzgerald, e-mail to Adm. Michael Mullen, Sept. 2, 2005, 5:53 p.m. Provided to Committee.

236 Lt. Gen. Honoré interview, Jan. 9, 2006, p. 48.

237 Lt. Gen. Honoré interview, Jan. 9, 2006, p. 46.

238 Col. Tom Muir, e-mail to Maj. Gen. Richard Rowe, Aug. 29, 2005, 4 p.m. Provided to Committee.

239 Lt. Gen. Honoré interview, Jan. 9, 2006, p. 33.

240 U.S. Department of Defense, First U.S. Army, Joint Task Force Katrina, "Hurricane Katrina Chronology." Provided to Committee.

241 Lt. Gen. Honoré interview, Jan. 9, 2006, p. 29.

242 U.S. Northern Command, Message to Chairman of the Joint Chiefs of Staff and others, "NORTHCOM Mod 4 to EXORD Katrina," Aug. 30, 2005, 0200 Z. Provided to Committee.

243 U.S. Northern Command, Message to Chairman of the Joint Chiefs of Staff and others, "NORTHCOM Mod 5 to EXORD Katrina," Aug. 30, 2005, 2100 Z. Provided to Committee.

244 U.S. Department of Defense, First U.S. Army, Joint Task Force Katrina, Hurricane Katrina Chronology. Provided to Committee.

245 Brig. Gen. Graham interview, Jan. 12, 2006, pp. 24-27.

246 Maj. Gen. Caldwell interview, Feb. 28, 2006, p. 8.

247 U.S. Forces Command, Message to III Corps and XVIII Corps, "FORSCOM Frago #8 Provides Support of BDE Size Forces ISO Hurricane Katrina Relief Operations," Sept. 1, 2005, 0039 Z. Provided to Committee.

248 Maj. Gen. Caldwell interview, Feb. 28, 2006, p. 20.

249 Maj. Gen. Caldwell interview, Feb. 28, 2006, pp. 25-26. Notes from the Forces Command teleconference at 8 a.m. correspond to this time frame, and state that the command was "just waiting for the trigger to deploy," and that a phased deployment plan was in place to commit the Brigade to the response. U.S. Forces Command, notes of FORSCOM Teleconference, Sept. 2, 2005. Provided to Committee.

250 Col. Michael Okita, e-mail to Maj. Gen. William Caldwell and others, Sept. 3, 2005, 10:02 a.m. Provided to Committee. According to Maj. Gen. Caldwell, "It was no longer be prepared now, it was on order. When you change to an on order, that means you need to plan on it occurring at some time in the future. It doesn't mean it will, but it just says you need now to plan on it. And they said, on order deploy your Division Headquarters [approx. 180 people] and a Brigade Task Force [approx. 3,200 people] in support of JTF Katrina…with the purpose of operating distribution centers, crowd control and security, in the New Orleans area." Maj. Gen. Caldwell interview, Feb. 28, 2006, pp. 23-24.

251 President George W. Bush, "President Addresses Nation, Discusses Hurricane Katrina Relief Efforts," radio address, Sept. 3, 2005, 10:06 a.m. ET. http://www.whitehouse.gov/news/releases/2005/09/20050903.html. Accessed on Apr. 21, 2006.

252 U.S. Forces Command, Message to Commanders of III Corps and others, "FORSCOM Exorder Deploys Units in Support of JTF-KAT," Sept. 3, 2005, 1729 Z. Provided to Committee.

253 Maj. Gen. Caldwell interview, Feb. 28, 2006, pp. 31-32.

254 Maj. Gen. Caldwell interview, Feb. 28, 2006, p. 36 ("The fact that we moved that force and did not kill, maim or injure a single person is absolutely incredible. They went from a cold start. I don't keep 1,383 vehicles prepped and ready to go on a key moment's notice. I keep about – I'd have to guess, about 180 to 240. So we literally were going across the Division grabbing vehicles, people, because we just realized the great need for command and control, logistics support, medical support, so we put that all on the road.").

255 Maj. Gen. Caldwell interview, Feb. 28, 2006, p. 49.

256 Maj. Gen. Caldwell interview, Feb. 28, 2006, pp. 50-53.

257 Col. Shanahan interview, Feb. 23, 2006.

258 U.S. Northern Command, Message to Chairman of the Joint Chiefs of Staff and others, "NORTHCOM Mod 8 to EXORD Katrina," Sept. 2, 3005, 0015 Z. Provided to Committee.

259 Col. Shanahan interview, Feb. 23, 2006.

260 Col. Shanahan interview, Feb. 23, 2006.

261 U.S. Forces Command, Message to III Corps and XVIII Corps, "Frago 8," contained in e-mail from First Army Joint Operations Center Watch Team to LTG Honoré and others, Sept. 1, 2005, 4:23 p.m. Provided to Committee.

262 Committee staff interview of Col. Bryan Roberts, U.S. Army, Commander, 2nd Brigade Combat Team, 1st Cavalry Division, U.S. Department of Defense, conducted on Feb. 23, 2006 (untranscribed).

263 Col. Roberts interview, Feb. 23, 2006.

264 President George W. Bush, "President Addresses Nation, Discusses Hurricane Katrina Relief Efforts," radio address, Sept. 3, 2005, 10:06 a.m. ET. http://www.whitehouse.gov/news/releases/2005/09/20050903.html. Accessed on Apr. 21, 2006.

265 Col. Roberts interview, Feb. 23, 2006.

266 U.S. Department of Defense, Hurricane Katrina Comprehensive Review Task Force, "Standing Rules for the Use of Force," Sept. 2, 2005. Provided to Committee.

267 Col. Roberts interview, Feb. 23, 2006.

268 Lt. Gen. Amos interview, Dec. 14, 2005, p. 10.

269 Second Marine Expeditionary Force, Hurricane Katrina Timeline. Provided to Committee; Lt. Gen. Amos interview,

Dec. 14, 2005, p. 14.

270 Lt. Gen. Amos interview, Dec. 14, 2005, pp. 15-16; Office of the Assistant Secretary of Defense for Homeland Defense, Timeline, What Marine forces were deployed, when were they deployed, and on what authority were they deployed? Provided to Committee (states that on Sept. 1, multiple aircraft "self-deploy to NAS Pensacola, FL").

271 Lt. Gen. Amos interview, Dec. 14, 2005, p. 21.

272 Lt. Gen. Amos interview, Dec. 14, 2005, p. 22. "JTF Katrina Commander's Assessment, Sept. 2, 2005" confirms that as of 7 a.m. Friday, "SPMAGTF assessment team in Belle Chase. ADVON COB today. CE 03 Sept. 130 Pax CE total," and also "Reserve AAV platoon closed on ISB Gulf Port, MS. BPT posture." JTF-Katrina, Commander's Assessment, Sept. 2, 2005. Provided to Committee.

273 Lt. Gen. Amos interview, Dec. 14, 2005, p. 75.

274 Lt. Gen. James Amos, e-mail to Lt. Gen. Honoré, via First Army JOC Watch Battle Captain, Sept. 1, 2005, 8:25 a.m. Provided to Committee.

275 Lt. Gen. Russel Honoré, e-mail to Lt. Gen. Amos, via 1A JOC Watch Battle Captain, Sept. 1, 2005, 7:48 p.m. Provided to Committee.

276 Lt. Gen. Russel Honoré, e-mail to Lt. Gen. James Amos, Sept. 2, 2005, 10:08 a.m. Provided to Committee.

277 Lt. Gen. Amos interview, Dec. 14, 2005, pp. 23-24.

278 Capt. Robert Reininger, e-mail to Maj. Gen. Richard Rowe, Sept. 2, 2005, 6:35 a.m. Provided to Committee.

279 Maj. Gen. O'Dell interview, Dec. 14, 2005, p. 28.

280 Lt. Gen. Amos interview, Dec. 14, 2005, p. 75.

281 Marine Forces Atlantic, Message to Commanding General, II MEF and Commander of Marine Forces Reserve, "COMMARFORLANT Deployment order," Sept. 2, 2005, 1850 Z. Provided to Committee.

282 Par. 3.A.2 of the COMMARFORLANT Deployment order states: "Concept of op. COMMARFORLANT requests ROMMARFORRES to ID, Prep, and deploy aviation assets into ISB NAS Pensacola, FL and det AAV vic Gulfport, MS for further movement into affected areas iso SPMAGTF GC. COMMARFORLANT dir CG II MEF to ID, prep and deploy a SPMAGTF iso comdr JTF Katrina HA/DR operations in and around the states of Louisiana, Mississippi, Alabama and Florida. SPMAGTF deploys via sea, land, and hcptr NLT 03 Sep 05." Marine Forces Atlantic, Message to Commanding General, II MEF and Commander of Marine Forces Reserve, "COMMARFORLANT Deployment order," Sept. 2, 2005, 1850 Z. Provided to Committee.

283 Maj. Gen. Rowe interview, Jan. 20, 2006, p. 80.

284 Lt. Gen. Amos interview, Dec. 14, 2005, p. 25.

285 Lt. Gen. Amos interview, Dec. 14, 2005, pp. 27-28.

286 Maj. Gen. O'Dell interview, Dec. 14, 2005, p. 32.

287 Maj. Gen. O'Dell interview, Dec. 14, 2005, p. 33.

288 Maj. Gen. O'Dell interview, Dec. 14, 2005, p. 34.

289 Brig. Gen. Selva interview, Feb. 16, 2006, pp. 12-15.

290 FEMA, Mission Assignment, 1603DR-LA-DOD-01, Aug. 30, 2005. Provided to Committee.

291 Committee staff interview of Col. Glen Joerger, U.S. Air Force, Former Vice Commander, 436th Airlift Wing, Dover Air Force Base, pre-designated Director of Mobility Forces, Air Mobility Command, U.S. Transportation Command, U.S. Department of Defense, conducted on Jan. 6, 2006, transcript p. 15.

292 Col. Joerger interview, Jan. 6, 2006, p. 17.

293 FEMA, Mission Assignment, 1603DR-LA-DOD-14, Sept. 1, 2005. Provided to Committee.

294 Col. Joerger interview, Jan. 6, 2006, p. 27.

295 Col. Joerger interview, Jan. 6, 2006, p. 20.

296 William Lokey, e-mail to Michael Lowder, Edward Buikema, Nicol Andrews and Thomas Bossert, Aug. 31, 2005, 12:30 a.m. Provided to Committee; filed as Bates no. DHS 0004688.

297 Col. Joerger interview, Jan. 6, 2006, p. 28.

298 Maj. Gen. Caldwell interview, Feb. 28, 2006, pp. 25-26.

299 Maj. Gen. Caldwell interview, Feb. 28, 2006, p. 34.

300 McHale, Committee hearing, Feb. 9, 2006.

301 Maj. Gen. Richard Rowe, U.S. Army, e-mail to Maj. Gen. Paul Sullivan, Sept. 1, 2005, 7:28 a.m.; Capt. Robert Reininger, U.S. Coast Guard, e-mail to Maj. Gen. Richard Rowe, Sept. 1, 2005, 10:54 a.m.

302 Adm. Keating interview, Feb. 3, 2006.

303 Maj. Gen. Rowe interview, Jan. 20, 2006, p. 84.

304 Maj. Gen. Richard Rowe, e-mail to Lt. Gen. Russel Honoré, Sept. 4, 2005, 10:47 p.m. Provided to Committee.

305 Brig. Gen. Moulton interview, Dec. 5, 2005, p. 24. NORTHCOM directed the deployment in message "Mod 12 to EXORD Katrina," Sept. 3, 2005, 1200 Z. Provided to Committee.

306 He and his Louisiana National Guard counterpart, Brig. Gen. Hunt Downer, who had taken on the task of Reception, Staging, Onward Movement and Integration of Guard forces, derived a draft solution of the problem: "So we sort of, on the back of a napkin, if you will, drew up a basic construct, which is we would try to take over some of the key mission sets to then probably utilize National Guard forces for those missions that Title 10 guys could not do." Brig. Gen. Moulton interview, Dec. 5, 2005, p. 42.

307 Brig. Gen. Moulton interview, Dec. 5, 2005, pp. 52-53.

308 Col. Woods interview, Dec. 7, 2005, p. 54.

309 Col. Woods interview, Dec. 7, 2005, pp. 54-55.

310 Col. Woods interview, Dec. 7, 2005, pp. 54-55.

311 Col. Woods interview, Dec. 7, 2005, p. 40. Woods and her staff were "aware of a need to get food into the Superdome," but did not interpret that as something the NORTHCOM staff had to work because they understood it was being worked at the state and JTF level. Col. Woods interview, Dec. 7, 2005, p. 40.

312 Col. Woods interview, Dec. 7, 2005, pp. 18, 40.

313 Col. Woods interview, Dec. 7, 2005, p. 20 ("Our ability to support is dependent upon a mission assignment which gives us that authority to provide the support.").

314 Col. Woods interview, Dec. 7, 2005, p. 41.

315 FEMA, Mission Assignment, 1603DR-LA-DOD-14, Sept. 1, 2005. Provided to Committee.

316 FEMA, Mission Assignment, 1603DR-LA-DOD-12, Sept. 1, 2005. Provided to Committee (requesting "DOD/NG (EMAC) provide 50,000 MRE's/Water to people located in the vicinity of the LA Superdome NLT [not later than] daybreak 01 Sept. 05. Also provide 1,000 MREs/water to people located in the vicinity of Clover Leaf" in the amount of $100,000.00); FEMA, Mission Assignment, 1603DR-LA-DOD-13, Sept. 1, 2005. Provided to Committee; filed as Bates no. DHS 0000525 (requesting "DOD/NG (EMAC) to air drop food (MRE) & water along Gulf Coast areas affected by Hurricane Katrina and City of New Orleans" in the amount of $300,000.00). These mission assignments are different from the one billion dollar mission assignment to have DOD take over logistics discussed below. The 50,000 cases of MREs delivered to Mississippi on Sept. 3-4, 2005 were delivered pursuant to the one billion dollar assignment, not these two assignments. Col. Woods interview, Dec. 7, 2005, pp. 46-47, 75-76.

317 Lokey interview, Jan. 20, 2006, pp. 133, 140.

318 Lokey interview, Jan. 20, 2006, p. 134. Lokey said that's when he told Brown, "that we needed to get help."

319 Committee staff interview of Michael Brown, former Director, FEMA, conducted on Jan. 23, 2006, transcript pp. 198-199.

320 For example, Ken Burris, FEMA's acting director of operations, told staff in his interview that, prior to Buikema's visit that Thursday morning, he did not believe DOD needed to play a larger role in logistics. Committee staff interview of Ken Burris, Chief of Operations, FEMA, conducted on Dec. 29, 2005, transcript p. 82. Col. Al Jones, a defense liaison who was assigned permanently to assist Brown and was with him on Thursday when Brown met with General Honoré stated that Brown told Honoré DOD "could possibly" help with logistics. Committee staff interview of Col. Al Jones, U.S. Army, Senior Army Advisor, Georgia Army National Guard, conducted on Mar. 2, 2006, transcript p. 36. Assistant Secretary of Defense for Homeland Defense Paul McHale said that he spoke with Brown on Wednesday, August 31, and that Brown did not mention that he wanted DOD to take over FEMA's logistics function. Committee staff interview of the Hon. Paul McHale, Assistant Secretary of Defense for Homeland Defense, U.S. Department of Defense, conducted on Feb. 17, 2005 (untranscribed).

321 Buikema interview, Nov. 21, 2005, pp. 156-157.

322 Buikema interview, Nov. 21, 2005, p. 166.

323 Buikema interview, Nov. 21, 2005, p. 169.

324 Buikema interview, Nov. 21, 2005, p. 169.

325 Buikema interview, Nov. 21, 2005, p. 170.

326 Burris interview, Dec. 29, 2005, p. 82. Initially, Burris stated that FEMA wanted DOD to "take over the process of distributing [commodities] into the forward operating areas." *Source*: Burris interview, Dec. 29, 2005, p. 117; however, after reviewing the actual mission assignment, Burris stated that DOD was being asked to assume FEMA's responsibility. *Source*: Burris interview, Dec. 29, 2005, p. 124.

327 Lokey interview, Jan. 20, 2006, p. 137.

328 Burris interview, Dec. 29, 2005, p. 112.

329 Lokey interview, Jan. 20, 2006, p. 138.

330 Lokey interview, Jan. 20, 2006, p. 134.

331 Lokey interview, Jan. 20, 2006, p. 137 ("At the time this took place, we did not need that help from them … As a matter of fact, I'm not sure they ever took over that.").

332 Brown interview, Jan. 23, 2006, p. 186 ("as I recall the meeting, it was more I want you to do logistics. I want you just to take over logistics completely"). Aside from Brown's statements in his staff interview, we have not found corroborating evidence that Brown made a request to Honoré on Wednesday that DOD take over all logistics. General Honoré did not mention it in connection with his staff interview when he discussed what he said was a brief "sidebar" meeting with Brown on this date. *Source*: Lt. Gen. Honoré interview, Jan. 9, 2006, p. 103. Honoré also does not include any meeting with Brown in his timeline of events for Wednesday August 31, but he does include a meeting with Brown the next day, Sept. 1, 2005. *Source*: U.S. Department of Defense, First U.S. Army, Joint Task Force Katrina, Hurricane Katrina Chronology. Provided to Committee. In addition, Brown testified to staff that he thought he met with Honoré on a different day than August 31, the day he had a telephone conversation with the General. *Source*: Brown interview, Jan. 23, 3005, p. 181. Thus, Brown may have made his request for logistics assistance the next day. This is consistent with the recollection of Col. Al Jones, who testified to Committee staff that Brown mentioned logistics to Honoré in a meeting with him on Thursday, Sept. 1, 2005. However, Jones remembered that Brown said DOD "could possibly" help with logistics, which is a different recollection from Brown's. *Source*: Col. Jones interview, Mar. 2, 2006, p. 36. In light of this conflicting testimony, we have not been able to resolve when Brown first raised this issue with DOD officials or what specific request he made when he did raise it.

333 Although a number of witnesses testified that this exchange and other events related to this assignment took place on Thursday, Sept. 1, the documentary evidence we have reviewed (cited below) suggests it may have taken place on Friday, Sept. 2.

334 Burris interview, Dec. 29, 2005, pp. 82, 84.

335 Col. Richard Chavez, e-mail to Thomas Kuster, Sept. 2, 2005, 9:38 a.m. Provided to Committee. In his staff interview, Chavez recalled the request as "take over all logistical operations for FEMA." *Source*: Col. Chavez interview, Nov. 9, 2005, pp. 118-119. Assistant Secretary of Defense for Homeland Defense Paul McHale recalled the initial request as "full logistics support throughout the entire area of responsibility." *Source*: McHale, Senate Committee hearing, Feb. 9, 2006.

336 Col. Chavez interview, Nov. 9, 2005, p. 121.

337 Col. Chavez interview, Nov. 9, 2005, p. 133.

338 Col. Richard Chavez, e-mail to Thomas Kuster, Sept. 2, 2005, 9:38 a.m. Provided to Committee; Col. Chavez interview, Nov. 9, 2005, pp. 119, 121.

339 ESF-1 – Transportation, for example, includes as a "function" that DOD "Provides military transportation capacity from the U.S. Transportation Command (USTRANSCOM) to move essential resources and assist in the contracting for civilian airlift when requested and approval by the Secretary of Defense." *NRP*, p. ESF #1–4.

340 Captain Mike McDaniel, e-mail to the DOD Joint Directorate of Military Support and others, Sept. 2, 2005, 10:48 a.m. ("I received a hard copy of an e-mail from Mr. Ken Burris just now with the following wording:

> Gentlemen,
>
> This is the request that was made of DOD this morning. I spoke with Col. Chaves [sic] in the Dep Sec office of DOD that instructed me that the request must come from Secretary to Secretary.
>
> 'FEMA request that DOD provide the support the planning and execution of the full logistical support to the Katrina disaster in all declared states in coordination with FEMA.'
>
> We currently have DOD lashed up with our Response Division to make this happen and our DOD reps are moving forward.

Mr. Burris indicated to me that the wording was very important.").

See also: Col. Chavez interview, Nov. 22, 2005, p. 134 ("From that point on, again, there were a number of e-mails, as we saw … that went between Mr. Burris and Chertoff saying that the Secretaries should talk. Whatever happened in the interim, the next e-mail I got from Ken Burris and phone call was okay, I'm revising the request for assistance, and the request for assistance now stated that DOD provide support to FEMA for procurement and distribution of ice, food, water, fuel, and medical supplies."). Col. Chavez thought it was significant that the request submitted on Friday requested DOD's "support" in the Katrina response in "specific areas" rather than the initial request which requested that DOD take over logistics from FEMA. Col. Chavez interview, Nov. 22, 2005, pp. 122-123.

341 Burris interview, Dec. 29, 2005, p. 83. We have not been able to establish whether Secretary Chertoff called Secretary of Defense Rumsfeld. However, an e-mail establishes that Assistant Secretary of Defense for Homeland Defense Paul McHale spoke with Chertoff's Deputy Michael Jackson, so the matter ultimately may have been handled at a level below the Secretaries. Paul McHale, e-mail to Michael Jackson, Sept. 2, 2005, 7:41 p.m. Provided to Committee ("Thought you might be interested in reading this follow-up to our conversation.").

342 McHale, Senate Committee hearing, Feb. 9, 2006; Adm. Keating interview, Feb. 3, 2006.

343 Office of the Assistant Secretary of Defense (Homeland Defense), Hurricane Katrina/Rita/Ophelia Interim Timeline, Nov. 2, 2005, p. 8. Provided to Committee; Col. Chavez interview, Nov. 22, 2005, p. 118.

344 Col. Chavez interview, Nov. 22, 2005, pp. 118, 114.

345 FEMA, Mission Assignment, 1604DR-MS-DOD-19, Sept. 2, 2005.

346 FEMA, Mission Assignment, 1604DR-MS-DOD-19, Sept. 2, 2005. As discussed below, this amount was an estimate.

347 Col. Woods interview, Dec. 7, 2005, pp. 82-83. Although some amount of this assignment was de-obligated, this had no effect on DOD's logistics operation. Col. Woods interview, Dec. 7, 2005, p. 83; Lokey interview, Jan. 20, 2006, pp. 134, 137 (Assignment was to "cover the eventualities.").

348 Written Statement of Paul McHale, Assistant Secretary of Defense for Homeland Defense, U.S. Department of Defense, for the U.S. Senate, Committee on Homeland Security and Governmental Affairs, hearing on Hurricane Katrina: The Defense Department's Role in the Response, Feb. 9, 2006, p. 8; McHale, Senate Committee hearing, Feb. 9, 2006.

349 U.S. Department of Defense, "DOD FEMA Mission Assignment Summary," as of Feb. 28, 2006, p. 1. Provided to Committee. Although FEMA de-obligated $500 million dollars from this mission and then re-obligated the same amount, we have not been able to discern any effect on DOD's activities in carrying out the mission from those fiscal decisions.

350 McHale interview, Jan. 4, 2006, pp. 43-45; McHale, Senate Committee hearing, Feb. 9, 2006.

351 Paul McHale, e-mail to Michael Jackson, Sept. 2, 2005, 7:41 p.m. Provided to Committee ("Michael – Thought you might be interested in reading this follow-up to our conversation. SECDEF has agreed to support your RFA for broad logistics support, throughout the entire four state AOR. We're working on the specific language – and a planning staff to implement it. We may actually be able to do more than you have requested. We will get back to you with written confirmation tomorrow AM. Keep up the good work. Paul").

352 U.S. Department of Defense, "MOD 8 to EXORD for DOD Support to FEMA for Hurricane Katrina," signed by Peter F. Verga, Deputy Assistant Secretary of Defense for Homeland Defense, and others, Sept. 3, 2005. Provided to Committee. MOD 8 ordered NORTHCOM to begin logistical support operations, "upon CJCS approval of CONOPS."

353 On that Friday morning, Gary Moore, the Director of Logistics for FEMA, spoke with Col. Roberta Woods, Chief of Plans and Operations in NORTHCOM's Logistics Division in Colorado Springs, Colorado, and said, "Robbie I need help. … We need help with commodity distribution: food, water, ice. … We're sending a mission assignment to … DOD for this." Woods' impression was that the Moore's request was "Pretty much open-ended, start to finish." Source: Col. Woods interview, Dec. 7, 2005, p. 36. Woods said that this call was a major turning point. "That's when life changed for me personally and for the bulk of the J4 staff." Source: Col. Woods interview, Dec. 7, 2005, p. 36. Woods asked Moore, "Who do I talk to … to figure out what's going on and what's needed?" Source: Col. Woods interview, Dec. 7, 2005, p. 43. She got the information and "immediately began doing detailed tracking as best we could, understanding processes, systems. I mean, we were … massively in the information gathering mode at this time because we had not had direct access to information. We had sort of eavesdropped." Source: Col. Woods interview, Dec. 7, 2005, p. 44.

354 Col. Woods interview, Dec. 7, 2005, p. 44.

355 Col. Woods interview, Dec. 7, 2005, p. 57.

356 Col. Woods interview, Dec. 7, 2005, p. 51.

357 Col. Woods interview, Dec. 7, 2005, p. 52.

358 Col. Woods interview, Dec. 7, 2005, p. 46.

359 Col. Woods interview, Dec. 7, 2005, p. 59; Brig. Gen. Mike Lally, e-mail to Brig. Gen. Paul Selva, Sept. 4, 2005, 12:34 p.m. Provided to Committee (discussing difficulties of having too many aircraft converge on Norfolk. Virginia to airlift MREs because it was difficult to put the MREs on pallets "in this short amount of time").

360 Col. Woods interview, Dec. 7, 2005, pp. 46, 53-53.

361 Col. Woods interview, Dec. 7, 2005, p. 62 ("And … that's what … our experience … in military logistics taught us, is you prioritize. Everything can't be all the same equal importance right now because it requires all the same kinds of transportation.").

362 Col. Woods interview, Dec. 7, 2005, pp. 46-48.

363 NRP; Col. Woods interview, Dec. 7, 2005, p. 50.

364 Col. Woods interview, Dec. 7, 2005, p. 50.

365 Col. Woods interview, Dec. 7, 2005, p. 45 ("We tried to grasp the magnitude of the task, you know, what is it you really want us to do, because FEMA did not step out. And … for a little while, we were in the is FEMA going to completely back out and DOD has it all, or is FEMA staying and we're just going to assist?"). See also: JTF-Katrina, Commander's Assessment, Sept. 2, 2005, 7 p.m. Provided to Committee.

366 NORTHCOM's logistics staff thought it likely that the distribution infrastructure at the state level – in other words, after the operational staging area managed by FEMA – "would remain in place to execute that piece of the task." Source: Col. Woods interview, Dec. 7, 2005, p. 63. Admiral Keating said NORTHCOM did not want to take over distributing commodities for the last part of the distribution chain because DOD could not legally command National Guard forces involved in that task. Source: Admiral Keating interview, Feb. 3, 2006. Col. Jones, the military advisor to PFO Brown, who was involved with developing DOD's commodities distribution plan during the first weekend after the storm, told the Committee that the National Guard advised they would remain in control of distribution from the PODs. Source: Col. Jones interview, Mar. 2, 2006, p. 40.

367 Rear Adm. Steven Maas, e-mail to Lt. Gen. Robert Dail, Sept. 3, 2005, 2:59 p.m. Provided to Committee; Col. Roberta Woods, e-mail to Col. James Hodge, Sept. 5, 2005, 8:24 p.m. Provided to Committee ("NORTHCOM Headquarters have responsibility for distribution management from the depot (either DLA or USACE contract, etc) to the Forward Operational Staging Area [FOSA] – that's from the strategic level into the J[oint] O[perating] A[rea]. J[oint] T[ask] F[orce]-Katrina

… has responsibility for management at the FOSA (in coordination with FEMA) down to the state designated distribution points. (That's the operational level.) The state has responsibility for the tactical level distribution to individuals.").

368 Col. James Hodge, e-mail to Rear Adm. Steven Maas, Sept. 6, 2005, 9:18 p.m. Provided to Committee.

369 Col. James Hodge, e-mail to Rear Adm. Steven Maas, Sept. 6, 2005, 9:18 p.m. Provided to Committee. *See also*: Lt. Gen. Robert Dail, e-mail to Lt. Gen. Duncan McNabb, Sept. 3, 2005, 11:56 a.m. Provided to Committee (DOD "will not execute 'tactical distribution'.").

370 Wells interview, Nov. 15, 2005, p. 91 ("I don't recall distribution of supplies being I'll call it, a red item. Maybe an amber item, but it was working. We had the op – we had the staging area at Beauregard working; we had an oversight feeding that [was] working, and then we were putting stuff forward. Now, from that point forward, we had problems. But people were getting food, people were getting water, people in the Superdome got food and water every day.").

371 Col. Woods interview, Dec. 7, 2005, pp. 45-46.

372 Paul McHale, e-mail to Michael Jackson, Sept. 2, 2005, 7:41 p.m. Provided to Committee.

373 McHale interview, Jan. 4, 2006, p. 16.

374 Committee staff interview of Michael Jackson, Deputy Secretary, U.S. Department of Homeland Security, conducted on Jan. 27, 2006, transcript p. 25.

375 Jackson interview, Jan. 27, 2006, p. 26.

376 McHale interview, Jan. 4, 2006, pp. 15-16.

377 Jackson interview, Jan. 27, 2006, pp. 26-27.

378 McHale interview, Jan. 4, 2006, p. 16. Edward Buikema, the acting Director of FEMA's Response Division was present at the meeting and described England's view of whether DOD was willing to take on large portions of the response effort: "He was – he was more than willing to help out, as I recall. He was very positive, very much no resistance. It was a very frank discussion. As I mentioned, Deputy Secretary Jackson was there. I was there, but just observing more than anything, but it was a positive, very positive discussion." Buikema interview, Nov. 21, 2005, p. 259. The colloquy continued, "Q: So people at the top level seemed to want to get this done. A: Yes, sir."

379 Col. Darryl Roberson, e-mail to Maj. Gen. Rich Rowe, Sept. 3, 2005, 10:39 p.m. Provided to Committee; filed as Bates no. DHS-HSOC-0004-0003817; Buikema interview, Nov. 21, 2005, pp. 160-162.

380 This requirement appears redundant vis a vis the earlier $1 billion logistics mission assignment, and indeed, one draft version of this mission assignment indicates "portions of which may already be covered on MS-DOD 19," the logistics mission assignment. Col. Darryl Roberson, e-mail to Maj. Gen. Rich Rowe, Sept. 3, 2005, 10:39 p.m. Provided to Committee; filed as Bates no. DHS-HSOC-0004-0003817.

381 Paul McHale, e-mail to Matthew Broderick and others, Sept. 5, 2005, 5:07 p.m. Provided to Committee (including e-mail chain among DHS and DOD officials regarding the large FEMA Mission Assignment attached to this e-mail); Col. Darryl Roberson, e-mail to Maj. Gen. Rich Rowe, Sept. 3, 2005, 10:39 p.m. Provided to Committee; filed as Bates no. DHS-HSOC-0004-0003817 (enclosing a very similar list that appears to have been drafted earlier in the process but which contains substantially the same list of missions, and which states "Sir, there was a meeting this evening with representatives of DHS, FEMA, OSD, JS, and COE to craft a RFA/mission statement that would reflect the increased responsibilities DoD is taking on with Hurricane Katrina. The following two products [one an organization chart and one a list of the missions described above] have been agreed to at the ASD level.").

382 This original list was approved by the Deputy Secretaries of Defense and Homeland Security in the evening on Saturday, Sept. 3, 2005. *Source*: Matthew Broderick, e-mail to Gail Kulisch and Admiral Timothy Sullivan, Sept. 4, 2005, 12:30 p.m. Provided to Committee (referencing the attachment and stating, "Results are a series of meetings between both Dep Secs and lower level staffing actions"). On Sunday, Sept. 4, Deputy Secretary England sent a memorandum to the Secretary of Defense setting forth the draft in written text. *Source*: Deputy Secretary of Defense and Vice Chairman Joint Chiefs of Staff, memorandum to Secretary of Defense, Chairman Joint Chiefs of Staff, and Admiral Keating, Sept. 4, 2005, 1:30 p.m. Provided to Committee ("If you agree with the draft it will be sent to DHS to be put on the normal RFA form. It will then be processed and appear in an orders book for your final approval."). The Secretary of Defense, who was traveling to the Gulf Coast when he received this memorandum via facsimile, "responded favorably to the substantive content of this document" but instructed that the various requests be broken out into "more logical and operationally effective component parts" because "the topics included … related resources." *Source*: McHale interview, Jan. 4, 2006, p. 19. McHale stated that there was "no resistance on the part of this department to the underlying substance of the RFA." Rather, "The Secretary instructed me to disaggregate a very brief, very broad single RFA into more logical and operationally effective component parts so that mission areas that were discretely defined would not be illogically folded into a single document."

383 Written Statement of McHale, Senate Committee hearing, Feb. 9, 2006, p. 9.

384 McHale interview, Jan. 4, 2006, p. 20. *See also*: Frank DiFalco, e-mail to Ken Burris, Sept. 5, 2005, 7:28 p.m. Provided to Committee ("please process the attached RFAs and submit to DOD this evening."). Although we cannot pinpoint the time of approval, these two sources indicate that the Secretary of Defense approved the RFAs after 7:28 p.m. the evening of Sept. 5, 2005, although he vocally approved them earlier. Paul McHale, e-mail to Frank DiFalco, Sept. 5, 2005, 7:37 p.m. Provided to Committee ("SecDef gave VOCO to the draft RFA we sent you.").

385 Maj. Gen. Caldwell interview, Feb. 28, 2006, p. 36.

386 Michael Jackson, e-mail to Paul McHale, Sept. 6, 2005, 11:17 a.m. Provided to Committee.

387 Written Statement of McHale, Senate Committee hearing, Feb. 9, 2006, p. 9; Keating interview, Feb. 3, 2006.

388 Jackson interview, Jan. 27, 2006, pp. 27-28.

389 The USS *Bataan* launched helicopters for search and rescue and logistics missions at 6 p.m. ET, Tues. Aug 30, 2005, in coordination with U.S. Coast Guard District Eight. Capt. Snyder interview, Nov. 14, 2005.

390 Brig. Gen. Graham interview, Jan. 12, 2006, pp. 25-28, 44-45.

391 U.S. Northern Command, USNORTHCOM Hurricane Katrina Timeline (Draft), p. 11. Provided to Committee (indicates Wednesday, Aug. 31, 2005.: Aeromedical Evacuation mission (47 patients).).

392 U.S. Joint Forces Command, Hurricane Katrina Comprehensive Timeline, Nov. 15, 2006, p. 8. Provided to Committee (indicates Friday, Sept. 2: "Navy P-3 conduct streaming video mission to assess hurricane impact.").

393 U.S. Joint Forces Command, Hurricane Katrina Comprehensive Timeline, Nov. 15, 2006, p. 7. Provided to Committee (indicates Thursday, Sep 1: "468,000 MREs shipped.").

394 Col. Joerger interview, Jan. 6, 2006, pp. 13-16; U.S. Northern Command, USNORTHCOM Hurricane Katrina Timeline (Draft), p. 15. Provided to Committee (indicates that on Friday, Sept. 2, 2005: "Navy CH-53 helos dumping sand bags [in] levee breaches.").

395 U.S. Northern Command, USNORTHCOM Hurricane Katrina Timeline (Draft), p. 17. Provided to Committee (indicates that on Saturday, Sept. 3, 2005: "Slingload of MRE's are made along the Gulf Coast.").

396 Lokey interview, Jan. 20, 2006, p. 135 (Q: So they were already helping with this [the one billion dollar logistics request]? A: Oh heavens, yes. Oh, yes.).

397 Lokey interview, Jan. 20, 2006, p. 136 ("But what I will speak to is Col. [Daskevich] and his people. They busted their ass to do anything I asked them to do. Our bureaucratic processes are slow."). Lokey described DOD's assistance in evacuating the Superdome, stating "They did the planning for it and their people – they had people down at the bus distribution, or the collection points, staging areas, and at the Dome, they were helping organize the National Guard folks and the other folks on scene, lined the people up and get them on the buses. They did it for us and I thought they did an excellent job." Lokey interview, Jan. 20, 2006, p. 140. *See also*: Lokey interview, Jan. 20, 2006, p. 205 ("Honoré's a guy, he makes things happen. … He was picking up garbage, he was rescuing people, he was doing all sorts of stuff that he had the people and the stuff to do.").

 U.S. Joint Forces Command, Hurricane Katrina Comprehensive Timeline, Nov. 15, 2005, p. 8. Provided to Committee (indicates Friday, Sept. 2: "Navy P-3 conduct streaming video mission to assess hurricane impact.").

 U.S. Joint Forces Command, Hurricane Katrina Comprehensive Timeline, Nov. 15, 2005, p. 7. Provided to Committee (indicates Thursday, Sept. 1: "468,000 MREs shipped.").

 U.S. Northern Command, USNORTHCOM Hurricane Katrina Timeline (Draft), p. 15. Provided to Committee (indicates that on Friday, Sept. 2, 2005: "Navy CH-53 helos dumping sand bags in levee breaches.").

 U.S. Northern Command, USNORTHCOM Hurricane Katrina Timeline (Draft), p. 17. Provided to Committee (indicates that on Saturday, Sept. 3, 2005: "Slingload of MRE's are made along the Gulf Coast.").

Lokey interview, Jan. 20, 2006, p. 135.

Lokey interview, Jan. 20, 2006, p. 136 ("But what I will speak to is Col. [Daskevich] and his people. They busted their ass to do anything I asked them to do. Our bureaucratic processes are slow"). Lokey described DOD's assistance in evacuating the Superdome, stating "They did the planning for it and their people – they had people down at the bus distribution, or the collection points, staging areas, and at the Dome, they were helping organize the National Guard folks and the other folks on scene, lined the people up and get them on the buses. They did it for us and I thought they did an excellent job." *Source*: Lokey interview, Jan. 20, 2006, p. 140. *See also*: Lokey interview, Jan. 20, 2006, p. 205 ("he makes things happen, and quite frankly, when he started making things happen, I didn't care because he was making things happen and he was picking up garbage, he was rescuing people, he was doing all sorts of stuff that he had the people and the stuff to do."); Buikema interview, Nov. 21, 2005, p. 181 ("I believe they did" fulfill all mission assignments that FEMA gave them; "In terms of the communications and cooperation between us, it was good … it was good."); Committee staff interview of Maj. Gen. Bennett Landreneau, U.S. Army, Adjutant General, Louisiana, conducted on Jan. 11, 2006, transcript p. 78 ("I believe he [Brig. Gen. Graham] was helping a lot.").

398 Wells interview, Nov. 14, 2005, pp. 122, 123.

399 Lokey interview, Jan. 20, 2006, p. 135.

400 Testimony of Gov. Haley Barbour, Mississippi, before the U.S. Senate, Committee on Homeland Security and Governmental Affairs, hearing on *Hurricane Katrina: The Role of the Governors in Managing the Catastrophe*, Feb. 2, 2006 ("Ultimately, the United States military provided us 1.5 million MREs that – I remember them flying in C-17s, if I remember right, there at Gulfport, Biloxi, and started unloading tens of thousands of cases of MREs. Again, I don't know whether to attribute that to FEMA being agile or the military just filling in for them, but for us, it was a godsend.").

401 Gov. Haley Barbour, Mississippi, Executive Order 939, Aug. 26, 2005; Written Statement of Maj. Gen. Harold A. Cross, Adjutant General, Mississippi Army and Air National Guard, before the U.S. House, Select Bipartisan Committee to Investigate the Preparation for and Response to Hurricane Katrina, hearing on *Hurricane Katrina: Preparedness and Response by the State of Mississippi*, Dec. 7, 2005.

402 Joint Force Headquarters, Mississippi National Guard, Memorandum, "Hurricane Katrina Narrative," Oct. 20, 2005, p.

1. Provided to Committee.

403 Written Statement of Maj. Gen. Cross, House Select Committee hearing, Dec. 7, 2005.

404 Written Statement of Maj. Gen. Cross, House Select Committee hearing, Dec. 7, 2005.

405 Joint Force Headquarters, Mississippi National Guard, Memorandum, "Hurricane Katrina Narrative," Oct. 20, 2005, p. 9. Provided to Committee.

406 Joint Force Headquarters, Mississippi National Guard, Memorandum, "Hurricane Katrina Narrative," Oct. 20, 2005, p. 7. Provided to Committee.

407 Gov. Barbour, Senate Committee hearing, Feb. 2, 2006.

408 Committee staff interview of Maj. Gen. Harold Cross, Adjutant General, Mississippi Army and Air National Guard, conducted on Jan. 26, 2006, transcript p. 12.

409 These forces included the Seabee base in Gulfport, Keesler Air Force Base in Biloxi, and Columbus Air Force Base. General Cross interview, Jan. 26, 2006, p. 15.

410 Written Statement of Maj. Gen. Cross, House Select Committee hearing, Dec. 7, 2005.

411 Committee staff interview of Col. Joe Spraggins, U.S. Air Force, Director, Harrison County Emergency Management Agency, MS, conducted on Nov. 17, 2005, transcript pp. 131-132.

412 Maj. Gen. Cross interview, Jan. 26, 2006, pp. 38-39.

413 Maj. Gen. Cross interview, Jan. 26, 2006, p. 41.

414 Joint Force Headquarters, Mississippi National Guard, Memorandum, "Hurricane Katrina Narrative," Oct. 20, 2005, p. 4. Provided to Committee.

415 Theodore Roosevelt, First Annual Message to Congress, Dec. 3, 1901. 14 Messages and Papers of the President 6672.

416 Louisiana Office of the Governor, Response to the U.S. Senate Committee on Homeland Security and Governmental Affairs Document and Information Request Dated October 7, 2005 and to the U.S. House of Representatives Select Committee to Investigate the Preparation for and Response to Hurricane Katrina, Overview of Gov. Kathleen Babineaux Blanco's Actions in Preparation for and Response to Hurricane Katrina, Dec. 2, 2005, p. 7 [hereinafter Louisiana Office of the Governor, Governor's Timeline]. *See also*: Eric Lipton, Eric Schmitt, and Thom Shanker, "Political Issues Snarled Plans for Troop Aid," *The New York Times*, Sept. 9, 2005, Section A, p. 1.

417 Louisiana Office of the Governor, Governor's Timeline, p. 7.

418 *See*: Eric Lipton, Eric Schmitt, and Thom Shanker, "Political Issues Snarled Plans for Troop Aid," *The New York Times*, Sept. 9, 2005, , p. 1; Robert Travis Scott, "Politics delayed troops dispatch to N.O.," New Orleans *Times-Picayune*, Dec. 11, 2005, p. 1; Susan B. Glasser and Michael Grunwald, "The Steady Buildup to a City's Chaos; Confusion Reigned At Every Level of Government," *The Washington Post*, Sept. 11, 2005, p. A01; Nicole Gaouette, and others, "Katrina's Aftermath, The Response; Put to Katrina's Test; After 9/11, a master plan for disasters was drawn. It didn't weather the storm," *Los Angeles Times*, Sept. 11, 2005, p. 1.

419 *NRP*, p. 34.

420 The National Response Plan (NRP) describes the Joint Field Office (JFO) as "a multiagency coordination center established locally. It provides a central location for coordination of Federal, State, local, tribal, nongovernmental, and private-sector organizations with primary responsibility for threat response and incident support. The JFO enables the effective and efficient coordination of Federal incident-related prevention, preparedness, response, and recovery actions." *NRP*, p. 28.

421 The NRP designates the Defense Coordinating Officer (DCO) as "DOD's single point of contact in the JFO," and assigns him the responsibility to "coordinate and process" requests for assistance, "orchestrate the accomplishment of approved mission assignments," and "refer problematic or contentious issues" to higher military authorities. *NRP*, p. 42. The NRP excepts three types of requests for assistance from the requirement to coordinate through the Defense Coordinating Officer: (1) requests to the Army Corps of Engineers, which itself is considered a primary supporting agency under the Plan; (2) requests to the Army and Air National Guard, which under the NRP "are not part of Federal military response efforts"; and (3) requests for support to the Federal Bureau of Investigation for law enforcement and domestic counterterrorism activities. The NRP states that the DCO "may continue to perform all duties" in the NRP even if a Joint Task Force is established. *NRP*, p. 42.

422 McHale, House Select Committee hearing, Oct. 27, 2005.

423 Col. Daskevich interview, Jan. 10, 2006, p. 132.

424 Col. Daskevich interview, Jan. 10, 2006, p. 132. William Lokey, the FEMA Federal Coordinating Officer, also stated FEMA did not make requests for large numbers of troops. Committee staff interview of William Lokey, Federal Coordinating Officer for Hurricane Katrina in Louisiana, FEMA, conducted on Nov. 4, 2005, transcript p. 224.

425 U.S. Library of Congress, Congressional Research Service, *Hurricane Katrina: DOD Disaster Response*, by Steve Bowman, Lawrence Kapp, and Amy Belasco, Jan. 24, 2006, p. CRS-8.

426 10 U.S.C. §§ 12301, 12302, 12304. The Congressional Research Service states that in the event of a catastrophic natural disaster, 10 U.S.C. § 12302 – which permits the President to activate the National Guard "in time of war or of national emergency declared by the President or when otherwise authorized by law" – "would probably be the authority that would be most useful for calling large numbers of National Guard personnel and other reservists to federal active

duty for an extended period of time. … Historically, however, 10 U.S.C. § 12302 has only been used for national security purposes and it could be controversial to use this authority for disaster relief purposes." U.S. Library of Congress, Congressional Research Service, *Hurricane Katrina: DOD Disaster Response*, by Steve Bowman, Lawrence Kapp, and Amy Belasco, Jan. 24, 2006, p. CRS-10.

427 10 U.S.C. §§ 331-335.

428 10 U.S.C. § 12406. This section requires such an order to be issued through the governors of the affected states.

429 U.S. Library of Congress, Congressional Research Service, *The Use of Federal Troops for Disaster Assistance: Legal Issues*, by Jennifer K. Elsea, Sept. 16, 2005, p. CRS-3.

430 DOD Directive 3025.12, MACDIS.

431 *NRP*, p. 42.

432 The National Response Plan states:

> Nothing in this plan alters or impedes the ability of federal, State, local, or tribal departments and agencies to carry out their specific authorities or perform their responsibilities under all applicable laws, Executive orders, and directives. Additionally, nothing in this plan in intended to impact or impede the ability of any Federal department or agency head to take an issue of concern directly to the President, the Assistant to the President for Homeland Security, the Assistant to the President for National Security, or any other member of the President's staff. *NRP*, p. 2.

433 Article II of the Emergency Management Assistance Compact (EMAC) Articles of Agreement states:

> The prompt, full, and effective utilization of resources of the participating states, including any resources onhand or available from the Federal Government or any other source, that are essential to the safety, care and welfare of the people in the event of any emergency or disaster declared by a party state, shall be the underlying principle on which all articles of this compact shall be understood.

National Emergency Management Association, "EMAC Articles of Agreement." http://www.emacweb.org/?146. Accessed on May 18, 2006.

434 Louisiana National Guard, Timeline of Significant Events Hurricane Katrina, Dec. 7, 2005; National Guard Bureau, Hurricane Katrina Update Brief, Sept. 11, 2005, 11 a.m. Provided to Committee.

435 10 U.S.C. §§ 10501, 10502. Lt. Gen. Blum interview, Jan. 19, 2006, p. 23.

436 Lt. Gen. Steven Blum, memorandum for Secretary of Defense, through Assistant Secretary of Defense (Homeland Defense), Sept. 5, 2005, p. 1. Provided to Committee.

437 Lt. Gen. Steven Blum, memorandum for Secretary of Defense, through Assistant Secretary of Defense (Homeland Defense), Sept. 5, 2005, p. 1. Provided to Committee.

438 Lt. Gen. Steven Blum, memorandum for Secretary of Defense, through Assistant Secretary of Defense (Homeland Defense), Sept. 5, 2005, p. 1. Provided to Committee.

439 Gordon England, memorandum for Secretary of the Army and Acting Secretary of the Air Force, Sept. 7, 2005. Provided to Committee.

440 David S. Addington, e-mail to William J. Haynes, Aug. 28, 2005, 8:41 p.m. Provided to Committee; filed as Bates no. 000007. Mr. Addington recommended that Mr. Haynes prepare a "Proclamation to Disperse," whereby the President would "immediately order the insurgents to disperse and retire peaceably within their abodes" (10 U.S.C. §334), and executive orders for 10 U.S.C. 332, "Use of militia and armed forces to enforce Federal authority," and 10 U.S.C. §334, "Interference with State and Federal Law."

441 Maj. Gen. Richard Rowe, e-mail to Maj. Gen. Thomas Miller, Aug. 31, 2005, 7:46, a.m. Provided to Committee.

442 Maj. Gen. Terry Scherling, e-mail to Maj. Gen. Rowe and others, Aug. 31, 2005, 10:25 a.m. Provided to Committee.

443 Committee staff interview of Col. Thomas Beron, Commander, 61st Troop Command, Louisiana Army National Guard, and Lt. Col. Douglas Mouton, Commander, 225th Engineering Group, Louisiana National Guard, conducted on Dec. 1, 2005, transcript p. 102.

444 Louisiana Office of the Governor, Governor's Timeline, p. 9.

445 For an explanation of Lt. Gen. Honoré's activities prior to being designated Commander of Joint Task Force Katrina, see prior text regarding the "First Army" and "Army Commanders."

446 *See*: National Guard Bureau, After Action Review, "Hurricane Response September 2005," Dec. 21, 2005, p. 13. Provided to Committee (second entry for "31 August Wednesday": "CNGB asks to talk with MG Landreneau, TAG LA"). Lt. Gen. Blum's recollection and the NGB timeline is consistent with notes dated at 7:21 a.m. on Wednesday the 31st taken by National Guard Bureau Major Karl Konzelman, of a conversation between Maj. Gen. Landreneau, Army National Guard Director Lt. Gen. Clyde A. Vaughn, and Lt. Gen. Blum, as well as the recollection of Lt. Gen. Vaughn. Major Konzelman's notes are reprinted in: U.S. House, Select Bipartisan Committee to Investigate the Preparation for and Response to Hurricane Katrina, *A Failure of Initiative*. Washington: Government Printing Office, 2006, p. 206 [hereinafter U.S. House, *A Failure of Initiative*]. *See also*: Committee staff interview of Lt. Gen. Clyde A. Vaughn, U.S. Army, Director, Army National Guard, U.S. Department of Defense, conducted on Jan. 18, 2006, transcript pp. 22-23.

447 Testimony of Maj. Gen. Bennett C. Landreneau, U.S. Army, Adjutant General, Louisiana, before the U.S. Senate,

Committee on Homeland Security and Governmental Affairs, hearing on *Hurricane Katrina: The Defense Department's Role in the Response*, Feb. 9, 2006. In his interview with the Committee staff, Maj. Gen. Landreneau said he requested an active-duty division. "I told him that we felt like we needed active-duty support in the state. I felt like we needed an active-duty division to help us – to help with the planning and execution of the movement of displaced persons out of New Orleans." *Source*: Maj. Gen. Landreneau interview, Jan. 11, 2006, p. 9. Maj. Gen. Landreneau's testimony that he requested an active-duty headquarters element rather than an entire division is consistent with the recollections of other LANG officers, see below. Maj. Gen. Landreneau also told the Committee staff he informed FEMA Director Brown and FCO Lokey of his request to Lt. Gen. Honoré for a headquarters division of active-duty troops. Brown "turned to his staff and said we need to make sure we log that request and that it's properly funneled through the right request chain." *Source*: Maj. Gen. Landreneau interview, Jan. 11, 2006, pp. 56-57. Neither Brown nor Lokey could recall that conversation or any other conversation in which Maj. Gen. Landreneau requested federal active-duty troops. *Source*: Lokey interview, Jan. 20, 2006, p. 98 (Q. "At any time, did General Landreneau relate to you any request that he made to General Honoré for Federal troops?" A. "I don't recall it."); Brown interview, Jan. 23, 2006, p. 188 (Q. "Do you remember the first time you learned of a request for significant numbers of troops, National Guard or Federal active-duty?" A. "You know, counsel, I don't."); *Compare with*: Committee staff interview of Col. Steven Dabadie, Former Chief of Staff, Louisiana National Guard, conducted on Jan. 12, 2006, transcript p. 118 ("He told me that the first conversation that he had shortly after I talked to him was with General Honoré, and they talked about a division headquarters and tasking that division headquarters with planning, coordinating, executing evacuation.").

448 "I told him the need for troops and that I needed his [help] with the EMAC [Emergency Management Assistance Compact] push, and gave him an assessment of what I thought we needed at that time. … At that time that we were talking about 10,000 or more, and then I called him back later and I said it's going to be more." General Landreneau interview, Jan. 11, 2006, pp. 12-14. *See also*: Task Force Pelican, Louisiana National Guard Timeline of Significant Events Hurricane Katrina, Dec. 7, 2005, p. 6 (sixth entry for "30 Aug 05": "Requested additional EMAC assistance through NGB"). Maj. Gen. Landreneau's testimony that he first sought assistance from the National Guard Bureau on Tuesday, August 30, is consistent with the recollections of Lt. Gen. Honoré and three of his subordinate officers in the Louisiana National Guard: Brig. Gen. Gary Jones, the Commander of the LANG's Joint Task Force Pelican, Brig. Gen. Brod Veillon, Assistant Adjutant General for the Louisiana National Guard and Commander of the Louisiana Air National Guard, and Col. Steve Dabadie, Chief of Staff for Maj. Gen. Landreneau. (All witnesses interviewed by the Committee were instructed not to discuss their testimony with other potential witnesses and agreed to abide by this instruction.)

Maj. Gen. Landreneau also stated that in a subsequent conversation he relayed the substance of his conversation with Lt. Gen. Blum to Lt. Gen. Honoré. *Source*: Maj. Gen. Landreneau interview, Jan. 11, 2006, General Honoré. *Source*: General Landreneau interview, Jan. 11, 2006, p. 12. As a result of differing recollections, the Committee is unable to determine whether Maj. Gen. Landreneau had more than one conversation with Lt. Gen. Honoré on Tuesday, or the precise time when any such conversation occurred.

449 Lt. Gen. Honoré interview, Jan. 9, 2006, pp. 72-74.

450 Lt. Gen. Honoré interview, Jan. 9, 2006, p. 67.

451 Lt. Gen. Honoré interview, Jan. 9, 2006, pp. 67, 75. Lt. Gen. Honoré also said he told Maj. Gen. Landreneau that "We had about 5,000 troops that possibly could be ready to deploy," including the 82nd Airborne Division and the 1st Cavalry Division of the 5th Army. Lt. Gen. Honoré interview, Jan. 9, 2006, p. 67. Maj. Gen. Landreneau recalled this conversation occurring on Wednesday, August 31, when Lt. Gen. Honoré arrived at the Superdome. *Source*: Maj. Gen. Landreneau interview, Jan. 11, 2006, pp. 8-9.

452 Referring to the NGB's timeline, which reports a request for 5,000 troops from Maj. Gen. Landreneau first occurring early Wednesday morning, Lt. Gen. Blum stated, "I talked to him at home one night before that, which probably was Tuesday night, but I don't see that in here [the NGB timeline], because this is generated from my operations center, not from my home phone." Lt. Gen. Blum interview, Jan. 19, 2006, p. 33.

453 Louisiana National Guard Brig. Gen. Brod Veillon recounted how his concerns over security became magnified when the rising waters flooded the generator providing power to the Superdome:

> About 11 on Tuesday night, they came to us and said, "Boys, the water is rising. The generator has about a foot to go. You will lose the generator when the water tops the wall." I asked the man, "What happens when we lose a generator?" He said, "All the lights go out." I said, "Every light in the Dome?" "Every light." So I knew the Dome would go dark, and I was concerned at that point for what we were going to do if the whole place went black.

Committee staff interview of Brig. Gen. Brod Veillon, Assistant Adjutant General – Air, Louisiana National Guard, conducted on Nov. 29, 2005, transcript p. 58.

454 A number of witnesses, including Col. Dabadie, provided conflicting and inconsistent accounts of when this conversation and other conversations about the need for additional troops occurred. Col. Dabadie interview, Jan. 12, 2006, pp. 99-103, 107. The Committee cannot rule out the possibility that there was more than one related conversation on this subject at different times from early Tuesday to early Wednesday. The weight of the evidence and testimony indicates that this particular conversation occurred in the wee hours of Wednesday morning.

455 Committee staff interview of Brig. Gen. Gary Jones, Assistant Joint Forces Commander/Army, Louisiana Army National Guard, conducted on Dec. 7, 2005, transcript pp. 92-93, 139-40.

456 Col. Dabadie interview, Jan. 12, 2006, pp. 99-100. According to Col. Dabadie, "a little bit after" that conversation, Maj. Gen. Landreneau told him that he had asked Lt. Gen. Honoré "about a division type headquarters." Col. Dabadie added:

"And I think that is kind of where General Graham came into the picture, and then the rest of the forces were National Guard – conversation with General Blum and the rest of the forces were National Guard through EMAC." Col. Dabadie interview, Jan. 12, 2006, pp. 102-103, 118.

457 Brig. Gen. Veillon interview, Nov. 29, 2005, p. 191.

458 Lt. Gen. Blum interview, Jan. 19, 2006, p. 34. Referring to notes taken by his assistant, Major Karl Konzelman of the Army National Guard, Lieutenant General Clyde Vaughn, Director of the Army National Guard, provided a similar recollection of this conversation. Lt. Gen. Vaughn understood Maj. Gen. Landreneau's primary need was for additional security forces. *Source*: Lt. Gen. Vaughn interview, Jan. 18, 2006, p. 23. Major General Harold Cross, the Adjutant General of the Mississippi National Guard, called General Blum about the same time, and also asked the National Guard Bureau to expedite the EMAC process for Mississippi. *Source*: Maj. Gen. Cross interview, Jan. 26, 2006, pp. 12-14. *See also*: Maj. Gen. Landreneau interview, Jan. 11, 2006, pp. 49-50; Lt. Gen. Vaughn interview, Jan. 18, 2006, p. 49.

459 Lt. Gen. Blum interview, Jan. 19, 2006, p. 36.

460 National Guard Bureau, Hurricane Katrina Update Brief, Sept. 10, 2005, 10 a.m. Provided to Committee.

461 Lt. Gen. Vaughn interview, Jan. 18, 2006, p. 31. The Committee asked Lt. Gen. Vaughn:

> Q: Is it correct to characterize the process as follows, that initially General Landreneau, when he called and said I need 5,000 that he was saying this is big, I'm going to need a lot; I don't know exactly what I'm going to need, but I'm going to need a lot. And then, on the Guard's end, you interpreted that … [t]hey're going to need a lot, let's just send whatever we've got in, and we'll refine it? Was that what you were doing?

> LT. GEN. VAUGHN: I think that's right on the money. I think it's exactly like that.

Lt. Gen. Vaughn interview, Jan. 18, 2006, p. 33.

462 National Guard Bureau, Hurricane Katrina Update Brief, Sept. 10, 2005, 10 a.m. Provided to Committee.

463 National Guard Bureau, After Action Review, "Hurricane Response September 2005," Dec. 21, 2005, p. 6. Provided to Committee.

464 National Guard Bureau, After Action Review, "Hurricane Response September 2005," Dec. 21, 2005, p. 6. Provided to Committee.

465 Lt. Gen. Blum interview, Jan. 19, 2006, p. 54.

466 National Guard Bureau, After Action Review, "Hurricane Response September 2005," Dec. 21, 2005, p. 20. Provided to Committee.

467 Lt. Gen. Blum interview, Jan. 19, 2006, p. 54

468 National Guard Bureau, After Action Review, "Hurricane Response September 2005," Dec. 21, 2005, p. 20. Provided to Committee.

469 Lt. Gen. Blum interview, Jan. 19, 2006, pp. 54-55.

470 McHale, House Select Committee hearing, Oct. 27, 2005.

471 Maj. Gen. Rowe interview, Jan. 20, 2006, pp. 125-126.

472 Adm. Keating interview, Feb. 3, 2006.

473 Gen. Myers interview, Feb. 28, 2006.

474 U.S. Department of Defense, First U.S. Army, Joint Task Force Katrina, "Hurricane Katrina Chronology." Provided to Committee.

475 Lt. Gen. Honoré interview, Jan. 9, 2006, pp. 71-72.

476 Maj. Gen. Landreneau interview, Jan. 11, 2006, pp. 43-44.

477 Wells interview, Nov. 15, 2005, p. 121; Lt. Gen. Honoré interview, Jan. 9, 2006, pp. 76-77. Although Gen. Honoré talks about evacuation planning, he does not state that he was asked to take over the evacuation.

478 Committee staff interview of Phil Parr, Federal Coordinating Officer, Region I, FEMA, conducted on Nov. 16, 2005, transcript p. 47.

479 Parr interview, Nov. 16, 2005, p. 69. There were similar uninformed expectations in FEMA headquarters. Col. Don Harrington, the lead DOD liaison to FEMA, was asked whether at FEMA there was "any expectation that [Lt. Gen. Honoré] would be bringing a large number of forces with him?" "Yes, yes," Col Harrington responded and then explained:

> I had to kind of let them know that the troop presence he brought, he didn't control the Guard. They had to understand that. But that he was not necessarily going to bring a huge number of troops initially. You know, he had to get an assessment, and plus you had a large number of National Guard troops.

Col. Harrington interview, Jan. 6, 2006, p. 100.

480 Maj. Gen. Landreneau interview, Jan. 11, 2006, p. 44.

481 Committee staff interview of Col. Glenn Curtis, Chief of Staff, Louisiana National Guard, and Lt. Col. Jacques Thibodeaux, Joint Director of Military Support to Civilian Authorities and Branch Chief, Louisiana National Guard, conducted on Dec. 6, 2006, transcript pp. 270-271.

482 Lt. Gen. Honoré interview, Jan. 9, 2006, pp. 131-134.

483 Wells interview, Nov. 15, 2005, p. 67. Lt. Col. Jacques Thibodeaux of the Louisiana National Guard, the Joint Director of Military Support during Katrina, responded to Mr. Wells's concern, as raised by Committee staff during the interview, by stating that it was Mayor Nagin, not Lt. Gen. Honoré, who was at all times in charge of the evacuation of the Superdome and New Orleans:

> Mayor Nagin was also there and Col. Ebert, who is his emergency operations manager – I think Col. Ebert's title is Director of Homeland Security for New Orleans – were both also involved in that meeting. … So it was, once again, not a break in protocol. It was a civilian entity, a civilian representative trying to facilitate the evacuation of his city. And General Landreneau and General Honoré were both there in any attempt to facilitate that. Basically a unified command system; a meeting amongst commanders of certain areas to facilitate DOD support, both National Guard and active component.

Lt. Col. Thibodeaux interview, Dec. 6, 2006, pp. 267-269.

484 Louisiana Office of the Governor, Governor's Timeline, p. 9.

485 Committee staff interview of Terry Ryder, Executive Counsel, Office of the Governor, LA, conducted on Jan. 10, 2006, transcript pp. 192-194. Andy Kopplin, Chief of Staff to Governor Blanco, recalled a similar conversation with Senator Vitter:

> Either Mr. Ryder or Senator Vitter mentioned to me Senator Vitter wanted to visit with the Governor about his conversation with Mr. Rove about federalization in regard to the Governor's conversation that morning with Ms. Townsend, the Homeland Security advisor. And the question was, did the Governor's request for additional federal assistance constitute a request for federalization, because that was the way it had been reported to the Senator per his – at some point, whether it was Senator Vitter first or Terry or – well, I talked to both Terry, and I talked to Senator Vitter about that.

Committee staff interview of Andy Kopplin, former Chief of Staff, Office of the Governor, LA, conducted on Jan. 6, 2006, transcript p. 122.

486 Ryder interview, Jan. 10, 2006, p. 202.

487 Ryder interview, Jan. 10, 2006, p. 203.

488 Ryder interview, Jan. 10, 2006, p. 203. Andy Kopplin, Governor Blanco's Chief of Staff, expounded on the Governor's comments regarding the appropriate command structure for the response. After receiving Senator Vitter's question whether the Governor's request for additional federal assistance constituted a request for federalization, Kopplin sought the advice of Col. Smith, the Deputy Director of LOHSEP, on the consequences of federalization:

> I think the conclusions were fairly clear that the Governor's request, which was for additional federal assistance to help in particular with the evacuation, would not benefit from federalization but, in fact, the law enforcement functions of the guard could, in fact be compromised. … So the Governor took immediate action to clarify by placing a second call of the day looking for the President. This time, she got him, and she made the point that she's looking for assistance, that she needed assistance, but the unified command she felt was the appropriate structure to continue to use.

Kopplin interview, Jan. 6, 2006, pp. 122-125.

489 Ryder interview, Jan. 10, 2006, p. 203.

490 Ryder interview, Jan. 10, 2006, p. 203. The Governor's timeline characterizes the conversation between the Governor and the President as follows:

> She stresses to him that the situation is extremely grave and asks for additional resources. Governor Blanco also specifically stresses that she wants to continue to be his partner in a unity of effort as is called for under the National Response Plan. To relay the urgency and magnitude of the need at that point in time, the Governor tells the President she estimates 40,000 troops would be needed, and again reiterates her frustration about the FEMA buses.

Louisiana Office of the Governor, Governor's Timeline, p. 10.

491 Testimony of Gov. Kathleen Blanco, Louisiana, before the U.S. Senate, Committee on Homeland Security and Governmental Affairs, hearing on *Hurricane Katrina: The Role of the Governors in Managing the Catastrophe*, Feb. 2, 2006.

492 Lokey interview, Jan. 20, 2006, p. 71. Lokey provided a similar recollection at another point during the interview:

> I went to Brown and said, we've got to do something, sir. This is more than we can do. Our programs aren't designed for this. Our resources aren't there, so whatever. … We had to do something, and the only group I know that knows how to do stuff that big and has done it before was the United States military.

Lokey interview, Jan. 20, 2006, p. 91.

493 Lokey interview, Jan. 20, 2006, pp. 88-89.

494 Brown interview, Jan. 23, 2006, p. 198.

495 Committee staff interview of Michael Brown, former Director, FEMA, conducted on Feb. 23, 2006, transcript p. 113.

496 Brown interview, Feb. 23, 2006, pp. 115-116. Dolph Diemont, the U.S. Department of Transportation's representative at the state EOC, described how Brown communicated his frustration to the federal staff at the EOC:

When he came in and they closed the door he turned beet red and said this is unaccceptable. You guys are all incompetent. This is not going the way we want. We've got to change it. You know, I don't know what the hell's going on. You know, screaming and yelling at us, at everybody. It was hard to take because we were pouring our hearts out, trying to get the job done, and instead of encouragement, we got that kind of – it was … demoralizing.

Committee staff interview of Dolph Diemont, Region X Regional Emergency Transportation Representative, Office of Intelligence, Security and Emergency Response, U.S. Department of Transportation, conducted on Jan. 6, 2006, transcript p. 80.

497 Brown interview, Feb. 23, 2006, p. 114.

498 Brown interview, Feb. 23, 2006, pp. 114-115.

499 Brown interview, Feb. 23, 2006, p. 123.

500 Lt. Gen. Honoré interview, Jan. 9, 2006, p. 141.

501 This point is discussed in the Logistics portion earlier in this chapter.

502 McHale interview, Jan. 4, 2006, pp. 57-62.

503 McHale interview, Jan. 4, 2006, p. 61. Lt. Gen. Inge, U.S. Army, Deputy Commander of U.S. Northern Command, stated in a press conference following the President's deployment orders on Sept. 3, 2005, that the Title 10 Troops "will not take on a law enforcement role [nor] have they been directed in any way to do so. They will provide security. They will … be available to relieve National Guard soldiers who are in state status should there be a requirement for National Guard guys to do law enforcement. … I am not aware of any discussion of waiver of Posse Comitatus that's taken place." Lt. Gen. Joseph Inge, U.S. Northern Command, "Defense Department Briefing on Ongoing DoD Response to Hurricane Katrina," news briefing, Sept. 3, 2005. http://www.defenselink.mil/transcripts/2005/tr20050903-3849.html. Accessed on May 16, 2006.

504 Lokey interview, Jan. 20, 2006, p. 71.

505 The Posse Comitatus Act restrictions do not apply if the National Guard troops are activated under the Insurrection Act. *See*: U.S. Library of Congress, Congressional Research Service, *The Posse Comitatus Act and Related Matters: A Sketch*, by Jennifer Elsea, June 6, 2005.

506 Gov. Blanco, Senate Committee hearing, Feb. 2, 2006.

507 Lokey interview, Jan. 20, 2006, p. 72.

508 Lokey interview, Jan. 20, 2006, p. 72. Although Lokey recalled the state's reaction as unambiguously negative, Brown interpreted it differently: "There was enough ambiguity that I thought we might actually be able to pull it off, that she might actually agree to this. And she did say…she needed more time; she needed to talk to her staff about it, which I fully understood and respected, but I really thought I had kind of made some inroads there." Brown interview, Jan. 23, 2006, p. 201.

509 FEMA Director Brown telephoned Lt. Gen. Honoré prior to his arrival in Baton Rouge. According to Brown, "[Lt. Gen. Honoré] already had a litany of things he wanted to do, and I had to back him down and say, "I may want all of those things done, but until we get federalized or however we work this out, I'm still in control, and you need to let me know what you want to do." *Source*: Testimony of Michael Brown, former Director, FEMA, before the U.S. Senate, Committee on Homeland Security and Governmental Affairs, hearing on *Hurricane Katrina: The Roles of DHS and FEMA Leadership*, Feb. 10, 2006. Maj. Gen. Landreneau recalled a similar conversation after General Honoré arrived at the EOC in Baton Rouge. According to Maj. Gen. Landreneau, Brown told General Honoré "that he was the primary federal official, P.F.O., and General Honoré was not going to anything in the way of marshalling resources or doing anything without his concurrence." "Yes, sir," Lt. Gen. Honoré replied. *Source*: Maj. Gen. Landreneau interview, Jan. 11, 2006, p. 54. In his second interview with the Committee, Brown related that he was not dissatisfied with Lt. Gen. Honoré's performance; in fact, Brown believed that Lt. Gen. Honoré was doing an excellent job of operating within DOD's role under the unified command. Rather, according to Brown, he engaged in this colloquy with Lt. Gen. Honoré in order to strengthen the unified command that Lt. Gen. Honoré and Maj. Gen. Landreneau were attempting to establish. *Source*: Brown interview, Feb. 23, 2006, pp. 118-119.

510 Louisiana Office of the Governor, Governor's Timeline, p. 10. Lt. Gen. Honoré stated that the Governor's timeline fairly reflected the substance of this conversation. Lt. Gen. Honoré interview, Jan. 9, 2006, pp. 121-122.

511 Brig. Gen. Graham interview, Jan. 12, 2006, pp. 22-26.

512 Brig. Gen. Graham interview, Jan. 12, 2006, pp. 27-28. General Graham had begun his assignment at the 5th Army headquarters on August 15. From that time until his assignment in Hurricane Katrina, General Graham's duties had focused on the 5th Army's transition to its newly focused mission of homeland defense and defense support to civil authorities. Brig. Gen. Graham interview, Jan. 12, 2006, pp. 5-10, 24-26.

513 Louisiana Office of the Governor, Governor's Timeline, p. 10; Col. Curtis and Lt. Col. Thibodeaux interview, Dec. 6, 2006, pp. 270-271.

514 Maj. Gen. Landreneau interview, Jan. 11, 2006, pp. 57-58.

515 Maj. Gen. Landreneau interview, Jan. 11, 2006, p. 58.

516 Maj. Gen. Landreneau interview, Jan. 11, 2006, p. 58.

517 Maj. Gen. Landreneau interview, Jan. 11, 2006, p. 61.

518 Col. Anthony Daskevich, the Defense Coordinating Officer in Baton Rouge also was present at this meeting and re-

called that the Governor did not make a specific request for additional federal ground troops. *Source*: Col. Daskevich interview, Jan. 10, 2006, pp. 130-132. General Graham also stated that the Governor did not make any request for federal troops during the part of the conversation in which he was present. *Source*: Brig. Gen. Graham interview, Jan. 12, 2006, pp. 29-30.

519 Lt. Gen. Honoré interview, Jan. 9, 2006, pp. 103-105.

520 Lt. Gen. Honoré interview, Jan. 9, 2006, p. 130. At another point during the Committee's interview Lt. Gen. Honoré identified several other types of assets that DOD provided during that first week:

> We knew we needed helicopters. We knew we needed COMs [communications] capability. We knew we needed MEDEVAC. And these started to flow…This is Wednesday morning, and we're doing this without an open request. We've got no request for any specific capability, but what we have done is an assessment that these types of capabilities could be used, and started to flow them.

Lt. Gen. Honoré interview, Jan. 9, 2006, pp. 123-124.

Lt. Gen. Honoré addressed why he did not call on the 82nd Airborne Division for the deployment of a large number of ground troops on day one: "The type of capability we needed wasn't necessarily the 82nd. They'd jump in and secure for us, recon for us. The type of capability we needed at that time was evacuation capability. … I don't recall any serious conversation on why we didn't have the 82nd Airborne there on day one." *Source*: Lt. Gen. Honoré interview, Jan. 9, 2006, p. 127. General Richard Myers, Chairman of the Joint Chiefs of Staff during Katrina, told the Committee that another consideration was the primary mission of the 82nd Airborne was to be prepared for potential overseas missions. *Source*: Gen. Myers interview, Feb. 28, 2006, pp. 33-34. Col. Don Harrington, the DOD liaison to FEMA, explained, "There is a reticence, too, to deploy the 82nd down range. It's not something really – keep in mind, that next year, the [terrorists] may take advantage of this. You know, that's a very big concern. So do you want to kick everybody out in, what I call the Hindenburg disaster mode? Everybody goes out, the Hindenburg is burning. Everybody goes down range, and you don't realize that some people may be taking advantage of that." *Source*: Col. Harrington interview, Jan. 6, 2006, p. 101. Assistant Secretary McHale commented, "We don't want to turn the 82nd Airborne into a first responder, always available on a moment's notice for law enforcement activity throughout the United States. To be prepared for such a mission would require a change in the training and equipment of the 82nd. It would also produce a significant change in the historically defined role of the military within domestic American society." *Source*: McHale interview, Jan. 4, 2006, pp. 90-91.

521 Brig. Gen. Graham interview, Jan. 12, 2006, pp. 143-145.

522 Maj. Gen. Richard Rowe, e-mail to Col. James Hickey, Aug. 31, 2005, 6:05 p.m. Provided to Committee. General Honore was cc'd on the e-mail and the subject was "LA Security mission." Col. Hickey was General Honoré's executive officer. In the context of this e-mail, the term federal troops appears to refer to federal troops that are not National Guard troops – in other words, active-duty troops.

523 Maj. Gen. Richard Rowe, e-mail to Col. James Hickey, Aug. 31, 2005, 6:05 p.m. Provided to Committee.

524 U.S. Army Forces Command, Message to Commander, First Army, and others, "FORSCOM FRAGO #8," Sept. 1, 2005, 0039 Z. Provided to Committee. *See also*: JTF-Katrina, Commander's Assessment, Sept. 3, 2005. Provided to Committee.

525 82nd Airborne Division, "82nd Airborne Division Mission." http://www.bragg.army.mil/82dv/Mission.html. Accessed on Apr. 13, 2006.

526 1st Cavalry Division, "Reorganization." http://pao.hood.army.mil/1stcavdiv/index.htm. Accessed on Apr. 13, 2006.

527 U.S. Department of Defense, Hurricane Katrina Major Events Timeline, Draft, Dec. 28, 2005, 12:52 p.m. Provided to Committee.

528 Lt. Gen. Russel Honoré, e-mail to Maj. Gen. Rowe, Sept. 1, 2005, 11:46 a.m. Provided to Committee; Lt. Gen. Honoré interview, Jan. 9, 2006, p. 139.

529 Lt. Gen. Blum interview, Jan. 19, 2006, p. 78.

530 Lt. Gen. Russel Honoré, e-mail to Lt. Gen. James Amos, Sept. 1, 2005, 1:46 p.m. Provided to Committee.

531 Lt. Gen. Blum interview, Jan. 19, 2006, p. 288.

532 Adm. Keating, Senate Committee hearing, Feb. 9, 2006.

533 Lt. Gen. Blum interview, Jan. 19, 2006, p. 139.

534 Lt. Gen. Blum interview, Jan. 19, 2006, pp. 250-251.

535 Maj. Gen. Richard Rowe, e-mail to Lt. Gen. Russel Honoré, Sept. 1, 2005, 1:50 p.m. Provided to Committee. Approximately 15 minutes later, Lt. Gen. Honoré responded, "GOT IT."

536 U.S. Department of Defense, *Strategy for Homeland Defense and Civil Support*, June 2005, p. 35.

537 McHale interview, Jan. 4, 2006, p. 56.

538 Gen. Myers interview, Feb. 28, 2006, pp. 30-31. Gen. Myers stated that DOD continued to hold this view on Friday afternoon, even after the Governor made an additional request to the President for more federal troops on Friday morning aboard Air Force One. Nonetheless, according to Gen. Myers, DOD sent additional troops requested by the Governor. The troops already were on high alert status, Gen. Myers noted, "so you said okay, if the Governor thinks we need more, we'll send more." *Source*: Gen. Myers interview, Feb. 28, 2006, p. 39. Lt. Gen. Blum, who met with both the President and the Governor on that Friday, stated, "It was clear in my mind that by 3:00 on Sept. 2 that there were sufficient forces in Louisiana to manage the security condition, to complete the search and rescue operation, and that the Governor of Louisiana

agree to that assessment and personally expressed it to me as well as Mayor Nagin." *Source*: Lt. Gen. Blum interview, Jan. 19, 2005, p. 72.

539 Louisiana Office of the Governor, Governor's Timeline, pp. 11-12; Lt. Gen. Honoré interview, Jan. 9, 2006, pp. 183-184.

540 "I don't recall a specific request from the governor for Title X troops at that time." Lt. Gen. Honoré interview, Jan. 9, 2006, p. 184.

541 Ryder interview, Jan. 10, 2006, pp. 213-215.

542 Lt. Gen. Blum interview, Jan. 19, 2006, p. 57; Louisiana Office of the Governor, Governor's Timeline, p. 12.

543 Lt. Gen. Blum interview, Jan. 19, 2006, p. 57.

544 Louisiana Office of the Governor, Governor's Timeline, p. 12. Lt. Gen. Blum told the Committee that this description of his views is "entirely consistent with my recollection." Lt. Gen. Blum interview, Jan. 19, 2006, p. 68.

545 Brown interview, Feb. 23, 2006, p. 125.

546 Office of the Assistant Secretary of Defense (Homeland Defense), Hurricane Katrina/Rita/Ophelia Interim Timeline, Oct. 31, 2005, p. 9; Office of the Assistant Secretary of Defense (Homeland Defense), Hurricane Katrina/Rita/Ophelia Interim Timeline, Nov. 2, 2005, p. 9. Earlier that morning the President met with Secretary of Defense Rumsfeld and Lt. Gen. Blum to receive "a hurricane status brief." U.S. Department of Defense, Draft Hurricane Katrina Major Events Timeline, Dec. 28, 2005, 12:52 p.m. Provided to Committee.

547 Gen. Myers interview, Feb. 28, 2006, p. 43; England interview, Feb. 3, 2006.

548 McHale, Senate Committee hearing, Feb. 9, 2006.

549 Louisiana Office of the Governor, Governor's Timeline, p. 14.

550 Testimony of Mayor C. Ray Nagin, New Orleans, LA, before the U.S. Senate, Committee on Homeland Security and Governmental Affairs, hearing on *Hurricane Katrina: Managing the Crisis and Evacuating New Orleans*, Feb. 1, 2006. When asked by the Committee whether he was advocating that the National Guard be federalized, Mayor Nagin replied, "It was just a question of who had final authority. I'm not sure of the details of what they were debating." *Source*: Mayor Nagin, Senate Committee hearing, Feb. 1, 2006. It is not clear what "final authority" would have meant other than federal control of the National Guard, since the mayor, as head of the local government, was the incident commander. "He's the civilian, the lead civilian authority in charge of that municipality. He is really the only one that can control that operation." *Source*: Lt. Col. Thibodeaux interview, Dec. 6, 2006, pp. 268-269. *See also*: Mayor Nagin, Senate Committee hearing, Feb. 1, 2006 (affirming role as incident commander for New Orleans).

551 Mayor Nagin, Senate Committee hearing, Feb. 1, 2006. Governor Blanco testified, "the Mayor was not in our meeting that I had with the President, per se. ... At that point in time, Mayor Nagin had not been in good communication with us. You know, the communication system had fallen down." Gov. Blanco, Senate Committee hearing, Feb. 2, 2006.

552 Gov. Blanco, Senate Committee hearing, Feb. 2, 2006. The Governor also sent a letter to the President on Sept. 2, requesting additional federal troops and other resources:

> Based on our initial assessment, I have previously requested significant federal support to include: an additional 40,000 troops; trailers of water, ice and food; commercial buses; base camps; staging areas; amphibious personnel carriers; deployable morgues; urban search and rescue teams; airlift; temporary housing; and communications systems. Even if these initial requests had been fully honored, these assets would not be sufficient to address our critical, immediate needs.

Governor Kathleen Babineaux Blanco, letter to President George W. Bush, Sept. 2, 2005.

553 Gov. Blanco, Senate Committee hearing, Feb. 2, 2006. The Governor's timeline elaborated:

> The Governor has a private conversation with President Bush about the command structure of the operations, and reiterates her need for a significant number of federal troops. The President asks Governor Blanco to put her troops, the Louisiana National Guard and EMAC National Guard, under control of a Department of Defense appointed General. By the time of Friday's conversation, the situation has evolved and the immediate needs on the ground are far different than the needs when federal troops were first requested earlier in the week.

Louisiana Office of the Governor, Governor's Timeline, p. 14.

554 Gov. Blanco, Senate Committee hearing, Feb. 2, 2006.

555 Robert Travis Scott, "Politics delayed troops dispatch," New Orleans *Times-Picayune*, Dec. 11, 2005, National, p. 1.

556 In particular, elements of the 24 Marine Expeditionary Unit (MEU) were prepared to deploy and could have deployed on Friday. Lt. Gen. Amos told the Committee:

> I anticipated [the Special Air Contingency Marine Air Ground Task Force] leaving on Friday. I figured the DEP [deploy] order was going to be signed on Friday. ... I kind of expected the DEP order was going to happen on Friday, and that's because all the news was reporting the President was going to make an announcement on one of his public things while he was going around New Orleans. ... So I expected them to actually start moving out on Friday. So I put them on their what we call, affectionately, put them on their packs probably – I either did that Wednesday afternoon, the 31st, or the first.

Lt. Gen. Amos interview, Dec. 14, 2005, p. 75.

557 White House Briefing to Committee, given by Kenneth Rapuano, Deputy Assistant to the President for Homeland Security, Dec. 12, 2005.

558 The Governor's timeline addresses this issue:

> Erroneous reports have been circulated that she denied federal troops or delayed help for 24-hours. The facts are clear and evidence confirms that the Governor requests early and often the need for additional federal military presence, including a federal military presence and assets. At no time does anyone from the federal government tell her that federal troops are withheld because the existing structure was inadequate. In fact, the new proposal is first presented to her aboard Air Force One on Friday, four days after the storm struck on Monday, and the President never suggests that federal troops were reliant on this new structure nor did he convey that the joint command structure is insufficient.

Source: Louisiana Office of the Governor, Governor's Timeline, p. 15. Regarding the Mayor's charge that the Governor's position delayed the deployment of federal troops and impeded the overall response in Louisiana, the Governor testified, "I will tell you at that point in time, Mayor Nagin had not been in good communication with us. You know the communication system had fallen down." *Source*: Gov. Blanco, Senate Committee hearing, Feb. 2, 2006.

559 Lt. Gen. Blum interview, Jan. 19, 2006, pp. 100-101.

560 Gen. Myers interview, Feb. 28, 2006, pp. 38-43.

561 Brown interview, Feb. 23, 2006, p. 121.

562 Thomas Kuster, e-mail to Col. Richard Chavez, Sept. 2, 2005, 5:31 p.m. Provided to Committee.

563 Ryder interview, Jan. 10, 2006, pp. 237-238. Witt was serving as a consultant to the Governor.

564 Kopplin interview, Jan. 6, 2006, pp. 159-160.

565 Kopplin interview, Jan. 6, 2006, p. 153.

566 According to Governor Blanco, "It was Blum, Blum, Blum, and then Card came in on the third." Gov. Blanco, Senate Committee hearing, Feb. 2, 2006.

567 Gov. Blanco, Senate Committee hearing, Feb. 2, 2006. The Governor's timeline summarizes these exchanges:

> Close to midnight on Friday, Gov. Blanco receives phone calls from Gen. Steve Blum, just after his return to DC, and White House Chief of Staff Andrew Card, who want to discuss with her their proposed organizational restructuring. She hears them out, but continues to believe, given the stabilization now underway and the massive National Guard buildup on the ground, that bringing in the federal forces and putting them under the command of Gen. Honoré to coordinate with Gen. Landreneau who leads the Guard forces is the most effective solution.

Louisiana Office of the Governor, Governor's Timeline, p. 15.

568 Gov. Blanco, Senate Committee hearing, Feb. 2, 2006.

569 Lt. Gen. Blum interview, Jan. 19, 2006, pp. 83-86.

570 McHale, Senate Committee hearing, Feb. 9, 2006.

571 President George W. Bush, "President Addresses Nation, Discusses Hurricane Katrina Relief Efforts," radio address, Sept. 3, 2005, 10:06 a.m. ET. http://www.whitehouse.gov/news/releases/2005/09/20050903.html Accessed on May 16, 2006.

572 Gov. Blanco, Senate Committee hearing, Feb. 2, 2006.

573 Committee staff interview of Col. Terry Ebbert, U.S. Marine Corps (Ret.), Director, New Orleans Office of Homeland Security, LA, conducted on Jan. 10, 2006, transcript pp. 170-171.

574 Adm. Timothy J. Keating, "Defense Department Briefing on Ongoing DoD Response to Hurricane Katrina," news briefing, Sept. 5, 2005. http://www.dod.mil/transcripts/2005/tr20050905-3851.html. Accessed on May 16, 2006. At a press conference on Tuesday, Sept. 6, Gen. Myers was asked whether the response would have been quicker had it been federalized:

GEN. MYERS: I think the response by the National Guard, which is under state authority in both Louisiana and Mississippi, and I assume Alabama and Florida as well, was, I think, very quick. I think if you asked the TAGs of that state, I think they responded very quickly.

Sec. Donald Rumsfeld and Gen. Richard Myers, "Defense Department Operational Update Briefing," news briefing, Sept. 6, 2005. http://www.defenselink.mil/transcripts/2005/tr20050906-secdef3862.html. Accessed on May 16, 2006.

575 Committee staff interview of Lt. Col. Gordon Ellis, U.S. Army, former Commander of First Battalion, 148th Infantry, Ohio National Guard, conducted on Feb. 16, 2006, transcript pp. 88-89.

576 McHale interview, Jan. 4, 2006, pp. 88, 110.

577 Gov. Barbour, Senate Committee hearing, Feb. 2, 2006 ("I made very plain from day one that we didn't … need the federal government to run our National Guard. … I was very emphatic it was the wrong thing to do."); Gov. Blanco, Senate Committee hearing, Feb. 2, 2006 ("It's very important for a governor to be able to retain control of the National Guard precisely for its law enforcement capabilities.").

Admiral Allen giving Principal
Federal Officer's views for TV
U.S. Coast Guard photo

Failures in National Response Plan: Unified Command

Failures in Design, Implementation, and Execution of the National Response Plan

The National Response Plan (NRP) aims to be a comprehensive framework for managing domestic incidents, whether terrorist attacks or natural disasters. It seeks to delineate the mechanisms for coordinating federal support to states, localities, and tribes; for interacting with nongovernmental and private-sector entities; and for directly exercising federal authority when appropriate.

The Department of Homeland Security (DHS) developed the NRP pursuant to Homeland Security Presidential Directive-5[1] and in accordance with section 502(6) of the Homeland Security Act.[2] DHS released the NRP on January 6, 2005.[3] It was to be "fully implemented" by April 14, 2005; at that date, response plans that had remained in effect during the implementation period were superseded.[4] Implementation of the NRP (and the associated National Incident Management System) was deemed a "national priority" in DHS's Interim National Preparedness Goal.[5]

The NRP was set up to guide the national response to actual and potential Incidents of National Significance – "high-impact events that require a coordinated and effective response by an appropriate combination of federal, state, local, tribal, private sector, and nongovernmental entities in order to save lives, minimize damage, and provide the basis for long-term community recovery and mitigation activities."[6] The NRP applies to all federal agencies that may be requested to provide assistance or conduct operations during an actual or potential Incident of National Significance.[7] The heads of 30 federal agencies and two nongovernmental organizations signed the document. [8]

Incidents of National Significance include all Presidentially declared disasters and emergencies under the Stafford Act, which establishes the most commonly used programs for disaster and emergency assistance to states, local governments and individuals.[9] Incidents of National Significance can also include incidents not covered by the Stafford Act, such as high-profile "National Special Security Events" like national political conventions or the Super Bowl.[10]

Although smaller incidents warranting a Stafford Act declaration occurred in the months after the NRP was issued, Hurricane Katrina was the first major test of the NRP. The response to Katrina exposed flaws in the design and pre-storm implementation of the NRP as well as in its execution during the disaster. Some of the more prominent of these problems are discussed below.[11]

Failures in the Design and Implementation of the NRP

Insufficient Training and Exercises

The NRP was publicly issued with fanfare in January 2005. Tom Ridge, then DHS Secretary, said, "America is better prepared today, thanks to the National Response Plan."[12] He contrasted the NRP with other plans and reports routinely issued in Washington: "Instead of promising results in the future, it is a deliverable that we believe will bring definite results now."[13]

The NRP, however, was not a self-executing document. It is a complex, ambitious, 400-plus-page, high-level plan that was well described in a document produced to the Committee by the Office of the Vice President as "a very detailed, acronym-heavy document that is not easily accessible to the first-time user."[14] The NRP, moreover, entails significant departures from the primary plan it replaced, the Federal Response Plan,[15] including shifting leadership from FEMA to the new Department of Homeland Security; introducing a new lead coordinating figure, the Principal Federal Official (PFO), to supplement the existing Federal Coordinating Official (FCO) position; and assigning new emergency-support functions to federal agencies, including, for the first time, public-safety and security responsibilities.

Without a systematic training and implementation effort, the NRP was unlikely to be widely or readily understood, and unlikely to offer effective guidance, just four months after its implementation, for the massive federal, state, and local response necessary for Katrina.

DHS's implementation effort appears to have been entirely inadequate. After the NRP was issued, DHS conducted a wave of training for headquarters staff of component agencies.[16] Beyond that, it appears no one at DHS was charged with ensuring that the NRP would be well implemented. The National Incident Management System (NIMS) Integration Center is responsible for federal, state, and local NRP awareness training as an adjunct to its primary mission of fostering the widespread adoption of the NIMS, a nationwide approach for different jurisdictions and levels of government to work together in domestic incidents, but its staffing (fewer than 10 people) inherently limited its impact.[17] The Integration Center relies largely on self-administered online training, in which sessions could last as little as 15-20 minutes.[18]

Only one large-scale exercise of the NRP took place before Katrina, the Top Officials 3 exercise (TOPOFF 3) in April 2005, at about the time the NRP was to take full effect and supersede other plans. TOPOFF 3, sponsored by DHS, involved responders from all levels of government. A report by the DHS Inspector General in November 2005 found that "the exercise highlighted – at all levels of government – a fundamental lack of understanding for the principles and protocols set forth in the NRP and NIMS."[19] It appears that little was done to correct this shortcoming, and that widespread unfamiliarity with the NRP persisted.[20]

In addition, the absence of any other exercises of the NRP meant that there were no further formal opportunities to understand and flesh out the roles allocated by the plan, to clarify ambiguities, to identify potential problems, and to incorporate lessons recognized back into the NRP as lessons learned. DHS's lack of substantial and sustained effort to familiarize officials and responders with the NRP and to exercise the NRP under simulated conditions meant, as one expert testified, that "the NRP was only a plan – it was not a functioning, practiced, operable, system."[21]

Principal Federal Official and Federal Coordinating Officer Roles

The NRP does not clearly define the role of the PFO or distinguish it from that of the FCO. This was an obstacle to an effective, coordinated response to Katrina.

The FCO position, authorized by the Stafford Act, predates the NRP. The Stafford Act requires that the President appoint an FCO immediately upon issuing a major disaster or emergency declaration.[22] The FCO is to appraise the types of relief most urgently needed, establish field offices, coordinate the administration of relief, and take other necessary action to help citizens and public officials obtain proper assistance.[23] Before the NRP, the FCO led the federal response on the ground.

The NRP created a new PFO position that is not explicitly provided for in the Stafford Act, so the PFO remains a non-statutory position. According to the NRP, the PFO is to be "personally designated" by the Secretary of Homeland Security and is to represent the Secretary as "the lead federal official."[24] The PFO is also, among other things, to ensure overall coordination of federal incident-management activities and of resource allocation and serve as a "primary, though not exclusive" point of contact for state and local officials, the media, and the private sector.[25] But the NRP also says that the PFO is not to "direct or replace" the incident-command structure, and that the PFO does not have "directive authority" over the FCO or other federal and state officials.[26]

Tasked with leading the federal response but lacking authority to direct others, the PFO position has inherent challenges. Moreover, the division of responsibilities between the PFO and the FCO – who leads the federal response in Stafford Act situations where no PFO has been assigned[27] – is not clear. Both positions have coordination responsibilities, but they are not clearly distinguished.[28] Their relationship is also unclear: the PFO can "coordinate" but not direct the FCO, who is to "work closely with" the PFO.[29]

Bruce Baughman, President of the National Emergency Management Association and Director of the Alabama Emergency Management Agency, testified that "basically, in Louisiana, we had two people in charge. … And it wasn't real clear what the roles and responsibilities of each were.[30]

Comptroller General David Walker, the head of the Government Accountability Office (GAO), found that "shifting roles and responsibilities" of the PFO, FCO and the DHS Secretary (who is to provide strategic, national leadership) resulted in "disjointed efforts of many federal agencies involved in the response, a myriad of approaches and processes for requesting and providing assistance, and confusion about who should be advised of requests and what resources would be provided within specific time frames."[31] William Lokey, FCO for Louisiana during Katrina, and Colonel Jeff Smith, Deputy Director of the Louisiana Office of Homeland Security and Emergency Preparedness, each testified that problems arose due to the unclear chain of command.[32]

Vice Admiral Thad Allen of the U.S. Coast Guard, who succeeded then-FEMA Director Michael Brown as PFO during Katrina, acknowledged the difficulties in sorting out the PFO and FCO roles: "If you need to invoke the Stafford Act for whatever reason, you're always going to have an issue with the relationship of the PFO and the FCO together."[33] Approximately three weeks after he was designated PFO, Allen accepted an appointment to be FCO for Katrina in each of the three Gulf Coast states as well – effectively merging the two roles.[34]

Potentially Overlapping Agency Roles

Another NRP design flaw revealed by Katrina was the failure to delineate areas of potentially overlapping responsibility among federal agencies. The NRP includes 15 Emergency Support Functions (ESF), groupings of substantive capabilities – communications or urban search and rescue, for example – that may be needed in a disaster. Each of these ESFs has a designated primary agency, which is to lead that ESF's mission in an incident; a list of other support agencies, which are to provide support for that mission in an incident; and a designated coordinating agency, which coordinates the efforts and planning of the primary agency or agencies and support agencies on an ongoing basis.[35]

A striking example of the problem of overlapping responsibilities, discussed at greater length in the law-enforcement portion of this report (see Chapter 25), is the NRP's assignment of both the coordinating-agency role and the primary-agency role for ESF-13, public safety and security, jointly to DHS and the Department of Justice. Nowhere does the ESF-13 Annex to the NRP spell out the respective roles of the two agencies, how they are to divide or share responsibilities or circumstances where one or the other is to have primacy.[36] Compounding this lack of NRP guidance were the agencies' own failures to clarify the ambiguities prior to a major disaster. Such activities should have been completed during the initial 60-day "transitional period" after the NRP was issued.[37] Predictably, this led to significant confusion, and ultimately contributed to a delayed federal law-enforcement response in the Gulf Coast.

Greater clarity in the responsibilities of Primary and Support Agencies for Emergency Support Functions (ESFs) might also have helped avoid other conflicts. For instance, the NRP assigns lead responsibility for ESF-8, public health and medical services, to the federal Department of Health and Human Services (HHS).[38] But one of the response mechanisms, the National Disaster Medical System (NDMS), is part of FEMA, a DHS agency that deploys NDMS's Disaster Medical Assistance Teams as FEMA assets. In the response to Katrina, FEMA and HHS engaged in minimal coordination on pre-positioning and deploying Disaster Medical Assistance Teams.[39]

Contingency and Catastrophic Planning

The NRP is a high-level plan, with a core set of principles meant to apply to a wide range of possible events. It was not designed to address specific scenarios or geographic areas, or to provide operational details. The NRP does contemplate that such plans may be developed, but it sets neither a process nor a timetable for doing so.[40] More detailed planning, particularly for catastrophic events, might have made possible a more effective response to Katrina.

Under the Federal Response Plan, the NRP's predecessor, FEMA developed plans adapted to each FEMA region; each plan could then be tailored to individual states.[41] The plan for FEMA Region VI, based in Denton, TX, and covering Arkansas, Louisiana, New Mexico, Oklahoma, and Texas, included a hurricane plan for Louisiana.[42] This investigation found no indication that equivalent work has been done under the NRP, nor any indication that earlier regional plans have been updated.[43]

It also appears that no plans have been developed under the NRP to deal with specific risk scenarios such as the 15 homeland-security planning scenarios developed by the White House Homeland Security Council in 2004, which included a hurricane situation.[44] Admiral Allen suggested using more specific "sub-plans" to flesh out how plans would actually be executed. He observed:

> This [NRP] is a high-level document. I think as you're able to establish the parameters of almost a spectrum of an all hazards type of an approach to things that you need to be more detailed planning on how you would respond to it ... a natural disaster is one thing; a natural disaster with a radiological event is an entirely different issue.[45]

Detailed, more specific planning is likely to be particularly important in responding to catastrophes. Comptroller General Walker has stressed the crucial need for strong planning for catastrophic events, and recommended that the NRP and its Catastrophic Incident Annex – the portion of the NRP that provides for a proactive, national response to a catastrophe – "should be supported and supplemented by more detailed and robust operational implementation plans."[46]

Certainly the NRP, as it had been implemented and without the necessary associated planning to support it, was found inadequate to the catastrophe of Katrina. Though the NRP was intended to address a wide spectrum of events of varying size, in an actual situation where upwards of a million people were affected – tens of thousands of whom continued to face serious danger to life, health or safety after the storm itself had passed – and in which the capabilities of local responders had been decimated, the NRP's procedures were not yet ready for use and simply fell short. As Admiral Allen noted, the NRP as written "doesn't contemplate" an event on the massive scale of Katrina: "When it goes off the scale, you know, you need a separate plan for how to deal with something that massive. In this case, there were some things that were unique to this event that can only be handled by an almost different approach to what you're doing."[47]

The NRP's Catastrophic Incident Annex and its associated but still-to-be-released Catastrophic Incident Supplement were intended to provide this separate plan for a catastrophe, but, incomplete and largely untested, they went unused. The Catastrophic Incident Annex sets out the broad principles of a proactive response; the Catastrophic Incident Supplement was supposed to fill in significant, operational details.[48] Unfortunately, when Katrina hit, nearly nine months after the NRP had been announced, the Supplement still had not been issued.

According to David Garratt, Acting Director of FEMA's Recovery Division, who had chaired the interagency Catastrophic Incident Planning Group that was charged with developing the Catastrophic Incident Supplement, the Supplement had been 99 percent completed by late 2004,[49] roughly the same time the NRP itself was finished. Garratt explained that when it came time to get the concurrence of the relevant federal agencies to the Catastrophic Incident Supplement, all approved except the Department of Defense (DOD). DOD had concerns about a Memorandum of Agreement related to the National Disaster Medical System and, in particular, provisions related to reimbursement for certain costs of care in a public-health emergency.[50] The Memorandum of Agreement (to which DOD, FEMA, the Department of Health and Human Services, and the Department of Veterans Affairs were parties) went unresolved and unsigned until approximately September 6, 2005[51] – eight days after Katrina made landfall and apparently only after the White House's Homeland Security Council got involved.[52] The Supplement, meanwhile, has never been issued.[53]

The delay in issuing the Catastrophic Incident Supplement – and developing the agency plans and procedures that were required to support it – deprived the federal government of a potential tool in its response to Hurricane Katrina. The heart of the Supplement is an Execution Schedule that provides an agency-by-agency (and hour-by-hour) list of the assets various federal agencies are to deploy automatically to the affected area once the Secretary of Homeland Security orders implementation.[54] Had it been issued and high-priority resources pre-identified and made ready to deploy, the Catastrophic Incident Supplement might have sped delivery of supplies and personnel to mobilization centers close to the disaster or, in certain circumstances, directly to the incident scene without a need for requests from state and local authorities, or from any other federal agency.

Even if the Supplement had been implemented, however, it is not clear that it would have been adequate to the task at hand. The Execution Schedule is essentially a method of pre-prioritizing a certain set of assets – an important and potentially very useful function, but not by itself likely to constitute a sufficient response to an event of catastrophic magnitude. Garratt, chair of the Catastrophic Incident Planning Group, characterized the Supplement as "basically just an acceleration model for resources that are already identified under the NRP."[55] Indeed, the fact that the Catastrophic Incident Supplement, while complete, has not yet been issued, apparently reflects questions about whether it needs further modification.[56] To be truly effective, the Supplement would need to move beyond its important but narrowly focused Execution Schedule, and incorporate more robust, catastrophe-focused planning.[57]

Failures in the Execution of the NRP

Declaration of an Incident of National Significance

Under the NRP, every event that provokes a Presidential declaration under the Stafford Act automatically becomes an Incident of National Significance.[58] Thus, when the President issued an emergency declaration for portions of Louisiana on Saturday, August 27, 2005, Hurricane Katrina became an Incident of National Significance. Despite this, on the afternoon of Tuesday, August 30, Secretary Chertoff issued a memorandum "declaring" Katrina an Incident of National Significance as well as appointing Brown PFO.[59] The next day, Secretary Chertoff appeared at a press conference at which he reiterated his declaration and noted that this was the first time that such a declaration had been made.[60]

The superfluous Tuesday "declaration" has caused confusion. In testimony before the House of Representatives, the Secretary said, "I did it because we were going to have a Cabinet meeting the next day and I wanted to have some kind of a documented notification of the steps I had taken. I didn't have to do it."[61] He echoed this explanation in testimony before the Committee, again citing the pending Cabinet meeting and saying, "In truth, I didn't need to do it. I was told I didn't need to do it. But I just did it to formalize it." He also stated that "my understanding of the plan and my reading of the plan then and now is that by dint of declaring the emergency, it automatically made it an Incident of National Significance."[62]

At minimum, the Secretary's redundant declaration of an Incident of National Significance confused an already difficult situation and suggested a lack of familiarity with core concepts of the NRP within the Secretary's office. Robert Stephan, Assistant Secretary for Infrastructure Protection, and the individual who led the Department's development of the NRP, also addressed the Tuesday "declaration." In an account similar to that provided by the Secretary's Chief of Staff, John Wood, Stephan explained that his staff produced the initial draft of the Tuesday announcement, and that as originally written it only addressed the appointment of Brown as PFO. According to Stephan, the "declaration" of an Incident of National Significance was subsequently added to the statement by someone in the Secretary's office. When, in the wake of press coverage raising questions about the declaration, Stephan realized that this language had been added, he contact the Secretary's office and explained the issue.[63] Stephan further testified that he "got the sense" that the Secretary's front office staff did not realize the error until he told them, and he noted that the Secretary was "not very excited" when informed that the error had occurred.[64]

Appointment of Michael Brown as Principal Federal Official

Secretary Chertoff also departed from the NRP in his appointment of a PFO. In Chapter 12, this report discusses the advantages that might have been gained by appointing a PFO prior to Katrina's landfall. Questions have also been raised about the wisdom of appointing Brown, who had little experience as an emergency manager, as PFO. But apart from these issues of judgment, Brown's appointment as PFO violated the literal requirements of the NRP.

It is inadvisable to appoint any FEMA Director PFO. The NRP prohibits the PFO from being "dual-hatted" – that is, from occupying another position or having another set of conflicting or distracting obligations at the same time. Specifically, the NRP states that, "Once formally designated, the PFOs relinquish the conduct of all normal duties and functions. PFOs may not be 'dual-hatted' with any other roles or responsibilities that could detract from their overall incident management responsibilities."[65] Notwithstanding this requirement, at the time of his appointment as PFO, Brown also served as Under Secretary for Emergency Preparedness and Response and as the Director of FEMA. Some of his duties appeared to be assumed by his Deputy, Patrick Rhode, but he took no formal steps, nor was he asked to take any, to relinquish his other responsibilities.[66]

Michael Jackson, Deputy Secretary of Homeland Security,[67] and Secretary Chertoff defended Brown's "dual-hatted" role, arguing that the PFO and FEMA responsibilities complemented each other.[68] FEMA Director and PFO responsibilities, however, are far from identical. The FEMA Director has responsibilities for managing an organization that are distinct from overseeing any individual incident, however large. Not only may administrative issues – of personnel, budget, contracting, and the like – arise back in Washington that will either distract from the incident coordination or be neglected, but other disasters may occur as well that will demand attention from the FEMA Director. Indeed, on September 1, 2005 – three days after Katrina made landfall – an earthquake struck California.[69] Though fortunately minor, it demonstrates that potential problems that can occur where the FEMA Director is also assigned the day-to-day responsibilities as the PFO for a specific incident. The development of another potentially devastating hurricane, Hurricane Rita, a mere four weeks after Katrina further underscores the problems inherent in tying the Director to the management of a single, specific incident.

Brown also failed to satisfy the NRP requirement that individuals – except in "extenuating" circumstances – must complete a formal training program before serving as PFO,[70] as he had never participated in such training.[71]

Another form of "dual-hatting" occurred after Coast Guard Vice Admiral Thad Allen replaced Brown as PFO. As discussed above (and at greater length in the unified-command section), approximately three weeks after his appointment as PFO, Adm. Allen was also appointed to be the FCO for Louisiana, Mississippi, and Alabama. These dual appointments appear to be inconsistent with the NRP, which clearly envisions the PFO as separate and distinct from the FCO position. Robert Stephan confirmed that the "dual-hatting" of the PFO and FCO "was never contemplated" by the NRP.[72]

Non-Implementation of the Catastrophic Incident Annex

In failing to implement the National Response Plan's Catastrophic Incident Annex (NRP-CIA), Secretary Chertoff ignored a potentially powerful tool that might have alleviated difficulties in the federal response to Katrina.

As discussed above, the Catastrophic Incident Supplement, with its detailed Execution Schedule, had not been issued at the time Katrina came ashore, but the NRP-CIA, released in January 2005, provides important tools on its own for a faster and more effective response.[73]

The NRP-CIA explicitly provides for a proactive federal response to catastrophic events.[74] The NRP defines a catastrophic event as "any natural or manmade incident, including terrorism, that results in extraordinary levels of mass casualties, damage, or disruption severely affecting the population, infrastructure, environment, economy, national morale, and/or government functions."[75] The Secretary of Homeland Security or the Secretary's designee may initiate implementation of the NRP-CIA.[76] The NRP-CIA was not accompanied by changes in the Stafford Act or other legislation and thus does not provide new authority to federal officials. It does, however, set a policy and tone for an urgent and proactive response that moves beyond the usual procedures in responding to an "ordinary" disaster.[77] For a "typical" disaster, the standard practice is that the federal government does not extend aid until a state requests assistance. During a catastrophe, however, NRP-CIA activation prompts the government to help without waiting for requests.

The NRP-CIA recognizes that, in a catastrophe, "Federal and/or national resources are required to augment overwhelmed state, local, and tribal response efforts" and therefore provides for the identification and rapid deployment of essential resources expected to be urgently needed to save lives and contain incidents.[78] Upon notification that the NRP-CIA has been implemented, federal agencies are to "take immediate actions to protect life, property, and critical infrastructure under their jurisdiction, and provide assistance within the affected area."[79] In addition, the NRP provides that normal procedures for certain Emergency Support Functions (ESFs) may be "expedited or streamlined to address the magnitude of urgent requirements of the incident."[80] And while the federal government must still notify and coordinate with states, "the coordination process should not delay or impede the rapid mobilization and deployment of critical Federal resources."[81]

In short, the NRP-CIA turns what is traditionally a "pull" system, in which the federal government waits to receive requests from state and local officials, or from other federal agencies, into a "push" system, where federal authorities proactively deploy resources to mobilization centers close to the disaster or, in certain circumstances, directly to the incident scene to assist in responding to the incident.

When the President issued an emergency declaration in the days before landfall, it should have been apparent that Katrina had significant potential to cause a "catastrophe" as defined by the NRP-CIA. After landfall, it should have been immediately apparent that the catastrophe had occurred. Indeed, Secretary Chertoff would eventually describe Katrina as an "ultra catastrophe."[82] But the NRP-CIA was never activated. It is unknown whether DHS leaders ever considered activating the NRP-CIA, although both Secretary Chertoff's Chief of Staff Wood, and Garratt, a FEMA employee who headed the Catastrophic Incident Planning Group, were unaware of any discussions concerning the NRP-CIA in the days before Katrina made landfall.[83]

In the aftermath of Hurricane Katrina, DHS and other federal officials have suggested that it was not appropriate to invoke the NRP-CIA to respond to the hurricane because the NRP-CIA was intended only for "no-notice" events – for which there is no time to go through normal procedures – whereas there was notice that Katrina was heading toward the Gulf Coast.[84] The Catastrophic Incident Annex itself, however, does not contain any language that would limit it to no-notice events. The yet-to-be-issued Catastrophic Incident Supplement was somewhat more explicit, stating that it is intended to apply to "no-notice" or "short-notice" events.[85] These terms are left undefined in the Supplement. While DHS officials contend that Hurricane Katrina was not a no-notice or a short-notice event, a contrary view is just as plausible. Specifically, it could be argued that a massive hurricane hurtling towards a major American city with two or three days' notice meets some common-sense definition of a short-notice event.

Indeed, the Catastrophic Incident Supplement's Execution Schedule makes specific reference to hurricanes, events for which there is typically some notice, suggesting further that these documents would apply to an event such as Katrina.[86] Nonetheless, federal officials have argued that Katrina provided too much notice to qualify as a "short-notice" event.[87] The basis for this argument is respect for the states – with prior notice the normal NRP process of consultation with the states about their needs should apply. There are, of course, countervailing considerations: some known events can still be so overwhelming and urgent that the NRP-CIA may be the appropriate tool. If it were deliberate policy to exclude an event such as Katrina from the purview of the Catastrophic Incident Annex, there may be a significant flaw in the policy underlying the NRP-CIA and the Catastrophic Supplement. As Comptroller General David Walker testified, "the idea that we would be less proactive in dealing with a known natural disaster [than with a no-notice event] just defies common sense."[88]

Failures to Establish an Incident Command System Structure or Unified Command

Background: Incident Command System and Unified Command

Emergencies create confusion. Even in the case of a minor incident involving a single response agency, response personnel must quickly determine what is happening and then coordinate and control many separate activities at the scene to ensure everyone is working toward a common, productive goal. If the incident is a disaster or catastrophe, the failure to coordinate multiple agencies from different jurisdictions, each with its own internal lines of communication and authority, can seriously degrade the capabilities of the government as a whole to respond effectively. The absence of interoperable communications or an effectively trained and exercised plan will further undermine the response.

In the event that an emergency or disaster necessitates a response from more than one entity or jurisdiction, use of the Incident Command System (ICS) and establishment of a unified command will normally greatly improve chances of an effective response.

Hurricane Katrina brought about an attempt to establish a unified command among multiple agencies during a significant natural disaster. The story of that effort points to the need for agreement on goals and strategies, for understanding and training, for communication and coordination – and illustrates the practical difficulties of becoming ready and maintaining readiness with the NIMS-ICS doctrine including the concept of unified command.

The NRP, which utilizes ICS as part of the National Incident Management System (NIMS), the system that provides a nationwide approach for federal, state, and local governments and others to work together in domestic incidents, states that a unified command should be established:

> when there is more than one agency with incident jurisdiction or when incidents cross political jurisdictions. Agencies work together through the designated members of the Unified Command to establish their designated Incident Commanders at a single [location] and to establish a common set of objectives and strategies and a single Incident Action Plan.[89]

Unified command does not mean that a single person or agency directs others involved in a response (an arrangement known as "unity of command") Unified command, in the words of the NIMS manual, "allows agencies with different legal, geographic, and functional authorities and responsibilities to work together effectively without affecting individual agency authority, responsibility, or accountability."[90]

The challenges faced by the City of New York's emergency response agencies immediately after the attacks on the World Trade Center on September 11, 2001, demonstrate the need for a common incident-command system and a unified command in a major disaster. As reported by the National Commission on Terrorist Attacks Upon the United States (the "9/11 Commission"), deficiencies in the City's unified-command structure significantly impaired the ability of the New York Fire Department, the New York Police Department, and the Port Authority to coordinate their responses.[91] Exacerbating and complicating the lack of a unified-command structure were the poor communications systems and separate command posts that failed to effectively share information among the various emergency-response agencies.[92]

To ensure that different agencies work well together in a disaster, the 9/11 Commission recommended:

> Emergency response agencies nationwide should adopt the Incident Command System (ICS). When multiple agencies or multiple jurisdictions are involved, they should adopt a unified command. Both are proven frameworks for emergency response.[93]

Even before the 9/11 Commission made this recommendation, the federal government had begun developing the NRP, as well as NIMS. The Incident Command System, the incident-management component of NIMS, embraces the concept of unified command. Homeland Security Presidential Directive/HSPD-5, issued in February 2003, directed the Secretary of the Department of Homeland Security to develop a National Response Plan, as well as a National Incident Management System "to provide a consistent nationwide approach for Federal, State, and local governments to work effectively and efficiently together to prepare for, respond to, and recover from domestic incidents, regardless of cause, size, or complexity."[94] The Presidential directive specified that NIMS should incorporate the concepts of the Incident Command System.[95]

DHS issued NIMS in March 2004. NIMS identifies the advantages of utilizing ICS and specifically of establishing a unified command:

- a single set of objectives,
- a collective approach to develop strategies to achieve incident objectives,
- improved information flow and coordination between all jurisdictions and agencies involved,
- all involved agencies have an understanding of joint priorities and restrictions,
- protection from the compromise of each participating agency's legal authorities, and
- optimization of combined efforts through a single Incident Action Plan.[96]

Unified command is achieved through a team approach to incident management. The precise nature of a unified command structure will depend on particulars of the incident, but in general, each agency with jurisdictional authority or functional responsibility will participate in a collaborative process.[97] That is, each of the responding agencies with incident jurisdiction shares in the responsibility to establish a unified command.

Homeland Security Presidential Directive-5 directed federal departments and agencies to "make adoption of the NIMS a requirement ... for providing federal preparedness assistance through grants, contracts, or other activities."[98]

The NRP, which incorporates NIMS, was to be "fully implemented" 120 days after issuance.[99] During this period, which ended April 15, 2005, states and local governments were requested to "modify [their] existing incident management and emergency operations plans ... to ensure proper alignment with NRP coordinating structures."[100] DHS, however, did not require states to be in full compliance with NIMS until the fiscal year beginning October 1, 2006.[101] Federal compliance was to have been met by October 1, 2005.[102]

Gil Jamieson, Director of the NIMS Integration Center at FEMA, explained the rationale for this multi-year, phased approach for the states to adopt NIMS:

> You're asking for a cultural change in terms of the way that people do business. The National Incident Management System and ICS grew up from the fire service [due to the frequent need to coordinate firefighting of wildfires ranging across many jurisdictions]. There's still a tendency on the part of law enforcement to view it as a fire-centered process. Health and medical folks, while they want to comply with it, are just not familiar with it. So as opposed to having a knee-jerk reaction to a very hard-hitting federal mandate, we thought it was an appropriate response to phase it in over time, do the cultural awareness, migrate; while there were negative incentives in there in terms of provision of grant assistance, where we were trying to get to was that we were moving in that direction because it was a good idea, not because it was a federal mandate.[103]

At the time the NRP became effective in early 2005, it was apparent that many local, state, and federal agencies still were unfamiliar with the plan and NIMS. This lack of familiarity was observed in April 2005, during DHS's Top Officials Exercise (TOPOFF) 3, "by any measure the most ambitious civilian terrorism response exercise ever conducted."[104] Involving representatives from 27 federal departments, 30 state, 44 local, and 156 private-sector organizations, TOPOFF 3 simulated the simultaneous outbreak of pneumonic plague in Union and Middlesex Counties, New Jersey, and the dispersal of mustard gas and high-yield explosives in the city of New London, Connecticut.[105] TOPOFF 3 was the first national preparedness exercise that used the NRP and NIMS as the framework for the incident response and management.[106]

In a Quick Look Report on TOPOFF 3 issued in May 2005, DHS recognized that the exercise had revealed a fundamental lack of understanding of unified command.[107] The Report noted that "confusion at all levels regarding identification and clarification of roles and levels of responsibilities."[108] In November 2005, the DHS's Inspector General found that while "overall, objectives were addressed and met," the TOPOFF 3 exercise demonstrated "at all levels of government – a fundamental lack of understanding for the principles and protocols set forth in the NRP and NIMS."[109] The Inspector General highlighted "confusion over the different roles and responsibilities performed by the Principal Federal Official (PFO) and the Federal Coordinating Officer (FCO),"[110] an issue that also plagued the Katrina response.

In light of the incomplete understanding of the NRP and NIMS "at all levels of government" just prior to the 2005 hurricane season, it is not surprising that a number of the deficiencies in understanding and implementing the NRP surfaced in the wake of Katrina. It was the first time that the NRP and NIMS were used in a real-life major-disaster response.[111]

Difficulties in Establishing an ICS Structure and Unified Command

Louisiana

In the days surrounding Hurricane Katrina's assault on the Gulf Coast, FEMA's top operatives in Louisiana struggled to establish a unified-command structure with the state and other entities. But the efforts did not succeed. Although FEMA was contending with its own staffing and training issues, the main problem was the state's lack of emergency-management capacity. As Deputy FCO Scott Wells put it, "at some point we saw there was . . . nothing for the federal government to stick on to."[112]

As envisioned under the NRP and NIMS, a unified command should include:

- the FCO who, in the absence of a PFO, serves as the lead federal official;
- the State Coordinating Officer (SCO), the lead state official; and
- representatives of a variety of other entities who have authorities or resources important to the response, including the Department of Defense (DOD) (through a Defense Coordinating Officer (DCO)) and other federal and state agencies.[113]

Together, the individuals in the unified command are to make collective decisions about priorities and plans in responding to the disaster. In Louisiana, FEMA's William Lokey served as FCO, Scott Wells was his deputy, and Colonel Jeff Smith of the Louisiana Office of Homeland Security and Emergency Preparedness served as the SCO.

Lokey, Wells, and Colonel Smith worked alongside one another in the State Emergency Operations Center in Baton Rouge. Later, they moved to the Joint Field Office (JFO).[114]

But a unified command was not achieved. As Lokey frankly noted, "I can pretty much honestly say I was not in charge of all the federal operations in the field."[115] Complicating the situation, many requests for assistance were addressed outside the unified-command structure. For instance, Major General Bennett Landreneau, the Adjutant General and head of Louisiana's National Guard, requested troops through the interstate Emergency Management Assistance Compact, the National Guard Bureau, and the commander of the DOD forces responding to Katrina, General Honoré. According to the DOD's DCO for Louisiana, requests for large numbers of active-duty forces did not come to FEMA or to him, as a representative of DOD.[116] Although Lokey did not think General Landreneau's actions were inappropriate,[117] he was frustrated that, overall, many requests for assistance did not go through the unified command and thought this impaired the response to Katrina:

> People down there were asking everybody for everything, so when the final analysis is done, and everybody gets all the records of who asked who when, there's a tremendous amount of duplication and there's a tremendous amount of gaps.[118]

The geographic scope and physical intensity of the devastation, and the urgent human needs that faced responders in the immediate aftermath of Katrina in Louisiana, created a level of challenge not seen before in this country. The storm's decimation of much of the incident-command structure beneath the state-level unified command also undermined effective top-level command. The ICS incorporates the expectation that most incidents will be managed at the most local level possible, but the storm and its massive flooding largely incapacitated local responders. As William Carwile, the FCO for Mississippi, explained, "In a situation, a catastrophic disaster, it is very difficult to build from the bottom up if there is no bottom."[119]

This situation was exacerbated by the destruction of vast swaths of communication infrastructure in New Orleans and the surrounding parishes, substantially undermining the ability of those in the EOC in Baton Rouge to communicate with responders in the hardest-hit parts of the state.[120] The lack of communication limited the unified command's ability to form an accurate picture of what has happened in the affected areas, to receive and act on requests for assistance, and to fully understand what some of the goals and objectives for response should be.

The result was that essential features of a unified command were not achieved. The DHS Inspector General found that the FCO and SCO in Louisiana did not establish joint priorities and objectives for the response – a requirement of NIMS and effective unified command – until September 11 and did not develop the first joint incident-action plan until September 14.[121] Katrina had made landfall on August 29.

A catastrophe, of course, is exactly when the need for unified command and an effective incident-command structure is most acute. The failure in Louisiana reflects not only the overwhelming difficulties of the moment, but longer-term problems such as insufficient training; widespread lack of understanding of the NRP, NIMS-ICS and unified command; and an overall lack of preparation. Katrina, like the TOPOFF 3 national preparedness exercise just a few months earlier, exposed – at all levels of government – differing levels of knowledge, training, and ability to implement the principles of the ICS and unified command. During the response to Katrina, these abstract weaknesses became very real liabilities.

Perhaps the most significant reason for the failure to establish unified command in Louisiana is the lack of NIMS and NRP training. While FEMA as an institution must do a better job of training its emergency managers,[122] the top FEMA officials in Louisiana – including Lokey and Wells – appear to have been well-versed in the doctrine needed to establish unified command. The real problem was that Louisiana's emergency managers were unfamiliar with the NRP and NIMS. Indeed, the state brought in consultants a few days *after* Katrina made landfall to give basic ICS courses to EOC participants and to members of the Louisiana National Guard.[123] Both Lokey and Wells expressed frustration with the Louisiana's lack of training and the problems this caused. As Wells put it:

> Two days after the storm hit [Louisiana emergency-management staff] had a consultant come in and show them ICS, explain ICS. In the middle of a catastrophic disaster. This is how ICS works. There was no unified command under the National Response Plan. They didn't understand it. They had no idea. … My point is we have an architecture, we have [the] National Response

Plan. The states agreed to use NIMS. They agreed to ICS. What does it tell you when two days into a catastrophic disaster a state gets somebody in to explain ICS to them?[124]

Louisiana also lacked both adequate staff to support the needed ICS structure and appropriate resources to support the unified command. "Louisiana Office of Homeland Security and Preparedness is a small organization, 44, 47 people," Tony Robinson, FEMA's Deputy FCO for Special Projects, explained. "So I think this event challenged them to build an ICS organization to respond and to field geographic teams or liaisons. … It stretched their staff extremely thin."[125]

Staffing was a problem for FEMA as well, though it is not clear to what extent the staffing shortfalls impacted the ability to establish unified command. The National Emergency Response Team (ERT-N) was to form the nucleus of support for the FCO in Baton Rouge. Yet, according to Lokey, prior to landfall, only about half of the 25 members of the ERT-N team had arrived.[126] An internal after-action review by FEMA after Katrina estimated that the ERT team had only 25 percent of the needed staff.[127] FEMA's Chief of Planning, who was responsible for producing each day's Incident Action Plan (IAP) – a fundamental requirement of NIMS-ICS and integral to an effective unified command – did not arrive at the Baton Rouge EOC until after landfall.[128]

Inadequate physical space also presented obstacles. According to Lokey, lack of meeting space at the Louisiana EOC hindered the ability of state and federal officials to work together. "We had much better communication and coordination among everybody when we could [get everybody around the table], because the State EOC was very crowded and we had a lot of our staff meetings in the hallways."[129] Although a JFO is normally set up within three days, the JFO established by FEMA in Louisiana was not operational until 12 days after landfall.[130] Brown had reserved "Red October," the large FEMA tractor-trailer with meeting space and communications equipment, for his work, so Lokey and his team were rarely able to use it for their meetings with state officials.[131]

The combined effect of these problems was that unified command and an incident-command structure were not established in Louisiana until, at the earliest, weeks after the disaster.[132] This failure had unfortunate consequences. As put succinctly by Wells, "if we can't do ICS, we cannot manage disasters."[133]

Mississippi

Federal and state officials in Mississippi, spared the continuing dangers that afflicted southeastern Louisiana even after Katrina had passed, were able to successfully implement a unified-command system more quickly, though they confronted some of the same challenges.

Carwile was asked if he had found enough qualified people to staff his command. "Absolutely not," he said.[134] Like Lokey, his counterpart in Louisiana, Carwile attributed these deficiencies to the failure of DHS to approve funding requests for training and exercises. Beginning in 2004, according to Carwile, there was "no more money to plan; no more money to exercise; no more money for equipment; that money went away."[135] "You know, I honestly felt bad," Carwile told the Committee, "because the [emergency response] teams were reported as ready, and I didn't feel that they really were."[136]

Robert Latham, Executive Director of the Mississippi Emergency Management Agency, was particularly critical of federal agencies' weak knowledge of the NIMS and the ICS:

> I don't think most people understood it at all. I don't think anybody read the
> National Response Plan. … It's just too many agencies. They didn't understand

unified command. I mean, you almost had to learn it on the job. They didn't understand NIMS. I almost hate to bring this up … but I don't think people understood what a PFO was, what an FCO was, what the authority of an FCO was.[137]

Nevertheless, Carwile and Latham both believed that after a period of "chaos" that lasted two to three days after landfall, they were able to establish in Mississippi a successful ICS structure and a broadened unified command that included the State's Adjutant General and its Commissioner of Public Safety.[138] Carwile and Latham attributed this success, in part, to the extensive prior training on the Incident Command System received by state and local responders in Mississippi.[139] Carwile also had people on his team who had taught ICS; one member of his team had written an ICS handbook.[140]

Carwile also credited his pre-landfall relationship with Latham and Latham's deputy.[141] Latham described himself and Carwile as "joined at the hip from Saturday … I mean, neither one of us did anything or made a decision that the other one didn't know about."[142] Before Katrina's landfall in Mississippi, Carwile had also strengthened his coordination with the state by assigning a FEMA employee to be with state and local officials at each of three local EOC sites in areas expected to be hardest hit.[143]

The joint planning pre-landfall served federal and state managers well in the chaos that followed the storm. As in Louisiana, storm damage hindered maintenance of an ICS structure for several days. For 48 to 72 hours after the disaster, the primary response agencies for Mississippi, MEMA, the National Guard, and the Department of Public Safety, were engaged in their own areas of response. Since the different agencies had representatives at MEMA's Mobile Command Center, officials at MEMA had some idea of what the different agencies were doing, but poor communications prevented them from achieving a fully functioning ICS structure and a broadened unified command that included each of these agencies for the first few days after landfall.[144]

Latham described the difficulty of establishing an ICS structure in the immediate aftermath of any major disaster:

> I think that it's important to understand that in any disaster there is a period of chaos. And I don't care how good your plan is. … And what you hope is that at some period of time, as quick as possible, that you can shorten the period of chaos and the plan kicks in.[145]

Despite his overall conclusion that Mississippi was able to operate an effective ICS structure and unified command, Latham said that "it wasn't easy."[146] He echoed Carwile's observation that keeping the other participating federal agencies within the unified command was "like herding cats."[147]

Moreover, Admiral Allen's appointment as PFO, after which he began to exercise operational command, highlighted the NRP's ambiguity about the respective roles of the PFO and FCO, which had been evident during the TOPOFF 3 exercise. Admiral Allen, Lokey, Colonel Smith, and various other observers have commented that the appointment of a PFO in effect meant that there were "two people in charge" in each state.[148]

To resolve this ambiguity, approximately three weeks after he was designated PFO, Admiral Allen was concurrently appointed FCO for each of the three Gulf Coast states as well – effectively merging the PFO and FCO positions. Admiral Allen's concurrent appointment resulted in the simultaneous revocation of the appointments of the existing FCOs in Louisiana, Mississippi, and Alabama; they became Deputy FCOs. From the perspective of Carwile, the FCO in Mississippi prior to the concurrent appointment, the appointment of a single PFO-

FCO created other problems, including the impairment of the unified command where it already had been solidly established. Carwile found it "extraordinarily unusual" to designate a single FCO for three states, "knowing that at least in my view that a Federal Coordinating Officer had to be a full participant in the unified command." Although, according to Carwile, an FCO "belongs in a state working closely as part of that unified command," prior to his appointment Admiral Allen had devoted "none of his attention on Mississippi."[149]

Conclusion

Establishing a unified command and incident-command structure can be tremendously important in coordinating a large incident that involves officials and responders from many different jurisdictions and different levels of government.

The situation on the Gulf Coast presented many challenges to establishing a broad, unified command and effective incident-management structure, particularly in the early days after the storm including: the size and chaos of the situation itself; the severely impaired ability to communicate across agencies or with front-line first responders; and the disruption to the potential supporting incident-command structure when many responders became victims. The Gulf Coast experience demonstrated that, despite the many challenges of the incident, additional experience with and training on NIMS-ICS, an adequate number of sufficiently trained support personnel, and the discipline in adhering to the doctrine of the incident command system made a difference in the success of the efforts to establish a unified command and incident-command structure in the response where these circumstances existed.

1 The White House, Homeland Security Presidential Directive-5: Management of Domestic Incidents, Feb. 28, 2003, Section 16. http://www.whitehouse.gov/news/releases/2003/02/20030228-9.html. Accessed on Apr. 7, 2006.

2 6 U.S.C. § 312(6).

3 Tom Ridge, former Secretary, U.S. Department of Homeland Security, "Remarks by Secretary of Homeland Security Tom Ridge at a Press Conference Announcing the National Response Plan," Jan. 6, 2005. http://www.dhs.gov/dhspublic/display?content=4301. Accessed on Feb. 28, 2006. As discussed in greater detail below, DHS also developed the National Incident Management System (NIMS) as the incident management system to be used for incidents under the NRP. NIMS was released by DHS in Mar. 2004. U.S. Department of Homeland Security, "Department of Homeland Security Secretary Tom Ridge Approves National Incident Management System (NIMS)," press release, Mar. 1, 2004.

4 U.S. Department of Homeland Security, *National Response Plan*. Washington: Government Printing Office, Dec. 2004, p. ix (Letter of Instruction) [hereinafter *NRP*]. Although the NRP was released publicly on Jan. 6, 2005, it is dated, and was completed in, December 2004. The 120-day implementation period provided for in the NRP was calculated based on the December date and officially ended on Apr. 14, 2005.

5 U.S. Department of Homeland Security, *Interim National Preparedness Goal*, Mar. 31, 2005, p. 10. http://www.ojp.usdoj.gov/odp/docs/InterimNationalPreparednessGoal_03-31-05_1.pdf. Accessed on Apr. 6, 2006. The Interim Preparedness Goal was prepared pursuant to Homeland Security Presidential Directive-8 and is intended to establish the "national vision and priorities" that are to guide preparedness efforts.

6 *NRP*, p. 3. The NRP bases its definition of an Incident of National Significance on the four criteria set forth in HSPD-5 to describe the situations when the Secretary of Homeland Security is to coordinate the Federal Government's resources in response to or recovery from terrorists attacks, major disaster or other emergencies:

> 1. A Federal department or agency acting under its own authority has requested the assistance of the Secretary of Homeland Security.

> 2. The resources of State and local authorities are overwhelmed and Federal assistance has been requested by the appropriate State and local authorities. Examples include:
> • Major disasters or emergencies as defined under the Stafford Act; and
> • Catastrophic incidents (as defined elsewhere in the NRP).

> 3. More than one Federal department or agency has become substantially involved in responding to an incident. Examples include:
> • Credible threats, indications or warnings of imminent terrorist attack, or acts of terrorism

directed domestically against the people, property, environment, or political or legal institutions of the United States or its territories or possessions; and

• Threats or incidents related to high-profile, large-scale events that present high-probability targets such as National Special Security Events (NSSEs) and other special events as determined by the Secretary of Homeland Security, in coordination with other Federal departments and agencies.

4. The Secretary of Homeland Security has been directed to assume responsibility for managing a domestic incident by the President. *NRP*, p. 4.

7 *NRP*, p. 3.

8 *NRP*, pp. v-viii.

9 *NRP*, p. 7. Note that "emergencies" under the Stafford Act include "any occasion or instance" for which federal assistance is needed, whether man-made or the result of natural disaster. *Source*: 42 U.S.C. § 5122 (1). In contrast, "major disasters" under the Stafford Act include "any natural catastrophe . . . or, regardless of cause, any fire, flood, or explosion," suggesting that events other than natural disasters, including terrorist events, are covered only insofar as they result in fire, flood or explosion. *Source*: 42 U.S.C. § 5122(2). DHS's Inspector General has raised concerns that the definition of "major disaster" does not cover all WMD events. *See*: Department of Homeland Security, Office of Inspector General, "A Review of the Top Officials 3 Exercise," Nov. 2005, p. 30. http://www.dhs.gov/interweb/assetlibrary/OIG_06-07_Nov05. pdf. Accessed on Feb. 28, 2006 [hereinafter "TOPOFF 3," Nov. 2005].

10 *NRP*, p. 4.

11 The discussion in this section is not intended to constitute a comprehensive assessment of the development and functioning of the National Response Plan. The Committee, for example, has not looked at the initial development process of the NRP, which reportedly encountered some difficulties, nor has the Committee conducted a systematic assessment of the ways in which the NRP interacts with state-to-state assistance mechanisms such as the Emergency Management Assistance Compact (EMAC). Rather, this section is intended to touch on some of the more conspicuous problems that came to light in the preparations for and response to Katrina.

12 U.S. Department of Homeland Security, "Remarks by Secretary of Homeland Security Tom Ridge at a Press Conference Announcing the National Response Plan," Jan. 6, 2005. http://www.dhs.gov/dhspublic/display?content=4301. Accessed on Feb. 28, 2006.

13 U.S. Department of Homeland Security, "Remarks by Secretary of Homeland Security Tom Ridge at a Press Conference Announcing the National Response Plan," Jan. 6, 2005. http://www.dhs.gov/dhspublic/display?content=4301. Accessed on Feb. 28, 2006.

14 Office of the Vice President, "National Response Plan and Response Structure." Provided to Committee; filed as Bates nos. OVP 003422 through 003424.

15 FEMA, *Federal Response Plan*, Apr. 1999.

16 Committee staff interview of Robert Stephan, Assistant Secretary of Homeland Security for Infrastructure Protection, Preparedness Directorate, U.S. Department of Homeland Security, conducted on Jan. 13, 2006, transcript pp. 126-128. Stephan, who led the development of the NRP at DHS, stated that other agencies that were signatories to the NRP were also required, in the NRP's 120-day implementation period to conduct appropriate training and awareness courses for the NRP. Stephan interview, Jan. 13, 2006, pp. 126-127. The Committee has not investigated to what extent other federal agencies carried out such NRP training.

17 Committee staff interview of Gil Jamieson, Acting Director, National Incident Management System Integration Center, Federal Emergency Management Agency (FEMA), conducted on Dec. 20, 2005, transcript p. 29. Mr. Jamieson indicated that the NIC was authorized for 10 employees but that only seven slots were filled.

18 Jamieson interview, Dec. 20, 2005, pp. 37-39. Jamieson recognized that such training was not sufficient and that additional training tailored to specific jobs, as well as exercises and actual field assignments, were important as well. In explaining why more had not been done, Jamieson indicated that they were at the beginning of a gradual process and that FEMA needed additional resources. Jamieson interview, Dec. 20, 2005, pp. 8-10.

19 "TOPOFF 3," Nov. 2005, p. 2.

20 Various officials acknowledged to us their lack of familiarity with the NRP. For example, ICE official Michael Vanacore who was sent down to the Gulf Coast to address DHS's public safety and security responsibilities under ESF-13, stated: "I . . . had a fleeting familiarity with it. To be honest, wasn't something that was high on my radar screen with my particular responsibilities." *Source*: Committee staff interview of Michael Vanacore, Director, Office of International Affairs, Immigration and Customs Enforcement, U.S. Department of Homeland Security, conducted on Jan. 27, 2006, transcript p. 8. During his first three days in Baton Rouge, "a lot of it seemed to be in a foreign language there because that whole National Response Plan had a language all its own, which I had never heard up until that point." *Source*: Vanacore interview, Jan. 27, 2006, p. 35. Brig. Gen. Graham, Deputy Commanding General for Army North, Fifth U.S. Army who worked for General Honoré in Joint Task Force Katrina testified that he read the NRP on his way to Louisiana. Committee staff interview of Brig. Gen. Mark Graham, Deputy Commanding General, Fifth U.S. Army, conducted on Jan. 12, 2006, transcript p. 26.

21 Written Statement of Herman B. Leonard, Professor, John F. Kennedy School of Government and Harvard Business School, Harvard University, and Arnold M. Howitt, Professor, John F. Kennedy School of Government, Harvard University, for the U.S. Senate, Committee on Homeland Security and Governmental Affairs, hearing on *Hurricane Katrina:*

Recommendations for Reform, Mar. 8, 2006, p. 3.

22 42 U.S.C. § 5143. Pursuant to Executive Order 12148 (July 20 1979 – Sec. 4-203), as amended by Executive Orders 13286 (68 Fed. Reg. 10619, Feb. 28, 2003), Sec. 52 and 12673 (54 Fed. Reg. 12573, Mar. 29, 1989 – Sec. 1) the responsibility to appoint an FCO is delegated to the Secretary of Homeland Security, though traditionally the President has continued to make the initial appointment that accompanies a disaster or emergency declaration, based upon the recommendation of FEMA.

23 42 U.S.C. § 5143.

24 *NRP*, p. 33. Depending on the magnitude of the disaster, a PFO need not always be designated for an incident covered by the Stafford Act; if no PFO is designated, then, according to the NRP, the FCO is to serve as the federal lead. *NRP*, pp. 29, 34.

25 *NRP*, pp. 33-34.

26 *NRP*, p. 33.

27 *NRP*, p. 34.

28 According to the NRP, the FCO is to "coordinate Federal resource support activities," while the PFO is to ensure "overall coordination of Federal domestic incident management and resource allocation activities." *NRP*, pp. 33-34.

29 *NRP*, p. 34. Not surprisingly, the DHS Office of Inspector General found, in its review of the Department's Apr. 2005 TOPOFF-3 exercise that there was confusion over the different roles and responsibilities of the PFO and FCO; the IG suggested that developing a better understanding of these roles would enhance implementation of the NRP. "TOPOFF 3," Nov. 2005, p. 13.

30 Testimony of Bruce Baughman, President, National Emergency Management Association and Director, Alabama State Emergency Management Agency, before the U.S. Senate, Committee on Homeland Security and Governmental Affairs, hearing on *Hurricane Katrina: Recommendations for Reform*, Mar. 8, 2006.

31 Written Statement of David M. Walker, Comptroller General of the United States, for the U.S. Senate, Committee on Homeland Security and Governmental Affairs, hearing on *Hurricane Katrina: Recommendations for Reform*, Mar. 8, 2006, p. 11.

32 Committee staff interview of William Lokey, Federal Coordinating Officer for Hurricane Katrina in Louisiana, FEMA, conducted on Jan. 20, 2006, transcript pp. 191-192. *See also*: Written Statement of Col. Jeff Smith, Deputy Director, Louisiana Office of Homeland Security and Emergency Preparedness (LOHSEP), before the U.S. House, Select Bipartisan Committee to Investigate the Preparation for and Response to Hurricane Katrina, hearing on *Hurricane Katrina: Preparedness and Response by the State of Louisiana*, Dec. 14, 2005, p. 16 ("One of the complaints in the testimony before the House that Jeff Smith had was he had three chains of command to deal with. He had the PFOs, he had mine, and he had headquarters. Well, I'm working as much as I can with the whole, now that PFO is operational, which it wasn't supposed to be. You know, the ERT-N ought to be working for that person, not having them create a separate thing. They were doing their own plans and all that kind of stuff like that and made it very confusing.").

33 Committee staff interview of Vice Adm. Thad Allen, U.S. Coast Guard, Chief of Staff, conducted on Feb. 3, 2006, transcript p. 76.

34 70 Fed. Reg. 56929 (Sept. 29, 2005) (Louisiana); 70 Fed. Reg. 57308 (Sept. 30, 2005) (Alabama); 70 Fed. Reg. 57309 (Sept. 30, 2005) (Mississippi).

35 *NRP*, pp. ESF–iii through ESF–iv.

36 *NRP*, p. ESF–13.

37 *NRP*, pp. ix-x.

38 *NRP*, p. ESF–8.

39 *See*: Chapter 24: Medical Assistance for more information.

40 *NRP*, pp. 60-62.

41 Committee staff interview of David Garratt, Acting Director of Recovery, FEMA, conducted on Jan. 9, 2006, transcript pp. 170-171.

42 FEMA, *Hurricane Plan for Louisiana: An Attachment to the Regional Supplement to the Federal Response Plan*, May 2002. Provided to Committee; filed as Bates nos. DHS-FEMA-0058-0001773 through 0001785.

43 The NRP does appear to contemplate that certain regional plans may be developed. *Source*: *NRP*, p. 61. David Garratt, a 10-year veteran of FEMA who chaired the interagency Catastrophic Incident Planning Group, said he couldn't say whether he had seen a regional supplement for the NRP, but stated that he "would be shocked if there were not regional supplements to the NRP." *Source*: Garratt interview, Jan. 9, 2006, p. 174.

44 Homeland Security Council and U.S. Department of Homeland Security, *National Planning Scenarios*, Version 20.2 Draft, Apr. 2005. Provided to Committee; Homeland Security Council and U.S. Department of Homeland Security, *National Planning Scenarios*, "Scenario 10: Natural Disaster – Major Hurricane," Version 20.2 Draft, Apr. 2005. Provided to Committee; filed as Bates nos. WHK 17500 through 17511; *See also*: U.S. Library of Congress, Congressional Research Service, *The National Preparedness System: Issues in the 109th Congress*, by Keith Bea, Mar. 10, 2005, pp. 8-10.

45 Vice Adm. Allen interview, Feb. 3, 2006, p. 122. Elsewhere in the interview Adm. Allen gives an example of a "natural disaster with a radiological event" as a disaster that somehow impacted a nuclear power plant. *Source*: Vice Adm. Allen

interview, Feb. 3, 2006, pp. 89-90 ("I think there are a spectrum of hazards that we have to deal with, and I think we need better clarity and maybe some more detail about the types of incidents PFOs are likely to encounter, and we need to plan against those particular threats rather than just having the three generics, you know, the NSSE, the natural disaster, and the terrorist attack."). Adm. James Loy, former Deputy Secretary of Homeland Security, suggested a similar approach in a non-transcribed interview with Committee Staff, proposing that more specific plans should be developed around particular scenarios. *Source*: Committee staff interview of Adm. James Loy, former Deputy Secretary, U.S. Department of Homeland Security, conducted on Nov. 16, 2005 (untranscribed).

46 Written Statement of Walker, Senate Committee hearing, Mar. 8, 2006, p. 13.

47 Vice Adm. Allen interview, Feb. 3, 2006, p. 106.

48 U.S. Department of Homeland Security, *National Response Plan, Catastrophic Incident Annex*. Washington: Government Printing Office, Dec. 2004, p. CAT-1 [hereinafter *NRP-CIA*].

49 Garratt interview, Jan. 9, 2006, pp. 9-12. In the interview, Garratt initially stated that the final draft of the Catastrophic Incident Supplement was completed in September 2004, but subsequently modified that estimate to "sometime approaching the end of 2004."

50 Garratt interview, Jan. 9, 2006, pp. 12-13; *See also*: Jamieson interview, Dec. 20, 2005, pp. 24-25; U.S. Department of Homeland Security, *National Response Plan, Catastrophic Incident Supplement*, "National Disaster Medical System, Memorandum of Agreement Among the Departments of Homeland Security, Health and Human Services, Veterans Affairs, and Defense," Draft for Official Use Only, Sept. 2005, p. 2. Both Mr. Garratt and Mr. Jamieson described the dispute as involving payment for definitive medical care, defined in the Memorandum of Agreement as "medical treatment or services beyond emergency care, initiated upon inpatient admission to an NDMS treatment facility and provided for injuries or illnesses resulting directly from a specified public health emergency, or for injuries, illnesses and conditions requiring non-deferrable medical treatment or services to maintain health when such medical treatment and services are temporarily not available as a result of the public health emergency."

51 Jamieson interview, Dec. 20, 2005, p. 25. The signature pages to the Memorandum of Agreement reflect fax dates of Sept. 5 and 6, 2005. The version of the Catastrophic Incident Supplement produced to the Committee and attaching the Catastrophic Incident Supplement is dated Sept. 2005.

52 Rajeev Vankayya, e-mail to Tom Sizemore and Brian Kamoie, Sept. 2, 2005, 7:36 p.m. Provided to Committee; filed as Bates no. OPHEP 24179. This e-mail between the Senior Director for Biodefense at the Homeland Security Council and HHS officials said in part "Could you give me a call to discuss the MOU [Memorandum of Understanding]? We discussed in the DC this morning and there was agreement that it should be signed immediately." An e-mail from Mr. Kamoie to Mr. Sizemore and Robert Claypool of HHS sent approximately one hour later forwarded Dr. Vankayya's e-mail message and said, in part, "I assume from this the Deputies want this document signed immediately. We did not get to work through the issues Monday. You will recall our concerns as discussed last Friday. Bob, I suggest you raise this with Stewart and get guidance on whether in the middle of all of this he wants us to go to the mat and work through the document or wait until response activities allow a meeting." *Source*: Brian Kamoie, e-mail to Tom Sizemore and Robert Claypool, Sept. 2, 2005, 8:31 p.m. Provided to Committee; filed as Bates no. OPHEP 24179. The "DC" and "Deputies" referred to in the e-mail messages are presumably references to the Homeland Security Council's Deputies Committee, the "senior sub-cabinet interagency forum for consideration of policy issues affecting homeland security" and made up of the Deputy Secretaries of Treasury, Defense, Health and Human Services, Transportation, Homeland Security; the Deputy Attorney General; the Deputy Directors of Central Intelligence, FBI, FEMA, and OMB; and the Chief of Staff to the Vice President, as its regular members. *Source*: The White House, Homeland Security Presidential Directive-1: Organization and Operation of the Homeland Security Council, Oct. 29, 2001. http://www.whitehouse.gov/news/releases/2001/10/20011030-1.html. Accessed on Apr. 7, 2006.

53 Even once issued, the Catastrophic Incident Supplement was not designed to take effect immediately. Instead, it was to be phased in over a number of months, to allow agencies to make the preparations necessary to be able to comply with the provisions of the Supplement. Garratt interview, Jan. 9, 2006, pp. 37-38; U.S. Department of Homeland Security, *National Response Plan, Catastrophic Incident Supplement*, Draft for Official Use Only, Sept. 2005, p. 2. Provided to Committee; filed as Bates no. DHS-FEMA-0109-0000003 (providing for a 120-day "process institutionalization period") [hereinafter *Catastrophic Incident Supplement*].

54 *Catastrophic Incident Supplement*, Annex 1. The Execution Schedule varies depending on the nature of the catastrophic incident – *i.e.,* whether it is a natural disaster, biological incident, explosion, etc.

55 Garratt interview, Jan. 9, 2006, p. 44.

56 Jamieson interview, Dec. 20, 2005, p. 60. Asked what had happened since to the Catastrophic Incident Supplement since the Memorandum of Understanding had been signed on Sept. 6, 2005, Mr. Jamieson stated "I think the whole issue has been put on hold in terms of the revision of the NRP and whether or not what we're doing is still relevant in the context of the post-Katrina environment." *See also*: U.S. Assistant to the President for Homeland Security and Counterterrorism, *The Federal Response to Hurricane Katrina: Lessons Learned*. Washington: Government Printing Office, Feb. 2006, p. 163 ("our experience in Katrina suggests [the Catastrophic Incident Supplement] must now be reconsidered to make it more robust in ensuring the Federal assistance arrives as soon as possible.") [hereinafter The White House, *Hurricane Katrina Lessons Learned*].

57 One possible starting point for such planning may be the 15 National Planning Scenarios which have already been developed under the auspices of the Homeland Security Council. The Scenarios represent a diverse array of plausible, high-consequence all-hazards events, ranging from a biological attack to a major hurricane; they are currently used as a preparedness

tool to help identify necessary capabilities for first responders. One measure of an effective catastrophic plan is that it should be capable of addressing these or similar scenarios. *See*: Homeland Security Council and U.S. Department of Homeland Security, *National Planning Scenarios*, Version 20.2 Draft, Apr. 2005; U.S. Library of Congress, Congressional Research Service, *The National Preparedness System: Issues in the 109th Congress*, by Keith Bea, Mar. 10, 2005, pp. 8-10.

58 *NRP*, p. 7.

59 Sec. Chertoff, memorandum to various DHS officials, "Designation of Principal Federal Official for Hurricane Katrina," Aug. 30, 2005. Provided to Committee; filed as Bates nos. DHS-FRNT-0010-0000768 through 0000769 ("In accordance with the guidance provided in the National Response Plan (NRP), I hereby declare Hurricane Katrina an Incident of National Significance.").

60 Sec. Chertoff, "Press Conference with Officials from Homeland Security, the Environmental Protection Agency, and the Departments of Health and Human Services, Energy, Transportation, and Defense," Aug. 31, 2005. http://www.dhs. gov/dhspublic/display?content=4773. Accessed on Mar. 15, 2006 ("The Department of Homeland Security has declared this an Incident of National Significance, the first ever use of this designation under the new National Response Plan.").

61 Testimony of Sec. Michael Chertoff, U.S. Department of Homeland Security, before the U.S. House, Select Bipartisan Committee to Investigate the Preparation for and Response to Hurricane Katrina, hearing on *Hurricane Katrina: The Role of the Department of Homeland Security*, Oct. 19, 2005.

62 Testimony of Sec. Michael Chertoff, U.S. Department of Homeland Security, before the U.S. Senate, Committee on Homeland Security and Governmental Affairs, hearing on *Hurricane Katrina: The Homeland Security Department's Preparation and Response*, Feb. 15, 2006.

63 Stephan interview, Jan. 13, 2006, pp. 88-92. Mr. Wood identified Scott Weber, Counselor to the Secretary, as the individual who he believed had inserted the language about an Incident of National Significance into the statement. According to Mr. Wood, Mr. Weber was the individual responsible for FEMA matters in the Secretary's Office. Committee staff interview of John Wood, Chief of Staff, U.S. Department of Homeland Security, conducted on Jan. 27, 2006, transcript pp. 34-38.

64 Stephan interview, Jan. 13, 2006, pp. 92-93.

65 *NRP*, p. 33.

66 Testimony of Patrick Rhode, former Acting Deputy Director and Chief of Staff, FEMA, before the U.S. Senate, Committee on Homeland Security and Governmental Affairs, hearing on *Hurricane Katrina: The Roles of DHS and FEMA Leadership*, Feb. 10, 2006. Rhode stated: "I'm not certain as I sit here that I was made aware that Mr. Brown's title as Director had been removed, even temporarily. I honestly can't say that I remember hearing that. … I'm not aware during the time of the early days of Katrina, as Brown was initially named Principal Federal Officer, I'm not aware of any additional impacts to me or how I was conducting myself in the office." Asked if he gave up his role as FEMA Director when appointed PFO, Brown replied "Great question. I don't know. I tried not to, and I tried to keep the FCOs – I tried to keep them in the traditional mode of operations; you guys keep doing what you need to do, and when you have policy issues or questions, feed those to me, and I will just deal with those, and the same with the NRCC. Everybody just keep operating as you think we normally should, and I'll just try to deal with this PFO designation on my own." He also stated that no one asked him to relinquish his role as Director of FEMA. *Source*: Committee staff interview of Michael Brown, former Director, FEMA, conducted on Jan. 23, 2006, transcript p. 75. When asked whether Michael Brown's designation as PFO was consistent with his remaining director of FEMA, Robert Stephan, who led DHS's development of the NRP, stated "Well you could remain director of FEMA, but you would have had to have passed of the duties associated with being the director of FEMA to whoever his deputy was, so that Michael Brown could have focused exclusively on the duties as principal Federal official." *Source*: Stephan interview, Jan. 13, 2006, p. 123.

67 Committee staff interview of Michael Jackson, Deputy Secretary, U.S. Department of Homeland Security, conducted on Jan. 27, 2006, transcript pp. 49-50. When asked about the NRP and whether Brown was not supposed to continue on as Director of FEMA after being named PFO, Jackson stated: "There is this unique relationship … between the FEMA Director managing an event like this and a PFO managing an event like this in which their existing organizational and legal responsibilities are aligned very directly and where there is really, it seems to me, not the inherent conflict that might be anticipated by some portion of this text with a different fact set."

68 Questions for the Record of Sec. Michael Chertoff, U.S. Department of Homeland Security, for the U.S. Senate, Committee on Homeland Security and Governmental Affairs, hearing on *Hurricane Katrina: The Homeland Security Department's Response*, Feb. 15, 2006, p. 8.

69 [69] FEMA Operations Center, e-mail to Michael Brown and others, Sept. 1, 2005, 9:07 p.m. Provided to Committee; filed as Bates no. DHS 003140; "Swarm of Small Earthquakes Shakes Calif," The Associated Press, Sept. 1, 2005.

70 *NRP*, p. 34.

71 Brown interview, Jan. 23, 2006, p. 132. Vice Adm. Thad Allen, who replaced Brown as PFO, also had not participated in the requisite PFO training prescribed by the NRP. However, Vice Adm. Allen's many years of experience in response efforts with the Coast Guard makes his lack of specific PFO training far less troubling. Vice Adm. Allen interview, Feb. 3, 2006, p. 5.

72 Stephan interview, Jan. 13, 2006, p. 105. Stephan nonetheless declined to criticize the decision to make Allen simultaneously PFO and the FCO of three states, stating "if that's what [Admiral Allen] said needed to be done and the Secretary supported him . . . the dumbest thing I ever did would be to second-guess that."

73 One expert noted to Committee staff that "only a lawyer" would look at the NRP-CIA, even without the Catastrophic

Incident Supplement, and not recognize it as an excellent tool for an emergency response manager to create a "sense of urgency." Committee staff interview of Chuck Mills, Vice President, Emergency Management Services International, Inc., conducted on Feb. 14, 2006 (untranscribed). Mills is a 30-year veteran and Type-I Incident Commander with the U.S. Forest Service.

74 *NRP-CIA*, p. CAT–1; *NRP*, p. 43.

75 *NRP*, p. 43; *NRP-CIA*, p. CAT–1.

76 *NRP-CIA*, p. CAT–1.

77 For an example of the tone set by the NRP-CIA, see Chapters 13 and 24, describing how, even in the absence of the formal activation of the Catastrophic Incident Annex, officials at the Department of Health and Human Services invoked the Annex in requesting assistance from the Department of Defense and in "leaning forward" to begin to deploy significant medical assets in anticipation of the needs on the Gulf Coast.

78 *NRP-CIA*, pp. CAT–1 through CAT–3 (recognizing that "[t]he response capabilities and resources of the local jurisdiction . . . may be insufficient and quickly overwhelmed. Local emergency personnel who normally respond to incidents may be among those affected and unable to perform their duties.").

79 *NRP-CIA*, p. CAT–4.

80 *NRP-CIA*, p. CAT–2.

81 *NRP-CIA*, p. CAT–4.

82 Sec. Chertoff, House Select Committee hearing, Oct. 19, 2005.

83 Two days before landfall, David Garratt, the Deputy Director of FEMA's Recovery Division and the chair of the Catastrophic Incident Planning Group charged with developing the Catastrophic Incident Supplement, told Janet Benini, a former Homeland Security Council official who had worked with him to develop the Catastrophic Incident Supplement, that he had heard no talk activating of the NRP-CIA. David Garratt, e-mail to Janet Benini, Aug. 27, 2005, 12:36 p.m. Provided to Committee; filed as Bates no. DHS-FEMA-0096-0000395. *See also*: Wood interview, Jan. 27, 2006, pp. 54-55.

84 *See*: Altshuler interview, Dec. 15, 2005, pp. 55-59; Wood interview, Jan. 27, 2006, pp. 46-47; Questions for the Record of Sec. Chertoff, Senate Committee hearing, Feb. 15, 2006, p. 3; Jamieson interview, Dec. 20, 2005, pp. 67-71. In written answers to questions posed by the Committee, Secretary Chertoff also asserted that "With regard to Katrina, the Department's analysis suggests that 100% of the assets called for by the [Castasthic Incident Supplement] in the first 48 hours *after* landfall were, in fact, deployed *prior* to landfall." Therefore, the Secretary stated, "any conclusion that use of the CIA would have improved FEMA's performance in Katrina is mistaken and contradicted by the facts." *Source*: Questions for the Record of Sec. Chertoff, Senate Committee hearing, Feb. 15, 2006, pp. 3-4 (emphasis in original). A table provided by DHS that purports to demonstrate that the requirements of the Supplement had been fully complied with, however, contains inaccurate entries and, with respect to certain items, is misleading in its portrayal of the extent of DHS's pre-landfall efforts as well as the difference implementing the Catastrophic Incident Annex (including, if available, the execution schedule in the Catastrophic Incident Supplement) might have made.

For example, the Supplement specifies that the Interagency Incident Management Group (IIMG) is to be activated within 15 minutes of an incident and a PFO is to be designated within one hour; though these entries are marked as completed in the table submitted by DHS, in fact, as described elsewhere in this report, the IIMG was not activated nor the PFO designated until Tuesday, Aug. 30, the day after landfall. Another entry – juxtaposed against a requirement that DHS initiate deployment of 11 Disaster Medical Assistance Teams (DMATs) – indicates that 18 DMATs were "in theater" on Aug. 25, 2005; in fact, as of late on Sunday, Aug. 28, only four full DMAT teams and two partial DMAT teams had been pre-staged and, with the exception of one team in Baton Rouge, these DMATs were outside the affected states of Louisiana and Mississippi. In addition, in entries corresponding to the Supplement's requirement that DHS initiate action to immediately deploy various quantities of everything from ice and water to tents and sleeping bags, DHS's chart notes that each of these items were "loaded at Logistics Centers and available." Such items, however, are permanently stored at such logistics centers throughout the country; their inclusion in this table therefore does not reflect any action on DHS's part in response to Katrina nor does it necessarily indicate items that were quickly transported to the Gulf Coast. *Source*: Committee staff interview of Gary Moore, Director, Logistics, FEMA, conducted on Dec. 9, 2005, transcript p. 10. Finally, DHS's table does not reflect the many actions that the Catastrophic Incident Supplement would have directed other agencies to undertake had it been completed and the Annex activated.

85 *NRP-CIA*, p. CAT–5.

86 *Catastrophic Incident Supplement*, p. 1-1.

87 Jamieson interview, Dec. 20, 2005, pp. 67-71.

88 Walker, Senate Committee hearing, Mar. 8, 2006. "Because it is possible to respond to incidents maturing to catastrophic magnitude in a more proactive manner than surprise catastrophic incidents, it does not make sense to exclude evolving catastrophic incidents from the scope of the annex's coverage." Written Statement of Walker, Senate Committee hearing, Mar, 8, 2006, p. 12.

89 *NRP*, p. 73. The NRP also explains that the Unified Command "provides direct on-scene control of tactical operations and utilizes a NIMS ICS incident management team organization." *Source*: *NRP*, p. 39. The Unified Command concept "utilized by civil authorities is distinct from the military chain of command." *Source*: *NRP*, p. 10.

90 U.S. Department of Homeland Security, *National Incident Management System*, Mar. 1, 2004, pp. 11-12 [hereinafter

NIMS].

91 The deficiencies in unified command reported by the 9/11 Commission included the Fire Department's inability to coordinate excess personnel from West Street to support Fire Chiefs that needed more personnel at the South Tower, and the Police department's inability to control non-Emergency Service Unit personnel inside the towers. National Commission on Terrorist Attacks upon the United States, *The 9/11 Commission Report*. Washington: Government Printing Office, 2004, pp. 319-320 [hereinafter *The 9/11 Commission Report*].

92 *The 9/11 Commission Report*, p. 321.

93 *The 9/11 Commission Report*, p. 397.

94 The White House, Homeland Security Presidential Directive-5: Management of Domestic Incidents, Feb. 28, 2003.

95 The White House, Homeland Security Presidential Directive-5: Management of Domestic Incidents, Feb. 28, 2003.

96 *NIMS*, pp. 14, 15.

97 The National Incident Management System explains:

> As a team effort, [Unified Command] overcomes much of the inefficiency and duplication of effort that can occur when agencies at different functional and geographic jurisdictions, or agencies at different levels of government, operate without a common system or organizational framework. All agencies with jurisdictional authority or functional responsibility for any or all aspects of an incident and those able to provide specific resource support participate in the [Unified Command] structure and contribute to the process of determining overall incident strategies; selecting objectives; ensuring that joint planning for tactical activities is accomplished in accordance with approved incident objectives; ensuring the integration of tactical operations; and approving, committing, and making optimum use of all assigned resources.

NIMS, p. 14.

98 The White House, Homeland Security Presidential Directive-5: Management of Domestic Incidents, Feb. 28, 2003. In 2004, the 9/11 Commission recommended more specifically that DHS "should consider making funding contingent on aggressive and realistic training in accordance with incident command system and unified command procedures." *The 9/11 Commission Report*, p. 397.

99 The National Response Plan is dated Dec. 2004, but was issued – i.e. released – by the Secretary of the Department of Homeland Security on Jan. 6, 2005. The NRP became effective upon issuance but its implementation was phased in over a one-year period:

> Phase I – Transitional Period (0 to 60 days): This 60-day timeframe was intended to provide a transitional period for departments and agencies and other organizations to modify training, designate staffing of NRP organizational elements, and become familiar with NRP structures, processes and protocols. Day 60 was Feb. 13, 2005.

> Phase II – Plan Modification (60 to 120 days): This second 60-day timeframe was intended to provide departments and agencies the opportunity to modify existing federal interagency plans to align with the NRP and conduct necessary training. Day 120 was Apr. 14, 2005.

> Phase III – Initial Implementation and Testing (120 days to 1 year): Four months after its issuance, the NRP was to be fully implemented and the Initial NRP, Federal Response Plan, U.S. Government Domestic Terrorism Concept of Operations Plan, and Federal Radiological Emergency Response Plan were superseded. Other existing plans remained in effect, modified to align with the NRP. During this timeframe, DHS is to conduct systematic assessments of NRP coordinating structures, processes and protocols implemented for actual Incidents of National Significance, national-level homeland security exercises, and National Special Security Events. These assessments are to gauge the plan's effectiveness in meeting specific objectives outlined in Homeland Security Presidential Directive-5. At the end of this period, DHS is to conduct a one-year review to assess the implementation process and make recommendations to the DHS' Secretary on necessary NRP revisions. Following this initial review, the NRP was to begin a deliberate four-year review and re-issuance cycle. The one-year date was Dec. 15, 2005.

NRP, ix.

100 *NRP*, x.

101 U.S. Department of Homeland Security, "Fiscal Year 2005 Homeland Security Grant Program: Program Guidelines and Application Kit," p. 49.

102 U.S. Department of Homeland Security, "Text of Secretary Ridge's Letter to National Response Plan (NRP) Federal Departments and Agencies Regarding NIMS Implementation in FY 2005." http://www.fema.gov/doc/nims/nrp_letter_from_secretary_ridge.doc. Accessed on Apr. 30, 2006 ("All Federal departments and agencies are required to adopt the NIMS and use it in their individual domestic incident management and emergency prevention, preparedness, response, recovery, and mitigation activities, as well as in support of all actions taken to assist State or local entities.").

103 Jamieson interview, Dec. 20, 2005, pp. 10-11.

104 "TOPOFF 3," Nov. 2005, p. 1.

105 "TOPOFF 3," Nov. 2005, pp. 1, 4.

106 "TOPOFF 3," Nov. 2005, p. 5.

107 U.S. Department of Homeland Security, "Top Officials 3 (TOPOFF 3) Full Scale Exercise: Quick Look Report," Draft, May 26, 2005, p. 5.

108 Specifically, the Quick Look Report found:

> • "… autonomous UCP [Unified Command Post] often circumvented the state [Emergency Operations Center] EOC and the PFO highlighting the confusion at all levels regarding identification and clarification of roles and responsibilities."
>
> • "The UCP lost track of overall site management and personnel accountability at the site became inconsistent."
>
> • "The PFO worked within the framework of the unified command structure however the physical separation of the FCO and the Secretary's Emergency Response Team representative within the JFO impacted effective communication and coordination."

U.S. Department of Homeland Security, "Top Officials 3 (TOPOFF 3) Full Scale Exercise: Quick Look Report," Draft, May 26, 2005, p. 5. Similar deficiencies in establishing an effective command had previously been observed in FEMA's responses to Hurricanes Charley, Frances, and Ivan in 2004. *See*: William L. Carwile III, FEMA White Paper: The 2004 Hurricane Season, Issues and Recommendations, Apr. 2, 2005.

109 The Inspector General's recommendations included "more emphasis on training and exercising NRP and NIMS; developing standard operating procedures to define roles, clarifying Incident of National Significance designations; developing systems to track and share information more openly and efficiently."

"TOPOFF 3," Nov. 2005, p. 2.

110 "TOPOFF 3," Nov. 2005, p. 12.

111 Written Statement of William Carwile III, Federal Coordinating Officer for Hurricane Katrina in Mississippi, FEMA, before the U.S. Senate, Committee on Homeland Security and Governmental Affairs, hearing on *Hurricane Katrina: Perspectives of FEMA's Operations Professionals*, Dec. 8, 2005, p. 3.

112 Committee staff interview of Scott Wells, Deputy Federal Coordinating Officer for Hurricane Katrina in Louisiana, FEMA, conducted on Nov. 14, 2005, transcript p. 224.

113 *NRP*, p. 29.

114 Lokey interview, Nov. 4, 2005, pp. 41-43, 128.

115 Testimony of William Lokey, Federal Coordinating Officer for Hurricane Katrina in Louisiana, FEMA, before the U.S. House, Select Bipartisan Committee to Investigate the Preparation for and Response to Hurricane Katrina, hearing on *Hurricane Katrina: Preparedness and Response by the State of Louisiana*, Dec. 14, 2005.

116 Committee staff interview of Col. Anthony Daskevich, U.S. Army, Louisiana Defense Coordinating Officer, conducted on Jan. 10, 2006, transcript p. 132. Scott Wells, the Deputy Federal Coordinating Officer, related how the separate process for requesting and deploying military resources bypassed the unified command:

> It was about 6:00 or 7:00 [Wednesday] morning, and [Maj. Gen. Landreneau] says, I called General Honore up and asked him for help. I said, what? And he said, yeah, I asked him for help. I said, you did?
>
> And then I talked to Jeff Smith right after that. And I said, Jeff, he shouldn't have done that. And he said, why? And I said, the state does not go to DOD directly, you're supposed to come to Bill Lokey, to the FCO, we will go to DOD to get whatever support you need.
>
> That breaks – that not only violates protocol, but it breaks the whole unified command approach, when you go out to another agency and then this three star general just shows up.

Wells interview, Nov. 14, 2005, p. 67. Lt. Col. Jacques Thibodeaux of the Louisiana National Guard, the Joint Director of Military Support during Katrina, responded that after Lt. Gen. Honore arrived his activities at the Superdome were coordinated through the unified command. Committee staff interview of Lt. Col. Jacques Thibodeau, Joint Director of Military Support to Civilian Authorities and Branch Chief, Louisiana National Guard, conducted on Dec. 6, 2006, transcript pp. 267-269.

117 Lokey interview, Jan. 20, 2006, pp. 67-68.

118 Lokey interview, Jan. 20, 2006, p. 81; Lokey attributed these problems in part to the difficulties in communications, noting "one thing that frustrated me was nobody could call the Louisiana Emergency Operations Center, but nobody had a problem calling the White House or their Senator's office."

119 Testimony of William Carwile III, Federal Coordinating Officer for Hurricane Katrina in Mississippi, FEMA, before the U.S. Senate, Committee on Homeland Security and Governmental Affairs, hearing on *Hurricane Katrina: Perspectives of FEMA's Operations Professionals*, Dec. 8, 2005. Carwile also noted that, as currently constructed, the NRP "calls for unified command only at the top of a few people" but that it was his view that "unified command has to go all the way down the structure, and we have got to be able to use State and Federal personnel to prop up local communities that have been totally destroyed by something like Katrina." Carwile, Senate Committee hearing, Dec. 8, 2005.

120 Although the lack of a communications infrastructure does not eliminate the ability to form either an Incident Command Post (ICP) at the local level or a Unified Command at the state level, NIMS emphasizes the importance of

functioning communications infrastructure to support the overall ICS structure which in turn supports the unified command. "On activation of a local EOC [Emergency Operations Center], communications and coordination must be established between the [Incident Command] or [unified command] and the EOC, when they are not collocated. ICS field organizations must also establish communications with the activated local EOC, either directly or through their parent organization. Additionally, EOCs at all levels of government and across functional agencies must be capable of communicating appropriately with other EOCs during incidents." *NIMS*, pp. 26-27.

121 Written Statement of Richard Skinner, Inspector General, U.S. Department of Homeland Security, before the U.S. Senate, Committee on Homeland Security and Governmental Affairs, hearing on *Hurricane Katrina: Recommendations for Reform*, Mar. 8, 2006, p. 5.

122 Lokey interview, Jan. 20, 2006, p. 192. At the time Katrina hit, FEMA had not yet produced an Incident Management Handbook to adapt ICS to FEMA operations. *Source*: Lokey interview, Jan. 20, 2006, p. 194; FEMA, Draft ERT-N Concept of Operations, June 6, 2005. Provided to Committee; filed as Bates nos. DHS-FEMA-0115-0000010 through 0000011. Lokey partially attributed the gaps in training to lack of funding. "We've had no training dollars. We've had no opportunity to bring the folks together." Lokey interview, Jan. 20, 2006, p. 193.

123 Lokey interview, Jan. 20, 2006, p. 193; Wells interview, Nov. 14, 2005, pp. 225-226 ("We didn't really have a unified command in the EOC. Two days after – we didn't have a unified command in the EOC. Two days after, the EOC is getting training in ICS. Two days after the storm hit they had a consultant come in and show them ICS, explain ICS. In the middle of a catastrophic disaster. … There was no unified command under the National Response Plan. They didn't understand it. They had no idea. [State emergency management staff] were getting training in the middle of a disaster response operation. … My point is we have an architecture, we have [the] National Response Plan. The states agreed to use NIMS. They agreed to ICS. What does it tell you when 2 days into a catastrophic disaster a state gets somebody in to explain ICS to them?").

Although training individuals on ICS during a disaster may seem like a sign of dysfunction, in fact, William Carwile has subsequently recommended that staff at JFOs all receive basic ICS training as a short-term measure. When Adm. Allen arrived in Louisiana, he tasked one of his assistants with training those who inevitably arrived without ICS knowledge. *See*: William Carwile III, White Paper, "The Response and Initial Recovery to Hurricane Katrina in Mississippi: A Field Perspective," Feb. 22, 2006, p. 19. Provided to Committee.

124 Wells interview, Nov. 14, 2005, pp. 225-226.

125 Tony Robinson also noted there were a number of state officials at the EOC who did not appear to be familiar with the ICS. Committee staff interview of Tony Robinson, Director, Response and Recovery Division, Region VI, FEMA, conducted on Nov. 15, 2005, transcript pp. 42-43. The DHS IG also found that Louisiana did not have sufficient trained emergency management staff to be able to provide a counterpart to all federal ICS positions. U.S. Department of Homeland Security, Office of Inspector General, "A Performance Review of FEMA's Disaster Management Activities in Response to Hurricane Katrina," Mar. 2006, p. 21.

126 Lokey interview, Jan. 20, 2006, pp. 41-42.

127 FEMA, *DHS/FEMA Initial Response Hotwash: Hurricane Katrina in Louisiana*, Feb. 13, 2006, p. 32.

128 Committee staff interview of William King, Branch Chief, Region V, FEMA, conducted on Jan. 17, 2006, transcript pp. 9-11, 95-96.

129 Lokey interview, Jan. 20, 2006, p. 25.

130 Committee staff interview of Lucy Brooke, Emergency Management Program Specialist, FEMA, conducted on Jan. 24, 2006, transcript p. 16.

131 Lokey interview, Jan. 20, 2006, pp. 24-25.

132 Vice Adm. Allen interview, Feb. 3, 2006, pp. 27-29.

133 Testimony of Scott Wells, Deputy Federal Coordinating Officer for Hurricane Katrina in Louisiana, FEMA, before the U.S. Senate, Committee on Homeland Security and Governmental Affairs, hearing on *Hurricane Katrina: Perspectives of FEMA's Operations Professionals*, Dec. 8, 2005.

134 Committee staff interview of William Carwile III, Federal Coordinating Officer for Hurricane Katrina in Mississippi, FEMA, conducted on Dec. 6, 2005, transcript p. 76.

135 Carwile interview, Dec. 6, 2005, pp. 39, 46.

136 Carwile interview, Dec. 6, 2005, p. 39.

137 Committee staff interview of Robert Latham, Executive Director, MEMA, conducted on Jan. 27, 2006, transcript pp. 149-50. This lack of understanding of the basic principles of the National Response Plan, ICS and the concept of unified command surfaced during the Committee's interview of Patrick Rhode, the Acting Deputy Director of FEMA during Katrina and at the same time Chief of Staff to FEMA Director Brown. During the interview, Rhode stated he believed "there was difficulty in establishing a unified chain of command within those early days, particularly within Louisiana." In a unified command involving multiple jurisdictions, however, there is no single "chain of command." Rhode was unable to elaborate on what he meant by a "unified chain of command:"

> Q. Unity of command and unity of effort, are you familiar with the distinction between those two concepts?

A. Maybe, not, No.

Q. Do you know whether Louisiana, the State, at the time of the incident was trying to establish unity of command or unity of effort? Do you know in the Emergency Operations Center [whether] they were trying to establish a unity of effort or a unity of command?

A. I'm not – I'm not certain, going back to your last question, that I understand what you mean by unity of effort.

Committee staff interview of Patrick Rhode, former Acting Deputy Director, FEMA, conducted on Dec. 22, 2005, transcript p. 147.

138 Carwile, Senate Committee hearing, Dec. 8, 2005; Latham interview, Jan. 27, 2006, pp. 92-93, 95-96.

139 Carwile, Senate Committee hearing, Dec. 8, 2005; Testimony of Robert Latham, Executive Director, MEMA, before the U.S. House, Select Bipartisan Committee to Investigate the Preparation for and Response to Hurricane Katrina, hearing on *Hurricane Katrina: Preparedness and Response by the State of Mississippi*, Dec. 7, 2005.

140 Carwile interview, Dec. 6, 2005, p. 49.

141 Carwile interview, Dec. 6, 2005, pp. 98-99

142 Latham interview, Jan. 27, 2006, p. 147.

143 Carwile interview, Dec. 6, 2005, pp. 97-98. State officials are sometimes reluctant to allow federal officials direct access to local officials and their operations. Robert Block and Amy Schatz, "Local and Federal Authorities Battle to Control Disaster Relief," *The Wall Street Journal*, Dec. 8, 2005, p. A1.

144 Committee staff interview of Thomas McAllister, Director of Response and Recovery, MEMA, conducted on Jan. 27, 2006, transcript pp. 87-90.

145 Latham interview, Jan. 27, 2006, p. 95.

146 Latham interview, Jan. 27, 2006, p. 146.

147 Latham interview, Jan. 27, 2006, p. 146.

148 See earlier discussion in this chapter.

149 Carwile interview, Dec. 6, 2005, pp. 102-104.

FEMA trailers in transit
AP/Wide World photo

FEMA Waste and Fraud

Poor Controls and Decisions in FEMA Spending

Besides overwhelming many government emergency-response capabilities, Hurricane Katrina severely affected the government's ability to purchase goods and services and properly track and verify its costs when it contracted for them.

It takes money to prepare, respond, and recover from a disaster. As of March 8, 2006, the federal government has committed $88 billion to the response, recovery, and rebuilding efforts for Katrina.[1] Unfortunately, not all of this money has been wisely spent. Precious taxpayer dollars have been lost to fraud, waste, and abuse.

The Committee did not specifically include pre- and post-Hurricane Katrina spending by FEMA and other federal agencies as part of its investigation. However, almost from the time Katrina hit, the Committee was aware of wasteful, and sometimes fraudulent and abusive, spending practices and fiscal decision making. The Committee carefully followed reports of wasteful spending, conducting a number of oversight activities to understand how funds were being spent and to encourage measures to prevent wasteful spending. The full Committee held two hearings on Hurricane Katrina spending by FEMA, and its Federal Financial Management, Government Information, and International Security Subcommittee held another.[2]

Wasteful Spending: Nothing New

What is particularly troubling about the wasteful practices in the wake of Katrina is the similarity to wasteful spending examined by this Committee in a May 18, 2005, hearing, "FEMA's Response to the 2004 Florida Hurricanes: A Disaster for Taxpayers?"[3]

In the span of just six weeks in August and September 2004, Florida was hit by four powerful hurricanes: Charley, Frances, Ivan, and Jeanne. Parts of Florida suffered tremendous devastation. More than 10 percent of the state's housing stock was damaged or destroyed by the hurricanes, affecting more than 700,000 residents. Property damage exceeded $21 billion and 117 Floridians lost their lives. A disaster of this scale required a rapid and substantial response. FEMA distributed more than $2 billion in immediate relief to Floridians as they rebuilt their battered state.[4]

In the wake of these hurricanes, however, it became clear to the Committee that FEMA's provision of assistance was marred by payments for fraudulent claims, wasteful spending, and ineffective internal and management controls. When scarce resources are wasted, fraudulent claims are paid, and safeguards are ignored, there are new victims – the taxpayers. Then Under Secretary for Emergency Preparedness and Response and Director of FEMA, Michael Brown, said:

Among the many challenges we face when responding to disasters, the most difficult often involves balancing the tradeoff between ensuring a timely and effective response to those in need, and the responsibility to protect the fiscal integrity of the program. It is a classic competing tension between the provision of immediate disaster assistance and administrative perfection. As you move closer to one, you move farther away from the other.[5]

The Committee rejects this argument. Saying that government cannot protect taxpayers while responding effectively to the urgent needs of disaster victims is a false dichotomy.

Subsequent to the May 18, 2005, hearing, the Chairman and the Ranking Member of the Committee, Senator Collins and Senator Lieberman, sent a letter to Brown, urging FEMA to address some of the serious issues revealed by the 2004 Florida hurricanes.[6] In his response, Brown wrote, "FEMA is always seeking to improve upon its successes as well as improve upon other practices to best serve our stakeholders."[7] This echoed his statement at the hearing that "We take the opportunity after every major disaster to review and analyze our performance so we can institutionalize best practices, identify issues and concerns, and correct problems, all to face the next disaster better prepared."[8] Unfortunately, the response to Katrina showed that FEMA was still inadequately prepared to exercise good stewardship of taxpayer dollars while carrying out its mission of assisting disaster victims.

Hurricane Katrina: Same Story

On February 13, 2006, the Committee held a hearing, "Hurricane Katrina: Waste, Fraud, and Abuse Worsen the Disaster."[9] Like the May 18, 2005, hearing, this one revealed that taxpayer dollars intended to help hurricane victims were once again being lost to waste, fraud, and abuse.

The U.S. Government Accountability Office (GAO) testified about its preliminary review of some Hurricane Katrina expenditures, recognizing that it will be many months, and perhaps years, before a complete assessment can be conducted. However, GAO concluded from its initial work that weak controls in the Individuals and Households Program (IHP) that provides temporary help with housing and financial aid for other needs, left FEMA vulnerable to waste, fraud, and abuse.

GAO testified that there were flaws, including weaknesses or outright failures of controls and safeguards, in the process of registering those receiving assistance under the IHP. For instance, GAO found that when applying for benefits over the Internet, applicants were screened by checking for valid Social Security numbers before benefits were approved. When people applied by telephone, however, FEMA did not perform this screening before paying initial IHP benefits, which allowed thousands of false and fraudulent applications. Of the more than 2.5 million registrations recorded in FEMA's database, 60 percent (more than 1.5 million) were not subject to identity verification because they were submitted via the telephone; some of these registrations were found to be fraudulent.

GAO outlined several other examples of fraud, abuse, or poor management, including the following:

> • FEMA made expedited-assistance payments to tens of thousands of individuals whose registrations contained false or duplicative information, including Social Security numbers that had never been issued, or had been issued to another individual, or to an individual since deceased. It is important to note that not all duplicate information was submitted fraudulently. GAO is continuing to investigate both payments resulting from individuals intentionally trying to defraud the government and those resulting from errors in FEMA's system or registration process.

> • GAO found thousands of Social Security numbers that were used on more than one registration associated with the same disaster. A Social Security number is a unique number assigned to an individual. Because individuals are eligible to receive disaster relief only on their primary residence, the same Social Security Number should not be used more than once to receive assistance for the same disaster.

- GAO found that $10 million in duplicate payments were made when 5,000 registrants received both a debit card and a check worth $2,000 each, when they should have received either a debit card or a check.[10]

The Inspector General of the Department of Homeland Security (DHS IG) has conducted oversight of Katrina response and recovery activities, and testified about some specific examples of wasteful spending by FEMA. One of the most egregious examples presented, as discussed more fully below, is the purchase of approximately 25,000 manufactured homes that are virtually useless to Katrina victims because FEMA's own regulations prohibit their installation in a flood plain. At the time of the hearing, at least 10,000 of these homes were sitting unused in Hope, AK.[11] Making one bad decision after another, FEMA decided to make sure that no home had better amenities than others, so they removed some equipment, including microwaves and televisions. The DHS IG indicated that in the immediate aftermath of Katrina, decision making was mostly reactive, lacking planning or coordination.[12]

Another area of waste occurred in temporarily housing evacuees in hotels. As evacuees were moved out of shelters, FEMA instructed hotels across the country to allow anyone with a driver's license from the affected areas to check in and then send FEMA the bill. There were virtually no controls in place. The DHS IG found hotels charging for empty rooms, individuals holding multiple rooms, hotel rooms being used as storage units for personal goods, individuals staying at resorts, and hotels charging rates above even the "rack rate" (the maximum or full price the hotel will charge for the room) – at times costing taxpayers up to $400 per night.[13]

The DHS IG indicated that his investigators had seen more waste in contracts than actual fraud at that point, but attributed this partly to the fact that FEMA was in the very early stages of the major contracting activity. At the time of the February 13, 2006, hearing, DHS had reported awarding contracts valued at over $5 billion, with other federal agencies reporting an additional $4.2 billion. The DHS IG indicated that the federal Inspectors General will continue their oversight activities through the life of these contracts.

As government agencies rushed to meet requirements in the immediate aftermath of Katrina, they used expedited contracting methods authorized by the Federal Acquisition Regulations. The DHS IG found cases in which procurement personnel authorized contractors to begin work without a definitive statement of work, sometimes on a sole-source basis with no attempt to independently estimate costs. Some of the contractors performed the work efficiently and in good faith, but some did not. Under some of the most questionable contracts, the government may have little legal recourse to recoup payments made to contractors who did not perform required work or who overcharged for work they did perform.[14]

On September 8, 2005, the Department of Justice established the Hurricane Katrina Fraud Task Force to deter, investigate, and prosecute hurricane-related fraud in the wake of Hurricane Katrina, stating "The message of our collective effort is clear: we will not tolerate this kind of behavior in our compassionate society. Fraud will not go unpunished."[15] U.S. Attorneys have never before implemented a "zero tolerance" policy with respect to disaster-related assistance and contracting fraud. The chair of the Task Force indicated that this policy did have an impact. She reported that individuals returned payments to FEMA or requested to arrange repayment plans, coincident with publicized arrests for fraud.[16]

The Odyssey of the Ice

In the immediate aftermath of a disaster, some of the commodities most in demand include water, food, and ice. FEMA's problems in moving commodities are well known. In the case of ice, plenty of movement occurred – but not always to places one would expect.

FEMA ordered 182 million pounds of ice to respond to Hurricane Katrina. After a typical hurricane, evacuees soon return to their homes, but may be without electric power for some time. Ice helps keep food and medicine cold until power is restored. After Katrina, however, hundreds of thousands of evacuees were sent to shelters across the country and did not return home for days and weeks after the storm. Thus, the household need for ice was much lower in some areas than anticipated.[17] While there was a severe shortage of ice in some affected areas, and many hurricane victims who remained in the area did not have access to ice,[18] in the end FEMA had excess ice and used less than 50 percent of what it had ordered.[19]

Some of the ice ended up in Portland, ME – 1,600 miles from the disaster area. The cost of handling and storing the 200-plus truckloads of ice that went to Portland was approximately $275,000.[20] More ice went to other distant locations around the country because FEMA decided it made more sense to move the ice to cold-storage facilities for use in new disasters than to let it melt.[21] It is not clear that this was the most cost-effective choice, given the lack of planning that resulted in trucks being rerouted multiple times, and sometimes sitting idle for days, while costs to the government were mounting.

On September 16, NBC News reported that it had found trucks full of ice in locations such as Maryland, Missouri, Georgia, and Tennessee. Some of the trucks had been driving and/or sitting idle with their full loads for two weeks. One truck driver reported that he had begun his trip in Oshkosh, Wisconsin, traveled to Louisiana, then was sent to Georgia, but was rerouted to South Carolina, before being sent to Cumberland, MD.[22] NBC News later reported that the truck was then sent to Iowa, where the ice was put into cold storage.[23] The driver reported that this cost taxpayers at least an extra $9,000.[24] When multiplied by hundreds of truckloads that also took circuitous routes to cold storage, the wasted taxpayer dollars begin to add up.

Some of the ice shipped to cold-storage facilities around the country has already been used for other disasters. But one truckload ended up at the Reid Park Zoo in Tucson, AZ, to be enjoyed by the polar bears and other animals. The truck driver who donated the ice to the zoo did so after traveling through 22 states without delivering a single bag of ice to hurricane victims.[25]

No-Bid Contracts

FEMA typically has a contingency Individual Assistance Technical Assistance Contract (IATAC) in place to assist when disaster strikes. When Katrina hit, FEMA was "competing" this contract – bids had been solicited and evaluated, and contract negotiations had begun, but the process was not complete, so no competitively awarded IATAC was in place. Faced with an overwhelming demand for technical assistance, FEMA contracted with four major engineering firms to provide technical assistance to the Individual Assistance Program, the scope of which included "supporting staging areas for housing units (travel trailers and mobile homes), installation of housing units, maintenance and upkeep, site inspections and preparations, site restoration, group site design, group site construction, site assessments, property and facility management, as well as housing unit deactivation and rehabilitation."[26]

One of the contracts was awarded on the basis of competition (Fluor had won, but the contract had not yet been negotiated), and the other three contracts (awarded to Shaw Group, Bechtel, and CH2M Hill) were awarded as letter-contracts based on FEMA's critical need for expedited assistance.[27] Essentially, these were sole-source contracts. Each had an original ceiling value of $100 million, but this was raised to $500 million late in 2005.[28] The ceiling on two of the contracts was raised again in early 2006.[29]

On October 6, 2005, Acting FEMA Director R. David Paulison pledged in a Committee hearing to "compete" the requirements covered by the contracts,[30] holding an open competition, as normally required by federal contracting regulations, where all companies can compete for the work. It is generally accepted that only through full and open competition is the government assured of getting the best price for supplies and services. The Committee was disappointed that this was not done. FEMA did compete a subset of the requirements for future work, such as maintenance and deactivation of the travel trailers, but these awards were not made until April 2006.[31] FEMA decided to allow the four contractors to continue work under the sole-source contracts. To respond to future disasters, FEMA officials have said the agency intends to competitively award a number of national IATACs before the 2006 hurricane season.

Unusable Manufactured Housing

As part of its Individual Assistance Program, FEMA typically provides travel-trailers to house individuals whose homes have been badly damaged or destroyed while they rebuild or find alternative housing. When Hurricane Katrina hit and FEMA realized the scope of temporary-housing needs, the agency began buying all of the travel trailers it could find. Unfortunately, in this buying frenzy, FEMA purchased approximately $900 million worth of manufactured homes and modular homes that could not be used because FEMA's own regulations do not allow for these types of homes to be placed in flood plains. Further, some of the homes purchased did not fit FEMA's size standards.[32]

The Committee held a hearing on the manufactured housing in Hope, Arkansas, on April 21, 2006, and learned more about FEMA's poor decision making and wasteful spending. FEMA purchased 24,967 manufactured homes and 1,295 modular homes in response to the need for transitional housing to assist displaced evacuees.[33] However, FEMA seemingly had no plans for how the homes would be used when the purchases were made. FEMA issued a mission assignment to the U.S. Forest Service to set up eight emergency storage sites, including one in Hope, Arkansas.[34] To house some of the manufactured and modular homes, FEMA leased a staging area at the Hope Municipal Airport at a cost of $25,000 per *month* – equivalent to a rent of $300,000 per year. The Committee learned that prior to the lease with FEMA, the City of Hope had rented the same site to a hay farmer for $5,000 per year.[35]

As of the April hearing, there were 15,603 manufactured and modular homes as well as 7,229 travel trailers staged at the eight emergency housing sites. While FEMA was able to use some of the homes in other disasters, and had plans to use more, they still had no plan for thousands of manufactured and modular homes. The Committee learned that FEMA had already hired sales staff to sell the homes as surplus property if they are not eventually used,[36] but typically this type of sale recoups only pennies on the dollar.[37] The manufactured and modular homes purchased represent some of the most serious waste discovered to date.

Conclusion

The Committee is not the only organization looking into the fraud, waste, and abuse issues related to Katrina. The DHS IG, GAO, and other federal Inspectors General are investigating these issues as well. It may well be years before the full scope of taxpayer dollars lost to waste, fraud, and abuse is determined, but the preliminary findings should be noted as the more expensive recovery and rebuilding phases proceed. New natural or man-made disasters are inevitable, but they need not also become fiscal disasters where taxpayer funds meant to provide speedy, effective relief are lost to fraud, waste, and abuse.

1 The White House, "Fact Sheet: Gulf Coast Update: Hurricane Relief, Recovery, and Rebuilding Continues," press release, Mar. 8, 2006. http://www.whitehouse.gov/news/releases/2006/03/20060308-8.html. Accessed on Apr. 21, 2006.

2 U.S. Senate, Committee on Homeland Security and Governmental Affairs, hearing on *Hurricane Katrina: Waste, Fraud, and Abuse Worsen the Disaster*, Feb. 13, 2006; U.S. Senate, Committee on Homeland Security and Governmental Affairs, hearing on *FEMA's Manufactured Housing Program: Haste Makes Waste*, Apr. 21, 2006; U.S. Senate, Committee on Homeland Security and Governmental Affairs, Subcommittee on Federal Financial Management, Government Information, and International Security, hearing on *Katrina and Contracting: Blue Roof, Debris Removal, Travel Trailer Case Studies*, Apr. 10, 2006.

3 U.S. Senate, Committee on Homeland Security and Governmental Affairs, hearing on *FEMA's Response to the 2004 Florida Hurricanes: A Disaster for Taxpayers?*, May 18, 2005.

4 Written Statement of Sen. Susan M. Collins, for the U.S. Senate, Committee on Homeland Security and Governmental Affairs, hearing on *FEMA's Response to the 2004 Florida Hurricanes: A Disaster for Taxpayers?*, May 18, 2005.

5 Written Statement of Michael Brown, then-Director, Federal Emergency Management Agency (FEMA), for the U.S. Senate, Committee on Homeland Security and Governmental Affairs, hearing on *FEMA's Response to the 2004 Florida Hurricanes: A Disaster for Taxpayers?*, May 18, 2005, pp. 5-6.

6 Senators Susan M. Collins and Joseph I. Lieberman, letter to Michael Brown, July 8, 2005.

7 Michael Brown, letter to Chairman Susan M. Collins and Senator Joseph I. Lieberman, Aug. 4, 2005, p. 1.

8 Written Statement of Brown, Senate Committee hearing, May 18, 2005, p. 7.

9 U.S. Senate, Committee on Homeland Security and Governmental Affairs, hearing on *Hurricane Katrina: Waste, Fraud, and Abuse Worsen the Disaster*, Feb. 13, 2006.

10 Written statement of Gregory D. Kutz, Managing Director, Forensic Audits and Special Investigations, U. S. Government Accountability Office, for the U.S. Senate, Homeland Security and Governmental Affairs Committee, hearing on *Hurricane Katrina: Waste, Fraud, and Abuse Worsen the Disaster*, Feb. 13, 2006.

11 Written Statement of Richard L. Skinner, Inspector General, U.S. Department of Homeland Security, for the U.S. Senate, Homeland Security and Governmental Affairs Committee, hearing on *Hurricane Katrina: Waste, Fraud, and Abuse Worsen the Disaster*, Feb. 13, 2006, p. 7.

12 Written Statement of Skinner, Senate Committee hearing, Feb. 13, 2006.

13 U.S. Department of Homeland Security, Office of the Inspector General, briefing by Richard L. Skinner, Inspector General, U.S. Department of Homeland Security, given to Committee staff, Jan. 31, 2006.

14 Written Statement of Skinner, Senate Committee hearing, Feb. 13, 2006.

15 Alberto R. Gonzales, "Remarks at the Hurricane Katrina Fraud Task Force Conference," Oct. 20, 2005. http://www.usdoj.gov/ag/speeches/2005/ag_speech_0510201.html. Accessed on Apr. 21, 2006.

16 Written Statement of Alice S. Fisher, Assistant Attorney General, Criminal Division, Chairman, Hurricane Katrina Fraud Task Force, U.S. Department of Justice, for the U.S. Senate, Homeland Security and Governmental Affairs Committee, hearing on *Hurricane Katrina: Waste, Fraud, and Abuse Worsen the Disaster*, Feb. 13, 2006.

17 "FEMA Responds to Ice Issues," MSNBC, Oct. 11, 2005. http://www.msnbc.msn.com/id/9665486/from/RL.1. Accessed on Apr. 19, 2006.

18 Matthew Brown, "The Ice Trucks Cometh to the Relief of Many; For Those in Their Homes, the Cubes are 'Like Gold'," New Orleans *Times-Picayune*, Sept. 6, 2006, p. A06; Arnold Lindsay, "Firms Work to Relieve Scarcity of Ice," *The Clarion-Ledger*, Sept. 2, 2006. http://www.clarionledger.com/apps/pbcs.dll/article?AID=/20050902/NEWS0110/509020352/1260. Accessed on May 25, 2006.

19 "FEMA Responds to Ice Issues," MSNBC, Oct. 11, 2005. http://www.msnbc.msn.com/id/9665486/from/RL.1. Accessed on Apr. 19, 2006.

20 Michael W. Lowder, letter to Senator Susan M. Collins, Nov. 4, 2005, p. 1.

21 "FEMA Responds to Ice Issues," MSNBC, Oct. 11, 2005. http://www.msnbc.msn.com/id/9665486/from/RL.1. Accessed on Apr. 19, 2006.

22 Lisa Myers and the NBC Investigative Unit, NBC News, "The FEMA Ice Follies: How come ice can't efficiently reach those in need?" Sept. 16, 2005. http://www.msnbc.msn.com/id/9369937/print/1/displaymode/1098. Accessed on Apr. 19, 2006.

23 Lisa Myers and the NBC Investigative Unit, NBC News, "The FEMA Ice Follies Revisited: Agency Opts to store millions of pounds for next disaster," Oct. 11, 2005. http://www.msnbc.msn.com/id/9665434/print/1/displaymode/1098.

Accessed on Apr. 19, 2006.

24 Lisa Myers and the NBC Investigative Unit, NBC News, "The FEMA Ice Follies: How come ice can't efficiently reach those in need?" Sept. 16, 2005. http://www.msnbc.msn.com/id/9369937/print/1/displaymode/1098. Accessed on Apr. 19, 2006.

25 Lisa Myers and the NBC Investigative Unit, NBC News, "The FEMA Ice Follies Revisited: Agency Opts to store millions of pounds for next disaster," Oct. 11, 2005. http://www.msnbc.msn.com/id/9665434/print/1/displaymode/1098. Accessed on Apr. 19, 2006.

26 Written Statement of Skinner, Senate Committee hearing, Feb. 13, 2006, p. 12

27 Written Statement of Skinner, Senate Committee hearing, Feb. 13, 2006, p. 12

28 Committee staff interview of Elaine Duke, Chief Procurement Officer, U.S. Department of Homeland Security, conducted on Feb. 24, 2006 (untranscribed).

29 Duke interview, Feb. 24, 2006.

30 Testimony of R. David Paulison, Acting Undersecretary of Homeland Security for Emergency Preparedness and Response and Acting Director, FEMA, before the U.S. Senate, Committee on Homeland Security and Governmental Affairs, hearing on *FEMA Status Report on Recovery Efforts in the Gulf States*, Oct. 6, 2005.

31 U.S. Department of Homeland Security, "FEMA, Small Business Administration Work Together to Award Hurricane Katrina Recovery Contracts to Small and Minority-Owned Businesses," press release, Mar. 31, 2006. http://www.fema.gov/news/newsrelease.fema?id=24682. Accessed on May 9, 2006.

32 Skinner, Senate Committee hearing, Feb. 13, 2006.

33 Testimony of Richard L. Skinner, Inspector General, U.S. Department of Homeland Security, before the U.S. Senate, Committee on Homeland Security and Governmental Affairs, hearing on *FEMA's Manufactured Housing Program: Haste Makes Waste*, Apr. 21, 2006.

34 Skinner, Senate Committee hearing, Apr. 21, 2006.

35 Committee staff interview of Mayor Dennis Ramsey, City of Hope, AR, conducted on Apr. 6, 2006 (untranscribed); Andy Davis, "Hope Airport to See 5,000 Homes Go, Rest Stay: FEMA Has Long-Term Emergency Supply Plans for Site," *Arkansas Democrat-Gazette*, Mar. 22, 2006. Accessed on LexisNexis.

36 Written Statement of Skinner, Senate Committee hearing, Apr. 21, 2006, p. 5.

37 Skinner, Senate Committee hearing, Feb. 13, 2006.

Overview: Conclusions and Findings

1. Four overarching factors contributed to the failures of Hurricane Katrina:

(i) long-term warnings went unheeded and government officials neglected their duties to prepare for a forewarned catastrophe;

(ii) government officials took insufficient actions or made poor decisions in the days immediately before and after landfall;

(iii) systems on which officials relied to support their response efforts failed, and

(iv) government officials at all levels failed to provide effective leadership.

These individual failures, moreover, occurred against a backdrop of failure, over time, to develop the capacity for a coordinated, national response to a truly catastrophic event, whether caused by nature or man-made.

2. During a catastrophe, which by definition almost immediately exceeds state and local resources and significantly disrupts governmental operations and emergency services, the role of the federal government is particularly important.

3. It has long been standard practice that emergency response begins at the lowest possible jurisdictional level – typically the local government, with state government becoming involved at the local government's request when the resources of local government are (or are expected to be) overwhelmed. Similarly, while the federal government provides ongoing financial support to state and local governments for emergency preparedness, ordinarily it becomes involved in responding to a disaster at a state's request when resources of state and local governments are (or are expected to be) overwhelmed. Louisiana's Emergency Operations Plan explicitly lays out this hierarchy of response.

4. While several engineering analyses continue, the Committee has found deeply disturbing evidence of flaws in the design and construction of the levees protecting New Orleans. For instance, two major drainage canals – the 17th Street and London Avenue Canals – failed at their foundations. Equally troubling was the revelation of serious disagreement – still unresolved months after Katrina – among officials of several government entities over who had responsibility, and when, for key levee issues including emergency response and levee repair. Such conflicts prevented any meaningful emergency plans from being put in place and, at the time of Katrina, none of the relevant government agencies had a plan for responding to a levee breach.

5. Top officials at every level of government – despite strongly worded advisories – did not appear to truly grasp the magnitude of the storm's potential for destruction before it made landfall. Over the weekend, there was a drumbeat of warnings: FEMA held video-teleconferences on both days, where the danger of Katrina and the particular risks to New Orleans were discussed; Max Mayfield of the National Hurricane Center called the governors of the affected states, something he had only done once before in his 33-year career; President Bush took the unusual step of declaring in advance an emergency for the states in the impact zone; numerous media reports noted that New Orleans was a "bowl" and could be left submerged by the storm; the Department of Homeland Security's Simulation and Analysis

Group generated a report stating that the levees protecting New Orleans were at risk of breaching and overtopping; and internal FEMA slides stated that the projected impacts of Katrina could be worse than those in the "Hurricane Pam" exercise.

6. Beginning in 2004, the federal government sponsored a planning exercise with participation from federal, state, and local officials, based on a scenario whose characteristics foreshadowed most of Katrina's impacts. While this hypothetical "Hurricane Pam" exercise resulted in draft plans beginning in early 2005, they were incomplete when Katrina hit. Nonetheless, some officials took the initiative to use concepts developed in the drafts, with some success in the critical aspects of the Katrina response. However, many of its admonitory lessons were either ignored or inadequately applied.

7. The City of New Orleans, with primary responsibility for evacuation of its citizens, had language in its plan stating the city's intent to assist those who needed transportation for pre-storm evacuation, but had no actual plan provisions to implement that intent.

8. The Louisiana Department of Transportation and Development, whose secretary had personally accepted departmental responsibility under the state's emergency-operations plan to arrange for transportation for evacuation in emergencies, had done nothing to prepare for that responsibility prior to Katrina.

9. Some coastal towns in Mississippi went to extraordinary lengths to get citizens to evacuate, including sending people door-to-door to convince residents to move out of harm's way. The State of Louisiana activated more than twice the number of National Guard troops called to duty in any prior hurricane, and achieved the largest evacuation of a threatened population ever to occur. The City of New Orleans issued its first-ever mandatory evacuation order.

10. The U.S. Coast Guard conducted extensive planning and training for disasters, and put that preparation to use when disaster struck, leading to the successful and heroic search-and-rescue efforts that saved more than 33,000 people.

11. FEMA was unprepared for a catastrophic event of the scale of Katrina. Well before Katrina, FEMA's relationships with state and local officials, once a strength, had been eroded in part because certain preparedness grant programs were transferred elsewhere in the Department of Homeland Security; with its importance to state and local preparedness activities reduced, FEMA's effectiveness was diminished.

12. FEMA's Director, Michael Brown, lacked the leadership skills that were needed for his critical position. Before landfall, Brown did not direct the adequate pre-positioning of critical personnel and equipment, and willfully failed to communicate with Secretary Chertoff, to whom he was supposed to report.

13. The Department of Homeland Security (DHS) leadership failed to bring a sense of urgency to the federal government's preparation for Hurricane Katrina, and Secretary Chertoff himself should have been more engaged in preparations over the weekend before landfall. Secretary Chertoff made only top-level inquiries into the state of preparations, and accepted uncritically the reassurances he received. He did not appear to reach out to the other Cabinet secretaries to make sure that they were readying their departments to provide whatever assistance DHS – and the people of the Gulf Coast – might need.

14. Had Secretary Chertoff invoked the Catastrophic Incident Annex (CIA) of the National Response Plan, he could have helped remove uncertainty about the federal government's need and authority to take initiative before landfall and signaled that all federal government

agencies were expected to think – and act – proactively in preparing for and responding to Katrina.

15. DHS was slow to recognize the scope of the disaster or that FEMA had become over-whelmed. On the day after landfall, DHS officials were still struggling to determine the "ground truth" about the extent of the flooding despite the many reports it had received about the catastrophe; key officials did not grasp the need to act on the less-than-complete information that is to be expected in a disaster. DHS leaders did not become fully engaged in recovery efforts until Thursday, when, in Deputy Secretary Michael Jackson's words, they "tried to kick it up a notch"; after that, they did provide significant leadership within DHS (and FEMA) as well as coordination across the federal government. But this effort should have begun sooner.

16. Problems with obtaining, communicating, and managing information plagued many other aspects of the response as well. FEMA lacked the tools to track the status of ship-ments, interfering with the management of supplying food, water, ice, and other vital com-modities to those in need across the Gulf Coast. So, too, did the incompatibility of the elec-tronic systems used by federal and state authorities to manage requests for assistance, which made it necessary to transfer requests from the state system to the federal system manually.

17. Katrina resulted in the largest National Guard deployment in U.S. history, with 50,000 troops and supporting equipment arriving from 49 states and four territories within two weeks. These forces participated in every aspect of emergency response, from medical care to law enforcement and debris removal, and were considered invaluable by Louisiana and Mississippi officials. However, the deployments of National Guard troops were not coordi-nated with the federal Northern Command, which was overseeing the large-scale deploy-ments and operations of the active-duty military.

18. While large numbers of active-duty troops did not arrive until the end of the first week following landfall – although National Guard troops did – the Department of Defense (DOD) contributed in other important ways during that period. Early in the week, DOD or-dered its military commanders to push available assets to the Gulf Coast. They also stream-lined their ordinarily bureaucratic processes for handling FEMA requests for assistance and emphasized movement based on vocal commands with the paperwork to follow, though some FEMA officials believe that DOD's approval process continued to take too long. They provided significant support to search-and-rescue missions, evacuee airlifts, logistics man-agement of buses arriving in the State for evacuation, and other matters.

19. Pervasive and widespread communications failures substantially hampered rescue and response efforts.

20. Law enforcement was a problem, and was fueled by several contributing factors, includ-ing erroneous statements by top city officials that inflamed the public's perception of the lawlessness in New Orleans. Without effective law enforcement, real or imagined safety threats interrupted virtually every aspect of the response.

21. Federal law-enforcement assistance was too slow in coming, in large part because the two federal departments charged under the NRP with providing such assistance – DHS and the Department of Justice (DOJ) – had done almost no pre-storm planning. In fact, they failed to determine even well into the post-landfall period which of the two departments would assume the lead for federal law enforcement under the NRP. As a result, later in the week, as federal law-enforcement officers did arrive, some were distracted by a pointless "turf war" between DHS and DOJ over which agency was in the lead. In the end, federal as-sistance was crucial, but should have arrived much sooner.

22. While both FEMA and the Department of Health and Human Services made efforts to activate the federal emergency health capabilities of the National Disaster Medical System (NDMS) and the U.S. Public Health Service, only a limited number of federal medical teams were actually in position prior to landfall to deploy into the affected area. Only one such team was in a position to provide immediate medical care in the aftermath of the storm.

23. The Committee also identified significant planning failures that predated Katrina. One of the most remarkable stories from this investigation is the history of planning for the 100,000 people in New Orleans believed to lack the means to evacuate themselves.

24. Almost exactly four years after 9/11, Katrina showed that the nation is still unprepared to respond to a catastrophe.

Findings

Emergency Management Along The Gulf Coast: Federal, State, And Local – Louisiana

1. First responders in Louisiana played an indispensable role in the response to Hurricane Katrina.

2. The Louisiana state government failed to provide sufficient resources to the Louisiana Office of Homeland Security and Emergency Preparedness (LOHSEP). Its planning, preparedness and response to Katrina suffered as a result.

3. LOHSEP failed to ensure that state agencies adequately understood their emergency-response obligations.

Emergency Management On The Gulf Coast: State And Local – Mississippi

4. First responders in Mississippi played an indispensable role in the response to Katrina.

5. Mississippi's use of the Emergency Management Assistance Compact interstate mutual-aid arrangement was vital to its response to Hurricane Katrina.

6. Many residents found shelter conditions quite difficult because of shortages of food and water, and sanitation problems. Though their challenges regarding mass care were formidable, state and local governments and the American Red Cross could have prepared better for a catastrophic disaster on the scale of Hurricane Katrina. In addition, state and local governments in Mississippi could have been better prepared to shelter the special-needs population on the Mississippi Gulf Coast.

Hurricane Pam: Katrina Is Predicted

7. Hurricane Pam was an elaborate planning exercise that anticipated many of the challenges of responding to Katrina.

8. Hurricane Pam and other planning exercises put federal, state, and local officials on notice of the potential consequences of a hurricane of the magnitude of Katrina.

9. Louisiana should have given greater consideration to filling gaps in federal funding of the Hurricane Pam exercise.

Legacy Effects Of Environmental, Engineering Changes

10. Changes in Louisiana's coastal landscape, including wetlands loss and soil subsidence, have made New Orleans and coastal Louisiana more vulnerable to hurricanes and may have contributed to damage from Hurricane Katrina. These changes are in large part an unintended consequence of human activities that have altered the natural flow of the Mississippi River and other coastal processes.

11. Until addressed, the continued subsidence, loss of wetlands, and other changes to the coastal landscape will make New Orleans and other regions of the Louisiana deltaic plain increasingly vulnerable to hurricanes.

12. The building of the Mississippi River Gulf Outlet (MRGO) and the combined Gulf Intracoastal Waterway (GIWW/MRGO) channel resulted in substantial environmental damage, including a significant loss of wetlands which had once formed a natural barrier against hurricanes threatening New Orleans from the east.

13. MRGO and the combined GIWW/MRGO provided a connection between Lake Borgne and Lake Pontchartrain that allowed the much greater surge from Lake Borgne to flow into both New Orleans and Lake Pontchartrain. These channels further increased the speed and flow of the Katrina surge into New Orleans East and the Ninth Ward/St. Bernard Parish, increasing the destructive force against adjacent levees and contributing to their failure. As a result, MRGO and the combined GIWW/MRGO resulted in increased flooding and greater damage from Hurricane Katrina.

Levees

14. Confusion, ambiguity, and uncertainty characterized the perceptions of the Army Corps of Engineers, the local levee boards, and other agencies with jurisdiction over the levee system of their respective responsibilities, leading to failures to carry out comprehensive inspections, rigorously monitor system integrity, or undertake needed repairs.

15. Louisiana law imposes on local levee boards the responsibility to protect their respective jurisdictions from flooding and gives them extraordinary taxing authority to carry out that duty.

16. Congress tasked the Army Corps of Engineers with designing and constructing a levee system in and around New Orleans, but that responsibility does not diminish the Orleans Levee District's statutory duty to protect its jurisdiction from flooding.

17. The Orleans Levee District performed modest maintenance of the levees, such as mowing the grass. Nevertheless, ambiguities, confusion, and disputes between the Orleans Levee District and Army Corps of Engineers over responsibility led to inadequate maintenance of the levee system and to a lack of effective emergency plans and preparations.

18. Local levee districts, including the Orleans Levee District, did not have the engineering expertise or diagnostic equipment to ensure that the hurricane-protection systems provided the level of protection for which they were designed.

19. The Louisiana Department of Transportation and Development failed to fully carry out its responsibilities under state statutes, such as the need to: (a) train levee-board members and their appointed inspectors or watchmen on how to care for and inspect levees; and (b) review the emergency plans of local levee districts to ensure that the levee districts could adequately respond to emergency situations.

20. The Orleans Levee District focused time, attention, and resources on business interests unrelated to levees, such as casinos, restaurants, a karate club, and a beautician school, to the detriment of flood protection.

21. Inspections of the Lake Pontchartrain Project administered jointly by the Army Corps of Engineers and the Orleans Levee District failed to ensure that the project provided the level of protection for which it was designed and constructed.

22. The forensic teams investigating the flooding have concluded that: (a) the flood walls along the 17th Street and London Avenue Canals failed in that they did not withstand the forces for which they were supposedly designed or constructed; and (b) flooding was exacerbated as many levees and floodwalls were breached because of design and construction deficiencies, including not having protection against the scour and erosion caused by overtopping.

23. In designing, constructing, and maintaining the hurricane-protection system, the Corps did not adequately address: (a) the effects of local and regional subsidence of land upon which the protection system was built; and (b) then-current information about the threat posed by storm surges and hurricanes in the region.

24. For several years, the Corps has inaccurately represented to state and local officials and to the public the level of protection that the hurricane system provided. The Corps claimed the system protected against a fast-moving Category 3 storm even though: (a) there was no adequate study or documentation to support this claim; and (b) information known to or provided to the Corps demonstrated that the claim was not accurate.

Preparing For The Storm: State And Local Governments

25. Governor Blanco and Mayor Nagin failed to meet expectations set forth in the National Response Plan to coordinate state and local resources "to address the full spectrum of actions" needed to prepare for and respond to Hurricane Katrina. Funding shortages and inadequacies in long-term planning doomed Louisiana's preparations for Katrina.

26. Governor Blanco submitted an inadequate and erroneous request for assistance to the President and generally failed to ask the federal government for sufficient assistance before the storm.

27. The Louisiana National Guard pre-positioned too many resources at Jackson Barracks in the lower Ninth Ward, where many of them were lost to flooding.

Preparing For The Storm: Federal Government

28. DHS, the agency charged with preparing for and responding to domestic incidents, whether terrorist attacks or natural disasters, failed to effectively lead the federal response to Hurricane Katrina.

29. In advance of landfall, Secretary Chertoff failed to make ready the full range of federal assets pursuant to DHS's responsibilities under the National Response Plan (NRP).

30. DHS leaders failed to bring a sense of urgency to the federal government's preparation for Hurricane Katrina.

31. Secretary Chertoff failed to appoint a Principal Federal Official (PFO), the official charged with overseeing the federal response under the NRP, until 36 hours after landfall.

32. The Interagency Incident Management Group (IIMG), intended to coordinate the federal response to a catastrophe, was not activated until the day after landfall, and then added little value to the federal response effort, leaving federal agencies without an intermediate inter-agency dispute resolution mechanism.

33. Secretary Chertoff failed to activate the Catastrophic Incident Annex (CIA) of the NRP, which could have led to a more proactive federal response.

34. Secretary Chertoff appointed a field commander, Michael Brown, who was hostile to the federal government's agreed-upon response plan and therefore was unlikely to perform effectively in accordance with its principles. Some of Secretary Chertoff's top advisors were aware of these issues but Secretary Chertoff has indicated that he was not. Secretary Chertoff should have known of these problems and, as a result, should have appointed someone other than Brown as Principal Federal Official.

35. Although the Hurricane Pam exercise, among other things, put FEMA on notice that a storm of Katrina's magnitude could have catastrophic impact on New Orleans, Michael Brown and FEMA leadership failed to do the necessary planning and preparations:

> a. to train or equip agency personnel for the likely needed operations;
>
> b. to adequately prearrange contracts to transport necessary commodities;
>
> c. to pre-position appropriate communications assets; or
>
> d. to consult with DOD regarding back-up capability in the event a catastrophe materialized, among other deficiencies.

36. National Hurricane Center (NHC) and National Weather Service (NWS) warnings –including a video-conference appearance by NHC Director Max Mayfield – put FEMA on notice as of August 26, 2005, for Katrina's catastrophic potential as the hurricane moved toward the Gulf Coast. DHS notified the White House of that potential.

37. FEMA did not adequately pre-position critical personnel and equipment before landfall.

38. Despite pre-positioning unprecedented amounts of relief supplies, FEMA's efforts were inadequate.

39. FEMA's inadequate preparations for Katrina were in part a consequence of insufficient long-term catastrophic planning.

40. Before landfall, it does not appear that FEMA asked the Department of Defense (DOD) to employ its assets.

DHS's Roles And Responsibilities

41. Statutory authorities and presidential directives establish the Department of Homeland Security (DHS) as the central federal entity for preparedness for and response to disasters.

42. The Secretary of Homeland Security has a clear duty to lead and manage the federal response to disasters such as Katrina.

43. When effective response is beyond the capabilities of the state and the affected local governments, the Stafford Act provides for federal assistance upon the request of the state and local governments.

44. Under our system of federalism, state and local governments bear the primary responsibility for responding to emergencies. As such, they generally manage the response to an incident in the first instance.

45. Following a catastrophic disaster, the traditional mode of operation may not work if state and local governments are so overwhelmed that they can't effectively make specific

requests for assistance. In such circumstances the National Response Plan's Catastrophic Incident Annex provides for a more proactive federal response.

46. The United States Coast Guard distinguished itself during the Hurricane Katrina emergency by protecting its vessels and aircraft from the initial attack of the storm, by anticipating the critical missions it would need to conduct, by immediately moving in as soon as conditions allowed, and by heroically sustaining a massive effort that rescued more than 33,000 people from danger of death.

Federal Emergency Management Agency (FEMA)

47. FEMA was unprepared – and has never been prepared – for a catastrophic event of the scale of Katrina.

48. FEMA had been operating at a more than 15 percent staff-vacancy rate for over a year before Katrina struck.

49. FEMA's senior political appointees, including Director Michael Brown and Deputy Director Patrick Rhode, had little or no prior relevant emergency-management experience before joining FEMA.

50. FEMA's emergency-response teams were inadequately trained, exercised, and equipped.

51. FEMA failed to adequately develop emergency-response capabilities assigned to it under the National Response Plan.

52. FEMA had budget shortages that hindered its preparedness.

53. Michael Brown, FEMA's Director, was insubordinate, unqualified, and counterproductive, in that he:

> a. sent a single employee, without operational expertise or equipment and from the New England region to New Orleans before landfall;
>
> b. circumvented his chain of command and failed to communicate critical information to the Secretary;
>
> c. failed to deliver on commitments made to Louisiana's leaders for buses;
>
> d. traveled to Baton Rouge with FEMA public-affairs and congressional-relations employees and a personal aide, and no operational experts;
>
> e. failed to organize FEMA's or other federal efforts in any meaningful way; and
>
> f. failed to adequately carry out responsibilities as FEMA's lead official in the Gulf before landfall and when he was appointed as the Principal Federal Official after landfall.

Government Response: The Role Of The White House

54. The White House knew or should have known that Hurricane Katrina could turn into the long-feared "New Orleans Scenario," and could wreak devastation throughout the Gulf region. The White House also may have been aware that FEMA was not prepared for such a catastrophe.

55. The President did take extraordinary steps to prepare for the storm – such as issuing emergency declarations in advance of landfall – but could have done more to marshal federal resources.

56. Despite receiving information from multiple sources on the extent of the damage in New Orleans, the White House does not appear to have been aware that levees had broken and the city was flooding on the day of the storm and, indeed, appears to have been under the misimpression, for some time, that the levees did not break until the day after Katrina made landfall.

57. The initial response to Katrina was halting and inadequate, in part due to poor situational awareness. Ultimately, the President and his team brought the full resources of the federal government to bear on the catastrophe.

Evacuations: Pre-Storm

58. Before landfall, Louisiana successfully evacuated people with vehicles who wanted to leave.

59. Prior to Katrina, New Orleans officials did not fulfill a commitment in their emergency plan to provide transportation for people without vehicles.

60. Mayor Nagin wasted time in waiting to order a mandatory evacuation until Sunday morning, while his staff worked out details of the order that should have been settled long before the crisis.

61. The City of New Orleans, the State of Louisiana, and the federal government failed to retain drivers for the pre-landfall evacuation, even though city officials informed state and federal officials of this need over a month before landfall.

62. Governor Blanco missed opportunities to ask the federal government to help evacuate New Orleans before landfall. For example, she failed to ask for transportation assistance in her request for an emergency declaration, which was promptly granted by the President.

63. The state's lead agency for transportation, the Louisiana Department of Transportation and Development, failed to meet its responsibility under the state's emergency operations plan as lead agency for identifying, mobilizing, and coordinating transportation to assist with a pre-landfall evacuation.

64. The Louisiana Office of Homeland Security and Emergency Preparedness did not exercise sufficient oversight to ensure that the Louisiana Department of Transportation and Development would fulfill its responsibilities under the state's April 2005 plan.

65. The federal government did not engage state or local authorities about transportation alternatives for those lacking means for pre-landfall evacuation.

66. The federal government could have offered assistance with pre-landfall evacuation without waiting for requests from state and local government.

67. Hurricane Katrina revealed that consideration of the needs of those with pets should be a factor in emergency planning for evacuations and sheltering.

Communications Voids

68. Hurricane Katrina resulted in a pervasive and widespread breakdown in communications, significantly affecting the ability of first responders and government officials in their rescue and response efforts.

69. The National Communications System failed to develop plans to support first-responder communications, assess the damage to the communications systems, and maintain awareness of the federal government's available communications assets. Local governments either had inadequate plans or were unable to rapidly repair damage to their first responder communications systems.

70. The response to Katrina was also hampered by the lack of data interoperability – that is, responders' inability to electronically share data including patient medical records and information needed to track missing children and adults, to coordinate search-and-rescue operations, and to verify eligibility for benefits.

71. During Katrina, many of the 911 systems citizens call first during emergencies failed. Because of widespread destruction of call centers, many calls could not be rerouted; when they were rerouted, there were no systems in place to share critical data, for example, about the call's point of origin. Officials also had no plans to provide additional 911 operators needed to field thousands of calls for help.

72. When terrestrial-based communications networks were damaged or destroyed, some responders were able to use satellite phones for limited communications capabilities. For example, the Mississippi Emergency Management Agency provided satellite phones to all of its employees in the field; it also had a mobile communications unit with satellite capability.

73. The private sector deployed massive resources to restore their communications infrastructure, but their efforts were hampered because (a) government did not provide repair workers with uniform credentials to gain access to devastated areas; (b) government sometimes diverted fuel resources needed for generators; and (c) industry was justifiably reluctant to go into some areas without security, a principal responsibility of the government.

Lack Of Situational Awareness

74. Michael Brown willfully failed to report key information directly to DHS leadership, instead reporting straight to White House officials.

75. The Homeland Security Operations Center (HSOC) failed to take timely steps to create a system to identify and acquire all available, relevant information.

76. The HSOC failed in its responsibility under the National Response Plan (NRP) to provide "general situational awareness" and a "common operational picture," particularly concerning the failure of the levees, the flooding of New Orleans, and the crowds at the Convention Center.

77. On the day of landfall, senior DHS officials received numerous reports that should have led to an understanding of the increasingly dire situation in New Orleans, yet they were not aware of the crisis until Tuesday morning.

78. Louisiana was not equipped to process the volume of information received by its emergency operations center after landfall.

79. Lack of situational awareness regarding the status of deliveries created difficulties in managing the provision of needed commodities in Louisiana and Mississippi.

Critical Infrastructure; ESF-15, Public Affairs

80. Hurricane Katrina demonstrated that it is an enormous and complex task for government to assess damage to critical infrastructure and work with the private sector to coordinate its restoration. At the time Katrina struck, the Department of Homeland Security had not completed its planning and assessment work to prioritize the protection of critical infrastructure; this plan might have been helpful in coordinating the restoration of critical infrastructure.

81. Federal and state officials failed to fulfill their responsibilities under federal and state plans to disseminate timely and accurate information to the public.

Search And Rescue

82. Federal, state, and local agencies rescued approximately 60,000 people in the aftermath of Katrina. Of this 60,000, the Coast Guard missions alone accounted for 33,000 rescues. The Louisiana Department of Wildlife & Fisheries (W&F), along with the out-of-state agencies that assisted the Department through the EMAC process, accounted for 21,000 rescues. The Coast Guard, DOD and the National Guard conducted an extensive helicopter search-and-rescue mission.

83. The NRP does not adequately address the organizational structure and the assets needed for search and rescue in a large-scale, multi-environment catastrophe. Under the NRP, Emergency Support Function 9 (ESF-9, Urban Search and Rescue) is focused on missions to rescue people in collapsed structures. ESF-9 gives the U.S. Coast Guard a support role for water rescue. However, the NRP does not provide a comprehensive structure for water and air rescues, which constituted a significant portion of the necessary search-and-rescue missions in the Katrina response.

84. The lack of a strategic intergovernmental plan to address search and rescue in a disaster environment that required tactical planning and organization, communications, air traffic control, and the reception of victims, led to inefficient employment of resources, hazardous flight conditions, and protracted waits by victims in need of rescue.

85. The City of New Orleans left the New Orleans Fire Department (NOFD) and the New Orleans Police Department (NOPD) unprepared to conduct water search-and-rescue missions by repeatedly denying budget requests by those departments for watercraft. Consequently, the NOFD entered Katrina with no boats, and the NOPD entered Katrina with five boats.

86. The Louisiana National Guard stationed many boats and high water vehicles at Jackson Barracks, one of the lowest points in the city. Jackson Barracks flooded during Katrina and rendered many of these assets unavailable for search-and-rescue missions.

87. The individuals working on behalf of federal, state, and local agencies to rescue victims worked in chaotic situations often at great risk to themselves. Yet search-and-rescue resources, including boats and helicopters, were insufficient despite their accelerated deployment through the first week of landfall.

88. Despite the large number of helicopters in the Gulf by the end of the first week, the number of helicopters capable of performing search and rescue – the most critical of all missions – was still inadequate for the number of victims in immediate need of rescue.

89. Regarding the need for additional boats, the state asked for rubber rafts, but FEMA did not provide them because FEMA decided rubber rafts would not be sturdy enough to maneuver in debris-laden water. However, state officials disagree and believe these rafts would have been valuable for such things as towing groups of rescued victims behind regular boats.

90. Planning and coordination by the designated lead federal and state agencies, FEMA, and the Louisiana Department of Wildlife & Fisheries, were inadequate and impaired the overall effectiveness of the search-and-rescue mission.

91. The Hurricane Pam exercise predicted flooding in New Orleans and called for boat- and helicopter-based rescues, but emergency planners at all levels of government did not anticipate before landfall the need for large-scale rescue operations.

92. FEMA did not equip or train its SAR teams for water search and rescue. FEMA SAR teams did not begin search-and-rescue missions until Tuesday morning.

93. Communications failures abounded at the local, state, and federal level, undermining the ability of agencies and rescuers to coordinate their work.

94. The Emergency Management Assistance Compact proved to be a valuable resource for Louisiana to obtain necessary equipment and teams. However, bureaucracy related to and confusion over the approval process delayed its utility to the State of Louisiana.

95. Concerns about lawlessness forced some FEMA and NOFD search-and-rescue teams to pull back their operations temporarily because they lacked security.

96. The Department of Homeland Security was slow to deploy equipment that could have assisted in the response to Katrina. For example, the Department did not deploy, until nearly a week after the storm, pre-positioned equipment "pods," each of which was capable of providing lifesaving equipment to 150 first responders. DHS waited until at least two days after landfall to advise either Louisiana or Mississippi of their availability.

Search And Rescue For Mississippi

97. The number of communities and the geographic area affected by Katrina created manpower and logistical difficulties for search-and-rescue operations, especially given the time-sensitive nature of the work.

98. The amount of debris hindered search-and-rescue operations. Mississippi National Guard engineering unit and others often had to clear debris before rescuers could access areas to conduct operations.

99. The collapse of communications along the Gulf Coast made coordination difficult from the start and presented challenges for the duration of search-and-rescue missions.

100. Despite the many challenges, search-and-rescue operations proceeded successfully along the Mississippi Gulf Coast, with operations beginning even before the flood waters had receded. Search-and-rescue responders and assets were effectively marshaled from

the ranks of Mississippi communities, FEMA, EMAC states, the Coast Guard, Mississippi National Guard, and other sources.

Post-Landfall Evacuation

101. The failure to effect a complete pre-landfall evacuation amplified the challenges of the post-landfall evacuation.

102. While the need for post-landfall evacuation of New Orleans was foreseeable, no level of government took the steps necessary to prepare for it.

103. FEMA Director Michael Brown failed to follow through on his promise to Louisiana officials to arrange for speedy delivery of buses to evacuate New Orleans.

104. Lack of communication among city officials resulted in the missed opportunity to use as many as 200 safely positioned city buses to begin the evacuation of New Orleans shortly after Katrina passed.

105. The Louisiana Department of Transportation and Development's lack of preparedness contributed to the delay in locating in-state buses to evacuate New Orleans.

106. Delays in arranging transportation to evacuate New Orleans led to unnecessary suffering of people stranded there.

107. Provisions for sheltering were inadequate, and the State of Louisiana was at least partially responsible.

108. Concerns about security slowed the post-landfall evacuation.

109. No level of government addressed the evacuation of the Convention Center until Friday, two days after large numbers of people began congregating there.

Logistics

110. DHS leaders knew or should have known that FEMA's logistics system suffered from significant and long-standing problems, yet they did not take sufficient steps to fix the system.

111. Prior to landfall, FEMA failed to pre-stage enough commodities in either Mississippi or Louisiana.

112. FEMA's logistics system failed out of the box, but with revisions and assistance from DOD logistics specialists, the FEMA system began to improve in the second week after landfall.

113. Louisiana's failure to adequately prioritize its requests to FEMA wasted FEMA's time and limited resources.

114. Louisiana's Office of Homeland Security and Emergency Preparedness failed to effectively coordinate the distribution of commodities.

115. The ARF and E-Team methods by which response resources were requested were incompatible and ill-equipped to handle a disaster of this magnitude.

116. FEMA lacked the ability to track the shipment of commodities. The lack of visibility disrupted the ability to respond effectively to the aftermath of Katrina.

117. Fuel is a crucial commodity during the response to any disaster. In Katrina's immediate aftermath, a shortfall in the fuel supply hindered the response as early attempts to mitigate the disruptions appear to have been inadequate.

118. The Louisiana National Guard (LANG) failed to anticipate and adequately plan for the large-scale commodity distribution necessitated by Katrina. LANG did not have enough manpower and equipment available to complete its distribution mission.

119. During approximately the first ten days following the storm, the federal logistics system was unable to provide the requested level of Meals Ready to Eat (MRE) rations, water, and ice in Mississippi.

120. The commodity pipeline Florida set up to bring supplies into south Mississippi was crucial to alleviating additional suffering in that area.

121. Early in the response, Mississippi recognized how severely Katrina had disrupted the state's infrastructure, and the resulting inability of many residents of south Mississippi to travel to the Points of Distribution to acquire life-saving supplies. The resulting "push" of supplies by the National Guard to residents was crucial to preventing additional hardship in south Mississippi.

Medical Assistance

Federal

122. The federal government's medical response suffered from a lack of planning, coordination, and cooperation, particularly between the U.S. Department of Health and Human Services (HHS) and the Department of Homeland Security.

123. Despite its lead role as the primary agency in charge of coordinating the federal medical response, HHS did not deploy its on-scene response-coordination teams as rapidly as it should have, and lacked adequate emergency-coordination staff and resources.

124. The federal agencies involved in providing medical assistance did not have adequate resources or the right type or mix of medical capabilities to fully meet the medical needs arising from Katrina, such as the needs of large evacuee populations, and were forced to use improvised and unproven techniques to meet those needs.

125. Unlike Disaster Medical Assistance Teams, the U.S. Public Health Service is not organized or equipped to serve as medical first responders and have no pre-established, readily deployable teams, personnel practices, transportation and other logistical difficulties.

126. Although FEMA eventually deployed virtually all of its National Disaster Medical System resources – having started with only a single team – there was a greater need for such teams than could be filled, and those teams that did deploy experienced difficulties in obtaining necessary logistical, communications, security, and management support.

127. Despite efforts by both FEMA and HHS to activate federal emergency-health capabilities of the National Disaster Medical System (NDMS) and the U.S. Public Health Service as Katrina approached the Gulf Coast, only a limited number of federal medical teams were actually in position prior to landfall to deploy into the affected area, of which only one (the

Oklahoma – 1 Disaster Medical Assistance Team) was in a position to provide immediate medical care in the aftermath of the storm.

128. Although a shipment of medical supplies was dispatched from the Strategic National Stockpile to Louisiana late on Sunday, August 28, in response to a last-minute request from the City of New Orleans, it was not possible to get it to Louisiana before landfall, and no other federal medical supplies were pre-positioned in the Gulf region.

Louisiana

129. The State of Louisiana failed to ensure that nursing homes and hospitals were incorporated into the state's emergency-planning process, and as a result failed to ensure that they had effective evacuation plans or were genuinely prepared to shelter their critical-care patients in place, causing loss of life and avoidable suffering.

130. Louisiana failed to plan for known emergency medical-response needs, such as post-storm evacuation of patients from hospitals or moving large numbers of patients to medical-treatment facilities.

131. Louisiana State University failed to carry out its responsibilities under the state emergency-operations plan to ensure adequate emergency preparedness for health-care facilities, and the Louisiana Office of Homeland Security and Emergency Preparedness failed to ensure that its functions were implemented.

Public Safety And Security

132. Actual and perceived lawlessness hampered the emergency response during Katrina.

133. In statements to the media, New Orleans officials perpetuated unsubstantiated rumors about violent crimes that had not occurred.

134. The NOPD was overwhelmed by Katrina. Under extraordinarily difficult circumstances, most of its officers performed their duties.

135. The NOPD failed to adequately provision personnel or coordinate fully the pre-staging and pre-positioning of its assets, which reduced its effectiveness.

136. DHS and DOJ's failure to understand, plan for, and implement their ESF-13 responsibilities in natural disasters prior to Katrina led to delays in providing law enforcement assistance.

137. Neither DHS nor DOJ planned for or coordinated their joint ESF-13 roles and responsibilities relating to a natural disaster.

138. The lack of advance planning by DHS and DOJ delayed the deployment of federal law enforcement into the Gulf region and New Orleans, in particular.

139. Inadequate planning by local officials for the evacuation of detention facilities and the identification of back-up facilities for new arrests contributed to the public-safety problems in New Orleans.

140. There was insufficient coordination of the processes that procured and deployed National Guard and civilian law-enforcement assistance.

Military Operations

Overall

141. The National Guard and active-duty military troops and assets deployed during Katrina constituted the largest domestic deployment of military forces since the Civil War. The National Guard and active-duty military response saved lives; provided urgent food, water, shelter, and medical care to many hurricane victims; and helped restore law and order, re-establish communications, and rebuild damaged roads.

142. Although the Department of Defense's preparations for Katrina were consistent with its procedures and prior practices in civil-support missions, they were not sufficient for a storm of Katrina's magnitude. Additional preparations in advance of specific requests for support could have enabled a more rapid response.

143. The deployments of National Guard and active-duty forces were not well coordinated. A major cause of this was that there was no pre-existing plan or process for the large-scale deployment of National Guard forces from multiple states in response to a catastrophic disaster. NORTHCOM did not have full and timely information on the capabilities of National Guard troops deploying to the Gulf Coast.

144. In part because of the lack of a pre-existing plan for large scale deployments, some National Guard units arrived before there was established an adequate command-and-control structure for the number of forces deployed, resulting in a failure to efficiently employ all available troops.

145. While some active-duty and National Guard units are designed and structured to deploy rapidly as part of their military missions, the Department of Defense is not organized, funded, or structured to act as a first responder for all domestic catastrophic disasters.

146. The dual military-command structure in Katrina exposed a fundamental tension – inherent in our system of government – between the principles of unity of command and federalism.

147. DOD has unique resources and capabilities to provide humanitarian relief in a catastrophe. FEMA's failure to request these assets sooner delayed the Department's delivery of these critical assets.

148. On the whole, the performance of the individual Coast Guard personnel, sailors, soldiers, airmen, and Marines – active, Guard, and Reserve – was in keeping with the high professional standards of the United States military, and these men and women are proud of their service to help the victims of this natural disaster.

Pre-Landfall Preparation

149. The Department of Defense prepared for Hurricane Katrina in a manner consistent with its interpretation of DOD's role under the National Response Plan, which is to respond to requests for assistance from FEMA. However, this approach was inadequate to prepare for a catastrophe of the magnitude of Katrina.

150. The Department of Defense's preparations prior to landfall largely consisted of deploying Defense Coordinating Officers and Defense Coordinating Elements, identifying staging bases, identifying some assets and units for potential disaster support, participating in conference calls and meetings led by FEMA, monitoring the progress of the storm, and identifying available commodities.

151. Based on their previous experience in hurricanes, prior to landfall a number of commanders took additional actions to prepare assets for deployment in advance of any specific request or order for those assets.

152. NORTHCOM and First Army commanders requested that certain DOD assets be identified before landfall in anticipation of requirements, but the Joint Directorate of Military Support failed to respond in a timely manner.

153. Because the Department has denied the Committee access to NORTHCOM's plans for its preparation for and response to domestic catastrophes, even though they are not classified, the Committee was unable to assess their status and adequacy. The Committee has received directly contradictory testimony as to whether these plans are complete, so it is unclear to what extent the Department, especially NORTHCOM, had planned its response to Katrina or whether the plans would have addressed the problems of coordination identified by this investigation.

Initial Response After Landfall

154. During the initial 24 hours after landfall, the Department of Defense lacked timely and accurate information about the immediate impact of Hurricane Katrina. DOD and DHS did not coordinate adequately for the use of DOD assets to make such assessments during this period.

155. During this initial period after landfall, a number of military commanders within the services were proactive, identifying, alerting, and positioning assets for potential response, prior to receiving requests from FEMA or specific orders. Many of these preparations proved essential to the overall response; however, they reflected the individual initiative of various commanders rather than a pre-planned, coordinated response as is necessary for a disaster of this magnitude.

156. During this initial period after landfall, the office of the Joint Director of Military Support took the position that DOD should provide support or mobilize assets only after DOD had received, evaluated, and approved a specific request for assistance from FEMA. As a result, DOD did not act quickly to process and approve the first request it received from FEMA for two helicopters for rapid needs assessment.

157. On Tuesday, August 30, as DOD officials became concerned about the extent of the damage, DOD prepared and mobilized many assets to be able to respond quickly to requests for assistance and provide military support to the hurricane response. The Acting Deputy Secretary of Defense gave direction that eliminated much of the internal review and approval process, and encouraged the deployment of assets that commanders deemed potentially necessary prior to receiving requests for such assets. The Chairman of the Joint Chiefs of Staff provided guidance to the Service Chiefs on Tuesday to exercise their own judgment in pushing assets forward. The services followed this guidance. Some commanders moved quickly to mobilize and position assets for potential deployments in advance of formal requests or approvals.

158. Not all deployments were fully coordinated among the services, NORTHCOM, and the Joint Task Force. NORTHCOM did not have a complete picture of the movement of troops and resources within its area of responsibility.

Responses to FEMA's Requests for Assistance

159. DOD's normal, "21 step" process for accepting assignments from FEMA to assist in responding to a disaster is cumbersome and unlike the processes followed by all other fed-

eral agencies. It also caused tension between DOD and FEMA and slowed certain of DOD's initial efforts in the response.

160. On Tuesday, August 30, in an effort to speed DOD's response, the Acting Deputy Secretary of Defense suspended the regular approval process, including the requirement that formal written approval by the Secretary of Defense precede the actual execution of a mission. Following this decision, DOD appears to have responded quickly to FEMA requests for assistance.

161. Despite the assignment of numerous DOD liaison officers, some FEMA officials still did not have a good understanding of the assets and resources that DOD could provide. Similarly, some FEMA officials did not have a good understanding of the DOD's processes for responding to FEMA requests for assistance.

162. In many instances, discussions between FEMA or DHS officials and DOD officials were necessary to clarify requests for assistance or to ensure that DOD would be providing the most effective resources in response to the request. Some FEMA officials believed that these discussions and DOD's approval process took too long.

National Guard Troop Deployments

163. There is no established process for the large-scale, nationwide deployment of National Guard troops in response to a governor's request for large-scale deployment of troops for civil support.

164. During Katrina, neither the State of Louisiana, the State of Mississippi, nor the Emergency Management Assistance Compact was able to manage the large-scale deployments of National Guard troops from all 50 states and four other jurisdictions.

165. The National Guard Bureau solicited the rapid deployment of National Guard troops from all 50 states and four other jurisdictions. Although this process successfully deployed a large number of National Guard troops, it did not proceed efficiently, or according to any pre-existing plan or process.

Federal Troop Deployments

166. Some active-duty units, including elements of the 82nd Airborne Division and the Second Marine Expeditionary Force, are maintained on alert for rapid deployment, and were placed on higher alert on Wednesday, August 31. These forces could have deployed sooner into Louisiana had the President or the Department of Defense made a decision to deploy them.

167. Due to the restrictions placed by the White House and DOD on the Committee's ability to interview White House and senior civilian and military officials within DOD about deployment decisions, the Committee has been unable to conclude why the President ordered the deployment of federal active-duty troops on Saturday, September 3, including reasons why the President did not order the deployment of federal active-duty troops sooner. However, the Committee has been able to make findings about DOD officials' views on these topics.

168. The deployment of National Guard forces before active-duty troops was consistent with the DOD Strategy for Homeland Defense and Civil Support, which relies on the National Guard in the first instance for civil support.

169. The large numbers of National Guard troops that were deploying into Louisiana were a major factor in the Department of Defense's decision not to deploy additional active-duty

troops prior to Saturday, September 3. DOD officials said that the choice to deploy National Guard troops first was correct because the National Guard is designated as the first military responder under the DOD Strategy for Homeland Defense and Civil Support, and because National Guard forces, unlike active duty troops, are not restricted from performing law-enforcement duties under the federal Posse Comitatus Act.

170. Federal and state officials did not coordinate well the requests and consideration of requests for National Guard and active-duty troop deployments. The Governor of Louisiana asked for 40,000 troops, but federal officials did not interpret this as a specific request for active-duty troops.

171. Local, state, and federal officials had differing perceptions of the numbers of federal troops that would be arriving and the appropriate command structure for all troops, causing confusion and diverting attention from response activities. In Louisiana, a stronger unified command might have avoided this confusion and diversion of attention.

Poor Controls And Decisions In FEMA Spending

172. Taxpayer dollars meant for relief and recovery were lost to waste and fraud.

173. Wasteful practices and program-control weaknesses that FEMA indicated it had identified and was addressing after the 2004 Florida hurricanes were not remedied prior to Katrina.

174. Due to a lack of planning and preparation, much of FEMA's initial spending was reactive and rushed, resulting in costly purchase decisions and utilization of no-bid, sole-source contracts that put the government at increased risk of not getting the best price for goods and services.

Failures In Design, Implementation, And Execution Of The National Response Plan

175. DHS did not effectively implement the National Response Plan, although it was released in January 2005 and required to be implemented in April 2005.

176. The NRP lacked clarity on a number of points, including the role and authorities of the Principal Federal Official and the allocation of responsibilities among multiple agencies under the Emergency Support Functions, which led to confusion in the response to Katrina. Plan ambiguities were not resolved or clarified in the months after the NRP was issued, either through additional operational planning or through training and exercises.

177. Although DHS was charged with administering the plan and leading the response under it, DHS officials made decisions that appeared to be at odds with the NRP, failed to fulfill certain responsibilities under the NRP on a timely basis, and failed to make effective use of certain authorities under the NRP.

178. By not implementing the NRP's Catastrophic Incident Annex (NRP-CIA) in response to Hurricane Katrina, the Secretary of DHS did not utilize a tool that may have alleviated some of the difficulties with the federal response. The Secretary's activation of the NRP-CIA could have increased the urgency of the federal response and led the federal government to respond more proactively rather than waiting for formal requests from overwhelmed state and local governments.

179. DHS had not completed the Catastrophic Incident Supplement referred to in the NRP-CIA, had not engaged in adequate catastrophic planning, and had not developed regional or situation specific plans that could have improved the usefulness of the NRP in a catastrophe.

180. In the absence of additional operational planning and without adequate implementation, the NRP was insufficient to address this catastrophic event.

181. The Incident Command System doctrine includes the concept of Unified Command, which is designed to allow all agencies with responsibility for an incident to work together effectively. It establishes a process through which strategies and objectives are determined collectively so that agencies under different jurisdictional control can work under a single incident action plan toward common objectives.

182. FEMA, as well as other federal agencies, did not have an adequate number of personnel familiar with and trained in the Incident Command System and the principles of unified command to be able to respond to a catastrophe of the magnitude of Katrina.

183. The Louisiana Office of Homeland Security and Emergency Preparedness suffered problems such as inadequate funding; not enough staff; insufficient training, (demonstrated by the need of Louisiana officials to hire consultants to train EOC participants and National Guard members in basic NIMS ICS courses two days after Katrina made landfall); widespread lack of understanding of NIMS ICS and unified command; an overall lack of preparation, and a lack of emergency-management capacity to respond effectively to Katrina. Together, these were the primary reasons for the failure to establish unified command and establish an incident-command structure in Louisiana.

184. Mississippi established a unified command with FEMA, conducted joint planning prior to landfall, and was able to broaden the unified command and establish an incident-command structure after a short period of chaos following Katrina.

185. Senior leaders and individuals in Mississippi with responsibilities for emergency management had been given extensive prior training on NIMS ICS, and FEMA's senior personnel in Mississippi possessed a very high level of knowledge and understanding of NIMS ICS.

186. Where and when personnel with experience and training on NIMS ICS were in control with an adequate number of trained support personnel, coupled with the discipline to adhere to the doctrine of NIMS ICS, it made a positive difference in the quality and success of implementing an incident command structure, establishing a unified command, and the response.

Recommendations

In the recommendations that follow, we set out seven core recommendations meant to help establish a sturdy underpinning for the nation's emergency-management structure. Based on the weaknesses and challenges we uncovered in our investigation, we believe the core recommendations are the essential first steps in the successful construction of an effective system.

These recommendations are then followed by what will be the building blocks for the structure, the more tactical actions that must be taken – by federal, state, and local governments, non-governmental organizations, the private sector, and individual citizens – to make the system strong, agile, effective, and robust. The foundation is crucial, and every building block we can add will make the system stronger. We believe these measures, if implemented, will significantly improve the nation's ability to prepare for and respond to disasters and catastrophes, providing better safety and security for our citizens.

Core Recommendations

Core Recommendation #1 – Create a New, Comprehensive Emergency-Management Organization within DHS to Prepare for and Respond to All Disasters and Catastrophes.

Hurricane Katrina exposed flaws in the structure of the Federal Emergency Management Agency (FEMA) and the Department of Homeland Security (DHS) that are too substantial to mend. We propose to abolish FEMA and build a stronger, more capable structure within DHS. The structure will form the foundation of the nation's emergency-management system. It will be an independent entity within DHS, but will draw on the resources of the Department and will be led and staffed by capable, committed individuals.

We must create a robust National Preparedness and Response Authority (NPRA) within the Department of Homeland Security. The NPRA would fuse the Department's emergency-management, preparedness, and critical-infrastructure assets into a powerful new organization that can confront the challenges of natural or man-made catastrophes. It will provide critical leadership for preparedness and response by combining key federal personnel and assets, as well as federal partnerships with state and local officials and the private sector to prepare for and respond to terror attacks or natural disasters.

National Preparedness and Response Authority

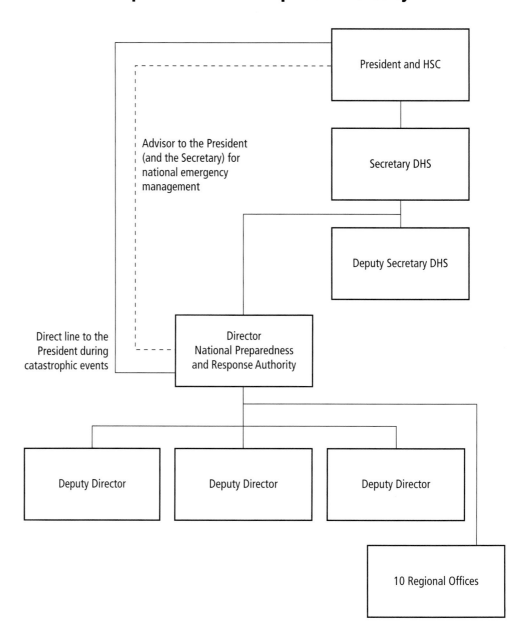

The NPRA Will Have the Following Characteristics:[1]

Distinct Entity within DHS, with Access to the Full Resources of the Department. It is essential that NPRA be located within DHS, but it should be situated as a "distinct entity" – the same status accorded the U.S. Coast Guard and the U.S. Secret Service. The organization's mission and components should also be protected from internal reorganizations or diminution by the Department.

DHS is the central agency in the federal government for protecting the nation from the effects of terrorist attacks and natural disasters, and NPRA's mission is a necessary part of that. Maintaining NPRA within DHS allows the new organization to take full advantage of the substantial range of resources DHS has at its disposal – the Coast Guard, the National Communications System, SAFECOM (which provides research and support for interoperable communications), and one of the largest bodies of law-enforcement agents in any federal agency. DHS's prevention and intelligence resources also represent potentially valuable assets, as more effective identification of risks and vulnerabilities can lead to better and more targeted preparedness. In short, DHS has a substantially greater and wider range of resources that can be brought to bear on the challenge of natural or man-made catastrophes in a disaster than was or would be the case with an independent FEMA; what was formerly the responsibility of a small 2,500-person independent agency is now the responsibility of a 180,000 person, Cabinet-level department.

Removing NPRA (or FEMA as it currently exists) from the Department, moreover, would do nothing to solve the key problems that Katrina has revealed, including a lack of resources and weak and ineffective leadership. Separating NPRA from DHS could, in fact, cause new difficulties, including the need to replicate a number of key functions, such as facilities to maintain situational awareness, in two different agencies. It would also place a hardship on states that would have to coordinate their preparedness and response efforts through two separate federal agencies. Katrina has made it clear that we need more integration in federal preparedness and response, not less, and that we need to effectively integrate, not bifurcate, prevention, preparedness, protection and response initiatives with state, local, and non-governmental and private-sector partners.

It is important to distinguish between preventing a terrorist attack and preventing damage from a terrorist attack or natural disaster. Prevention activities related directly to preventing a terrorist incident from occurring – largely a law-enforcement and intelligence function – are not included in the NPRA. Neither would be the grants that support this function.

Director with Sufficient Access and Clout. The Director of National Preparedness and Response should be a Level II official – that is, of the same rank as the Deputy Secretary – and would report directly to the Secretary of DHS. The Director would also serve as the Advisor to the President for national emergency management, in a manner akin to the Chairman of the Joint Chiefs of Staff. The Director would have a direct line of communication to the President during catastrophes.

The Director should also have the political authority to direct appropriate personnel within DHS and in other departments and agencies of the federal government to carry out their assigned emergency-management responsibilities under the Stafford Act, the National Response Plan (NRP), Emergency Support Functions (ESFs), and other appropriate emergency-management doctrine.

Capable and Qualified Leadership. Those leading NPRA should have skills commensurate with the organization's critically important mission of protecting American lives and property in the event of a terrorist attack or natural disaster. The three Deputy Directors – for Preparedness and Mitigation, Response, and Recovery – would serve under the Director and would be Level III, Senate-confirmed appointees. Each of the ten regional offices would be headed by a Senior Executive Service-level Regional Director qualified to act as a senior Federal Coordinating Officer (FCO) to provide strategic oversight of incident management when needed.

The Director and each of the three Deputy Directors should have significant experience in crisis management, in addition to substantial management and leadership experience, whether in the public, private, or nonprofit sector. For example, appropriate experience could include a military career with broad leadership experience; emergency-management experience and a proven track record of leading complex preparedness and response efforts; or private-sector experience successfully leading a company or organization through a crisis.

Those with direct technical and operational responsibilities during disasters should be individuals with emergency or crisis-management knowledge, training, and experience. The nation's preparedness and response agency requires a cadre of seasoned professionals with knowledge of crisis management and government operations, who have exhibited leadership and commitment and will build trusted relationships with other federal agencies, state and local governments, non-governmental organizations (NGOs), volunteer organizations, and the private sector.

Core Recommendation #2 – From the Federal Level Down, Take a Comprehensive All-Hazards Plus Approach to Emergency Management.

The new organization should bring together the full range of responsibilities that are core to preparing for and responding to disasters. These include the four central functions of comprehensive emergency management – preparedness, response, recovery and mitigation – which need to be integrated. Actions in recent years that removed preparedness grants from FEMA and separated preparedness from response weakened FEMA's relationship with state officials and undermined its ability to utilize "the power of the purse," in the form of grant funding, to encourage states to improve their preparedness and response functions. A more comprehensive approach should be restored. If NPRA is going to effectively respond to major events, for example, it needs to have been involved in the preparations for such events. The Director, moreover, must be responsible for administering and distributing preparedness grants to state and local governments and for national preparedness training, as these are key tools for ensuring a consistent and coordinated national response system.

All-Hazards Plus. NPRA would adopt an "all-hazards plus" strategy for preparedness. In preparing our nation to respond to terrorist attacks and natural disasters, NPRA must focus on building those common capabilities – for example survivable, interoperable communications and evacuation plans – that are necessary regardless of the incident. At the same time, it must not neglect to build those unique capabilities – like mass decontamination in the case of a radiological attack, or water search and rescue in the case of flooding – that will be needed for particular types of incidents.

Common Emergency Management Elements

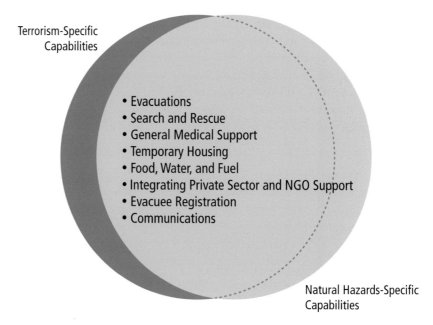

Terrorism-Specific
Capabilities

- Evacuations
- Search and Rescue
- General Medical Support
- Temporary Housing
- Food, Water, and Fuel
- Integrating Private Sector and NGO Support
- Evacuee Registration
- Communications

Natural Hazards-Specific
Capabilities

Protect Critical Infrastructure. NPRA's mandate would also include overseeing protection of critical infrastructure, such as energy facilities and telecommunications systems, both to protect such infrastructure from harm and to ensure that such infrastructure is restored as quickly as possible after a natural disaster or terrorist attack – an essential part of an effective response. The critical-infrastructure programs would work with the Department's intelligence arm and other Department assets to help prevent terror attacks, and should establish priorities for the protection and restoration of critical infrastructure during an emergency and should help support restorative efforts.

Core Recommendation #3 – Establish Regional Strike Teams and Enhance Regional Operations to Provide Better Coordination Between Federal Agencies and the States.

Most of the essential work of emergency management does not happen in Washington, D.C., but on the front lines, with state and local officials and first responders having lead responsibility in a disaster. Regional offices – building on FEMA's 10 existing regional offices – should play a key role in coordinating with and assisting states and localities in preparing for and responding to disasters. Regional offices can facilitate planning tailored to the specific risks and needs of a particular geographic area: for example, the risks faced, and the types of preparedness necessary, in Gulf Coast states may differ markedly from that of cities along the Northeast Corridor that were attacked on 9/11, or of those areas that lie along the New Madrid seismic fault in the central Mississippi Valley.

Federal Strike Teams. The regional offices should provide the federal government's first-line response to a disaster when a state requests assistance. A critical feature of the regional structure should be a robust, deployable, multi-agency Strike Team at each of the regional offices that consists of, at a minimum: a designated FCO; personnel trained in incident management, public affairs, response and recovery, and communications support; a Defense Coordinating Officer (DCO); and liaisons to other federal agencies. These regional Strike Teams should coordinate their training and exercises with the state and local officials and the private-sector entities they will support when disasters occur.

Coordination and Assistance to States. The regional offices should provide coordination and assist in planning, training, and exercising of emergency preparedness and response activities; work with states to ensure that grant funds are spent most effectively, based on the specific risks and weaknesses identified at the regional level; coordinate and develop inter-state agreements; enhance coordination with NGOs and the private sector; and provide personnel and assets, in the form of Strike Teams, to be the federal government's first line of response to a disaster.

Adequate Regional Staffing. Regional offices would be staffed based on the needs in that region, but would likely include any or all of the following: a regional Strike Team; a dedicated staff and FCO for each state in the region; regional grants administration and oversight coordinator(s); regional and interstate planning; training, and exercise support and coordination officer(s); a federal interagency liaison; an interstate cooperation coordinator; designated state DCOs and National Guard liaisons; a private-sector, NGO, and volunteer-organization coordinator; mitigation specialist(s); and response-and-recovery specialist(s).

Multi-Agency Regional Efforts. The regional offices should coordinate with personnel from other components of DHS as well as from federal agencies outside DHS who are likely to be called upon to respond to a significant disaster in the region, including the Coast Guard, and the Departments of Health and Human Services (HHS), Defense (DOD), Transportation (DOT), Justice (DOJ), and others.

Core Recommendation #4 – Build a True, Government-Wide Operations Center to Provide Enhanced Situational Awareness and Manage Interagency Coordination in a Disaster.

During Katrina, the Homeland Security Operations Center (HSOC) had difficulty maintaining accurate situational awareness and failed to ensure that those in DHS's leadership had an accurate picture of the situation on the Gulf Coast, particularly about the failing levee system in New Orleans. Currently, a multiplicity of interagency coordinating structures with overlapping missions attempt to facilitate an integrated federal response. Three of these structures – the Homeland Security Operations Center (HSOC), the National Response Coordination Center (NRCC), and the Interagency Incident Management Group (IIMG) – should be consolidated into a single, integrated entity – a new National Operations Center (NOC).

Common Operating Picture. The NOC, housed within DHS, should include representatives from all relevant federal agencies. In an actual or potential disaster, the operations center should supply government-wide situational awareness, facilitate information sharing, and provide overall operational coordination through agency mission assignments and the NRP's Emergency Support Function (ESF) process. All federal and relevant state and local command centers would feed relevant information to the NOC, which would develop a common operating picture not just for DHS, but for the entire federal government, as well as states and local jurisdictions involved in an incident. The NOC should provide for one clearly defined emergency-management line of communication from the states to the federal government and from the federal government to the states. DHS should work with the NOC to develop protocols for disseminating information on the status of relief efforts to decisionmakers, responders, the private sector, and affected individuals.

Replace the IIMG. The IIMG would be disbanded and replaced by a permanent policy staff composed of detailees from relevant federal agencies who would conduct planning for emergencies and would help resolve conflicts among different federal entities. Conflicts that could not be resolved at this level would be forwarded to higher-level agency officials or the HSC for resolution. The NOC would include a strong analytic team capable of sorting through and assessing information and determining which pieces would become part of the common operating picture.

Improved Performance. To improve its performance in future disasters, the NOC should establish clear protocols and procedures to ensure that reports are received and reviewed, at appropriate levels, in a timely manner. When there is notice of a potential major disaster, the NOC should implement plans, including one for securing information from DOD, for obtaining post-disaster situational awareness, including identifying sources of information and data particular to the region in which the disaster may occur and, where appropriate, bringing in individuals with particular knowledge or expertise about that region.

Core Recommendation #5 – Renew and Sustain Commitments at All Levels of Government to the Nation's Emergency Management System.

Commitment from State and Local Government. Although the federal government should play a more proactive role in responding to catastrophic events when state and local officials may be overwhelmed, states and localities will continue to provide the backbone of response – the first response – for all disasters, catastrophic or not. State and local officials must take responsibility for their citizens' welfare and conduct the planning, training, and exercising that will prepare them to meet this obligation.

Commitment Commensurate with the Mission. The importance of providing for the safety of American citizens in the event of a natural disaster or terrorist attack can hardly be over-stated. Yet this investigation showed that FEMA did not have the resources to fulfill the mission and respond effectively in a catastrophic event. Resources are needed for additional planning, more frequent and ambitious training and exercises, enhancement of regional offices, staffing and preparation of regional Strike Teams, better development of a trained cadre of reservists, and development of new logistics capabilities. If the federal government is to improve its performance and be prepared to respond effectively to the next disaster, it must give NPRA – and the other federal agencies with central responsibilities under the NRP – the necessary resources to accomplish this. NPRA funding must be commensurate with the significance of its mission, with assurance that those funds are well-spent.

To be full partners in the national preparedness effort, states and localities will need additional resources as well. The pattern over the last three years of steadily declining funds for state and local preparedness needs to be reversed. NPRA should be given sufficient funds for homeland security and emergency-management grants to assist state and local governments in developing and exercising emergency plans, providing training, and attaining and maintaining essential capabilities, such as survivable and interoperable communications. But the states and localities must do their part as well. Every homeland security dollar, whether provided by the federal government or through state and local resources, must be spent only on those things that truly support the homeland-security mission. The new NPRA regional offices should be tasked with working with states to ensure that homeland-security expenditures are based on the risks and needs identified for that state or locality.

Federal Commitment. The President, DHS, and Congress must ensure that the NPRA is funded, staffed and equipped consistent with the range of risks facing American citizens. The federal government must provide protection no less robustly for all domestic hazards than it does for the defense from threats abroad.

The Administration and DHS must ensure that federal leaders understand their key responsibilities under the NRP and the resources they need to effectively carry out the comprehensive planning required, while also training and exercising on the National Incident Management System (NIMS), NRP and other operational plans. Each agency that has a role under an ESF, whether primary, coordinating, or supporting, should have a sufficient number of full-time staff whose primary responsibilities are to prepare for executing the agency's responsibilities under the ESF. Such preparedness activities should include training people who will be deployed to DHS's operational center for disaster response or to the disaster scene. These individuals must have sufficient authority and experience to be able to efficiently and effectively execute the agency's responsibilities under the ESFs.

State and Local Advisory Council. Any attempt to develop a full-fledged national system of preparedness and response must fully integrate state and local officials into the system. There should be established an advisory council to NPRA made up of state and local officials and first responders. The advisory council should play an integral role in ensuring that the full range of activities of the new organization – including developing response plans, conducting training and exercises, formulating preparedness goals, and effectively managing grants and other resources – are done in full consultation and coordination with, and take into account the needs and priorities of, states and localities.

Better Integrate Non-Governmental Organizations (NGOs) and the Private Sector. After Katrina struck, private companies and their employees provided important and even life-saving, relief to citizens across the Gulf Coast region; many other companies sought to offer assistance. Yet there was no system in place to effectively incorporate many private-sector resources into the response effort. Nor was there a system to efficiently incorporate important contributions from faith-based and other charitable and community organizations that sought to offer assistance.

DHS and NPRA should more fully integrate the private and nonprofit sectors into their planning and preparedness initiatives. Among other things, they should designate specific individuals at the national and regional levels to work directly with private-sector organizations. Where appropriate, private-sector representatives should also be included in planning, training, and exercises. In all cases, advance planning for how to most effectively utilize these nongovernmental resources is essential.

Core Recommendation #6 – Strengthen the Plans and Systems for the Nation's Response to Disasters and Catastrophes.

Despite their shortcomings and imperfections, the NRP and National Incident Management System (NIMS), including the ESF structure that has taken years to develop, currently represent the best approach available to respond to multi-agency, multi-jurisdictional emergencies of any kind, and should be retained and improved. Federal, state and local officials and other responders must commit to supporting the NRP and NIMS and work together to improve the performance of the national emergency-management system. We must undertake further refinements of the NRP and NIMS, develop operational plans, and engage in training and exercises to ensure that everyone involved in disaster response understands them and is prepared to carry them out.

The NRP should be amended to add an ESF responsible for assessing the damage to critical infrastructure, taking measures to mitigate the impact on the economy and national security, and restoring critical infrastructure. DHS should be responsible for leading this ESF, but it should have the involvement of the private sector, other federal agencies, and state and local governments, as appropriate.

Successfully implementing the NIMS during a disaster or catastrophe requires a true unity of effort. Katrina showed that a unity of effort generates much better outcomes than the lack thereof. The NRP should be strengthened to make the unity of effort concept very clear, so that everyone understands the concept and their roles in establishing unity. The NRP should clearly demonstrate the importance of establishing a unified command in which the principal incident-management organizations – the Federal Joint Field Office (JFO), the DOD Joint Task Force (JTF), and the State Emergency Operations Center (EOC) – are co-located where the Incident Command System (ICS) and ESF staffs can be fully integrated. The NRP should also be revised to further clarify the importance of integrating agencies with ESF responsibilities into the ICS, rather than their operating in "stovepipes." Agencies should not function as independent "cells," but should be represented by functional areas throughout the ICS. For example, agency representatives working on transportation issues should be sitting together, whether they are from DOT, NPRA, or DOD. Likewise, agencies supporting ESF-13 (Public Safety and Security), which may include the DOJ, NPRA, the Coast Guard, and the State Police, should all be physically located and working together in a unity of effort.

The roles and responsibilities of the Principal Federal Official (PFO) and the FCO overlap and were a source of confusion during Hurricane Katrina. The Stafford Act should be amended to clarify the roles and responsibilities of the FCO, and the NRP should be revised to eliminate the PFO position for Stafford Act-declared emergencies and disasters.

DHS should work with state and local governments to clarify expectations for such governments within the NRP. For the federal response to be effective, all levels of government must follow the same game plan. This did not always occur in Katrina.

The Stafford Act should be amended to address responses to all disasters and catastrophes, whether natural or man-made.

Core Recommendation #7 – Improve the Nation's Capacity to Respond to Catastrophic Events.

As documented in this report, FEMA does not have the capacity to respond to large-scale disasters and catastrophes. The United States was, and is, ill-prepared to respond to a catastrophic event of the magnitude of Hurricane Katrina. Catastrophic events are, by their nature, difficult to imagine and to adequately plan for, and the existing plans and training proved inadequate in Katrina. Yet it is precisely events of such magnitude – where local responders may be rendered victims, where hundreds of thousands of citizens are rendered homeless and thousands may need medical attention, where normal communications systems may fail, and where the usual coordination mechanisms may not be available – that most require advance planning. As stated previously, preparation for domestic incidents must be done as robustly as that for foreign threats. We would not tolerate a DOD that was not prepared for a worst-case catastrophic attack, nor should we tolerate a FEMA that is unprepared for domestic catastrophes.

Catastrophic Incident Annex and Supplement. DHS should ensure that the Catastrophic Incident Annex (NRP-CIA) is fully understood by the federal departments and agencies with associated responsibilities. The NRP-Catastrophic Incident Supplement (NRP-CIS) should be clarified and published, and the supporting operational plans for departments and agencies with responsibilities under the NRP-CIA should be completed. These plans should be reviewed and coordinated with the states, and on a regional basis, to ensure they are understood, trained, and exercised prior to an emergency. In addition, ambiguities in the plans – such as whether commodities are to be pre-positioned to mobilization centers or directly to incident sites absent a state request – must be clarified. The NRP-CIS itself should also be continuously reviewed and revised based upon the lessons of Katrina and future catastrophes.

DHS should define the circumstances under which the NRP-CIA and NRP-CIS may be invoked, both for known and no-notice events. Finally, the Stafford Act should be amended to more clearly reflect the proactive responsibility of the federal government for catastrophic events represented in the NRP-CIA, including authorizing funding for federal agencies to pre-deploy necessary assets before a disaster when the NRP-CIA is activated by the Secretary or NPRA Director.

Surge Capacity. DHS must develop the national capabilities – especially surge capacity – it needs to respond to catastrophic disasters, ensuring it has sufficient full-time staff, response teams, contracting personnel, and adequately trained and sufficiently staffed reserve corps to ramp up capabilities, as needed. These capabilities must be scalable so that NPRA can draw on the appropriate resources from supporting ESF agencies to respond to a disaster regardless of cause, size, or complexity. The Disaster Assistance Employee (DAE) corps should be modified/revamped so that it more closely resembles a reserve corps that can quickly and reliably respond with trained personnel in the case of a large-scale catastrophic event. Funds should be made available to ensure that these reservists receive appropriate and regular training, as well as adequate compensation for their time when called upon. DHS should investigate cross-training some of its 180,000 employees to become part of this reserve cadre.

Building the Nation's Emergency-Management System

Readiness

Planning, Training, Exercising (39-41)

Waste/Fraud/Abuse (42-43)

Evacuation and Sheltering (44-50)

Search and Rescue (51-52)

Mitigation (53-55)

Credentialing (56-58)

Education (59-62)

Special Needs Awareness (63-64)

Military Preparations (65-72)

State and Local (73-83)

Levees (84-88)

Coordination

Stafford Act/NRP/NIMS (8-14)

Interagency Coordination (15-22)

NGO/Private Sector Involvement (23-25)

Technological Support

Communications/Interoperability (26-31)

Information Systems (32-38)

New Structure

Core Recommendations (1-4)

Commitment

Core Recommendations (5-7)

Building Blocks: Coordination

Reviewing, Aligning and Improving the Stafford Act, the National Response Plan, and the National Incident Management System

Recommendation 8: The NRP should be reviewed and revised to provide clear guidance to federal agencies and clear information to state, local, and tribal officials, private-sector organizations and non-governmental organizations, eliminating ambiguities. The NRP should be a clear and accessible document that can be readily understood by those preparing for or participating in the response to a disaster. DHS should build commitment to the National Incident Management System (NIMS) from federal, state, and local officials, and other responders.

Recommendation 9: The Stafford Act and the NRP should be updated to better address and provide guidance for short- and long-term recovery activities, so that DHS, the Executive Branch, and Congress are not forced to react, but will already have plans and a structure in place to guide short- and long-term recovery efforts. Within the Recovery Branch of the new organization, there should be a long-term recovery office, able to ramp up and coordinate the federal government's long-term recovery assistance, as needed.*Recommendation 10:* The Stafford Act should be reviewed, and if, appropriate, amended, to provide statutory authority for committing resources and technical assistance to enable state and local governments and eligible non-profits to conduct short-term assessments and long-term recovery activities to meet the environmental mitigation needs of affected communities.

Recommendation 11: The scope of ESF-8 (Public Health and Medical Services), as defined in the NRP, should be expanded to clearly include the public-health and medical needs not only of victims of an emergency, but also those of evacuees, special-needs populations, and the general population who may be impacted by the event or may need to be evacuated or sheltered in place. The NRP should also clarify that responsibility for all mortuary activities, including collection of victims, resides with ESF-8, and appropriate mass fatality plans and capabilities should be developed.

Recommendation 12: The NRP should be revised to include language assigning a single federal maritime-salvage coordinator who will be responsible for responses to maritime-salvage needs during times of national disasters (man-made or natural) and clarify federal-agency responsibilities (NPRA, U.S. Coast Guard, U.S. Navy, U.S. Army Corps of Engineers).

Recommendation 13: DHS should amend the NRP to designate which agency should have primary responsibility for ESF-13 (Public Safety and Security) in which circumstances, and clarify relationships between the Senior Federal Law Enforcement Official (SFLEO) designation and ESF-13 functions described in the NRP support annex.

Recommendation 14: The NRP should be revised to reflect the broad range of search and rescue requirements that may arise in a disaster or catastrophe. ESF-9 (currently Urban Search and Rescue) should be expanded to encompass the multiple environments and requirements that may arise in a disaster or catastrophe, and should designate the appropriate lead agency and supporting agencies, as determined by the nature of the disaster.

Interagency Coordination

Recommendation 15: DOD and DHS should improve their coordination.

- DOD should continue to provide experienced officers to assist DHS officials in the execution of their responsibilities during an incident or disaster;

- DHS and NPRA officials should receive better training as to the capabilities and authorities of DOD during an emergency;

- DOD should streamline its existing, cumbersome process for Mission Assignments (MAs), particularly as applied in the event of a catastrophe;

- Key DOD personnel who may be called to participate in DOD's response efforts should receive training on the NRP, NIMS, and ICS;

- DOD should coordinate with the Secretary of DHS to develop a plan for commodities distribution in the event that DOD is called upon to augment DHS's commodities distribution in a catastrophic event.

- DOD and DHS should coordinate to expand the presence of DHS officials at U.S. Northern Command (NORTHCOM) and, as appropriate, U.S. Pacific Command (PACOM), and integrate DHS officials into NORTHCOM and PACOM's planning, training, exercising, and responding to an incident or disaster.

- DOD and DHS should develop an inventory of assets under DOD's control that are most likely to be needed in response to a disaster in order to enable expeditious deployment should they be required. Such assets may include, for example, utility and heavy-lift helicopters, medium-lift helicopters capable of performing search and rescue, shallow-draft boats, communications equipment, medical equipment and personnel, and engineering equipment.

Recommendation 16: DHS and HHS should improve their coordination.

- The Secretary of HHS should strengthen the Department's emergency preparedness and response organization (Office of Public Health Emergency Preparedness) by giving it greater authority to coordinate and integrate programs across HHS that relate to emergency, bioterrorism- and public-health preparedness. In addition, the Secretary of HHS should increase the capabilities of the regional emergency-coordination officers in the field and direct them to coordinate efforts with the regional NPRA offices.

• The Secretary of DHS and the Secretary of HHS should enter into a formal memorandum of understanding between the two agencies specifically describing how the departments will coordinate ESF-8 (Public Health and Medical Services) resources on all aspects of preparedness and deployment, as well as clearly defining responsibility for logistical, security, and other support, including mortuary activities, required by health care facilities and organizations providing emergency medical care in a disaster or catastrophe.

• DHS, in conjunction with HHS, should develop and implement a system to identify, deploy and track federal public health and medical assets (human, fixed, and materiel) used in preparation for or response to national disasters and catastrophes.

• The National Disaster Medical System (NDMS) is a critical medical-response asset whose capabilities must be increased. In particular, the Secretary of DHS should develop a strategic plan and a management structure that recognizes the unique nature of NDMS teams (i.e., highly skilled, all-volunteer staff and outside-sponsor relationships). This should include providing adequate resources to equip, staff, and train NDMS teams; improving transportation, logistics, and communications capabilities; and developing more effective management-support team capability. NDMS should remain in DHS – possibly reporting to the Chief Medical Officer (CMO) – but should coordinate closely with HHS in preparing for disaster response.

Recommendation 17: DOJ and DHS should inventory their law-enforcement assets and identify other available assets, including units with particular skill sets, in advance of a domestic incident. Planning for the deployment of law-enforcement personnel should include how to transport officers to the affected region, which may require coordination with the Department of Defense and the Department of Transportation. Planning also should include arrangements to provide personnel with food, sheltering, supplies, and vehicles once they arrive. Federal law-enforcement units should be self-sustaining so that they do not impose any additional burden on state and local responders.

Recommendation 18: Federal agencies and departments, including DOD, HHS, and DOJ, should work with DHS to create an inventory of physical and support assets within the agencies and departments that can be used in responding to disasters. For assets most likely to be used in responding to future disasters, DHS should develop pre-scripted Mission Assignments/Requests for Assistance (MAs/RFAs). The purpose of the pre-scripted MAs/RFAs should be to expedite the submission and approval of MAs/RFAs and the provision of commonly requested assets and support in the event of a disaster. These MAs/RFAs should include provisions to pre-position assets and personnel.

Recommendation 19: The NPRA, through the National Communications System (NCS), should develop a database for monitoring the inventory of all federal, including DOD and, where appropriate, private-sector communications equipment that can be deployed following a catastrophic incident to assist first responders and restore commercial communications services. In addition, DHS should maintain an inventory of what federal resources are necessary to support the deployment and operation of such assets.

Recommendation 20: DHS should work with all federal departments and agencies with responsibilities under the NRP, including the ESFs, to pre-identify areas in policy, doctrine, and guidance that can be streamlined, or that provide an opportunity for regulatory flexibility, where appropriate or necessary during a disaster or catastrophe. DHS should ensure that policies and procedures provide emergency-management experts sufficient regulatory and policy flexibility so that they are empowered to make decisions that are critical to a quick and effective response during a catastrophic event. For example, during a catastrophe, it may be appropriate to waive certain training requirements.

Recommendation 21: NPRA should develop data-sharing arrangements with other federal agencies and other appropriate organizations, prior to the next disaster, to more effectively respond to disasters, while protecting privacy and protecting against waste, fraud, and abuse. For example:

> • A data-sharing agreement between NPRA, HHS, DOJ, and other appropriate organizations (such as the National Center for Missing and Exploited Children) could facilitate tracking missing children and adults and reunifying families separated during evacuation. These data-sharing arrangements should have protections in place to address privacy concerns and to comply with child-custody agreements.
>
> • A data-sharing agreement between NPRA and the Social Security Administration would allow NPRA to ensure that a disaster victim registering for assistance is using a valid Social Security number, helping to prevent fraudulent registrations.

Recommendation 22: The lack of easily understandable, policy-based, field operations guides available to responders at all levels contributed to misunderstandings and inefficiencies, and degraded overall operations. DHS should develop and publish a comprehensive Federal Disaster Field Operations Guide and make the guide available to all federal, state, and local response officials, so that all responders are better informed of what to expect from federal agency operations.

NGO and Private-Sector Involvement

Recommendation 23: DHS should coordinate with the private sector and NGOs at the state, regional, and national level to incorporate those entities, where appropriate, into their planning, training, and exercises, to the greatest extent possible.

Recommendation 24: There needs to be a balance, even in a time of disaster, between procuring essential goods and services and maintaining fairness and reasonableness in the procurement process to the extent possible.

> • The federal government should establish pre-negotiated contracts for priority resources prior to disasters, especially in the areas of food, water, ice, fuel distribution, and housing. DHS should include provisions in pre-negotiated contracts to provide the surge capacity needed to respond to catastrophic disasters.
>
> • The federal government, working with the private sector, should develop standard-form agreements tailored for various needs to facilitate faster procurement for disaster relief operations.
>
> • The federal government should consider expanding the cooperative purchasing authority of state and local governments to use all of the General Services Administration (GSA) Schedules (not just Information Technology Schedule 70), for the purchase of goods and services that are designed to facilitate response to and recovery from a presidentially declared disaster or catastrophe. Under the expanded authority, state and local governments would use the same procedures as GSA already has adopted for IT Schedule 70 cooperative purchasing.

Recommendation 25: DHS should develop a policy for accepting and directing corporate in-kind donations. The U.S. Department of State, in coordination with DHS, should develop a policy for accepting and directing foreign donations.

Technological Support

Communications and Interoperability

Recommendation 26: DHS should develop a national strategy, including timeframes, for implementing a survivable and resilient national interoperable-communications network. DHS should establish a plan to migrate to the use of (1) interoperable platforms for communications networks; (2) equipment that permits sharing of resources in times of crisis; and (3) systems to promote high-precedence data communications and interoperability during disasters so that information such as medical, victim registration, and Geographic Information Systems (GIS) data can be electronically shared among responders, as needed, at all levels of government. This process of developing a national strategy should recognize existing state plans and provide a mechanism for states to collaborate on interoperability and the ability to provide emergency assistance to other states through shared communications resources. DHS should condition the award of grants for public-safety communications equipment on their being used to purchase interoperable communications systems that operate under open-architecture standards developed by the SAFECOM unit within DHS.

Recommendation 27: The NPRA, through the regional Strike Teams, should coordinate with NCS, state-level ESF-2 (Communications) agencies, and private-sector partners to be prepared to deploy in an emergency to facilitate reestablishment of public and private communications systems that work across jurisdictions. This should be done with the recognition that maintaining and/or reestablishing communications capabilities is critical to an effective emergency response. Although most of the physical damage to telecommunications equipment may occur in a central area, it can adversely affect large portions of the surrounding areas. DHS should take a lead role to facilitate and encourage cooperation among local jurisdictions to address mutual restoration and redundant routing that will help create a more resilient network to aid public-safety first responders.

Recommendation 28: DHS should strengthen its mobile emergency-response teams' (now incorporated into the regional Strike Teams) ability to provide communications support during disasters. DHS should acquire and position at regional offices mobile-communications suites or caches of secure, interoperable emergency-communications equipment and systems that can be deployed when normal land line, mobile, and radio systems are disrupted or destroyed, as does the National Interagency Fire Center.

Recommendation 29: The NPRA, through NCS, should work with all communications providers to encourage development of and adherence to best practices to ensure reliability in the event of a disaster, or quick restoration of services and facilities in the event service is disrupted. These best practices should address, among other things, (1) maintaining service during extended commercial power outages through the use of back-up generators and equipment; (2) building communications towers, transmitters, and repeaters to withstand a severe storm; and (3) implementing regional, interoperable communications networks that would increase the survivability of communications by allowing first responders' radios to operate via towers in a neighboring jurisdiction that survived the disaster. DHS and state and local governments should develop plans for better direct, redundant lines of communications between the emergency-operations centers used by all levels of government.

Recommendation 30: States should be encouraged to purchase communications systems such as satellite phones that can operate when land-based infrastructures are damaged or destroyed.

Recommendation 31: DHS should work with state and local officials to encourage 911 call centers to develop plans to route calls to other centers in case the center is not functional and should encourage the inclusion of 911 communicators in Emergency Management Assistance Compacts (EMACs).

Information Systems

Recommendation 32: DHS should adopt a common computer-software standard for use by all federal and state entities involved in incident management that will serve as the information architecture for shared situational and operational awareness. Based on this standard, the Homeland Security Information Network (HSIN) may be improved, or a new system may need to be developed. The system might include a Geographic Information System capability to support functions such as tracking commodities, Search and Rescue (SAR), and status of evacuation shelters, among others.

Recommendation 33: DHS should refine and streamline the Action Request Form (ARF) system (through which state and local governments request disaster-related assistance from the federal government) and work with state and local governments to ensure that federal and state systems are compatible and provide for seamless interfacing.

Recommendation 34: DHS should complete and/or adopt technology and information-management systems to effectively manage disaster-related activities. DHS should develop an efficient ordering system that minimizes delays and provides order-status visibility and accurate, timely commodity tracking, and a transportation protocol that moves commodities and resources directly from the supplier to the usage area.

Recommendation 35: The states, in coordination with DHS, DOJ, HHS and other appropriate agencies and organizations, should establish evacuee-registration systems to facilitate reunification of family members separated as a result of a disaster or catastrophe. DHS should work with the states to encourage development of systems that can share data across states, including the use of a model intake form with standard information to be collected.

Recommendation 36: Given the importance of providing as much warning as possible to coastal populations in the event of a major hurricane, the National Oceanographic and Atmospheric Administration (NOAA) and the National Hurricane Center (NHC) should review their protocols for issuing hurricane advisories and related forecast products to ensure that critical information is made available to the public as soon as possible, in a form that is as complete and understandable as possible. Further, NOAA and the NHC should identify any technical or resource constraints that limit their ability to do so.

Recommendation 37: Because storm surge is historically the most deadly element in major hurricanes, NOAA and the NHC should examine the use of additional forecasting models, such as the Advanced Circulation Model (ADCIRC) sponsored by the U.S. Army Corps of Engineers (the Corps), to provide additional confidence and perspective to their periodic modeling and publication of storm-surge projections and pre-landfall storm-surge forecasts, as is currently done for forecasting hurricane intensity and track. As part of this review, the NHC should also reexamine its practice of making pre-landfall storm-surge forecasts for major hurricanes no earlier than 24 hours before landfall.

Recommendation 38: NOAA, utilizing expertise within the NWS, the NHC, and the National Geodetic Survey, should routinely revise its models and published impacts of hurricane storm-surge projections to take into account changes in modeling and forecasting technology and regional conditions, such as regional subsidence, loss of coastal wetlands, and sea-level rise. Changes in projected impacts as a result of such revisions should be clearly documented and published.

Readiness

Planning, Training, and Exercising

Recommendation 39: DHS should ensure that the NRP becomes more than just words on paper – it must be operationalized if it is to be effectively executed in response to disasters and catastrophes. In doing so, DHS should direct all federal departments and agencies with responsibilities in the NRP, including DOD, in the completion of a coordinated, operational, federal disaster-response plan that is then exercised, with lessons learned incorporated into a revised plan. DHS should simultaneously coordinate with the states to ensure that the states' emergency-response plans are aligned with the NRP, including ESF responsibilities, to the highest degree possible and exercised, with lessons learned incorporated into a revised plan, and should provide necessary support for any additional planning required to achieve this level of preparedness. DHS should lead an effort, coordinated with the states, to develop response plans for specific geographic regions and for specific types of high-risk events that will augment the NRP and provide additional operational detail.

Recommendation 40: Federal departments and agencies with responsibilities under the NRP should be required to conduct exercises to ensure that their plans are continually revised and updated. The exercises should include broad, all-encompassing federal disaster and catastrophic exercises. DHS, in conjunction with DOD, other federal agencies, and state and local participants should stage exercises simulating a large-scale catastrophe to improve the training for all personnel, familiarize responding agencies with one another's personnel and capabilities, address issues of command and control, and improve the working relationships between DHS and other response agencies.

Recommendation 41: Emergency agencies at the federal, state, and local levels of government, as well as first-responder groups outside of government, should receive regular training on NRP and NIMS, integrating the ESF structure, including statutorily required exercises and simulations to expose unaddressed challenges, provide feedback about progress, and maintain pressure to improve. These exercises and simulations should be objectively assessed by an independent evaluator. DHS should consider tying future cost-share requirements for preparedness grant funds to performance and results of these exercises.

Protecting Against Waste, Fraud, and Abuse

Recommendation 42: Fraud related to disaster assistance and contracting is not tolerable. DHS should work with DOJ and other federal agencies to ensure that a cooperative effort is made to investigate and prosecute fraud. DHS should also strengthen controls on the Individuals and Households Program (IHP), and other programs where appropriate, to reduce fraud and abuse, while continuing to offer speedy assistance and relief to the true victims of a disaster.

Recommendation 43: In a disaster where the government is entering into contracts and other procurement vehicles (grants, cooperative agreements, direct purchase orders, etc.) quickly and with expedited procedures and oversight, it is all the more important that the agencies making these procurements be thoroughly committed to full transparency. This transparency must occur from the outset so that waste, fraud, abuse, or simple mismanagement or inefficiency can be identified before additional financial liability is incurred by the taxpayers. There is no federal dollar that is spent on disaster relief and recovery for which the government is not accountable to taxpayers. DHS should:

- Ensure that NPRA has sufficient contracting staff to handle the flow of disaster assistance and should identify and train procurement staff from other agencies who can provide additional surge capacity.

- Develop procurement plans, based on past experience, for a variety of disaster scenarios and use those plans as a guide in future disasters so that spending is not simply reactive.

- Engage in more rigorous procurement planning and execution to ensure that one or more competitively awarded technical-assistance contracts are always in place.

- Improve acquisition-process accountability post-disaster, discouraging and strictly reviewing sole-source and no-bid contracts (where necessary), as well as reviewing purchase decisions by the government that appear excessive, unwise, or poorly managed.

- Make non-proprietary information related to disaster-related procurements available to the general public in an easily accessible format.

Evacuation and Sheltering

Recommendation 44: As the primary federal agency under ESF-1 (Transportation), the Department of Transportation, in coordination with DHS, should:

- Develop plans to assist in conducting mass evacuations when an effective evacuation is beyond the capabilities, or is likely to be beyond the capabilities, of the state and affected local governments. DOT should develop plans to quickly deploy transportation assets to an area in need of mass evacuation. DHS should, in coordination with DOT, assist state and affected local governments in evacuating populations when requested.

- In coordination with the states, plan, train, and exercise for evacuations including medical patients and others with special needs, in coordination with other relevant federal agencies, the American Red Cross, and state and local partners. DOT should consider using a variety of transportation modes, including air medical services.

- Work with state and local emergency planners – in particular, state and local agencies charged with ESF-1 responsibilities – to help them assess the resources needed to assist with evacuations, those that are locally available, and what shortfalls exist; determine unique geographical/demographic obstacles to evacuation in particular areas; and develop catalogues of regionally available evacuation-related assets, including transit agencies from various municipalities.

- Establish liaisons with ESF-6 (Mass Care, Housing, and Human Services) to coordinate sheltering destinations for evacuees from various areas, and work with ESF-13 (Public Safety and Security) to ensure that air, bus, and other transportation providers have appropriate security escorts to ensure safety during evacuation activities.

Recommendation 45: All evacuation plans must provide for populations that do not have the means to evacuate. DHS and DOT should make available assistance to state and local governments for developing plans to ensure that the nation's most vulnerable citizens are not left behind in a disaster.

Recommendation 46: DHS should support state and local governments in planning, training, and exercising evacuation plans and ensure that these plans address the challenges posed by evacuating hospitals, nursing homes, and individuals with special needs.

Recommendation 47: DHS, in conjunction with HHS, DOD, the U.S. Department of Veterans Affairs (VA), and state and local partners in the patient-movement system, should develop a specific concept of operations (CONOP), training and outreach programs, and patient triage and tracking capabilities to execute domestic patient movement/evacuations utilizing the NDMS patient-movement capability. Non-governmental emergency-response and emergency-management entities, including private air medical services, should be integrated into the planning and response process.

Recommendation 48: DHS and DOT should support state and local governments in developing evacuation plans that prevent, to the extent practicable, families being separated from one another during an evacuation and that facilitate rapid reunification in the event that families are separated.

Recommendation 49: DHS should coordinate with DOT to annually evaluate state evacuation plans, as well as evacuation plans for large urban areas.

Recommendation 50: DHS should encourage individuals, and state and local governments to plan for evacuating and sheltering pets.

> • Due to various health, safety, and other concerns, pets may be separated from their owners during transportation or sheltering. State and local agencies should work with animal-welfare organizations to develop procedures for animal identification and processing to facilitate the return of the pets to their owners.
>
> • State and local agencies should establish memorandums of understanding with animal- welfare organizations to ensure their assistance with the transport, sheltering, and rescue of pets.
>
> • State and local evacuation plans should include consideration of transportation and sheltering of pets owned by residents in need of transportation or shelter themselves.

Search and Rescue

Recommendation 51: Signatory agencies to the National Search and Rescue Plan should develop a comprehensive plan for search and rescue in a multi-environment disaster. The plan should provide for a unified coordination structure, with subordinate coordination of air, land, and water-borne assets, and should establish the means for obtaining the necessary assets and personnel. The plan should also provide for a unified communications network, a common grid-reference system, and standardized procedures and methods for utilizing and sharing local situational awareness acquired by search and rescue operational units.

Recommendation 52: Policies, plans, and procedures, as defined by the National Search and Rescue Plan, need to be incorporated into personnel recovery training at the operational and strategic levels of NORTHCOM and, as appropriate, PACOM, so that DOD can more effectively participate in future domestic mass-rescue operations.

Mitigation

Recommendation 53: In order to protect coastal areas from becoming increasingly vulnerable to damage from hurricanes, ecological-restoration efforts must be integrated into hurricane protection in a comprehensive manner that addresses the root causes of ongoing ecological and geological processes, such as the loss of coastal wetlands and regional subsidence.

Recommendation 54: Future decision making regarding the Mississippi River-Gulf Outlet (MRGO) and other navigation channels should recognize, account for, and mitigate not only the direct role that navigation channels can play in increasing, speeding, or transferring storm surges, but also the impact of the channels on wetland loss and the coastal environment, and the resulting long-term implications for hurricane vulnerability.

Recommendation 55: DHS, with the participation of the Corps, the U.S. Department of the Interior, NOAA, and other relevant agencies, should establish an interagency review board, including state and local officials, to examine the level of vulnerability of communities located in floodplains and coastal regions to hurricanes and floods, and specifically examine the adequacy of existing and planned flood and hurricane protection for levees and flood-control structures, the contribution of environmental and ecological conditions, and the impact of non-structural programs, such as the federal flood-insurance program and pre- and post-disaster mitigation programs.

Credentialing

Recommendation 56: DHS should ensure that all federal emergency-response personnel from federal departments and agencies with responsibilities under the NRP have a standard credential (a Red Card system) that details the emergency-management positions the person is qualified for based on measurable criteria, performance, objectives and standards so that they may easily integrate into emergency response operations. DHS should coordinate with state governments to ensure that all state emergency-response personnel from departments and agencies with responsibilities under the state emergency-response plan, and volunteers, also have a standard credential based on the same credentialing system.

Recommendation 57: HHS, in conjunction with DHS, should lead a federal, state, and local initiative to roster and credential, in a centralized or linked manner, medical personnel and volunteers (National Disaster Medical System, Medical Reserve Corps, U.S. Public Health Service, etc.) to ensure that in case of national emergencies, properly qualified medical providers are quickly identified and are able to gain appropriate access to the affected area.

Recommendation 58: Private-sector telecommunications, utility, critical infrastructure, and other private entities should be included in emergency-response planning and be assured appropriate access to disaster areas to repair critical infrastructure and restore essential services. DHS should coordinate with federal, state, local, and other emergency management officials to develop a standardized national credential that would allow emergency management professionals, first responders, and other response personnel from the private sector access to disaster areas, as appropriate.

Professional and Public Education

Recommendation 59: DHS should, during the transition to the NPRA organizational structure, conduct an agency-wide training assessment (inventory) of the current state of capabilities to meet the FEMA/NPRA mission. Based on this assessment, DHS should develop and implement strategies, including appropriate incentives and rewards, to recruit, retain, and build a cadre of trained, practiced, and experienced professional emergency-response professionals; develop career paths that reward and promote individuals who have served in multiple state and federal agencies with emergency-management responsibilities; and, as part of the NPRA career track, require all personnel to engage in continuous learning and education.

Recommendation 60: DHS should establish and maintain a Homeland Security Academy to:

- Develop and provide a course of instruction on Homeland Security matters, including the nation's emergency-preparedness and response system, to meet the specific needs of political officials (Cabinet officials, agency heads, governors, mayors, and other federal, state and local officials) who must provide leadership during emergency-response operations; and

• Develop and provide a course of instruction, and maintain a Web-based "lessons recognized-lessons learned" and best-practices program that can be accessed by emergency-management professionals at the federal, state, and local levels.

Recommendation 61: DHS should strengthen and expand the Emergency Management Institute's (EMI) courses for emergency-management personnel. In order to reach the widest audience, EMI should develop "train the trainer" courses to expedite building a cadre of emergency-management experts around the country. Course schedules should be designed around the heaviest emergency "seasons," so that experienced instructors are available to teach the courses.

Recommendation 62: DHS should develop and implement a comprehensive strategy to develop a culture of preparedness in America. DHS should coordinate with state and local officials to ensure that emergency plans are community-based and include outreach and education to the public, through community and faith-based organizations and other institutions to promote individual preparedness based on the risks in their communities. This information should be widely distributed in languages appropriate to the relevant constituencies.

Special Needs Awareness

Recommendation 63: DHS should ensure and direct that all federal departments and agencies with responsibilities under the NRP, including the ESFs, take into consideration the special needs of persons with physical, mental, and other disabilities, the most vulnerable and those least able to help themselves, in their response and recovery plans. DHS should coordinate with state and local governments to ensure that their response and recovery plans also address persons with special needs.

Recommendation 64: DHS should coordinate with the private sector and NGOs, including the American Red Cross, to ensure that the response and recovery plans of those participating in emergency-preparedness and response operations take into consideration the special needs of persons with physical, mental, and other disabilities.

Military Preparations

Recommendation 65: DOD should continue to provide the Commander, U.S. Northern Command (NORTHCOM) and, as appropriate, the Commander, U.S. Pacific Command (PACOM), with authority to assign DCOs and Defense Coordinating Elements, and identify staging bases as necessary and prudent, to provide anticipated support for a domestic emergency or catastrophe. DOD should expand this authority to include the ability to deploy pre-packaged or pre-identified basic response assets (such as helicopters, boats, medical supplies and personnel, food and water, and communications equipment). DOD should develop procedures and guidelines for pre-positioning assets.

Recommendation 66: DOD should make the position of DCO in NPRA regional offices a full-time assignment for senior officers. The DCO should receive training and education on DOD's role under the NRP, and should coordinate closely with DHS, NORTHCOM, and PACOM, as appropriate, and state officials in plans, training, and exercises.

Recommendation 67: NPRA should work with DOD and the state governors to assist them in developing an integrated plan for the deployment of National Guard units and personnel in state status when large-scale military support is requested by a state to respond to a catastrophic incident or disaster. The plan should include a process for identification of National Guard units with the capabilities required to respond to the incident or disaster, and should take into account the availability of National Guard units for mobilization for national-defense missions. The plan should include expedited procedures for requesting and approving federal funding under Title 32, United States Code, for National Guard forces employed in accordance with the plan, and procedures for DOD and the governors, during a catastrophe, to coordinate the process of matching units and capabilities of National Guard forces with the requirements of the governors. The integrated plan should ensure that there is sufficient command and control and reception, staging and onward integration capability for any such large-scale National Guard deployment.

Recommendation 68: In developing a federal catastrophic-disaster response plan, DHS should work with DOD to develop a plan for the employment of active-duty units and personnel when wide-scale military support is requested by a state or ordered by the President to respond to a catastrophic incident or disaster. The plan should include a process for identification of active-duty units with the capabilities required to respond to the incident or disaster, include planning for reception, staging and onward integration of the active-duty forces and commodities distribution, and should, via the National Guard Bureau, take into account the availability and capability of National Guard units.

Recommendation 69: DHS, DOD, and the states should develop detailed operational plans for Defense Support to Civil Authorities (DSCA) missions, including specific plans for response to hurricanes, wildfires, earthquakes, pandemics, and other natural disasters.

Recommendation 70: DOD and the States should develop the systems and processes of communication, coordination, and command and control, to ensure unity of effort when National Guard and Title 10 forces are deployed in integrated disaster-response missions.

Recommendation 71: NORTHCOM and the National Guard Bureau should coordinate to expand the presence of the National Guard Bureau at NORTHCOM and integrate National Guard Bureau officials into NORTHCOM's planning, training, exercising, and responding to an incident or disaster.

Recommendation 72: DOD should require that officers selected for general-officer or flag rank are trained on the NRP, NIMS, ICS, and DOD's Defense Support to Civil Authorities (DSCA) missions.

State and Local Preparations

Recommendation 73: At least annually, state emergency-preparedness offices should audit plans of agencies with ESF responsibilities under the state's emergency-operations plan to ensure they: (1) take an all-hazards approach to emergency management; (2) comprehensively address the agency's ESF responsibilities; (3) are up-to-date; and (4) include provisions for regular training and exercising. Governors should require their state emergency-preparedness offices to then report to them the state of the emergency-preparedness office, all supporting agencies, and the state emergency-operations plan. The audit should review, at a minimum:

- Realistic, comprehensive evacuation plans to provide for the safety of the state's population in a disaster, especially those who lack their own transportation or have physical, mental, or other disabilities;

- The staffing needs of agencies with emergency-operations responsibilities and long-range plans to attract and maintain qualified staff;

- Laws, regulations, and plans to ensure clear responsibilities for ordering evacuations and to address liability issues that may be impediments to evacuation orders;

• Laws, regulations, and plans that clarify the governor's authority to assume control of emergency response where local governments' response capabilities are significantly damaged;

• Pre-contracting for emergency supplies to address needs of shelters in disaster-stricken areas; plans for sheltering and then evacuating people who have remained in an area struck by a disaster; and evaluations of the capacity, suitability, and structural strength of shelters in the state;

• Plans for alternative means of distributing commodities in situations where distribution through central distribution points may not be possible;

• Plans that outline resource needs, such as volunteers for emergency support functions, transportation providers, and medical supplies, and where they will be obtained when disaster strikes;

• Plans under ESF-9 (Urban Search and Rescue) of the state emergency operations plan, to ensure there is appropriate equipment and resources, based on the state's terrain and risks, to effectively carry out this function; and

• Plans for ensuring the protection of vital records, whether paper or electronic, such as property titles, court-case files, and driver's license and voter information.

Recommendation 74: States should coordinate with the NPRA to assess or upgrade their logistics-management capabilities and address any asset-tracking deficiencies.

Recommendation 75: States should coordinate through the NPRA regional offices to develop plans adequate to address shelter needs in a catastrophe or when needs exceed a state's capacity.

Recommendation 76: State and local governments should review and resolve, to the extent possible, legal and operational issues incident to the issuance of evacuation orders, and should be prepared to issue a mandatory-evacuation order quickly in the event of a disaster.

Recommendation 77: States with high-risk urban areas should develop multi-phased evacuation plans that provide for the speediest evacuation of residents most at risk, particularly those who lack the means to evacuate on their own. States with high-risk urban areas should consider whether a contraflow plan is advisable, and if so, should develop agreements with bordering states to secure their participation in the contraflow plan. Neighboring political entities should work together to coordinate evacuation plans in advance, and state and local governments should publicize their evacuation plans and ensure that citizens are familiar with one or more evacuation options. States whose location puts them at high risk of recurring hurricanes and tropical storms should use updated storm-surge estimates to establish evacuation zones and evacuation-clearance times. States whose locations put them at risk of other types of natural disasters should evaluate those risks and consider evacuation zones and clearance times in line with them.

Recommendation 78: States should develop estimates of populations that will require short-term sheltering in the event of a catastrophic event. This estimate should particularly focus on special-needs populations. In consultation with NPRA, states should then develop plans for providing shelter for these estimated populations. Such plans should include a way to create a voluntary database of people in the shelters so victims can be accounted for. States should develop a catastrophic medical-response plan that is integrated with its evacuation and shelter plan and documents the availability of nurses and health-care professionals with emergency medical and trauma training in the state.

Recommendation 79: States should establish neighborhood pre- and post-disaster information centers at schools, shopping centers, places of worship, and other community institutions, to provide information on evacuations and the location of disaster assistance sites.

Recommendation 80: States should ensure that effective communications lines and information-sharing systems exist between the state emergency operations centers and all facilities or mobile units that provide medical care or other assistance to victims of a catastrophic event.

Recommendation 81: State agencies responsible for licensing of hospitals and nursing homes should ensure those facilities have evacuation plans and audit them annually, including evaluation of availability of transportation resources, to verify that they are viable.

Recommendation 82: State agencies responsible for special-needs shelters, working with local counterparts and emergency-support organizations, should consider developing and maintaining a voluntary database of special-needs persons residing in the area.

Recommendation 83: The EMAC system should (1) be refined to pre-certify qualified out-of-state first responders, such as those with specialized skills like search and rescue or medical services, in order to shorten the response time; (2) develop National Guard civil affairs support teams trained in continuity of government operations (these could be the same teams that are already constituted for a weapons of mass destruction (WMD) event); (3) streamline the required paperwork process; and (4) streamline the deputization process with regard to various law-enforcement agencies that may assist during the disaster response.

Levees

Recommendation 84: The Interagency Performance Evaluation Taskforce (IPET), along with the American Society of Civil Engineers (ASCE) External Review Panel (ERP), should be continued beyond the scope of the current task and should have the ongoing responsibility to evaluate and review the design, construction, operation, reconstruction, and improvements to the hurricane-protection levee system in southeast Louisiana. Formal charters for the IPET and the ASCE ERP should be created for this purpose and should ensure that the IPET process is independent from the U.S. Army Corps of Engineers' operational organizations. The independent review task forces should be extended to other levee systems that protect significant population centers throughout the country.

Recommendation 85: The Corps, in conjunction with the State of Louisiana, the local levee districts, and other relevant federal, state, and local agencies, should assume responsibility for development of a comprehensive emergency plan for the hurricane-protection and Mississippi River levees systems, including high-water accidents, breaches, and floods. Current plans, including, but not limited to, the New Orleans Unwatering Plan, must be re-examined and brought into conformance with this comprehensive plan. The emergency plan must address incident command, interoperable communications, repair, and flood-fighting resources, monitoring of levee conditions, the acquisition of assets or alternative arrangements that allow the Corps to have real-time (or close to real-time) situational awareness of levee and flood conditions in the New Orleans area, and reporting and exercise procedures.

Recommendation 86: The Corps and local levee sponsors should immediately clarify and memorialize responsibilities and procedures for the turn-over of projects to local sponsors, and for operations and maintenance, including, but not limited to, procedures for the repair or correction of levee conditions that reduce the level of protection below the original design level (due to subsidence or other factors) and also emergency response. It must always be clear – to all parties involved – which entity is ultimately in charge of each stage of each project. The Corps should also provide real-time information to the public on the level of protection afforded by the levee system. A mechanism should be included for the public to report potential problems and provide general feedback to the Corps.

Recommendation 87: In states where applicable, governors should ensure that the equivalent of ESF-3 (Public Works and Engineering) of the state emergency plan is clarified to ensure that hurricane-protection levee systems and other flood-control infrastructures within the state are included within the definition of critical infrastructure, that a designated state agency is responsible for ensuring that state and local agencies and levee districts prepare for, and are able to respond to, emergencies involving these structures, whether they are directly owned by the state or not, and that the designated state agency executes this responsibility.

Recommendation 88: State statutes governing the operation of levee districts, such as preparation of emergency plans and training for levee board members and staff, must be re-examined and revised to ensure that levee districts exercise state-of-the art care and inspection of levees and are prepared to meet their primary obligation of flood protection and respond to emergencies. The inspection regime should include the use of advanced inspection techniques that are commensurate with the potential threat to life and property posed by the failure of a flood control project.

---

1 While the entirety of DHS's Preparedness Directorate would become part of NPRA, we continue to review the appropriate placement of individual offices (e.g., Infrastructure Protection, the Chief Medical Officer, and Cyber- and Telecommunications).

Appendix 1
Common Acronyms

(All agencies named are federal, unless otherwise noted)

ARF	Action Request Form
ATF	Bureau of Alcohol, Tobacco, Firearms and Explosives
CBP	Customs and Border Protection (DHS)
CDC	Centers for Disease Control and Prevention
CDT	Central Daylight Time
CEMP	Comprehensive Emergency Management Plan
CT	Central Time
DAE	Disaster Assistance Employee (FEMA)
DCO	Defense Coordinating Officer
DHH	Department of Health and Hospitals (Louisiana)
DHS	Department of Homeland Security
DLA	Defense Logistics Agency
DMAT	Disaster Medical Assistance Team
DMORT	Disaster Mortuary Operational Response Team
DOD	Department of Defense
DOI	Department of the Interior
DOJ	Department of Justice
DOT	Department of Transportation
DOTD	Department of Transportation and Development (Louisiana)
DSCA	Defense Support to Civil Authorities
DTE	Disaster Temporary Employees
EDT	Eastern Daylight Time
EMAC	Emergency Management Assistance Compact
EMS	Emergency Medical Services
EOC	Emergency Operations Center
EOP	Emergency Operations Plan
ERT	Emergency Response Team
ERT-A	Emergency Response Team, Advance Element
ERT-N	Emergency Response Team, National
ESF	Emergency Support Function
ESG	Expeditionary Strike Group
ET	Eastern Time
FBI	Federal Bureau of Investigation
FCO	Federal Coordinating Officer

FEMA . . . . Federal Emergency Management Agency

FIRST . . . . First Incident Response Support Team

FMS . . . . Federal Medical Shelter

FOSA . . . . Federal Operational Staging Area

FPS . . . . Federal Protective Service

FRAGO . . . . Fragmentary Order

FRP . . . . Federal Response Plan

GAO . . . . Government Accountability Office (pre-2004, the General Accounting Office)

GIWW . . . . Gulf Intracoastal Waterway

GSA . . . . General Services Administration

HHS . . . . Department of Health and Human Services

HQ . . . . Headquarters

HRSA . . . . Health Resources and Services Administration

HSC . . . . Homeland Security Council

HSGAC . . . . Homeland Security and Governmental Affairs Committee

HSOC . . . . Homeland Security Operations Center

HSPD . . . . Homeland Security Presidential Directive

IATAC . . . . Individual Assistance Technical Assistance Contract

ICCOH . . . . Interagency Coordinating Committee on Hurricanes

ICE . . . . Immigration and Customs Enforcement

ICS . . . . Incident Command System

IEM . . . . Innovative Emergency Management, Inc.

IIMG . . . . Interagency Incident Management Group

IPET . . . . Interagency Performance Evaluation Taskforce

JDOMS . . . . Joint Directorate of Military Support

JFO . . . . Joint Field Office

JIC . . . . Joint Information Center

JIS . . . . Joint Information System

JOC . . . . Joint Operations Center

JTF . . . . Joint Task Force

LA DOTD . . . . Louisiana Department of Transportation and Development

LANG . . . . Louisiana Army National Guard

LEEP . . . . Louisiana Emergency Evacuation Plan

LNHA . . . . Louisiana Nursing Home Association

LOEP . . . . Louisiana Office of Emergency Preparedness (became LOHSEP in 2003)

LOHSEP . . . . Louisiana Office of Homeland Security and Emergency Preparedness (as of March 2006, Governor's Office of Homeland Security and Emergency Preparedness, or GOHSEP)

LSP . . . . Louisiana State Police

LSU . . . . Louisiana State University

MACDIS . . . . Military Assistance for Civil Disturbances

MA . . . . Mission Assignment

MDH . . . . Mississippi Department of Health

MDHS . . . . Mississippi Department of Human Services

MDOT . . . . Mississippi Department of Transportation

MEMA . . . . Mississippi Emergency Management Agency

MERS . . . . Mobile Emergency Response Support

MEU . . . . Marine Expeditionary Unit

MOU . . . . Memorandum of Understanding

MRE . . . . Meal Ready to Eat

MRGO . . . . Mississippi River Gulf Outlet

MST . . . . Management Support Team

NCS . . . . National Communications System

NDMS . . . . National Disaster Medical System

NEMA . . . . National Emergency Management Association

NEMS . . . . National Emergency Management System

NGO . . . . Non-governmental organization

NHC . . . . National Hurricane Center

NIMS . . . . National Incident Management System

NOAA . . . . National Oceanic and Atmospheric Administration

NOC . . . . National Operations Center

NOFD . . . . New Orleans Fire Department

NOOEP . . . . New Orleans Office of Emergency Planning

NOPD . . . . New Orleans Police Department

NORTHCOM . . . . Northern Command

NRCC . . . . National Response Coordination Center

NRP-CIA . . . . National Response Plan – Catastrophic Incident Annex

NRP-CIS . . . . National Response Plan – Catastrophic Incident Supplement

NSF . . . . National Science Foundation

NWC . . . . National Weather Center

NWS . . . . National Weather Service

O&M . . . . Operations & Maintenance

OEP . . . . Office of Emergency Preparedness

OFRD . . . . Office of Force Readiness and Deployment (HHS)

OPHEP . . . . Office of Public Health and Emergency Preparedness (HHS)

PACOM . . . . Pacific Command

PFO . . . . Principal Federal Official

PHS . . . . Public Health Service

POD . . . . Point of Distribution

PSA. . . . . Protective Security Advisor

RFA. . . . . Request for Assistance

RRCC . . . . Regional Response Coordination Center

RTA. . . . . Regional Transit Authority (New Orleans)

SAC. . . . . Special Agent in Charge

SAR . . . . Search and Rescue

SARBOO. . . . . Search-and-Rescue Base of Operations

SERT. . . . . Secretary's Emergency Response Team (HHS)

SFLEO. . . . . Senior Federal Law Enforcement Officials

SLOSH . . . . Sea, Lake, and Overland Surges from Hurricanes (NHC software)

SNS. . . . . Strategic National Stockpile

SPH. . . . . Standard Project Hurricane

TMOSA. . . . . Temporary Medical-and-Operations Staging Area

TOPOFF 3. . . . . Top Officials 3 (DHS Conference)

TRANSCOM . . . . Transportation Command

USAR . . . . Urban Search and Rescue

USPHS . . . . U.S. Public Health Service

UTC. . . . . Universal Time Coordinated, Coordinated Universal Time (See Z)

VMAT . . . . Veterinary Medical Assistance Team

VOAD . . . . Voluntary Organizations Active in Disaster

VTC. . . . . Video teleconference

W&F . . . . Department of Wildlife & Fisheries (Louisiana)

WFO . . . . Weather Forecast Office

WLF . . . . Department of Wildlife and Fisheries

Z . . . . Zulu Time (also known as Greenwich Mean Time and UTC; standard time at zero degrees longitude, five hours later than U.S. East Coast time; usually given on a 24-hour clock basis where 7 a.m. is 0700 hours, noon is 1200 hours, 10:30 p.m. is 2030 hours, etc.)

Appendix 2
Emergency Support Functions (ESFs)

"The ESFs provide the structure for coordinating Federal interagency support for Incidents of National Significance. The ESF structure includes mechanisms used to provide Federal support to States and Federal-to-Federal support, both for declared disasters and emergencies under the Stafford Act and for non-Stafford Act incidents. ... The ESF structure provides mechanisms for interagency coordination during all phases of incident management. ... The National Response Coordination Center (NRCC), a component of the Homeland Security Operations Center (HSOC), develops and issues operation orders to activate individual ESFs based on the scope and magnitude of the threat or incident. ... ESF primary agencies notify and activate support agencies as required for the threat or incident, to include support to specialized teams. Each ESF is required to develop standard operating procedures (SOPs) and notification protocols and to maintain current rosters and contact information."

– *National Response Plan,* "Emergency Support Function Annexes: Introduction" (Washington, D.C.: Department of Homeland Security, December 2004), ESF–i.

ESF-1: Transportation
• Federal and civil transportation support
• Transportation safety
• Restoration/recover of transportation infrastructure
• Movement restrictions
• Damage and impact assessment

ESF-2: Communications
• Coordination with telecommunications and industry
• Restoration/repair of telecommunications infrastructure
• Protection, restoration, and sustainment of national cyber and information technology resources

ESF-3: Public Works and Engineering
• Infrastructure protection and emergency repair
• Infrastructure restoration
• Engineering services, construction management
• Critical infrastructure liaison

ESF-4: Firefighting
• Firefighting activities on Federal lands
• Resource support to rural and urban firefighting operations

ESF-5: Emergency Management
• Coordination of incident management efforts
• Issuance of mission assignments
• Resource and human capital
• Incident action planning
• Financial management

ESF-6: Mass Care, Housing, and Human Services
• Mass care
• Disaster housing
• Human services

ESF-7: Resource Support
• Resource support (facility space, office equipment and supplies, contracting services, etc.)

ESF-8: Public Health and Medical Services
• Public health
• Medical
• Mental health services
• Mortuary services

ESF-9: Urban Search and Rescue
• Life-saving assistance
• Urban search and rescue

ESF-10: Oil and Hazardous Materials Response
• Oil and hazardous materials (chemical, biological, radiological, etc.) response
• Environmental safety and short- and long-term cleanup

ESF-11: Agriculture and Natural Resources
• Nutrition assistance
• Animal and plant disease/pest response
• Food safety and security
• Natural and cultural resources and historic-properties protection and restoration

ESF-12: Energy
• Energy-infrastructure assessment, repair, and restoration
• Energy-industry utilities coordination
• Energy forecast

ESF-13: Public Safety and Security
• Facility and resource security
• Security planning and technical-resource assistance
• Public safety/security support
• Support to access, traffic, and crowd control

ESF-14: Long-Term Community Recovery and Mitigation
• Social and economic community-impact assessment
• Long-term community recovery assistance to states, local governments, and the private sector

ESF-15: External Affairs
• Emergency public information and protective-action guidance
• Media and community relations
• Congressional and international affairs
• Tribal and insular affairs

Appendix 3
Committee Hearings on Hurricane Katrina

Date: Sept. 14, 2005

Title: Recovering from Hurricane Katrina: The Next Phase
Witnesses:

Hon. Pete Wilson, former Governor, California

Hon. Patricia A. Owens, former Mayor, Grand Forks, North Dakota

Hon. Marc H. Morial, President and CEO, National Urban League, and former Mayor, New Orleans, Louisiana

Iain B. Logan, Operations Liaison, International Federation of Red Cross and Red Crescent Societies

Date: Sept. 28, 2005

Title: Recovering from Hurricane Katrina: Responding to the Immediate Needs of Its Victims
Witnesses:

Hon. Robert A. Eckels, County Judge, Harris County, Texas

Hon. Melvin L. Holden, Mayor/President, Baton Rouge, Louisiana

Hon. Robert V. Massengill, Mayor, Brookhaven, Mississippi

Hon. Dan Coody, Mayor, Fayetteville, Arkansas

Date: Oct. 6, 2005

Title: Hurricane Katrina: How is FEMA Performing Its Mission at This Stage of Recovery?
Witness:

R. David Paulison, Acting Undersecretary for Emergency Preparedness and Response, U.S. Department of Homeland Security, and Acting Director, Federal Emergency Management Agency

Date: Oct. 20, 2005

Title: Hurricane Katrina in New Orleans: A Flooded City, a Chaotic Response
Witness:

Marty J. Bahamonde, Regional Public Affairs Director, Region I, Federal Emergency Management Agency, U.S. Department of Homeland Security

Date: Nov. 2, 2005

Title: Hurricane Katrina: Why Did the Levees Fail?
Witnesses:

Ivor van Heerden, Ph.D., Head, State of Louisiana Forensic Data Gathering Team

Paul F. Mlakar, Ph.D., P.E., Senior Research Scientist, U.S. Army Engineer Research and Development Center

Raymond B. Seed, Ph.D., Professor, University of California at Berkeley, on behalf of the National Science Foundation

Peter Nicholson, Ph.D., P.E., Associate Professor, University of Hawaii, on behalf of the American Society of Civil Engineers

Date: Nov. 9, 2005

Title: Always Ready: The Coast Guard's Response to Hurricane Katrina
Witnesses:

Rear Admiral Robert F. Duncan, U.S. Coast Guard, Commander, Eighth Coast Guard District

Captain Frank M. Paskewich, U.S. Coast Guard, Commander, Coast Guard Sector New Orleans

Captain Bruce C. Jones, U.S. Coast Guard, Commanding Officer, Coast Guard Air Station New Orleans

Date: Nov. 16, 2005

Title: Hurricane Katrina: What Can Government Learn from the Private Sector's Response?
Witnesses:

David M. Ratcliffe, President and CEO, Southern Co.

Stanley S. Litow, Vice President, Corporate Community Relations, and President, IBM International Foundation, IBM Corp.

Kevin T. Regan, Regional Vice President, Hotel Operations, Starwood Hotels and Resorts Worldwide, Inc.

Jason F. Jackson, Director of Business Continuity, Global Security Division, Wal-Mart Stores, Inc.

Date: Dec. 8, 2005

Title: Hurricane Katrina: Perspectives of FEMA's Operations Professionals
Witnesses:

Scott Wells, Federal Coordinating Officer, Federal Emergency Management Agency, Joint Field Office, Baton Rouge, Louisiana

Philip E. Parr, Deputy Federal Coordinating Officer, Federal Emergency Management Agency, Joint Field Office, Austin, Texas

William L. Carwile III, former Federal Coordinating Officer, Federal Emergency Management Agency, Joint Field Office, Biloxi, Mississippi

Date: Dec. 15, 2005

Title: Hurricane Katrina: Who's In Charge of the New Orleans Levees?
Witnesses:

Col. Richard P. Wagenaar, District Engineer, New Orleans District, U.S. Army Corps of Engineers

Alfred C. Naomi, Senior Project Manager, New Orleans District, U.S. Army Corps of Engineers

Gerard A. Colletti, Operations Manager, Completed Works, New Orleans District, U.S. Army Corps of Engineers

Edmond J. Preau Jr., Assistant Secretary, Public Works and Inter-Modal Transportation, Louisiana Department of Transportation and Development

James P. Huey, former President, Board of Commissioners, Orleans Levee District

Max L. Hearn, Executive Director, Orleans Levee District

Date: Jan. 17, 2006

Title: Hurricane Katrina: Mississippi's Recovery

Witnesses:

Panel 1

Hon. Donald E. Powell, Coordinator of Recovery and Rebuilding in the Gulf Coast Region, U.S. Department of Homeland Security

Panel 2

Hon. Gene Taylor, U.S. Representative, U.S. House of Representatives

Hon. Brent E. Warr, Mayor, Gulfport, Mississippi

Hon. Edward Favre, Mayor, Bay St. Louis, Mississippi

Dr. Gavin Smith, Director, Governor's Office of Recovery and Renewal, State of Mississippi

Date: Jan. 24, 2006

Title: Preparing for a Catastrophe: The Hurricane Pam Exercise

Witnesses:

Wayne Fairley, Chief, Response Operations Branch, Federal Emergency Management Agency, Region VI, Denton, TX

Sean R. Fontenot, former Chief, Planning Division, Louisiana Office of Homeland Security and Emergency Preparedness, Baton Rouge, LA

Jesse St. Amant, Director, Plaquemines Parish Homeland Security and Office of Emergency Preparedness

Madhu Beriwal, President and CEO, Innovative Emergency Management Inc.

Date: Jan. 30, 2006

Title: Hurricane Katrina: Urban Search and Rescue in a Catastrophe

Witnesses:

William M. Lokey, Chief, Operations Branch, Response Division, Federal Emergency Management Agency, U.S. Department of Homeland Security

Brigadier General Brod Veillon, Assistant Adjutant General, Louisiana National Guard

Lietenant Colonel Keith LaCaze, Assistant Administrator, Law Enforcement Division, Louisiana Department of Wildlife and Fisheries

Captain Tim Bayard, Commander, Vice Crimes and Narcotics Section, New Orleans Police Department

Date: Jan. 31, 2006

Title: Challenges in a Catastrophe: Evacuating New Orleans in Advance of Hurricane Katrina

Witnesses:

Panel 1:

Hon. Johnny B. Bradberry, Secretary, Louisiana Department of Transportation and Development

Colonel Terry J. Ebbert, Director, New Orleans Office of Homeland Security

Walter S. Maestri, Ph.D., Director, Jefferson Parish Department of Emergency Management

Panel 2:

Jimmy Guidry, M.D., Medical Director and State Health Officer, Louisiana Department of Health and Hospitals

Kevin U. Stephens, M.D., J.D., Director, New Orleans Health Department

Joseph A. Donchess, Executive Director, Louisiana Nursing Home Association

Date: Feb. 1, 2006

Title: Hurricane Katrina: Managing the Crisis and Evacuating New Orleans
Witnesses:
Panel 1:

Hon. C. Ray Nagin, Mayor, New Orleans, Louisiana

Panel 2:

Brigadier General Mark A. Graham, Deputy Commanding General, Fifth U.S. Army

Vince Pearce, Manager, National Response Program, U.S. Department of Transportation

Dwight Brashear, CEO and General Manager, Capital Area Transit System, Baton Rouge, Louisiana

Date: Feb. 2, 2006

Title: Hurricane Katrina: The Role of the Governors in Managing the Catastrophe
Witnesses:

Hon. Haley Barbour, Governor of Mississippi

Hon. Kathleen Babineaux Blanco, Governor of Louisiana

Date: Feb. 6, 2006

Title: Hurricane Katrina: Managing Law Enforcement and Communications in a Catastrophe
Witnesses:

Michael J. Vanacore, Assistant Director, Office of Investigations, U.S. Immigration and Customs Enforcement, U.S. Department of Homeland Security

Kenneth W. Kaiser, Special Agent in Charge, Boston Field Office, Federal Bureau of Investigation

Warren J. Riley, Superintendent of Police, New Orleans Police Department

Peter M. Fonash, Ph.D., Deputy Manager, National Communications System, U.S. Department of Homeland Security

Colonel FG Dowden, Regional Liaison, New Orleans Department of Homeland Security and Public Safety

William L. Smith, Chief Technology Officer, Bell South Corp.

Date: Feb. 9, 2006

Title: Hurricane Katrina: The Defense Department's Role in the Response
Witnesses:
Panel 1:

Hon. Paul McHale, Assistant Secretary of Defense for Homeland Defense, U.S. Department of Defense

Admiral Timothy J. Keating, Commander, North American Aerospace Defense Command and U.S. Northern Command

Lieutenant General H. Steven Blum, Chief, National Guard Bureau

Panel 2:

Lieutenant General Russel L. Honoré, Commanding General, First U.S. Army

Major General Bennett C. Landreneau, Adjutant General, Louisiana National Guard, and Director, Louisiana Office of Homeland Security and Emergency Preparedness

Date: Feb. 10, 2006

Title: Hurricane Katrina: The Roles of DHS and FEMA Leadership
Witnesses:
Panel 1:

Hon. Michael D. Brown, former Under Secretary for Emergency Preparedness and Response, and Director, Federal Emergency Management Agency, U.S. Department of Homeland Security

Patrick J. Rhode, former Acting Deputy Director and Chief of Staff, Federal Emergency Management Agency, U.S. Department of Homeland Security

Panel 2:

Robert B. Stephan, Assistant Secretary for Infrastructure Protection, U.S. Department of Homeland Security

Matthew E. Broderick, Director for Operations Coordination, U.S. Department of Homeland Security

Date: Feb. 13, 2006

Title: Hurricane Katrina: Waste, Fraud, and Abuse Worsen the Disaster
Witnesses:

Gregory D. Kutz, Managing Director, Forensic Audits and Special Investigations, U.S. Government Accountability Office

Richard L. Skinner, Inspector General, U.S. Department of Homeland Security

Alice S. Fisher, Assistant Attorney General, Criminal Division, and Chairwoman, Hurricane Katrina Fraud Task Force, U.S. Department of Justice

Date: Feb. 15, 2006

Title: Hurricane Katrina: The Homeland Security Department's Preparation and Response
Witness:

Hon. Michael Chertoff, Secretary, U.S. Department of Homeland Security

Date: Mar. 8, 2006

Title: Hurricane Katrina: Recommendations for Reform
Witnesses:
Panel 1:

Hon. Barbara A. Mikulski, U.S. Senator, Maryland

Panel 2:

Hon. David M. Walker, Comptroller General, U.S. Government Accountability Office

Richard L. Skinner, Inspector General, U.S. Department of Homeland Security

Panel 3:

Bruce P. Baughman, President, National Emergency Management Association and Director, Alabama State Emergency Management Agency

Frank J. Cilluffo, Associate Vice President for Homeland Security and Director, Homeland Security Policy Institute, The George Washington University

Herman B. Leonard, Ph.D., Professor of Public Management, John F. Kennedy School of Government, and Professor of Business Administration, Harvard Business School, Harvard University

Date: Apr. 21, 2006
Title: FEMA's Manufactured Housing Program: Haste Makes Waste
(Field Hearing in Hope, Arkansas)
Witnesses:
Panel 1:

Hon. Mike Ross, U.S. House of Representatives, 4th Congressional District, Arkansas

Panel 2:

David Garratt, Acting Director of Recovery Efforts, Federal Emergency Management Agency, U.S. Department of Homeland Security

Richard L. Skinner, Inspector General, U.S. Department of Homeland Security

Panel 3:

Hon. Dennis Ramsey, Mayor, City of Hope, Arkansas

J. D. Harper, Executive Director, Arkansas Manufactured Housing Association

Appendix 4
HSGAC Interviews

The following people were interviewed as part of the Committee's investigation. Titles listed are as of Aug. 31, 2005, unless otherwise indicated. (Abbreviations: USA = U.S. Army, USCG = U.S. Coast Guard, USMC = U.S. Marine Corps, USN = U.S. Navy, USNR = U.S. Navy Reserve, USAF = U.S. Air Force, ANG = Army National Guard, AirNG = Air National Guard, LANG = Louisiana National Guard .)

Name	Date of Interview	Title
Accordo, Dexter	Nov. 9, 2005	Director, Emergency Management and Homeland Security, St. Tammany Parish, Louisiana
Acton, Rear Adm. John, USCG	Jan. 23, 2006	Deputy Area Commander, Mobilization and Reserve Affairs, Coast Guard Atlantic Area
Adam, Brian	Nov. 16, 2005	Director, Emergency Management Agency, and Director of Homeland Security, Fire Marshal/Investigator, Hancock County, Mississippi
Adams, Steve	Feb. 14, 2006	Deputy Director, Strategic National Stockpile, Centers for Disease Control and Prevention, U.S. Department of Health and Human Services
Aiken, James, M.D.	Jan. 11, 2006	Medical Director, Office of Emergency Preparedness, Medical Center of Louisiana in New Orleans
Allen, Vice Adm. Thad, USCG	Feb. 3, 2006	Chief of Staff, U.S. Coast Guard
Altshuler, Brooks	Dec. 15, 2005	Acting Deputy Chief of Staff and Policy Director, Federal Emergency Management Agency
Amos, Lt. Gen. James, USMC	Dec. 14, 2005	Commanding General, Second Marine Expeditionary Force, U.S. Marine Forces Atlantic Command
Andrews, Nicol	Oct. 26, 2005; Nov. 8, 2005	Deputy Director of Public Affairs, Federal Emergency Management Agency
Attaway, James	Jan. 13, 2006	Telecommunications Specialist, Mobile Emergency Response System, Region VI, Federal Emergency Management Agency
Atterberry, Linda	Nov. 16, 2005	Director, Biloxi Emergency Management, Mississippi
Aycock, Col. David	Jan. 4, 2006	Operations Officer, Louisiana National Guard

Babb, Rear Adm. John	Feb. 8, 2006	Director, Office of Force Readiness and Deployment, U.S. Public Health Service, U.S. Department of Health and Human Services
Bahamonde, Marty	Oct. 14, 2005; Oct. 7, 2005	Regional Director, External Affairs, Region I, Federal Emergency Management Agency
Ballow, James	Dec. 21, 2005; Jan. 4, 2006	Senior Operations Officer, Louisiana Office of Homeland Security and Emergency Preparedness
Barbour, Marsha	Jan. 26, 2006	First Lady, Mississippi
Barksdale, Jim	Jan. 10, 2006	Chairman, Governor's Commission on Recovery, Rebuilding, and Renewal, Mississippi (named on Sept. 20, 2005)
Baumy, Walter, Jr.	Nov. 15, 2005	Chief of Engineering Division, New Orleans District, U.S. Army Corps of Engineers
Bayard, Capt. Tim	Nov. 21, 2005	Commander, Vice Crimes and Narcotics Section, New Orleans Police Department, Louisiana
Beall, Jack	Jan. 10, 2006	Chief, National Disaster Medical System, Federal Emergency Management Agency
Beeman, Michael	Jan. 20, 2006	Director, National Preparedness Division, Region II, Federal Emergency Management Agency
Ben-Iesau, Lt. Cmdr. Shari, USCG	Oct. 18, 2005; Nov. 18, 2005	Public Affairs Officer, New Orleans Sector, U.S. Coast Guard
Bennett, Jean	Mar. 1, 2006	Regional Emergency Coordinator, Region VI, Office of Public Health and Emergency Preparedness, U.S. Department of Health and Human Services
Bennett, Paul	Dec. 8, 2005	Deputy Chief of Police, Gulfport Police Department, Mississippi
Berkely, Vince	Feb. 16, 2006	Acting Deputy Director and Chief Medical Officer, Phoenix (AZ) Area, Indian Health Service, U.S. Department of Health and Human Services
Bernazzani, James	Jan. 25, 2006	Special Agent in Charge, New Orleans Division, Federal Bureau of Investigation
Beron, Col. Thomas	Dec. 1, 2005	Commander, 61st Troop Command, Louisiana Army National Guard
Besser, Rich	Feb. 14, 2006	Director, Coordinating Office for Terrorism Preparedness and Emergency Response, Centers for Disease Control and Prevention, U.S. Department of Health and Human Services

Blankenship, Maj. Walter	Jan. 25, 2006	State Partnership Program Coordinator, Mississippi Air National Guard
Blitzer, Robert	Feb. 2, 2006	Deputy Assistant Secretary, Operations and Security Program, Office of Public Health Emergency Preparedness, U.S. Department of Health and Human Services
Blong, Clair, Ph.D.	Dec. 8, 2005	Liaison to U.S. Northern Command, Federal Emergency Management Agency
Blum, Lt. Gen. H. Steven, USA	Jan. 19, 2006	Chief, National Guard Bureau, U.S. Department of Defense
Bohnert, Roger	Dec. 2, 2005	Acting Director, Office of Intelligence, Security and Emergency Response, U.S. Department of Transportation
Bookert, Rear Adm. Reubin, USN	Nov. 16, 2005	Commander, Amphibious Group 2
Booth, Lt. Col. Joseph	Oct. 12, 2005; Dec. 9, 2005	Deputy Superintendent, Crisis Response and Special Operations, Louisiana State Police
Bossert, Thomas	Dec. 20, 2005	Deputy Director of Legislative Affairs, Federal Emergency Management Agency
Bottcher, Denise	Jan. 9, 2006	Press Secretary, Office of the Governor, Louisiana
Bouchard, Michael	Jan. 24, 2006	Assistant Director For Field Operations, Bureau of Alcohol, Tobacco, and Firearms and Explosives, U.S. Department of Justice
Boudreaux, Jill	Oct. 12, 2005	Deputy Undersecretary, Public Safety Services, Louisiana
Boyd, Lt. Valerie, USCG	Nov. 7, 2005	Command Center Watch Officer, 8th District Office Headquarters, New Orleans, Louisiana
Bradberry, Johnny	Nov. 17, 2005; Dec. 21, 2005	Secretary, Louisiana Department of Transportation and Development
Brashear, Dwight	Jan. 5, 2006	Chief Executive Officer and General Manager, Capital Area Transit System, Baton Rouge, Louisiana
Bridges, Jim	Dec. 1, 2005	Director, Southern Antiterrorist Regional Training Academy
Brinson, Jim	Dec. 14, 2005	Response Coordinator, Office of Homeland Security, Mississippi Department of Public Safety

Brock, George	Feb. 27, 2006	Chief of Plans and Policies Division, Plans, Policies and Strategies Directorate, National Guard Bureau, U.S. Department of Defense
Broderick, Matthew	Jan. 19, 2006	Director, Homeland Security Operations Center, U.S. Department of Homeland Security
Brommel, Ty	Jan. 10, 2006	Executive Director, Governor's Office of Rural Development, Louisiana
Brooke, Lucy	Jan. 24, 2006	Emergency Management Program Specialist, Federal Emergency Management Agency
Broun, Laurence	Mar. 21, 2006	Emergency Coordinator, U.S. Department of the Interior
Brown, Michael	Jan. 23, 2006; Feb. 23, 2006	Director, Federal Emergency Management Agency; (Resigned September 2005)
Brown, Randy	Dec. 8, 2005	Support Bureau Commander, Gulfport Police Department, Mississippi
Brown, William	Jan. 26, 2006	Operations Branch Chief, Mississippi Emergency Management Agency
Buikema, Edward	Nov. 21, 2005	Regional Director, Region V, Federal Emergency Management Agency
Burris, Ken	Dec. 29, 2005	Former Acting Director of Operations, Federal Emergency Management Agency
Butcher, Tim	Jan. 20, 2006	Former Emergency Management Director, Medical Center of Louisiana in New Orleans
Caldwell, Maj. Gen. William, USA	Feb. 28, 2006	Commander, 82nd Airborne Division, U.S. Department of Defense
Cardwell, Jeff	Nov. 16, 2005	Area 13 Coordinator, Western Branch Office, North Carolina Division of Emergency Management
Carwile, William, III	Dec. 6, 2005	Federal Coordinating Officer for Hurricane Katrina in Mississippi, Federal Emergency Management Agency
Cerise, Fred, M.D.	Oct. 26, 2005; Dec. 2, 2005; Dec. 6, 2005	Secretary, Louisiana Department of Health and Hospitals
Cerveny, Lt. Steve, USCG	Oct. 26, 2005	Pilot, Aviation Special Operations Division, Aviation Training Center Mobile, Alabama
Chapman, Bob	Dec. 13, 2005; Dec. 14, 2005	State Transportation Emergency Coordinator, Mississippi Department of Transportation

Chatelain, Myron	Jan. 9, 2006	Manger, Louisiana Nursing Home Service Corporation
Chavez, Col. Richard, USAF	Nov. 9, 2005; Nov. 22, 2005	Senior Military Advisor for Civil Support, Office of the Assistant Secretary of Defense for Homeland Defense, U.S. Department of Defense
Claypool, Robert, M.D.	Feb. 15, 2006	Deputy Assistant Secretary, Director of Mass Casualty Planning, Office of Public Health Emergency Preparedness, U.S. Department of Health and Human Services
Coachman, Sandy	Nov. 15, 2005	Federal Coordinating Officer, Region VI, Federal Emergency Management Agency
Colletti, Jerry	Nov. 22, 2005; Dec. 9, 2005	Operations Manager for Completed Projects, New Orleans District, U.S. Army Corps of Engineers
Compass, Eddie	Jan. 12, 2006	Superintendent of Police, New Orleans Police Department, Louisiana
Cooper, Lt. Cmdr. Tom, USCG	Oct. 18, 2005	Helicopter Pilot and Engineering Officer, Air Station New Orleans, Louisiana
Costello, Capt. John, USN	Nov. 15, 2005	Assistant Chief of Operations, Commander Task Force 20
Craig, Jim	Jan. 25, 2006	Director, Office of Health Protection, Mississippi Department of Health
Crea, Vice Adm. Vivien, USCG	Jan. 3, 2006	Commander, Coast Guard Atlantic Area and Commander, Maritime Defense Zone Atlantic
Crosbie, William	Feb. 17, 2006	Senior Vice-President of Operations, The National Railroad Passenger Corporation (Amtrak)
Cross, Maj. Gen. Harold	Jan. 26, 2006	Adjutant General, Mississippi Army and Air National Guard
Crumholt, Kenneth	Nov. 16, 2005	Resident Engineer, Construction Division, West Bank Hurricane Protection Project, New Orleans District, U.S. Army Corps of Engineers
Cuber, Bruce	Jan. 9, 2006	Former Disaster Management Director, Southeast Louisiana, American Red Cross
Cucolo, Brig. Gen. Tony, USA	Nov. 17, 2005	Director of Joint Center for Operational Analysis, Joint Forces Command, U.S. Department of Defense
Curtis, Col. Glenn	Dec. 6, 2005	Deputy Chief of Staff, Louisiana National Guard
Dabadie, Col. Steven	Jan. 12, 2006	Chief of Staff, Louisiana National Guard

Dancer, Maj. David	Dec. 21, 2005; Dec. 22, 2005	Operations Officer, Military Support Division, Louisiana National Guard
Daskevich, Col. Anthony, II, USA	Jan. 10, 2006	Commander, 4th Brigade, 75th Division Training Support, Fort Sill, Oklahoma
Dawkins, Richard	Dec. 13, 2005	Program Manager, Division of Economic Assistance, Mississippi Department of Human Services
Day, Don	Jan. 17, 2006	Region VI Regional Emergency Transportation Representative, Office of Intelligence, Security and Emergency Response, U.S. Department of Transportation
Delacroix, Scott, M.D.	Feb. 21, 2006	PGY-2 Urology Resident, Department of Urologic Surgery, Ochsner Clinic Foundation, New Orleans, Louisiana; PGY-2 Urology Resident, Department of Urologic Surgery, Louisiana State University, New Orleans, Louisiana
DeLorenzo, Mike	Feb. 9, 2006	Bureau Chief, Bureau of Preparedness and Response, Florida Division of Emergency Management
Deville, William	Nov. 22, 2005	General Manager and Chief Executive Officer, Regional Transit Authority of New Orleans, Louisiana
Diemont, Dolph	Jan. 6, 2006	Region X Regional Emergency Transportation Representative, Office of Intelligence, Security and Emergency Response, U.S. Department of Transportation
DiFalco, Frank	Jan. 13, 2006	Deputy Director, Homeland Security Operations Center, U.S. Department of Homeland Security
Donchess, Joseph	Jan. 9, 2006	Executive Director, Louisiana Nursing Home Service Corporation
Doran, Lt. Col. William, Louisiana AirNG	Dec. 2, 2005; Dec. 8, 2005	Chief, Operations Division, Louisiana Office of Homeland Security and Emergency Preparedness
Dowden, FG	Nov. 8, 2005	Regional Liaison, New Orleans Department of Homeland Security, Louisiana
Downey, Erin	Jan. 20, 2006	Louisiana Hospital Association, Director of Emergency Preparedness (Liaison to Health and Resources Services Administration)
Drake, Chris	Oct. 20, 2005	Program Manager for Interoperability, Mayor's Office of Technology, City of New Orleans, Louisiana
Duke, Elaine	Feb. 4, 2006	Chief Procurement Officer, U.S. Department of Homeland Security

Dunagan, Bruce	Jan. 18, 2006	Chief of Police, Biloxi Police Department, Mississippi
Duncan, Rear Adm. Robert, USCG	Oct. 18, 2005; Oct. 29, 2005	Commander, Eighth Coast Guard District
Duthu, Robert	Dec. 8, 2005	Enforcement Captain, Louisiana Department of Wildlife and Fisheries
Ebbert, Col. Terry, USMC (Ret.)	Oct. 6, 2005; Oct. 13, 2005; Oct. 14, 2005; Jan. 10, 2006	Director, New Orleans Office of Homeland Security, City of New Orleans, Louisiana
Eller, Ronald	Jan. 23, 2006	Liaison to North American Aerospace Defense Command, U.S. Army Corps of Engineers
Ellis, Lt. Col. Gordon, USA	Feb. 16, 2006	Commander, First Battalion, 148th Infantry, Ohio National Guard
England, Gordon	Feb. 3, 2006	Deputy Secretary of Defense, U.S. Department of Defense
English, Patricia	Jan. 5, 2006	Senior Procurement Executive, Federal Emergency Management Agency
Fairley, Wayne	Jan. 18, 2006	Response Operations Branch Chief, Region VI, Federal Emergency Management Agency
Farlow, Matt	Dec. 1, 2005	Information Technology Division Chief, Louisiana Office of Homeland Security and Emergency Preparedness
Favre, Eddie	Jan. 9, 2006	Mayor, City of Bay St. Louis, Mississippi
Fenton, Robert	Dec. 22, 2005	Response Branch Chief, Region IX, Federal Emergency Management Agency
Fincher, Capt. Joseph	Nov. 7, 2005	Captain, Engine 18, Third Platoon, Fifth District, New Orleans Fire Department, Louisiana
Fitzgerald, Allison	Nov. 12, 2005	Attorney, Louisiana Department of Public Safety
Fitzgerald, Vice Adm. Mark, USN	Nov. 15, 2005	Commander, U.S. Second Fleet, U.S. Department of Defense
Flores-Arias, Saraya	Dec. 19, 2005	Executive Assistant to the Director, New Orleans Office of Emergency Preparedness, Louisiana
Fonash, Peter, Ph.D.	Jan. 27, 2006	Deputy Manager, National Communications System, U.S. Department of Homeland Security

Fontenot, Sean	Jan. 10, 2006	Former Chief, Preparedness Division, Louisiana Office of Homeland Security and Emergency Preparedness
Foran, Michael	Jan. 17, 2006	Region IV Regional Emergency Transportation Representative, Office of Intelligence, Security and Emergency Response, U.S. Department of Transportation
Forman, Sally	Jan. 10, 2006	Communications Director, Office of the Mayor, City of New Orleans, Louisiana
Fowler, Erin	Jan. 30, 2006	Senior Analyst, Regional Emergency Coordinator Program, Office of Public Health and Emergency Preparedness, U.S. Department of Health and Human Services
Frazier, Tami	Dec. 19, 2005	Press Secretary, Office of the Mayor, City of New Orleans, Louisiana
Frels, Col. Mary, USA	Dec. 7, 2005	Command Force Protection Officer, U.S. Northern Command, U.S. Department of Defense
French, Capt. Art, M.D.	Mar. 2, 2006	Officer, U.S. Public Health Service, U.S. Department of Health and Human Services
Fudge, Lt. Robert, LANG	Dec. 21, 2005; Jan. 6, 2006	Chief, Preparedness Division, Louisiana Office of Homeland Security and Emergency Preparedness
Garratt, David	Jan. 9, 2006	Acting Director of Recovery, Federal Emergency Management Agency
Glick, Jeffrey	Feb. 3, 2006	Chief, Critical Infrastructure Protection Division, National Communications System, U.S. Department of Homeland Security
Glynn, Capt. Steve	Dec. 20, 2005	Chief of Special Operations Division, New Orleans Fire Department, Louisiana
Graham, Brig. Gen. Mark, USA	Jan. 12, 2006	Deputy Commanding General, Fifth U.S. Army, U.S. Department of Defense
Grass, Brig. Gen. Frank, USA	Jan. 18, 2006	Deputy Director, Army National Guard (Army National Guard Bureau)
Gray, Avis	Dec. 8, 2005	Regional Administrator, Region I, Office of Public Health, Louisiana Department of Health and Hospitals
Gray, Richard	Jan. 20, 2006	Acting Chief, National Response Coordination Center, Federal Emergency Management Agency
Guidry, Jimmy, M.D.	Dec. 20, 2005	Medical Director and State Health Officer, Louisiana Department of Health and Hospitals

Guidry, Roland	Jan. 11, 2006	Oil Spill Coordinator, Office of the Governor, Louisiana
Gusman, Marlin	Jan. 10, 2006	Criminal Sheriff, Office of the Criminal Sheriff, City of New Orleans, Louisiana
Guttman-McCabe, Christopher	Jan. 24, 2006	Vice President for Regulatory Affairs, Cellular Telecommunications and Internet Association
Hall, Michael	Nov. 28, 2005; Dec. 1, 2005	Acting Director of Human Resources, Federal Emergency Management Agency
Harrald, John, Ph.D.	Feb. 14, 2006	Co-Director, The George Washington University Institute for Crisis, Disaster, and Risk Management
Harrington, Col. Don, USA	Jan. 6, 2006	Liaison to National Response Coordination Center, U.S. Department of Defense
Harris, Julie	Dec. 21, 2005	Director of Federal and State Programs and Deputy Director of Intergovernmental Relations, Mayor's Office, City of New Orleans, Louisiana
Harry, Jim	Jan. 24, 2006	Policy Director, Office of the Governor, Mississippi
Hatfield, Brenda, Ph.D.	Dec. 21, 2005	Chief Administrative Officer, City of New Orleans, Louisiana
Hearn, Max	Nov. 14, 2005; Dec. 8, 2005	Executive Director, Orleans Levee District
Heath, Michael	Nov. 10, 2005	Special Assistant, Office of the Director, Federal Emergency Management Agency
Hellmers, Capt. Paul	Nov. 7, 2005	Captain Engine 18, Second Platoon, Fifth District, New Orleans Fire Department, Louisiana
Hitchings, Daniel	Nov. 15, 2005	Regional Business Director and Task Force HOPE, Mississippi Valley Division, U.S. Army Corps of Engineers
Holloway, A.J.	Jan. 5, 2006	Mayor, City of Biloxi, Mississippi
Holman, Rear Adm. Brenda	Feb. 9, 2006	Regional Director, Food and Drug Administration – Pacific Region, and Officer, U.S. Public Health Service, U.S. Department of Health and Human Services
Honoré, Lt. Gen. Russel, USA	Jan. 9, 2006	Commanding General, First U.S. Army, U.S. Department of Defense
Hornsby, Irby	Jan. 5, 2006	Special Needs Shelter Manager, New Orleans Region, Louisiana Department of Social Services

Huey, James	Nov. 29, 2005	Former President, Board of Commissioners, Orleans Levee District, Louisiana
Huff, Willie	Dec. 14, 2005	Director, Enforcement, Mississippi Department of Transportation
Hurst, Jules	Jan. 27, 2006	Transportation Supervisor, Logistics Branch, Federal Emergency Management Agency
Hurst, Paul	Jan. 30, 2006	Chief Counsel, Office of the Governor, Mississippi
Ingargiola, Larry	Oct. 26, 2005	Director, Department of Homeland Security and Emergency Preparedness, St. Bernard Parish, Louisiana
Jackson, Michael	Jan. 27, 2006	Deputy Secretary, U.S. Department of Homeland Security
James, Lt. Gen. Daniel, III	Jan. 3, 2006	Director, Air National Guard; Vice Chief of Staff, Department of the Air Force, U.S. Department of Defense
Jamieson, Gil	Dec. 20, 2005	Acting Director, National Incident Management System Integration Center, Federal Emergency Management Agency
Joerger, Col. Glen, USAF	Jan. 6, 2006	Wing Commander, Charleston Air Force Base
Johnson, Edward	Nov. 29, 2005	Safety and Training Manager, New Orleans Public Schools, City of New Orleans
Jones, Col. Al, USA	Mar. 2, 2006	Senior Army Advisor, Georgia Army National Guard
Jones, Art	Dec. 8, 2005	Chief, Disaster Recovery Division, Louisiana Office of Homeland Security and Emergency Preparedness
Jones, Capt. Bruce, USCG	Oct. 12, 2005; Nov. 12, 2005	Commanding Officer, Air Station New Orleans, Louisiana
Jones, Gary	Jan. 11, 2006	Acting Regional Director, Region VI, Federal Emergency Management Agency
Jones, Brig. Gen. Gary	Dec. 7, 2005	Director, Standing Joint Headquarters-North, U.S. Northern Command, U.S. Department of Defense
Jones, Greg	Jan. 6, 2006	Federal Highway Administration, U.S. Department of Transportation
Jones, Reggie	Jan. 17, 2006	ESF-1 Program Manager, Office of Intelligence and Emergency Response, U.S. Department of Transportation
Jones, Wayne	Feb. 9, 2006	Forest Area Supervisor, Florida Division of Forestry

Jordan, Col. John, USA	Feb. 28, 2006	Inspector General, Florida National Guard
Joseph, Capt. Michael	Nov. 8, 2005	Liaison to New Orleans Office of Homeland Security, New Orleans Fire Department, Louisiana
Jowett, Jack	Oct. 31, 2005	Chair, Emergency Management Assistance Compact
Kaiser, Ken	Jan. 25, 2006	Special Agent in Charge, Boston Field Office, Federal Bureau of Investigation
Keating, Adm. Timothy, USN	Feb. 3, 2006	Commander, North American Aerospace Defense Command and U.S. Northern Command, U.S. Department of Defense
Keeling, Col. Barry,	Oct. 18, 2005	Commander, State Aviation Command, Louisiana Army National Guard
Kessler, Gary	Jan. 27, 2006	Executive Vice President, Operations, Carey International, Inc.
Kilkenny, Rear Adm. Joseph, USN	Nov. 30, 2005	Commander, Carrier Strike Group Ten, U.S. Department of Defense
King, William	Jan. 17, 2006	Branch Chief, Region V, Radiological Emergency Preparedness Program, Technical Services Branch, Federal Emergency Management Agency
Kirkpatrick, Col. Tom	Dec. 7, 2005	Citizen Corps Coordinator, Louisiana Office of Homeland Security and Emergency Preparedness
Kleinpeter, Leonard	Jan. 11, 2006	Special Assistant to the Governor, Office of the Governor and Director, Office of Community Programs, Louisiana
Kohlman, Col. James	Dec. 6, 2005	Deputy, J6, U.S. Northern Command and North American Aerospace Defense Command, U.S. Department of Defense
Kopplin, Andy	Jan. 6, 2006	Chief of Staff, Office of the Governor, Louisiana
Kruse, Margaret	Nov. 16, 2005	Head of White House Pacific Command, Counter-Drug and Force Protection Division, Joint Forces Command, U.S. Department of Defense
LaBuda, Capt. Gary, USN	Dec. 2, 2005	Emergency Preparedness Liaison Officer to National Response Coordination Center, U.S. Department of Defense
LaCaze, Lt. Col. Keith	Nov. 30, 2005	Assistant Administrator, Law Enforcement Division, Louisiana Department of Wildlife and Fisheries
Lampard, Patrick	Jan. 11, 2006	Chief, Fifth District, New Orleans Fire Department, Louisiana

Landreneau, Maj. Gen. Bennett, USA	Jan. 11, 2006	Adjutant General, Louisiana, Director, LOHSEP
Landreneau, Dwight	Nov. 30, 2005	Secretary, Louisiana Department of Wildlife and Fisheries
Lapeyrolerie, Kitty	Dec. 20, 2005	Regional Manager, Louisiana Rehabilitative Services and Emergency Preparedness Coordinator, Louisiana Department of Social Services
Latham, Robert	Jan. 27, 2006	Executive Director, Mississippi Emergency Management Agency
Lavender, Robert, Jr.	Feb. 3, 2006	Deputy Director of Information Technology Communications, Office of Public Health and Emergency Preparedness, U.S. Department of Health and Human Services
Lee, Harry	Jan. 10, 2006	Sheriff, Jefferson Parish, Louisiana
Lloyd, Rear Adm. Dan, USCG	Dec. 8, 2005	Division Chief, Joint Inter-Agency Coordination Group, U.S. Northern Command, U.S. Department of Defense
Lokey, William	Nov. 4, 2005; Jan. 20, 2006	Federal Coordinating Officer for Hurricane Katrina in Louisiana, Federal Emergency Management Agency
Loper, Butch	Dec. 6, 2005	Director, Emergency Management Agency, Jackson County, Mississippi
Lowder, Michael	Nov. 10, 2005	Deputy Director of Response, Federal Emergency Management Agency
Lowe, Michael	Nov. 15, 2005	Emergency Manager, New Orleans District Corps of Engineers, U.S. Army Corps of Engineers
Loy, Adm. James, USCG (Ret.)	Nov. 16, 2005	Former Deputy Secretary, U.S. Department of Homeland Security
Ludgood, Gary	Jan. 20, 2006	Vice President for Integrated Network Planning and Implementation, BellSouth Corp.
Lumpkin, Dee	Nov. 16, 2005	Deputy Director of Emergency Management Agency, Hancock County, Mississippi
Lyle, Mary Ann	Jan. 25, 2006	Night Manager, National Response Coordination Center, Federal Emergency Management Agency
Maestri, Walter, Ph.D.	Oct. 26, 2005; Oct. 27, 2005	Director, Jefferson Parish Office of Emergency Management, Louisiana
Maner, Andrew	Feb. 2, 2006	Acting Chief Financial Officer, U.S. Department of Homeland Security

Markham, Capt. Brett, USN	Dec. 7, 2005	Deputy Director of Intelligence, U.S. Northern Command and North American Aerospace Defense Command, U.S. Department of Defense
Martin, Bruce	Nov. 10, 2005	Deputy of Administration, New Orleans Fire Department, Louisiana
Martin, Ronald	Jan. 13, 2006	Deputy Commander, Management Support Team, National Disaster Medical System, Federal Emergency Management Agency
Mason, Maj. Gen. James	Feb. 14, 2006	Commander, 35th Infantry Division, Kansas Army National Guard
Massengill, Robert	Sept. 16, 2005	Mayor, City of Brookhaven, Mississippi
Matthews, Joseph	Oct. 14, 2005; Nov. 23, 2005; Jan. 10, 2006	Director, New Orleans Office of Emergency Preparedness, Louisiana
Mayeaux, Jadwin, Col., LANG (Ret.)	Nov. 29, 2005	Deputy Director, Homeland Security, Louisiana Office of Homeland Security and Emergency Preparedness
Mayer, Matt	Jan. 26, 2006	Chief of Staff and Senior Policy Advisor, Office of Domestic Preparedness Security and Acting Executive Director, Office of Domestic Preparedness, U.S. Department of Homeland Security
Mayfield, Max, Ph.D.	Jan. 27, 2006	Director, Tropical Prediction Center and National Hurricane Center, National Weather Service, National Oceanic and Atmospheric Administration
Mayne, Jeff	Nov. 30, 2005	Supervisor, Special Investigator Section, and Legislative Liaison, Louisiana Department of Wildlife and Fisheries
McAllister, Tom	Jan. 25, 2006; Jan. 27, 2006	Director of Response and Recovery, Mississippi Emergency Management Agency
McCall, Jim	Nov. 30, 2005	Director, Youth Challenge Program, Carville, Louisiana
McClellan, Col. Wesley	Jan. 23, 2006	Division Chief, Joint Interagency Coordination Group, U.S. Northern Command, U.S. Department of Defense
McDaniel, Capt. Michael, USNR	Dec. 2, 2005	Navy Emergency Preparedness Liaison to Federal Emergency Management Agency, U.S. Department of Defense
McHale, Paul	Jan. 4, 2006; Feb. 3, 2006; Feb. 17, 2006	Assistant Secretary of Defense for Homeland Defense, U.S. Department of Defense

McKeon, Capt. Tom, USN	Nov. 14, 2005	Deputy Director of Operations (N3A) for U.S. Fleet Forces Command, U.S. Department of Defense
Mercer, William	Jan. 26, 2006; Feb. 23, 2006	Principal Associate Deputy Attorney General, Office of the Attorney General and U.S. Attorney, Montana District, Executive Office for United States Attorneys, U.S. Department of Justice
Milani, William	Jan. 12, 2006	Chief, Mobile Operations Section, Logistics Branch, Federal Emergency Management Agency
Miller, Maj. John	Dec. 14, 2005	Chief Inspector (Southern Region), Highway Safety Patrol, Mississippi Public Safety Department
Mills, Chuck	Feb. 14, 2006	Vice President, Emergency Management Services International, Inc.
Misczak, Mark	Nov. 14, 2005	Individual Assistance Branch Chief, Region VI, Federal Emergency Management Agency
Modicut, Joseph	Jan. 5, 2006	Emergency Services Coordinator, Operations Office, Louisiana Department of Transportation and Development
Monette, Ted	Nov. 15, 2005	Acting Director, Response and Recovery Division, Region I, Federal Emergency Management Agency
Montz, Cindy	Jan. 12, 2006	Senior Planner, Louisiana Office of Homeland Security and Emergency Preparedness
Moore, Gary	Dec. 9, 2005	Director, Logistics Branch, Federal Emergency Management Agency
Moulton, Brig. Gen. Harold, USAF	Dec. 5, 2005	Director, Standing Joint Headquarters-North, U.S. Northern Command, U.S. Department of Defense
Mouton, Lt. Col. Doug	Dec. 1, 2005	Commander, 225th Engineering Group, Louisiana National Guard
Muir, Col. Thomas, USA	Dec. 6, 2005	Deputy Chief, Current Operations, U.S. Northern Command, U.S. Department of Defense
Murillo, Luis	Dec. 7, 2005	Deputy Director, New Orleans Office of Emergency Preparedness, Louisiana
Myers, Gen. Richard, USAF	Feb. 28, 2006	Chairman, Joint Chiefs of Staff, U.S. Department of Defense
Naomi, Alfred	Nov. 16, 2005; Dec. 9, 2005	Senior Project Manager, Lake Pontchartrain and Vicinity Hurricane Protection Project, New Orleans District, U.S. Army Corps of Engineers
Neely, Daryl	Jan. 24, 2006	Policy Advisor, Office of the Governor, Mississippi

Nelms, Bill	Jan. 6, 2006	Acquisitions Branch Manager, Federal Aviation Administration Southwest Region, Federal Aviation Administration, U.S. Department of Transportation
Nelson, Gordon	Jan. 6, 2006	Assistant Secretary for Operations, Louisiana Department of Transportation and Development
Noble, Ellen	Dec. 13, 2005	Chapters Solution Manager, Southeast Service Area, American Red Cross
O'Dell, Maj. Gen. Douglas, USMC	Dec. 14, 2005	Commanding General, 4th Marine Division, U.S. Department of Defense
Oliver, Col. Cliff	Nov. 30, 2005	Installation Commander, Gillis W. Long Center, Louisiana National Guard
Otterstedt, Col. Chuck, USA	Nov. 16, 2005	Deputy Director of Operations, Joint Forces Command, U.S. Department of Defense
Oxley, Col. Mark	Oct. 12, 2005; Dec. 9, 2005; Mar. 13, 2006	Chief of Staff, Louisiana State Police
Parent, Charles	Nov. 10, 2005	Superintendent, New Orleans Fire Department, Louisiana
Parker, Gerald, D.V.M., Ph.D.	Feb. 10, 2006	Principal Deputy Assistant Secretary, Office of Public Health Emergency Preparedness, U.S. Department of Health and Human Services
Parr, Philip	Nov. 16, 2005	Federal Coordinating Officer, Region I, Federal Emergency Management Agency
Paskewich, Capt. Frank, USCG	Oct. 12, 2005	Commander, Coast Guard Sector New Orleans, U.S. Coast Guard
Payne, Maj. Wayne	Dec. 6, 2005	Director of Operations, Harrison County Sheriff's Department, Mississippi
Pearce, Vince	Jan. 6, 2006	Manager, National Response Program, Office of Intelligence, Security and Emergency Response, U.S. Department of Transportation
Penoyer, Lt. Cmdr. Brian	Mar. 2, 2006	Operations Integration Staff, U.S. Department of Homeland Security
Petillo, Jay	Feb. 13, 2006	Operations Officer, Office of Public Health and Emergency Preparedness, U.S. Department of Health and Human Services
Pevey, Lt. Joe	Dec. 6, 2005	Deputy Director, Southern Regional Public Safety Institute, Harrison County Sheriff's Department, Mississippi

Phillips, George	Jan. 26, 2006	Commissioner, Mississippi Department of Public Safety
Phillips, Jeff	Nov. 1, 2005	Director, Emergency Operations Center, Office of Emergency Management, New Mexico
Pinner, Richard	Nov. 16, 2005	Section Chief, Geotech Branch, Engineering Division, New Orleans District, U.S. Army Corps of Engineers
Powell, Don	Jan. 11, 2006	Coordinator of Recovery and Rebuilding in the Gulf Coast Region, U.S. Department of Homeland Security (named Nov. 1, 2005)
Pratts, Roseanne	Jan. 31, 2006	Director of Emergency Preparedness, Louisiana Department of Health and Hospitals
Preau, Edmond, Jr.	Nov. 17, 2005	Assistant Secretary, Public Works and Inter-Modal Transportation, Louisiana Department of Transportation and Development
Prechter, Col. Pat	Jan. 6, 2006	State Chief Nurse, Louisiana Army National Guard and Deputy Commander, Louisiana Medical Command
Prevo, Dan	Jan. 17, 2006	Former Region VI Regional Emergency Transportation Representative, Office of Intelligence, Security and Emergency Response, U.S. Department of Transportation
Quinn, Cmdr. Tom, USN	Nov. 15, 2005	Director of Operations, Naval Air Forces, Atlantic
Ramsey, Dennis	Apr. 4, 2006	Mayor, City of Hope, Arkansas
Reese, Lou	Oct. 14, 2005; Nov. 21, 2005	Assistant to the Director, New Orleans Office of Emergency Preparedness, Louisiana
Reininger, Capt. Bob, USCG	Dec. 5, 2005	Chief, Future Operations Division, Operational Planning Group, U.S. Northern Command, U.S. Department of Defense
Rembert, Brenda	Jan. 26, 2006	Director, Planning, Training and Exercise Bureau, Mississippi Emergency Management Agency
Reppel, Charles, Sr.	Oct. 18, 2005	Special Assistant to the Parish President, St. Bernard Parish
Rhode, Patrick	Dec. 22, 2005; Jan. 4, 2006; Jan. 10, 2006	Acting Deputy Director, Federal Emergency Management Agency
Rice, Joseph	Oct. 4, 2005	Director of Operations, Carson Helicopters, Inc
Riemann, Kris	Dec. 8, 2005	Director of Public Works, City of Gulfport, Mississippi

Riley, Warren	Dec. 20, 2005; Jan. 12, 2006	Former Deputy Superintendent, New Orleans Police Department, Louisiana
Roberson, Col. Darryl, USAF	Nov. 10, 2005	Assistant Deputy Director, Antiterrorism and Homeland Defense, Joint Staff, U.S. Department of Defense
Roberts, Col. Bryan, USA	Feb. 23, 2006	Commander, 2nd Brigade Combat Team, 1st Cavalry Division, U.S. Department of Defense
Roberts, David	Jan. 18, 2006	Director, Biloxi Fire Department, Mississippi
Robinson, Tony	Nov. 15, 2005	Director, Response and Recovery Division, Region VI, Federal Emergency Management Agency
Rodriguez, Junior	Oct. 18, 2005	President, St. Bernard Parish, Louisiana
Rowe, Maj. Gen. Richard, USA	Jan. 20, 2006	Director of Operations, U.S. Northern Command, U.S. Department of Defense
Russo, Nick	Dec. 21, 2005	Federal Coordinating Officer, Region I, Federal Emergency Management Agency
Ryder, Terry	Jan. 10, 2006	Executive Counsel, Office of the Governor, Louisiana
Sanders, Rev. Torrin	Nov. 23, 2005	President, Orleans Parish School Board, Louisiana
Santos, Col. Earl	Dec. 21, 2005	Joint Director of Military Support, Louisiana National Guard
Scherling, Maj. Gen. Terry, USAF	Jan. 19, 2006	Deputy Director for Antiterrorism and Homeland Defense, and Joint Director for Military Support, Operations Directorate, Joint Staff, U.S. Department of Defense
Selva, Brig. Gen. Paul, USAF	Feb. 16, 2006	Director of Operations, U.S. Transportation Command, U.S. Department of Defense
Sexton, Alfred	Dec. 19, 2005	Commander of Administration, Gulfport Police Department, Mississippi
Shaffer, Wilson, Ph.D.	Feb. 24, 2006	Chief, Evaluations Branch, National Weather Service, National Oceanic and Atmospheric Administration
Shanahan, Col. Dan, USA	Feb. 23, 2006	Commander, 1st Air Cavalry Brigade, 1st Cavalry Division, U.S. Department of Defense
Shingler, Wendell	Jan. 31, 2006; Feb. 14, 2006	Director, Office of Federal Protective Service, Border and Transportation Security, U.S. Department of Homeland Security

Simonson, Stewart	Feb. 16, 2006	Assistant Secretary, Office of Public Health and Emergency Preparedness, U.S. Department of Health and Human Services
Sloan, Marie	Mar. 1, 2006	Section Chief, Disaster Workforce, Response Division, Federal Emergency Management Agency
Smith, Jeffrey, Jr.	Jan. 13, 2006	Acting Deputy Director, Emergency Management, Louisiana Office of Homeland Security and Emergency Preparedness
Smith, Gavin	Jan. 11, 2006	Director, Governor's Office of Recovery and Renewal, Mississippi
Smith, Col. George, USAF	Dec. 6, 2005	Chief, Joint Planning Group, J5, U.S. Northern Command, U.S. Department of Defense
Smith, John	Sept. 16, 2005	Mayor, City of Meridian, Mississippi
Smith, Kenya	Dec. 20, 2005	Executive Assistant, Division of Intergovernmental Relations, Office of the Mayor, City of New Orleans, Louisiana
Smith, Patricia	Jan. 11, 2006	Director of Scheduling and Administration, Office of the Mayor, City of New Orleans, Louisiana
Smith, William	Jan. 20, 2006	Chief Technology Officer, BellSouth Corp
Smithburg, Don	Feb. 7, 2006	Executive Vice President and Chief Executive Officer, Health Care Services Division, Louisiana State University
Smithson, Lt. Col. Lee	Jan. 25, 2006	Director of Military Support, Mississippi Army National Guard
Snyder, Capt. Rick, USN	Nov. 14, 2005	Executive Officer, USS *Bataan*
Spangenburg, Clayton	Jan. 24, 2006	Program Specialist, Preparedness Division, Federal Emergency Management Agency
Spencer, Stevan, P.E.	Nov. 14, 2005	Chief Engineer, Orleans Levee District, Louisiana
Spohrer, Gerry	Nov. 15, 2005	Executive Director, West Jefferson Levee District, Louisiana
Spraggins, Col. Joseph,	Nov. 17, 2005	Director, Harrison County Emergency Management Agency, Mississippi
St. Amant, Jesse	Nov. 9, 2005	Director, Homeland Security Office of Emergency Preparedness, Plaquemines Parish, Louisiana
St. Martin, Marcia	Dec. 9, 2005	Executive Director, New Orleans Sewerage and Water Board, Louisiana

Stack, Michael	Nov. 17, 2005	Engineer, New Orleans District Design Water Resources, Louisiana Department of Transportation and Development
Stanley, Ron	Jan. 27, 2006	President, Landstar Express America, Inc.
Stanton, Larry	Feb. 6, 2006	Deputy Director, Risk Management Division, Office of Infrastructure Protection, Preparedness Directorate, U.S. Department of Homeland Security
Stephan, Robert	Jan. 13, 2006	Assistant Secretary of Homeland Security for Infrastructure Protection, Preparedness Directorate, U.S. Department of Homeland Security
Stephens, Kevin, M.D.	Nov. 9, 2005; Nov. 10, 2005	Director, New Orleans Health Department, Louisiana
Strickland, Jim	Jan. 25, 2006	Team Member, Urban Search and Rescue, Federal Emergency Management Agency
Sullivan, Pat	Dec. 7, 2005	Fire Chief, Gulfport Fire Department, Mississippi
Swain, Lonnie	Nov. 9, 2005	Assistant Superintendent, New Orleans Police Department, Louisiana
Taylor, Cynthia	Oct. 14, 2005; Oct. 17, 2005	Deputy Director, Office of Public Affairs, Federal Emergency Management Agency
Thibodeaux, Lt. Col. Jacques	Dec. 6, 2005; Jan. 12, 2006	Joint Director of Military Support to Civilian Authorities, Louisiana National Guard
Tillie, James	Dec. 19, 2005	Safety Director, Regional Transit Authority, New Orleans, Louisiana
Tolbert, Eric	Nov. 8, 2005; Dec. 1, 2005	Former Director, Response Division, Federal Emergency Management Agency
Torres, Lt. Roberto, USCG	Oct. 18, 2005	Pilot, Air Station New Orleans, Louisiana
Tullier, Terry	Nov. 22, 2005	Director, New Orleans Office of Emergency Preparedness and former Deputy Director, New Orleans Fire Department, Louisiana
Turner, Fredrick	Nov. 23, 2005	Transportation Manager, Transportation Department, Orleans Parish School Board, Louisiana
Vallarautto, Terry	Dec. 2, 2005	Interoperability Coordinator, Louisiana Office of Homeland Security and Emergency Preparedness
Vanacore, Michael	Jan. 27, 2006	Director, Office of International Affairs and Assistant Director, Office of Investigations, Immigration and Custom Enforcement, U.S. Department of Homeland Security

Vanderwagen, Rear Adm. Craig	Feb. 7, 2006	Acting Chief Medical Officer, Indian Health Service, and Officer, U.S. Public Health Service, U.S. Department of Health and Human Service
Vaughn, Lt. Gen. Clyde., USA	Jan. 18, 2006	Director, Army National Guard, U.S. Department of Defense
Veillon, Brig. Gen. Brod, Louisiana AirNG	Nov. 29, 2005	Assistant Adjutant General, Louisiana Air National Guard
Villar, Chris	Jan. 26, 2006	Owner, Go-Cans, LLC
Vislay, Lt. Cmdr. Mark, USCG	Oct. 26, 2005	HH-60J Instructor Pilot, Training Division, Aviation Training Center Mobile, Alabama, U.S. Coast Guard
Wagenaar, Col. Richard, USA	Nov. 15, 2005	District Engineer, New Orleans District, U.S. Army Corps of Engineers
Waguespack, Leslie	Nov. 16, 2005	Task Force Guardian, New Orleans District Support Team, Mississippi Valley Division, U.S. Army Corps of Engineers
Wainwright, Sherry	Jan. 23, 2006	Assessment and Exercise Branch Chief, Region VI, Federal Emergency Management Agency
Wallace, Mark	Jan. 20, 2006	Region VI, Operations Officer, Federal Emergency Management Agency
Warr, Brent	Nov. 15, 2005; Nov. 17, 2005; Jan. 9, 2006	Mayor, City of Gulfport, Mississippi
Weatherford, Alan	Dec. 8, 2005	Operations Bureau Commander, Gulfport Police Department, Mississippi
Webb, David	Feb. 7, 2006	Program Specialist, Program Office, National Search and Rescue, Urban Search and Rescue Response System, Federal Emergency Management Agency
Wells, Scott	Nov. 15, 2005	Deputy Federal Coordinating Officer for Hurricane Katrina in Louisiana, Federal Emergency Management Agency
White, Marva	Nov. 23, 2005	Director, Transportation Department, Orleans Parish School Board, Louisiana
Whitehorn, Col. Henry	Nov. 29, 2005	Superintendent, Louisiana State Police and Deputy Secretary, Public Safety Services and Corrections, Louisiana
Wiley, Jeffery	Nov. 4, 2005	Sheriff, Sheriff's Office, Ascension Parish, Louisiana

Wilkins, Kay	Dec. 20, 2005	Chief Executive Officer, Southeast Louisiana Chapter, American Red Cross
Williamson, Ann	Dec. 7, 2005	Secretary, Louisiana Department of Social Services
Willow, Capt. Mark	Nov. 9, 2005	Commander, Homeland Security Division, New Orleans Police Department, Louisiana
Womack, Thomas	Jan. 27, 2006	Deputy Director, Mississippi Emergency Management Agency
Wood, John	Jan. 27, 2006	Chief of Staff, U.S. Department of Homeland Security
Woods, Col. Roberta, USA	Dec. 7, 2005	Chief, Plans and Operations Division, U.S. Northern Command, U.S. Department of Defense
Young, Maj. Gen. Ronald	Jan. 17, 2006	Acting Director, Joint Staff, National Guard Bureau, U.S. Department of Defense
Ziegler, D.J.	Dec. 9, 2005	Harbor Master, Gulfport Harbor, Mississippi

Appendix 5
Additional Views

Senator Susan M. Collins, Senator Ted Stevens,
Senator Norm Coleman, Senator Tom Coburn, M.D.,
Senator Robert F. Bennett, and Senator Pete V. Domenici.

On White House and Department of Homeland Security Cooperation

The Committee's seven-month investigation into the preparedness for and response to Hurricane Katrina, by all levels of government, has been an extraordinary undertaking. The Committee has held 22 hearings with 85 witnesses, has received and analyzed 838,000 pages of documents, and has formally interviewed more than 325 individuals. This investigation has been the most comprehensive of the Katrina reviews, each of which has been useful in advancing the public's understanding.

The Committee has been relentless in its efforts to secure the information it has needed to ensure that the investigation is thorough and comprehensive. And we have succeeded. On October 7, 2005, the Committee sent extensive requests for documents and information to the White House and the Office of the Vice President. On January 12, 2006, the Committee sent another letter to the White House prioritizing the requests and asking for more documents and information. Throughout the process, we have been in direct communications with the White House to secure the documents and information that we required.

The Committee has been similarly adamant in its pursuit of documents and information from federal departments and agencies. The Department of Homeland Security alone has produced 350,000 pages of documents and made available more than 70 witnesses for interviews.

Moreover, when one federal entity refused to make key witnesses available for interviews, the Committee issued five subpoenas for Department of Justice personnel, who were promptly interviewed by Committee staff.

The Executive Office of the President has produced more than 17,000 pages of documents. These documents include memos, policy analyses, and e-mails with electronic attachments sent to individuals in the White House. The Committee also has received transcripts of the FEMA-hosted video teleconferences, including those in which the President or other White House officials participated. Collectively, these documents show us the information that the White House was receiving from various agencies before landfall and during the response phase. The production contains documents relating to the White House Task Force Katrina and includes lists of individuals attending White House-organized meetings and summaries of agency efforts. Also produced were documents that included information provided to the most senior officials within the White House during the critical period.

In addition to the documents, the White House has provided two extensive briefings on its role in the preparation for and response to Hurricane Katrina, and a third briefing on the White House *Lessons Learned* report. All three briefings were presented by Ken Rapuano, the Deputy Assistant to the President for Homeland Security, who was deeply involved in the response to Hurricane Katrina at the White House. These briefings included significant question-and-answer sessions where Committee staff had the opportunity to explore issues in depth.

In addition to the information the Committee has received from the White House document productions and briefings, the Committee has analyzed the *Lessons Learned* report, which further details the White House's involvement in – and shortcomings relating to – the response to Hurricane Katrina. The 125 specific recommendations in the report include several suggestions that recognize problems with the White House's role before or following the catastrophe.

The Office of the Vice President (OVP), too, produced documents that have helped us piece together its role, and that of the White House, with respect to Hurricane Katrina. Among the more than 6,300 pages of documents produced are substantive e-mails, policy memos, and reports on the economic impact of Hurricane Katrina. Some of the e-mails were from David Addington, Counsel to the Vice President (and now Chief of Staff). The OVP also produced daily reports of the White House Hurricane Katrina Task Force and Homeland Security Council agendas.

Finally, the Committee has gained insight into the White House role through the testimony and subsequent interview of former FEMA Director Michael Brown. In his February 10, 2006, testimony before the Committee and interview with Committee staff two weeks later, as well as through documents he produced directly to the Committee, Mr. Brown gave us his detailed view into the workings and deliberations of the White House during this critical period. As a result, the Committee has a well-developed picture of the White House's interaction with the top federal official on the ground before and during the critical days after Katrina made landfall. We know that, through Mr. Brown's communications with Deputy White House Chief of Staff Joseph Hagin, the White House was aware, on the day of the storm, of the devastation that New Orleans had suffered. And we know, from documents produced to us by Mr. Brown, that White House Chief of Staff Andy Card was aware of what Mr. Brown had told Mr. Hagin.

While, as noted, the Committee has received extensive briefings from Homeland Security Council staff as well as more than 23,000 pages of documents from the White House and OVP, much of the Committee's information on alleged communications between Mr. Brown and the President and his staff comes from Mr. Brown, and Mr. Brown alone. The White House staff declined the opportunity to be interviewed, which would have allowed for an even more complete understanding of what transpired.

As a result of the Committee's efforts, we have a clear window into the functioning and role of the White House in the days before and after Hurricane Katrina made landfall. The Committee had ample evidence to draw conclusions on how to strengthen our nation's ability to prepare for and respond to future catastrophes.

Additional Views

Senator Joseph I. Lieberman, Senator Carl Levin,
Senator Daniel K. Akaka, Senator Thomas R. Carper,
Senator Frank R. Lautenberg, and Senator Mark L. Pryor

On White House Katrina Failures, Administration Lack of Cooperation With the Investigation, and Failure to Establish Unified Command

As it did with the investigation that preceded the issuing of this Report, the Committee has produced a thorough and thoughtful piece of work, which we are proud to have worked on and wholeheartedly support. Indeed, the conduct of this investigation and the drafting of the Report should serve as a model for future such endeavors. In its comprehensiveness and non-partisanship, the Homeland Security and Governmental Affairs Committee's Hurricane Katrina investigation did exactly what the American people have a right to expect from a Congressional investigation. For that, we are very grateful to Chairman Collins and Ranking Member Lieberman, who have worked closely since they first announced, last September, their intent to investigate the tragedy that Katrina – and the flawed government response to it – wrought upon the citizens of the Gulf Coast.

We write separately here to express our additional views on three matters on which the Chairman and the Ranking Member were ultimately unable to reach a meeting of the minds: The role of the White House and the President in the events leading to and following last August's storm; the level of cooperation provided by the Administration to this investigation; and the failure to establish a unified command in Louisiana to respond to Katrina.

The Committee's efforts to understand the role the White House played in events leading up to and following the catastrophe were severely hindered by the White House's failure to comply with Committee requests for information, documents, and interviews. As a result, we learned much too little about what the White House and the Executive Office of the President were doing during the critical days before and after Katrina struck.

Based on the information the Committee was able to obtain, we have reached the following conclusions:

> 1. As the head of the federal government, the President has a unique responsibility to ensure government preparedness and response at critical times. For Hurricane Katrina, the President failed to provide critical leadership when it was most needed, and that contributed to a grossly ineffective federal response to Hurricane Katrina.

> 2. The White House was aware long before Katrina struck that FEMA did not have the capability to handle a catastrophe, but failed to adequately address the critical shortcomings in preparedness.

> 3. The White House had been aware of the "New Orleans Scenario," a catastrophic hurricane hitting New Orleans. Despite this awareness, the White House failed to ensure that the federal government was prepared to respond to this catastrophic scenario.

> 4. Despite the clear warnings before landfall that Katrina would be catastrophic, the President and the White House staff were not sufficiently engaged and failed to initiate a sufficiently strong and proactive response.

5. Although the President and the White House were following events after landfall, they seemed surprisingly detached until two days later, Wednesday, August 31, 2005.

6. After the hurricane, the White House continued to demonstrate a lack of understanding of the magnitude of the catastrophe.

7. The White House's failure to cooperate with this Committee's investigation wrongly deprived the Committee and the American people of the ability to assess a key aspect of the federal government's response to Hurricane Katrina.

Part I: The Role of the White House

As the head of the federal government, the President has a unique responsibility to ensure government preparedness and response at critical times. For Hurricane Katrina, the President failed to provide critical leadership when it was most needed, and that contributed to a grossly ineffective federal response to Hurricane Katrina.

A catastrophic event in the United States requires clear, decisive, and constant Presidential leadership.

The President is the head of the federal government. The Constitution vests executive power in him. He is personally charged with taking care that the nation's laws are faithfully executed. And while he has the apparatus of the entire federal government to aid him in discharging his Constitutional functions, he is no titular head of government. To the contrary, only he – or those working in the White House on his behalf – has the authority to order all federal agencies to take action, to resolve disputes among participating federal agencies, and to ensure that the government *as a whole* functions as it should in a time of crisis and catastrophe.

He has another, more symbolic role, which is also very important. As Presidential scholar Clinton Rossiter has written, the President is "the one-man distillation of the American people."[1] President Bush showed the power of that role in the wake of 9/11, when he made clear to the nation that he was in control of the response.

But in the events leading up to and following Hurricane Katrina's landfall, the President and his staff did not provide early, urgent, and strong public leadership, and the nation suffered.

The White House was aware long before Katrina struck that FEMA did not have the capability to handle a catastrophe, but failed to adequately address the critical shortcomings in preparedness.

Throughout his term as FEMA Director, Michael Brown sounded the alarm to White House officials about the degradation of FEMA's capabilities and that the agency was not prepared to handle a catastrophe. For example, after the tsunami that struck Southeast Asia in 2004, Brown told President Bush that FEMA did not have the resources to respond to a catastrophe of that magnitude.[2]

Brown also repeatedly told then-White House Chief of Staff Andrew Card, Deputy Chief of Staff Joe Hagin, and then-Office of Management and Budget Director Josh Bolten that FEMA did not have the capabilities to respond adequately to a catastrophe and sought additional resources.[3] Brown said that he told these officials several times that "We [FEMA] weren't getting the money we needed; we weren't getting the personnel that we needed, that DHS was – I don't think I ever used with them the word emaciating us, but I described to them, you know, DHS was not really following the Homeland Security Act and giving [emergency preparedness and response] the muscle that it was supposed to have."[4]

We do not know what the White House did with Brown's requests, but we do know that FEMA was underfunded and unprepared heading into the 2005 hurricane season. As the chief executive of the federal government, the President bears responsibility for FEMA's lack of preparedness.

> The White House had been aware of the "New Orleans Scenario," a catastrophic hurricane hitting New Orleans. Despite this awareness, the White House failed to ensure that the federal government was prepared to respond to this catastrophic scenario.

As discussed in the Committee's report, the threat of a Category 3 storm to New Orleans was well known, and the White House was among those who clearly knew of it. In early 2004, for example, Assistant to the President and Homeland Security Advisor General John A. Gordon traveled to New Orleans to receive a briefing on the region's catastrophic-hurricane planning efforts. The briefing was comprehensive and detailed. Gen. Gordon learned about the catastrophic consequences of a Category 3 hurricane striking New Orleans, and reported the information to the White House with a request for funding that resulted in the Hurricane Pam exercise, the first inter-governmental exercise to test preparation for and response to such a contingency.[5]

Another White House aide, Janet Benini, Director of Response and Planning for the White House Homeland Security Council, attended the Hurricane Pam exercise (although she did not work at the White House during the Katrina response).[6] Benini also chaired the group that developed the National Planning Scenarios, a set of 15 plausible, high-consequence events used by the federal government to come up with preparedness goals and lists of emergency-response capabilities necessary for federal, state, and local responders. One of the scenarios was a hurricane hitting New Orleans.[7]

Both Benini and Kirstjen Nielsen, the Senior Director for Preparedness and Response at the White House Homeland Security Council, received an e-mail in February 2005 indicating that flooding in New Orleans "could cause similar devastation" as the tsunami did in Southeast Asia.[8]

When Katrina landed in the United States in August 2005, we found a federal government that was unprepared for a catastrophic hurricane. The White House's failure to ensure such preparedness is therefore particularly profound, in light of its understanding of the catastrophic New Orleans scenario for close to two years before Katrina hit.

> Despite the clear warnings before landfall that Katrina would be catastrophic, the President and the White House staff were not sufficiently engaged and failed to initiate a sufficiently strong and proactive response.

The White House's – and the President's – knowledge of the risk of a massive storm to New Orleans became even more specific in the days leading up to Hurricane Katrina. Katrina was a lesser challenge to the nation's emergency-management apparatus than the 9/11 attacks in one critical way: It was preceded by 72 hours of increasingly dire predictions. In the days before landfall, the White House received repeated warnings from top officials at the National Weather Service and the National Hurricane Center that Katrina's impact would be catastrophic. FEMA and DHS's National Infrastructure Simulation and Analysis Center echoed the alarm in direct messages to the White House, as did senior state officials.[9]

Saturday, August 27, 2005 (Two Days before Landfall)

These warnings began on Saturday, August 27, 2005, two days before landfall. FEMA Director Brown says he spoke directly to President Bush, saying that Katrina could be catastrophic – "the big one" that meteorologists, emergency-management experts, and government officials had feared for years.[10]

On Saturday, White House staff in Crawford, Texas, where the President was vacationing, members of the White House Homeland Security Council, and other White House offices participated in a noon video teleconference call organized by FEMA. The potentially catastrophic nature of Katrina was discussed during this conversation as well.[11] Brown said:

> I know I am preaching to the choir on this one, but I've learned over the past four and a half, five years, to go with my gut on a lot of things, and I've got to tell you my gut hurts on this one. It hurts. I've got cramps. So, we need to take this one very, very seriously.[12]

During the same call, a National Hurricane Center forecaster discussed the danger of Katrina's storm surge:

> Well, obviously, where it's headed, you're at the worst possible locations for storm surge. You remember [Hurricane] Camille and its 26 feet. I would advise all the folks that are in the potential path of this storm to be looking at their maximum off the storm surge models, the meows [maximum envelopes of water] and whatnot off of a Category 4 or 5 storm, and plan accordingly.[13]

Yet White House Deputy Chief of Staff Joe Hagin, the senior White House official participating in the FEMA video teleconference, asked no questions after Brown's severe forecast. Instead, Hagin limited himself to a perplexingly optimistic assessment of FEMA's readiness: "We're here, and anything we can do, obviously, to support you, but it sounds like the planning, as usual, is in good shape, and good luck to the States and just know that we're watching, and we'll do the right thing as fast as we can."[14]

The warnings continued through the night. At 11:24 p.m., the White House received a National Weather Service–National Hurricane Center report which said: "The bottom line is that Katrina is expected to be an intense and dangerous hurricane heading towards the North Central Gulf Coast … and this has to be taken very seriously."[15]

Sunday, August 28, 2005 (Day before Landfall)

There was another FEMA video teleconference at noon on Sunday. This time, President Bush took part, along with officials from DHS, FEMA, Louisiana, and Mississippi.[16] Dr. Max Mayfield, Director of the National Hurricane Center, predicted Katrina would be a "very dangerous hurricane," adding that the possibility that levees could be overtopped was a "very, very grave concern.[17]

FEMA Director Michael Brown reiterated his concern: "My gut tells me – I told you guys my gut was that this [missing] is a bad one and a big one," and that Katrina could be "a catastrophe within a catastrophe."[18] Bill Doran, the Chief of Operations for Louisiana's Office of Homeland Security and Emergency Preparedness, said that the state was undergoing "planning for a catastrophic event."[19]

Neither the President nor his staff made any inquiries. The President offered only the following statement:

> I want to assure the folks at the state level that we are fully prepared to not only help you during the storm, but we will move in whatever resources and assets

we have at our disposal after the storm to help you deal with the loss of property. And we pray for no loss of life, of course.

Unfortunately, we've had experience at this in recent years, and I – the FEMA folks have done great work in the past, and I'm confident, Mike, that you and your team will do all you can to help the good folks in these affected states.

Again, I want to thank [Louisiana] Governor [Kathleen] Blanco and [Alabama] Governor [Bob] Riley and [Mississippi] Governor [Haley Barbour], Governor [Jeb] Bush of Florida, for heeding these warnings, and doing all you can possibly do with your state folks and local folks to prepare the citizenry for this storm.

In the meantime, I know the nation will be praying for the good folks in the affected areas, and we just hope for the very best.[20]

The White House continued to receive warnings about the storm's projected force throughout the day.[21] Early Sunday morning, it had been notified that Katrina had been upgraded to a Category 5 storm; at approximately 5 p.m. ET, DHS's Homeland Security Operations Center sent to the White House a report that included a National Oceanic and Atmospheric Administration update, which repeated Dr. Mayfield's warning about floodwaters overtopping New Orleans' levees.[22]

The warnings continued throughout late Sunday night and early Monday morning, just hours before landfall. At 1:47 a.m. ET, the Homeland Security Operations Center sent the White House a report from DHS's National Infrastructure Simulation and Analysis Center, which predicted: "Any storm rated Category 4 or greater on the Saffir-Simpson scale will likely lead to severe flooding and/or levee breaching. This could leave the New Orleans area being submerged for weeks or months. … The magnitude of this storm is expected to cause massive flooding."[23]

To his credit, the President did take at least two steps that showed some understanding of the urgency of the impending crisis: First, at the requests of Governors Blanco, Barbour, and Riley, the President issued a pre-storm declaration of emergency for the Gulf Coast states, which ensured that the federal government would finance many pre-landfall and post-landfall activities undertaken by state and local officials.[24] This had only been done once in the previous 15 years, when President Clinton issued four pre-landfall declarations, all for Hurricane Floyd in 1999. Second, on the day before landfall, at the urging of FEMA Director Brown,[25] the President called Governor Blanco to urge a mandatory evacuation of New Orleans; however, that call occurred "just before she walk[ed] into the news conference" with Mayor Nagin to announce the evacuation of New Orleans.[26] Therefore, the President's call came too late, as the Governor and Mayor had already decided to announce the mandatory evacuation.

With the exception of these two steps, in the face of dire warnings of the catastrophe before landfall, there was a failure of presidential leadership and initiative.

Although the President and the White House were following events after landfall, they seemed surprisingly detached until two days later, Wednesday, August 31, 2005.

Secretary of Homeland Security Michael Chertoff has said that the President was "acutely aware of Katrina and the risk it posed" during the weekend before landfall.[27] "[W]e went into the weekend before," Secretary Chertoff said, "with an understanding and with warnings that this was potentially the nightmare scenario that I think people have talked about for years in terms of New Orleans."[28]

Unfortunately, the President's behavior didn't reflect this awareness. Instead of exercising the actual and symbolic leadership of the President, he seemed detached.

The President didn't return to Washington until two days after Katrina hit,[29] sending a clear message to the rest of the federal government about the storm's perceived importance in the federal hierarchy, and depriving the government of the clear and significant focus the storm required at that point. As Congressman Tom Davis, Chairman of the House Select Bipartisan Committee to Investigate the Preparation for and Response to Hurricane Katrina aptly put it, "The director … of the National Hurricane Center said this was the big one," but "when this happened … Bush is in Texas. Card is in Maine. The vice president is fly-fishing. I mean, who's in charge here?"[30]

The White House's failure to set in motion a more proactive set of pre-landfall preparations by the federal government was part of the reason the response was so ineffective.

This presidential detachment is particularly unacceptable because of the flow of specific information coming into the White House about the growing catastrophe that was occurring on America's Gulf Coast.

Monday, August 29, 2005 (Day of Landfall)

Katrina came ashore in Louisiana at 6:10 a.m. CT, Monday morning, August 29, 2005.[31] As early as 11:13 a.m. ET, the White House's own Homeland Security Council circulated a report with the following information:

- A levee in New Orleans had broken;
- Based on a report from the Homeland Security Operations Center, water was rising in the city's Lower Ninth Ward;
- Based on a report from Governor Blanco, water was rising at one foot per hour; and
- Based on a report from Mayor Nagin, problems with a pumping station were undermining the city's ability to relieve flooding.[32]

Minutes later, the Homeland Security Operations Center e-mailed the White House that at 7:30 a.m. CT, Mayor Nagin had announced that there was "water coming over the levee system in the Lower Ninth Ward;"[33] that the State of Louisiana's Adjutant General, Maj. Gen. Bennett Landreneau, had confirmed that water was rising in the Lower Ninth Ward;[34] and that local officials had said that "floodwaters are encroaching on roads in the lower-lying parishes of St. Bernard and Plaquemines."[35]

At noon, White House Deputy Chief of Staff Hagin, who was traveling with the President on Air Force One, participated in a conference call with state and local officials who reported flooding of eight to 10 feet in St. Bernard Parish.[36] The President did not take part in the call.

The White House, and Hagin in particular, also received direct reports from FEMA Director Brown.[37] According to Brown, he informed Hagin no later than 6 p.m. CT Monday that New Orleans' 17th Street levee had broken, and that the city was flooding.[38] Brown testified that he was certain that the information reached the President: "I never worried about whether I talked directly to the President because I knew that in speaking to Joe [Hagin], I was talking directly to the President."[39]

FEMA Director Brown testified that he made some 30 calls to the President, White House Chief of Staff Andrew Card, Deputy Chief of Staff Joe Hagin, and other senior White House officials throughout the weekend before landfall.[40] Because the White House refused to cooperate with the Committee's requests, we don't know what the President and his staff did with the information about the impending disaster from Brown and others. What questions did they ask? What instructions did they give? Card and Hagin were getting direct and unequivocal assessments of a catastrophe from the federal official charged with coordinating the response to the storm. Brown recalls telling Hagin in a Sunday afternoon call "how bad this one was going to be" and was "adamant" that the White House should understand his concern about New Orleans.[41] Did Hagin tell the President, as Brown assumed? Were there discussions about marshaling federal assets? Were calls made from the White House to Secretary Chertoff? Did Card or Hagin reach out to other Cabinet secretaries? Did they contact Secretary Rumsfeld about the readiness of the military to enter the Gulf Coast to help? The White House has declined to answer such important questions, and so the Committee therefore is unable to offer any insights into these critical issues.

What we do know is that instead of responding to the ominous reports from the Gulf Coast, the President spent the day of landfall discussing Medicare in Arizona and California, as well as joining Arizona Senator John McCain at his birthday celebration.[42]

At 4:40 p.m. New Orleans time, as Hurricane Katrina was flooding and battering the city, the President was in Rancho Cucamonga, California, delivering a speech on Medicare and new prescription-drug benefits. He offered only this brief assessment of the unfolding crisis in the Gulf during a 30-minute speech:

> We're in constant contact with the local officials down there. The storm is moving through, and we're now able to assess damage, or beginning to assess damage. ... For those of you who are concerned about whether or not we're prepared to help, don't be. We are. We're in place. We've got equipment in place, supplies in place. And once the – once we're able to assess the damage, we'll be able to move in and help those good folks in the affected areas.[43]

President Bush had offered similar assurances to survivors of the storm earlier in the day, during a "Conversation on Medicare" at the Pueblo El Mirage RV Resort and Country Club in El Mirage, Arizona:

> When the storm passes, the federal government has got assets and resources that we'll be deploying to help you.[44]

As we now know – and the President should have known then – this was not the case: As the Committee has demonstrated throughout this report, various levels of government were not prepared to help.

The White House received additional reports that the levees had broken in the early hours of Tuesday, August 30 (the day after landfall), but continued to operate as if it hadn't. At 12:02 a.m. ET, the White House received a report from the Homeland Security Operations Center that included this chilling assessment by the lone official FEMA had sent to New Orleans, public-affairs officer Marty Bahamonde: "There is a quarter-mile breech (sic) in the levee near the 17th Street Canal about 200 yards from Lake Pontchartrain allowing water to flow into the City ... an estimated 2/3 to 75% of the city is under water."[45]

Another DHS situation report, at 6:33 a.m. ET, confirmed the extent of flooding and damage in New Orleans:

> Widespread and significant flooding has occurred throughout the city of New Orleans, extending eastward, across the Mississippi gulf coast into coastal Alabama. The following flood reports have been received for the city of New Orleans:
>
> • Industrial Canal at Tennessee St.: levee has been breached, with water to a depth of 5 feet at Jackson Barracks
>
> • 17th St. at Canal Blvd.: levee has been breached – breach extends several 100 meters in length
>
> • Much of downtown and east New Orleans is underwater, depth unknown at this time.
>
> The U.S. Army Corps of Engineers estimates are in progress and project that it could take months to dewater the City of New Orleans.[46]

A 10:23 a.m. ET report from the Homeland Security Operations Center detailed the locations of the breached levees and noted specific concerns about the 17th Street Canal and Tennessee Street levees.[47]

These reports notwithstanding, no one from the White House participated in an inter-governmental conference call at noon organized by FEMA. Instead, the President was at a naval base in San Diego, where, once again, he offered a falsely reassuring assessment of the crisis: "Our teams and equipment are in place and we're beginning to move in the help that people need."[48]

In fact, it seems as if President Bush and, consequently, the Administration, did not grasp that Katrina was a catastrophe until later in the day – a full day and a half after landfall – when Michael Brown informed President Bush, Vice-President Cheney, Secretary Chertoff, and Deputy Chief of Staff Karl Rove in a telephone call that at least 90 percent of New Orleans's population had been displaced and that responders "needed military assets; this was the big one."[49] He added that FEMA "needed the help of the entire cabinet ... DOD and HHS and everybody else."[50]

Brown testified that this, at last, may have been the turning point in the President's comprehension of the catastrophe:

> And as I recall my first statement to him was, you know, Mr. President, I estimate right now that 90 percent of the population of New Orleans has been displaced. And he is like, My God you mean it is that bad? Yes, sir, it was that bad.[51]

Brown added that he thought the officials on the call continued to fail to grasp how badly FEMA and the state were overwhelmed,[52] but Brown's alarm seems to have prompted a "discussion about convening the Cabinet."[53]

On Tuesday morning, while in California, White House Press Secretary Scott McClellan announced that the President would return to Washington, D.C., on Wednesday in order to "oversee the response efforts from there."[54]

Soon after, the President began to take steps to amplify and organize the government's response. At 5:11 p.m., nearly 60 hours after landfall, President Bush, surrounded by his Cabinet, addressed the nation from the Rose Garden, announcing that he had convened the Cabinet and "directed Secretary of Homeland Security Mike Chertoff to chair a Cabinet-level task force to coordinate all our assistance from Washington."[55] Notably, the task force demanded a list of available resources from each federal agency assigned responsibility in a disaster under the National Response Plan.[56] For example, FEMA was asked for "the inventory of all department agency operations/activity. ... Are [there] any Federal powers or other processes that could be implemented to expedite the response or make it more efficient. ... What are the plans for providing housing to ... displaced people by hurricane damage?"[57] These questions were being asked for the first time more than two days after landfall.

When Hurricane Rita threatened the Gulf Coast weeks later, the nation saw what can happen when the White House becomes more actively engaged in catastrophe preparedness before landfall. For example, on September 20, 2005, three days before landfall, the President participated in a hurricane briefing shortly after Rita had become a Category 1 hurricane.[58] After the briefing, the President announced that a Coast Guard admiral would be stationed in Texas to coordinate the response[59] and later that day made an emergency declaration for the State of Florida at the request of its Governor. On September 21, two days before Rita made landfall, the President also issued disaster declarations for Louisiana and Texas.[60] On September 22, the day before the storm hit, the President visited Texas to "get a firsthand look at the preparations"[61] and then traveled to Northern Command, the domestic military headquarters in Colorado, where he participated in a series of briefings detailing the response and coordination between DOD, other government agencies, and state and local governments[62]

In the case of Katrina, the President did not take equally meaningful action until two days after landfall. The President should have made these critical moves – returning to Washington, convening the Cabinet, taking stock of the federal government's readiness for Katrina, making sure key White House staff were at their posts, and directly addressing the people of the Gulf Coast – before landfall.

After the hurricane, the White House continued to demonstrate a lack of understanding of the magnitude of the catastrophe.

Even several days after landfall, statements from the President and the White House suggested that they still did not understand or appreciate what had happened to New Orleans.

On the Thursday, September 1, edition of "Good Morning America," the President said that "I don't think anybody anticipated the breach of the levees."[63] He was later given an opportunity to correct his statement. The President said he was not misinformed and affirmed his view, continuing:

> When that storm came by, a lot of people said we dodged a bullet. When that storm came through at first, people said, Whew. There was a sense of relaxation, and that's what I was referring to. And I, myself, thought we had dodged a bullet. You know why? Because I was listening to people, probably over the [airwaves], say, the bullet has been dodged. And that was what I was referring to. Of course, there were plans in case the levee had been breached. There was a sense of relaxation in the moment, a critical moment.[64]

But the President was wrong.

The levees breached soon after the storm came ashore,[65] as was noted in the reports that arrived at the White House.[66] The vulnerability of the levees to a catastrophic storm was known long before Katrina.[67] Besides, the city was threatened as much by flooding from overtopping as it was from breaches, a danger forewarned in the years before Katrina and reiterated in the months before landfall by federal agencies.[68]

During a press conference in Mobile, Alabama on Friday following landfall, President Bush infamously said of Brown, "Brownie, you're doing a heck of a job."[69] Brown's performance was anything but worthy of praise. This comment was totally at odds with what was apparent to all – that the federal government's response, which was supposed to have been led in part by then FEMA Director Brown, was grossly inadequate. It serves as an example of just how disengaged President Bush was from the failed response. It illustrates the President's failure to understand Katrina's devastation and the suffering of Katrina's victims.

The White House received a massive amount of information from a wide range of authoritative sources describing in dire terms the catastrophe unfolding in the Gulf.[70] While some media reports inaccurately described the storm as a near-miss that had mostly spared the city, the President of the United States should have been fully and accurately informed and should have acted urgently on that information.

Decisive presidential leadership before and immediately after Katrina was missing. How much it could have mitigated the loss of life and anguish of survivors in the Gulf Coast will never be known.

Part II: Lack of Administration Cooperation in Investigation

The Administration's failure to cooperate with the Committee's investigation had regrettable consequences. In too many instances, the Committee faced agencies and Departments that saw its efforts as a nuisance – and their own response as up to their discretion. And the worst offender was the entity that should have stood above the fray and worked hardest with the Committee to uncover the government's failings in Katrina: the White House.

Despite President Bush's pronouncement early on that he recognized that "Congress also has an important oversight function to perform" and his commitment that "I will work with members of both parties to make sure this effort is thorough,"[71] our Committee faced a White House less willing to cooperate with a Senate investigation than any we have witnessed in our many years in this body. That is why we ultimately concluded that the Committee should issue subpoenas to the White House to produce the material that the Committee asked for during its investigation. Unfortunately, the Chairman disagreed with Senator Lieberman's request to issue subpoenas, and so, the Committee did not obtain all that we believe was necessary for a comprehensive investigation.

There are matters that we could not fully explore because of agency and Administration recalcitrance and, in some cases, intransigence. We don't know what we don't know – for example, as a result of the Justice Department's failure to produce large volumes of what the Committee had requested. But one thing we do know is that because we were denied the opportunity to fully explore the role the White House played in preparing for and responding to Katrina, we have little insight into how the President and his staff monitored, managed, and directed the government's disaster preparedness in the post-9/11 world, how they coordinated the rest of the federal bureaucracy in response to Katrina, or how leadership was exercised by the only entity in the federal government with the authority to order all the others to act. Without this information, the Committee's investigation necessarily lacked the ability to fully and fairly analyze and assess a critical element of the response to Katrina.

We have plenty of circumstantial evidence to believe that there were significant failures of leadership at the top and actions that should have been taken but were not. That evidence is discussed in the previous section of these additional views. But there remain too many important questions that cannot be answered conclusively because the White House did not provide the information necessary to do so.

Clearly, our government was unprepared to deal with the catastrophe of Katrina. Only through a thorough and comprehensive investigation of what went wrong could we be assured that the government will know what steps are necessary to get it right the next time. Full cooperation in this investigation was critical, but was denied.

The White House

A Chronology of Efforts to Obtain Information from the White House

On October 7, 2005, the Committee sent a letter, signed by Chairman Collins and Senator Lieberman, to White House Chief of Staff Andrew H. Card, Jr. The letter was similar to those sent to over twenty federal agencies and Departments, as well as to the Governors of Louisiana, Mississippi and Alabama, the Mayors of New Orleans, Biloxi, Gulfport, and Mobile, and a number of other state and local agencies. The goal of these letters was to help the Committee collect a comprehensive set of documents and information that would allow it to understand what those at all levels of all relevant governments did or didn't do to prepare for and respond to Hurricane Katrina.

The White House letter sought a variety of documents and information. Some requests were basic, like those that asked the White House to identify its various components with emergency-preparedness and response responsibilities, to explain how the White House learns of and monitors hurricanes, and to provide an organizational chart of the relevant White House components. Others sought more detailed, Katrina-specific information, such as how the White House and the President first learned about the storm, who was responsible for processing requests from the Governors for emergency declarations, how much the White House understood about the vulnerability of New Orleans to flooding, and, perhaps most importantly, a description of what the White House specifically did to prepare for and respond to the hurricane. The Committee also asked for documents related to all of these issues.

The closest cognates we have to the White House – the governors of the affected states – responded well to similar letters. Louisiana Governor Kathleen Blanco's office, for example, produced over 8,000 pages of substantive documents, including a large number of e-mails to or from the Governor herself, and granted the Committee access to all six members of her staff with whom it requested interviews. Similarly, Mississippi Governor Haley Barbour's office provided the information that the Committee asked for, including material directly involving the Governor's office and his staff, and the Committee interviewed both members of the Governor's staff for whom it asked. The cooperation the Committee received from these offices greatly enhanced the Committee's ability to understand what happened, and helped ensure that it could be confident in the Committee report's findings and conclusions.

The White House was an entirely different story. On November 3, 2005, the Committee received its initial response. In a letter signed by Deputy Counsel to the President William K. Kelley, the White House started off well, pledging that "[t]he Administration is committed to cooperating with your Committee." Unfortunately, it then offered very little to show for that commitment. Kelley's letter and the accompanying documents made clear that the White House had little intention of giving the Committee what it had requested. His letter noted that the Committee had sought information and documents from other Executive Branch agencies and observed:

> As is customary for any examination of an issue addressed by many components of the federal Government, the Administration's principal form of

assistance will be through the production of information from those agencies and departments most directly involved in preparing for and responding to Hurricane Katrina. . . . As is traditional for responses to Congressional Committee requests for information, the [White House] stands ready to assist your Committee in appropriate ways once the scope and content of the agencies' and departments' production of information can be assessed in relation to your Committee's remaining requirements.

As discussed further below, the views expressed by Kelley were neither customary nor traditional, but given them, it was not surprising that the near entirety of the nearly 4,000 accompanying pages of documents were publicly available. In fact, a portion of this production – White House press releases, copies of press conferences, and copies of press gaggles – could be found on the White House's web site. The production also included situation reports and updates that were sent to many recipients, only one of which was the White House, from other federal agencies and departments, as well as widely circulated e-mails sent by DHS as part of its responsibility under the National Response Plan to disseminate information throughout the federal government. These latter e-mails primarily consisted of DHS and FEMA press releases as well as Department "Talking Points." In sum, not only did Kelley's letter decline to answer a single one of the questions posed in the Committee's October 7 letter; it also did not bring with it much in the way of responsive or informative documents.

To make matters worse, the Committee soon learned that despite the White House's suggestion that the Committee seek its information elsewhere, the White House was in fact directing the federal agencies that were producing documents and witnesses for the Committee's investigation to withhold from the Committee any material or testimony relating to the agencies' or witnesses' interactions with the White House.

The Committee spent the next two months attempting to work these matters out at a staff level. Committee pressure yielded marginally more documents and a three-hour briefing from the White House's Deputy Homeland Security Advisor, Ken Rapuano. Many of the additional documents were of the same type as previously produced. The White House provided several e-mails, updates, and reports it had received from DHS's Homeland Security Operations Center (HSOC), consisting primarily of repackaged material that other agencies, including federal and state entities, sent to the HSOC. In many cases, the White House produced multiple copies of the same widely distributed material. As for material actually generated within the White House, though the Committee did receive a small number of substantive e-mails from a very small number of lower-level White House Homeland Security Council (HSC) staff, those e-mails offered little insight into what the White House was actually doing, and the Committee received nothing from the files of those in higher-level positions.

In short, the Committee did not receive information or documents showing what actually was going on within the White House and was still left with little insight into the White House's substantive actions in preparation for and response to Hurricane Katrina. And Rapuano's briefing, while informative, focused primarily on what the White House had learned about the federal response writ large; it did not address roles played by specific White House officials or specific actions taken by the Executive Office of the President (EOP).

Frustrated by the White House's omissions (its failure to produce what the Committee had requested), as well as its commissions (its interference with productions and testimony from other agencies), the Committee sent Card a second letter on January 12, 2006. The letter, again signed by both Chairman Collins and Senator Lieberman, expressed concern about the White House's response to the investigation. It assessed the status of the White House production this way:

> We have received several boxes of documents, which we do appreciate. However, a majority of that material was either publicly available or originated in other agencies, offering little insight into what the EOP knew or did during this catastrophic event. We also received a briefing from the Homeland Security Counsel (HSC), which we view as a constructive and useful attempt to convey to the Committee some information about the HSC's "Lessons Learned Review" as well as, generally, some of the key events the EOP was aware of in the days leading up to and following Hurricane Katrina. The briefing did not, however, address roles played by specific EOP officials or specific actions taken by the EOP. As a result, to date, we have yet to receive the bulk of what we requested, and the Committee is unable to fully understand and assess actions involving White House personnel during the preparations for and response to Hurricane Katrina.

The Committee's letter saved its harshest language for its assessment of the White House's directions to agency counsel to keep White House-related information from the Committee: "This practice," Senators Collins and Lieberman wrote, "simply must cease." They continued:

> We are willing to discuss claims of executive privilege asserted by the White House, either directly or through a federal agency. But we will not stand for blanket instructions to refuse answering any questions concerning any communications with the EOP.

The Committee's letter also took issue with another of the White House's arguments: That the White House was acting within tradition by telling the Committee that it must wait for the White House's response until after other agencies provided theirs: "Respectfully," Chairman Collins and Senator Lieberman wrote:

> We are aware of no such tradition. Indeed, this Committee, as well as others, has repeatedly conducted investigations of matters involving this and previous White Houses and has never held White House requests in abeyance.

In an effort to end the impasse, the Committee offered the White House a significantly pared-down list of priorities and asked that it produce particular documents and provide specific individuals for interviews by January 23, 2006.

On January 27, 2006, the White House responded. In a letter again signed by Kelley, the White House once again paid homage to "Congress's important role in examining events surrounding Hurricane Katrina and the need for the Executive Branch to assist those inquiries." Then, once again, it declined to provide what the Committee had asked for. Instead, it offered to address the Committee's requests through a combination of a briefing and additional documents. It declined to furnish any of the requested witnesses.

As for the complaint about the White House's hindering of Committee efforts to obtain from other agencies information related to the White House, Kelley explained that the White House was allowing agency personnel to "discuss factual and operational communications involving nearly all EOP personnel other than a relatively small number of officials most directly involved in supporting the President's actions and determinations." This category was later described to Committee staff as including all individuals at the level of Deputy Assistant to the President and above and all individuals, regardless of level, in the Chief of Staff's office. While Kelley's letter suggested that this left a wide area of inquiry open to the Committee, the reality was that it walled off documents and testimony involving virtually anyone in the White House who had any level of responsibility or involvement with Katrina, regardless of whether that person actually had anything to do with advising the President.

On February 3, 2006, the Committee received its second briefing from Rapuano, and by February 8, it had in hand the additional documents the White House promised in its January 27 letter. Rapuano's briefing, while again helpful in answering questions about the activities of some of the federal agencies and about the White House, offered few of the additional specific details the Committee had sought about the White House's actions. The documents did not differ markedly in type from those received already: The Committee had obtained virtually all of them previously from other agencies; consequently, they offered little new insight. As an example, the Committee asked for all White House documents related to the deployment of federal troops to the Gulf region. Given the weighty implications of deploying our premier fighting force on domestic soil, and the controversies surrounding the timing of those deployments and the allegations that Governor Blanco was responsible for the delay, the Committee believed that access to this information from the White House was critical to understanding and informing the American people of this important part of the Katrina story. But the documents provided by the White House consisted mainly of situation reports, most of which already had been produced to the Committee by the Pentagon, and did not address the issue of troop deployment.

Around the time of this exchange, the Committee gained virtually its only significant insight into what actually happened within the White House immediately before and after Katrina's landfall. It learned this information only because former FEMA Director Michael Brown refused to decline to answer the Committee's questions about his communications with the White House absent an assertion of executive privilege by the President. When the President declined to invoke that privilege, Brown testified before the Committee on Friday, February 10, and shortly thereafter sat for a more detailed, transcribed interview with Committee staff. In both instances, Brown made clear that he saw the White House as a critical player in the preparations for and response to Hurricane Katrina.

Brown testified that, before landfall, he had conveyed to the President that, depending on where it struck, the storm could be catastrophic.[72] He also told the Committee that he believed that on Monday, August 29, the day of Katrina's landfall, he spoke with Deputy White House Chief of Staff Joe Hagin on at least two occasions to inform him of the situation on the ground in New Orleans.[73] Brown testified that in a call with Hagin – placed after Brown received FEMA employee Marty Bahamonde's eyewitness account of the extent of the devastation – "I think I told [Hagin] that we were realizing our worst nightmare, that everything we had planned about, worried about, that FEMA, frankly, had worried about for 10 years, was coming true."[74] According to Brown's interview, by Monday evening there was no doubt that Hagin knew from Brown that the 17th Street Canal levee had broken and that New Orleans was flooding.[75] Additionally, at approximately 10 p.m. that night, White House Chief of Staff Andy Card informed Brown in an e-mail exchange that Hagin had kept him "well-informed" of Brown's reports. Brown reiterated to Card that "this is a bad one."[76]

Just as importantly, Brown made clear that he believed that informing and seeking action from the White House was capable of producing faster results than contacting the designated leader of the federal response, Homeland Security Secretary Michael Chertoff.[77] Brown's testimony made clear that he believed that the White House had a significant role to play in coordinating and helping to manage the response to Katrina. After putting that testimony together with what the investigation had already revealed about the federal government's activities during the week after landfall, Senator Lieberman concluded that the Committee would be remiss if it did not follow up on the multiple questions regarding White House action left unanswered by Brown's testimony and the rest of our investigation.

In sum, despite the Committee's detailed requests, intended to enable an understanding of the actions taken by the White House during Hurricane Katrina, the Committee had received interviews with none of the requested White House witnesses, written answers to none of the questions posed in the October 7, 2005, letter to the White House, and roughly 17,000 pages of documents, the vast majority of which consisted of publicly available material, material otherwise generated by other agencies, and reports and updates from DHS's Homeland Security Operations Center. In addition, the Committee failed to receive from federal agencies an unknown volume of responsive material as a result of White House orders to withhold anything related to or referencing virtually anyone of significance in the White House.

After reviewing that response, Senator Lieberman wrote Chairman Collins on March 15, 2006, asking her to issue subpoenas to (1) the White House for the documents requested in their joint January 12, 2006, letter; (2) to five members of the White House staff most involved in the response, ordering them to sit for Committee depositions; and (3) to each federal agency to which they previously sent request letters, compelling them to produce previously withheld White House-related material.[78] The Chairman declined. And we believe that the investigation is the worse for it.

Analysis of the White House's Arguments

We do not believe that the White House, or any Executive Branch agency, must automatically turn over material to a Congressional committee simply because it has been asked to do so. What we do believe – indeed, know – is that Congressional committees have significant authority to seek and obtain material from the White House and Executive Branch agencies when they are conducting legitimate oversight or investigations on matters within their jurisdiction, absent an assertion of a valid privilege to the contrary. During the Committee's months of efforts to obtain the information sought from the White House, the White House provided no satisfactory reason for its limited response.

We have already referenced the fallacy of the White House's assertion that it appropriately directed the Committee elsewhere for its information. As noted above, Chairman Collins and Senator Lieberman rejected that argument in their January 12, 2006, letter to Card. And, in a November 29, 2005, report, the non-partisan Congressional Research Service (CRS) agreed that the White House was wrong to assert that custom or tradition allows it to point Congressional investigative committees elsewhere to seek information or that the White House is permitted to defer answers to specific requests until *it* has assessed the Committee's needs:

> Without question, under Senate rules, your Committee has jurisdictional responsibility and authority to conduct an investigation of the preparations for and response to Hurricane Katrina by all governmental entities that had roles, responsibilities and authorities in dealing with that catastrophic event. That investigative authority reaches the White House and concerned elements of the Executive Office of the President. We are aware of no legal authority that allows a targeted entity, whether it is a government agency, including the EOP, or private party, to dictate to a jurisdictional committee the manner, order or timing of the exercise of its exercise of investigative authority.[79]

Kelley's January 27, 2006, letter also suggested that our requests implicated "very important Executive Branch interests," including "avoiding the burden on officials most directly supporting the President, threatening to impair the President's ability to discharge his constitutional duties; preserving the confidentiality required to support Presidential decision-making; and adhering to the course of dealings between the branches, in analogous contexts, regarding the occasions for broad inquiry into EOP policymaking and deliberations."

But the Committee tried to accommodate those interests to the extent they were legitimate. In informal conversations throughout the fall and then in the Chairman's and Senator Lieberman's January 12, 2006, letter, the Committee sought to prioritize its requests, but that prioritization yielded precious little additional information in return. Perhaps even more importantly, the virtually complete immunity from our inquiry claimed by the White House to protect its asserted interests was far out of proportion with those interests and highly inconsistent with the manner in which Congressional investigations have been conducted in the past.

This Committee has repeatedly conducted investigations touching on or directly involving the White House. But never before have we seen a White House that not only denies the Committee most relevant information, but also precludes the Committee from receiving from other agencies most material relating to the White House's involvement. In his January 27, 2006, letter, Kelley asserted that the White House was giving the Committee access to material involving "factual and operational communications involving nearly all EOP personnel other than a relatively small number of officials most directly involved in supporting the President's actions and determinations." But, as already discussed, this exception neutralized the rule: Virtually anyone in the White House whose actions had operational significance to the preparation for and response to Katrina falls into the category made off-limits to the Committee.

And, of course, the Committee was denied requested interviews with even those lower-level employees about whom the White House said it was willing to give us information. This left the Committee unable to obtain any real sense of what the White House did or didn't do to direct or assist the federal response to Katrina. And it kept the Committee from obtaining key information from Executive Branch agencies about the government's response to Katrina. For months, Committee staff repeatedly asked White House staff for precedent for the White House's sweeping assertion of near-immunity from inquiry. They were given none.

The Congressional Research Service confirmed that the White House position was wrong. According to a February 9, 2006, CRS memorandum prepared for the Committee:

> The Supreme Court has held that "the scope of [Congress'] power of inquiry ... is as penetrating and far-reaching as the potential power to enact and appropriate under the Constitution," "encompasses inquiries concerning the administration of existing laws as well as proposed or possibly needed statutes," and is at its peak when the subject is alleged waste, fraud, abuse or maladministration. [citations omitted] In the last 80 years, Congress has consistently sought and obtained documents and testimony that reflects deliberations in agencies, including almost every office and bureau in the Department of Justice and the Executive Office of the President (EOP). *There have been some 75 instances in which EOP officials have testified before congressional committees, a list that includes chiefs of staff to the President, White House counsels and National Security Advisers.*[80]

In short, while we certainly recognize that there are important Executive Branch interests at stake whenever the Congress seeks to conduct oversight – interests which we believe the Committee tried to accommodate – the White House failed to recognize in return that there are countervailing and constitutionally based Legislative Branch interests at stake as well, namely the uncontested authority of the Congress to inquire into the Executive Branch's administration of federal programs.

It is the traditional view of the Congress that the only basis on which the Executive Branch may ultimately resist providing information requested by a Congressional committee is an assertion by the President of executive privilege. This Constitutional safeguard ensures that the Legislative Branch's determination that its constitutional functions require certain information may be outweighed only if the President is willing to conclude and assert that his constitutional interests demand otherwise. Of course, even then, the privilege is a qualified one and may be overcome, but the competing interests can't even be weighed if the President is unwilling to meet Congress's assertion of Constitutional authority with an equivalent assertion of his own. In the words of this Committee's former Chairman Fred Thompson, when addressing the previous Administration's efforts to resist a document request on a basis short of executive privilege:

> If the President is claiming special status because he is President, then his assertion is really one of executive privilege and not attorney-client privilege. While I can still remember [Watergate Committee chair] Sam Ervin's repeated admonitions that no man is above the law and that we are entitled to every man's evidence, I still concede that executive privilege can be a valid claim, under some circumstances. However, *the President must assert it.*[81]

This is a point the Committee itself recognized when Brown testified. Having asked the White House whether the President wished to assert executive privilege and having heard that it did not, the Chairman instructed Brown to answer questions regarding his contacts with the White House.[82]

It is due to this experience with Brown that we must respectfully disagree with one of the reasons the Chairman provided for declining Senator Lieberman's request to issue subpoenas, namely that it would merely force the President to assert executive privilege.[83] Based on the experience with Brown – and the fact that a significant portion of the material the Committee requested likely falls outside any legitimate claim of privilege – we firmly believe a subpoena would have been met with at least a modicum of compliance that would have aided the Committee's investigation significantly. After all, previous Administrations repeatedly have been willing to provide information of this sort to Congress. The current Administration also has provided to investigators even material that clearly could have been subject to a claim of privilege. Both the President and the Vice-President, for example, sat for a personal interview with the 9/11 Commission. Surely, the White House would have provided the Committee with more information than it did had it faced a Congressional subpoena.

Before leaving this topic, we want to comment on one more issue raised by at least some Administration representatives in response to the Committee's information and document requests. In seeking to justify the demonstrably lower level of cooperation seen from this Administration than from its predecessor, we heard that a different standard should apply in this investigation because of the absence of any allegations of criminal conduct.

We could not disagree more. Congress surely has a role to play in the investigation of conduct that may violate the law, and we have supported such investigations in the past, regardless of the political affiliation of the Administration. But if the case for White House cooperation is more persuasive for one type of investigation than the other, surely it would be for an investigation like the one into Katrina.

To the extent Congressional investigations involve allegations of criminal wrongdoing, a Congressional investigation simply isn't necessary to discover facts or hold perpetrators responsible, as it is likely to be accompanied by a parallel investigation by the Department of Justice, as we've seen with many of the recent scandal investigations.

Thankfully, there has been no such criminality on the part of government workers alleged here; instead, this was an investigation into wholesale errors, and, in many cases, incompetence. No other independent investigator with the authority to go fully where the facts lead has or will review this matter, and so the need for a full and fair review by the Congress is absolutely critical.[84]

The Department of Homeland Security

The Department of Homeland Security (DHS) presents a different case from the White House. In contrast to the White House, DHS did provide the Committee with a significant amount of information and access to a large number of witnesses – material without which the Committee could not have conducted its investigation or issued its report. But the Department did so in an often slow, spotty, and incomplete manner. On one hand, the Committee received a large amount of information and many witnesses from the Federal Emergency Management Agency (FEMA). But on the other, when we sought documents and witnesses from elsewhere in the Department, and particularly from DHS leadership, the Department frequently dragged its feet, taking an adversarial posture and ultimately producing only a small fraction of the documents and witnesses that reasonably could have been expected. For example, it took until January 13, 2006, for the Department to produce a single witness from outside FEMA or the Coast Guard. Similarly, the Committee did not receive documents from the Homeland Security Operations Center (HSOC)– an entity at the center of DHS's emergency-response mandate – until January 12, 2006. And despite increasingly urgent requests for the document, it took the Department until January 11, 2006, to give the Committee the Catastrophic Incident Supplement to the National Response Plan, a foundational document that the Committee could have used to question witnesses more knowledgeably had it only had it sooner. When combined with the Department's practice of waiting until the last minute to tell the Committee who it would supply as witnesses and providing a witness's e-mails and documents as late as the night before a scheduled interview, there is no doubt that the way in which the Department responded to the Committee's document, information, and witness requests significantly hampered the Committee's ability to conduct its investigation. As a result, though the Committee has gathered key facts, it still does not have as complete a picture as we would have liked of DHS's preparations and response to Katrina. Given Secretary Chertoff's public statements asserting the importance of learning the lessons, "even painful lessons," from Katrina, reasonably we had hoped for more.[85]

Chronology of DHS's Production

It was clear from the start that much of this Committee's investigation would turn on information provided by and about the Department of Homeland Security. DHS is the Department given the official responsibility to lead and coordinate preparations for and response to disasters, whether natural or man-made. Various DHS component agencies had significant operational responsibilities in the response as well; eventually, some 16 DHS offices became involved in the response.[86] This included not only the high-profile involvement of agencies such as FEMA and the U.S. Coast Guard, but also the National Communications System (NCS), an agency charged with coordinating the federal government's disaster communications support, and the Department's law enforcement assets – Immigration and Customs Enforcement (including the Federal Protective Service), the U.S. Secret Service,

Customs and Border Patrol, among others – many of which provided assistance with public safety and security in the Gulf Coast after Katrina.

Therefore, on September 28, 2005, the Committee sent four letters to DHS: (1) to FEMA; (2) to the Coast Guard; (3) to NCS (through the Assistant Secretary for Infrastructure Protection); and (4) to Secretary Chertoff for the remainder of the Department. These letters asked for a range of information and documents related to the Department's and its components' response to Katrina. In addition, in the weeks and months that followed, the Committee sought to interview witnesses with relevant knowledge from throughout the Department.

Responses to the Committee's four request letters to DHS were due October 27, 2005. The following day, FEMA produced its first documents to the Committee; the Coast Guard followed with a small production approximately a week later. And even before these documents arrived, the Committee began interviewing FEMA witnesses, beginning with Marty Bahamonde, an External Affairs employee who was stationed in New Orleans during the storm, on October 7, 2005. Interviews with Coast Guard witnesses began not long thereafter.

During this time, however, the Committee received no response at all to its two other request letters, to the National Communications System and to Secretary Chertoff for the remainder of DHS. Concerned as time continued to pass, in November, Committee staff sent to DHS a short list of initial witnesses from other parts of the Department that we thought it important to interview.

Notwithstanding this request, no witnesses from outside FEMA or the Coast Guard were made available for interviews at that time. And by the end of the year – three months after the request letters had been sent – only a small number of documents had been produced in response to the letter to Secretary Chertoff. No documents related to NCS had been produced at all. On December 30, 2005, Senators Collins and Lieberman expressed their concerns directly to Secretary Chertoff. They wrote him that the Committee lacked the "documents, information, and access to Department personnel that we need to conduct a thorough and timely investigation" and included a prioritized list of documents, information, and witnesses that they wanted in the following two weeks.

On January 9, 2006, the Committee received a disappointing response from Philip Perry, the General Counsel of DHS, in which Perry offered little that was new, but made clear that much of what the Committee asked for would not be forthcoming in the requested time frame. Specifically, he indicated that the Department was declining to respond to any of the information requests the Committee had submitted and stated only that the Department "should" be able to provide the Committee with a "substantial number" of the priority documents by the revised January 13, 2006, deadline (in fact, only a small number were provided by that date). He indicated that three of the twelve priority non-FEMA witnesses the Committee had requested would be made available for interviews, but made no further commitments on the remaining ones.

Finding little reassurance in Perry's response, Senator Lieberman wrote to Chairman Collins on January 12, 2006, requesting that the Committee issue subpoenas to DHS. Three and a half months after sending the Committee's initial request letter and with three weeks of intensive Committee hearings on Hurricane Katrina rapidly approaching, the letter argued, the time had come to insist on the additional documents, information, and witnesses that were crucial if the Committee were to attain an accurate understanding of what occurred in the days leading up to and following Katrina, and how the government's response could be improved in the future. Chairman Collins declined to issue a subpoena to DHS, but she did personally intervene with the Secretary and insisted upon greater cooperation.

DHS's cooperation in the following weeks – effectively the final weeks of the investigation before attention would turn to crafting the report – improved, somewhat, with some additional witnesses and documents produced to the Committee. With respect to non-FEMA matters, however, it never reached the level the Committee had the right to expect from the Department.

In the end, 300,000 of the approximately 344,000 pages of documents that DHS produced to the Committee – 87 percent – were produced by FEMA. The National Communications Systems (NCS) produced approximately 3,100 pages of documents (roughly one box's worth), with its first materials not provided to the Committee until January 18, 2006. The Coast Guard provided a total of some 7,400 pages of documents. Approximately 33,000 pages of documents – the rough equivalent of fewer than a dozen boxes – were produced in response to the Committee's letter to Secretary Chertoff from the remainder of DHS, including its law enforcement components, the Homeland Security Operations Center, and front-office personnel.

Interviews broke down in somewhat the same fashion: The Committee conducted formal interviews with 46 FEMA, or ex-FEMA, employees; 11 representatives of the Coast Guard; 2 NCS employees; and 12 individuals from the remainder of DHS.

Apart from the numbers, it is clear that DHS failed to fully comply with the majority of the requests for documents and information contained in all but one of the Committee's original letters. The same goes for a significant portion of even the priority requests set out in the Committee's letter of December 30, 2005.[87] DHS did eventually make available all but one of the non-FEMA witnesses on the Committee's December 30, 2005 priority list,[88] although subsequent requests for additional non-FEMA DHS witnesses were, with two exceptions, ignored.

Specific Concerns

Limitations on witness interviews

Significant delays in producing witnesses. The Department did not provide the Committee with any witnesses from its leadership staff, from the HSOC, from NCS – indeed, from any component outside FEMA or the Coast Guard – until January 13, 2006, a full three months after the Committee began to conduct investigative interviews. In contrast, by mid-October, the Committee staff had already begun to speak to state and local officials in Louisiana and Mississippi, as well as to FEMA and Coast Guard personnel. By mid-November, interviews were underway with Department of Defense personnel, as well as with the U.S. Army Corps of Engineers, among others. The significant delay in providing witnesses from DHS's leadership, the HSOC, NCS, and the Department's law enforcement components inevitably constrained the Committee's investigation. The late start in interviewing these important witnesses, as intensive weeks of hearings were underway and the investigation was coming to a close, meant that there was simply insufficient time to follow up effectively on new information that invariably and predictably came to light in those interviews. Unlike the Committee's scrutiny of the performance of FEMA or the State of Louisiana, for example, the examination of the actions of other parts of DHS was not permitted to evolve organically based on what was learned at each stage. Although the Committee was ultimately able to uncover important and enlightening facts even from the limited number of witnesses and documents made available, we simply cannot know where those facts would have led if the Committee had been allowed greater time to pursue leads to their logical conclusions.

Failure to produce additional witnesses. Even within the significant time constraints, the Committee staff was able to identify a relatively small number of additional DHS witnesses who appeared to have information important to the investigation; efforts to bring in these additional non-FEMA, non-Coast Guard witnesses were largely ignored.[89]

For example, as discussed in Chapter 19 of the report, the Committee discovered during the course of its investigation that the HSOC, the central organization within DHS charged with maintaining situational awareness, issued a report at 6 p.m. on the day Katrina made landfall stating that preliminary reports indicated that the levees had not been breached.[90] This unfortunate report, issued despite considerable evidence to the contrary, may have falsely reassured a variety of government officials, who went home Monday, August 29, ignorant of the ongoing catastrophe in New Orleans, and it may well have contributed to a delayed federal response. Therefore, Committee staff sought to interview the HSOC's Senior Watch Officer who was on duty at the time and who would have been responsible for issuing that erroneous report. Notwithstanding Committee staff's request, the individual was never made available. The Department, moreover, has never provided any explanation for not complying with the Committee's request.

DHS also failed, without explanation, to produce, in response to a Committee staff request, Scott Weber, Senior Counselor to the Secretary and the member of the Secretary's immediate staff responsible for FEMA-related issues.[91]

DHS limitations on the terms under which witness interviews were conducted. Even when DHS made witnesses available, it often did so under conditions that limited the effectiveness of the interview. It became routine for DHS counsel to produce witnesses with unreasonably short notice, limiting Committee staff's ability to prepare. In one case, for example, staff was informed only Tuesday morning that a FEMA witness would be made available that afternoon; when questioned, the witness revealed that *he* had been informed of the interview by the previous Thursday or Friday and had arrived in Washington on Monday afternoon.[92] In some cases, none of the witness's e-mails or other documents were made available to the Committee before the interview.

Perhaps the practice that most directly restricted the ability of staff to gather information was DHS Counsel's unilateral insistence, in almost all the interviews with DHS employees outside of FEMA and the Coast Guard, on limiting the time the witness would be made available to a single session lasting three to four hours.[93] This artificial time constraint was not imposed (or accepted) by other agencies or in other contexts. Thus, for example, staff conducting interviews with state and local officials in Louisiana were routinely given access to significant witnesses for extended periods of time: Among others, Major General Bennett Landreneau, Adjutant General of Louisiana, was interviewed for approximately eight hours and Terry Ebbert, Director of New Orleans' Office of Homeland Security and Public Safety, sat three times for interviews for a total of approximately 10 hours. The Department of Defense, for its part, made Lieutenant General Russel Honoré, Commander of First Army and Commander of Joint Task Force-Katrina, available for a seven-hour interview. But with high-level staff at DHS, relatively short time limits were almost always imposed.

A particularly notable example of this was the interview Committee staff conducted with Robert Stephan. By his own count, Stephan wore five "hats" at DHS at the time Katrina hit. Among others, he was Acting Under Secretary for Information Analysis and Infrastructure Protection; Director of the Interagency Incident Management Group; and Manager of the National Communications System. He also had led the development of the National Response Plan, the central document guiding the federal response. By virtue of these various responsibilities, Stephan appeared to possess a wealth of information important to the Committee's investigation, and as the relatively short period that had been allotted for his interview came to a close, it was obvious that the range of critical topics had only begun to be explored. Appropriately, the Committee's Minority staff asked to continue the interview at another time.[94] Stephan, however, was not made available again to Committee staff.

Inadequate Document Production

As outlined above, DHS produced only a fraction of the documents and information requested by the Committee – particularly in response to those requests contained in the three letters that were sent to components of the Department other than FEMA – and failed to fully comply even with many of the Committee's priority requests. Notably, DHS at no time asserted any basis for withholding the material from a legitimate Congressional inquiry, nor, in most cases, did its lawyers seek to reach agreement with the Committee on the scope of the material to be produced. Rather, it frequently appeared to be the case that DHS simply unilaterally decided what material it would and would not produce to the Committee. As a result, there are gaps, perhaps significant, in the materials (and, in particular, the non-FEMA materials) that the Committee has in its possession. A handful of prominent ones are noted below.

FEMA budget documents. Although DHS produced a substantial number of documents the Committee requested from FEMA, the Department largely refused to provide documents related to FEMA's budget. As the report discusses, concerns were raised by several FEMA witnesses that FEMA's budget was not sufficient to fulfill its mission and about DHS's "taxing" of FEMA to support the overall operations of the Department, and how these budget matters may have affected FEMA's preparedness for a catastrophic disaster such as Katrina. DHS refused to provide all but a very few of the relevant requested documents – a request made in the Committee's original September 28, 2005, letter and reiterated in the priority list submitted to DHS on December 30, 2005. As with other areas in which DHS declined to produce documents, information, or witnesses, the Department did not cite any authority that would exempt it from the Committee's oversight jurisdiction other than its own preference. This refusal has prevented the Committee from fully addressing and resolving these issues.[95]

HSOC documents. As is evident from the Committee's report, the problems in maintaining accurate situational awareness during the storm became a focus of the investigation. For that reason, both in the Committee's original September 28, 2005, letter and in its December 30, 2005, priority request, we sought all the communications into or out of the HSOC that related to Katrina in the days immediately before and after landfall. DHS, however, chose to produce to the Committee only e-mails that were sent from or to a computer account associated with the Senior Watch Officer on duty;[96] although some 45 agencies staff desks at the HSOC, information coming in to these individuals was ignored.

The significance of this came to light in one instance where the Committee obtained, through other sources, an e-mail that the Coast Guard had sent to the HSOC at 1:51 pm on the day of landfall, informing the HSOC that a levee in New Orleans had breached;[97] this e-mail, though obviously important and clearly within both the Committee's original and priority requests, had not been produced to the Committee.

In another area of concern, though sources at the Coast Guard indicated to the Committee that the Coast Guard had produced documents to DHS responsive to many of the Committee's requests, DHS had not turned all of them over to the Committee. Because DHS has not produced a log of withheld documents, however, we do not know if DHS is deliberately withholding documents, based on a claim of privilege or otherwise, or whether it simply determined that the documents were not responsive.

No answers to information requests. Finally, DHS declined to answer any of the requests for information contained in each of the four letters that were sent to the Department – even basic information such as which components of the Department were involved in the response to Katrina,[98] or the identities of key personnel at NCS. DHS has not posed any objection to the questions raised, although in his January 9, 2006, letter, Perry asserted that DHS "cannot fully respond to several of these questions before it completes its lessons learned process and has a trustworthy understanding of the underlying facts" – though he did not identify to which questions he objected on these grounds. He also argued that so much information has already been provided to staff through documents and interviews that the Committee already had much of the information it sought; and that if the Committee would provide access to transcripts of witness interviews, DHS would produce responses more quickly. These arguments are unpersuasive, especially when they apply across the board even to requests to which the Department surely knows the answer and to which none of its objections apply. For example, the Committee asked for a statement of when the National Response Plan was activated and which annexes were activated. There is no reason why that information cannot have been provided by the Department during the past six months.

The Department of Justice

The Department of Justice (DOJ) was highly uncooperative with the Committee. DOJ has important responsibilities under the National Response Plan, most significantly for maintaining security during a disaster when local and state law enforcement personnel are overwhelmed. In addition, the Department, as the Executive Branch's principal legal advisor, surely played a role in offering advice on the very controversial issues involved in deploying the military to aid the Katrina response, among other matters. DOJ was necessarily a critical part of the Committee's investigation.

Yet DOJ was utterly uncooperative throughout the Committee's investigation. The Committee sent its initial request letter on October 7, 2005, asking for information and documents by November 3, 2005. On October 24, 2005, the Committee received its first communication back from the Department, in which the Department simply acknowledged receipt. Not until November 18, 2005, did DOJ produce its first installment of documents. The Department ultimately produced a very limited quantity of documents (approximately 2,000 pages) and answered only some of the questions that the Committee asked in its October 7, 2005, letter and none of those asked in its February 21, 2006, follow-up list of prioritized items. Most disturbingly, DOJ's refusal to make any witnesses available for transcribed interviews ultimately required the Committee to serve its only witness subpoenas of the investigation on the Department.

These deficiencies seriously impeded the Committee's ability to investigate DOJ's preparations for and response to Hurricane Katrina. Most significantly, the delay in providing information or interviews necessarily kept the Committee from pursuing important leads generated by the little information it had received. For example, on August 30, 2005, the head of the Louisiana State Police, Colonel Henry Whitehorn, wrote to FBI Director Robert Mueller requesting "any assistance you can provide," noting that New Orleans had "suffered massive damage"; that the state police were "utilizing all state assets to stabilize the situation" but that "looting continues to be a significant problem."[99] Yet at his January 26, 2006, interview, William Mercer, Principal Associate Deputy Attorney General, said that DOJ was limited in its ability to provide law-enforcement assistance because the request did not come sooner, and from the Governor.[100] This assertion made us especially interested in DOJ's response to the Committee's request to identify all requests for assistance that it received and its response to those requests, including "the date and time orders were issued to fulfill the request"; "the entity within the Department tasked to provide the assistance"; and "the key personnel involved in processing and responding to the request." But DOJ never answered this question, nor did it provide the documents the Committee requested that would have shed light on DOJ's reaction to the Whitehorn letter at the time. As a result, the Committee is left unable to fully understand why DOJ did not respond to the letter from Col. Whitehorn, either by soliciting the letter from the Governor it claims was required or otherwise,[101] and why it took the position that it hadn't received an adequate request.

As for the documents the Committee did receive, the production was, plainly, incomplete. For example, the Committee received documents from Mercer's files reflecting communications with individuals in the Attorney General's office and showing the significant – albeit belated – involvement of that office in the Katrina response, but received virtually no materials originating in the Attorney General's office itself.[102] Mercer's documents also show discussions on the National Response Plan with Senior Counsel for National Security Affairs James McAtamney, but McAtamney's files were not produced.[103] The Committee received no after-action reports or similar documents examining the response of the Department or its various components to Katrina, raising the troubling possibility that DOJ has made no systematic efforts to examine its own conduct for future benefit.

Equally disturbingly, the Committee received a scant amount of e-mails from many component agencies involved in the response, including, notably, the FBI. FBI e-mails likely would have offered insight into the circumstances under which the FBI operated in the first days of the response. Hundreds of FBI agents were deployed to the area, but the Committee has no e-mails concerning this deployment exchanged between personnel at FBI headquarters; between agents in the field; or between headquarters personnel and agents in the field. E-mails produced by DHS law-enforcement officials convey a sense of confusion about the respective roles of DOJ, FBI, and DHS, and suggest that there was, at least for a time, a "turf war" between the FBI and DHS.[104] This investigation is not complete without full insight into these issues.

Finally, because the Department has attempted to excuse its tardy response to Katrina by claiming that its authority to provide the types of support contemplated under the National Response Plan is limited by federal statute,[105] it is important that the Committee see any internal DOJ documents that analyze DOJ's authority and that reflect when this issue was researched and/or resolved.

In short, DOJ's response was one of the investigation's true disappointments. By treating the requests of a duly authorized Congressional investigative committee so cavalierly, we cannot but conclude that DOJ obstructed the Committee's investigation and prevented the Committee – and, through it, the American people – from knowing the full story of the government's failed response to this catastrophe.

The Department of Health and Human Services

The Department of Health and Human Services (HHS) also did not cooperate with Committee efforts to obtain information. HHS plays a significant role in the federal response to disasters. The National Response Plan charges it with coordinating the federal government's health and medical assistance to state and local authorities. During Katrina, HHS deployed over 2,100 U.S. Public Health Officers to assist in the response. HHS also sent over $38 million of medical supplies to affected states through its Division of the Strategic National Stockpile at the Centers for Disease Control and Prevention, providing essential supplies to a region where large parts of the health-care system were damaged or destroyed. As the federal government's primary agency for public health and medical assistance, HHS was also responsible for ensuring that other federal medical assets, such as the National Disaster Medical System, were used effectively.

The Committee raised serious questions about the federal government's fulfillment of its mandate, ranging from the role it played in evacuating hospital and other acutely ill patients from New Orleans to recovering the bodies of Katrina's victims. The Committee could not truly assess the adequacy of the federal medical response to Katrina nor make informed judgments for future recommendations without a comprehensive assessment of HHS's actions. For that, the Committee needed HHS to have answered the questions and provided the documents the Committee had requested in its September 28, 2005, letter.

Yet, HHS was often unresponsive to the Committee's requests and, to this day, its production remains incomplete. Key witnesses have not been interviewed and important information remains undelivered. Delays in providing access to information and witnesses severely hampered the ability of investigators to fully examine HHS's performance prior to and during Katrina.

Perhaps most disturbingly, HHS did not respond to the Committee's September 28, 2005, information request until February 24, 2006.[106] Even then, the HHS response had major gaps and shortcomings. For example, the Committee's original request asked HHS to provide all emergency and contingency plans for all Department elements and relevant regional offices that were in effect at the time of Katrina. What HHS gave the Committee included, in essence, only one headquarters-level plan.[107] The Committee requested after-action reports for emergency events and drills for the past five years. While the Department's response identified 60 events and drills in this time frame, not a single after-action report was provided until April 7, 2006. In several cases, such as two Committee questions about the provision of mental-health services, there was no response whatsoever. Similarly, the Committee asked HHS to describe the extent to which two volunteer credentialing systems were used to help process volunteer medical personnel seeking to provide medical care in Mississippi and Louisiana during Katrina, but no response was provided.

The Committee's original request also requested "copies of all communications, including, but not limited to, all records or logs of such communications" for numerous activities related to HHS's response. HHS did not begin to provide relevant documents until December 2, 2005. Without exception, the responses for "all communications" were incomplete. For example, no records or logs of communications were provided. This was true even with regard to information logged into the HHS electronic incident-tracking system described by the Department (at the Committee's request). Even documents produced by HHS were incomplete. For example, numerous e-mails provided in response to the Committee's request did not include attachments – even when the sole purpose of the e-mail was to transmit the attachment.

Frustrated by this unacceptable lack of compliance, Chairman Collins and Senator Lieberman wrote to HHS Secretary Michael Leavitt on January 13, 2006, expressing concern about the Department's response. The letter noted that HHS "has been slow and disorganized – failing to provide attachments to e-mails, preparatory or pre-landfall materials, interrogatory responses, and basic situation reports."[108] The letter went on to identify priority items for production and stated that "[a]t this point, nearly four months after we first requested the Department's assistance, we must insist on a production of the requested documents by Wednesday, January 25, 2006." Not having received a satisfactory answer, on February 17, 2006, they again wrote to Secretary Leavitt asking for a status report, no later than February 24, 2006, detailing when final production would be complete. Some of the priority materials were finally provided on February 24, 2005. Still, a great deal of material remained outstanding.

HHS's response to requests to interview Department employees was also unsatisfactory. Although two informational briefings were provided to Committee investigators on December 9, 2005, by staff of the Office of Public Health Emergency Preparedness, and on January 12, 2006, by officers of the U.S. Public Health Service who deployed to Katrina, HHS resisted efforts to schedule staff interviews. The first did not take place until Monday, January 30, 2006. Ultimately, the Department did make a number of requested witnesses available. However, the delay in initiating the process hampered the ability of investigators to conduct a thorough investigation and left inadequate time to interview several important witnesses.

Part III: Failure to Establish a Unified Command

We want to comment on one more issue. The report places primary blame on the State of Louisiana for the inability of all the response agencies to establish a unified command in that state during the first week after landfall. In our view, the issue is far more complex.

We believe that the failure to establish a unified command resulted from three factors: The severity of the disaster; the failure of FEMA to have adequate numbers of personnel with sufficient expertise and training to cope with a disaster of this magnitude; and the failure of the State of Louisiana to have sufficient expertise and trained personnel to cope with a disaster of this magnitude.

As the report acknowledges, local, state, and federal response agencies were responsible for establishing a unified command under the Incident Command System (ICS). As the lead federal response agency, FEMA shared this responsibility. The evidence before the Committee is that the ability of many of the local responders to participate in a unified command was severely impaired by extensive flooding and the destruction of much of the communications infrastructure. Neither FEMA nor Louisiana had a sufficient number of trained personnel to establish an Incident Command System and a unified command in the face of such extensive damage and the incapacitation of local officials. Both FEMA and Louisiana had to train additional personnel during the crisis.

William Lokey, the FEMA Federal Coordinating Officer in Louisiana, told the Committee, "The locals were overwhelmed. We were going to be overwhelmed. There was no way, with my experience and what I had to bring to the table, I was taking a knife to a gunfight."[109] Lokey said that FEMA employees, including those in Baton Rouge responding to Katrina, had not had sufficient ICS training,[110] and that FEMA's requirement that National Emergency Response Team (ERT-N) members be proficient in ICS by January 1, 2006, was just "wishful thinking" because "we've had no training dollars [and] we've had no opportunity to bring the folks together."[111] William Carwile, FEMA's Federal Coordinating Officer in Mississippi, testified similarly: "Those of us who were somehow responsible for the teams felt very uncomfortable that the teams weren't really ready to go."[112] As a result, William King, FEMA's Chief of Planning in Louisiana during Katrina, reported, FEMA had to train its own people in the midst of the response: "We had to what I call 'crawl, walk, run' it and do the training of people and implement it over several days."[113] Tony Robinson, FEMA's Operations Section Chief in Louisiana during Katrina, agreed that FEMA would have been able to respond better if it had more personnel available for deployment.[114]

This testimony leads us to conclude that neither FEMA nor Louisiana had a sufficient number of trained personnel to establish the appropriate command-and-control structure in Louisiana. As FEMA and Louisiana shared the responsibility to establish a unified command, FEMA and Louisiana share the accountability for the failure to do so.

1 Clinton Rossiter, *The American Presidency*, 2nd Ed. New York: Harcourt, Brace & World, Inc., 1960, p. 4.

2 Commitee staff interview of Michael Brown, former Director, FEMA, conducted on Feb. 23, 2006, transcript p. 141.

3 Brown interview, Feb. 23, 2006, transcript p. 143.

4 Brown interview, Feb. 23, 2006, transcript pp. 137-138, 141. Brown did not address these concerns publicly or in writing with Congress. However, during his appearance in front of the U.S. House Select Bipartisan Committee to Investigate Preparation for and Response to Hurricane Katrina on Sept. 27, 2005, Brown alluded to having had some conversations with Members of Congress, though not with any Members of this Committee, regarding FEMA's emaciation. When asked about the "emaciation" of FEMA, Brown suggested that for several years, he privately discussed how FEMA would become extremely limited in both personnel and financial resources hindering its capacity to handle a disaster. In response to a question about Brown expressing his concerns about FEMA privately, but not publicly, Brown stated: "I can go to bed at night and sleep because I know I fought that battle." In addition, later in the hearing when asked why he expressed his views about FEMA's emaciation privately versus publicly, Brown testified that he wanted to work within the system to make the needed changes. *Source:* Testimony of Michael Brown, former Director, FEMA, before the U.S. House, Select Bipartisan Committee to Investigate Preparation for and Response to Hurricane Katrina, hearing on *Hurricane Katrina: The Role of the Federal Emergency Management Agency,* Sept. 27, 2005.

5 Committee staff interview of Gary Jones, Acting Director, Region VI, FEMA, conducted on Jan. 11, 2006, transcript pp. 48-49, 149-152; Committee staff interview of Wayne Fairley, Response Operations Branch Chief, Region VI, FEMA conducted on Jan. 18, 2006, pp. 2, 57-58.

6 Eric Tolbert, e-mail to Janet Benini and Ron Castleman, July 1, 2004, 4:24 p.m. ET. Provided to Committee; filed as Bates no. DHS-0058-0000261.

7 Janet Benini, e-mail to Eric Tolbert and Ron Castleman, July 1, 2004, 4 p.m. ET. Provided to Committee; filed as Bates no. DHS-0058-0000261 ("The Louisiana Hurricane is one of the potentially 'catastrophic' scenarios we've been working on at HSC").

8 Stephen Black, e-mail to Kirstjen Nielsen and Janet Benini, Feb. 22, 2005, 4:41 p.m. Provided to the Committee; filed as Bates nos. WHK 001059 through 001061.

9 The White House does not dispute that the President received these warnings and communications before landfall: "The President 'received regular briefings, had countless conversations with Federal, State, and local officials, and took extraordinary steps prior to landfall.'" *Source*: U.S. Assistant to the President for Homeland Security and Counterterrorism, *The Federal Response to Hurricane Katrina: Lessons Learned*. Washington: Government Printing Office, Feb. 2006, pp. 28-29 [hereinafter The White House, *Hurricane Katrina: Lessons Learned*]. But the White House did not detail in either its report, *The Federal Response to Hurricane Katrina: Lessons Learned,* Frances Fragos Townsend's February 13, 2006, speech at the National Emergency Management Association's mid-year conference, or elsewhere, any specific details about the briefings or conversations. *Source:* The White House, *Hurricane Katrina: Lessons Learned*, pp. 28-29, 174.

10 Testimony of Michael Brown, former Director, FEMA, before the U.S. Senate, Committee on Homeland Security and Governmental Affairs, hearing on Hur*ricane Katrina: The Roles of U.S Department of Homeland Security and Federal Emergency Management Agency Leadership*, Feb. 10, 2006; Deposition of Michael Brown, before U.S. House Select Committee staff, Feb. 11, 2006, p. 11 (testifying that during a call to the President, he said that Hurricane Katrina could be "the big one").

11 FEMA Daily Video Teleconference, Aug. 27, 2005, transcript pp. 22-23. Provided to Committee; filed as Bates nos. DHS-FEMA-0105-000061 through 0000062.

12 Michael Brown, FEMA Daily Video Teleconference, Aug. 27, 2005, transcript p. 22. Provided to Committee; filed as Bates no. DHS-FEMA-0105-00000061.

13 Bill Reed, FEMA Daily Video Teleconference, Aug. 27, 2005, transcript pp. 5-6. Provided to Committee; filed as Bates nos. DHS-FEMA-0105-0000044 through 0000045.

14 Joseph Hagin, FEMA Daily Video Teleconference, Aug. 27, 2005, transcript p. 24. Provided to Committee; filed as Bates no. DHS-FEMA-0105-0000063.

15 Andrew Akers, e-mail to Homeland Security Operations Center Senior Watch Officer and others, Aug. 27, 2005, 11:24 p.m. Provided to the Committee; filed as Bates nos. WHK 05865 through 05867. The other addressees for the e-mail are DL-NSC-WHSR, Bethany Nichols, Elliot Langer, Kirstjen Nielsen, Joel Bagnal, Elizabeth Farrell, Julie Bentz, Daniel Kaniewski, Matthew Broderick, Frank DiFalco, Bob Stephan, John Chase, Tom Dinanno, Edward McDonald, Gail Kulish, Tom Paar, Michael Jackson, John Wood, National Interagency Coordination Center, Secretary Briefing Staff, Homeland Security Operations Center, Homeland Security Information Network. Attached to that e-mail was "Fast Analysis Report (Update to Reflect Category 5 Status) to DHS IP on Hurricane Katrina, Gulf Coast," the Department of Homeland Security's National Infrastructure Simulation and Analysis Center, Aug. 28, 2005, p. 1.

16 FEMA Daily Video Teleconference, Aug. 28, 2005, transcript pp. 1, 14-16, 20. Provided to Committee; filed as Bates no. DHS-FEMA-0105-0000066, -0000079 through 0000081, 0000085.

17 Max Mayfield, FEMA Daily Video Teleconference, Aug. 28, 2005, transcript pp. 2, 6. Provided to Committee; filed as Bates no. DHS-FEMA-0105-0000067, 0000071.

18 Michael Brown, FEMA Daily Video Teleconference, Aug. 28, 2005, transcript p. 37. Provided to the Committee; filed as Bates no. DHS-FEMA-0105-0000102. During his staff interview on February 23, 2006, Brown discussed a telephone call with Joe Hagin after the noon VTC. He described the conversation as follows: "And Hagin and I were having a conversation just about . . . how bad this one was going to be and, you know, dad-gamut all the – I mean, I was really bitching at Hagin about all of the planning I'd been asking for and you know, the catastrophic planning we'd been wanting to do, you know, now – and now here we are, and, you know, saying to him, you know, dad-gamut, why didn't I quit earlier – then, you know, you guys knew I wanted to quit. I mean, we're having this sparring match about all of this stuff that I was really mad about because I knew I was walking into this hornets' nest . . . I'm really ticked off, because I know how bad this thing's going to be." Brown further described the conversation: " . . . I'm just adamant that they understand my concern about New Orleans. I mean, I don't know how to get this across to people that I have pushed and pushed for catastrophic disaster planning; we had chosen New Orleans as the first place to do catastrophic disaster planning; and now, damn it, here was a, you know, a Cat 5 bearing down on – on New Orleans." Brown interview, Feb. 23, 2006, pp. 34, 36-37.

19 Bill Doran, FEMA Daily Video Teleconference, Aug. 28, 2005, transcript pp. 16-17. Provided to Committee; filed as Bates no. DHS-FEMA-0105-0000081 through -0000090.

20 President Bush, FEMA Daily Video Teleconference, Aug. 28. 2005, transcript pp. 14-15. Provided to Committee; filed as Bates no. DHS-FEMA-0105-0000079 through 0000080. The White House's own report, *The Federal Response to Hurricane Katrina: Lessons Learned*, describes the President as actively engaged the weekend prior to landfall, communicating with state and local officials and offering federal assets. The White House's report also cites the August 28 video teleconference as the mechanism used by the President to communicate with officials and offer federal assets. *Source:* The White House, *Hurricane Katrina: Lessons Learned*, pp. 28, 174. But on March 2, 2006, Trent Duffy, a spokesman for the President, downplayed the utility of that call: "I hope people don't draw conclusions from the president getting a single briefing … He received multiple briefings from multiple officials, and he was completely engaged at all times." *Source:* Robert Block, "Tape of Pre-Katrina Briefing Shows Bush Was Warned Of Dangers," *Wall Street Journal*, Mar. 2, 2006, p. A3.

21 breakingnews@foxnews.com, e-mail to BREAKINGNEWS Subscribers, Aug. 28, 2005, 7:51 a.m., Provided to Committee; Bates no. WHK-08489 (printed out by Landon Gibbs).

22 Steven York, e-mail to Andrew Akers and others, Aug. 28, 2005, 5:21 p.m. Provided to Committee; filed as Bates nos. WHK 05319 through 05320. The other addressees of this e-mail are Homeland Security Operations Center Senior Watch Officer, DL-NSC-WHSR, Bethany Nichols, Elliott Langer, Kirstjen Nielsen, Joel Bagnal, Elizabeth Farrell, Julie Bentz, Daniel Kaniewski and copied to Matthew Broderick, Frank DiFalco, Bob Stephan, John Chase, Tom Dinanno, Edward McDonald, Gail Kulisch, Tom Paar, Michael Jackson (DepSec), John Wood, NICC, Secretary Briefing Staff, Homeland Security Operations Center Homeland Security Information Network; breakingnews@foxnews.com, e-mail to BREAKINGNEWS Subscribers, Aug. 28, 2005, 7:51 a.m. Provided to Committee; Bates no. WHK-08489.

23 Andrew Akers, e-mail to Homeland Security Operations Center Senior Watch Officer, Aug. 29, 2005, 1:47 a.m. Provided to Committee; filed as Bates nos. WHK 15894 through 15937. The other addresses of the e-mail are DL-NSC-WHSR, Bethany Nichols, Elliott Langer, Kirstjen Nielsen, Joel Bagnal, Elizabeth Farrell, Julie Bentz, Daniel Kaniewski, Richard Davis, Michael Barton, Matthew Broderick, Frank DiFalco, Bob Stephan, John Chase, Tom Dinanno, Edward McDonald, Gail Kulisch, Tom Paar, Michael Jackson (DepSec), John Wood, NICC, Secretary Briefing Staff, HSOC HSIN.

24 The White House lauded the President's issuance of the emergency declarations as "extremely rare, and indicative of the recognition that Katrina had the potential to be particularly devastating." The White House, *Hurricane Katrina: Lessons Learned*, p. 27.

25 Brown interview, Feb. 23, 2006, p. 33; White House Briefing to Committee, conducted by Kenneth Rapuano, Deputy Assistant to the President for Homeland Security, Dec. 13, 2005.

26 Louisiana Office of the Governor, Response to the U.S. Senate Committee on Homeland Security and Governmental Affairs Document and Information Request dated October 7, 2005, and to the U.S. House of Representatives Select Committee to Investigate the Preparation for and Response to Hurricane Katrina, Overview of Governor Kathleen Babineaux Blanco's Actions in Preparation for and Response to Hurricane Katrina, Dec. 2, 2005, p. 6 [hereinafter Louisiana Office of the Governor, Governor's Timeline]. (Stating that she received the call from the President "just before she walks into the news conference," at which she announced with Mayor Nagin the mandatory evacuation of New Orleans).

27 Testimony of Sec. Michael Chertoff, Department of Homeland Security, before the U.S. Senate, Committee on Homeland Security and Governmental Affairs, hearing on *Hurricane Katrina: The Homeland Security Department's Preparation and Response*, Feb. 15, 2006.

28 Sec. Chertoff, Senate Committee hearing, Feb. 15, 2006.

29 The White House, "President Outlines Hurricane Katrina Relief Efforts," press release, Aug. 31, 2005. http://www.whitehouse.gov/news/releases/2005/08/print/20050831-3.html. Accessed on Mar. 29, 2006.

30 Spencer Hsu and Amy Goldstein, "Administration Faulted on Katrina," *Washington Post*, Feb. 2, 2006, p. A5.

31 Richard D. Knabb, Jamie Rhome, and Daniel Brown, National Hurricane Center, *Tropical Cyclone Report, Hurricane Katrina*, Dec. 20, 2005, p. 3. http://www.nhc.noaa.gov/pdf/TCR-AL122005_Katrina.pdf. Accessed on Mar. 30, 2006.

32 Daniel Kaniewski, e-mail to Dan Bartlett and others, Aug. 29, 2005, 11:13 a.m. Provided to Committee; filed as Bates no. OVP 004795. The other addressees are Todd Beyer, Bill Burck, Trent Duffy, Joseph Hagin, Brian Hook, Brett Kavanaugh, Emily Kropp, William McGurn, Stephen McMillin, Harriet Miers, Bruce Miller, Susan Ralston, Kenneth Rapuano, Scott Sforza, Kristen Silverberg, Heidi Smith, Frances Townsend, and copied to Steven Atkiss, Jessica Bennett,

Stephen Black, Jamie Brown, John Burke, Shannon Burkhart, John Currin, Robert DeServi, DL-HSC-BTS, DL-HSC-CHEM-BIO, DL-HSCEXECSEC, DL-HSC-Front, DL-HSC-PPR, DL-NSC-WHSR, Lindsey Drouin, Debbie Fiddelke, Erin Healy, Taylor Hughes, Lauren Kane, Karyn Richman Kendall, Matthew Kirk, Ross Kyle, Jeannie Mamo, Christopher Michel, Alexander Mistri, John Mitnick, Derrick Morgan, Erin Nagle, Neil Patel, Dana Perino, Douglas Pitkin, Heather Roebke, Daniel Wilmot, Candace Wysocki, DeWitt Zemp. ("Flooding significant throughout the region and a levee in New Orleans has reportedly been breached sending 6 to 8 feet of water throughout the 9th Ward area of the city. Per the Governor, water is rising at 1 foot per hour and the New Orleans mayor reports problems with a pumping station, causing flooding. HSOC reports that due to the rising water in the 9th Ward, residents are in their attics and on their roofs."). The President's knowledge of when New Orleans' levees breached has been the subject of much media attention. In the week after landfall, the President himself made statements regarding the levee breaches. For instance, on Friday, September 2, 2005, during a press conference in Biloxi, Mississippi, the President stated: "The levees broke on Tuesday in New Orleans. On Wednesday, we – and Thursday we started evacuating people. A lot of people have left that city. A lot of people have been pulled out on buses. It's – I am satisfied with the response. I'm not satisfied with all the results. They started pulling people off roofs immediately. They started rallying – we started rallying choppers to get people off rooftops, started savings lives. I mean, thousands of peoples' lives have been saved immediately, and that's good news. This is one of the worst storms in our nation's history. New Orleans got hit by two storms, one the hurricane, and then the flood. And it's going to take a monumental effort to continue moving forward, but we will." The White House, "President Tours Biloxi, Mississippi, Hurricane Damaged Neighborhoods," press release, Sept. 2, 2005. Provided to Committee; filed as Bates nos. WHK 01656, 01658. As set forth herein, the President's statements contradict the reality of the situation as several pieces of evidence show the levees breached on Monday.

33 Insung Lee, e-mail to Kirstjen Nielsen, Aug. 29, 2005, 11:16 a.m. Provided to the Committee; filed as Bates no. WHK 16111. The other addressees of the e-mail are Homeland Security Operations Center Senior Watch Officer, Matthew Broderick, Frank DiFalco, Interagency Incident Management Group, and Homeland Security Operations Center-All-Desks.

34 Insung Lee, e-mail to Homeland Security Operations Center Senior Watch Officer, Aug. 29, 2005, 11:32 a.m. Provided to the Committee; filed as Bates no. WHK 11923. The other addressees of the e-mail are DL-NSC-WHSR; Bethany Nichols, Elliott Langer, Kirstjen Nielsen, Joel Bagnal, Elizabeth Farrell, Julie Bentz, Daniel Kaniewski, Richard Davis, Michael Barton, Matthew Broderick, Frank DiFalco, Bob Stephan, John Chase, Tom Dinanno, Edward McDonald, Gail Kulisch, Tom Paar, Michael Jackson (DepSec), John Wood, NICC, Secretary Briefing Staff, HSOC.HSIN.

35 Insung Lee, e-mail to Homeland Security Operations Center Senior Watch Officer, Aug. 29, 2005, 11:32 a.m. Provided to the Committee; filed as Bates no. WHK 11923. The other addressees of the e-mail are DL-NSC-WHSR; Bethany Nichols, Elliott Langer, Kirstjen Nielsen, Joel Bagnal, Elizabeth Farrell, Julie Bentz, Daniel Kaniewski, Richard Davis, Michael Barton, Matthew Broderick, Frank DiFalco, Bob Stephan, John Chase, Tom Dinanno, Edward McDonald, Gail Kulisch, Tom Paar, Michael Jackson (DepSec), John Wood, NICC, Secretary Briefing Staff, HSOC.HSIN.

36 FEMA Daily Video Teleconference, Aug. 29, 2005, transcript p. 24. Provided to Committee.

37 On the noon video teleconference, Brown said he spoke with President Bush at least twice on the day of landfall, likely prior to noon. Brown stated: "I talked to the President twice today, once in Crawford and then again on Air Force One." Michael Brown, FEMA Daily Video Teleconference, Aug. 29, 2005, transcript p. 14. Provided to Committee. Brown also testified that he spoke to White House Deputy Chief of Staff Joe Hagin on at least two occasions on the day of landfall. Testimony of Michael Brown, former Director, FEMA, before the U.S. Senate, Committee on Homeland Security and Governmental Affairs, hearing on *Hurricane Katrina: The Roles of DHS and FEMA Leadership,* Feb. 10, 2006; Andrew Card, e-mail to Michael Brown, Aug. 29, 2005, 9:51 p.m. Provided to Committee (showing that Brown spoke with Hagin on August 29 to provide updates of the situation in New Orleans.). Interestingly, when asked whether he spoke directly to the President on the night of landfall concerning Bahamonde's over flight, Brown said he could not recall if he spoke to the President then. Brown stated: "I really don't recall if the President got – normally during my conversations with Deputy Chief of Staff Hag[i]n, sometimes the President would get on the phone for a few minutes, sometimes he wouldn't, and I don't recall specifically that night whether he did or not." Testimony of Michael Brown, former Director, FEMA, before the U.S. S*enate, Committee on Homeland Security and Governmental Affairs, hearing on Hurricane Katrina: The Roles of DHS and FEMA Leadership,* Feb. 10, 2006.

38 Brown interview, Feb. 23, 2006, transcript pp. 23-25 ("Question: Is there any reason for us to doubt that after you talked to Joe Hagin 5 or 6 o'clock on Monday evening, August 29th, that he then knew from you that the 17th Street Canal levee had broke and the city was flooding? Answer: I don't think there is any reason for any of us to doubt that they knew that. Question: Okay. And that they knew that at least in part from your phone conversation with Joe Hagin, correct? Answer: That's correct."). The substance of the Brown's reports to the White House on August 29 concerned the situation on the ground in New Orleans, including the early reports from Marty Bahamonde, a FEMA Public Affairs official and the only FEMA official on the ground in New Orleans the day of landfall. More specifically, Brown said he spoke with Hagin on Monday evening to discuss Bahamonde's report of his New Orleans flyover over New Orleans, but could not recall whether he specifically told Hagin in that call that the levees had broken. Brown interview, Feb. 23, 2006, transcript p. 21 ("I think I used the phrase to Joe that, you know, our – the worst nightmare is occurring. … I can't recall all of the words I used other than, this is, you know, our worst – this is the worst scenario; this is, you know my worst fears are coming true. You know, I used the phrase, you know we have breaches of the canals."); Testimony of Michael Brown, former Director, FEMA, before the U.S. Senate, Committee on Homeland Security and Governmental Affairs, hearing on *Hurricane Katrina: The Roles of U.S. DHS and FEMA Leadership,* Feb. 10, 2006 ("I think I told him that we were realizing our worst nightmare, that everything we had planned about, worried about, that FEMA, frankly, had worried about for 10 years was coming true."). Brown said he told Hagin or White House Chief of Staff Andrew Card about the levee breaches late in the afternoon on Monday because he recalled they were "debating" at the state Emergency Operations Center whether the levees were breached or overtopped. Testimony of Michael Brown, former Director, FEMA, before the U.S. Senate, Com-

mittee on Homeland Security and Governmental Affairs, *Hurricane Katrina: The Roles of U.S. DHS and FEMA Leadership,* Feb. 10, 2006; Brown interview, Feb. 23, 2006, transcript pp. 15-16; Deposition of Michael Brown, before the House Katrina Select Committee Staff, Feb. 11, 2006, p. 114. Brown also received an e-mail from White House Chief of Staff Andrew Card at 9:51 p.m., Monday, in which Card acknowledged Brown's continued contact with White House Deputy Chief of Staff Joe Hagin and said: "Joe Hagin has kept me well-informed of your reports." Andrew Card, e-mail to Michael Brown, Aug. 29, 2005, 9:51 p.m. Provided to Committee. Brown responded and stated: "Thanks for writing, Andy. This is a bad one." Michael Brown, e-mail to Andrew Card, Aug. 29, 2005, 10 p.m. Provided to Committee.

39 Testimony of Michael Brown, former Director, FEMA, before the U.S. Senate, Committee on Homeland Security and Governmental Affairs, *Hurricane Katrina: The Roles of U.S. DHS and FEMA Leadership,* Feb. 10, 2006.

40 Testimony of Michael Brown, former Director, FEMA, before the U.S. Senate, Committee on Homeland Security and Governmental Affairs, *Hurricane Katrina: The Roles of U.S. DHS and FEMA Leadership,* Feb. 10, 2006.

41 Brown interview, Feb. 23, 2006, transcript pp. 34-36.

42 The White House, "President Participates in Conversation on Medicare," press release, Aug. 29, 2005. http://www.whitehouse.gov/new/releases/2005/08/print/20050829-5.html. Accessed on Apr. 26, 2006; The White House, "President Discusses Medicare, New Prescription Drug Benefits," press release, Aug. 29, 2005. http://www.whitehouse.gov/news/releases/2005/08/print/20050829-11.html. Accessed on Apr. 26, 2006; The White House, "Recent Photo Essay," Aug. 29, 2005. http://www.whitehouse.gov/news/releases/2005/08/images/20050829-5_p082905pm-0125-515h.html. Accessed on Apr. 26, 2006 (including a picture of the President with Senator McCain holding a birthday cake and the caption, "President George W. Bush joins Arizona Senator John McCain in a small celebration of McCain's 69th birthday.").

43 The White House, "President Discusses Medicare, New Prescription Drug Benefits," press release, Aug. 29, 2005. http://www.whitehouse.gov/news/releases/2005/08/20050829-11.html. Accessed on Mar. 7, 2006.

44 The White House, "President Participates in Conversation on Medicare," press release, Aug. 29, 2005. http://www.whitehouse.gov/news/releases/2005/08/20050829-5.html Accessed on Mar. 7, 2006.

45 HSOC Spot Report #13: The Report further stated: "Only one of the main pumps is reported to still be working but cannot keep up with the demand and its longevity is doubtful." The White House received this report at 12:02 a.m., Tuesday, Aug. 30, 2005. Michael Izner, e-mail to Homeland Security Operations Center – Homeland Security Information Network and others, Aug. 30, 2005, 12:02 a.m. Provided to Committee; filed as Bates nos. WHK 07158 through 07160. The other addressees for the e-mail are DL-NSC-WHSR, the National Interagency Coordination Center, as well as the following officials, Bethany Nichol, Elliott Langer, Kirstjen Nielsen, Joel Bagnal, Elizabeth Farrell, Julie Bentz, Daniel Kaniewski, Richard Davis, Michael Barton and copied to Matthew Broderick, Frank DiFalco, Bob Stephan, John Chase, Tom Dinanno, Edward McDonald, Gail Kulish, Tom Parr, Michael Jackson, and John Wood.

46 Michael Izner, e-mail to DL-NSC-WHSR, Aug. 30, 2005, 6:33 a.m. Provided to Committee; filed as Bates no. WHK 06264. The other addresses of the e-mail are Bethany Nichols, Elliott Langer, Kirstjen Nielsen, Joel Bagnal, Elizabeth Farrell, Julie Bentz, Daniel Kaniewski, Richard Davis, Michael Barton, and copied to Matthew Broderick, Frank DiFalco, Bob Stephan, John Chase, Tom Dinanno, Edward McDonald, Gail Kulisch, Tom Paar, Michael Jackson, (DepSec), John Wood, (COS), NICC, Secretary Briefing Staff, HSOC.HSIN, HSOC.SWO.

47 E-mail from Insung Lee to DL-NSC-WHSR and others, Aug. 30, 2005, 10:23 a.m. Provided to Committee; filed as Bates no. WHK 07910. The other addressees of the e-mail are Bethany Nichols, Elliott Langer, Kirstjen Nielsen, Joel Bagnal, Elizabeth Farrell, Julie Bentz, Daniel Kaniewski, Richard Davis, Michael Barton, Matthew Broderick, Frank DiFalco, Bob Stephan, John Chase, Tom Dinanno, Edward McDonald, Gail Kulisch, Tom Paar, Michael Jackson, John Wood, (COS), NICC, Secretary Briefing Staff; HSOC.HSIN, HSOC.SWO, HSOC.FEMA, HSOC.DOD, HSOC.State&Local.

48 The White House, "President Commemorates 60th Anniversary of V-J Day," press release, Aug. 30, 2005. http://www.whitehouse.gov/news/releases/2005/08/images/20050830-1.html. Accessed on Mar. 11, 2005.

49 Brown interview, Feb. 23, 2006, transcript pp. 89-90; Deposition of Michael Brown before the House Katrina Select Committee, Feb. 11, 2006, pp. 111-112 (warning the President, Vice President, Secretary Chertoff, and Deputy Chief of Staff Karl Rove that "probably 90 percent of the population of New Orleans had been displaced, that we had a true catastrophic disaster on our hands, that this was probably one of the most serious things that the country had faced; that it was. We needed to be doing everything possible.").

50 Brown interview, Feb. 23, 2006, transcript pp. 89-90.

51 Brown interview, Feb. 23, 2006, transcript pp. 97-98.

52 Brown interview, Feb. 23, 2006, transcript pp. 97-98.

53 Brown interview, Feb. 23, 2006, transcript pp. 89-91.

54 The White House. "Press Gaggle by Scott McClellan, Naval Air Station North Island, San Diego, California," press release, Aug. 30, 2005. Provided to Committee; filed as Bates nos. WHK 01632 through 01633. ("QUESTION: This is more – this is more symbolic. Cutting short his vacation is more symbolic because he can do all this from the ranch, right? McCLELLAN: No, I think – no, I disagree. Like I said, this is one of the most devastating storms in our nation's history, and the President, after receiving a further update this morning, made the decision that he wanted to get back to D.C. and oversee the response efforts from there.").

55 The White House, "President Outlines Hurricane Katrina Relief Efforts," press release, Aug. 31, 2005. Provided to Committee; filed as Bates nos. WHK 01636 through 01637.

56 Committee staff interview with Laurence Broun, Emergency Coordinator, U.S. Department of the Interior, conducted on Mar. 21, 2006, transcript pp. 15-16.

57 Insung Lee, e-mail to Homeland Security Operations Center, Senior Watch Officer, Aug. 31, 2005, 12:41 p.m. Provided to Committee; filed as Bates nos. WHK 12588 through 12598. The other addressees of the e-mail are DL-NSC-WHSR, Bethany Nichols, Elliott Langer, Kirstjen Nielsen, Joel Bagnal, Elizabeth Farrell, Julie Bentz, Daniel Kaniewski, Richard Davis, Michael Barton, Matthew Broderick, Frank DiFalco, Bob Stephan, John Chase, Tom Dinanno, Edward McDonald, Gail Kulisch, Tom Paar, Michael Jackson, (DepSec), John Wood, (COS), NICC, Secretary Briefing Staff, HSOC.HSIN, IMD.

58 The White House, "President's Remarks to the Travel Pool in Louisiana," press release, Sept. 20, 2005. http://www.whitehouse.gov/news/releases/2005/09/20050920-2.html. Accessed on Apr. 26, 2006.

59 Remarks by President George W. Bush to the travel pool in Louisiana. White House Regular Briefing, Sept. 20, 2005; http://www.whitehouse.gov/news/releases/2005/09/20050920-3.html. Accessed on Apr. 24, 2006.

60 The White House, "Press Briefing by Scott McClellan," press release, Sept. 22, 2005. http://www.whitehouse.gov/news/releases/2005/print/20050922-2.html. Accessed on Apr. 26, 2006.

61 The White House, "President Briefed on Hurricane Rita Preparations at FEMA," press release, Sept. 23, 2005. http://whitehouse.gov/news/releases/2005/09/print/20050923.html. Accessed on Apr. 26, 2006.

62 White House Press Gaggle (as released by the White House), Sept. 24, 2005 aboard Air Force One en route to Austin, Texas http://www.whitehouse.gov/news/releases/2005/09/20050924-8.html. Accessed on Apr. 26, 2006.

63 President George W. Bush, *Good Morning America*, ABC, "President George W. Bush Exclusive Interview," Sept. 1, 2005. Transcript accessed on LexisNexis.

64 The White House. "President, Lieutenant General Honoré Discuss Hurricane Relief in Louisiana," press release, Sept. 12, 2005. Provided to Committee; filed as Bates no. WHK 01723.

65 Richard D. Knabb, Jamie Rhume, and Daniel Brown, National Hurricane Center, *Tropical Cyclone Report, Hurricane Katrina*, Dec. 20, 2005, p.9. http://www.nhc.noaa.gov/pdf/TCR-AL122005_Katrina.pdf. Accessed on Mar. 30, 2006. ("The surge overtopped large sections of the levees during the morning of 29 August east of New Orleans, in Orleans Parish and St. Bernard Parish, and it also pushed water up the Intracoastal Waterway and into the Industrial Canal. The water rise in Lake Pontchartrain strained the floodwalls along the canals adjacent to its southern shore, including the 17th Street Canal and the London Avenue Canal. Breaches along both the Industrial Canal east of downtown New Orleans and the 17th Street Canal northwest of downtown appear to have occurred during the early morning on 29 August, possibly even before the eye made initial landfall in Louisiana. Breaches along the London Avenue Canal north of downtown appear to have occurred later that night.").

66 Daniel J. Kaniewski, Director of Response and Recovery Homeland Security Council, e-mail to Dan Bartlett and others. The White House, Aug. 29, 2005, 11:13 a.m., p.1. Provided to Committee. Filed as Bates no. WHK 004795. ("Currently Katrina has 127 mph sustained winds, making it a Category 3 storm. Katrina is moving northward, located 22 miles to the east of New Orleans. Flooding is significant throughout the region and a levee in New Orleans has reportedly been breached sending 6 to 8 feet of water throughout the 9th Ward area of the city. Per the Governor, water is rising at 1 foot per hour and the New Orleans mayor reports problems with a pumping station, causing flooding. HSOC reports that due to the rising water in the 9th ward, residents are in their attics and on their roofs.")

67 *Southeast Louisiana Hurricane Preparedness Study,* prepared by U. S. Army Corps of Engineers, Federal Emergency Management Agency, and National Weather Service, 1994, p. 5–2 ("Although designed to provide substantial levels of protection, these levees and floodwalls are subject to overtopping during catastrophic events. The surge inundation maps show that for slow moving category 3, category 4, or category 5 storms, only those reaches of St. Tammany Parish located north of I-12 would be outside of the potential limits of storm surge."); Federal Emergency Management Agency, "Background Information to Accompany Region VI Hurricane Plan For New Orleans, Corps of Engineers Analysis of the Flood Problem in New Orleans," p. 1 ("The most dangerous storm would be a slow-moving category 3 or stronger hurricane on a path that carries it northward 20 to 30 miles west of and parallel to the Mississippi River until it is near New Orleans. The worst case would be if a storm on that path then re-curved to the north and continued inland. … There could be extensive and severe erosion of levees and perhaps complete breaches. … Each of the affected parishes has a series of one or more levees which normally form a protective ring around the inhabited area, although, if a severe hurricane produces flooding higher than the levees are designed for, the surge could overtop the levees and cause massive flooding. Storm surge, rain water, and natural run-off can fill these bowl-shaped areas after a hurricane. Some areas do not have hurricane protection levees, and in those areas, storm surge can rise and recede quickly. But when a hurricane storm surge overtops ring-levees and fills the bowl, the protective levees may actually trap flood-water, prevent it from draining out, and prolong the flooding."); in Sherry Wainwright, FEMA Region VI, "Hurricane Plan for Louisiana, Attachment to the Regional Supplement to the Federal Response Plan," May 2002. Provided to the Committee; Southeast Louisiana Hurricane Evacuation and Sheltering Plan, Jan. 2000, p. II-1 ("… worst case Category 3, 4 or 5 Hurricane Scenario for the Greater New Orleans Metropolitan Area, as determined by the National Weather Service (NWS) Sea, Lake, and Overland Surge from Hurricanes (SLOSH) Model, could cause a maximum inundation of 20 feet above sea level in some of the parishes in the Region, not including tidal effects, wind waves and storm rainfall."); State of Louisiana Hazard Mitigation Strategy – Volume I State of Louisiana Hazard Mitigation Plan, Apr. 15, 2005, p. I-46 ("In Louisiana, storm surges are large waves of Gulf waters that sweep across coastlines where a tropical storm makes landfall. Generally the more intense the storm, the greater the height of the storm surge; the higher the storm surge, the greater the damage to the coastline. … Shallow coastal bathymetry increases the magnitude of a storm surge. The coastal

bathymetry of southeastern Louisiana, with its low, flat topography and land surface elevations that in many places dip below sea level, can experience storm surges up to 100 miles inland. Category 3 storms can bring depths up to 24 feet as far north as the City of New Orleans. Category 5 storms can produce depths as high as 36 feet. Furthermore, lakes along the coast, namely, Lake Maurepas, Lake Borgne, and Lake Pontchartrain, exacerbate the effects of coastal flooding because of wave effects that can regenerate over inland lakes.").

68 Committee staff interview with Wilson Shaffer, Ph.D., National Weather Service, conducted on Feb. 24, 2006, transcript p. 56 (Sea, Lake, and Overland Surge from Hurricane (SLOSH) storm surge studies in New Orleans reported to emergency preparedness officials in 2004 and 2005, stating that "The big change that we saw was that we were going to start seeing some flooding now with a few category 2 hurricanes," without any mention of levee breaches); "Hurricanes: Nature's Weapons of Mass Destruction," presentation by Wilson Shaffer, Ph.D., National Weather Service to the Louisiana Emergency Preparedness Association, June 1, 2005 (including a computer projection showing extensive overtopping of New Orleans levees from composite of Category 3 hurricanes, as well as a slide entitled, "Louisiana's Vulnerability to Hurricane Storm Surge"); Brett Herr, e-mail to Jay Baker, Mar. 15, 2004. Provided to Committee; filed as Bates no. DHS-FEMA-0025-0002638 ("New surge inundation maps show significant portions of Orleans and Jefferson Parish that are susceptible to flooding from slow-moving Category 2 and fast Category 3 hurricanes. We had previously thought that the city would … fare pretty well for these types of storm. The new maps will result in significantly longer [evacuation] clearance times for these scenarios.").

69 President George W. Bush, *CNN Live Today*, CNN, "President Bush Visits Gulf Coast: Early Warnings – Part 2," Sept. 2, 2005, 10 a.m. Transcript, accessed on LexisNexis.

70 White House Briefing to Committee, conducted by Kenneth Rapuano, Deputy Assistant to the President for Homeland Security, Feb. 3, 2006.

71 Speech of President George W. Bush, Jackson Square, New Orleans, Louisiana, Sept. 15, 2005.

72 Testimony of Michael Brown, former Director, FEMA, before the U.S. Senate, Committee on Homeland Security and Governmental Affairs, hearing on *The Roles of DHS and FEMA Leadership,* Feb. 10, 2006.

73 Testimony of Michael Brown, former Director, FEMA, before the U.S. Senate, Committee on Homeland Security and Governmental Affairs, hearing on "*The Roles of DHS and FEMA Leadership,* Feb. 10, 2006; Andrew Card, e-mail to Michael Brown, Aug. 29, 2005, 9:51 p.m. Provided to Committee.

74 Testimony of Michael Brown, former Director, FEMA, before the U.S. Senate, Committee on Homeland Security and Governmental Affairs, hearing on *The Roles of DHS and FEMA Leadership,* Feb. 10, 2006; Brown interview, Feb. 23, 2006, transcript p. 21.

75 Brown interview, Feb. 23, 2006, transcript pp. 24-25. The following exchange occurred: Question: Is there any reason for us to doubt that after you talked to Joe Hagin 5 or 6 o'clock on Monday evening, August 29th, that he then knew from you that the 17th Street Canal levee had broke and the city was flooding? Answer: I don't think there is any reason for any of us to doubt that they knew that. Question: Okay. And that they knew that at least in part from your phone conversation with Joe Hagin, correct? Answer: That's correct.

76 Andrew H. Card, Jr., e-mail to Michael Brown, Aug. 29, 2005, 9:51 p.m. Provided to the Committee; Michael Brown, e-mail to Andrew Card, Aug. 29, 2005, 10 p.m. Provided to the Committee.

77 Testimony of Michael Brown, former Director, FEMA, before the U.S. Senate, Committee on Homeland Security and Governmental Affairs, hearing on *The Roles of DHS and FEMA Leadership,* Feb. 10, 2006.

78 Senator Lieberman stated: At the time, I did not seek a subpoena to the Office of the Vice President (OVP), to which the Committee sent a separate request letter, because that Office provided, in some respects, more responsive and useful material than did the rest of the White House. The OVP produced to the Committee a variety of material referencing or originating with its high-level staff, and it did not seek to assert the absolutist position put forth by the White House Counsel's office on behalf of the rest of the White House. While I am skeptical that we received a full production from the OVP and believe that the Committee should have pushed harder for a larger production, I nonetheless did not include the OVP in my subpoena request because I did not conclude that its response reached the level of egregiousness demonstrated by the rest of the White House. Ranking Member Lieberman, letter to Chairman Collins, Mar. 15, 2006.

79 Congressional Research Service, Memorandum to Senate Homeland Security and Governmental Affairs Committee, Nov. 29, 2005, p. 13.

80 Congressional Research Service, Memorandum to Senate Homeland Security and Governmental Affairs Committee, Feb. 9, 2006, p. 3. (Emphasis added.)

81 Congressional Record, Dec. 20, 1995 p. S18972. (Emphasis added).

82 Testimony of Michael Brown, former Director, FEMA, before the U.S. Senate, Committee on Homeland Security and Governmental Affairs, hearing on "*The Roles of DHS and FEMA Leadership,* Feb. 10, 2006.

83 Chairman Collins, letter to Ranking Member Lieberman, Mar. 15, 2006, p. 1.

84 True, the General Accountability Office and some agency Inspectors General have conducted their own investigations, but none, to our knowledge, are as comprehensive as the Committee's, nor have any received greater cooperation from the White House (to the extent that they have even asked for it).

85 Testimony of Sec. Michael Chertoff, U.S. Department of Homeland Security, before the U.S. House, Select Bipartisan Committee to Investigate the Preparation for and Response to Hurricane Katrina, hearing on *Hurricane Katrina: The*

Role of the Department of Homeland Security, Oct. 19, 2005 ("it is important as we go forward that we learn lessons, even painful lessons, from past experiences, things that worked well and things that didn't work well.").

86 Questions for the Record of Sec. Michael Chertoff, U.S. Department of Homeland Security, for the U.S. Senate, Committee on Homeland Security and Governmental Affairs, hearing on *Hurricane Katrina: The Homeland Security Department's Preparation and Response,* Feb. 15, 2006, p. 33.

87 Because only individuals at DHS know if they have produced to us all the responsive documents they have, it can be difficult for a requestor to state definitively whether a request has been fully complied with. However, there are areas where the nonresponsiveness is obvious – for instance, in the case of information requests that there has been no attempt to answer or in requests, such as that for Secretary Chertoff's schedule or documents in his possession, for which clearly no material has been produced. In other cases, a small fraction of the material requested may have been produced but the request has nonetheless clearly not been complied with. Thus, for example, in a January 30, 2006 letter to the majority staff director, which was shared with Senator Lieberman's staff, Gus Coldebella, Deputy General Counsel of DHS attached a table purporting to show the extent of DHS's compliance with the priority document requests included in the Committee's December 30, 2005 letter. A cursory look at the table might suggest that most of the requests have been complied with, but in fact any such suggestion would be highly misleading. For example, the December 30 letter asked for all documents related to the Federal Protective Service's preparation for or response to Hurricane Katrina, including any actions taken at the Superdome and the Convention Center; what Coldebella's letter lists as produced in response comprises simply the e-mails for a single individual, the head of the Federal Protective Service. Gus P. Coldebella, letter to Michael Bopp, Senate Committee staff member, Jan. 30, 2006.

88 Committee staff agreed to forego interviewing the remaining individual on the list.

89 The Committee was permitted to interview only two individuals who were not on the December 30, 2005, priority list: the Director of the Federal Protective Service and the Chief of the Critical Infrastructure Protection Division of the National Communications System – both in preparation for a hearing focused on law enforcement and communications issues, respectively.

90 U.S. Department of Homeland Security, SITREP #7, Aug. 29, 2005, 6 p.m. Provided to Committee; filed as Bates no. DHS 0001181.

91 Committee staff interview of John Wood, Chief of Staff, U.S. Department of Homeland Security, conducted on Jan. 27, 2006, transcript p. 38.

92 Committee staff interview of William E. King, Branch Chief, Region V, Radiological Emergency Preparedness Program, Technical Services Branch, FEMA, conducted on Jan. 17, 2006, transcript pp. 178-179.

93 The only exceptions to this were Matthew Broderick, Director of the HSOC, whose interview lasted for approximately a total of six hours over the course of two sessions in a single day, and Wendell Shingler, Director of the Federal Protective Service, who was interviewed in a second session lasting less than 40 minutes two weeks after his initial interview, in order to clarify a particular issue.

94 Specifically, at the end of the session with Robert Stephan, the General Counsel for the Minority stated: "If I may, and I don't mean this in any way – there are a whole lot of – we are sort of circumscribed by time here, and I must tell you, you have been most informative, extremely insightful in a lot of ways. But it doesn't begin to get to a whole lot of other issues that we want to spend time with, with somebody who is so central to so many aspects of DHS in connection with a catastrophe. I would like to meet with you again. I would like to ask that this be continued. I would like to get documents, particularly e-mails, from you. And that's central to any good investigation. So while we may finish here today, it's a very strong position of the minority that we really do have to speak with you again, and we need to have documents that are central to what you were doing, particularly the e-mails. And I would like to have this session be continued on that basis." Committee staff interview of Robert Stephan, Assistant Secretary for Infrastructure Protection, U.S. Department of Homeland Security, conducted on Jan. 13, 2006, transcript pp. 148-149. Stephan's interview represented a convergence of a number of DHS's uncooperative practices. In addition to unreasonably limiting the time of the interview, DHS counsel also produced Stephan several hours before he had been scheduled to appear and in lieu of another witness who had been scheduled for that time. Moreover, none of Stephan's e-mails had been produced before his appearance for the interview.

95 Although DHS eventually made the then-Chief Financial Officer, Andrew Maner, available for an interview on February 2, 2006, the virtual absence of any budget-related documents significantly limited the effectiveness of any questioning Committee staff could pursue.

96 Subsequently, DHS also produced to the Committee documents that were posted on the Homeland Security Information Network (HSIN) portal.

97 Lt. Robert Walls, e-mail to LANTMHLS Watch, RCCAlameda, CommandCenPAC, Command Center - D1, CC1, Command Center - LANTD5, D7CommandCenter, D8 Command Center, Ninth District Command Center, CommandCenD11, D13(cc), D14ccDutyOfficer, D17-PF-Jun-Command Center, hsoc.uscg@dhs.gov, fldr-NRC, D05-SMB-D5MHLSWatch, D05-SMB-LANTCmdCtr, D05-SMB-LANTMHLSWatch, D8IMTWatch, tsoc.st@dhs.gov, est-mcc-dot@dhs.gov, CMC-01@rspa.dot.gov, cmc-02@dot.gov, uscg.iimg@dhs.gov, Aug. 29, 2005. Provided to the Committee.

98 The Committee recently received information in answer to this specific question only by including it, in a modified form, in a question for the record to Secretary Chertoff after his appearance before the Committee. Questions for the Record of Sec. Chertoff, Feb. 15, 2006, pp. 33-41. Other questions remain unanswered, however.

99 Col. Henry Whitehorn, letter to FBI Director Robert Mueller, Aug. 30, 2005. Provided to Committee; filed as Bates no. FBI 000000003.

100 Committee staff interview of William Mercer, Principal Associate Deputy Attorney General, Department of Justice, conducted on Jan. 26, 2006, transcript pp. 29-30 ("But I guess if the question is how did the requests come in, let me turn to those. Because that's a very significant part of the Federal statute here. In Title 42 – and I think the provision is 42 U.S.C. § 10501 – a governor, not a state attorney general, not a mayor – a governor can ask the Attorney General of the United States to deploy Federal law enforcement resources if the governor makes a proffer saying, 'We can't meet the responsibilities that we need to carry out for public safety, and I request that you deploy Federal resources to assist.' And we got a letter from Governor Barbour on Saturday the 3rd. And we responded that same day. It was faxed in on the 3rd, we met with the Attorney General on Saturday. He issued the order on Saturday. . . . And Governor Blanco faxed us a letter the next day."). Mr. Mercer also said that the Office of the Deputy Attorney General did not receive "any direct requests from a state or local official until [it] got the letter from Governor Barbour on the 3rd of September." Mercer interview, Jan. 26, 2006, p. 24. Apparently, Mercer also did not consider a request addressed to the head of the FBI to be a "direct request" to the appropriate office. Mercer interview, Jan. 26, 2006, pp. 30-31.

101 Mercer, when asked whether anyone from DOJ had spoken with the governor's office about the requirement of a gubernatorial request, responded that he did not know. Mercer interview, Jan. 26, 2006, pp. 44-45.

102 *See, e.g.,* William Mercer, e-mail to Ted Ulloyt, Kyle Sampson, and Jeffrey Taylor, Sept. 1, 2005, 1:30 a.m. Provided to Committee; filed as Bates no. DAG 000000064 (forwarding a memorandum written by Mercer that has never been produced. In the transmittal e-mail, Mercer offers to put the information into bullet points and notes that "there are some important things to pass along to the AG" concerning Mercer's discussions with the U.S. Attorneys from Baton Rouge and New Orleans).

103 *See, e.g.,* James McAtamney, Senior Counsel for National Security Affairs, Transmittal slip with cover notes and ESF-13 excerpt to Ted Ullyot and Bill Mercer. Provided to Committee; filed as Bates nos. DAG 000000100 through 000000106. The Committee does not have McAtamney's e-mails except to the extent they were produced as part of Mercer's files.

104 *See, e.g.,* Matthew Broderick, e-mail to John Clark, Sept. 4, 2005, 4:23 p.m. Provided to Committee; filed as Bates no. DHS-HSOC-0004-0006525. ("The dispute is whether FBI or ICE is the lead. I believe we have designated the ICE SAC as the lead. DHS and DOJ co-share this ESF and usually (terrorist related) FBI is lead. This is a good chance for us to be.").

105 42 U.S.C. § 10501 ("Emergency Federal Law Enforcement Assistance Program").

106 U.S. Department of Health and Human Services, "U.S. Department of Health and Human Services Response to the Senate Homeland Security and Governmental Affairs Questions regarding Katrina," undated, received by the Committee on Feb. 24, 2006.

107 U.S. Department of Health and Human Services, "Concept of Operations Plan (CONOPS) for Public Health and Medical Emergencies," Jan. 2005. Provided to Committee; filed as OPHEP 16285 through OPHEP 16315.

108 Chairman Collins and Sen. Lieberman, letter to Sec. Michael Leavitt, Jan. 13, 2006.

109 Committee staff interview of William M. Lokey, Federal Coordinating Officer for Hurricane Katrina in Louisiana, FEMA, conducted on Jan. 20, 2006, transcript pp. 75-76.

110 Lokey interview, Jan. 20, 2006, pp. 192-193. At the time Katrina hit, FEMA had not yet produced an Incident Management Handbook to adapt ICS to FEMA operations. Lokey interview, Jan. 20, 2006, p. 194. *See* FEMA ERT-N Draft Concept of Operations (6-6-05). Provided to Committee; filed as Bates no. DHS-FEMA-0115-0000010.

111 Lokey interview, Jan. 20, 2006, p. 191. William Carwile III, the FCO for Mississippi, also complained about the lack of training dollars for ERT-N teams. Committee staff interview of William Carwile, Federal Coordinating Officer for Hurricane Katrina in Mississippi, FEMA, conducted on Dec. 6, 2005, transcript pp. 22-23, 43.

112 Carwile interview, Dec. 6, 2005, p. 47.

113 King interview, Jan. 17, 2006, p. 28.

114 Committee staff interview of Tony Robinson, Director, Response and Recovery Division, Region VI, FEMA, conducted on Nov. 15, 2005, transcript p. 40.

Additional Views

Senator George V. Voinovich

I commend Senators Collins and Lieberman and their investigative staff for producing a thorough examination of the government's response to Hurricane Katrina.

It is clear there were serious and regrettable deficiencies in the response at every level of government during the days leading up to and following the unprecedented catastrophe in the Gulf Coast. This country can and must improve its capabilities in preparing for and responding to future disasters, whether natural or man-made.

The Senate Committee on Homeland Security and Governmental Affairs has produced a substantial report, which I am confident will contribute positively to the future of emergency management. I wholeheartedly agree with the following recommendations detailed in the report:

- Commitment to emergency management across federal, state, and local governments must be strengthened;

- The Department of Homeland Security (DHS) must develop a true all-hazards focus and strike the appropriate balance between addressing terrorism and natural disasters;

- A stronger regional DHS/Federal Emergency Management Agency (FEMA) framework is necessary;

- Collaboration and coordination must be improved among federal agencies and between federal, state, and local governments;

- FEMA – or the proposed National Preparedness and Response Authority (NPRA) – must have capable and qualified leadership with a robust and well-trained workforce; and

- Our nation's plans and systems for responding to disasters and catastrophes should be improved and clarified to establish clear lines of authority, roles, and responsibilities by all appropriate federal, state, and local parties.

While I concur with many of the Chairman and Ranking Member's findings and recommendations, I appreciate the opportunity to express my differing opinion on several key matters.

I believe too much emphasis has been placed upon reconsidering the organizational structure of FEMA. Whether FEMA is an independent, Cabinet-level agency or reorganized within DHS is not the most critical factor. The key to FEMA's effectiveness is ensuring the agency has capable and qualified leadership, is fully staffed with a well-trained and experienced workforce, and has the necessary budgetary resources. As this Report details, FEMA did not have the appropriate leadership, staffing levels, or budgetary resources necessary for optimal readiness prior to Hurricane Katrina.

This Report declares that FEMA is beyond repair. I do not share that assessment. Nor do I agree at this time that reorganizing and renaming FEMA is the answer. I am concerned that yet another reorganization of FEMA and DHS would be disruptive and could cause more harm than good. Instead of "moving boxes around" yet again, I believe this Committee should focus its oversight authority and legislative efforts on ensuring that DHS and FEMA are working as effectively as possible to strengthen institutional capabilities, assemble the appropriate leadership team with the optimal staffing levels, and make the best use of budgetary resources.

In the past months, DHS Secretary Michael Chertoff, Acting FEMA Director R. David Paulison, and Under Secretary for Preparedness George Foresman have assured this Committee that they are rehabilitating FEMA and improving preparedness and response capabilities throughout DHS for the impending hurricane season and beyond. DHS is already implementing many of the recommendations in this Committee's Report. However, Secretary Chertoff does not support the Report's reorganization proposal. As a former government executive, I believe the Secretary's views are critical and deserve serious consideration in this matter. Congress must hold DHS accountable for its performance, but should refrain from micromanaging the agency.

Much attention has been paid in this Report to the link between the emergency preparedness and response functions within DHS. While I agree these two functions are necessarily interdependent, I am not presently convinced the agency must be reorganized to achieve coordination. When Secretary Chertoff conducted his management review of the agency last year, he determined that the preparedness and response offices should be separated – but work together closely – because the two functions require different core competencies. Therefore, he proposed creating a Preparedness Directorate to focus exclusively on grants, training, and exercises; while allowing FEMA to focus entirely on its response and recovery missions. The new Preparedness Directorate became operational only months ago, in October 2005, following Hurricane Katrina. Therefore, I believe judgments regarding the current structure of the preparedness and response functions within DHS are premature.

I also have reservations regarding the proposed dual-reporting structure for the Director of NPRA. The chain of command recommended in this report would allow the Director of the proposed NPRA to bypass the DHS Secretary and report directly to the President. Following the leadership failures during Hurricane Katrina, a dual-reporting structure is a tempting recommendation, but one that would ultimately harm accountability and the effectiveness and coherence of the chain of command. If the DHS Secretary is to be held fully accountable for the actions of his Department, the NPRA Director should not be allowed to circumvent the Secretary's authority, even during times of crisis.

Overall, it seems that the recommendations in this Report could entail shifting an increased burden to the federal government for emergency management, which has historically been recognized as a shared responsibility between federal, state, and local governments. In an environment of limited federal budgetary resources, I would urge that where possible, improvements in emergency preparedness and response capabilities should primarily be achieved through better management, training, coordination, and leveraging of existing resources at all levels of government.

I feel strongly that we in Congress have an obligation to exercise our oversight capacity to ensure our nation develops a more robust and effective emergency-management system in order to prevent future devastation and suffering on the scale of Hurricane Katrina. I support the spirit in which this Report is offered, however, I would caution my colleagues that Congress should avoid being overly prescriptive toward the Executive Branch or the States. Certain recommendations in this report denote a specificity with which I am uncomfortable.

In total, I believe the Chairman and Ranking Member of the Committee have produced a solid Report, and I greatly appreciate their efforts. I hope the Congress and the Administration can work cooperatively in the coming months to identify and implement the appropriate modifications to improve our nation's disaster preparedness and response capabilities.

Additional Views

Senator Tom Coburn, M.D.

I commend the Committee Chairman, Ranking Member, and investigative staff for their arduous investigation into the Hurricane Katrina disaster and the work that went into the voluminous Report. To a large extent, this Report provides a detailed account of the events leading up to, during and after the landfall of Hurricane Katrina. I am concerned, however, that the main recommendation of the Report – to abolish FEMA and reconstitute it as the National Preparedness and Response Authority – does not adequately address the root cause of the disaster. That root cause, in my view, was a lack of accountability for performance (both before and after the hurricane), rather than a flawed organizational or management structure. I would argue that by overemphasizing organizational change rather than performance improvement, these somewhat conflicting recommendations miss the point.

Misplaced Focus: Organization v. Outcomes

The Report recommendations focus on micromanaging the "how" and "who" of emergency preparedness and response rather than the "what." Rearranging organization and prescribing certain qualities for, tasks of, and relationships between managers, and creating new teams and task forces, is not the appropriate role of Congress. We should ensure that taxpayers are getting the "product" they pay for with tax revenues, rather than dictating the specifics of how it is obtained. In other words, the Report recommendations should have focused more on developing an accountability system based on meeting actual preparedness and response indicators and benchmarks *as a condition* for receiving federal, state or local funds, using whatever management and organizational structures are preferred by a given President, Governor, and Mayor or County Executive. Different Executives will naturally have different personalities, management styles and operating procedures. They should be permitted to operate and organize in whatever lawful manner they choose. The key matter of importance to the Congress is that they deliver the level of performance on pre-legislated preparedness and response outcomes, improving after each exercise and real-life emergency.

The Committee's investigation did not adequately address this aspect of accountability for performance over the long term. It uncovered the *symptoms* of the disease rather than the disease itself. I would argue that under-funding of emergency-planning activities is not a root cause, but rather, the result of consistent inattention to meeting emergency-planning goals.

Lack of oversight by accountable government officials, including Congress, is the reason behind any funding deficiency. When elected officials fail to recognize a dangerous lack of readiness, they are unlikely to have either the political will to increase funding or the attention span required to identify which underperforming functions require a redirection of existing funding streams. Perhaps, if adequate oversight were being performed, it would have been recognized that funding levels were saturated in some areas, but that more important or worse-performing areas needed targeted funding redirection. A non-specific accusation of "under-funding" does not explain why nobody with the power of the purse at the local, state, or federal level noticed that preparedness was not being achieved, or if it was noticed, nobody took the steps necessary to remedy the situation. Funding was provided over a period of years to achieve preparedness, but it took the massive real-life test of Hurricane Katrina to expose what should have been exposed and fixed by simulated or smaller-scale real-life tests such as the 2004 Florida hurricane season or the Hurricane Pam simulated exercise.

I believe that the reason why preparedness was not achieved is that measurable indicators of that preparedness were not demanded at any level of government by elected officials. If preparedness is operationalized using measurable indicators (such as performance during drills, testing of communications equipment and systems, testing of staff on certain aspects of a plan, and actual performance during smaller disasters), then officials have a way of targeting funds to where they are most needed, or conditioning funds on actual performance. Instead, the usual process involves automatic funding every year without any reference to what the American people are getting for those dollars. I suspect that Americans don't care how the Department of Homeland Security delivers adequate disaster planning and response; they simply want the Department to deliver at the point of crisis. Congress should take the same approach. A useful model can be found in New Zealand, which reorganized its federal legislative and oversight approach during the 1980s and 1990s to become entirely outcomes-focused, conditioning funding on performance on certain outcomes that were legislated in advance. The result was radical improvement in federal performance.

Misplaced Focus: Timeframe

Another weakness of the Report is the timeframe of its focus, which may be why the recommendations miss the mark. The primary failure of all levels of government in the Katrina disaster occurred years before landfall, and no amount of brilliant performance immediately before or after the hurricane would have overcome that neglect. That the performance wasn't satisfactory (far from it) is indeed relevant to the observed outcomes, but only marginally so. It should hardly have been the primary focus of the report and its recommendations. There is simply only so much a local, state, or federal government, with its layers of bureaucracies, rules, regulations, and systems, can do to help people during a disaster if the years of planning and drilling (until all systems and plans have been *demonstrably and measurably* tested) have been neglected.

As a primary example, the report acknowledges that without the breaking of the levee, most of the significant problems would have had far less of an impact on the city of New Orleans. Yet, the problems with the city's levee system go back 40 years or more. In fact, the very likelihood of a situation exactly like the one that occurred was predicted *for decades* by experts inside and outside the government. While it is keenly important to obtain the lessons learned from those that commanded the response and recovery activities, it is far more important to understand the long-term failures to prepare for this event.

Misplaced Focus: Expectations of Federal Government

Finally, the Report places too much blame on "last responders" in this disaster, that is, the federal government. Unwieldy, distant, slow, and inefficient *by nature*, the federal government is rightly the responder of last resort to any disaster. However, as the biggest source of funding for local and state preparedness activities, the federal government has the critical obligation to serve as a quality-assurance monitor in advance of any disaster. It is essential that the federal government conduct thorough, regular, and well-publicized oversight of state, local, and federal officials' performance, to observe whether they are performing in a way that reduces the need for a massive federal engagement following an emergency. If performance is substandard, then the well-publicized nature of such oversight can serve to generate public demand and political will for the conditioning of funds and other "tough love" measures that may be the only means of motivating improvement.

Given that the federal government is not designed to be a fast or first responder in a disaster, any federal bail-out of states and localities in a disaster would itself be a disaster. That means that the best and most effective federal role is to demand excellence, indeed, to condition funding on it, over the years prior to a disaster, ensuring that state and local officials are so prepared as to preempt the need for federal intervention, and certainly to preempt the need for *quick and efficient* intervention. That the federal government had to *take over* Hurricane Katrina recovery and response, rather than simply help coordinate it, represents the real tragedy of the Katrina narrative. The Report fails to recognize the inherent inability of the federal government to respond well in a situation like this and instead castigates it for being what it must be: a large, slow bureaucracy.

Conclusion

The Congress often resorts to rearranging agencies in reaction to disasters and then criticizing the very agencies they organized and oversaw for being organized poorly. The Department of Homeland Security itself was the product of Congressional bureaucratic reshuffling after 9/11. Perhaps the problem is not flawed federal organization, but flawed oversight by local, state, and federal legislative and executive officials. All Americans, especially the victims of Hurricane Katrina, deserve better from us in the future.

Additional Views

Senator Pete V. Domenici

On Corps of Engineers and Levee Issues

Hurricane Katrina: A Nation Still Unprepared develops its conclusion based on available, albeit incomplete, data. The Army Corps of Engineers is continuing to collect and synthesize data on the storm. The Interagency Performance Evaluation Task Force (IPET) established by the Chief of Engineers to provide credible and objective scientific and engineering answers to fundamental questions about the performance of the hurricane protection and flood damage-reduction system in the New Orleans metropolitan area has not yet completed their analysis. Their report is scheduled for completion in June 2006. The IPET team consists of more than 150 experts from more than 50 federal, state, and local agencies, as well as international, academia and industry groups.

As this team was established by the Corps, outside oversight was considered essential to validate the team's results. The oversight is set up as follows: the Corps IPET team will collect the facts, the National Research Council Committee on New Orleans Regional Hurricane Protection Projects will synthesize the facts, and the American Society of Civil Engineers is the external review panel to verify the data and develop conclusions.

The IPET Mission has five focus areas. They are:

> The Flood Protection System – What were the design criteria for the pre-Katrina hurricane protection system, and did the design, as-built construction, and maintained condition meet these criteria?

> The Storm – What were the storm surges and waves used as the basis of design, and how do those compare to the storm surges and waves generated by Hurricane Katrina?

> The Performance – How did the floodwalls, levees, pumping stations, and drainage canals, individually and acting as an integrated system, perform in response to Hurricane Katrina, and why?

> The Consequences – What have been the societal-related consequences of the Katrina-related damage?

> The Risk – Following the immediate repairs, what will be the quantifiable risk to New Orleans and vicinity from future hurricanes and tropical storms?

The hurricane and flood damage-reduction projects in the New Orleans metropolitan area were designed for a compact, relatively fast-moving Category 3 storm. This was the so-called standard project hurricane.

Katrina was a huge, powerful, relatively slow-moving hurricane. The United States Geological Survey (USGS) says that the storm surge from Hurricane Katrina was the largest recorded storm surge ever to hit the United States.

Some of the preliminary information from the report shows that levee subsidence had caused some levee segments to be lower than designed, and consequently did not provide the protection level intended. For instance, the levees along the Industrial Canal were nearly three feet below the design elevation due solely to subsidence.

Unanticipated failure mechanisms in the I-wall design resulted in catastrophic failure of the I-walls along two of the interior drainage canals with water levels below the tops of the floodwalls. These failure modes had been modeled, but had not been incorporated in the design as they were not anticipated to occur at these locations.

Earthen levees were subjected to long-period ocean waves. This type of wave is not usually associated with more compact hurricanes typical of the Gulf of Mexico. These long-period waves carry tremendous energy and ripped huge chunks out of the levees as the waves overtopped the structures. Vivid images of this destruction were captured showing waves breaking over the levee along the Mississippi River Gulf Outlet during Hurricane Katrina as well as pictures created after the storm showing the same levee section and how it was damaged by these breaking waves. This type of wave action was not incorporated in the design of the earthen levees.

While these preliminary results from the IPET team do not absolve the Corps of Engineers, the State of Louisiana, or local officials from blame in design and maintenance of the levees, Katrina was a huge storm when it made landfall. It packed a Category 5 storm surge even though wind speed may have been as low as Category 3 when it made landfall. The storm surge was the devastating factor on the flood-control infrastructure. Further, the interior drainage system, developed over a 100-year period mostly by non-Federal interests, proved to be inadequate to deal with the flooding caused by the storm surge and attendant flooding.

The preliminary information from the IPET study shows that the design assumptions that were made when the project was authorized and throughout the 40-year period of construction were likely faulty, in hindsight. However, as a storm like Katrina was not considered typical for Gulf hurricanes, the same design decisions may well have been repeated if we were building the project today, had this storm not occurred.

Somewhat as a validation of the above statement is that FEMA was in the process of revising the 100-year flood plain maps for New Orleans prior to Katrina. Had Katrina not occurred, these maps would have, in all likelihood, validated existing, but faulty, conclusions. However, after Katrina occurred, FEMA reworked their analysis to incorporate the data from Katrina. The result was drastically altered 100-year flood plain maps for the New Orleans metro area. These new maps indicate that the levees currently in place do not provide protection from a 100-year flooding event. Prior to Katrina, it was believed the same levees provided a 200-year level of protection. This revised analysis demonstrates the power and magnitude of Katrina by showing how drastically it altered the hydraulic assumptions in the metro area.

Supplemental appropriations to date have provided the Corps necessary funding to respond to immediate disaster needs and restore the hurricane and flood-protection system to pre-Katrina conditions before the start of this year's hurricane season on June 1st. Additionally, funding has been provided to complete the hurricane and flood-protection system as originally conceived and designed.

The latest supplemental proposal is intended to strengthen the obvious weaknesses in this system by closing off the interior drainage canals and the Industrial Canal to storm surge. This will provide increased protection to the central area of New Orleans. Proposed levee raisings will increase protection levels for the New Orleans metropolitan area. Armoring of the levees will protect many of the levees in St. Bernard and other hard-hit areas from the wave action that was so devastating during Katrina. Restoration of coastal areas will provide protection by reducing storm surge, and storm-proofing the interior pump stations should allow this vital system to continue operating during hurricane events.

Studies by the Corps are on-going to determine the ultimate level of protection that should be provided for the greater New Orleans and south Louisiana area. These studies will provide preliminary interim recommendations in June 2006, with a final report scheduled for December 2007. These studies are anticipated to provide the basis for additional investments in hurricane and flood-system improvements to the greater New Orleans and south Louisiana area.

Additional Views

Senator John Warner

The investigation conducted by this Committee represents a remarkable undertaking in contemporary Senate history – 22 investigative hearings calling 85 witnesses, formal interviews of 325 witnesses, and nearly 1 million pages of documentation have led to the Committee report. The enormity of this task cannot be overstated and I wish to applaud the tireless work of Chairman Collins, Senator Lieberman, and their staff on their efforts. All Americans share the same goal to prepare for the future and respond when called upon to help our fellow citizens. It is the responsibility of all levels of government to serve its people.

Department of Defense Response

After these investigative hearings and extensive additional interviews, it is my personal view that the Department of Defense (DOD) active-duty personnel, National Guard, and Reserves performed with professional distinction in the days and weeks following the landfall of Hurricane Katrina. There are many stories of individual service, persons or small groups accepting personal risks in helping the victims of this tragic natural disaster.

The Department of Defense response to Hurricane Katrina represents the largest and most rapid "domestic" deployment of the military in contemporary military history. Even while over 75,000 National Guard and Reserves were deployed overseas fighting for freedom in Iraq and Afghanistan, an additional 50,000 troops were deployed in response to Hurricane Katrina.

At the peak of the Department of Defense deployment there were 20 ships; 346 helicopters; 68 fixed-wing aircraft; and 72,614 Active Duty, Reserves, and National Guardsmen assisting the recovery effort. In addition, the DOD delivered 26.6 million Meals Ready to Eat, treated 26,304 patients, and flew 16,525 sorties.[1] While the Committee report deservedly singles out the contributions of the Coast Guard in performing 33,000 rescues, it bears mentioning that the National Guard and Reserve saved 11,000 people from their rooftops.[2]

The Department takes seriously its civil-support mission and provided unprecedented support to the response to Hurricane Katrina, as noted by the testimony of Assistant Secretary Paul McHale February 9, 2006:

> The Department of Defense's deployment of military resources in support of civil authorities after Hurricane Katrina exceeded, in speed and size, any other domestic disaster relief mission in the history of the United States. The ability of our military forces – Active Duty, Reserves, and the National Guard – to respond quickly and effectively to an event of this magnitude is a testament to their readiness, agility, and professionalism. It is also a reflection of the resources provided by Congress that enable them to organize, train, and equip to meet the full range of DOD's missions.[3]

Over 72,000 Federal military and National Guard personnel were deployed in response to Hurricane Katrina, more than twice the number deployed in response to Hurricane Andrew in 1992 (over 29,000).[4]

As President Bush,[5] DHS Deputy Secretary Michael Jackson,[6] LTG General Russel Honoré,[7] former FEMA Director Michael Brown,[8] and FEMA federal coordinating officer William Lokey[9] stated in their public statements, interviews, and testimony, the Department of

Defense performed commendably and responded effectively to every request made by FEMA for assistance to the Department. As a personal observation, Lieutenant General Honoré served with great distinction.

On the whole, the performance of the individual soldiers, sailors, Marines, and airmen – active, Guard, and Reserve – was in keeping with the high professional standards of the United States Military, and these men and women are proud of their service to help the victims of this natural disaster.

The Senate as a whole should be proud of these men and women in uniform who responded with courage and untiring professionalism on behalf of their fellow citizens who fell victim to the destruction of Hurricane Katrina.

National Preparedness and Response Authority and Organizational Recommendations

The movement of the Federal Emergency Management Agency (FEMA) into the Department of Homeland Security (DHS) with its creation in 2003 has led to criticism that this organizational structure impedes the ability of FEMA to adequately prepare for and respond to incidents. The Senate Katrina Report calls for the reorganization of FEMA into a quasi-independent agency that would combine preparedness and response functions under a "National Preparedness Response Authority" (NPRA) with direct reporting to the President during national emergencies.

It is my belief that the combination of preparedness and response functions can lead to a potential for focus on one of the two missions, leaving the other neglected. Certainly both missions are of extreme importance, as adequate preparedness efforts can contribute significantly to our ability to respond when emergencies take place. The current separation of these duties in the Department's framework enables the Department of Homeland Security to provide significant resources and attention to both functions without leading to a situation choosing one over the other.

In addition, my experience in government has shown that a strong reporting structure can only serve to strengthen the ability of any organization to work effectively in times of crisis. Certainly the FEMA Director has the authority to execute his or her mission during national emergencies as granted by the Stafford Act.[10] A dual reporting structure where the FEMA or NPRA Director reports to the Secretary of Homeland Security and the President simultaneously would inject confusion into the chain of command. However, as with all chains of command, should the President call on the Director, he or she is responsible to act. The most important factor in the success or failure of any organization rests on the shoulders of the individuals in that organization. Experienced leaders and talented staff are essential to the ability of FEMA to execute its mission.

For these reasons, I believe that the creation of the NPRA and elevation of the Director position above the Under Secretary level would not provide a more effective organizational structure for the Department of Homeland Security.

---

1 Department of Defense, Assistant Secretary of Defense for Homeland Defense, After Action Report.

2 Testimony of Lieutenant General H. Steven Blum, Chief, National Guard Bureau, before the House Appropriations Subcommittee on Defense, Sept. 28, 2005.

3 Testimony of Paul McHale, Assistant Secretary of Defense for Homeland Defense, Feb. 9, 2006, p. 2.

4 Testimony of Paul McHale, Assistant Secretary of Defense for Homeland Defense, Feb. 9, 2006, p. 4.

5 Statement of President George W. Bush, Aug. 31, 2005.

6 Interview of Michael Jackson, Jan. 27, 2006, pp. 27-28.

7 Testimony of Lieutenant General Russel Honoré, Commander, First U.S. Army, Feb. 9, 2006, pp. 5-9.

8 Interview of former FEMA Director Michael Brown, Jan. 23, 2006, pp. 206-207.

9 Interview of William Lokey, FEMA Federal Coordinating Officer, Nov. 4, 2005, pp. 80-87, 136.

10 Robert T. Stafford Disaster Relief and Emergency Assistance Act, 42 U.S.C. § 5143.

Additional Views

Senator Carl Levin

Committee Chairman Collins and Ranking Member Lieberman deserve the nation's gratitude for their determined efforts in conducting the most detailed Congressional investigation of the events surrounding Hurricane Katrina. Congressional oversight is critical if we are to learn from the mistakes made in this disaster and strengthen the nation's emergency management capabilities.

The televised pictures of Americans dislodged from their homes and stranded for days at the New Orleans Superdome and Convention Center, without adequate food, water, or basic necessities, continue to haunt the public and raise questions about the competency of government. The Committee Report provides needed factual information about what actually happened, and important recommendations for reforms. It is clear, as the Report recommends, that we need to choose leaders for federal emergency-management programs based on experience and qualifications, not cronyism. We need to create a central command post that gets and disseminates accurate, real-time information during emergency conditions. We need to restore emergency-preparedness and mitigation initiatives in our federal emergency-management programs. It is also painfully clear that Presidential leadership is essential during an unfolding disaster.

FEMA Reorganization

One of the Report's primary recommendations, the proposed reorganization of FEMA, raises difficult issues. Clearly, FEMA needs to be strengthened. It needs qualified leadership. It needs adequate funding. It needs to regain control of the state emergency-preparedness grant programs. It needs to address all types of hazards, including natural disasters.

Whether FEMA should remain in DHS or return to independent-agency status, however, is a complex issue that depends to a large extent on how the legislation reorganizing the agency will define its mission, its authorities, its assets, and its funding. Giving FEMA independent status would not automatically cure its ills. While it performed well under President Clinton as an independent agency, under President George H.W. Bush, it lost effectiveness as evidenced by FEMA's bungling response to the 1992 Hurricane Andrew. On the other hand, keeping FEMA within DHS would require it to continue to compete against a host of important programs, including those to promote border security and prevent terrorism. FEMA lost out to those other programs in the past, and the Committee Report does not identify reforms that would ensure FEMA would obtain a priority status or be able to protect its budget while within DHS.

Another problem involves issues of accountability and the chain of command. The Committee Report recommends that, during "catastrophes," the head of the newly reconstituted FEMA report directly to the President.[1] The Report does not, however, define "catastrophe," specify when this direct reporting relationship should take effect, or clarify the authority of the DHS Secretary during such catastrophes. Moreover, the head of FEMA presumably continues to report to the DHS Secretary on routine matters such as the agency's annual budget, long-term priorities, and programs to assist states to prepare for, mitigate, and recover from emergencies. The Report also recommends that the head of FEMA serve as a national emergency-management advisor to the President, in a capacity that presumably bypasses the DHS Secretary. These alternative chains of command could create confusion and blur accountability.

For these and other reasons, I plan to wait to see the actual legislative proposals for reorganizing FEMA and consider the pros and cons at hearings before taking a position on this issue.

National Guard Coordination

I strongly endorse the finding in the Report that the "National Guard and active-duty military response saved lives; provided urgent food, water, shelter, and medical care to many hurricane victims; and helped restore law and order, re-establish communications, and rebuild damaged roads." Additionally, the Report finds that as soon as the DOD leadership recognized the severity of the disaster, it adopted an energetic, forward-looking posture that brought critical expertise and personnel to support the beleaguered state and federal first responders. I also fully agree with the findings and recommendations of the Report on how the response of DOD and the National Guard can be improved in the event of a future catastrophe or major disaster.

In particular, it is imperative that both DOD and the National Guard improve their planning and co-ordination in the event a large military response is needed for another catastrophe.

With respect to the deployment of National Guard forces, there is a clear need to better plan for large-scale deployments. As the Report recommends, the Governors should work with the Department of Defense to develop a coordinated, integrated process for the large-scale deployment of National Guard forces when such a large-scale deployment is requested by a Governor during a catastrophe.

Communications. I also endorse the Report's focus on the importance of emergency communications. The Report states: "The problems of operability and interoperability of communications were a central part of the failures in the governments' response to Hurricane Katrina." To address this problem, I support the enactment of legislation providing a dedicated funding source for the purchase of interoperable communications equipment. States cannot afford to correct this problem on their own; they need federal assistance. I will continue to work with Senators Collins and Lieberman to ensure that any legislation arising out of this investigation includes dedicated funding for interoperability equipment.

Separated Families

One particularly disturbing aspect of the Katrina disaster involves the failure of federal, state, and local governments to deal effectively with the problem of family members who became separated during the disaster. During evacuation and search-and-rescue efforts, some family members became separated, ending up in different places within the same state and sometimes in different states. Over 5,000 children were reported missing by family members, as well as over 13,000 adults. While the reported cases of missing children have since been characterized as resolved, it took nearly seven months for the last child to be reunited with her family.[2]

DHS and FEMA failed to take the lead in addressing this devastating problem. FEMA, for example, failed for a substantial period of time to make use of an existing database to assist in reuniting families. It did not set standards for states to use in evacuation efforts so that, for example, the name, origin, and destination of each evacuated individual was recorded. Instead, the Department of Justice tasked a single nonprofit agency, experienced in locating missing persons, to set up a hotline for reporting missing children and adults and to devise ways to try to reunite them with friends or family. In addition, charitable organizations, businesses, ad hoc groups, and even the media set up websites to help persons locate their loved ones.

One Web site identified 52 other Web sites with lists of Katrina survivors and missing persons.[3] This Web site explained that it was providing the list of these databases to help people find missing friends and family members. It also pointed out the obvious: "There needs to be a way to pool this data so that people don't have to go from database to database looking for the information they seek."

FEMA not only failed to utilize a central database to track Katrina survivors and missing persons, it also failed to cooperate fully with the nonprofit agency tasked with reuniting families.[4] Citing privacy issues that could have been resolved, FEMA declined to provide needed assistance and allowed the problem to fester for months.

Some have argued that, during the next disaster, state and local governments should assume responsibility for tracking evacuees, resolving missing-person reports, and reuniting separated family members. I disagree. People go missing when there are disasters of such magnitude that they overwhelm state and local capacity. The Committee Report states in the "Conclusions and Findings" section: "During a catastrophe, which by definition almost immediately exceeds state and local resources and significantly disrupts governmental operations and emergency services, the role of the federal government is particularly important."

Catastrophic events also often affect multiple states. Even disasters confined to a single state may see persons evacuated to multiple states, as in the case of the New Orleans flood. It is unlikely that states will know ahead of time which of them will be involved in a particular disaster or in evacuation efforts. Even if they did, it is naive to think that multiple states facing imminent disaster can work out an effective plan for tracking evacuated individuals. Logic dictates that DHS should take responsibility for addressing the problem beforehand by developing standards and forms for collecting evacuee information, providing a common database or means for linking multiple databases to track evacuees and identify missing persons, and resolving privacy issues. Assigning this responsibility to the states instead, without a lead federal agency, is impractical and likely to ensure another round of confusion and heartache for misplaced persons and their families.

The House Committee report does not address this problem.[5] The White House report briefly mentions it, but does not hold anyone accountable for the confused and inadequate response during Katrina, nor does it recommend corrective actions.[6] Every day that families are separated during a disaster brings loss and sadness. Each separation consumes federal resources in the search for the missing. Each lost child, suffering alone without family or friends, is a tragedy. This is an issue that deserves our full attention.

Preventive action can avert much of the problem. Forms to track evacuees and identify missing persons, designation of a central database to accept and organize this information, standards for resolving privacy concerns, and methods to make appropriate information accessible are matters which can be worked out before disaster strikes, and then used to prevent tens of thousands of future cases of missing persons during disasters. These systems need to be developed before the next emergency. Where necessary, Congress needs to appropriate the funds needed to put these systems in place. I urge DHS to take on and complete this task prior to the upcoming hurricane season.

Unified Command

I agree with the points made by Senator Lieberman in his additional views, which I have joined, that FEMA must share the blame for the absence of a unified command in Louisiana during Katrina. It is abundantly clear from the record before the Committee that FEMA lacked an adequate number of trained personnel in Louisiana to establish a fully functional Incident Command System and a unified command for the response to Katrina. Under the National Response Plan, FEMA was the lead federal agency responsible for establishing a unified command in partnership with the state; neither FEMA nor the state had an adequate number of trained personnel to deal with a catastrophe of this magnitude. The absence of a unified command contributed to confusion and delays. Among the lessons learned from Katrina is the need for FEMA to take stronger action to ensure a unified command in future disasters.

Waste, Fraud, and Abuse. I am disappointed that the Committee's investigation did not more fully tackle the issue of contract waste, fraud, and abuse. Our Committee has jurisdiction over federal procurement issues, and multiple examples of procurement failings came up during the Katrina hearings, including allegations involving no-bid contracts, inflated prices, unqualified contractors, and wasteful purchasing. More aggressive Congressional oversight could have helped identify the many problems and suggest needed reforms.

Active involvement by this Committee in Katrina procurement matters could still provide a significant boost to efforts to prevent contract problems during the Katrina recovery effort. I hope the Committee will redouble its efforts to prevent, expose, and remedy contract waste, fraud and abuse during the Katrina recovery.

FEMA and DOD

Finally, I would like to note one matter that merits a clarification. The Report's Executive Summary states that even after DOD Deputy Secretary England issued a "blank check" to Admiral Keating to provide DOD assistance in the Katrina disaster, and the Chairman of the Joint Chiefs of Staff, General Myers, directed DOD commanders to move potentially useful assets in advance of FEMA requests, "some FEMA officials believe that DOD's approval process continued to take too long." As the Report implies, however, the majority of FEMA officials were satisfied with DOD's approval process and the efforts it made to assist FEMA during the Katrina disaster. As FEMA Federal Coordinating Officer William Lokey said: "What I will speak to is Colonel Daskevich and his people. They … [did] anything I asked them to do … everything they could for the people in Louisiana."[7]

---

1 The Democratic Staff of the House Committee on Homeland Security recently made a similar recommendation, but specifically defined when the FEMA Director would report to the President. The report explains: "We recommend requiring a direct line of reporting between the Director of FEMA and the President of the United States during incidents of national significance." *Redirecting FEMA Toward Success: A Report and Legislative Solution*, Prepared for Congressman Bennie G. Thompson, Ranking Member, by the Democratic Staff of the Committee on Homeland Security, Feb. 2006, page 35.

2 "National Center for Missing and Exploited Children Reunites Last Missing Child Separated By Hurricane Katrina and Rita," press release, Mar. 17, 2006, http://www.missingkids.com/missingkids, accessed on May 4, 2006.

3 www.rexblog.com/2005/09/03, accessed on May 4, 2006.

4 "FEMA Restricts Evacuee Data, Citing Privacy," *The Washington Post*, October 12, 2005, page A01; "FEMA Slows Search for Kids From Katrina," *The Washington Post*, Dec. 23, 2005, page A06; "Coordinated search for the missing; Reuniting children separated from families after Hurricane Katrina should be a FEMA priority," *The Grand Rapids Press*, Grand Rapids, MI, Dec. 31, 2005, p. A12.; "FEMA stymies Katrina searches: Agency cites privacy laws in preventing efforts to find missing children," *Charleston Daily Mail*, Charleston, WV, Dec. 27, 2005, page 7A.

5 *A Failure of Initiative: Final Report*, U.S. House of Representatives, Select Bipartisan Committee to Investigate the Preparation for and Response to Hurricane Katrina, Feb. 15, 2006.

6 The White House, *The Federal Response to Hurricane Katrina: Lessons Learned*, Feb. 2006.

7 Interview of William Lokey, FEMA Federal Coordinating Officer, Nov. 4, 2005, p. 136.

Additional Views

Senator Daniel Akaka, Senator Frank Lautenberg, and Senator Mark Pryor

On Maintaining the Functions of the Federal Emergency Management Agency (FEMA) within the Department of Homeland Security

While we subscribe to the majority of the Committee Report, we do not believe the Committee's recommendation for restructuring the Federal Emergency Management Agency (FEMA) within the Department of Homeland Security (DHS) adequately addresses the chain of command and budget problems made evident by Hurricane Katrina. We believe FEMA was more effective and robust as an independent, Cabinet-level agency, and we recommend returning FEMA to that status.

When the Homeland Security Act of 2002, which created DHS, was being debated in Congress, the inclusion of FEMA in the new Department was a controversial subject. Members of Congress from both sides of the aisle and emergency-management experts questioned the wisdom of folding FEMA into DHS. The Brookings Institution issued a study in July 2002, *Assessing the Department of Homeland Security*, stating that only agencies "where the function would not be performed as well in its current agency or would provide a useful synergy with other entities" should be included in DHS. "Furthermore, mergers should enhance, not detract, from the ability to fulfill stated agency missions. The merger of a consolidated FEMA into a larger Department of Homeland Security does not meet any of these criteria."[1]

James Lee Witt, Director of FEMA, 1993-2001, recommended creating the new Department slowly, arguing that DHS should first assume responsibility for critical infrastructure protection and intelligence analysis instead of assuming FEMA's emergency-management responsibilities, which "were not broken and didn't need fixing."[2]

Members of Congress questioned whether FEMA would lose its ability to respond to natural disasters. For example, at the confirmation hearing for Michael Brown to be Deputy Director of FEMA, Senator Akaka stated:

> The President's proposal for a new Department of Homeland Security will include the Federal Emergency Management Agency (FEMA). A key question is how will this new role for FEMA in homeland security affect its traditional mission? … Many of the agencies impacted by this proposal, including FEMA, have a number of core responsibilities unrelated to their homeland security missions. Most of what FEMA does every day, and what Americans expect from FEMA, does not fall under the category of homeland security.[3]

However, these arguments did not prevail, and four years later Hurricane Katrina has made evident to us that incorporating FEMA into DHS was a mistake.

There are three main reasons that FEMA must be an independent agency in order to function effectively: chain of command, budget integrity, and flexibility.

Chain of Command

The Director of FEMA should have a direct – not a dotted – line to the President. In 1996, recognizing the importance of emergency response, President Bill Clinton elevated the FEMA Director position to the Cabinet level. Being a member of the President's Cabinet enabled the FEMA Director to task other federal agencies more effectively during a disaster and provided an established and direct line of communication to the President.

This status was eliminated in 2003 when FEMA was folded into DHS and the FEMA Director was reduced to the rank of Undersecretary requiring that he report to the Secretary of Homeland Security instead of the President.

Under the Robert T. Stafford Disaster Relief and Emergency Assistance Act (P.L. 93-288), the FEMA Director has the authority to task other federal agencies to provide specific assistance to states overwhelmed by disaster. In today's current structure, this means that an Undersecretary of DHS is tasking Cabinet-level Secretaries, who clearly outrank the FEMA Director. In addition, the FEMA Director must go through the DHS Secretary to communicate with the President. Former FEMA Director Michael Brown was criticized heavily for at times reporting directly to the White House during Katrina.

Hurricane Katrina provided countless examples of federal assets not being deployed quickly enough, such as the delayed arrival of active-duty military in a chaotic New Orleans,[4] possibly due to the lack of authority and clarity in the tasking orders. The Department of Defense (DOD) describes FEMA's tasks as "requests" that are evaluated by the Department before a decision is made as to whether they will be fulfilled.[5] The FEMA Director should speak for the President in order to inspire an expedient and effective response. In the wake of Hurricane Katrina, former FEMA Director Witt made the comparison between an independent FEMA and today's structure: "We had all the resources of the federal government. We didn't have to ask anyone to activate the Department of Defense. I did that. I called up the President."[6]

Because FEMA's primary function is to provide fast, coordinated relief to often unforeseen disasters, a speedy response is essential. This is no time for red tape, which is why the FEMA Director must have a clear, direct reporting line to the President.

Budget Integrity

DHS has an annual budget of over $40 billion, of which FEMA receives approximately $5 billion or 12 percent. However, the majority of FEMA's funding is for the National Flood Insurance Fund and the Disaster Relief Fund, which is accessed only after a federal disaster is declared. FEMA's annual operating budget is less than $1 billion.

During this Committee's Hurricane Katrina hearings, Michael Brown testified that when FEMA joined DHS, the Agency was forced to pay a "tax" of approximately 14 percent of its budget to fund shared services in the Department such as information technology (IT) systems and the Secretary's office. He further testified that this funding was taken disproportionately from mitigation programs instead of other FEMA accounts because the Bush Administration gave mitigation funding "a backseat."[7] Mr. Brown told the House Select Katrina Response Investigation Committee that FEMA requested additional funding for preparedness after the Hurricane Pam exercise, and that the request was denied by DHS.

Congress and the American public never knew about these funding shortfalls because FEMA was buried within DHS. Mr. Brown testified that instead of taking his budget proposal to the President, the FEMA Director first cleared it with another Undersecretary at DHS, then the Secretary, and then the President.

FEMA needs to be an independent agency to avoid having its budget siphoned off for other homeland security functions. In addition, as a Cabinet member, the FEMA Director can better present the funding needs of FEMA to the President and Congress.

Flexibility

When FEMA was folded into DHS it went from being a small, independent agency of 3,000 employees to becoming part of a Department of 180,000 employees. FEMA went from a nimble and agile agency, to one bogged down in a new, extended chain of command.

During the hearings, we heard numerous examples of information and initiative getting lost in DHS during the Hurricane Katrina response. Witnesses described sending information updates and requests out to the Department, never knowing where those messages went or if action had been taken. DHS appeared to be a black hole where information and accountability were lost, not an asset that enhanced FEMA's performance.

Being a part of DHS did provide FEMA with access to more resources during a disaster, but it is not clear that FEMA was able to draw effectively upon the additional DHS resources in the immediate aftermath of Katrina. The senior DHS leadership appeared disengaged from the hurricane preparation and response until days after the hurricane when the failed response had garnered national attention. Furthermore, under the Stafford Act the FEMA Director has the authority to draw upon the resources of other federal agencies during a disaster, leaving no reason why an independent FEMA could not tap into DHS for assistance. Former FEMA officials have stated publicly that they believe an independent FEMA would have been much better equipped to coordinate the resources of the federal government during Hurricane Katrina.

Conclusion

We acknowledge that the Committee Report makes recommendations that would improve upon the current emergency management structure, such as reuniting preparedness and response. However, keeping these functions under the DHS umbrella is a mistake. The proposed National Preparedness and Response Authority (NPRA) would be a super-agency within a super-agency. Creating more layers is not the solution. We strongly urge our colleagues in Congress and the Administration to consider separating FEMA from the DHS and restoring the FEMA Director to a Cabinet-level position.

---

1 Ivo Dalde et al., *Assessing the Department of Homeland Security* (Washington, D.C.: Brookings Institution, July 2002), p. 23.

2 Statement of James Lee Witt, before the U.S. House of Representatives, Subcommittee on National Security, Emerging Threats and International Relations, Committee on Government Reform, hearing on *The Homeland Security Department's Plan to Consolidate and Co-locate Regional and Field Offices: Improving Communication and Coordination,* Mar. 24, 2002.

3 Nomination Hearing of Michael D. Brown, Committee on Governmental Affairs, S. Hrg. 107-616 (2002), p. 6.

4 Committee on Homeland Security and Governmental Affairs, *Hurricane Katrina: A Nation Still Unprepared*, 2006, Ch. 26.

5 *Hurricane Katrina: A Nation Still Unprepared*, Ch. 26-7.

6 Bill Walsh, "Tug of war being played out over who has FEMA control," New Orleans *Times-Picayune*, Apr. 13, 2006.

7 Testimony of Michael D. Brown, before the U.S. Senate, Committee on Homeland Security and Governmental Affairs, hearing on *Hurricane Katrina: The Roles of DHS and FEMA Leadership,* Feb. 10, 2006.

Additional Views

Senator Mark Dayton

I voted not to approve the draft Report in Committee, because it is seriously incomplete without the information, documents, and testimony denied by the White House. According to the Ranking Member's "Additional Views," on March 15, 2006, he asked the Chairman to subpoena the withheld documents and witnesses. She declined.

Earlier this year, on January 12, 2006, the Chairman and Ranking Member wrote then-White House Chief of Staff, Mr. Andrew Card, regarding the information they had previously requested. Their letter stated, in part, "This practice (of withholding information) must cease."

It continued, "We are willing to discuss claims of executive privilege asserted by the White House, either directly or through a federal agency. But we will not stand for blanket instructions to refuse answering any questions concerning any communications with the EOP [Executive Office of the President]."

Their insistence that either Administration officials comply with this oversight committee's rightful demands, or the President invoke his Executive Privilege not to do so, was entirely appropriate. Unfortunately, when Mr. Card and his subordinates still refused to comply, the Chairman denied the Ranking Member's request to issue subpoenas. Regrettably, other Committee Members (at least, this Member) were not informed of their previous attempts to obtain information, or of the decision to give in to the Administration's recalcitrance.

Unfortunately, at its mark-up of the draft report, the Committee failed to support my motion to subpoena those documents and witnesses, which were being withheld by the White House without claim to Executive Privilege, and which were being wrongfully denied by executive agencies.

The Administration's refusal to comply and cooperate with this investigation is deplorable, as is the Committee's failure to back the Chairman's and Ranking Member's proper insistence that the White House do so. This Committee is charged by the full Senate with the responsibility to oversee the agencies, programs, and activities that are related to homeland security. The Committee was expressly directed by the Senate Majority Leader to examine the Bush Administration's failure to respond quickly or effectively to the disasters caused by Hurricane Katrina. This investigation is not complete without all of the information requested from the Administration by the Chairman, the Ranking Member, or their staffs. Furthermore, its findings and conclusions can hardly be considered reliable, if the White House has decided what information to provide, and what information to withhold, from the Committee.

This unfortunate acquiescence confirms the judgment of the Senate Democratic Leader that an independent, bi-partisan Commission was necessary to ensure a complete and unbiased investigation into the federal, state, and local responses to Hurricane Katrina. His request has been repeatedly denied by the Majority, with the assurance that this Committee would fulfill its responsibilities. Tragically and reprehensibly, it has failed to do so. Thus, the Committee failed the Senate's Constitutional obligations to be an independent, co-equal branch of government from the Executive. It also failed the long-suffering victims of Hurricane Katrina, who deserve to know why their governments failed them, and all the American people, who depend upon their elected representatives to protect their lives and their interests, without regard to partisan political considerations. That partisanship includes unjustified protection of an administration of the same political party, as much as undue criticism of one from another party.

Given the information provided to the Committee, the Chairman, the Ranking Member, and the Committee staff deserve commendation for their dedication to this undertaking. They held 22 hearings, and they arranged for Committee members to tour afflicted sites in Mississippi and Louisiana. The hearings established an extensive public record, which informed Committee members and provided the solid foundation of this Report.

Our January 17, 2006, trip to Gulfport, Mississippi, and New Orleans, Louisiana, allowed us to visually inspect areas devastated by Hurricane Katrina and to meet with state and local officials. Almost five months after the hurricane, the observed and reported lack of progress in clean-up, repair, and reconstruction, provided further evidence of the federal government's continuing failure to respond efficiently or effectively. There is no time in which the helping hand of government is more urgently needed and more surely deserved than during and after a disaster. Victims are damaged or devastated – physically, emotional, and financially. Local officials and their public services are overwhelmed, if not destroyed. They need a federal emergency-response organization composed of experienced, dedicated professionals, who have the resources necessary to alleviate short-term suffering and commence long-term recovery, and also the authority to expeditiously commit those resources.

What the failed federal response to Hurricane Katrina showed is the utter ineptitude of the Federal Emergency Management Agency. Even worse, FEMA's indifference and incompetence in the aftermath of Hurricane Katrina was not an isolated instance. In the direct experience of this Senator with FEMA's disaster-relief responses in Minnesota, the agency is too often a major obstruction to recovery projects, rather than a principal ally.

I agree with this Report's "Core Recommendation #1 – Create a New, Comprehensive Emergency Management Organization … to Prepare for and Respond to all Disasters and Catastrophes." I remain open-minded whether this new entity should remain within the DHS, as this Recommendation intends, or be established as a separate federal agency. The challenge for the Committee, for all of Congress, and for the Administration will be to actually "re-create" an existing federal agency that has become dysfunctional and non-functional. Merely "reforming" FEMA by rearranging some boxes and lines on its organizational chart, revising it, and giving its head a new title, will be usefully inadequate. The new organization must be more streamlined, centralized, and compact than its predecessor. It must be less bureaucratic, less consumed with regulatory minutiae, and less resistant to local recovery initiatives. It must spend less time creating complex plans and cumbersome procedures, and more time in training and perfecting action responses to emergency situations.

This new organization cannot be effective, however, without a clear definition of its role in national disasters. Inter-governmental, and even inter-agency, coordination is an oxymoron in an emergency. Someone must be in charge. And that "someone" must be clearly understood by everyone in advance of the crisis. It is no coincidence that the most effective "First Responders" immediately after Hurricane Katrina were military organizations: the U.S. Coast Guard and the National Guard. They are trained to act in crisis situations. They have clear, pre-established chains of command. They act.

That is why I am concerned about "Core Recommendation #5," which states, "Although the federal government should play a more proactive role in responding to catastrophic events, when state and local officials may be overwhelmed, states and localities will continue to provide the backbone of response – the first response – for all disasters, catastrophic or not."

While that approval may be appropriate for "typical disasters" (itself an oxymoron!), Hurricane Katrina exposed its fatal flaws in an extreme or widespread disaster. Lines of communication are disrupted, if not temporarily destroyed, in such a catastrophe, which makes inter-governmental "coordination" extremely difficult, inefficient, and delayed. If the situation deteriorates in the disaster's aftermath, as has occurred in New Orleans, attempts to avoid responsibilities and to blame others for failed responses, override efforts of coordination and cooperation.

A large-scale catastrophe requires a federally led response. Invoking what is presently termed the "Catastrophic Incident Annex of the National Response Plan" should place this new organization's head as the "Situation Commander," operating directly under, and reporting directly to, the President of the United States. All of the other federal, state, local, and private emergency-response operations should then become subordinate to, and under the direction of, the "Situation Commander," for as long as the President deems necessary.

History shows that "If the student does not learn the lesson, the teacher reappears." This Report describes some of the most important lessons from the failed response to Hurricane Katrina. This Committee's and the Congress's subsequent actions to correct those serious deficiencies before the next catastrophe will indicate whether those lessons will be learned.

Additional Views

Senator Frank R. Lautenberg

1: On Establishing an Independent, Bi-Partisan Katrina Commission

I commend the efforts of Chairman Collins and Ranking Member Lieberman and their staffs in putting together a solid, thoughtful, and comprehensive report which chronicles in great and grave detail the failures of all levels of government in preparing for and responding to Hurricane Katrina and the subsequent flooding. I fully believe that the Chairman and the Ranking Member did the best they could, given the difficult political circumstances the Homeland Security and Governmental Affairs Committee faced during this seven-month investigation.

I say that the Committee labored under difficult circumstances because the Administration refused to cooperate fully. On page 13 of his dissenting views, Senator Lieberman stated that the "worst offender ... that should have stood above the fray and worked hardest with the Committee to uncover the government's failings in Katrina: the White House."[1] Senator Lieberman added that "not once in his Senate career of nearly 18 years has he engaged a White House less willing to cooperate with a Senate investigation." The Committee investigation was the best it could have been given White House intransigence, but what is required now is an independent, bi-partisan Katrina Commission with subpoena power.

We all know that the Administration repeatedly failed – or refused – to cooperate with the Committee's Katrina investigation, even after assurances by President Bush in September 2005 to "work with members of both parties to make sure this effort is thorough."[2] In fact, the White House became an obstacle to this Committee's investigation by not producing large quantities of information or witnesses the Committee requested. The White House opposed Committee efforts to interview their personnel and interfered with the Committee's ability to get much-needed information from other federal agencies regarding White House actions vis-à-vis Hurricane Katrina. Again, in his additional views, Senator Lieberman explicitly stated that:

The Committee's efforts to understand the role the White House played in events leading up to and following the catastrophe were severely hindered by the White House's failure to comply with the Committee requests for information, documents, and interviews. As a result, we learned much too little about what the White House and the Executive Office of the President were doing during the critical days before and after Katrina struck.[3]

For these reasons, I strongly believe and recommend that an independent commission – with subpoena power – should be established immediately to investigate the federal, state, and local government preparation for and response to Hurricane Katrina and its aftermath. I concur with Senator Lieberman that:

The one thing we do know is that because we were denied the opportunity to fully explore the role the White House played in preparing for and responding to Katrina, we have little insight into how the President and his staff monitored, managed, and directed the government's disaster preparedness in the post-9/11 world, how they coordinated the rest of the federal bureaucracy in response to Katrina. ... Without this information, the Committee's investigation necessarily lacked the ability to fully and fairly analyze and assess a critical element of the response to Katrina.[4]

Although Senator Lieberman does not concur with my view that an independent Katrina Commission should be established without further delay, his dissenting views eloquently make the best arguments for its creation.

From the beginning of this investigation, I – along with Senator Clinton and others – called for the creation of a Katrina Commission that would be bi-partisan, modeled very closely after the National Commission on Terrorist Attacks Upon the United States (the so-called 9/11 Commission), which was so successful. This commission would be charged with examining the federal, state, and local responses to the devastation wrought by Hurricane Katrina in the Gulf Region of the United States, specifically in the states of Louisiana, Mississippi, and Alabama, and other affected areas. The Commission would then make recommendations on immediate corrective measures to improve preparedness for and responses to future disasters.

The Katrina Commission would be modeled very closely after the 9/11 Commission, but would place its primary emphasis on emergency-services preparedness, mitigation, response, and recovery. The President would appoint the Chair, and the remaining members would be appointed by the Republican and Democrat leadership of the House and Senate with no more than five individuals from the same political party. The Commission would report on its findings within six months of its establishment. The Commission would begin its work as soon as practicable.

This independent approach of the 9/11 Commission served this nation well in the aftermath of the worst terrorist attack upon the United States and will serve the nation well in the aftermath of one of the worst natural disasters to strike the United States.

The many findings and 88 recommendations in the Committee's Katrina Report are very useful, but Americans want and deserve more. The government failed its citizens before, during, and after this disaster. Let's not fail the American people again by denying them access to what the White House knew and when they knew it. Let's listen to them, and appoint an independent, bi-partisan Katrina Commission to complete an investigation into what went wrong and why.

2: On the Need to Account for People with Pets in Emergency Planning

One of the many disturbing and heart-rending developments we saw unfold after Hurricane Katrina was the peril many people found themselves in because they could not bear to evacuate without their pets, and the anguish of those people who were forced to leave their pets behind.

There was much media coverage, both in print and on television, of distraught pet owners and of abandoned animals going hungry, thirsty, and full of fear as their world was washed away. Millions of people heard or saw the distressing story of one young boy who was so traumatized after his dog was taken from him when he boarded a bus to leave the Superdome that he became physically ill. One distraught woman reportedly offered her wedding ring to a shelter aide if he would find out what had happened to her dog, which she was not allowed to bring inside with her.

The evidence suggests that the attachment people have to their pets was a key reason why many decided not to evacuate. According to a recent survey of people affected by Hurricane Katrina who were living in Louisiana, Mississippi, or Alabama, 44 percent of those who did not evacuate by choice (as opposed to those who lacked the means to do so), did not leave in part because they weren't willing to abandon their pets.[5]

These were life-and-death decisions, and for some of these people, the decision to stay with their pets cost them their lives. The Mississippi *Sun-Herald* recently identified seven individuals who died during or after Hurricane Katrina because they did not want to leave a beloved pet, and so they stayed in harm's way.[6]

Moreover, some of the animals left behind, agitated by hunger, thirst, and fear, presented threats to the rescue and response personnel who went door-to-door looking for survivors.

As with other aspects of the disjointed and incomplete preparation for and response to Hurricane Katrina, there was no plan in place to help people with pets evacuate, or to ensure there were adequate shelters that could accommodate people and their pets.

I agree with the Committee Report's finding that the needs of those with pets and service animals should be a factor in emergency planning for evacuations and sheltering. While I support the Committee's recommendation that the Department of Homeland Security (DHS) should encourage individuals as well as state and local governments to plan for evacuating and sheltering pets, I also think it is important that we do more to address this issue. To that end, I joined Senator Stevens in introducing the "Pets Evacuation and Transportation Standards (PETS) Act," S. 2548.

Our bill would require state and local emergency-preparedness plans to take into account the needs of individuals with household pets and service animals. In addition, our bill would authorize the Federal Emergency Management Agency (FEMA) to provide technical assistance in developing these plans and financial assistance for purchasing, constructing, leasing, or renovating emergency shelter facilities that can accommodate people with pets and service animals. Finally, our bill would include people with pets and service animals among those for whom FEMA may provide essential assistance in response to a major disaster.

I hope that our bill will be included as part of any legislation that this Committee develops in response to Hurricane Katrina and its aftermath.

In addition, I am concerned by reports that despite FEMA's deployment of more than 200 veterinarians to assist in the Gulf Coast – the largest simultaneous deployment of veterinary relief in U.S. history – the veterinary teams were ill-equipped because of FEMA policies. Apparently, FEMA prohibits veterinarians from using their own equipment, accepting donations, or buying supplies. As a result, Veterinary Medical Assistance Teams (VMATs) – which are identified in the National Response Plan as the source of federal veterinary medical treatment during an emergency – did not have what they needed to carry out their mission.[7]

I believe the Committee should work with FEMA, DHS, and other interested parties to address problems like this to ensure that, like the rest of FEMA, VMATs will be appropriately staffed, equipped, and otherwise prepared to fulfill their role within the National Response Plan.

Conclusion

It is important to note that what happened in the Gulf Coast could happen anywhere in the United States the next time disaster strikes. According to the Humane Society of the United States (HSUS), Americans currently have over 358 million pets. Sixty-three percent of all American households have one or more pets. So wherever a natural or manmade disaster could occur, many of the people who would be affected will be pet owners – 61 percent of whom told national pollsters they would refuse to evacuate ahead of a disaster if they could not take their pets with them.[8]

One of the most important lessons to be learned from Hurricane Katrina is that planning and preparedness are essential to avoid aggravating whatever disasters may strike in the future. By accounting for the very strong ties that millions of Americans have to their pets in preparing for future emergencies, we can ensure a better response and actually save lives. As HSUS executive vice president Michael Markarian has said, Hurricane Katrina and its aftermath "made people recognize that helping pets during a disaster is helping people during a disaster."

---

1 *See*, in this Report, Additional Views of Senators Lieberman, Levin, Akaka, Carper, Lautenberg and Pryor on White House Katrina Failures, Administration Lack of Cooperation with the Investigation, and Failure to Establish Unified Command.

2 Speech, President George W. Bush, Jackson Square, New Orleans, LA, Sept. 15, 2005.

3 *See*, in this Report, Additional Views of Senators Lieberman, Levin, Akaka, Carper, Lautenberg and Pryor on White House Katrina Failures, Administration Lack of Cooperation with the Investigation, and Failure to Establish Unified Command.

4 *See*, in this Report, Additional Views of Senators Lieberman, Levin, Akaka, Carper, Lautenberg and Pryor on White House Katrina Failures, Administration Lack of Cooperation with the Investigation, and Failure to Establish Unified Command.

5 Fritz Institute, "Hurricane Katrina: Perceptions of the Affected," Apr. 26, 2006.

6 Karen Nelson, "Staying with animals in Katrina was a deadly choice for some, and the hurricane left other owners seeking shelter from the storm," SunHerald.com, posted Apr. 30, 2006. http://www.sunherald.com/mld/sunherald/news/local/14464093.htm.

7 William Wan, "A Lesson from Katrina: Pets Matter," *The Washington Post*, Jan. 2, 2006.

8 http://www.zogby.com/news/ReadNews.dbm?ID=1029.